TWELFTH EDITION

Basic
MARKETING
A Global-Managerial Approach

William D. Perreault, Jr., Ph.D.
UNIVERSITY OF NORTH CAROLINA

E. Jerome McCarthy, Ph.D.
MICHIGAN STATE UNIVERSITY

Lindsay Meredith
SIMON FRASER UNIVERSITY

Lynne Ricker
UNIVERSITY OF CALGARY

Toronto   Montréal   Boston   Burr Ridge, IL   Dubuque, IA   Madison, WI   New York
San Francisco   St. Louis   Bangkok   Bogotá   Caracas   Kuala Lumpur   Lisbon   London
Madrid   Mexico City   Milan   New Delhi   Santiago   Seoul   Singapore   Sydney   Taipei

Basic Marketing
A Global-Managerial Approach
Twelfth Canadian Edition

ISBN-13: 978-0-07-097425-8
ISBN-10: 0-07-097425-X

1 2 3 4 5 6 7 8 9 10 VH 0 9 8 7

Editorial Director: Joanna Cotton
Publisher: Lynn Fisher
Senior Sponsoring Editor: Leanna MacLean
Senior Marketing Manager: Joy Armitage Taylor
Developmental Editor, Freelance: Tracey Haggert
Editorial Associate: Stephanie Hess
Senior Supervising Editor: Margaret Henderson
Copy Editor: Evan Turner
Senior Production Coordinator: Madeleine Harrington
Cover Design: Sharon Lucas Design
Cover Image: Getty Images
Interior Design: Kiera Pohl/Sharon Lucas
Typeface: 10.5/12 Goudy
Composition: Liz Harasymczuk Design
Printer: Von Hoffmann Press, Inc.

Library and Archives Canada Cataloguing in Publication

    Basic marketing : a global-managerial approach / William D. Perreault Jr. ... [et al.]. — 12th Canadian ed.

E. Jerome McCarthy listed first on 1st-7th Canadian eds.; 8th-9th Canadian eds. by Stanley J. Shapiro, William D. Perreault, E. Jerome McCarthy.
Includes bibliographical references and index.
ISBN 978-0-07-097425-8

    1. Marketing—Management—Textbooks. I. Perreault, William D. II. Shapiro, Stanley J. Basic marketing.

HF5415.13.B38 2007   658.8   C2006-906856-9

About the Authors

William D. Perreault, Jr.

William D. Perreault, Jr. is currently Kenan Professor at the University of North Carolina Kenan-Flagler Business School. He has also taught at Stanford University, the University of Georgia, and North Carolina State University and has been an invited speaker at over 80 universities. During 1997 he was the Arthur Andersen Distinguished Visitor at Cambridge University.

Dr. Perreault is the recipient of the two most prestigious awards in his field: the American Marketing Association Distinguished Educator Award and the Academy of Marketing Science Outstanding Educator Award. He also was selected for the Churchill Award, which honors career impact on marketing research. He was editor of the *Journal of Marketing Research* and has been on the review board of the *Journal of Marketing* and other journals. His research has also been published in many journals, and one *Journal of Marketing* article was recently voted one of the most influential articles on sales and sales management of the twentieth century.

The Decision Sciences Institute has recognized Dr. Perreault for innovations in marketing education, and at UNC he has received several awards for teaching excellence. His books include two other widely used texts: *Essentials of Marketing* and *The Marketing Game!*

Dr. Perreault is a past president of the American Marketing Association Academic Council and twice served on the AMA board. He was chair of an advisory committee to the U.S. Bureau of the Census, a trustee of the Marketing Science Institute, and on the Council of the Decision Sciences Institute. He is a Fellow of the Society for Marketing Advances. He has also worked as a consultant to organizations that range from GE and IBM to the Federal Trade Commission and Venezuelan Ministry of Education. He is on the advisory board for Copernicus: The Marketing Investment Strategy Group.

E. Jerome McCarthy

E. Jerome McCarthy received his Ph.D. from the University of Minnesota. He has taught at the Universities of Oregon, Notre Dame, and Michigan State. He was honored with the American Marketing Association's Trailblazer Award in 1987, and he was voted one of the "top five" leaders in Marketing Thought by marketing educators.

He has been deeply involved in teaching and developing new teaching materials. Besides writing various articles and monographs, he is the author of textbooks on data processing and social issues in marketing.

Dr. McCarthy is active in making presentations to business meetings and academic conferences. He has worked with groups of teachers throughout the country and has addressed international conferences in South America, Africa, and India.

He was also a Ford Foundation Fellow in 1963–64, studying the role of marketing in global economic development. In 1959–60 he was a Ford Foundation Fellow at the Harvard Business School working on mathematical methods in marketing.

Besides his academic interests, Dr. McCarthy has been involved in consulting for, and guiding the growth of, a number of businesses—both in the U.S. and overseas. He has worked with top managers from Steelcase, Dow Chemical, 3M, Bemis, Grupo Industrial Alfa, and many other companies. He has also been active in executive education and is a director of several organizations. However, through out his career his primary interests have been in (1) "converting" students to marketing and effective marketing strategy planning and (2) preparing teaching materials to help others do the same. This is why he has spent a large part of his career developing, revising, and improving marketing texts to reflect the most current thinking in the field.

About the Authors

Lindsay Meredith

Lindsay Meredith is a professor of marketing in the Faculty of Business Administration at Simon Fraser University. His doctoral education consists of training in both marketing and economics. Dr. Meredith's articles include publications in *The Journal of Business and Industrial Marketing*, *The Journal of Industrial Marketing Management*, *The Journal of Business Research*, *International Journal of Advertising*, *The Columbia Journal of World Business*, and Harvard's *Review of Economics and Statistics*. He has co-authored an international textbook in Business Marketing that was sold in Canada, the United States, United Kingdom, India, Sweden, Belgium, Africa, New Zealand, Australia, and Southeast Asia. Dr. Meredith has 25 years of consulting experience with major multinational corporations and senior levels of government including work as an expert witness in marketing for Canada's Competition Tribunal. He has completed over 1,100 media interviews on marketing and economics. Radio broadcasts include Canadian provincial and national radio, American Public (national) Radio, CBC International Radio, and two interviews on *Voice of America*—Southeast Asia. Television broadcasts include CBC *News World International*, CBC *National* broadcasts (*Venture*, *Newsmagazine*, *Canada Now*, *Canada AM*, and a one-hour national documentary on CBC's *Marketplace*), CTV's international broadcast *Newsnet*, CTV *National News* and their national program *Digital Desk*, Global TV *National News*, and BCTV documentary programming. Regional TV includes numerous interviews for CBC, BCTV-Global, VTV, Rogers TV, Shaw TV, Fairchild Television, CTV, Channel M, The Women's Network (W Network), and the Knowledge Network. Newspaper interviews have been completed for *The Globe and Mail*, *Financial Post*, *National Post*, *Ottawa Citizen*, *New York Observer*, *Liberation* (French national daily paper), *Telegraph* (London, U.K.), *Sing Tao*, *Sing Pao*, and numerous provincial papers. Magazine interviews have been included in articles for *Time*, *National Post Business*, *Canadian Business*, *Maclean's*, *Atlantic Progress*, *Profit*, *Enterprise*, *Ad Blitz*, *Stockwatch*, *Strategy*, *Edge*, and *BCBusiness*. National and international news wire stories include numerous interviews for the Canadian Press and CanWest Global Wire services, and Bloomberg's Business News Wire (New York). In-depth interviews for Internet news stations have been done for *My Radio Dot Com*, a U.S.-based operation, and BCTV's new *Internet News Desk*.

Lynne Ricker

Lynne Ricker is a senior instructor in the Haskayne School of Business at the University of Calgary. For the past 25 years, Lynne has taught introductory marketing, marketing strategy, marketing communications, and retail management. Her business experience includes work in the fields of retail management, professional services marketing, training, and communications. As a senior partner with Piper Hill Marketing, she worked with clients ranging from small local businesses to large international corporations. Since spending time as the Associate Dean responsible for several undergraduate degree programs, Lynne's publications have focused on managing undergraduate education and integrating theory with practice in business education in publications such as the *Journal of Management Education*. She is also the co-author of a retailing textbook. Lynne does regular interviews with media such as *The Globe and Mail*, *Calgary Herald*, *National Post*, CBC Radio, *Marketing Magazine*, CBC TV, *Alberta Venture*, *Calgary Inc.*, and other specialized publications such as *Progressive Grocer*.

Brief Contents

Contents

CHAPTER ONE

Marketing for Consumers, Firms, and Society

CHAPTER TWO

Strategic Planning

CHAPTER NINE

Product Planning for Goods and Services

CHAPTER TEN

Product Management and New-Product Development

CHAPTER ELEVEN

Place—Distribution Management

CHAPTER TWELVE

Retailing and Wholesaling

CHAPTER THIRTEEN

Promotion—Integrated Marketing Communications

CHAPTER FOURTEEN

Personal Selling

CHAPTER FIFTEEN

Advertising, Publicity, and Sales Promotion

CHAPTER SIXTEEN

Pricing Objectives and Policies

Preface

The Twelfth Canadian edition of *Basic Marketing* is all about new beginnings: a new author team, a new design, a new streamlined text. However, this has not been undertaken at the expense of the elements that have made *Basic Marketing* such a successful brand. Quite the contrary. Using a managerial approach, this new edition builds on the pioneering framework of the "four Ps." This framework has been so well received because it organizes the best ideas about marketing in such a way that readers can both understand and apply them. The unifying focus of these ideas has always been on how to make marketing decisions that a manager must make in deciding what customers to focus on and how best to meet their needs.

This book is about marketing and marketing strategy planning. And, at its essence, marketing strategy planning is about figuring out how to do a superior job of satisfying customers. This is a point of view we take very seriously, and we have created this edition to satisfy your needs.

What's New—the Macro View

The four Ps framework, managerial orientation, and strategy planning focus have proved to be foundation pillars that are remarkably robust for supporting developments in the field and innovations in the text. This new edition of *Basic Marketing* features a number of innovative changes designed to provide a flexible, high-quality text that allows instructors and students to accomplish their learning objectives including:

- Leaner, crisper coverage throughout the whole text—resulting in fewer chapters, and significantly less text material to read while maintaining interesting and thorough coverage of all of the basics of marketing strategy planning.
- Extensive revisions to the first three chapters, to introduce marketing orientation and customer value earlier and to introduce the marketing strategy planning process in the context of an integrative model that sets the stage for the rest of the text.
- A sharper focus, throughout the text, on how the strategy planning process should lead to decisions about a target market and marketing mix that represents the best opportunity and competitive advantage for the firm and superior value for

consumers. In today's dynamic marketing environment it's not enough to simply figure out an attractive opportunity and an effective marketing mix. Our objective is to prepare students to analyze marketing situations, zero in on the target market, figure out the best blend of the four Ps for the firm, and develop exceptional marketing strategies.

- A commitment to clear and interesting communication to make it easy, interesting, and fast for students to grasp the key concepts of marketing, including careful explanations to ensure that students understand the "basics" of marketing strategy planning.
- A wider variety of examples to back up the strategy and theory, because this variety reinforces the point that effective marketing is critical to all organizations. Examples have been drawn from a diverse range of large and small firms, profit and nonprofit organizations, organizations that have moved to e-commerce and those that have found other ways to innovate, Canadian and international settings, services, and ideas or "causes," as well as physical goods, established products, and new technologies.
- Special attention on changes taking place in today's dynamic markets. Some textbooks treat "special" topics like those listed below in separate chapters. We deliberately avoid doing that because we are convinced that treating such topics separately leads to an unfortunate compartmentalization of ideas. We think that they are too important to be isolated. So, we have chosen instead to interweave and illustrate these topics throughout the text to emphasize that marketing thinking is crucial in all aspects of our society and economy. Therefore, throughout every chapter of the text we have integrated discussion and examples of:

- Lifetime customer value and equity
- Best practices in marketing, and how to avoid the mistakes of death-wish marketing (including errors and omissions all too common among many failed dot-com operators)
- Effective e-commerce innovations and changes in marketing over the Internet
- The costs and benefits of different approaches for customer acquisition and retention

- Relationship building in marketing
- Services marketing
- Social impacts of marketing and macro-marketing
- The importance of providing superior customer value as the means to achieve customer satisfaction and competitive advantage
- International perspectives
- Ethical issues and social impacts of marketing

- Similarly, we have also integrated new material on many important and fast-evolving topics. For example:

  - Multichannel marketing
  - Integrated marketing communications, direct-response promotion, and customer-initiated interactive marketing communications
  - Promotional campaigns that build "buzz" among consumers ("buzz" and "viral" marketing)
  - Impact of economic fluctuations, changes in international exchange rates, and other topics central to how the economy impacts marketing
  - The growth of business-to-business (B2B) exchanges on the Web and the expanding use of reverse auctions and interactive bidding
  - The circumstances when using a Web site for direct distribution or dual distribution makes sense and when it doesn't
  - The expanding role of sales technologies and self-service technology
  - The increasing channel power of large retail chains
  - Competitor analysis and how to develop a competitive advantage
  - How to use flexible pricing and evaluate price sensitivity
  - Marketing control, including marketing cost analysis

A Look at Each Chapter

The emphasis of *Basic Marketing* is on marketing strategy planning. Eighteen chapters introduce the important concepts in marketing management and help the student see marketing through the eyes of the marketing manager. The organization of the chapters and topics is carefully planned, but we took special care in writing so that:

- It is possible to rearrange and use the chapters in many different sequences to fit different needs. For example, some professors prefer to cover marketing research after covering the marketing mix chapters, and this reordering should cause students no problem. Similarly, some professors

prefer to cover Price topics (Chapters 16 and 17) immediately after introducing Product concepts (Chapters 9 and 10), or to save the Place chapter until other marketing mix decisions have been covered. *Basic Marketing* is carefully written to be flexible in this regard, so changes in order can be made quite readily.

- All of the topics and chapters fit together into a clear, overall framework for the marketing strategy and planning process.

The chapters of the text fall into three broad groupings. The first 8 chapters introduce marketing and a broad view of the marketing strategy planning process. They cover topics such as segmentation, differentiation, the marketing environment, and buyer behaviour, as well as how marketing information systems and research provide information about these forces to improve marketing decisions. The next 9 chapters go into the details of planning the four Ps, with specific attention to the key strategy decisions in each area. Then, the final chapter concludes the coverage with consideration of overarching topics such as implementation and control (including quality management), and an assessment of marketing's challenges and opportunities.

Chapter 1—Marketing for Consumers, Firms, and Society deals with the important role of marketing—focusing not only on how a marketing orientation guides a business or nonprofit organization in the process of providing superior value to customers but also on the role of macro-marketing and how a market-directed economy shapes choices and quality of life for consumers.

Chapter 2—Strategic Planning builds on these ideas with a focus on the marketing strategy planning process and why it involves narrowing down to selection of a specific target market and blending the four Ps into a marketing mix to meet the needs of those customers. With that foundation in place, the chapter introduces an integrative model of the marketing strategy planning process that serves as an organizing framework for the rest of the text.

Chapter 3—Segmenting and Positioning Market Strategy shows how analysis of the market and external market environment relate to segmentation and differentiation decisions as well as the criteria for narrowing down to a specific target market and marketing mix. This strategic view alerts students to the importance of evaluating opportunities in the external environments affecting marketing—and these are discussed in **Chapter 4—Evaluating Market Opportunities**. This chapter also highlights the critical role of screening criteria in narrowing down from possible opportunities to those that the firm will pursue.

You have to understand customers to understand marketing, segment markets, and satisfy target market needs. So the next three chapters take a closer look at customers. **Chapter 5—Demographics, Consumers, and Markets** introduces the demographic dimensions of the global consumer market and provides up-to-date coverage on important geodemographic trends. The next chapter, **Chapter 6—Consumer Behaviour**, studies the behavioural aspects of the final consumer market. **Chapter 7—Marketing to Businesses and Organizations** looks at how business and organizational customers—like manufacturers, channel members, and government purchasers—are using e-commerce and how they are similar to and different from final consumers.

Chapter 8—Improving Decisions with Marketing Information is a contemporary view of getting information, through marketing information systems and marketing research, for marketing management planning. This chapter includes discussion of how information technology—ranging from intranets and speedy collection of market research data—is transforming the marketing manager's job. This sets the stage for discussions in later chapters about how research and marketing information improve each area of marketing strategy planning.

The next group of chapters, Chapters 9 to 17, is concerned with developing a marketing mix out of the four Ps: Product, Place (involving channels of distribution, logistics, and distribution customer service), Promotion, and Price. These chapters are concerned with developing the "right" Product and making it available at the "right" Place with the "right" Promotion and the "right" Price to satisfy target customers and still meet the objectives of the business. These chapters are presented in an integrated, analytical way—as part of the overall framework for the marketing strategy planning process—so students' thinking about planning marketing strategies develops logically.

Chapter 9—Product Planning for Goods and Services and **Chapter 10—Product Management and New-Product Development** focus on product planning for goods and services as well as new-product development and the different strategy decisions that are required at different stages of the product life cycle. We emphasize the value of developing really new products that propel a firm to competitive advantage and long-run profitable growth.

Chapter 11 and Chapter 12 focus on Place. **Chapter 11—Place—Distribution Management** introduces decisions a manager must make about using direct distribution (for example, selling from the firm's own Web site) or working with other firms in a channel of distribution. We put special emphasis on the need for channel members to cooperate and coordinate to better meet the needs of customers. This chapter also focuses on the fast-changing arena of logistics and the strides that firms are

making in using e-commerce to reduce the costs of storing and transporting products while improving the distribution service they provide customers. **Chapter 12—Retailing and Wholesaling** provides a clear picture of retailers, wholesalers, and their strategy planning—including exchanges taking place via the Internet. This composite chapter helps students see why the big changes taking place in retailing are reshaping the channel systems for many consumer products.

Chapters 13 to 15 deal with Promotion. These chapters build on the concepts of integrated marketing communications, direct-response promotion, and customer-initiated digital communication, which are introduced in **Chapter 13—Promotion—Integrated Marketing Communications**. Then, **Chapter 14—Personal Selling** deals with the role of personal selling and sales technology in the promotion blend. **Chapter 15—Advertising, Publicity, and Sales Promotion** covers advertising and sales promotion, including the ways that managers are taking advantage of the Internet and other highly targeted media to communicate more effectively and efficiently.

Chapters 16 and 17 deal with Price. **Chapter 16—Pricing Objectives and Policies** focuses on pricing objectives and policies, including use of information technology to implement flexible pricing, pricing in the channel, and the use of discounts, allowances, and other variations from a list price. **Chapter 17—Price Setting in the Business World** covers cost-oriented and demand-oriented pricing approaches and how they fit in today's competitive environments. The careful coverage of marketing costs helps equip students to deal with the cost-conscious firms they will join.

Chapter 18—Marketing Plans and Controls offers up-to-date coverage of how information technology is reshaping marketing implementation and control. This chapter also details how quality management approaches can improve implementation, including implementation of better customer service. Finally, this chapter reinforces the integrative nature of marketing management and reviews the marketing strategy planning process that leads to creative marketing plans and programs.

The text concludes with two appendices to aid student learning with what has often been deemed particularly challenging aspects of marketing—math and economics. **Appendix A—Economics Fundamentals** explains some of the economist's tools including demand and supply curves, elasticity and inelasticity of demand and supply, and competitive market situations. **Appendix B—Marketing Arithmetic** discusses some of the accountant's tools including operating statements, operating ratios, stockturn rates, markups, markdowns, and ROI and ROA.

PEDAGOGY—HELPING STUDENTS UNDERSTAND MARKETING STRATEGY AND MAKE BETTER MARKETING DECISIONS

Visual Elements—Exhibits, Photos, Ads, and Illustrations

We've already mentioned the new design for the Twelfth Canadian edition of *Basic Marketing*, which includes hundreds of new photographs and ads from Canadian and international sources. We have placed these annotated photos and ads near the concepts they illustrate to provide a visual reminder of ideas and to show vividly how they apply in the current business world. We've also created many new exhibits—conceptual organizers, charts, and tables—and updated pieces from past editions, all with a fresh new design. The aim of all of this revising, refining, editing, and illustrating is to make important concepts and points even clearer to you. We want to make sure that you get a really good feel for a market-directed system and how you can help it, and some company, run better.

Exhibit 1-5 The Canadian Marketing Association Code of Ethics

CODE OF ETHICS

The Canadian Marketing Association (CMA) sets ethical standards of practice and prescribes a code of professional conduct for its members. Ethical issues in marketing are wide ranging and apply to consumer and business-to-business marketing as well as nonprofit organizations and international marketing. Exhibit 1-6 shows just a few of the major ethical issues in marketing. The CMA's Web site features their Code of Ethics and Standards of Practice in its entirety. Topics (which are edited for brevity) include the following:

Overarching Ethical Principles

1. Personal Information Practices

Marketers must promote responsible and transparent personal information management practices.

2. Truthfulness

Marketing communications must be clear and truthful. Marketers must not knowingly make a representation to a consumer or business that is false or misleading.

3. Campaign Limitations

- Marketers must not participate in any campaign involving the disparagement or exploitation of any person or group on the grounds of race, colour, ethnicity, religion, national origin, gender, sexual orientation, marital status or age.
- Marketers must not participate in the dissemination of unsolicited material that is sexually explicit, vulgar or indecent in nature.
- Marketers must not participate in the dissemination of any material that unduly, gratuitously and without merit exploits sex, horror, mutilation, torture, cruelty, violence or hate.
- Marketers must not knowingly exploit the credulity, lack of knowledge or inexperience of any consumer.

Universal Marketing Practices

- Support for Claims: Test or survey data referred to in any marketing communication must be reliable, accurate and current and must support the specific claim being made.
- Disguise: Marketers must not engage in marketing communications in the guise of one purpose when the intent is for a different purpose like selling a product or obtaining a donation.
- Testimonials: Testimonials and endorsements must be authorized by the person or organization quoted, positioned as opinion, not fact (unless supported by valid research) and not taken out of context.
- Availability: Unless the promotional material advises the consumer or business of limited stock, marketers must have adequate quantities to meet reasonably foreseeable demand.

- Comparative Advertising: Comparisons included in marketing communications must be factual, verifiable and not misleading.
- Complaints: Marketers must establish and communicate fair, effective and timely procedures to handle complaints from consumers or businesses.

Protection of Personal Privacy

CMA Members must obey federal and provincial privacy laws that affect how information about consumers is collected, stored, reviewed and transferred. Because of rising concerns about the right to privacy, CMA also requires its members to comply with their Do Not Contact Service for consumers who don't want mail, fax and phone calls from marketers.

Special Considerations in Marketing to Kids and Teenagers

Teens and children have special status under CMA regulations. Information can't be collected without consent from parents. Marketing to children must not exploit children's credulity, lack of experience or sense of loyalty. Marketing to teenagers must not unduly exploit teenagers' impressionability, or susceptibility to peer pressure and members must use language that is age appropriate when marketing to teens and kids.

Sub-Disciplines and Specific Marketing Practices

- E-commerce: Online marketers must, provide a clear order confirmation process with a separate e-mail to confirm the customer's order. An online "click-through" mechanism for consumers to contact the marketer must also be provided.
- Contests: Marketers must present all terms and conditions of a contest in a manner that is clear, visible, easy to find, easy to read and easy to understand.
- Public Relations (PR): Firms providing PR services must disclose the identity of their client when operating in the public domain.

Media-Specific Standards of Practice

The CMA Code requires truthfulness and transparency in all media communications. This means for example that infomercials and ads in print media are clearly identified.

CMA members must respect the CMA's "do not contact" lists and are prohibited from sending unsolicited faxes, text messages and e-mails. Other marketers can subscribe to the lists but are not obliged to follow them.

Members who refuse to abide by CMA's Code of Ethics face the potential risk of having their membership revoked.

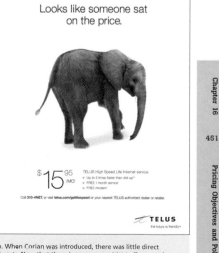

DuPont Corian, a solid countertop material, was costly to develop. When Corian was introduced, there was little direct competition and a premium price helped to recover development costs. Now that there is more competition, discounted prices are sometimes available. Telus has reduced their price for high-speed Internet service to gain market share.

Chapter-Opening Vignettes—Fourteen New Vignettes!

Each chapter of *Basic Marketing* opens with a short case study designed specifically to highlight real-life examples of the specific marketing decision areas covered in the chapter. From Starbucks to Roots, BlackBerry to Ben & Jerry's, each chapter-opening case features a company you know or product that you use.

Special Case Reports—Revised and Updated for this Edition!

Each chapter features a special case report in a highlighted box that illustrates how companies handle a topic of special interest covered in the chapter. These examples and scenarios give you a close-up look at how marketing decisions are made in the real world.

Marketing Ethically—NEW!

In keeping with our philosophy of integrating key topics like ethics and social responsibility, each of the four Ps chapters (9–17) has a boxed feature that discusses the ethics of marketing practices and asks you how you feel about how marketers are behaving. Topics include: privacy, buzz marketing, the uses of customer information, the tactics used for information gathering, knock-offs stealing market share from legitimate brands, and outsourcing goods to sweatshops.

MARKETING ETHICALLY

Legitimate companies spend considerable amounts of money in promoting their brand names. Consumers put trust in a brand name such as Sony or BlackBerry or Roots. Counterfeit products take advantage of the value of brand names by using them on their products.

Counterfeit goods can legally enter Canada if they are declared, due to a loophole in the country's laws. This has upset trading partners because Canada has the most lax laws in the developed world when it comes to protecting consumers and markets from bogus goods. Those selling legitimate goods face unfair competition from those selling marked-down fakes. There's also the issue of public health and safety. Recent seizures in Canada include expired baby food with counterfeit best-before dates attached, counterfeit, brand name batteries containing elevated levels of dangerous chemicals, children's stuffed toys filled with hair and fibreglass, and safety boots with inadequate protection and fake safety logos. The trade of fake goods is estimated to cost Canada $20 billion to $30 billion a year.

Anthony Toderian, spokesman for the Canadian Standards Association, says the traditional concept of counterfeiting has expanded from simply knock-off T-shirts and handbags to medicines, cleaning solutions, electronics, and toothbrushes—basically, anything that bears a brand name. According to Toderian, Metropolitan centres, such as Vancouver and Toronto, are the hottest markets for counterfeit products.

Knock-offs fall under two categories, counterfeit and copyright infringement, according to Vancouver lawyer Michael Manson, a partner at law firm Smart and Biggar. Exact duplicates are considered counterfeits, and violators can be brought to Canadian court under either criminal or civil law, he said. Goods like the "oK" watches, which bear a striking resemblance to Calvin Klein's "cK" logo but are slightly different, are copyright infringements. Infringements are typically not criminal violations, but can be taken to court under civil law. It's illegal to make, sell, and use fake products, and punishments range from jail terms to fines or statutory damages up to $20,000 per infringement, according to Manson. But he points out that the law is difficult to enforce, noting that Canadian police and customs officials lack resources, while Canadian legislation is weak. Would it bother you to purchase a fake Rolex watch? Why or why not?[15]

Internet Exercises

The Internet Exercises in each chapter of the text provide you with a great opportunity to see how marketing concepts are being applied on the Internet and serve as an excellent basis for in-class discussions. These exercises are integrated with the discussion of important ideas as they are developed, so you learn about marketing while surfing interesting Web sites.

INTERNET EXERCISE

Consumers interested in finding deals such as coupons, special offers, and more can check out the Frugalshopper Web site (www.frugalshopper.ca). Frugalshopper offers freebies, coupons, and contests as well as many sponsored links to other deals. For example, HBC has a link via dealsoutlet.ca. Check out a few links to see what kinds of deals you can find. Do you think the password system used for coupons on the site will prevent coupon fraud?

End-of-Chapter Questions and Problems

These questions and problems are a great way for you to review what you have learned in the chapter and to apply that knowledge to real-world marketing situations.

www.mcgrawhill.ca/olc/perreault

QUESTIONS AND PROBLEMS

1. Discuss the concept of a marketing information system and why it is important for marketing managers to be involved in planning the system.

2. In your own words, explain why a decision support system (DSS) can add to the value of a marketing information system. Give an example of how a decision support system might help.

3. If a firm's intranet and marketing decision support system do not include a search engine, would they still be useful to a marketing manager? Why?

4. Discuss how output from a marketing information system (MIS) might differ from the output of a typical marketing research department for a company like Rogers Video.

5. Discuss some of the likely problems facing the marketing manager in a small firm that has just purchased a personal computer with a cable modem to search the Internet for information on competitors' marketing plans.

6. Explain the key characteristics of the scientific method and show why these are important to managers concerned with research.

7. How is the situation analysis different from the data collection step? Can both these steps be done at the same time to obtain answers sooner? Is this wise?

8. Distinguish between primary data and secondary data and illustrate how Bell Canada in Ontario would use the data.

Computer-Aided Problems

Unique to *Basic Marketing*, the computer-aided problems have been designed to deepen your understanding about specific marketing concepts, theories, and frameworks. And, because the exercises require you to work with marketing "numbers," you will see how they relate to the details of the situation and the marketing problem. The problems help you realize that marketing managers don't make decisions just on hunches and intuition, but with careful analysis of strategies. With *Basic Marketing*'s computer-aided problems, you are learning to work with the type of analysis that managers often use.

www.mcgrawhill.ca/olc/perreault

COMPUTER-AIDED PROBLEM

5. Demographic Analysis

RESOURCE REMINDER

Stylco Inc., is a producer of specialty clothing. To differentiate its designs and appeal to its Chinese-Canadian target market, Stylco uses authentic Asian materials. Originally, it just focused on designs targeted at adults in the 35–44 age range. However, in the late 1990s, when sales to these middle-aged adults started to level off, Stylco added a more conservative line of clothes for older consumers. Most buyers of the conservative styles are in the 45–59 age group.

Stylco has focused on distributing its products through select fashion boutiques in metropolitan market areas with the highest concentrations of Chinese-Canadian consumers. This approach has reduced Stylco's personal selling expense; as a result, however, only a percentage of the total Chinese population is served by current Stylco retailers. For example, about half of the consumers in the 35–44 age group are in the market areas served by Stylco retailers.

In the fall of 2006, Naomi Davis, Stylco's marketing manager, read an article about the "greying of Canadians." This left her wondering how shifts in the age distribution might affect her market and sales.

To get a long-run view of these trends, she looked at census data on Chinese consumers by age group. She also looked up estimates of the expected percent rate of change in the size of each group through the year 2007. By multiplying these rates by the size her target markets were in 2000, she can estimate how large they are likely to be in the year 2007. Further, from analysis of past sales data, she knows that the number of units the firm sells is directly proportional to the size of each age group. Specifically, the ratio of units sold to target market size has been about 5 units per 1,000 people (that is, a ratio of .005). Finally, she determined the firm's average unit profit for each of the lines. To see how changes in population are likely to affect Stylco units sold and future profits from each line, Davis programmed all of these data, and the relationships discussed above, into a spreadsheet.

a. Briefly compare the profit data for 2000 and estimated profit for 2007 as it appears on the initial spreadsheet. What is the likely reason for the expected shift? What are the implications of these and other data in the spreadsheet for Stylco's marketing strategy planning?

b. The rate of growth or decline for different Chinese-Canadian age groups tends to vary from one geographic region to another. Davis thinks that in the market areas that Stylco serves the size of the 35–44 age group may decrease by as much as 10 to 12 percent by 2007. However, the government estimates that the decline of the 35–44 age group for the whole country will only be about –1.7 percent. If the decline in the target market size for Davis' market areas turns out to be –1.7 percent rather than the 10.1 she has assumed, what is the potential effect on profits from the young adult line? On overall profits?

c. Because more firms are paying attention to fast-growing ethnic markets, Davis thinks competition may increase in lines targeted at affluent Chinese Canadians in the 45–59 age group. Because of price competition, the line targeted at this group already earns a lower average profit per unit. Further, as more firms compete for this business, she thinks that her "ratio of units sold to market size" may decrease. Use the what-if analysis to prepare a table showing how percent of profit from this group, as well as total profit, might change as the ratio of units sold to market size varies between a minimum of .001 and a maximum of .010. Explain the implications to the firm.

If you want to read the cases and view the video cases that accompany this chapter, visit the *Basic Marketing* Online Learning Centre at: **www.mcgrawhill.ca/olc/perreault**. Along with these cases and video cases, the OLC also has the software and user guide for this chapter's Computer-Aided Problem, as well as exercises, quizzes, articles, links, and other *interactive* content that will help you with your studies.

Student Support

Student Online Learning Centre (OLC)

Visit the OLC at www.mcgrawhill.ca/olc/perreault for a complete set of learning and study tools that will help you improve your grades in Marketing. The OLC includes self-grading quizzes and flashcards, marketing plan and career resources, Marketing Cases, streaming Video Cases, the software that accompanies the Computer-Aided Problems in the text, access to *Marketing Magazine*, the student Integrator, and E-STAT. You will also find a series of podcasts featuring Canadian marketing professionals talking about what they do, and how the marketing strategy you have learned about in the text is implemented in the real world.

Marketing Magazine **Marketing**

Get free access to *Marketing Magazine*'s archives with purchase of the text. This real-world complement to *Basic Marketing* is a great way to keep up to date with what is happening in the Canadian marketing scene.

E-STAT **Σ-STAT**

E-STAT is an educational resource designed by Statistics Canada and made available to Canadian educational institutions. Using 450,000 current CANSIM (Canadian Socio-economic Information Management System) Time Series and the most recent—as well as historical—census data, E-STAT lets you bring data to life in colourful graphs and maps. Access to E-STAT is made available to purchasers of this book, via the *Basic Marketing* Online Learning Centre, by special agreement between McGraw-Hill Ryerson and Statistics Canada. The Online Learning Centre provides additional information.

Student Integrator **integrator**

Improve your grades! The Student Integrator is a tool that will help you find all the student support material that relates to a particular learning objective in *Basic Marketing*, Twelfth Canadian Edition. Access the student integrator at www.mcgrawhill.ca/olc/perreault.

Instructor Support

Basic Marketing, Twelfth Canadian Edition, offers a complete, integrated, and updated supplements package for instructors to meet your needs no matter what your teaching style.

Superior Service

Your **Integrated Learning Sales Specialist** is a McGraw-Hill Ryerson representative who has the experience, product knowledge, training, and support to help you assess and integrate all of the *Basic Marketing* supplements, technology, and services into your course for optimum teaching and learning performance. Whether it's using our test bank software, helping your students improve their grades, or putting your entire course online, your *i*Learning Sales Specialist is there to help you do it. Contact your local *i*Learning Sales Specialist today to learn how to maximize all of McGraw-Hill Ryerson's resources!

*i*Learning Services Program

McGraw-Hill Ryerson offers a unique *i*Services package designed for Canadian faculty. Our mission is to equip providers of higher education with superior tools and resources required for excellence in teaching. For additional information visit http://www.mcgrawhill.ca/highereducation/iservices.

Teaching, Technology, & Learning Conference Series

The educational environment has changed tremendously in recent years, and McGraw-Hill Ryerson continues to be committed to helping you acquire the skills you need to succeed in this new milieu. Our innovative Teaching, Technology, & Learning Conference Series brings faculty together from across Canada with 3M Teaching Excellence award winners to share teaching and learning best practices in a collaborative and stimulating environment. Pre-conference workshops on general topics, such as teaching large classes and technology integration, are also offered. We will also work with you at your own institution to customize workshops that best suit the needs of your faculty at your institution.

Instructor Supplements

Instructor's Online Learning Centre (OLC)

The OLC at www.mcgrawhill.ca/olc/perreault includes a password-protected Web site for instructors. The site offers downloadable supplements, including an Instructor's Manual, Microsoft® PowerPoint® slides, Cases, streaming Video Cases, and Case Teaching Notes, as well as access to the integrator, *Marketing Magazine*, and

PageOut—the McGraw-Hill Ryerson Web site development centre.

Instructor's CD-ROM

The CD-ROM contains the Instructor's Manual, Test Bank in Rich Text Format, Computerized Test Bank, and Microsoft® PowerPoint® slides:

- *Instructor's Manual*
  The Instructor's Manual contains perspectives on teaching each chapter. These include summaries of the chapter's boxed features, suggested answers to the end-of-chapter review and questions, and comments on and suggested answers to the Learning Aid problems and the Computer-Aided Problems that accompany each chapter.

- *Test Bank in Rich Text Format*
  The Test Bank contains an extensive array of multiple-choice questions and essay items categorized by level of learning (definition, conceptual, application) and learning objective.

- *Computerized Test Bank*
  This flexible and easy-to-use electronic testing program allows instructors to create tests from book-specific items. It accommodates a wide range of question types and instructors may add their own questions. Multiple versions of the test can be created and printed.

- *Microsoft® PowerPoint® Slides*
  These robust presentations offer high-quality visuals to bring key marketing concepts to life.

Video Case Studies

A unique series of contemporary marketing cases are available on DVD, as well as for download from the Online Learning Centre.

Marketing Cases

Twenty-five cases can be found on the Online Learning Centre, providing even more opportunities to bring the course content to life for students.

Case and Video Case Teaching Notes

This manual, available for download from the Online Learning Centre, includes helpful teaching suggestions for the cases and video cases.

The Integrator

Keyed to the chapters and learning objectives of *Basic Marketing*, Twelfth Canadian edition, the Integrator ties together all of the elements in your resource package, guiding you to where you'll find corresponding coverage in each of the related support package components—be it the Instructor's Manual, Computerized Test Bank, PowerPoint® slides, Case Studies, or Online Learning Centre. Link to the Integrator via the Online Learning Centre at www.mcgrawhill.ca/olc/perreault.

Course Management

Visit www.mhhe.com/pageout to create a Web page for your course using our resources. PageOut is the McGraw-Hill Ryerson Web site development centre. This Web page-generation software is free to adopters and is designed to help faculty create an online course, complete with assignments, quizzes, links to relevant Web sites, and more—all in a matter of minutes.

In addition, content cartridges are available for the course management systems **WebCT and Blackboard**. These platforms provide instructors with user friendly, flexible teaching tools. Please contact your local McGraw-Hill Ryerson *i*Learning Sales Specialist for details.

Team Learning Assistant

The Team Learning Assistant (TLA) is a Web-based set of tools that promotes effective classroom teaming for faculty and students alike. TLA is organized into two toolboxes, one for students and one for faculty. The faculty toolbox contains teaching notes, helpful hints, and proven materials, designed for instructors who use teams in their courses. The professor determines how students will use the student toolbox, and then are able to track student performance data generated by each class. Located at http://www.mhhe-tla.com, the Team Learning Assistant features such important advice on integrating teams into the syllabus and grading process, the importance of having a team contract and how to write one, details on peer and instructor evaluations, as well as meeting and conflict management.

Acknowledgments

The Twelfth Canadian edition of *Basic Marketing* has been influenced and improved through the input of a number of individuals and we would like to acknowledge their efforts here. Lynne would like to thank her long-time colleagues Debi Andrus and Carolyn Guichon for their inspired ideas and suggestions.

Many of the improvements, updates, and additions to this edition were stimulated by feedback from a number of colleagues from around the country. The following list of those who participated is substantial because we tried to practice what we preach. Rather than produce a text we thought you might like, we set out to directly involve your participation so that we could offer a book that reflected your product preferences. Kind of like letting the customer help design the car. Our gratitude to the following designers of this book:

Onur Bodur, Concordia University

Brahm Canzer, John Abbott College

Alan Chappelle, Malaspina University-College

Mark Cleveland, University of Western Ontario

Brad Davis, Wilfrid Laurier University

Craig Dyer, Red River College

Robert Grieve, Loyalist College

Dwight Heinrichs, University of Regina

Sarah Holding, Malaspina University-College

Ruth Jaglowitz, Seneca College

Marianne Marando, Seneca College

Brent McKenzie, University of Western Ontario

Zahaf Mehdi, Lakehead University

Kalyani Menon, Wilfrid Laurier University

Don Shiner, Mount St. Vincent University

David Smith, Lakehead University

Taras Wasyliw, Red River College

Lisa Watson, University of Regina

As with any major project there is always a cast of unsung heroines and heroes without whom progress would be impossible. The McGraw-Hill Ryerson staff has provided outstanding guidance and help throughout the whole process. Beginning with the family team of Leanna MacLean as Senior Sponsoring Editor through Jeff MacLean, Director of Sales, our interactions with McGraw-Hill Ryerson have been productive and efficient. In between there has been a host of professionals who ensured things went smoothly. First to start was Denise Foote, Senior Development Editor. Then, Tracey Haggert as Freelance Developmental Editor was indispensable in moving the whole text along in record time against some pretty tight deadlines. Thanks also go to Christina Beamish, Photo Researcher, for tracking down and managing many of the visuals that appear in the text. Next came Kim Fussell as *i*Learning Sales Specialist, and Evan Turner, Copy Editor, who carefully searched for those loose ends and tied them up. Margaret Henderson as Senior Supervising Editor did a great job of organizing the myriad details of production so that we could review our material in a timely fashion.

The Twelfth Canadian edition of *Basic Marketing* is built on the dedication of its previous authors. Certainly William Perreault and Jerome McCarthy have laboured long and hard over all those previous editions. Ken Wong put his name on the book for two editions and finally Stan Shapiro whose name is synonymous with the text after he participated in eleven previous editions. To all of you we are most grateful since our inheritance was produced by your dedication and hard work.

Finally, we would like to thank all of our colleagues who contributed to the pedagogy within the text and to those who created the supplemental materials that accompany this edition:

Scott Follows, Acadia University

Sarah Holding, Malaspina University-College

Al Juzukonis, Seneca College

Marianne Marando, Seneca College

Brent McKenzie, University of Western Ontario

Harvey Skolnick, Sheridan College Institute of Technology and Advanced Learning

Lindsay Meredith

Lynne Ricker

Basic

MARKETING

A Global-Managerial Approach

**WHEN YOU FINISH
THIS CHAPTER,
YOU SHOULD**

1. Know what
   marketing is and why
   you should learn
   about it.

2. Know the marketing
   functions and why
   marketing
   specialists—including
   intermediaries and
   facilitators—develop
   to perform them.

3. Know what the
   marketing concept
   is—and how it should
   guide a firm or
   nonprofit
   organization.

4. Know how social
   responsibility and
   marketing ethics
   relate to the
   marketing concept.

Marketing for Consumers, Firms, and Society

When it's time to roll out of bed in the morning, does your Sony alarm clock wake you with a buzzer—or by playing your favourite radio station? Is the station playing rock, classical, or country music—or perhaps a Red Cross ad asking for a contribution? Will you slip into your Levi's jeans, your sweatshirt from Roots, and your Nikes, or does the day call for your Tommy Hilfiger interviewing suit? Will breakfast be Timbits from Tim Hortons or Kellogg's Frosted Flakes—made with grain from the Prairies—or some extra-large eggs and Maple Leaf bacon cooked in a Panasonic microwave oven imported from Japan? Will you mix up some Tang instant juice and brew a pot of President's Choice coffee—or is this a day to meet a friend at the local Starbucks, where you'll pay someone else to fix you a Frappuccino while you use the Internet connection to log on to sympatico.msn.ca to check your e-mail? After breakfast, will you head off to school or work in a Toyota Prius, on your Rollerblade inline skates, or on the bus that the city bought from General Motors?

When you think about it, you can't get very far into a day without bumping into marketing—and what the whole marketing system does for you. It affects every aspect of our lives—often in ways we don't even consider.

In other parts of the world, people wake up each day to different kinds of experiences. A family in China may have little choice about what food they will eat or where their clothing will come from. A consumer in a large city like Tokyo may have many choices but not be familiar with products that have names like Schneider's or Roots.

What's more, each element in the descriptions above could be viewed in more detail and through a different lens. Consider, for example, that visit to Tim Hortons or to Starbucks. How do these firms make so many customers so satisfied? Why do they come back time and again when they could get a cup of coffee almost anywhere—and without the lines you see at Tim's

or the prices you see at Starbucks? Do loyal customers use the Starbucks card because it allows them to participate in sweepstakes and get e-mail notices of in-store promotions and new products? Or is it because the card makes it fast and easy to order and pay? Why does Starbucks offer wi-fi at many locations—and, by the way, who dreamed up the idea of calling that tasty icy thing a Frappuccino? In the world of advertising, how did Tim Hortons manage to make "Roll up the rim to win" a household phrase in Canada. Twenty years ago, Starbucks was just another tiny company in Seattle; now it operates over 5,000 coffee bars, has expanded into distribution through supermarkets, and is one of the best-known brand names in the world (yes, even in Tokyo). Tim Hortons started out as a little operation in 1964 and has grown into a classic Canadian icon that has now expanded into the U.S. market as well. If this is such a simple (and profitable) business idea, why didn't somebody else think of it earlier? And if you were going to build your own marketing success, what would it be and how would you do it?[1]

In this text, we'll answer questions like these. In this chapter, you'll see what marketing is all about and why it's important to you as a consumer. We'll also explore why it is so crucial to the success of individual firms and nonprofit organizations and the impact that it has on the quality of life in different societies.

MARKETING—WHAT'S IT ALL ABOUT?

Marketing is more than selling or advertising

Many people think that marketing means "selling" or "advertising." It's true that these are parts of marketing. But *marketing is much more than selling and advertising.*

Why the wide variety of bicycles?

To illustrate some of the other important things that are included in marketing, think about all the bicycles being peddled with varying degrees of energy by cyclists around the world. Most of us don't make our own bicycles. Instead, they are made by firms like Devinci (http://www.devinci.com/), Rocky Mountain (http://www.bikes.com/index.aspx), and Oryx (http://www.oryxbicycles.ca/2004/).

Most bikes were originally designed to do one thing—get the rider from point "A" to point "B." Things changed however as marketers realized people were using bicycles in different ways and for more than just transportation. Road bikes like CCM gave way to racing bikes designed for speed, BMX bikes for trick riding, and mountain bikes intended for rugged trail riding. You can find bicycles in the $100 range at Canadian Tire or custom-made machines that cost well over $8000—more than some used cars.

A whole new world of accessories has developed as well since they are sold in conjunction with the bicycles. Everything from clothing and mountain bike armour to chariot carriers for babies are sold as complementary products to the bicycle. Type http://www.canadianmade.com/bikes.htm into your browser and look at the shopping list.

Below are just a few of the marketing decisions that have to be made before and after a firm sells a bike.

1. Analyze the needs of potential buyers and find out how they intend to use the bike. Do they want a downhill or a cross-country mountain bike? The uses are different so the designs have to be different as well.
2. Predict what types of bikes—handlebar styles, types of wheels, brakes, and frames—different customers want and decide which groups the firm will try to satisfy. Sometimes it is dangerous to target everybody in the market because you may end up producing a product that appeals to none of them.
3. Estimate how many of the potential customers want to purchase bicycles and when. Bicycles are a seasonal product so the firm needs the right amount of inventory for the start of the spring season but they have to sell it all by the end of fall when the season closes.

Selling and advertising are important parts of marketing, but modern marketing involves more. For example, to better satisfy its customers' needs and make travelling more enjoyable, this French railroad's service includes door-to-door delivery of the passenger's luggage. The ad says, "Your luggage is old enough to travel by itself. It's up to us to ensure you'd rather go by train "

4. Determine where in the world these bike riders are and how to get the product to them. When Cannondale became the cool product to own in the Whistler mountain bike community, demand skyrocketed and local retailers had to scramble in order to quickly increase their inventories of the brand.

5. Estimate what price buyers will pay and determine if the firm can make a profit at that price. The company can "sell a little for a lot or a lot for a little," but they have to get the price right or the customers may not buy.

6. Decide what kind of promotion should be used to tell potential customers about the firm's bikes. Would you try to sell a road bike (plus a chariot carrier for her baby) to a thirty-year-old mom the same way you would sell a heavy-duty mountain bike to a twenty-year-old male?

7. Determine what kind of warranty, parts, servicing, and Web site are needed to support the customer after the bike has been sold to them.

The above activities are not part of **production**—actually making goods or performing services. Rather, they are part of a larger process—called *marketing*—that provides needed direction for production and helps make sure that the right goods and services are produced and find their way to consumers.

You'll learn much more about marketing activities in the next chapter. For now, it's enough to see that marketing plays an essential role in providing consumers with need-satisfying goods and services and, more generally, in creating customer satisfaction. Simply put, **customer satisfaction** is the extent to which a firm fulfills a customer's needs, desires, and expectations.

MARKETING IS IMPORTANT TO YOU

Marketing is important to every consumer

As a consumer, you pay for the cost of marketing activities. In advanced economies, marketing costs comprise about 50 cents of each consumer dollar. For some goods and services, the percentage is much higher. Marketing affects almost every aspect of your daily life. All the goods and services you buy, the stores where you shop, and the radio and TV programs paid for by advertising are there because of marketing. Even your job résumé is part of a marketing campaign to sell yourself to some employer! Some courses are interesting when you take them but never relevant again once they're over. Not so with marketing—you'll be a consumer dealing with marketing for the rest of your life.

Marketing means opportunities

Another reason for studying marketing is that it offers many exciting and rewarding career opportunities. Throughout this book you will find information about opportunities in different areas of marketing.

Even if you're aiming for a nonmarketing job, knowing something about marketing will help you do your own job better. Throughout the book, we'll discuss ways that marketing relates to other functional areas. Further, marketing is important to the success of every organization. The same basic principles used to sell soap are also used to "sell" ideas, politicians, mass transportation, health care services, conservation, museums, and even colleges.[2]

Marketing affects standard of living and economic growth

An even more basic reason for studying marketing is that marketing plays a big part in economic growth and development. One key reason is that marketing encourages research and **innovation**—the development and spread of new ideas, goods, and services. As firms offer new and better ways of satisfying consumer needs, customers have more choices among products and this fosters competition for consumers' money. This competition drives down prices. Moreover, when firms develop products that really satisfy customers, fuller employment and higher incomes can result. The combination of these forces means that marketing has a big impact on consumers' standard of living—and it is important to the future of all nations.[3]

HOW SHOULD WE DEFINE MARKETING?

Micro- or macro-marketing?

In our bicycle example, we saw that a producer of bicycles has to perform many customer-related activities besides just making bikes. The same is true for an insurance company, an art museum, or a family-service agency. This supports the idea of marketing as a set of activities done by an individual organization to satisfy the customers that it serves.

In advanced economies, it takes goods and services from thousands of organizations to satisfy the many needs of society. A typical Wal-Mart supercentre carries more than 120,000 different items. A society needs some sort of marketing system to organize the efforts of all the producers and middlemen needed to satisfy the varied needs of all its citizens. So marketing is also an important social process.

INTERNET EXERCISE

You can check out the online shopping experience of Wal-Mart on the Web by going to the Wal-Mart home page (www.walmart.ca) and clicking on a tab for one of the product categories. How many different manufacturers' products are shown? Would consumers be better off if each manufacturer just sold directly from its own Web site?

So *marketing is both a set of activities performed by organizations and a social process.* In other words, marketing exists at both the micro and macro levels. Therefore, we will use two definitions of marketing—one for micro-marketing and another for

The aim of marketing is to identify customers' needs—and to meet those needs so well that the product almost sells itself.

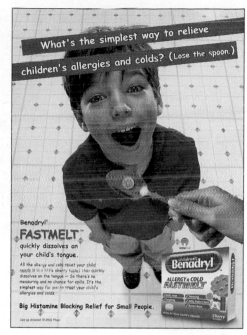

macro-marketing. Micro-marketing looks at customers and the organizations that serve them. Macro-marketing takes a broad view of our whole production–distribution system.

Micro-marketing defined

Micro-marketing is the performance of activities that seek to accomplish an organization's objectives by anticipating customer or client needs and directing a flow of need-satisfying goods and services from producer to customer or client.

Let's further explore this definition.[4]

Applies to profit and nonprofit organizations

Marketing applies to both profit and nonprofit organizations. Profit is the objective for most business firms. But other types of organizations may seek more members—or acceptance of an idea. Customers or clients may be individual consumers, business firms, nonprofit organizations, government agencies, or even foreign nations. While most customers and clients pay for the goods and services they receive, others may receive them free of charge or at a reduced cost through private or government support.

More than just persuading customers

Marketing isn't just selling and advertising. Unfortunately, many executives still think it is. They feel that the job of marketing is to "get rid of" whatever the company happens to produce. In fact, the aim of marketing is to identify customers' needs and meet those needs so well that the product almost "sells itself." This is true whether the product is a physical good, a service, or even an idea. If the whole marketing job has been done well, customers don't need much persuading. They should be ready to buy. And after they do buy, they'll be satisfied and ready to buy the same way again the next time.

Begins with assessing customer needs

Marketing should begin with assessing potential customer needs—not with the production process. Marketing should try to anticipate needs. And then marketing, rather than production, should determine what goods and services are to be developed— including decisions about product design and packaging; prices or fees; credit and collection policies; use of middlemen; transporting and storing policies; advertising and sales policies; and, after the sale, installation, customer service, warranty, and perhaps even disposal policies.

Does not do it alone	This does not mean that marketing should try to take over production, accounting, and financial activities. Rather, it means that marketing—by interpreting customers' needs—should provide direction for these activities and try to coordinate them.
Marketing involves exchanges	The idea that marketing involves a flow of need-satisfying offerings from a producer to a customer implies that there is an exchange of the need-satisfying offering for something else, such as the customer's money. Marketing focuses on facilitating exchanges. In fact, *marketing doesn't occur unless two or more parties are willing to exchange something for something else*. For example, in a **pure subsistence economy**—when each family unit produces everything it consumes—there is no need to exchange goods and services and no marketing is involved. (Although each producer–consumer unit is totally self-sufficient in such a situation, the standard of living is typically relatively low.)
Marketing means customer relationships	Keep in mind that a marketing exchange may be part of an ongoing relationship, not just a single transaction. When marketing helps everyone in a firm really meet the needs of a customer before and after a purchase, the firm doesn't just get a single sale. Rather, it has a sale and an ongoing *relationship* with the customer. Then, in the future, when the customer has the same need again—or some other need that the firm can meet—other sales will follow. Often, the marketing *flow* of need-satisfying goods and services is not just for a single transaction but rather is part of building a long-lasting relationship that benefits both the firm and the customer.

Much of Tim Hortons' and Starbucks' success discussed in our opening vignette is due to their ability to generate satisfied loyal customers who return repeatedly to buy their products. In effect, these marketers understand the role of customer relationship management, and focus not on the sale of a single cup of coffee, but rather on a long-term relationship that involves the sale of multiple products and multiple transactions with their customers. The companies win because their consistent ability to produce high levels of customer satisfaction promotes high customer loyalty that in turn fosters customer retention. Consequently, they don't have to fight to attract new customers (which is always more difficult and costly) and the customers win because they are consistently pleased with Tim Hortons' and Starbucks' brands and their outlets.

The focus of this text—management-oriented micro-marketing	Since you are probably preparing for a career in management, the main focus of this text will be on micro-marketing. We will see marketing through the eyes of the marketing manager.

The marketing ideas we will be discussing throughout this text apply to a wide variety of situations. They are important for new ventures started by one person as well as big corporations, in domestic and international markets, and regardless of whether the focus is on marketing physical goods, services, or an idea or cause. They are equally critical whether the relevant customers or clients are individual consumers, businesses, or some other type of organization. For editorial convenience, we will sometimes use the term *firm* as a shorthand way of referring to any type of organization, whether it is a political party, a religious organization, a government agency, or the like. However, to reinforce the point that the ideas apply to all types of organizations, throughout the book we will illustrate marketing concepts in a wide variety of situations.

Although micro-marketing is the primary focus of the text, marketing managers must remember that their organizations are just small parts of a larger macro-marketing system. Therefore, next we will briefly look at the macro view of marketing. Then, we will develop this idea more fully in later chapters.

MACRO-MARKETING

Macro-marketing is a social process that directs an economy's flow of goods and services from producers to consumers in a way that effectively matches supply and demand and accomplishes the objectives of society.[5]

Emphasis is on whole system

With macro-marketing we are still concerned with the flow of need-satisfying goods and services from producer to consumer. However, the emphasis with macro-marketing is not on the activities of individual organizations. Instead, the emphasis is on *how the whole marketing system works*. This includes looking at how marketing affects society and vice versa.

Separation between producers and consumers

Effective marketing in an advanced economy is difficult because producers and consumers are often separated in several ways. As Exhibit 1-1 shows, exchange between producers and consumers is hampered by spatial separation, separation in time, separation of information and values, and separation of ownership. You may love your MP3 player, but you probably don't know when or where it was produced or how it got to you. The people in the factory that produced it don't know about you or how you live.

Marketing functions help narrow the gap

The purpose of a macro-marketing system is to overcome these separations and discrepancies. The "universal functions of marketing" help do this.

The **universal functions of marketing** are buying, selling, transporting, storing, standardization and grading, financing, risk taking, and market information. They must be performed in all macro-marketing systems. *How* these functions are performed—and *by whom*—may differ among nations and economic systems. But they are needed in any macro-marketing system. Let's take a closer look at them now.

Any kind of exchange usually involves buying and selling. The **buying function** means looking for and evaluating goods and services. Canadian Tire for example, has to evaluate the quality of suppliers and their products before making the decision to carry their stock as a regular store item. The **selling function** involves promoting the product. It includes the use of personal selling, advertising, and other direct and mass selling methods. This is probably the most visible function of marketing.

The **transporting function** means the movement of goods from one place to another. Companies like Dofasco and Alcan ship their steel and aluminum products worldwide so that foreign manufacturers can convert their raw metals into finished products—which may then be transported back to Canada for sale to consumers.

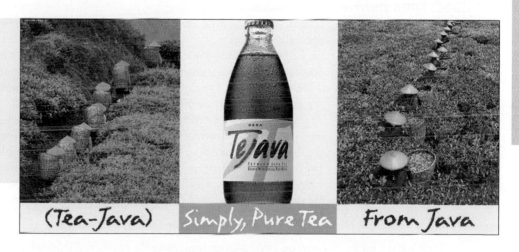

Most consumers who drink tea live far from where it is grown. To overcome this spatial separation, someone must first perform a variety of marketing functions, like standardizing and grading the tea leaves, transporting and storing them, and buying and selling them.

(Tea-Java) Simply, Pure Tea From Java

Exhibit 1-1 Marketing Facilitates Production and Consumption

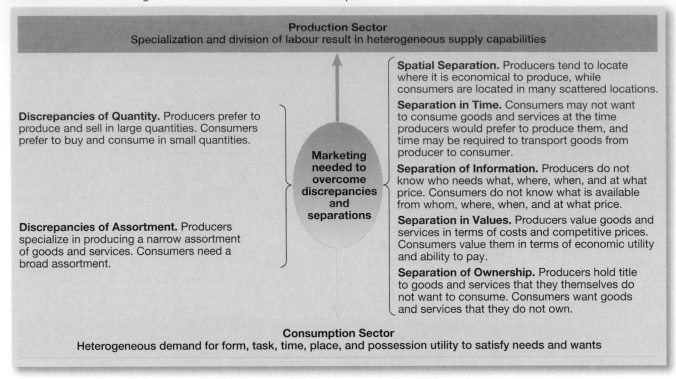

The **storing function** involves holding goods until customers need them. One look at the size of the warehouses used by a large retailer like The Bay gives you an idea of the massive inventory they need to support their retail stores.

Standardization and grading involve sorting products according to size and quality. This makes buying and selling easier because it reduces the need for inspection and sampling. **Financing** provides the necessary cash and credit to produce, transport, store, promote, sell, and buy products. **Risk taking** involves bearing the uncertainties that are part of the marketing process. A firm can never be sure that customers will want to buy its products. Products can also be damaged, stolen, or outdated. The **market information function** involves the collection, analysis, and distribution of all the information needed to plan, carry out, and control marketing activities, whether in the firm's own neighbourhood or in a market overseas.

Intermediaries help the exchange process

Producers and consumers sometimes handle some of the marketing functions themselves. However, exchanges are often easier or less expensive when a marketing specialist performs some of the marketing functions. For example, both producers and consumers may benefit when an **intermediary** (or a **middleman**)—someone who specializes in trade rather than production—plays a role in the exchange process.

A wide variety of marketing specialists may help smooth exchanges between producers, consumers, or intermediaries. These specialists are **facilitators**—firms that provide one or more of the marketing functions other than buying or selling. These facilitators include advertising agencies, marketing research firms, independent product-testing laboratories, Internet service providers, public warehouses, transporting firms, communications companies, and financial institutions (including banks). Consider for example what would happen to all that Ontario car production if the Royal Bank, CIBC, or Toronto Dominion did not provide financing for consumer car loans.

Some marketing specialists perform all the functions. Others specialize in only one or two. Marketing research firms, for example, specialize only in the market

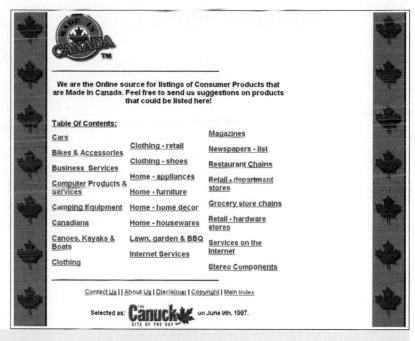

Intermediaries and facilitators develop and offer specialized services that facilitate exchange between producers and customers.

information function. Further, technology may make a certain function easier to perform. For example, the buying process may require that a customer first identify relevant sellers and where they are. Even though that might be accomplished quickly and easily with an online search of the Internet, the function hasn't been cut out.

New specialists develop to fill market needs

As the Internet example suggests, new types of marketing specialists develop or evolve when new opportunities arise for someone to make exchanges between producers and consumers more efficient or effective. Such changes can come quickly, as is illustrated by the speed with which firms have adopted e-commerce. **E-commerce** refers to exchanges between individuals or organizations—and activities that facilitate these exchanges—based on applications of information technology. New types of Internet-based intermediaries—like chapters.indigo.ca and eBay.ca—are helping to cut the costs of many marketing functions. Similarly, Internet service providers like sympatico.msn.ca and canada.aol.com that also operate Web sites are a new type of facilitator. They make it easier for many firms to satisfy their customers with Web-based information searches or transactions. Collectively, these developments have had a significant impact on the efficiency of our macro-marketing system. At the same time, many individual firms take advantage of these innovations to improve profitability and customer satisfaction.[6]

Through innovation, specialization, or economies of scale, marketing intermediaries and facilitators are often able to perform the marketing functions better—and at a lower cost—than producers or consumers can. This allows producers and consumers to spend more time on production, consumption, or other activities—including leisure.

Functions can be shifted and shared

From a macro-marketing viewpoint, all of the marketing functions must be performed by someone—an individual producer or consumer, an intermediary, a facilitator, or, in some cases, even a nation's government. Regardless of who performs the marketing functions, in general they must be performed effectively and efficiently or the performance of the whole macro-marketing system will suffer and impact the larger economic system with which it interacts.

All societies must provide for the needs of their members. Therefore, every society needs some sort of economic system—the way an economy organizes to use scarce resources to produce goods and services and distribute them for consumption by various people and groups in the society.

How an economic system operates depends on a society's objectives and the nature of its political institutions.[7] But regardless of what form these take, all economic systems must develop some method—along with appropriate economic institutions—to decide what and how much is to be produced and distributed by whom, when, to whom, and why.

There are two basic kinds of economic systems: planned systems and market-directed systems. Actually, no economy is entirely planned or market-directed. Most are a mixture of the two extremes.

Government planners may make the decisions

In a planned economic system, government planners decide what and how much is to be produced and distributed by whom, when, to whom, and why. Producers generally have little choice about what goods and services to produce. Their main task is to meet their assigned production quotas. Prices are set by government planners and tend to be very rigid—not changing according to supply and demand. Consumers usually have some freedom of choice—it's impossible to control every single detail! But the assortment of goods and services may be quite limited. Activities such as market research, branding, and advertising usually are neglected. Sometimes they aren't done at all.

Government planning may work fairly well as long as an economy is simple and the variety of goods and services is small. It may even be necessary under certain conditions—during wartime, drought, or political instability, for example. However, as economies become more complex, government planning becomes more difficult. It may even break down. Countries such as North Korea and Cuba still rely primarily on planned economic systems. Even so, around the world there is a broad move toward market-directed economic systems—because they are more effective in meeting consumer needs.

A market-directed economy adjusts itself

In a market-directed economic system, the individual decisions of the many producers and consumers make the macro-level decisions for the whole economy. In a pure market-directed economy, consumers make a society's production decisions when they make their choices in the marketplace. They decide what is to be produced and by whom—through their dollar "votes."

Price is a measure of value

Prices in the marketplace are a rough measure of how society values particular goods and services. If consumers are willing to pay the market prices, then apparently they feel they are getting at least their money's worth. Similarly, the cost of labour and materials is a rough measure of the value of the resources used in the production of goods and services to meet these needs. New consumer needs that can be served profitably—not just the needs of the majority—will probably be met by some profit-minded businesses.

Greatest freedom of choice

Consumers in a market-directed economy enjoy great freedom of choice. They are not forced to buy any goods or services, except those that must be provided for the good of society—things such as national defence, schools, police and fire protection, highway systems, and public-health services. These are provided by the community—and the citizens are taxed to pay for them.

COLGATE BRUSHES UP ON MARKETING IN RURAL INDIA

Two-thirds of the people in India still live in rural farm areas. Many don't have life's basic comforts. For example, three out of four use wood as fuel to cook. Only about 40 percent have electricity, and less than 20 percent have piped water. Most can't afford a refrigerator. A person who works in the sugarcane fields, for example, only earns about $1 a day.

While these rural villagers do not have much money, there are about 1 *billion* of them. So they are an important potential market for basic products like toothpaste and shampoo. Marketing managers for Colgate know that. However, many rural Indians have never even held a tube of toothpaste. Rather, they clean their mouths with charcoal powder and the stem of a local plant. But Colgate can't rely on U.S.-style ads—or the local drugstore—to do the selling job. Half of the rural population can't read, and very few have a TV. They also don't go to stores. Rather, once a week the men go to a central market in a nearby village to get basic supplies they can't grow themselves.

In spite of these challenges, in the past decade Colgate has about doubled its sales—and rural Indians are now buying over 17,000 tons of toothpaste a year. What's the trick? Colgate sends a van that is equipped with a generator and video gear into a village on market day. Music attracts the shoppers, and then an entertaining half-hour video (infomercial) explains the benefits (including increased sex appeal!) of using Colgate toothpaste. The van reaches only about 100 people at a time, but many of those who see the video try the toothpaste. Of course, not many want to spend a day's wages to buy a standard tube. So Colgate offers a small (30 gram) tube for six rupees (about 18 cents). Colgate's approach is expensive, but managers in the firm are wisely thinking about the long-run return on the marketing investments.

Where did this idea come from? The video vans were first used in 1987 to spread propaganda for a political party that was denied airtime on state-run television. Between elections the vans were idle, so the owner decided to become a marketing specialist—and offered to rent the vans to firms like Colgate that wanted to reach rural consumers.[8]

Similarly, producers are free to do whatever they wish—provided that they stay within the rules of the game set by government *and* receive enough dollar "votes" from consumers. If they do their job well, they earn a profit and stay in business. But profit, survival, and growth are not guaranteed. For now, however, we'll return to our general emphasis on micro-marketing and a managerial view of the role of marketing in individual organizations.

MARKETING'S ROLE HAS CHANGED A LOT OVER THE YEARS

It's clear that marketing decisions are very important to a firm's success. But marketing hasn't always been so complicated. In fact, understanding how marketing thinking has evolved makes the modern view clearer. So we will discuss five stages in marketing evolution: (1) the simple trade era, (2) the production era, (3) the sales era, (4) the marketing department era, and (5) the marketing company era. We'll talk about these eras as if they applied generally to all firms—but keep in mind that *some managers still have not made it to the final stages*. They are stuck in the past with old ways of thinking.

Specialization permitted trade— and middlemen met the need

When societies first moved toward some specialization of production and away from a subsistence economy where each family raised and consumed everything it produced, traders played an important role. Early "producers for the market" made products that were needed by themselves and their neighbours. As bartering became more difficult, societies moved into the simple trade era—a time when families traded

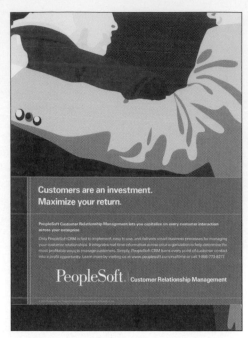

or sold their "surplus" output to local middlemen. These specialists resold the goods to other consumers or distant middlemen. This was the early role of marketing—and it is still the focus of marketing in many of the less-developed areas of the world.

From the production to the sales era

From the Industrial Revolution until the 1920s, most companies were in the production era. The production era is a time when a company focuses on production of a few specific products—perhaps because few of these products are available in the market. "If we can make it, it will sell" is management thinking characteristic of the production era.

By about 1930, most companies in the industrialized Western nations had more production capability than ever before. Now the problem wasn't just to produce— but to beat the competition and win customers. This led many firms to enter the sales era. The sales era is a time when a company emphasizes selling because of increased competition.

To the marketing department era

For most firms in advanced economies, the sales era continued until at least 1950. By then, sales were growing rapidly in most areas of the economy. The problem was deciding where to put the company's effort. Someone was needed to tie together the efforts of research, purchasing, production, shipping, and sales. As this situation became more common, the sales era was replaced by the marketing department era. The marketing department era is a time when all marketing activities are brought under the control of one department to improve short-run policy planning and to try to integrate the firm's activities.

To the marketing company era

Since 1960, most firms have developed at least some managers with a marketing management outlook. Many of these firms have even graduated from the marketing department era into the marketing company era. The marketing company era is a time when, in addition to short-run marketing planning, marketing people develop long-range plans—sometimes five or more years ahead—and the whole company effort is guided by the marketing concept.

WHAT DOES THE MARKETING CONCEPT MEAN?

The **marketing concept** means that an organization aims *all* its efforts at satisfying its *customers*—at a *profit*. The marketing concept is a simple but very important idea. See Exhibit 1-2.

The marketing concept is not a new idea—it's been around for a long time. But some managers show little interest in customers' needs. These managers still have a **production orientation**—making whatever products are easy to produce and *then* trying to sell them. They think of customers existing to buy the firm's output rather than of firms existing to serve customers and—more broadly—the needs of society.

Well-managed firms have replaced this production orientation with a marketing orientation. A **marketing orientation** means trying to carry out the marketing concept. Instead of just trying to get customers to buy what the firm has produced, a marketing-oriented firm tries to offer customers what they need.

Three basic ideas are included in the definition of the marketing concept: (1) customer satisfaction, (2) a total company effort, and (3) profit—not just sales—as an objective. These ideas deserve more discussion.

Customer satisfaction guides the whole system

"Give the customers what they need" seems so obvious that it may be hard for you to see why the marketing concept requires special attention. However, people don't always do the logical—especially when it means changing what they've done in the past. In a typical company 40 years ago, production managers thought mainly about getting out the product. Accountants were interested only in balancing the books. Financial people looked after the company's cash position. And salespeople were mainly concerned with getting orders for whatever product was in the warehouse. Each department thought of its own activity as the centre of the business. Unfortunately, this is still true in many companies today.

Work together to do a better job

Ideally, all managers should work together as a team. Every department may directly or indirectly impact customer satisfaction. But some managers tend to build "fences" around their own departments. There may be meetings to try to get them to work together—but they come and go from the meetings worried only about protecting their own turf.

Exhibit 1-2
Organizations with a Marketing Orientation Carry Out the Marketing Concept

We use the term *production orientation* as a shorthand way to refer to this kind of narrow thinking—and lack of a central focus—in a business firm. But keep in mind that this problem may be seen in sales-oriented sales representatives, advertising-oriented agency people, finance-oriented finance people, directors of nonprofit organizations, and so on. It is not a criticism of people who manage production. They aren't necessarily any more guilty of narrow thinking than anyone else.

The fences come down in an organization that has accepted the marketing concept. There may still be departments because specialization often makes sense. But the total system's effort is guided by what customers want—instead of what each department would like to do.

The marketing concept provides a guiding focus that *all* departments adopt. It should be a philosophy of the whole organization, not just an idea that applies to the marketing department.

Survival and success require a profit

Firms must satisfy customers. But keep in mind that it may cost more to satisfy some needs than any customers are willing to pay. Or it may be much more costly to try to attract new customers than it is to build a strong relationship with—and repeat purchases from—existing customers. So profit—the difference between a firm's revenue and its total costs—is the bottom-line measure of the firm's success and ability to survive. It is the balancing point that helps the firm determine what needs it will try to satisfy with its total (sometimes costly!) effort.

ADOPTION OF THE MARKETING CONCEPT HAS NOT BEEN EASY OR UNIVERSAL

The marketing concept was first accepted by consumer products companies such as General Electric and Procter & Gamble. Competition was intense in their markets—and trying to satisfy customers' needs more fully was a way to win in this competition. Widespread publicity about the success of the marketing concept at these companies helped spread the message to other firms.[9]

Producers of industrial commodities—steel, coal, paper, glass, and chemicals—have accepted the marketing concept slowly if at all. Similarly, many traditional retailers have been slow to accept the marketing concept.

Service industries are catching up

Service industries—including airlines, power and telephone companies, banks, investment firms, lawyers, physicians, accountants, and insurance companies—were slow to adopt the marketing concept, too. But in recent years this has changed dramatically. This is partly due to changes in government regulations that forced many of these businesses to be more competitive. For example, the Canadian government has deregulated areas of the banking and insurance industries, as well as the airlines. The Canadian Radio-Television and Telecommunications Commission (CRTC) continues to remove competitive barriers between the telephone and cable companies, so Telus has moved into the Internet and television signal business while competitors like Rogers now offer home telephone services.

Banks used to be open for limited hours that were convenient for bankers—not customers. Many closed during lunch hour! But now banks stay open longer and also offer more services for their customers—automated teller machines, banking over the Internet, or a "personal banker" to give financial advice.[10]

What caused the transition to the marketing orientation? Competition. The credit unions in provinces like British Columbia and Quebec now have the major share of the residential mortgage market while other financial intermediaries like trust companies and life-insurance firms are active in financing the commercial sector.

Exhibit 1-3 Some Differences in Outlook between Adopters of the Marketing Concept and the Typical Production-Oriented Managers

Topic	Marketing Orientation	Production Orientation
Attitudes toward customers	Customer needs determine company plans.	They should be glad we exist, trying to cut costs and bringing out better products.
An Internet Web site	A new way to serve customers.	If we have a Web site customers will flock to us.
Product offering	Company makes what it can sell.	Company sells what it can make.
Role of marketing research	To determine customer needs and how well company is satisfying them.	To determine customer reaction, if used at all.
Interest in innovation	Focus is on locating new opportunities.	Focus is on technology and cost cutting.
Importance of profit	A critical objective.	A residual, what's left after all costs are covered.
Role of packaging	Designed for customer convenience and as a selling tool.	Seen merely as protection for the product.
Inventory levels	Set with customer requirements and costs in mind.	Set to make production more convenient.
Focus of advertising	Need-satisfying benefits of goods and services.	Product features and how products are made.
Role of sales force	Help the customer to buy if the product fits customer's needs, while coordinating with rest of firm.	Sell the customer, don't worry about coordination with other promotion efforts or rest of firm.
Relationship with customer	Customer satisfaction before and after sale leads to a profitable long-run relationship.	Relationship ends when a sale is made.
Costs	Eliminate costs that do not give value to customer.	Keep costs as low as possible.

It's easy to slip into a production orientation

The marketing concept may seem obvious, but it's very easy to slip into a production-oriented way of thinking. For example, a company might rush a new product to market—rather than first finding out if it will fill an unsatisfied need. Many firms in high-technology businesses fall into this trap. Consider the thousands of new dot-com firms that failed. They may have had a vision of what the technology could do, but they didn't stop to figure out all that it would take to satisfy customers or make a profit. As an example, think about your MP3 player. Apple wasn't the first mover in that market but we all buy their iPod because they got the product features, the marketing, and the user-friendly nature of the product correct. It might be the early bird that gets the worm, but in marketing, sometimes it's the second mouse that gets the cheese. Imagine how parents felt when eToys.com failed to deliver online purchases of Christmas toys on time. If you had that experience, would you ever shop there again? What would you tell others?

Take a look at Exhibit 1-3. It shows some differences in outlook between adopters of the marketing concept and typical production-oriented managers. As the exhibit suggests, the marketing concept forces the company to think through what it is doing—and why. And it motivates the company to develop plans for accomplishing its objectives.

THE MARKETING CONCEPT AND CUSTOMER VALUE

Take the customer's point of view

A manager who adopts the marketing concept sees customer satisfaction as the path to profits. And to better understand what it takes to satisfy a customer, it's useful to take the customer's point of view.

A customer may look at a market offering from two views. One deals with the potential benefits of that offering; the other concerns what the customer has to give up to get those benefits. Consider a student who has just finished an exam and is thinking about getting a cup of mocha latte from Starbucks. Our coffee lover might see this as a great-tasting beverage, a personal reward, a quick pick-me-up, and even as a way to get to know an attractive classmate. Clearly, different needs are associated with these different benefits. The cost of getting these benefits would include the price of the coffee and any tip, but there might be other nondollar costs. For example, how difficult it will be to park is a convenience cost. Slow service would be an aggravation. And you might worry about another kind of cost if the professor whose exam you have the next day sees you "wasting time" at Starbucks.

Customer value reflects benefits and costs

As this example suggests, both benefits and costs can take many different forms, perhaps ranging from economic to emotional. They also may vary depending on the situation. However, it is the customer's view of the various benefits and costs that is important. This leads us to the concept of **customer value**—the difference between the benefits a customer sees from a market offering and the costs of obtaining those benefits. A consumer is likely to be more satisfied when the customer value is higher—when benefits exceed costs by a larger margin. On the other hand, a consumer who sees the costs as greater than the benefits isn't likely to become a customer.

Some people think that low price and high customer value are the same thing. But that may not be the case at all. A good or service that doesn't meet a consumer's needs results in low customer value, even if the price is very low. Yet a high price may be more than acceptable when it obtains the desired benefits. Think again about our Starbucks example. You can get a cup of coffee for a much lower price, but Starbucks offers more than *just* a cup of coffee. Similarly, think about fashion. Ladies, you can buy jeans for a lot less than you paid for that pair of Seven Jeans or Juicy Jeans. So why did you spend the big bucks? Sometimes wearing the right brand that is currently "in" can add value to a product and, as a result, you'll pay more.

Build relationships with customer value

Firms that embrace the marketing concept seek ways to build a profitable long-term relationship with each customer. Even the most innovative firm faces competition sooner or later. And trying to get new customers by taking them away from a competitor is usually more costly than retaining current customers by really satisfying their needs. Satisfied customers buy again and again. This makes their buying job easier, and it also increases the selling firm's profits.

Building relationships with customers requires that everyone in a firm work together to provide customer value before *and after* each purchase. If there is a problem with a customer's bill, the accounting people can't just leave it to the salesperson to straighten it out or, even worse, act like it's "the customer's problem." The long-term relationship with the customer—and the lifetime value of the customer's future purchases—is threatened unless everyone works together to make things right for the customer. Similarly, the firm's advertising people can't just develop ads that try to convince a customer to buy once. If the firm doesn't deliver on the benefits promised in its ads, the customer is likely to go elsewhere the next time the need arises. And the same ideas apply whether the issue is meeting promised delivery dates, resolving warranty problems, giving a customer help on how to use a product, or even making it easy for the customer to return a purchase made in error.

Exhibit 1-4
Satisfying Customers with
Superior Customer Value to
Build Profitable
Relationships

In other words, any time the customer value is reduced—because the benefits to the customer decrease or the costs increase—the relationship is weakened.[11]

Exhibit 1-4 summarizes these ideas. In a firm that has adopted the marketing concept, everyone focuses on customer satisfaction. They offer superior customer value. That helps attract customers in the first place—and keeps them satisfied after they buy. Because customers are satisfied, they want to purchase from the firm again. The relationship with customers is profitable, so the firm is encouraged to find better ways to offer superior customer value. In other words, when a firm adopts the marketing concept, it wins and so do its customers. This is another example of **relationship marketing** that you learned about earlier—and you will hear even more about it shortly. The idea behind attracting a lifetime customer is that you gain their loyalty and often that of their family and friends—for a long time. An ophthalmologist told of a woman whose prescription for glasses he had to change six times. Each time, LensCrafters replaced her glasses free of charge. They certainly made no money on that woman. The ophthalmologist who had already taken some marketing training promptly pointed out that the company didn't necessarily want the woman's business—they wanted to get her entire family's business. Treating the woman well was just the first step on the way to that objective.

Mountain Equipment Co-op
(MEC) has always focused on
customer satisfaction and
customer value as a way to
build long-term relationships
with customers.

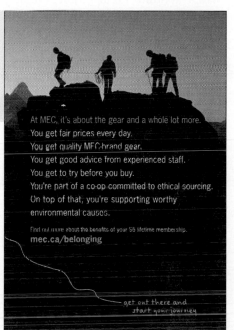

Mountain Equipment Co-op delivers value in a long-term customer relationship

Mountain Equipment Co-op is another company that illustrates these ideas. It is a firm that builds enduring relationships with its customers. It offers good customer value to consumers who are interested in enjoying the outdoors. MEC's products are well suited to a wide variety of outdoor needs—whether it's clothing for hikers or equipment for kayakers. While they may not be the cheapest in town, the product quality is there to match their prices. The product-price positioning used by the company has proven to be very successful at attracting a substantial group of loyal consumers from Vancouver to Halifax. Their selling strategy uses a national chain of retail stores, mail order, online shopping, and an "outdoor gear swap" Web site where members of MEC can buy and sell used equipment.

INTERNET EXERCISE

The MEC Web site (mec.ca) offers consumers a lot of information, including a section with information about trails, equipment mainte-nence, and trip planning. Do you think that this helps MEC to build relationships with its target customers?

THE MARKETING CONCEPT APPLIES IN NONPROFIT ORGANIZATIONS

Newcomers to marketing thinking

The marketing concept is as important for nonprofit organizations as it is for business firms. In fact, marketing applies to all sorts of public and private nonprofit organizations—ranging from government agencies, health care organizations, educational institutions, and religious groups to charities, political parties, and fine arts organizations.

Support may not come from satisfied "customers"

As with any business firm, a nonprofit organization needs resources and support to survive and achieve its objectives. Yet support often does not come directly from those who receive the benefits the organization produces. For example, the World Wildlife Fund protects animals. If supporters of the World Wildlife Fund are not satisfied with its efforts—don't think the benefits are worth

Marketing is now widely accepted by many nonprofit organizations including the Girl Guides of Canada. This ad reminds girls and their families "Why Girls Need Guides."

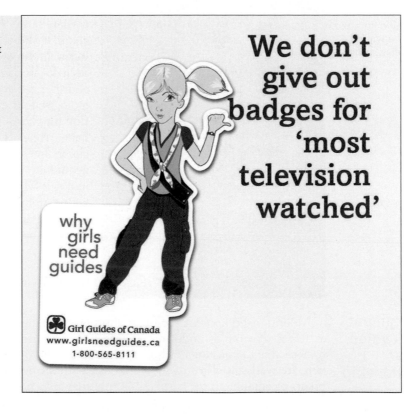

We don't give out badges for 'most television watched'

why girls need guides

Girl Guides of Canada
www.girlsneedguides.ca
1-800-565-8111

what it costs to provide them—they will, and should, put their time and money elsewhere.

Just as most firms face competition for customers, most nonprofits face competition for the resources and support they need. The Canadian military faces a big problem if it can't attract new recruits. A shelter for the homeless may fail if supporters decide to focus on some other cause, such as AIDS education.

What is the "bottom line"?

As with a business, a nonprofit must take in as much money as it spends or it won't survive. However, a nonprofit organization does not measure "profit" in the same way as a firm. And its key measures of long-term success are also different. The YMCA, colleges, symphony orchestras, and the post office, for example, all seek to achieve different objectives and need different measures of success.

Profit guides business decisions because it reflects both the costs and benefits of different activities. In a nonprofit organization, it is sometimes more difficult to be objective in evaluating the benefits of different activities relative to what they cost. However, if everyone in an organization agrees to *some* measure(s) of long-run success, it helps serve as a guide to where the organization should focus its efforts.

May not be organized for marketing

Some nonprofits face other challenges in organizing to adopt the marketing concept. Often no one has overall responsibility for marketing activities. Even when some leaders do the marketing thinking, they may have trouble getting unpaid volunteers with many different interests to all agree with the marketing strategy. Volunteers tend to do what they feel like doing![12]

Nonprofits achieve objectives by satisfying needs

A simple example shows how marketing thinking helped a small town reduce robberies. Initially the chief of police asked the town manager for a larger budget—for more officers and patrol cars. Instead of a bigger budget, the town manager suggested a different approach. She put two officers in charge of a community watch program. They helped neighbours to organize and notify the police of any suspicious situations. They also set up a program to engrave ID numbers on belongings. And new signs warned thieves that a community watch was in effect. Break-ins all but stopped—without increasing the police budget. What the town *really* needed was more effective crime prevention—not just more police officers.

Throughout this book, we'll be discussing the marketing concept and related ideas as they apply in many different settings. Often we'll simply say "in a firm" or "in a business"—but remember that most of the ideas can be applied in *any* type of organization.

THE MARKETING CONCEPT, SOCIAL RESPONSIBILITY, AND MARKETING ETHICS

Society's needs must be considered

The marketing concept is so logical that it's hard to argue with it. Yet when a firm focuses its efforts on satisfying some consumers—to achieve its objectives—there may be negative effects on society. For example, producers and consumers making free choices can cause conflicts and difficulties. This is called the **micro-macro dilemma**. What is "good" for some firms and consumers may not be good for society as a whole.

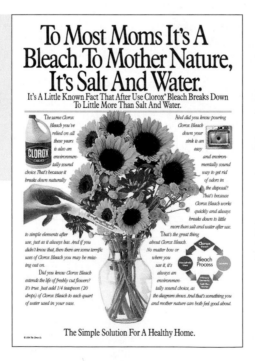

For example, many Canadians want the convenience of disposable products and products in easy-to-use, small-serving packages. But these same "convenient" products and packages often lead to pollution of the environment and inefficient use of natural resources. Should future generations be left to pay the consequences of pollution that is the result of free choice by today's consumers?

Questions like these are not easy to answer. The basic reason is that many different people may have a stake in the outcomes—and social consequences—of the choices made by individual managers *and* consumers in a market-directed system. This means that marketing managers should be concerned with **social responsibility**—a firm's obligation to improve its positive effects on society and reduce its negative effects. As you read this book and learn more about marketing, you will also learn more about social responsibility in marketing—and why it must be taken seriously. You'll also see that being socially responsible sometimes requires difficult trade-offs.

Consider, for example, the environmental problems created by CFCs, chemicals that were used in hundreds of critical products, including fire extinguishers, cooling systems, and electronic circuit boards. When it was learned that CFCs deplete the earth's ozone layer, it was not possible to immediately stop producing and using all CFCs. For many products critical to society, there was no feasible short-term substitute. Du Pont and other producers of CFCs worked hard to balance these conflicting demands until substitute products could be found. Yet you can see that there are no easy answers for how such conflicts should be resolved.[13]

The issue of social responsibility in marketing also raises other important questions—for which there are no easy answers.

Socially responsible marketing managers are concerned about the environmental impact of their decisions, and some firms are finding innovative ways to both help the environment and improve customer satisfaction at the same time.

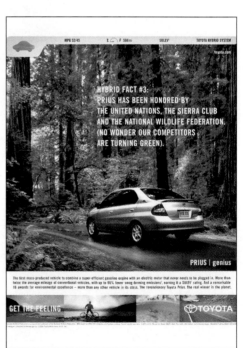

Should all consumer needs be satisfied?

Some consumers want products that may not be safe or good for them in the long run. Some critics argue that businesses should not offer high-heeled shoes, alcoholic beverages, or sugar-coated cereals because they aren't "good" for consumers in the long run.

Similarly, bicycles and inline skates are among the most dangerous products on the market. Who should decide if these products will be offered to consumers?

What if it cuts into profits?

Being more socially conscious often seems to lead to positive customer response. For example, many consumers praise Wal-Mart as a "safe haven" for kids to shop because it does not carry CDs that are not suitable for children, lewd videos, plastic guns that look authentic, and video games judged to be too violent. And some consumers buy only from firms that certify that their overseas factories don't rely on child labour.[14]

Yet as the examples above show, there are times when being socially responsible conflicts with a firm's profit objective. Concerns about such conflicts have prompted critics to raise the basic question: Is the marketing concept really desirable?

Many socially conscious marketing managers are trying to resolve this problem. Their definition of customer satisfaction includes long-range effects—as well as immediate customer satisfaction. They try to balance consumer, company, *and* social interests.

The marketing concept guides marketing ethics

Certainly some concerns about social responsibility and marketing arise because some individual firm or manager was intentionally unethical and cheated the market. Of course, a manager cannot be truly consumer-oriented and at the same time intentionally unethical. However, at times, problems and criticism may arise because a manager did not fully consider the ethical implications of a decision. In either case, there is no excuse for sloppiness when it comes to **marketing ethics**—the moral standards that guide marketing decisions and actions. Each individual develops moral standards based on his or her own values. That helps explain why opinions about what is right or wrong often vary from one person to another, from one society to another, and among different groups within a society. It is sometimes difficult to say whose opinions are "correct." Even so, such opinions may have a very real influence on whether an individual's (or a firm's) marketing decisions and actions are accepted or rejected. So marketing ethics are not only a philosophical issue, they are also a pragmatic concern.

Problems may arise when some individual manager does not share the same marketing ethics as others in the organization. One person operating alone can damage a firm's reputation and even survival.

To be certain that standards for marketing ethics are as clear as possible, many organizations have developed their own written codes of ethics. These codes usually state—at least at a general level—the ethical standards that everyone in the firm should follow in dealing with customers and other people. Many professional societies also have such codes. For example, the Canadian Marketing Association's code of ethics—see Exhibit 1-5—sets specific ethical standards for many aspects of marketing.[15]

Throughout the text, we will be discussing the types of ethical issues individual marketing managers face. But we won't be moralizing and trying to tell you how you should think on any given issue. Rather, by the end of the course we hope that *you* will have some firm personal opinions about what is and is not ethical in micro-marketing activities.[16]

Fortunately, the prevailing practice of most businesspeople is to be fair and honest. However, not all criticisms of marketing focus on ethical issues.

Exhibit 1-5   The Canadian Marketing Association Code of Ethics

CODE OF ETHICS

The Canadian Marketing Association (CMA) sets ethical standards of practice and prescribes a code of professional conduct for its members. Ethical issues in marketing are wide ranging and apply to consumer and business-to-business marketing as well as nonprofit organizations and international marketing. Exhibit 1-6 shows just a few of the major ethical issues in marketing. The CMA's Web site features their Code of Ethics and Standards of Practice in its entirety. Topics (which are edited for brevity) include the following:

Overarching Ethical Principles

1. Personal Information Practices

Marketers must promote responsible and transparent personal information management practices.

2. Truthfulness

Marketing communications must be clear and truthful. Marketers must not knowingly make a representation to a consumer or business that is false or misleading.

3. Campaign Limitations

- Marketers must not participate in any campaign involving the disparagement or exploitation of any person or group on the grounds of race, colour, ethnicity, religion, national origin, gender, sexual orientation, marital status or age.

- Marketers must not participate in the dissemination of unsolicited material that is sexually explicit, vulgar or indecent in nature.

- Marketers must not participate in the dissemination of any material that unduly, gratuitously and without merit exploits sex, horror, mutilation, torture, cruelty, violence or hate.

- Marketers must not knowingly exploit the credulity, lack of knowledge or inexperience of any consumer.

Universal Marketing Practices

- Support for Claims: Test or survey data referred to in any marketing communication must be reliable, accurate and current and must support the specific claim being made.

- Disguise: Marketers must not engage in marketing communications in the guise of one purpose when the intent is for a different purpose like selling a product or obtaining a donation.

- Testimonials: Testimonials and endorsements must be authorized by the person or organization quoted, positioned as opinion, not fact (unless supported by valid research) and not taken out of context.

- Availability: Unless the promotional material advises the consumer or business of limited stock, marketers must have adequate quantities to meet reasonably foreseeable demand.

- Comparative Advertising: Comparisons included in marketing communications must be factual, verifiable and not misleading.

- Complaints: Marketers must establish and communicate fair, effective and timely procedures to handle complaints from consumers or businesses.

Protection of Personal Privacy

CMA Members must obey federal and provincial privacy laws that affect how information about consumers is collected, stored, reviewed and transferred. Because of rising concerns about the right to privacy, CMA also requires its members to comply with their Do Not Contact Service for consumers who don't want mail, fax and phone calls from marketers.

Special Considerations in Marketing to Kids and Teenagers

Teens and children have special status under CMA regulations. Information can't be collected without consent from parents. Marketing to children must not exploit children's credulity, lack of experience or sense of loyalty. Marketing to teenagers must not unduly exploit teenagers' impressionability, or susceptibility to peer pressure and members must use language that is age appropriate when marketing to teens and kids.

Sub-Disciplines and Specific Marketing Practices

- E-commerce: Online marketers must, provide a clear order confirmation process with a separate e-mail to confirm the customer's order. An online "click-through" mechanism for consumers to contact the marketer must also be provided.

- Contests: Marketers must present all terms and conditions of a contest in a manner that is clear, visible, easy to find, easy to read and easy to understand.

- Public Relations (PR): Firms providing PR services must disclose the identity of their client when operating in the public domain.

Media-Specific Standards of Practice

The CMA Code requires truthfulness and transparency in all media communications. This means for example that infomercials and ads in print media are clearly identified.

CMA members must respect the CMA's "do not contact" lists and are prohibited from sending unsolicited faxes, text messages and e-mails. Other marketers can subscribe to the lists but are not obliged to follow them.

Members who refuse to abide by CMA's Code of Ethics face the potential risk of having their membership revoked.

Exhibit 1-6   Sample Criticisms of Marketing

- Advertising is everywhere, and it's often annoying, misleading, or wasteful.
- The quality of products is poor and often they are not even safe.
- There are too many unnecessary products.
- Packaging and labelling are often confusing and deceptive.
- Middlemen add too much to the cost of distribution and just raise prices without providing anything in return.
- Marketing serves the rich and exploits the poor.

- Service stinks, and when a consumer has a problem nobody cares.
- Marketing creates interest in products that pollute the environment.
- Private information about consumers is collected and used to sell them things they don't want.
- Marketing makes people too materialistic and motivates them toward "things" instead of social needs.
- Easy consumer credit makes people buy things they don't need and can't afford.

Marketing has its critics

We must admit that marketing—has many critics. Marketing activity is especially open to criticism because it is the part of business most visible to the public.

A number of typical complaints about marketing are summarized in Exhibit 1-6. Think about these criticisms and whether you agree with them or not. What complaints do you have that are not covered by one of the categories in Exhibit 1-6?

Such complaints should not be taken lightly. They show that many people are unhappy with some parts of the marketing system. Certainly, the strong public support for consumer protection laws proves that not all consumers feel they are being treated fairly.

As you consider the various criticisms of marketing, keep in mind that not all of them deal with the marketing practices of specific firms. Some of the complaints about marketing really focus on the basic idea of a market-directed macro-marketing system—and these criticisms often occur because people don't understand what marketing is—or how it works.[17] As you go through this book, we'll discuss some of these criticisms. Then in our final chapter, we will return to a more complete appraisal of marketing in our consumer-oriented society.

CONCLUSION

In this chapter, we highlighted the value of marketing for consumers, firms, and society. There are two levels of marketing: micro-marketing and macro-marketing. Micro-marketing focuses on the activities of individual firms. Macro-marketing is concerned with the way the whole marketing system works in a society or economy. We discussed the functions of marketing and who performs them, including marketing specialists who serve as intermediaries between producers and consumers and other specialists who are facilitators. We'll consider macro-marketing issues throughout the text but the major thrust of this book is on micro-marketing.

The marketing concept provides direction to a marketing-oriented firm. The marketing concept stresses that the company's efforts should focus on satisfying some target customers—at a profit. Production-oriented firms tend to forget this. The various departments within a production-oriented firm let their natural conflicts of interest get in the way of customer satisfaction. Satisfaction relates to customer value, and superior customer value is crucial in attracting customers and in building beneficial long-term relationships with them. Having learned this theory you now understand why Starbucks has been so successful. They understand customer relationship management, and are in there for the "long haul" when it comes to holding on to their loyal clientele. And finally, you now know why you keep going back to them when you know you can buy cheaper coffee elsewhere.

We also covered ways that social responsibility and marketing ethics relate to the marketing concept, and ended with the criticisms of marketing—both of the way individual firms work and of the whole macro system.

KEY TERMS

QUESTIONS AND PROBLEMS

1. List your activities for the first two hours after you woke up this morning. Briefly indicate how marketing affected your activities.

2. It is fairly easy to see why people do not beat a path to a mousetrap manufacturer's door, but would they be similarly indifferent if some food processor developed a revolutionary new food product that would provide all necessary nutrients in small pills for about $100 per year per person?

3. If a producer creates a really revolutionary new product and consumers can learn about it and purchase it at a Web site on the Internet, is any additional marketing effort really necessary? Explain your thinking.

4. Explain, in your own words, why this text emphasizes micro-marketing.

5. Distinguish between macro- and micro-marketing. Then explain how they are interrelated, if they are.

6. Refer to Exhibit 1-1, and give an example of a purchase you made recently that involved separation of information and separation in time between you and the producer. Briefly explain how these separations were overcome.

7. Describe a recent purchase you made. Indicate why that particular product was available at a store and, in particular, at the store where you bought it.

8. Define the functions of marketing in your own words. Using an example, explain how they can be shifted and shared.

9. Online computer shopping at Web sites on the Internet makes it possible for individual consumers to get direct information from hundreds of companies they would not otherwise know about. Consumers can place an order for a purchase that is then shipped to them directly. Will growth of these services ultimately eliminate the need for retailers and wholesalers? Explain your thinking, giving specific attention to what marketing functions are involved in these "electronic purchases" and who performs them.

10. Explain why a small producer might want a marketing research firm to take over some of its information-gathering activities.

11. Define the marketing concept in your own words, and then explain why the notion of profit is usually included in this definition.

12. Define the marketing concept in your own words, and then suggest how acceptance of this concept might affect the organization and operation of your college or university.

13. Distinguish between production orientation and marketing orientation, illustrating with local examples.

14. Explain why a firm should view its internal activities as part of a total system. Illustrate your answer for (a) a large grocery products producer, (b) a plumbing wholesaler, (c) a department store chain, and (d) a cell phone service.

15. Give examples of some of the benefits and costs that might contribute to the customer value of each of the following products: (a) a wristwatch, (b) a weight-loss diet supplement, (c) a cruise on a luxury liner, and (d) a chequing account from a bank.

16. Give an example of a recent purchase you made where the purchase wasn't just a single transaction but rather part of an ongoing relationship with the seller. Discuss what the seller has done (or could do better) to strengthen the relationship and increase the odds of you being a loyal customer in the future.

www.mcgrawhill.ca/olc/perreault

17. Discuss how the micro-macro dilemma relates to each of the following products: high-powered engines in cars, nuclear power, bank credit cards, and pesticides that improve farm production.

18. Marketing has been defined as "the process of planning and executing the conception, pricing, promotion, and distribution of ideas, goods, and services to create exchanges that satisfy individual and organizational objectives." Does this definition consider macro-marketing? Explain your answer.

COMPUTER-AIDED PROBLEM

1. Revenue, Cost, and Profit Relationships

RESOURCE REMINDER

In Exhibits 1-2 and 1-3 we presented the ideas that marketers have to consider things like customer satisfaction and inventory levels—but they also have to generate a profit. This problem introduces you to the computer-aided problem (CAP) software—which is a feature of this text's Online Learning Centre. It gets you started with the use of spreadsheet analysis so you can understand how costs, sales, and the selling price all fit together to produce a profit.

This problem is simple. In fact, you could work it without the software. But by starting with a simple problem, you will learn how to use the program more quickly and see how it will help you with more complicated problems. Instructions for the software are available on the Online Learning Centre at www.mcgrawhill.ca/olc/perreault.

Sue Cline, the business manager at Magna University Student Bookstore, is developing plans for the next academic year. The bookstore is one of the university's non-profit activities, but any "surplus" (profit) it earns is used to support the student activities centre.

Two popular products at the bookstore are the student academic calendar and notebooks with the school name. Sue Cline thinks that she can sell calendars to 90 percent of Magna's 3,000 students, so she has had 2,700 printed. The total cost, including artwork and printing, is $11,500. Last year the calendar sold for $5.00, but Sue is considering changing the price this year.

Sue thinks that the bookstore will be able to sell 6,000 notebooks if they are priced right. But she knows that many students will buy similar notebooks (without the school name) from stores in town if the bookstore price is too high.

Sue has entered the information about selling price, quantity, and costs for calendars and notebooks in the spreadsheet program so that it is easy to evaluate the effect of different decisions. The spreadsheet is also set up to calculate revenue and profit, based on

$$\text{Revenue} = (\text{Selling price}) \times (\text{Quantity sold})$$

$$\text{Profit} = (\text{Revenue}) - (\text{Total cost})$$

Use the program to answer the questions below. Record your answers on a separate sheet of paper.

a. From the Spreadsheet Screen, how much revenue does Sue expect from calendars? How much revenue from notebooks? How much profit will the store earn from calendars? From notebooks?

b. If Sue increases the price of her calendars to $6.00 and still sells the same quantity, what is the expected revenue? The expected profit? (Note: Change the price from $5.00 to $6.00 on the spreadsheet and the program will recompute revenue and profit.) On your sheet of paper, show the calculations that confirm that the program has given you the correct values.

c. Sue is interested in getting an overview of how a change in the price of notebooks would affect revenue and profit, assuming that she sells all 6,000 notebooks she is thinking of ordering. Prepare a table—on your sheet of paper—with column headings for three variables: selling price, revenue, and profit. Show the value for revenue and profit for different possible selling prices for a notebook—starting at a minimum price of $1.60 and adding 8 cents to the price until you reach a maximum of $2.40. At what price will selling 6,000 notebooks contribute $5,400.00 to profit? At what price would notebook sales contribute only $1,080.00? (Hint: Use the What If analysis feature to compute the new values. Start by selecting "selling price" for notebooks as the value to change, with a minimum value of $1.60 and a maximum value of $2.40. Select the revenue and profit for notebooks as the values to display.)

If you want to read the cases and view the video cases that accompany this chapter, visit the *Basic Marketing* Online Learning Centre at: **www.mcgrawhill.ca/olc/perreault**. Along with these cases and video cases, the OLC also has the software and user guide for this chapter's Computer-Aided Problem, as well as exercises, quizzes, articles, links, and other *interactive* content that will help you with your studies.

Strategic Planning

As you saw in Chapter 1, marketing and marketing management are important in our society—and in business firms and nonprofit organizations. To get you thinking about the marketing strategy planning ideas we will be developing in this chapter and the rest of the book, let's consider Dell Computers.

As a freshman in college, Michael Dell started buying and reselling computers from his dorm room. At that time, the typical marketing mix for PCs emphasized distribution through specialized computer stores that sold to business users and some final consumers. Often the dealers' service quality didn't justify the high prices they charged, the features of the PCs they had in stock didn't match what customers wanted, and repairs were a hassle.

Dell decided there was a target market of price-conscious customers who would respond to a different marketing mix. He used direct-response advertising in computer magazines—and customers called a toll-free number to order a computer with the exact features they wanted. Dell built computers to match the specific orders that came in and used UPS to quickly ship orders directly to the customer. Prices were low, too—because the direct channel meant there was no retailer markup and the build-to-order approach reduced inventory costs. This approach also kept Dell in constant contact with customers. Problems could be identified quickly and corrected. Dell also implemented the plan well—with constant improvements—to make good on its promise of reliable machines and superior service. For example, Dell pioneered a system of guaranteed on-site service—within 24 hours. Dell also set up ongoing programs to train all employees to work together to please customers.

Of course, it's hard to satisfy everyone all of the time. For example, profits fell when one of Dell's laptop designs didn't measure up. Customers simply didn't see them as a good value. However, smart marketers learn from and fix mistakes. Dell quickly got its product line back on the bull's eye.

As sales grew, Dell put more money into advertising. Its ad agency crafted ads to position Dell in consumers' minds as an aggressive, value-oriented source of computers. At the same time, Dell added a direct sales force to call on big government and corporate buyers—because they expected in-person selling and a relationship, not just a telephone contact. And when these important customers said they wanted Dell to offer high-power machines to run their corporate networks, Dell put money into R&D to create what they needed.

Dell also saw the prospect for international growth. Many firms moved into Europe by exporting. But Dell set up its own operations there. Dell knew it would be tough to win over skeptical European buyers. They had never bought big-ticket items such as PCs on the phone. Yet in less than five years, sales in Europe grew to 40 percent of Dell's total revenue and Dell pushed into Asian markets for more growth. That also posed challenges, so Dell's advertising manager invited major ad agencies to make presentations on how Dell could be more effective with its $80 million global advertising campaign.

By the mid 1990s, IBM and other firms were trying to imitate Dell's direct-order approach. However, the retailers who were selling the bulk of IBM's PCs were not happy about facing price competition from their own supplier! So IBM couldn't simply copy Dell's strategy. It was in conflict with the rest of IBM's marketing program.

As computer prices fell, many firms were worried about how to cope with slim profits. But Dell saw an opportunity for profitable growth by extending its direct model to a Web site (www.dell.com). Moreover, online selling lowered expenses and reduced supply and inventory costs. For example, when a customer ordered a PC produced in one factory and a monitor produced in another, the two pieces were brought together enroute to the customer. This cost cutting proved to be especially important when the economy softened and demand for PCs fell off. Building on its strengths, Dell cut prices in what many competitors saw as an "irrational" price war. But the design of Dell's Web site and sales system allowed it to charge different prices to different segments to match demand with supply. For example, high-margin laptops were priced lower to educational customers—to stimulate demand—than to government buyers who were less price sensitive. Similarly, if the supply of new 17-inch flat-screen monitors fell short, Dell could use an online promotion for 19-inch monitors and shift demand. To earn more profit from existing customers, Dell also put more emphasis on selling extended-care service agreements.

As PC sales taper off, Dell is seeking new growth with strategies that will enhance its marketing program. For example, Dell's new kiosks in retail stores and malls should reach new customers who want to shop and buy "in person." And product-development efforts include new lines of printers, handhelds, and network servers. In contrast, after screening the opportunity for new tablet computers, Dell decided *not* to be one of the earliest firms in that market.[1]

We've mentioned only a few of many decisions marketing managers at Dell had to make in developing marketing strategies, but you can see that each of these decisions affects the others. Further, making marketing decisions is never easy and strategies may need to change. Yet knowing what basic decision areas to consider helps you to plan a more successful strategy. This chapter will get you started by giving you a frame-work for thinking about marketing strategy planning—which is what the rest of this book is all about.

THE MANAGEMENT JOB IN MARKETING

In Chapter 1 you learned about the marketing concept—a philosophy to guide the whole firm toward satisfying customers at a profit. From the Dell case, it's clear that marketing decisions are very important to a firm's success. So let's look more closely at how a marketing manager helps a firm to achieve its objectives. Because the marketing manager is a manager, let's look at the marketing management process.

The **marketing management process** is the process of (1) *planning* marketing activities, (2) directing the *implementation* of the plans, and (3) *controlling* these plans. Planning, implementation, and control are basic jobs of all managers—but here we will emphasize what they mean to marketing managers.

Exhibit 2-1 shows the relationships among the three jobs in the marketing management process. The jobs are all connected to show that the marketing management process is continuous. In the planning job, managers set guidelines for the implementing job and specify expected results. They use these expected results in the control job to determine if everything has worked out as planned. The link from the control job to the planning job is especially important. This feedback often leads to changes in the plans or to new plans.

Marketing managers should seek new opportunities

Marketing managers cannot be satisfied just planning present activities. Markets are dynamic. Consumers' needs, competitors, and the environment keep changing. Consider Parker Brothers, a company that seemed to have a "Monopoly" in family games. While it continued selling board games, firms like Sega, Sony, and Nintendo zoomed in with video game competition. Of course, not every opportunity is good for every company. Really attractive opportunities are those that fit with what the whole company wants to do and is able to do well.

Exhibit 2-1
The Marketing
Management Process

Strategic management planning concerns the whole firm	The job of planning strategies to guide a whole company is called **strategic (management) planning**—the managerial process of developing and maintaining a match between an organization's resources and its market opportunities. This is a top-management job. It includes planning not only for marketing but also for production, finance, human resources, and other areas.

Although marketing strategies are not whole-company plans, company plans should be market-oriented. And the marketing plan often sets the tone and direction for the whole company. So we will use *strategy planning* and *marketing strategy planning* to mean the same thing.[2]

WHAT IS MARKETING STRATEGY PLANNING?

Exhibit 2-2
A Marketing Strategy

Marketing strategy planning means finding attractive opportunities and developing profitable marketing strategies. But what is a "marketing strategy"? We have used these words rather casually so far. Now let's see what they really mean.

What is a marketing strategy?

A **marketing strategy** specifies a target market and a related marketing mix. It is a big picture of what a firm will do in some market. Two interrelated parts are needed:

1. A **target market**—a fairly homogeneous (similar) group of customers to whom a company wishes to appeal.
2. A **marketing mix**—the controllable variables the company puts together to satisfy this target group.

The importance of target customers in this process can be seen in Exhibit 2-2, where the target customer—the "C"—is at the centre of the diagram. The customer is surrounded by the controllable variables that we call the "marketing mix." A typical marketing mix includes some product, offered at a price, with some promotion to tell potential customers about the product, and a way to reach the customer's place.

Tim Hortons successfully developed a target market of loyal consumers by providing the right assortment of coffees, light lunch products, and fresh bakery items. That is only part of the story however, because their pricing structure and promotional programs as well as store design and locations all work together so that a unique offering is provided to their customers. Does the unique combination of controllable variables work? Take a look at their lineups.

SELECTING A MARKET-ORIENTED STRATEGY IS TARGET MARKETING

Target marketing is not mass marketing	Note that a marketing strategy specifies some *particular* target customers. This approach is called "target marketing" to distinguish it from "mass marketing." **Target marketing** says that a marketing mix is tailored to fit some specific target customers. In contrast, **mass marketing**—the typical production-oriented approach—vaguely aims at "everyone" with the same marketing mix. Mass marketing assumes that everyone is the same—and it considers everyone to be a potential customer. It may help to think of target marketing as the "rifle approach" and mass marketing as the "shotgun approach." See Exhibit 2-3.
Mass marketers may do target marketing	Commonly used terms can be confusing here. The terms *mass marketing* and *mass marketers* do not mean the same thing. Far from it! *Mass marketing* means trying to sell to "everyone," as we explained above. *Mass marketers* like Kraft Foods and Wal-Mart are aiming at clearly defined target markets. The confusion with mass marketing occurs because their target markets usually are large and spread out.

Exhibit 2-3
Production-Oriented and
Marketing-Oriented
Managers Have Different
Views of the Market

Production-oriented manager sees
everyone as basically similar and
practices "mass marketing"

Marketing-oriented manager sees
everyone as different and
practices "target marketing"

Target marketing can mean big markets and profits

Target marketing is not limited to small market segments—only to fairly homogeneous ones. A very large market—even what is sometimes called the "mass market"—may be fairly homogeneous, and a target marketer will deliberately aim at it. For example, a very large group of parents of young children are homogeneous on many dimensions—including their attitudes about changing baby diapers. In Canada alone, this group spends about $600 million a year on disposable diapers—so it should be no surprise that it is a major target market for companies like Kimberly-Clark (Huggies) and Procter & Gamble (Pampers).

The basic reason to focus on some specific target customers is so that you can develop a marketing mix that satisfies those customers' *specific* needs better than they are satisfied by some other firm. For example, E*Trade uses an Internet site (www.etrade.com) to target knowledgeable investors who want a convenient, low-cost way to buy and sell stocks online without a lot of advice (or pressure) from a salesperson.

When a firm carefully targets its marketing mix, it is less likely to face direct competitors. So superior customer value is achieved with the benefits provided by the whole marketing mix rather than just by relying on a lower price. Consider a big box retailer like Costco. They don't have the cheapest prices in town but their product assortment of consumer durables together with their selection of food products has allowed them to attract customers from both the supermarket competition like Safeway and Loblaws as well as from the department stores like The Bay and Sears. Costco usually sell larger volume sizes than their competitors but they link that with name brand products of good quality at reasonably competitive prices. This unique combination has allowed them to develop a target market that differs from that offered by their traditional competitors.

DEVELOPING MARKETING MIXES FOR TARGET MARKETS

There are many marketing mix decisions

There are many possible ways to satisfy the needs of target customers. A product might have many different features. Customer service levels before or after the sale can be adjusted. The package, brand name, and warranty can be changed. Various advertising media—newspapers, magazines, cable, the Internet—may be used. A company's own sales force or other sales specialists can be used. The price can be changed, discounts can be given, and so on. With so many possible variables, is there any way to help organize all these decisions and simplify the selection of marketing mixes? The answer is yes.

The four "Ps" make up a marketing mix

It is useful to reduce all the variables in the marketing mix to four basic ones. These variables along with the chapters where you can explore them in more detail are:

Product (Chapter 10)
Place (Chapter 11 & 12)
Promotion (Chapter 16)
Price (Chapter 17)

It helps to think of the four major parts of a marketing mix as the "four Ps." Exhibit 2-4 emphasizes their relationship and their common focus on the target customer—"C."

Exhibit 2-4
A Marketing Strategy—Showing the Four Ps of a Marketing Mix

Customer is not part of the marketing mix

The customer is shown surrounded by the four Ps in Exhibit 2-4. Some students assume that the customer is part of the marketing mix—but this is not so. The customer should be the *target* of all marketing efforts. The customer is placed in the centre of the diagram to show this. The C stands for some specific customers—the target market.

Exhibit 2-5 shows some of the strategy decision variables organized by the four Ps. These will be discussed in later chapters. For now, let's just describe each P briefly.

Product—the good or service for the target's needs

The Product area is concerned with developing the right "product" for the target market. This offering may involve a physical good, a service, or a blend of both. Keep in mind that Product is not limited to physical goods. For example, the Product of H & R Block is a completed tax form. The Product of a political party is the set of causes it will work to achieve. The important thing to remember is that your good or service should satisfy some customers' needs.

Along with other Product-area decisions like branding, packaging, and warranties, we will talk about developing and managing new products and whole product lines.

Place—reaching the target

Place is concerned with all the decisions involved in getting the "right" product to the target market's Place. A product isn't much good to a customer if it isn't available when and where it's wanted.

Exhibit 2-5
Strategy Decision Areas Organized by the Four Ps

Product	Place	Promotion	Price
Physical good	Objectives	Objectives	Objectives
Service	Channel type	Promotion blend	Flexibility
Features	Market exposure	Salespeople	Level over
Benefits	Kinds of	Kind	product life
Quality level	middlemen	Number	cycle
Accessories	Kinds and	Selection	Geographic terms
Installation	locations of	Training	Discounts
Instructions	stores	Motivation	Allowances
Warranty	How to handle	Advertising	
Product lines	transporting	Targets	
Packaging	and storing	Kinds of ads	
Branding	Service levels	Media type	
	Recruiting	Copy thrust	
	middlemen	Prepared by	
	Managing	whom	
	channels	Sales promotion	
		Publicity	

A firm's product may involve a physical good, a service, or a combination of both.

A product reaches customers through a channel of distribution. A **channel of distribution** is any series of firms (or individuals) that participate in the flow of products from producer to final user or consumer.

Sometimes a channel system is quite short. It may run directly from a producer to a final user or consumer. This is especially common in business markets and in the marketing of services. The channel is direct when a producer uses an online Web site to handle orders by target customers, whether the customer is a final consumer or an organization. So direct channels have become much more common since the development of the Internet. Let's return to our opening discussion about Dell. They found a huge target market because the Internet allowed them to sell direct at very competitive prices. Sometimes the unique application of just one of the marketing mix variables (in this case direct distribution) will allow you to adjust other control variables like price so that you can develop valuable new target segments even when the big players like IBM and Apple seem to have the computer market sewn up.

On the other hand, often the channel system is much more complex—involving many different retailers and wholesalers. See Exhibit 2-6 for some examples. When a marketing manager has several different target markets, several different channels of distribution may be needed.

We will also see how physical distribution service levels and decisions concerning logistics (transporting, storing, and handling products) relate to the other Place decisions and the rest of the marketing mix.

Promotion—telling and selling the customer

The third P—Promotion—is concerned with telling the target market or others in the channel of distribution about the "right" product. Sometimes promotion is focused on acquiring new customers, and sometimes it's focused on retaining current customers. Promotion includes personal selling, mass selling, and sales promotion. It is the marketing manager's job to blend these methods of communication.

Personal selling involves direct spoken communication between sellers and potential customers. Personal selling usually happens face-to-face, but sometimes the communication occurs over the telephone or even via a video conference over the Internet. Personal selling lets the salesperson adapt the firm's marketing mix to each potential customer. But this individual attention comes at a price; personal selling can be very expensive. Often this personal effort has to be blended with mass selling and sales promotion.

Mass selling is communicating with large numbers of customers at the same time. The main form of mass selling is **advertising**—any *paid* form of nonpersonal presentation of ideas, goods, or services by an identified sponsor. **Publicity**—any *unpaid* form of nonpersonal presentation of ideas, goods, or services—is another important form of mass selling. The launch of the last edition of *Harry Potter* is a classic example of using media publicity to sell a book. A number of copies found their way into the hands of consumers prior to the heavily hyped midnight launch of the latest book. This happened in Canada as well as a number of other countries. The media coverage of the leaked copies was massive and literally international in scope. The publisher didn't have to pay a penny for all the media attention and because it was presented as news, consumers paid more attention than if it was just another ad. Mass selling may involve a wide variety of media, ranging from newspapers and billboards to the Internet.

Sales promotion refers to those promotion activities—other than advertising, publicity, and personal selling—that stimulate interest, trial, or purchase by final customers or others in the channel. This can involve use of coupons, point-of-purchase materials, samples, signs, contests, catalogues, novelties, and circulars.

Price—making it right

In addition to developing the right Product, Place, and Promotion, marketing managers must also decide the right Price. Price setting must consider the kind of competition in the target market and the cost of the whole marketing mix. Consider for example the intense competition in the Canadian phone market. Bell and Telus have been waging a protracted marketing war based on price per minute for calling charges, but things have become even more price competitive with the entry of Rogers into the same market. A manager must also try to estimate customer reaction to possible prices. Besides this, the manager must know current practices as to markups, discounts, and other terms of sale. And if customers won't accept the Price, all of the planning effort is wasted.

Each of the four Ps contributes to the whole

All four Ps are needed in a marketing mix. In fact, they should all be tied together. But is any one more important than the others? Generally speaking, the answer is no—all contribute to one whole. When a marketing mix is being developed, all (final) decisions about the Ps should be made at the same time. That's why the four Ps are arranged around the customer (C) in a circle—to show that they all are equally important.

LIFETIME VALUE OF CUSTOMERS CAN BE VERY HIGH— OR VERY LOW

Investors lost millions when stock market values of dot-com firms collapsed after an initial, frenzied run-up. But why did values get so high in the first place, especially when most dot-coms were not yet profitable? The stock went up because many investors expected that the firms would earn profits in the future as more consumers went online and the early dot-coms accumulated customers. These hopes were fuelled by dot-coms that made optimistic predictions about the lifetime value of the customers they were acquiring. The lifetime value of the customer concept is not new. For decades General Motors has known that a consumer who buys a GM car and is satisfied is likely to buy another one the next time. If that happens again and again, over a lifetime the happy customer would spend $250,000 on GM cars. Of course, this only works if the firm's marketing mix attracts the target customers and the relationship keeps them satisfied before, during, and after every purchase. If you don't satisfy and retain customers they don't have high lifetime value and don't generate sales. Of course, sales revenue alone does not guarantee profits. For example, a firm can't give away products—or spend so much on promotion to acquire new customers (or keep the ones it has)—that the revenue will never be able to offset the costs. Unfortunately, that is what happened with many of the dot-coms. They saw how the financial arithmetic might work—*assuming* that new customers kept buying and costs came under control. But without a sensible marketing strategy, that assumption was not realistic.[3]

Let's sum up our discussion of marketing mix planning thus far. We develop a *Product* to satisfy the target customers. We find a way to reach our target customers' *Place*. We use *Promotion* to tell the target customers (and others in the channel) about the product that has been designed for them. And we set a *Price* after estimating expected customer reaction to the total offering and the costs of getting it to them.

Strategy jobs must be done together

It is important to stress—it cannot be overemphasized—that selecting a target market *and* developing a marketing mix are interrelated. Both parts of a marketing strategy must be decided together. It is *strategies* that must be evaluated against the company's objectives—not alternative target markets or alternative marketing mixes.

Understanding target markets leads to good strategies

The needs of a target market often virtually determine the nature of an appropriate marketing mix. So marketers must analyze their potential target markets with great care. This book will explore ways of identifying attractive market opportunities and developing appropriate strategies.

These ideas can be seen more clearly with an example in the children's fashion market.

Market-oriented strategy planning at Toddler University

The case of Jeff Silverman and Toddler University (TU) Inc., a shoe company he started, illustrates the strategy planning process. During high school and college, Silverman worked as a salesperson at local shoe stores. He also gained valuable experience during a year working for Nike. From these jobs he learned a lot about customers' needs and interests. He also realized that some parents were not satisfied when it came to finding shoes for their preschool children.

Silverman thought that there was a large, but hard to describe, mass market for general-purpose baby shoes—perhaps 60 or 70 percent of the potential for all kinds of baby shoes. Silverman did not focus on this market because it didn't make sense for his small company to compete head on with many other firms where he had no particular advantage. However, he identified four other markets that were quite different. In the following description of these markets, note that useful marketing mixes come to mind immediately.

They fit like Toddler U's. They just don't wear as well.

The "shoes" above are probably the best-fitting kids' shoes in the world. Toddler U's are a close second. Because when it comes to fit, Toddler U's are different from any other kids' shoes you can buy.

Most shoes are fitted by measuring just the length and width of the foot. This covers two dimensions. Feet occupy three.

Toddler U solves this problem through a process unsurprisingly named Tri-Dimensional Fit. As our illustration indicates, we measure not just length and width, but *girth*—the distance around the foot.

Then, to make sure the shoes fit all three dimensions, we use something no one else does: a system of custom-fitted footbeds.

Fit, Comfort, Mobility.

These form-fitting terry cloth cushions come in three different sizes. When the right size footbed is inserted, the shoe fits snugly to the precise contours of the foot.

But these footbeds definitely aren't designed for feet to sleep on. Toddler U's also come with a unique Flex Zone in the soles that lets feet flex as effortlessly as though barefoot. And the upper portions of our shoes are stitched (not glued) to the soles, a feature we call Natural Construction," which permits still more fluidity of movement.

The reasons are obvious: Shoes also have to fit when you aren't standing still, especially with people as intolerant of standing still as kids.

The Toddler U Guarantee.

In all, Toddler U makes everything from shoes for newborns to grade-schoolers. From athletic shoes to hiking shoes to arguably the world's most comfortable dress shoes.

But they're all designed in the same belief. At Toddler University' shoes are molded to feet, instead of vice versa.

In fact, if you're ever dissatisfied with the way Toddler U's fit or wear, call us and we'll send you a replacement pair without charge.

For more information, call 1-800-237-6751, and we'll send along a free sample footbed.

TODDLER UNIVERSITY'

Higher education for younger feet'

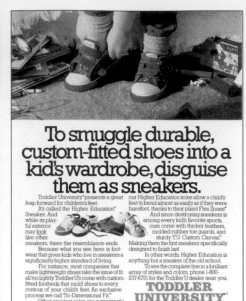

To smuggle durable, custom-fitted shoes into a kid's wardrobe, disguise them as sneakers.

Toddler University' presents a great leap forward for children's feet.

It's called the Higher Education" Sneaker. And while its playful exterior may look like other sneakers, there the resemblance ends.

Because what you see here is footwear that gives kids who live in sneakers a significantly higher standard of living.

For instance, most companies that make lightweight shoes take the issue of fit all too lightly. Toddler U's come with custom-fitted footbeds that mold shoes to every contour of your child's feet. An exclusive process we call Tri-Dimensional Fit."

Other sneaker soles are surprisingly inflexible when it comes to bending. But our Higher Education soles allow a child's feet to bend almost as easily as if they were barefoot, thanks to their pliant Flex Zones"

And since destroying sneakers is among every kid's favorite sports, ours come with thicker leathers, molded rubber toe guards, and sturdy T.U. Custom Canvas." Making them the first sneakers specifically designed to finish last.

In other words, Higher Education is anything but a sneaker of the old school.

To see the complete line in a brilliant array of styles and colors, phone 1-800-237-6751 for the Toddler U dealer near you.

TODDLER UNIVERSITY'

Higher education for younger feet'

The *Traditionalists* seemed to be satisfied with a well-manufactured shoe that was available from "quality" stores where they could seek help in selecting the right size and fit. They didn't mind if the design was old-fashioned and didn't change. They wanted a well-known brand that had a reputation for quality, even if it was a bit more expensive.

Many of the *Economy Oriented* parents were in the lower income group. They wanted a basic shoe at a low price. They saw baby shoes as all pretty much the same—so a "name" brand didn't have much appeal. They were willing to shop around to see what was on sale at local discount, department, or shoe stores.

The *Fashion Conscious* were interested in dressing up baby in shoes that looked like smaller versions of the latest styles that they bought for themselves. Fit was important, but beyond that a colourful design is what got their attention. They were more likely to look for baby-size shoes at the shop where they bought their own athletic shoes.

The *Attentive Parents* wanted shoes that met a variety of needs. They wanted shoes to be fun and fashionable and functional. They didn't want just a good fit but also design and materials that were really right for baby play and learning to walk. These well-informed, upscale shoppers were likely to buy from a store that specialized in baby items. They were willing to pay a premium price if they found the right product.

The market was meeting the needs of the Traditionalists quite well. The Economy Oriented and Fashion Conscious customers were also satisfied with shoes from a variety of other companies, including Nike. But Silverman saw a way to get a toe up on the competition by targeting the Attentive Parents with a marketing mix that combined, in his words, "fit and function with fun and fashion." He developed a detailed marketing plan that attracted financial backers, and at age 24 his company came to life.

TU didn't have its own production facilities, so Silverman contracted with a producer in Taiwan to make shoes with his brand name and to his specs. And his specs were different—they improved the product for his target market. Unlike most rigid high-topped infant shoes, he designed softer shoes with more comfortable rubber soles. The shoes lasted longer because they are stitched rather than glued. An extrawide opening made fitting easier on squirming feet. He also patented a special insert so parents could adjust the width. This change also helped win support from retailers. Since there are 11 sizes of children's shoes—and five widths—retailers usually need to stock 55 pairs of each model. TU's adjustable width reduced this stocking problem and made it more profitable for retailers to sell the line. It also made it possible for TU to resupply sold-out inventory faster than competitors. Silverman's Product and Place decisions worked together well to provide customer value and also to give him a competitive advantage.

For promotion, Silverman developed print ads with close-up photos of babies wearing his shoes and informative details about their special benefits. Creative packaging also helped promote the shoe and attract customers in the store. For example, he put one athletic-style shoe in a box that looked like a grey gym locker. Silverman also provided the stores with "shoe rides"—electric-powered rocking replicas of its shoes. The rides not only attracted kids to the shoe department, but since they were coin-operated, they paid for themselves in a year.

TU priced most of its shoes at $35 to $40 a pair. This is a premium price, but with today's smaller families, the Attentive Parents are willing to spend more on each child.

In just four years, TU's sales jumped from $100,000 to over $40 million. To keep growth going, Silverman expanded distribution to reach new markets in Europe. To take advantage of TU's relationship with its satisfied target customers, he also added shoes for older kids to the Toddler University product assortment. Then Silverman made his biggest sale of all: He sold his company to Genesco, one of the biggest firms in the footwear business.[4]

You've seen how Silverman managed to target and capture a premium priced market segment of "Attentive Parents." Type www.robeez.ca into your browser to see how a Canadian business was able to tap into the same market of quality baby shoes—with the same remarkable level of success. The marketing strategies between the two firms are similar in that ROBEEZ correctly determined that higher-income level parents were prepared to pay a premium price to get the best shoes for their baby.

THE MARKETING PLAN IS A GUIDE TO IMPLEMENTATION AND CONTROL

Marketing plan fills out marketing strategy

As the Toddler University case illustrates, a marketing strategy sets a target market and a marketing mix. It is a big picture of what a firm will do in some markets. A marketing plan goes farther. A **marketing plan** is a written statement of a marketing strategy *and* the time-related details for carrying out the strategy. It should spell out the following in detail: (1) what marketing mix will be offered, to whom (that is, the target market), and for how long; (2) what company resources (shown as costs) will be needed at what rate (month by month perhaps); and (3) what results are expected (sales and profits perhaps monthly or quarterly, customer satisfaction levels, and the like). The plan should also include some control procedures—so that whoever is to carry out the plan will know if things are going wrong. This might be something as simple as comparing actual sales against expected sales—with a warning flag to be raised whenever total sales fall below a certain level.

Later we will take a closer look at what is in a marketing plan. At that point, you will have learned about all of the major strategy decision areas (Exhibit 2-5) and how to blend them into an innovative strategy.

Implementation puts plans into operation

After a marketing plan is developed, a marketing manager knows *what* needs to be done. Then the manager is concerned with **implementation**—putting marketing plans into operation.

Strategies work out as planned only when they are effectively implemented. Many **operational decisions**—short-run decisions to help implement strategies—may be needed.

Marketing Mix Decision Area	Strategy Policies	Likely Operational Decisions
Product	Carry as limited a line of colours, styles, and sizes as will satisfy the target market.	Add, change, or drop colours, styles, and/or sizes as customer tastes dictate.
Place	Distribute through selected "baby-products" retailers that will carry the full line and provide good in-store sales support and promotion.	In market areas where sales potential is not achieved, add new retail outlets and/or drop retailers whose performance is poor.
Promotion	Promote the benefits and value of the special design and how it meets customer needs.	When a retailer hires a new salesperson, send current training package with details on product line; increase use of local newspaper print ads during peak demand periods (before holidays, etc.).
Price	Maintain a "premium" price, but encourage retailers to make large-volume orders by offering discounts on quantity purchases.	Offer short-term introductory price "deals" to retailers when a new style is first introduced.

Managers should make operational decisions within the guidelines set down during strategy planning. They develop product policies, place policies, and so on as part of strategy planning. Then operational decisions within these policies probably will be necessary—while carrying out the basic strategy. Note, however, that as long as these operational decisions stay within the policy guidelines, managers are making no change in the basic strategy. If the controls show that operational decisions are not producing the desired results, however, the managers may have to reevaluate the whole strategy—rather than just working harder at implementing it.

It's easier to see the difference between strategy decisions and operational decisions if we illustrate these ideas using our Toddler University example. Possible four-P or basic strategy policies are shown in the left-hand column in Exhibit 2-7, and examples of operational decisions are shown in the right-hand column.

It should be clear that some operational decisions are made regularly—even daily—and such decisions should not be confused with planning strategy. Certainly, a great deal of effort can be involved in these operational decisions. They might take a good part of the sales or advertising manager's time. But they are not the strategy decisions that will be our primary concern.

Our focus in this text is on developing marketing strategies. But eventually marketing managers must control the marketing plans that they develop and implement.[5]

Control is analyzing and correcting what you've done

The control job provides the feedback that leads managers to modify their marketing strategies. To maintain control, a marketing manager uses a number of tools—like computer sales analysis, marketing research surveys, and accounting analysis of expenses and profits.

In addition, as we talk about each of the marketing decision areas, we will discuss some of the control problems. This will help you understand how control keeps the firm on course—or shows the need to plan a new course.

All marketing jobs require planning and control

At first, it might appear that only high-level management or large companies need be concerned with planning and control. This is not true. Every organization needs planning—and without control it's impossible to know if the plans are working.

Several plans make a whole marketing program

Most companies implement more than one marketing strategy—and related marketing plan—at the same time. They may have several products—some of them quite different—that are aimed at different target markets. The other elements of

Exhibit 2-8
Elements of a Firm's
Marketing Program

the marketing mix may vary too. Gillette's Right Guard deodorant, its Mach3 razor blades, and its Venus razors all have different marketing mixes. Yet the strategies for each must be implemented at the same time.[6] While this is complicated, Gillette gets a real benefit because there are efficiencies when all of their different products are shipped through the same distribution system. Even more important, all those different products use the same Gillette name and that helps promote consumer brand recognition.

A **marketing program** blends all of the firm's marketing plans into one "big" plan. See Exhibit 2-8. This program, then, is the responsibility of the whole company. Typically, the whole *marketing program* is an integrated part of the whole-company strategic plan we discussed earlier.

We will emphasize planning one marketing strategy at a time, rather than planning—or implementing—a whole marketing program. This is practical because it is important to plan each strategy carefully. Too many marketing managers fall into sloppy thinking. They try to develop too many strategies all at once—and don't develop any very carefully. However, when new strategies are evaluated, it makes sense to see how well they fit with the existing marketing program.

THE IMPORTANCE OF MARKETING STRATEGY PLANNING

We emphasize the planning part of the marketing manager's job for a good reason. The "onetime" strategy decisions—the decisions that decide what business the company is in and the strategies it will follow—usually determine success, or failure. An extremely good plan might be carried out badly and still be profitable, while a poor but well-implemented plan can lose money. The case history that follows shows the importance of planning and why we emphasize marketing strategy planning throughout this text.

Time for new strategies in the watch industry

The conventional watchmakers—both domestic and foreign—had always aimed at customers who thought of watches as high-priced, high-quality symbols to mark special events, like graduations or retirement. Advertising was concentrated around Christmas and graduation time and stressed a watch's symbolic appeal. Expensive jewellery stores were the main retail outlets.

This commonly accepted strategy of the major watch companies ignored people in the target market that just wanted to tell the time and were interested in a reliable, low-priced watch. So the U.S. Time Company developed a successful strategy around its Timex watches and became the world's largest watch company. Timex completely upset the watch industry—both foreign and domestic—not only by offering a good product (with a one-year repair or replace guarantee) at a lower price, but also by using new, lower-cost channels of distribution. Its watches were widely available in drugstores, discount retailers, and nearly any other retail stores that would carry them.

Marketing managers at Timex soon faced a new challenge. Texas Instruments, a new competitor in the watch market, took the industry by storm with its low-cost but very accurate electronic watches—using the same channels Timex had originally developed. But other firms quickly developed a watch that used a more stylish liquid crystal display for the digital readout. Texas Instruments could not change quickly enough to keep up, and the other companies took away its customers. The competition became so intense that Texas Instruments stopped marketing watches altogether.

While Timex and others were focusing on lower-priced watches, Japan's Seiko captured a commanding share of the high-priced gift market for its stylish and accurate quartz watches by obtaining strong distribution. All of this forced many traditional watchmakers—like some of the once-famous Swiss brands—to close their factories.

Then Switzerland's Swatch launched its colourful, affordable plastic watches and changed what consumers see when they look at their watches. Swatch promoted its watches as fashion accessories and set them apart from those of other firms, whose ads squabbled about whose watches were most accurate and dependable. Swatch was also able to attract new retailers by focusing its distribution on upscale fashion and department stores. The total size of the watch market increased because many consumers bought several watches to match different fashions.

The economic downturn in the early 1990s brought more changes. Consumers were more cost conscious and less interested in expensive watches like those made by Rolex that were the "in" status symbol a few years earlier. The reemergence of value-seeking customers prompted Timex to return to its famous advertising tagline of the 1960s: "It takes a licking and keeps on ticking." Its position as the inexpensive-but-durable choice has helped it strengthen its distribution and has given it a leg up in getting shelf space for new products, such as its Indiglo line of watches.

By the turn of the century, the total market for watches was growing at only about 5 percent a year. To spark higher sales of its lines, Timex pushed to introduce more watches that combine time-telling and other needs. For example, Timex watches include heart-rate monitors, GPS systems to compute a runner's distance and speed, personal digital assistant functions (including data links to a computer), and Internet messenger capabilities so a watch can receive short text messages, like an alert from the wearer's stockbroker that it's time to sell. Of course, all the new features can make a watch more complicated to use, so Timex has promoted its I-control technology, which makes its watches "ridiculously easy to use." However, the competition is on the move as well. For example, Fossil Inc., and Citizen Watch Company were the first watch companies to incorporate Microsoft's new operating system for SPOT (Small Personal Objective Technology). These watches connect to a wireless network to provide a variety of information services, including traffic and weather reports. With such changes always underway, marketing strategies at Timex must be constantly updated and revised.[7]

CREATIVE STRATEGY PLANNING NEEDED FOR SURVIVAL

Dramatic shifts in strategy—like those described above—may surprise conventional, production-oriented managers. But such changes should be expected. Managers who embrace the marketing concept realize that they cannot just define their line of business in terms of the products they currently produce or sell. Rather, they have to think about the basic consumer needs they serve, how those needs may change in the future, and how they can improve the value they offer to customers. If they are too nearsighted, they may fail to see what's coming until too late.

Creative strategy planning is becoming even more important. Domestic and foreign competition threatens those who can't provide superior customer value and find ways to build stronger relationships with customers. New markets, new customers, and new ways of doing things must be found if companies are to operate profitably in the future—and contribute to the macro-marketing system.

Focus on "best practices" for improved results

The case studies and concepts in this chapter highlight effective marketing thinking. Throughout the text, we will continue with this thrust—focusing on marketing frameworks and concepts that produce good results. Some of these are new and innovative, and others are well established. What they have in common is that they all work well.

Sometimes we will warn you about marketing errors—so you can avoid them. But we won't just give you laundry lists of different approaches and then leave it to you to guess what might work. Rather, our focus will be on "best-practices" marketing.

There is an important reason for this approach. In too many firms, managers do a poor job planning and implementing marketing strategies and programs. The discount airline industry in Canada saw some marketing disasters when the number of new customers they attracted was insufficient to make up for the losses they encountered on deep price-cut seat sales. And, as shown in Exhibit 2-9, this type of "death-wish" marketing is both costly and ineffective. In fact, you can see that even the average marketing program isn't producing great results—and that accounts for the majority of firms!

Exhibit 2-9 was developed by experts at Copernicus, one of the premier marketing research and consulting firms in the world. As these experts indicate in the chart, some managers are creating marketing programs that produce exceptional results for their companies. This book will help you do exactly that.

WHAT ARE ATTRACTIVE OPPORTUNITIES?

Effective marketing strategy planning matches opportunities to the firm's resources (what it can do) and its objectives (what top management wants to do). Successful strategies get their start when a creative manager spots an attractive market

Exhibit 2-9 Distribution of Different Firms Based on Their Marketing Performance

MARKETING PERFORMANCE:	TOTAL FAILURE	POOR	FAIR	GOOD	EXCEPTIONAL
Marketing Share	Dramatic Decline	Significant Decline	Modest Decline	Increase	Dramatic Increase
New Product Success	0%	5%	10%	25%	40%+
Advertising ROI	Negative	0%	1–4%	5–10%	20%
Customer Satisfaction	0–59%	60–69%	70–79%	80–89%	90–95%
Customer Retention/Loyalty	0–44%	45–59%	60–74%	75–89%	90–94%

opportunity. Yet an opportunity that is attractive for one firm may not be attractive for another. Attractive opportunities for a particular firm are those that the firm has some chance of doing something about—given its resources and objectives.

Breakthrough opportunities are best

Throughout this book, we will emphasize finding **breakthrough opportunities**—opportunities that help innovators develop hard-to-copy marketing strategies that will be very profitable for a long time. That's important because there are always imitators who want to "share" the innovator's profits—if they can. Recall the earlier example about Timex. Switzerland's Swatch was successful at imitating the Timex strategy of introducing a cheaper watch sold through lower-priced distribution channels. It's hard to continuously provide *superior* value to target customers if competitors can easily copy your marketing mix.

Competitive advantage is needed—at least

Even if a manager can't find a breakthrough opportunity, the firm should try to obtain a competitive advantage to increase its chances for profit or survival. **Competitive advantage** means that a firm has a marketing mix that the target market sees as better than a competitor's mix. A competitive advantage may result from efforts in different areas of the firm—cost cutting in production, innovative R&D, more effective purchasing of needed components, or financing for a new distribution facility. Similarly, a strong sales force, a well-known brand name, or good dealers may give it a competitive advantage in pursuing an opportunity. Whatever the source, an advantage only succeeds if it allows the firm to provide superior value and satisfy customers better than some competitor.

Sometimes a firm can achieve breakthrough opportunities and competitive advantage by simply fine-tuning its current marketing mix(es) or developing closer relationships with its customers. Other times it may need new facilities, new people in new parts of the world, and totally new ways of solving problems. But every firm needs some competitive advantage—so the promotion people have something unique to sell and success doesn't just hinge on offering lower and lower prices.[8]

Avoid hit-or-miss marketing with a logical process

You can see why a manager *should* seek attractive opportunities. But that doesn't mean that everyone does—or that everyone can turn an opportunity into a successful strategy. As Exhibit 2-9 shows, too many firms settle for the sort of death-wish marketing that doesn't satisfy customers or make a profit—to say nothing about

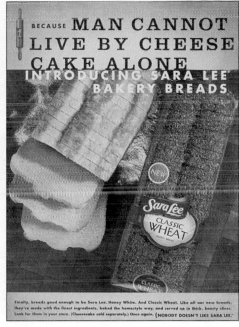

Attractive new opportunities are often fairly close to markets the firm already knows.

achieving a breakthrough or providing superior value. Looking at the percentages under the standard normal curve in Exhibit 2-9 for example, indicates that the people from Copernicus estimate that the marketing performance of 16 percent of the firms is considered to be below or well below average. Other items from their study show the importance of good marketing practices on the success of key variables. Look at the dramatic improvement on the success of new product introductions, return on investment for advertising dollars spent, or customer satisfaction and loyalty statistics. It's all too easy for a well-intentioned manager to react in a piece-meal way to what appears to be an opportunity. Then by the time the problems are obvious, it's too late.

Developing a successful marketing strategy doesn't need to be a hit-or-miss proposition. And it won't be if you learn the marketing strategy planning process developed in this text. Exhibit 2-10 summarizes the marketing strategy planning process we'll be developing throughout the rest of the chapters.

MARKETING STRATEGY PLANNING PROCESS HIGHLIGHTS OPPORTUNITIES

We've emphasized that a marketing strategy requires decisions about the specific customers the firm will target and the marketing mix the firm will develop to appeal to that target market. We can organize the many marketing mix decisions (review Exhibit 2-5) in terms of the four Ps—Product, Place, Promotion, and Price. Thus, the "final" strategy decisions are represented by the target market surrounded by the four Ps. However, the idea isn't just to come up with *some* strategy. After all, there are hundreds or even thousands of combinations of marketing mix decisions and target markets (i.e., strategies) that a firm might try. Rather, the challenge is to zero in on the best strategy.

Process narrows down from broad opportunities to specific strategy

As Exhibit 2-10 suggests, it is useful to think of the marketing strategy planning process as a narrowing-down process. Later in this chapter and in the next two chapters we will go into more detail about strategy decisions relevant to each of the terms in this figure. Then, throughout the rest of the book, we will present a variety of concepts and "how to" frameworks that will help you improve the way you

Exhibit 2-10
Overview of Marketing
Strategy Planning Process

Narrowing down to focused strategy with quantitative and qualitative screening criteria

Customers
Needs and Other
Segmenting
Dimensions

Company
Objectives
and
Resources

Competitors
Current
and
Prospective

S.
W.
O.
T.

Segmentation
& Targeting

Differentiation
& Positioning

Product　Place
Target
Market
Price　Promotion

External Market Environment
Technological　Political and Legal　Cultural and Social　Economic

make these strategy decisions. As a preview of what's coming, let's briefly overview the general logic of the process depicted in Exhibit 2-10.

The process starts with a broad look at the market. The external market environment affects the entire strategic plan. Technological, political, legal, cultural, social, and economic factors all set the stage for influencing how customers, competitors, and the marketer's firm will interact. Failing to appreciate how Internet technology or the differing cultures of Canada can affect consumer buying behaviour would hurt the marketing efforts of high-tech companies like Research in Motion with their BlackBerry, all the way through to large national retailers like The Bay for example.

The strategic plan gains focus when we look at customer needs, the company's competitive advantages and costs, and competitors. These are referred to as the Cs so that you will remember them just like the four Ps. You already understand the importance of focusing on your customers, but you also need to consider your company's competitive advantages compared to others and also your costs because these limit the kind and amount of marketing you can do. Last, but very important, is the need to consider your competitors and their strengths and weaknesses because these will also play a key role in guiding your planning. Remember how Dell Computers developed a large price sensitive market through the direct-order business. That approach helped them control costs. Additionally, they knew their competitive advantages lay both in underpricing their competition as well as being able to custom produce for their market.

The C's help to identify new and unique opportunities that might be overlooked if the focus is narrowed too quickly. They also help to warn you of dangers in the marketplace that you should consider when planning your strategy. When ING Direct entered the banking business in Canada, they knew better than to take on established Canadian banks by opening branches. Instead they used Internet technology to tap into a computer literate market niche.

Segmentation helps pinpoint the target

A key objective of marketing is to satisfy the needs of some group of customers that the firm serves. Broadly speaking, then, in the early stages of a search for opportunities we're looking for customers with needs that are not being satisfied as well as they might be. Of course, potential customers are not all alike. They don't all have the same needs—nor do they always want to meet needs in the same way. Part of the reason is that there are different possible types of customers with many different characteristics. For example, individual consumers often have different needs than organizations, and

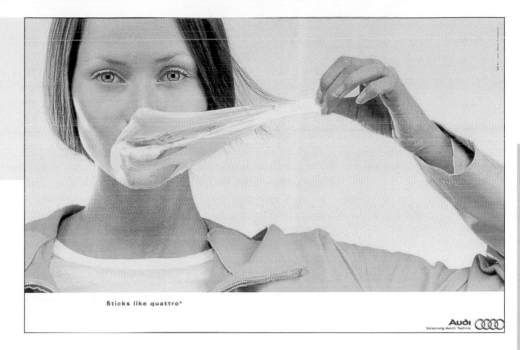

This Norwegian ad for the Audi quattro simply says, "Sticks like quattro." Although it doesn't show the car at all, it helps to differentiate the Audi and its four-wheel drive system that holds the road especially well, even in the snow.

Sticks like quattro*

Audi ⨀⨀
Vorsprung durch Technik

people with certain attitudes or interests have different preferences for how they spend their time, what shows they watch, and the like. In spite of the many possible differences, there often are subgroups (segments) of consumers who are similar and could be satisfied with the same marketing mix. Thus, we try to identify and understand these different subgroups—with market segmentation. We will explain approaches for segmenting markets later in Chapter 3. Then, in Chapters 5 to 7, we delve into the many interesting aspects of customer behaviour. For now, however, you should know that really understanding customers is at the heart of using market segmentation to narrow down to a specific target market. In other words, segmentation helps a manager decide to serve some segment(s)—subgroup(s) of customers—and not others.

Narrow down to a superior marketing mix

A marketing mix must meet the needs of target customers, but a firm isn't likely to get a competitive advantage if it *just* meets needs in the same way as some other firm. So in evaluating possible strategies, the marketing manager should think about whether there is a way to differentiate the marketing mix. **Differentiation** means that the marketing mix is distinct from and better than what is available from a competitor. Sometimes the difference is based mainly on one important element of the marketing mix—say, an improved product or faster delivery. However, differentiation often requires that the firm fine-tune all of the elements of its marketing mix to the specific needs of a distinctive target market. Differentiation is also more obvious to target customers when there is a consistent theme integrated across the four Ps decision areas. That emphasizes the difference so target customers will think of the firm as being in a unique position to meet their needs. For example, in Norway many auto buyers are particularly concerned about safety in the snow. So Audi offers a permanent four-wheel drive system, called quattro, that helps the car to hold the road. Audi ads emphasize this differentiation. Rather than show the car, however, the ads feature things that are very sticky (like bubblegum!) and the only text is the headline "sticks like quattro" and the Audi brand name. Of course, handling is not Audi's only strength, but it is an important one in helping to position Audi as better than competing brands with this target market. In contrast, consider General Motors' decision to discontinue the 100-year-old Oldsmobile line. In spite of repeated efforts, marketers for Oldsmobile were no longer able to develop a differentiated position in the crowded U.S. auto market. And when target customers don't see an advantage with a firm's marketing mix, they just move on.[9]

In Chapter 3, we'll introduce concepts relevant to this sort of positioning. Then, in Chapters 9 to 18, we'll cover the many ways in which the four Ps of the marketing mix can be differentiated. For now you can see that the thrust is to narrow down from all possible marketing mixes to one that is differentiated to meet target customers' needs particularly well. Of course, finding the best differentiation requires that we understand competitors as well as customers.

Screening criteria make it clear why you select a strategy

There are usually more different opportunities—and strategy possibilities—than a firm can pursue. Each one has its own advantages and disadvantages. Trends in the external market environment may make a potential opportunity more or less attractive. These complications can make it difficult to zero in on the best target market and marketing mix. However, developing a set of specific qualitative and quantitative screening criteria can help a manager define what business and markets the firm wants to compete in. It can also help eliminate potential strategies that are not well suited for the firm. We will cover screening criteria in more detail in Chapter 4. For now, you should realize that the criteria you select in a specific situation grow out of an analysis of the company's objectives and resources.

S.W.O.T. analysis highlights advantages and disadvantages

A useful aid for identifying relevant screening criteria and for zeroing in on a feasible strategy is **S.W.O.T. analysis**—which identifies and lists the firm's strengths and weaknesses and its opportunities and threats. The name S.W.O.T. is simply an abbreviation for the first letters of the words strengths, weaknesses, opportunities, and threats. A good S.W.O.T. analysis helps the manager focus on a strategy that takes advantage of the firm's opportunities and strengths while avoiding its weaknesses and threats to its success. These can be compared with the pros and cons of different strategies that are considered.

The marketing strategy developed by Amilya Antonetti illustrates the basic ideas behind a S.W.O.T. analysis. Her son was allergic to the chemicals in standard detergents—and her research showed that many other children had the same problem. So she started SoapWorks and developed a line of hypoallergenic cleaning products to pursue this opportunity. Unlike the big firms, she didn't have relations with grocery chains or money for national TV ads. To get around these weaknesses, she used inexpensive radio ads in local markets and touted SoapWorks as a company created for moms by a mom who cared about kids. She had a credible claim that the big corporations couldn't make. Her ads also helped her get shelf space because they urged other mothers to ask for SoapWorks products and to tell friends about stores that carried them. This wasn't the fastest possible way to introduce a new product line, but her cash-strapped strategy played to her unique strengths with her specific target market.[10]

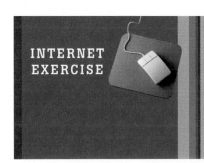

INTERNET EXERCISE

Go to lululemon athletica (lululemon.com) and surf the whole site. Using the Web site information and a S.W.O.T. analysis, can you define the lululemon strategy in developing the youth female sports fashion market? Now consider the SoapWorks example we just discussed. Are there any similarities in the way these two small start-up companies managed to develop their markets—even though they were faced with much larger well-established competitors?

Exhibit 2-10 focuses on planning each strategy carefully. Of course, this same approach works well when several strategies are to be planned. Then, having an organized evaluation process is even more important. It forces everyone involved to think through how the various strategies fit together as part of an overall marketing program.[11]

TYPES OF OPPORTUNITIES TO PURSUE

Some alert marketers seem to be able to spot attractive opportunities everywhere they look. This seems reasonable when you recognize that most people have unsatisfied needs. Unfortunately, many opportunities seem "obvious" only after someone else identifies them. So, early in the marketing strategy planning process it's useful for marketers to have a framework for thinking about the broad kinds of opportunities they may find. Exhibit 2-11 shows four broad possibilities: market penetration, market development, product development, and diversification. We will look at these separately, but some firms pursue more than one type of opportunity at the same time.

Market penetration

Market penetration means trying to increase sales of a firm's present products in its present markets—probably through a more aggressive marketing mix. The firm may try to strengthen its relationship with customers to increase their rate of use or repeat purchases, or try to attract competitors' customers or current nonusers. Coleman got a 50 percent increase in sales of its outdoor equipment, like camping lanterns and stoves, by reaching its target market with special promotional displays at outdoor events like concerts, fishing tournaments, and NASCAR races. For example, about 250,000 auto racing fans camp on-site at NASCAR races each year—so a display at the campground is an effective way to reach customers when they have leisure time to browse through product displays and demos.[12]

New promotion appeals alone may not be effective. A firm may need to make it easier for customers to place repeat orders on the Internet. Or it may need to add more stores in present areas for greater convenience. Short-term price cuts or coupon offers may help.

Many firms try to increase market penetration by developing closer relationships with customers so that they will be loyal. Frequent buyer clubs use this approach. Similarly, firms often analyze customer databases to identify "cross-selling" opportunities. For example, when a customer goes online to register Adobe's Photoshop, the Web page promotes other related products, including its popular Acrobat Reader.

Market development

Market development means trying to increase sales by selling present products in new markets. This may involve searching for new uses for a product. E-Z-Go, a producer of golf carts, has done this. Its carts are now a quiet way for workers to get around malls, airports, and big factories. The large units are popular as utility vehicles on farms, at outdoor sports events, and at resorts. E-Z-Go even fits carts with ice compartments and cash drawers so they can be used for mobile food services.

Firms may also try advertising in different media to reach new target customers. Or they may add channels of distribution or new stores in new areas, including overseas. For example, to reach new customers, McDonald's has opened outlets in airports, zoos, casinos, and military bases. And it's rapidly expanded into international markets with outlets in places like Russia, Brazil, and China.[13]

Product development

Product development means offering new or improved products for present markets. By knowing the present market's needs, a firm may see new ways to satisfy customers. For example, kids are the big consumers of ketchup. So Heinz figured out how ketchup could be more fun. Producing ketchup in gross green and funky purple colours—in an EZ Squirt dispenser molded to fit little hands—increased sales so much that the factory had to run 24/7. Ski resorts have developed trails for hiking and biking to bring their winter ski customers back in the summer. Nike moved beyond shoes and sportswear to offer its athletic target market a running watch, digital audio player, and even a portable heart-rate monitor. And of course Intel boosts sales by developing newer and faster chips.[14]

Exhibit 2-11
Four Basic Types of
Opportunities

	Present products	New products
Present markets	Market penetration	Product development
New markets	Market development	Diversification

Diversification

Diversification means moving into totally different lines of business—perhaps entirely unfamiliar products, markets, or even levels in the production-marketing system. Products and customers that are very different from a firm's current base may look attractive to the optimists—but these opportunities are usually hard to evaluate. That's why diversification usually involves the biggest risk. McDonald's, for example, opened two hotels in Switzerland. The plan was to serve families on the weekend, but business travellers were the target during the week. Business travellers are not the group that McDonald's usually serves, and an upscale hotel is also very different from a fast-food restaurant. This helps to explain why operation of the Golden Arch hotels was taken over by a hospitality management company after two years. On the other hand, diversification can be successful—especially when the new strategy fits well with the firm's resources and marketing program.[15]

Which opportunities come first?

Usually firms find attractive opportunities fairly close to markets they already know. This may allow them to capitalize on changes in their present markets—or more basic changes in the external environment. Moreover, many firms are finding that the easiest way to increase profits is to do a better job of hanging on to the customers that they've already won—by meeting their needs so well that they wouldn't consider switching to another firm. This is why business-to-business (B2B) marketers like Alcan, Dofasco, and Teck Cominco developed customer relationship management programs, intranet sites, and joint research projects with their customers. International commodity competitors in South America and Asia would otherwise have poached their customers based on cheaper commodity prices.

For these reasons, most firms think first of greater market penetration. They want to increase profits where they already have experience and strengths. On the other hand, many firms are proving that market development—including the move into new international markets—is another profitable way to take advantage of current strengths.

INTERNATIONAL OPPORTUNITIES SHOULD BE CONSIDERED

It's easy for a marketing manager to fall into the trap of ignoring international markets, especially when the firm's domestic market is prosperous. Yet there are good reasons to go to the trouble of looking elsewhere for opportunities.

The world is getting smaller

International trade is increasing all around the world, and trade barriers are coming down. In addition, advances in e-commerce, transportation, and communications are making it easier and cheaper to reach international customers. With an Internet Web site and e-mail, even the smallest firm can provide international customers with a great deal of information—and easy ways to order—at very little expense. E-commerce ordering can be fast and efficient whether the customer is a mile away or in another country. Around the world, potential customers have needs and money to spend. The real question is whether a firm can effectively use its resources to meet these customers' needs at a profit.

McDonald's pursues growth in a variety of ways including new product development efforts, like its Grilled Chicken Flatbread sandwich and McGriddles breakfast sandwich, to offer customers more reasons to eat at McDonald's.

Develop a competitive advantage at home and abroad

If customers in other countries are interested in the products a firm offers—or could offer—serving them may improve economies of scale. Lower costs (and prices) may give a firm a competitive advantage both in its home markets *and* abroad. Black and Decker, for example, uses electric motors in many of its tools and appliances. By selling overseas as well as in Canada, it gets economies of scale and the cost per motor is very low.

Marketing managers who are only interested in the "convenient" customers in their own backyards may be rudely surprised to find that an aggressive, low-cost foreign producer is willing to pursue those customers—even if doing it is not convenient. Many companies that thought they could avoid the struggles of international competition have learned this lesson the hard way. A small air purification equipment manufactuer puts it this way: "If I'm not [selling to an oil refinery] in Saudi Arabia, somebody else is going to solve their problem, then come attack me on my home turf."[16]

Get an early start in a new market

Different countries are at different stages of economic and technological development, and their consumers have different needs at different times.

A company facing tough competition, thin profit margins, and slow sales growth at home may get a fresh start in another country where demand for its product is just beginning to grow. A marketing manager may be able to transfer marketing know-how—or some other competitive advantage—the firm has already developed. Consider JLG, a producer of equipment used to lift workers and tools at construction sites. Faced with tough competition, JLG's profits all but evaporated. By cutting costs, the company improved its domestic sales. But it got an even bigger boost from expanding overseas. By 2000 its international sales were greater than its total sales five years before. Now JLG is adding distribution in China. So international sales could soon account for half of its business.[17]

Find better trends in variables

Unfavourable trends in the marketing environment at home—or favourable trends in other countries—may make international marketing particularly attractive. For example, population growth in North America has slowed and income is levelling off. In other places in the world, population and income are increasing rapidly. Many firms can no longer rely on the constant market growth that once drove increased domestic sales. Growth—and perhaps even survival—will come

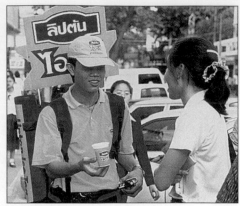

Lipton is pursuing new customers and growth in over 100 countries. For example, its multilingual Web site in Belgium explains how to make exotic cocktails from Ice Tea, and in Asia it encourages consumer trial with free samples.

only by aiming at more distant customers. It doesn't make sense to casually assume that all of the best opportunities exist "at home."[18]

Screening must consider risks as well as benefits

International opportunities should be considered in the strategy planning process, but they don't always survive as the most attractive ones that are turned into strategies. As with local opportunities, managers should consider international opportunities relative to the firm's objectives and resources—as well as its strengths and weaknesses.

Screening criteria for international market development may include a variety of factors ranging from expected rate of population growth or cultural challenges to political instability or other economic risks. Risks are often higher with international opportunities. For example, while the 9/11 attack on the World Trade Center shows that horrible terrorist acts are not limited to overseas markets, most managers find it more difficult to protect a firm's employees—and its financial interests—in a remote market if the political structure, laws, resources, and culture are very different.

ETHICAL PLANNING AND STRATEGY

Planning and strategy are long-term concepts. So is ethical behaviour. Good strategists realize the importance of ethical issues and recognize that good planning incorporates them. Aside from "doing the right thing," developing a strong ethical position in your marketing plan makes good business sense. Ask lululemon or The Body Shop. Both companies have used their ethical strategic commitments as a strong marketing positioning strategy—very successfully.

Let's consider a few of the major ethical issues impacting today's markets and our need to incorporate them in strategic planning.

We need more social responsibility

Good business managers put themselves in the consumer's position. A useful rule to follow might be: Do unto others as you would have others do unto you. In practice, this means developing satisfying marketing mixes for specific target markets. It may mean building in more quality or more safety. The consumer's long-run satisfaction should be considered too. How will the product hold up in use? What about service guarantees? While trying to serve the needs of some target market, does the marketing strategy disregard the rights and needs of other consumers or create problems that will be left for future generations?[19]

We need to welcome international competition

Marketers can't afford to bury their heads in the sand and hope that international competition will go away. Rather, they must realize that it is part of today's marketing environment. It creates even more pressure on marketing managers to figure out what it takes to gain a competitive advantage—both at home and in foreign markets. But with the challenge comes opportunities. The forces of competition in and among market-directed economies will help speed the diffusion of marketing advances to consumers everywhere. As macro-marketing systems improve worldwide, more consumers will have income to buy products—from wherever in the world those products come.

We need to use technology wisely

We live in a time of dramatic new technologies. Many marketers hate the idea that what they've learned from years of on-the-job experience may no longer apply when a technology like the Internet comes along. Or they feel that it's the job of the technical specialist to figure out how a new technology can help the firm serve its customers. But marketers can't just pawn that responsibility off on "somebody else." If that means learning about new technologies, then that is just part of the marketing job.

At a broader level, firms face the challenge of determining what technologies are acceptable and which are not. For example, gene research has opened the door to life-saving medicines, genetically altered crops that resist drought or disease, and even cloning of human beings. Yet in all of these arenas there is intense conflict among different groups about what is appropriate. How should these decisions be made? There is no simple answer to this question, but it's clear that old production-oriented views are *not* the answer. Perhaps we will move toward developing answers if some of the marketing ideas that have been applied to understanding individual needs can be extended to better understand the needs of society as a whole.

The environment is everyone's need

Marketers need to work harder and smarter at finding ways to satisfy consumer needs without sacrificing the environment. All consumers need the environment, whether they realize it yet or not. We are only beginning to understand the consequences of the environmental damage that's already been done. Acid rain, depletion of the ozone layer, global warming, and toxic waste in water supplies—to mention but a few current environmental problems—have catastrophic effects.

In the past, most firms didn't pass on the cost of environmental damage to consumers in the prices that they paid. Pollution was a hidden and unmeasured cost for most companies. That is changing rapidly. Firms are already paying billions of dollars to correct problems, including problems created years ago. The government isn't accepting the excuse that "nobody knew it was a big problem."[20]

We need to pay attention to consumer privacy

Marketers must also be sensitive to consumers' rights and privacy. Today, sophisticated marketing research methods, the Internet, and other technologies make it easier to abuse these rights. For example, credit card records—which reveal much about consumers' purchases and private lives—are routinely computerized and sold to anybody who pays for the list. And these problems, if ignored in the short-term, create a consumer backlash in the long run. Remember our discussion about the Canadian Marketing Association's "do not call" lists in Chapter 1? Consumers are demanding protection from Canadian telemarketers who invade their privacy.

We need laws when ethics fail

One of the advantages of a market-directed economy is that it operates automatically. In Canada however, the government also institutes laws on behalf of consumers and businesses in those situations where fair and honest trade practices fail. Type the words "Competition Act" into your browser to see some examples of laws that govern fair marketing practices and competitive behaviour. Unethical marketing practices may generate some short-term profits but they may also attract some long-term criminal charges.

What's the best policy to guide your ethical marketing planning? When you are considering something you would prefer to hide from other people—chances are you are considering something unethical.

CONCLUSION

The marketing manager must constantly study the market environment—seeking attractive opportunities and planning new strategies. A marketing strategy specifies a target market and the marketing mix the firm will offer to provide that target market with superior customer value. A marketing mix has four major decision areas: the four Ps—Product, Place, Promotion, and Price.

There are usually more opportunities than a firm can pursue, so possible target markets must be matched with marketing mixes the firm can offer. Then attractive strategies—really, whole marketing plans—are chosen for implementation. In the opening case, Dell was well aware it couldn't go head-to-head with the established computer manufacturers so its marketing plan called for a low priced market penetration strategy designed to capture the price sensitive target market. Controls are needed to be sure that the plans are carried out successfully. If anything goes wrong along the way, continual feedback should cause the process to be started over again—with the marketing manager planning more attractive marketing strategies. When Dell introduced a laptop design that the market didn't want the company's marketing control system quickly detected the problem, the product was pulled, and the error corrected. Thus, the job of marketing management is one of continuous planning, implementing, and control.

Firms need effective strategy planning to survive in our increasingly competitive markets. The challenge isn't just to come up with *some* strategy, but to zero in on the strategy that is best for the firm given its objectives and resources—and taking into consideration its strengths and weaknesses and the opportunities and threats that it faces. To improve your ability in this area, this chapter introduces a framework for marketing strategy planning. The rest of this text is organized to deepen your understanding of this framework and how to use it to develop profitable marketing mixes for clearly defined target markets. After several chapters on analyzing target markets, we will discuss each of the four Ps in greater detail.

While market-oriented strategy planning is helpful to marketers, it is also needed by financial managers, accountants, production and personnel people, and all other specialists. A market-oriented plan lets everybody in the firm know what ballpark they are playing in and what they are trying to accomplish.

We will use the term *marketing manager* for editorial convenience, but really, when we talk about marketing strategy planning, we are talking about the planning that a market-oriented manager should do when developing a firm's strategic plans. Without a clearly defined strategic plan, carrying out major target market shifts is suicidal. Dell had well-defined plans both for moving into the network manufacturing business in order to capture North American government and corporate customers but also for moving into the totally new European PC market. This kind of thinking should be done—or at least understood—by everyone in the organization. And this means even the entry-level salesperson, production supervisor, retail buyer, or personnel counsellor.

Good strategic planning includes good ethics. Marketers today are much more sensitive to the ethical implications of their plans. It makes good long-run business sense, the market demands it, and it's the right thing to do.

KEY TERMS

marketing management process, 31

strategic (management) planning, 32

marketing strategy, 32

target market, 32

marketing mix, 32

target marketing, 32

mass marketing, 32

channel of distribution, 35

personal selling, 35

mass selling, 36

advertising, 36

publicity, 36

sales promotion, 36

marketing plan, 39

implementation, 39

operational decisions, 39

marketing program, 41

breakthrough opportunities, 44

competitive advantage, 44

differentiation, 47

S.W.O.T. analysis, 48

market penetration, 49

market development, 49

product development, 49

diversification, 50

QUESTIONS AND PROBLEMS

1. Distinguish clearly between a marketing strategy and a marketing mix. Use an example.

2. Distinguish clearly between mass marketing and target marketing. Use an example.

3. Why is the customer placed in the centre of the four Ps in the text diagram of a marketing strategy (Exhibit 2-4)? Explain, using a specific example from your own experience.

4. If a company sells its products only from a Web site, which is accessible over the Internet to customers from all over the world, does it still need to worry about having a specific target market? Explain your thinking.

5. Explain, in your own words, what each of the four Ps involves.

6. How does the Body Shop's marketing strategy set the details for its implementation?

7. Distinguish between strategy decisions and operational decisions, illustrating for a local retailer.

8. Distinguish between a strategy, a marketing plan, and a marketing program, illustrating for a local retailer.

9. Outline a marketing strategy for each of the following new products: (a) a radically new design for a toothbrush, (b) a new fishing reel, (c) a new wonder drug, and (d) a new industrial stapling machine.

10. Provide a specific illustration of why marketing strategy planning is important for all the employees at Radisson Hotels & Resorts, not just for those in the marketing department.

11. Exhibit 2-9 shows that only about three out of every four customers are, on average, satisfied by a firm's marketing programs. Give an example of a purchase you made where you were not satisfied and what the firm could have changed to satisfy you. If customer satisfaction is so important to firms, why don't they score better in this area?

12. Distinguish between an attractive opportunity like Bell's cell phone service and a breakthrough opportunity like SKYPE's Internet-based telephone system.

13. Did WestJet define its market more precisely than Air Canada when it entered the airline business?

14. In your own words, explain why the book suggests that you should think of marketing strategy planning as a narrowing-down process.

15. Explain the major differences among the four basic types of growth opportunities discussed in the text and cite examples for two of these types of opportunities.

16. Explain why a firm may want to pursue a market penetration opportunity before pursuing one involving product development or diversification.

17. In your own words, explain several reasons why a marketing manager should consider international markets when evaluating possible opportunities.

18. Explain why you shop at Wal-Mart. Now explain why you shop at The Bay. Do the reasons for shopping at each store differ?

COMPUTER-AIDED PROBLEM

2. Target Marketing

RESOURCE REMINDER

Marko Inc. manufactures and distributes a game for use on hand-held computer devices. The target market is young people who are price sensitive but still ready to spend a modest amount for extra gaming capability on their wireless computers.

Marko Inc.'s managers are comparing the profitability of a target marketing strategy with a mass marketing "strategy." The spreadsheet gives information about both approaches.

The mass marketing strategy is aiming at a much bigger market. But a smaller percent of the consumers in the market will actually buy this product—because not everyone needs or can afford it. Moreover, because this marketing mix is not tailored to specific needs, Marko will get a smaller share of the business from those who do buy than it would with a more targeted marketing mix.

Just trying to reach the mass market will take more promotion and require more retail outlets in more locations—so promotion costs and distribution costs are higher than with the target marketing strategy. On the other hand, the cost of producing each unit is higher with the target marketing strategy—to build in a more satisfying set of features. But because the more targeted marketing mix is trying to satisfy the needs of a specific target market, those customers will be willing to pay a higher price.

In the spreadsheet, "quantity sold" (by the firm) is equal to the number of people in the market who will actually buy one each of the product—multiplied by the share of those purchases won by the firm's marketing mix. Thus, a change in the size of the market, the percent of people who purchase, or the share captured by the firm will affect quantity sold. And a change in quantity sold will affect total revenue, total cost, and profit.

a. On a piece of paper, show the calculations that prove that the spreadsheet "total profit" value for the target marketing strategy is correct. (Hint: Remember to multiply unit production cost and unit distribution cost by the quantity sold.) Which approach seems better—target marketing or mass marketing? Why?

b. If the target marketer could find a way to reduce distribution cost per unit by $.25, how much would profit increase?

c. If Marko Inc., decided to use the target marketing strategy and better marketing mix decisions increased its share of purchases from 50 to 60 percent—without increasing costs—what would happen to total profit? What does this analysis suggest about the importance of maketing managers knowing enough about their target markets to be effective target marketers?

If you want to read the cases and view the video cases that accompany this chapter, visit the *Basic Marketing* Online Learning Centre at: **www.mcgrawhill.ca/olc/perreault**. Along with these cases and video cases, the OLC also has the software and user guide for this chapter's Computer-Aided Problem, as well as exercises, quizzes, articles, links, and other *interactive* content that will help you with your studies.

Segmenting and Positioning Market Strategy

It's a good thing that everyone doesn't think the same way. Otherwise, we would all shop at the same stores, eat all the same food, wear the same clothes, and buy all the same toys. An example of thinking differently is Coast Mountain Sports who sell top-of-the-line, technologically advanced outdoor gear and higher-end clothing versus SportChek who also sell outdoor recreational equipment and clothing—but at lower price points than Coast Mountain. The SportChek customers probably think that the Coast Mountain shoppers are paying too much for the high-end products when cheaper alternatives are available. Conversely, the Coast Mountain buyers may feel that paying big bucks for top-of-the-line advanced equipment is well worth the investment. Thinking differently doesn't mean that one person is right and the other is wrong. It just means that the target market or type of customer that Coast Mountain goes after is different than the SportChek target market.

Why do some people like wearing clothes with designer labels, such as Roots or Tommy Hilfiger? This target market feels that they have good taste and that it is worth the extra money to buy the designer label. The group of people who shun designer labels may feel that the other group is pretentious and unwise for paying an inflated price just for the privilege of wearing a designer label.

While we are on the subject of what people think, let's look at the concept of positioning or how people perceive brands. What is the first thing that comes to mind when you hear the word Xerox? Most people would say *photocopier* or *photocopy*. So it's probably not a good idea for Xerox to market a computer with the brand name Xerox. But this is exactly what Xerox did many years ago. As you can imagine, it failed, not because it was an inferior product but because it was positioned incorrectly in people's minds.

Having said that, marketers on some occasions can change a brand's positioning successfully. Take Oil of Olay, which was introduced in 1970 by a company called Richardson-Vicks Inc. It was positioned as a skin moisturizer for older women. Procter & Gamble acquired the brand in 1985 and has successfully expanded the line to include a full range of skin care products aimed at a younger demographic. Research showed that the word oil was negative, implying grease. As a result, P & G has eliminated the word oil from its brand in North America. Today's Olay product line includes top-performing beauty bar soaps, facial cleansers, facial moisturizers, hand and body lotions, and body washes.

In this chapter, we will look more deeply into the area of market segmentation, target markets, and positioning.

SEARCH FOR OPPORTUNITIES CAN BEGIN BY UNDERSTANDING MARKETS

Find breakthrough opportunities

The marketing strategy planning process involves careful evaluation of the market opportunities available before narrowing down to focus on the most attractive target market and marketing mix (review Exhibit 2-10). As the introductory cases illustrate, a manager who develops an understanding of the needs and characteristics of specific groups of target customers within the broader market may see new, breakthrough opportunities. But it's not always obvious how to identify the real needs of a target market—or the marketing mix that those customers will see as different from, and better than, what is available from a competitor. This chapter covers concepts and approaches that will help you to succeed in the search for those opportunities.

What is a company's market?

Identifying a company's market is an important but sticky issue. In general, a **market** is a group of potential customers with similar needs who are willing to exchange something of value with sellers offering various goods or services—that is, ways of satisfying those needs. However, within a general market, marketing-oriented managers develop marketing mixes for *specific* target markets. Getting the firm to focus on specific target markets is vital.

Don't just focus on the product

Some production-oriented managers don't understand this narrowing-down process. They get into trouble because they ignore the tough part of defining markets. To make the narrowing-down process easier, they just describe their markets in terms of *products* they sell. For example, producers and retailers of greeting cards might define their market as the "greeting-card" market. But this production-oriented approach ignores customers—and customers make a market! This also leads to missed opportunities. Hallmark isn't missing these opportunities. Instead, Hallmark aims at the "personal-expression" market. Hallmark stores offer all kinds of products that can be sent as "memory makers"—to express one person's feelings toward another. And as opportunities related to these needs change, Hallmark changes too. For example, at the Hallmark Web site (www.hallmark.com) it is easy to get shopping suggestions from an online "gift assistant," to order flowers, or to personalize an electronic greeting card to send over the Internet.[1]

From generic markets to product-markets

To understand the narrowing-down process, it's useful to think of two basic types of markets. A **generic market** is a market with *broadly* similar needs—and sellers offering various, *often diverse,* ways of satisfying those needs. In contrast, a **product-market** is a market with *very* similar needs and sellers offering various *close substitute* ways of satisfying those needs.[2]

A generic market description looks at markets broadly and from a customer's viewpoint. Entertainment-seekers, for example, have several very different ways to satisfy their needs. An entertainment-seeker might buy a Panasonic digital video recorder and plasma screen TV, sign up for a cruise on the Carnival Line, or reserve season tickets for the symphony. Any one of these *very different* products may satisfy this entertainment need. Sellers in this generic entertainment-seeker market have to focus on the need(s) the customers want satisfied—not on how one seller's product (digital TV system, vacation, or live music) is better than that of another producer.

It is sometimes hard to understand and define generic markets because *quite different product types may compete with each other.* For example, a person on a business trip to Italy might want a convenient way to record memories of the trip. Minolta's digital camera, Sony's video camcorder, Kodak's PalmPix digital

The Olympus pocket camera competes directly with other 35 mm cameras, but it may also compete in a broader product-market against Vivitar's digital camera for kids or even Samsung's innovative DigitAll mobile phone that takes photos with a built-in digital camera and then wirelessly sends them by e-mail.

accessory for a Palm, and even postcards from local shops may all compete to serve our traveller's needs. If customers see all these products as substitutes—as competitors in the same generic market—then marketers must deal with this complication.

Suppose, however, that our traveller decides to satisfy this need with a digital camera. Then—in this product-market—Minolta, Kodak, HP, Nikon, and many other brands may compete with each other for the customer's dollars. In this *product-*market concerned with digital cameras *and* needs to conveniently record memories, consumers compare similar products to satisfy their image needs.

Broaden market definitions to find opportunities

Broader market definitions—including both generic market definitions and product-market definitions—can help firms find opportunities. But deciding *how* broad to go isn't easy. Too narrow a definition limits a firm's opportunities—but too broad a definition makes the company's efforts and resources seem insignificant. Consider, for example, the mighty Coca-Cola Company. It has great success and a huge market share in the North American cola-drinkers' market. On the other hand, its share of all beverage drinking worldwide is very small.

Here we try to match opportunities to a firm's resources and objectives. So the *relevant market for finding opportunities* should be bigger than the firm's present product-market—but not so big that the firm couldn't expand and be an important competitor. A small manufacturer of screwdrivers in Mexico, for example, shouldn't define its market as broadly as "the worldwide tool users market" or as narrowly as "our present screwdriver customers." But it may have the production or marketing potential, or both, to consider "the handyman's hand-tool market in North America." Carefully naming your product-market can help you see possible opportunities.

Later we'll study the many possible dimensions for segmenting markets. But for now you should see that defining markets only in terms of current products is not the best way to find new opportunities. Instead, the most effective way to find opportunities is to use market segmentation.

MARKET SEGMENTATION DEFINES POSSIBLE TARGET MARKETS

Market segmentation is a two–step process

Market segmentation is a two-step process of (1) *naming* broad product-markets and (2) *segmenting* these broad product-markets in order to select target markets and develop suitable marketing mixes.

This two-step process isn't well understood. First-time market segmentation efforts often fail because beginners start with the whole mass market and try to find one or two demographic characteristics to divide up (segment) this market. Customer behaviour is usually too complex to be explained in terms of just one or two demographic characteristics. For example, not all elderly men buy the same products or brands. Other dimensions usually must be considered—starting with customer needs.

Naming broad product–markets is disaggregating

The first step in effective market segmentation involves naming a broad product-market of interest to the firm. Marketers must break apart—disaggregate—all possible needs into some generic markets and broad product-markets in which the firm may be able to operate profitably. See Exhibit 3-1. No one firm can satisfy everyone's needs. So the naming—disaggregating—step involves brainstorming about very different solutions to various generic needs and selecting some broad areas— broad product-markets—where the firm has some resources and experience. This means that a car manufacturer would probably ignore all the possible opportunities in food and clothing markets and focus on the generic market, "transporting people in the world," and probably on the broad product-market, "cars, trucks, and utility vehicles for transporting people in the world."

Disaggregating, a practical rough-and-ready approach, tries to narrow down the marketing focus to product-market areas where the firm is more likely to have a competitive advantage or even to find breakthrough opportunities.

Market grid is a visual aid to market segmentation

Assuming that any broad product-market (or generic market) may consist of sub-markets, picture a market as a rectangle with boxes that represent the smaller, more homogeneous product-markets.

Exhibit 3-2, for example, represents the broad product-market of bicycle riders. The boxes show different submarkets. One submarket might focus on people who

Initially the Clorox brand name became well known as laundry bleach, but now the brand is used with other products related to the broader product-market for household cleaning needs.

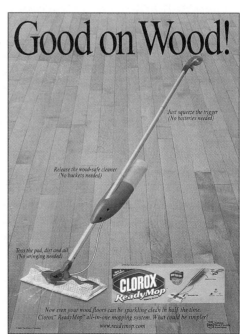

Exhibit 3-1
Narrowing Down to Target
Markets

Segmenting is an aggregating process

want basic transportation, another on people who want exercise, and so on. Alternatively, in the generic "transporting market" discussed above, we might see different product-markets of customers for bicycles, motorcycles, cars, airplanes, ships, buses, and "others."

Marketing-oriented managers think of **segmenting** as an aggregating process—clustering people with similar needs into a "market segment." A **market segment** is a (relatively) homogeneous group of customers who will respond to a marketing mix in a similar way.

This part of the market segmentation process (see Exhibit 3-1) takes a different approach from the naming part. Here we look for similarities rather than basic differences in needs. Segmenters start with the idea that each person is one of a kind but that it may be possible to aggregate some similar people into a product-market.

Segmenters see each of these one-of-a-kind people as having a unique set of dimensions. Consider a product-market in which customers' needs differ on two important segmenting dimensions: need for status and need for dependability. In Exhibit 3-3A, each dot shows a person's position on the two dimensions. While each person's position is unique, many of these people are similar in terms of how much status and dependability they want. So a segmenter may aggregate them into three (an arbitrary number) relatively homogeneous submarkets—A, B, and C. Group A might be called "status-oriented" and Group C "dependability-oriented." Members of Group B want both and might be called the "demanders."

Exhibit 3-2
A Market Grid Diagram with
Submarkets

Exhibit 3-4
Every Individual Has His or
Her Own Unique Position in
a Market—Those with
Similar Positions Can Be
Aggregated into Potential
Target Markets

A. Product-market showing three segments

B. Product-market showing six segments

How far should the aggregating go?

The segmenter wants to aggregate individual customers into some workable number of relatively homogeneous target markets and then treat each target market differently.

Look again at Exhibit 3-3A. Remember we talked about three segments. But this was an arbitrary number. As Exhibit 3-3B shows, there may really be six segments. What do you think—does this broad product-market consist of three segments or six?

Another difficulty with segmenting is that some potential customers just don't fit neatly into market segments. For example, not everyone in Exhibit 3-3B was put into one of the groups. Forcing them into one of the groups would have made these segments more heterogeneous and harder to please. Further, forming additional segments for them probably wouldn't be profitable. They are too few and not very similar in terms of the two dimensions. These people are simply too unique to be catered to and may have to be ignored—unless they are willing to pay a high price for special treatment. And when they are, these small defined market niches can sometimes be very profitable.

The number of segments that should be formed depends more on judgment than on some scientific rule. But the following guidelines can help.

Criteria for segmenting a broad product-market

Ideally, "good" market segments meet the following criteria:

1. *Homogeneous (similar) within*—the customers in a market segment should be as similar as possible with respect to their likely responses to marketing mix variables *and* their segmenting dimensions.
2. *Heterogeneous (different) between*—the customers in different segments should be as different as possible with respect to their likely responses to marketing mix variables *and* their segmenting dimensions.
3. *Substantial*—the segment should be big enough to be profitable.
4. *Operational*—the segmenting dimensions should be useful for identifying customers and deciding on marketing mix variables.

It is especially important that segments be *operational*. This leads marketers to include demographic dimensions such as age, sex, income, location, and family size. In fact, it is difficult to make some Place and Promotion decisions without such information.

Avoid segmenting dimensions that have no practical operational use. For example, you may find a personality trait such as moodiness among the traits of heavy buyers of a product, but how could you use this fact? Salespeople can't give a personality test to each buyer. Similarly, advertising couldn't make much use of this information. So although moodiness might be related in some way to previous purchases, it would not be a useful dimension for segmenting.

Competitive Review in Toronto

Base: 5 day cume

Adults 18+ · Age 25-54, HHI $100K+ · Business Purchase Influence

Legend: 24 hours · The Globe and Mail · Metro · National Post · Toronto Star · The Toronto Sun

Source: NADbank 2005

Across the country, daily newspapers use information supplied by NADbank to identify the demographic characteristics of their readers. Using this information, the four major dailies in Toronto, for example, can then provide data on the demographic characteristics of their audiences to convince advertisers that these are effective media for reaching specific markets. This practice is common to most major media outlets including CNN, who use their data to show advertisers that their station reaches affluent markets.

Target marketers aim at specific targets

Once you accept the idea that broad product-markets may have submarkets, you can see that target marketers usually have a choice among many possible target markets.

There are three basic ways to develop market-oriented strategies in a broad product-market.

1. The **single target market approach**—segmenting the market and picking one of the homogeneous segments as the firm's target market.
2. The **multiple target market approach**—segmenting the market and choosing two or more segments, then treating each as a separate target market needing a different marketing mix.
3. The **combined target market approach**—combining two or more submarkets into one larger target market as a basis for one strategy.

Note that all three approaches involve target marketing. They all aim at specific, clearly defined target markets. See Exhibit 3-4. For convenience, we call people who follow the first two approaches the "segmenters" and people who use the third approach the "combiners."

Combiners try to satisfy "pretty well"

Combiners try to increase the size of their target markets by combining two or more segments. Combiners look at various submarkets for similarities rather than differences. Then they try to extend or modify their basic offering to appeal to these "combined" customers with just one marketing mix. See Exhibit 3-4. For example, combiners may try a new package, more service, a new brand, or new flavours. But even if they make product or other marketing mix changes, they don't try to satisfy unique smaller submarkets. Instead, combiners try to improve the general appeal of their marketing mix to appeal to a bigger "combined" target market.

A combined target market approach may help achieve some economies of scale. It may also require less investment than developing different marketing mixes for different segments—making it especially attractive for firms with limited resources.

Exhibit 3-4
Target Marketers Have
Specific Aims

In a product-market area

A segmenter

Using single target market approach—can aim at one submarket with one marketing mix

Using multiple target market approach—can aim at two or more submarkets with different marketing mixes

A combiner

Using combined target market approach—can aim at two or more submarkets with the same marketing mix

The strategy

Strategy one

Strategy three

Strategy two

The strategy

Too much combining is risky

It is tempting to aim at larger combined markets instead of using different marketing mixes for smaller segmented markets. But combiners must be careful not to aggregate too far. As they enlarge the target market, individual differences within each submarket may begin to outweigh the similarities. This makes it harder to develop marketing mixes that can satisfy potential customers.

A combiner faces the continual risk of innovative segmenters chipping away at the various segments of the combined target market—by offering more attractive marketing mixes to more homogeneous submarkets. ATI Technologies, a firm that is a leader in making graphics chips for PCs, saw this happen. It produced high-quality products with features desired by a very wide variety of computer users. But then ATI lost business to more specialized competitors like Nvidia Corp. Nvidia focused on the needs of video-game lovers who don't want to compromise when it comes to realistic special effects. Nvidia developed chips that did fewer things, but by doing those specialized things really well it captured much of the video-game lovers' business—until ATI did more segmenting.

Segmenters try to satisfy "very well"

Segmenters aim at one or more homogeneous segments and try to develop a different marketing mix for each segment. Segmenters usually adjust their marketing mixes for each target market—perhaps making basic changes in the product itself—because they want to satisfy each segment very well.

Instead of assuming that the whole market consists of a fairly similar set of customers (like the mass marketer does) or merging various submarkets together (like the combiner), a segmenter sees submarkets with their own demand curves—as shown in Exhibit 3-5. Segmenters believe that aiming at one, or some, of these smaller markets makes it possible to provide superior value and satisfy them better. This then provides greater profit potential for the firm.

Segmenting may produce bigger sales

Note that segmenters are not settling for a smaller sales potential or lower profits. Instead, they hope to increase sales by getting a much larger share of the business in the market(s) they target. A segmenter that really satisfies the target market can often build such a close relationship with customers that it faces no real competition. A segmenter that offers a marketing mix precisely matched to the needs of the target market can often charge a higher price that produces higher profits.

Compared to the competition Sony's PlayStation video gaming system commanded a premium price in the market. Not only that, in addition to their teenage target market they sold well in a related segment of older video gaming males too.

Exhibit 3-5
There May Be Different
Demand Curves in Different
Market Segments

How did they do it? High-end hardware and graphics plus a strong base of video games compared to their competition allowed Sony to charge a premium price while continuing to maintain strong demand within their market segment.

Should you segment or combine?

Which approach should a firm use? This depends on the firm's resources, the nature of competition, and—most important—the similarity of customer needs, attitudes, and buying behaviour.

In general, it's usually safer to be a segmenter—that is, to try to satisfy some customers *very* well instead of many just *fairly* well. That's why many firms use the single or multiple target market approach instead of the combined target market approach. Procter & Gamble, for example, offers many products that seem to compete directly with each other (e.g., Tide versus Cheer or Joy versus Ivory). However, P&G offers tailor-made marketing mixes to each submarket large and profitable enough to deserve a separate marketing mix. Though extremely effective, this approach may not be possible for a smaller firm with more limited resources. A smaller firm may have to use the single target market approach—focusing all its efforts at the one submarket niche where it sees the best opportunity.[3] Just be careful how far you take your segmentation process. CityTV in Vancouver tried to target young singles in the inner-city market with their evening newscast. The 6:00 p.m. news show was dropped because the segment was so narrow there were insufficient viewers to make the time slot financially viable.

Toothpaste marketers often fine-tune their marketing mixes to appeal to the specific needs of different target market segments.

Profit is the balancing point

In practice, cost considerations probably encourage more aggregating—to obtain economies of scale—while demand considerations suggest less aggregating—to satisfy needs more exactly.

Profit is the balancing point. It determines how unique a marketing mix the firm can afford to offer to a particular group.

WHAT DIMENSIONS ARE USED TO SEGMENT MARKETS?

Segmenting dimensions guide marketing mix planning

Market segmentation forces a marketing manager to decide which product-market dimensions might be useful for planning marketing strategies. The dimensions should help guide marketing mix planning. Exhibit 3-6 shows the basic kinds of dimensions we'll be talking about in Chapters 5 and 6—and their probable effect on the four Ps. Ideally, we want to describe any potential product-market in terms of all three types of customer-related dimensions—plus a product type description—because these dimensions help us develop better marketing mixes.

Exhibit 3-6 Relation of Potential Target Market Dimensions to Marketing Strategy Decision Areas

Potential Target Market Dimensions	Effects on Strategy Decision Areas
1. Behavioural needs, attitudes, and how present and potential goods and services fit into customers' consumption patterns.	Affects *Product* (features, packaging, product line assortment, branding) and *Promotion* (what potential customers need and want to know about the firm's offering, and what appeals should be used).
2. Psychographic or lifestyle analysis considers a person's activities, interests, and opinions.	Affects *Advertising Themes* (targets communications to specific market segments).
3. Urgency to get need satisfied and desire and willingness to seek information, compare, and shop.	Affects *Place* (how directly products are distributed from producer to customer, how extensively they are made available, and the level of service needed) and *Price* (how much potential customers are willing to pay).
4. Geographic location and other demographic characteristics of potential customers.	Affects size of *Target Markets* (economic potential), *Place* (where products should be made available), and *Promotion* (where and to whom to target advertising and personal selling).

Any hiking boot should repel water, and a product that doesn't meet that "qualifying need" probably wouldn't appeal to many hikers. Sorel wants its target customers to know that its boots go further in keeping feet dry because that difference may determine which brand of boot they buy.

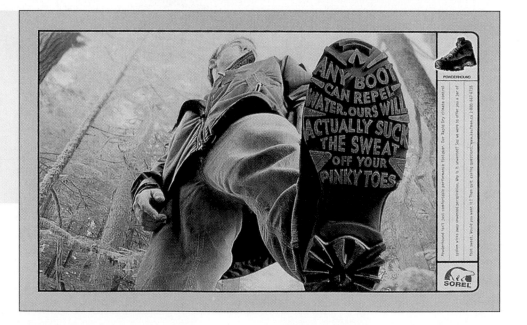

Behavioural and Psychographic

Needs	Economic, functional, physiological, psychological, social, and more detailed needs.
Benefits sought	Situation specific, but to satisfy specific or general needs.
Thoughts	Favourable or unfavourable attitudes, interests, opinions, beliefs.
Rate of use	Heavy, medium, light, nonusers.
Purchase relationship	Positive and ongoing, intermittent, no relationship, bad relationship.
Brand familiarity	Insistence, preference, recognition, nonrecognition, rejection.
Kind of shopping	Convenience, comparison shopping, specialty, none (unsought product).
Type of problem-solving	Routinized response, limited, extensive.
Information required	Low, medium, high.

Geographic

Region of world, country	North America (Canada, United States), Europe (France, Italy, Germany), and so on.
Region in country	(Examples in Canada): Atlantic, Maritimes, Quebec, Ontario, Prairies, and British Columbia.
Size of city	No city; population under 5,000; 5,000–19,999; 20,000–49,999; 50,000–99,999; 100,000–249,999; 250,000–499,999; 500,000–999,999; 1,000,000–3,999,999; 4,000,000 or over.

Demographic

Income	Under $5,000; $5,000–9,999; $10,000–14,999; $15,000–19,999; $20,000–29,999; $30,000–39,999; $40,000–59,999; $60,000 and over.
Sex	Male, female.
Age	Infant; under 6; 6–11; 12–17; 18–24; 25–34; 35–49; 50–64; 65 or over.
Family size	1, 2, 3–4, 5 or more.
Family life cycle	Young, single; young, married, no children; young, married, youngest child under 6; young, married, youngest child over 6; older, married, with children; older, married, no children under 18; older, single; other variations for single parents, divorced, etc.
Occupation	Professional and technical; managers, officials, and proprietors; clerical sales; craftspeople; forepersons; operatives; farmers; retired; students; housewives; unemployed.
Education	Grade school or less; some high school; high school graduate; some college; university graduate.
Ethnicity	French Canadian, Black, Indo-Canadian, Native Canadian, White, Asian.
Social class	Lower-lower, upper-lower, lower-middle, upper-middle, lower-upper, upper-upper.
Religion	Christian, Muslim, Buddhist

Note: Terms used in this table are explained in detail later in the text.

Many segmenting dimensions may be considered

Customers can be described by many specific dimensions. Exhibit 3-7 shows some dimensions useful for segmenting consumer markets. A few are behavioural and psychographic dimensions, others are geographic and demographic. Exhibit 3-8 shows some additional dimensions for segmenting markets when the customers are businesses, government agencies, or other types of organizations. Regardless of whether customers are final consumers or organizations, segmenting a broad product-market *usually* requires using several different dimensions at the same time.[4]

What are the qualifying and determining dimensions?

To select the important segmenting dimensions, think about two different types of dimensions. **Qualifying dimensions** are those relevant to including a customer type in a product-market. **Determining dimensions** are those that actually affect the customer's purchase of a specific product or brand in a product-market.

A prospective car buyer, for example, has to have enough money—or credit—to buy a car and insure it. Our buyer also needs a driver's license. This still doesn't

Kind of relationship	Weak loyalty → strong loyalty to vendor Single source → multiple vendors "Arm's length" dealings → close partnership No reciprocity → complete reciprocity
Type of customer	Manufacturer, service producer, government agency, military, nonprofit, wholesaler or retailer (when end user), and so on.
Demographics	Geographic location (region of world, country, region within country, urban → rural); Size (number of employees, sales volume); Primary business or industry (North American Industry Classification System); Number of facilities
How customer will use product	Installations, components, accessories, raw materials, supplies, professional services
Type of buying situation	Decentralized → centralized Buyer → multiple buying influence Straight rebuy → modified rebuy → new-task buying
Purchasing methods	Vendor analysis, purchasing specifications, Internet bids, negotiated contracts, long-term contracts, e-commerce Web sites

Note: Terms used in this table are explained in detail later in the text.

guarantee a purchase. He or she must have a real need—like a job that requires "wheels" or kids who have to be carpooled. This need may motivate the purchase of *some* car. But these qualifying dimensions don't determine what specific brand or model car the person might buy. That depends on more specific interests—such as the kind of safety, performance, or appearance the customer wants. Determining dimensions related to these needs affect the specific car the customer purchases. If safety is a determining dimension for a customer, a Volvo wagon that offers side impact protection, air bags, and all-wheel drive might be the customer's first choice.

Determining dimensions may be very specific

How specific the determining dimensions are depends on whether you are concerned with a general product type or a specific brand. See Exhibit 3-9. The more specific you want to be, the more particular the determining dimensions may be. In a particular case, the determining dimensions may seem minor. But they are important because they *are* the determining dimensions.

Marketers at General Mills know this. Lots of people try to check e-mail or drive a car while eating breakfast or lunch. General Mills has figured out that for many

Exhibit 3-9   Finding the Relevant Segmenting Dimensions

Segmenting dimensions become more specific to reasons why the target segment chooses to buy a particular brand of the product

All potential dimensions	Qualifying dimensions	Determining dimensions (product type)	Determining dimensions (brand specific)
Dimensions generally relevant to purchasing behaviour	Dimensions relevant to including a customer type in the product-market	Dimensions that affect the customer's purchase of a specific type of product	Dimensions that affect the customer's choice of a specific brand

of these target customers the real determining dimension in picking a snack is whether it can be eaten "one-handed."[5]

Qualifying dimensions are important too

The qualifying dimensions help identify the "core features" that must be offered to everyone in a product-market. Qualifying and determining dimensions work together in marketing strategy planning.

Different dimensions needed for different submarkets

Note that each different submarket within a broad product-market may be motivated by a different set of dimensions. In the snack food market, for example, health food enthusiasts are interested in nutrition, dieters worry about calories, and economical shoppers with lots of kids may want volume to "fill them up."

Ethical issues in selecting segmenting dimensions

Marketing managers sometimes face ethical decisions when selecting segmenting dimensions. Problems may arise if a firm targets customers who are somehow at a disadvantage in dealing with the firm or who are unlikely to see the negative effects of their own choices. For example, some people criticize shoe companies for targeting poor, inner-city kids who see expensive athletic shoes as an important status symbol. Many firms, including producers of infant formula, have been criticized for targeting consumers in less-developed nations. Encyclopedia publishers have been criticized for aggressive selling to less-educated parents who don't realize that the "pennies a day" credit terms are more than they can afford. Some nutritionists criticize firms that market soft drinks, candy, and snack foods to children.

Sometimes a marketing manager must decide whether a firm should serve customers it really doesn't want to serve. For example, banks sometimes offer marketing mixes that are attractive to wealthy customers but that basically drive off low-income consumers.

People often disagree about what segmenting dimensions are ethical in a given situation. A marketing manager needs to consider not only his or her own view but also the views of other groups in society. Even when there is no clear "right" answer, negative publicity may be very damaging. This is what Amazon.com encountered when it was revealed that it was charging some regular customers higher prices than new customers at its site.[6]

International marketing requires even more segmenting

Success in international marketing requires even more attention to segmenting. There are over 228 nations with their own unique cultures! And they differ greatly in language, customs (including business ethics), beliefs, religions, race, and income distribution patterns. (We'll discuss some of these differences in Chapters 5 and 6.) These additional differences can complicate the segmenting process. Even worse, critical data is often less available—and less dependable—as firms move into international markets. This is one reason why some firms insist that local operations and decisions be handled by natives. They, at least, have a feel for their markets.

There are more dimensions—but there is a way

Segmenting international markets may require more dimensions. But one practical method adds just one step to the approach discussed above. First, marketers segment by country or region—looking at demographic, cultural, and other characteristics, including stage of economic development. This may help them find regional or national submarkets that are fairly similar. Then—depending on whether the firm is aiming at final consumers or business markets—they apply the same basic approaches discussed earlier.

A BEST PRACTICE APPROACH TO SEGMENTING PRODUCT MARKETS

Most marketing managers embrace the idea of using market segmentation to narrow down from a broad set of opportunities to a specific target market and marketing strategy (review Exhibit 2-10). There are also hundreds of books and articles about different approaches and tools for market segmentation that a manager might consider. Yet many managers don't do a good job with market segmentation. One reason is that they are often unclear where to start or how to fit the ideas together. So that *you* don't have this knowledge gap, here we introduce a logical seven-step approach to market segmentation. Later in Chapter 8 you'll learn more about how marketing research can help to fine-tune some of the decisions made with this approach. But even without additional research, *this approach works*—and it has led to successful strategies. It is especially useful for finding the determining dimensions for product types. However, when you want to find dimensions for specific brands—especially when there are several competing brands—you may need more sophisticated techniques.

To be sure you understand this approach, we will review each step separately and use an ongoing example to show how each step works. The example concerns people who need a place to stay—in particular, the market for motel guests in a big urban area.

1: Name the broad product-market

First, decide what broad product-market the firm wants to be in. This may be stated in the firm's objectives. Or if the firm is already successful in some product-market, its current position might be a good starting point. Try to build on the firm's strengths and avoid its weaknesses and competitors' strengths. Available resources, both human and financial, will limit the possibilities—especially if the firm is just getting started.

Example

A firm has been building small motels around the edges of a large city and renting rooms to travellers. A narrow view—considering only the firm's current products and markets—might lead the firm to think only of more small motels. A bigger view might see such motels as only a small part of the larger "overnight lodging needs" market in the firm's geographic area. Taking an even bigger view, the firm could consider expanding to other geographic areas—or moving into other kinds of products (like apartment buildings, retirement centres, or even parks for people who travel in their own recreational vehicles).

There has to be some balance between naming the product-market too narrowly (same old product, same old market) and naming it too broadly (the whole world and all its needs). Here the firm decides on the whole market of motel users in one city—because this is a city where the number of visitors is growing and where the firm has some experience.

2: List potential customers' needs

Write down as many relevant needs as you can—considering all of the potential customers in the broad product-market. This is a brainstorming step. The list doesn't have to be complete yet, but it should provide enough input to help stimulate your thinking in the next steps. To see possible needs, think about *why* some people buy the present offerings in this broad product-market. At this point, focus on the basic needs—but begin to consider what a company could offer to meet those needs.

Example

In the broad motel guest market, you can easily list some possible needs: privacy (including a private room and furnishings), safety and security (security guards, lighted parking lots with video coverage), comfort (a good bed and nice furnishings), space for activities (exercise, work, socializing), entertainment (TV, radio, video games), convenience (registration, check-out, reservations, access to highways), economy (costs), communicating (phone, messages, fax, voice mail, Internet service), and the like.

3: Form homogeneous submarkets—narrow product-markets

Assuming that some people have (or emphasize) different needs than others, form different submarkets based on each submarket's specific needs. This step will most likely need some marketing research—perhaps in the form of some guest surveys. Start by forming one submarket around some typical type of customer (perhaps even yourself), and then aggregate similar people into this segment as long as they can be satisfied by the same marketing mix. Write down the important need dimensions and customer-related characteristics (including demographic characteristics) of each submarket to help you decide whether each new customer type should be included in the first segment. This will also help later—when you name the submarkets.

For example, if the people in one market are young families looking for a good place to stay on vacation, this will help you understand what they want and why—and will help you name the market (perhaps as "family vacationers").

Put people who are not homogeneous—who don't fit in the first segment—in a new submarket. List their different need dimensions on another line. Continue this classifying until three or more submarkets emerge.

Example

A young family on a vacation probably wants a motel to provide a clean room large enough for adults and children, convenient parking, a location near tourist attractions, a pool for recreation with a lifeguard for safety, entertainment in the room (a TV and video movies), and perhaps a refrigerator or vending machine for snacks. A travelling executive, on the other hand, has quite different interests—a room with a desk, but *also* a nice restaurant, fast transportation to and from an airport, more services (room service, dry cleaning, a way to send and receive a fax, and fast check-in)—without distracting noise from children. See Exhibit 3·10.

Exhibit 3-10   Segmenting the Broad Product-Market for Motel Guests in a Large Urban Area

Nickname of Product-Market	Need Dimensions (benefits sought)	Customer-Related Characteristics
1 Family vacationers	Comfort, security, privacy, *family fun, recreation (playground, pool), entertainment (video games, movies), child care, and snacks*	Couples and single parents with children who want a fun family experience: young, active, and energetic.
2 Upscale executives	Comfort, security, privacy, *distinctive furnishings, attentive staff, prestige status, easy access to airport and business meetings, express check-in and check-out, quality dining, business services (copying, fax, wi-fi Internet)*	Senior business executives with a big expense account who want to be pampered with "very important person" service and accommodations; often repeat guests.
3 Budget-oriented travellers	Comfort, security, privacy, *economy, (no extras that increase cost), convenience (to low-cost restaurants, highways), free parking*	Young people, retirees, and salespeople who travel by car, pay their own expenses, and want a simple place for one night—before moving on.
4 Long-stay guests	Comfort, security, privacy, *homelike amenities (kitchenette, separate living room), laundry and exercise facilities, pleasant grounds, entertainment, staying "connected" (e-mail, etc.)*	Businesspeople, out-of-town visitors, and others who stay in the same motel for a week or more; want many of the comforts they have at home.
5 Event-centred visitors	Comfort, security, privacy, *socializing (lounges and public areas), conference facilities (including catering of group meals), message and transportation services*	Individuals who are attending events scheduled at the motel (a business meeting or conference, family reunion, wedding, etc.) often for several days.
6 Resort seekers	Comfort, security, privacy, *relaxation (golf, whirlpool bath), pleasure (fine dining, nice views), fun, variety information (arrangements for theatre, activities)*	Sophisticated couples with leisure time to relax and have "adult" fun; they want to show their individuality and have discretionary income to spend.

Note. Comfort, security, and privacy are core qualifying needs. Determining dimensions for each segment are in italic.

4: Identify the determining dimensions

Review the list of need dimensions for each possible segment and identify the determining dimensions (perhaps by putting an asterisk beside them). Although the qualifying dimensions are important—perhaps reflecting "core needs" that should be satisfied—they are not the *determining* dimensions we are seeking now.

To help identify the determining dimensions, think carefully about the needs and attitudes of the people in each possible segment. They may not seem very different from market to market, but if they are important to those people then they *are* determining dimensions.

Example

With our motel customers, basic comfort needs (heating and cooling, a good bed, a clean bathroom), a telephone for communicating, and safety and security are probably not determining. Everyone has these qualifying needs. Looking beyond these common needs helps you see the determining dimensions—such as different needs with respect to recreation, restaurant facilities, services, and so on. See the needs highlighted in italic in Exhibit 3-10.

5: Name (nickname) the possible product-markets

Review the determining dimensions—market by market—and name (nickname) each one based on the relative importance of the determining dimensions (and aided by your description of the customer types). A market grid is a good way to help visualize this broad product-market and its narrow product-markets.

Draw the market grid as a rectangle with boxes inside representing smaller, more homogeneous segments. See Exhibit 3-10. Think of the whole grid as representing the broad product-market and each of the rows as a different (narrower) product-market. Since the markets within a broad product-market usually require very different segmenting dimensions, don't try to use the same dimensions to name every submarket. Then label each segment with its nickname.

Example

Exhibit 3-10 identifies the following overnight guest submarkets: (1) family vacationers, (2) upscale executives, (3) budget-oriented travellers, (4) long-stay guests, (5) event-centred visitors, and (6) resort seekers. Note that each segment has a different set of determining dimensions (benefits sought) that follow directly from customer type and needs.

6: Evaluate why product-market segments behave as they do

After naming the markets as we did in step 5, think about what else you know about each segment to see how and why these markets behave the way they do. Different segments may have similar, but slightly different, needs. This may explain why some competitive offerings are more successful than others. It can also mean you have to split and rename some segments.

Example

The resort seekers might have been treated as family vacationers in step 5 because the "family" characteristic did not seem important. But with more thought, we see that while some of the resort seekers are interested in the same sort of fun and recreation as the family vacationers, resort seekers focus on adult fun—not activities with children. For them, getting away from the family vacationer's children may be part of the escape they want. Further, although the resort seekers are a higher income group who are similar to the upscale executives, they have different needs than the executives and probably should be treated as a separate market. The point is that you might discover these market differences only in step 6. At this step you would name the "resort seekers" market—and create a related row in the grid to describe the new segment.

7: Make a rough estimate of the size of each product-market segment

Remember, we are looking for profitable opportunities. So now we must try to tie our product-markets to demographic data—or other customer-related characteristics—to make it easier to estimate the size of these markets. We aren't trying to estimate our likely sales yet. Sales depend on the competition as well as the particulars of the marketing mix. Now we only want to provide a basis for later forecasting and marketing mix planning. The more we know about possible target markets, the easier those jobs are. That's where marketing research will help.

Fortunately, we can obtain a lot of data on the size of markets—especially demographic data. And bringing in demographics adds a note of economic reality. Some possible product-markets may have almost no market potential. Without hard facts, we risk aiming at such markets.

To refine the market grid, you might want to change the height of the rows so that they give a better idea of the size of the various segments. This will help highlight the larger, and perhaps more attractive, opportunities. Remember, the relative sizes of the markets might vary depending on what geographic areas you consider. The market sizes might vary from city to city or from one country to another.

Example

We can tie the family vacationers to demographic data. Most of them are between 21 and 45. Statistics Canada publishes detailed data by age, family size, and related information. Moreover, a provincial tourist bureau or city Chamber of Commerce might be able to provide estimates of how many families vacation in a specific city during a year and how long they stay. Given this information, it's easy to estimate the total number of nights family vacationers will need motel rooms in a certain city.

Market dimensions suggest a good mix

Once we follow all seven steps, we should be able to outline the kinds of marketing mixes that would appeal to the various markets. For example, based on the determining dimensions (benefits sought) in Exhibit 3-10, a motel designed to appeal to the upscale executives might offer rooms with quality furniture (including a desk and chair for reading and an extra comfortable bed with special luxury sheets and pillows), a high-quality restaurant with all-hours room service, special business services (copying, fax, wireless Internet access) on an extra-cost basis, limousine pickup at the airport, someone to help with travel problems, and precleared check-in and check-out. The motel might also provide a quiet bar and exercise room and extras such as thick bath towels and a valet service for free shoe shines. It might also offer a business library for after-hours reading and a free copy of *The Wall Street Journal* delivered every morning. Of course, the price could be high to pay for this special treatment. It's also useful to think about what the executives would *not* want: noisy facilities shared by families with young children!

While the discussion above focuses on the upscale executives, profitable marketing mixes can be developed for the other segments as well. For example, Super 8 has done very well by targeting budget-oriented travellers. Similarly, Residence Inns cater to the needs of long-stay guests with kitchens, fireplaces, and convenient recreation areas. Courtyard by Marriott has been successful with facilities designed for event-centred visitors. During the week, many of its customers are there for business conferences, but on the weekend the focus often shifts to family events—such as meals and receptions related to a wedding or family reunion.[7] Using this strategy allows the Marriott to service two different market segments based on different days of the week. Monday through Friday serves the business travel segment but on the weekends when the executives have returned home, rather than suffer the cost of empty rooms, the hotel can advertise to the family vacationer segment.

Improve the marketing mix for current customers

Our motel example highlights an approach to identify new target market and marketing mix opportunities. However, the same approaches provide a basis for identifying new ways to serve existing customers and strengthen the relationship with them. Too often, firms let their strategies get stagnant. For example, special business services related to the determining needs of upscale executives (like voice mail) might initially help a motel win this business with superior customer value. However, the motel loses its competitive edge if other motels start to offer the same benefits. Or the benefit might disappear if customer needs change; executives who carry a cell phone don't need voice mail at the motel. Then the determining dimensions change. To retain the base of customers it has built or attract new ones, the motel needs to find new and better ways to meet the executives' needs. Reevaluating the need dimensions and customer-related characteristics, perhaps in greater detail, may point to new opportunities. For example, our motel might equip rooms with a wireless access point to a high-speed Internet connection.

MORE SOPHISTICATED TECHNIQUES MAY HELP IN SEGMENTING

Marketing researchers and managers often turn to computer-aided methods for help with the segmenting job. A detailed review of the possibilities is beyond the scope of this book. But a brief discussion will give you a flavour of how computer-aided methods work. In addition, the computer-aided problem for this chapter (3, Segmenting Customers) on the Online Learning Centre gives you a hands-on feel for how managers use them.

Clustering usually requires a computer

Clustering techniques try to find similar patterns within sets of data. Clustering groups customers who are similar on their segmenting dimensions into homogeneous segments. Clustering approaches use computers to do what previously was done with much intuition and judgment.

The data to be clustered might include such dimensions as demographic characteristics, the importance of different needs, attitudes toward the product, and past buying behaviour. The computer searches all the data for homogeneous groups of people. When it finds them, marketers study the dimensions of the people in the

It is usually better to focus on customer needs satisfied by products rather than on the product characteristics themselves groups to see why the computer clustered them together. The results sometimes suggest new, or at least better, marketing strategies.[8]

A cluster analysis of the toothpaste market, for example, might show that some people buy toothpaste because it tastes good (the sensory segment), while others are concerned with the effect of clean teeth and fresh breath on their social image (the sociables). Still others worry about decay or tartar (the worriers), and some are just interested in the best value for their money (the value seekers). Each of these market segments calls for a different marketing mix—although some of the four Ps may be similar.

Customer database can focus the effort

A variation of the clustering approach is based on customer relationship management methods. With **customer relationship management (CRM)**, the seller fine-tunes the marketing effort with information from a detailed customer database. This usually includes data on a customer's past purchases as well as other segmenting information. For example, an auto-repair garage that keeps a database of customer oil changes can send a reminder postcard when it's time for the next oil change. Similarly, a florist that keeps a database of customers who have ordered flowers for Mother's Day or Valentine's Day can call them in advance with a special offer. Firms that operate over the Internet may have a special advantage with these database-focused approaches. They are able to communicate with customers via a Web site or e-mail, which means that the whole effort is not only targeted but also very inexpensive. Further, it's fast and easy for a customer to reply.[9]

Amazon.com takes this even further. When a customer orders a book, the Amazon CRM system at the Web site recommends other related books that have been purchased by other customers who bought that book.

INTERNET EXERCISE

Visit the Web site for onContact Software (www.oncontact.com), and from the demo link at the top of the page select *Screenshot Tour* (*note:* the interactive tour requires that you register). Select the links to review the different examples of the firm's client management software. Give several examples of how this software could help a salesperson be more effective in working with customers.

DIFFERENTIATION AND POSITIONING TAKE THE CUSTOMER POINT OF VIEW

Differentiate the marketing mix—to serve customers better

As we've emphasized throughout, the reason for focusing on a specific target market—by using marketing segmentation approaches or tools such as cluster analysis or CRM—is so that you can fine-tune the whole marketing mix to provide some group of potential customers with superior value. By *differentiating* the marketing mix to do a better job meeting customers' needs, the firm builds a competitive advantage. When this happens, target customers view the firm's position in the market as uniquely suited to their preferences and needs. Further, because everyone in the firm is clear about what position it wants to achieve with customers, the Product, Promotion, and other marketing mix decisions can be blended better to achieve the desired objectives.

Although the marketing manager may want customers to see the firm's offering as unique, that is not always possible. Me-too imitators may come along and copy

CDW TARGETS THE SMALL BUSINESS SEGMENT WITH UNCOMMON SERVICE

Sellers in business markets often rely on customer size as a key segmentation dimension. When potential profit from serving a big customer is high, the selling firm may even treat that customer as a "segment of one"—and develop a unique marketing mix targeted to win and keep its business. Even if a unique marketing mix isn't justified, big customers in these segments often get volume discounts, extra services, and personalized attention. By contrast, smaller customers are often left to get information and handle orders themselves—at a seller's Web site. This can be efficient, reduce costs for both the seller and customer, and serve the need. But that is not always the case.

CDW is a wholesaler that sells all sorts of computer gear produced by many manufacturers. Most of its 360,000 business customers are too small to command much attention from equipment manufacturers. Yet they also have smaller IT departments and know less about buying IT equipment. CDW has enjoyed rapid growth because it offers a marketing mix that is atypical for these customers. Even the smallest customer gets a dedicated account manager (AM). These salespeople don't just take orders; they go through months of CDW training so that they really understand a customer's needs and can help the buyer make the right purchases. The AM is a single point-of-contact with the account over time and is encouraged to act almost as an extension of the client's IT department. This relationship helps the AM anticipate client needs; the AM is also supported with customer relationship management databases that help predict when an upgrade is needed—rather than wait for the customer to ask. This is especially helpful to small customers who don't have backup systems in place to tide them over if something goes wrong. This is also why CDW fills orders fast—usually on the same day they are received. To provide that level of service with 17,000 orders a day, CDW operates a 450,000-square-foot distribution centre and keeps about $130 million in inventory on hand. CDW's "high-touch" strategy is costly, but high volume keeps its prices competitive. And CDW's sales volume is high because CDW delivers superior customer value that wins a large share of its target customers' business.[10]

the firm's strategy. Further, even if a firm's marketing mix is different, consumers may not know or care. They're busy and, simply put, the firm's product may not be that important in their lives. Even so, in looking for opportunities it's important for the marketing manager to know how customers *do* view the firm's offering. It's also important for the marketing manager to have a clear idea about how he or she would like for customers to view the firm's offering. This is where another important concept, *positioning,* comes in.

Positioning is based on customers' views

Positioning refers to how customers think about proposed or present brands in a market. And they often think about them relative to competing brands so a marketing manager also has to consider the competition when positioning a product. A marketing manager needs a realistic view of how customers think about offerings in the market. Without that, it's hard to differentiate. At the same time, the manager should know how he or she *wants* target customers to think about the firm's marketing mix. Positioning issues are especially important when competitors in a market appear to be very similar. For example, many people think that there isn't much difference between one brand of TV and another. But Sony wants TV buyers to see its Wega flatscreen as offering the best picture and brightest colours.

Once you know what customers think, then you can decide whether to leave the product (and marketing mix) alone or reposition it. This may mean *physical changes in the product* or simply *image changes based on promotion*. A word to the wise. Sometimes when you try to reposition a product or service, you may not manage to attract

Firms often use promotion to help "position" how a marketing mix meets target customers' specific needs. For example, Bic ads along the roadside in Thailand highlight an ultraclose shave.

the new segment you targeted—and you may risk alienating your existing target market because you changed your positioning from what they were used to. Some time back, The Bay tried to attract a younger upscale market with a new "Bayman" campaign. They missed. The repositioning attempt didn't attract the youth market because they considered The Bay a place where their parents and grandparents shopped. The Bay's existing target market of older shoppers would only have been confused (and possibly alienated) by the youth-focused "Bayman" campaign. Sometimes repositioning can be downright dangerous.

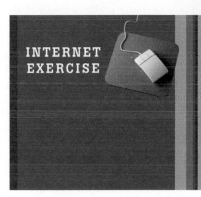

INTERNET EXERCISE

For many years, Michelin's marketing mix emphasized the safety of Michelin tires. To highlight that positioning, scores of ads showed the "Michelin baby" surrounded by a tire with the tagline "because so much is riding on your tires." Ads still use this tagline, but the baby is no longer used. Now most promotion highlights another icon, the "Michelin Man." Go to the Michelin Web site (www.michelin.com), select the country where you live, and review the site. Does the Web site reinforce the safety positioning suggested by the tagline? Explain your thinking.

Positioning and the unique selling proposition

How do you actually set about positioning your product or service? Creating a unique selling proposition is an important first step.

A **unique selling proposition** tells a target audience why they should buy the given product—or choose it—over others in the market. These propositions determine the overall theme of the positioning statement. There are a number of ways to express a value proposition to help position the product:

- *Product/service attributes*: In this case, positioning is based on a specific aspect that is most valued by the target market. For example, Sensodyne toothpaste offers relief to users with sensitive teeth.

- *Overall value*: Value is determined by customers based on the relationship between quality and price. Wal-Mart consistently competes on this dimension with its "Everyday low price guarantee," that is coupled to a product quality level sufficient to make it a major threat to Canada's other department store chains.

- *Class of user*: Marketers often position their product based on the personality of their target market. In this case, the product offers a particular lifestyle image, or attitude—such as Nike, which wants buyers to think of themselves as winners and not just average competitors.

- *Product class*: Usually there is an entrenched standard or technology that a company is trying to challenge. For example, the manufacturers of Blu-ray position their product as producing a superior TV picture compared to old DVD technology.

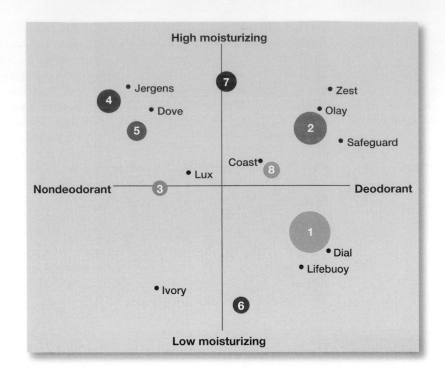

- *End-use application*: This type of positioning is based on the user's situation. Maple Leaf Foods is trying to reposition its bacon and sausage products by making them microwave reheatable for quick and convenient use by families on the move.
- *Specific competitor*: Competition-based positioning tries to target an area of dissatisfaction with a competing brand. This tactic is most often used with packaged goods such as laundry detergent, like Tide, that make claims of cleaning superiority compared to competing brands.

Figuring out what customers really think about competing products isn't easy either, but there are approaches that help. Most of them require some formal marketing research. The results are usually plotted on graphs to help show how consumers view the competing products. Usually, the products' positions are related to two or three product features that are important to the target customers.

Managers make the graphs for positioning decisions by asking consumers to make judgments about different brands—including their "ideal" brand—and then use computer programs to summarize the ratings and plot the results. The details of positioning techniques—sometimes called *perceptual mapping*—are beyond the scope of this text. But Exhibit 3-11 shows the possibilities.[11]

Exhibit 3-11 shows the "product space" for different brands of bar soap using two dimensions—the extent to which consumers think the soaps moisturize and deodorize their skin. For example, consumers see Dove as quite high on moisturizing but low on deodorizing. Dove and Jergens are close together—implying that consumers think of them as similar on these characteristics. Dial is viewed as different and is further away on the graph. Remember that positioning maps are based on *customers' perceptions*—the actual characteristics of the products (as determined by a chemical test) might be different!

Each segment may have its own preferences

The circles in Exhibit 3-11 show different sets (submarkets) of consumers clustered near their ideal soap preferences. Groups of respondents with a similar ideal product are circled to show apparent customer concentrations. In this graph, the size of the circles suggests the size of the segments for the different ideals.

Ideal clusters 1 and 2 are the largest and are close to two popular brands—Dial and Olay. It appears that customers in cluster 1 want more moisturizing than they see in Dial. However, exactly what this brand should do about this isn't clear. Perhaps Dial should leave its physical product alone—but emphasize moisturizing more in its promotion to make a stronger appeal to those who want moisturizers. A marketing manager talking about this approach might simply refer to it as "positioning the brand as a good moisturizer." Of course, whether the effort is successful depends on whether the whole marketing mix delivers on the promise of the positioning communication.

Note that ideal cluster 7 is not near any of the present brands. This may suggest an opportunity for introducing a new product—a strong moisturizer with some deodorizers. A firm that chooses to follow this approach would be making a segmenting effort.

Combining versus segmenting

Positioning analysis may lead a firm to combining—rather than segmenting—if managers think they can make several general appeals to different parts of a "combined" market. For example, by varying its promotion, Coast might try to appeal to segments 8, 1, and 2 with one product. These segments are all quite similar (close together) in what they want in an ideal brand. On the other hand, there may be clearly defined submarkets—and some parts of the market may be "owned" by one product or brand. In this case, segmenting efforts may be practical—moving the firm's own product into another segment of the general market area where competition is weaker.

Positioning as part of broader analysis

A positioning analysis helps managers understand how customers see their market. It is a visual aid to understanding a product-market. The first time such an analysis is done, managers may be shocked to see how much customers' perceptions of a market differ from their own. For this reason alone, positioning analysis may be crucial. But a positioning analysis usually focuses on specific product features and brands that are close competitors in the product-market. Thus, it is a product-oriented approach. Important *customer*-related dimensions—including needs and attitudes—may be overlooked.

Premature emphasis on product features is dangerous in other ways as well. As our bar soap example shows, starting with a product-oriented definition of a market and how bar soaps compete against other bar soaps can make a firm miss more basic shifts in markets. For example, bars have lost popularity to liquid soaps. Other products, like bath oils or body shampoos for use in the shower, are now part of the relevant competition also. Managers wouldn't see these shifts if they looked only at alternative bar soap brands—the focus is just too narrow.

It's also important to realize that the way consumers look at a product isn't just a matter of chance. Let's return to our bar soap example. While many consumers do think about soap in terms of moisturizing and deodorizing, other needs shouldn't be overlooked. For example, some consumers are especially concerned about wiping out germs. Marketers for Dial soap recognized this need and developed ads that positioned Dial as "the choice" for these target customers. This helped Dial win new customers, including those who switched from Lifebuoy—which was otherwise similar to Dial (see Exhibit 3-11). In fact, what happened to Lifebuoy highlights what happens if managers don't update their marketing strategy as customer needs and competition change. Lifebuoy was the first deodorant soap on the market; it was a leading brand for over 100 years. But it gradually lost sales to competitors with stronger marketing mixes (clearer differentiation, better positioning, and superior customer value) until 2002, when Lever stopped selling it.

As we emphasize throughout the text, you must understand potential needs and attitudes when planning marketing strategies. If customers treat different products as substitutes, then a firm has to position itself against those products too. Customers won't always be conscious of all of the detailed ways that a firm's marketing mix might be different, but careful positioning can help highlight a unifying theme or benefits that relate to the determining dimensions of the target market. Thus, it's useful to think of positioning as part of the broader strategy planning process—because the purpose is to ensure that the whole marketing mix is positioned for competitive advantage.

CONCLUSION

In this chapter we saw that carefully defining generic markets and product-markets can help find new opportunities. Using our opening example you should now recognize that Coast Mountain Sports and SportChek shared a similar generic market in supplying consumer demand for outdoor recreational gear and clothing. The product-markets through which they met that demand were very different however. Coast Mountain opted for the high-end, technologically advanced gear while SportChek focused on less expensive, less "state of the art" clothing and equipment that sold to a more price-sensitive market segment.

There are many ways to define market segments however. The sports marketing companies focused on products but in the vignette example Tommy Hilfiger or Roots successfully targeted segments based on the appeal of fashion and designer labels. Segments can differ drastically in terms of their dimensions however. That approach would not sell well with the Army and Navy crowd who are much more inclined to buy on the basis of price.

By now, you are also aware of positioning and how important that is in defining a product or service for your target market. The example of Xerox trying to move into the computer business was a good example of how not to do it. So using your new knowledge of clustering and positioning, return to our opening example and identify two different target market segments for Xerox copiers.

KEY TERMS

market, 60

generic market, 60

product-market, 60

market segmentation, 62

segmenting, 63

market segment, 63

single target market approach, 65

multiple target market approach, 65

combined target market approach, 65

combiners, 65

segmenters, 66

qualifying dimensions, 69

determining dimensions, 69

clustering techniques, 76

customer relationship management (CRM), 77

positioning, 78

unique selling proposition, 79

QUESTIONS AND PROBLEMS

1. Distinguish between a generic market and a product-market. Illustrate your answer.

2. How does CBC radio segment its market versus your favourite rock station?

3. List the types of potential segmenting dimensions, and explain which you would try to apply first, second, and third in segmenting the BMW sports model market versus the SUV market.

4. Explain why segmentation efforts based on attempts to divide the mass market using a few demographic dimensions may be very disappointing.

5. Illustrate the concept that segmenting is an aggregating process by referring to the admissions policies of your own college and a nearby college or university.

6. Review the types of segmenting dimensions listed in Exhibits 3-7 and 3-8, and select the ones you think should be combined to fully explain the market segment you personally would be in if you were planning to buy a new watch today. List several dimensions and try to develop a shorthand name, like "fashion-oriented," to describe your own personal market segment. Then try to estimate what proportion of the total watch market would be accounted for by

your market segment. Next, explain if there are any offerings that come close to meeting the needs of your market. If not, what sort of a marketing mix is needed? Would it be economically attractive for anyone to try to satisfy your market segment? Why or why not?

7. Identify the determining dimension or dimensions that explain why you bought the specific brand you did in your most recent purchase of a *(a)* soft drink, *(b)* shampoo, *(c)* shirt or blouse, and *(d)* larger, more expensive item, such as a bicycle, camera, or boat. Try to express the determining dimension(s) in terms of your own personal characteristics rather than the product's characteristics. Estimate what share of the market would probably be motivated by the same determining dimension(s).

8. Consider the market for off-campus apartments in your city. Identify some submarkets that have different needs and determining dimensions. Then evaluate how well the needs in these market segments are being met in your geographic area. Is there an obvious breakthrough opportunity waiting for someone?

9. Explain how positioning analysis can help a marketing manager identify target market opportunities in the MP3 player market.

10. How would you position a cottage brewery beer like Sleeman's or Keith's versus a national brand like Canadian?

11. How would you position Canadian wines to compete against French import wines?

COMPUTER–AIDED PROBLEM

3. Segmenting Customers

RESOURCE
REMINDER

The marketing manager for Audiotronics Software Company is seeking new market opportunities. He is focusing on the voice recognition market and has narrowed down to three segments: the Fearful Typists, the Power Users, and the Professional Specialists. The Fearful Typists don't know much about computers—they just want a fast way to create e-mail messages, letters, and simple reports without errors. They don't need a lot of special features. They want simple instructions and a program that's easy to learn. The Power Users know a lot about computers, use them often, and want a voice recognition program with many special features. All computer programs seem easy to them—so they aren't worried about learning to use the various features. The Professional Specialists have jobs that require a lot of writing. They don't know much about computers but are willing to learn. They want special features needed for their work—but only if they aren't too hard to learn and use.

The marketing manager prepared a table summarizing the importance of each of three key needs in the three segments (see table below).

Market Segment	Importance of Need (1 = not important; 10 = very important)		
	Features	Easy to Use	Easy to Learn
Fearful typists	3	8	9
Power users	9	2	2
Professional specialists	7	5	6

Audiotronics' sales staff conducted interviews with seven potential customers who were asked to rate how important each of these three needs were in their work. The manager prepared a spreadsheet to help him cluster (aggregate) each person into one of the segments—along with other similar people. Each person's ratings are entered in the spreadsheet, and the clustering procedure computes a similarity score that indicates how similar (a low score) or dissimilar (a high score) the person is to the typical person in each of the segments. The manager can then "aggregate" potential customers into the segment that is most similar (that is, the one with the *lowest* similarity score).

a. The ratings for a potential customer appear on the first spreadsheet. Into which segment would you aggregate this person?

b. The responses for seven potential customers who were interviewed are listed in the table below. Enter the ratings for a customer in the spreadsheet and then write down the similarity score for each segment. Repeat the process for each customer. Based on your analysis, indicate the segment into which you would aggregate each customer. Indicate the size (number of customers) of each segment.

c. In the interview, each potential customer was also asked what type of computer he or she would be using. The responses are shown in the table along with the ratings. Group the responses based on the customer's segment. If you were targeting the Fearful Typists segment, what type of computer would you focus on when developing your software?

d. Based on your analysis, which customer would you say is least like any of the segments? Briefly explain the reason for your choice.

| Potential Customer | Importance of Need (1 = not important; 10 = very important) | | | |
	Features	Easy to Use	Easy to Learn	Type of Computer
A.	8	1	2	Dell laptop
B.	6	6	5	IBM desktop
C.	4	9	8	Apple
D.	2	6	7	Apple
E.	5	6	5	IBM desktop
F.	8	3	1	Dell laptop
G.	4	6	8	Apple

If you want to read the cases and view the video cases that accompany this chapter, visit the *Basic Marketing* Online Learning Centre at: **www.mcgrawhill.ca/olc/perreault**. Along with these cases and video cases, the OLC also has the software and user guide for this chapter's Computer-Aided Problem, as well as exercises, quizzes, articles, links, and other *interactive* content that will help you with your studies.

Evaluating Market Opportunities

Marketers have to be quick on their feet. Things are always changing around them. Take the movie theatre business, for example. It's facing challenges from home-theatre systems and DVDs. People are spending thousands of dollars on wide-screen, high-definition TVs, top-of-the-line DVD players, and surround-sound systems. Films are being rushed into DVD release faster than ever and are widely available on the Internet and through on-demand television.

The trend is hurting movie chains such as Famous Players and Cineplex and independent theatres. So much so, that Festival Cinemas, a small chain of theatres and a Toronto landmark since 1974, is planning to close four out of its five theatres.

How can theatre marketers respond to such overwhelming odds against them? They are pinning their hopes on digital cinema. Thirty-five millimetre projectors will eventually be phased out and replaced with digital projectors. This results in a crystal-clear picture that won't degrade over time as film images do when they pass through the projector. There are also more practical reasons to switch to digital. It will cut exhibition costs since theatres will no longer have to order multiple prints, and they will be able to get films easily via satellite or computer. Filmmaker George Lucas, has this to say about film versus digital technology. "Making a big movie, a *Harry Potter* or a *Spiderman*, you're spending $20 to $30 million for the prints to strike them and ship them to theaters. Smaller movies have to spend a huge part of their budgets on prints."

As box-office revenues continue to fall, theatres are looking for creative ideas to turn around the situation.

Cineplex, for example, is promoting its theatres for private use. The giant screens are often rented for corporate presentations and private screenings.

In this chapter, we will be looking at external variables that can affect a company's business and how companies deal with them.[1]

The movie theatre case shows that a marketing manager must analyze customer needs and choose marketing strategy variables within the framework of the marketing environment and how it is changing.

A large number of forces shape the marketing environment. To help organize your thinking, it's useful to classify the various forces as falling into either (1) the direct market environment or (2) the external market environment. The direct environment includes customers, the company, and competitors. The external market environment is broader and includes four major areas:

1. Economic environment.
2. Technological environment.
3. Political and legal environment.
4. Cultural and social environment.

The marketing manager can't control the variables of the marketing environment. That's why it's useful to think of them as uncontrollable variables. On the other hand, the marketing manager should carefully analyze the environmental variables when making decisions that can be controlled. For example, a manager can select a strategy that leads the firm into a product-market where competition is not yet strong. In this chapter, we'll look at the marketing environment variables in more detail. We'll see how they shape opportunities—limiting some possibilities and making others more attractive.

In its stores, Recreational Equipment Inc. (REI) has added Internet kiosks with access to the REI Web site to help meet the objective of providing customers with easy access to information—whether it's to check for an out-of-stock item or to find a new hiking trail.

OBJECTIVES SHOULD SET FIRM'S COURSE

A company must decide where it's going, or it may fall into the trap expressed so well by the quotation: "Having lost sight of our objective, we redoubled our efforts." Company objectives should shape the direction and operation of the whole business.

It is difficult to set objectives that really guide the present and future development of a company. The marketing manager should be heard when the company is setting objectives. But setting whole-company objectives—within resource limits—is ultimately the responsibility of top management. Top management must look at the whole business, relate its present objectives and resources to the external environment, and then decide what the firm wants to accomplish in the future. Consider the following near disaster.

The sales analyst of a large Canadian multinational recognized a marketer's dream when a paint products manufacturer approached his firm to distribute their product coast to coast. The product was a dream because it was a top seller and it had one of the highest markups in the business. You can imagine the sales analyst's consternation when the executive committee turned down the proposal. The problem? The multinational's lawyers discovered evidence of stock manipulation by the paint products owner. The deal was perfect from a marketing standpoint but the corporate-wide objective of maintaining a stellar business reputation would have been trashed by a potential police investigation involving stock fraud. The shareholders would not have been pleased.

Three basic objectives provide guidelines

The following three objectives provide a useful starting point for setting a firm's objectives. They should be sought *together* because in the long run a failure in even one of the three areas can lead to total failure of the business. A business should

1. Engage in specific activities that will perform a socially and economically useful function.
2. Develop an organization to carry on the business and implement its strategies.
3. Earn enough profit to survive.[2]

Should be socially useful

The first objective isn't just a "do-gooder" objective. Businesses can't exist without the approval of consumers. If a firm's activities appear to be contrary to the consumer "good," the firm can be wiped out almost overnight by political or legal action—or consumers' own negative responses.[3]

Should earn some profit

A firm must make a profit to survive. But just saying that a firm should try to make a profit isn't enough. Management must specify the time period involved since many plans that maximize profit in the long run lose money during the first few years. Thousands of new dot-com firms went belly-up after a year or two of losses because they could not even cover their expenses in the short run.

On the other hand, seeking only short-term profits may steer the firm from opportunities that would offer larger long-run profits. For example, Fruit of the Loom struggled to maximize profits with its men's underwear and other clothing lines, but in those intensely competitive markets the maximum possible profit margins were so thin that it ultimately had to reorganize under the bankruptcy law. In a situation like this, it might be better to set a *target* rate of profit that will lead the firm into areas with more promising possibilities.

A mission statement helps set the course

Our three general objectives provide guidelines, but a firm should develop its own objectives. This is important, but top executives often don't state their objectives clearly. If objectives aren't clear from the start, different managers may hold unspoken and conflicting objectives.

Many firms try to avoid this problem by developing a **mission statement**, which sets out the organization's basic purpose for being. For example, one library's mission statement is "to serve the minds of the citizens in our community by providing easy access to resources that meet their informational and recreational needs." Ideally, a good mission statement should reflect a marketing orientation and not a production orientation as can easily happen. It should be customer-need focused and stated in marketing terms that are intended to meet those needs. The mission statement should also focus on a few key goals rather than trying to be everything to everybody and finally, it should supply guidelines when managers face difficult decisions. For example, if an employee of the library is trying to decide whether or not to write a proposal for the funding of a French language story time or new computers that provide Internet access, it should be clear that these services are within the scope of the library's stated mission. A mission statement may need to be revised as new market needs arise or as the marketing environment changes. But this would be a fundamental change and not one that is made casually.[4]

The whole firm must work toward the same objectives

A mission statement is important, but it is not a substitute for more specific objectives that provide guidance in screening possible opportunities. For example, top management might set objectives such as "earn 25 percent annual return on investment" and "introduce at least three innovative and successful products in the next two years."

Of course, when there are a number of specific objectives stated by top management, it is critical that they be compatible. For example, the objective of introducing new products is reasonable. However, if the costs of developing and introducing the new products cannot be recouped within one year, the return on investment objective is impossible.[5]

Company objectives should lead to marketing objectives

To avoid such problems, the marketing manager should at least be involved in setting company objectives. Company objectives guide managers as they search for and evaluate opportunities—and later plan marketing strategies. Particular *marketing* objectives should be set within the framework of larger company objectives. As shown in Exhibit 4-1, firms need a hierarchy of objectives—moving from company objectives to marketing department objectives. For each marketing strategy, firms also need objectives for each of the four Ps—as well as more detailed objectives. For example, in the Promotion area, we need objectives for advertising, sales promotion, *and* personal selling.

Exhibit 4-1   A Hierarchy of Objectives

Toyota provides a good example. One of its company objectives is to achieve high customer satisfaction. So the R&D people design vehicles to meet specific reliability objectives. Similarly, the production people work to cut manufacturing defects. The marketing department, in turn, sets specific customer satisfaction objectives for every product. That leads to specific promotion objectives to ensure that the sales and advertising people don't promise more than the company can deliver. Dealers' service people, in turn, work to fix any problem the first time it's reported.

Both company objectives and marketing objectives should be realistic and achievable. Overly ambitious objectives are useless if the firm lacks the resources to achieve them.

COMPANY RESOURCES MAY LIMIT SEARCH FOR OPPORTUNITIES

Every firm has some resources—hopefully some unique ones—that set it apart. Breakthrough opportunities—or at least some competitive advantage—come from making use of these strengths while avoiding direct competition with firms having similar strengths.

To find its strengths, a firm must evaluate its functional areas (production, human relations, research and engineering, marketing, general management, and finance) as well as its present products and markets. The knowledge of people at the firm and the organization's culture can also be unique resources. By analyzing successes or failures in relation to the firm's resources, management can discover why the firm was successful—or why it failed—in the past.

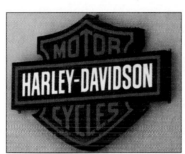

Harley-Davidson's motorcycle business was on the ropes, and it was losing customers to Japanese competitors. Studying the Japanese firms helped Harley identify ways to produce higher quality motorcycles at lower cost. With these resource-use problems resolved, Harley was again on the road to achieving its objectives. As its sales and reputation grew, its close relationship with Harley owners became a resource that helped Harley introduce a profitable line of accessories. The Harley case highlights both manufacturing quality and relationships with existing customers as resources. Other resources that should be considered as part of an evaluation of strengths and weaknesses are discussed in the following sections.[6]

Financial strength

Some opportunities require large amounts of capital just to get started. Money may be required for R&D, production facilities, marketing research, or advertising before a firm makes its first sale. And even a really good opportunity may not be profitable for years. So lack of financial strength is often a barrier to entry into an otherwise attractive market.

Producing capability and flexibility

In many businesses, the cost of producing and selling each unit decreases as the quantity increases. Therefore, smaller firms can be at a great cost disadvantage if they try to win business from larger competitors.

On the other hand, new—or smaller—firms sometimes have the advantage of flexibility. They are not handicapped with large, special-purpose facilities that are obsolete or poorly located. Large steel producers once enjoyed economies of scale. But today they have trouble competing with producers using smaller, more flexible plants.

Some firms are finding that they have the greatest flexibility by not having any "in house" manufacturing at all. Sara Lee, the company that markets brands like

Hanes and L'Eggs, is a good example. Sara Lee sold its manufacturing facilities for many of these textile-related markets. Sara Lee says it doesn't have a competitive advantage in manufacturing. Further, as its needs change in various markets around the world it will buy products from whatever suppliers are best able to meet its specifications.

Marketing strengths	Our marketing strategy planning framework (Exhibit 2-10) helps in analyzing current marketing resources. In the product area, for example, a familiar brand can be a big strength. Starbucks is famous for its coffee beverages. When Starbucks introduced its Coffee Ice Cream, many people quickly tried it because they knew what Starbucks flavour meant.[7] A new idea or process may be protected by a *patent*. A patent owner has a 20-year monopoly to develop and use its new product, process, or material. If one firm has a strong patent, competitors may be limited to second-rate offerings—and their efforts may be doomed to failure.[8]

Good relations with established channel intermediaries—or control of good locations—can be important resources. When marketing managers at Microsoft decided to introduce the Xbox game console, Microsoft software and computer accessories had already proved profitable for retailers like Best Buy and Wal-Mart that could reach the target market. So these retailers were willing to give the new product shelf space even if they were already carrying competing products from Nintendo or Sony.[9]

Similarly, existing computer systems that effectively share information in the channel, speed delivery of orders, and control inventory can be a big advantage. When P&G adds a new type of detergent, the systems to manage distribution are already in place.

Promotion and price resources must be considered too. The Source by Circuit City already has a skilled sales force. Marketing managers know these sales reps can handle new products and customers. And expertise to create an Internet Web site for online orders may enable a firm to expand its market and undercut competitors' prices.

Finally, thorough understanding of a target market can give a company an edge. Many companies fail in new product-markets because they don't really understand the needs of the new customers or the new competitive environment.

ANALYZING COMPETITORS AND THE COMPETITIVE ENVIRONMENT

Choose opportunities that avoid head-on competition	The **competitive environment** affects the number and types of competitors the marketing manager must face and how they may behave. Although marketing managers usually can't control these factors, they can choose strategies that avoid head-on competition. And where competition is inevitable, they can plan for it. When WestJet made a bid for market share it didn't go against Air Canada on expensive long-haul routes. Instead, it concentrated initially on short hauls in Western Canada where Air Canada was not such a formidable competitor.

Economists describe four basic kinds of market (competitive) situations: pure competition, oligopoly, monopolistic competition, and monopoly. Understanding the differences among these market situations is helpful in analyzing the competitive environment.

Most product-markets head toward pure competition—or oligopoly—over the long run. In these situations, competitors offer very similar products. Because customers see the different available products (marketing mixes) as close substitutes, managers just compete with lower and lower prices, and profit margins shrink. Sometimes managers do this much too quickly, without really thinking through the question of how to add more customer value. The marketing mix that offers the best customer value is not necessarily the one with the lowest price. Once WestJet became a market threat, Air Canada retaliated by creating its own discount airline

Rogers wants to limit head-on price competition with this ad claiming the new BlackBerry 8700 can only be obtained through them. Dirt Devil wants to convince customers that its Scorpion Hand Vac has more power than competitors, so its ad gives the specific amp and watt rating. However, a consumer who does not know the ratings for other brands may not know that this is an advantage.

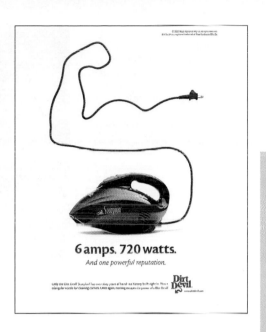

(Zip) and the price war was on. WestJet was not eliminated however because customers saw value that went beyond getting the cheapest seat available. WestJet created customer value with such marketing extras as better schedules and seating as well as a reputation for friendly flight crews.

Avoiding pure competition is sensible and certainly fits with our emphasis on target marketing and the need to find a competitive advantage on which to differentiate the firm's marketing mix. This is why effective target marketing is fundamentally different from effective decision making in other areas of business. Accounting, production, and financial managers for competing firms can learn about and use the same standardized approaches—and they will work well in each case. By contrast, marketing managers can't just adopt the same "good" marketing strategy being used by other firms. That just leads to head-on competition and a downward spiral in prices and profits. So target marketers try to offer a marketing mix better suited to customers' needs than competitors' offerings.

Competitor-free environments are rare

Most marketing managers would like to have such a strong marketing mix that customers see it as uniquely able to meet their needs. This competitor-free ideal guides the search for breakthrough opportunities. Yet monopoly situations, in which one firm completely controls a broad product-market, are rare in market-directed economies. Further, governments commonly regulate monopolies. For example, in many parts of the world prices set by utility companies like Hydro or Enbridge Gas must be approved by a government agency. Although most marketing managers can't expect to operate with complete control in an unregulated monopoly, they can move away from head-on competition.

Monopolistic competition is typical—and a challenge

In monopolistic competition, a number of different firms offer marketing mixes that at least some customers see as different. Each competitor tries to get control (a monopoly) in its "own" target market. But competition still exists because some customers see the various alternatives as substitutes. Most marketing managers in developed economies face monopolistic competition.

In monopolistic competition, marketing managers sometimes try to differentiate very similar products by relying on other elements of the marketing mix. For example, Clorox Bleach uses the same basic chemicals as other bleaches. But marketing managers for Clorox may help to set it apart from other bleaches by offering an improved pouring spout, by producing ads that demonstrate its stain-killing power,

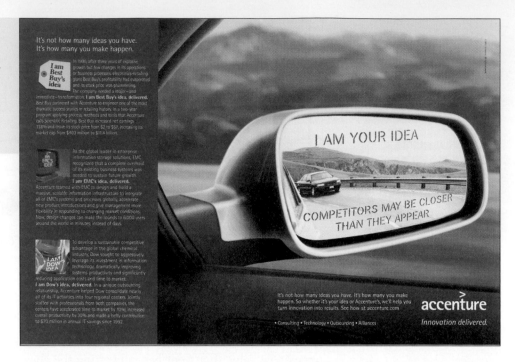

or by getting it better shelf positions in supermarkets. Yet such approaches may not work, especially if competitors can easily imitate each new idea.

Analyze competitors to find a competitive advantage

The best way for a marketing manager to avoid head-on competition is to find new or better ways to satisfy customers' needs and provide value. The search for a breakthrough opportunity—or some sort of competitive advantage—requires an understanding not only of customers but also of competitors. That's why marketing managers turn to **competitor analysis**—an organized approach for evaluating the strengths and weaknesses of current or potential competitors' marketing strategies.

The basic approach to competitor analysis is simple. You compare the strengths and weaknesses of your current (or planned) target market and marketing mix with what competitors are currently doing or are likely to do in response to your strategy.

The initial step in competitor analysis is to identify potential competitors. It's useful to start broadly and from the viewpoint of target customers. Companies may offer quite different products to meet the same needs, but they are competitors if customers see them as offering close substitutes. For example, disposable diapers, cloth diapers, and diaper rental services all compete in the same generic market concerned with baby care. Identifying a broad set of potential competitors helps marketing managers understand the different ways customers are currently meeting needs and sometimes points to new opportunities. For example, even parents who usually prefer the economy of cloth diapers may be interested in the convenience of disposables when they travel.

Usually, however, marketing managers quickly narrow the focus of their analysis to the set of **competitive rivals**—firms that will be the closest competitors. Rivals offering similar products are usually easy to identify. However, with a really new and different product concept, the closest competitor may be a firm that is currently serving similar needs with a different type of product. Although such firms may not appear to be close competitors, they are likely to fight back—perhaps with a directly competitive product—if another firm starts to take away customers.

Anticipate competition that will come

A successful strategy attracts copycats who jump in for a share of the profit. Sometimes a creative imitator figures out a way to provide customers with superior value. Then sales may disappear before the pioneer even knows what's happened.

	P&G's Current and Planned Strategy	Kao's Strengths (+) and Weaknesses (−)	Uni-Charm's Strengths (+) and Weaknesses (−)
Target Market(s)	Upscale, modern parents who can afford disposable diapers	Same as for P&G	Same as for P&G, but also budget-conscious segment that includes cloth diaper users (+)
Product	Improved fit and absorbency (+); brand name imagery weak in Japan (−)	Brand familiarity (+), but no longer the best performance (−)	Two brands—for different market segments—and more convenient package with handles (+)
Place	Distribution through independent wholesalers to both food stores and drugstores (+), but handled by fewer retailers (−)	Close relations with and control over wholesalers who carry only Kao products (+); computerized inventory reorder system (+)	Distribution through 80% of food stores in best locations (+); shelf space for two brands (+)
Promotion	Heaviest spending on daytime TV, heavy sales promotion, including free samples (+); small sales force (−)	Large efficient sales force (+); lowest advertising spending (−) and out-of-date ad claims (−)	Advertising spending high (+); effective ads that appeal to Japanese mothers (+)
Price	High retail price (−), but lower unit price for larger quantities (+)	Highest retail price (−), but also best margins for wholesalers and retailers (+)	Lowest available retail price (+); price of premium brand comparable to P&G (−)
(Potential) Competitive Barriers	Patent protection (+), limits in access to retail shelf space (−)	Inferior product (−), excellent logistics support system (+)	Economies of scale and lower costs (+); loyal customers (+)
Likely Response(s)	Improve wholesaler and retailer margins; faster deliveries in channel; change package to require less shelf space	Press retailers to increase in-store promotion; change advertising and/or improve product	Increase short-term sales promotions; but if P&G takes customers, cut price on premium brand

Finding a sustainable competitive advantage requires special attention to competitor strengths and weaknesses. For example, it is very difficult to dislodge a firm that is already a market leader simply by attacking with a similar strategy. The leader can usually defend its position by quickly copying the best parts of what a new competitor is trying to do. On the other hand, an established competitor may not be able to defend quickly if it is attacked where it is weak. For example, Sony Walkman CD players had a large market share. When RCA added a new feature to its CD players that enabled them to also handle MP3 files, Sony was slow to respond. Sony executives were worried that more widespread use of MP3 files would hurt profits from the firm's music recording business.[10]

Watch for competitive barriers

In a competitor analysis, you also consider **competitive barriers**—the conditions that may make it difficult, or even impossible, for a firm to compete in a market. Such barriers may limit your own plans or, alternatively, block competitors' responses to an innovative strategy.

For example, Exhibit 4-2 summarizes a competitor analysis in the Japanese market for disposable diapers. P&G was about to replace its original Pampers, which were selling poorly, with a new version that offered improved fit and better absorbency. Kao and Uni-Charm, the two leading Japanese producers, both had better distribution networks. Kao also had a better computer system to handle reorders. Because most Japanese grocery stores and drugstores are very small, frequent restocking by wholesalers is critical. So getting cooperation in the channel was a potential competitive barrier for P&G. To overcome this problem, P&G changed its packaging to take up less space and offered wholesalers and retailers better markups.[11]

Seek information about competitors

A marketing manager should actively seek information about current or potential competitors. Although most firms try to keep the specifics of their plans secret, much public information may be available. Sources of competitor information include trade publications, alert sales reps, middlemen, and other industry experts. In business markets, customers may be quick to explain what competing suppliers are offering.

The Internet is a powerful way to get information about competitors. A firm that puts all of its marketing information on a Web site for customers also makes it readily available to competitors. Similarly, it's easy to search through thousands of online publications and databases for any mention of a competitor. It's also increasingly common to specify what you want and instruct a software "robot" to send you a copy as soon as it's available.

INTERNET EXERCISE

If you were a new marketing manager at Rubbermaid, you might be interested in finding out more about Tupperware, an important competitor in some markets. What type of relevant information could you get by going to the Tupperware Canada Web site (www.tupperware.ca)?

Ethical issues may arise

The search for information about competitors sometimes raises ethical issues. For example, people who change jobs and move to competing firms may have a great deal of information about the competitor, but is it ethical for them to use it? Similarly, some firms have been criticized for going too far—like waiting at a landfill for competitors' trash to find copies of confidential company reports. And the high-tech version of that occurs when computer "hackers" use the Internet to break into a competitor's computer network.

Beyond the moral issues, spying on competitors to obtain trade secrets is illegal. Damage awards can be huge. In a settlement with Air Canada over an espionage scandal, WestJet issued a press release admitting its involvement and agreed to pay $5 million in legal and investigation fees. They also agreed to donate $10 million to various charities in Air Canada's and WestJet's names.

Competition may vary from country to country

A firm that faces very stiff competition may find that the competitive environment—and the opportunities—are much better in another region or country. For instance, eight years of slow growth and deregulation made the Japanese market extremely competitive. So the Iris Ohyama Company, a maker of plastic storage containers, started exporting to North America. Within three years, its sales to U.S. retailers like Staples were $60 million.[12]

Direct competition cannot always be avoided

Despite the desire to avoid highly competitive situations, a firm may find that it can't. Some firms are already in an industry before it becomes intensely competitive. For example, Rubbermaid was one of the first firms to introduce sturdy, low-cost plastic housewares. Now it is a respected brand name but faces competition from hundreds of other firms. As competitors fail, new firms enter the market, possibly because they don't see more attractive alternatives. This is a common pattern with small retailers and wholesalers in less-developed economies. New entrants may not even know how competitive the market is—but they stick it out until they run out of money.

THE ECONOMIC ENVIRONMENT

The **economic and technological environment** affects the way firms—and the whole economy—use resources. We will treat the economic and technological environments separately to emphasize that the technological environment provides a

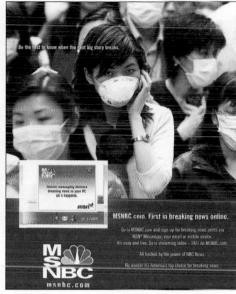

Managers who compete in global markets need to be aware of how changes in the global economy will impact their strategies and opportunities.

base for the economic environment. Technical skills and equipment affect the way companies convert an economy's resources into output. The economic environment, on the other hand, is affected by the way all of the parts of a macro-economic system interact. This then affects such things as national income, economic growth, and inflation. The economic environment may vary from one country to another, but economies around the world are linked.

Economic conditions change rapidly

The economic environment can, and does, change quite rapidly. The effects can be far-reaching and require changes in marketing strategy.

Even a well-planned marketing strategy may fail if a country or region goes through a rapid business decline. As consumers' incomes drop, they must shift their spending patterns. They may simply have to do without some products. When this happens, many businesses collapse or have big losses. You can see how quickly this happens by considering what happened in Thailand in the late 1990s. In a few months, the buying power of Thai money (the baht) was cut by half. Imagine how *your* life would change if you suddenly had half as much money. If this happened to you and most of the people you know, what would its effect be on businesses where you buy?

Economic changes are not always this dramatic. Consider the recent growth spurt of the Canadian economy. Increased economic activity in Canadian and international markets has created a strong job market, increased incomes, and focused attention on the rising value of investments. Many consumers feel like they are well off. Purchases of pricey items and luxuries have trended up because of this "wealth effect." This behaviour will quickly disappear however when the economic cycle turns, but for most products, demand will decline more gradually. Even so, many companies aren't strong enough to survive such downturns.

Interest rates and inflation affect buying

Changes in the economy are often accompanied by changes in the interest rate—the charge for borrowing money. Interest rates directly affect the total price borrowers must pay for products. So the interest rate affects when, and if, they will buy. This is an especially important factor in some business markets. But it also affects consumer purchases of homes, cars, and other items usually bought on credit.

Interest rates usually increase during periods of inflation, and inflation is a fact of life in many economics. In some Latin American countries, inflation has run in

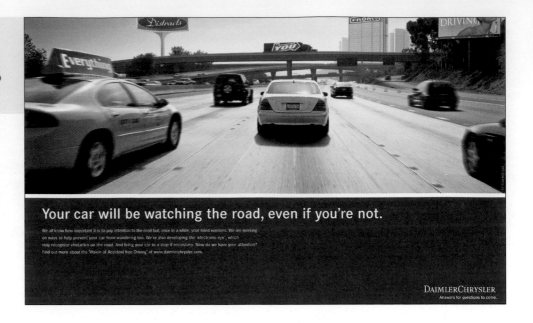

Your car will be watching the road, even if you're not.

We all know how important it is to pay attention to the road but, once in a while, your mind wanders. We are working
on ways to help prevent your car from wandering too. We're also developing the 'electronic eye', which
may recognize obstacles on the road. And bring your car to a stop if necessary. Now do we have your attention?
Find out more about the 'Vision of Accident free Driving' at www.daimlerchrysler.com.

DAIMLERCHRYSLER
Answers for questions to come.

the 20–30 percent range in recent years. In contrast, current Canadian levels of around 2 percent seem low. Still, inflation must be considered in strategy planning. When costs are rising rapidly and there are no more cost-cutting measures to take, a marketing manager may have to increase prices.

The global economy is connected

The economies of the world are connected—and changes in one economy quickly affect others. One reason for this is that the amount of international trade is increasing—and it is affected by changes in and between economies. For example, International Harvester (IH) was very successful selling its earth-moving equipment in Asia when construction was booming. However, when an economic downturn spread across Asia, many customers could no longer make payments. IH faced big losses—and the cost of retrieving equipment that was 13,000 miles away!

Changes in the *exchange rate*—how much one country's money is worth in another country's money—have an important effect on international trade. When the dollar is strong, it's worth more in foreign countries. This sounds good—but it makes Canadian products more expensive overseas and foreign products cheaper in Canada. New domestic competition arises as foreign products gain a competitive edge with lower prices. A country's whole economic system can change as the balance of imports and exports shifts—affecting jobs, consumer income, and national productivity.

Marketing managers must watch the economic environment carefully. In contrast to the cultural and social environment, economic conditions can move rapidly and require immediate strategy changes.[13]

THE TECHNOLOGICAL ENVIRONMENT

Technology affects opportunities

Technology is the application of science to convert an economy's resources to output. Technology affects marketing in two basic ways: with new products and with new processes (ways of doing things). For example, advances in information technology make it possible for people in different parts of the world to communicate with satellite video-conferencing and to send complex design drawings over the Internet. Web sites enable sophisticated e-commerce exchanges between remote firms. These process changes are accompanied by an exciting explosion of high-tech products—from genome-based medicines to cars that contact the police if they are stolen.

Technology transfer is rapid

New technologies have created important industries that didn't even exist a few years ago. Ten years ago eBay didn't exist. Now it's one of the best known firms in the world. With such big opportunities at stake, you can also see why there is such rapid transfer of technology from one part of the world to another. But technology transfer is not automatic. Someone—perhaps you—has to see the opportunity.

Internet technologies are reshaping marketing

Many of the big advances in business have come from early recognition of new ways to do things. There is perhaps no better example of this than the World Wide Web and the Internet. The Internet is a system for linking computers around the world. The idea of linking computers in a network is not new. Even so, the Internet expands the network concept to include any computer anywhere and the World Wide Web makes the exchange of information easy. As a result, this technology is radically changing just about every aspect of marketing. We'll be discussing these changes in more detail throughout the text, but for now we'll just illustrate the impact.

Consider the arena of promotion. The invention of TV changed marketing because it suddenly made it possible for a sponsor to broadcast a vivid message to millions of people at the same time. Now, the Internet makes it possible for that sponsor to select any of millions of messages and to simultaneously narrowcast any of them to millions of different individuals. It is just as easy for customers to request the information in the first place, or to respond electronically once they have it. Thus, the Internet's capability radically changes our ideas about how firms communicate with customers, and vice versa. Similarly, the Internet is creating totally different approaches to pricing. Airlines run online auctions of seats that might otherwise go unsold. If you sell every seat to the highest bidder, you are really pricing precisely to match supply and demand. To check out an online auction, go to www.ebay.ca.

In hindsight, new approaches such as these seem obvious—given that the technology is available. But they are not obvious up front—unless you're really looking for them.[14]

Technology also poses challenges

Technological change opens up new opportunities, but it also poses challenges for marketers. For some firms, success hinges on how quickly new ideas can be brought to market. But it's easy for a firm to slip into a production orientation in the flush of excitement that comes from a new idea or R&D discovery. That makes it more important than ever for marketing thinking to guide the production process—starting at the beginning with decisions about what customers will really value and where development efforts should be focused.

Technology and ethical issues

Marketers often must help their firms decide what technological developments are ethically acceptable. For example, many firms track information about who "hits" the company Web page and what Web site they came from. The firm can then sell this information to whoever wants to use it to send promotional e-mail. Yet uninvited e-mail is just another form of invasion of privacy.

Some attractive technological developments may be rejected because of their long-run effects on the environment. Aseptic drink boxes, for example, are convenient but difficult to recycle. In a case like this, what's good for the firm and some customers may not be good for the cultural and social environment or acceptable in the political and legal environment. Being close to the market should give marketers a better feel for current trends and help firms avoid serious mistakes.[15]

THE POLITICAL ENVIRONMENT

The attitudes and reactions of people, social critics, and governments all affect the political environment. Consumers in the same country usually share a common political environment, but the political environment can also affect opportunities at a local or international level. Some business managers have become very successful by studying the political environment and developing strategies that take advantage of opportunities related to changing political dimensions.

Nationalism can be limiting in international markets

Strong sentiments of **nationalism**—an emphasis on a country's interests before everything else—affect how macro-marketing systems work. They can affect how marketing managers work as well. Nationalistic feelings can reduce sales—or even block all marketing activity—in some international markets. For many years, Japan has made it difficult for outside firms to do business there—in spite of the fact that Japanese producers of cars, TVs, digital cameras, and other products have established profitable markets in Canada, the United States, Europe, and other parts of the world.

The "Buy American" policy in many government contracts and business purchases reflects this same attitude in the United States. There is broad support for protecting U.S. producers—and jobs—from foreign competition.[16] Consider for example the pressure on U.S. employment brought about by the Ontario auto manufacturers under the North American Free Trade Agreement (NAFTA).

Nationalistic feelings can determine whether a firm can enter markets because businesses often must get permission to operate. In some political environments, this is only a routine formality. In others, a lot of red tape and personal influence are involved, and bribes are sometimes expected. This raises ethical issues for marketing managers—and legal issues too, since it's illegal for Canadian firms to offer such bribes. Clearly, that can make it difficult for a Canadian firm to compete with a company from a country that doesn't have similar laws.

Regional groupings are becoming more important

Important dimensions of the political environment are likely to be similar among nations that have banded together to have common regional economic boundaries. The move toward the unification of Europe and free trade among the nations of North America are outstanding examples of this sort of regional grouping.

The unification of European markets

In the past, each country in Europe had its own unique trade rules and regulations. These differences made it difficult and expensive to move products from one country to the others. Now, the member countries of the European Union (EU) are reducing conflicting laws, taxes, and other obstacles to trade within Europe. This, in turn, is reducing costs and the prices European consumers pay and creating new jobs. Even bigger changes may come if Britain decides to join other countries that have moved to the euro, a new unified money system for the EU. With the currencies of countries in the euro-zone phased out, transactions no longer involve the extra uncertainty and cost of converting payments from one currency to another.

NAFTA is building trade cooperation

The international competition fostered by the moves to unify Europe provided impetus for Canada, the United States, and Mexico to develop more cooperative trade agreements. The **North American Free Trade Agreement (NAFTA)** lays out a plan to reshape the rules of trade among Canada, the United States, and Mexico. NAFTA basically enlarges the free-trade pact that had already knocked down most barriers to Canadian–American trade, and over a 15-year period it will eliminate most such barriers with Mexico.

The long-term economic impact of NAFTA is yet to be seen. However, tariffs that have already dropped are having a significant impact on specific businesses. Many firms have moved production—and jobs—to Mexico where labour is cheaper. NAFTA is creating a free-trade region that encompasses over 400 million people and three economies that produce over $9 trillion worth of goods and services annually. Thus, the changes that result from NAFTA may ultimately be as significant as those in Europe. Talks are underway to explore the concept of expanding NAFTA to create a free-trade zone for 34 countries across North, South, and Central America.

Of course, removal of some economic and political barriers—whether across all of the Americas or Europe—will not eliminate the need to adjust strategies to reach submarkets of consumers. Centuries of cultural differences will not disappear overnight. Some may never disappear.[17]

Some dramatic changes in the political environment—like the fall of communism in Eastern Europe—happen fast and are hard to predict. Yet many important political changes—both within and across nations—evolve more gradually. The development of consumerism is a good example.

Marketing consumerism, environmentalism, and ethics

Consumerism is a social movement that seeks to increase the rights and powers of consumers. The consumer movement really became high profile in the 1960s when concerns focused on product safety and the full disclosure of product information. Embedded in the movement was—and to a considerable degree still is—the issue of increasing consumer power relative to corporations through the widespread dissemination of information about products. Publications like *Consumer Reports* and *Lemon-Aid* reflect this. Consumerism today has however, taken on a larger mandate with environmental and ethical issues added to the movement. The effect of consumer protests and boycotts is not to be underestimated and the list of corporate targets is substantial. Greenpeace for example, have successfully pressured the Japanese and Norwegian whaling industries, and the U.S. tuna fishery because of their incidental dolphin catch. In BC, MacMillan Bloedel suffered some serious damage to their European forest products markets because of boycotts organized by environmentalists over their old-growth logging practices, and in Newfoundland the harvest of white seal coats was devastated by European organized boycotts.

Similarly, the ethical consumer movement has brought pressure to bear on companies accused of manufacturing their products in Third World "sweatshop" factories. Major corporations like Nike and Wal-Mart have been targeted by consumer groups.

Whether the issues focus on environmental or ethically driven consumerism or on complaints about products and services, the Internet has exerted a profound impact by providing a mass-market public forum for consumerism in all of its various manifestations. Blogs, rightly or wrongly (and sometimes customer complaints are wrong) mean individual angry consumers can now gain access to the same mass-market exposure for their messages as corporations. This type of mass-market negative advertising can have important ramifications for a company's product reputation and ultimately their sales. It would be foolhardy in the extreme for a marketer to underestimate the potential impact of this newest manifestation of Internet technology on product or service sales.

INTERNET EXERCISE

Check out the site belonging to the Consumers' Association of Canada at www.consumer.ca. From the menu on left, click on *Links* under the Resources section. From the Links page, click on *Consumer Complaints and Information*. Note the spectrum of product and service categories for which they collect complaints. Next, type "sweatshops" into a search engine like www.google.ca and note the numerous sites that are listed.

Based on the Internet blogs and complaint sites it is easy to reach the very incorrect conclusion that consumers everywhere are on the ethical warpath and marketers are running for cover. You should notice however that when you clicked on "sweatshops" there is also a site called the Fair Labor Association. These marketers position and successfully sell their products based on the claim that they explicitly do not use sweatshops in manufacturing their products. Among others, Eddie Bauer, Mountain Equipment Co-op, and about 190 universities who sell clothing are listed there. The point is marketing can be used just as easily to promote the causes of ethics, consumerism, and environmentalism as it can less desirable products like cigarettes.

THE LEGAL ENVIRONMENT

Changes in the political environment often lead to changes in the legal environment and in the way existing laws are enforced. The legal environment sets the basic rules for how a business can operate in society. The legal environment may severely limit some choices, but changes in laws and how they are interpreted also create new opportunities. To illustrate the effects of the legal environment, let's look at some of its effects on Canadian marketing and business.

The Competition Bureau of Canada (www.competitionbureau.gc.ca) administers four federal acts that have important implications for marketers. Exhibit 4-3 describes some of the laws governing business and how they affect marketing.

Trying to encourage competition

Canadian economic and legislative thinking is based on the idea that competition among many small firms helps the economy. Therefore, attempts by business to limit competition are considered contrary to the public interest. Much of the **Competition Act** was initially concerned with limiting monopolistic behaviour that could be damaging to smaller competitors. Subsequently, sections were also added to the act with the specific intent of protecting consumers as well.

In later chapters we will specifically apply the Competition Act to the four Ps. For now, Exhibit 4-4 will give you a brief idea of some offenses that the Competition Bureau outlines in lay terms for businesses—and marketers in particular.

Exhibit 4-3   Marketing and the Law

Law	Governs
Competition Act	These are federal laws governing most of the business conduct in Canada. Both criminal and civil provisions are aimed at preventing anticompetitive practices in the marketplace. The laws are designed to protect both consumers as well as other firms from anticompetitive behaviour.
Consumer Packaging and Labelling Act	This is another criminal statute that governs the packaging, labelling, sale, importation, and advertising of products. The act prohibits misleading advertising but also specifies mandatory labelling that includes product name, net quantity, and dealer identification.
Textile Labelling Act	A criminal statute relating to the labelling sale importation and advertising of consumer textile articles which must bear accurate information about the generic name of each fibre present as well as the dealer's full identification.
Precious Metals Marketing Act	This Criminal Code Act requires the description and quality markings of articles made from precious metals like gold or silver. It prohibits false or misleading advertising related to articles made from precious metals.

Exhibit 4-4   Deceptive Marketing Offences

Advertising Dos and Don'ts	
Dos	**Don'ts**
• Do avoid fine print disclaimers. They often fail to change the general impression conveyed by an advertisement. If you do use them, make sure the overall impression created by the ad and the disclaimer is not misleading.	• Don't confuse "regular price" or "ordinary price" with "manufacturer's suggested list price" or a like term. They are often not the same.
• Do fully and clearly disclose all material information in the advertisement.	• Don't use "regular price" in an advertisement unless the product has been offered in good faith for sale at that price for a substantial period of time, or a substantial volume of the product has been sold at that price within a reasonable period of time.
• Do avoid using terms or phrases in an advertisement that are not meaningful and clear to the ordinary person.	• Don't use the words "sale" or "special" in relation to the price of a product unless a significant price reduction has occurred.
• Do charge the lowest of two or more prices appearing on a product.	• Don't run a "sale" for a long period or repeat it every week.
• Do ensure that you have reasonable quantities of a product advertised at a bargain price.	• Don't increase the price of a product or service to cover the cost of a free product or service.
	• Don't use illustrations that are different from the product being sold.
• Do, when conducting a contest, disclose all material details required by the Act before potential participants are committed to it.	• Don't make a performance claim unless you can prove it, even if you think it is accurate. Testimonials usually do not amount to adequate proof.
	• Don't sell a product above your advertised price.
• Do ensure that your sales force is familiar with these "Dos and Don'ts." Advertisers may be held responsible for representations made by employees.	• Don't unduly delay the distribution of prizes when conducting a contest.
	• Don't forget that no one actually needs to be misled for a court to find that an advertisement is misleading.

Prosecution is serious—you can go to jail

Businesses and *individual managers* are subject to both criminal and civil laws. Penalties for breaking civil laws are limited to blocking or forcing certain actions—along with fines. Where criminal law applies, jail sentences can also be imposed. For example, misleading advertising can draw a fine of $200,000 and one year in jail, but consider this news release from the Competition Bureau on January 9, 2006:

"Competition Bureau Investigation Leads to Record Fine in Domestic Conspiracy—Fine Paper Merchants Sentenced to pay $37.5 Million; Key Personnel to be Removed."[18]

Current high-priority targets for the Competition Bureau are telemarketers who are misrepresenting products and services and those involved in "cyber fraud" and misrepresentation on the Internet. Prison sentences are common for those marketers who are found guilty.

Consumer protection laws are not new

Although antimonopoly laws focus on protecting competition, the wording of the acts in Exhibit 4-3 has, over time, moved toward protecting consumers. Some consumer protections are also built into the English and U.S. common law systems. A seller has to tell the truth (if asked a direct question), meet contracts, and stand behind the firm's product (to some reasonable extent). Beyond this, it is expected that vigorous competition in the marketplace will protect consumers—*so long as they are careful*.

Yet focusing only on competition didn't protect consumers very well in some areas. So the government found it necessary to pass other laws. For example, various laws regulate packaging and labels, credit practices, and environmental issues. Usually, however, the laws focus on specific types of products.

Product safety is controlled

As long as product safety and consumer protection attract the high-profile media coverage that is the current norm, governments will insist on the right to force a product off the market or require expensive recalls because consumers now insist that safety must be considered in product design. And safety must be treated seriously by marketing managers. There is no more tragic example of this than the recent recall of Firestone tires used as original equipment on Ford's Explorer SUV. Hundreds of consumers were killed or seriously injured in accidents.[19]

INTERNET EXERCISE

Go to the *Consumer Reports* Web site (www.consumerreports.org); from the *Cars* page, select the link for *Recalls*. Then check to see if there has been a recall on a year and model of car or truck that is of interest to you (say, one owned by your family).

Provincial and local laws vary

Besides federal legislation marketers must be aware of provincial and local laws. There are provincial and city laws regulating minimum prices and the setting of prices, regulations for starting up a business (licenses, examinations, and even tax payments), and in some communities, regulations prohibiting certain activities—such as selling on Sundays or during evenings.

Often laws are vaguely phrased—to convey intent but not specific detail. As a result, a law may be interpreted and enforced differently over time.

Consumerists and the law say "let the seller beware"

Given current trends in government enforcement and court decisions it appears that the old rule about buyer–seller relations—*let the buyer beware*—has changed to *let the seller beware*. The current shift to proconsumer laws and court decisions suggests that lawmakers are more interested in protecting consumers. This may upset production-oriented managers. But times have changed—and managers must adapt to this new political and legal environment.[20] Yes, sometimes that's difficult—but then again look at how Volvo and BMW Xdrive have positioned their cars to compete on the basis of providing extra driver safety. For some managers changing trends are a threat. For a good marketing manager those threats can often be turned into an opportunity.

THE CULTURAL AND SOCIAL ENVIRONMENT

The **cultural and social environment** affects how and why people live and behave as they do— which affects customer buying behaviour and eventually the economic, political, and legal environment. As a consequence, the importance of culture and social class cannot be overstated when considering their impact on the marketing environment. Many variables make up the cultural and social environment. Some examples are the languages people speak, the type of education they have, their religious beliefs, what type of food they eat, the style of clothing and housing they have, and how they view work, marriage, and family. Because the cultural and social environment has such broad effects, most people don't stop to think about it, or how it may be changing, or how it may differ for other people.

A marketing manager can't afford to take the cultural and social environment for granted. Although changes tend to come slowly, they can have far-reaching effects. A marketing manager who sees the changes early may be able to identify big opportunities. Further, within any broad society, different subgroups of people may be affected by the cultural and social environment in different ways. In most countries, the trend toward multiculturalism is making such differences even more important to marketers. Consider for example the regional concentrations of different ethnic groups in our provinces—from French Canadians in Quebec to Chinese and South Asians in British Columbia. They require special attention when segmenting markets. In fact, dealing with these differences is often one of the greatest challenges managers face when planning strategies, especially for international markets.

Since we will discuss details of how the cultural and social environment relates to buying behaviour in Chapters 5 through 7, here we will just use an example to illustrate its impact on marketing strategy planning.

Changing women's roles

The shifting roles of women in society illustrate the importance of the cultural and social environment on marketing strategy planning. Fifty years ago, most people felt that a woman's role was in the home—first and foremost as a wife and mother. Women had less opportunity for higher education and were completely shut out of many of the most interesting jobs. Obviously, there have been big changes in that stereotyped thinking. With better job opportunities, more women are delaying marriage, and once married they are likely to stay in the workforce and have fewer children. Current statistics show 81 percent of Canadian women aged 25–54

Realizing that more and more consumers are interested in the benefits of a healthy diet, Kellogg uses humour to remind consumers that its Nutri-Grain bar is a healthy (and not so fattening) choice for breakfast. Similarly, Orville Redenbacher's Smart Pop reminds snackers that "now you can eat all you want" because its new flavour is 94 percent fat free.

HYBRID CARS PLUG INTO A PITCH FOR CONVENIENCE AND POWER

For 100 years, gasoline-powered vehicles have been the king of the road. And unlike in some cultures, people in North America drive everywhere they go. Yet this has created problems. The high cost of gasoline, its environmental impact, and reliance on oil from the politically volatile Middle East long ago led to federal laws that required automakers to improve gas mileage. In response, during the 1980s and 90s automakers redesigned vehicles to improve mileage. Even so, progress was slow. Many consumers preferred big gas-guzzler SUVs that were a better match for their suburban lifestyles. A decade ago, to help curb smog in cities like Los Angeles, desperate California lawmakers even told automakers that by 2003, 10 percent of the autos and trucks they sell must produce zero emissions. To nudge toward that target, a few manufacturers offered electric vehicles. Yet battery-powered cars, like GM's EV1, were very costly, had a drive-range less than 100 miles, and were generally underpowered. A few wealthy celebrities drove them for publicity or to make an environmental "statement." But for most consumers, electric cars were too expensive and the need to plug them into an electric outlet was a real obstacle.

Now sales of hybrid vehicles (which combine power from gasoline and electric motors) are beginning to grow. Competition among producers is encouraging innovations based on this new technology. Costs are lower, mileage is higher, and power is better. For example, both Toyota and Honda enjoyed a dramatic jump in sales when they introduced their new Prius and Civic hybrids. This jump occurred in spite of a weak economy—when many consumers postpone big purchases. Initial sales might have been even higher if it were not for a problem that was revealed by Toyota's marketing research. Even after thousands of hybrids were on the road, about half of all consumers wrongly believed that you still have to plug in a hybrid (or said that they just didn't know). In light of this, Toyota worked with its ad agency to develop promotions to constantly remind consumers that "you never have to plug it in." Yet many consumers are still not very motivated to pay extra to buy a "green" vehicle. This may explain why Ford's promotion focuses on the increased power of its new hybrid SUVs and trucks rather than on an environmental appeal.[21]

are now in the paid workforce. Not everything has changed, though. The median income for women still lags behind that of men.

Still, the flood of women into the job market boosted economic growth and changed society in many other ways. Many in-home jobs that used to be done primarily by women—ranging from family shopping to preparing meals to doing volunteer work—still need to be done by someone. Husbands and children now do some of these jobs, a situation that has changed the target market for many products. Or a working woman may face a crushing "poverty of time" and look for help elsewhere, creating opportunities for producers of frozen meals, child care centres, dry cleaners, financial services, and the like.

Although there is still a big wage gap between men and women, the income working women generate gives them new independence and purchasing power. For example, women now purchase about half of all cars. Not long ago, many car dealers insulted a woman shopper by ignoring her or suggesting that she come back with her husband. Now car companies have realized that women are important customers. It's interesting that Japanese car dealers, especially Mazda and Toyota, were the first to really pay attention to women customers. In Japan, fewer women have jobs or buy cars—the Japanese society is still very much male-oriented. Perhaps it was the extreme contrast with Japanese society that prompted these firms to pay more attention to women buyers in their overseas markets.[22]

Women's changing role has created opportunities for marketing but also complications. A marketing mix targeted at women, for example, may require a real balancing act. Advertising showing a woman at the office may attract some customers but alienate housewives who feel that their job doesn't command as much status as it should. Conversely, an ad that shows a woman doing housework might be criticized for encouraging stereotypes.

Changes come slowly

Most changes in basic cultural values and social attitudes come slowly. An individual firm can't hope to encourage big changes in the short run. Instead, it should identify current attitudes and work within these constraints—as it seeks new and better opportunities.[23]

USING SCREENING CRITERIA TO NARROW DOWN TO STRATEGIES

A progressive firm constantly looks for new opportunities. Once the opportunities are identified, the firm must screen and evaluate them. Usually, a firm can't pursue all available opportunities, so it must try to match its opportunities to its resources and objectives. First, management must quickly screen out obvious mismatches so other opportunities can be analyzed more carefully. Let's look at some approaches for screening and evaluating opportunities.

Developing and applying screening criteria

After you analyze the firm's resources (for strengths and weaknesses), the environmental trends the firm faces, and the objectives of top management, you merge them all into a set of product-market screening criteria. These criteria should include both quantitative and qualitative components. The quantitative components summarize the firm's objectives: sales, profit, and return on investment (ROI) targets. The qualitative components summarize what kinds of businesses the firm wants to be in, what businesses it wants to exclude, what weaknesses it should avoid, and what resources (strengths) and trends it should build on.[24]

Developing screening criteria is difficult but worth the effort. They summarize in one place what the firm wants to accomplish—in quantitative terms—as well as roughly how and where it wants to accomplish it. When a manager can explain the specific criteria that are relevant to selecting (or screening out) an opportunity, others can understand the manager's logic. Thus, marketing decisions are not just made or accepted based on intuition and gut feel.

The criteria should be realistic—that is, they should be achievable. Opportunities that pass the screen should be able to be turned into strategies that the firm can implement with the resources it has.

Exhibit 4-5 illustrates some product-market screening criteria for a small retail and wholesale distributor. These criteria help the firm's managers eliminate unsuitable opportunities and find attractive ones to turn into strategies and plans.

Whole plans should be evaluated

You need to forecast the probable results of implementing a marketing strategy to apply the quantitative part of the screening criteria because only implemented plans generate sales, profits, and return on investment. For a rough screening, you only need to estimate the likely results of implementing each opportunity over a logical planning period. If a product's life is likely to be three years, for example, a good strategy may not produce profitable results for 6 to 12 months. But evaluated over the projected three-year life, the product may look like a winner. When evaluating the potential of possible opportunities (product-market strategies), it is important to evaluate similar things—that is, *whole* plans.

Opportunities that pass the screening criteria should be evaluated in more detail before being accepted as *the* product-market strategic plans for implementation. Usually, a firm has more opportunities than resources and has to choose among them—to match its opportunities to its resources and objectives. The following approaches help firms select among possible plans.

Exhibit 4-5 An Example of Product-Market Screening Criteria for a Small Retail and Wholesale Distributor ($10 million annual sales)

1. **Quantitative criteria**
   a. Increase sales by $1,500,000 per year for the next five years.
   b. Earn ROI of at least 25 percent before taxes on new ventures.
   c. Break even within one year on new ventures.
   d. Opportunity must be large enough to justify interest (to help meet objectives) but small enough so company can handle with the resources available.
   e. Several opportunities should be pursued to reach the objectives—to spread the risks.

2. **Qualitative criteria**
   a. Nature of business preferred.
      (1) Should take advantage of our Internet order system and Web site promotion.
      (2) New goods and services for present customers to strengthen relationships and revenue.
      (3) "Quality" products that do not cannibalize sales of current products.
      (4) Competition should be weak and opportunity should be hard to copy for several years.
      (5) There should be strongly felt (even unsatisfied) needs—to reduce promotion costs and permit "high" prices.
   b. Constraints.
      (1) Nature of businesses to exclude.
         (a) Manufacturing.
         (b) Any requiring large fixed capital investments.
         (c) Any requiring many support people who must be "good" all the time and would require much supervision.
      (2) Geographic.
         (a) Canada, United States, and Mexico only.
      (3) General.
         (a) Make use of current strengths.
         (b) Attractiveness of market should be reinforced by more than one of the following basic trends: technological, demographic, social, economic, political.
         (c) Market should not be bucking any basic trends.

Total profit approach can help evaluate possible plans

In the total profit approach, management forecasts potential sales and costs during the life of the plan to estimate likely profitability.

Managers may evaluate the prospects for each plan over a five-year planning period, using monthly and/or annual sales and cost estimates. This is shown graphically in Exhibit 4-6.

Note that managers can evaluate different marketing plans at the same time. Exhibit 4-6 compares a much improved product and product concept (Product A) with a "me-too" product (Product B) for the same target market. In the short run, the me-too product will make a profit sooner and might look like the better choice—if managers consider only one year's results. The improved product, on the other hand, will take a good deal of pioneering—but over its five-year life will be much more profitable.

Return-on-investment (ROI) approach can help evaluate possible plans too

Besides evaluating the profit potential of possible plans, firms may also calculate the return on investment of resources needed to implement plans. ROI analyses can be useful for selecting among possible plans because equally profitable plans may require vastly different resources and offer different rates of return on investment. One plan may require a heavy investment in advertising and channel development,

Exhibit 4-6
Expected Sales and Cost Curves of Two Strategies over Five-Year Planning Periods

for example, while another relies primarily on lower price. Some firms are very concerned with ROI, especially those that borrow money for working capital. There is little point in borrowing to implement strategies that won't return enough to meet the cost of borrowing.

PLANNING GRIDS HELP EVALUATE A PORTFOLIO OF OPPORTUNITIES

When a firm has many possibilities to evaluate, it usually has to compare quite different ones. This problem is easier to handle with graphical approaches—such as the nine-box strategic planning grid developed by General Electric and used by many other companies. Such grids can help evaluate a firm's whole portfolio of strategic plans or businesses.

General Electric looks for green positions

General Electric's strategic planning grid—see Exhibit 4-7—forces company managers to make three-part judgments (high, medium, and low) about the business strengths and industry attractiveness of all proposed or existing product-market plans. As you can see from Exhibit 4-7, this approach helps a manager organize information about the company's marketing environments (discussed earlier in this chapter) along with information about its strategy and translate it into relevant screening criteria.

The industry attractiveness dimension helps managers answer the question: Does this product-market plan look like a good idea? To answer that question, managers have to judge such factors (screening criteria) as the size of the market and its growth rate, the nature of competition, the plan's potential environmental or social impact, and how laws might affect it. Note that an opportunity may be attractive for *some* company—but not well suited to the strengths (and weaknesses) of a particular firm. That is why the GE grid also considers the business strengths dimension.

The business strengths dimension focuses on the ability of the company to pursue a product-market plan effectively. To make judgments along this dimension, a manager evaluates whether the firm has people with the right talents and skills to implement the plan, whether the plan is consistent with the firm's image and profit objectives, and whether the firm could establish a profitable market share given its technical capability, costs, and size. Here again, these factors suggest screening criteria specific to this firm and market situation.

GE feels opportunities that fall into the green boxes in the upper left-hand corner of the grid are its best growth opportunities. Managers give these opportunities

Exhibit 4-7
General Electric's Strategic Planning Grid

high marks on both industry attractiveness and business strengths. The red boxes in the lower right-hand corner of the grid, on the other hand, suggest a no-growth policy. Existing red businesses may continue to generate earnings, but they no longer deserve much investment. Yellow businesses are borderline cases—they can go either way. GE may continue to support an existing yellow business but will probably reject a proposal for a new one. It simply wouldn't look good enough on the relevant screening criteria.

GE's "stoplight" evaluation method is a subjective, multiple-factor approach. It avoids the traps and possible errors of trying to use oversimplified, single-number criteria—like ROI or market share. Instead, top managers review detailed written summaries of many different screening criteria that help them make summary judgments. Then they can make a collective judgment. This approach helps everyone understand why the company supports some new opportunities and not others.[25]

General Electric considers factors that reflect its objectives. Another firm might modify the evaluation to emphasize other screening criteria—depending on its objectives and the type of product-market plans it is considering.

MULTIPRODUCT FIRMS HAVE A DIFFICULT STRATEGY PLANNING JOB

Multiproduct firms, like General Electric, obviously have a more difficult strategic planning job than firms with only a few products or product lines aimed at the same target markets. Multiproduct firms have to develop strategic plans for very different businesses. And they have to balance plans and resources so the whole company reaches its objectives. This means they must approve plans that make sense for the whole company—even if it means getting needed resources by milking some businesses and eliminating others.

Details on how to manage a complicated multiproduct firm are beyond our scope. But you should be aware that the principles in this text are applicable—they just have to be extended. For example, some multiproduct firms form strategic business units (SBUs), and some use portfolio management.

  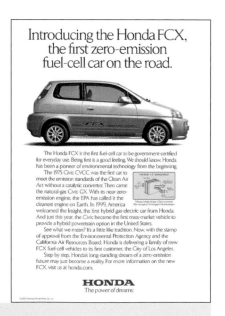

Large multiproduct firms, like Honda, evaluate and pursue a varied portfolio of strategic opportunities all around the world.

Strategic business units may help

A **strategic business unit (SBU)** is an organizational unit (within a larger company) that focuses on some product-markets and is treated as a separate profit centre. By forming SBUs, a company formally acknowledges its very different activities. One SBU of Sara Lee, for example, produces baked goods for consumers and restaurants; another produces and markets Hanes brand T-shirts and underwear.

Some SBUs grow rapidly and require a great deal of attention and resources. Others produce only average profits and should be *milked*—that is, allowed to generate cash for the businesses with more potential. Product lines with poor market position, low profits, and poor growth prospects should be dropped or sold.

Some firms use portfolio management

Some top managements handle strategic planning for a multiproduct firm with an approach called **portfolio management**—which treats alternative products, divisions, or strategic business units as though they were stock investments, to be bought and sold using financial criteria. Such managers make trade-offs among very different opportunities. They treat the various alternatives as investments that should be supported, milked, or sold off—depending on profitability and return on investment. In effect, they evaluate each alternative just like a stock market trader evaluates a stock.[26]

This approach makes some sense if alternatives are really quite different. Top managers feel they can't become very familiar with the prospects for all of their alternatives. So they fall back on the easy-to-compare quantitative criteria. And because the short run is much clearer than the long run, they place heavy emphasis on *current* profitability and return on investment. This puts great pressure on the operating managers to deliver *in the short run*—perhaps even neglecting the long run.

Neglecting the long run is risky—and this is the main weakness of the portfolio approach. This weakness can be overcome by enhancing the portfolio management approach with market-oriented strategic plans. They make it possible for managers to more accurately evaluate the alternatives' short-run and long-run prospects.

EVALUATING OPPORTUNITIES IN INTERNATIONAL MARKETS

Evaluate the risks

The approaches we've discussed so far apply to international markets just as they do to domestic ones. But in international markets it is often harder to fully understand the marketing environment variables. This may make it harder to see the risks

Some products, like industrial motors made by Baldor, are used the same way all over the world. Other products are much more sensitive to cultural differences.

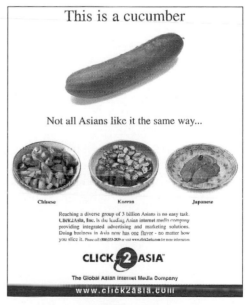

Exhibit 4-8
Continuum of
Environmental Sensitivity

Insensitive		Sensitive
Industrial products	Basic commodity-type consumer products	Consumer products that are linked to cultural variables

involved in particular opportunities. Some countries are politically unstable; their governments and constitutions come and go. An investment safe under one government might become a takeover target under another.

To reduce the risk of missing some basic variable that may help screen out a risky opportunity, marketing managers sometimes need a detailed analysis of the market environment they are considering entering. Such an analysis can reveal facts about an unfamiliar market that a manager in a distant country might otherwise overlook. Further, a local citizen who knows the marketing environment may be able to identify an "obvious" problem ignored even in a careful analysis. Thus, it is very useful for the analysis to include inputs from locals—perhaps cooperative middlemen.[27]

Risks vary with environmental sensitivity

The farther you go from familiar territory, the greater the risk of making big mistakes. But not all products, or marketing mixes, involve the same risk. Think of the risks as running along a "continuum of environmental sensitivity." See Exhibit 4-8.

Some products are relatively insensitive to the economic and cultural environment they're placed in. These products may be accepted as is—or they may require just a little adaptation to make them suitable for local use. Most industrial products are near the insensitive end of this continuum.

At the other end of the continuum, we find highly sensitive products that may be difficult or impossible to adapt to all international situations. Consumer products closely linked to other social or cultural variables are at this end. For example, some cultures view dieting as unhealthy; that explains why products like Diet Pepsi that are popular in North America have done poorly there. "Faddy" type consumer products are also at this end of the continuum. It's sometimes difficult to understand why such products are well accepted in a home market. This, in turn, makes it even more difficult to predict how they might be received in a different environment.

This continuum helps explain why many of the early successes in international marketing were basic commodities such as gasoline, soap, transportation vehicles, mining equipment, and agricultural machinery. It also helps explain why some consumer products firms have been successful with basically the same promotion and products in different parts of the globe.

Yet some managers don't understand the reason for these successes. They think they can develop a global marketing mix for just about *any* product. They fail to see that firms producing and/or selling products near the sensitive end of the continuum should carefully analyze how their products will be seen and used in new environments—and plan their strategies accordingly.[28]

What if risks are still hard to judge?

If the risks of an international opportunity are hard to judge, it may be wise to look first for opportunities that involve exporting. This gives managers a chance to build experience, know-how, and confidence over time. Then the firm will be in a better position to judge the prospects and risks of taking further steps.

CONCLUSION

Businesses need innovative strategy planning to survive in our increasingly competitive markets. In this chapter, we discussed the variables that shape the environment of marketing strategy planning and how they may affect opportunities. First we looked at how the firm's own resources and objectives may help guide or limit the search for opportunities. Then we went on to look at the need to understand competition and how to do a competitive analysis. Then we shifted our focus to the external market environments. They are important because changes in these environments present new opportunities, as well as problems, that a marketing manager must deal with in marketing strategy planning. We saw in the opening case that movie theatre attendance is suffering as a result of home entertainment systems. Notice how many and how quickly the technological home entertainment substitutes for movie theatres impacted companies like Cineplex and Famous Players. It was also pointed out that movie theatres are looking for creative solutions to their problems. That's why the vignette opens with the line "Marketers have to be fast on their feet."

The economic environment—including chances of recessions or inflation—also affects the choice of strategies. And the marketer must try to anticipate, understand, and deal with these changes—as well as changes in the technology underlying the economic environment.

The marketing manager must also be aware of legal restrictions and be sensitive to changing political climates. The acceptance of consumerism has already forced many changes.

The cultural and social environment affects how people behave and what marketing strategies will be successful.

Developing good marketing strategies within all these environments isn't easy. You can see that marketing management is a challenging job that requires integration of information from many disciplines.

Eventually, managers need procedures for screening and evaluating opportunities. We explained an approach for developing qualitative and quantitative screening criteria—from an analysis of the strengths and weaknesses of the company's resources, the environmental trends it faces, and top management's objectives. We also discussed ways for evaluating and managing quite different opportunities—using the GE strategic planning grid, SBUs, and portfolio management.

Now we can go on in the rest of the book to discuss how to turn opportunities into profitable marketing plans and programs.

KEY TERMS

mission statement, 90

competitive environment, 92

competitor analysis, 94

competitive rivals, 94

competitive barriers, 95

economic and technological environment, 96

nationalism, 100

North American Free Trade Agreement (NAFTA), 100

consumerism, 101

competition act, 102

cultural and social environment, 105

strategic business unit (SBU), 111

portfolio management, 111

QUESTIONS AND PROBLEMS

1. Do you think it makes sense for a firm to base its mission statement on the type of product it produces? For example, would it be good for a division that produces electric motors to have as its mission: "We want to make the best (from our customers' point of view) electric motors available anywhere in the world"?

2. Explain how a firm's objectives may affect its search for opportunities.

3. Specifically, how would various company objectives affect the development of a marketing mix for a new type of Internet browser software? If this company were just being formed by a former programmer with limited financial resources, list the objectives the programmer might have. Then discuss how they would affect the development of the programmer's marketing strategy.

4. Explain how a firm's resources may limit its search for opportunities. Cite a specific example for a specific resource.

5. Discuss how a company's financial strength may have a bearing on the kinds of products it produces. Will it have an impact on the other three Ps as well? If so, how? Use an example in your answer.

6. In your own words, explain how a marketing manager might use a competitor analysis to avoid situations that involve head-on competition.

7. The owner of a small hardware store—the only one in a medium-sized town in the mountains—has just learned that a large home improvement chain plans to open a new store nearby. How difficult will it be for the owner to plan for this new competitive threat? Explain your answer.

8. Discuss the probable impact on your hometown if a major breakthrough in air transportation allowed foreign producers to ship into any Canadian market for about the same transportation cost that domestic producers incur.

9. Will the elimination of trade barriers between countries in Europe eliminate the need to consider submarkets of European consumers? Why or why not?

10. Which way does the Canadian political and legal environment seem to be moving (with respect to consumer-related affairs)?

11. Why is it necessary to have so many laws regulating business? Why doesn't government just pass one set of laws to take care of business problems?

12. What and who is the Canadian government attempting to protect in its effort to preserve and regulate competition?

13. Explain the components of product-market screening criteria that can be used to evaluate opportunities.

14. Explain the differences between the total profit approach and the return-on-investment approach to evaluating alternative plans.

15. How could Bombardier use General Electric's Planning Grid to evaluate the opportunities it faces in selling its transit systems to various countries?

16. Now that Internet blogging allows consumers to post their own Web site complaints, how will that affect the sales of Ford in Canada?

COMPUTER-AIDED PROBLEM

4. Competitor Analysis

RESOURCE REMINDER

Mediquip Inc., produces medical equipment and uses its own sales force to sell the equipment to hospitals. Recently, several hospitals have asked Mediquip to develop a laser-beam "scalpel" for eye surgery. Mediquip has the needed resources, and 200 hospitals will probably buy the equipment. But Mediquip managers have heard that Laser Technologies—another quality producer—is thinking of competing for the same business. Mediquip has other good opportunities it could pursue—so it wants to see if it would have a competitive advantage over Laser Tech.

Mediquip and Laser Tech are similar in many ways, but there are important differences. Laser Technologies already produces key parts that are needed for the new laser product—so its production costs would be lower. It would cost Mediquip more to design the product—and getting parts from outside suppliers would result in higher production costs.

On the other hand, Mediquip has marketing strengths. It already has a good reputation with hospitals—and its sales force calls on only hospitals. Mediquip thinks that each of its current sales reps could spend some time selling the new product and that it could adjust sales territories so only four more sales reps would be needed for

good coverage in the market. In contrast, Laser Tech's sales reps call on only industrial customers, so it would have to add 14 reps to cover the hospitals.

Hospitals have budget pressures—so the supplier with the lowest price is likely to get a larger share of the business. But Mediquip knows that either supplier's price will be set high enough to cover the added costs of designing, producing, and selling the new product—and leave something for profit.

Mediquip gathers information about its own likely costs and can estimate Laser Tech's costs from industry studies and Laser Tech's annual report. Mediquip has set up a spreadsheet to evaluate the proposed new product.

a. The initial spreadsheet results are based on the assumption that Mediquip and Laser Tech will split the business 50/50. If Mediquip can win at least 50 percent of the market, does Mediquip have a competitive advantage over Laser Tech? Explain.

b. Because of economies of scale, both suppliers' average cost per machine will vary depending on the quantity sold. If Mediquip had only 45 percent of the market and Laser Tech 55 percent, how would their costs (average total cost per machine) compare? What if Mediquip had 55 percent of the market and Laser Tech only 45 percent? What conclusion do you draw from these analyses?

c. It is possible that Laser Tech may not enter the market. If Mediquip has 100 percent of the market, and quantity purchases from its suppliers will reduce the cost of producing one unit to $6,500, what price would cover all its costs and contribute $1,125 to profit for every machine sold? What does this suggest about the desirability of finding your own unsatisfied target markets? Explain.

If you want to read the cases and view the video cases that accompany this chapter, visit the *Basic Marketing* Online Learning Centre at: **www.mcgrawhill.ca/olc/perreault**. Along with these cases and video cases, the OLC also has the software and user guide for this chapter's Computer-Aided Problem, as well as exercises, quizzes, articles, links, and other *interactive* content that will help you with your studies.

**WHEN YOU FINISH
THIS CHAPTER,
YOU SHOULD**

1. Understand how
   population growth is
   shifting in different
   areas and for
   different age groups.

2. Know how consumer
   spending is related to
   family life cycle and
   other demographic
   dimensions.

3. Know why ethnic
   markets are
   important—and why
   increasingly they are
   the focus of
   multicultural
   marketing strategies.

Demographics, Consumers, and Markets

Starting in the 1970s and 80s the financial services sector in Canada underwent a transition that changed it forever. Firms began to realize that many people wanted to direct their own investments—without a lot of advice and fees from bankers or stockbrokers. Enter the "no frills" financial products and services provided at discounted prices. Banks offered direct computer trading and discount brokerage firms emerged to serve a new demographic group of consumers who were computer literate and well enough versed in investments to carry out online trades. BMO Investorline, RBC Action Direct, and Scotia Discount Brokerage to name just a few, began to target the markets traditionally dominated by the investment houses.

Of course the innovative and targeted marketing strategies didn't stop there. Just as the large group of middle-aged baby boomers were beginning to worry about retirement, the financial services industry again evolved to give them a lot of choices in a big "supermarket" of mutual funds. This time life insurance companies like Great-West Life and Sun Life made the transition from their traditional products into the world of selling mutual funds, segregated funds, RRSPs, and other retirement targeted products.

The financial services industry has become even more fragmented with the evolution of low-cost Web site-based trading companies like E*Trade Canada and "no branch" computer-based bankers like ING Direct. These firms have also discovered that important demographic niche of younger computer literate customers who are prepared to sacrifice the personal human interaction component in return for convenience and attractive term-deposit rates.

Today, the financial services industry no longer see investors in the retail banking sector as just one big market. Rather, they develop different marketing mixes to meet different needs. Consider, for example, the senior citizen group. Canadians over 65 control about 70 percent of the country's investment assets, but Internet use among this group is low compared to younger people. To better meet the needs of this group—and others who prefer personal contact—companies supplemented their online services by adding more call-in advisors as well as opening new branch investment centres in high-growth areas. They also introduced advisors to help with ancillary services like estate planning for their older more affluent customers who still valued the "personal touch."

Affluent investors, with the most wealth to manage, often have special needs when it comes to expert advice, objective research, and a personal relationship. To provide this group with the choices they want, some of Canada's largest investment companies introduced "wealth management teams" to provide these high-income clients with the attention they demand while allowing them to stay involved and in control.

Similarly, a number of Canada's major banks developed distinct strategies to reach fast-growing ethnic markets. It's no accident that branch offices in cities like Vancouver and Toronto have investment consultants who speak Mandarin and Cantonese. Many older Chinese like to converse with an advisor in their native language—and these customers are a key target market because they account for a substantial volume of wealth. While the Chinese segment is proportionately a small percentage of the total population, the median income of their households is higher than that of many Canadian households and they are more likely to have a university degree and own their own businesses.

The finance industry has also developed strategies to sharpen its focus on the growing number of women who manage their own investments. Importantly, the needs and interests of these women are sometimes different. Coast Capital Savings introduced a "No Haggle" policy over the rates they offered on deposit accounts. The reason? Their market research showed that the female demographic did not enjoy negotiating deposit rates on their bank accounts. About 60–65 percent of females found it stressful. Was it a dumb strategy to give women a higher rate on deposits than they had to? Not at all. Many women are becoming

small-business owners and also comprise a significant percentage of single-family households. Those demographic groups will require loans. And guess who will be first in line to provide them because they already hold the deposits of these women?

One thing is certain. The finance industry will never be the same. Countless new competitors have fragmented the old world that was once dominated by the major banks with their decidedly nonmarketing orientation. These newcomers took market share by focusing on demographic groups and marketing to their needs. Today, some of the biggest competitors in the residential mortgage market come from the credit union movement such as the BC Central Credit Union in British Columbia. The banks however have learned quickly and now realize that they have many different kinds of customers that can be targeted and served effectively with the help of demographics. TD Canada Trust has recently focused on a market niche of small-business owners who want later banking hours so branches now stay open until 8:00 p.m. in many locations.

TARGET MARKETERS FOCUS ON THE CUSTOMER

Target marketers believe that the *customer* should be the focus of all business and marketing activity. These marketers hope to develop unique marketing strategies by finding unsatisfied customers and offering them superior value with more attractive marketing mixes. They want to work in less-competitive markets with more inelastic demand curves. Finding these attractive opportunities takes real knowledge of potential customers and what they want. This means finding those market dimensions that make a difference—in terms of population, income, needs, attitudes, and buying behaviour.

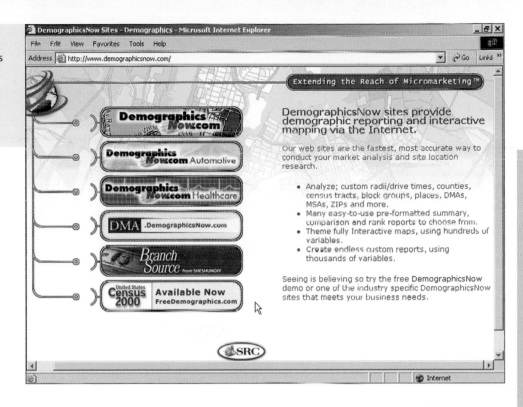

Marketers need to answer three important questions about any potential market:

1. What are its relevant segmenting dimensions?
2. How big is it?
3. Where is it?

The first question is basic. Management judgment—perhaps aided by analysis of existing data and new findings from marketing research—is needed to pick the right dimensions.

To help build your judgment regarding buying behaviour, this chapter and the next two will discuss what we know about various kinds of customers and their buying behaviour. Keep in mind that we aren't trying to make generalizations about average customers or how the mass market behaves—but rather how *some* people in *some* markets behave. You should expect to find differences.

In this chapter we focus on demographic dimensions. Demographic dimensions provide marketing managers with critical information about the size, location, and characteristics of target markets. Marketing managers must also be alert to demographic trends. They often provide an early warning about new opportunities—or the need to adjust existing strategies.

There are some very good reasons why marketers are concerned with demographics. First, demographics can tell you if there are enough of the "right kind of consumers" in a geographic area or a particular kind of segment. When some of Canada's major banks opened facilities in Vancouver, they placed Mandarin· and Cantonese-speaking tellers in certain branches because they served predominantly Chinese neighbourhoods. Without the demographic data on ethnicity, they would have made a fatal error by trying to use English only tellers. Second, demographic data can be correlated with psychographic and behavioural variables that help to define our segments. In the opening vignette, Coast Capital Savings had good demographic data about the number of females and their income levels. That information was correlated with their market research indicating women didn't like to bargain over term deposit rates at their bank. The demographic data tied to the psychographic and behavioural market research allowed Coast Capital to launch their "no haggle" advertising campaign specifically targeted at women.

Get the facts straight—for good marketing decisions

Everybody "knows" that there is a vast and largely untapped market in China and that many people in Somalia live in desperate poverty. It's also clear that demographic dimensions vary within countries: Many Albertans are politically conservative and the population in BC's Okanagan region is rapidly driven in part by the immigration of retiring baby boomers. Generalities like these may be partly true—but "partly true" isn't good enough when it comes to making marketing strategy decisions.

Fortunately, much useful information is available on the demographic dimensions of consumer markets around the world. Most of it is free because it has been collected by government agencies. With valid data available, managers have no excuse for basing their decisions on guesses. Look at the data in the next few chapters in terms of selecting relevant market dimensions—and estimating the potential in different market segments. Also, check your own assumptions against these data. Now is a good time to get your facts straight!

PEOPLE WITH MONEY MAKE MARKETS

Markets consist of people with money to spend. So it makes sense to start with a broad view of how population, income, and other key demographic dimensions vary for different countries around the world. This will help you to see why so many firms pursue opportunities in international markets. And our examples will illustrate why companies can't depend on half-truths in increasingly competitive international markets.

Marketers search for growing markets

Some marketing managers never consider opportunities outside of their own country. That may make sense in some cases, but it may also lead to missed opportunities. For example, crowded cities in North America may seem to offer great potential, but the entire population makes up less than 5 percent of the total world population, which is now over 6 billion.

Although a country's current population is important, it provides only a snapshot of the market. The population trend is also important.

Between 1950 and 2000, world population doubled. Early in that period, global population growth was over 2 percent per year. Now it's down to about 1.2 percent. Long-term world population growth is expected to come from countries in South Asia and the Far East. The populations of India and China, which are each over one billion, are expected to become even larger. Perhaps even more importantly for Canada, they are going to quickly progress from Third World economies to developed economic status and in all likelihood will shift the balance of economic power away from the Western economies. That means a massive demand for Canada's natural resources like minerals and fossil fuels can be expected to develop as well. You can see why so many firms from all over the world want to reach consumers in these countries now that trade barriers are relaxing. Although many of the countries in South America and Africa have much smaller populations, they too are growing at a rapid rate.[1]

Over the long term population growth is expected in most countries. But how rapidly? And will output and income increase faster than population? These are important questions for marketers. The answers affect how quickly a country moves to higher stages of development and becomes a new market for different kinds of products.

Population, income, and other demographic dimensions help to answer these questions. And population growth varies dramatically from country to country. In

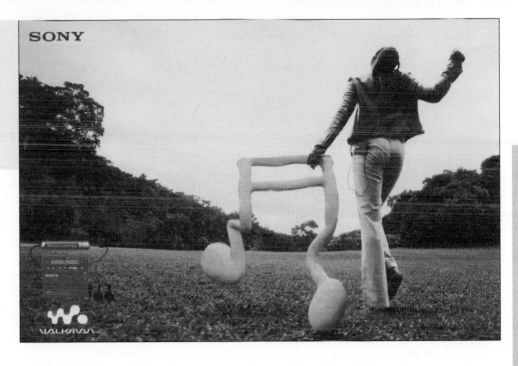

Marketers who are interested in the rapidly growing teen market often find that teens in different parts of the world have many common interests, values, and needs. This Sony Walkman ad was developed by its ad agency in Malaysia.

general, less-developed countries experience the fastest rate of growth. The populations of Pakistan, Nicaragua, Nigeria, and Saudi Arabia are expected to nearly double by 2025. The population of the United States will grow by only about 22 percent in that time period. Population growth is even slower in Canada, Japan, and the European countries.[2]

Population is becoming more concentrated

The population in some countries is spread over a very large area. Population density is important to marketers. If the population is very spread out, as it is in many of the African countries, it is difficult and expensive for marketers to adjust time and place discrepancies between producers and consumers. This is especially a problem in countries without efficient highway and rail systems. Similarly, a widely spread population may make promotion more difficult, especially if there are language differences or communication systems are poor. Of course, even in countries with low population density, major cities may be packed with people.

The extent to which a country's population is clustered around urban areas varies a lot. In the United Kingdom, Argentina, Australia, Israel, and Singapore, for example, more than 85 percent of people live in urban areas. By contrast, in Ethiopia, Nepal, and Uganda less than 17 percent of the people live in major urban areas.

People everywhere are moving off the farm and into industrial and urban areas. Shifts in population—combined with already dense populations—have led to extreme crowding in some parts of the world. And the crowding is likely to get worse.

The worldwide trend toward urbanization has prompted increased interest in international markets. For many firms, the concentration of people in major cities simplifies Place and Promotion strategy decisions, especially for major cities in the wealthiest nations. Affluent, big-city consumers often have similar lifestyles and needs. Thus, many of the products successful in Toronto, New York, or Paris are likely to be successful in Caracas and Tokyo. The spread of the Internet, satellite TV, and other communication technologies will accelerate this trend.

However, keep in mind that many of the world's consumers—whether crowded in cities or widely spread in rural areas—live in deplorable conditions. These people have little hope of escaping the crush of poverty. They certainly have needs—but they don't have the income to do anything about the needs.

For firms interested in pursuing international markets, the growing concentration of population and income in major cities often simplifies Place and Promotion strategy decisions.

There's no market when there's no income

Profitable markets require income—as well as people. The amount of money people can spend affects the products they are likely to buy. When considering international markets, income is often one of the most important demographic dimensions.

There are a variety of different measures of national income. One widely used measure is **gross domestic product (GDP)**—the total market value of all goods and services provided in a country's economy in a year by both residents and nonresidents of that country. *Gross national income (GNI)* is a measure that is similar to GDP, but GNI does not include income earned by foreigners who own resources in that nation. By contrast, GDP does include foreign income. (Note: Until recently, GNI was called gross national product or GNP, so many government documents still include that label.)

When you compare countries with different patterns of international investment, the income measure you use can make a difference. For example, Ford has a factory in Thailand. The GDP measure for Thailand would include the profits from that factory because they were earned in that country. However, Ford is not a Thai firm and most of its profit will ultimately flow out of Thailand. Thus, the Thai GNI would not include those profits. You should see that using GDP income measures can give the impression that people in less-developed countries have more income than they really do. In addition, in a country with a large population the income of the whole nation must be spread over more people. So GNI *per capita* (per person) is a useful figure because it gives some idea of the income level of people in the country. Finally, marketers also like to look at **Purchasing Power Parity, (PPP)** because it provides an approximation of the purchasing power that consumers hold. It is most helpful for comparing consumer standards of living among different economies and allows marketers to roughly compare what it would cost a consumer in Canada for example, to buy a standard basket of goods with a consumer in the U.S. buying the same basket.

Developed economies have most of the income

The more developed industrial nations account for the biggest share of the world's GDP. In these countries the GNI per capita is also quite high. This explains why so much trade takes place between these countries—and why many firms see them as the more important markets. In general, markets like these offer the best potential for products that are targeted at consumers with higher income levels.

China has the largest population in the world, and its culture and economy are undergoing rapid changes. For example, consumers in China buy more cell phones than in any other country. Their Internet use is also growing; it is predicted that by 2007, Chinese will be the number one language on the Web. Managers who ignore such changes may miss out on attractive opportunities.

Many managers, however, see great potential—and less competition—where GNI per capita is low. For example, Mars is making a big push to promote its candy in the countries of Eastern Europe. As with many other firms, it hopes to establish a relationship with consumers now, and then turn strong brand loyalty into profitable growth as consumer incomes increase.

A business and a human opportunity

The large number of countries with low GNI per capita is a stark reminder that much of the world's population lives in extreme poverty. You see some sign of this even among some countries with large overall GDP. For example, GNI per capita in China is only about $890 per year (in U.S. dollars) and in India it is about half that at $460.

Many countries are in the early stages of economic development. Most of their people work on farms and live barely within the money economy. At the extreme, in Ethiopia GNI per capita per year is only about $100. To put this in perspective, 60 percent of the world's population—in 61 countries—receives only about 6 percent of the world's total income, or about $2 a day.

These people, however, have needs, and many are eager to improve themselves. But they may not be able to raise their living standards without outside help. This presents a challenge and an opportunity to the developed nations—and to their business firms. Some companies are trying to help the people of less-developed countries. Corporations such as Pillsbury, Monsanto, and Coca-Cola have developed nutritious foods that can be sold cheaply, but still profitably, in poorer countries.[3]

What do Third World consumers really need?

Marketing managers from developed nations sometimes face an ethical dilemma about whether their products help or hurt consumers in less-developed nations. For example, a United Nations report criticized Coke and Pepsi for expanding their soft-drink sales in the Philippines. The study concluded that consumers had shifted to soft drinks from local beverages—such as a mixture of lime juice and coconut water—that provided needed vitamins.

In another much publicized case, producers of infant formula were criticized for giving free samples to hospitals. Nestlé and other big suppliers in this market say that they only gave the free samples to children who were in need—and at the request of hospitals. But critics argued that the practice encouraged new mothers to give up breast feeding. Away from the hospital, mothers would rely on unsanitary water supplies. Such improper use of the formula could lead to malnutrition and other illnesses. So Nestlé and the others pledged to stop giving away free samples. Although that step stopped some misuse, now the formula is not available to many people who really need it. For example, over a million babies have been infected with AIDS from breast feeding. To help fight this staggering epidemic, Nestlé said it was willing to donate formula, but not unless the World Health Organization agreed that it was not a violation of its pledge.

In cases like these, a marketing manager may need to weigh the benefits and risks of trying to serve Third World markets. For example, in the United States, Quicksilver Enterprises sells its 250-pound aluminum and fibreglass "ultralight" airplanes—which look like go-carts with wings—to wealthy hobbyists. However, Quicksilver found a growing market for ultralights in developing nations, where farmers use them for crop dusting. They help farmers increase production of much needed foods. So what's the problem? In the U.S. the government bans ultralights as not being safe enough for crop dusting. Some critics argue that a firm shouldn't sell its products in foreign markets if they are illegal in the U.S. But ultimately, the marketing manager often must decide what to do.[4]

Reading, writing, and marketing problems

The ability of a country's people to read and write has a direct influence on the development of its economy—and on marketing strategy planning. The degree of literacy affects the way information is delivered, which in marketing means promotion. Unfortunately, only about three-fourths of the world's population can read and write. Data on illiteracy rates is inexact because different countries use different measures.

Illiteracy sometimes causes difficulties with product labels and instructions, for which we normally use words. This was one issue in the infant formula conflict. In an even more extreme case, some producers of baby food found that consumers misinterpreted a baby's picture on their packages. Illiterate natives believed that the product was just that—a ground-up baby! Many companies meet this lack of literacy with instructions that use pictures instead of words. Singer used this approach with its sewing machines.

Even in Latin America—which has generally higher literacy rates than Africa or Asia—a large number of people cannot read and write. Marketers have to use symbols, colours, and other nonverbal means of communication if they want to reach the masses.[5]

Much segmenting may be required

Marketers can learn a great deal about possible opportunities in different countries by studying available demographic data and trends. The examples we considered here give you a feel, but much more useful data is available. For example, *The World Factbook* is prepared by the Central Intelligence Agency (CIA) for the use of U.S. government officials, but it is available to everyone. It gives facts and statistics on each country in the world. This book can be accessed at the CIA's Web site (www.odci.gov/cia/publications/factbook). The World Bank publishes *The World Development Indicators*, another excellent source for statistics on individual countries. It is available at the World Bank's Web site (www.worldbank.org/data/wdi). The International Programs Center of the U.S. Census Bureau also publishes an analysis on world population and related topics called *World Population Profile*. You can also access useful statistics for individual countries at the Census Bureau's Web site (www.census.gov/ipc).

INTERNET EXERCISE

Visit the Web site for the CIA (www.odci.gov). Scroll down to *Library and Reference* and click on *The World Factbook*. Compare the profile data for Canada and Australia. How are they similar and how are they different?

After finding some countries or regions of possible interest (and eliminating unattractive ones), much more segmenting may be required. To illustrate how useful demographic dimensions can be in this effort, we will consider specific characteristics of the Canadian market in some detail. For additional data on the Canadian market, you can go to the Statistic Canada Web site (www.statscan.gc.ca). Similar ideas apply to other markets around the world.

POPULATION TRENDS IN THE CANADIAN CONSUMER MARKET

Where does your province stand?

Exhibit 5-1 is a map of Canada showing the relative population for each province and the percentage increase or decrease of that population from 1994 to 2004. Colour codes on the map emphasize the concentration of population in the different geographic regions. Note that the heavy concentration of people in Central Canada (Ontario and Quebec) makes this market larger than the rest of Canada combined.

Population figures for a single year don't show the dynamic aspects of markets however. In 2004, based on our last census, Canada's population was over 31 million (up from 28 million in 1994). By 2014 the population is projected to be approximately 34 million. Note the percentage change in provincial populations in Exhibit 5-1. The fast growth areas are BC, Alberta, and Nunavut. Marketers like fast-growing markets. They want to know where the growth has occurred recently and where it is likely to occur in the future. The first thing a marketing manager would want to know about these demographic trends is what kind of socio-economic factors are driving the population growth in each of these regions. What's your opinion—are the growth drivers all the same for each of these areas? The reasons could be important because they have an impact on the kind of goods and services people want.

Other regions are growing more slowly. Look at Quebec with a 10-year growth of around 5 percent—but it is right next door to Ontario with a growth of 14.6 percent. Still others have a net out-migration. Why do you think people are leaving Newfoundland–Labrador and Saskatchewan?

These different rates of growth are especially important to marketers. Sudden growth in one area may create a demand for many new shopping centres —while retailers in declining areas face tougher competition for a smaller number of customers. In growing areas, demand may increase so rapidly that profits may be good even in poorly planned facilities.

Although Canada is the world's second largest country by area, due to climate conditions, the vast majority of the population lives within a very narrow belt close to the U.S. border. As is the case in many countries, the most populated areas developed near inexpensive water transportation—on ocean harbours (East and West Coasts), or in the Great Lakes region. Obviously, these markets are attractive to many marketers. But this can also mean tough competition, as in the big urban markets.

Marketers anxious to avoid the extremely competitive central Canadian markets are beginning to view other Canadian cities as unique target markets. Note, too, the smaller populations in other regions of Canada, which explains why some national marketers pay less attention to these areas.

The map in Exhibit 5-1 summarizes provincial level data to give the big picture. However, much more detailed population data are available. You can obtain detailed census data—or updated estimates—for very small geographic areas. Just as we mapped population changes at the provincial level, a local marketer can divide a big metropolitan area into many smaller areas to see where the action is. As this decade continues, census data may become outdated—but by then local and provincial government planning groups will be able to provide updates.

YUKON TERRITORY
31
(5.1%)

NORTHWEST TERRITORIES
43
(5.5%)

NUNAVUT
30
(21.4%)

BRITISH COLUMBIA
4,196
(12.4%)

ALBERTA
3,202
(18.6%)

MANITOBA
1,117
(4.2%)

SASKATCHEWAN
995
(-1.4%)

ONTARIO
12,392
(14.6%)

QUEBEC
7,543
(4.9%)

NEWFOUNDLAND
517
(-10%)

PRINCE EDWARD ISLAND
138
(3.3%)

NOVA SCOTIA
939
(1.1%)

NEW BRUNSWICK
751
(0.2%)

Population 2003
◻ 0–100 ◼ 100–1,000 ◼ 1,000–5,000 ◼ 5,000–10,000 ◼ 10,000+

Population will keep growing, but . . .

Despite the large increases, the *rate* of population growth has slowed dramatically—to about 1 percent a year during the last decade. In fact, many marketers who enjoyed rapid and profitable growth in the 1970s and 1980s know that the domestic picnic is over. They now turn to international markets where population—and sales revenues—continue to grow.

In Canada, as in the U.S., most of our future growth is expected to come from immigration. In fact, even now the total North American population would start to decline if immigration stopped. Let's look at some of these trends and what they mean to marketing managers.[6]

Birthrate—boom or bust?

The Canadian **birthrate**—the number of babies born per 1,000 people—fluctuated greatly in the last 50 years. Exhibit 5-2 shows a clear pattern. A post–World War II **baby boom** began as returning soldiers started families, and it lasted about 15 years into the early 1960s. In the 1970s, the situation changed to a "baby bust" as more women stayed in the workforce and couples waited longer to have children. When you see the dip in the birthrate—and think about the declining market for baby products—you can understand why Johnson & Johnson promotes its baby shampoo to adults who want a gentle product. You can also understand why Johnson & Johnson looks for opportunities in Asia and Latin America where the birthrate is higher.

The Canadian birthrate decreased until the 1980s when it temporarily began to stabilize. Since then however, its consistent decline has resumed—until the last few years when it appears to have levelled off at around 10.5 births per thousand population. These shifts are easy to explain. As the baby boom generation entered its child-bearing years, there were more women to have babies. However, as the boomers aged this baby "boomlet" passed and turned to what some have called a

Exhibit 5-2
Changes in Canadian Birth
Rate, 1935–2002

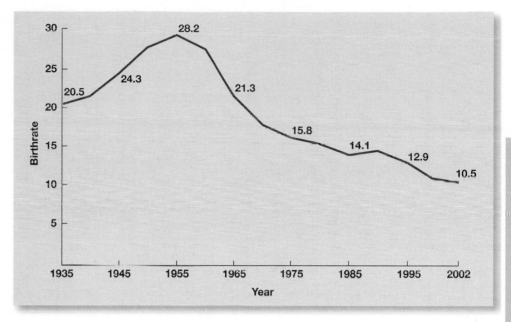

"baby bust." In addition, Canadian couples are having fewer children. There may be more demand for small apartments, in-home entertainment, travel, and smaller food packages.

With fewer children, parents can spend more money on each child. For example, expensive bikes, video game consoles, MP3 players, and designer clothes for children have all sold well in recent years because parents can indulge one or two children more easily than a houseful.

The greying of Canada

Because our population is growing slowly, the average age is rising. In 1970, the average age of the population was 28—but by the year 2001 the average age jumped to about 36.

Stated another way, the percentage of the population in different age groups is changing. Exhibit 5-3 shows the number of people in different age groups in 1994 and 2004—and how the size of these groups will look in 2014. Note the big increases in the 45–64 age group from 1994 to 2004 and also 2004 to 2014.

Highly targeted advertising media are proving especially effective at targeting messages to specific demographic groups. For example, TBS Superstation targets its Comedy Block to a particular group, and *Automobile Magazine* targets people who love cars.

Exhibit 5-3
Population by Age Group for Different Ten-Year Periods

Age Group		
65+	5,363.1 (15.8%)	4,141.0 (13.0%)	3,438.2 (10.0%)
45–64	9,795.4 (28.8%)	8,192.6 (25.6%)	5,969.7 (19.0%)
25–44	9,289.2 (27.3%)	9,535.4 (29.8%)	9,651.8 (31.5%)
15–24	4,345.7 (12.8%)	4,349.1 (13.6%)	3,981.0 (18.0%)
5–14	3,520.8 (10.4%)	4,032.4 (12.6%)	3,949.7 (14.3%)
Under 5	1,691.9 (5.0%)	1,695.9 (5.3%)	2,008.5 (7.2%)

■ Year 2014
■ Year 2004
■ Year 1994

Size of Age Group (population in 000's with percentage of population shown in brackets)

The major reason for the changing age distribution is that the post–World War II baby boom produced about one-fourth of the present population. This large group crowded into the schools in the 1950s and 60s—and then into the job market in the 1970s. In the 1980s, they swelled the middle-aged group. And early in the 21st century, they will reach retirement—still a dominant group in the total population. According to one population expert, "It's like a goat passing through a boa constrictor."

Some of the effects of this big market are very apparent. For example, recording industry sales exploded—to the beat of rock and roll music and the Beatles—as the baby boom group moved into their record-buying teens. Soon after, universities added facilities and faculty to handle the surge. With the increasing population of seniors, universities are now adding special courses and programs for adults to attract the now-aging baby boom students. The fitness industry and food producers who offer low-calorie foods are also reaping the benefit of a middle-aged "bulge" in the population.

Medical advances help people live longer and are also adding to the proportion of the population in the senior citizen group. Note from Exhibit 5-3 that the over-65 age group will increase to 15.8 percent by 2014. This ongoing growth creates new opportunities for such industries as tourism, health care, and financial services.[8]

The youth cycle has started again

While society, and many marketers have been fixated on the aging baby boomers, the 15–24 age group has started to grow again as a consequence of the "baby boom-let" that developed in the 1980s and early 90s. By 2014, the 15–24 age group is projected to grow to 4.3 million—up over 9 percent from 1994. This will create new marketing opportunities targeted at the "youth segment." However, marketers who simultaneously try to appeal to aging baby boomers and to the 15–24 age group may find themselves right in the middle of a real clash of generational cultures.[9]

Household composition is changing

Many people incorrectly think of the "typical" Canadian household as a married couple with two children—living in the suburbs. This might have been true 40 years ago, but it isn't now. Only about 29 percent of census families have children at home. Approximately 16 percent of households are now headed by a single parent, while about 22 percent of marriages end in separation or divorce. Common-law couples have increased quickly over the last decade and now make up around 14 percent of the households.

HOW TO GET A BOOST IN MOBILE PHONE SALES TO TEENS

When cell phones first came out 30 years ago they were pricey tools for high-income executives. They were sold at prices around $800 (with $1-a-minute service plans) by dealers who could explain their value and close the deal. Even at those prices, service was often limited to big metro business areas. Of course, that quickly changed as costs came down; before long, mass-merchandisers were giving away phones to customers who would sign a one-year service contract or a family plan. And companies like Sprint even bypassed the retailer with credit card sales from their own Web sites. Yet until recently, wireless carriers have had trouble hooking up with Generation Y—the group of "tweens," teens, and twenty-somethings born between 1977 and 1995. Gen Y is famed for its skepticism, and they have proved a difficult target market to woo. The calling plans offered by the big firms left them cold, and most didn't yet have the income (or credit rating) required by firms like Bell or Telus.

Now, however, cell phone companies have figured out how to crack the code and get sales penetration with this group and the following generation as well. No more binding contracts, credit checks, or monthly billing for the "tweens," teens, and twenties markets. The current model is an extension of products introduced years ago like Telus's "Pay and Talk." These customers (or their parents) buy a chunk of prepaid airtime. When that is gone, they top it up. The pricing component change played a big role in cracking these markets. But so did the product changes in the marketing mix. A cell phone isn't just a cell phone anymore. It's a camera, video game player, and more importantly, it has "morphed" over into an MP3 player with downloading capabilities as well. Finally, the cell phone companies adjusted their distribution and promotion strategies so their younger customers could identify with a brand image that was much cooler than the boring old telephone company.[10]

Nonfamily households are increasing

Some of these household arrangements are temporary—as in university towns or in large cities where recent graduates go for their first "real" job. But the majority are older couples who choose not to get married. The number of these non-traditional households is still relatively small. But marketers pay special attention to them because they are growing at a much higher rate than the traditional family households. And they have different needs and attitudes than the stereotypical family. To reach this market, some banks changed their policies about loans to unmarried couples for homes, cars, and other major purchases. And some insurance companies designed coverage for unmarried couples.

Single-adult households are also on the rise, and they account for about half of all households! These include young adults who leave home when they finish school, as well as separated, divorced, or widowed people who live alone. These people need smaller apartments, smaller cars, smaller food packages, and, in some cases, less-expensive household furnishings because many singles don't have much money. Other singles have ample discretionary income and are attractive markets for top-of-the-line clothing, expensive electronic gadgets, status cars, travel, nice restaurants, and trendy bars.[11] For example Synovate, a global research company, even suggests there is a new market segment of roughly 465,000 working-class youths aged 18–25. This new demographic of singles has been named the **Gold-Collar Segment** because they often live at home to minimize rent and spend most of their earnings on luxury products like Prada sunglasses, electronics, expensive cars, and generally high-end brand name products.

The shift to urban and suburban areas

Migration from rural to urban areas has occurred throughout much of Canada's history. The move to cities from rural areas began to increase with the Great Depression in the 1930s, and by the 1960s the farm population for example, had shrunk to a fraction of its original size.[12]

"IF YOU WANT MY MONEY, STOP SHOWING ME PICTURES OF MY DAUGHTER IN UNDERWEAR."

And stop pretending you think she's me. That's not "aspirational," that's obnoxious. It's your decision.

Since World War II, there has been a continuous flight to the suburbs by middle-income consumers. By 1970, more people lived in the suburbs than in the central cities. Retailers moved too—following their customers. Lower-income consumers—often with varied ethnic backgrounds—moved in, changing the nature of markets in the centre of the city.

Industries too have been fleeing the cities, moving many jobs closer to the suburbs. Today's urban economic system is not as dependent on central cities. A growing population must go somewhere—and the suburbs can combine pleasant neighbourhoods with easy transportation to higher-paying jobs nearby or in the city.

Purchase patterns are different in the suburbs. And in some areas, it almost seems that an SUV or a minivan—to carpool kids and haul lawn supplies or pets—is a necessity.

Local political boundaries don't define market areas

These continuing shifts—to and from urban and suburban areas—mean that the usual practice of reporting population by city and county boundaries can result in misleading descriptions of markets. Marketers are more interested in the size of homogeneous *marketing* areas than in the number of people within political boundaries. To meet this need, Statistics Canada has developed a separate population classification based on metropolitan statistical areas. Much data is reported on the characteristics of people in these areas. The technical definition of these areas has changed over time. But basically a **Census Metropolitan Area (CMA)** is an integrated economic and social unit with a large population nucleus. Generally, CMA centres on one city or urbanized area of 100,000 or more inhabitants.

The vast majority of Canadians of course live within a CMA, and detailed data regarding anything from ethnicity to income information can be acquired for aggregated groups. Statistics Canada provides some of the best data libraries in the world that also allow you to disaggregate data down to areas as small as a neighbourhood. This is provided as block census data that can be related to a geographical map of the area and can be very useful in deciding where to locate a small business for example.

Big targets are attractive—but very competitive	Some national marketers sell only in these metro areas because of their large, concentrated populations. They know that having so many customers packed into a small area can simplify the marketing effort. They can use fewer middlemen and still offer products conveniently. One or two local advertising media—a city newspaper or TV station—can reach most residents. If a sales force is needed, it will incur less travel time and expense because people are closer together.
Metro areas are also attractive markets because they offer greater sales potential than their large population alone suggests. Consumers in these areas have more money to spend because wages tend to be higher. In addition, professionals—with higher salaries—are concentrated there. But remember that competition for consumer dollars is usually stiff in a CMA.[13]
The mobile ones are an attractive market	Of course, none of these population shifts is necessarily permanent. People move, stay awhile, and then move again. Often people who move in the same city trade up to a bigger or better house or neighbourhood. They tend to be younger and better educated people on the way up in their careers. Their income is rising—and they have money to spend. Buying a new house may spark many other purchases too. The old sofa may look shabby in the new house. And the bigger yard may require a new lawn mower, or even a yard service.
Many long-distance moves are prompted by the search for a better lifestyle. Many affluent retirees, for example, move to find a more comfortable life. Young people also hop from place to place, attracted by better job opportunities. This applies to graduates moving to high-paying, new-economy jobs as well as recent immigrants whose only choice may be a low-wage service job.
Regardless of why someone moves, many market-oriented decisions have to be made fairly quickly after a move. People must find new sources of food, clothing, medical and dental care, and household products. Once they make these basic buying decisions, they may not change for a long time. Alert marketers try to locate these potential customers early—to inform them of offerings before they make their purchase decisions. Retail chains, "national" brands, and franchised services available in different areas have a competitive advantage with mobiles. The customer who moves to a new town may find a familiar Blockbuster sign down the street and never even try their local competitors.[14]

INCOME DIMENSIONS OF THE CANADIAN MARKET

	So far, we have been concerned mainly with the *number* of different types of people—and *where* they live.
More people are in middle- and upper-income levels	Earlier in this chapter you saw how GNI (Gross National Income) figures can be helpful in analyzing markets. But GNI figures are more meaningful to marketing managers when converted to family or household income and its distribution. Family incomes generally increased with GNI. But even more important to marketers, the *distribution* of income changed drastically over time.
Fifty years ago, the income distribution looked something like a pyramid. Most families were bunched together at the low end of the income scale—just over a subsistence level—to form the base of the income pyramid. There were many fewer families in the middle range, and a relative handful formed an elite market at the top. This pattern still exists in many nations.
By the 1970s, real income (buying power) had risen so much that most families even those near the bottom of the income distribution—could afford a comfortable standard of living. And the proportion of people with middle incomes was much larger. Such middle-income people enjoyed real choices in the marketplace.

Marketers are very aware that spending varies with income and other demographic dimensions.

This revolution broadened markets and drastically changed the marketing system. Products viewed as luxuries in most parts of the world sell to "mass" markets in Canada. And these large markets lead to economies of scale, which boost our standard of living even more. Similar situations exist in the United States, many Western European countries, Australia, New Zealand, and Japan.

Real income growth has slowed—but for how long?

Trends in median family income from 1960 to 2001 reflected an upward shift in the income distribution—and an increased number of families with more money to spend. Real median income (Exhibit 5-4) however has had a slight downward trend over the period 1980–2003.

There is heated debate about what will happen to consumer incomes—and income distribution—in the future. Some business analysts feel that the lack of significant income growth signals worse things to come. They think that a decline in the manufacturing sector of the economy threatens middle-class standards of living. These analysts argue that in industries with traditionally high wages, firms are replacing workers with technology—to be able to compete with low-cost foreign producers. At the same time, new jobs are coming from growth of the lower-paying service industries. But other analysts are not so pessimistic. They agree that the percentage of the workforce earning middle-income wages has declined recently— but they think this is a temporary shift, not a long-term trend, and that over time the efficiencies that come from new information technologies will "lift" the whole economy.

What happens to income levels will be critical to you and to consumers in general. It is easy for both consumers and marketing managers to be lulled by the promise of a constantly increasing standard of living. Both consumer thinking and marketing strategy will have to adjust if growth does not resume.

The higher-income groups receive a big share

Higher-income groups in Canada receive a very large share of total income. For example, those in the highest bracket received about 47 percent of the total family income in the country. This gives them extra buying power, especially for luxury items like memberships in country clubs and yachts.

At the lower end of the scale, are families earning less than $28,500 income. They account for 20 percent of all families but receive only 4.2 percent of total income.

Exhibit 5-4
Median Total Income of
Economic Family Type in
Constant Dollars

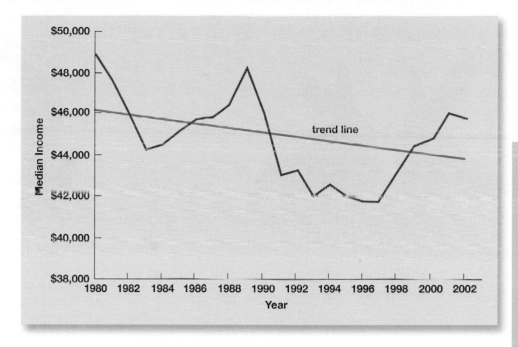

Even this low-income group is an attractive market for some basic commodities, especially food and clothing. Some of these consumers may receive welfare and housing assistance, which increases their buying power. Marketers target this group, usually with a lower-price marketing mix.

How much income is "enough"?

We can't stress the importance of income distribution too much. Many companies make serious marketing strategy errors by overestimating the amount of income in various target markets. Marketers can easily make such errors because of the natural tendency for people to associate with others like themselves and to assume that almost everyone lives like they do. A marketing manager who earns $135,000 a year may have no clue what life is like for a family that lives on $25,000 a year.

The 2003 average family income of about $73,000 is a useful reference point because some university graduates approach this level within a short period of time. And a young working couple together can easily go way over this figure. This may seem like a lot of money at first—but it is surprising how soon needs and expenses rise and adjust to available income. Middle-income consumers have been hit hard by the spiralling costs of insurance, housing, energy, cars, taxes, and tuition bills. More than ever, these consumers look for purchases that offer good value for the money spent. Some high-living marketers may not understand that these consumers *need* to pinch their pennies, but that practical reality now explains much of the buying behaviour of lower- and middle-income markets in Canada and the U.S.[15]

Can low-income consumers protect themselves?

In considering statistics such as these, it is important for all of us to think about the enormous problems of poverty that low-income consumers face. They often can't afford enough to eat, clothing for their children, or even a safe place to live. With little income, education, or opportunity to become informed, many consumers in the lowest income groups have few real choices. Some marketing managers struggle over whether to serve these markets. A credit company, for example, may find customers willing to pay a high finance charge to borrow money. And the high rate may be needed to cover the risk of unpaid loans. But is it exploitation to charge a higher rate to those who can least afford it and who really have no other choice?[16]

"I heard they're good for family planning."

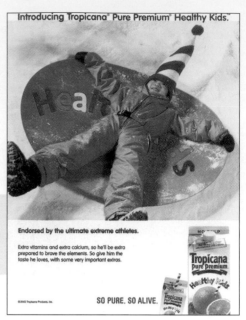

Telus offers phone and service packages that are designed to appeal to a whole family. Similarly, Tropicana Healthy Kids orange juice appeals to kids with a great taste—but its extra vitamins and calcium give parents added reasons to buy it.

SPENDING VARIES WITH INCOME AND OTHER DEMOGRAPHIC DIMENSIONS

We've been using the term *family income* because consumer budget studies show that many consumers spend their incomes as part of family or household units. They usually pool their incomes when planning major expenditures. So most of our discussion will concern how families or households spend their income.

Disposable income is what you get to spend

Families don't get to spend all of their income. **Disposable income** is what is left after taxes. Out of this disposable income—together with gifts, pensions, cash savings, or other assets—the family makes its expenditures. Some families don't spend all their disposable income—they save part of it. Therefore, when trying to estimate potential sales in target markets, we should distinguish among income, disposable income, and what consumers actually spend.

Discretionary income is elusive

Most families spend a good portion of their income on such "necessities" as food, rent or mortgage payments, car and home furnishings payments, and insurance. A family's purchase of "luxuries" comes from **discretionary income**—what is left of disposable income after paying for necessities.

Discretionary income is an elusive concept because the definition of necessities varies from family to family and over time. It depends on what they think is necessary for their lifestyle. A cable TV service might be purchased out of discretionary income by a lower-income family but be considered a necessity by a higher-income family. But if many people in a lower-income neighbourhood subscribe to cable TV, it might become a "necessity" for the others—and severely reduce the discretionary income available for other purchases.

Many families do not have enough discretionary income to afford the lifestyles they see on TV and in other mass media. On the other hand, some young adults and older people without family responsibilities have a lot of discretionary income. They may be especially attractive markets for electronic gear, digital cameras, new cars, foreign travel, designer fashions, and various kinds of recreation—tennis, skiing, boating, concerts, and fine restaurants.[17]

Spending varies over the family life cycle

Income has a direct bearing on spending patterns, but many other demographic dimensions are also useful in understanding consumer buying. Marital status, age, and

Exhibit 5-5 Stages in Modern Family Life Cycles

→ Usual flow   ---→ Recycled flow   * Traditional family flow

the age of any children in the family have an especially important effect on how people spend their income. Put together, these dimensions tell us about the life-cycle stage of a family. Exhibit 5-5 shows a summary of stages in the **family life cycle**. In our discussion, we will focus on the traditional flow from one stage to the next—as shown in the middle of the diagram. However, as shown at the top and bottom of the exhibit, divorce does interrupt the flow for many people; after a divorce, they may recycle through earlier stages.[18]

Young people and families accept new ideas

Singles and young couples seem to be more willing to try new products and brands—and they are careful, price-conscious shoppers. Younger people often earn less than older consumers, but they spend a greater proportion of their income on discretionary items because they don't have the major expenses of home ownership, education, and family rearing. Although many young people are waiting longer to marry, most do tie the knot eventually. These younger families—especially those with no children—are still accumulating durable goods, such as automobiles and home furnishings. They spend less on food. Only as children arrive and grow does family spending shift to soft goods and services, such as education and personal care. This usually happens when the family head reaches the 35–49 age group. To meet expenses, people in this age group often make more purchases on credit, and they save less of their income.

Divorce—increasingly a fact of life—disrupts the family life-cycle pattern. Divorced parents don't spend like other singles. The mother usually has custody of the children, and the father may pay child support. The mother and children typically have much less income than two-parent families. Such families spend a larger percent of their income on housing, child care, and other necessities—with little left for discretionary purchases. If a single parent remarries, the family life cycle may start over again.[19]

Reallocation for teenagers

Once children become teenagers, further shifts in spending occur. Teenagers eat more, want to wear expensive clothes, and develop recreation and education needs that are hard on the family budget. The parents—or increasingly, the single parent—may be forced to reallocate expenditures to cover these expenses—spending less on durable goods, such as appliances, automobiles, household goods, and housing. The fast-rising expense of sending a son or daughter to university can create a major financial crisis.

For many firms, teens are an important and attractive market. To this very substantial segment we can also add the "**tween**" market, which captures kids who are moving into their teen years. Marketers are concentrating more on both of these segments because their spending patterns have moved well into the billions of dollars. Further, in today's families with a single parent or with two wage earners, teens play an increasingly important role in shopping and shaping family purchases. With teens spending more money, they are a target for many firms. For example, Siemens added an MP3 player to its wireless phone to help it win teen preference away from Nokia. Similarly, MasterCard is targeting teens with its credit card promotions and Bausch & Lomb's contact-lens sales hit record levels when the firm refocused its marketing efforts on teens.[20]

Selling to the empty nesters

Another important category is the **empty nesters**—people whose children are grown and who are now able to spend their money in other ways. Usually these people are in the 50–64 age group. But this is an elusive group because some people marry later and are still raising a family at this age. And in recent years lots of empty nesters have been surprised when adult singles move back in to avoid the big costs of housing.

Empty nesters are an attractive market for many items. Often they have paid for their homes, and the big expenses of raising a family are behind them. They are more interested in travel, sports cars, and other things they couldn't afford before. Much depends on their income, of course. But this is a high-income period for many workers, especially white-collar workers.[21]

Senior citizens are a big market

Finally, marketers should not neglect the senior citizens—people over 65. The number of people over 65 is increasing rapidly because of modern medicine, improved sanitary conditions, and better nutrition. This group now makes up over 12 percent of the population.

Our senior citizens are more prosperous than ever before. Their income is lower than in their peak earning years, but most do have money to spend. Older people also have very different needs. Many firms already cater to senior citizens—and more will be serving this market. For example, some companies have developed housing and "life care" centres designed to appeal to older people. Casio makes a calculator with large, easy-to-read numbers. *Reader's Digest* long ago had the good marketing sense to publish an easy-to-read "big print" edition of its magazine because they realized that seniors were one of their major market segments. The cruise lines operating out of Vancouver have for years successfully targeted seniors for their Alaskan summer run. This market has, over the years, generated hundreds of millions of dollars and is one of BC's most important tourism programs. Other companies offer diet supplements and drug products, often in special easy-to-open packages. And senior citizen discounts at drugstores are more than just a courtesy—the elderly make up the biggest market for medicines.

Keep in mind, however, that older people are not all the same. With a group this large, generalities and stereotypes can be dangerous. Within that relatively well-off seniors group for example, there is a segment that have very limited income. Single females in their senior years are a group that can be vulnerable to poverty. Different senior citizen target markets have different needs and require different marketing strategies.[22]

ETHNIC DIMENSIONS OF THE CANADIAN MARKET

Do ethnic groups buy differently?

The ethnic composition of Canada has changed markedly over the last three decades. For years marketing distinguished between the two major and distinct cultures of English and French Canada. Things have gotten more complex from a

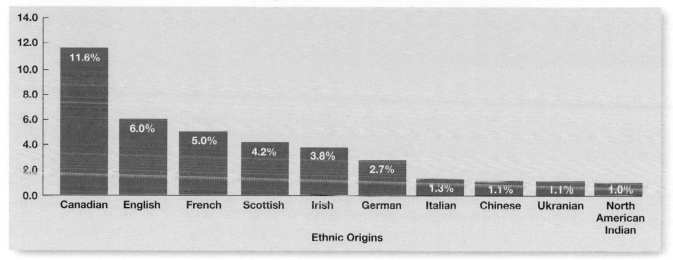

Ethnic Origins

marketing standpoint because Canada has become much more of an ethnic mosaic with significant cultures that sometimes merit their own distinct marketing mixes. We sometimes give these ethnic groups special attention because they may be influenced by very different cultural variables and have quite different needs from those in other segments.

Exhibit 5-6 shows just some of our larger populations by ethnic origin and gives an idea of the cultural melting pot that now characterizes Canada. Some of these segments continue to speak their mother tongue at home, often because seniors may not adapt as quickly to our languages or because newly arrived immigrants are initially more comfortable with their own language. This obviously affects promotion planning. Similarly, brand preferences vary for some ethnic groups. For example, cosmetic companies offer products tailored to different skin tones. But ethnic groups don't just differ in the colour of their skin. Differences in attitudes, experiences, and values, as well as where they shop and what advertising appeals they attend to, come together to shape differences in buying behaviour.

Many firms are developing new strategies to appeal to fast-growing ethnic markets in the U.S. The T&T Supermarket in Vancouver not only targets a very large Chinese segment with ads and information on their Web site, but also offers products that are specific to their Chinese customers as well.

Stereotypes are common—and misleading

A marketer needs to study ethnic dimensions very carefully because they can be subtle and fast-changing. This is also an area where stereotyped thinking is the most common—and misleading. Many firms make the mistake of treating all consumers in a particular ethnic group as homogeneous. For example, the first Canadian born generation of immigrants very quickly assimilates into Canadian culture so their preference patterns become very similar to those of Canadians—not those of their parents. The same ethnic group could well show different responses to the same promotional appeal based on the gap between the two different generations.

Ethnic markets are becoming more important

More marketers pay attention to ethnic groups now because the number of ethnic consumers is growing at a much faster rate than the overall society. Much of this growth results from immigration, but differing birth rates among ethnic groups play a role as well.

The French-Canadian segment is, based on size, one of the largest ethnic markets in the country and therefore of great interest to marketers. Not only do language issues require changes in both product packaging and advertising communications but French-Canadians also differ in some of the products and services they consume. The major banks dominate much of the financial market in Canada but in Quebec, Dejardins is one of the dominant players. For example, the caisse populaire movement in Quebec is an important force in their financial market and it shows up in their consumer preferences. French Canadians also differ in some of their consumption patterns; spending proportionately more on clothing, food, and entertainment and less on housing and financial products than other Canadians. Marketers have to understand these nuances and realize that brand positioning has to account for cultural differences among ethnic groups. This is a major reason for the increase of mass media targeted at ethnic minorities. The process had its roots in the development of French-Canadian TV and radio stations but has rapidly expanded to provide mass media content for all major ethnic groups.

Strategy changes may be needed

Ethnic shifts are changing the face of the Canadian market. Many companies will need separate strategies for these ethnically or racially defined markets. Some may only require changes in Place and Promotion. But many companies have had difficulty developing strategies and segmenting ethnic submarkets. For example, Asians emigrated from China, Japan, the Philippines, India, Korea, Vietnam, Pakistan, and Indonesia to name a few. Many come from very different backgrounds with no common language, religion, or culture. That adds to the marketing challenge; it means marketers must really understand the basic needs that motivate specific target markets to think and act as they do. This is important with any consumer market, regardless of people's ethnic or racial background or where in the world they live. We'll deal with that important issue in more detail in the next chapter.[23]

CONCLUSION

In this chapter, we studied population, income, and other demographic dimensions of consumer markets. We learned that the potential of a given market cannot be determined by population figures alone. Geographic location, income, stage in life cycle, ethnic background, and other factors are important too. We talked about some of the ways these dimensions—and changes in them—affect marketing strategy planning. Now that you know something about demographics—and thinking back to the opening vignette—what kind of variables should the marketers at Visa consider if they were to persuade consumers just like you to apply for their credit card?

We also noted how the high concentration of population and spending power in large metropolitan areas of Canada has made them attractive target markets. However, competition in these markets is often tough.

Canadian consumers are among the most affluent in the world. They have more discretionary income and can afford a wide variety of products that people in other parts of the world view as luxuries. However, in Canada, as in most other societies, income is distributed unevenly among different groups. Consumers at the top income levels have a disproportionately large share of the total buying power.

The kind of data discussed in this chapter can be very useful for estimating the market potential within possible target markets. But, unfortunately, it is not very helpful in explaining specific customer behaviour—why people buy *specific* products and *specific* brands. Yet such detailed forecasts are important to marketing managers. Better forecasts can come from a better understanding of consumer behaviour—the subject of the next chapter.

KEY TERMS

gross domestic product (GDP), 122

purchasing power parity (PPP), 122

birthrate, 126

baby boom, 126

gold-collar segment, 129

Census Metropolitan Area (CMA), 130

disposable income, 134

discretionary income, 134

family life cycle, 135

tweens, 136

empty nesters, 136

QUESTIONS AND PROBLEMS

1. Describe the demographic group targeted by Roots. Who does The Bay target?

2. Discuss the value of gross domestic product and gross national income per capita as measures of market potential in consumer markets. Try to give examples in your answer.

3. Discuss how slower population growth will affect businesses in your local community.

4. Discuss the impact of the new teen cycle on marketing strategy planning in Canada.

5. Name three specific examples of firms that developed a marketing mix to appeal to senior citizens. Name three examples of firms that developed a marketing mix to appeal to teenagers.

6. Some demographic characteristics are more important than others in determining market potential. For each of the following characteristics, identify two products for which this characteristic is *most* important: (a) size of geographic area, (b) population, (c) income, (d) stage of life cycle.

7. Name three specific examples (specific products or brands—not just product categories) and explain how demand in Canada will differ by geographic location *and* urban–rural location.

8. Explain how the continuing mobility of Canadian consumers—as well as the development of big metropolitan areas—should affect marketing strategy planning in the future. Be sure to consider the impact on the four Ps.

9. Explain why the concept of the Census Metropolitan Area was developed. Is it the most useful breakdown for retailers?

10. Describe the target market who watch the Shaw TV Golf channel.

11. Explain how the redistribution of income in the U.S. has affected marketing planning thus far and its likely impact in the future.

12. Why are marketing managers paying more attention to ethnic dimensions of consumer markets in Canada?

13. Name three categories of products marketed in Canada that are influenced by ethnic minorities.

14. Describe who CBC TV target with their hockey programming.

15. What is the difference between a beer drinker loyal to Sleeman's versus one who is loyal to Molson Canadian?

COMPUTER-AIDED PROBLEM

5. Demographic Analysis

RESOURCE REMINDER

Stylco Inc., is a producer of specialty clothing. To differentiate its designs and appeal to its Chinese-Canadian target market, Stylco uses authentic Asian materials. Originally, it just focused on designs targeted at adults in the 35–44 age range. However, in the late 1990s, when sales to these middle-aged adults started to level off, Stylco added a more conservative line of clothes for older consumers. Most buyers of the conservative styles are in the 45–59 age group.

Stylco has focused on distributing its products through select fashion boutiques in metropolitan market areas with the highest concentrations of Chinese-Canadian consumers. This approach has reduced Stylco's personal selling expense; as a result, however, only a percentage of the total Chinese population is served by current Stylco retailers. For example, about half of the consumers in the 35–44 age group are in the market areas served by Stylco retailers.

In the fall of 2006, Naomi Davis, Stylco's marketing manager, read an article about the "greying of Canadians." This left her wondering how shifts in the age distribution might affect her market and sales.

To get a long-run view of these trends, she looked at census data on Chinese consumers by age group. She also looked up estimates of the expected percent rate of change in the size of each group through the year 2007. By multiplying these rates by the size her target markets were in 2000, she can estimate how large they are likely to be in the year 2007. Further, from analysis of past sales data, she knows that the number of units the firm sells is directly proportional to the size of each age group. Specifically, the ratio of units sold to target market size has been about 5 units per 1,000 people (that is, a ratio of .005). Finally, she determined the firm's average unit profit for each of the lines. To see how changes in population are likely to affect Stylco units sold and future profits from each line, Davis programmed all of these data, and the relationships discussed above, into a spreadsheet.

a. Briefly compare the profit data for 2000 and estimated profit for 2007 as it appears on the initial spreadsheet. What is the basic reason for the expected shift? What are the implications of these and other data in the spreadsheet for Stylco's marketing strategy planning?

b. The rate of growth or decline for different Chinese-Canadian age groups tends to vary from one geographic region to another. Davis thinks that in the market areas that Stylco serves the size of the 35–44 age group may decrease by as much as 10 to 12 percent by 2007. However, the government estimates that the decline of the 35–44 age group for the whole country will only be about −1.7 percent. If the decline in the target market size for Davis' market areas turns out to be −1.7 percent rather than the −10.1 she has assumed, what is the potential effect on profits from the young adult line? On overall profits?

c. Because more firms are paying attention to fast-growing ethnic markets, Davis thinks competition may increase in lines targeted at affluent Chinese Canadians in the 45–59 age group. Because of price competition, the line targeted at this group already earns a lower average profit per unit. Further, as more firms compete for this business, she thinks that her "ratio of units sold to market size" may decrease. Use the what-if analysis to prepare a table showing how percent of profit from this group, as well as total profit, might change as the ratio of units sold to market size varies between a minimum of .001 and a maximum of .010. Explain the implications to the firm.

If you want to read the cases and view the video cases that accompany this chapter, visit the *Basic Marketing* Online Learning Centre at: **www.mcgrawhill.ca/olc/perreault**. Along with these cases and video cases, the OLC also has the software and user guide for this chapter's Computer-Aided Problem, as well as exercises, quizzes, articles, links, and other *interactive* content that will help you with your studies.

Consumer Behaviour

In the 1970s, yogourt was a popular food in Europe but was not as "mainstream" in Canada. All of that changed when Dannon and other firms more actively began to promote their products here. Sales grew slowly at first, but that changed in the 1980s as more adults became interested in healthy eating. For lots of on-the-go workers, yogourt was an economical lunch that tasted good and saved time. It didn't require preparation or cleanup, and it could be eaten almost anywhere. All you needed was a plastic spoon.

By the 1990s, many brands and flavours of yogourt were on the market. Most consumers couldn't tell the difference between brands. When it was time to buy, they just picked up their routine brand or perhaps whatever was on sale. Most marketers felt that growth in the yogourt category was pretty much tapped out. But by carefully studying consumer behaviour, Ian Friendly and others on his marketing team at Yoplait changed all of that. Their U.S. marketing plan for a new product, Go-Gurt, racked up $100 million in sales in the first year. Yoplait Tubes were introduced as the Canadian version of Go-Gurt and met with the same popularity in the kids' segment. Much of the increase in sales represented new demand in the yogourt category because the percentage of kids eating yogourt doubled. That was no accident. The product was designed to have kid appeal.

Kids need nutritious food, but research showed that what they want in snacks is great taste, convenience, and fun. Traditional yogourt was convenient, but it still took one hand for the spoon and one to hold the carton. And a carton of yogourt didn't exactly impress the other kids as a cool thing to eat. Yoplait took care of that. It did away with the spoon by putting the yogourt in a 9-inch-long, one handed squeeze tube. The creaminess of the product was adjusted to make it just right for on-the-go eating. Kids didn't have a very positive attitude about most standard yogourt flavours, so the Yoplait tube was filled with flavours kids could learn to love—like Cyber Strawberry and Volcanik Blueberry.

Yoplait's introductory ads were placed on media so they'd reach kids directly. Then it was up to them to ask their parents to buy Tubes at the store. The ads positioned Tubes not just as a food but as a lifestyle accessory for kids. To build awareness of the benefits of the package and interest in the product, the ads conveyed the idea that it was OK to play with your food. For example, in one American TV spot, a young skateboarder holding a Go-Gurt blasts past another kid who looks bored eating from a carton of yogourt as the announcer asks, "Why eat yogourt like this when you can eat with your hands, not a spoon? Go-Gurt comes in a totally cool squeeze tube you can squeeze and slurp, grab and glurp." The Go-Gurt slurping skateboarder tells the other boy, "Hey, lose the spoon."

The Canadian Web site for Tubes uses an interactive page that lets kids and teenagers send messages to their friends using different voices and sound effects. It also contains a list of flavours as well as nutritional information for parents. The strategy is to create high traffic on the site that will continue to give their target market exposure to the brand name. Check it out by entering Yoplait Tubes on your browser.

Other food companies quickly imitated Yoplait's tube packaging. Yet none was able to copy their big success. Hunt's Squeez 'n Go pudding, Mott's Fruit Blasters apple sauce, and Skippy peanut butter in a tube were among the brands that did not sell well. Why? Moms complained that the tubes created a big mess on kids' clothes and furniture, so retailers lost interest and would not provide shelf-space support. One critic argued that the costly failures could have been avoided—because the "knee-jerk reaction" to imitate the tubes packaging resulted in products that were rushed to market without adequate research to gather insights from consumers.[1]

CONSUMER BEHAVIOUR—WHY DO THEY BUY WHAT THEY BUY?

In the last chapter, we discussed basic data on population, income, and consumer spending patterns. This information can help marketers predict basic *trends* in consumer spending patterns. For example, the average person in Canada or the U.S. consumes 5 times more than a Mexican person, 10 times more than a Chinese person, and 30 times more than a person from India. Unfortunately, when many firms sell similar products, demographic analysis isn't much help in predicting which specific products and brands consumers will purchase—and why. Our Yoplait case shows that many other variables can influence consumers and their buying behaviour.

Economic needs affect many buying decisions, but for some purchases the behavioural influences on a consumer are more important.

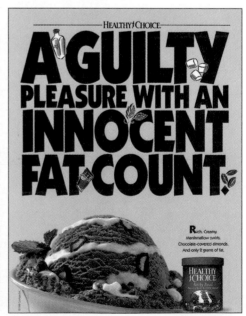

144

To better understand why consumers buy as they do, many marketers turn to the behavioural sciences for help. In this chapter, we'll explore some of the thinking from economics, psychology, sociology, and the other behavioural disciplines.

Specific consumer behaviours vary a great deal for different products and from one target market to the next. In today's global markets, the variations are countless. That makes it impractical to catalogue all the possibilities for every different situation. For example, how and why a given consumer buys a specific brand of cookies may be very different from how that same consumer buys a DVD recorder; and customers in different countries may have very different reactions to either product. But there are *general* behavioural principles—frameworks—that marketing managers can apply to learn more about their specific target markets. Our approach focuses on developing your skill in working with these frameworks.

THE BEHAVIOURAL SCIENCES HELP YOU UNDERSTAND THE BUYING PROCESS

Economic needs affect most buying decisions

Most economists assume that consumers are **economic buyers**—people who know all the facts and logically compare choices to get the greatest satisfaction from spending their time and money. A logical extension of the economic-buyer theory led us to look at consumer income patterns. This approach is valuable because consumers must at least have income to be in a market. Further, most consumers don't have enough income to buy everything they want, so they must make choices.

This view assumes that economic needs guide most consumer behaviour. **Economic needs** are concerned with making the best use of a consumer's time and money—as the consumer judges it. Some consumers look for the lowest price. Others will pay extra for convenience. And others may weigh price and quality for the best value. Some economic needs are

1. Economy of purchase or use.
2. Convenience.
3. Efficiency in operation or use.
4. Dependability in use.
5. Improvement of earnings.

Clearly, marketing managers must be alert to new ways to appeal to economic needs. Most consumers appreciate firms that offer them improved economic value for the money they spend. But improved value does not just mean offering lower and lower prices. For example, products can be designed to work better, require less service, or last longer. Promotion can inform consumers about product benefits in terms of measurable factors like operating costs, the length of the guarantee, or the time a product will save. Carefully planned Place decisions can make it easier and faster for customers who face a poverty of time to make a purchase.

Economic value is an important factor in many purchase decisions. But most marketing managers think that buyer behaviour is not as simple as the economic-buyer model suggests. A product that one person sees as a good value—and is eager to buy—is of no interest to someone else. So we can't expect to understand buying behaviour without taking a broader view.

How we will view consumer behaviour

Many behavioural dimensions influence consumers. Let's try to combine these dimensions into a model of how consumers make decisions. Exhibit 6-1 shows that psychological variables, social influences, and the purchase situation all affect a person's buying behaviour. We'll discuss these topics in the next few pages. Then we'll expand the model to include the consumer problem-solving process.

Exhibit 6-1
A Model of Buyer Behaviour

Marketing mixes   All other stimuli

Person making decision

Psychological variables
- Motivation
- Perception
- Learning
- Attitude
- Personality/lifestyle

Social influences
- Family
- Social class
- Reference groups
- Culture

Purchase situation
- Purchase reason
- Time
- Surroundings

Problem-solving process

Person does or does not purchase (response)

PSYCHOLOGICAL INFLUENCES WITHIN AN INDIVIDUAL

Here we will discuss some variables of special interest to marketers—including motivation, perception, learning, attitudes, and lifestyle. Much of what we know about these *psychological (intrapersonal) variables* draws from ideas originally developed in the field of psychology.

Needs motivate consumers

Everybody is motivated by needs and wants. **Needs** are the basic forces that motivate a person to do something. Some needs involve a person's physical well-being, others the individual's self-view and relationship with others. Needs are more basic than wants. **Wants** are "needs" that are learned during a person's life. For example, everyone needs water or some kind of liquid, but some people also have learned to want Clearly Canadian's raspberry-flavoured sparkling water on the rocks.

When a need is not satisfied, it may lead to a drive. The need for liquid, for example, leads to a thirst drive. A **drive** is a strong stimulus that encourages action to reduce a need. Drives are internal—they are the reasons behind certain behaviour patterns. In marketing, a product purchase results from a drive to satisfy some need.

Some critics imply that marketers can somehow manipulate consumers to buy products against their will. But marketing managers can't create internal drives. Most marketing managers realize that trying to get consumers to act against their will is a waste of time. Instead, a good marketing manager studies what consumer drives, needs, and wants already exist and how they can be satisfied better.

Consumers seek benefits to meet needs

We're all a bundle of needs and wants. Exhibit 6-2 lists some important needs that might motivate a person to some action. This list, of course, is not complete. But thinking about such needs can help you see what *benefits* consumers might seek from a marketing mix.

When a marketing manager defines a product-market, the needs may be quite specific. For example, the food need might be as specific as wanting a Domino's thick-crust pepperoni pizza—delivered to your door hot and ready to eat.

Several needs at the same time

Consumer psychologists often argue that a person may have several reasons for buying—at the same time. Maslow is well known for his five-level hierarchy of needs. We will discuss a similar four-level hierarchy that is easier to apply to consumer

Exhibit 6-2   Possible Needs Motivating a Person to Some Action

Types of Needs	Specific Examples			
Physiological needs	Hunger Sex Rest	Thirst Body elimination	Activity Self-preservation	Sleep Warmth/coolness
Psychological needs	Aggression Family preservation Nurturing Playing-relaxing Self-identification	Curiosity Imitation Order Power Tenderness	Being responsible Independence Personal fulfillment Pride	Dominance Love Playing-competition Self-expression
Desire for . . .	Acceptance Affiliation Comfort Esteem Knowledge Respect Status	Achievement Appreciation Leisure Fame Prestige Retaliation Sympathy	Acquisition Beauty Distance "space" Happiness Pleasure Self-satisfaction Variety	Affection Companionship Distinctiveness Identification Recognition Sociability Fun
Freedom from . . .	Fear Pain Harm	Depression Stress Ridicule	Discomfort Loss Sadness	Anxiety Illness Pressure

behaviour. Exhibit 6-3 illustrates the four levels along with an advertising slogan showing how a company has tried to appeal to each need. The lowest-level needs are physiological. Then come safety, social, and personal needs. As a study aid, think of the PSSP needs.[2]

Physiological needs are concerned with biological needs—food, drink, rest, and sex. **Safety needs** are concerned with protection and physical well-being (perhaps involving health, food, medicine, and exercise). **Social needs** are concerned with love, friendship, status, and esteem—things that involve a person's interaction with others. **Personal needs**, on the other hand, are concerned with an individual's need for personal satisfaction—unrelated to what others think or do. Examples include self-esteem, accomplishment, fun, freedom, and relaxation.

Most products must fill more than one need at the same time.

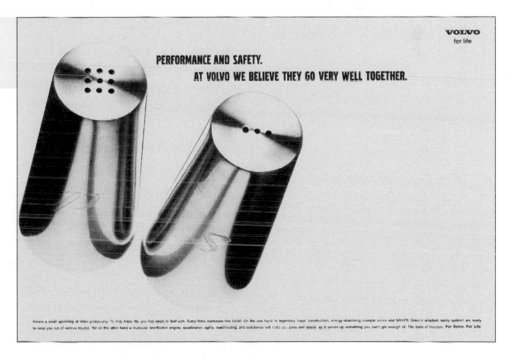

Exhibit 6-3 The PSSP Hierarchy of Needs

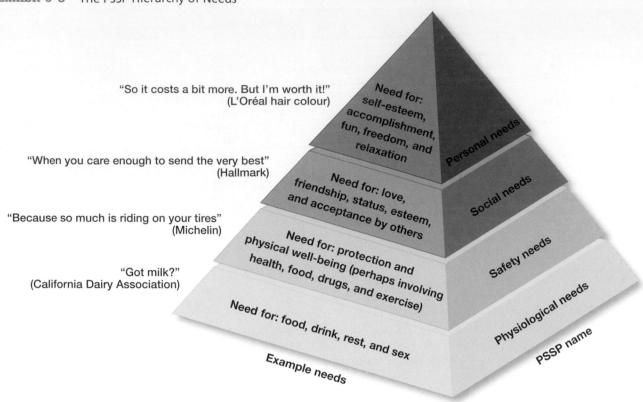

"So it costs a bit more. But I'm worth it!"
(L'Oréal hair colour)

"When you care enough to send the very best"
(Hallmark)

"Because so much is riding on your tires"
(Michelin)

"Got milk?"
(California Dairy Association)

Need for: self-esteem, accomplishment, fun, freedom, and relaxation — Personal needs

Need for: love, friendship, status, esteem, and acceptance by others — Social needs

Need for: protection and physical well-being (perhaps involving health, food, drugs, and exercise) — Safety needs

Need for: food, drink, rest, and sex — Physiological needs

Example needs

PSSP name

Motivation theory suggests that we never reach a state of complete satisfaction. As soon as we get our lower-level needs reasonably satisfied, those at higher levels become more dominant. This explains why marketing efforts targeted at affluent consumers in advanced economies often focus on higher-level needs. It also explains why these approaches may be useless in parts of the world where consumers' basic needs are not being met.

It is important to see, however, that a particular product may satisfy more than one need at the same time. In fact, most consumers try to fill a *set* of needs rather than just one need or another in sequence.

Obviously marketers should try to satisfy different needs. Yet discovering these specific consumer needs may require careful analysis. Consider, for example, the lowly vegetable peeler. Marketing managers for OXO International realized that many people, especially young children and senior citizens, have trouble gripping the handle of a typical peeler. OXO redesigned the peeler with a bigger handle that addressed this physical need. OXO also coated the handle with dishwasher-safe rubber. This makes cleanup more convenient—and the sharp peeler is safer to use when the grip is wet. The attractively designed grip also appeals to consumers who get personal satisfaction from cooking and who want to impress their guests. Even though OXO priced the peeler much higher than most kitchen utensils, it has sold very well because it appeals to people with a variety of needs. Since that initial success, OXO has redesigned many everyday utensils, including its new scoop colander. The colander's long handle makes it safe and easy to scoop and drain cooked pasta—without handling a hot pan or boiling water.[3]

There are other perspectives on motivation in addition to those of Maslow. Sigmund Freud, suggested that our behaviour is also determined by unconscious cues. It's not just the physical characteristics of the product that drive our decision making but also the less conscious emotions that they trigger. This leads market

How consumers perceive a product or marketing communication may depend on consumer interest and the urgency of the need.

researchers to conduct in-depth interviews and to use associative techniques in order to uncover the deeper emotions that are generated by the product. The objective is to then use those psychological associations in an attempt to influence the consumer's motivations toward the product. You might like to drive a BMW not only for its performance, but also because you feel it connotes status and the ads make you feel a sense of adventure and fun in driving it.

Herzberg took yet another approach by focusing on how satisfiers and dissatisfiers influence motivation. The implication for marketers is that we must avoid the presence of dissatisfiers in our product because they will be sufficient to block the sale—even in the presence of satisfiers. Microsoft for example encountered some serious consumer resistance when its early e-mail products turned out to be very prone to hackers. At the same time we must identify and incorporate satisfiers into the product because they are necessary to induce the customer to buy.[4]

Customer dissatisfaction as a motivating issue in consumer behaviour appears to be gaining in importance. Both the Internet and the media may be contributing to a reemergence of consumerism. Media are providing more coverage of customer dissatisfaction with products and services through news shows like CBC's *Market Place*, the W Network's TV show *The Shopping Bags*, and Rogers TV's *Goldhawk Live*. The shows seem to be resonating with consumers because TV ratings are good enough for them to remain on the air.

The Internet may have an even bigger impact on providing a forum for customers to express their dissatisfaction. At the height of its consumer service problems, the Internet-posted complaints about Air Canada were impressive. Blogs (personal Web logs) and organized complaint sites are springing up to provide very public discussions of real or perceived product shortcomings. This information is exposed to wide audiences who scan the Web looking for complaints that voice dissatisfaction with products they are thinking about purchasing. Try surfing www.complaints.com.

Which is the "right" theory of motivation? All of them may have relevance in the appropriate buying situation. What is necessary, is to be aware of them and to use the necessary discretion in their application when the appropriate situations arise.

Perception determines what consumers see and feel

Consumers select varying ways to meet their needs sometimes because of differences in **perception**—how we gather and interpret information from the world around us.

We are constantly bombarded by stimuli—ads, products, stores—yet we may not hear or see anything. This is because we apply the following selective processes:

1. **Selective exposure**—our eyes and minds seek out and notice only information that interests us. How often have you closed a pop-up ad at a Web site without even noticing what it was for?

2. **Selective perception**—we screen out or modify ideas, messages, and information that conflict with previously learned attitudes and beliefs. Consider the long hard media campaign waged by McDonald's and Wendy's. They both made substantial nutritional changes to their products and spent big dollars advertising that fact; but ask yourself if you still see them as "fast food" outlets selling the same old burgers and fries.

3. **Selective retention**—we remember only what we want to remember. If you like the Ford Taurus you will tend to retain information about the car that supports your attitudes and beliefs. Conversely, you will tend to forget advertising information about the good points of a competing brand that doesn't appeal to your attitudes and beliefs.

These selective processes help explain why some people are not affected by some advertising—even offensive advertising. They just don't see or remember it! Even if they do, they may dismiss it immediately. Some consumers are skeptical about any advertising message.

These selective processes are stronger than many people realize. For example, to make their positioning efforts memorable, many companies use a common slogan ("tag line") on all of their ads. However, when researchers showed consumers the tag lines for 22 of the biggest advertisers (over $100 million a year), only 6 were recognized by more than 10 percent of the consumers. Three slogans were not recognized by anyone in the sample. One of those was Circuit City's "We're with you" slogan that had been running in ads for two years. (Wal-Mart's "Always low prices, Always," with 64 percent recognition, was the only slogan recognized by more than half of the sample.)[5]

Our needs affect these selective processes. And current needs receive more attention. For example, Goodyear tire retailers advertise some sale in the newspaper almost weekly. Most of the time we don't even notice these ads—until we need new tires. Only then do we tune in to Goodyear's ads.

Marketers are interested in these selective processes because they affect how target consumers get and retain information. This is also why marketers are interested in how consumers *learn*.

Learning determines what response is likely

Learning is a change in a person's thought processes caused by prior experience. Learning is often based on direct experience: A little girl tastes her first cone of Ben & Jerry's Uncanny Cashew flavour ice cream, and learning occurs! Learning may also be based on indirect experience or associations. If you watch an ad that shows other people enjoying Ben & Jerry's Chocolate Fudge Brownie low-fat frozen yogourt, you might conclude that you'd like it too.

Consumer learning may result from things that marketers do, or it may result from stimuli that have nothing to do with marketing. Either way, almost all consumer behaviour is learned.[6]

Experts describe a number of steps in the learning process. We've already discussed the idea of a drive as a strong stimulus that encourages action. Depending on the **cues**—products, signs, ads, and other stimuli in the environment—an individual chooses some specific response. A **response** is an effort to satisfy a drive. The specific response chosen depends on the cues and the person's past experience.

Exhibit 6-4
The Learning Process

Reinforcement of the learning process occurs when the response is followed by satisfaction—that is, reduction in the drive. Reinforcement strengthens the relationship between the cue and the response. And it may lead to a similar response the next time the drive occurs. Repeated reinforcement leads to development of a habit—making the individual's decision process routine. Exhibit 6-4 shows the relationships of the important variables in the learning process.

The learning process can be illustrated by a thirsty person. The thirst *drive* could be satisfied in a variety of ways. But if the person happened to walk past a vending machine and saw a Mountain Dew sign—a *cue*—then he might satisfy the drive with a *response*—buying a Mountain Dew. If the experience is satisfactory, positive *reinforcement* occurs, and our friend may be quicker to satisfy this drive in the same way in the future. This emphasizes the importance of developing good products that live up to the promises of the firm's advertising. People can learn to like or dislike Mountain Dew—reinforcement and learning work both ways. Unless marketers satisfy their customers, they must constantly try to attract new ones to replace the dissatisfied ones who don't come back.

Good experiences can lead to positive attitudes about a firm's product. Bad experiences can lead to negative attitudes that even good promotion won't be able to change.

Positive cues help a marketing mix

Sometimes marketers try to identify cues or images that have positive associations from some other situation and relate them to their marketing mix. Many people associate the smell of lemons with a fresh, natural cleanliness. So companies often add lemon scent to household cleaning products—Clorox bleach and Pledge furniture polish, for example—because it has these associations. Similarly, firms like Calvin Klein use ads suggesting that people who use their products have more appeal to the opposite sex. Simple cues may even be important for a big purchase. Some consumers draw conclusions about the quality of a car at a dealer's showroom from the "thunk" of the door when it closes. Luxury-car makers try for a "new car smell" with an aroma of leather and wood, even though the car would really smell more like metal and adhesives as it comes off the production line in a factory.[7]

Many needs are culturally learned

Many needs are culturally (or socially) learned. The need for food, for instance, may lead to many specific food wants. Many Japanese enjoy sushi (raw fish), and their children learn to like it. Fewer Canadians, however, have learned to enjoy it.

Some critics argue that marketing efforts encourage people to spend money on learned wants totally unrelated to any basic need. For example, Europeans are less concerned about perspiration, and many don't buy or use antiperspirants. Yet Canadians spend millions of dollars on such products. Advertising says that using Ban deodorant "takes the worry out of being close." But is marketing activity the cause of the difference in the two cultures? Most research says that advertising can't convince buyers of something contrary to their basic attitudes and values.

Attitudes relate to buying

An **attitude** is a person's point of view toward something. The "something" may be a product, an advertisement, a salesperson, a firm, or an idea. Attitudes are an important topic for marketers because attitudes affect the selective processes, learning, and eventually the buying decisions people make.

Because attitudes are usually thought of as involving liking or disliking, they have some action implications. Beliefs are not so action-oriented. A **belief** is a person's opinion about something. Beliefs may help shape a consumer's attitudes but don't necessarily involve any liking or disliking. It is possible to have a belief—say, that Listerine PocketPak strips have a medicinal taste—without really caring what they taste like. On the other hand, beliefs about a product may have a positive or negative effect in shaping consumers' attitudes. For example, promotion for Splenda, a new no-cal sweetener in a yellow packet, informs consumers that it's "made from sugar so it tastes like sugar." A dieter who believes that Splenda will taste better

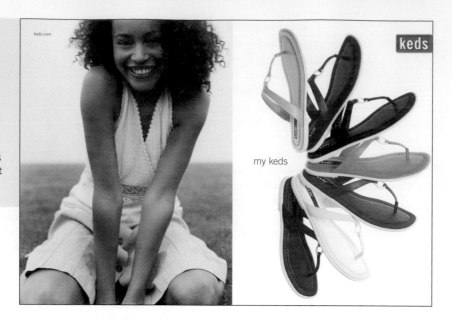

Many consumers (and retailers) still think of Keds as white sneakers. This ad is trying to change that perception by showcasing the brand's expansion into colourful new styles, such as slides, mules, and thongs. While the Keds marketing mix has changed, sometimes it takes time to change what and how consumers think.

because it is made from sugar might try it instead of just routinely rebuying another brand, like Equal. On the other hand, a person with diabetes might believe that he should avoid Splenda—like he avoids other products made from sugar—even though Splenda is actually suitable for people with diabetes.[8]

In an attempt to relate attitude more closely to purchase behaviour, some marketers stretched the attitude concept to include consumer "preferences" or "intention to buy." Managers who must forecast how much of their brand customers will buy are particularly interested in the intention to buy. Forecasts would be easier if attitudes were good predictors of intentions to buy. Unfortunately, the relationships usually are not that simple. A person may have positive attitudes toward Jacuzzi whirlpool bathtubs but no intention of buying one.

Try to understand attitudes and beliefs

Research on consumer attitudes and beliefs can sometimes help a marketing manager get a better picture of markets. For example, consumers with very positive attitudes toward a new product idea might provide a good opportunity—especially if they have negative attitudes about competitors' offerings. Or they may have beliefs that would discourage them from buying a product.

Marketing managers for Purina Dog Chow faced this challenge. Research showed that one segment of consumers thought that Purina was a great dog food, but they didn't buy it all of the time. They believed that their dogs would get bored with it. After all, people don't like eating the same thing all of the time. But dogs are not people. Vets have found dogs benefit from a good, consistent diet. So Purina developed an ad campaign to convince these dog owners that what they believed was not true. Each ad gave a dog's-eye-view reaction to being fed a different dog food. In one ad, after taking a few bites, the dog looks into the camera with a pained expression and walks away. He returns with a packet of antacid, which he drops in his water bowl. Advertising research and sales results both showed that the soft-sell ad hit the bull's-eye in convincing occasional customers that switching foods was not good. Many bought Purina more regularly, and Dog Chow sales increased by $36 million. Consumer beliefs—right or wrong—can have a significant impact on whether a strategy succeeds.[9]

Most marketers work with existing attitudes

Purina's efforts were successful in changing beliefs. But marketers generally try to understand the attitudes of their potential customers and work with them. Because attitudes tend to be enduring, it's usually more economical to work with consumer attitudes than to try to change them.

Marketing managers for new Olay Cleansing Cloths (and other Olay skin care products) wanted to take advantage of the familiar Oil of Olay brand name, but they realized that many consumers didn't have a positive association between "oil" and beauty. So the brand name was updated to just Olay and the logo of a woman's figure was changed slightly to appeal to younger women.

Changing negative attitudes may be necessary

Yet changing present attitudes—especially negative ones—is sometimes necessary. Consider the plight of auto companies that rely heavily on revenue from sales of minivans. It's hard to find a vehicle that is less hip than a minivan; most people associate them with carpooling, hauling groceries, and other not-so-glamorous activities. It's no wonder that lots of buyers who need passenger space have opted for the more rugged sport-utility vehicles. Even if they don't need a rugged vehicle, it helps their self-image. That may help explain why GM now refers to its minivans as "crossover sports vans" and why Nissan is pushing to make its minivan more sexy. Its recently redesigned Quest sports a lush interior and stylish lines, the ride is smoother, the handling is better, and ads position it as not just for moms, but for hot mamas. One two-page ad says "Passion built it. Passion will fill it up." Perhaps these efforts will help differentiate Quest from other minivans. And if other firms continue to spruce up their minivans attitudes may slowly change. But this is likely to be a slow, expensive effort. Changing negative attitudes is probably the most difficult job marketers face.[10]

Ethical issues may arise

Part of the marketing job is to inform and persuade consumers about a firm's offering. An ethical issue sometimes arises, however, if consumers have *inaccurate* beliefs. For example, many consumers are confused about what foods are really healthy. Marketers for a number of food companies have been criticized for packaging and promotion that take advantage of inaccurate consumer perceptions about the meaning of the words *lite* or *low-fat*. A firm's lite donuts may have less fat or fewer calories than its other donuts—but that doesn't mean that the donut is *low* in fat or calories. Similarly, promotion of a "children's cold formula" may play off parents' fears that adult medicines are too strong—even though the basic ingredients in the children's formula are the same and only the dosage is different. And when Lance Armstrong's winning smile appears in a Subaru ad, it's easy to forget that he's paid for his endorsement.

Marketers must also be careful about promotion that might encourage false beliefs, even if the advertising is not explicitly misleading. For example, ads for Ultra Slim-Fast low-fat beverage don't claim that anyone who buys the product will lose all the weight they want or look like the slim models who appear in the ads—but some critics argue that the advertising gives that impression.[11]

Meeting expectations is important

Attitudes and beliefs sometimes combine to form an **expectation**—an outcome or event that a person anticipates or looks forward to. In our Planters' peanuts example on the next page we learn that the words "Fresh Roast" and the type of package that

WOULD YOU LIKE THOSE PEANUTS WITH SUGAR AND CREAM?

Marketing managers for Planters' peanuts wanted a new package that would keep peanuts fresh. They also wanted the package to be a cue to promote freshness to consumers. They thought that they had the right idea when they put Planters Fresh Roast Salted Peanuts in a vacuum-packed bric-pac, like the ones that coffee comes in. They were confident that when consumers saw the vacuum-packed peanuts it would remind them that they were fresh roasted, just like with fresh-roasted coffee. To reinforce that message, Planters put the words "Fresh Roast" in large print on the front of the package—right under the Planters name and over the words "salted peanuts." The familiar Mr. Peanut trademark character was there too. He looked dapper with his top hat and cane pointing toward the words "Fresh Roast." This all seemed like a good idea, but it didn't work as planned.

One problem was that the peanuts weren't the same size and shape as coffee, so the bags were pretty lumpy. That made the words harder to read on supermarket shelves. The bags were supposed to be resealable. But that didn't work well because of the lumps. So once the bag was opened, the peanuts got stale. Consumers who expected extra freshness were disappointed. But other shoppers had a bigger surprise before they even left the store.

Some consumers opened the bag and put the contents into the grocery store's coffee grinder. You can imagine the gooey peanut butter mess that made. You can also imagine that the store manager was not happy with Planters. Were the consumers trying to make peanut butter? No. Everything on the bag made it clear that it was peanuts. However, the link of the bag with coffee was so strong that consumers didn't stop to think about it. Moreover, the new package came out at about the same time that flavoured coffees were just becoming popular. Hey, if some ad is telling you to try hazelnut-flavoured coffee, why not peanut-flavoured coffee too? No, Planters doesn't want to compete with Starbucks, so this package is off the market.[12]

mimicked coffee bags created an expectation so strong that people simply ignored the other cues on the bag like the Mr. Peanut logo and the brand name Planters. Consumer expectations often focus on the benefits or value that the consumer expects from a firm's marketing mix. This is an important issue for marketers because a consumer is likely to be dissatisfied if his or her expectations are not met. For example, when Dryel home dry-cleaning kits were introduced, ads portrayed Dryel as an alternative to expensive dry-cleaner services. Many consumers who tried it were disappointed because it failed to get out some stains and clothing still needed to be pressed.[13]

A key point here is that consumers may evaluate a product not just on how well it performs, but on how it performs *relative to their expectations*. When expectations are surpassed consumers are delighted but a product that otherwise might get high marks from a satisfied consumer may be a disappointment if there's a gap between what the consumer gets and what the consumer expects. Promotion that over-promises what the rest of the marketing mix can really deliver leads to problems in this area. Finding the right balance, however, can be difficult. Consider the challenge faced by marketing managers for Van Heusen shirts. A few years ago Van Heusen came up with a new way to treat its shirts so that they look better when they come out of the wash than previous wash-and-wear shirts. Van Heusen promoted these shirts as "wrinkle-free" and the label showed an iron stuffed in a garbage can. Most people agree that the new shirt is an improvement. Even so, consumers who buy a shirt expecting it to look as crisp as if it had just been ironed are disappointed. For them, the improvement is not enough.[14]

Personality affects how people see things

Many researchers study how personality affects people's behaviour, but the results have generally been disappointing to marketers. A trait like neatness can be associated with users of certain types of products—like cleaning materials. But marketing

Dimension		Examples	
Activities	Work	Vacation	Surfing Web
	Hobbies	Entertainment	Shopping
	Social events	Club membership	Sports
Interests	Family	Community	Food
	Home	Recreation	Media
	Job	Fashion	Achievements
Opinions	Themselves	Business	Products
	Social issues	Economics	Future
	Politics	Education	Culture
Demographics	Income	Geographic area	Occupation
	Age	Ethnicity	Family size
	Family life cycle	Dwelling	Education

managers have not found a way to use personality in marketing strategy planning.[15] As a result, they've stopped focusing on personality measures borrowed from psychologists and instead developed lifestyle analysis.

Psychographics focus on activities, interests, and opinions

Psychographics or **lifestyle analysis** is the analysis of a person's day-to-day pattern of living as expressed in that person's Activities, Interests, and Opinions— sometimes referred to as AIOs. Exhibit 6-5 shows a number of variables for each of the AIO dimensions—along with some demographics used to add detail to the lifestyle profile of a target market.

Lifestyle analysis assumes that marketers can plan more effective strategies if they know more about their target markets. Understanding the lifestyle of target customers has been especially helpful in providing ideas for advertising themes. Let's see how it adds to a typical demographic description. It may not help Toyota marketing managers much to know that an average member of the target market for a Highlander SUV is 34.8 years old, married, lives in a three-bedroom home, and has 2.3 children. Lifestyles help marketers paint a more human portrait of the target market. For example, lifestyle analysis might show that the 34.8-year-old is also a community-oriented consumer with traditional values who especially enjoys spectator sports and spends much time in other family activities. An ad might show the Highlander being used by a happy family at a ball game so the target market could really identify with the ad. And the ad might be placed on a TSN show whose viewers match the target lifestyle profile.[16]

Marketing managers for consumer products firms who are interested in learning more about the lifestyle of a target market sometimes turn to outside specialists for help. For example, SRI Consulting Business Intelligence (SRIC-BI), a research firm, offers a service called geoVALS (VALS is an abbreviation for values, attitudes, and lifestyles). GeoVALS uses psychographics to show where customers live and why they behave as they do; it is especially useful for targeting direct-mail ad campaigns. With another VALS service, SRIC-BI describes a firm's target market in terms of a set of typical VALS lifestyle groups (segments). An advantage of this approach is that SRIC-BI has developed very detailed information about the various VALS groups. For example, the VALS approach has been used to profile consumers in the United Kingdom, Germany, Japan, and Canada as well as the United States. However, the disadvantage of VALS—and other similar approaches—is that it may not be very specific to the marketing manager's target market.[17]

This type of segmentation profiling is destined to increase and become ever more sophisticated. Environics Analytics promotes one of their products with the following Web site introduction:

The Harley-Davidson marketing mix often emphasizes the lifestyle and psychographics of its target customers, not just the features of its popular motorcycles.

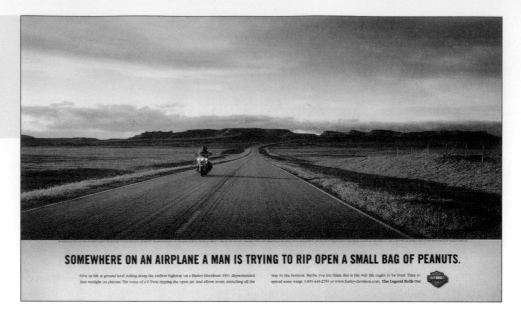

The Harley-Davidson marketing mix often emphasizes the lifestyle and psychographics of its target customers, not just the features of its popular motorcycles.

PRIZMCE is a new consumer segmentation system that classifies all Canadians into one of 66 lifestyle types—with names like Cosmopolitan Elite, Electric Avenues, Les Chics and Lunch at Tim's. The system marks the first time that a Canadian segmentation model has linked geodemographics to psychographics, incorporating "Social Values" data from Environics Research with demographics and product preferences to explain consumer behaviour.

PRIZMCE targets Canadian consumers using a cluster analysis of 2001 census demographics and exhaustive survey data on how Canadians spend their time and their money. The system can be used to improve the execution of many business strategies: customer profiling and acquisition, cross-selling and site selection, strategic planning and media buying. It has wide application for marketers in a variety of industries, including financial services, packaged goods, retail, telecommunications, government agencies, not-for-profits, media and automotive industries.[18]

INTERNET EXERCISE

Go to the SRIC-BI Internet site (www.sric-bi.com), click on *VALS Survey*, and then click on *Take the Survey* to review the VALS questionnaire. If you wish, complete the short questionnaire online. If you provide your e-mail address, SRIC-BI will provide you with your VALS profile.

SOCIAL INFLUENCES AFFECT CONSUMER BEHAVIOUR

We've been discussing some of the ways needs, attitudes, and other psychological variables influence the buying process. Now we'll see that these variables—and the buying process—are often affected by relations with other people too. We'll look at how the individual interacts with family, social class, and other groups who may have influence.

Who is the real decision maker in family purchases?

Relationships with other family members influence many aspects of consumer behaviour. We saw specific examples of this in Chapter 5 when we considered the effects of the family life cycle on family spending patterns. Family members may also share many attitudes and values, consider each other's opinions, and divide various buying tasks. In years past, most marketers targeted the wife as the family purchasing agent. Now, with sex-role stereotypes changed and with night and weekend shopping more popular, men and older children take more responsibility for shopping and decision making. In other countries, family roles vary. For example, in Norway women still do most of the family shopping.

Although only one family member may go to the store and make a specific purchase, when planning marketing strategy it's important to know who else may be involved. Other family members may have influenced the decision or really decided what to buy. Still others may use the product.

You don't have to watch much Saturday morning TV to see that Kellogg's knows this. Cartoon characters like Tony the Tiger tell kids about the goodies found in certain cereal packages and urge them to remind Dad or Mom to pick up that brand at the store. Kids also influence grown-up purchases. Surveys show that kids often have a big say in a family's choice of products such as apparel, cars, vacations, electronics, and health and beauty aids. Many parents say they choose vacations based on kids' opinions.

Family considerations may overwhelm personal ones

A husband and wife may jointly agree on many important purchases, but sometimes they may have strong personal preferences. However, such individual preferences may change if the other spouse has different priorities. One might want to take a family vacation to Disneyland—when the other wants a new Sony DVD recorder and high-definition large-screen TV. The actual outcome in such a situation is unpredictable. The preferences of one spouse might change because of affection for the other or because of the other's power and influence.

Buying responsibility and influence vary greatly depending on the product and the family. A marketer trying to plan a strategy will find it helpful to research the specific target market. Remember, many buying decisions are made jointly, and thinking only about who actually buys the product can misdirect the marketing strategy.[19]

Social class affects attitudes, values, and buying

Up to now, we've been concerned with individuals and their family relationships. Now let's consider how society looks at an individual and perhaps the family—in terms of social class. A **social class** is a group of people who have approximately equal social position as viewed by others in the society.

Almost every society has some social class structure. For example just a few of the many social class clusters defined by Environics Research are:

1. Lunch at Tim's—Working-class old and young in industrial towns and cities.
2. South Asian Society—Young upper-middle-class South Asian families.
3. Electric Avenues—Young upper-middle-class urban singles.[20]

In most countries, social class is closely related to a person's occupation, but it may also be influenced by education, community participation, where a person lives, income, possessions, social skills, and other factors—including what family a person is born into. Because of such differences, people in different social classes tend to have different beliefs and feelings.

In most countries there is *some* general relationship between income level and social class. But the income level of people within the same social class can vary greatly, and people with the same income level may be in different social classes. So income by itself is usually not a good measure of social class. And people in different social classes may spend, save, and borrow money in very different ways. For example, spending for clothing, housing, home furnishings, and leisure activities, as well as choices of where and how to shop, often vary with social class.

The Canadian class system is far less rigid than those in most countries. Children start out in the same social class as their parents—but they can move to a different social class depending on their educational levels or the jobs they hold. By contrast, India's social structure is much more rigid, and individuals can't easily move up in the class system.

Marketers want to know what buyers in various social classes are like. In Canada, simple approaches for measuring social class groupings are based on a person's *occupation, education,* and *type and location of housing.* By using marketing research surveys or available census data, marketers can get a feel for the social class of a target market.

What do these classes mean?

Many people think of Canada as a middle-class society. In fact, when asked to classify themselves, most people just say that they're middle class or working class. But social class studies suggest that in many marketing situations the social class groups are more distinct than that suggests. Various classes shop at different stores. Consider the difference between the shoppers you will find at Holt Renfrew versus those at The Bay. They prefer different treatment from salespeople. They buy different brands of products—even though prices are about the same. And they have different spending–saving attitudes, even when they have the same income level.

Reference groups are relevant too

A **reference group** is the people to whom an individual looks when forming attitudes about a particular topic. These reference groups can also change over time. Family and friends may dominate at one point but these may give way to reference groups you later form at university or with co-workers. People normally have several reference groups for different topics. Some they meet face-to-face. Others they just wish to imitate. In either case, they may take values from these reference groups and make buying decisions based on what the group might accept.

We're always making comparisons between ourselves and others. So reference groups are more important when others will be able to "see" which product or brand we're using. That's why hockey stars for example are sometimes used to endorse clothing or sports equipment. Kids can associate with their NHL heroes through buying the team jersey while "making a statement" to their friends. Influence is stronger for products that relate to status in the group. For one group, owning an expensive fur coat may be a sign of "having arrived." A group of animal lovers might view it as a

Bombardier have changed the designs and performance characteristics of their Ski-Doos as consumer attitudes and lifestyles have changed over time.

sign of bad judgment. In either case, a consumer's decision to buy or not buy a fur coat might depend on the opinions of others in that consumer's reference group.[21]

Reaching the opinion leaders who are buyers

An **opinion leader** is a person who influences others. Opinion leaders aren't necessarily wealthier or better educated. And opinion leaders on one subject aren't necessarily opinion leaders on another. For example, you may have a friend who is ahead of the curve in knowing about computer products, but you might not want that friend's opinion about new clothing styles and cosmetics. On the other hand, sometimes a leader in one area earns respect in another. Arnold Schwarzenegger became influential as an entertainer, but then he became an opinion leader in politics.

Each social class and age group tends to have its own opinion leaders. Some marketing mixes aim especially at these people since their opinions affect others and research shows that they are involved in many product-related discussions with "followers." Favourable word-of-mouth publicity from opinion leaders can really help a marketing mix. But the opposite is also true. If opinion leaders aren't satisfied, they're likely to talk about it and negatively influence others.[22]

Culture surrounds the other influences

Culture is the whole set of beliefs, attitudes, and ways of doing things of a reasonably homogeneous set of people. In Chapters 4 and 5, we looked at the broad impact of culture.

We can think of the Canadian culture, the French culture, or the Chinese-Canadian culture. People within these cultural groupings tend to be more similar in outlook and behaviour. But often it is useful to think of subcultures within such groupings. For example, within the Canadian culture, there are various religious and ethnic subcultures; also different cultural forces tend to prevail in different regions of the country.

Failure to consider cultural differences, even subtle ones, can result in problems. Even political parties use market research on ethnic cultures to help decide which candidates to run in various ridings. Political parties in Canada learned long ago the value of running candidates who shared the same ethnic and cultural background as the constituents in the electoral district they were trying to win. Voters like the idea of being able to communicate with a representative they feel shares their culture and language and understands their concerns.

Culture varies in international markets

Planning strategies that consider cultural differences in international markets can be even harder—and such cultures usually vary more. Each foreign market may need to be treated as a separate market with its own submarkets. Ignoring cultural differences—or assuming that they are not important—almost guarantees failure in international markets.

For example, Japanese consumers tend to snap up the latest gadgets, but only about 7 percent of Japanese households have a dishwasher. Appliance manufacturers who have tried to export their standard models to Japan have met with failure. One reason is that Japanese kitchens are much too small. Another problem is that fermented soybeans and other common Japanese foods tend to be very sticky. A standard dishwasher won't clean the dishes well. To address these cultural differences, manufacturers have developed small countertop machines with powerful jets to do the cleaning. But another obstacle remains. Many traditional Japanese feel that it is the woman's duty to wash the dishes. For many housewives, the guilt of having dishes done by a machine is worse than the aggravation of doing the job. Foreign firms had missed that, but Matsushita, a Japanese firm, got big increases in sales by focusing its promotion on conserving hot water and hygiene—rather than convenience—as the important reasons to buy a dishwasher.[23]

From a target marketing point of view, a marketing manager probably wants to aim at people within one culture or subculture. A firm developing strategies for two cultures often needs two different marketing plans.[24]

The attitudes and beliefs that we usually associate with culture tend to change slowly. Consider something as unemotional as a cup of tea. For a long time, tea has been a basic part of British culture. Taking a break for a cup of hot tea is tradition—a social moment with friends. In striking contrast, few British consumers ever drink iced tea. Lipton, Nestea, and other iced-tea makers would like to change that and ask, "Why not in Britain?" But they face tough odds—and it's not just the cooler weather in England. Consumers there associate iced tea with the dregs left in the bottom of the teapot after it's cooled off. It's not an appealing image, and it isn't likely to change quickly. Iced-tea sales won't pick up until it does.[25]

Because cultural forces tend to change slowly, marketers can often avoid problems by getting help from someone who already has a good understanding of the culture of the target customers. This helps to avoid problems. A Canadian high-tech company was set to enter the Latin American market with some very impressive accounting software. They even had their name selected for it—until their new technical writer who just happened to have spent some time in Latin America pointed out that their new name translated as the Latin American slang term for AIDS.

INDIVIDUALS ARE AFFECTED BY THE PURCHASE SITUATION

Needs, benefits sought, attitudes, motivation, and even how a consumer selects certain products all vary depending on the purchase situation. So different purchase situations may require different marketing mixes—even when the same target market is involved. Let's briefly consider some of the ways that the purchase situation can vary.

Purchase reason can vary

Why a consumer makes a purchase can affect buying behaviour. For example, a student buying a pen to take notes might pick up an inexpensive Bic. But the same student might choose a Cross pen as a gift for a friend. And a gadget-lover with

The nature of the purchase situation and the problem-solving processes that consumers use are typically different when they are shopping for a gift instead of an everyday item.

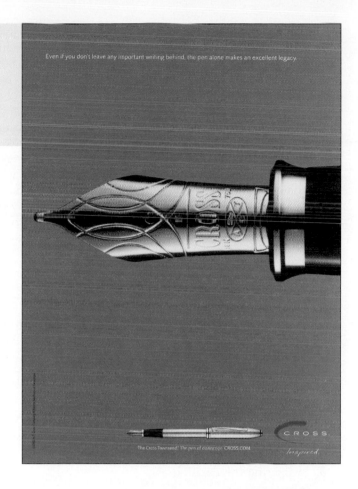

Even if you don't leave any important writing behind, the pen alone makes an excellent legacy.

The Cross Townsend™ The pen of distinction CROSS.COM

Inspired.

some free time on his hands might buy a digital pen that transfers handwritten notes to a tablet computer—just for the fun of trying it.

Time affects what happens

Time influences a purchase situation. *When* consumers make a purchase—and the time they have available for shopping—will influence their behaviour. A leisurely dinner or socializing with friends at a Starbucks induces different behaviour than grabbing a quick cup of 7-Eleven coffee on the way to work.

The urgency of the need is another time-related factor. A sports buff who needs a digital video recorder with an "instant replay" feature in time for the Super Bowl—that evening—might spend an hour driving across town in heavy traffic to get the right unit. In a different circumstance, the same person might order a unit online from a Web site and figure that the extra time for it to be shipped is well worth the money saved.

On the other hand, how long something takes may be relative. Our online shopper might be frustrated by a Web page that takes two minutes to load and abandon his virtual shopping cart after the digital video recorder is already selected. This happens all of the time online. On the other hand, you don't often see a consumer walk away from a shopping cart because of a two-minute wait in a checkout line at a store.

Surroundings affect buying too

Surroundings can affect buying behaviour. The excitement at an on-site auction may stimulate impulse buying. Checking out an auction online might lead to a different response.

Surroundings may discourage buying too. For example, some people don't like to stand in a checkout line where others can see what they're buying—even if the other shoppers are complete strangers.[26]

The rise of digital marketing	The purchasing situation has of course been heavily impacted by the huge increase of Internet usage by consumers. Internet purchases are clearly on the rise all over the world and they will continue to erode the sales generated by "bricks and mortar" retailers. In Canada, many consumers do not necessarily complete the transaction digitally, rather, they carry out all their research on the Internet and then buy the product at a retail store. Will we move more in the direction of pure Internet transactions? Most likely—as consumers learn to trust the electronic retailers (e-tailers), their shipping policies, and their security provisions.

This shift in buying behaviour is creating a whole new learning curve and a host of related problems for marketers. The challenges will focus on creating more consumer-oriented Web sites, increasing click-throughs and battling the problem of abandoned e-shopping carts. And those are just the beginning of many more marketing problems that will have to be researched and overcome.

CONSUMERS USE PROBLEM-SOLVING PROCESSES

The variables discussed affect *what* products a consumer finally decides to purchase. Marketing managers also need to understand *how* buyers use a problem-solving process to select particular products.

Most consumers seem to use the following five-step problem-solving process:

1. Becoming aware of, or interested in, the problem.
2. Recalling and gathering information about possible solutions.
3. Evaluating alternative solutions—perhaps trying some out.
4. Deciding on the appropriate solution.
5. Evaluating the decision.[27]

Exhibit 6-6 presents an expanded version of the buyer-behaviour model shown in Exhibit 6-1. Note that this exhibit integrates the problem-solving process with the whole set of variables we've been reviewing.

When consumers evaluate information about purchase alternatives, they may weigh not only a product type in relation to other types of products but also differences in brands within a product type *and* the stores where the products may be available. Future Shop and Costco both sell electronics, but consumers may choose one store over the other depending upon how much brand information they require. This can be a very complicated evaluation procedure, and, depending on their choice of criteria, consumers may make seemingly irrational decisions. If convenient service is crucial, for example, a buyer might pay list price for an unexciting car from a very convenient dealer. Marketers need a way to analyze these decisions.

It is important to understand the stages in the consumer's problem-solving process because it creates the opportunity to intervene at each level. If consumers are at the "awareness" stage in step one of the process, that suggests more advertising to make sure they know about your product. If they are at step three and evaluating alternatives, your advertising might change to communicate the superiority of your product's features versus those of competitors. It is vital that marketers adjust their marketing mix to match their target market's various stages in the problem-solving process.

Grid of evaluative criteria helps	On the basis of studies of how consumers seek out and evaluate product information, researchers suggest that marketing managers use an evaluative grid showing features common to different products (or marketing mixes). For example, Exhibit 6-7 shows some of the features common to three different cars a consumer might consider.

The first thing to notice about this sample grid is that it lists information about only a few cars. For a marketer, making it into a consumer's **consideration set**—the

Exhibit 6-6
An Expanded Model of the
Consumer Problem-Solving
Process

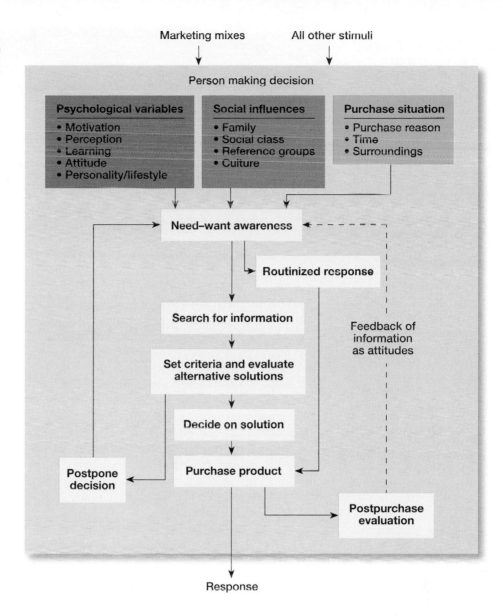

list of potential choices that a consumer will actually consider buying—can be critically important. When making purchase decisions, even important ones, consumers often save time and effort by first narrowing down to a few alternatives that they will evaluate more carefully. Sometimes they just narrow down based on a familiar brand name or because they remember an interesting ad. Other times a product might be suggested by a friend or get attention because it is displayed by a local retailer or shows up in an Internet search for information. But brands that don't at least make it into the consumer's consideration set are not likely to get close attention—or in the end be what the consumer chooses to buy.

The grid in Exhibit 6-7 encourages marketing managers to view each product in the consideration set as a bundle of features or attributes. The pluses and minuses in Exhibit 6-7 indicate one consumer's attitude toward each feature of each car. If members of the target market don't rate a feature of the marketing manager's brand with pluses, it may indicate a problem. The manager might want to change the product to improve that feature or perhaps use more promotion to emphasize an already acceptable feature. The consumer in Exhibit 6-7 has a minus under gas mileage for the Nissan. If the Nissan really gets better gas mileage than the other

Exhibit 6-7
Grid of Evaluative Criteria
for Three Car Brands

Brands	Common features			
	Gas mileage	Ease of service	Comfortable interior	Styling
Nissan	[−]	+	+	−
Saab	+	[−]	+	+
Subaru	+	+	[+]	[−]

Note: Pluses and minuses indicate a consumer's evaluation of a feature for a brand.

cars, promotion might focus on mileage to improve consumer attitudes toward this feature and toward the whole product.

Some consumers will reject a product if they see *one* feature as substandard—regardless of how favourably they regard the product's other features. The consumer in Exhibit 6-7 might avoid the Saab, which he saw as less than satisfactory on ease of service, even if it were superior in all other aspects. In other instances, a consumer's overall attitude toward the product might be such that a few good features could make up for some shortcomings. The comfortable interior of the Subaru (Exhibit 6-7) might make up for less exciting styling—especially if the consumer viewed comfort as really important.

Of course, most consumers don't use a grid like this. However, constructing such a grid helps managers think about what evaluative criteria target consumers consider really important, what consumers' attitudes are toward their product (or marketing mix) on each criteria, and how consumers combine the criteria to reach a final decision. Having a better understanding of the process should help a manager develop a better marketing mix.[28]

Three levels of problem solving are useful

The basic problem-solving process shows the steps consumers may go through trying to find a way to satisfy their needs—but it doesn't show how long this process will take or how much thought a consumer will give to each step. Individuals who have had a lot of experience solving certain problems can move quickly through some of the steps or almost directly to a decision.

It is helpful, therefore, to recognize three levels of problem solving: extensive problem solving, limited problem solving, and routinized response behaviour. See Exhibit 6-8. These problem-solving approaches are used for any kind of product. Consumers use **extensive problem solving** for a completely new or important need—when they put *much* effort into deciding how to satisfy it. For example, a music lover who wants to download music might decide to buy an MP3 player—but not have any idea what model to buy. After talking with friends to find out about their experiences with different models, she might do a search on the Internet to see if highly recommended models were still available, to get the details about features, and even to look for published product reviews. She might also compare prices listed by firms selling the players over the Internet. After thinking about her needs some more, she might want to visit a local dealer to listen to a Sony unit with an optional memory card to hold more tracks. And if she likes the sound—and the store has a good extended service guarantee at the right price—she'll buy it. This is not exactly an impulse purchase!

Consumers use **limited problem solving** when they're willing to put *some* effort into deciding the best way to satisfy a need. Limited problem solving is typical when a consumer has some previous experience in solving a problem but isn't certain

Exhibit 6-8   Problem-Solving Continuum

Low involvement
Frequently purchased
Inexpensive
Little risk
Little information needed

| Routinized response behaviour | Limited problem solving | Extensive problem solving |

High involvement
Infrequently purchased
Expensive
High risk
Much information desired

which choice is best at the current time. If our music lover also wanted some new compact discs for her car CD player, she would already know what type of music she enjoys. She might go to a familiar store and evaluate what new CDs they had in stock for her favourite types of music.

Consumers use **routinized response behaviour** when they regularly select a particular way of satisfying a need when it occurs. Routinized response behaviour is typical when a consumer has considerable experience in how to meet a need and has no need for additional information. For example, our music lover might routinely buy the latest recording by her favourite band as soon as it's available.

Most marketing managers would like their target consumers to buy their products in this routinized way. Some firms provide special services for frequent buyers, encourage repeat business with discounts, or do other things to build a good relationship so that the customer purchases from them in a routinized way.

Routinized response behaviour is also typical for **low-involvement purchases**—purchases that have little importance or relevance for the customer. Let's face it, buying a box of salt is probably not one of the burning issues in your life.[29]

Problem solving is a learning process

The reason problem solving becomes simpler with time is that people learn from experience—both positive and negative things. As consumers approach the problem-solving process, they bring attitudes formed by previous experiences and social training. Each new problem-solving process may then contribute to or modify this attitude set.

New concepts require an adoption process

When consumers face a really new concept, their previous experience may not be relevant. These situations involve the **adoption process**—the steps individuals go through on the way to accepting or rejecting a new idea. Although the adoption process is similar to the problem-solving process, learning plays a clearer role and promotion's contribution to a marketing mix is more visible.

In the adoption process, an individual moves through some fairly definite steps:

1. *Awareness*—the potential customer comes to know about the product but lacks details. The consumer may not even know how it works or what it will do.
2. *Interest*—if the consumer becomes interested, he or she will gather general information and facts about the product.
3. *Evaluation*—a consumer begins to give the product a mental trial, applying it to his or her personal situation.
4. *Trial*—the consumer may buy the product to experiment with it in use. A product that is either too expensive to try or isn't available for trial may never be adopted.
5. *Decision*—the consumer decides on either adoption or rejection. A satisfactory evaluation and trial may lead to adoption of the product and regular use. According to psychological learning theory, reinforcement leads to adoption.
6. *Confirmation*—the adopter continues to rethink the decision and searches for support for the decision—that is, further reinforcement.[30]

PepsiCo had to work with the adoption process when it introduced Pepsi One, a low-calorie cola. Many consumers are interested in staying trim, but diet sodas have an image of bad taste. In light of that, Pepsi's initial ads didn't directly say that Pepsi One was a diet drink. Rather, they used the slogan "True Cola Taste. One Calorie." But that confused a lot of consumers who couldn't tell what made it different from Diet Pepsi. As a result, consumer interest was not as great as Pepsi had expected. Because awareness and interest were low among consumers, retailers didn't devote much shelf space to Pepsi One, so it often wasn't even there for a consumer to consider. Even after a year on the market, trial was low. To help more consumers through the adoption process, Pepsi made changes. To build awareness and interest, new ads explained that Pepsi One was using a new sweetener, recently approved by the government, which tasted better than the sweetener used in other diet drinks. The ads showed consumers drinking Pepsi One and not being able to taste the difference from a regular cola; they used the tagline "Too good to be one calorie, but it is." Pepsi also changed the packaging graphics to put more emphasis on the sweetener at the point of purchase. To generate more trial, Pepsi pushed to get Pepsi One promoted in special end-aisle displays and stepped up its sampling program with taste-testing booths on campuses, in office cafeterias, and at movie theatres. Of course, consumers who tried Pepsi One would seek it out again only if they were satisfied with the taste.[31]

INTERNET EXERCISE

To make it easier for consumers to visualize how certain fashions will look, the Lands' End Web site (www.landsend.com) has an interactive "virtual model" feature. Go to the Lands' End Web site, click on *My Virtual Model*, and check out this feature. Do you think that it makes it easier to evaluate a potential purchase?

Dissonance may set in after the decision

A buyer may have second thoughts after making a purchase decision. The buyer may have chosen from among several attractive alternatives—weighing the pros and cons and finally making a decision. Later doubts, however, may lead to **dissonance**—tension caused by uncertainty about the rightness of a decision. Dissonance may lead a buyer to search for additional information to confirm the wisdom of the decision and so reduce tension. Without this confirmation, the adopter might buy something else next time or not comment positively about the product to others.[32]

Marketers know dissonance can be dangerous—even leading consumers to return the product to the store. That is why you sometimes get a phone call or a letter congratulating you on your new purchase and reinforcing your perception that you made a good decision in buying the product.

Exhibit 6-9
Relation of Problem-Solving Process, Adoption Process, and Learning (given a problem)

Problem-solving steps	Adoption process steps	Learning steps
1. Becoming aware of or interested in the problem	Awareness and interest	Drive
2. Gathering information about possible solutions	Interest and evaluation	Cues
3. Evaluating alternative solutions, perhaps trying some out	Evaluation, maybe trial	Reinforcement
4. Deciding on the appropriate solution	Decision	Response
5. Evaluating the decision	Confirmation	

SEVERAL PROCESSES ARE RELATED AND RELEVANT TO STRATEGY PLANNING

Exhibit 6-9 shows the interrelation of the problem-solving process, the adoption process, and learning. It is important to see this interrelation and to understand that promotion can modify or accelerate it. Also note that the potential buyers' problem-solving behaviour should affect how firms design their distribution systems. Similarly, customers' attitudes may determine how price sensitive they are and what price the firm should charge. Knowing how target markets handle these processes helps companies with their marketing strategy planning.

CONSUMER BEHAVIOUR IN INTERNATIONAL MARKETS

All the influences interact—often in subtle ways

You're a consumer, so you probably have very good intuition about the many influences on consumer behaviour that we've been discussing. For many different purchase situations you also know from experience which variables are most important. That's good, but it's also a potential trap—especially when developing marketing mixes for consumers in international markets. The less a marketing manager knows about the *specific* social and intrapersonal variables that shape the behaviour of target customers, the more likely it is that relying on intuition or personal experience will be misleading. We all have a tendency to try to explain things we don't understand by generalizing from what we do know. Yet when it comes to consumer behaviour, many of the specifics do not generalize from one culture to another.

Cadbury's effort to develop a Japanese market for its Dairy Milk Chocolate candy bar illustrates the point. Cadbury marketing managers conducted marketing research to find out more about candy preferences among Japanese consumers. The consumers said that they didn't like the high milk-fat content of Cadbury's bar. Cadbury's managers, however, reasoned that this reaction must be from lack of opportunity to

In Saudi Arabia, McDonald's modifies its marketing mix to adapt to the local culture. For example, the McDonald's in Riyadh is segregated by sex with a separate section for women and children.

become accustomed to the candy. After all, in most other countries it's the rich taste of the candy that turns consumers into "chocoholics." When Cadbury introduced the bar in Japan, it was a real flop. Taste preferences in other countries simply didn't generalize to Japan. It also wasn't just a matter of opportunity. The whole diet in Japan is different enough that eating the candy was unpleasant. By contrast, Dannon was successful because it took similar research findings to heart and dramatically modified its yogourt dairy desserts until they satisfied Japanese tastes.[33]

Sometimes an understanding of local cultural influences points to new ways to blend the four Ps. For example, Nestlé knew that free samples would be a good way to kick start the adoption process when it wanted to introduce a new line of food flavourings in Brazil. In the United States, it's common to distribute samples at stores. But local Nestlé managers knew a more effective approach. In Brazil, cooks rely on stoves that run on gas rather than electricity, so local deliverymen regularly bring canisters of gas into consumers' kitchens. Nestlé paid the deliverymen to offer their customers samples of the flavourings and explain how to use them. Consumers showed more interest in the samples when they were offered by someone they knew and trusted—and the conversation usually took place right by the stove where the flavourings would be used.[34]

Watch out for stereotypes, and change

Consumers in a foreign culture may be bound by some similar cultural forces, but that doesn't mean that they are all the same. So it's important to watch out for oversimplifying stereotypes. Further, changes in the underlying social forces may make outdated views irrelevant.

Many Westerners believe that the typical Japanese executive works very long hours and devotes very little time to family life. That stereotype has been highlighted in the Western media. It's still partly true. Yet many young Japanese executives now want a more balanced family life; they don't want to continue the almost total dedication to business accepted by the previous generation. A marketer who didn't recognize this change probably wouldn't fully understand these people, their needs, or buying behaviour in their families.

Developing a marketing mix that really satisfies the needs of a target market takes a real understanding of consumer behaviour and the varied forces that shape it. That holds whether the target market is local or halfway around the world. So when planning strategies for international markets, it's best to involve locals who have a better chance of understanding the experience, attitudes, and interests of your customers. Many companies, even very sophisticated ones, have faltered because they failed to heed that simple advice.

CONCLUSION

In this chapter, we analyzed the individual consumer as a problem solver who is influenced by psychological variables, social influences, and the purchase situation. All of these variables are related, and our model of buyer behaviour helps integrate them into one process. Marketing strategy planning requires a good grasp of this material.

Assuming that everyone behaves the way you do—or even like your family or friends do—can lead to expensive marketing errors.

Consumer buying behaviour results from the consumer's efforts to satisfy needs and wants. We discussed some reasons why consumers buy and saw that consumer behaviour can't be fully explained by only a list of needs.

You now realize that buying decisions can be pretty complex. Think about the Yoplait opening case. Why would they bother to put up a Web site for kids to become familiar with the brand name when it's mom who actually has to shell out the cash for the purchase?

We also saw that most societies are divided into social classes, a fact that helps explain some consumer behaviour. And we discussed the impact of reference groups and opinion leaders.

We presented a buyer-behaviour model to help you interpret and integrate the present findings—as well as any new data you might get from marketing research. As of now, the behavioural sciences can only offer insights and theories, which the marketing manager must blend with intuition and judgment to develop marketing strategies.

Companies may have to use marketing research to answer specific questions. But if a firm has neither the money nor the time for research, then marketing managers have to rely on available descriptions of present behaviour and guesstimates about future behaviour. Popular magazines and TV shows often reflect the public's shifting attitudes. And many studies of the changing consumer are published regularly in the business and trade press. That material—coupled with the information in this book—will help your marketing strategy planning.

Remember that consumers—with all their needs and attitudes—may be elusive, but they aren't invisible. Research has provided more data and understanding of consumer behaviour than business managers generally use. Applying this information may help you find your breakthrough opportunity.

KEY TERMS

economic buyers, 145

economic needs, 145

needs, 146

wants, 146

drive, 146

physiological needs, 147

safety needs, 147

social needs, 147

personal needs, 147

perception, 150

selective exposure, 150

selective perception, 150

selective retention, 150

learning, 150

cues, 150

response, 150

reinforcement, 151

attitude, 151

belief, 151

expectation, 153

psychographics, 155

QUESTIONS AND PROBLEMS

1. Can you apply any parts of Exhibit 6-9 that summarizes the problem-solving adoption or learning models to explain how Yoplait Tubes caught on in the Canadian market?

2. In your own words, explain economic needs and how they relate to the economic-buyer model of consumer behaviour. Give an example of a purchase you recently made that is consistent with the economic-buyer model. Give another that is not explained by the economic-buyer model. Explain your thinking.

3. Explain what is meant by a hierarchy of needs and provide examples of one or more products that enable you to satisfy each of the four levels of need.

4. Cut out or photocopy two recent advertisements: one full-page colour ad from a magazine and one large display from a newspaper. In each case, indicate which needs the ads are appealing to.

5. Explain how an understanding of consumers' learning processes might affect marketing strategy planning. Give an example.

6. Briefly describe your own *beliefs* about the potential value of wearing automobile seat belts, your *attitude* toward seat belts, and your *intention* about using a seat belt the next time you're in a car.

7. Give an example of a recent purchase experience in which you were dissatisfied because a firm's marketing mix did not meet your expectations. Indicate how the purchase fell short of your expectations—and also explain whether your expectations were formed based on the firm's promotion or on something else.

8. Explain psychographics and lifestyle analysis. Explain how they might be useful for planning marketing strategies to reach college students, as opposed to average consumers.

9. How should social class influences affect the planning of a new restaurant in a large city? How might the four Ps be adjusted?

10. Illustrate how the reference group concept may apply in practice by explaining how you personally are influenced by some reference group for some product. What are the implications of such behaviour for marketing managers?

11. Give two examples of recent purchases where the specific purchase situation influenced your purchase decision. Briefly explain how your decision was affected.

12. Give an example of a recent purchase in which you used extensive problem solving. What sources of information did you use in making the decision?

13. On the basis of the data and analysis presented in Chapters 5 and 6, what kind of buying behaviour would you expect to find for the following products: *(a)* a haircut, *(b)* a shampoo, *(c)* a digital camera, *(d)* a tennis racket, *(e)* a dress belt, *(f)* a cell phone, *(g)* life insurance, *(h)* an ice cream cone, and *(i)* a new chequing account? Set up a chart for your answer with products along the left-hand margin as the row headings and the following factors as headings for the columns: *(a)* how consumers would shop for these products, *(b)* how far they would travel to buy the product, *(c)* whether they would buy by brand, *(d)* whether they would compare with other products, and *(e)* any other factors they should consider. Insert short answers—words or phrases are satisfactory—in the various boxes. Be prepared to discuss how the answers you put in the chart would affect each product's marketing mix.

14. Review the Yoplait case that introduces this chapter, and identify the key terms (that appear in red) from the text of the chapter that you think are illustrated in the case. Write down each key term you identify and briefly explain how it is illustrated.

15. In a company's promotional messages is it better to under promise and over deliver or over promise and under deliver? How do these notions relate to customer recruitment and retention?

16. Give two examples of how marketing mixes might need to be adapted to reflect cultural differences.

17. Given the rise of electronic music download sites like iTunes and MP3 players, what impact do you think that will have on the sales of CDs by big music distributors like SONY BMG?

18. Before you buy an expensive high-involvement product do you surf the Net to look at Blogs? Why?

19. Would you buy an expensive high-definition TV from an online auction site like eBay Canada? Why or why not?

COMPUTER-AIDED PROBLEM

6. Selective Processes

RESOURCE REMINDER

Subma Inc., uses direct-mail promotion to sell magazine subscriptions. Magazine publishers pay Submag $3.12 for each new subscription. Submag's costs include the expenses of printing, ad dressing, and mailing each direct-mail advertisement plus the cost of using a mailing list. There are many suppliers of mailing lists, and the cost and quality of different lists vary.

Submag's marketing manager, Shandra Debose, is trying to choose between two possible mailing lists. One list has been generated from phone directories. It is less expensive than the other list, but the supplier acknowledges that about 10 percent of the names are out-of-date (addresses where people have moved away.) A competing supplier offers a list of active members of professional associations. This list costs 4 cents per name more than the phone list, but only 8 percent of the addresses are out-of-date.

In addition to concerns about out-of-date names, not every consumer who receives a mailing buys a subscription. For example, *selective exposure* is a problem. Some target customers never see the offer—they just toss out junk mail without even opening the envelope. Industry studies show that this wastes about 10 percent of each mailing—although the precise percentage varies from one mailing list to another.

Selective perception influences some consumers who do open the mailing. Some are simply not interested. Others don't want to deal with a subscription service. Although the price is good, these consumers worry that they'll never get the magazines. Submag's previous experience is that selective perception causes more than half of those who read the offer to reject it.

Of those who perceive the message as intended, many are interested. But *selective retention* can be a problem. Some people set the information aside and then forget to send in the subscription order.

Submag can mail about 25,000 pieces per week. Shandra Debose has set up a spreadsheet to help her study effects of the various relationships discussed above and to choose between the two mailing lists.

a. If you were Debose, which of the two lists would you buy based on the initial spreadsheet? Why?

b. For the most profitable list, what is the minimum number of items that Submag will have to mail to earn a profit of at least $3,500?

c. For an additional cost of $.01 per mailing, Submag can include a reply card that will reduce the percent of consumers who forget to send in an order (Percent Lost—Selective Retention) to 45 percent. If Submag mails 25,000 items, is it worth the additional cost to include the reply card? Explain your logic.

If you want to read the cases and view the video cases that accompany this chapter, visit the *Basic Marketing* Online Learning Centre at: **www.mcgrawhill.ca/olc/perreault**. Along with these cases and video cases, the OLC also has the software and user guide for this chapter's Computer-Aided Problem, as well as exercises, quizzes, articles, links, and other *interactive* content that will help you with your studies.

WHEN YOU FINISH THIS CHAPTER, YOU SHOULD

1. Understand why business purchases are influenced by a number of people.

2. Understand the problem-solving behaviour of organizational buyers.

3. Understand the different types of buyer–seller relationships.

4. Know the basic e-commerce methods used in organizational buying.

5. Know how buying by service firms, retailers, wholesalers, and governments is similar to—and different from—buying by manufacturers.

Marketing to Businesses and Organizations

METOKOTE CORP. SPECIALIZES IN PROTECTIVE COATING APPLICATIONS, LIKE POWDER-COAT AND LIQUID PAINT, THAT OTHER MANUFACTURERS NEED FOR THE PARTS AND EQUIPMENT THEY MAKE. FOR EXAMPLE, WHEN YOU SEE JOHN DEERE AGRICULTURAL, CONSTRUCTION, OR LAWN AND GROUNDS-CARE EQUIPMENT, MANY of the components have likely been coated (painted) in a MetoKote facility. In fact, Deere & Company and MetoKote have a close buyer–seller relationship. While Deere uses a variety of methods to identify suppliers and get competitive bids for many items it needs, it's different with MetoKote. Deere isn't going to switch to some other supplier just because other options provide cheaper coatings. MetoKote not only provides protective coatings for many John Deere products, it has built facilities right next to some Deere plants. When it's time for a component to be coated, a conveyer belt moves the part out of the John Deere plant and into the MetoKote facility. A short time later it's back—and it's green or yellow.

Deere favours this type of arrangement. It lets MetoKote's experts keep up with all of the environmental regulations and new technologies for coatings.

For a manufacturer, this type of relationship allows its facilities to be smaller and less costly to build and maintain, as the space isn't required for large spray booths. With MetoKote's facilities located nearby, newly coated parts for Deere do not have to be shipped, resulting in fewer scratches and dents—which results in higher quality parts with less rework required.

The decision to purchase coating services this way wasn't made casually. And it takes ongoing coopera-tion and good communication by many people in both organizations to make the relationship work. The decision additionally indicates that the choice of vendor rests on a variety of operational responsibilities within an organization—not exclusively with the purchasing department, but with finance, quality control, and in some cases even the production employees themselves.

John Deere needs high-quality protective finishes because its customers want durable, long-lasting equipment. Like John Deere, they want good value. Upholding Deere & Company's long reputation for quality service is equally as important as the company's reputation for a quality product.

For example, if a huge commercial farm in Brazil needs a repair part, workers can contact the local John Deere dealer, or at any hour, visit the company's Web site (www.johndeere.com) to access JDParts.com (www.jdparts.com), the online service that allows customers to learn which dealers have a needed part in inventory, check the price, and place an order for fast delivery. But helping John Deere customers and dealers earn better profits doesn't stop there.

For example, some John Deere farm equipment now includes a global positioning device that tracks exactly where the equipment goes when it is plowing, seeding, or cutting. The company's GreenStar™ system, which can easily be moved from machine to machine, uses advanced technology to measure average farm and field yields, and facilitate documentation of tillage practices, planting, spraying, weather, and more. These Deere innovations can help a farmer make better management decisions, increase productivity, and provide better value to the entire operation. Of course, a farmer who wants to buy a new tractor with global positioning may want a Deere dealer to take used equipment in trade. To help its dealers sell trade-ins, Deere runs a Web site that tracks used equipment its dealers have for sale (www.machinefinder.com). If a customer wants a used machine that the local dealer doesn't have, the local dealer can quickly find it at another Deere dealer. And dealers who are not worrying about getting rid of used inventory can focus more on sales of new equipment. Customers can also access several other online resources to find used John Deere equipment across all of its divisions. An important part of business-to-business marketing also involves supplying rapid access to parts and service for business customers. Downtime for industrial equipment is expensive. That's why John Deere maintains an extensive dealer network in Canada. Type "John Deere Canada" into your browser then click on dealer locator and follow the prompts. It is benefits like these that make Deere the supplier of choice for many business customers.[1]

BUSINESS AND ORGANIZATIONAL CUSTOMERS—A BIG OPPORTUNITY

Most of us think about individual final consumers when we hear the term *customer*. But many marketing managers aim at customers who are not final consumers. In fact, the total dollar value of purchases made by businesses greatly exceeds that made by consumers. As the John Deere case illustrates, the buying behaviour of these organizational customers can be very different from the buying behaviour of final consumers. Developing marketing strategies for these markets requires a solid understanding of who these customers are and how they buy. That is the focus of this chapter.

What types of customers are involved?

Business and organizational customers are any buyers who buy for resale or to produce other goods and services. Exhibit 7-1 shows the different types of customers in these markets. As you can see, not all of the organizational customers in these

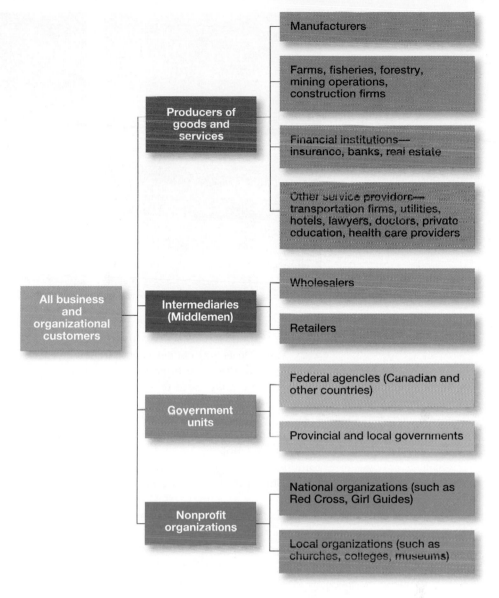

markets are business firms. Even so, to distinguish them from the final consumer market, managers sometimes refer to them collectively as the "business-to-business" market, or simply the *B2B market*.

Many characteristics of buying behaviour are common across these varied types of organizations. That's why the different kinds of organizational customers are sometimes loosely called "business buyers," "intermediate buyers," or "industrial buyers." As we discuss organizational buying, we will intermix examples of buying by many different types of organizations. Later in the chapter, however, we will highlight some of the specific characteristics of the different customer groups.

ORGANIZATIONAL CUSTOMERS ARE DIFFERENT

Organizations buy for a basic purpose

Like final consumers, organizations make purchases to satisfy needs. As a result, some of the initial issues for the marketing manager are the same. Questions like "Who are the buyers, what are their needs and characteristics and, what are the external environment factors that govern how they purchase?" still have to be

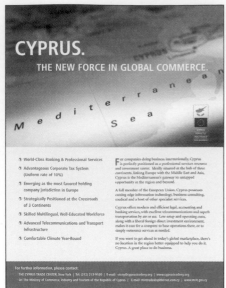

addressed. And, just as with consumer markets, the manager still has to contend with competitors and concerns about their strengths and weaknesses. But it's often easier to understand an organization's needs because most organizations make purchases for the same basic reason. They buy goods and services that will help them meet the demand for the goods and services that they in turn supply to their markets. In other words, their basic need is to satisfy their own customers and clients. A producer buys because it wants to earn a profit by making and selling goods or services. A wholesaler or retailer buys products it can profitably resell to its customers. A town government wants to meet its legal and social obligations to citizens. Similarly, a country club wants to help its members enjoy their leisure time.

Basic purchasing needs are economic

Organizational buyers are usually less emotional in their buying than final consumers. They typically focus on economic factors when they make purchase decisions.

Buyers try to consider the total cost of selecting a supplier and its particular marketing mix, not just the initial price of the product. For example, a hospital that needs a new type of digital X-ray equipment might look at both the original cost and ongoing costs, how it would affect doctor productivity, and of course the quality of the images it produces. The hospital might also consider the seller's reliability and general cooperativeness; the ability to provide speedy maintenance and repair, steady supply under all conditions, and reliable and fast delivery; and any past and present relationships (including previous favours and cooperation in meeting special requests).

The matter of dependability deserves further emphasis. An organization may not be able to function if purchases don't arrive when they're expected. For example, there's nothing worse to a manufacturer than shutting down a production line because sellers haven't delivered the goods. Dependable product quality is important too. For example, a bug in e-commerce software purchased by a firm might cause the firm's online order system to shut down. The costs of finding and correcting the problem—to say nothing about the cost of the lost business—could be completely out of proportion to the original cost of the software.

Even small differences are important

Understanding how the buying behaviour of a particular organization differs from others can be very important. Even seemingly trivial differences in buying behaviour may be important because success often hinges on fine-tuning the marketing mix.

Business buyers make purchases that help them satisfy the needs of their own customers. In this ad, Intel is targeting decision makers who make or influence all decisions with regard to the direction and operation of the business. Intel chose to feature GEOTrac, a small Canadian company less than two years old, to show how Intel technology has helped GEOTrac satisfy their customers' needs for efficient and reliable management of equipment and personnel in remote and northern parts of the country.

with intel built in, GEOTrac has
reliability built in

Sellers often approach each organizational customer directly, usually through a sales representative. This gives the seller more chance to adjust the marketing mix for each individual customer. A seller may even develop a unique strategy for each individual customer. Canadair for example will customize its regional jets to meet the needs of individual buyers. This approach carries target marketing to its extreme. But sellers often need unique strategies to compete for large-volume purchases.

In such situations, the individual sales rep takes much responsibility for strategy planning. The sales rep often coordinates the whole relationship between the supplier and the customer. That may involve working with many people—including top management—in both firms. This is relevant to your career planning since these interesting jobs are very challenging, and they pay well too.

Serving customers in international markets

Many marketers discover that there are good opportunities to serve business customers in different countries around the world. Specific business customs do vary from one country to another—and the differences can be important. For example, a salesperson working in Japan must know how to handle a customer's business card with respect. Japanese consider it rude to write notes on the back of a card or put it in a wallet while the person who presented it is still in the room. But the basic approaches marketers use to deal with business customers in different parts of the world are much less varied than those required to reach individual consumers.

This is probably why the shift to a global economy has been so rapid for many firms. Their business customers in different countries buy in similar ways and can be reached with similar marketing mixes. Moreover, business customers are often willing to work with a distant supplier who has developed a superior marketing mix.

Specifications describe the need

Organizational buyers often buy on the basis of a set of **purchasing specifications**— a written (or electronic) description of what the firm wants to buy. When quality is highly standardized, as is often the case with manufactured items, the specification may simply consist of a brand name or part number. With products like agricultural commodities, where there is more variation, the specification may include information about the grade of the product. Often, however, the purchase requirements are more complicated; then the specifications may set out detailed information about the performance standards the product must meet. Magna International Inc. is a major player in supplying parts as well as R&D to the automotive business in Canada. As a consequence, technical specifications need to be very exact so that Magna can provide detailed engineering requirements to their suppliers. Purchase specifications for services tend to be detailed because services are less standardized and usually are not performed until after they're purchased.

Customers may expect quality certification

Organizational customers considering a new supplier or one from overseas may be concerned about product quality. However, this is becoming less of an obstacle because of the International Standards Organization (ISO). **ISO 9000** is a way for a supplier to document its quality procedures according to internationally recognized standards. Organizations like the Canadian Space Agency who are responsible for the Canadarm used on the space shuttle and on space stations would be very interested in suppliers with ISO certification because the cost of substandard quality in parts and software could be catastrophic.

ISO 9000 assures a customer that the supplier has effective quality checks in place, without the customer having to conduct its own costly and time-consuming audit. Some customers won't buy from any supplier who doesn't have it. To get ISO 9000 certified, a company basically must prove to outside auditors that it documents in detail how the company operates and who is responsible for quality every step of the way.[2]

MANY DIFFERENT PEOPLE MAY INFLUENCE A DECISION

Purchasing managers are specialists

Many organizations, especially large ones, rely on specialists to ensure that purchases are handled sensibly. These specialists have different titles in different firms (such as procurement officer, supply manager, purchasing agent, or buyer), but basically they are all **purchasing managers**—buying specialists for their employers. In large organizations, they usually specialize by product area and are real experts.

Some people think purchasing is handled by clerks who sit in cubicles and do the paperwork to place orders. That view is out-of-date. Today, most firms look to their procurement departments to help cut costs and provide competitive advantage. In this environment, purchasing people have a lot of clout. And there are good job opportunities in purchasing for capable business graduates.

Salespeople often have to see a purchasing manager first—before they contact any other employee. These buyers hold important positions and take a dim view of sales reps who try to go around them. Rather than being "sold," these buyers want salespeople to provide accurate information that will help them buy wisely. They like information on new goods and services, and tips on potential price changes, supply shortages, and other changes in market conditions. Sometimes all it takes for a sales rep to keep a buyer up-to-date is to send an occasional e-mail. But a buyer can tell when a sales rep has the customer firm's interest at heart.

 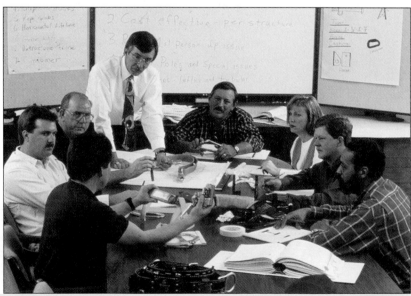

A person who works on a utility firm's high-power wires needs safe, durable climbing gear. A number of different people may influence the decision about which gear the firm should buy.

Exhibit 7-2
Roles Played in the Buying
Process

Stage of the buying proccess	Role
1. Need awareness	Users
2. Search for information	Influencers/gatekeepers
3. Set criteria and evaluate alternative solutions	Deciders
4. Purchases the product	Buyers
5. Use and post purchase evaluation of the product	Users

Although purchasing managers usually coordinate relationships with suppliers, other people may also play important roles in influencing the purchase decision.[3]

Multiple buying influence in a buying centre

Multiple buying influence means that several people—perhaps even top management—share in making a purchase decision. Possible buying influences include:

1. *Users*—perhaps production line workers or their supervisors.
2. *Influencers*—perhaps engineering or R&D people who help write specifications or supply information for evaluating alternatives.
3. *Buyers*—the purchasing managers who have the responsibility for working with suppliers and arranging the terms of the sale.
4. *Deciders*—the people in the organization who have the power to select or approve the supplier—often a purchasing manager but perhaps top management for larger purchases.
5. *Gatekeepers*—people who control the flow of information within the organization—perhaps a purchasing manager who shields users or other deciders. Gatekeepers can also include receptionists, secretaries, research assistants, and others who influence the flow of information about potential purchases.

Depending on how important the purchase is the organizational buying process, as outlined in Exhibit 7-2, moves through a number of stages just as it did with consumer buying behaviour.

An example shows how the different buying influences work. Suppose Electrolux, the Swedish firm that produces vacuum cleaners, wants to buy a machine to stamp out the various metal parts it needs. An assistant to the purchasing manager does an Internet search to identify possible vendors. However, the list that the assistant (a gatekeeper) prepares for the manager excludes a few vendors on the basis of an initial evaluation of information from their Web sites. The manager e-mails a description of the problem to vendors on the list. It turns out that each of them is eager to get the business and submits a proposal. Several people (influencers) at Electrolux help to evaluate the vendors' proposals. A finance manager worries about the high cost and suggests leasing the machine. The quality control people want a machine that will do a more accurate job—although it's more expensive. The production manager is interested in speed of operation. The production line workers and their supervisors want the machine that is easiest to use so workers can continue to rotate jobs.

The company president (the decider) asks the purchasing department to assemble all the information but retains the power to select and approve the supplier. The purchasing manager's assistant schedules visits for salespeople. After all these buying influences are considered, one of the purchasing agents for the firm (the buyer) will be responsible for making recommendations and arranging the terms of the sale.

It is helpful to think of a **buying centre** as all the people who participate in or influence a purchase. Different people may make up a buying centre from one decision to the next. This makes the marketing job difficult.

Exhibit 7-3
Multiple Influence and Roles
in the Buying Centre

The salesperson must study each case carefully. Just learning who to talk with may be hard, but thinking about the various roles in the buying centre can help. See Exhibit 7-3.

The salesperson may have to talk to every member of the buying centre—stressing different topics for each. That can be a pretty daunting and sometimes flat-out impossible task to do effectively. The dangerous part is that if you "turn off" one or more of those buying centre people with poor answers to their concerns you can kill the whole deal. The solution? On the really complicated deals, the sales rep acts as a "traffic cop" for her own organization's staff. She coordinates the seller's technical specialists with the potential buyer's specialists so that the appropriate sophisticated responses are given to the buying centre's influencers. When negotiations move to higher levels she makes sure her own senior people are there to interact with the buyer's deciders so that assurances are provided by the seller's CEO to the buyer's CEO if necessary—and it certainly will be when the deals get into the multimillions of dollars. (And you thought a sales rep was just a sales rep.)

This multilevel promotion process can not only complicate the job but also lengthen it. Approval of a routine order may take anywhere from a day to several months. On very important purchases—a new computer system, a new building, or major equipment—the selling period may take a year or more.[4]

Vendor analysis considers all of the influences

Considering all of the economic factors and influences relevant to a purchase decision is sometimes complex. A supplier or product that is best in one way may not be best in others. To try to deal with these situations, many firms use **vendor analysis**—a formal rating of suppliers on all relevant areas of performance. The purpose isn't just to get a low price from the supplier on a given part or service. Rather, the goal is to lower the *total costs* associated with purchases. Analysis might show that the best vendor is the one that helps the customer reduce costs of excess inventory, retooling of equipment, or defective parts.[5]

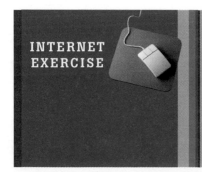

INTERNET EXERCISE

Hewlett-Packard is often praised for having a Web site (www.hp.ca) that is helpful to buyers for small and medium business. Visit the site and click on the link for *Small & Medium Business*. At the bottom of the page under *Learn & Use*, on the lower left-hand corner of the page click on *Business Templates*. On the right-hand side under *How-to Guides*, click on *Direct Marketing How-to Guide* and read the material that is available. Do you think that these types of resources help HP win new customers? Why or why not?

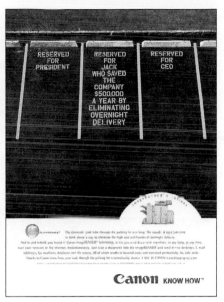

A seller's marketing mix may need to consider both the needs of the customer company as well as the needs of individuals who influence the purchase decision.

Behavioural needs are relevant too

Vendor analysis tries to focus on economic factors, but purchasing in organizations may also involve many of the same behavioural dimensions we discussed in Chapter 6. Purchasing managers and others involved in buying decisions are human, and they want friendly relationships with suppliers.

The purchasing people in some firms are eager to imitate progressive competitors or even to be the first to try new products. Such "innovators" deserve special attention when new products are being introduced.

The different people involved in purchase decisions are also human with respect to protecting their own interests and their own position in the company. That's one reason people from different departments may have different priorities in trying to influence what is purchased. Similarly, purchasing managers may want to avoid taking risks that might reflect badly on their decisions. They have to buy a wide variety of products and make decisions involving many factors beyond their control. If a new source delivers late or quality is poor, you can guess who will be blamed. Marketers who can help the buyer avoid risk have a definite appeal. In fact, this may make the difference between a successful and unsuccessful marketing mix.

A seller's marketing mix should satisfy *both* the needs of the customer company as well as the needs of individuals who influence the purchase. Therefore, sellers need to find an overlapping area where both can be satisfied. See Exhibit 7-4 for a summary of this idea.

Exhibit 7-4
Overlapping Needs of Individual Influencers and the Customer Organization

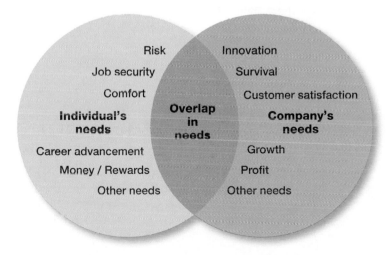

Ethical conflicts may arise

Although organizational buyers are influenced by their own needs, most are serious professionals who are careful to avoid a conflict between their own self-interest and company outcomes. Marketers must be careful here. A salesperson who offers one of his company pens to a prospect may view the giveaway as part of the promotion effort—but the customer firm may have a policy against any employee accepting *any* gift from a supplier. For example, General Motors developed an ethics policy that forbids employees from accepting anything of value from a vendor. It specifically includes entertainment—like a golf outing, a steak dinner, or tickets to a sporting event.

Most organizational buyers do their work ethically and expect marketers to do the same. Yet there have been highly publicized abuses. For example, some members of the site selection committee for the 2000 Olympic Games asked for personal gifts that may have influenced where the games were held. Several years ago, it was common practice for some shipping companies to take the purchasing managers of their best customers on fishing trips for trophy BC salmon. Similarly, some dairy products marketers used to run competitions—with substantial prizes for the dairy managers of supermarkets who could build the best displays using their products. These practices are now considered to be questionable—and often are banned outright—because they arguably compromise the role of the purchasing manager who is supposed to act on behalf of the company, not their own self-interest. Abuses of this sort have prompted many organizations to set up policies that prohibit a buyer or other employees from accepting anything from a potential supplier.

Marketers need to take concerns about conflict of interest very seriously. Part of the promotion job is to persuade different individuals who may influence an organization's purchase. Yet the whole marketing effort may be tainted if it even *appears* that a marketer has encouraged a person who influences a decision to put personal gain ahead of company interest.[6]

Purchasing may be centralized

If a large organization has facilities at many locations, much of the purchasing work may be done at a central location. With centralized buying, a sales rep may be able to sell to facilities all over a country—or even across several countries—without leaving a base city. In fact because Wal-Mart is the single largest purchaser of Procter & Gamble products, a group of several hundred employees are retained by P&G at Wal-Mart's headquarters to ensure their biggest customer is well served. Many purchasing decisions for agencies of the Canadian government are handled in Ottawa.

Many firms also have centralized controls on who can make purchases. A person who needs to purchase something usually completes a **requisition**—a request to buy something. This is frequently handled online to cut time and paper shuffling. Even so, there may be delays before a supervisor authorizes the requisition and a purchasing manager can select the "best" seller and turn the authorization into a purchase order. The process may take a few hours for a simple purchase—but it may turn into months for a complex purchase.

ORGANIZATIONAL BUYERS ARE PROBLEM SOLVERS

Three kinds of buying processes are useful

In Chapter 6, we discussed problem solving by consumers and how it might vary from extensive problem solving to routine buying. In organizational markets, we can adapt these concepts slightly and work with three similar buying processes: a new-task buying process, a modified rebuy process, or a straight rebuy.[7] See Exhibit 7-5.

Exhibit 7-5
Organizational Buying
Processes

Characteristics	Type of Process		
	New-Task Buying	Modified Rebuy	Straight Rebuy
Time Required	Much	Medium	Little
Multiple Influence	Much	Some	Little
Review of Suppliers	Much	Some	None
Information Needed	Much	Some	Little

New-task buying occurs when an organization has a new need and the customer wants a great deal of information. New-task buying can involve setting product specifications, evaluating sources of supply, and establishing an order routine that can be followed in the future if results are satisfactory. Multiple buying influence is typical in new-task buying. When Air Canada added Embraer light jets to their fleet the new-task buying procedure was very intense because the Brazilian based company and its jet were completely new to Air Canada and the purchase also represented a substantial long-term financial and strategic commitment.

A **straight rebuy** is a routine repurchase that may have been made many times before. Buyers probably don't bother looking for new information or new sources of supply. Most of a company's small or recurring purchases are of this type—but they take only a small part of an organized buyer's time. Important purchases may be made this way too—but only after the firm has decided what procedure will be "routine." Canadian National Railways (CN) for example might elect to buy grease and even larger purchases like fuel for its diesels on a straight rebuy basis because these products are routinely needed factor inputs for operating their trains.

The **modified rebuy** is the in-between process where some review of the buying situation is done—though not as much as in new-task buying. Sometimes a competitor will get lazy enjoying a straight rebuy situation. An alert marketer can turn these situations into opportunities by providing more information or a better marketing mix. A modified rebuy could also come into effect if Canadian National decided that there was a need to reevaluate its supplier at the end of their contract to provide fuel. This is because diesel fuel would constitute such a large portion of CN's operating overhead that they would occasionally review their purchasing to make sure they were getting the best deal from their suppliers.

New-task buying requires information

Customers in a new-task buying situation are likely to seek information from a variety of sources. See Exhibit 7-6. Keep in mind that many of the impersonal sources are readily available in electronic form online as well as in other formats. How much information a customer collects depends on the importance of the purchase and the level of uncertainty about what choice might be best. The time and expense of searching for information may not be justified for a minor purchase. But a major purchase often involves real detective work by the buyer.

Of course, the flip side of the new-task buying situation is that a seller's promotion has much more chance to have an impact. At the very least, the marketer needs to be certain that his or her firm will turn up in the buyer's search. In this regard, a good Web site is a crucial piece of insurance. Later we will talk more about the role of e-commerce at this stage, but for now you should see that even a simple Web site is likely to turn up in a buyer's Internet search.[8]

Exhibit 7-6
Major Sources of
Information Used by
Organizational Buyers

	Marketing sources	Nonmarketing sources
Personal sources	• Salespeople • Others from supplier firms • Trade shows	• Buying centre members • Outside business associates • Consultants and outside experts
Impersonal sources	• Advertising in trade publications • Sales literature • Sales catalogues • Web page	• Rating services • Trade associations • News publications • Product directories • Internet news pointcasts

What buying procedure becomes routine is critical

Once a buying firm gets beyond the early stages of a new-task buying decision, it needs to make important decisions about how it is going to deal with one or more suppliers to meet its needs. At one extreme, a buyer might want to rely on competition among all available vendors to get the best price on each and every order it places. At the other extreme, it might just routinely buy from one vendor with whom it already has a good relationship. In practice, there are common variations between these extremes.

BUYER–SELLER RELATIONSHIPS IN BUSINESS MARKETS

Close relationships may produce mutual benefits

There are often significant benefits of a close working relationship between a supplier and a customer firm. And such relationships are becoming common. Many firms are reducing the number of suppliers with whom they work—expecting more in return from the suppliers that remain. The best relationships involve real partnerships where there's mutual trust and a long-term outlook.

Closely tied firms can often share tasks at lower total cost than would be possible working at arm's length. Costs are sometimes reduced simply by reducing uncertainty and risk. A supplier is often able to reduce its selling price if a customer commits to larger orders or orders over a longer period of time. A large sales volume may produce economies of scale and reduce selling costs. The customer benefits from lower cost and also is assured a dependable source of supply.

A firm that works closely with a supplier can resolve joint problems. For example, it may cost both the supplier and the customer more to resolve the problems of a defective product after it is delivered than it would have cost to prevent the problem. Large metals producers like Alcan and Dofasco work closely with their customers to develop the very best fit between the alloys they produce and the metals application needs of their customers. Therefore it is better to develop the right alloy for the job at the outset than have the customer suffer the grief of having to issue product recalls later because of parts failures.

An important aspect of relationship marketing is that the buyer and the seller sometimes incur **switching costs**. These are costs that develop when the seller has to "customize" their product or service to meet the buyer's specific needs or when the buyer has to reconfigure their operations so they can be adapted to the seller's offering. Either way, switching costs make it more difficult to abandon the buyer–seller relationship so the linkage between both parties becomes harder to break. This can work to the seller's advantage because it becomes more difficult for a competitor to poach their customer. It can also work the other way and scare off a potential customer who may not want to commit to the switching costs. Switching costs can work to the buyer's advantage because the seller may have to configure their production or logistics systems to meet a particular customer's needs. The seller then incurs switching costs if they want to break from the relationship later.

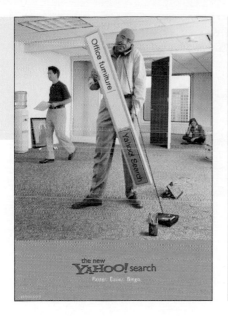

In business-to-business markets, the Internet is making it faster, easier, and less expensive for firms to search for and identify suppliers who can meet their needs.

The classic example of B2B switching costs occurred in the Canadian financial services sector. When global financing sources made it easier for customers to move their loans overseas in order to save just a few tenths of one percent in interest, customers became disloyal and the competition became intense. When banks began to offer other services like employee payroll or interactive financial computer systems however, companies thought twice about moving for a few extra basis points on their loan because they would also have to reconfigure important parts of their computer systems if they left their bank.

The same principle has been applied in the B2C (business-to-consumer) sector for Internet, phone, and TV services. If you become unhappy with your TV choices and wish to switch to a Star Choice satellite TV connection you may also have to make decisions about switching your Internet and phone service providers as well—not to mention the modem you may have purchased which now becomes surplus. By packaging your electronic services it becomes easier for you to buy—but also more difficult for you to change providers because you now have switching costs.

Switching costs are just one key component of Customer Relationship Management (CRM) that is designed to tie the customer more closely to the marketer. The whole idea of finding and retaining the best customers has spawned a major trend in the last decade. CRM software has been developed on a wide-scale basis to help B2B marketers create a closer linkage with customers and their needs on a corporate-wide basis and to provide customized personal service to their most preferred buyers. Among many features, CRM software can track customers' purchases, allow buyers to check shipments and inventory levels, and provide interactive real time links with the supplier's technical staff for on the spot problem solving.

At the opposite end of the spectrum from relationship marketing is transactions-based marketing. The buyer–seller interaction is dominated by distributive bargaining that focuses on highly competitive market prices where both parties try to make the best deal for themselves. Unlike the long-term trust-based interaction that characterizes the collaborative nature of relationship marketing, neither buyer nor seller are particularly interested in creating a loyal relationship. Commodity exchanges where raw resources like minerals or forest products are traded anonymously on a daily basis are a good example of **transactional marketing**.

Of course it is possible to have buyer–seller exchanges that fall between relationship-based and transactions-based interactions. It is also possible for the same marketer to have a relationship marketing interaction with one customer and a transactional interaction with another.

Relationships may not make sense

Although close relationships can produce benefits, they are not always best. A long-term commitment to a partner may reduce flexibility. When competition drives down prices and spurs innovation, the customer may be better off letting suppliers compete for the business. It may not be worth the customer's investment to build a relationship for purchases that are not particularly important or made that frequently.

It may at first appear that a seller would *always* prefer to have a closer relationship with a customer, but that is not so. Some customers may place orders that are too small or require so much special attention that the relationship would never be profitable for the seller. Also, in situations where a customer doesn't want a relationship, trying to build one may cost more than it's worth. Further, many small suppliers have made the mistake of relying too heavily on relationships with too few customers. One failed relationship may bankrupt the business.[9]

Powerful customer may control the relationship

Although a marketing manager may want to work in a cooperative partnership, that may be impossible with large customers who have the power to dictate how the relationship will work. For example, Duall/Wind, a plastics producer, was a supplier of small parts for Polaroid instant cameras. But when Duall/Wind wanted to raise its prices to cover increasing costs, Polaroid balked. Polaroid's purchasing manager demanded that Duall/Wind show a breakdown of all its costs, from materials to labour to profit. As Duall/Wind's president said, "I had a tough time getting through my head that Polaroid wanted to come right in here and have us divulge all that." But Polaroid is a big account—and it got the information it wanted. Polaroid buyers agreed to a price increase only after they were confident that Duall/Wind was doing everything possible to control costs.[10]

Buyers may still use several sources to spread their risk

Even if a marketing manager develops the best marketing mix possible and cultivates a close relationship with the customer, the customer may not give *all* of its business to one supplier. Buyers often look for several dependable sources of supply to protect themselves from unpredictable events such as strikes, fires, or floods in one of their suppliers' plants. A good marketing mix is still likely to win a larger share of the total business—which can prove to be very important. From a buyer's point of view, it may not seem like a big deal to give a particular supplier a 30 percent share of the orders rather than a 20 percent share. But for the seller that's a 50 percent increase in sales![11]

Reciprocity may influence relationship

We've emphasized that most buyer–seller relationships are based on reducing the customer's total procurement costs. However, for completeness we should mention that some relationships are based on reciprocity. **Reciprocity** means trading sales for sales—that is, "if you buy from me, I'll buy from you." If a company's customers also can supply products that the firm buys, then the sales departments of both buyer and seller may try to trade sales for sales. Purchasing managers generally resist reciprocity but often face pressure from their sales departments.

When prices and quality are otherwise competitive, an outside supplier seldom can break a reciprocity relationship. The outside supplier can only hope to become an alternate source of supply and wait for the competitor to let its quality slip or prices rise.

Reciprocity is often a bigger factor in other countries than it is in Canada. In Japan, for example, reciprocity is very common.[12]

The decision of which interaction to use with your customer deserves some serious thought. There are good reasons for choosing relationship marketing, transactional marketing, or something in between. A careful evaluation of the customer and their objectives is required before making your choice however. If you mistakenly take a relationship marketing approach with a transactional buyer, disaster awaits because you will negotiate on a cooperative basis where compromise is part of your strategy and your customer will bargain to get the best deal for himself—at your expense. Choose carefully.

We've been discussing some of the differences in how customer firms and their suppliers relate to each other. How a customer uses e-commerce is also related to these differences.

INTERNET E-COMMERCE IS RESHAPING MANY BUSINESS MARKETS

The Internet and new types of B2B e-commerce Web sites have changed the way that many purchase decisions are made. The Web is making it possible for all types of information to flow back and forth between buyers and sellers much more quickly and efficiently. This lowers the cost of the search for market information and, in many cases, the cost of transactions. For example, online order systems can cut out paper-shuffling bottlenecks, speed the delivery of purchases, and reduce inventory costs. We'll discuss distribution service related issues in more detail in Chapter 11.

Here, we'll consider basic e-commerce Web site resources that many buyers use and the role that they play. We'll describe them separately, but often one Web site (or linked set of Web sites) combines them.

Community sites mainly offer digital information

Like online trade magazines (or online trade associations), community sites offer information and communications of interest for specific industries. A Web site may focus on a single "community" or feature different sections for different industries. Community sites were among the first on the Web because many just put in digital form information that was already being distributed in other ways. Initially they relied on advertising revenue to operate, but now some of them charge fees or try to earn commissions based on sales referrals. The Council of Forest Industries (www.cofi.org) for example, represents 120 forest products facilities that produce about 80 percent of BC's softwood lumber shipments.

Catalogue sites make it convenient to search for products

Catalogue sites, as the name implies, offer digital product catalogues, usually for a number of different sellers. For example, PlasticsNet.com focuses on polymers and resins used in the plastics industry. The basic benefit of catalogue sites is that they make it easy for industrial buyers to search for a product and do one-stop shopping. For example, Grainger.com features a vast array of supply items that are used across many different industries. Catalogue sites are upgrading their service to make it easier for a buyer to place an order, track delivery status, and update inventory information. Many are improving the quality of the information available. For instance, rather than just give a basic description of an electric motor, a site might also provide a link so the buyer can download detailed engineering drawings and electrical details.

Exchanges bring buyers and sellers together

Exchanges operate much like a stock exchange (for example, the Toronto Stock Exchange) by bringing buyers and sellers together to agree on prices for commodities such as energy or chemicals (see, for example, www.chemconnect.com). Exchanges are sometimes independent intermediaries or they may be backed by major firms in the industry. Either way, an exchange must maintain a neutral role and not favour either buyers or sellers if it expects return visits.

Procurement hubs operate for the benefit of buyers

Procurement hub sites direct suppliers to particular companies (or divisions of a company) that need to make purchases. In some industries, recognized leaders have banded together to create procurement hubs. The big three automakers in the U.S. are doing this. These hubs make it easier for a larger number of suppliers to find out about the purchasing needs of customers in target industries. As a result, the number of suppliers competing for a buyer's business increases, and this tends to drive down selling prices or provide benefits to the buyer with respect to other terms of the sale. On the other hand, procurement hubs are a way for a seller to find out about and pursue sales opportunities with new customers (or new markets) without a lot of additional research or selling expense. The Canadian Public Tenders Gateway (www. marcan.net) helps companies identify public sector Internet sites that may publish notices for procurement opportunities. This provides a good source of one-stop shopping that helps Canadian firms quickly find governments looking for suppliers.

Interactive competitive bidding systems drive down prices

Most procurement hubs incorporate an interactive system to get competitive bids. **Competitive bids** are the terms of sale offered by different suppliers in response to the purchase specifications posted by the buyer. Usually, the focus is on the supplier's price. Firms have used the competitive bidding process for a long time. However, before the Internet it was usually too slow and too inconvenient to go through several rounds of bids. Now, however, it is fast and easy for a customer firm to run a *reverse auction*. Vendors are invited (via e-mail or at the procurement hub) to place a bid for a purchase with a given specification. Usually the bidding still focuses on price, but sometimes other terms of sale (like warranty period or delivery time) are considered as well. Each bid, and who made it, is typically visible to all potential bidders via the Web site. That way, other bidders can decide whether or not to offer the customer a lower price. Depending on the preferences of the customer, the bidding can be limited by a specific deadline.

Exhibit 7-7
Examples of Different B2B E-Commerce Sites Used by Organizational Buyers and Sellers

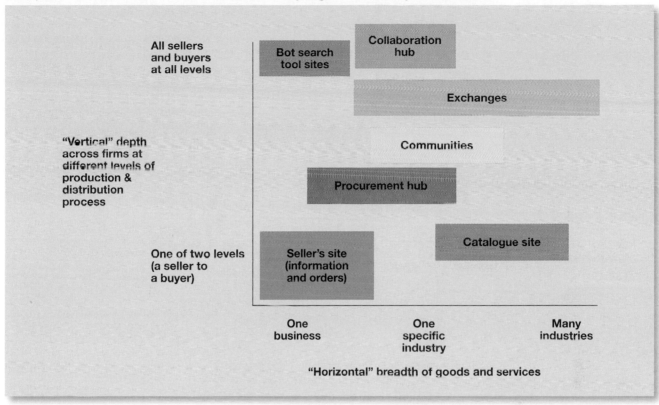

Auction sites focus on unique items

Auction sites tend to be more seller-driven and are especially popular for used items, surplus inventory, and perishable products (such as unsold advertising space or produce) that are unique and only available for sale once. For example, www.avbid.net runs auctions related to aircraft parts and services. At these auctions the seller lists and describes what's for sale, and potential buyers place their bids (what they would pay) at a Web site. Auctions use a variety of formats, but in general the highest bidder (prior to the deadline) purchases the product. Some auction sites also handle reverse auctions for the benefit of buyers. FreeMarkets (www.freemarkets.com) is a popular site that operates this way.

Collaboration hubs support cooperation

Collaboration hubs go beyond matching buyers and sellers for a one-time transaction and instead are designed to help firms work together. The collaboration might involve design, manufacturing, and distribution. Many of these sites focus on the needs of smaller firms, usually within a vertical industry. For instance, Citadon (www.citadon.com) provides a single online workplace for construction contractors to collaborate with architects, store blueprints, work through building permit requirements, and purchase building materials.

Web sites within and across industries

As the examples above suggest, some B2B e-commerce Web sites are specialized for firms at different levels of production and distribution within a particular industry. For example, one of these "vertical" sites that specializes in the plastics industry might be of interest to firms that make the basic chemicals from which plastics are formed, firms that create plastic injection molding equipment, and firms that use that equipment to make finished goods. On the other hand, some Web sites are designed to serve a broad ("horizontal") cross section of firms from different industries. For example, a horizontal site might serve manufacturers regardless of whether they produce bearings, truck frames, or construction equipment. See Exhibit 7-7.

Linking Buyers, Products, and Distributors

NATIONAL SEMICONDUCTOR DESIGNED its Web site to serve several key audiences. Purchasers from large customers who buy directly from the company's salespeople have private extranets with tailored information. National's other customers buy through distributors, but they can use National's site to research products and link directly to distributors' sites to buy. National also allows engineers and purchasing agents to look at information in ways that suit their individual needs.

National's LARGEST CUSTOMERS log on to private extranets that show their purchasing history and the shipping status of products they have ordered.

www.national.com

ENGINEERS click to look at lists of products in different categories.

PURCHASERS can create and save a list of products needed for a project...

...and then check the inventory of different distributors and link directly to their individual sites.

Each product has a page with detailed information...

...and links to distributors' individual pages.

On the DISTRIBUTOR's page, buyers can purchase a product with a credit card.

National Semiconductor's Web site, for example, creates easy e-commerce links between its customers, products, and distributors.

Internet (ro)bots search for products— by description

Purchasing managers often use Internet search engines to find what they need. For example, if a purchasing manager can specify a certain model of a product the search **"bot"** (short for *robot*) looks for Web sites where that product is mentioned. Some bots take things further and assemble price comparisons or e-mail distribution lists.

Bots can also help purchasing people figure out exactly how to describe what they want. By searching for descriptions of products in a broad product category, it is often possible to develop a better understanding not only of what alternatives exist but also of what specs are best for the particular need. Some purchasing managers are using this basic approach to locate hard-to-find, off-the-shelf products that eliminate the need for custom-produced items.

GE LIGHTS THE WAY FOR E-COMMERCE

General Electric is a true pioneer in e-commerce—and its successes provide evidence of what is possible. Even so, some of its early efforts didn't work. When it first tried to solicit bids from vendors over the Internet, it only focused on price. So it got a lot of lowball quotes from firms that didn't have the ability to fill orders. By 1995 GE was on a smarter track. It developed an Internet-based system called the Trading Process Network (TPN) that eliminated the delays of traditional purchasing approaches still using paper documents and snail mail. With TPN, a buyer for GE's lighting division could search the Net to find possible suppliers for the custom-made machine tools it needed. To eliminate the paper shuffle, electronic blueprints could be sent with a bid request via e-mail. As a GE purchasing manager put it, they could "simply point and click and send out a bid package to suppliers around the world." Suppliers could respond quickly, too. So a bid process that previously took about a month could be reduced to only days, or even hours.

When GE executives saw how e-commerce was improving their purchasing, they decided to offer the TPN service to outside companies. A small firm could try the TPN Web (www.getradeweb.com) for a fee of only $65 a month. However, the monthly fee for a large company was $70,000. That pricing gives a hint of the kind of savings big purchasers could reap—and why GE's Global eXchange Services (GXS) division pushed to develop a full-service Internet portal. GSX quickly grew to become one of the largest B2B e-commerce networks in the world—linking 100,000 trading partners involved in 1 billion exchanges a year worth $1 trillion in goods and service.

In 2002, GE sold GSX (except for a 10 percent share) for a whopping $800 million and now it operates as an independent e-commerce service provider. But GE has continued to drive down its own purchasing costs with e-commerce. To put this in perspective, in the first six months that GE used real-time, online competitive bidding, GE saved $480 million. However, GE does not purchase everything this way. And even when it relies on online competitive bidding it does not always select the lowest bid. A supplier with a higher bid may get the business when it offers a service or other value that meets GE's needs.[13]

More progress is needed

When everything else about a supplier's marketing mix is the same, a buyer would obviously prefer low prices. But "everything else" is not always the same. We considered examples of this earlier when we reviewed why a buyer might prefer closer relationships with fewer sellers. So Internet tools that focus primarily on lowering the purchase price do not necessarily lower total purchasing costs or provide a benefit in all types of purchases.

On the other hand, many firms are developing Web sites and Internet-based systems that help buyers and sellers work together in more efficient and effective relationships. National Semiconductor's Web site, for example, creates easy links between its customers, products, and distributors. Large customers get special services, like access to a secure Web site that shows specific purchase histories and production or shipping status of their orders. Smaller customers can get all the product information they need and then link directly to the order page for the distributor that serves them. This system does not go as far as some, but it illustrates how shared information and cooperation over the Internet is helping to create better relationships.[14]

E-commerce order systems like GE's are common

We've been discussing ways that managers use the Web. But some e-commerce computer systems *automatically* handle a large portion of routine order-placing. Buyers program decision rules that tell the computer how to order and leave the details of following through to the computer. For example, when an order comes in that requires certain materials or parts, the computer system automatically orders them from the appropriate suppliers, the delivery date is set, and production is scheduled.

If economic conditions change, buyers modify the computer instructions. When nothing unusual happens, however, the computer system continues to routinely rebuy as needs develop—electronically sending purchase orders to the regular supplier.

Obviously, it's a big sale to be selected as the major supplier that routinely receives all of a customer's electronic orders for the products you sell. Often this type of customer will be more impressed by an attractive marketing mix for a whole *line* of products than just a lower price for a particular order. Further, it may be too expensive and too much trouble to change the whole buying system just because somebody is offering a low price on a particular day.

It pays to have an ongoing relationship

In this sort of routine order situation, it's very important to be one of the regular sources of supply. For straight rebuys, the buyer (or computer) may place an order without even considering other potential sources. However, if a buyer believes that there are several suppliers who could meet the specs, the buyer may request competitive bids. If different suppliers' quality, dependability, and delivery schedules all meet the specs, the buyer will select the low-price bid. But a creative marketer needs to look carefully at the purchaser's specs—and the need—to see if other elements of the marketing mix could provide a competitive advantage.

Sellers' sales reps (and perhaps whole teams of people) regularly call on these customers, but *not* to sell a particular item. Rather, they want to maintain relations, become a preferred source, or point out new developments that might cause the buyer to reevaluate the present straight rebuy procedure and give more business to the sales rep's company.

Variations in buying by customer type

We've been discussing aspects of relationships and e-commerce that generally apply with different types of customer organizations—in both Canada and internationally. However, it's also useful to have more detail about specific types of customers.

MANUFACTURERS ARE IMPORTANT CUSTOMERS

There are not many big ones

One of the most striking facts about manufacturers is how few there are compared to final consumers. This is true in every country. The majority of Canadian manufacturing establishments are quite small with well over half employing less than 50 workers. While these smaller establishments are large in number, they are small in terms of the total manufacturing value that is produced. In small plants, the owners often do the buying. And they buy less formally than buyers in the relatively few large manufacturing plants—which employ most of the workers and produce a large share of the value added by manufacturing.

In other countries, the size distribution of manufacturers varies. But across different countries, the same general conclusion holds: Marketers often segment industrial markets on the basis of customer size because large firms do so much of the buying.

Customers cluster in geographic areas

In addition to concentration by company size, industrial markets are concentrated in certain geographic areas. Internationally, industrial customers are concentrated in countries that are at the more advanced stages of economic development.

Within a country, there is often further concentration in specific areas. In Canada, many factories are concentrated in big metropolitan areas—especially in the manufacturing corridor stretching between Quebec city and Windsor.

There is also concentration by industry. In Germany, for example, the steel industry is concentrated in the Ruhr Valley. In Canada it is again concentrated in the Ontario–Quebec region in proximity to most of the factory-based manufacturers that are the prime users of steel.

A firm like Alcoa Aluminum is likely to find that the majority of its customers are concentrated within a few industries that it can identify by North American Industry Classification System code number.

Business data often classifies industries

The products an industrial customer needs to buy depend on the business it is in. Because of this, sales of a product are often concentrated among customers in similar businesses. For example, apparel manufacturers are the main customers for zippers. Marketing managers who can relate their own sales to their customers' type of business can focus their efforts.

Detailed information is often available to help a marketing manager learn more about customers in different lines of business. The Canadian, Mexican, and U.S. governments collect and publish data by the **North American Industry Classification System (NAICS) codes**—groups of firms in similar lines of business. (NAICS is pronounced like "nakes.") The number of establishments, sales volumes, and number of employees—broken down by geographic areas—are given for each NAICS code. A number of other countries collect similar data, and some of them try to coordinate their efforts with an international variation of the NAICS system. However, in many countries data on business customers is incomplete or inaccurate.

The NAICS is a recent development that is being phased in over time. The phase-in makes it easier to use the system because in the past data were reported using Standard Industrial Classification (SIC) codes. Many of the codes are similar; check the Web site at www.naics.com for details. However, the move to the new system is helping business marketers. The NAICS system is suited for identifying new or fast-changing industries—and for marketers that spells opportunity. NAICS is also more detailed than SIC and works better for services such as financial institutions, health care providers, and firms in the entertainment business. The general logic of NAICS and SIC is similar. So let's take a closer look at how the NAICS codes work.

The NAICS code breakdowns start with broad industry categories such as construction (23), manufacturing (31), wholesale trade (42), finance and insurance (52), and so on. Within each two-digit industry breakdown, much more detailed data may be available for three-digit industries (that is, subindustries of the two-digit industries). For example, within the two-digit manufacturing industry (code 31) there are manufacturers of food (311), apparel (315) and others. Then each three-digit group of firms is further subdivided into more detailed four-, five-, and six-digit classifications. For instance, within the three-digit (315) apparel manufacturers there are four-digit subgroups for knitting mills (3151), cut and sew firms (3152), and producers of apparel accessories (3159). Exhibit 7-8 illustrates that breakdowns are more detailed as you move to codes with more digits. However, detailed data (say, broken down at the four-digit level) isn't available for all industries in every geographic area.

The government does not provide detail when only one or two plants are located in an area.

INTERNET EXERCISE

Comprehensive information about NAICS codes is available online (www.naics.com). At the Web site select *Code Search* and when the search page appears submit a query for the keyword "welding." If your firm was interested in selling its lasers to manufacturers of laser welding equipment, what is the NAICS code of the industry for which you would want to get a list of manufacturers?

Many firms find their *current* customers' NAICS codes and then look at NAICS-coded lists for similar companies that may need the same goods and services. Other companies look at which NAICS categories are growing or declining to discover new opportunities.

If companies aiming at business target markets in Canada know exactly who they are aiming at, readily available data organized by NAICS codes can be valuable. Most trade associations and private organizations that gather data on business markets also use these codes.

The NAICS codes are an improvement over the old approach, but they are not perfect. Some companies have sales in several categories but are listed in only one—the code with the largest sales. In addition, some businesses don't fit any of the categories very well. So although a lot of good information is available, the codes must be used carefully.[15]

PRODUCERS OF SERVICES—SMALLER AND MORE SPREAD OUT

The service side of the Canadian economy is large and has been growing fast. Service operations are also growing in some other countries. There are many good opportunities to provide these service companies with the products they need to support their operations. But there are also challenges.

Many firms are developing new strategies to target small businesses, a fast-growing sector of the economy. For example, Hertz offers double Frequent Flyer Miles and a free year of Club Gold membership to small businesses.

BMO Bank of Montreal® targets small businesses by offering customized products that meet their unique banking needs as well as by being the only bank in Canada to offer AIR MILES®†TM Reward Miles.

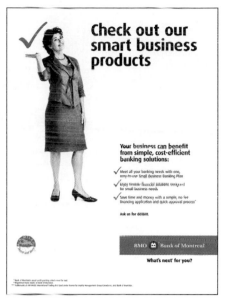

As with manufacturers, there is a large spread among the sizes of firms in the services field. The large service companies include the major banks like BMO Bank of Montreal®, major hotel chains like Delta or Sheraton, and insurance companies such as Sun Life. Given the size of Canada's land mass it is no accident that the transportation sector contains shipping services companies like Canadian Pacific and Canadian National Railways. These firms have purchasing departments that are like those in large manufacturing organizations. But as you might guess given the large number of service firms, most of them are small. They're also more spread out around the country than manufacturing concerns. Factories often locate where transportation facilities are good, raw materials are available, and it is less costly to produce goods in quantity. Service operations, in contrast, often have to be close to their customers.

Buying may not be as formal

Purchases by small service firms are often handled by whoever is in charge. This may be a doctor, lawyer, owner of a local insurance agency, or manager of a hotel. Suppliers who usually deal with purchasing specialists in large organizations may have trouble adjusting to this market. Personal selling is still an important part of promotion, but reaching these customers in the first place often requires more advertising. And small service firms may need much more help in buying than a large corporation.

Canon, the familiar name in office copiers, was very successful serving the needs of smaller service firms like law offices. Canon developed promotion materials to help first-time buyers understand differences in copiers. It emphasized that its machines were easy to use and maintain. And Canon also used retail channels to make the copiers available in smaller areas where there wasn't enough business to justify using a sales rep.[16]

RETAILERS AND WHOLESALERS BUY FOR THEIR CUSTOMERS

Most retail and wholesale buyers see themselves as purchasing agents for their target customers—remembering the old saying that "Goods well bought are half sold." Typically, retailers do *not* see themselves as sales agents for particular manufacturers. They buy what they think they can profitably sell. For example, Costco

® registered trademark of Bank of Montreal
®†TM Trademark of AIR MILES International Trading B.V. Used under license by Loyalty Management Group of Canada Inc. and Bank of Montreal.

not only change their selections among their outlets but you will notice their products and brands within one store are changed over time as well. Costco is a successful "big box" wholesaler in the B2B market but also a major retailer. The company is very aware of the differing target markets that each of their stores serve and how the needs of their segments change over the course of the year. The winter tires are replaced by the lawn mowers. Additionally however, Costco also have the good sense to work with manufacturers by offering promotional discounts on brands when it benefits both themselves and the manufacturer.

Similarly, wholesalers buy what they think their retailers can sell. In other words, they focus on the needs and attitudes of *their* target customers. This is where we introduce an important concept you will hear much more about later. **Derived demand** refers to the idea of looking at your "customer's customers." The idea being that whatever changes in customer demand affect a retailer for example, will eventually affect the wholesaler who sells to that retailer. A good marketing manager is always looking past his direct customer to watch that "downstream demand" so that he can anticipate any changes in final consumer demand. That helps him select products that he thinks consumers will like so that he can more easily sell to his retailers—because if the retailer does well, so does the wholesaler.

Committee buying is impersonal

Some buyers—especially those who work for big retail chains—are annoyed by the number of wholesalers' and manufacturers' representatives who call on them. Space in their stores is limited, and they simply are not interested in carrying every product that some salesperson wants them to sell. Consider the problem facing grocery chains. In an average week, 150 to 250 new items are offered to the buying offices of a large chain like Loblaws. If the chain accepted all of them, it would add 10,000 new items during a single year! Obviously, these firms need a way to deal with this overload.[17]

Decisions to add or drop lines or change buying policies may be handled by a *buying committee*. The seller still calls on and gives a pitch to a buyer—but the buyer does not have final responsibility. Instead, the buyer prepares forms summarizing proposals for new products and passes them on to the committee for evaluation. The seller may not get to present her story to the buying committee in person. This rational, almost cold-blooded approach certainly reduces the impact of a persuasive salesperson. On the other hand, it may favour a firm that has hard data on how its whole marketing mix will help the retailer to attract and keep customers.

| Buyers watch computer output closely | Most larger firms now use sophisticated computerized inventory replenishment systems. Scanners at retail checkout counters keep track of what goes out the door—and computers use this data to update the records. Safeway's checkout scanners can individually track the thousands of items they sell and automatically update inventory figures so they know what has to be reordered and when. This has been one of the biggest productivity boosters to ever hit the supermarket business. Even small retailers and wholesalers use automated control systems that create daily reports showing sales of every product. Buyers with this kind of information know, in detail, the profitability of the different competing products. If a product isn't moving, the retailer isn't likely to be impressed by a salesperson's request for more in-store attention or added shelf space. |

| Reorders are straight rebuys | Retailers and wholesalers usually carry a large number of products. A drug wholesaler, for example, may carry up to 125,000 products. Because they deal with so many products, most middlemen buy their products on a routine, automatic reorder basis—straight rebuys—once they make the initial decision to stock specific items. Automatic computer ordering is a natural outgrowth of computerized checkout systems. Sellers to these markets must understand the size of the buyer's job and have something useful to say and do when they call. |

| Some are not "open to buy" | Retail buyers are sometimes controlled by a miniature profit and loss statement for each department or merchandise line. In an effort to make a profit, the buyer tries to forecast sales, merchandise costs, and expenses. The figure for "cost of merchandise" is the amount buyers have budgeted to spend over the budget period. If the money has not yet been spent, buyers are **open to buy**—that is, the buyers have budgeted funds that can be spent during the current period. However, if the budget has been spent, they are no longer in the market and no amount of special promotion or price-cutting is likely to induce them to buy.[18] |

| Buying and selling are closely related | In wholesale and retail firms, there is usually a very close relationship between buying and selling. Buyers are often in close contact with their firm's salespeople and with customers. The housewares buyer for a local department store, for example, may even supervise the salespeople who sell housewares. Salespeople are quick to tell the buyer if a customer wants a product that is not available—especially if the salespeople work on commission. |

THE GOVERNMENT MARKET

| Size and diversity | Some marketers ignore the government market because they think that government red tape is more trouble than it's worth. They probably don't realize how big the government market really is. Government is the largest customer group in many countries—including Canada where they buy almost every kind of product and service. Governments run not only schools, police departments, and military organizations, but also public utilities, research laboratories, offices, hospitals, and liquor stores. These huge government expenditures cannot be ignored by an aggressive marketing manager. Collectively, all levels of government in Canada contribute about 40 percent of the country's GDP. |

| Competitive bids may be required | Government buyers in Canada are expected to spend money wisely—in the public interest—so their purchases are usually subject to much public review. To avoid charges of favouritism, most government customers buy by specification using a mandatory bidding procedure. Often the government buyer must accept the lowest |

I AM A POLICE OFFICER.

I HAVE X-RAY VISION. I HAVE THE POWER TO SEE A BANK ROBBERY FROM ACROSS TOWN. I HAVE THE POWER TO SEE HOW MANY PEOPLE ARE ROBBING THE BANK. I EVEN HAVE THE POWER TO SEE WHICH ONE IS WEARING THE SKI MASK. I AM MORE THAN A POLICE OFFICER.

I AM A NETWORK.

I AM THE X-RAY GLASSES. I AM A WIRELESS NETWORK. I HAVE THE POWER TO SEND VIDEO AND DATA WITHOUT THE USE OF WIRES. I HAVE THE POWER TO LINK A BANK'S SURVEILLANCE CAMERA TO A SQUAD CAR EN ROUTE TO A ROBBERY. I HAVE THE POWER TO SHOW COPS WHAT THEY'RE UP AGAINST. I AM HERE TO PROTECT AND SERVE. I AM MORE THAN A NETWORK.

CISCO SYSTEMS

THIS IS THE POWER OF THE NETWORK. now.
cisco.com/powernow

bid that meets the specifications. You can see how important it is for the buyer to write precise and complete specifications. Otherwise, sellers may submit a bid that fits the specs but doesn't really match what is needed.

Writing specifications is not easy—and buyers usually appreciate the help of well-informed salespeople. Salespeople *want* to have input on the specifications so their product can be considered or even have an advantage. One company may get the business—even with a bid that is not the lowest—because the lower bids don't meet minimum specifications.

Rigged specs are an ethical concern

At the extreme, a government customer who wants a specific brand or supplier may try to write the description so that no other supplier can meet all the specs. The buyer may have good reasons for such preferences—a more reliable product, prompt delivery, or better service after the sale. This kind of loyalty sounds great, but marketers must be sensitive to the ethical issues involved. Laws that require government customers to get bids are intended to increase competition among suppliers, not reduce it. Specs that are written primarily to defeat the purpose of these laws may be viewed as illegal bid rigging.

The approved supplier list

Specification and bidding difficulties aren't problems in all government orders. Some items that are bought frequently—or for which there are widely accepted standards—are purchased routinely. The government unit simply places an order at a previously approved price. To share in this business, a supplier must be on the list of approved suppliers. The list is updated occasionally, sometimes by a bid procedure. Government units buy school supplies, construction materials, and gasoline this way. Buyers and sellers agree on a price that will stay the same for a specific period—perhaps a year.

Negotiated contracts are common too

Contracts may be negotiated for items that are not branded or easily described, for products that require research and development, or in cases where there is no effective competition. Depending on the government unit involved, the contract may be subject to audit and renegotiation, especially if the contractor makes a larger profit than expected.

Negotiation is often necessary when there are many intangible factors. Unfortunately, this is exactly where favouritism and influence can slip in. And such influence is not unknown—especially in provincial and federal government. Nevertheless, negotiation is an important buying method in government sales—so a marketing mix should emphasize more than just low price.[19]

Learning what government wants

Keeping on top of all the federal, provincial, and local government agencies that buy goods and services is nearly impossible. Potential suppliers should focus on the government units they want to cater to and learn the bidding methods of those units. Then it's easier to stay informed since most government contracts are advertised. Target marketing can make a big contribution here—making sure the marketing mixes are well matched with the different bid procedures. In addition, good timing can be very important—because an agency may not be able to make a purchase if money isn't already set aside in its budget. Agencies often plan their budgets before the start of a new fiscal year. On the other hand, at the end of a fiscal year an agency may have some flexibility to use leftover funds to make purchases.

A marketer can learn a lot about potential government target markets from various government publications and by using the Internet. Type "supplier contracts Canada," "supplier contracts British Columbia," or "supplier contracts Newfoundland" into your browser. This will give you an idea of how easy it has now become to learn about the various protocols federal or provincial governments use to encourage supplier bidding on contracts. Governments at all levels are now interested in making it easier for businesses to supply them because of past criticisms about how complicated their bidding systems were and because of common sense—the more suppliers you have bidding on a contract to supply you—the better.

Trade magazines and trade associations provide information on how to reach schools, hospitals, highway departments, park departments, and so on. These are unique target markets and must be treated as such when developing marketing strategies.

Dealing with foreign governments

Selling to government units in foreign countries can be a real challenge. In many cases, a firm must get permission from the government in its own country to sell to a foreign government. Moreover, most government contracts favour domestic suppliers if they are available. Even if such favouritism is not explicit, public sentiment may make it very difficult for a foreign competitor to get a contract. Or the government bureaucracy may simply bury a foreign supplier in so much red tape that there's no way to win.

Is it unethical to "buy help"?

In some countries, government officials expect small payments (grease money) just to speed up processing of routine paperwork, inspections, or decisions from the local bureaucracy. Outright influence peddling—where government officials or their friends request bribe money to sway a purchase decision—is common in some markets. In the past, marketers from some countries have looked at such bribes as a cost of doing business. However, the Corruption of Foreign Public Officials Act now prohibits Canadian firms from paying bribes to foreign officials. The act does allow for "facilitation payments," to expedite business under certain conditions. Also, if the payments are legal in the foreign jurisdiction, that is also a defence for the Canadian firm. It would be naive to believe that all foreign markets view the "cost of doing business" the way we do in Canada. As one North American telecommunications president said privately, "It's a simple as this—does our company want to be allowed to even bid on [that] foreign contract? If we do we have to pay." That may be reality—but it doesn't make it ethical.

CONCLUSION

In this chapter, we considered the number, size, location, and buying behaviour of various types of organizational customers—to try to identify logical dimensions for segmenting markets and developing marketing mixes. We looked at who makes and influences organizational buying decisions, and how multiple influences may make the marketing job more difficult. We also saw that the nature of the buyer and the buying situation are relevant and that the problem-solving models of buyer behaviour introduced in Chapter 6 apply here, with modifications.

Buying behaviour—and marketing opportunities—may change when there's a close relationship between a supplier and a customer. Some buyers and sellers however don't want relationship marketing and prefer to work on a transactional marketing basis. Still others may prefer a relationship in between these two extremes. Looking back to the interaction between John Deere and Metokote at the start of this chapter, what are the switching costs and benefits for each of the parties of the relationship?

We also looked at how buyers use e-commerce in the buying process. Some capabilities, like interactive competitive bidding, have already had a major impact. And much progress is underway toward fostering more efficient relationships.

The chapter focuses on aspects of buying behaviour that often apply to different types of organizational customers. However, we discussed some key differences in the manufacturer, services, intermediary, and government markets.

A clear understanding of organizational buying habits, needs, and attitudes can aid marketing strategy planning. And since there are fewer organizational customers than final consumers, it may even be possible for some marketing managers (and their salespeople) to develop a unique strategy for each potential customer.

This chapter offers some general principles that are useful in strategy planning—but the nature of the products being offered may require adjustments in the plans. Different product classes are discussed in Chapter 9. Variations by product may provide additional segmenting dimensions to help a marketing manager fine-tune a marketing strategy.

KEY TERMS

business and organizational customers, 174
purchasing specifications, 177
ISO 9000, 177
purchasing managers, 178
multiple buying influence, 179
buying centre, 179
vendor analysis, 180

requisition, 182
new-task buying, 183
straight rebuy, 183
modified rebuy, 183
switching costs, 184
transactional marketing, 185
reciprocity, 186
procurement hub, 188

competitive bids, 188
auction sites, 189
"bot," 190
North American Industry Classification System (NAICS) codes, 193
derived demand, 196
open to buy, 197

QUESTIONS AND PROBLEMS

1. Should customer relationship marketing be used with all of your buyers?

2. In buying a computer how would your purchasing behaviour differ from that of a manager buying a computer for a corporation?

3. Briefly discuss why a marketing manager should think about who is likely to be involved in the buying centre for a particular purchase. Is the buying centre idea useful in consumer buying? Explain your answer.

4. If a hospital were planning to buy expensive MRI scanning equipment (to detect tumours), who might be involved in the buying centre? Explain your answer and describe the types of influence that different people might have.

5. Describe the situations that would lead to the use of the three different buying processes for a particular product—lightweight bumpers for a pickup truck.

6. Why would an organizational buyer want to get competitive bids? What are some of the situations when competitive bidding can't be used?

7. What do you think of the Internet site for used equipment run by John Deere (www.machinefinder.com)? How would this help the company recruit more dealers to retail their equipment?

8. Explain why a customer might be willing to work more cooperatively with a small number of suppliers rather than pitting suppliers in a competition against each other. Give an example that illustrates your points.

9. Would a tool manufacturer need a different marketing strategy for a big retail chain like RONA than for a single hardware store run by its owner? Discuss your answer.

10. How do you think a furniture manufacturer's buying habits and practices would be affected by the specific type of product to be purchased? Consider fabric for upholstered furniture, a lathe for the production line, cardboard for shipping cartons, and lubricants for production machinery.

11. Discuss the importance of target marketing when analyzing organizational markets. How easy is it to isolate homogeneous market segments in these markets?

12. Explain how NAICS codes might be helpful in evaluating and understanding business markets. Give an example.

13. Considering the nature of retail buying, outline the basic ingredients of promotion to retail buyers. Does it make any difference what kinds of products are involved? Are any other factors relevant?

14. The government market is obviously an extremely large one, yet it is often slighted or even ignored by many firms. Red tape is certainly one reason, but there are others. Discuss the situation and be sure to include the possibility of segmenting in your analysis.

15. Some critics argue that the Corruption of Foreign Public Officials Act puts Canadian businesses at a disadvantage when competing in foreign markets with suppliers from other countries that do not have similar laws. Do you think that this is a reasonable criticism? Explain your answer.

COMPUTER-AIDED PROBLEM

7. Vendor Analysis

RESOURCE REMINDER

CompuTech Inc., makes circuit boards for microcomputers. It is evaluating two possible suppliers of electronic memory chips.

The chips do the same job. Although manufacturing quality has been improving, some chips are always defective. Both suppliers will replace defective chips. But the only practical way to test for a defective chip is to assemble a circuit board and "burn it in"— run it and see if it works. When one chip on a board is defective at that point, it costs $2.00 for the extra labour time to replace it. Supplier 1 guarantees a chip failure rate of not more than 1 per 100 (that is, a defect rate of 1 percent). The second supplier's 2 percent defective rate is higher, but its price is lower.

Supplier 1 has been able to improve its quality because it uses a heavier plastic case to hold the chip. The only disadvantage of the heavier case is that it requires CompuTech to use a connector that is somewhat more expensive.

Transportation costs are added to the price quoted by either supplier, but Supplier 2 is farther away so transportation costs are higher. And because of the distance, delays in supplies reaching CompuTech are sometimes a problem. To ensure that a sufficient supply is on hand to keep production going, CompuTech must maintain a backup inventory—and this increases inventory costs. CompuTech figures inventory costs— the expenses of finance and storage—as a percentage of the total order cost.

To make its vendor analysis easier, CompuTech's purchasing agent has entered data about the two suppliers on a spreadsheet. He based his estimates on the quantity he thinks he will need over a full year.

a. Based on the results shown in the initial spreadsheet, which supplier do you think CompuTech should select? Why?

b. CompuTech estimates it will need 100,000 chips a year if sales go as expected. But if sales are slow, fewer chips will be needed. This isn't an issue with Supplier 2; its price is the same at any quantity. However, Supplier 1's price per chip will be $1.95 if CompuTech buys less than 90,000 during the year. If CompuTech only needs 84,500 chips, which supplier would be more economical? Why?

c. If the actual purchase quantity will be 84,500 and Supplier 1's price is $1.95, what is the highest price at which Supplier 2 will still be the lower-cost vendor for CompuTech? (Hint: You can enter various prices for Supplier 2 in the spreadsheet—or use the analysis feature to vary Supplier 2's price and display the total costs for both vendors.)

If you want to read the cases and view the video cases that accompany this chapter, visit the *Basic Marketing* Online Learning Centre at: **www.mcgrawhill.ca/olc/perreault**. Along with these cases and video cases, the OLC also has the software and user guide for this chapter's Computer-Aided Problem, as well as exercises, quizzes, articles, links, and other *interactive* content that will help you with your studies.

WHEN YOU FINISH THIS CHAPTER, YOU SHOULD

1. Know about marketing information systems.

2. Understand a scientific approach to marketing research.

3. Know how to define and solve marketing problems.

4. Know about getting secondary and primary data.

5. Understand the role of observing, questioning, and using experimental methods in marketing research.

Improving Decisions with Marketing Information

When you see the array of products—strips, gels, swabs, and more—on drugstore shelves to make your smile whiter and brighter, it's easy to forget that just a few years ago this category of products—for a combination of oral care and beauty needs—didn't exist. Movie stars would pay Hollywood dentists thousands of dollars for special whitening treatments, but the rest of us would just envy their pearly smiles.

That changed after research convinced marketing managers for Crest oral care products that this unmet need was a big opportunity. A variety of marketing research approaches were employed. For example, focus group interviews suggested that consumers would be excited about a do-it-yourself whitening treatment that was effective, simple to use, and affordable. Responses by representative samples of consumers to survey questionnaires confirmed that this was a large market. Online product concept tests revealed that there would be demand even at a price around $50, which would cover development and introductory promotion costs. On the other hand, research also revealed that dentists, who

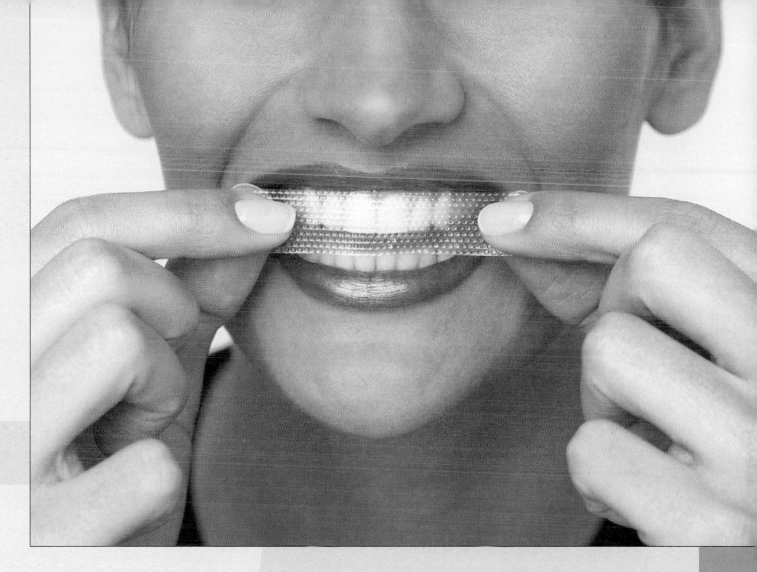

are influential in recommending oral care products, were concerned that the product might eat into their business.

When the R&D people came up with the idea of using a clear, tape-like strip that works by sticking to the teeth, product effectiveness tests confirmed that consumers could see a difference in whiteness. Research also showed that 30 minutes was the consumer limit for wearing the strips. Research even helped in selecting a brand name, Crest Whitestrips, and in focusing the positioning with advertising copy on "easy to use" and "superior whitening versus toothpaste" benefits.

Rather than work with traditional test markets in retail stores, marketing managers used infomercials and ads in consumer magazines to explain the product and direct consumers to a Web site (www.whitestrips.com) where they could buy Whitestrips. That approach not only produced sales quickly but also showed retailers that there was strong demand, even at a $44 retail price. Moreover, by doing studies on the Internet, researchers were able to deliver consumer test market input to marketing managers within days. For example, when researchers found that 80 percent of customers were female rather than the 50/50 split of men and women that was expected, the ad agency refined the focus of the advertising media.

When Whitestrips went into national distribution, the new product launch was one of the most successful in 20 years. Within a year, sales of Whitestrips surpassed $200 million and the product became the category leader. A professional version of Whitestrips for dentists to sell contributed to this success. Some dentists reported that the strips even helped increase interest in other types of cosmetic dentistry.

Competitors weighed in quickly with entries such as Colgate's Simply White, and that increased price competition. But research continues to play a crucial role in shaping Whitestrips marketing. For example, three years after introducing the original Whitestrips, research data from Information Resources Inc., showed that Crest Whitestrips was still the leader in the category with more than half of total sales. To maintain that lead, Crest introduced new products. One was Crest Night Effects, a lower-priced product, which is dabbed on the teeth and worn while sleeping. The other was a premium version of Whitestrips. It has a higher concentration of the whitening ingredient, but perhaps the bigger selling point is that it works in half the time. Many retailers took shelf space away from competitors to stock all three of Crest's whitening products. Based on internal sales data, they knew competitors were losing sales to both Colgate and Crest.[1]

The Whitestrips case shows that successful marketing strategies require information about potential target markets and their likely responses to marketing mixes as well as about competition and other marketing environment variables. Managers also need information for implementation and control. Without good information, managers are left to guess—and in today's fast-changing markets, that invites failure.

RADICAL CHANGES ARE UNDERWAY IN MARKETING INFORMATION

Marketing managers for some companies make decisions based almost totally on their own judgment—with very little hard data. The manager may not even know that he or she is about to make the same mistake that the previous person in that job already made! When it's time to make a decision, they may wish they had more information. But by then it's too late, so they do without.

MIS makes information available and accessible

Many firms realize that it doesn't pay to wait until you have important questions you can't answer. They anticipate the information they will need. They work to develop a *continual flow of information* that is available and quickly accessible when it's needed.

A **marketing information system (MIS)** is an organized way of continually gathering, accessing, and analyzing information that marketing managers need to make decisions.

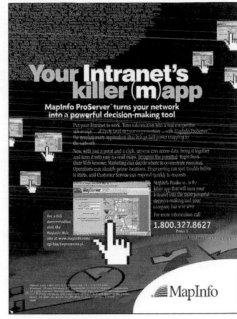

We won't cover all of the technical details of planning for an MIS. But you should understand what an MIS is so you know some of the possibilities. So we'll be discussing the elements of a complete MIS as shown in Exhibit 8-1. As part of that review, we'll highlight how technology is changing MIS use.

Get more information—faster and easier

Basic MIS concepts are not very different today than they were 20 years ago. However, advances in information technology have ushered in *radical* improvements. Now it is easy to set up and use an MIS. A short time ago, exchanging data among remote computers was very difficult. Now, it's standard. Managers have access to much more information. It's instantly available, and often just a mouse click away.

The *type* of information available is also changing dramatically. Until recently, marketing managers relied on computers mainly for number crunching. The multimedia revolution in computing lifted that limitation. Now it doesn't matter whether marketing information takes the form of a report, spreadsheet, database, presentation, photo, graphic, video, or table of statistics. It is all being created on computer. So it

Exhibit 8-1
Elements of a Complete Marketing Information System

can be easily stored and accessed by computer. When we talk about a "database" of marketing information, it may include all types of information, not just numbers.

An intranet is easy to update

Many firms, even very small ones, have their own **intranet**—a system for linking computers within a company. An intranet works like the Internet. However, to maintain security, access to Web sites or data on an intranet is usually limited to employees. Even so, information is available on demand. Further, it's a simple matter to "publish" new information to a Web site as it becomes available.

In any case, you seldom have all the information you need. Both customers and competitors can be unpredictable. Getting the precise information you want may cost too much or take too long. For example, data on international markets is often incomplete, outdated, or difficult to obtain. So a manager often must decide what information is really critical and how to get it.

Marketing managers must help develop an MIS

Computers are getting easier to use, but setting up and supporting an MIS still requires technical skill. In fact, converting an existing MIS to take advantage of Internet capabilities can be a real challenge. So in some companies, an MIS is set up by a person or group that provides *all* departments in the firm with information technology support. Or it may be set up by marketing specialists.

These specialists are important, but the marketing manager should play an important role, too. Marketing managers know what data they've routinely used or needed in the past. They can also foresee what types of data might be useful. They should communicate these needs to the specialists so the information will be there when they want it and in the form they want it.

Decision support systems put managers online

An MIS system organizes incoming information into a **data warehouse**—a place where databases are stored so that they are available when needed. You can think of a data warehouse as a sort of electronic library, where all of the information is indexed extremely well. Firms with an MIS often have information technology specialists who help managers get specialized reports and output from the warehouse. However, to get better decisions, most MIS systems now provide marketing managers with a decision support system. A **decision support system (DSS)** is a computer program that makes it easy for a marketing manager to get and use information *as he or she is making decisions*.

A decision support system usually involves some sort of **search engine**—a computer program that helps a marketing manager find information that is needed. For example, a manager who wants sales data for the previous week or day might search for any database or computer file that references the term *unit sales* as well as the relevant data. The search engine would identify any files where that term appeared. If there were many, the manager could narrow the search further (say by specifying the product of interest).

When the search is focused on numerical data, simply finding the information may not go far enough. Thus, a DSS typically helps change raw data—like product sales for the previous day—into more *useful information*. For example, it may draw graphs to show relationships in data—perhaps comparing yesterday's sales to the sales on the same day in the last four weeks. The MIS that managers at Frito-Lay use illustrates the possibilities.

All of Frito-Lay's salespeople are equipped with hand-held computers. Throughout the day they input sales information at the stores they visit. In the evening they send all the data over telephone lines to a central computer, where it is analyzed. Within 24 hours marketing managers at headquarters and in regional offices get reports and graphs that summarize how sales went the day before—broken down by brands and locations. The information system even allows a manager to zoom in and take a closer look at a problem in Regina or a sales success in Halifax.[2]

Some decision support systems go even further. They allow the manager to see how answers to questions might change in various situations. For example, a manager at Kraft Foods may want to estimate how much sales will increase if the firm uses a certain type of promotion in a specific market area. The DSS will ask the manager for a *personal* judgment about how much business could be won from each competitor in that market. Then, using this input and drawing on data in the database about how the promotion had worked in other markets, the system will make a sales estimate using a marketing model. A **marketing model** is a statement of relationships among marketing variables. For example, the adoption or problem-solving processes you learned about in Chapter 6 are used by sales people in electronics stores like The Source By Circuit City when you are considering an expensive purchase such as one of their laptops. They know you are going to move through a series of psychological stages and their job is to supply you with the right information at the right time to help in your decision.

In short, the decision support system puts managers online so they can study available data and make better marketing decisions—faster.[3]

Information for planning, implementation, and control

Once marketing managers use an MIS—and perhaps a DSS—they are eager for more information. They realize that they can improve all aspects of their planning—blending individual Ps, combining the four Ps into mixes, and developing and selecting plans. Further, they can monitor the implementation of current plans, comparing results against plans and making necessary changes more quickly. For example, LensCrafters is one of the largest chains of eyewear stores in Canada and the U.S. Each of its stores carries a very large selection of frame styles, lenses, and sunglasses tailored not only to the age, gender, and ethnic makeup of the local market but also to what is selling at that particular store. Shifts in eyewear fashions can come fast. So managers at LensCrafters routinely analyze sales data available in the firm's marketing information system. By breaking down sales by product, store, and time period, they can spot buying trends early and plan for them.[4]

Many firms are not there yet

Of course, not every firm has a complete MIS system. And in some firms that do, managers don't know how to use what's there. A major problem is that many managers are used to doing it the old way—and they don't think through what information they need.

One sales manager thought he was progressive when he asked his assistant for a report listing each sales rep's sales for the previous month and the current month. The assistant quickly found the relevant information on the firm's intranet, put it into an Excel spreadsheet, and printed out the report. Later, however, she was surprised to see the sales manager working on the list with a calculator. He was figuring the percentage change in sales for the month and ranking the reps from largest increase in sales to smallest. The spreadsheet software could have done all of that—instantly—but the sales manager got what he *asked for,* not what he really needed. An MIS can provide information—but only the marketing manager knows what problem needs solving. It's the job of the manager—not the computer or the MIS specialist—to ask for the right information in the right form.

MIS use is growing rapidly

Some people think that only large firms can develop an effective MIS. In fact, just the opposite may be true. Big firms with complicated marketing programs often face a challenge trying to develop an MIS from scratch. And once a large firm has a system in place it may be very costly to switch to something better. It can be easier for small firms because they are often more focused. They can get started with a simple system and then expand it as needs expand. There is a lot of opportunity in this area for students who are able and willing to apply computer skills to solve real marketing problems.[5]

New questions require new answers

MIS systems tend to focus on recurring information needs. Routinely analyzing such information can be valuable to marketing managers. But it shouldn't be their only source of information for decision making. They must try to satisfy ever-changing needs in dynamic markets. So marketing research must be used—to supplement data already available and accessible through the MIS.

WHAT IS MARKETING RESEARCH?

Research provides a bridge to customers

The marketing concept says that marketing managers should meet the needs of customers. Yet today, many marketing managers are isolated in company offices—far from potential customers.

This means marketing managers have to rely on help from **marketing research**—procedures to develop and analyze new information to help marketing managers make decisions. One of the important jobs of a marketing researcher is to get the "facts" that are not currently available. Ultimately however, the objective of marketing research is to help make better marketing decisions.

Who does the work?

Most large companies have a separate marketing research department to plan and carry out research projects. These departments often use outside specialists—including interviewing and tabulating services—to handle technical assignments. Further, they may call in specialized marketing consultants and marketing research organizations to take charge of a research project.

Small companies (those with less than $4 or $5 million in sales) usually don't have separate marketing research departments. They often depend on their salespeople or managers to conduct what research they do.

Some nonprofit organizations have begun to use marketing research—usually with the help of outside specialists. For example, many politicians rely on research firms to conduct surveys of voter attitudes.[6]

Ethical issues in marketing research

The basic reason for doing marketing research is to get information that people can trust in making decisions. But research often involves many hidden details. A person who wants to misuse marketing research to pursue a personal agenda can often do so.

Perhaps the most common ethical issues concern decisions to withhold certain information about the research. For example, a manager might selectively share only those results that support his or her viewpoint. Others involved in a decision might never know that they are getting only partial truths. Or during a set of interviews, a researcher may discover that consumers are interpreting a poorly worded question many different ways. If the researcher doesn't admit the problem, an unknowing manager may rely on meaningless results.

Another problem involves more blatant abuses. It is unethical for a firm to contact consumers under the pretense of doing research when the real purpose is to sell something. For example, some political organizations have been criticized for surveying voters to find out their attitudes about various political candidates and issues. Then, armed with that information, someone else calls back to solicit donations. Legitimate marketing researchers don't do this!

Another major issue that has developed, especially in the last few years, is the right to consumer privacy and the ethical handling of data about people. Canada has federal privacy laws governed by the Personal Information Protection and Electronic Documents Act (PIPEDA). Some of the highlights of the act deal with the following issues regarding consumer privacy:

1. Information has to be used for the purposes to which the consumer originally agreed.
2. The right to know what information has been collected and the ability to see and correct that information is established.
3. The researcher has to gain informed consent from the consumer before using the information and it can't be passed to someone else without the consumer's permission.
4. Information on consumers must be current, accurate as possible, and protected from unauthorized access by outsiders.
5. The information can only be kept for the purposes collected.
6. The market researcher has to maintain a formal system for dealing with consumer complaints that includes someone in the organization specifically responsible for dealing with the elements of PIPEDA.

These are only a few of the sections in the act and they have been much reduced for brevity. It is strongly suggested you type PIPEDA into a search engine like google.ca and review the entire act. The fines for contravention of the act are substantial.

The relationship between the researcher and the manager sometimes creates an ethical conflict. Managers must be careful not to send a signal that the only acceptable results from a research project are ones that confirm their existing viewpoints. Researchers are supposed to be objective, but that objectivity may be swayed if future jobs depend on getting the "right" results.[7]

Effective research usually requires cooperation

Good marketing research requires cooperation between researchers and marketing managers. Researchers must be sure their research focuses on real problems.

Marketing managers must be able to explain what their problems are and what kinds of information they need. They should be able to communicate with specialists in the specialists' language. Marketing managers may only be "consumers" of research. But they should be informed consumers—able to explain exactly what they want from the research. They should also know about some of the basic decisions made during the research process so they know the limitations of the findings.

For this reason, our discussion of marketing research won't emphasize mechanics but rather how to plan and evaluate the work of marketing researchers.[8]

THE SCIENTIFIC METHOD AND MARKETING RESEARCH

The scientific method—combined with the strategy planning framework we discussed in Chapter 2—can help marketing managers make better decisions.

The **scientific method** is a decision-making approach that focuses on being objective and orderly in *testing* ideas before accepting them. With the scientific method, managers don't just *assume* that their intuition is correct. Instead, they use their intuition and observations to develop **hypotheses**—educated guesses about the relationships between things or about what will happen in the future. Then they test their hypotheses before making final decisions.

A manager who relies only on intuition might introduce a new product without testing consumer response. But a manager who uses the scientific method might say, "I think (hypothesize) that consumers currently using the most popular brand will prefer our new product. Let's run some consumer tests. If at least 60 percent of the consumers prefer our product, we can introduce it in a regional test market. If it doesn't pass the consumer test there, we can make some changes and try again."

The scientific method forces an orderly research process. Some managers don't carefully specify what information they need. They blindly move ahead—hoping that research will provide "the answer." Other managers may have a clearly defined problem or question but lose their way after that. These hit-or-miss approaches waste both time and money.

FIVE-STEP APPROACH TO MARKETING RESEARCH

The **marketing research process** is a five-step application of the scientific method that includes:

1. Defining the problem.
2. Analyzing the situation.
3. Getting problem-specific data.
4. Interpreting the data.
5. Developing conclusions.

Exhibit 8-2 shows the five steps in the process. Note that the process may lead to a solution before all of the steps are completed. Or as the feedback arrows show, researchers may return to an earlier step if needed. For example, the interpreting step may point to a new question—or reveal the need for additional information— before a final decision can be made.

DEFINING THE PROBLEM—STEP 1

Defining the problem is often the most difficult step in the marketing research process. But it's important for the objectives of the research to be clearly defined. The best research job on the wrong problem is wasted effort.

Exhibit 8-2
Five-Step Scientific Approach to Marketing Research Process

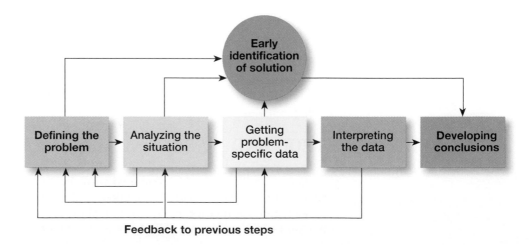

Finding the right problem level almost solves the problem

The strategy planning framework introduced in Chapter 2 can be useful here. It can help the researcher identify the real problem area and what information is needed. Do we really know enough about our target markets to work out all of the four Ps? Do we know enough to decide what celebrity to use in an ad or how to handle a price war in Montreal or Tokyo? If not, we may want to do research rather than rely on intuition.

The importance of understanding the problem—and then trying to solve it—can be seen in the introduction of Fab One Shot, a laundry product developed to clean, soften, and reduce static cling all in one step. Marketing managers were sure that Fab One Shot was going to appeal to heavy users—especially working women with large families. Research showed that 80 percent of these women used three different laundry products for the family wash, but they were looking for more convenience.

When marketing managers found that other firms were testing similar products, they rushed Fab One Shot into distribution. To encourage first-time purchases, they offered introductory price discounts, coupons, and rebates. And they supported the sales promotion with heavy advertising on TV programs that research showed the heavy users watched.

However, research never addressed the problem of how the heavy user target market would react. After the introductory price-off deals were dropped, sales dropped off too. While the product was convenient, heavy users weren't willing to pay the price—about 25 cents for each washload. For the heavy users, price was a qualifying dimension. And these consumers didn't like Fab's premeasured packets because they had no control over how much detergent they could put in. The competing firms recognized these problems at the research stage and decided not to introduce their products.

After the fact, it was clear that Fab One Shot was most popular with college students, singles, and people living in small apartments. They didn't use much—so the convenience benefit offset the higher price. But the company never targeted those segments. It just assumed that it would be profitable to target the big market of heavy users.[9]

The moral of this story is that our strategy planning framework is useful for guiding the problem definition step—as well as the whole marketing research process. First, a marketing manager should understand the target market and what needs the firm can satisfy. Then the manager can focus on lower-level problems—namely, how sensitive the target market is to a change in one or more of the marketing mix ingredients. Without such a framework, marketing researchers can waste time, and money, working on the wrong problem.

Don't confuse problems with symptoms

The problem definition step sounds simple—and that's the danger. It's easy to confuse symptoms with the problem. Suppose a firm's MIS shows that the company's sales are decreasing in certain territories while expenses are remaining the same—resulting in a decline in profits. Will it help to define the problem by asking: How can we stop the sales decline? Probably not. This would be like fitting a hearing-impaired patient with a hearing aid without first trying to find out why the patient was having trouble hearing.

It's easy to fall into the trap of mistaking symptoms for the problem. When this happens, the research objectives are not clear, and researchers may ignore relevant questions—while analyzing unimportant questions in expensive detail. The key is to accurately assess the symptoms so as to correctly diagnose the underlying problem.

Setting research objectives may require more understanding

Sometimes the research objectives are very clear. A manager wants to know if the targeted households have tried a new product and what percent of them bought it a second time. But research objectives aren't always so simple. The manager might also want to know why some didn't buy or whether they had even heard of the product. Companies rarely have enough time and money to study everything. A manager must narrow the research objectives. One good way is to develop a list of research questions that includes all the possible problem areas. Then the manager can consider the items on the list more completely—in the situation analysis step—before narrowing down to final research objectives.

ANALYZING THE SITUATION—STEP 2

What information do we already have?

When the marketing manager thinks the real problem has begun to surface, a situation analysis is useful. A **situation analysis** is an informal study of what information is already available in the problem area. It can help define the problem and specify what additional information, if any, is needed.

Pick the brains around you

The situation analysis usually involves informal talks with informed people. Informed people can be others in the firm, a few good middlemen who have close contact with customers, or others knowledgeable about the industry. In industrial markets—where relationships with customers are close—researchers may even call the customers themselves.

Situation analysis helps educate a researcher

The situation analysis is especially important if the researcher is a research specialist who doesn't know much about the management decisions to be made or if the marketing manager is dealing with unfamiliar areas. They both must be sure they understand the problem area—including the nature of the target market, the marketing mix, competition, and other external factors. This is where a careful S.W.O.T. analysis can help as a kind of background check to make sure all the relevant issues are considered. Otherwise, the researcher may rush ahead and make costly mistakes or simply discover facts that management already knows. The following case illustrates this danger.

A marketing manager at the home office of a large retail chain hired a research firm to do in-store interviews to learn what customers liked most, and least, about some of its stores in other cities. Interviewers diligently filled out their questionnaires. When the results came in, it was apparent that neither the marketing manager nor the researcher had done their homework. No one had even talked with the local store managers! Several of the stores were in the middle of some messy remodelling—so all the customers' responses concerned the noise and dust from the construction. The research was a waste of money.

Secondary data may provide the answers—or some background

The situation analysis should also find relevant **secondary data**—information that has been collected or published already. Later, in Step 3, we will cover **primary data**—information specifically collected to solve a current problem. Too often researchers rush to gather primary data when much relevant secondary information is already available—at little or no cost! See Exhibit 8-3. One caution is in order. Make sure the secondary data are current and actually appropriate for the market with which you are concerned.

Much secondary data is available

Ideally, much secondary data is already available from the firm's MIS. Data that has not been organized in an MIS may be available from the company's files and reports. Secondary data also is available from libraries, trade associations, government agencies, and private research organizations; increasingly, these organizations are putting their information online. So one of the first places a researcher should look for secondary data is on the Internet.

Exhibit 8-3   Sources of Secondary and Primary Data

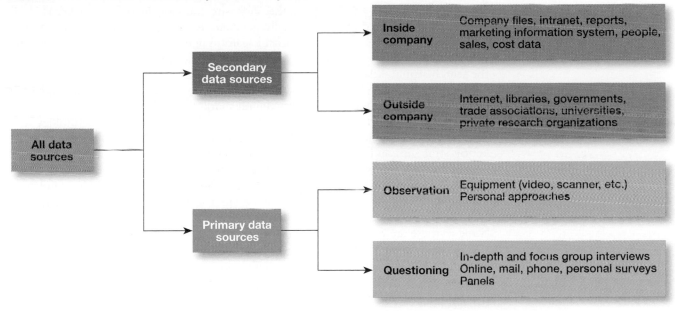

Inside company	Company files, intranet, reports, marketing information system, people, sales, cost data
Outside company	Internet, libraries, governments, trade associations, universities, private research organizations
Observation	Equipment (video, scanner, etc.) Personal approaches
Questioning	In-depth and focus group interviews Online, mail, phone, personal surveys Panels

Search engines find information on the Internet

Although much information relevant to your situation analysis may be on the Internet, it won't do you much good if you can't find it. Fortunately, there are a number of good tools for searching on the Internet and reference books that explain the details of the different tools. However, the basic idea is simple. And, usually, the best way to start is to use a search engine.

Most popular Internet browsers, like Firefox and Microsoft Internet Explorer, have a menu selection or button to activate an Internet search. In addition, there are hundreds of more specialized search engines. In general, a user specifies words or a phrase to find and the search engine produces a list of hyperlinks to Web sites where that search string is found. Usually, all you do is click on the hyperlink of interest and the browser shows the relevant page on screen. If you want, you can go back to the list and check out other links.

The Internet is dramatically changing how marketing managers get both primary and secondary data.

One of the most popular and useful search engines is at the Web site for Google (www.google.ca). It is especially good at searching for Web pages. Another very useful search engine is at the AltaVista Web site (www.altavista.ca); it does a good job of classifying online documents that include the search string. A Web site using Google that is particularly useful for locating specific people or businesses is at www.lycos.ca. With two offices in Canada, 24/7 Real Media (www.247realmedia.ca) offers digital marketing solutions to advertisers and publishers in 20 countries throughout the world. Products include technology and services that allow marketers to develop and manage highly effective digital marketing strategies and campaigns, including highly effective Search Engine Marketing solutions. Keep in mind, however, that these are just a few of the popular search engines. In fact, if you want to get an idea of how many are available—and how they are different—go to www.yahoo.ca and do a search on the term *search engine*.[10]

Most computerized database and index services are now available over the Internet. Some of these are provided by libraries and private firms. For instance, for a fee a user can use Dow Jones' interactive news retrieval system (www.djnewswires.com) to search the full text of hundreds of publications, including newspapers from around the world. ProQuest Direct, at www.proquest.ca, is another valuable research tool. It provides access to one of the world's largest collections of information, including summaries of articles from over 5,000 publications. Many articles are available in full text, full image format.

INTERNET EXERCISE

Assume that your boss has asked you to do a customer satisfaction survey. As part of a situation analysis, you want to get ideas about what others have done in this area. Go to the Web site for the Google search engine (www.google.ca). In the dialogue box type 'customer satisfaction survey' (include the single quote marks) and click on Google search. Look at some of the Web sites identified. How helpful is this? How could it be improved?

Government data is inexpensive

Federal, provincial, and local governments publish data on many subjects. Government data is often useful in estimating the size of markets. In Chapter 5 we gave a number of examples of the different types of data that are available and suggested some Web sites. Distribution of government data is not limited to the Internet, however. Almost all government data is available in inexpensive publications. Much of it is also available in computer form ready for further analysis.

Sometimes it's more practical to use summary publications for leads to more detailed reports. For the Canadian market, a great starting point for quick access to data is E-STAT (estat.statcan.ca). This is a Statistics Canada product ideal for educational institutions that allows students access to information for which they would normally have to pay a fee. Among other articles and databanks, it includes census information as well as Cansim (cansim2.statcan.ca)—a multidimensional database with over 2,400 tables. Strategis (strategis.ic.gc.ca) is also a valuable business and consumer site with data as well as articles on business, industrial, and economic activity. You can also sign up for weekly e-mail headline updates from Strategis. Similarly, the *United Nations Statistical Yearbook* is one of the finest summaries of worldwide data; like many other international statistical references, it is available on CD-ROM and online (www.un.org/depts/unsd).

Secondary data is very limited on some international markets. However, most countries with advanced economies have government agencies that help researchers get the data they need. For example, Statistics Canada (www.statcan.ca) compiles a great deal of information on the Canadian market. Eurostat (europa.eu.int/ comm/eurostat), the statistical office for the European Union countries, and the Organization for Economic Cooperation (in Paris) offer many publications packed with data on Europe. In the United States, the Department of Commerce (www.doc.gov) distributes statistics compiled by all other federal departments. Some city and provincial governments have similar agencies for local data. The Yahoo Web site (www.yahoo.ca) provides an index to a large amount of information about different governments.

Private sources are useful too

Many private research organizations—as well as advertising agencies, newspapers, and magazines—regularly compile and publish data. A good business library is valuable for sources such as *Sales & Marketing Management*, *Advertising Age*, *Journal of Global Marketing*, and the publications of the Conference Board of Canada.

The *Encyclopedia of Associations* lists 75,000 international trade and professional associations that can be a good source of information. For example, the Canadian and American Marketing Associations have information centres with many marketing publications.

Most trade associations compile data from and for their members. Some also publish magazines that focus on important topics in the industry. *Chain Store Age*, for example, has much information on retailing (www.chainstoreage.com).

Standard & Poor's Industry Surveys is another source of information on whole industries. And the local telephone company or your library usually has copies of the Yellow Pages for many cities; Yellow Page listings are also available on the Internet. Similarly, a number of firms sell computer CD-ROMs that include all of the businesses in the country. Resources such as these may be a big help in estimating the amount of competition in certain lines of business and where it is located.[11]

Situation analysis yields a lot—for very little

The virtue of a good situation analysis is that it can be very informative but takes little time. And it's inexpensive compared with more formal research efforts—like a large-scale survey. Situation analysis can help focus further research or even eliminate the need for it entirely. The situation analyst is really trying to determine the exact nature of the situation and the problem.

Determine what else is needed

At the end of the situation analysis, you can see which research questions—from the list developed during the problem definition step—remain unanswered. Then you have to decide exactly what information you need to answer those questions and how to get it.

This may require discussion between technical experts and the marketing manager. Often companies use a written **research proposal**—a plan that specifies what information will be obtained and how—to be sure no misunderstandings occur later. The research plan may include information about costs, what data will be collected, how it will be collected, who will analyze it and how, and how long the process will take. Then the marketing manager must decide if the time and costs involved are worthwhile. It's foolish to pay $100,000 for information to solve a $50,000 problem!

GETTING PROBLEM-SPECIFIC DATA—STEP 3

Gathering primary data

The next step is to plan a formal research project to gather primary data. There are different methods for collecting primary data. Which approach to use depends on the nature of the problem and how much time and money are available.

In most primary data collection, the researcher tries to learn what customers think about some topic or how they behave under some conditions. There are two basic methods for obtaining information about customers: *questioning* and *observing*.

The real value of questioning is that it links the market research to the marketing concept and orientation. It is a great way to find out about unmet customer needs and how to better meet them or even how a proposed new product might be received. Questioning can range from qualitative to quantitative research. And many kinds of observing are possible.

Qualitative questioning— open-ended with a hidden purpose

Qualitative research seeks in-depth, open-ended responses, not yes or no answers. The researcher tries to get people to share their thoughts on a topic—without giving them many directions or guidelines about what to say.

A researcher might ask different consumers, "What do you think about when you decide where to shop for food?" One person may talk about convenient location, another about service, and others about the quality of the fresh produce. The real advantage of this approach is *depth*. Each person can be asked follow-up questions so the researcher really understands what *that* respondent is thinking. The depth of the qualitative approach gets at the details—even if the researcher needs a lot of judgment to summarize it all.

Some types of qualitative research don't use specific questions. For example, a consumer might simply be shown a product or an ad and be asked to comment.

Focus groups stimulate discussion

The most widely used form of qualitative questioning in marketing research is the **focus group interview**, which involves interviewing 6 to 10 people in an informal group setting. The focus group also uses open-ended questions, but here the interviewer wants to get group interaction—to stimulate thinking and get immediate reactions.

A skilled focus group leader can learn a lot from this approach. A typical session may last an hour, so participants can cover a lot of ground. Sessions are often videotaped (or broadcast over the Internet or by satellite) so different managers can form their own impressions of what happened. Some research firms create electronic focus groups in which participants log onto a specified Web site and with others participate in a chat session; each person types in comments that are shared on the computer screen of each of the other participants. What they type is the record of the session.[12]

Focus groups are also popular in business markets. For example, IBM used 27 focus groups as part of its research to better identify who in large companies makes buying decisions for e-commerce equipment and how they thought about the issues of selecting a vendor.[13]

Regardless of how a focus group is conducted, conclusions reached from a session usually vary depending on who watches it. A typical problem—and serious limitation—with qualitative research is that it's hard to measure the results objectively. The results seem to depend largely on the viewpoint of the researcher. In addition, people willing to participate in a focus group—especially those who talk the most—may not be representative of the broader target market. Ideally of course, focus group participants should be representative of the market that the manager is trying to reach.

Focus groups can be conducted quickly and at relatively low cost—an average of about $3,500 each. This is part of their appeal. But focus groups are probably being overused. It's easy to fall into the trap of treating an idea arising from a focus group as a "fact" that applies to a broad target market. For example, Consumers Gas (now Enbridge) showed one of their focus groups a test advertisement that featured a middle-aged couple getting amorous on the rug in front of a fireplace. It went over well. While the focus group loved it the larger target market were offended and felt it was too risqué for their age group. The ad was pulled, the public relations disaster dealt with, and the expensive production costs of the ad written off because a focus group doesn't necessarily represent a whole target market. To avoid this kind of problem, the qualitative opinions from the focus group should have been used as input to prepare for quantitative research of a larger more representative sample.

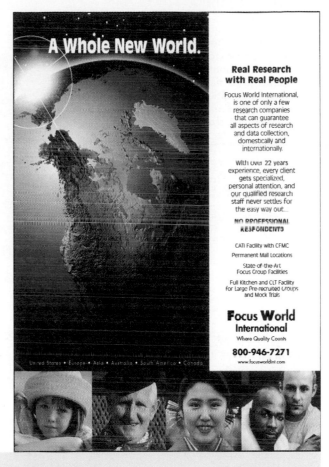

Focus groups are popular, and well-run groups can provide a lot of useful information. As with any type of marketing research, a marketing manager should be aware of both the advantages and limitations of this approach when drawing conclusions and making decisions.

You also have to be wary of "professionals" who respond to the ads requesting focus group members because these people get paid for their time. As one woman in a CBC *Venture* program on focus groups put it, "They are paying me so I tell them what they want to hear."

Focus groups can be very helpful as long as the researcher and the sponsor are aware of the potential misinformation they can generate. That's where a sharp researcher conducting the focus group earns their money. In one televised segment the facilitator conducting a focus group for the launch of Happy Planet's new organic line of juices was quick to spot a "pro" who knew far too much about the business. The man was ejected before he could unduly influence the opinions of the other focus group members.

Qualitative research can provide good ideas—hypotheses. But we need other approaches—perhaps based on more representative samples and objective measures—to *test* the hypotheses.

Structured questioning gives more objective results

When researchers use identical questions and response alternatives, they can summarize the information quantitatively. Samples can be larger and more representative, and various statistics can be used to draw conclusions. For these reasons, most survey research is **quantitative research**—which seeks structured responses that can be summarized in numbers, like percentages, averages, or other statistics. For example, a marketing researcher might calculate what percentage of respondents have tried a new product and then figure an average score for how satisfied they were.

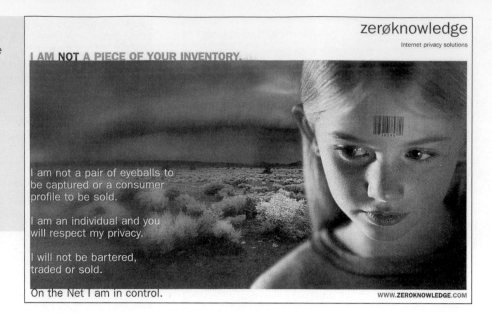

Fixed responses speed answering and analysis

Survey questionnaires usually provide fixed responses to questions to simplify analysis of the replies. This multiple-choice approach also makes it easier and faster for respondents to reply. Simple fill-in-a-number questions are also widely used in quantitative research. Fixed responses are also more convenient for computer analysis, which is how most surveys are analyzed. Sometimes however, open-ended questions are also used so the respondent can make extra comments or suggestions.

Quantitative measures of attitudes too

One common approach to measuring consumers' attitudes and opinions is to have respondents indicate how much they agree or disagree with a questionnaire statement. A researcher interested in what target consumers think about frozen pizzas, for example, might include a statement like "I add extra toppings when I prepare frozen pizza." The respondent might check off a response such as (1) strongly disagree, (2) disagree, (3) agree, or (4) strongly agree.

Another approach is to have respondents *rate* a product, feature, or store. For example, a questionnaire might ask consumers to rate the taste of a pizza as *excellent, good, fair,* or *poor.*

Surveys come in many forms

Decisions about what specific questions to ask and how to ask them usually depend on how respondents will be contacted—by mail (or electronic mail), via a Web site, on the phone, or in person. What question and response approach is used may also affect the survey. There are many possibilities. For example, whether the survey is self-administered or handled by an interviewer, the questionnaire may be on paper or in an interactive computer format (perhaps distributed on a CD or disk or displayed on a Web site). The computer can be programmed to skip certain questions, depending on answers given. Computerized questionnaires also allow the research to show pictures or play audio/video clips (for example, to get reactions to an advertising jingle). In an automated telephone interview, questions may be prerecorded on an audio tape or computer and the subject responds by pushing touch-tone buttons on the phone.

Mail and online surveys are common and convenient

A questionnaire distributed by mail, e-mail, or online is useful when extensive questioning is necessary. Respondents can complete the questions at their convenience. They may be more willing to provide personal information—since a questionnaire can be completed anonymously. But the questions must be simple and easy to follow since no interviewer is there to help. If the respondent is likely to be a computer user,

Online surveys provide fast feedback and often at a lower cost than the old-fashioned way. Of course, the manager needs to be certain that the online sample is representative. This is also an issue with mail or telephone surveys. For example, some consumers are so aggravated by calls from telemarketers that they won't accept calls from legitimate research organizations.

In head-to-head ice cream tests, online panel beats mall intercept

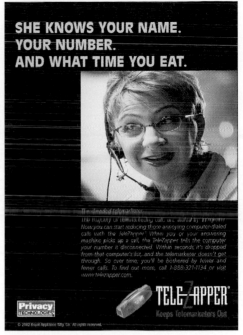

SHE KNOWS YOUR NAME. YOUR NUMBER. AND WHAT TIME YOU EAT.

it may be possible to send the questionnaire on a disk (or put it on a Web site) and include a help feature with additional directions for people who need them.

A big problem with questionnaires is that many people don't complete them. Another problem is the researcher sometimes has little control over who completes the questionaire. The **response rate**— the percentage of people contacted who complete the questionnaire—is often low and respondents may not be representative. There is particular concern about the representativeness of people who complete online questionnaires. The response rates tend to be even lower than by mail. In addition, online respondents may be younger, better educated, or different in other ways that impact how they answer. Mail, e-mail, and online surveys are economical if a large number of people respond. But they may be quite expensive if the response rate is low. Worse, the results may be misleading if the respondents are not representative.

Distributing questionnaires by e-mail, or at a Web site, is popular. It is quick, and the responses come back in computer form. Surveys sent by regular mail usually take a lot longer. In business markets, questionnaires can sometimes be sent by fax.

Regardless of how quickly a questionnaire is distributed, it often takes a month or more to get the data back. That is too slow for some decisions. Moreover, it is difficult to get respondents to expand on particular points. In markets where illiteracy is a problem, it may not be possible to get any response. In spite of these limitations, the convenience and economy of self-administered surveys makes them popular for collecting primary data.

INTERNET EXERCISE

Perseus Development Corporation sells software that allows a user to create online questionnaires that can be distributed by e-mail or used on the Internet. To see samples of online questions, go to the Perseus Web site (www.perseus.ca), click on *Surveysolutions Express,* and then click on *Sample Surveys*. Review several of the samples. Do you think that it's more convenient for a consumer to complete a survey online or with pencil and paper?

Telephone surveys—fast and effective

Telephone interviews are also popular. They are effective for getting quick answers to simple questions. Telephone interviews allow the interviewer to probe and really learn what the respondent is thinking. In addition, with computer-aided telephone interviewing, answers are immediately recorded on a computer, resulting in fast data analysis. On the other hand, many consumers find calls intrusive—and about a third refuse to answer any questions. Moreover, respondents can't be certain who is calling or how personal information might be used.

Personal interview surveys—can be in-depth

A personal interview survey is usually much more expensive per interview than e-mail, mail, or telephone surveys. But it's easier to get and keep the respondent's attention when the interviewer is right there. The interviewer can also help explain complicated directions and perhaps get better responses. For these reasons, personal interviews are commonly used for research on business customers. To reduce the cost of locating consumer respondents, interviews are sometimes done at a store or shopping mall. This is called a mall intercept interview because the interviewer stops a shopper and asks for responses to the survey.

Researchers have to be careful that having an interviewer involved doesn't affect the respondent's answers. Sometimes people won't give an answer they consider embarrassing. For instance, they may lie when asked something personal like how much alcohol they drink. Or they may try to impress or please the interviewer. Further, in some cultures people don't want to give any information. For example, many people in Africa, Latin America, and Eastern Europe are reluctant to be interviewed. This is also a problem in many low-income, inner-city areas in the United States; even Census Bureau interviewers have trouble getting cooperation.[15]

It is important to remember that any kind of survey work can be subject to bias. Sometimes it's because only certain kinds of people will respond to the survey and they do not represent the views of many other people who didn't answer the questions. Other times the interviewer or the way the questions are phrased, can introduce bias. The results can be worse than no information—you may get, and subsequently analyze and interpret, the wrong information.

Sometimes questioning has limitations. Then observing may be more accurate or economical.

Observing—what you see is what you get

Observing—as a method of collecting data—focuses on a well-defined problem. Here we are not talking about the casual observations that may stimulate ideas in the early steps of a research project. With the observation method, researchers try to see or record what the subject does naturally. They don't want the observing to *influence* the subject's behaviour, and in many cases that is easier said than done.

A museum director wanted to know which of the many exhibits was most popular. A survey didn't help. Visitors seemed to want to please the interviewer and usually said that all of the exhibits were interesting. Putting observers near exhibits—to record how long visitors spent at each one—didn't help either. The curious visitors stood around to see what the observer was recording, and that messed up the measures. Finally, the museum floors were waxed to a glossy shine. Several weeks later, the floors around the exhibits were inspected. It was easy to tell which exhibits were most popular—based on how much wax had worn off the floor!

In some situations, consumers are recorded on video. This may be in a store, at home, or out with friends. Later, researchers can study the tape by running the film at very slow speed or actually analyzing each frame. Researchers use this technique to study the routes consumers follow through a grocery store or how they select products in a department store. Similarly, firms that have online shopping services on the Internet can use software to "watch" how consumers use the Web site, how much time they spend at each display, and the like.

Data from electronic scanners helps retailers decide what brands are selling and helps their suppliers plan ahead so that products arrive at the store in time to prevent stock-outs.

Mystery shoppers are also widely used by firms that want to maintain their service quality levels or improve their profitability. The observation method is used by "undercover mystery shoppers" who work for companies like ACNielsen on behalf of clients that include retailers, oil companies, grocery stores, and restaurants to name a just a few. Westin Hotels (hospitality), Cineplex Odeon (theatres), and Pioneer Petroleum (gas stations) are just some of the companies concerned about maintaining good service and profitability. Mystery shoppers report back to their clients using everything from written reports to digital still pictures and even video.

Observing is common in advertising research

Observation methods are common in advertising research. For example, Nielsen Media Research (www.nielsenmedia.com) uses a device called the "people meter" that adapts the observation method to television audience research. This device is attached to the TV set in the homes of selected families. It records when the set is on and what station is tuned in. The fact that the TV networks sometimes criticize Nielsen's "counts" of audience size is a reminder that conclusions based on observing are sometimes subject to interpretation, even when a device of some sort is involved.

Checkout scanners see a lot

Computerized scanners at retail checkout counters, a major breakthrough in observing, help researchers collect very specific, and useful, information. Often this type of data feeds directly into a firm's MIS. Managers of a large chain of stores can see exactly what products have sold each day and how much money each department in each store has earned. But the scanner also has wider applications for marketing research.

Information Resources Inc. (www.infores.com), ACNielsen (acnielsen.ca), Decima Research (decima.ca), and Ipsos Reid (ipsos.ca/reid), one of Canada's largest research firms, use **consumer panels**—a group of consumers who provide information on a continuing basis. Whenever a panel member shops for groceries, he or she gives an ID card to the clerk, who scans the number. Then the scanner records every purchase—including brands, sizes, prices, and any coupons used. The scanner data can also be combined with other information that is specific to the person using the scanned ID card in order to create a very complete consumer profile. Department store credit cards, Safeway Air Miles, and Shoppers Drug Mart Optimum are just a few of the myriad scanner cards that all provide extremely valuable marketing data about consumer shopping behaviour and brand preferences. Retailers, grocery product producers, manufacturers, financial institutions, and pharmaceutical manufacturers are just some of the marketers who find scanner data very useful because it helps with just about every aspect of designing the four Ps.

In a variation of this approach, consumers use a hand-held scanner to record purchases once they get home. For a fee, clients can evaluate actual customer purchase patterns and answer questions. For example, if a consumer switched from another brand, did she go back to her old brand the next time?

WHIRLPOOL HEATS UP SALES WITH MARKETING RESEARCH

Marketing managers at Whirlpool want to satisfy customers. So they do a lot of research to find out how satisfied customers really are. For example, each year Whirlpool sends an appliance satisfaction survey to 180,000 households. Respondents rate all of their appliances on dozens of dimensions. When a competing product scores higher, Whirlpool engineers take it apart to see why and build the best ideas into their new models. However, they don't just wait for competitors to figure things out first.

A recently introduced oven, now one of Whirlpool's hottest sellers, illustrates their approach. A survey showed that consumers wanted an oven with easy-to-clean controls. That didn't seem consistent with previous sales patterns; the firm's MIS showed that models with knobs consistently outsold models with easier-to-clean push buttons. Rather than disregard the survey, Whirlpool designed a range with touch pad controls by listening to consumers at every step along the way. Consumers who played with computer simulations of the touch pad explained what they liked and didn't like. Videos of consumers who tried proto-type models in mall intercept interviews provided ideas to further refine the design. The result is a touch pad control that is easy to clean and so easy to use that consumers don't even need to read the manual.

Consumer research has been an even more important factor in Whirlpool's growth overseas. For example, until recently only about one-third of European households had a microwave oven. Whirlpool researchers learned that more people would buy a microwave oven if it could crisp food as it heated the food. Whirlpool designed a microwave with a broiler coil and other innovations. The result is an oven that is popular in Britain for frying bacon and eggs and in Italy for crisping pizza crusts.

Research also guided the design of a washing machine that sells for under $200 in developing nations. In Brazil, for example, workers earn an average of $220 a month, so few households have been able to afford a washer until now. Researchers who visited homes and observed manual washing realized that many Brazilians do laundry frequently and in small batches. As a result, automatic washers could be small, less powerful, and less costly to produce. However, focus groups revealed many low-income consumers saw the washer as a status symbol, so Whirlpool used stylish, colourful trim, four legs rather than the usual boxy styling, and a clear plastic lid that allows people to watch the washer operate.[16]

Some members of the consumer panel are also tied into a special TV cable system. With this system, a company can direct advertisements to some houses and not others. Then researchers can evaluate the effect of the ads by comparing the purchases of consumers who saw the ads with those who didn't.

The use of scanners to "observe" what customers actually do has changed consumer research methods. Companies can turn to firms like Information Resources as a *single source* of complete information about customers' attitudes, shopping behaviour, and media habits.

For example, Ocean Spray was seeing sales slip to competitors. Analysis of panel data revealed that households with kids are the heaviest purchasers of juice. Yet they purchased Ocean Spray on a less frequent basis. Further research with these panel members revealed this was due to its "too tart" taste and tendency to stain. To combat this, the company focused its energies on developing White Cranberry Juice Drinks by harvesting the berries before they develop their traditional red colour and pungent taste. An ad for the new product depicted a mom and her small son enjoying the taste of the new White Cranberry juice. When the boy accidentally spills it on the floor, it's also clear that it doesn't stain.[17]

Data captured by electronic scanners is equally important to e-commerce in business-to-business markets. Increasingly, firms mark their shipping cartons and packages with computer-readable bar codes that make it fast and easy to track inventory, shipments, orders, and the like. As information about product sales or shipments becomes available, it is instantly included in the MIS and accessible over the Internet.[18]

Simmons' ad agency used an experiment to improve a new print ad for the Beautyrest mattress. Groups of consumers saw two different ads. The ads were the same, except that one featured a father holding a baby and the other featured a mother. The ad with the father earned higher recall scores.

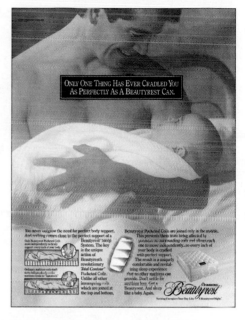

Customer relationship management (CRM) software is also designed to track the purchasing behaviour of buyers and is particularly useful in business-to-business marketing. The data can help marketers decide what other products might be of interest to the buyer if two products are used together—like coffee and sugar (called **complementary products**). For example, if a customer uses a Visa card for their small business, their banker could ask whether they might also be interested in a small business line of credit.

Experimental method controls conditions

A marketing manager can get a different kind of information—with either questioning or observing—using the experimental method. With the **experimental method**, researchers compare the responses of two (or more) groups that are similar except on the characteristic being tested. Researchers want to learn if the specific characteristic—which varies among groups—*causes* differences in some response among the groups. For example, a researcher might be interested in comparing responses of consumers who had seen an ad for a new product with consumers who had not seen the ad. The "response" might be an observed behaviour—like the purchase of a product—or the answer to a specific question—like "How interested are you in this new product?" See Exhibit 8-4.

Exhibit 8-4 Illustration of Experimental Method in Comparing Effectiveness of Two Ads

A firm's own data on customers' past purchases, if properly analyzed, can be an important source of information for evaluating new opportunities.

Marketing managers for Mars—the company that makes Snickers candy bars—used the experimental method to help solve a problem. They wanted to know if making their candy bar bigger would increase sales enough to offset the higher cost. To decide, they conducted a marketing experiment in which the company carefully varied the size of candy bars sold in *different* markets. Otherwise, the marketing mix stayed the same. Then researchers tracked sales in each market area to see the effect of the different sizes. They saw a big difference immediately: The added sales more than offset the cost of a bigger candy bar.

Test-marketing of new products is another type of marketing experiment. In a typical approach, a company tries variations on its planned marketing mix in a few geographic market areas. The results of the tests help to identify problems or refine the marketing mix—before the decision is made to go to broader distribution. However, alert competitors may disrupt such tests—perhaps by increasing promotion or offering retailers extra discounts. To avoid these problems, firms sometimes conduct tests in foreign markets.

Researchers don't use the experimental method as often as surveys and focus groups. Many managers don't understand the valuable information they can get from this method. Further, they don't like the idea of some researcher "experimenting" with their business.[19]

Syndicated research shares data collection costs

Some private research firms specialize in collecting data and then sell it to managers in many different client firms. Often the marketing manager subscribes to the research service and gets regular updates. About 40 percent of marketing research spending is for syndicated research, and this helps explain why it can

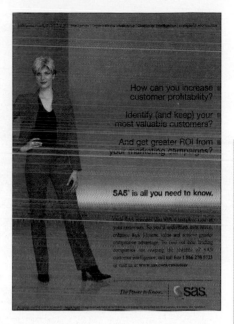

be an economical approach when marketing managers from many different firms need the same type of data. For example, Ipsos Reid (ipsos.ca/reid) is a Canadian syndicated market research provider with expertise in automotive, telecommunications, and travel among other areas of specialization. Simmons Market Research Bureau (www.smrb.com) does extensive research on consumer media habits and then sells its data to many advertising agencies. Many different auto producers use J. D. Power's (www.jdpower.ca) surveys of customer satisfaction—often as the basis for advertising claims. Subscription data services are available for many different industries—ranging from food service to prescription drugs to micro electronic devices.[20]

INTERPRETING THE DATA—STEP 4

What does it really mean?

After someone collects the data, it has to be analyzed to decide what it all means. In quantitative research, this step usually involves statistics. **Statistical packages**—easy-to-use computer programs that analyze data—have made this step easier. As we noted earlier, some firms provide *decision support systems* so managers can use a statistical package to interpret data themselves. More often, however, technical specialists are involved at the interpretation step.

Cross-tabulation is one of the most simple and frequently used approaches for analyzing and interpreting marketing research data. It shows the relationship of answers to two different questions. Exhibit 8-5 is an example. The cross-tab analysis showed

Exhibit 8-5
Cross-Tabulation Breakdown of Responses to a Phone Company Consumer Survey

		Have You Moved in the Last Year?		
	Answers:	No	Yes	Total
Do you have "Caller ID" on your phone at home?	Yes	10.2%	23.4%	15.5%
	No	89.8	76.6	84.5
	Total	100.0%	100.0%	100.0%

Interpretation: 15.5 percent of people in the survey said that they had "Caller ID" on their phone at home. However, the percentage was much higher (23.4%) among people who had moved in the last year, and lower (10.2%) among people who had not moved.

that customers who had moved in the last year were much more likely than non-movers to have adopted "Caller ID" on their phones at home.

There are many other approaches for statistical analysis—the best one depends on the situation. The details of statistical analysis are beyond the scope of this book. But a good manager should know enough to understand what a research project can and can't do.[21]

Is your sample really representative?

It's usually impossible for marketing managers to collect all the information they want about everyone in a **population**—the total group they are interested in. Marketing researchers typically study only a **sample**, a part of the relevant population. How well a sample *represents* the total population affects the results. Results from a sample that is not representative may not give a true picture.

The manager of a retail store might want a phone survey to learn what consumers think about the store's hours. If interviewers make all of the calls during the day, consumers who work outside the home during the day won't be represented. Those interviewed might say the limited store hours are "satisfactory." Yet it would be a mistake to assume that *all* consumers are satisfied.

Random samples tend to be representative

You can see that getting a representative sample is very important. One method of doing so is **random sampling**, where each member of the population has the same or known chance of being included in the sample. Great care must be used to ensure that sampling is really random, not just haphazard.

If a random sample is chosen from a population, it will tend to have the same characteristics and be representative of the population. "Tend to" is important because it is only a tendency—the sample is not exactly the same as the population.

Much marketing research is based on nonrandom sampling because of the high cost and difficulty of obtaining a truly random sample. Sometimes nonrandom samples give very good results—especially in industrial markets where the number of customers may be relatively small and fairly similar. But results from nonrandom samples must be interpreted, and used, with care.

Random and nonrandom samples both play a role in market research. The important point is to tell consumers how confident they can be about the accuracy of the information. That is why voter opinion polls conducted by Ipsos Reid prior to our federal and provincial elections always come with a qualification about how statistically trustworthy they are.

Research results are not exact

An estimate from a sample, even a representative one, usually varies somewhat from the true value for a total population. Managers sometimes forget this. They assume that survey results are exact. Instead, when interpreting sample estimates, managers should think of them as *suggesting* the approximate value.

If random selection is used to develop the sample, researchers can use various methods to help determine the likely accuracy of the sample value. This is done in terms of **confidence intervals**—the range on either side of an estimate that is likely to contain the true value for the whole population. Some managers are surprised to learn how wide that range can be.

Consider a wholesaler who has 1,000 retail customers and wants to learn how many of these retailers carry a product from a competing supplier. If the wholesaler randomly samples 100 retailers and 20 say yes, then the sample estimate is 20 percent. But with that information the wholesaler can only be 95 percent confident that the percentage of all retailers is in the confidence interval between 12 and 28 percent.[22]

The larger the sample size, the greater the accuracy of estimates from a random sample. With a larger sample, a few unusual responses are less likely to make a big difference.

Validity problems can destroy research

Even if the sampling is carefully planned, it is also important to evaluate the quality of the research data itself.

Managers and researchers should be sure that research data really measures what it is supposed to measure. Many of the variables marketing managers are interested in are difficult to measure accurately. Questionnaires may let us assign numbers to consumer responses, but that still doesn't mean that the result is precise. An interviewer might ask "How much did you spend on soft drinks last week?" A respondent may be perfectly willing to cooperate—and be part of the representative sample—but just not be able to remember.

Validity concerns the extent to which data measures what it is intended to measure. Validity problems are important in marketing research because many people will try to answer even when they don't know what they're talking about. Further, a poorly worded question can mean different things to different people and invalidate the results. Often, pretests of a research project are required to evaluate the quality of the questions and measures and to ensure that potential problems have been identified.

Poor interpretation can destroy research

Besides sampling and validity problems, a marketing manager must consider whether the analysis of the data supports the *conclusions* drawn in the interpretation step. Sometimes technical specialists pick the right statistical procedure—their calculations are exact—but they misinterpret the data because they don't understand the management problem. In one survey, car buyers were asked to rank five cars in order from "most preferred" to "least preferred." One car was ranked first by slightly more respondents than any other car so the researcher reported it as the "most liked car." That interpretation, however, ignored the fact that 70 percent of the respondents ranked the car *last*!

Interpretation problems like this can be subtle but crucial. Some people draw misleading conclusions on purpose to get the results they want. Marketing managers must decide whether *all* of the results support the interpretation and are relevant to their problem.

Marketing manager and researcher should work together

Marketing research involves many technical details. But you can see that the marketing researcher and the marketing manager must work together to be sure that they really do solve the problem facing the firm. If the whole research process has been a joint effort, then the interpretation step can move quickly to decision making—and solving the problem.

DEVELOPING CONCLUSIONS—STEP 5

The last step is developing conclusions and making decisions to solve the problem

In this final step, conclusions based on interpretation of the research results are developed so that decisions regarding the originally defined problem can be addressed. A number of possibilities can develop at this point. When all goes as anticipated, the research results yield exactly the kind of information needed to resolve the originally identified problem and the appropriate management action decisions can be taken. Sometimes the research will reveal unanticipated results with new and interesting marketing information that requires further work to explore the management implications. Sometimes however, the research fails to provide the necessary insights about the original problem for management to draw the firm conclusions that will make for good solid decision making. When that happens the research problem may not have been properly defined at the outset and/or errors in the other research steps may have occurred.

When things work properly and the research process is complete, the manager should be able to apply the findings in marketing strategy planning—the choice of a target market or the mix of the four Ps.

The key issue is that the research process must be designed at the outset and all the steps in the process must be carried out with a view to providing useable information for management to make the best decision possible about the problem they set out to address.

INTERNATIONAL MARKETING RESEARCH

Research contributes to international success

Marketing research on overseas markets is often a major contributor toward international marketing success. Conversely, export failures are often due to a lack of home office expertise concerning customer interests, needs, and other segmenting dimensions as well as environmental factors such as competitors' prices and products. Effective marketing research can help to overcome these problems.

Avoid mistakes with local researchers

Whether a firm is small and entering overseas markets for the first time or already large and well established internationally, there are often advantages to working

There are a large number of international marketing research firms that offer specialized services to marketing managers.

with local market research firms. They know the local situation and are less likely to make mistakes based on misunderstanding the customs, language, or circumstances of the customers they study.

Many large research firms have a network of local offices around the world to help with such efforts. Similarly, multinational or local advertising agencies and middlemen can often provide leads on identifying the best research suppliers.

Some coordination and standardization makes sense

When a firm is doing similar research projects in different markets around the world, it makes sense for the marketing manager to coordinate the efforts. If the manager doesn't establish some basic guidelines at the outset, the different research projects may all vary so much that the results can't be compared from one market area to another. Such comparisons give a home office manager a better chance of understanding how the markets are similar and how they differ.

Companies with operations in various countries often attempt to centralize some market research functions. One reason is to reduce costs or achieve research economies of scale. The centralized approach also improves the firm's ability to transfer experience and know-how from one market area or project to another. For example, one of Eastman Kodak's International Divisions appointed a market research specialist in each subsidiary company throughout the Asian region. The specialists report to local marketing managers but also receive research direction from expert research managers in the head office in the U.S.

There is even greater opportunity and need to standardize and coordinate elements of a marketing information system in an international marketing operation. Computer databases and information systems are most useful when they are designed to include the same variables organized consistently over time. Without this, it is impossible for the manager to go into much depth in comparing and contrasting data from different markets.[23]

While cultural heterogeneity will be a barrier to the standardization of some marketing variables and products, in other cases, standardization will continue to increase given the current trend of offering uniform products across different international markets. The sound system you recently bought is most likely sold in three or four different countries. That's because companies want to sell the same model in many different markets so they can maximize their economies of scale.

HOW MUCH INFORMATION DO YOU NEED?

What is the value of information?

We have been talking about the benefits of good marketing information, but dependable information can be expensive. For example, the continuing research available from multinational marketing research companies can cost a company well over $100,000 a year.

The high cost of good information must be balanced against its probable value to management. Managers never get all the information they would like to have. Very detailed surveys or experiments may be "too good" or "too expensive" or "too late" if all the company needs is a rough sampling of retailer attitudes toward a new pricing plan by tomorrow. Money is also wasted if research shows that a manager's guesses are wrong and the manager ignores the facts.

Marketing managers must take risks because of incomplete information. That's part of their job and always will be. But they must weigh the cost of getting more data against its likely value. If the risk is not too great, the cost of getting more information may be greater than the potential loss from a poor decision. A decision to expand into a new territory with the present marketing mix, for example, might be made with more confidence after a $50,000 survey. But just sending a sales rep into the territory for a few weeks to try to sell potential customers would be a lot cheaper. And, if successful, the answer is in and so are some sales.[24]

CONCLUSION

Marketing managers face difficult decisions in selecting target markets and managing marketing mixes. And managers rarely have all the information they would like to have. This problem is usually worse for managers who work with international markets. But they don't have to rely only on intuition. They can usually obtain good information to improve the quality of their decisions.

Both large and small firms are taking advantage of the Internet and intranets to set up marketing information systems (MIS)—to be certain that routinely needed data is available and accessible quickly.

Marketing managers deal with rapidly changing environments. Available data is not always adequate to answer the detailed questions that arise. Then a marketing research project may be required to gather new information.

Marketing research should be guided by the scientific method. The scientific approach to solving marketing problems involves five steps: defining the problem, analyzing the situation, obtaining data, interpreting data, and developing conclusions to solve the problem. This objective and organized approach helps to keep research on target—reducing the risk of doing costly research that isn't necessary or doesn't solve the problem.

Our strategy planning framework can be helpful in finding the real problem. By finding and focusing on the real problem, the researcher and marketing manager may be able to move quickly to a useful solution—without the cost and risks of gathering primary data in a formal research project. With imagination, they may even be able to find the answers in their MIS or in other readily available secondary data.

KEY TERMS

marketing information system (MIS), 204

intranet, 206

data warehouse, 206

decision support system (DSS), 206

search engine, 206

marketing model, 207

marketing research, 208

scientific method, 209

hypotheses, 210

marketing research process, 210

situation analysis, 212

secondary data, 212

primary data, 212

research proposal, 215

qualitative research, 216

focus group interview, 216

quantitative research, 217

response rate, 219

consumer panels, 221

complementary product, 223

experimental method, 223

statistical packages, 225

population, 226

sample, 226

random sampling, 226

confidence intervals, 227

validity, 227

QUESTIONS AND PROBLEMS

1. Discuss the concept of a marketing information system and why it is important for marketing managers to be involved in planning the system.

2. In your own words, explain why a decision support system (DSS) can add to the value of a marketing information system. Give an example of how a decision support system might help.

3. If a firm's intranet and marketing decision support system do not include a search engine, would they still be useful to a marketing manager? Why?

4. Discuss how output from a marketing information system (MIS) might differ from the output of a typical marketing research department for a company like Rogers Video.

5. Discuss some of the likely problems facing the marketing manager in a small firm that has just purchased a personal computer with a cable modem to search the Internet for information on competitors' marketing plans.

6. Explain the key characteristics of the scientific method and show why these are important to managers concerned with research.

7. How is the situation analysis different from the data collection step? Can both these steps be done at the same time to obtain answers sooner? Is this wise?

8. Distinguish between primary data and secondary data and illustrate how Bell Canada in Ontario would use the data.

9. With so much secondary information now available free or at low cost over the Internet, why would a firm ever want to spend the money to do primary research?

10. If a firm were interested in estimating the distribution of income in the province of Quebec, how could it proceed? Be specific.

11. If a firm were interested in estimating sand and clay production in New Brunswick, how could it proceed? Be specific.

12. Why does the Canadian government supply international marketing studies and data to Canada's businesses? What kind of marketing information would be most useful to a company like Teck Cominco if they were trying to export zinc to China?

13. Explain why a company might want to do focus group interviews rather than individual interviews with the same people. Apply this to Electronic Arts video games for online players

14. Distinguish between qualitative and quantitative approaches to research—and give some of the key advantages and limitations of each approach.

15. Define response rate and discuss why a marketing manager might be concerned about the response rate achieved in a particular survey. Why would Rogers Sugar care if it got markedly different response rates from a survey of Quebec consumers versus Alberta consumers?

16. Prepare a table that summarizes some of the key advantages and limitations of mail, e-mail, telephone, and personal interview approaches for administering questionnaires.

17. Would a firm want to subscribe to a shared cost data service if the same data were going to be available to competitors? Discuss your reasoning.

18. You are considering launching a new car engine oil. What types of market research would you use and why?

19. Marketing research involves expense—sometimes considerable expense. Why does the text recommend the use of marketing research even though a highly experienced marketing executive is available?

20. A marketing manager is considering opportunities to export her firm's current consumer products to several different countries. She is interested in getting secondary data that will help her narrow down choices to countries that offer the best potential. The manager then plans to do more detailed primary research with consumers in those markets. What suggestions would you give her about how to proceed?

21. Discuss the concept that some information may be too expensive to obtain in relation to its value. Illustrate.

22. In the Crest Whitestrips vignette, the managers were surprised that market research showed 80 percent of the customers were female when they expected a 50/50 split of both men and women. Can you generate any hypotheses that might explain this? Based on your explanations how would you develop a marketing campaign to capture that large untapped male market for Whitestrips?

COMPUTER-AIDED PROBLEM

8. Marketing Research

RESOURCE REMINDER

Texmac Inc., has an idea for a new type of weaving machine that could replace the machines now used by many textile manufacturers. Texmac has done a telephone survey to estimate how many of the old-style machines are now in use. Respondents using the present machines were also asked if they would buy the improved machine at a price of $10,000.

Texmac researchers identified a population of about 5,000 textile factories as potential customers. A sample of these were surveyed, and Texmac received 500 responses. Researchers think the total potential market is about 10 times larger than the sample of respondents. Two hundred twenty of the respondents indicated that their firms used old machines like the one the new machine was intended to replace. Forty percent of those firms said that they would be interested in buying the new Texmac machine.

Texmac thinks the sample respondents are representative of the total population, but the marketing manager realizes that estimates based on a sample may not be exact when applied to the whole population. He wants to see how sampling error would affect profit estimates. Data for this problem appears in the spreadsheet. Quantity estimates for the whole market are computed from the sample estimates. These quantity estimates are used in computing likely sales, costs, and profit contribution.

a. An article in a trade magazine reports that there are about 5,200 textile factories that use the old-style machine. If the total market is really 5,200 customers not 5,000 as Texmac originally thought—how does that affect the total quantity estimate and profit contribution?

b. Some of the people who responded to the survey didn't know much about different types of machines. If the actual number of old machines in the market is really 200 per 500 firms—not 220 as estimated from survey responses—how much would this affect the expected profit contribution (for 5,200 factories)?

c. The marketing manager knows that the percentage of textile factories that would actually buy the new machine might be different from the 40 percent who said they would in the survey. He estimates that the proportion that will replace the old machine might be as low as 36 and as high as 44 percent—depending on business conditions. Use the analysis feature to prepare a table that shows how expected quantity and profit contribution change when the sample percent varies between a minimum of 36 and a maximum of 44 percent. What does this analysis suggest about the use of estimates from marketing research samples? (Note: Use 5,200 for the number of potential customers and use 220 as the estimate of the number of old machines in the sample.)

If you want to read the cases and view the video cases that accompany this chapter, visit the *Basic Marketing* Online Learning Centre at: **www.mcgrawhill.ca/olc/perreault**. Along with these cases and video cases, the OLC also has the software and user guide for this chapter's Computer-Aided Problem, as well as exercises, quizzes, articles, links, and other *interactive* content that will help you with your studies.

WHEN YOU FINISH
THIS CHAPTER,
YOU SHOULD

1. Understand what "Product" really means.

2. Know the key differences between goods and services.

3. Know the differences among the various consumer and business product classes.

4. Understand how the product classes can help a marketing manager plan marketing strategies.

5. Understand what branding is and how to use it in strategy planning.

6. Understand the importance of packaging in strategy planning.

7. Understand the role of warranties in strategy planning.

Product Planning for Goods and Services

This chapter deals with Product planning and what better way to start than with an example of a huge Canadian success story, the BlackBerry. The BlackBerry hand-held device is a product designed and built by Research In Motion (RIM), a company founded in 1984 and based in Waterloo, Ontario. Now RIM operates offices in North America, Europe, and Asia. In 1984, RIM was known for being a geeky company that came out with interesting inventions that didn't always translate into financial success, hence its derisive nickname "Research in Slow Motion."

Although the BlackBerry is RIM's claim to fame, the company developed different products in its early days, including a film bar code reader for which it won an Academy Award in 1999.

In the mid-1990s, the company introduced the "RIM Inter@ctive Pager," the forerunner to today's BlackBerry hand-held devices. In 1999, RIM's marketing focus changed. The pager became part of the "BlackBerry Wireless Email Solution." The new BlackBerry platform integrated RIM's wireless hand-held devices directly and securely with corporate e-mail servers. The slimmed-down version sported a radio, address book, calculator, and links to the user's office e-mail system—all powered by just one AA battery. Still, RIM was largely unknown at the time, and market leader Palm had the kind of buzz not seen since Apple's Macintosh hit the market a decade earlier.

BlackBerry's success story is less a case of unseating a rival than burrowing into the right niche for the company. RIM, unlike Palm, stuck to its strategy to market the BlackBerry to the business market. In retrospect, it was a good idea. The consumer market would implode mightily in 2001 and Palm was stuck with tons of old inventory after demand plummeted, leaving RIM all alone in serving the corporate market.

The early print ads played on the word "Berry" as in "Berry Liberating" and "Berry Productive," using renderings of the BlackBerry outfitted with cartoon wings. The ads had a consumer look, but RIM's strategy was to market the BlackBerry solely to the business market.

The origin of the name BlackBerry started with a brand consulting company Lexicon hired by RIM to come up with a name. One of the naming experts at Lexicon thought the miniature buttons on RIM's product looked like the tiny seeds in a strawberry. A linguist at the firm thought straw was too slow sounding. Someone else suggested Black-Berry and the rest is history.

While including the usual PDA applications (address book, calendar, to-do lists, etc.) as well as telephone capabilities on newer models, the BlackBerry is primarily known for its ability to send and receive e-mail anywhere it has access to an appropriate wireless network, as well as for its built-in keyboard optimized for "thumbing," or using only the thumbs to type. System navigation is primarily accomplished by the trackwheel (or "thumb-wheel"), a scrolling wheel with a "click" function, located on the right side of the device.

Just as cell phones are status symbols to teens, the BlackBerry is certainly a status symbol to executives. Executives say the wireless devices help them stay connected to work around the clock, from anywhere in the world. The devices allow them to get out of the office and still get their work done. If an on-the-job crisis strikes, the devices keep them accessible. Among financial analysts and IT professionals, the product has been nicknamed "CrackBerry" because of its addictive qualities. BlackBerry's following of avid users includes such captains of industry as Dell Computer's Michael Dell, General Electric's Jack Welch, Mi-crosoft's Bill Gates, former U.S. vice president Al Gore, and celebrities Matt Damon, Ben Affleck, and Howard Stern.

A patent holding company, NTP, sued RIM over patent infringements and tried to prevent RIM from selling BlackBerry in the U.S. RIM and NTP ended their bitter battle recently by settling the matter with a one-time payment by RIM to NTP for $612.5 million. In exchange, RIM was granted a license that enables it to continue its BlackBerry mobile e-mail service. RIM gets unfettered rights to sell its products without threat of further litigation from NTP. The court case has been officially dismissed. It also liberates RIM's Black-Berry partners, including wireless service carriers, from the threat of lawsuits from NTP.[1]

THE PRODUCT AREA INVOLVES MANY STRATEGY DECISIONS

The BlackBerry case highlights some important topics we'll discuss in this chapter and the next. Here we'll start by looking at how customers see a firm's product. Then we'll talk about product classes to help you better understand marketing strategy planning. We'll also talk about branding, packaging, and warranties. As shown in Exhibit 9-1, there are many strategy decisions related to the Product area.

WHAT IS A PRODUCT?

Customers buy satisfaction, not parts

When Nikon sells a Coolpix digital camera, is it just selling a certain number of switches and buttons, a plastic case, a lens, and megapixels of memory?

When Air Canada sells a ticket for a flight to the Caribbean, is it just selling so much wear and tear on an airplane and so much pilot fatigue?

The answer to these questions is *no*. Instead, what these companies are really selling is the satisfaction, use, or benefit the customer wants.

All consumers care about is that their Coolpix cameras make it easy to take cool pictures. And when they take a trip on Air Canada, they really don't care how hard it is on the plane or the crew. They just want a safe, comfortable trip. In the same way, when producers and middlemen buy a product, they're interested in the profit they can make from its purchase—through use or resale.

Exhibit 9-1
Strategy Planning for
Product

Target
market

| Product | Place | Promotion | Price |

| Product idea | Brand | Package | Warranty |

Physical
good/service
Features
Benefits
Quality level
Accessories
Installation
Instructions
Product line

Type of brand:
Individual or
family
Manufacturer or
dealer

Protection
Promotion
Enhancement

None, limited,
full, extended

Product means the need-satisfying offering of a firm. The idea of "Product" as potential customer satisfaction or benefits is very important. Many business managers get wrapped up in the technical details involved in producing a product. But that's not how most customers view the product. Most customers think about a product in terms of the total satisfaction it provides. That satisfaction may require a "total" product offering that is really a combination of excellent service, a physical good with the right features, useful instructions, a convenient package, a trustworthy warranty, and perhaps even a familiar name that has satisfied the consumer in the past.

Product quality is not always a life or death matter, but a firm that provides customers with superior customer value is likely to have a competitive advantage.

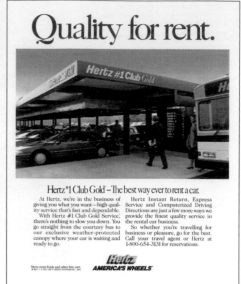

Product quality and customer needs

Product quality should also be determined by how customers view the product. From a marketing perspective, **quality** means a product's ability to satisfy a customer's needs or requirements. This definition focuses on the customer—and how the customer thinks a product will fit some purpose. For example, the "best" satellite TV service may not be the one with the highest number of channels but the one that includes a local channel that a consumer wants to watch. Similarly, the best-quality clothing for casual wear on campus may be a pair of jeans, not a pair of dress slacks made of a higher-grade fabric.

Among different types of jeans, the one with the strongest stitching and the most comfortable or durable fabric might be thought of as having the highest grade or *relative quality* for its product type. Marketing managers often focus on relative quality when comparing their products to competitors' offerings. However, a product with better features is not a high-quality product if the features aren't what the target market wants.

Quality and satisfaction depend on the total product offering. If potato chips get stale on the shelf because of poor packaging, the consumer will be dissatisfied. A broken button on a shirt will disappoint the customer—even if the laundry did a nice job cleaning and pressing the collar. A full-featured digital video recorder is a poor-quality product if it's hard for a consumer to program a recording session.[2]

Goods and/or services are the product

We want to think of a product in terms of the needs it satisfies. If a firm's objective is to satisfy customer needs, service can be part of its product—or service alone may *be* the product—and must be provided as part of a total marketing mix.

Exhibit 9-2 shows this bigger view of Product. It shows that a product can range from a 100 percent emphasis on physical goods—for commodities like steel pipe—to a 100 percent emphasis on service, like Internet access. Regardless of the emphasis involved, the marketing manager must consider most of the same elements in planning products and marketing mixes. Given this, we usually won't make a distinction between goods and services but will call all of them *Products.* Sometimes, however, understanding the differences in goods and services can help fine-tune marketing strategy planning. So let's look at some of these differences next.

Exhibit 9-2
Examples of Possible Blends
of Physical Goods and
Services in a Product

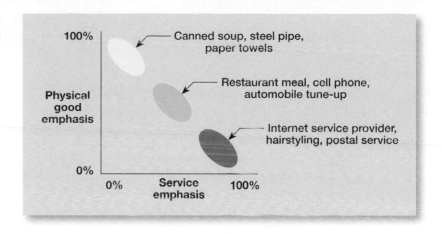

DIFFERENCES IN GOODS AND SERVICES

How tangible is the product?

Because a good is a physical thing, it can be seen and touched. You can try on a pair of Timberland shoes, thumb through the latest issue of *Rolling Stone* magazine, or smell Colombian coffee as it brews. A good is a *tangible* item. When you buy it, you own it. And it's usually pretty easy to see exactly what you'll get.

On the other hand, a **service** is a deed performed by one party for another. When you provide a customer with a service, the customer can't keep it. Rather, a service is experienced, used, or consumed. You go see a DreamWorks Pictures movie, but afterward all you have is a memory. You ride on a ski lift in the Rockies, but you don't own the equipment. Services are not physical—they are *intangible*. You can't "hold" a service. And it may be hard to know exactly what you'll get when you buy it.

Most products are a combination of tangible and intangible elements. A Domino's pizza is tangible, but the fast home delivery is not.

Is the product produced before it's sold?

Goods are usually produced in a factory and then sold. A Sony flat-screen TV may be stored in a warehouse or store waiting for a buyer. By contrast, services are often sold first, then produced. And they're produced and consumed in the same time frame. Thus, goods producers may be far away from the customer, but service providers often work in the customer's presence.

Hairstylists offer an intangible service. Haircuts cannot be stored up for busy times!

A worker in a Sony TV factory can be in a bad mood—and customers will never know. But a rude bank teller can drive customers away. The service and the service provider are *inseparable*.

Services can't be stored or transported

Services are *perishable*—they can't be stored. This makes it harder to balance supply and demand. An example explains the problem.

Bell sells long-distance telephone services. Even on Mother's Day when demand is high, customers expect the service to be available. They don't want to hear "Sorry, all lines are busy." So Bell must have enough equipment and employees to deal with peak demand times. But when customers aren't making many calls, Bell's facilities are idle and the unused capacity (equipment and people) can't be saved and sold later.

It's often difficult to have economies of scale when the product emphasis is on service. *Services often have to be produced in the presence of the customer.* So service suppliers often need duplicate equipment and staff at places where the service is actually provided. RBC Dominion Securities sells investment advice along with financial products. That advice could, perhaps, be produced more economically in a single building in Toronto and made available only on its Web site. But RBC has offices all across Canada. Many customers want a personal touch from the stockbroker telling them how to invest their money.[3] As a result, services may often be *inconsistent* or *variable*. Different advisors will give different advice.

Think about the whole product

Providing the right product—when and where and how the customer wants it—is a challenge. This is true whether the product is primarily a service, primarily a good, or as is usually the case, a blend of both. Marketing managers must think about the "whole" Product they provide, and then make sure that all of the elements fit together and work with the rest of the marketing strategy. Sometimes a single product isn't enough to meet the needs of target customers. Then assortments of different products may be required.

WHOLE PRODUCT LINES MUST BE DEVELOPED TOO

A **product assortment** is the set of all product lines and individual products that a firm sells. A **product line** is a set of individual products that are closely related. The seller may see the products in a line as related because they're produced or operate in a similar way, sold to the same target market, sold through the same types of outlets, or priced at about the same level. Sara Lee, for example, has many product lines in its product assortment—including coffee, tea, luncheon meats, desserts, snacks, hosiery, sportswear, lingerie, and shoe polish. But Enterprise has one product line—different types of vehicles to rent. An **individual product** is a particular product within a product line. It usually is differentiated by brand, level of service offered, price, or some other characteristic. For example, each size and scent of a brand of soap is an individual product. Middlemen usually think of each separate product as a stock-keeping unit (SKU) and assign it a unique SKU number.

Each individual product and target market may require a separate strategy. For example, Sara Lee's strategy for selling its Café Pilão coffee in Brazil is different from its strategy for selling Hanes men's underwear in Canada. We'll focus mainly on developing one marketing strategy at a time. But remember that a marketing manager may have to plan *several* strategies to develop an effective marketing program for a whole company.

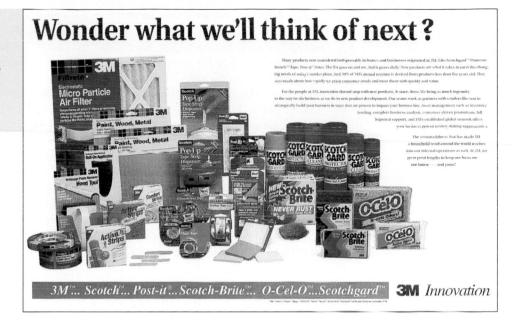

At companies like 3M, managers must develop marketing plans for individual products that are consistent with the marketing program for the whole product assortment.

PRODUCT CLASSES HELP PLAN MARKETING STRATEGIES

You don't have to treat *every* product as unique when planning strategies. Some product classes require similar marketing mixes. These product classes are a useful starting point for developing marketing mixes for new products and evaluating present mixes.

Product classes start with type of customer

All products fit into one of two broad groups—based on the type of customer that will use them. **Consumer products** are products meant for the final consumer. **Business products** are products meant for use in producing other products.

The same product—like Bertolli Olive Oil—*might* be both a consumer product and a business product. Consumers buy it to use in their own kitchens, but food processing companies and restaurants buy it in large quantities as an ingredient in the products they sell. Selling the same product to both final consumers and business customers requires (at least) two different strategies.

There are product classes within each group. Consumer product classes are based on *how consumers think about and shop for products*. Business product classes are based on *how buyers think about products and how they'll be used*.

INTERNET EXERCISE

Go to the Aldo Shoes Web site (www.aldoshoes.com) and click on *Shoes*. Then choose either men's or women's. You will see the major product lines listed. Click on each to view the depth of assortment, variety of styles, number of sizes, and colours available. Is this product offering appropriate for the target market? Why or why not?

CONSUMER PRODUCT CLASSES

Consumer product classes divide into four groups: (1) convenience, (2) shopping, (3) specialty, and (4) unsought. *Each class is based on the way people buy products.* See Exhibit 9-3 for a summary of how these product classes relate to marketing mixes.[4]

Convenience products—purchased quickly with little effort

Convenience products are products a consumer needs but isn't willing to spend much time or effort shopping for. These products are bought often, require little service or selling, don't cost much, and may even be bought by habit. A convenience product may be a staple, impulse product, or emergency product.

Staples are products that are bought often, routinely, and without much thought—like breakfast cereal, canned soup, and most other packaged foods used almost every day in almost every household.

Impulse products are products that are bought quickly—as *unplanned* purchases—because of a strongly felt need. True impulse products are items that the customer hadn't planned to buy, decides to buy on sight, may have bought the same way many times before, and wants right now. If the buyer doesn't see an impulse product at the right time, the sale may be lost.[5]

Emergency products are products that are purchased immediately when the need is great. The customer doesn't have time to shop around when a traffic accident occurs, a thunderstorm begins, or an impromptu party starts. The price of the ambulance service, raincoat, or ice cubes won't be important.

Shopping products—are compared

Shopping products are products that a customer feels are worth the time and effort to compare with competing products. Shopping products can be divided into two types, depending on what customers are comparing: (1) homogeneous or (2) heterogeneous shopping products.

Exhibit 9-3   Consumer Product Classes and Marketing Mix Planning

Consumer Product Class	Marketing Mix Considerations	Consumer Behaviour
Convenience products		
Staples	Maximum exposure with widespread, low-cost distribution; mass selling by producer; usually low price; branding is important.	Routinized (habitual), low effort, frequent purchases; low involvement.
Impulse	Widespread distribution with display at point of purchase.	Unplanned purchases bought quickly.
Emergency	Need widespread distribution near probable point of need; price sensitivity low.	Purchase made with time pressure when a need is great.
Shopping products		
Homogeneous	Need enough exposure to facilitate price comparison; price sensitivity high.	Customers see little difference among alternatives, seek lowest price.
Heterogeneous	Need distribution near similar products; promotion (including personal selling) to highlight product advantages; less price sensitivity.	Extensive problem solving; consumer may need help in making a decision (salesperson, Web site, etc.).
Specialty products	Price sensitivity is likely to be low; limited distribution may be acceptable, but should be treated as a convenience or shopping product (in whichever category product would typically be included) to reach persons not yet sold on its specialty product status.	Willing to expend effort to get specific product, even if not necessary; strong preferences make it an important purchase; Internet becoming important information source.
Unsought products		
New unsought	Must be available in places where similar (or related) products are sought; needs attention-getting promotion.	Need for product not strongly felt; unaware of benefits or not yet gone through adoption process.
Regularly unsought	Requires very aggressive promotion, usually personal selling.	Aware of product but not interested; attitude toward product may even be negative.

Many consumers shop for plates and other tableware as if they were homogeneous products, but Crate & Barrel wants customers to see its distinctive offerings as heterogeneous shopping products, or perhaps even specialty items.

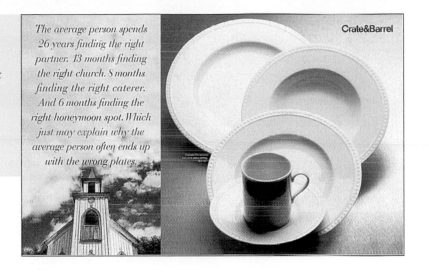

Homogeneous shopping products are shopping products the customer sees as basically the same and wants at the lowest price. Some consumers feel that certain sizes and types of computers, television sets, washing machines, and even cars are very similar. So they shop for the best price. For some products, the Internet has become a way to do that quickly.

Firms may try to emphasize and promote their product differences to avoid head-to-head price competition. For example, Rustoleum says that its spray paint goes on smoother and does a better job of preventing rust. But if consumers don't think the differences are real or important in terms of the value they seek, they'll just look at price.

Heterogeneous shopping products are shopping products the customer sees as different and wants to inspect for quality and suitability. Furniture, clothing, and membership in a spa are good examples. Often the consumer expects help from a knowledgeable salesperson. Quality and style matter more than price. In fact, once the customer finds the right product, price may not matter as long as it's reasonable. For example, you may have asked a friend to recommend a good dentist without even asking what the dentist charges.

Branding may be less important for heterogeneous shopping products. The more carefully consumers compare price and quality, the less they rely on brand names or labels. Some retailers carry competing brands so consumers won't go to a competitor to compare items.

Specialty products—no substitutes please!

Specialty products are consumer products that the customer really wants and makes a special effort to find. Shopping for a specialty product doesn't mean comparing—the buyer wants that special product and is willing to search for it. It's the customer's *willingness to search*—not the extent of searching—that makes it a specialty product.

Any branded product that consumers insist on by name is a specialty product. Examples include the Apple iPod and Dom Perignon champagne. Marketing managers want customers to see their products as specialty products and ask for them over and over again. Building that kind of relationship isn't easy. It means satisfying the customer every time. However, that's easier and a lot less costly than trying to win back dissatisfied customers or attract new customers who are not seeking the product at all.

Unsought products—need promotion

Unsought products are products that potential customers don't yet want or know they can buy. So they don't search for them at all. In fact, consumers probably won't buy these products if they see them—unless Promotion can show their value.

Businesses buy the goods and services they need to produce products for their own customers, so the demand for GE's special plastic resins, used to make lightweight and impact-resistant body panels, is derived from consumer demand for VW's unique car.

There are two types of unsought products. **New unsought products** are products offering really new ideas that potential customers don't know about yet. Informative promotion can help convince customers to accept the product, ending its unsought status. Dannon's yogourt, and Netscape's browser are popular items now, but initially they were new unsought products.

Regularly unsought products are products—like gravestones and life insurance—that stay unsought but not unbought forever. There may be a need, but potential customers aren't motivated to satisfy it. For this kind of product, personal selling is *very* important.

Many nonprofit organizations try to "sell" their unsought products. For example, the Canadian Blood Services regularly holds blood drives to remind prospective donors of how important it is to give blood.

One product may be seen several ways

The same product might be seen in different ways by different target markets at the same time. For example, a product viewed as a staple by most consumers in Canada, the United States, or some similar affluent country might be seen as a heterogeneous shopping product by consumers in another country. The price might be much higher when considered as a proportion of the consumer's budget, and the available choices might be very different. Similarly, a convenient place to shop often means very different things in different countries. In Japan, for example, retail stores tend to be smaller and carry smaller selections of products.

BUSINESS PRODUCTS ARE DIFFERENT

Business product classes are also useful for developing marketing mixes—since business firms use a system of buying related to these product classes.

Before looking at business product differences, however, we'll note some important similarities that affect marketing strategy planning.

One demand derived from another

The big difference in the business products market is derived demand—the demand for business products derives from the demand for final consumer products. For example, car manufacturers buy about one-fifth of all steel products. But if demand for cars drops, they'll buy less steel. Then even the steel supplier with the best marketing mix is likely to lose sales.[6]

| Price increases might not reduce quantity purchased | Total *industry* demand for business products is fairly inelastic. Business firms must buy what they need to produce their own products. Even if the cost of basic silicon doubles, for example, Intel needs it to make computer chips. However, sharp business buyers try to buy as economically as possible. So the demand facing *individual sellers* may be extremely elastic—if similar products are available at a lower price. |

BUSINESS PRODUCT CLASSES—HOW THEY ARE DEFINED

Business product classes are based on how buyers see products and how the products will be used. The classes of business products are (1) installations, (2) accessories, (3) raw materials, (4) components, (5) supplies, and (6) professional services. Exhibit 9-4 relates these product classes to marketing mix planning.

Installations—a boom-or-bust business

Installations—such as buildings, land rights, and major equipment—are important capital items. One-of-a-kind installations—like office buildings and custom-made machines—generally require special negotiations for each sale. Negotiations often involve top management and can stretch over months or even years. Standardized major equipment is treated more routinely.

Installations are a boom-or-bust business. During growth periods, firms may buy installations to increase capacity. But during a downswing, sales fall off sharply.[7]

Exhibit 9-4   Business Product Classes and Marketing Mix Planning

Business Product Classes	Marketing Mix Considerations	Buying Behaviour
Installations	Usually requires skillful personal selling by producer, including technical contacts, or understanding of applications; leasing and specialized support services may be required.	Multiple buying influence (including top management) and new-task buying are common; infrequent purchase, long decision period, and boom-or-bust demand are typical.
Accessory equipment	Need fairly widespread distribution and numerous contacts by experienced and sometimes technically trained personnel; price competition is often intense, but quality is important.	Purchasing and operating personnel typically make decisions; shorter decision period than for installations; Internet sourcing.
Raw materials	Grading is important, and transportation and storing can be crucial because of seasonal production and/or perishable products; markets tend to be very competitive.	Long-term contract may be required to ensure supply; online auctions.
Component parts and materials	Product quality and delivery reliability are usually extremely important; negotiation and technical selling typical on less-standardized items; replacement after market may require different strategies.	Multiple buying influence is common; online competitive bids used to encourage competitive pricing.
Maintenance, repair, and operating (MRO) supplies	Typically require widespread distribution or fast delivery (repair items); arrangements with appropriate middlemen may be crucial.	Often handled as straight rebuys, except important operating supplies may be treated much more seriously and involve multiple buying influence.
Professional services	Services customized to buyer's need; personal selling very important; inelastic demand often supports high prices.	Customer may compare outside service with what internal people could provide; needs may be very specialized.

Magna produces component parts used by automobile original equipment manufacturers (OEMs). It also sells car owners add-on parts they want for their vehicles, such as VideoMirror™, which uses a video screen to show a view of the blind zone behind the vehicle. The marketing mix for the two target markets is different, but Magna can meet the needs of both markets. ADP, by contrast, sells professional services. It wants potential customers to see that it makes sense to have ADP handle human resource administrative tasks that might otherwise be handled by a firm's own employees.

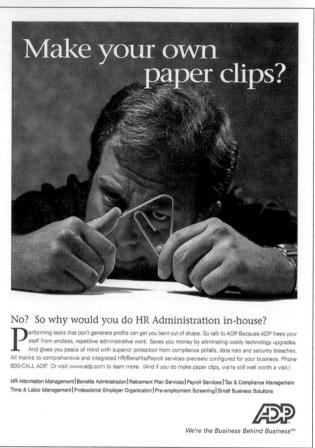

Specialized services are needed as part of the product

Suppliers sometimes include special services with an installation at no extra cost. A firm that sells (or leases) equipment to dentists, for example, may install it and help the dentist learn to use it.

Accessories— important but short-lived capital items

Accessories are short-lived capital items—tools and equipment used in production or office activities—like Canon's small copy machines, Rockwell's portable drills, and Steelcase's filing cabinets.

Since these products cost less and last a shorter time than installations, multiple buying influence is less important. Operating people and purchasing agents, rather than top managers, may make the purchase decision. As with installations, some customers may wish to lease or rent—to expense the cost.

Accessories are more standardized than installations. And they're usually needed by more customers. For example, IBM sells its robotics systems, which can cost over $2 million, as custom installations to large manufacturers. But IBM's ThinkPad computers, which are now made by China's Lenovo Group, are accessory equipment for just about every type of modern business all around the world.

Raw materials become part of a physical good

Raw materials are unprocessed expense items—such as logs, iron ore, and wheat—that are moved to the next production process with little handling. Unlike installations and accessories, *raw materials become part of a physical good and are expense items.*

There are two types of raw materials: (1) farm products and (2) natural products. Farm products are grown by farmers—examples are oranges, sugar cane, and cattle. Natural products are products that occur in nature—such as timber, iron ore, oil, and coal.

Most buyers of raw materials want ample supplies in the right grades for specific uses—fresh vegetables for Green Giant's production lines or logs for Weyerhaeuser's paper mills. To ensure steady quantities, raw materials customers often sign long-term contracts, sometimes at guaranteed prices.

Component parts and materials must meet specifications

Components are processed expense items that become part of a finished product. Component *parts* are finished (or nearly finished) items that are ready for assembly into the final product. ATI's graphics cards included in personal computers, TRW's air bags in cars, and Pratt and Whitney engines for airplanes are examples. Component *materials* are items such as wire, plastic, or textiles. They have already been processed but must be processed further before becoming part of the final product. Quality is important with components because they become part of the firm's own product.

Components are often produced in large quantity to meet standard specifications. However, some components are custom-made. Then teamwork between the buyer and seller may be needed to arrive at the right specifications. So a buyer may develop a close partnership with a dependable supplier. And top management may be involved if the price is high or the component is extremely important to the final product. In contrast, standardized component materials are more likely to be purchased online using a competitive bidding system.

Since component parts go into finished products, a replacement market often develops. This *after market* can be both large and very profitable. Car tires and batteries are two examples of components originally sold in the OEM (*original equipment market*) that become consumer products in the after market. The target markets are different—and different marketing mixes are usually necessary.[8]

Supplies for maintenance, repair, and operations

Supplies are expense items that do not become part of a finished product. Buyers may treat these items less seriously. When a firm cuts its budget, orders for supplies may be the first to go. Supplies can be divided into three types: (1) maintenance, (2) repair, and (3) operating supplies—giving them their common name: MRO supplies.

Maintenance and small operating supplies are like convenience products. The item will be ordered because it is needed—but buyers won't spend much time on it. Branding may become important because it makes buying easier for such "nuisance" purchases. Breadth of assortment and the seller's dependability are also important. Middlemen usually handle the many supply items. They are often purchased via online catalogue sites.[9]

Professional services—pay to get it done

Professional services are specialized services that support a firm's operations. They are usually expense items. Engineering or management consulting services can improve the plant layout or the company's efficiency. Information technology services can maintain a company's networks and Web sites. Design services can suggest a new look for products or promotion materials. Advertising agencies can help promote the firm's products. And food services can improve morale.

Managers compare the cost of buying professional services outside the firm (*outsourcing*) to the cost of having company people do them. Further, many firms try to cut costs by downsizing the number of people that they employ. In many cases, work that was previously done by an employee is now purchased from an independent supplier. Clearly, the number of service specialists is growing in our complex economy.

Exhibit 9-5   Recognized Trademarks and Symbols Help in Promotion

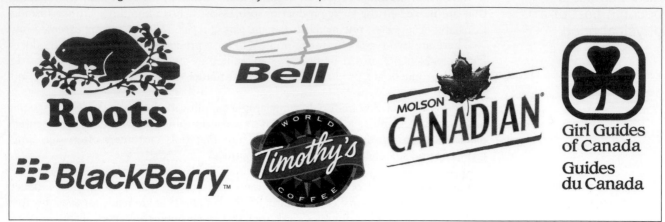

BRANDING NEEDS A STRATEGY DECISION TOO

There are so many brands—and we're so used to seeing them—that we take them for granted. But branding is an important decision area, so we will treat it in some detail.

What is branding?

Branding means the use of a name, term, symbol, or design—or a combination of these—to identify a product. It includes the use of brand names, trademarks, and practically all other means of product identification.

Brand name has a narrower meaning. A **brand name** is a word, letter, or a group of words or letters. Examples include WD-40, 3M Post-its, and PT Cruiser.

Trademark is a legal term. A **trademark** includes only those words, symbols, or marks that are legally registered for use by a single company. A **service mark** is the same as a trademark except that it refers to a service offering.

The word *FedEx* can be used to explain these differences. The FedEx overnight delivery service is branded under the brand name FedEx (whether it's spoken or printed in any manner). When "FedEx" is printed in a certain kind of script, however, it becomes a trademark. A trademark need not be attached to the product. It need not even be a word—it can be a symbol. Exhibit 9-5 shows some common trademarks.

These differences may seem technical. But they are very important to business firms that spend a lot of money to protect and promote their brands. Sometimes a firm's brand name is the only element in its marketing mix that a competitor can't copy.

Brands meet needs

Well-recognized brands make shopping easier. Think of trying to buy groceries, for example, if you had to evaluate each of 25,000 items every time you went to a supermarket. Many customers are willing to buy new things—but having gambled and won, they like to buy a sure thing the next time.

Brand promotion has advantages for branders as well as customers. A good brand reduces the marketer's selling time and effort. Good brands can also improve the company's image—speeding acceptance of new products marketed under the same name. For example, many consumers quickly tried Listerine PocketPaks breath fresheners when they appeared because they already knew they liked Listerine mouthwash.[10]

CONDITIONS FAVOURABLE TO BRANDING

Can you recall a brand name for file folders, bed frames, electric extension cords, or nails? As these examples suggest, it's not always easy to establish a respected brand.

The following conditions are favourable to successful branding:

1. The product is easy to label and identify by brand or trademark.
2. The product quality is easy to maintain and the best value for the price.
3. Dependable and widespread availability is possible. When customers start using a brand, they want to be able to continue using it.
4. Demand is strong enough that the market price can be high enough to make the branding effort profitable.
5. There are economies of scale. If the branding is really successful, costs should drop and profits should increase.
6. Favourable shelf locations or display space in stores will help. This is something retailers can control when they brand their own products.

In general, these conditions are less common in less-developed economies, and that may explain why efforts to build brands in less-developed nations often fail.

ACHIEVING BRAND FAMILIARITY IS NOT EASY

Some of the first brands started in the 1860s and 1870s (and still going strong) are Borden's Condensed Milk, Quaker Oats, Pillsbury's Best Flour, and Ivory Soap. Today, familiar brands exist for most product categories, ranging from crayons (Crayola) to real estate services (Century 21). However, what brand is familiar often varies from one country to another.

Brand acceptance must be earned with a good product and regular promotion. **Brand familiarity** means how well customers recognize and accept a company's brand. The degree of brand familiarity affects the planning for the rest of the marketing mix—especially where the product should be offered and what promotion is needed.

Five levels of brand familiarity

Five levels of brand familiarity are useful for strategy planning: (1) rejection, (2) nonrecognition, (3) recognition, (4) preference, and (5) insistence.

Some brands have been tried and found wanting. Brand rejection means that potential customers won't buy a brand unless its image is changed. Rejection may suggest a change in the product or perhaps only a shift to target customers who have a better image of the brand. Overcoming a negative image is difficult and can be very expensive.

It takes time and money to build brand awareness, so sometimes brands can be extended to new product offerings and different product categories. Dove has recently introduced new products that benefit from its well-recognized brand name.

Nutrition Bar

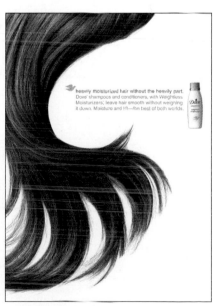

Marketing managers for Pepsi Bottling are seeking new customers. The traditional competition with Coke and retailers' private-label colas continues to be a challenge. However, another battle is brewing over the new generation of youthful soda drinkers—the "heavy users." They are less homogeneous than in the past. Many don't find big brands as appealing, and some don't see *any* cola as "their" drink. They want something different. So Pepsi developed a number of new products to appeal to different segments of this market. One of these was Code Red, a cherry-flavoured, caffeine-loaded, extension of Pepsi's Mountain Dew brand. The new-product team relied on a form of marketing experiment to develop Code Red. A large sample of consumers—including urban youth from different ethnic groups, computer geeks, and others in the target market—tested and rated different combinations of product features over time. This helped to fine-tune Code Red's packaging, candy-red colour, and cherry taste. Then, before Code Red was even available in stores, Pepsi used grassroots promotion to build brand awareness and word-of-mouth publicity. For example, an online game, "Mission: Code Red," gave players the chance to win free samples; similarly, a million samples were handed out at youth-oriented events like the Winter X Games and college basketball games.

Efforts like these helped Code Red achieve first-year sales that were even bigger than expected. So Pepsi quickly introduced other brand extensions, including lemon-flavoured Pepsi Twist, Vanilla Pepsi, and Pepsi Blue. The taste of Pepsi Blue, described as a "berry/cola fusion," and its Windex-like colour were selected because they appealed to youth who were bored with ordinary cola.

It will take time to see if Pepsi's efforts to target niche markets will be profitable. One risk is that these brand extensions will just siphon shelf space and sales away from regular Pepsi and Mountain Dew. Initially, about one-fourth of Code Red sales came from Mountain Dew. In addition, this is not the first time that Pepsi has tried to introduce new products under its well-known family brand. In the 1990s, Pepsi Crystal, a clear-coloured soda, and Pepsi AM both lost their fizz after the introductory promotion ended.[11]

Brand rejection is a big concern for service-oriented businesses because it's hard to control the quality of service. A business traveller who gets a dirty room in a Hilton Hotel in Caracas, Venezuela, might not return to a Hilton anywhere. Yet it's difficult for Hilton to ensure that every maid does a good job every time.

Some products are seen as basically the same. Brand nonrecognition means final consumers don't recognize a brand at all—even though middlemen may use the brand name for identification and inventory control. Examples include school supplies, inexpensive dinnerware, many of the items that you'd find in a hardware store, and thousands of dot-coms on the Internet.

Brand recognition means that customers remember the brand. This may not seem like much, but it can be a big advantage if there are many "nothing" brands on the market. Even if consumers can't recall the brand without help, they may be reminded when they see it in a store among other less familiar brands. Tide laundry detergent is a recognizable brand on the supermarket shelf.

Most branders would like to win **brand preference**—which means that target customers usually choose the brand over other brands, perhaps because of habit or favourable past experience. Consumers may prefer Coke to Pepsi—it's their "usual brand."

Brand insistence means customers insist on a firm's branded product and are willing to search for it. This is an objective of many target marketers. Heinz has been successful with brand insistence in ketchup.

The right brand name can help

A good brand name can help build brand familiarity. It can help tell something important about the company or its product. Exhibit 9-6 lists some characteristics of a good brand name. Some successful brand names seem to break all these rules, but many of them got started when there was less competition.

Exhibit 9-6
Characteristics of a Good
Brand Name

• Short and simple	• Suggestive of product benefits
• Easy to spell and read	• Adaptable to packaging/labelling needs
• Easy to recognize and remember	• No undesirable imagery
• Easy to pronounce	• Always timely (does not go out-of-date)
• Can be pronounced in only one way	• Adaptable to any advertising medium
• Can be pronounced in all languages (for international markets)	• Legally available for use (not in use by another firm)

Companies that compete in international markets face a special problem in selecting brand names. A name that conveys a positive image in one language may be meaningless in another. Or, worse, it may have unintended meanings. GM's Nova car is a classic example. GM stuck with the Nova name when it introduced the car in South America. It seemed like a sensible decision because *nova* is the Spanish word for star. However, Nova also sounds the same as the Spanish words for "no go." Consumers weren't interested in a no-go car, and sales didn't pick up until GM changed the name.[12]

A respected name builds brand equity

Because it's costly to build brand recognition, some firms prefer to acquire established brands rather than try to build their own. The value of a brand to its current owner or to a firm that wants to buy it is sometimes called **brand equity**—the value of a brand's overall strength in the market. For example, brand equity is likely to be higher if many satisfied customers insist on buying the brand and if retailers are eager to stock it. That almost guarantees ongoing profits.

The financial value of the Yahoo brand name illustrates the brand equity idea. In 1994, Yahoo was just a tiny start-up trying to make it with a directory site on the Internet. Most people had never heard the name, and few even knew what the Internet was or why you'd need a directory site. As interest in the Internet grew, Yahoo promoted its brand name on TV and in magazines. It was often the only Web site name that newcomers to the Web knew, so for many it was a good place from which to start their surfing. Within a few years, Yahoo was attracting 30 million different people a month. Since Yahoo charged fees to advertisers eager to reach these users, the familiarity of its brand translated directly into ad revenues.[13]

PROTECTING BRAND NAMES AND TRADEMARKS

Canadian firms may legally protect their trademarks and brand names under the **Trademark Act**. This act protects the company from other firms using trademarks or brand names that could be confused with the company's own. Note that registration is not required under Canadian law. Although ownership of brand names and trademarks is generally established by use, registration is a good idea. This action gives the company legal protection for a valuable asset.

You must protect your own

A brand can be a real asset to a company. Each firm should try to see that its brand doesn't become a common descriptive term for its kind of product. When this happens, the brand name or trademark becomes public property—and the owner loses all rights to it. This happened with the names cellophane, zipper, shredded wheat, and kerosene.[14]

Counterfeiting is accepted in some cultures

Even when products are properly registered, counterfeiters may make unauthorized copies. Many well-known brands—ranging from Levi's jeans to Rolex watches to Zantax ulcer medicine—face this problem. Of course, pirated digital copies of songs, movies, and books are also routinely shared over the Internet. Counterfeiting is especially

Legitimate companies spend considerable amounts of money in promoting their brand names. Consumers put trust in a brand name such as Sony or BlackBerry or Roots. Counterfeit products take advantage of the value of brand names by using them on their products.

Counterfeit goods can legally enter Canada if they are declared, due to a loophole in the country's laws. This has upset trading partners because Canada has the most lax laws in the developed world when it comes to protecting consumers and markets from bogus goods. Those selling legitimate goods face unfair competition from those selling marked-down fakes. There's also the issue of public health and safety. Recent seizures in Canada include expired baby food with counterfeit best-before dates attached, counterfeit, brand name batteries containing elevated levels of dangerous chemicals, children's stuffed toys filled with hair and fibreglass, and safety boots with inadequate protection and fake safety logos. The trade of fake goods is estimated to cost Canada $20 billion to $30 billion a year.

Anthony Toderian, spokesman for the Canadian Standards Association, says the traditional concept of counterfeiting has expanded from simply knock-off T-shirts and handbags to medicines, cleaning solutions, electronics, and toothbrushes—basically, anything that bears a brand name. According to Toderian, Metropolitan centres, such as Vancouver and Toronto, are the hottest markets for counterfeit products.

Knock-offs fall under two categories, counterfeit and copyright infringement, according to Vancouver lawyer Michael Manson, a partner at law firm Smart and Biggar. Exact duplicates are considered counterfeits, and violators can be brought to Canadian court under either criminal or civil law, he said. Goods like the "oK" watches, which bear a striking resemblance to Calvin Klein's "cK" logo but are slightly different, are copyright infringements. Infringements are typically not criminal violations, but can be taken to court under civil law. It's illegal to make, sell, and use fake products, and punishments range from jail terms to fines or statutory damages up to $20,000 per infringement, according to Manson. But he points out that the law is difficult to enforce, noting that Canadian police and customs officials lack resources, while Canadian legislation is weak. Would it bother you to purchase a fake Rolex watch? Why or why not?[15]

common in developing nations. In China, for example, many DVDs, CDs, and software programs are bootleg copies. As noted in this chapter's ethics box, counterfeiting can be big business, so efforts to stop it may meet with limited success. There are also differences in cultural values. In South Korea, for example, many people don't see counterfeiting as unethical.[16]

WHAT KIND OF BRAND TO USE?

Keep it in the family

Branders of more than one product must decide whether they are going to use a **family brand**—the same brand name for several products—or individual brands for each product. Examples of family brands are Sears' Kenmore appliances and Canadian Tire's Mastercraft tools.

The use of the same brand for many products makes sense if all are similar in type and quality. The main benefit is that the goodwill attached to one or two products may help the others. Money spent to promote the brand name benefits more than one product, which cuts promotion costs for each product. McCain Foods uses their brand across potato, beverage, and dessert categories.

A special kind of family brand is a **licensed brand**—a well-known brand that sellers pay a fee to use. For example, the familiar Sunkist brand name has been licensed to many companies for use on more than 400 products in 30 countries.[17]

Individual brands for outside and inside competition

A company uses **individual brands**—separate brand names for each product—when it's important for the products to each have a separate identity, as when products vary in quality or type.

As these trade ads suggest, both Del Monte and GE want retailers to remember that many consumers already know and trust their brand names.

If the products are really different, such as Tide and Crest toothpaste, individual brands can avoid confusion. Some firms use individual brands with similar products to make segmentation and positioning efforts easier. For example, when General Mills introduced a line of organic cereals, it used the Cascadian Farms name and the Big G logo was not on the box. The rationale was that consumers who try to avoid additives might not trust a big corporate brand.[18]

INTERNET EXERCISE

Go to the Procter & Gamble Web site (www.pg.ca) and click on *Products*, and then *Personal and Beauty*. Click on the *Choose by Brand* box to see a list of P&G brands. How many are brand names of the different shampoos that P&G makes? How are the different brands positioned, and what target markets do they appeal to?

Generic "brands"

Products that some consumers see as commodities may be difficult or expensive to brand. Some manufacturers and middlemen have responded to this problem with **generic products**—products that have no brand at all other than identification of their contents and the manufacturer or middleman. Generic products are usually offered in plain packages at lower prices. They are quite common in less-developed nations.[19]

WHO SHOULD DO THE BRANDING?

Manufacturer brands versus dealer brands

Manufacturer brands are brands created by producers. These are sometimes called *national brands* because the brand is promoted all across the country or in large regions. Note, however, that many manufacturer brands are now distributed globally. Such brands include Nabisco, Campbell's, Whirlpool, Ford, and IBM. Many creators of service-oriented firms—like McDonald's and the Royal Bank—promote their brands this way too.

Dealer brands, also called **private brands**, are brands created by middlemen or intermediaries. Examples of dealer brands include the brands of Loblaws, The Bay, Wal-Mart, and Sears. Some of these are advertised and distributed more widely than many national brands.

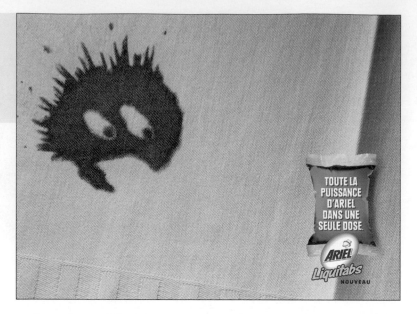

Innovative packaging turns Ariel's "Liquitabs" into a more convenient product. The copy on this French ad says "all the power of Ariel in a single dose."

From the middleman's perspective, the major advantage of selling a popular manufacturer brand is that the product is already presold to some target customers. The major disadvantage is that manufacturers normally offer lower gross margins than the middleman might be able to earn with a dealer brand. In addition, the manufacturer maintains control of the brand and may withdraw it from a middleman at any time. Customers, loyal to the brand rather than to the retailer or wholesaler, may go elsewhere if the brand is not available.

Dealer branders take on more responsibility and must promote their own product. They must be able to arrange a dependable source of supply and usually have to buy in fairly large quantities. This increases their risk and cost of carrying inventory. However, these problems are easier to overcome if the middleman deals in a large sales volume, as is the case with many large retail chains. Loblaws has been successful selling President's Choice brand products.

Who's winning the battle of the brands?

The **battle of the brands**, the competition between dealer brands and manufacturer brands, is just a question of whose brands will be more popular and who will be in control.

At one time, manufacturer brands were much more popular than dealer brands. Now sales of both kinds of brands are about equal—but sales of dealer brands are expected to continue growing. Middlemen have some advantages in this battle. With the number of large retail chains growing, they are better able to arrange reliable sources of supply at low cost. They can also give the dealer brand special shelf position or promotion.

Consumers benefit from the battle. Competition has already narrowed price differences between manufacturer brands and well-known dealer brands. And big retailers like Wal-Mart are constantly pushing manufacturers to lower prices—because national brands at low prices bring in even more customers than store brands.[20]

THE STRATEGIC IMPORTANCE OF PACKAGING

Packaging involves promoting, protecting, and enhancing the product. Packaging can be important to both sellers and customers. See Exhibit 9-7. It can make a product more convenient to use or store. It can prevent spoiling or damage. Good packaging makes products easier to identify and promotes the brand at the point of purchase and even in use.

Exhibit 9-7 Some Ways Packaging Benefits Consumers and Marketers

Opportunity to Add Value	Some Decision Factors	Examples
Promotion	Link product to promotion	The bunny on the Energizer battery package is a reminder that it "keeps going and going."
	Branding at point of purchase or consumption	Coke's logo greets almost everyone each time the refrigerator is opened.
	Product information	Kraft's nutrition label helps consumers decide which cheese to buy, and a UPC code reduces checkout time and errors.
Protection	For shipping and storing	Sony's MP3 player is kept safe by Styrofoam inserts.
	From spoiling	Tylenol's safety seal prevents tampering.
	From shoplifting	Cardboard hang-tag on Gillette razor blades is too large to hide in hand.
Enhance product	The environment	Tide detergent bottle can be recycled.
	Convenience in use	Squeezable tube of Yoplait Tubes is easy to eat on the go and in new situations.
	Added product functions	Plastic tub is useful for refrigerator leftovers after the Cool Whip is gone.

Packaging can enhance the product

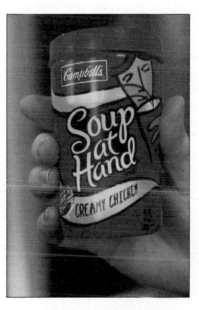

A new package can make *the* important difference in a new marketing strategy—by meeting customers' needs better. Sometimes a new package makes the product easier or safer to use. For example, most drug and food products now have special seals to prevent product tampering. And clever packaging is an important part of a new effort by Campbell's Soup to pump new life into an old product—soup. Campbell's developed its Soup at Hand with a package that doesn't require a can opener or a stirring pot and instead is microwavable. Soup at Hand is just right for today's on-the-go consumers who want a portable meal solution, so it also helps Campbell's get distribution in convenience stores and vending machines. Consumers value convenience, so the Soup at Hand price of $1.99 (versus $.99 for a traditional can of soup) also produces attractive profits.[21]

Packaging sends a message

Packaging can tie the product to the rest of the marketing strategy. Packaging for Energizer batteries features the pink bunny seen in attention-getting TV ads and reminds consumers that the batteries are durable. A good package sometimes gives a firm more promotion effect than it could get with advertising. Customers see the package in stores, when they're actually buying.

Packaging may lower distribution costs

Better protective packaging is very important to manufacturers and wholesalers. They sometimes have to pay the cost of goods damaged in shipment. Retailers need protective packaging too. It can reduce storing costs by cutting breakage, spoilage, and theft. Good packages also save space and are easier to handle and display.[22]

Universal product codes speed handling

To speed handling of fast-selling products, government and industry representatives have developed a **universal product code (UPC)** that identifies each product with marks readable by electronic scanners. A computer then matches each code to the product and its price. These codes speed the checkout process and reduce the need to mark the price on every item. They also reduce errors by cashiers and make it easy to control inventory and track sales of specific products.[23]

Radio frequency identification tags (RFIDs) will soon replace the universal product code. RFIDs allow firms to track merchandise through the distribution channel. Products can be scanned without being physically seen. Containers and boxes do not need to be unpacked. Many larger wholesalers and retailers are now implementing this technology.

WHAT IS SOCIALLY RESPONSIBLE PACKAGING?

Laws reduce confusion and clutter

Consumers desire socially responsible packaging—clearly labelled, not misleading, and often environmentally friendly. Canadian laws such as the Hazardous Products Act protect consumers. The **Consumer Packaging and Labelling Act** requires product packaging to be standardized. Bilingual labels are also required. Other laws, such as the Textile Labelling Act, provide labelling requirements for specific product categories. All packaging laws are designed to protect the consumer. Packaging laws change regularly to reflect changing consumer needs. For example, food product labels must now show the amount of fats and in particular the amount of trans fat in a serving.

Ethical decisions remain

Although various laws provide guidance on many packaging issues, many areas still require marketing managers to make ethical choices. For example, some firms have been criticized for designing packages that conceal a downsized product, giving consumers less for their money. Similarly, some retailers design packages and labels for their private-label products that look just like, and are easily confused with, manufacturer brands. Are efforts such as these unethical, or are they simply an attempt to make packaging a more effective part of a marketing mix? Different people will answer differently.

Empty packages litter our streets, and some plastic packages will lie in a city dump for decades. But some consumers like the convenience that accompanies

A study by the Internet Advertising Bureau showed that firms, like Kimberly-Clark (the producer of the Kleenex brand) and Colgate, are able to develop more brand awareness and purchase preference when they shift some of their ad budgets to online media.

these problems. Is it unethical for a marketing manager to give consumers with different preferences a choice? Some critics argue that it is. Others praise firms that give consumers choices.

Many critics feel that labelling information is too often incomplete or misleading. For example, what does it really mean if a label says a food product is "organic" or "low fat"? Do consumers really understand the nutritional information required by law? Further, some consumers want information that is difficult, perhaps even impossible, to provide. For example, how can a label accurately describe a product's taste or texture? But the ethical issues usually focus on how far a marketing manager should go in putting potentially negative information on a package. For example, should Häagen-Dazs affix a label that says "this product will clog your arteries"? That sounds extreme, but what type of information *is* appropriate?[24]

Unit-pricing is a possible help

Some retailers, especially supermarkets, make it easier for consumers to compare packages with different weights or volumes. They use **unit-pricing**— which involves placing the price per gram (or some other standard measure) on or near the product. This makes price comparison easier.[25]

WARRANTY POLICIES ARE A PART OF STRATEGY PLANNING

Warranty puts promises in writing

A **warranty** explains what the seller promises about its product. A marketing manager should decide whether to offer a specific warranty, and if so what the warranty will cover and how it will be communicated to target customers. This is an area where the legal environment—as well as customer needs and competitive offerings—must be considered. The Competition Act covers warranties.

Canadian law says that producers must stand behind their products—even if they don't offer a specific warranty. A written warranty provided by the seller may promise more than the law provides. However, it may actually *reduce* the responsibility a producer would have under common law.

A company has to make it clear whether it's offering a full or limited warranty—and the law defines what *full* means. Most firms offer a limited warranty if they offer one at all. In recent years, many firms have reduced the period of warranty cover-

In a competitive market, a product warranty or a service guarantee can be the critical difference in a firm's marketing mix.

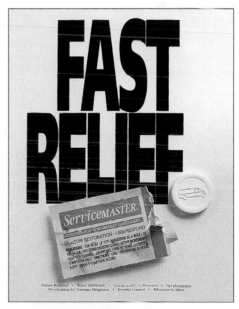

age. Apple's popular iPod music player and Sony's Clie hand-held organizer, for example, only have 90-day warranties. However, the Clie warranty is extended to one year if the owner registers the product.

Warranty may improve the marketing mix

Some firms use warranties to improve the appeal of their marketing mix. They design more quality into their goods or services and offer refunds or replacement, not just repair, if there is a problem. Xerox Corp. uses this approach with its copy machines. Its three-year warranty says that a customer who is not satisfied with a copier—for *any* reason—can trade it for another model. A strong warranty sends consumers a signal about brand quality.

Service guarantees

Customer service guarantees are becoming more common as a way to attract, and keep, customers. Pizza Hut guarantees a luncheon pizza in five minutes or it's free. General Motors set up a fast-oil-change guarantee to compete with fast-lube specialists who were taking customers away from dealers. If the dealer doesn't get the job done in 29 minutes or less, the next oil change is free. The Hampton Inn motel chain guarantees "100% satisfaction." If you're not totally satisfied with your stay, you're not expected to pay.

There's more risk in offering a service guarantee than a warranty on a physical product. An apathetic employee or a service breakdown can create a big expense. Front line staff may need to be empowered (allowed to make decisions) to effectively implement service guarantees. However, without the guarantee, dissatisfied customers may just go away mad without ever complaining. When customers collect on a guarantee, the company can fix the problem.

Warranty support can be costly

The cost of warranty support ultimately must be covered by the price that consumers pay. This has led some firms to offer warranty choices. The basic price for a product may include a warranty that covers a short time period or that covers parts but not labour. Consumers who want more or better protection pay extra for an extended warranty or a service contract.[26]

CONCLUSION

In this chapter, we looked at Product very broadly. We saw that a firm's Product is *what satisfies the needs of its target market*. The BlackBerry is a good example of a product that meets the needs of consumers. A product may be a physical good, a service, or some combination.

We introduced consumer product and business product classes and showed their effect on planning marketing mixes. Consumer product classes are based on consumers' buying behaviour. Business product classes are based on how buyers see the products and how they are used.

Branding and packaging can create new and more satisfying products. Packaging offers special opportunities to promote the product and inform customers. Variations in packaging can make a product attractive to different target markets.

Customers see brands as a guarantee of quality, and this leads to repeat purchasing. For marketers, such routine buying means lower promotion costs and higher sales.

Marketing managers use individual or family brands. In the end, however, customers express their approval or disapproval of the whole Product (including the brand). The degree of brand familiarity is a measure of the marketing manager's ability to carve out a separate market. And brand familiarity affects Place, Price, and Promotion decisions.

Warranties are also important in strategy planning. A warranty need not be strong—it just has to be clearly stated. But some customers find strong warranties attractive.

Product is concerned with much more than physical goods and services. To succeed in our increasingly competitive markets, the marketing manager must also be concerned about packaging, branding, and warranties.

KEY TERMS

QUESTIONS AND PROBLEMS

1. Define, in your own words, what a Product is.

2. Discuss several ways in which physical goods are different from pure services. Give an example of a good and then an example of a service that illustrates each of the differences.

3. What products are being offered by a shop that specializes in bicycles? By a travel agent? By a supermarket? By a new car dealer?

4. What kinds of consumer products are the following: (a) watches, (b) automobiles, and (c) toothpastes? Explain your reasoning.

5. Consumer services tend to be intangible, and goods tend to be tangible. Use an example to explain how the lack of a physical good in a pure service might affect efforts to promote the service.

6. How would the marketing mix for a staple convenience product differ from the one for a homogeneous shopping product? How would the mix for a specialty product differ from the mix for a heterogeneous shopping product? Use examples.

7. Give an example of a product that is a *new* unsought product for most people. Briefly explain why it is an unsought product.

8. In what types of stores would you expect to find (a) convenience products, (b) shopping products, (c) specialty products, and (d) unsought products?

9. Cite two examples of business products that require a substantial amount of service in order to be useful.

10. Explain why a new law office might want to lease furniture rather than buy it.

11. Would you expect to find any wholesalers selling the various types of business products? Are retail stores required (or something like retail stores)?

12. What kinds of business products are the following: (a) lubricating oil, (b) electric motors, and (c) a firm that provides landscaping and grass mowing for an apartment complex? Explain your reasoning.

13. How do raw materials differ from other business products? Do the differences have any impact on their marketing mixes? If so, what specifically?

14. For the kinds of business products described in this chapter, complete the following table (use one or a few well-chosen words).

    1. *Kind of distribution facility(ies) needed and functions they will provide.*
    2. *Calibre of salespeople required.*
    3. *Kind of advertising required.*

Products	1	2	3
Installations			
Buildings and land rights			
Major equipment			
Standard			
Custom-made			
Accessories			
Raw materials			
Farm products			
Natural products			
Components			
Supplies			
Maintenance and small operating supplies			
Operating supplies			
Professional services			

15. Is there any difference between a brand name and a trademark? If so, why is this difference important?

16. Is a well-known brand valuable only to the owner of the brand?

17. Suggest an example of a product and a competitive situation where it would *not* be profitable for a firm to spend large sums of money to establish a brand.

18. List five brand names and indicate what product is associated with the brand name. Evaluate the strengths and weaknesses of the brand name.

19. Explain family brands. Should Future Shop carry its own dealer brands to compete with some of the popular manufacturer brands it carries? Explain your reasons.

20. In the past, Sears emphasized its own dealer brands. Now it is carrying more well-known manufacturer brands. What are the benefits to Sears of carrying more manufacturer brands?

21. What does the degree of brand familiarity imply about previous and future promotion efforts? How does the degree of brand familiarity affect the Place and Price variables?

22. You operate a small hardware store with emphasis on manufacturer brands and have barely been breaking even. Evaluate the proposal of a large wholesaler who offers a full line of dealer-branded hardware items at substantially lower prices. Specify any assumptions necessary to obtain a definite answer.

23. Give an example where packaging costs probably (a) lower total distribution costs and (b) raise total distribution costs.

24. Is it more difficult to support a warranty for a service than for a physical good? Explain your reasons.

COMPUTER-AIDED PROBLEMS

9. Branding Decision

RESOURCE REMINDER

Wholesteen Dairy Inc., produces and sells Wholesteen brand condensed milk to grocery retailers. The overall market for condensed milk is fairly flat, and there's sharp competition among dairies for retailers' business. Wholesteen's regular price to retailers is $8.88 a case (24 cans). FoodWorld— a fast-growing supermarket chain and Wholesteen's largest customer—buys 20,000 cases of Wholesteen's condensed milk a year. That's 20 percent of Wholesteen's total sales volume of 100,000 cases per year.

FoodWorld is proposing that Wholesteen produce private label condensed milk to be sold with the FoodWorld brand name. FoodWorld proposes to buy the same total quantity as it does now, but it wants half (10,000 cases) with the Wholesteen brand and half with the FoodWorld brand. FoodWorld wants Wholesteen to reduce costs by using a lower-quality can for the FoodWorld brand. That change will cost Wholesteen $.01 less per can than it costs for the cans that Wholesteen uses for its own brand. FoodWorld

will also provide preprinted labels with its brand name— which will save Wholesteen an additional $.02 a can.

Wholesteen spends $70,000 a year on promotion to increase familiarity with the Wholesteen brand. In addition, Wholesteen gives retailers an allowance of $.25 per case for their local advertising, which features the Wholesteen brand. FoodWorld has agreed to give up the advertising allowance for its own brand, but it is only willing to pay $7.40 a case for the milk that will be sold with the FoodWorld brand name. It will continue under the old terms for the rest of its purchases.

Sue Glick, Wholesteen's marketing manager, is considering the FoodWorld proposal. She has entered cost and revenue data on a spreadsheet—so she can see more clearly how the proposal might affect revenue and profits.

a. Based on the data in the initial spreadsheet, how will Wholesteen profits be affected if Glick accepts the FoodWorld proposal?

b. Glick is worried that FoodWorld will find another producer for the FoodWorld private label milk if Wholesteen rejects the proposal. This would immediately reduce

Wholesteen's annual sales by 10,000 cases. FoodWorld might even stop buying from Wholesteen altogether. What would happen to profits in these two situations?

c. FoodWorld is rapidly opening new stores and sells milk in every store. The FoodWorld buyer says that next year's purchases could be up to 25,000 cases of Wholesteen's condensed milk. But Sue Glick knows that FoodWorld may stop buying the Wholesteen brand and want all 25,000 cases to carry the FoodWorld private label brand. How will this affect profit? (Hint: enter the new quantities in the "proposal" column of the spreadsheet.)

d. What should Wholesteen do? Why?

If you want to read the cases and view the video cases that accompany this chapter, visit the *Basic Marketing* Online Learning Centre at: **www.mcgrawhill.ca/olc/perreault**. Along with these cases and video cases, the OLC also has the software and user guide for this chapter's Computer-Aided Problem, as well as exercises, quizzes, articles, links, and other *interactive* content that will help you with your studies.

WHEN YOU FINISH THIS CHAPTER, YOU SHOULD

1. Understand how product life cycles and the adoption curve affect strategy planning.

2. Know what is involved in designing new products and what "new products" really are.

3. Understand the new-product development process.

4. See why product liability must be considered in screening new products.

5. Understand the need for product or brand managers.

Product Management and New-Product Development

MOTOROLA IS A LARGE COMPANY, BUT IT DIDN'T BEGIN THAT WAY. IT STARTED 75 YEARS AGO AS A TINY INNOVATOR IN ELECTRIC RADIOS WHEN BROADCAST COMMUNICATIONS WERE IN THEIR INFANCY. THEN IT CONTINUED TO GROW AS IT DEVELOPED RADIOS FOR "MOTOR CARS" (HENCE THE

Motorola name) and next moved on to become a pioneer in colour TV. Later, Motorola continued to enjoy profit growth from its role in developing the market for semiconductors—and in more recent times, Motorola has been a dominant brand in the explosive growth of the cell phone market. Now, however, Motorola is no longer involved in radios or TVs, parts of its semiconductor business are being sold off, and even its cell phone business is fighting for market share and profits against a host of worldwide competitors. It is still developing new and improved cell phones, but that is required just to stay in the game.

Firms that identify breakthrough market opportunities create exciting growth, but over time that growth is also what attracts competitors. Competition puts pressure on price levels and ultimately on profits. That's why Motorola's newest product development efforts are focused on meeting needs that other firms have not yet addressed. For example, Motorola is working on creating electronic display screens made out of thin plastic film. Plastic-based "organic light-emitting diodes" may ultimately lead to inexpensive TV and computer displays that are the size of a wall and applied like wallpaper. Another recent effort led to development of a "wearable" electronic device (similar to a wireless PDA) with its display screen built into the frame of a set of stylish eyewear. This device incorporates a heads-up display, digital camera, and an ear bud. The person wearing it can view 800×600 displays while simultaneously staying in touch with his or her surroundings. For example, a surgeon might use it to watch a display of a patient's MRI while doing sensitive surgery, or a test pilot could see a tutorial on the cockpit controls while flying a new airplane. Or later—if economies of scale bring down costs—kids might use it to watch music videos or play video games.

Motorola is a big company with technical strengths. But new-product development is equally important to smaller firms. Consider the case of Plantronics, a telephone headset maker. Revenues from sales to its core target market, operators in corporate call centres, were falling. Many customer firms were switching from human operators to digital voice mail systems. To offset the lost revenues, Plantronics looked at trends in the market to identify new opportunities. For example, when drivers using cell phones became a safety issue,

Plantronics developed a hands-free headset and worked with cell phone retailers to promote it. Now it is pursuing a similar initiative in England, which recently passed a hands-free law.

Customer satisfaction with the comfort, sound quality, and freedom of movement of Plantronics cell phone headsets has led to an opportunity to expand its product line into new products for home offices. Plantronics is also promoting its headsets to business firms—as a way to improve productivity and relieve stress among office workers.

Plantronics marketing managers have also capitalized on demographic trends like an aging population and diversified into products for the hearing impaired.

However, most of Plantronics new-product development efforts stick close to needs it already understands and capabilities it has in place. For example, it has developed a headset to be used with Microsoft's Xbox video console. Similarly, the growing use of multifunction wireless PDAs with built-in cell phones and cameras is another opportunity. Some consumers will prefer to use a headset with these devices because they are larger than a normal cell phone and awkward to hold up to your ear. Who knows, at some point in the future Plantronics may need to develop a headset with a microphone and a Bluetooth communications link that works with Motorola's heads-up display goggles.[1]

MANAGING PRODUCTS OVER THEIR LIFE CYCLES

The life and death cycle seen in our Motorola case is being repeated over and over again in product-markets worldwide. Cellular linkups over the Internet are coming on strong. Cassette tapes replaced vinyl records, and now CDs, digital minidiscs, and VHS tapes are challenged by DVD and downloaded MP3 digital files stored on miniature memory cards.

These innovations show that products, markets, and competition change over time. This makes marketing management an exciting challenge. Developing new products and managing existing products to meet changing conditions is important to the success of every firm. In this chapter, we will look at some important ideas in these areas.

Revolutionary products create new product-markets. But competitors are always developing and copying new ideas and products—making existing products out-of-date more quickly than ever. Products, like consumers, go through life cycles.

Product life cycle has four major stages

The **product life cycle** describes the stages a really new product idea goes through from beginning to end. The product life cycle is divided into four major stages: (1) market introduction, (2) market growth, (3) market maturity, and (4) sales decline. The product life cycle is concerned with new types (or categories) of products in the market, not just what happens to an individual brand.

A particular firm's marketing mix usually must change during the product life cycle. There are several reasons why customers' attitudes and needs may change over the product life cycle. The product may be aimed at entirely different target markets

Exhibit 10-1
Typical Life Cycle of a New-Product Concept

at different stages. And the nature of competition moves toward pure competition or oligopoly.

Further, total sales of the product—by all competitors in the industry—vary in each of its four stages. They move from very low in the market introduction stage to high at market maturity and then back to low in the sales decline stage. More important, the profit picture changes too. These general relationships can be seen in Exhibit 10-1. Note that sales and profits do not move together over time. *Industry profits decline while industry sales are still rising.*[2]

Market introduction—investing in the future

In the **market introduction** stage, sales are low as a new idea is first introduced to a market. Customers aren't looking for the product. Even if the product offers superior value, customers don't even know about it. Informative promotion is needed to tell potential customers about the advantages and uses of the new product concept.

Even though a firm promotes its new product, it takes time for customers to learn that the product is available. Most companies experience losses during the introduction stage because they spend so much money for Promotion, Product, and Place development. Of course, they invest the money in the hope of future profits. Bombardier, founded in 1942, started out with a tracked vehicle for transportation on snow-covered terrain.

Market growth—profits go up and down

In the **market growth** stage, industry sales grow fast—but industry profits rise and then start falling. The innovator begins to make big profits as more and more customers buy. But competitors see the opportunity and enter the market. Some just

Porter Airlines used ads to create interest in their product prior to introduction. These ads pique the curiosity of the consumer.

Innovative products, like Samsung's new 63-inch plasma high-definition TV and Transitions' new lens technology, are likely to get to the market growth stage of the product life cycle more quickly if customers see them as superior to products currently in use.

copy the most successful product or try to improve it to compete better. Others try to refine their offerings to do a better job of appealing to some target markets. The new entries result in much product variety.

This is the time of biggest profits *for the industry*. It is also a time of rapid sales and earnings growth for companies with effective strategies. *But it is toward the end of this stage when industry profits begin to decline* as competition and consumer price sensitivity increase. See Exhibit 10-1. By the late 1960s, snowmobiles were not just transportation, they were a new form of recreation. Bombardier listed on the stock exchange in 1969.

Some firms make big strategy planning mistakes at this stage by not understanding the product life cycle. They see the big sales and profit opportunities of the early market growth stage but ignore the competition that will soon follow. When they realize their mistake, it may be too late. This happened with many dot-coms during the late 1990s. Marketing managers who understand the cycle and pay attention to competitor analysis are less likely to encounter this problem.

Market maturity—sales level off, profits continue down

The **market maturity** stage occurs when industry sales level off and competition gets tougher. Many aggressive competitors have entered the race for profits—except in oligopoly situations. Industry profits go down throughout the market maturity stage because promotion costs rise and some competitors cut prices to attract business. Less efficient firms can't compete with this pressure—and they drop out of the market. There is a long-run downward pressure on prices.

New firms may still enter the market at this stage—increasing competition even more. Note that late entries skip the early life-cycle stages, including the profitable market growth stage. And they must try to take a share of the saturated market from established firms, which is difficult and expensive. The market leaders have a lot at stake, so they fight hard to defend their share. Customers who are happy with their current relationship won't switch to a new brand. So late entrants usually have a tough battle.

Persuasive promotion becomes even more important during the market maturity stage. Products may differ only slightly. Bombardier introduced new features, such as a reverse gear, to the snowmobile as a way to differentiate the Ski-Doo in a mature market. Most competitors have discovered effective appeals or just copied the leaders. As the various products become almost the same in the minds of potential consumers, price sensitivity is a real factor.[3]

The video game market vividly illustrates these competitive forces. By the time Microsoft introduced its Xbox game console, Nintendo's GameCube and Sony's PlayStation were already established leaders in the maturing market. Microsoft hoped to grab market share with a superior product designed to sell at a competitive price. To tout the advantages of the Xbox, it spent heavily on promotion. The others fought back with costly promotion of their own. Then Sony took advantage of its economies of scale and slashed the PlayStation II price by a third soon after Xbox hit the market. Nintendo followed with its own cuts. Experts estimate that, after matching the lower prices, Microsoft *lost* about $100 on each unit it sold. All the low prices did prompt renewed growth in unit sales. As the market leader, the added volume helped Sony make up for revenue lost from its price cut. However, for Microsoft, the expanded volume resulted in even greater total costs of coming into the market late. Time will tell if Microsoft's strengths will help it recoup profits by capturing share in video game software, a market that is still growing.[1]

In Canada, the markets for most cars and household appliances are in market maturity. This stage may continue for many years—until a basically new-product idea comes along—even though individual brands or models come and go. The growth of high-definition television (HDTV) will push older televisions into decline as it becomes increasingly popular.

Sales decline—a time of replacement

During the **sales decline** stage, new products replace the old. Price competition from dying products becomes more vigorous—but firms with strong brands may make profits until the end because they have successfully differentiated their products.

As the new products go through their introduction stage, the old ones may keep some sales by appealing to their most loyal customers or those who are slow to try new ideas. These conservative buyers might switch later—smoothing the sales decline. Consumers with VCRs may switch to DVDs, but some will be reluctant to do so. These consumers will keep buying VHS tapes as long as possible.

PRODUCT LIFE CYCLES SHOULD BE RELATED TO SPECIFIC MARKETS

Remember that product life cycles describe industry sales and profits for a *product idea* within a particular product-market. The sales and profits of an individual brand may not, and often do not, follow the life-cycle pattern. They may vary up and down throughout the life cycle—sometimes moving in the opposite direction of industry sales and profits. Further, a product idea may be in a different life-cycle stage in different markets.

Individual brands may not follow the pattern

A given firm may introduce or drop a specific product during *any* stage of the product life cycle. A "me-too" brand introduced during the market growth stage, for example, may never get sales at all and suffer a quick death. But market leaders may enjoy high profits during the market maturity stage—even though industry profits are declining. Weaker products, on the other hand, may not earn a profit during any stage of the product life cycle.

Strategy planners who naively expect sales of an individual product to follow the general product life-cycle pattern are likely to be rudely surprised. In fact, it might be more sensible to think in terms of "product-market life cycles" rather than product life cycles—but we will use the term *product life cycle* because it is commonly accepted and widely used.

Each market should be carefully defined

How we see product life cycles depends on how broadly we define a product-market. For example, microwave ovens are at the market maturity stage here. In many other countries they're still early in the growth stage. Even in European countries like Denmark, Italy, and Spain, fewer than 20 percent of all households own microwave ovens.[5] As this example suggests, a firm with a mature product can sometimes find new growth in international markets.

How broadly we define the needs of customers in a product-market also affects how we view product life cycles—and who the competitors are. Consider the needs related to storing and preparing foods. Wax paper sales started to decline when Dow introduced Saran Wrap. Then sales of Saran Wrap (and other similar products) fell sharply when small plastic storage bags became popular. However, sales picked up again later when microwave cooking became popular. Then resealable bags like those from Ziploc took over because they can be used in both the freezer and the microwave.

PRODUCT LIFE CYCLES VARY IN LENGTH

How long a whole product life cycle takes—and the length of each stage—varies a lot across products. The cycle may vary from 90 days—in the case of toys like the Finding Nemo line—to possibly 100 years for gas-powered cars.

The product life-cycle concept does not tell a manager precisely *how long* the cycle will last. But a manager can often make a good guess based on the life cycle for similar products. Sometimes marketing research can help too. However, it is more important to expect and plan for the different stages than to know the precise length of each cycle.

Some products move fast

A new-product idea will move through the early stages of the life cycle more quickly when it has certain characteristics. For example, the greater the *comparative advantage* of a new product over those already on the market, the more rapidly its sales will grow. Sales growth is also faster when the product is *easy to use* and if its advantages are *easy to communicate*. If the product *can be tried* on a limited basis—

IF AN EAR
THERMOMETER
SOUNDS PECULIAR,
IMAGINE THE
REACTION TO THE
FIRST RECTAL
THERMOMETER.

Until now, parents never had much choice. And kids had even less.

If there was a temperature to be taken, the standard rectal thermometer was the way to take it. An uncomfortable, messy, risky way. But the only accurate way.

That is, until we introduced the Thermoscan® Instant Thermometer. takes an accurate temperature at ear in one second. The same way many doctors' offices and hospitals do, millions of times each year.

Just position it and press a button. You'll get an easy-to-read temperature. With no struggle. No fear of injury. And no unhappy kid.

The first name in fast temperature.

THERMOSCAN.
INSTANT THERMOMETER

New products that do a better job of meeting the needs of specific target customers are more likely to move quickly and successfully through the introductory stage of the product life cycle.

without a lot of risk to the customer—it can usually be introduced more quickly. Finally, if the product is *compatible* with the values and experiences of target customers, they are likely to buy it more quickly.

The fast adoption of DVD players is a good example. The concept of renting or buying movies to view at home was already compatible with consumer lifestyles, but many consumers hesitated before buying a DVD player. They wanted to see if DVD movies would be readily available. As movies appeared, DVD player sales took off because they had advantages over VHS tape players. Consumers could clearly tell that the picture and audio quality were better from a store demo without buying anything. Further, ads highlighted DVD extras such as deleted scenes and interviews with directors. DVD players also met music listening needs because they worked with music CDs. Even though there is now high penetration of DVD players, many consumers still tape TV shows. However, now that the price of DVD recorders is falling, they will probably drive VHS recorders into the market decline stage of the product life cycle. Note, however, that DVD player adoption has not been as fast in less-developed countries. DVD players do not have the same comparative advantages in places where TV penetration is still low, movies are not available, and the costs are higher relative to consumer income.[6]

INTERNET EXERCISE

A number of software, hardware, and programming firms are working on products that deliver Internet information via TV. Explore the MSN TV Web site (www.msntv.com) to find out about one aspect of this idea and take the MSN Tour. How does MSN TV stack up when you consider the characteristics of an innovation reviewed earlier?

Product life cycles are getting shorter

Although the life of different products varies, in general product life cycles are getting shorter. This is partly due to rapidly changing technology. One new invention may make possible many new products that replace old ones. Tiny electronic microchips led to thousands of new products—from Texas Instruments calculators in the early days to microchip-controlled heart valves now.

Patents for a new product may not be much protection in slowing down competitors. Competitors can often find ways to copy the product idea without violating a specific patent. Worse, some unethical firms simply disregard the patent. This can be a big problem, especially for firms that rely on unique technology for competitive advantage. For example, Cisco Systems became suspicious when it learned that a Chinese competitor was selling computer network hardware that was similar. Even the model numbers and software commands were the same. It took a sting operation and six more months of detective work for Cisco to prove that its patent was being violated. In this case, the competitor took the product off the market and claimed the violation was unintentional. However, in other situations a product's life may be over before a case can get through patent-court bottlenecks. By then, the copycat competitor may even be out of business. These problems are even more severe in international cases because different governments, rules, and court systems are involved.[7]

Although life cycles keep moving in the developed economies, many advances bypass most consumers in less-developed economies. These consumers struggle at the subsistence level, without an effective macro-marketing system to stimulate innovation. However, some of the innovations and economies of scale made possible in the advanced societies do trickle down to benefit these consumers. Inexpensive antibiotics and drought-resistant plants, for example, are making a life-or-death difference.

The early bird usually makes the profits

The product life cycle means that firms must be developing new products all the time. Further, they must try to have marketing mixes that will make the most of the market growth stage—when profits are highest.

During the growth stage, competitors are likely to rapidly introduce product improvements. Fast changes in marketing strategy may be required here because profits don't necessarily go to the innovator. Sometimes fast copiers of the basic idea win in the market growth stage. General Motor's electric car, the EV1, was the first zero-emission vehicle on the market when it was first sold in California. However, Toyota and Honda leapfrogged past GM when they introduced hybrid vehicles powered by a combination of gas engine and electric motor. Their hybrids did not eliminate all emissions, but they met other needs better. They have more power, don't need to be plugged in, and are less expensive. With these changes, the market for low-emission hybrids is growing rapidly, and other producers are getting into the act. However, GM is still playing catch-up. In fact, some experts think that it will continue to trail its Japanese competitors because they are faster in adapting to market needs, even when they get their start by imitating an innovator. Marketers need to be innovative, but at the same time they must be flexible in adapting to the needs and attitudes of their target markets.[8]

The short happy life of fashions and fads

The sales of some products are influenced by **fashion**—the currently accepted or popular style. Fashion-related products tend to have short life cycles. What is currently popular can shift rapidly. A certain colour or style of clothing—baggy jeans, miniskirts, or four-inch-wide ties—may be in fashion one season and outdated the next. Marketing managers who work with fashions often have to make really fast product changes.

How fast is fast enough? Ask Le Chateau or Zara, a women's fashion retailer based in Spain that takes only about two weeks to go from a new fashion concept to having items on the racks of its stores. Zara's market-watching designers get a constant flow of new fashion ideas from music videos, fashion shows, and magazines. Zara quickly produces just enough of a design to test the waters and then sends it out for overnight delivery to some of its 876 stores around the world. Stores track consumer preferences every day through point-of-sale computers and designers get online summaries of what's selling and where. If an item is hot, more is produced and shipped. Otherwise it's dropped. With this system items are rarely on the shelves of Zara stores for more than a few weeks.[9] Le Chateau keeps pace with a similar fast product introduction.

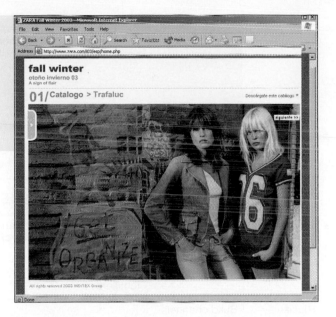

A certain colour or style may be in fashion one season and outdated the next. Zara, a fashion retailer, puts its catalogue on its Web site (www.zara.com) so it can be updated quickly each season.

Many present fashions are adaptations or revivals of previously popular styles. Designers are always looking for styles that will satisfy fashion innovators who crave distinctiveness. Lower-cost copies of the popular items may then catch on with other groups and survive for a while. Yet the constant changes increase the cost of producing and marketing fashion products and the costs to consumers. Fashion changes are a luxury that most people in less-developed countries simply can't afford.

A **fad** is an idea that is fashionable only to certain groups who are enthusiastic about it. But these groups are so fickle that a fad is even more short lived than a regular fashion. Many toys—whether it's a Hasbro *Lord of the Rings* plastic figure or a Toymax Paintball pack—are fads but do well during a short-lived cycle.[10]

PLANNING FOR DIFFERENT STAGES OF THE PRODUCT LIFE CYCLE

Length of cycle affects strategy planning

Where a product is in its life cycle—and how fast it's moving to the next stage—should affect marketing strategy planning. Marketing managers must make realistic plans for the later stages. Exhibit 10-2 shows the relationship of the product life cycle to the marketing mix variables. The technical terms in this figure are discussed later in the book.

Introducing new products

Exhibit 10-2 shows that a marketing manager has to do a lot of strategy planning to introduce a really new product. Even if the product is unique, this doesn't mean that everyone will immediately come running to the producer's door. The firm will have to build channels of distribution—perhaps offering special incentives to win cooperation. Promotion is needed to build demand *for the whole idea* not just to sell a specific brand. Because all this is expensive, it may lead the marketing manager to try to "skim" the market—charging a relatively high price to help pay for the introductory costs.

The correct strategy, however, depends on how quickly the new idea will be accepted by customers—and how quickly competitors will follow with their own versions of the product. When the early stages of the cycle will be fast, a low initial (penetration) price may make sense to help develop loyal customers early and keep competitors out.

	Market introduction	Market growth	Market maturity	Sales decline
Product	One or few	Variety—try to find best product Build brand familiarity	All "same" Battle of brands	Some drop out
Place	Build channels Maybe selective distribution	Move toward more intensive distribution →		
Promotion	Build primary demand Pioneering-informing	Build selective demand ——————→ Informing/Persuading —→ Persuading/Reminding (frantically competitive)		
Price	Skimming or penetration	Meet competition ——————————→ or Price dealing and price cutting ————→		
Competitive situation	Few competitors	More competitors	Maximum number of competitors	Declining number of competitors

Pioneer may need help from competitors

Sometimes it's not in the best interest of the market pioneer for competitors to stay out of the market. Building customer interest in a really new-product idea—and obtaining distribution to make the product available—can be too big a job for a single company. Two or more companies investing in promotion to build demand may help to stimulate the growth of the whole product-market. Similarly, a new product may languish if it is not compatible with other products that customers rely on. This is what happened with Digital Video Express (Divx) video disks. When Divx came out, many consumer-electronics firms were launching DVD format products. Divx had advantages over DVD, but it was not compatible with many of the ordinary DVD players that were already on the market. Video stores didn't want to stock movies in both formats so Divx fizzled.[11]

New product sales may not take off

Not all new-product ideas catch on. Customers or intermediaries may not be satisfied with the marketing mix, or other new products may meet the same need better. But the success that eludes a firm with its initial strategy can sometimes be achieved by modifying the strategy. David Mintz invented a soy-based frozen dessert and started Tofutti Brands Inc., to sell it. Tofutti was especially appealing to people who could not eat dairy products. To quickly reach his target market, Mintz's strategy was to offer a limited number of flavours and partner with a big company that already had national distribution in supermarkets. Häagen-Dazs agreed to the plan but wanted exclusive distribution rights. Sales grew quickly at

Some companies continue to do well in market maturity by improving their products or by finding new uses and applications. DuPont Textiles & Interiors' LYCRA® has expanded from personal apparel to furniture upholstery and McCain Foods appeals to kids with fun potato products like Smiles.

first but then plummeted when conflicts between Mintz and Häagen-Dazs ended the relationship. To keep consumers interested in Tofutti while he slowly rebuilt distribution through a dozen specialized wholesalers, Mintz had to constantly offer new flavours.[12]

How quickly a firm can change its strategy as the life cycle moves on is also relevant. Some firms are very flexible. They can compete effectively with larger, less adaptable competitors by adjusting their strategies more frequently.

Managing maturing products

It's important for a firm to have some competitive advantage as it moves into market maturity. Even a small advantage can make a big difference—and some firms do very well by carefully managing their maturing products. They are able to capitalize on a slightly better product or perhaps lower production or marketing costs. Or they are simply more successful at promotion—allowing them to differentiate their more or less homogeneous product from competitors. For example, graham crackers were competing in a mature market and sales were flat. Nabisco used the same ingredients to create bite-sized Teddy Grahams and then promoted them heavily. These changes captured new sales and profits for Nabisco.[13]

Industry profits are declining in market maturity. Top managers must see this, or they will expect the attractive profits that are no longer possible. Product life cycles keep moving. But that doesn't mean a firm should just sit by as its sales decline. There are other choices. A firm can improve its product or develop an innovative new product for the same market. Or it can develop a strategy for its product (perhaps with modifications) targeted at a new market. For example, it might find a market in a country where the life cycle is not so far along, or it might try to serve a new need. Or the firm can withdraw the product before it completes the cycle and refocus on better opportunities. See Exhibit 10-3.

Improve the product or develop a new one

When a firm's product has won loyal customers, it can be successful for a long time—even in a mature or declining market. However, continued improvements may be needed as customers' needs shift. An outstanding example is Procter & Gamble's Tide. Introduced in 1947, Tide led to a whole new generation of powdered laundry products that cleaned better with fewer suds. But Tide continues to change because of new washing machines and fabrics. The Tide sold today has had at least 55 modifications.

Do product modifications—like those made with powdered Tide—create a wholly new product that should have its own product life cycle? Or are they technical adjustments of the original product idea? We will take the latter position—focusing on the product idea rather than changes in features. This means that some of

Firm introduces an innovative new (or improved) product that starts a new cycle.

Firm introduces old (or modified) product in a new market with a different cycle.

Firm begins to phase out, and then withdraws, a dying product.

Tide to Go is a new product from an established company. Procter & Gamble realized the need to provide consumers with an instant version of laundry soap designed to remove stains immediately and without added water. Use of the Tide brand name helps establish the product in the mind of the consumer.

these Tide changes were made in the market maturity stage. But this type of product improvement can help to extend the product life cycle.

On the other hand, a firm that develops an innovative new product may move to a new product life cycle. For example, by 1985 new liquid detergents like Wisk were moving into the growth stage, and sales of powdered detergents were declining. To share in the growth-stage profits for liquid detergents and to offset the loss of customers from powdered Tide, Procter & Gamble introduced Liquid Tide.

Even though regular powdered detergents are in the decline stage, traditional powdered Tide continues to sell well because it still does the job for some consumers. But sales growth is likely to come from liquid detergents and the new low-suds detergents.[14] Product innovations such as the Tide to Go Instant Stain Remover will also help extend the life cycle.

Develop new strategies for different markets

In a mature market, a firm may be fighting to keep or increase its market share. But if the firm finds a new use for the product, it may stimulate overall demand. Arm & Hammer baking soda is a classic example. When sales declined due to a decline in home baking, Arm & Hammer repositioned their product. Advertising campaigns pushed the use of baking soda as a deodorizer, whitener, etc. Ads moved comsumers to use it in the refrigerator, on the rug, in the cat litter, and so on. DuPont's Teflon fluorocarbon resin is also a good example. It was developed more than 50 years ago and has enjoyed sales growth as a nonstick coating for cookware and as a lining for chemically resistant equipment. But marketing managers for Teflon are not waiting to be stuck with declining profits in those mature markets. They are constantly developing strategies for new markets. For example, Teflon is now selling well as a special coating for the wires used in high-speed communications between computers and as an additive that improves bathroom cleaning products.[15] Humpty Dumpty potato chips continue to come in new flavours such as Smokin' Bacon and Buffalo Wing Ripples.

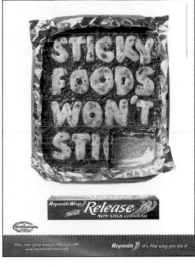

Humpty Dumpty potato chips introduces new flavours on a regular basis to keep repeat customers interested in their product and to lure new customers to try them. Similarly, Reynolds Wrap has introduced a new nonstick foil called Release.

Phasing out dying products

Not all strategies have to be exciting growth strategies. If prospects are poor in some product-market, a phase-out strategy may be needed. The need for phasing out becomes more obvious as the sales decline stage arrives. But even in market maturity, it may be clear that a particular product is not going to be profitable enough to reach the company's objectives. In any case, it is wise to remember that marketing plans are implemented as ongoing strategies. Salespeople make calls, inventory moves in the channel, advertising is scheduled for several months into the future, and so on. So the firm usually experiences losses if managers end a plan too abruptly. Because of this, it's sometimes better to phase out the product gradually.

Phasing out a product may involve some difficult implementation problems. But phase-out is also a *strategy*—and it must be market-oriented to cut losses. In fact, it is possible to milk a dying product for some time if competitors move out more quickly and there is ongoing (though declining) demand. Some customers are willing to pay attractive prices to get their old favourite. Video stores, for example, are switching from VCR tapes to DVDs—but some are switching more quickly than others. Many older consumers still want to rent movies on VCR technology.

ADOPTION PROCESSES CAN GUIDE PRODUCT PLANNING

Promotion must vary for different adopter groups

Research on how markets accept new product ideas has led to the adoption curve model. The **adoption curve** shows when different groups accept product ideas. It emphasizes the relations among groups and shows that individuals in some groups act as leaders in accepting a new idea. Promotion efforts usually need to change over time to adjust to differences among the adopter groups.

Exhibit 10-4 shows the adoption curve for a typical successful product. Some of the important characteristics of each of these customer groups are discussed below. Which one are you?

Innovators don't mind taking some risks

The **innovators** are the first to adopt. They are eager to try a new idea and willing to take risks. Innovators tend to be young and well educated. They are likely to be mobile and have many contacts outside their local social group and community. Young, well-educated consumers were the innovators for text messaging. Business firms in the innovator group are often specialized and willing to take the risk of doing something new.

Innovators tend to rely on impersonal and scientific information sources, or other innovators, rather than salespeople. They often search for information on

Exhibit 10-4
The Adoption Curve

Innovators (3–5%)	Early adopters (10–15%)	Early majority (34%)	Late majority (34%)	Laggards or nonadopters (5–16%)

the Internet, read articles in technical publications, or look for informative ads in special-interest magazines.

Early adopters are often opinion leaders

Early adopters are well respected by their peers and often are opinion leaders. They tend to be younger, more mobile, and more creative than later adopters. But unlike innovators, they have fewer contacts outside their own social group or community. Business firms in this category also tend to be specialized.

Of all the groups, this one tends to have the greatest contact with salespeople. Mass media are important information sources too. Marketers should be very concerned with attracting and selling the early adopter group. Their acceptance is crucial. The next group, the early majority, look to the early adopters for guidance. The early adopters can help the promotion effort by spreading *word-of-mouth* information and advice among other consumers.

The new "smart" LG refrigerator, which features a digital display on the door and an Internet connection, is likely to appeal to innovators who want to be among the first to adopt new products.

Opinion leaders help spread the word

Marketers know the importance of personal recommendations by opinion leaders. For example, some movie fans like to be the first to see new flicks. If they like a movie, they quickly tell their friends and word-of-mouth publicity does the real selling job. However, consumers are even more likely to talk about a negative experience than a positive experience. So if early groups reject the product, it may never get off the ground.

Some companies target promotion to encourage opinion leadership and word-of-mouth publicity. The Internet is one easy way to do this. For example, a retail shop called Hot Hot Hot, which carries a wide variety of hot sauces for food, established a Web site. It urged customers to click a link and e-mail the Web address to their friends.

MARKETING ETHICALLY

Marketers know the importance of personal recommendations made by opinion leaders. Marketers are now harnessing this fact under a process called buzz marketing. Picture this situation: undercover marketing representatives disguised as regular bar patrons, go to a trendy establishment. Flirting with real bar patrons, they subtly impart the beer sponsor's message when it's the right time. It's marketing by masquerade. And it's growing in popularity, but not without its critics. Not because it's illegal, but because it's unethical. Practitioners don't disclose they are being paid to promote a product. The practice is not going unnoticed by Canada's largest marketing association. The Canadian Marketing Association is so concerned with this growing trend and other similar marketing practices that a new section is being added to CMA's Code of Ethics. Mandatory for all CMA members, the code requires marketers to avoid undercover or word-of-mouth marketing campaigns that encourage a consumer or business to believe the marketer's agents are acting independently and without compensation when they are not.

On the flip side, legitimate word-of-mouth or experiential marketing is an increasingly popular and an ethical marketing tactic through which organizations work with satisfied consumers to spread the word about products and services they enjoy. Done properly, it creates the potential for exponential growth of a marketing message's exposure through the use of computer chat rooms and forums.

Word-of-mouth is becoming such an important marketing tool that a formal association called WOMMA has recently formed and can be found at www.womma.org. WOMMA is the first central resource for marketers who want to learn how to use word-of-mouth effectively and honestly. WOMMA is absolutely opposed to unethical word-of-mouth marketing tactics such as described above.

How would you feel if you found out that the person sitting next to you in the bar, telling you all the good things about a certain brand of beer, was getting paid to do it?[16]

Very quickly, largely because of word-of-mouth, 1,500 people were visiting the Web site each day.[17]

This chapter's Marketing Ethically discusses some of the issues surrounding the use of opinion leaders.

Early majority group is deliberate

The **early majority** avoid risk and wait to consider a new idea after many early adopters have tried it—and liked it. Average-sized business firms that are less specialized often fit in this category. If successful companies in their industry adopt the new idea, they will too.

The early majority have a great deal of contact with mass media, salespeople, and early adopter opinion leaders. Members usually aren't opinion leaders themselves.

Late majority is cautious

The **late majority** are cautious about new ideas. Often they are older and more set in their ways, so they are less likely to follow early adopters. In fact, strong social pressure from their own peer group may be needed before they adopt a new product. These consumers will purchase a DVD player after all their peers have one. Business firms in this group tend to be conservative, smaller-sized firms with little specialization.

The late majority make little use of marketing sources of information—mass media and salespeople. They tend to be oriented more toward other late adopters rather than outside sources they don't trust.

Laggards or nonadopters hang on to tradition

Laggards or **nonadopters** prefer to do things the way they've been done in the past and are very suspicious of new ideas. They tend to be older and less well educated. Laggards will only purchase a DVD player when VCRs are simply no longer available. The smallest businesses with the least specialization often fit this category. They cling to the status quo and think it's the safe way.

The main source of information for laggards is other laggards. This certainly is bad news for marketers. In fact, it may not pay to bother with this group.[18]

NEW-PRODUCT PLANNING

It is essential for a firm to develop new products or modify its current products to meet changing customer needs and competitors' actions. Not having an active new-product development process means that consciously, or subconsciously, the firm has decided to milk its current products and go out of business. New-product planning is not an optional matter. Motorola continues to innovate in today's dynamic markets.

What is a new product?

In discussing the introductory stage of product life cycles, we focused on the types of really new product innovations that tend to disrupt old ways of doing things. However, each year firms introduce many products that are basically refinements of existing products. So a **new product** is one that is new *in any way* for the company concerned.

A product can become "new" in many ways. A fresh idea can be turned into a new product and start a new product life cycle. For example, Alza Corporation's time-release skin patches are replacing pills and injections for some medications.

Variations on an existing product idea can also make a product new. For example, Logitech has improved the lowly computer mouse by making it wireless and Gatorade has made its bottle easier to grip. Even small changes in an existing product can make it new.[19] Industry Canada allows a product to be called *new* for twelve months after introduction.

Ethical issues in new-product planning

New-product decisions—and decisions to abandon old products—often involve ethical considerations. For example, some firms (including firms that develop drugs) have been criticized for holding back important new-product innovations until patents run out, or sales slow down, on their existing products.

At the same time, others have been criticized for "planned obsolescence"—releasing new products that the company plans to soon replace with improved new versions. Apple has introduced increasingly smaller versions of the iPod in a short time span. Similarly, wholesalers and middlemen complain that producers too often keep their new-product introduction plans a secret and leave middlemen with dated inventory that they can sell only at a loss.

Companies also face ethical dilemmas when they decide to stop supplying a product or the service and replacement parts to keep it useful. An old model of a Cuisinart food processor, for example, might be in perfect shape except for a crack in the plastic mixing bowl. It's sensible for the company to improve the design if the crack is a frequent problem, but if consumers can't get a replacement part for the model they already own, they're left holding the bag.

Criticisms are also levelled at firms that constantly release minor variations of products that already saturate markets. Consider what happened with disposable diapers. Marketing managers thought that they were serving some customers' needs better when they offered diapers in boys' and girls' versions and in a variety of sizes, shapes, and colours. But many retailers felt that the new products were simply a ploy to get more shelf space. Further, some consumers complained that the bewildering array of choices made shopping difficult. Some people would level the same criticism at Huggies Little Swimmers Disposable Swimpants. But unlike other disposables, this product doesn't swell in the water. They have been a success because they seem to fill a different need.

Product management decisions often have a significant effect on customers and middlemen. A too-casual decision may lead to a negative backlash that affects the firm's strategy or reputation.[20]

AN ORGANIZED NEW-PRODUCT DEVELOPMENT PROCESS IS CRITICAL

Identifying and developing new-product ideas—and effective strategies to go with them—is often the key to a firm's success and survival. But the costs of new-product development and the risks of failure are high. Experts estimate that consumer packaged-goods companies spend at least $20 million to introduce a new brand—and 70 to 80 percent of these new brands flop. That's a big expense—and a waste. In the service sector, the front-end cost of a failed effort may not be as high, but it can have a devastating long-term effect if dissatisfied consumers turn elsewhere for help.[21]

INTERNET EXERCISE

Marketing Intelligence Service Ltd., is a firm that tracks new consumer packaged-goods—both successes and failures. Enter its Web site (www.productscan.com) and click on the *What's New* button, then review its selections for new product innovations of the year. Do you think that these products offer customers superior value, or are they just me-too imitations?

A new product may fail for many reasons. Most often, companies fail to offer a unique benefit or underestimate the competition. Sometimes the idea is good but the company has design problems—or the product costs much more to produce than was expected. Some companies rush to get a product on the market without developing a complete marketing plan.[22]

But moving too slowly can be a problem too. With the fast pace of change for many products, speedy entry into the market can be a key to competitive advantage. Marketing managers at Xerox learned this the hard way. Japanese competitors were taking market share with innovative new models of copiers. It turned out that the competitors were developing new models twice as fast as Xerox and at half the cost. For Xerox to compete, it had to slash its five-year product development cycle. Many other companies—ranging from auto manufacturers like DaimlerChrysler to Internet service firms like E*Trade—are working to speed up the new-product development process.[23]

Generating innovative and profitable new products requires an understanding of customer needs—and an organized new-product development process.

Exhibit 10-5   New-Product Development Process

To move quickly and also avoid expensive new-product failures, companies should follow an organized new-product development process. The following pages describe such a process, which moves logically through five steps: (1) idea generation, (2) screening, (3) idea evaluation, (4) development (of product and marketing mix), and (5) commercialization.[24] See Exhibit 10-5.

Process tries to kill new ideas— economically

An important element in the new-product development process is continued evaluation of a new idea's likely profitability and return on investment. The hypothesis tested is that the new idea will *not* be profitable. This puts the burden on the new idea—to prove itself or be rejected. Such a process may seem harsh, but experience shows that most new ideas have some flaw. Marketers try to discover those flaws early, and either find a remedy or reject the idea completely. Applying this process requires much analysis of the idea *before* the company spends money to develop and market a product. This is a major departure from the usual production-oriented approach—in which a company develops a product first and then asks sales to "get rid of it."

Step 1: Idea generation

Finding new-product ideas can't be left to chance. Instead, firms need a formal procedure to generate a continuous flow of ideas. New ideas can come from a company's own sales or production staff, middlemen, competitors, consumer surveys, or other sources such as trade associations, advertising agencies, or government agencies. By analyzing new and different views of the company's markets and studying present consumer behaviour, a marketing manager can spot opportunities that have not yet occurred to competitors or even to potential customers. For example, ideas for new service concepts may come directly from analysis of consumer complaints.

No one firm can always be first with the best new ideas. So companies should pay attention to what competitors are doing. Some firms use what's called *reverse engineering*. For example, new-product specialists at Ford Motor Company buy other firms' cars as soon as they're available. Then they take the cars apart to look for new ideas or improvements. British Airways talks to travel agents to learn about new services offered by competitors. Many other companies use similar approaches.[25]

Many firms now "shop" in international markets for new ideas. For instance, food companies in Europe are experimenting with an innovation recently introduced in Japan—a clear, odourless, natural film for wrapping food. Consumers don't have to unwrap it; when they put the product in boiling water or a microwave, the wrapper vanishes.[26]

Research shows that many new ideas in business markets come from customers who identify a need they have. Then they approach a supplier with the idea and perhaps even with a particular design or specification. These customers become the lead users of the product, but the supplier can also pursue the opportunity in other markets.[27]

Step 2: Screening

Screening involves evaluating the new ideas with the type of S.W.O.T. analysis described in Chapter 2 and the product-market screening criteria described in

Exhibit 10-6
Types of New-Product
Opportunities

		Immediate satisfaction	
		High	**Low**
Long-run consumer welfare	**High**	Desirable products	Salutary products
	Low	Pleasing products	Deficient products

Chapter 4. Recall that these criteria include the combined output of a resources (strengths and weaknesses) analysis, a long-run trends analysis, and a thorough understanding of the company's objectives. Further, a "good" new idea should eventually lead to a product (and marketing mix) that will give the firm a competitive advantage—hopefully, a lasting one.

The life-cycle stage at which a firm's new product enters the market has a direct bearing on its prospects for growth. So screening should consider how the strategy for a new product will hold up over the whole product life cycle.

Some companies screen based on consumer welfare

Screening should also consider how a new product will affect consumers over time. Ideally, the product should increase consumer welfare, not just satisfy a whim. Exhibit 10-6 shows different kinds of new-product opportunities. Obviously, a socially responsible firm tries to find desirable opportunities rather than deficient ones. This may not be as easy as it sounds, however. Some consumers want pleasing products and give little thought to their own long-term welfare. And some competitors will offer consumers whatever they will buy.

Safety must be considered

Real acceptance of the marketing concept prompts managers to screen new products on the basis of how safe they are. Safety is not a casual matter. Under the Hazardous Products Act, the government can regulate the distribution and sale of unsafe products.

Product safety complicates strategy planning because not all customers—even those who want better safety features—are willing to pay more for safer products. Some features cost a lot to add and increase prices considerably. These safety concerns must be considered at the screening step because a firm can later be help liable for unsafe products.

Products can turn to liabilities

Product liability means the legal obligation of sellers to pay damages to individuals who are injured by defective or unsafe products. Product liability is a serious matter. Liability settlements may exceed not only a company's insurance coverage but its total assets!

Sellers may be held responsible for injuries related to their products no matter how the items are used or how well they're designed. In one widely publicized judgment, McDonald's paid a huge settlement to a woman who was burned when her coffee spilled. The court concluded that there was not enough warning about how hot the coffee was. Cases and settlements like this are common.

Sometimes there is incentive for lawyers to push liability cases to take a share of the payments. Juries sometimes give huge settlements based on an emotional reaction to the case rather than scientific evidence. That seems to have happened in lawsuits over silicon breast implants.

Product liability is a serious ethical and legal matter. Many countries are attempting to change their laws so that they will be fair to both firms and consumers. But until product liability questions are resolved, marketing managers must be even more sensitive when screening new-product ideas.[28]

ROI is a crucial screening criterion

Getting by the initial screening criteria doesn't guarantee success for the new idea. But it does show that at least the new idea is in the right ballpark *for this firm*. If many ideas pass the screening criteria, a firm must set priorities to determine which ones go on to the next step in the process. This can be done by comparing the ROI (return on investment) for each idea—assuming the firm is ROI-oriented. The most attractive alternatives are pursued first.

Step 3: Idea evaluation

When an idea moves past the screening step, it is evaluated more carefully. Note that an actual product has not yet been developed—and this can handicap the firm in getting feedback from customers. For help in idea evaluation, firms use **concept testing**—getting reactions from customers about how well a new-product idea fits their needs. Concept testing uses market research—ranging from informal focus groups to formal surveys of potential customers.

Companies can often estimate likely costs, revenue, and profitability at this stage. And market research can help identify the size of potential markets. Even informal focus groups are useful—especially if they show that potential users are not excited about the new idea. If results are discouraging, it may be best to kill the idea at this stage. Remember, in this hypothesis-testing process, we're looking for any evidence that an idea is *not* a good opportunity for this firm and should be rejected.

Product planners must think about wholesale and retail customers as well as final consumers. Middlemen may have special concerns about handling a proposed product. At the idea evaluation stage, companies often find that other members of the distribution channel won't cooperate or that cooperation costs.[29]

Idea evaluation is often more precise in business markets. Potential customers are more informed—and their needs focus on the economic reasons for buying rather than emotional factors. Further, given the derived nature of demand in business markets, most needs are already being satisfied in some way. So new products just substitute for existing ones. This means that product planners can compare the cost advantages and limitations of a new product with those currently being used. And by interviewing well-informed people, they can determine the range of product requirements and decide whether there is an opportunity.

For example, you've probably noticed that most new car designs use low-profile headlights. They allow sleeker styling and better gas mileage. Yet these lights were initially only used on high-priced cars. That's because the GE development team worked with engineers at Ford when they were first developing the bulbs for these headlights. Together they determined that the switch to the new bulb and headlight assembly would add about $200 to the price of a car. That meant that the bulb was initially limited to luxury cars—until economies of scale brought down the costs.[30]

Whatever research methods are used, the idea evaluation step should gather enough information to help decide whether there is an opportunity, whether it fits with the firm's resources, *and* whether there is a basis for developing a competitive advantage. With such information, the firm can estimate likely ROI in the various market segments and decide whether to continue the new-product development process.[31]

Step 4: Development

Product ideas that survive the screening and idea evaluation steps must now be analyzed further. Usually, this involves some research and development (R&D) and engineering to design and develop the physical part of the product. In the case of a new service offering, the firm will work out the details of what training, equipment, staff, and so on will be needed to deliver on the idea. Input from a firm's earlier efforts helps guide this technical work.

New computer-aided design (CAD) systems are sparking a revolution in design work. Designers can develop lifelike 3-D colour drawings of packages and products. Changes can be made almost instantly. They can be sent by e-mail to managers all over the world for immediate review. They can even be put on a Web site for marketing research with remote customers. Then once the designs are finalized, they feed directly into computer-controlled manufacturing systems. Companies like Motorola and Timex have found that these systems cut their new-product development time in half—giving them a leg up on many competitors.

Even so, **test marketing** is still useful for testing models and early versions of the product in the market. This process may have several cycles. A manufacturer may build a model of a physical product or produce limited quantities; a service firm may try to train a small group of service providers. Product tests with customers may lead to revisions—*before* the firm commits to full-scale efforts.

With actual goods or services, potential customers can react to how well the product meets their needs. Focus groups, panels, and larger surveys can react to specific features and to the whole product idea. Sometimes that reaction kills the idea. For example, Coca-Cola Foods believed it had a great idea with Minute Maid Squeeze-Fresh, frozen orange juice concentrate in a squeeze bottle. In tests, however, Squeeze-Fresh bombed. Consumers loved the idea but hated the product. It was messy to use, and no one knew how much concentrate to squeeze in the glass.[32]

In other cases, testing can lead to revision of product specifications for different markets. Sometimes months or even years of research may be necessary to focus on precisely what different market segments will find acceptable. For example, Gillette's Mach3 razor blade took over a decade and $750 million in development and tooling costs.[33]

Firms often use full-scale market testing to get reactions in real market conditions or to test variations in the marketing mix. For example, a firm may test alternative brands, prices, or advertising copy in different test cities. Note that the firm is testing the whole marketing mix, not just the product. For example, a hotel chain might test a new service offering at one location to see how consumers react.

Test-marketing can be risky because it may give information to competitors. Some companies monitor products in test markets and then sell the information to competing firms. Similar firms monitor markets in other countries.

But *not* testing is risky too. Frito-Lay was so sure it understood consumers' snack preferences that it introduced a three-item cracker line without market testing. Even with network TV ad support, MaxSnax met with overwhelming consumer indifference. By the time Frito-Lay pulled the product from store shelves, it had lost $52 million.[34]

Firms often take apart competitors' products to look for ideas that they can apply or adapt in their own products.

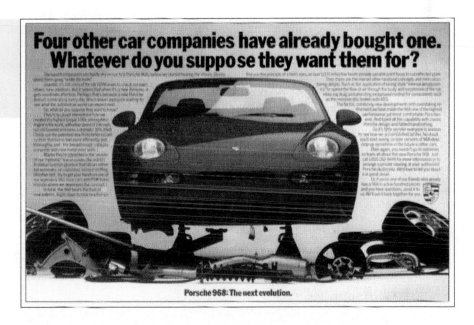

Porsche 968: The next evolution.

Market tests can be very expensive. Yet they can uncover problems that otherwise might go undetected and destroy the whole strategy. After the market test, the firm can estimate likely ROI for various strategies to determine whether the idea moves on to commercialization.

Some companies don't do market tests because they just aren't practical. In fashion markets, for example, speed is extremely important, and products are usually just tried in market. And durable products—which have high fixed production costs and long production lead times—may have to go directly to market. In these cases, it is especially important that the early steps be done carefully to reduce the chances for failure.[35]

Step 5:
Commercialization

A product idea that survives this far can finally be placed on the market. Putting a product on the market is expensive, and success usually requires cooperation of the whole company. Manufacturing or service facilities have to be set up. Goods have to be produced to fill the channels of distribution, or people must be hired and trained to provide services. Further, introductory promotion is costly—especially if the company is entering a very competitive market.

Because of the size of the job, some firms introduce their products city by city or region by region—in a gradual "rollout"—until they have complete market coverage. Rollouts also permit more market testing, but the main purpose is to do a good job implementing the marketing plan. But marketing managers also need to pay close attention to control—to ensure that the implementation effort is working and that the strategy is on target.

NEW-PRODUCT DEVELOPMENT: A TOTAL COMPANY EFFORT

We've been discussing the steps in a logical, new-product development process. However, as shown in Exhibit 10-7, many factors can impact the success of the effort.

Top-level support is vital

Companies that are particularly successful at developing new goods and services seem to have one key trait in common: enthusiastic top-management support for new-product development. New products tend to upset old routines that managers

Exhibit 10-7   New-Product Development Success Factors

of established products often try in subtle but effective ways to maintain. So someone with top-level support, and authority to get things done, needs to be responsible for new-product development.[36]

Put someone in charge

In addition, rather than leaving new-product development to someone in engineering, R&D, or sales who happens to be interested in taking the initiative, successful companies put someone in charge. It may be a person, department, or team.

A new-product development team with people from different departments helps ensure that new ideas are carefully evaluated and profitable ones are quickly brought to market. It's important to choose the right people for the job. Overly conservative managers may kill too many, or even all, new ideas. Or committees may create bureaucratic delays that make the difference between a product's success or failure.

Market needs guide R&D effort

Many new-product ideas come from scientific discoveries and new technologies. In many firms the new-product R&D effort is handled by scientists, engineers, and other technical specialists. Even service firms have technical specialists who help in development work. For example, a bank thinking about offering customers a new set of investment alternatives must be certain that it can deliver on its promises. Skillful R&D work can give a firm a competitive advantage—especially if it competes in high-tech markets. However, technical creativity by itself is not enough. The R&D effort must be guided by the type of market-oriented new-product development process we've been discussing.

From the idea generation stage to the commercialization stage, the R&D specialists, the operations people, and the marketing people must work together to evaluate the feasibility of new ideas. It isn't sensible for a marketing manager to develop elaborate marketing plans for goods or services that the firm simply can't produce—or produce profitably. It also doesn't make sense for R&D people to develop a technology or product that does not have potential for the firm and its markets. Clearly, a balancing act is involved here. But the critical point is the basic one we've been emphasizing throughout the whole book: Marketing-oriented firms seek to satisfy customer needs at a profit with an integrated, whole company effort. RIM's Black-Berry, discussed earlier in Chapter 9, reflects this approach.

Steps should not be skipped

Even with a careful development process, many new products do fail—usually because a company skips some steps in the process. Because speed can be important, it's always tempting to skip needed steps when some part of the process seems to indicate that the company has a "really good idea." But the process moves in steps—gathering different kinds of information along the way. By skipping steps, a firm may miss an important aspect that could make a whole strategy less profitable or actually cause it to fail.

NEED FOR PRODUCT MANAGERS

Product variety leads to product managers

Eventually, the new product is no longer new—it becomes just another product. In some firms, at this point the new-product people turn the product over to the regular operating people and go on to developing other new ideas. In other firms, the person who was the new-product champion continues with the product, perhaps taking on the broader responsibility for turning it into a successful business.

When a firm has only one or a few related products, everyone is interested in them. But when a firm has products in several different product categories, management may decide to put someone in charge of each category, or each brand,

HOW TO BE INNOVATIVE WHEN YOU'RE A HUNDRED YEARS OLD

3M is a 100-year-old company that has discovered its own "fountain of youth." Yet it is no secret what it does to constantly renew itself. 3M is fast and successful in spinning out new products that offer innovative and practical solutions to customers' problems. This doesn't happen by chance. It is an ongoing priority of top managers. For example, 3M's chief set an objective that 30 percent of sales should come from products that didn't exist four years earlier. You can see the emphasis on innovation in even the quickest visit to 3M's Web site (www.3m.com). Current 3M innovations include respirators, radiant light film (for uses ranging from brighter cell phone displays to glittery signage), elastomers (which seal in aggressive chemicals in high-temperature settings), and Filtrete electrostatic fibres (which filter dust out of heating vents). Everywhere you look there are past 3M innovations that are still being improved, including brands like Post-it Notes, Thinsulate outdoor wear, and Scotch Pop-Up Tape Strips.

3M motivates innovation by staying close to customers, rewarding new-product champions, and sharing ideas among divisions. Teams from marketing, operations, and R&D screen new-product concepts for the ones with the highest profit potential. Then everyone works to bring the best ones to market fast. 3M's Scotch-Brite Never Rust Wool Soap Pads show how this approach can succeed. Consumers told 3M marketing researchers that they wanted an improved soap pad. Ordinary steel wool pads leave rust stains on sinks and tiny metal splinters in dishpan hands. 3M screens new products for their environmental impact, so the R&D people developed a pad using plastic fibres from recycled plastic bottles. Experts from 3M's abrasives division figured out how to coat the fibres with fine abrasives and biodegradable soap. Further marketing research refined the shape of the pads, and test markets evaluated details of the marketing plan. For example, tests confirmed that consumers liked the colourful package made from recycled paper and would pay more for Never Rust pads than they did for Brillo.

The managers varied the marketing plan for different countries. In mature markets such as Canada, the U.S., and Brazil where steel wool pads already had a large consumer base, the objective was to capture share. In Japan, where steel wool is not commonly used, the objective was to pioneer the market and attract new customers. In a firm renowned for innovation, the launch of Never Rust pads was one of 3M's most profitable ever.

3M is also serious about how its innovations affect consumer welfare. When managers learned that traces of a chemical in 3M's Scotchgard fabric protector might persist in the environment, they didn't wait for scientists to do more tests. They voluntarily pulled the popular product off the market—before they even knew if R&D could find a substitute chemical.[37]

Consumer packaged-goods companies, like Nabisco, usually assign brand managers who are responsible for individual products. However, when there are a number of products in the same product category, there is often a higher-level manager who ensures that the marketing program for the whole category is effective.

to be sure that attention to these products is not lost in the rush of everyday business. **Product managers** or **brand managers** manage specific products—often taking over the jobs formerly handled by an advertising manager. That gives a clue to what is often their major responsibility—Promotion—since the products have already been developed by the new-product people. However, some brand managers start at the new-product development stage and carry on from there.

Product managers are especially common in large companies that produce many kinds of products. Several product managers may serve under a marketing manager. Sometimes these product managers are responsible for the profitable operation of a particular product's whole marketing effort. Then they have to coordinate their efforts with others, including the sales manager, advertising agencies, production and research people, and even channel members. This is likely to lead to difficulties if product managers have no control over the marketing strategy for other related brands or authority over other functional areas whose efforts they are expected to direct and coordinate.

To avoid these problems, in some companies the product manager serves mainly as a "product champion"—concerned with planning and getting the promotion effort implemented. A higher-level marketing manager with more authority coordinates the efforts and integrates the marketing strategies for different products into an overall plan.

The activities of product managers vary a lot depending on their experience and aggressiveness and the company's organizational philosophy. Today, companies are emphasizing marketing *experience*—because this important job takes more than academic training and enthusiasm. But it is clear that someone must be responsible for developing and implementing product-related plans, especially when a company has many products.[38]

CONCLUSION

New-product planning is an increasingly important activity in a modern economy because it is no longer very profitable to just sell me-too products in highly competitive markets. Markets, competition, and product life cycles are changing at a fast pace.

The product life-cycle concept is especially important to marketing strategy planning. It shows that a firm needs different marketing mixes—and even strategies—as a product moves through its cycle. This is an important point because profits change during the life cycle—with most of the profits going to the innovators or fast copiers.

We pointed out that a product is new to a firm if it is new in any way or to any target market. But Industry Canada takes a narrower view of what you can call "new."

The product life cycle depends upon new consumers adopting the product. As different groups of consumers adopt a product, the product moves through the life cycle. Motorola continually innovates new products for both current and new consumers.

New products are so important to business survival that firms need some organized process for developing them. We discussed such a process and emphasized that it requires a total company effort to be successful.

The failure rate of new products is high—but it is lower for better-managed firms that recognize product development and management as vital processes. Some firms appoint product managers to manage individual products and new-product teams to ensure that the process is carried out successfully.

KEY TERMS

product life cycle, 264

market introduction, 265

market growth, 265

market maturity, 266

sales decline, 267

fashion, 270

fad, 271

adoption curve, 275

innovators, 275

early adopters, 276

early majority, 277

late majority, 277

laggards, 277

nonadopters, 277

new product, 278

product liability, 281

concept testing, 282

test marketing, 283

product managers, 286

brand managers, 286

QUESTIONS AND PROBLEMS

1. Explain how industry sales and industry profits behave over the product life cycle.

2. Cite two examples of products that you feel are currently in each of the product life-cycle stages. Consider services as well as physical goods.

3. Explain how you might reach different conclusions about the correct product life-cycle stage(s) in the worldwide automobile market.

4. Explain why individual brands may not follow the product life-cycle pattern. Give an example of a new brand that is not entering the life cycle at the market introduction stage.

5. Discuss the life cycle of a product in terms of its probable impact on a manufacturer's marketing mix. Illustrate using personal computers.

6. What characteristics of a new product will help it to move through the early stages of the product life cycle more quickly? Briefly discuss each characteristic—illustrating with a product of your choice. Indicate how each characteristic might be viewed in some other country.

7. What is a new product? Illustrate your answer.

8. Explain the importance of an organized new-product development process and illustrate how it might be used for (a) a new hair care product, (b) a new children's toy, and (c) a new subscribers-only cable television channel.

9. Discuss how you might use the new-product development process if you were thinking about offering some kind of summer service to residents in a beach resort town.

10. Explain the role of product or brand managers. When would it make sense for one of a company's current brand managers to be in charge of the new-product development process? Explain your thinking.

11. If a firm offers one of its brands in a number of different countries, would it make sense for one brand manager to be in charge, or would each country require its own brand manager? Explain your thinking.

12. Discuss the social value of new-product development activities that seem to encourage people to discard products that are not all worn out. Is this an economic waste? How worn out is all worn out? Must a shirt have holes in it? How big?

13. Discuss the adoption curve as it relates to DVD players. Who buys the product at each stage? Who will buy next?

14. Laggards are not usually considered a good target market. Give two specific examples of company products that could target laggards. How would you do this?

COMPUTER-AIDED PROBLEM

10. Growth Stage Competition

RESOURCE REMINDER

AgriChem Inc., has introduced an innovative new product—a combination fertilizer, weed killer, and insecticide that makes it much easier for soybean farmers to produce a profitable crop. The product introduction was quite successful, with one million units sold in the year of introduction. And AgriChem's profits are increasing. Total market demand is expected to grow at a rate of 200,000 units a year for the next five years. Even so, AgriChem's marketing managers are concerned about what will happen to sales and profits during this period.

Based on past experience with similar situations, they expect one new competitor to enter the market during each of the next five years. They think this competitive pressure will drive prices down about 6 percent a year. Further, although the total market is growing, they know that new competitors will chip away at AgriChem's market share—even with the 10 percent a year increase planned for the promotion budget. In spite of the competitive pressure, the marketing managers are sure that familiarity with AgriChem's brand will help it hold a large share of the total market and give AgriChem greater economies of scale than competitors. In fact, they expect that the ratio of profit to dollar sales for AgriChem should be about 10 percent higher than for competitors.

AgriChem's marketing managers have decided the best way to get a handle on the situation is to organize the data in a spreadsheet. They have set up the spreadsheet so they can change the "years in the future" value and see what is likely to happen to AgriChem and the rest of the industry. The starting spreadsheet shows the current situation with data from the first full year of production.

a. Compare AgriChem's market share and profit for this year with what is expected next year—given the marketing managers' current assumptions. What are they expecting? (Hint: Set number of years in the future to 1.)

b. Prepare a table showing AgriChem's expected profit, and the expected industry revenue and profit, for the current year and the next five years. Briefly explain what happens to industry sales and profits and why. (Hint: Do an analysis to vary the number of years in the future value in the spreadsheet from a minimum of 0—the current year—to a maximum of 5. Display the three values requested.)

c. If market demand grows faster than expected—say, at 280,000 units a year—what will happen to AgriChem's profits and the expected industry revenues and profits over the next five years? What are the implications of this analysis?

If you want to read the cases and view the video cases that accompany this chapter, visit the *Basic Marketing* Online Learning Centre at: **www.mcgrawhill.ca/olc/perreault**. Along with these cases and video cases, the OLC also has the software and user guide for this chapter's Computer-Aided Problem, as well as exercises, quizzes, articles, links, and other *interactive* content that will help you with your studies.

WHEN YOU FINISH
THIS CHAPTER,
YOU SHOULD

1. Understand what product classes suggest about Place objectives.

2. Understand why some firms use direct channel systems while others rely on intermediaries and indirect systems.

3. Understand how and why marketing specialists develop to make channel systems more effective.

4. Understand how to develop cooperative relationships and avoid conflict in channel systems.

5. Know how channel members in vertical marketing systems shift and share functions to meet customer needs.

6. Understand the differences between intensive, selective, and exclusive distribution.

Place— Distribution Management

If you want a Coca-Cola, there's usually one close by—no matter where you might be in the world. And that's no accident. An executive for the best-known brand name in the world stated the objective simply: "Make Coca-Cola available within an arm's reach of desire." To achieve that objective, Coke works with many different channels of distribution. But that's just the start. Think about what it takes for a bottle, can, or cup of Coke to be there whenever you're thirsty. In warehouses and distribution centres, on trucks, in gyms and sports arenas, and thousands of other retail outlets, Coke handles, stores, and transports more than 400 billion servings of the soft drink a year. Getting all of that product to consumers could be a logistical nightmare, but Coke does it effectively and at a low cost.

Fast information about what the market needs helps keep Coke's distribution on target. Coke uses an Internet-based data system that links about one million retailers and other sellers to Coke and its bottlers. The system lets Coke bottlers and retailers exchange purchase orders, invoices, and pricing information online. Orders are processed instantly—so sales to consumers at the end of the channel aren't lost because of stock-outs. Similarly, computer systems show Coke managers exactly what's selling in each market; they can even estimate the effects of promotions as they plan inventories and deliveries. And Coke products move efficiently through the channel. In Cincinnati, for example, Coke built the beverage industry's first fully automated distribution centre. Forklifts were replaced with automatically guided vehicles that speed up the product flow and reduce labour costs. And when Coke's truck drivers get to the retail store, they efficiently stock the shelves.

Coke's strategies in international markets rely on many of the same ideas. But the stage of market development varies in different countries, so Coke's emphasis varies as well. To increase sales in France, for example, Coke installed thousands of soft-drink coolers in French supermarkets. In Great Britain, Coke emphasizes multipacks because it wants to have more inventory at the point of consumption—in consumers' homes. In Japan, by contrast, Coke has relied heavily on an army of truck drivers to constantly restock one million Coke vending machines, more per capita than anywhere else in the world. Coke is even testing vending machines that raise the price when it's hot or when few cans are left. And, in Australia, some Coke vending machines have built-in cell phone systems, a press of a button makes a call so customers can charge the Coke to their cell phone accounts.

In less-developed areas, the Place system is not always so sophisticated. In China, for example, Coke has done well in big cities, but most of the population lives in outlying areas, where high transportation costs made Coke too expensive. So Coke built more local bottling facilities in these areas and set up systems to recycle glass bottles. With these changes, a serving of Coke is now only about 12 cents. The market potential for Coke in India is also huge, but the per capita consumption of soft drinks at present is only about seven 237-ml servings per year. So, in India, Coke is increasing promotion and gearing up to handle more demand by investing $150 million to expand its bottling and distribution network.

Coke is also working to increase fountain-drink sales in domestic and international markets. As part of that effort, Coke equips restaurants and food outlets with Coke dispensers. Once a Coke dispenser is installed, the retailer usually doesn't have room for a competitor's dispenser. And when a consumer wants a fountain drink, Coke isn't just "the real thing," it's the only thing. The number of fountain outlets has grown so rapidly that one Coke account rep serves as many as 1,000 retail customers in a geographic area. That means that the little guys could get lost in the shuffle. However, to give them the service they need at a reasonable cost, Coke launched Coke.net, a password-protected Web portal where fountain customers can access account managers online, track syrup orders, request equipment repairs, or download marketing support materials.

Of course, Pepsi is a tough competitor and isn't taking all of this sitting down. It has added more noncola products, and its edgy ads for Code Red and other products are helping it gain market share—which means it gets more shelf space and more Pepsi stocked at the point of purchase. Coke is pushing on new fronts as well, so the competition is becoming even more intense. It's not just the "Cola Wars" anymore but rather the wars for cola, juice, water, sports drinks, tea, and many other beverages. And who wins customers and profits in this broader competition will depend on overall marketing programs—but clearly Place has an important role to play.[1]

PLACE DECISIONS ARE AN IMPORTANT PART OF MARKETING STRATEGY

Managers must think about **Place**—making goods and services available in the right quantities and locations—when customers want them. And when different target markets have different needs, a number of Place variations may be required. New Place arrangements can dramatically change the competition in a product-market. This is especially important in business today because many firms are using information technology, including Web sites and e-commerce, to reach customers more efficiently.

In the next two chapters, we'll deal with the many important strategy decisions that a marketing manager must make concerning Place. Exhibit 11-1 gives an

Motorola coordinates
marketing efforts for the
Razr with Rogers
Communications.

overview. We'll start in this chapter with a discussion of the type of channel that's
needed to meet customers' needs. We'll show why specialists are often involved and
how they come together to form a channel of distribution—any series of firms or
individuals who participate in the flow of products from producer to final user or
consumer. We'll also consider how to manage relations among channel members to
reduce conflict and improve cooperation.

Exhibit 11-1
Strategy Decision Areas
in Place

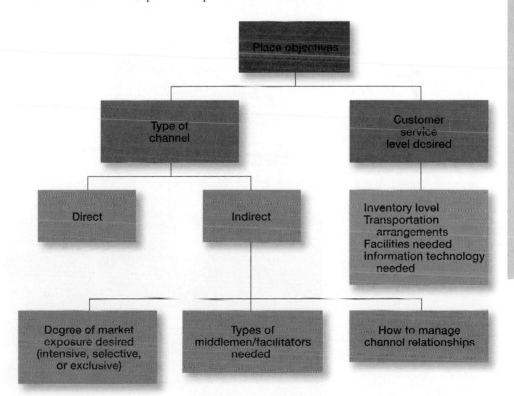

PLACE DECISIONS ARE GUIDED BY "IDEAL" PLACE OBJECTIVES

All marketing managers want to be sure that their goods and services are available in the right quantities and locations—when customers want them. But customers may have different needs with respect to when and where goods are made available as they make different purchases.

Product classes suggest Place objectives

In Chapter 9 we introduced the product classes, which summarize consumers' urgency to have needs satisfied and willingness to seek information, shop, and compare. Now you should be able to use the product classes to handle Place decisions.

Exhibit 9-3 showed the relationship between consumer product classes and ideal Place objectives. Similarly, Exhibit 9-4 showed the business product classes and how they relate to customer needs. Study these exhibits carefully. They set the framework for making Place decisions. In particular, the product classes help us decide how much market exposure we'll need in each geographic area.

Place system is not automatic

Several different product classes may be involved if different market segments view a product in different ways. Thus, marketing managers may need to develop several strategies, each with its own Place arrangements. There may not be one Place arrangement that is best.

Place decisions have long-run effects

The marketing manager must also consider Place objectives in relation to the product life cycle; see Exhibit 10-2. Place decisions often have long-run effects. They're usually harder to change than Product, Price, and Promotion decisions. Many firms that thought they could quickly establish effective Web sites for direct online sales, for example, found that it took several years and millions of dollars to

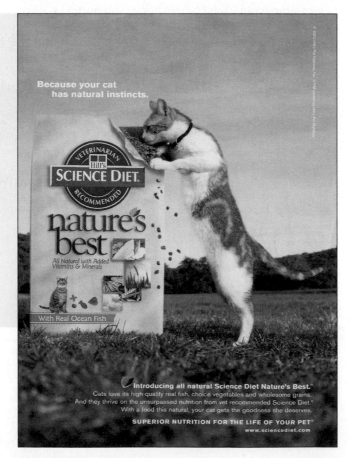

Most pet food companies focus on distribution through grocery stores, but Science Diet brand premium pet foods reach consumers in Canada, the U.S., Japan, France, and Italy through a different channel—veterinary offices and pet stores. Because Science Diet has developed cooperative relationships with members of this channel, Science Diet products often get special promotion support at the point of purchase. In addition, as shown in this ad, the package reminds customers that Science Diet is "Veterinarian Recommended."

work out the kinks. It can take even longer and cost more to develop effective working relationships with others in the channel. Legal contracts with channel partners may limit changes. And it's hard to move retail stores and wholesale facilities once they are set up. Yet as products mature, they typically need broader distribution to reach different target customers.

The distribution of premium pet foods followed this pattern. A decade ago, supermarkets wouldn't carry specialized pet foods because there wasn't much demand. So marketing managers for Science Diet products concentrated on getting distribution through pet shops and veterinary offices. Science Diet's sales in this channel grew rapidly. What's more, profit margins on the specialty foods were much higher than on traditional fare. Seeing this growth, Purina, Kal Kan, and other producers developed new products and worked with their supermarket channels to set up special "nutrition centers" on the pet food aisle. As market growth continued, P&G bought Iams and pushed for distribution in pet superstores, at mass-merchandisers, and online. But Science Diet is still competing well in its own channel. It's using the same approach in pet stores in Japan, France, and Italy.[2]

CHANNEL SYSTEM MAY BE DIRECT OR INDIRECT

One of the most basic Place decisions producers must make is whether to handle the whole distribution themselves—perhaps by relying on direct-to-customer e-commerce selling—or use wholesalers, retailers, and other specialists (see Exhibit 11-1). Middlemen, in turn, must select the producers they'll work with.

Why a firm might want to use direct distribution

Many firms prefer to distribute directly to the final customer or consumer because they want to control the whole marketing job. They may think that they can serve target customers at a lower cost or do the work more effectively than middlemen. Since middlemen often carry products of several competing producers, they might not give any one item the special emphasis its producer wants.

The Internet makes direct distribution easier

Web site-based e-commerce systems give many firms direct access to customers whom it would have been impossible to reach in the past. Even small, specialized firms may be able to establish a Web page and draw customers from all over the world. Of course, there are limitations. If a customer wants a salesperson to demonstrate a product, then a "virtual store" may not be adequate. However, distribution via the Internet is still evolving. Some firms now use live camera "feeds" while

In Canada and many other developed nations, Unilever relies primarily on indirect distribution through a variety of wholesalers and retailers. However, in Spain it delivers frozen foods directly to consumer homes, and in Vietnam a mobile store brings products to local consumers. And now some products are sold direct to consumers from an Internet Web site.

talking with the customer over an Internet video phone. Other innovations are being tested. Regardless, if it's with the help of technology or by other more traditional means, there often *are* great advantages in selling directly to the final user or consumer.

Direct contact with customers

If a firm is in direct contact with its customers, it is more aware of changes in customer attitudes. It is in a better position to adjust its marketing mix quickly because there is no need to convince other channel members to help. If a product needs an aggressive selling effort or special technical service, the marketing manager can ensure that salespeople receive the necessary training and motivation.

Suitable middlemen are not available

A firm may have to go direct if suitable middlemen are not available or will not cooperate. For example, Apple is again opening its own stores in hopes of getting more in-store promotional emphasis on what's different about its iMac computers.

Middlemen who have the best contacts with the target market may be hesitant to add unproven vendors or new products, especially really new products that don't fit well with their current business. Many new products die because the producer can't find willing middlemen and doesn't have the financial resources to handle direct distribution.

Common with business customers and services

Many business products are sold direct-to-customer. Alcan sells aluminum to General Motors direct. And Honda sells its motors direct to lawn mower producers. This is understandable since in business markets there are fewer transactions, orders are larger, and customers may be concentrated in one geographic area. Further, once relationships are established, e-commerce systems can efficiently handle orders, inventory replenishment, and routine information (such as delivery schedules).

Service firms often use direct channels. If the service must be produced in the presence of customers, there may be little need for middlemen. An accounting firm like PricewaterhouseCoopers, for example, must deal directly with its customers. However, many firms that produce physical goods turn to middlemen specialists to help provide the services customers expect. Maytag may hope that its authorized dealers don't get many repair calls, but the service is available when customers need it. Here the middleman produces the service.[3]

Some consumer products are sold direct

Many companies that produce consumer products have Web sites where a consumer can place a direct order. A few, such as cowboy boot manufacturer Alberta Boot, have retail storefronts at the factory as well as using intermediaries. But for most consumer products this is still a small part of total sales. Most consumer products are sold through intermediaries.

Of course, some consumer products are sold direct to consumers where they live or work. Mary Kay and Avon cosmetics, as well as Dell and Gateway computers are examples. These firms and many others are finding that this is a good way to crack open international markets ranging from India and China to Brazil and the U.K. Most of these firms rely on direct selling, which involves personal sales contact between a representative of the company and an individual consumer. However, most of these "salespeople" are *not* company employees. Rather, they usually work as independent middlemen, and the companies that they sell for refer to them as *dealers, distributors, agents,* or some similar term. So in a strict technical sense, this is not really direct producer-to-consumer distribution.[4]

Don't be confused by the term *direct marketing*

Even though most consumer products are sold through middlemen, an increasing number of firms rely on **direct marketing**—direct communication between a seller and an individual customer using a promotion method other than face-to-face personal selling. Sometimes direct marketing promotion is coupled with direct distribution from a producer to consumers. Park Seed Company, for example, sells the seeds it grows directly to consumers with a mail catalogue and Web site. However, many firms that use direct marketing promotion distribute their products through middlemen. So the term *direct marketing* is primarily concerned with the Promotion area, not Place decisions. We'll talk about direct marketing promotion in more detail in Chapter 13.[5]

When indirect channels are best

Even if a producer wants to handle the whole distribution job, sometimes it's simply not possible. Customers often have established buying patterns. For example, Square D, a producer of electrical supplies, might want to sell directly to electrical contractors. It can certainly set up a Web site for online orders or even open sales offices in key markets. But if contractors like to make all of their purchases in one convenient stop— at a local electrical wholesaler—the only practical way to reach them is through a wholesaler.

Consumers want convenience

Similarly, consumers are spread throughout many geographic areas and often prefer to shop for certain products at specific places. Some consumers, for instance, see Sears as *the* place to shop for appliances, so they'll only buy the brands that Sears carries. This is one reason most firms that produce consumer products rely so heavily on indirect channels (see Exhibit 2-6).[6]

Middlemen may invest in inventory

Direct distribution usually requires a significant investment in facilities, people, and information technology. A company that has limited financial resources or that wants to retain flexibility may want to avoid that investment by working with established middlemen.

Middlemen may further reduce a producer's need for working capital by buying the producer's output and carrying it in inventory until it's sold. If customers want a good "right now," there must be an inventory available to make the sale. And if customers are spread over a large area, it will probably be necessary to have widespread distribution.

Until recently, Levi Strauss jeans were not distributed by Wal-Mart. However, many shoppers prefer to buy their jeans at Wal-Mart and other mass-merchandisers. To reach this segment, Levi Strauss created the Signature line. It features lighter-weight denim and less detailing and is now available at Wal-Mart and Zellers.

Middlemen may reduce credit risk

Some middlemen play a critical role by providing credit to customers at the end of the channel. A middleman who knows local customers can help reduce credit risks. As sales via the Internet grow, sellers are looking for faster and better ways to check the credit ratings of distant customers. It's an unhappy day when the marketing manager learns that a customer who was shipped goods based on an online order can't pay the invoice.

The most important reason for using an indirect channel of distribution is that an intermediary can often help producers serve customer needs better and at lower cost. Remember that we discussed this briefly in Chapter 1. Now we'll go into more detail.

The assortment and quantity of products customers want may be different from the assortment and quantity of products companies produce. Producers are often located far from their customers and may not know how best to reach them. Customers in turn may not know about their choices. Specialists develop to adjust these discrepancies and separations.[7]

Middlemen may supply needed information

Specialists often help provide information to bring buyers and sellers together. For example, most consumers don't know much about the wide variety of home and auto insurance policies available. A local independent insurance agent may help them decide which policy, and which insurance company, best fits their needs.

Middlemen who are close to their customers are often able to anticipate customer needs and forecast demand more accurately. This information can help reduce inventory costs in the whole channel—and it may help the producer smooth out production.

Most producers seek help from specialists when they first enter international markets. Specialists can provide crucial information about customer needs and insights into differences in the marketing environment.

Discrepancies of quantity and assortment

Discrepancy of quantity means the difference between the quantity of products it is economical for a producer to make and the quantity final users or consumers normally want. For example, most manufacturers of golf balls produce large quantities—perhaps 200,000 to 500,000 in a given time period. The average golfer, however, wants only a few balls at a time. Adjusting for this discrepancy usually requires middlemen—wholesalers and retailers.

Producers typically specialize by product—and therefore another discrepancy develops. **Discrepancy of assortment** means the difference between the lines a

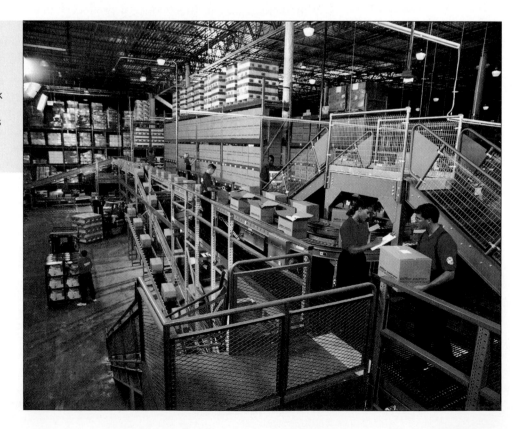

Office Depot, a large office supplies chain, accumulates products from many producers at its distribution centre and then breaks bulk to provide the convenient assortments that consumers expect to find at individual Office Depot stores.

To reach its Place objectives, TELUS sells PCS phones and its wireless services through authorized dealers, kiosks in retail outlets and malls, and at its own TELUS corporate stores.

typical producer makes and the assortment final consumers or users want. Most golfers, for example, need more than golf balls. They want golf shoes, gloves, clubs, a bag, and, of course, a golf course to play on. And they usually don't want to shop for each item separately. So, again, there is a need for wholesalers and retailers to adjust these discrepancies.

Channel specialists adjust discrepancies with regrouping activities

Regrouping activities adjust the quantities or assortments of products handled at each level in a channel of distribution.

There are four regrouping activities: accumulating, bulk-breaking, sorting, and assorting. When one or more of these activities is needed, a marketing specialist may develop to fill this need.

Adjusting quantity discrepancies by accumulating and bulk-breaking

Accumulating involves collecting products from many small producers. Much of the coffee that comes from Colombia is grown on small farms in the mountains. Accumulating the small crops into larger quantities is a way of getting the lowest transporting rate and making it more convenient for distant food processing companies to buy and handle it. Accumulating is especially important in less-developed countries and in other situations, like agricultural markets, where there are many small producers.

Accumulating is also important with professional services because they often involve the combined work of a number of individuals, each of whom is a specialized producer. A hospital makes it easier for patients by accumulating the services of a number of health care specialists, many of whom may not actually work for the hospital.

Many middlemen who operate from Internet Web sites focus on accumulating. Specialized sites for everything from Chinese art to Dutch flower bulbs bring together the output of many producers.

Bulk-breaking involves dividing larger quantities into smaller quantities as products get closer to the final market. The bulk-breaking may involve several levels of middlemen. Wholesalers may sell smaller quantities to other wholesalers or directly to retailers. Retailers continue breaking bulk as they sell individual items to their customers.

Adjusting assortment discrepancies by sorting and assorting

Different types of specialists adjust assortment discrepancies. They perform two types of regrouping activities: sorting and assorting.

Sorting means separating products into grades and qualities desired by different target markets. For example, an investment firm might offer its customers shares in a mutual fund made up only of stocks for companies that pay regular dividends. Similarly, a wholesaler that specializes in serving convenience stores may focus on smaller packages of frequently used products.

Assorting means putting together a variety of products to give a target market what it wants. This usually is done by those closest to the final consumer or user—retailers or wholesalers who try to supply a wide assortment of products for the convenience of their customers. Thus, a wholesaler selling Yazoo tractors and mowers to golf courses might also carry Pennington grass seed and Scott fertilizer. Wallace & Carey Ltd., Canada's largest independent distributor, offers retailers an assortment of products ranging from Blistex to Duracell to Tootsie Rolls.

Watch for changes

Sometimes these discrepancies are adjusted badly, especially when consumer wants and attitudes shift rapidly. When cell phones suddenly became popular, an opportunity developed for a new specialist. Cell phone dealers came on the scene to help customers figure out what type of cell phone and service would meet their needs. It cost the sellers of cell services up to $300 per customer to sell through dealers. However, as the market grew, competition for customers heated up and electronics stores wanted a piece of the action. They were willing to take a smaller markup. Now that the market is established, cell service providers are finding it cheaper to sell from a Web site or use their own salespeople.[8]

Specialists should develop to adjust discrepancies *if they must be adjusted*. But there is no point in having middlemen just because that's the way it's been done in the past. Sometimes a breakthrough opportunity can come from finding a better way to reduce discrepancies. Some manufacturers of business products can now reach more customers in distant markets with an Internet Web site than it was previously possible for them to reach with independent manufacturers' reps who sold on commission (but otherwise left distribution to the firm). The Web site cost advantage can translate to lower prices and a marketing mix that is a better value for some target segments.[9]

CHANNEL RELATIONSHIP MUST BE MANAGED

Marketing manager must choose type of channel relationship

Middlemen specialists can help make a channel more efficient. But there may be problems getting the different firms in a channel to work together well. How well they work together depends on the type of relationship they have. This should be carefully considered since marketing managers usually have choices about what type of channel system to join or develop.

The whole channel should have a product-market commitment

Ideally, all of the members of a channel system should have a shared *product-market commitment*—with all members focusing on the same target market at the end of the channel and sharing the various marketing functions in appropriate ways. When members of a channel do this, they are better able to compete effectively for the customer's business. Unfortunately, many marketing managers overlook this idea because it's not the way their firms have traditionally handled channel relationships.

Traditional channel systems involve weak relationships

In **traditional channel systems**, the various channel members make little or no effort to cooperate with each other. They buy and sell from each other—and that's the extent of their relationship. Each channel member does only what it considers to be in its own best interest. It doesn't worry about other members of the channel. This is shortsighted, but it's easy to see how it can happen. The objectives of the various channel members may be different. For example, General Electric wants a wholesaler of electrical building supplies to sell GE products. But a wholesaler who works with different producers may not care whose products get sold. The wholesaler just wants happy customers and a good profit margin.

A channel captain can improve the performance of the whole channel—by developing strategies that help everyone in the channel do a better job of meeting the needs of target customers at the end of the channel.

Traditional channel systems are still typical, and very important, in some industries. The members of these channels have their independence, but they may pay for it too. As we will see, such channels are declining in importance—with good reason.[10]

Conflict gets in the way

Specialization can make a channel more efficient—but not if the specialists are so independent that the channel doesn't work smoothly. Because members of traditional channel systems often have different objectives—and different ideas about how things should be done—conflict is common.

There are two basic types of conflict in channels of distribution. Vertical conflicts occur between firms at different levels in the channel of distribution. A vertical conflict may occur if a producer and a retailer disagree about how much shelf space or promotion effort the retailer should give the producer's product. For example, when Wherehouse Entertainment (a large retail music chain) started to sell used CDs—at about half the price of new ones—several recording companies said that they would halt cooperative advertising payments to any retailer that sold used CDs. The recording companies felt that the used CDs hurt their sales.[11]

Horizontal conflicts occur between firms at the same level in the channel of distribution. For example, a furniture store that keeps a complete line of furniture on display isn't happy to find out that a discount chain store down the street is offering customers lower prices on special orders of the same items. The discounter is getting a free ride from the competing store's investment in inventory. And nothing gets an independent retailer more charged up than finding out that a chain store is selling some product for less than the wholesale price the independent pays. Consumers may travel from one Ford dealership to another (especially in the same city) comparing prices, and horizontal conflict may occur if one dealer is selling the same model for a much lower price.

Cooperative relationships share common objectives

Usually the best way to avoid conflict is to get everyone in the channel working together in a cooperative relationship that is focused on the same basic objective—satisfying the customer at the end of the channel. This leads us away from traditional channels to cooperative channel relationships and the channel captain concept.

Channel captain can guide channel relationships

Each channel system should act as a unit, where each member of the channel collaborates to serve customers at the end of the channel. In this view, cooperation is everyone's responsibility. However, some firms are in a better position to take the lead in the relationship and in coordinating the whole channel effort. This situation calls for a **channel captain**—a manager who helps direct the activities of a whole channel and tries to avoid or solve channel conflicts.

For example, when Harley-Davidson wanted to expand sales of fashion accessories, it was difficult for motorcycle dealers to devote enough space to all of the different styles. Harley considered selling the items directly from its own Web site, but that would take sales away from dealers who were working hard to help Harley sell both cycles and fashions. So Harley's president asked a group of dealers and Harley managers to work together to come up with a plan they all liked. The result was a Web site that sells Harley products through the dealer that is closest to the customer.[12]

The concept of a single channel captain is logical. But most traditional channels don't have a recognized captain. The various firms don't act as a coordinated system. Yet firms are interrelated, even if poorly, by their policies. So it makes sense to try to avoid channel conflicts by planning for channel relations. The channel captain arranges for the necessary functions to be performed in the most effective way.

The situation faced by Goodyear is a good example. The Goodyear brand was sold almost exclusively through its own stores and its 2,500 independent tire dealers. But sales were falling. There were many reasons. France's Michelin and Japan's Bridgestone had aggressively expanded distribution in North America. Moreover, many consumers were shopping at discount outlets. Goodyear decided it had no choice but to expand distribution and sell Goodyear tires to other big retail chains. To reach the discount shoppers, Goodyear also converted many of its own auto-centres to no-frills stores operated under the Just Tires name. However, to reduce the conflict that these changes caused with its independent dealers, Goodyear introduced the new Aquatred line and other specialized tires that appealed to the dealers' target market. Goodyear also increased advertising and created the Gemini brand name to help promote service by Goodyear dealers. Because of this channel leadership, Goodyear's sales increased and so did the sales of its dealers.[13]

Some producers lead their channels

As the Goodyear case suggests, producers frequently take the lead in channel relations. Middlemen often wait to see what the producer intends to do and wants them to do. Then they decide whether their roles will be profitable and whether they want to join in the channel effort.

Some middlemen are channel captains

Sometimes wholesalers or retailers do take the lead. They are closer to the final user or consumer and are in an ideal position to assume the channel captain role. These middlemen analyze their customers' needs and then seek out producers who can provide these products at reasonable prices. With the growth of powerful chains, like Wal-Mart and Toys "R" Us, retailers now dominate the channel systems for many products in North America. In Japan, very large wholesalers (trading companies) are often the channel captains.

Retailers like Sears and wholesalers like Home Hardware who develop their own dealer brands in effect act like producers. They specify the whole marketing mix for a product and merely delegate production to a factory.

Made with pure botanical extracts and enriched with moisturizing ingredients and protective properties, our exclusive line of **Life Brand Botanicals** shampoos and conditioners cater to your hair's specific needs.

A fresh new addition to our extensive premium quality platinum line of products, these Amazonian-inspired blends work to naturally and effectively bring out the vibrancy and shine of your hair.

SHOPPERS DRUG MART

The growing number of retailer-led channel systems is prompting growth of private-label dealer brands in a wide variety of product categories. However, a retailer that carries its own store brands may want to give customers a choice by offering a national brand, especially when the manufacturer takes the lead in areas such as promotion and new-product development.

Some strong middlemen use their power to control channel relationships. For example, buyers for Wal-Mart look at the value added by a wholesaler. If they think Wal-Mart can be efficient without the wholesaler, they tell the producer that the chain will only buy direct—usually at a lower price than was paid to the wholesaler.[14]

VERTICAL MARKETING SYSTEMS FOCUS ON FINAL CUSTOMERS

Many marketing managers accept the view that a coordinated channel system can help everyone in the channel. These managers are moving their firms away from traditional channel systems and instead developing or joining vertical market systems. **Vertical marketing systems** are channel systems in which the whole channel focuses on the same target market at the end of the channel. Such systems make sense, and are growing, because if the final customer doesn't buy the product, the whole channel suffers. There are three types of vertical marketing systems—corporate, administered, and contractual. Exhibit 11-2 summarizes some characteristics of these systems and compares them with traditional systems.

Corporate channel systems shorten channels

Some corporations develop their own vertical marketing systems by internal expansion or by buying other firms, or both. With **corporate channel systems**—corporate ownership all along the channel—we might say the firm is going "direct." But actually the firm may be handling manufacturing, wholesaling, and retailing—so it's more accurate to think of the firm as a vertical marketing system.

Corporate channel systems may develop by **vertical integration**—acquiring firms at different levels of channel activity. Bridgestone, for example, has rubber plantations in Liberia, tire plants in Ohio, and wholesale and retail outlets all over the world. In England, most of the quaint local pubs are now actually owned and operated by the large beer breweries. In Canada, Weston bakeries supply products to Loblaws grocery stores and Real Canadian Superstores—which are owned by Weston.

Characteristics	Type of Channel			
		Vertical Marketing Systems		
	Traditional	Administered	Contractual	Corporate
Amount of cooperation	Little or none	Some to good	Fairly good to good	Complete
Control maintained by	None	Economic power and leadership	Contracts	Ownership by one company
Examples	Typical channel of "independents" such as a locally owned deli	General Electric, O.M. Scott & Sons (lawn products)	McDonald's, Holiday Inn, Coca-Cola, Chevrolet	Sherwin-Williams Paint, Sony Stores

Vertical integration has potential advantages—stable sources of supplies, better control of distribution and quality, greater buying power, and lower executive overhead. Provided that the discrepancies of quantity and assortment are not too great at each level in a channel, vertical integration can be profitable. However, many managers have found that it's hard to be really good at running manufacturing, wholesaling, and retailing businesses that are very different from each other. Instead, they try to be more efficient at what they do best and focus on ways to get cooperation in the channel for the other activities. Coca-Cola, for example, has moved from vertical integration to a focus on marketing the product.

Administered and contractual systems may work well

Firms can often gain the advantages of vertical integration without building a costly corporate channel. A manager can develop administered or contractual channel systems instead. In **administered channel systems**, the channel members informally agree to cooperate with each other. They can agree to routinize ordering, share inventory and sales information over computer networks, standardize accounting, and coordinate promotion efforts. In **contractual channel systems**, the channel members agree by contract to cooperate with each other. With both of these systems, the members retain some of the flexibility of a traditional channel system.

The opportunities to reduce costs and provide customers with superior value are growing in these systems because of help from information technology. For example, Costco has a system that it calls "vendor managed inventory" in which key suppliers take over responsibility for managing a set of products, often a whole product category. Costco uses this approach with Kimberly-Clark (KC), the firm that makes Huggies. Every day, an analyst at KC's headquarters studies Costco's online data that details Huggies' sales and inventory at every Costco store. The analyst studies how much is sold of each item in each store in the average week. If inventory is getting low, a new order is placed and shipping is scheduled. Shipping cartons with computer-readable bar codes track the status of shipments and reduce errors. This system reduces buying and selling costs, inventory management, lost sales from inventory stock-outs, and the consumer frustration that creates. Because KC does this job well, it makes more money and so does Costco. Costco could do the job itself, but it handles such a wide assortment of products that it would be costly to do all the work required in every high-volume category.[15]

Vertical marketing systems—dominant force in the marketplace

Vertical systems in the consumer products area have a healthy majority of retail sales and should continue to increase their share in the future. Vertical marketing systems are becoming the major competitive units in the North American distribution system—and they are growing rapidly in other parts of the world as well.[16]

MUSIC FIRMS FIDDLE AROUND WHILE CUSTOMERS SEARCH FOR DIGITAL TUNES

The music industry knew that its target market was the Internet generation, but it doggedly stuck to distribution of music on CDs through its traditional channels of distribution. Selling digital downloads was, at best, a piecemeal effort. With this head-in-the-sand approach, the Internet became a threat rather than an opportunity.

Napster's file-sharing service kick started the digital media revolution and attracted 60 million avid fans who downloaded pirated digital songs for free. Even after Napster was forced into liquidation in 2002, few music firms had come up with effective plans of their own for digital distribution. A year later, Napster was reinvented as a subscription service. For $9.95 a month, a user could legally download songs for 99 cents each.

However, by then Apple's iTunes online music jukebox and pay-per-song store had a head start. It had distribution agreements with most music labels. Also, iTunes was designed to be easy to use, but only with Apple's popular iPod MP3 player (although the iPod software was updated to reach Windows users later). Apple even formed an alliance with America Online so that AOL's 25 million users would be steered to iTunes.com for music purchases and billed directly on their AOL accounts for downloads. However, competition from new intermediaries for digital content is heating up, so consumers are likely to have many available choices not only for music but for movies, books, and other items.[17]

Short-term alliances are also popular

Firms that cooperate to build vertical marketing systems typically share a longer-term commitment. Sometimes, however, what a firm wants is a short-term collaboration to accomplish a specific objective. This may lead to an alliance, a partnership (usually informal) in which firms agree to work together to achieve an objective. An alliance may involve two firms, or a whole network of firms. The firms may be at the same level in the channel or at different levels. For example, a number of hardware, software, and service firms in the computer business have formed alliances to build a market for the Linux operating system. Some of these firms are even competitors (at least in some of their product-markets). Nevertheless, without the alliance it would be difficult for any of them to compete with Microsoft.[18]

Wal-Mart uses real-time data and works with vendors to ensure that the right assortment of products is always on hand, while reducing inventory levels and virtually eliminating lost sales because of out-of-stock items. Such cooperation among channel members can reduce costs and result in lower prices to the final consumer.

You may think that all marketing managers want their products to have maximum exposure to potential customers. This isn't true. Some product classes require much less market exposure than others. **Ideal market exposure** makes a product available widely enough to satisfy target customers' needs but not exceed them. Too much exposure only increases the total cost of marketing.

Ideal exposure may be intensive, selective, or exclusive

Intensive distribution is selling a product through all responsible and suitable wholesalers or retailers who will stock or sell the product. **Selective distribution** is selling through only those middlemen who will give the product special attention. **Exclusive distribution** is selling through only one middleman in a particular geographic area. As we move from intensive to exclusive distribution, we give up exposure in return for some other advantage—including, but not limited to, lower cost.

In practice, this means that Coke is available everywhere—through intensive distribution. But Rolls-Royces are handled, through exclusive distribution, by only a very limited number of middlemen across the country.

Intensive distribution—sell it where they buy it

Intensive distribution is commonly needed for convenience products and business supplies—such as laser printer cartridges, ring binders, and copier paper—used by all offices. Customers want such products nearby.

The seller's intent is important here. Intensive distribution refers to the desire to sell through *all* responsible and suitable outlets. What this means depends on customer habits and preferences. If customers preferred to buy Panasonic portable TVs only at electronics stores, you would try to sell through all electronics stores to achieve intensive distribution. Today, however, many customers buy small portable TVs at a variety of convenient outlets—including London Durgs, Wal-Mart, over the phone from the Sharper Image catalogue, or perhaps from a Web site on the Internet. This means that an intensive distribution policy requires use of all these outlets, and more than one channel, to reach one target market.

Rayovac batteries were not selling well even though their performance was very similar to other batteries. Part of that was due to heavier advertising for Duracell and Energizer. But consumers usually don't go shopping for batteries. They're purchased on impulse 83 percent of the time. To get a larger share of purchases, Rayovac had to be in more stores. It offered retailers a marketing mix with less advertising and a

To make products more readily available, a manufacturer may need to recruit additional middlemen and also be certain that it is convenient for consumers to purchase online.

lower price. In three years, the brand moved from being available in 36,000 stores to 82,000 stores—and that increase gave sales a big charge.[19]

Selective distribution—sell it where it sells best

Selective distribution covers the broad area of market exposure between intensive and exclusive distribution. It may be suitable for all categories of products. Only the better middlemen are used here. Companies commonly use selective distribution to gain some of the advantages of exclusive distribution—while still achieving fairly widespread market coverage.

Reduce costs and get better partners

A selective policy might be used to avoid selling to wholesalers or retailers that (1) place orders that are too small to justify making calls, (2) make too many returns or request too much service, (3) have a poor credit rating, or (4) are not in a position to do a satisfactory job.

Selective distribution is becoming more popular than intensive distribution as firms see that they don't need 100 percent coverage of a market to support national advertising. Often the majority of sales come from relatively few customers—and the others buy too little compared to the cost of working with them. This is called the 80/20 rule—80 percent of a company's sales often come from only 20 percent of its customers *until it becomes more selective in choosing customers*.

Esprit—a producer of women's clothing—was selling through about 4,000 department stores and specialty shops in North America. But Esprit's sales analysis showed that sales in Esprit's own stores were about four times better than sales in other outlets. Profits increased when Esprit cut back to about half as many outlets and opened more of its own stores and a Web site. Over time, competition from retailers like The Gap and Abercrombie & Fitch increased, so in recent years Esprit has selectively focused on building profitability in over 630 directly managed shops and 2,000 franchised shops in Europe and Asia.[20]

Get special effort from channel members

Selective distribution can produce greater profits not only for the producer but for all channel members. Wholesalers and retailers are more willing to promote products aggressively if they know they're going to obtain the majority of sales through their own efforts. They may carry wider lines, do more promotion, and provide more service—all of which lead to more sales.

Selective often moves to intensive as market grows

In the early part of the life cycle of a new unsought good, a producer may have to use selective distribution. Well-known middlemen may have the power to get such a product introduced, but sometimes on their own terms. That often means limiting the number of competing wholesalers and retailers. The producer may be happy with such an arrangement at first but dislike it later when more retailers want to carry the product.

Exclusive distribution sometimes makes sense

Exclusive distribution is just an extreme case of selective distribution—the firm selects only one middleman in each geographic area. Besides the various advantages of selective distribution, producers may want to use exclusive distribution to help control prices and the service offered in a channel.

Retailers of shopping products and specialty products often try to get exclusive distribution rights in their territories. Fast-food franchises often have exclusive distribution—and that's one reason they're popular. Owners of McDonald's franchises pay a share of sales and follow McDonald's strategy to keep the exclusive right to a market.

Unlike selective distribution, exclusive distribution usually involves a verbal or written agreement stating that channel members will buy all or most of a given product from the seller. In return, these middlemen are granted the exclusive rights to that product in their territories.

Is limiting market exposure legal?

Exclusive distribution is legal in Canada. Firms should take care, however, not to abuse a significant market position.

Horizontal arrangements among competitors are illegal

Horizontal arrangements—among *competing* retailers, wholesalers, or producers—to limit sales by customer or territory have consistently been ruled illegal under the Competition Act such arrangements normally reduce competition in the marketplace and are therefore not tolerated.

Vertical arrangements may or may not be legal

The Competition Act also regulates this area. Once again, unduly lessening competition is illegal if detrimental to consumers. Some exclusive deals are allowed. Examples include introducing new products or new technologies. Even these exclusive deals must, however, be only temporary to be legal. Thus, firms should be cautious about entering into any exclusive distribution agreement.

CHANNEL SYSTEMS CAN BE COMPLEX

Trying to achieve the desired degree of market exposure can lead to complex channels of distribution. Firms may need different channels to reach different segments of a broad product-market or to be sure they reach each segment. Sometimes this results in competition between different channels.

Consider the different channels used by a company that publishes computer books. See Exhibit 11-3. This publisher sells through a general book wholesaler who in turn sells to Internet book retailers and independent book retailers. The publisher may have some direct sales of its best-selling books to a large chain or even to consumers who order directly from its Web site. However, it might also sell through a computer supplies wholesaler that serves electronics superstores like Future Shop. This can cause problems because different wholesalers and retailers want different markups. It also increases competition, including price competition. And the competition among different middlemen may result in conflicts between the middlemen and the publisher.

Exhibit 11-3 An Example of Multichannel Distribution by a Publisher of Computer Books

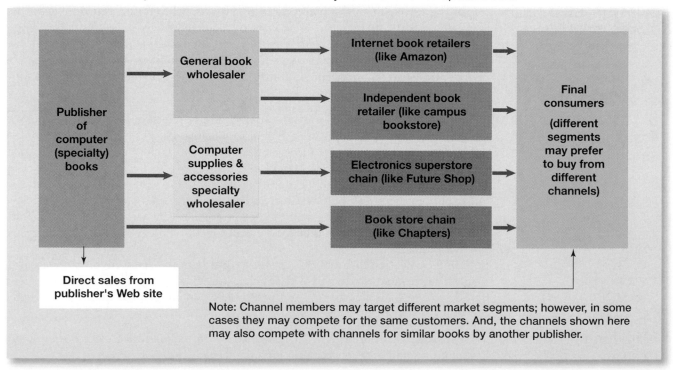

Note: Channel members may target different market segments; however, in some cases they may compete for the same customers. And, the channels shown here may also compete with channels for similar books by another publisher.

Multichannel distribution systems may be needed

Multichannel distribution (sometimes called **dual distribution**) occurs when a producer uses several competing channels to reach the same target market—perhaps using several middlemen in addition to selling directly. Multichannel distribution is becoming more common. For instance, big retail chains want large quantities and low prices. A producer may sell directly to retail chains and rely on wholesalers to sell to smaller accounts. Some established middlemen resent this because they don't appreciate *any* competition—especially price competition set up by their own suppliers.

Reebok

Other times, producers are forced to use multichannel distribution because their present channels are doing a poor job or aren't reaching some potential customers. For example, Reebok International had been relying on local sporting goods stores to sell its shoes to high school and college athletic teams. But Reebok wasn't getting much of the business. When it set up its own team-sales department to sell directly to the schools, it got a 30,000-unit increase in sales.[21]

Ethical decisions may be required

If competition changes or customers' Place requirements shift, the current channel system may not be effective. The changes required to serve customer needs may hurt one or more members of the channel. Ethical dilemmas in the channels area arise in situations like this—because not everyone in the channel can win.

For example, wholesalers and the independent retailers that they serve in a channel of distribution may trust a producer channel-captain to develop marketing strategies that will work for the whole channel. However, the producer may decide that consumers, and its own business, are best served by a change (say, dropping current middlemen and selling directly to big retail chains). A move of this sort, if implemented immediately, may not give current middlemen-partners a chance to make adjustments of their own. The more dependent they are on the producer, the more severe the impact is likely to be. It's not easy to determine the best or most ethical solution in these situations. However, marketing managers must think carefully about the consequences of Place strategy changes for other channel members. In channels, as in any business dealing, relationships of trust must be treated with care.[22]

Reverse channels should be planned

Most firms focus on getting products to their customers. But some marketing managers must also plan for **reverse channels**—channels used to retrieve products that customers no longer want. The need for reverse channels may arise in a variety of different situations. Toy companies, automobile firms, drug companies, and others sometimes have to recall products because of safety problems. A firm that makes an error in completing an order may have to take returns.

If a Viewsonic computer monitor breaks while it's still under warranty, someone needs to get it to the repair centre. Soft-drink companies may need to recycle empty bottles. Similarly, used inkjet and laser toner catridges are often recycled and reused. And, of course, consumers sometimes buy something in error and want to return it. This is common with online purchases where consumers can't see, touch, or try the product before purchasing it.[23] Gifts may also need to be exchanged.

Another problem arises from products that are damaged in shipping or discontinued. Most manufacturers take them back. A grocery products trade group says that the cost of such unsalable products, in total, may be as much as $4 billion a year. To reduce such costs, P&G has

MARKETING ETHICALLY

Wal-Mart wields its power for just one purpose: to bring the lowest possible prices to its customers. At Wal-Mart, that goal is never reached. The retailer has a clear policy for suppliers: on basic products that don't change, the price Wal-Mart will pay, and will charge shoppers, must drop year after year. But what almost no one outside the world of Wal-Mart and its 21,000 suppliers knows is the high cost of those low prices. Wal-Mart has the power to squeeze profit-killing concessions from vendors. To survive in the face of its pricing demands, makers of everything from bras to bicycles to blue jeans have had to lay off employees and close plants in favour of outsourcing products from overseas.

Of course, companies have been moving jobs offshore for decades; long before Wal-Mart was a retailing power. But, there is no question that the chain is helping accelerate the loss of jobs to low-wage countries such as China.

It is accepted wisdom that Wal-Mart makes the companies it does business with more efficient and focused, leaner and faster. Wal-Mart itself is known for continuous improvement in its ability to handle, move, and track merchandise. It expects the same of its suppliers. But the ability to operate at peak efficiency only gets you in the door at Wal-Mart. Then the real demands start. The public image Wal-Mart projects may be as cheery as its yellow smiley-face mascot, but there is nothing genial about the process by which Wal-Mart gets its suppliers to provide products at everyday low prices. Wal-Mart is legendary for forcing its suppliers to redesign everything from their packaging to their computer systems. It is also legendary for quite straightforwardly telling them what it will pay for their goods.

Do you feel that Wal-Mart is being ethical with its dealings with its suppliers?[24]

adopted a no-returns policy and instead gives retailers a payment for damaged items. Some retailers don't like P&G's policy, but it is important to see that it is a specific plan and part of an overall strategy.

When marketing managers don't plan for reverse channels, the firm's customers may be left to solve "their" problem. That usually doesn't make sense. So a complete plan for Place may need to consider an efficient way to return products—with policies that different channel members agree on. It may also require specialists who were not involved in getting the product to the consumer. But if that's what it takes to satisfy customers, it should be part of marketing strategy planning.[25]

PHYSICAL DISTRIBUTION GETS IT TO CUSTOMERS

Choosing the right channel of distribution is crucial in getting products to the target market's Place. But as the Coke case shows, that alone is usually not enough to ensure that products are available at the right time and in the right quantities. Whenever the product includes a physical good, Place requires logistics decisions. **Logistics** is the transporting, storing, and handling of goods to match target customers' needs with a firm's marketing mix—both within individual firms and along a channel of distribution. **Physical distribution (PD)** is another common name for logistics. PD provides time and place utility and makes possession utility possible. The physical distribution system must meet customers' needs with an acceptable service level and cost.

The physical distribution concept

The physical distribution (PD) concept says that all transporting, storing, and product-handling activities of a business and a whole channel system should be coordinated as one system that seeks to minimize the cost of distribution for a given customer service level. Both lower costs and better service help to increase customer

310

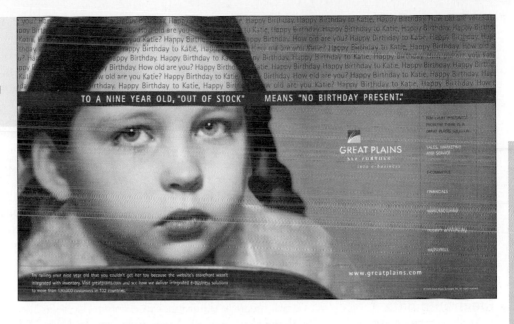

Logistics activities are often invisible to consumers, but a breakdown in distribution customer service can result in dissatisfied consumers and lost business.

value. It may be hard to see this as a startling development. But until just a few years ago, even the most progressive companies treated physical distribution functions as separate and unrelated activities.

Decide what service level to offer

With broader adoption of the physical distribution concept, this is changing. Firms work together to decide what aspects of service are most important to customers at the end of the channel. Then they focus on finding the least expensive way to achieve the target level of service.

Exhibit 11-4 shows a variety of factors that may influence the customer service level (at each level in the channel). The most important aspects of customer service depend on target market needs. Xerox might focus on how long it takes to deliver copy machine repair parts once it receives an order. When a copier breaks down, customers want the repair "yesterday." The service level might be stated as "we will deliver 90 percent of all emergency repair parts within 24 hours." This might require that commonly needed parts be available on the service truck, that order processing be very fast, and that parts not available locally be sent by airfreight. Obviously, supplying this service level will affect the total cost of the PD system. But it may also beat competitors.

COORDINATING LOGISTICS ACTIVITIES AMONG FIRMS

Supply chain management

In our discussion, we have taken the point of view of a marketing manager. **Supply chain management** focuses on how logistics should be coordinated to meet the

Exhibit 11-4
Examples of Factors that Affect PD Service Levels

- Advance information on product availability
- Time to enter and process orders
- Backorder procedures
- Where inventory is stored
- Accuracy in filling orders
- Damage in shipping, storing, and handling
- Online status information

- Advance information on delays
- Time needed to deliver an order
- Reliability in meeting delivery date
- Complying with customer's instructions
- Defect-free deliveries
- How needed adjustments are handled
- Procedures for handling returns

needs of customers at the end of the channel of distribution. Now, however, we should broaden the picture somewhat because the relationships within the distribution channel are sometimes part of a broader network of relationships in the **chain of supply**— the complete set of firms and facilities and logistics activities that are involved in procuring materials, transforming them into intermediate or finished products, and distributing them to customers. For example, Toyota not only works with dealers and customers but also with the supplier firms from which it buys parts. Those firms, in turn, coordinate with their own suppliers. What happens at each link can impact the whole chain. If the firm that produces seats for Toyota doesn't get the fabric from its supplier on time, the seats will be delayed en route to Toyota and the car will be slow getting to the dealer and consumer.

The concept of supply chain management has, ideally, all of the firms in the chain of supply working together to meet the needs of the customer at the very end of the chain. That way, at each link along the chain the shifting and sharing of logistics functions and costs are handled to result in maximum value for the final customer. Further, all of the firms in the whole chain of supply are able to do a better job of competing against competitors who are involved in other chains of supply.

Electronic data interchange sets a standard

Until recently, differences in computer systems from one firm to another hampered the flow of information. Many firms attacked this problem by adopting **electronic data interchange (EDI)**—an approach that puts information in a standardized format easily shared between different computer systems. In many firms, purchase orders, shipping reports, and other paper documents were replaced with computerized EDI. With EDI, a customer transmits its order information directly to the supplier's computer. The supplier's computer immediately processes the order and schedules production, order assembly, and transportation. Inventory information is automatically updated, and status reports are available instantly. The supplier might then use EDI to send the updated information to the transportation provider's computer. In fact, most international transportation firms rely on EDI links with their customers.

EDI systems were originally developed before the Internet gained widespread use. Traditional EDI systems are expensive to develop and rely on proprietary computer networks to exchange data securely. Newer alternatives to this approach that rely on the Internet and a standard format, called XML, for exchanging data are gaining popularity.[26]

Improved information flow and better coordination of PD activities is a key reason for the success of Pepperidge Farm's line of premium cookies. Most of the company's delivery truck drivers use hand-held computers to record the inventory at each stop along their routes. They use the Internet to instantly transmit the information into a computer at the bakeries, and cookies in short supply are produced. The right assortment of fresh cookies is quickly shipped to local markets, and delivery trucks are loaded with what retailers need that day. Pepperidge Farm moves cookies from its bakeries to store shelves in about three days; most cookie producers take about 10 days. That means fresher cookies for consumers and helps to support Pepperidge Farm's high-quality positioning and premium price.[27]

THE TRANSPORTING FUNCTION ADDS VALUE TO A MARKETING STRATEGY

Transporting aids economic development and exchange

Transporting is the marketing function of moving goods. Transportation provides time and place utilities—at a cost. But the cost is less than the value added to products by moving them or there is little reason to ship in the first place.

Transporting can help achieve economies of scale in production. If production costs can be reduced by producing larger quantities in one location, these savings may more than offset the added cost of transporting the finished products to

The cost of transportation adds little to the total cost of products—like pharmaceuticals—that are already valuable relative to their size and weight. But transporting costs can be a large part of the total cost for heavy products that are low in value, like sheet aluminum.

customers. Without low-cost transportation, both within countries and internationally, there would be no mass distribution as we know it today.

Transporting can be costly

Transporting costs limit the target markets a marketing manager can serve. Shipping costs increase delivered cost—and that's what really interests customers. Transport costs add little to the cost of products that are already valuable relative to their size and weight. A case of medicine, for example, might be shipped to a drugstore at low cost. But transporting costs can be a large part of the total cost for heavy products of low value—like many minerals and raw materials. You can imagine that shipping a massive roll of aluminum to a producer of soft-drink cans is an expensive proposition. Exhibit 11-5 shows transporting costs as a percent of total sales dollars for several products.[28]

Exhibit 11-5
Transporting Costs as a Percent of Selling Price for Different Products

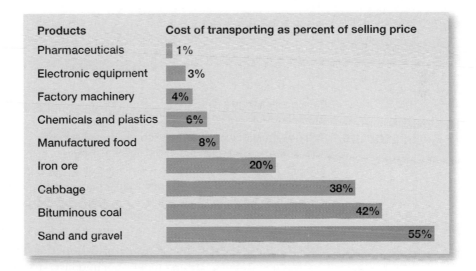

Products	Cost of transporting as percent of selling price
Pharmaceuticals	1%
Electronic equipment	3%
Factory machinery	4%
Chemicals and plastics	6%
Manufactured food	8%
Iron ore	20%
Cabbage	38%
Bituminous coal	42%
Sand and gravel	55%

WHICH TRANSPORTING ALTERNATIVE IS BEST?

Transporting function must fit the whole strategy

The transporting function should fit into the whole marketing strategy. But picking the best transporting alternative depends on the product, other physical distribution decisions, and what service level the company wants to offer. The

Exhibit 11-6 Benefits and Limitations of Different Transport Modes

			Transporting Features			
Mode	Cost	Delivery Speed	Number of Locations Served	Ability to Handle a Variety of Goods	Frequency of Scheduled Shipments	Dependability in Meeting Schedules
Truck	High	Fast	Very extensive	High	High	High
Rail	Medium	Average	Extensive	High	Low	Medium
Water	Very low	Very slow	Limited	Very high	Very low	Medium
Air	Very high	Very fast	Extensive	Limited	High	High
Pipeline	Low	Slow	Very limited	Very limited	Medium	High

best alternative should provide the level of service (for example, speed and dependability) required at as low a cost as possible. Exhibit 11-6 shows that different modes of transportation have different strengths and weaknesses.

Railroads—large loads moved at low cost

Railroads are still the workhorse of the transportation system. They carry more freight over more miles than any other mode. They carry heavy and bulky goods—such as coal, steel, and chemicals—over long distances at relatively low cost. Because railroad freight usually moves more slowly than truck shipments, it is not as well suited for perishable items or those in urgent demand. Railroads are most efficient at handling full carloads of goods. Less-than-carload (LCL) shipments take a lot of handling, which means they usually move more slowly and at a higher price per pound than carload shipments.[29]

INTERNET EXERCISE Canadian companies are served by two major railways—Canadian National and Canadian Pacific. Compare the two Web sites—www.cn.ca and www8.cpr.ca. Check the service maps on each site and tracking capabilities—such as *QuickTrace*. Which railroad has the most to offer companies wanting to transport goods by rail in your province?

Trucks are more expensive, but flexible and essential

The flexibility and speed of trucks make them better at moving small quantities of goods for shorter distances. They go where the rails can't. They are also reliable in meeting delivery schedules, which is an essential requirement for logistics systems that provide rapid replenishment of inventory after a sale. In combination these factors explain why at least 75 percent of consumer products travel at least part of the way from producer to consumer by truck. Trucks compete for high-value items. This is reflected in their competitve rates. Critics complain that trucks congest traffic and damage highways. But trucks are essential to our present macro-marketing system.[30] Trimac Transportation, headquartered in Calgary, Alberta, has 95 branches across North America. With over 2,200 tractors and 5,200 bulk trailers, Trimac moves commodities to industrial firms and consumers via highways.

Ship it overseas, but slowly

Water transportation is the slowest shipping mode, but it is usually the lowest-cost way of shipping heavy freight. Water transportation is very important for international shipments and often the only practical approach. This explains why port cities like Vancouver, New York City, Rotterdam, Osaka, and Singapore are important centres for international trade.

Mercedes recently introduced a new, smaller truck that is designed to be more flexible in making deliveries in congested cities like Istanbul, where this ad appeared.

Mercedes-Benz'in küçük kamyonu MB 800

Büyümüş de küçülmüş!

Inland waterways are important too

Inland waterways (such as the St. Lawrence Seaway in Eastern Canada and the Rhine and Danube in Europe) are also important, especially for bulky, nonperishable products such as iron ore, grain, and gravel. However, when winter ice closes freshwater harbours, alternate transportation must be used.

Pipelines move oil and gas

Pipelines are used primarily to move oil and natural gas. So pipelines are important both in the oil-producing and oil-consuming countries. Only a few major cities in Canada, the United States, Mexico, and Latin America are more than 300 kilometres from a major pipeline system. However, the majority of the pipelines in Canada are located in the West, connecting the oil fields and refineries.

Airfreight is expensive, but fast and growing

The most expensive cargo transporting mode is airplane—but it is fast! Airfreight rates are on average three times higher than trucking rates—but the greater speed may offset the added cost.

DHL offers a full range of logistics services, sometimes coordinating shipments across several modes of transportation, to better meet the needs of its clients.

High-value, low-weight goods—like high-fashion clothing and parts for the electronics industry—are often shipped by air. Perishable products that previously could not be shipped are now being flown across continents and oceans. Flowers and bulbs from Holland, for example, now are jet-flown to points all over the world. And airfreight has become very important for small emergency deliveries, like repair parts, special orders, and business documents that must be somewhere the next day.

But airplanes may cut the total cost of distribution

Using planes may reduce the cost of packing, unpacking, and preparing goods for sale and may help a firm reduce inventory costs by eliminating outlying warehouses. Valuable benefits of airfreight's speed are less spoilage, theft, and damage. Although the *transporting* cost of air shipments may be higher, the *total* cost of distribution may be lower. As more firms realize this, airfreight firms—like DHL Worldwide Express and FedEx—have enjoyed rapid growth.

These firms play an especially important role in the growth of international business. While the bulk of international cargo moves on ships, the speed of airfreight opens up global markets for many businesses that previously had only domestic opportunities. For example, DHL Worldwide Express offers 24-hour delivery service from Tokyo to Los Angeles, New York to Rome, and London to Chicago. For a firm whose products are valuable relative to their weight and size, the cost of air deliveries may seem trivial when compared to the sales potential of competing in new markets.[31]

Put it in a container—and move between modes easily

Products often move by several different modes and carriers during their journey. This is especially common for international shipments. Japanese firms, like Sony, ship stereos to Canada, the United States, and Europe by boat. When they arrive at the dock, they are loaded on trains and sent across the country. Then the units are delivered to a wholesaler by truck or rail.

Loading and unloading goods several times used to be a real problem. Parts of a shipment would become separated, damaged, or even stolen. And handling the goods, perhaps many times, raised costs and slowed delivery. Many of these problems are reduced with **containerization**—grouping individual items into an economical shipping quantity and sealing them in protective containers for transit to the final destination. This protects the products and simplifies handling during shipping. Some containers are as large as truck bodies.

Piggyback—a ride on two or more modes

Piggyback service means loading truck trailers—or flatbed trailers carrying containers—on railcars to provide both speed and flexibility. Railroads now pick up truck trailers at the producer's location, load them onto specially designed rail flatcars, and haul them as close to the customer as rail lines run. The trailers are then hooked up to a truck tractor and delivered to the buyer's door. Similar services are offered on oceangoing ships—allowing door-to-door service between cities around the world.

A change in the way that a product is packaged can help reduce shipping, storing, and product handling costs while at the same time improving benefits and value to the final consumer.

Transportation choices affect environmental costs too

Marketing managers must be sensitive to the environmental effects of transportation decisions. Some say trucks cause air pollution in already crowded cities. People who live near airports suffer from noise pollution. A damaged pipeline can spew thousands of gallons of oil before it can be repaired. The Exxon *Valdez* oil spill in Alaska is a dramatic example of the kind of environmental disaster that can happen when a transportation accident occurs.

Many firms are taking steps to reduce these problems. FedEx and UPS are revamping their fleets to reduce emissions. Some trucking and railroad firms have elaborate safety procedures for dealing with toxic cargo. Today, the public *expects* companies to manufacture, transport, sell, and dispose of products in an environmentally sound manner. Companies are even more sensitive to these issues in an era of terrorism. However, all these efforts increase the cost of distribution.[32]

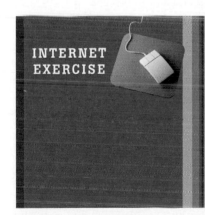

INTERNET EXERCISE

Companies and individuals shipping products across the Canada–U.S. border are interested in potential border delays and wait times. Go to www.purolator.ca. A tracking reference allows you to check your shipment status and whereabouts. Or, you can make a series of clicks (*About Cross Border, Ship To Canada, Border Info, Status of Border Points*) to check delays on commercial traffic flow. This site interfaces with the Canada Border Services Agency. Check out the St. Stephen, NB–Calais, Maine crossing, or the Detroit–Windsor tunnel, or the Surrey, BC–Blaine, Washington crossing. Very up-to-date information keeps you informed on shipments.

THE STORING FUNCTION AND MARKETING STRATEGY

Store it and smooth out sales, increase profits and consumer satisfaction

Storing is the marketing function of holding goods. It provides time utility. **Inventory** is the amount of goods being stored. Maintaining the right inventory level is difficult when it's hard to forecast likely demand. Even so, a firm that is stocked out when customers are ready to buy may not only lose the sale but also damage the relationship and the possibility of future sales.

Storing is necessary when production of goods doesn't match consumption. This is common with mass production. Dofasco Steel, for example, might produce thousands of steel bars of one size before changing the machines to produce another size. It's often cheaper to produce large quantities of one size, and store the unsold quantity, than to have shorter production runs. Thus, storing goods allows the producer to achieve economies of scale in production.

Some buyers purchase in large quantities to get quantity discounts from the producer or transporter. Then the extra goods must be stored until there is demand. And goods are sometimes stored as a hedge against future price rises, strikes, shipping interruptions, and other disruptions.

Storing varies the channel system

Storing allows producers and middlemen to keep stocks at convenient locations, ready to meet customers' needs. In fact, storing is one of the major activities of some middlemen.

Most channel members provide the storing function for some length of time. Even final consumers store some things for their future needs. Which channel members store the product, and for how long, affects the behaviour of all channel members. For example, the producer of Snapper lawn mowers tries to get wholesalers to inventory a wide selection of its machines. That way, retailers can carry smaller inventories since they can be sure of dependable local supplies from wholesalers. And the retailers might decide to sell Snapper—rather than Toro or some other brand that they would have to store at their own expense.

If final customers "store" the product, more of it may be used or consumed. Coke wants customers to buy six-packs and 2-litre bottles. Then consumers have an "inventory" in the refrigerator when thirst hits. Of course, consumers aren't always willing to hold the inventory. In China, for example, Coke had little success until it gave up pushing 2-litre bottles and switched to single-serving 75-ml bottles. Only 1 out of 10 Chinese families has a refrigerator—so they didn't have a good way to store a bottle once it was open.

Goods are stored at a cost

Storing can increase the value of goods, but *storing always involves costs* too. Different kinds of cost are involved. See Exhibit 11-7. Car dealers, for example, must store cars on their lots—waiting for the right customer. The interest expense of money tied up in the inventory is a major cost. In addition, if a new car on the lot

GE provides logistics-related services that help firms reduce costs and improve customer service.

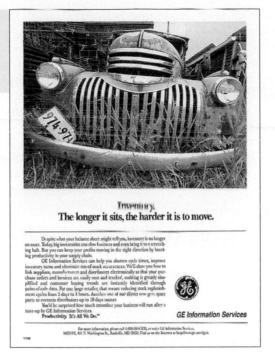

Inventory.
The longer it sits, the harder it is to move.

GE Information Services

is dented or scratched, there is a repair cost. If a car isn't sold before the new models come out, its value drops. There is also a risk of fire or theft—so the retailer must carry insurance. And, of course, dealers incur the cost of leasing or owning the display lot where they store the cars.

In today's competitive markets, most firms watch their inventories closely. Taken in total, the annual direct and indirect costs of inventory are typically 20 to 40 percent of the average value of the inventory.

Rapid response cuts inventory costs

Many firms are finding that they can cut inventory costs—and still provide the desired customer service—if they can reduce the time it takes to replace items that are sold. This is one important reason that JIT and Efficient Consumer Response (ECR) approaches have been widely adopted. ECR is a collaborative system between supermarket chains and producers that supply them that was established in the 1990s. The basic idea involves establishing paperless, computerized links between

Exhibit 11-7 Many Expenses Contribute to Total Inventory Cost the two, which leads to continuous replenishment of stock based on daily sales. The firms involved use EDI, the Internet, and similar computerized approaches to share information and speed up the order cycle and delivery process.

Information from JIT and ECR systems can also help firms see the benefit of dropping some of the items that they stock and sell. P&G is a vivid example. Between 1991 and 1996 it introduced many new products but cut its total number of SKUs (individual stock-keeping units) by 34 percent, mainly by cutting the number of sizes and colours for some of its brands. After the cuts, sales of the remaining products went up and costs came down. With fewer products, P&G put more marketing effort behind those it kept, and its retailers were more willing to push products that turn over quickly. Reducing the number of SKUs does reduce consumer choice, but there is a point where the value of additional choice doesn't justify the extra cost.[33]

SPECIALIZED STORING FACILITIES MAY BE REQUIRED

New cars can be stored outside on the dealer's lot. Fuel oil can be stored in a specially designed tank. Coal and other raw materials can be stored in open pits. But most products must be stored inside protective buildings. Often, firms can choose among different types of specialized storing facilities. The right choice may reduce costs and serve customers better.

Private warehouses are common

Private warehouses are storing facilities owned or leased by companies for their own use. Most manufacturers, wholesalers, and retailers have some storing facilities either in their main buildings or in a separate location. Firms use private warehouses when a large volume of goods must be stored regularly. Yet private warehouses can be expensive. If the need changes, the extra space may be hard, or impossible, to rent to others.

Public warehouses fill special needs

Public warehouses are independent storing facilities. They can provide all the services that a company's own warehouse can provide. A company might choose a public warehouse if it doesn't have a regular need for space. For example, Tonka Toys uses public warehouses because its business is seasonal. Tonka pays for the space only when it is used. Public warehouses are also useful for manufacturers that must maintain stocks in many locations, including foreign countries.

In most countries, public warehouses are located in all major metropolitan areas and many smaller cities. See Exhibit 11-8 for a comparison of private and public warehouses.[34]

Exhibit 11-8 A Comparison of Private Warehouses and Public Warehouses

Characteristics	Type of Warehouse	
	Private	Public
Fixed investment	Very high	No fixed investment
Unit cost	High if volume is low Very low if volume is very high	Low: charges are made only for space needed
Control	High	Low managerial control
Adequacy for product line	Highly adequate	May not be convenient
Flexibility	Low: fixed costs have already been committed	High: easy to end arrangement

Many firms are using innovative technologies to more quickly and accurately track the flow of products through distribution channels. For example, this scanner, worn on a worker's hand like a ring, uses Bluetooth wireless technology so that information in a bar code can be instantly transmitted to a firm's information system.

Warehousing facilities cut handling costs too

The cost of physical handling is a major storing cost. Bar codes and UPC (uniform product code) numbers make it easy for computers to monitor inventory, order needed stock, and track storing and shipping costs. Increasingly, this information flows over wireless networks and takes advantage of radio frequency identification (RFID) tags that precisely track where items are. Some warehouses have computer-controlled order-picking systems or conveyor belts that speed the process of locating and assembling the assortment required to fill an order.[35]

THE DISTRIBUTION CENTRE—A DIFFERENT KIND OF WAREHOUSE

Is storing really needed?

Discrepancies of assortment or quantity between one channel level and another are often adjusted at the place where goods are stored. It reduces handling costs to regroup and store at the same place—*if both functions are required*. But sometimes regrouping is required when storing isn't.

Don't store it, distribute it

A **distribution centre** is a special kind of warehouse designed to speed the flow of goods and avoid unnecessary storing costs. Anchor Hocking moves over a million pounds of its housewares products through its distribution centre each day. Faster inventory turnover and easier bulk-breaking reduce the cost of carrying inventory.

Today, the distribution centre concept is widely used by firms at all channel levels. Many products buzz through a distribution centre without ever tarrying on a shelf; workers and equipment immediately sort the products as they come in and then move them to an outgoing loading dock and the vehicle that will take them to their next stop.

CONCLUSION

In this chapter, we discussed the role of Place and noted that Place decisions are especially important because they may be difficult and expensive to change.

Marketing specialists, and channel systems, develop to adjust discrepancies of quantity and assortment. Their regrouping activities are basic in any economic system. And adjusting discrepancies provides opportunities for creative marketers.

Channel planning requires firms to decide on the degree of market exposure they want. The ideal level of exposure may be intensive, selective, or exclusive.

They also need to consider the legality of limiting market exposure to avoid having to undo an expensively developed channel system or face steep fines.

The importance of planning channel systems was discussed—along with the role of a channel captain. We stressed that channel systems compete with each other and that vertical marketing systems seem to be winning.

Marketing managers often want to improve service and may select a higher-cost alternative to improve their marketing mix. The total cost approach might reveal that it is possible *both* to reduce costs and to improve service—perhaps by identifying creative new distribution alternatives.

We discussed various modes of transporting and their advantages and disadvantages. We also discussed ways to reduce inventory costs. We explained why distribution centres are an important way to cut storing and handling costs, and we explained how computerized information links—within firms and among firms in the channel—are increasingly important in blending all of the activities into a smooth-running system.

KEY TERMS

place, 292

direct marketing, 296

discrepancy of quantity, 298

discrepancy of assortment, 298

regrouping activities, 299

accumulating, 299

bulk-breaking, 299

sorting, 299

assorting, 300

traditional channel systems, 300

channel captain, 302

vertical marketing systems, 303

corporate channel systems, 303

vertical integration, 303

administered channel systems, 304

contractual channel systems, 304

ideal market exposure, 306

intensive distribution, 306

selective distribution, 306

exclusive distribution, 306

multichannel distribution, 309

dual distribution, 309

reverse channels, 309

logistics, 310

physical distribution (PD), 310

supply chain management, 311

chain of supply, 312

electronic data interchange, 312

transporting, 312

containerization, 316

piggyback service, 316

storing, 317

inventory, 317

private warehouses, 320

public warehouses, 320

distribution centre, 321

QUESTIONS AND PROBLEMS

1. Review Exhibit 11-4. Indicate which factors are most likely to be improved by EDI links between a supplier and its customers.

2. Give two examples of service firms that work with other channel specialists to sell their products to final consumers. What marketing functions is the specialist providing in each case?

3. Discuss some reasons why a firm that produces installations might use direct distribution in its domestic market but use middlemen to reach overseas customers.

4. Explain discrepancies of quantity and assortment using the clothing business as an example. How does the application of these concepts change when selling steel to the automobile industry? What impact does this have on the number and kinds of marketing specialists required?

5. Explain the four regrouping activities with an example from the building supply industry (nails, paint, flooring, plumbing fixtures, etc.). Do you think that many specialists develop in this industry, or do producers handle the job themselves? What kinds of marketing channels would you expect to find in this industry, and what functions would various channel members provide?

6. Insurance agents are middlemen who help other members of the channel by providing information

and handling the selling function. Does it make sense for an insurance agent to specialize and work exclusively with one insurance provider? Why or why not?

7. Discuss the Place objectives and distribution arrangements that are appropriate for the following products (indicate any special assumptions you have to make to obtain an answer):
   a. A postal scale for products weighing up to 2 kilograms.
   b. Children's toys: (1) radio-controlled model airplanes costing $80 or more, (2) small rubber balls.
   c. Heavy-duty, rechargeable, battery-powered nut tighteners for factory production lines.
   d. Fibreglass fabric used in making roofing shingles.

8. Give an example of a producer that uses two or more different channels of distribution. Briefly discuss what problems this might cause.

9. Explain how a channel captain can help traditional independent firms compete with a corporate (integrated) channel system.

10. Find an example of vertical integration within your city. Are there any particular advantages to this vertical integration? If so, what are they? If there are no such advantages, how do you explain the integration?

11. What would happen if retailer-organized channels (either formally integrated or administered) dominated consumer product marketing?

12. Discuss the relative advantages and disadvantages of rail, truck, and air transporting methods.

13. Why would middlemen want to be exclusive distributors for a product? Why would producers want exclusive distribution? Would middlemen be equally anxious to get exclusive distribution for any type of product? Why or why not? Explain with reference to the following products: candy bars, batteries, golf clubs, golf balls, steak knives, televisions, and industrial woodworking machinery.

14. Explain the present legal status of exclusive distribution. Describe a situation where exclusive distribution is almost sure to be legal. Describe the nature and size of competitors and the industry, as well as the nature of the exclusive arrangement. Would this exclusive arrangement be of any value to the producer or middleman?

COMPUTER-AIDED PROBLEM

11. Intensive versus Selective Distribution

RESOURCE REMINDER

Hydropump Inc., produces and sells high-quality pumps to business customers. Its marketing research shows a growing market for a similar type of pump aimed at final consumers—for use with Jacuzzi-style tubs In home remodelling jobs. Hydropump will have to develop new channels of distribution to reach this target market because most consumers rely on a retailer for advice about the combination of tub, pump, heater, and related plumbing fixtures they need. Hydropump's marketing manager, Robert Black, is trying to decide between intensive and selective distribution. With intensive distribution, he would try to sell through all the plumbing supply, bathroom fixture, and hot-tub retailers who will carry the pump. He estimates that about 5,600 suitable retailers would be willing to carry a new pump. With selective distribution, he would focus on about 280 of the best hot-tub dealers (2 or 3 in the 100 largest metropolitan areas).

Intensive distribution would require Hydropump to do more mass selling—primarily advertising in home renovation magazines—to help stimulate consumer familiarity with the brand and convince retailers that Hydropump equipment will sell. The price to the retailer might have to be lower too (to permit a bigger markup) so they will be motivated to sell Hydropump rather than some other brand offering a smaller markup.

With intensive distribution, each Hydropump sales rep could probably handle about 300 retailers effectively.

With selective distribution, each sales rep could handle only about 70 retailers because more merchandising help would be necessary. Managing the smaller sales force and fewer retailers, with the selective approach, would require less manager overhead cost.

Going to all suitable and available retailers would make the pump available through about 20 times as many retailers and have the potential of reaching more customers. However, many customers shop at more than one retailer before making a final choice—so selective distribution would reach almost as many potential customers. Further, if Hydropump is using selective distribution, it would get more in-store sales attention for its pump and a larger share of pump purchases at each retailer.

Black has decided to use a spreadsheet to analyze the benefits and costs of intensive versus selective distribution.

a. Based on the initial spreadsheet, which approach seems to be the most sensible for Hydropump? Why?

b. A consultant points out that even selective distribution needs national promotion. If Black has to increase advertising and spend a total of $100,000 on mass selling to be able to recruit the retailers he wants for selective distribution, would selective or intensive distribution be more profitable?

c. With intensive distribution, how large a share (percent) of the retailers' total unit sales would Hydropump have to capture to sell enough pumps to earn $200,000 profit?

> If you want to read the cases and view the video cases that accompany this chapter, visit the *Basic Marketing* Online Learning Centre at: **www.mcgrawhill.ca/olc/perreault**. Along with these cases and video cases, the OLC also has the software and user guide for this chapter's Computer-Aided Problem, as well as exercises, quizzes, articles, links, and other *interactive* content that will help you with your studies.

Retailing and Wholesaling

Roots is one of Canada's leading lifestyle brands. Started in 1973, Roots now has more than 125 stores in Canada. Roots stores can be found in nine Canadian provinces, from British Columbia to Nova Scotia and PEI. Well known for their Olympic gear, they have expanded successfully into both the American and Asian markets.

In 1973, Roots co-founders Michael Budman and Don Green had one small store in Toronto that sold the now-famous negative-heel shoe. This innovation led Roots to their first Olympic contract. At the request of the Canadian Olympic Committee, Roots outfitted Team Canada with a negative heel quilted boot for the opening ceremonies in Innsbruck, Austria in 1976. Since then, Roots has been involved with several Canadian Olympic teams as well as teams from Jamaica, Great Britain, and the United States.

The Jamaican bobsled team wore jackets designed by Roots during the 1988 Olympic Winter Games in Calgary, Alberta. The story of the Jamaican bobsled team was made into the hit movie *Cool Running*. In the movie, John Candy wore the Roots Jamaican bobsled jacket. This great publicity helped Roots become very well known for their clothing products.

Roots, Roots Kids, Roots Home, and Roots Factory Outlet Stores in Canada carry sportswear, shoes, bags, jackets, luggage, furniture, linens, towels, and licensed products such as watches and fragrances. The ever-expanding product line reflects Roots' commitment to their customers. Over 2,000 Canadians now work at Roots.

In 1998, Roots became the official outfitter of the Canadian Olympic team. The red Canadian poor-boy style hat became the fashion hit of the Nagano Olympics. Athletes from every country coveted the stylish hat. Roots sold over 500,000 poor-boy hats, which sold out as quickly as they arrived at the retail stores.

Following the popularity of the Canadian Olympic team fashions, the United States Olympic Committee pursued Roots to outfit their team.

In 2002, Roots outfitted both the Canadian and American Olympic teams in Salt Lake City, Utah. The Team U.S.A. beret was the hit product in Salt Lake City. More than one million berets were sold. The Roots boutique in Park City, Utah did $10 million worth of business in 2002. The popularity of Roots products in America was a factor in their success on the American retail scene. Although many Canadian retailers have not fared well in America, Roots has successfully opened five stores to date in the United States.

Continuing as the official outfitter of the American Olympic team in 2006 in Italy, Roots lost the Canadian contract to the Hudson's Bay Company (HBC). However, Roots was able to counteract this deal by signing hockey star Wayne Gretzky to promote a new line of sports apparel. In keeping with the Roots commitment to their core values, a portion of the proceeds of the new line will be donated to the Wayne Gretzky Foundation.

Notably, Mr. Gretzky recently ended a deal with HBC that involved a namesake line of clothing. The new line of clothing, which includes sweatshirts, toques, hats, and jackets, debuted at the 2006 Olympics and gained significant exposure for Roots. Although no longer the official outfitter of the Canadian Olympic team, Roots has found an innovative way to stay connected to the Canadian public as a provider of cool fashion products. Celebrities such as Katie Couric and Kelly Clarkson wear the brand. Members of *The Sopranos* cast and The Black Eyed Peas have also been spotted in Roots fashions.

Roots has enjoyed considerable success across Canada. Importantly, they are also seeing good results from their forays into the global marketplace. Having lost the Olympic contract to HBC, Roots continues to look for ways to retain global exposure via the Olympics. They were a Community Contributor with the 2010 Vancouver Bid Corporation and have created merchandise for the successful Olympic bid.[1]

WHOLESALERS AND RETAILERS PLAN THEIR OWN STRATEGIES

Earlier, we discussed the vital role that wholesalers and retailers perform in channel systems. Now, we'll look at the decisions that retailers and wholesalers make in developing their own strategies. We'll also highlight how their strategies have evolved.

Understand how retailing and wholesaling are evolving

Understanding the how and why of these changes will help you know what to expect in the future. It will also make it clear that it is the whole strategy, not just one aspect of it, that ultimately is a success or failure. This may seem obvious, but it's a point that many people have ignored—at great cost.

Consider the dramatic changes prompted by the Internet. A few years ago many people were proclaiming that it would quickly change everything we thought about successful retailing. Yet many creative ideas for online retailing bombed precisely because managers of dot-coms failed to understand why retailing has evolved as it has. For many consumers and many types of purchases, it won't matter that an online retailer posts low prices for an incredible assortment if there's no way to get customer service, products are not actually available, or it's a hassle to return a green shirt that looked blue on the Web site. *You* want to avoid the trap of this sort of incomplete thinking!

THE NATURE OF RETAILING

Retailing covers all of the activities involved in the sale of products to final consumers. Retailers range from large chains of specialized stores, like Toys "R" Us, to individual merchants like the woman who sells baskets from an open stall in the central market in Ibadan, Nigeria. Some retailers operate from stores and others operate without a store—by selling online, on TV, with a printed catalogue, from vending machines, or even in consumers' homes. Most retailers sell physical goods produced by someone else. But in the case of service retailing—like dry cleaning, fast food, tourist attractions, online bank accounts, or one-hour photo processing—the retailer is also the producer. Because they serve individual consumers, even the largest retailers face the challenge of handling small transactions. And the total number of transactions with consumers is much greater than at other channel levels.

Retailing is crucial to consumers in every macro-marketing system. For example, consumers spend $347 billion (that's $347,000,000,000!) a year buying goods and services from retailers in Canada. The nature of retailing and its rate of change are generally related to the stage and speed of a country's economic development.

PLANNING A RETAILER'S STRATEGY

Retailers interact directly with final consumers—so strategy planning is critical to their survival. If a retailer loses a customer to a competitor, the retailer is the one who suffers. Producers and wholesalers still make *their* sale regardless of which retailer sells the product.

Consumers have reasons for buying from particular retailers

Different consumers prefer different kinds of retailers. But many retailers either don't know or don't care why. All too often, beginning retailers just rent a store and assume customers will show up. As a result, about three-fourths of new retailing ventures fail during the first year. Even an established retailer will quickly lose if its customers find a better way to meet their needs. To avoid this fate, a retailer should carefully identify possible target markets and try to understand why these people buy where they do. That helps the retailer fine-tune its marketing mix to the needs of specific target markets.[2]

Retailer's whole offering is its Product

Most retailers in developed nations sell more than one kind of product. So the brands and product assortment they carry can be critical to success. Yet it's best to take a broader view in thinking about the Product strategy decisions for a retailer's marketing mix. The retailer's *whole* offering—assortment of goods and services, advice from salesclerks, convenience, and the like—is its "Product."

Different consumers have different needs—and needs vary from one purchase situation to another. Which retailer's Product offers the best customer value depends on the needs that a customer wants to satisfy. Whatever the effect of other consumer needs, economic needs are usually very important in shaping the choice of a retailer. Social and individual needs may also come into play. Our discussion of consumer behaviour in Chapter 6 applies here.

Features of offering relate to needs

Features of a retailer's offering that relate to economic needs include:
- *Convenience* (available hours, finding needed products, fast checkout, location, parking).
- *Product selection* (width and depth of assortment, quality).

It's best to think of a retailer's Product as its whole offering—including its assortment of goods and services, advice from salespeople, the convenience of shopping, and hours it is available.

- *Special services* (special orders, home delivery, gift wrap, entertainment).
- *Fairness in dealings* (honesty, correcting problems, return privileges, purchase risks).
- *Helpful information* (courteous sales help, displays, demonstrations, product information).
- *Prices* (value, credit, special discounts, taxes or extra charges).

Some features that relate to social and emotional factors include:

- *Social image* (status, prestige, "fitting in" with other shoppers).
- *Shopping atmosphere* (comfort, safety, excitement, relaxation, sounds, smells).

In later chapters we'll go into much more detail on the price and promotion decisions that all firms, including retailers and wholesalers, make.

Strategy requires carefully set policies

In developing a strategy a retailer should consciously make decisions that set policies on *all* of the factors above. Each of them can impact a customer's view of the costs and benefits of choosing that retailer. And in combination they differentiate one retailer's offering and strategy from another. If the combination doesn't provide superior value to some target market, the retailer will fail.

Consumer needs relate to segmentation and positioning

Segmentation and positioning decisions are important to retailers. And ignoring either economic or social and emotional values in those decisions can lead to serious errors in a retailer's strategy planning.

Consider, for example, how the shopping atmosphere may have an emotional effect on a consumer's view of a retailer. How merchandise is displayed, what decorations, colours, and finishes are used, and even the temperature, sounds, and smell of a store all contribute to its "atmospherics" and store image. The right combination may attract more target customers and encourage them to spend more. Birks, for example, offers luxury surroundings and inventive displays to attract upscale consumers. But Holt Renfrew may also appeal to consumers who get an ego boost from Holt Renfrew's prestige image and very attentive staff. Of course, interesting surroundings are usually costly, and the prices that consumers pay must cover that expense. An online retailer avoids those costs but offers a completely different shopping experience and deals with a different set of needs. So a retailer's atmosphere and image may be a plus or a minus, depending on the target market. And there's no single right answer about which target market is best.

328

In spite of consumer interest in Western products and new retailing formats, most retailing in Asia is still handled by small limited-line stores, like this Chinese electronics store.

Different types of retailers emphasize different strategies

Retailers have an almost unlimited number of ways in which to alter their offerings—their marketing mixes—to appeal to a target market. Because of all the variations, it's oversimplified to classify retailers and their strategies on the basis of a single characteristic—such as merchandise, services, sales volume, or even whether they operate in cyberspace. But a good place to start is by considering basic types of retailers and some differences in their strategies.

Let's look first at conventional retailers. Then we'll see how other retailers successfully modify conventional offerings to better meet the needs of *some* consumers. Think about *why* the changes take place. That will help you identify opportunities and plan better marketing strategies.

CONVENTIONAL RETAILERS—TRY TO AVOID PRICE COMPETITION

Single-line, limited-line retailers specialize by product

Most conventional retailers are **single-line** or **limited-line stores**—stores that specialize in certain lines of related products rather than a wide assortment. Many specialize not only in a single line, such as clothing, but also in a *limited line* within the broader line. Within the clothing line, a retailer might carry *only* shoes, formal wear, or even neckties but offer depth in that limited line. Sunglass Hut offers only sunglasses. Bata sells only shoes.

Single-line, limited-line stores are being squeezed

The main advantage of limited-line retailers is that they can satisfy some target markets better. Perhaps some are just more conveniently located. But most adjust to suit specific customers. They build a relationship with their customers and earn a position as *the* place to shop for a certain type of product. But these retailers face the costly problem of having to stock some slow-moving items in order to satisfy their target markets. Many of these stores are small—with high expenses relative to sales. So they try to keep their prices up by avoiding competition on identical products.

Conventional retailers like this have been around for a long time and are still found in every community. They are a durable lot and clearly satisfy some people's needs. In fact, in most countries conventional retailers still handle the vast

Exhibit 12-1 Types of Retailers and the Nature of Their Offerings

majority of all retailing sales. However, this situation is changing fast. Conventional retailers are being squeezed by retailers who modify their mixes in the various ways suggested in Exhibit 12-1. Let's look closer at some of these other types of retailers.

EXPAND ASSORTMENT AND SERVICE—TO COMPETE AT A HIGH PRICE

Specialty shops usually sell shopping products

A **specialty shop**—a type of conventional limited-line store—is usually small and has a distinct "personality." Specialty shops sell special types of shopping products, such as high-quality sporting goods, exclusive clothing, cameras, or even antiques. They aim at a carefully defined target market by offering a unique product assortment, knowledgeable salesclerks, and better service.

Catering to certain types of customers whom the management and salespeople know well simplifies buying, speeds turnover, and cuts costs due to obsolescence and style changes. Specialty shops probably will continue to be a part of the retailing scene as long as customers have varied tastes and the money to satisfy them.[3] Mountain Equipment Co-op caters to consumers seeking products to support outdoor activities such as hiking, backpacking, and snowshoeing. Roots Canada is also a specialty store.

Department stores combine many limited–line stores and specialty shops

Department stores are larger stores that are organized into many separate departments and offer many product lines. Each department is like a separate limited-line store and handles a wide variety of shopping products, such as menswear or housewares. They are usually strong in customer services, including credit, merchandise return, delivery, and sales help.

Department stores (The Bay and Sears) are still a major force in big cities. But in Canada, the number of department stores, the average sales per store, and their share of retail business has declined continuously since the 1970s. Well-run limited-line stores compete with good service and often carry the same brands. In Canada and many other countries, mass-merchandising retailers have posed an even bigger threat.[4]

EVOLUTION OF MASS-MERCHANDISING RETAILERS

Mass-merchandising is different from conventional retailing

So far we've been describing retailers primarily in terms of their product *assortment*. This reflects traditional thinking about retailing. We could talk about supermarkets, discount houses, or online retailers in these terms too. But then we would miss some important differences—just as some conventional retailers did when mass-merchandising retailers first appeared.

Conventional retailers think that demand in their area is fixed—and they have a "buy low and sell high" philosophy. Many modern retailers reject this idea. They accept the **mass-merchandising concept**—which says that retailers should offer low prices to get faster turnover and greater sales volumes—by appealing to larger markets. The mass-merchandising concept applies to many types of retailers, including both those that operate stores and those that sell online. But to understand mass-merchandising better, let's look at its evolution from the development of supermarkets and discounters to modern mass-merchandisers like Wal-Mart in the U.S., Tesco in the U.K., and Amazon.ca on the Internet.

Supermarkets started the move to mass-merchandising

From a world view, most food stores are relatively small limited-line operations. Shopping for food is inconvenient and expensive. Many Italians, for example, still go to one shop for pasta, another for meat, and yet another for milk. This may seem outdated, but many of the world's consumers don't have access to **supermarkets**—large stores specializing in groceries with self-service and wide assortments.

The basic idea for supermarkets developed in the U.S. during the 1930s Depression. Some innovators introduced self-service to cut costs but provided a broad assortment in large bare-bones stores. Profits came from large-volume sales, not from high traditional markups.[5] Newer supermarkets carry 50,000 product items and stores now push close to 100,000 square feet.

To outsell competitors, supermarkets try to differentiate their offerings. Some have better produce, lower prices, a cleaner store, and so forth. But there are many things they all have to offer—like milk and eggs and cereal. In fact, an average family gets about 80 percent of its needs from only about 150 SKUs. The rub is that the particular 150 SKUs vary from family to family. In the end, a consumer makes a single choice in deciding to shop at a particular supermarket. But to come out on top in *that* choice, the supermarket must offer consumers many thousands of choices and at the same time keep costs low.[6]

Modern supermarkets are planned for maximum efficiency. Scanners at checkout make it possible to carefully analyze the sales of each item and allocate more shelf space to faster-moving and higher-profit items. *Survival* depends on efficiency. Net profits in supermarkets usually run a thin 1 percent of sales *or less!*

Some supermarket operators have opened "super warehouse" stores. These 50,000- to 100,000-square-foot stores carry more items than supermarkets, but they usually put less emphasis on perishable items like produce or meat. These efficiently run, warehouse-like facilities sell groceries at about 25 percent off the typical supermarket price.[7] Major Canadian supermarkets include Loblaws and Sobeys as well as regional chains such as Sav-On Foods.

Discount retailers upset some conventional retailers

After World War II, some retailers started to focus on discount prices. These **discount retailers** offered "hard goods" (cameras, TVs, appliances) at substantial price cuts to customers who would go to the discounter's low-rent store, pay cash, and take care of any service or repair problems themselves. These retailers sold at 20 to 30 percent off the list price being charged by conventional retailers.

In the early 1950s, with war shortages finally over, manufacturer brands became more available. The discount retailers were able to get any brands they wanted and to offer wider assortments. At this stage, many discounters turned respectable—

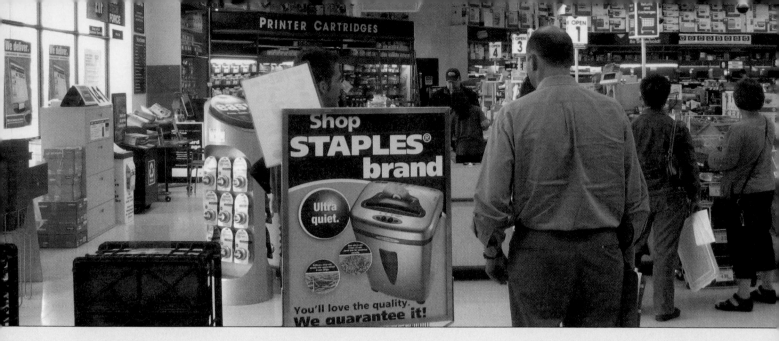

Although supermarkets were the first mass-merchandisers, the mass-merchandising concept has now been introduced by many retailers. Single-line mass-merchandisers like Staples Business Depot offer selections and prices that make it difficult for traditional retailers to compete.

moving to better locations and offering more services and guarantees. It was from these origins that today's mass-merchandisers developed. The Great Canadian Dollar Store is an example of a currently successful discounter.

Mass-merchandisers are more than discounters

Mass-merchandisers are large, self-service stores with many departments that emphasize "soft goods" (housewares, clothing, and fabrics) and staples (like health and beauty aids) but still follow the discount retailer's emphasis on lower margins to get faster turnover. Mass-merchandisers, like Wal-Mart and Zellers, have checkout counters in the front of the store and little sales help on the floor. Today, the average mass-merchandiser has nearly 60,000 square feet of floor space, but many new stores are 100,000 square feet or more. Mass-merchandisers grew rapidly—and they've become the primary place to shop for many frequently purchased consumer products.

By itself, Wal-Mart handles a large percentage of the total North American sales for whole categories of products. Even if you don't shop at Wal-Mart, Sam Walton (who started the company) has had a big impact on consumers' lives. He pioneered the use of high-tech systems to create electronic links with suppliers and take inefficiencies out of retailing logistics. That brought down costs *and* prices and attracted more customers, which gave Wal-Mart even more clout in pressuring manufacturers to lower prices. Other retailers are still scrambling to catch up. It was competition from Wal-Mart on staples such as health and beauty aids and household cleaning products that prompted firms in the supermarket supply chain to start the Efficient Consumer Response movement we discussed in the last chapter.

Although these mass-merchandisers are the driving force in much of retailing in the Canada today, in many areas they're no longer just taking customers from conventional retailers but instead are locked in head-to-head competition with each other.

Supercentres meet all routine needs

Some supermarkets and mass-merchandisers have moved toward becoming **supercentres (hypermarkets)**—very large stores that try to carry not only food and drug items but all goods and services that the consumer purchases *routinely*. Hypermarkets are more common in Europe, where French retailer Carrefour has had success with the format. Superstores look a lot like a combination of the supermarkets, drugstores,

Many retailers are looking for ways to make shopping faster and more convenient. With self-service scanners, shoppers save time and grocers save money. With ExxonMobil's Speedpass system, a miniature electronic device identifies the driver and turns on the pump; the customer doesn't need to swipe a credit card.

and mass-merchandisers from which they have evolved, but the concept is different. A supercentre is trying to meet *all* the customer's routine needs at a low price. Supercentre operators include Loblaws Real Canadian Superstore and Wal-Mart. In fact, Wal-Mart's supercentres have turned it into the largest food retailer in North America.

Supercentres average more than 150,000 square feet and carry about 60,000 items. Their assortment in one place is convenient, but many time-pressured consumers think that the crowds, lines, and "wandering around" time in the store are not.[8]

New mass-merchandising formats keep coming

The warehouse club is another retailing format that quickly gained popularity. Sam's Club and Costco are two of the largest. Consumers usually pay an annual membership fee to shop in these large, no-frills facilities. Among the 3,500 items per store, they carry food, appliances, yard tools, tires, and other items that many consumers see as homogeneous shopping items and want at the lowest possible price. The growth of these clubs has also been fuelled by sales to small-business customers. That's why some people refer to these outlets as wholesale clubs. However, when half or more of a firm's sales are to final consumers, it is classified as a retailer, not a wholesaler.[9]

Single-line mass-merchandisers are coming on strong

Since 1980, some retailers focusing on single product lines have adopted the mass-merchandisers' approach with great success. Toys "R" Us pioneered this trend. Similarly, Ikea (furniture), RONA (home improvements), Future Shop (electronics), and Staples Business Depot (office supplies) attract large numbers of customers with their vast assortment and low prices in a specific product category. These stores are called **category killers** because it's so hard for less specialized retailers to compete.[10] They are also often referred to as big box stores.

It's reasonable to think about the move to 24-hours-a-day online selling—by the established retailers, new firms that never relied on stores, or both—as a next step in the evolution of mass-merchandising. But we'll have a more complete basis for evaluating the strengths and limitations of selling and shopping on the Web if we first look at some retailers who have targeted consumers who want more convenience, even if the price is higher.

SOME RETAILERS FOCUS ON ADDED CONVENIENCE

Convenience (food) stores must have the right assortment

Convenience (food) stores are a convenience-oriented variation of the conventional limited-line food stores. Instead of expanding their assortment, however, convenience stores limit their stock to pickup or fill-in items like bread, milk, and eat-on-the-go snacks. Many also sell gas. Stores such as 7-Eleven and Mac's aim to fill consumers' needs between trips to a supermarket, and many of them are competing with fast-food outlets. They offer convenience, not assortment, and often charge prices 10 to 20 percent higher than nearby supermarkets. However, as many other retailers have expanded their hours, intense competition is driving down convenience store prices and profits.[11]

Vending machines are convenient

Automatic vending is selling and delivering products through vending machines. Although vending machine sales are a small percentage of retail sales, for some target markets this retailing method can't be ignored.

The major disadvantage to automatic vending is high cost. The machines are expensive to buy, stock, and repair relative to the volume they sell. So vendors must charge higher prices.[12] Vending machines are being used for more high-end products such as perfume, which offsets higher costs with higher margins. Think of the potential for campuses and airports—high-traffic areas with a need for 24/7 retailing.

Shop at home, in a variety of ways

In-home shopping started in the pioneer days with **door-to-door selling**—a salesperson going directly to the consumer's home. Variations on this approach are still important for firms like Avon and Mary Kay. It meets some consumers' need for convenient personal attention. It is also growing in popularity in some international markets, like China, where it provides salespeople with a good income. In Canada however it's getting harder to find someone at home during the day.

On the other hand, time-pressured, dual-career families are a prime target market for **telephone and direct-mail retailing** that allow consumers to shop at home—usually placing orders by mail or a toll-free long-distance telephone call and charging the purchase to a credit card. Typically, catalogues and ads on TV let customers see the offerings, and purchases are delivered by Canada Post. Some consumers really like this convenience, especially for products not available in local stores.

This approach reduces costs by using computer mailing lists to target specific customers and by using warehouse-type buildings and limited sales help. And shoplifting—a big expense for most retailers—isn't a problem. In recent years, many of these firms have faced increased competition, slower sales growth, and lower profits. As we will discuss, however, the Internet is opening up new growth opportunities for many of these firms.[13]

Put the catalogue on cable TV or computer

QVC, Home Shopping Network, and others are succeeding by devoting cable TV channels to home shopping. The explosion in the number of available cable channels and new interactive cable services will make sales from this approach grow even faster. In addition, QVC has opened a major Web site on the Internet. However, selling on the Internet is turning into something much more than just a variation of selling on TV or from a catalogue.[14]

RETAIL LOCATIONS

Location is crucial to success

A good retail location is crucial to the success of a bricks-and-mortar retailer. Although many types of retail locations are available, retailers need to consider their product mix and target market when choosing a location. The location decision is a big one—it's not easy to move your location and would be expensive to do so.

Historically, retailers were located in what we refer to as freestanding locations. If you wanted a retail store, you had to build one. Some retailers that require large stores, such as Costco, still use this type of location. Other convenience-based retailers such as McDonald's also use freestanding locations. However, this type of location is becoming harder and harder to find in most urban centres.

Unplanned centres are collections of retail stores that were not planned to be retail hubs. These centres started with one retail store. Gradually, several more stores located next door (or nearby) and created a draw for consumers. In most cities in Canada, the unplanned centre has become planned. Zoning regulations are often brought into play to contain the retail expansion and control issues such as parking.

Planned centres come in many sizes

Planned centres come in many sizes, from the small strip mall in your subdivision to large community-based centres. Strip malls appeal to convenience retailers such as Mac's and local video stores. Larger planned centres such as community centres draw consumers from a larger trading area and appeal to a greater variety of merchants. These centres normally have a larger anchor store such as Sobeys or Indigo along with a collection of smaller merchants.

Variations of the planned centre are the most common today. These include power centres and lifestyle centres. A power centre is a collection of the large big-box type stores such as Canadian Tire, RONA, Ikea, Toys "R" Us, Linens 'n Things, and Real Canadian Superstore. South Edmonton Common, Canada's largest power centre, has many of these merchants within its over 470,000 square metres of shopping space. The centre is a good draw for consumers wanting the convenience of direct access and a nice variety of stores in one area.

Lifestyle centres are growing rapidly

Lifestyle centres are somewhat new to Canada but are growing rapidly. Although some are small, the trend is definitely towards larger lifestyle centres. Lifestyle centres feature many of the same stores as power centres, but concentrate their merchant mix on meeting the needs of a particular target market more closely. They appeal to consumers that want to spend time shopping and enjoy the experience of purchasing products and service. The Village at Deerfoot Meadows in Calgary, Alberta is Canada's fastest growing lifestyle centre. When completed, this lifestyle centre will cover almost 14 hectacres.

Regional malls are the largest form of a planned centre. While very popular in the last quarter of the 1900s, regional malls fell from popularity in the 1990s and have only recently enjoyed resurgence. The traditional regional mall had two anchors, normally department stores. Now regional malls are bigger and in Canada in particular feature merchants other than department stores as anchors. The Toronto Eaton Centre is Canada's most successful regional mall. The West Edmonton Mall in Alberta, has more than 800 stores and services. This mega-mall is considered the world's largest shopping mall.

The central business district is returning to popularity

Also enjoying a return to popularity is the central business district. Every major urban centre and smaller town has a downtown business district. Downtown has traditionally been the focus of retail activity. However, the growth in regional malls during the 1970s and 1980s caused many downtown business districts to lose business. Recently, renovations and expansions have added to the popularity of the central business district. A more interesting mix of service businesses featuring restaurants and entertainment along with traditional fashion retailers draws more than just area workers to spend time downtown. Examples include Ste. Catherine Street in Montreal, Yonge Street in Toronto, and Robson Street in Vancouver.

RETAILING ON THE INTERNET

Most mass-merchandisers now sell on the Web, so one could view that development as just another aspect of how low-margin sellers try to appeal to a large target market with wide assortments at discount prices. Or one might view the Internet as just another way to add convenient in-home shopping, with an electronic catalogue and ordering on a remote computer. Yet both of these views are incomplete and probably misleading. Rather than just treat it as a new way that some types of retailers are incrementally varying their old strategies, let's look at what is *really* different about it.

It's still in its infancy but growing fast

Internet retailing is still in the growth stages. On the one hand, Internet usage continues to rise and consumer e-commerce sales have grown at a fast rate. In 1997, consumers spent about $2.7 billion worldwide on the Internet. To put that in perspective, it took about 3 percent of Wal-Mart's stores to rack up the same sales. By 2003 that number leaped to over $50 billion, and that does not include spending for travel or financial services, which more than double the amount. But don't confuse the effect that the Internet may have on retailing with the reality of its immediate economic impact. So far, it accounts for less than 2 percent of retailing sales dollars. So in absolute dollars, retailing on the Internet is in its infancy even as retailers such as Roots and The Bay offer consumers the option to buy online. Thus, it's useful to consider what's different about it today and how it will evolve. See Exhibit 12-2.

Moving information versus moving goods

Stripped to its essence, the Internet dramatically lowers the cost of communication and makes it faster. The Internet produces the biggest gains in businesses where better information flows result in more efficiency. That's what happens in much online B2B e-commerce. On the other hand, Place decisions for consumer markets need to deal with the challenge of getting many small purchases to the *consumer's* place. Much of the investment in Internet retailing systems has been directed toward

Exhibit 12-2   Some Illustrative Differences between Online and In-Store Shopping

Characteristics	Online Shopping	In-Store Shopping
Customer characteristics	Younger, better educated, more upscale	Cross section; depends on store
Day-of-week emphasis	Higher percent of purchases during weekdays	Higher percent of purchases on the weekend
Customer service	Weak but improving	Varies, but usually better than online
Products purchased	More emphasis on one-time purchases	More emphasis on routine purchases
Availability of product	Not available for inspection or immediate use	Usually available for inspection and immediate use
Comparative information about products	Much more extensive, but sometimes poorly organized	Often weak (for example, limited to what is on packages)
Entertainment value	A media experience	Often a social experience
Charges	Product prices often lower, but shipping and handling costly	Product prices and taxes higher, but usually no delivery expense
Shopping hours and preparation	Completely flexible if online access is available	Depends on store and available transportation to store

Buyarock.com created a Web site with a tongue-in-cheek 1950s design, animations, and information about buying a diamond ("Buyarock 101") to help appeal to male shoppers searching for an engagement ring. However, some shoppers are hesitant to make any big purchase online.

moving information (like orders), not physical goods. It takes, for example, about $25 million to build a world-class Web site for consumer e-commerce. But it costs about $150 million to build a distribution centre and systems to support a large-scale consumer Web operation. Therefore, much of the attention so far has been on the "front door" of the Internet "store" and not on the back end of retailing operations where more of the big costs accumulate. Canadacart offers retailers a turnkey approach to e-commerce (www.canadacart.ca).

INTERNET EXERCISE

Canadacart software allows companies to create "virtual stores" for Internet retailing. Go to the firm's Web site (www.canadacart.ca) and review the information provided. Do you think it would be easier for consumers if all Internet sellers used a common system, such as this one, rather than coming up with many different arrangements? Briefly explain your thinking.

The investments and innovations will come into balance over time, just as they have with other retailing innovations. But demand is what will shape investments in new supply capabilities. So far, the basic patterns of consumer demand have not changed that much.

Convenience takes on new meanings

Traditional thinking about retail stores looked at shopping convenience from the perspective of product assortments and location. On the Internet, by contrast, a consumer can get to a very wide assortment, perhaps from different sellers, by clicking from one Web site to another. The assortment moves toward being unlimited.

But the Internet makes shopping inconvenient in other ways. You have to plan ahead. You can't touch a product. When you buy something, you've actually just ordered it and you don't have it to use. Someone else has to deliver it, and that involves delays and costs.

Surfing around the Internet is convenient for people who are facile with computers, but many consumers are not. At present, people who actually shop on the Web are better educated, younger, and more well-to-do. It should be no surprise that the majority of retail dollars spent on the Internet so far are for computer-related stuff. That target market visits the Internet store. But many people don't.

There have been lots of retailing innovations, but most people wouldn't put flea markets or estate auctions in that category. Yet if you combine those ideas, attract about 28 million active buyers and sellers, use a state-of-the-art Web site to help them all complete exchanges worth $20 billion a year, then you'll have eBay. And given that eBay takes a cut of the $700 worth of deals that get made *every second,* it is not only an innovation but a very profitable one.

At the eBay.com "department store," sellers offer products ranging from one-of-a-kind antique collector cars or comic books to the latest designer wedding dresses (used only once!) and plasma screen HDTVs. And most of the time there's somebody, somewhere, who wants to buy what's listed. Imagine how managers at eBay must feel; they have little control over their vendors or who their target customers are. However, it is all about the customers. eBay is a self-directed marketplace where customer bids determine what will sell (and it also has "Buy It Now" items for customers who don't want to bid).

Of course, eBay has learned some things from traditional retailers. It doesn't have "greeters," but it has 2,000 customer service reps. It also constantly improves product categories so it is easier for shoppers to find what they want. eBay will even handle the bidding automatically and then link the buyer to PayPal to securely transfer payment to the seller. Of course, some sellers don't want to hassle with eBay. So for them eBay offers links to "trading assistants," independent specialists who handle eBay selling on a fee basis, much like an old-fashioned consignment shop.[15]

Of course, use of the Internet is growing. Cable and telephone companies are in a race to provide more consumers with faster access. Costs will continue to come down.

More and less information at the same time

On the Internet a consumer can't really inspect a product. Many consumers see that as a disadvantage. On the other hand, in a retail store it's often hard to get good information. At a Web site detailed product information is just a mouse-click away.

It's also possible to access a much broader array of information. Ziff-Davis Publishing, for example, has a comprehensive Web site (www.zdnet.com) with product reviews, feature comparisons, and performance tests on many computer-related products. Similar sites exist for everything from automobiles to vitamins. Better information can make many consumers better shoppers, even if they buy in a store rather than online. That's what many Web surfers do now. That reduces the risk of buying the wrong thing and the hassles of returning it if there's a problem.

More powerful computers are also opening up many more possibilities for multimedia information—pictures, product-demo videos, and audio explanations. The Internet is also a good medium for messaging and video conferencing. Many computers now come with an inexpensive videocam. So in the future it will be easier for consumers to get help from a real person while at a Web site. Many failed dotcom retailers figured out too late that cutting costs by dropping human customer service support was a big mistake. They ignored the lessons learned by mass-merchandisers when they tried to do the same thing in their early days. SportChek allows consumers to research products online but no longer has online buying for consumers. The site refers consumers to a bricks-and-mortar store.

Lost in the "aisles" of the Internet

If you know what you want, you can usually find it fast on the Internet. You can look for "Revo sunglasses" and get a list of sellers and see pictures of every style made. However, you may get too much information or the wrong information when you do a search. So there is a need for better "virtual malls"—databases with lots of information that can be viewed lots of ways—to make it easier to get information you want and avoid irrelevant clutter. Retailers like Amazon have improved their Web sites to make progress on this front.

Many established retailers, like Chapters, are combining "clicks and bricks" to meet consumers' needs better than would be possible with only an online Web site or a store.

The costs are still deceptive

The Internet makes it easy to compare products and prices from different sellers. That has put price pressure on Internet sellers who have not figured out how else to differentiate what they offer. For more expensive items, a discount price may offset delivery costs. That often isn't the case with less expensive items. Low-cost ways of handling post-purchase deliveries need to be developed for the Internet to be really practical for everyday purchases. We'll return to this issue at the end of the chapter. For now, though, we should note that a large number of people are working on that problem. For example, Tesco in England sells groceries from a Web site and delivers them within 24 hours. But other firms, like Webvan in the U.S., collapsed under the problems of trying to do that in a way that satisfies consumers' needs.

Another cost occurs if a product must be returned. That, of course, assumes you get what you order. The Internet is the ultimate weapon for fly-by-night operators. Fraud is already a big problem.

Competitive effects will influence other retailers

Retailers of every type are experimenting with selling on the Internet. They range from department stores like The Bay to discounters like Zellers to limited-line retailers like Lee Valley Tools (woodworking) to service providers like FTD (flower deliveries).

None of these retailers knows what longer-term impact Internet selling will have on their market. However, as new retailing formats and concepts are refined, they increase the competitive pressure on existing companies.[16]

RETAILING TYPES ARE EXPLAINED BY CONSUMER NEEDS FILLED

We've talked about many different types of retailers and how they evolved. No single characteristic provides a good basis for classifying all of them. However, Exhibit 12-3 positions different types of retailers in terms of three consumer-oriented dimensions: (1) width of assortment desired, (2) depth of assortment desired, and (3) a price/service combination. Price and service are combined because they are often indirectly related. Services are costly to provide. So retailers with a lot of service must charge prices that cover the added costs.

Exhibit 12-3 A Three-Dimensional View of the Market for Retail Facilities and the Probable Position of Some Present Offerings

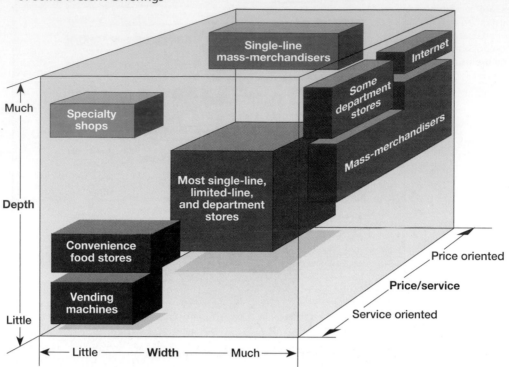

We can position most existing retailers within this three-dimensional market diagram. Exhibit 12-3, for example, suggests the *why* of vending machines. Some people—in the front upper left-hand corner—have a strong need for a specific item and are not interested in width of assortment or price. Note where Internet retailers are placed in the diagram. Does that position make sense to you?

WHY RETAILERS EVOLVE AND CHANGE

The wheel of retailing keeps rolling

The **wheel of retailing theory** says that new types of retailers enter the market as low-status, low-margin, low-price operators and then, if successful, evolve into more conventional retailers offering more services with higher operating costs and higher prices. Then they're threatened by new low-status, low-margin, low-price retailers—and the wheel turns again. Department stores, supermarkets, and mass-merchandisers went through this cycle. Some Internet sellers are on this path.

The wheel of retailing theory, however, doesn't explain all major retailing developments. Vending machines entered as high-cost, high-margin operations. Convenience food stores are high-priced. Suburban shopping centres don't emphasize low price. Current retailers who are adding Web sites are likely to face competitors who cut operating expenses even deeper. The West Edmonton Mall offers entertainment to keep consumers in the mall—restaurants, an ice rink, a wade pool, and Galaxyland.

Scrambled merchandising—mixing product lines for higher profits

Conventional retailers tend to specialize by product line. But most modern retailers are moving toward **scrambled merchandising**—carrying any product lines they think they can sell profitably. Supermarkets and drugstores sell anything they can move in volume—pantyhose, phone cards, one-hour photo processing, motor oil, potted

Some manufacturers have always had outlet stores near their factories, but outlet malls are emerging as a new retailing format that is popular with some consumers.

plants, and computer software. Mass-merchandisers don't just sell everyday items but also cell phones, computer printers, and jewellery.[17] Loblaws and Real Canadian Superstore offer patio furniture, financial services, and dinnerware as well as groceries.

Product life-cycle concept applies to retailer types too

Consumers' needs help explain why some kinds of retailers developed. But we can apply the product life-cycle concept to understand this process better. A retailer with a new idea may have big profits—for a while. But if it's a really good idea, the retailer can count on speedy imitation and a squeeze on profits. Other retailers will copy the new format or scramble their product mix to sell products that offer them higher margins or faster turnover. That puts pressure on the original firm to change or lose its market. London Drugs now sells computers and appliances.

Some conventional retailers are in decline as these life and death cycles continue. Recent innovators, like the Internet merchants, are still in the market growth stage. See Exhibit 12-4. Some retailing formats that are mature in North America are only now beginning to grow in other countries.

Exhibit 12-4
Retailer Life Cycles—
Timing and Years to
Market Maturity

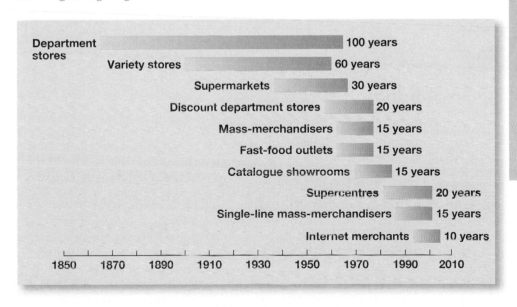

U.S. brand retailer American Apparel, which has outlets in Canada, has grown rapidly in the two years since it introduced its "no sweatshop" policy. Garments are not outsourced to Third World factories, some of which have a reputation for being sweatshops. All manufacturing is done in what happens to be the largest single garment factory in the U.S., which is located in downtown Los Angeles.

American Apparel is a vertically integrated manufacturer and retailer of clothing for men, women, kids, and dogs. The company has consolidated all stages of production under one roof at the Los Angeles factory—from the cutting and sewing, right through to the photography and marketing.

Dov Charney, a senior partner and native of Montreal, runs American Apparel. It's not your typical garment factory and Charney is not your typical garment factory boss. The energetic and wiry 37-year-old regularly stops by each department to greet his employees. Like nearly all of his 3,800 workers, Charney is an immigrant—though in his case, a Canadian with a green card. Charney's socially responsible initiatives have included affordable health care for employees and their families, immigration support, free English and computer classes, subsidized lunches and bus passes, as well as a commitment to paying decent wages (averaging over $12.50/hour) for the company's workers. He has been instrumental in propelling the company's growth to the status of being the largest and most profitable T-shirt manufacturing company in the United States. Recently, Charney also expanded the company's environmental policies by launching a new line of organic T-shirts and a program that recycles over a million pounds of fibre scraps annually. Through American Apparel, Charney has proven that the industry does not need to exploit its workforce to be cost-efficient, but rather has used innovation to produce the highest quality garments.

Would American Apparel's "no sweatshop" policy affect whether you would shop at this store or not?[18]

Ethical issues may arise

Most retailers face intense competitive pressure. The desperation that comes with such pressure has pushed some retailers toward questionable marketing practices.

Critics argue, for example, that retailers too often advertise special sale items to bring price-sensitive shoppers into the store or to a Web site but then don't stock enough to meet demand. Other retailers are criticized for pushing consumers to trade up to more expensive items. What is ethical and unethical in situations like these, however, is subject to debate. Retailers can't always anticipate demand perfectly, and deliveries may not arrive on time. Similarly, trading up may be a sensible part of a strategy—if it's done honestly.

The marketing concept should guide firms away from unethical treatment of customers. However, a retailer on the edge of going out of business may lose perspective on the need to satisfy customers in both the short and the long term.[19]

RETAILER SIZE AND PROFITS

The large number of retailers in Canada (over 227,200) might suggest that retailing is a field of small businesses. To some extent this is true. But the larger retail stores—such as Loblaws—also do a lot of the business. Department stores still do almost 7 percent of the retail trade in Canada.[20]

Big chains are building market clout

The main way for a retailer to achieve economies of scale is with a corporate chain. A **corporate chain** is a firm that owns and manages more than one store—and often it's many. Chains have grown rapidly and now account for about half of all retail sales. You can expect chains to continue to grow and take business from independent stores.

Large chains use such as Canadian Tire use central buying for different stores. They take advantage of quantity discounts and develop their own efficient distribution

Ich freue mich auf meinen grossen Auftritt im Streichelzoo vom 11.–23.2.

SHOPPI TIVOLI
Spreitenbach

Shoppi Tivoli is a shopping mall in Switzerland. The ad says: "I'm looking forward to my gig at the petting zoo between February 11 and 23." Shopping centres around the world are adding entertainment to draw customers and make shopping more enjoyable.

centres. They can use computer networks to control inventory costs and stock-outs. They may also spread promotion, information technology, and management costs to many stores. Retail chains also have their own dealer brands. Many of these chains are becoming powerful members, or channel captains, in their channel systems. In fact, the most successful of these big chains, like Home Depot and Wal-Mart, control access to so many consumers that they have the clout to dictate almost every detail of relationships with their suppliers.[21]

Franchisors form chains too

In a **franchise operation**, the franchisor develops a good marketing strategy, and the retail franchise holders carry out the strategy in their own units. Each franchise holder benefits from its relationship with the larger company and its experience, buying power, promotion, and image. In return, the franchise holder usually signs a contract to pay fees and commissions and to strictly follow franchise rules designed to continue the successful strategy.

Franchise holders' sales account for about half of all retail sales. One reason is that franchising is especially popular with service retailers, a fast-growing sector of the economy.[22] Examples include Subway and Tim Hortons.

DIFFERENCES IN RETAILING IN DIFFERENT NATIONS

New ideas spread across countries

New retailing approaches that succeed in one part of the world are often quickly adapted to other countries. Self-service approaches that started with supermarkets in North America are now found in retail operations worldwide. The supercentre concept, on the other hand, initially developed in Europe.

| Mass-merchandising requires mass markets | The low prices, selections, and efficient operations offered by mass-merchandisers might be attractive to consumers everywhere. But consumers in less-developed nations often don't have the income to support mass distribution. The small shops that survive in these economies sell in very small quantities, often to a small number of consumers. |

| Some countries block change | The political and legal environment severely limits the evolution of retailing in some nations. Japan is a prime example. For years its Large Store Law—aimed at protecting the country's politically powerful small shopkeepers—has been a real barrier to retail change. The law restricts development of large stores by requiring special permits, which are routinely denied. |

Japan is taking steps to change the Large Store Law. One such change allowed Toys "R" Us to move into the Japanese market. Even so, most experts believe that it will be years before Japan moves away from its system of small, limited-line shops. Many countries in other parts of Asia and South America impose similar restrictions. On the other hand, the European Union is prompting member countries to drop such rules.[23]

WHAT IS A WHOLESALER?

It's hard to define what a wholesaler is because there are so many different wholesalers doing different jobs. Some of their activities may even seem like manufacturing. As a result, some wholesalers describe themselves as "manufacturer and dealer." Some like to identify themselves with such general terms as *merchant, agent, dealer,* or *distributor.* And others just take the name commonly used in their trade—without really thinking about what it means.

Wholesaling is concerned with the *activities* of those persons or establishments that sell to retailers and other merchants, or to industrial, institutional, and commercial users, but that do not sell in large amounts to final consumers.

So **wholesalers** are firms whose main function is providing wholesaling activities. Wholesalers sell to all of the different types of organizational customers shown in Exhibit 7-1.

Wholesaling activities are just variations of the basic marketing functions—gathering and providing information, buying and selling, grading, storing, transporting, financing, and risk taking—we discussed in Chapter 1. You can understand wholesalers' strategies better if you look at them as members of channels. They add value by doing jobs for their customers and for their suppliers.

WHOLESALING IS CHANGING WITH THE TIMES

A hundred years ago wholesalers dominated distribution channels. The many small producers and small retailers needed their services. This situation still exists in less-developed economies. However, in the developed nations, as producers became larger many bypassed the wholesalers. Similarly, large retail chains often take control of functions that had been handled by wholesalers. Now e-commerce is making it easier for producers and consumers to "connect" without having a wholesaler in the middle of the exchange.

In light of these changes, many people have predicted a gloomy future for wholesalers. In the 1980s that seemed to be the pattern. Now, however, many wholesalers are adapting rapidly and finding new ways to add value in the channel. For example, some of the biggest B2B e-commerce sites on the Internet are wholesaler operations, and many wholesalers are enjoying significant growth.

Producing profits, not chasing orders

Progressive wholesalers are becoming more concerned with their customers and with channel systems. Many are using technology to offer better service. Others develop voluntary chains that bind them more closely to their customers.

Modern wholesalers no longer require all customers to pay for all the services they offer simply because certain customers use them. Many offer a basic service at minimum cost—then charge additional fees for any special services required. They've also streamlined their operations to cut unnecessary costs and improve profits. They use computers to track inventory and reorder only when it's really needed. Computerized sales analysis helps them identify and drop unprofitable products and customers. This sometimes leads to a selective distribution policy—when it's unprofitable to build relationships with too many small customers. Then they can fine-tune how they add value for their profitable customers.

Perhaps goodbye to some

Not all wholesalers are progressive, and less efficient ones will fail. Cost-conscious buyers for Wal-Mart, Lowe's, and other chains are refusing to deal with some of the middlemen who represent small producers. They want to negotiate directly with the producer. Similarly, producers see advantages in having closer direct relationships with fewer suppliers—and they're paring out weaker vendors. Efficient delivery services like Federal Express are also making it easy for many producers to ship directly to their customers, even ones in foreign markets. The Internet is putting pressure on wholesalers whose primary role is providing information to bring buyers and sellers together.[24]

Is it an ethical issue?

All of this is squeezing some wholesalers out of business. Some critics, including many of the wounded wholesalers, argue that it's unethical for powerful suppliers or customers to simply cut out wholesalers who spend money and time, perhaps decades, developing markets. Contracts between channel members and laws sometimes define what is or is not legal. But the ethical issues are often more ambiguous.

For example, Amana notified Cooper Distributing Co. that it intended to cancel their distribution agreement in 10 days. Cooper had handled Amana appliances for 30 years, and Amana products represented 85 percent of Cooper's sales. Amana's explanation to Cooper? "We just think we can do it better."

Situations like this arise often. They may be cold-hearted, but are they unethical? We argue that it isn't fair to cut off the relationship with such short notice. But most wholesalers realize that their business is *always* at risk—if they don't perform channel functions better or cheaper than their suppliers or customers can do themselves.[25]

Survivors will need effective strategies

The wholesalers who do survive will need to be efficient, but that doesn't mean they'll all have low costs. Some wholesalers' higher operating expenses result from the strategies they select, including the special services they offer to *some* customers.

WHOLESALERS ADD VALUE IN DIFFERENT WAYS

Exhibit 12-5 gives a big-picture view of the major types of wholesalers. There are lots more specialized types, but our discussion will give you a sense of the diversity. Note that a major difference between merchant and agent wholesalers is whether they *own* the products they sell. Before discussing these wholesalers, we'll briefly consider producers who handle their own wholesaling activities.

Manufacturers' sales branches are considered wholesalers

Manufacturers who just take over some wholesaling activities are not considered wholesalers. However, when they have **manufacturers' sales branches**—warehouses that producers set up at separate locations away from their factories—they're classified as wholesalers.

Exhibit 12-5 Types of Wholesalers

Manufacturer-owned branch operations are usually placed in the best market areas. This also helps explain why their operating costs, as a percent of sales, are often lower. It's also easier for a manufacturer to coordinate information and logistics functions with its own branch operations than with independent wholesalers.[26]

MERCHANT WHOLESALERS ARE THE MOST NUMEROUS

Merchant wholesalers own (take title to) the products they sell. They often specialize by certain types of products or customers. For example, Fastenal is a wholesaler that specializes in distributing threaded fasteners used by a variety of manufacturers. It owns (takes title to) the fasteners for some period before selling to its customers. If you think all merchant wholesalers are fading away, Fastenal is proof that they can serve a needed role. In the last decade Fastenal's profits have grown at about the same pace as Microsoft's.[27]

INTERNET EXERCISE Check out the different aspects of the Fastenal Web site (www.fastenal.com). Give examples of ways that the Web site is intended to help Fastenal's customers and suppliers.

A large majority of the wholesaling establishments in Canada are merchant wholesalers—and they handle more than half of wholesale sales. Merchant wholesalers are even more common in other countries. Japan is an extreme example. Products are often bought and sold by a series of merchant wholesalers on their way to the business user or retailer.[28]

Merchant wholesalers in Africa are often smaller, carry narrower product lines, and deal with fewer customers than their counterparts in North America.

Service wholesalers provide all the functions

Service wholesalers are merchant wholesalers that provide all the wholesaling functions. Within this basic group are three types: (1) general merchandise, (2) single-line, and (3) specialty.

General merchandise wholesalers are service wholesalers that carry a wide variety of nonperishable items such as hardware, electrical supplies, furniture, drugs, cosmetics, and automobile equipment. With their broad line of convenience and shopping products, they serve hardware stores, drugstores, and small department stores. *Mill supply houses* operate in a similar way, but they carry a broad variety of accessories and supplies to serve the needs of manufacturers.

Single-line (or general-line) wholesalers are service wholesalers that carry a narrower line of merchandise than general merchandise wholesalers. For example, they might carry only food, apparel, or certain types of industrial tools or supplies. In consumer products, they serve the single- and limited-line stores. In business products, they cover a wider geographic area and offer more specialized service.

Specialty wholesalers are service wholesalers that carry a very narrow range of products and offer more information and service than other service wholesalers. A consumer products specialty wholesaler might carry only health foods or oriental foods instead of a full line of groceries. Some limited-line and specialty wholesalers are growing by helping independent retailer-customers find better ways to compete with mass-merchandisers. But in general, many consumer-products wholesalers have been hit hard by the growth of retail chains that set up their own distribution centres and deal directly with producers. A specialty wholesaler of business products might limit itself to fields requiring special technical knowledge or service.

Limited-function wholesalers provide some functions

Limited-function wholesalers provide only *some* wholesaling functions. In the following paragraphs, we briefly discuss the main features of these wholesalers. Although less numerous in some countries, these wholesalers are very important for some products.

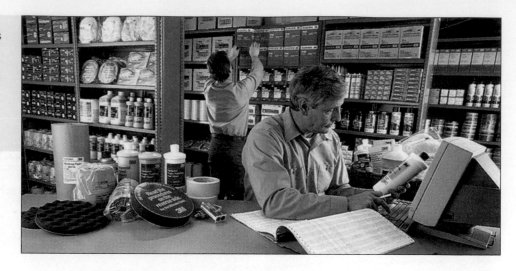

3M produces 1,600 products that are used by auto body repair shops in the U.S., Canada, Europe, Japan, and other countries. To reach this target market, 3M works with hundreds of specialty wholesalers.

Cash-and-carry wholesalers want cash

Cash-and-carry wholesalers operate like service wholesalers—except that the customer must pay cash. In North America, big warehouse clubs have taken much of this business. But cash-and-carry operators are common in less-developed nations where very small retailers handle the bulk of retail transactions. Full-service wholesalers often refuse to grant credit to small businesses that may have trouble paying their bills.

Drop-shippers do not handle the products

Drop-shippers own (take title to) the products they sell—but they do *not* actually handle, stock, or deliver them. These wholesalers are mainly involved in selling. They get orders and pass them on to producers. Then the producer ships the order directly to the customer. Drop-shippers commonly sell bulky products (like lumber) for which additional handling would be expensive and possibly damaging. Drop-shippers are already feeling the squeeze from buyers and sellers connecting directly via the Internet. But the progressive ones are fighting back by setting up their own Web sites and getting fees for referrals.

Truck wholesalers deliver—at a cost

Truck wholesalers specialize in delivering products that they stock in their own trucks. Their big advantage is that they promptly deliver perishable products that regular wholesalers prefer not to carry. A 7-Eleven store that runs out of potato chips on a busy Friday night doesn't want to be out of stock all weekend! They help retailers keep a tight rein on inventory, and they seem to meet a need.

Rack jobbers sell hard-to-handle assortments

Rack jobbers specialize in hard-to-handle assortments of products that a retailer doesn't want to manage—and rack jobbers usually display the products on their own wire racks. For example, a grocery store or mass-merchandiser might rely on a rack jobber to decide which paperback books or magazines it sells. The wholesaler knows which titles sell in the local area and applies that knowledge in many stores.

Catalogue wholesalers reach outlying areas

Catalogue wholesalers sell out of catalogues that may be distributed widely to smaller industrial customers or retailers that might not be called on by other middlemen. Customers place orders at a Web site or by mail, e-mail, fax, or telephone. These wholesalers sell lines such as hardware, jewellery, sporting goods, and computers. Most catalogue wholesalers quickly adapted to the Internet. It fits what they were already doing and makes it easier. But they're facing more competition too; the Internet allows customers to compare prices from more sources of supply.[29]

Innovative wholesalers are using multilingual bar codes to reduce costs and errors in overseas markets.

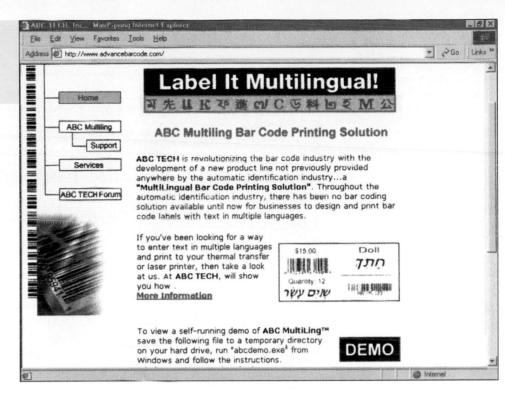

AGENT MIDDLEMEN ARE STRONG ON SELLING

They don't own the products

Agent middlemen are wholesalers who do *not* own the products they sell. Their main purpose is to help in buying and selling. Agent middlemen normally specialize by customer type and by product or product line. But they usually provide even fewer functions than the limited-function wholesalers. They operate at relatively low cost— sometimes 2 to 6 percent of their selling price—or less in the case of Web site-based agents who simply bring buyers and sellers together. Worldwide, the role of agent middlemen is rapidly being transformed by the Internet. Those who didn't get on board this fast-moving train were left behind.

They are important in international trade

Agent middlemen are common in international trade. Many markets have only a few well-financed merchant wholesalers. The best many producers can do is get local representation through agents and then arrange financing through banks that specialize in international trade.

Agent middlemen are usually experts on local business customs and regulations in their own countries. Sometimes a marketing manager can't work through a foreign government's red tape without the help of a local agent.

Manufacturers' agents— freewheeling sales reps

A **manufacturers' agent** sells similar products for several noncompeting producers—for a commission on what is actually sold. Such agents work almost as members of each company's sales force, but they're really independent middlemen. More than half of all agent middlemen are manufacturers' agents.

Their big plus is that they already call on some customers and can add another product line at relatively low cost—and at no cost to the producer until something sells! If an area's sales potential is low, a company may use a manufacturers' agent because the agent can do the job at low cost. Small producers often use agents everywhere because their sales volume is too small to justify their own sales force.

A few years ago, auctions were used for only a few specialized product categories, but now online services like eBay are making auctions a convenient and popular approach for buying and selling many different types of products (both new and used).

Agents can be especially useful for introducing new products. For this service, they may earn 10 to 15 percent commission. (In contrast, their commission on large-volume established products may be quite low—perhaps only 2 percent.) A 10 to 15 percent commission rate may seem small for a new product with low sales. Once a product sells well, however, a producer may think the rate is high and begin using its own sales reps. Agents are well aware of this possibility. That's why most try to work for many producers and avoid being dependent on only one line.

Export or import agents are basically manufacturers' agents who specialize in international trade. These agent middlemen operate in every country and help international firms adjust to unfamiliar market conditions in foreign markets.

Manufacturers' reps will continue to play an important role in businesses that need an agent to perform order-getting tasks. But manufacturers' reps everywhere are feeling pressure when it comes to routine business contacts. More producers are turning to telephone selling, Web sites, e-mail, teleconferencing, and faxes to contact customers directly.[30]

Brokers provide information

Brokers bring buyers and sellers together. Brokers usually have a *temporary* relationship with the buyer and seller while a particular deal is negotiated. They are especially useful when buyers and sellers don't come into the market very often. The broker's product is information about what buyers need and what supplies are available. If the transaction is completed, they earn a commission from whichever party hired them. **Export and import brokers** operate like other brokers, but they specialize in bringing together buyers and sellers from different countries. Smart brokers quickly saw new opportunities to expand their reach by using the Internet. As the Internet causes consolidation, it will also provide more value. A smaller number of cyberbrokers will cut costs and dominate the business with larger databases of buyers and sellers.

| Selling agents— almost marketing managers | **Selling agents** take over the whole marketing job of producers—not just the selling function. A selling agent may handle the entire output of one or more producers, even competing producers, with almost complete control of pricing, selling, and advertising. In effect, the agent becomes each producer's marketing manager. |

Financial trouble is one of the main reasons a producer calls in a selling agent. The selling agent may provide working capital but may also take over the affairs of the business. But selling agents also work internationally. A **combination export manager** is a blend of manufacturers' agent and selling agent—handling the entire export function for several producers of similar but noncompeting lines.

| Auction companies speed up the sale | **Auction companies** provide a place where buyers and sellers can come together and bid to complete a transaction. Traditionally they were important in certain lines—such as livestock, fur, tobacco, and used cars—where demand and supply conditions change rapidly. |

Auto Auction Network Limited (Aucsat), based in New Zealand, is a good example of a progressive auction company that put the bid process on the Internet. Its very successful used-car auction runs from a Web site (www.aucsat.co.nz). It provides bidders with a thorough online rating of the quality of each car. In the past, most auction companies said "What you see is what you get." Because the ratings add value and are credible, Aucsat attracts more dealers. The Internet has spurred growth of all sorts of auction companies in lines of business where auctions have previously not been common.[31]

WHAT WILL HAPPEN TO RETAILERS IN THE FUTURE?

Channels of distribution are in the midst of dynamic changes. There have been dramatic improvements in logistics, the Internet, and e-commerce. But before all of this, the evolution of retailing and wholesaling was ongoing. Middlemen that find new and better ways to add value prosper.

A variety of firms are trying to figure out how to have a presence on the Web. Many are reshaping competition in the product-markets in which they compete. On the other hand, much of the initial change has simply been an adjustment to what was done in the past. The catalogue becomes electronic. E-mail supplements toll-free phone orders. A retailer opens a new Web site instead of a new store. The technology is revolutionary and exciting, but much of what firms are doing with it so far is evolutionary.

In time, more revolutionary change may come. Imagine, for example, what it would take for you—and everyone you know—to do most of your routine shopping on the Internet. What new marketing functions would be needed, and who would provide them? Let's consider one scenario.

After you put products in your virtual shopping basket at several Web sites, the seller assembles your items in a carton with a bar code for your personal name, address, and account. Then that carton and cartons for all of the other orders that come into that Web site would be quickly taken in large economical batches to an intermediary. The computer-controlled sorting system going into the intermediary's 2-hectare facility would scan each carton's bar code and route it to the sorting area for a truck that serves you and each of your neighbours. After a night of accumulating all the cartons that are directed to you from different sellers, the intermediary would place the cartons on a delivery vehicle in the right sequence so they can be efficiently unloaded as the truck passes each customer on its route.[32]

Something like this probably isn't far off. Specialists will develop to make distribution *after* an Internet purchase more efficient, just as middlemen developed to make distribution more efficient *prior* to purchases in retail stores. What is described above isn't very different from what UPS does now, but the cost per package is much higher than it would be if everybody got deliveries everyday.

If the after-purchase distribution problem is handled, who will the seller be? Will the Internet merchants of tomorrow be an evolved form of the retailers of today? Or will current-day wholesalers be in a better position to catch that prize? Some wholesalers are already working with very large assortments. Or, in a world where you can conveniently surf from one specialized seller to another, will the breadth of assortment from any one seller be irrelevant? That could put producers in a stronger position. Perhaps none of these traditional forms of business will lead the way, but rather it will be a unique new type of specialist that is born on the Internet. The answers to these questions will take time, but already new intermediaries are coming on the scene.

Let's admit it. You can only speculate about where e-commerce will lead. But perhaps it's good to speculate a little. The way markets work in the future will depend on creative innovations that people like you imagine, analyze, and ultimately turn into profitable marketing strategies.

CONCLUSION

Modern retailing is scrambled—and we'll probably see more changes in the future. In such a dynamic environment, a producer's marketing manager must choose very carefully among the available kinds of retailers. And retailers must plan their marketing mixes with their target customers' needs in mind—while at the same time becoming part of an effective channel system.

We described many types of retailers—and we saw that each has its advantages and disadvantages. We also saw that modern retailers have discarded conventional practices. The old "buy low and sell high" philosophy is no longer a safe guide. Lower margins with faster turnover is the modern philosophy as more retailers move into mass-merchandising. But even this is no guarantee of success as retailers' life cycles move on.

A good retail location is key to the success of a retail business. Retail locations vary from free-standing stores to regional malls. Power and lifestyle centres are currently the fastest growing types of retail locations.

Growth of chains and scrambled merchandising will continue as retailing evolves to meet changing consumer demands. But important breakthroughs are possible—perhaps with the Internet—and consumers probably will continue to move away from conventional retailers.

The explosive growth within Internet retailing offers consumers many more options.

Wholesalers can provide functions for those both above and below them in a channel of distribution. These services are closely related to the basic marketing functions. There are many types of wholesalers. Some provide all the wholesaling functions—while others specialize in only a few. Eliminating wholesalers does not eliminate the need for the functions they now provide, but technology is helping firms to perform these functions in more efficient ways.

Merchant wholesalers are the most numerous and account for the majority of wholesale sales. Their distinguishing characteristic is that they take title to (own) products. Agent middlemen, on the other hand, act more like sales representatives for sellers or buyers—and they do not take title.

Despite dire predictions, wholesalers continue to exist. The more progressive ones are adapting to a changing environment. But some less progressive wholesalers will fail. The Internet is already taking its toll. On the other hand, new types of intermediaries are evolving. Some are creating new ways of helping producers and their customers achieve their objectives by finding new ways to add value.

KEY TERMS

QUESTIONS AND PROBLEMS

1. What sort of a "product" are specialty shops offering? What are the prospects for organizing a chain of specialty shops?

2. Distinguish among discount retailers, price-cutting by conventional retailers, and mass-merchandising. Forecast the future of low-price selling in food, clothing, and appliances. How will the Internet affect that future?

3. Discuss a few changes in the marketing environment that you think help to explain why telephone, mail-order, and Internet retailing have been growing so rapidly.

4. What are some advantages and disadvantages to using the Internet for shopping? What products would you consider buying online from Shopper's Drug Mart?

5. Apply the wheel of retailing theory to your local community. What changes seem likely? Will established retailers see the need for change, or will entirely new firms have to develop?

6. What advantages does a retail chain have over a retailer who operates with a single store? Does a small retailer have any advantages in competing against a chain? Explain your answer.

7. Many producers are now seeking new opportunities in international markets. Are the opportunities for international expansion equally good for retailers? Explain your answer.

8. Discuss how computer systems affect wholesalers' and retailers' operations.

9. Consider the evolution of wholesaling in relation to the evolution of retailing. List several changes that are similar, and several that are fundamentally different.

10. Do wholesalers and retailers need to worry about new-product planning just as a producer needs to have an organized new-product development process? Explain your answer.

11. How do you think a retailer of Maytag washing machines would react if Maytag set up a Web site, sold direct to consumers, and shipped direct from its distribution centre? Explain your thinking.

12. What risks do merchant wholesalers assume by taking title to goods? Is the size of this risk about constant for all merchant wholesalers?

13. Why would a manufacturer set up its own sales branches if established wholesalers were already available?

14. What is an agent middleman's marketing mix?

15. Why do you think that many merchant middlemen handle competing products from different producers, while manufacturers' agents usually handle only noncompeting products from different producers?

16. What alternatives does a producer have if it is trying to expand distribution in a foreign market and finds that the best existing merchant middlemen won't handle imported products?

17. Discuss the future growth and nature of wholesaling if chains, scrambled merchandising, and the Internet continue to become more important. How will wholesalers have to adjust their mixes? Will wholesalers be eliminated? If not, what wholesaling functions will be most important? Are there any particular lines of trade where wholesalers may have increasing difficulty?

COMPUTER-AIDED PROBLEM

12. Selecting Channel Intermediaries

RESOURCE REMINDER

Art Glass Productions, a producer of decorative glass gift items, wants to expand into a new territory. Managers at Art Glass know that unit sales in the new territory will be affected by consumer response to the products. But sales will also be affected by which combination of wholesalers and retailers Art Glass selects. There is a choice between two wholesalers. One wholesaler, Giftware Distributing, is a merchant wholesaler that specializes in gift items; it sells to gift shops, department stores, and some mass-merchandisers. The other wholesaler, Margaret Degan & Associates, is a manufacturers' agent that calls on many of the gift shops in the territory.

Art Glass makes a variety of glass items, but the cost of making an item is usually about the same—$5.20 a unit. The items would sell to Giftware Distributing at $12.00 each—and in turn the merchant wholesaler's price to retailers would be $14.00—leaving Giftware with a $2.00 markup to cover costs and profit. Giftware Distributing is the only reputable merchant wholesaler in the territory, and it has agreed to carry the line only if Art Glass is willing to advertise in a trade magazine aimed at retail buyers for gift items. These ads will cost $8,000 a year.

As a manufacturers' agent, Margaret Degan would cover all of her own expenses and would earn 8 percent of the $14.00 price per unit charged the gift shops. Individual orders would be shipped directly to the retail gift shops by Art Glass, using United Parcel Service (UPS). Art Glass would pay the UPS charges at an average cost of $2.00 per item. In contrast, Giftware Distributing would anticipate demand and place larger orders in advance.

This would reduce the shipping costs, which Art Glass would pay, to about $.60 a unit.

Art Glass' marketing manager thinks that Degan would only be able to sell about 75 percent as many items as Giftware Distributing—since she doesn't have time to call on all of the smaller shops and doesn't call on any department stores. On the other hand, the merchant wholesaler's demand for $8,000 worth of supporting advertising requires a significant outlay.

The marketing manager at Art Glass decided to use a spreadsheet to determine how large sales would have to be to make it more profitable to work with Giftware and to see how the different channel arrangements would contribute to profits at different sales levels.

a. Given the estimated unit sales and other values shown on the initial spreadsheet, which type of wholesaler would contribute the most profit to Art Glass Productions?

b. If sales in the new territory are slower than expected, so that the merchant wholesaler was able to sell only 3,000 units—or the agent 2,250 units—which wholesaler would contribute the most to Art Glass' profits? (Note: Assume that the merchant wholesaler only buys what it can sell; that is, it doesn't carry extra inventory beyond what is needed to meet demand.)

c. Prepare a table showing how the two wholesalers' contributions to profit compare as the quantity sold varies from 3,500 units to 4,500 units for the merchant wholesaler and 75 percent of these numbers for the manufacturers' agent. Discuss these results. (Note: Use the analysis feature to vary the quantity sold by the merchant wholesaler, and the program will compute 75 percent of that quantity as the estimate of what the agent will sell.)

If you want to read the cases and view the video cases that accompany this chapter, visit the *Basic Marketing* Online Learning Centre at: **www.mcgrawhill.ca/olc/perreault**. Along with these cases and video cases, the OLC also has the software and user guide for this chapter's Computer-Aided Problem, as well as exercises, quizzes, articles, links, and other *interactive* content that will help you with your studies.

13

CHAPTER

WHEN YOU FINISH THIS CHAPTER, YOU SHOULD

1. Know the advantages and disadvantages of the promotion methods a marketing manager can use in strategy planning.

2. Understand the integrated marketing communications concept and why most firms use a blend of different promotion methods.

3. Understand the importance of promotion objectives.

4. Know how the communication process affects promotion planning.

5. Understand how direct-response promotion is helping marketers develop more targeted promotion blends.

6. Understand how new customer-initiated interactive communication is different.

7. Know how typical promotion plans are blended to get an extra push from middlemen and help from customers in pulling products through the channel.

8. Understand how promotion blends typically vary over the product life cycle.

9. Understand how to determine how much to spend on promotion efforts.

Promotion—Integrated Marketing Communications

The classic MINI Cooper was a pop icon in England in the 1960s. John Lennon and Paul McCartney were MINI owners when they wrote "Baby, You Can Drive My Car." But the quirky MINI never made a splash in the U.S. (only 10,000 classic MINIs were sold from 1960–67). Now, however, all of that has changed—with the help of effective promotion.

After the BMW Group took ownership of the MINI brand, a new-product development team designed a new model. They gave it updated styling and high-tech features (including six standard airbags, Corner Brake Control, Dynamic Stability Control, ABS, heated seats, and a six-speaker CD stereo). Tiny compacts were already popular in Europe. Yet in North America, where SUVs rule, the new MINI was the smallest car on the road. The BMW Group hoped that the North American launch of the MINI would attract a segment of adventurous, fun-loving innovators who would change that. Kerri Martin, the Marketing Communications Manager for MINI U.S.A., planned the promotion to make that happen. Her team faced several challenges. The MINI brand had to be launched independently of any BMW brand association, so promotion had to simultaneously launch a new brand, two models, and a new small car segment. Further, Martin's team didn't have the big promotion budget typical for high-volume cars because first year production was limited to 20,000 units.

Martin needed distinctive promotion to appeal to prospects who saw the unique MINI as a form of self-expression, not just as a way to get to work. She selected the Crispin Porter + Bogusky (CPB) ad agency to help. They were creative—and not scared off by her warning to avoid costly TV campaigns and traditional ads.

Before the MINI'S introduction, they staged a series of sales promotion events to give the MINI a personality—and draw traffic to the newly created Web site. For ex-ample, they mounted a MINI on top of a jumbo SUV and drove it to auto shows and around major metropolitan cities like New York and San Francisco. A sign on the SUV said, "What are you doing for fun this weekend?" The big idea was that your fun stuff always goes on top, whether it be your skis, mountain bikes, or your MINI Cooper. Next they tore out seats at the Superdome in New Orleans and put a MINI right in with the fans for a game. The publicity stunts drew national TV coverage, including coverage on Monday Night Football. To get as much attention from TV ads would have cost millions of dollars. Before the rollout to dealers, CPB started to add cheeky billboard messages, like the one on the side of an urban parking garage that showed a picture of the MINI and the simple copy "Parking. How sad." Other ads just featured a simple headline such as "The SUV back-lash officially starts now," its "LET'S MOTOR" tagline, and the address for its Web site at www.MINIUSA.com.

In response to these attention-getting efforts, over 125,000 consumers flocked to the Web site—before cars even hit dealer showrooms. Thousands played the interactive video games and e-mailed electronic MINI greeting cards to friends—which helped spread the buzz. "MINI Insiders" signed up to receive e-mail newsletters about the MINI, and many used the dealer locator to find out where to see a MINI in person and take a test drive. MINI dealers added personal selling to the promotion blend. MINI Motoring Advisors (MINI doesn't use the term salesmen) explained MINI's options, negotiated prices, completed orders, and arranged for deliveries. Each MINI is delivered with a mint on the seat and a wrap on the steering wheel indicating that "Your MINI has been thoroughly inspected from boot to bonnet." Boot is a British term for a trunk and a bonnet is a hood.

Once cars were on dealer lots, CPB broadened the reach of the MINI message with more billboards, magazine ads and inserts, and 60-second ads in movie theatres. Some dealers ran the theatre ads on local TV. CPB created custom ads for some magazines taking advantage of the unique editorial environments. That was more expensive than just repeating the same ad month after month, but it generated much higher interest and ad recall. For example, an ad in *Playboy* featured a MINI in a centrefold format (along with a tongue-in-cheek list of "likes and dislikes" and a data sheet). An insert in another magazine allowed readers to customize their own MINI with accessory stickers. The MINI was featured in the movie *The Italian Job*, a product placement that generated attention for the car.

By the end of the year, 56 percent of U.S. consumers were aware of the MINI. More importantly, dealers had orders for 20 percent more MINIs than were available. The MINI was even named the 2003 "North American Car of the Year." In 2003, over 2,700 MINIs were sold in Canada. However, the successful introduction doesn't ensure that the MINI will become a long-run success. So promotion for the MINI will need to evolve with changes in the marketing environment while it remains true to the motoring spirit of the brand.[1]

SEVERAL PROMOTION METHODS ARE AVAILABLE

Promotion is communicating information between seller and potential buyer or others in the channel to influence attitudes and behaviour. The marketing manager's main promotion job is to tell target customers that the right Product is available at the right Place at the right Price.

As the Mini Cooper example shows, a marketing manager can choose from several promotion methods—personal selling, mass selling, and sales promotion (see

Exhibit 13-1
Basic Promotion Methods
and Strategy Planning

Exhibit 13-1). Further, because the different promotion methods have different strengths and limitations, a marketing manager usually uses them in combination. And, as with other marketing mix decisions, it is critical that the marketer manage and coordinate the different promotion methods as an integrated whole, not as separate and unrelated parts.

Personal selling—flexibility is its strength

Personal selling involves direct spoken communication between sellers and potential customers. Salespeople get immediate feedback, which helps them to adapt. Although some personal selling is included in most marketing mixes, it can be very expensive. So it's often desirable to combine personal selling with mass selling and sales promotion. We will discuss this topic in more detail in the next chapter.

Mass selling involves advertising and publicity

Mass selling is communicating with large numbers of potential customers at the same time. It's less flexible than personal selling, but when the target market is large and scattered, mass selling can be less expensive on a per contact basis.

Advertising is the main form of mass selling. Advertising is any paid form of nonpersonal presentation of ideas, goods, or services by an identified sponsor. It includes the use of traditional media like magazines, newspapers, radio and TV, signs, and direct mail as well as new media such as the Internet. While advertising must be paid for, another form of mass selling—publicity—is "free." Chapter 15 provides a greater discussion of advertising.

Publicity avoids media costs

Publicity is any *unpaid* form of nonpersonal presentation of ideas, goods, or services. Of course, personnel hired to generate publicity are paid. But they try to attract attention to the firm and its offerings *without having to pay media costs*. For example, movie studios try to get celebrities on TV talk shows because this generates a lot of interest and sells tickets to new movies without the studio paying for TV time. We revisit this topic in Chapter 15.

Sales promotion tries to spark immediate interest

Sales promotion refers to promotion activities—other than advertising, publicity, and personal selling—that stimulate interest, trial, or purchase by final customers or others in the channel. Sales promotion may be aimed at consumers, at middlemen, or at a firm's own employees. Examples are listed in Exhibit 13-2 and disussed in more detail in Chapter 15. Relative to other promotion methods, sales promotion can usually be implemented quickly and get results sooner. In fact, most sales promotion efforts are designed to produce immediate results.

Less is spent on advertising than personal selling or sales promotion

Many people incorrectly think that promotion money gets spent primarily on advertising—because advertising is all around them. The many ads you see on the Web, in magazines and newspapers, and on TV are impressive—and costly. But all the special sales promotions—coupons, sweepstakes, trade shows, and the like—add up to even more money. Similarly, much personal selling goes on in the channels

Exhibit 13-2
Example of Sales Promotion
Activities

Aimed at final consumers or users	Aimed at middlemen	Aimed at company's own sales force
Contests Coupons Online coupons Aisle displays Samples Trade shows Point-of-purchase materials Banners and streamers Frequent buyer programs Sponsored events	Price deals Promotion allowances Sales contests Calendars Gifts Trade shows Meetings Catalogues Merchandising aids Videos	Contests Bonuses Meetings Portfolios Displays Sales aids Training materials

and in other business markets. In total, firms spend less money on advertising than on personal selling or sales promotion.

We'll talk about individual promotion methods in more detail in the next two chapters. First, however, you need to understand the role of the whole promotion blend—personal selling, mass selling, and sales promotion combined—so you can see how promotion fits into the rest of the marketing mix.

Many different specialists help firms with special sales promotion needs. For example, Featherlite sells special trailers for use with event marketing and FloorGraphics helps firms with point-of-sale ads on the floors of retail stores.

INTEGRATING THE PROMOTION BLEND

Each promotion method has its own strengths and weaknesses. In combination, they complement each other. Each method also involves its own distinct activities and requires different types of expertise. As a result, it's usually the responsibility of specialists—such as sales managers, advertising managers, and promotion managers—to develop and implement the detailed plans for the various parts of the overall promotion blend. Refer to the Online Learning Centre for more information on careers in marketing.

Canada Post uses a blend of marketing communication tools to integrate their promotion strategy, including direct mail to end users, advertising to corporate users, and a comprehensive Web site.

Marketing manager talks to all, blends all

Although many specialists may be involved in planning for and implementing specific promotion methods, determining the blend of promotion methods is a strategy decision—and it is the responsibility of the marketing manager.

The various promotion specialists tend to focus on what they know best and their own areas of responsibility. A creative Web page designer or advertising copywriter in New York may have no idea what a salesperson does during a call on a wholesaler. In addition, because of differences in outlook and experience, the advertising, sales, and sales promotion managers often have trouble working with each other as partners. Too often they just view other promotion methods as using up budget money they want.

The marketing manager is responsible for intergrating all the marketing communication tools to create the ideal promotion strategy.

Send a consistent and complete message with integrated marketing communications

Effective blending of all of the firm's promotion efforts should produce **integrated marketing communications**—the intentional coordination of every communication from a firm to a target customer to convey a consistent and complete message.

The Mini Cooper case at the start of this chapter is a good example of integrated marketing communications. Different promotion methods handle different parts of the job. Yet the methods are coordinated so that the sum is greater than the parts. The separate messages are complementary, but also consistent. This integration effectively positions the Mini in the mind of the consumer.

INTERNET EXERCISE

Sony produces a very wide variety of products. Does the information available on its Web site (www.sony.ca) appear to be part of an integrated marketing communications effort? Explain your thinking.

It seems obvious that a firm's different communications to a target market should be consistent. However, when a number of different people are working on different promotion elements, they are likely to see the same big picture only if a marketing manager ensures that it happens. Getting consistency is harder when different firms handle different aspects of the promotion effort. For example, different firms in the channel may have conflicting objectives.

To get effective coordination, everyone involved with the promotion effort must clearly understand the plan for the overall marketing strategy. They all need to understand how each promotion method will contribute to achieve specific promotion objectives.[2]

WHICH METHODS TO USE DEPENDS ON PROMOTION OBJECTIVES

Overall objective is to affect behaviour

The different promotion methods are all different forms of communication. They should encourage customers to choose a *specific* product. Therefore, promotion must (1) reinforce present attitudes or relationships that might lead to favourable behaviour or (2) actually change the attitudes and behaviour of the firm's target market. The buyer behaviour model introduced in Chapter 6 showed the many influences on buying behaviour. You saw there that affecting buyer behaviour is a tough job—but that is exactly the objective of Promotion.

Informing, persuading, and reminding are basic promotion objectives

Promotion objectives must be clearly defined—because the right promotion blend depends on what the firm wants to accomplish. It's helpful to think of three basic promotion objectives: *informing, persuading,* and *reminding* target customers about the company and its marketing mix. All try to affect buyer behaviour by providing more information.

It's also useful to set more specific promotion objectives that state *exactly who* you want to inform, persuade, or remind, and *why.* This is unique to each company's strategy—and specific objectives vary by promotion method. We'll talk about more specific promotion objectives in the next two chapters. Here we'll focus on the three basic promotion objectives and how you can reach them.

Informing is educating

Potential customers must know something about a product if they are to buy at all. A firm with a really new product may not have to do anything but inform consumers about it and show that it meets consumer needs better than other products.

Persuading usually becomes necessary

When competitors offer similar products, the firm must not only *inform* customers that its product is available but also persuade them to buy it. A *persuading* objective means the firm will try to develop a favourable set of attitudes so customers

This trade ad for Simply White Clear Whitening Gel informs potential channel members that the new product is available and that market testing gives evidence that it will be profitable for the retailer. With its ad Beech-Nut wants to persuade parents that its natural baby food is superior to other products.

Exhibit 13-3
Relation of Promotion Objectives, Adoption Process, and AIDA Model

Promotion Objectives	Adoption Process	AIDA Model
Informing	Awareness	Attention
	Interest	Interest
Persuading	Evaluation	Desire
	Trial	
Reminding	Decision	Action
	Confirmation	

will buy, and keep buying, its product. A persuading objective often focuses on reasons why one brand is better than others. To convince consumers to buy Brawny paper towels, ads position Brawny as the towel that's best for tough cleanup jobs.

Reminding may be enough, sometimes

If target customers already have positive attitudes about a firm's marketing mix— or a good relationship with a firm—a *reminding* objective might be suitable. This objective can be extremely important. Customers who have been attracted and sold once are still targets for competitors' appeals. Reminding them of their past satisfaction may keep them from shifting to a competitor. Campbell realizes that most people know about its soup—so much of its advertising is intended to remind.

Promotion objectives relate to adoption process

In Chapter 6, we looked at consumer buying as a problem-solving process in which buyers go through steps on the way to adopting (or rejecting) an idea or product. The three basic promotion objectives relate to these steps. See Exhibit 13-3. *Informing* and *persuading* may be needed to affect the potential customer's knowledge and attitudes about a product and then bring about its adoption. Later promotion can simply *remind* the customer about that favourable experience and confirm the adoption decision.

The AIDA model is a practical approach

The basic promotion objectives and adoption process fit very neatly with another action-oriented model—called AIDA—that we will use in this and the next two chapters to guide some of our discussion.

The **AIDA model** consists of four promotion jobs: (1) to get *Attention*, (2) to hold *Interest*, (3) to arouse *Desire*, and (4) to obtain *Action*. (As a memory aid, note that the first letters of the four key words spell AIDA, the well-known opera.)

Exhibit 13-3 shows the relationship of the adoption process to the AIDA jobs. Getting attention is necessary to make consumers aware of the company's offering. Holding interest gives the communication a chance to build the consumer's interest in the product. Arousing desire affects the evaluation process, perhaps building preference. And obtaining action includes gaining trial, which may lead to a purchase decision. Continuing promotion is needed to confirm the decision and encourage an ongoing relationship and additional purchases.

PROMOTION REQUIRES EFFECTIVE COMMUNICATION

Communication can break down

Promotion is wasted when it doesn't communicate effectively. There are many reasons why a promotion message can be misunderstood or not heard at all. To understand this, it's useful to think about a whole **communication process**—which means a source trying to reach a receiver with a message. Exhibit 13-4 shows the elements of the communication process. Here we see that a **source**—the sender of a message—is trying to deliver a message to a **receiver**—a potential customer. Customers evaluate both the message and the source of the message in terms of

Exhibit 13-4
The Traditional
Communication Process

trustworthiness and credibility. For example, American Dental Association (ADA) studies show that Listerine mouthwash helps reduce plaque buildup on teeth. Listerine mentions the ADA endorsement in its promotion to help make the promotion message credible.

A major advantage of personal selling is that the source—the seller—can get immediate feedback from the receiver. It's easier to judge how the message is being received and to change it if necessary. Mass sellers usually must depend on marketing research or total sales figures for feedback—and that can take too long. Many marketers include toll-free telephone numbers and Web site addresses as ways of building direct-response feedback from consumers into their mass-selling efforts.

The **noise**—shown in Exhibit 13-4—is any distraction that reduces the effectiveness of the communication process. Conversations and snack-getting during TV ads are noise. The clutter of competing ads on the Internet is noise. Advertisers who plan messages must recognize that many possible distractions—noise—can interfere with communications.

Encoding and decoding depend on a common frame of reference

The basic difficulty in the communication process occurs during encoding and decoding. **Encoding** is the source deciding what it wants to say and translating it into words or symbols that will have the same meaning to the receiver. **Decoding** is the receiver translating the message. This process can be very tricky. The meanings of various words and symbols may differ depending on the attitudes and experiences of the two groups. People need a common frame of reference to communicate effectively. Maidenform encountered this problem with its promotion aimed at working women. The company ran a series of ads depicting women stockbrokers and doctors wearing Maidenform lingerie. The men in the ads were fully dressed. Maidenform was trying to show women in positions of authority, but some women felt the ad presented them as sex objects. In this case, the promotion people who encoded the message didn't understand the attitudes of the target market and how they would decode the message.[3]

Message channel is important too

The communication process is complicated even more because the message is coming from a source through some **message channel**—the carrier of the message. A source can use many message channels to deliver a message. The salesperson does it in person with voice and action. Advertising must do it with media such as magazines, TV, e-mail, or Internet Web sites. A particular message channel may enhance or detract from a message. A TV ad, for example, can *show* that Dawn dishwashing detergent "takes the grease away"; the same claim might not be convincing if it arrived in a consumer's e-mail. On the other hand, a receiver may attach value to a product if the message comes in a well-respected magazine. For instance, many people who are interested in herbal supplements have concerns about safety since the government does not regulate them like it does drugs. Some of these consumers might buy herbal supplements that advertise in *Good Housekeeping* magazine—because they have faith in its seal.[4]

JVC's ad for its mobile stereo gear features tattooed rock star Nikki Sixx and appears in print media that are specially tuned to its youthful, music-loving target market.

The same message may be interpreted differently

Different audiences may interpret a message differently. Such differences are common in international marketing when cultural differences or translation are problems. In Taiwan, the translation of the Pepsi slogan "Come alive with the Pepsi Generation" came out as "Pepsi will bring your ancestors back from the dead." Worse, a campaign for Schweppes Tonic Water in Italy translated the name into Schweppes Toilet Water. Many firms run into problems like this.[5]

Problems occur even when there is no translation. For example, a new children's cough syrup was advertised as extra strength. The advertising people thought they were assuring parents that the product worked well. But moms and dads avoided the product because they feared that it might be too strong for their children.

Ethical issues in marketing communications

Promotion is one of the most often criticized areas of marketing. Many criticisms focus on whether communications are honest and fair. Marketers must sometimes make ethical judgments in considering these charges and in planning their promotion.

For example, when a TV news program broadcasts a video publicity release, consumers don't know it was prepared to achieve marketing objectives. They think the news staff is the source. That may make the message more credible, but is it fair? Many say yes—as long as the publicity information is truthful. But grey areas still remain.

Critics raise similar concerns about the use of celebrities in advertisements. A person who plays the role of an honest and trustworthy person on a popular TV series may be a credible message source in an ad, but is using such a person misleading to consumers? Some critics believe it is. Others argue that consumers recognize advertising when they see it and know celebrities are paid for their endorsements.

The most common criticisms of promotion relate to exaggerated claims. If an ad or a salesperson claims that a product is the "best available," is that just a personal opinion or should every statement be backed up by proof? What type of proof should be required? Some promotions do misrepresent the benefits of a product. However, most marketing managers want relationships with, and repeat purchases from, their customers. They realize that customers won't come back if the marketing mix doesn't deliver what the promotion promises. Further, many consumers are skeptical about all the claims they hear and see. As a result, most marketing managers work to make promotion claims specific and believable.[6]

Is it ethical for fashion designers to continue showing extremely thin models in ads? Many women, especially teens, feel that this is the ideal they should espouse to. Some women are starving themselves to achieve that ideal thin look.

Dove researched women's attitudes toward their body shapes and found that women felt intimidated and depressed by the prevalence of "stick-thin" models. The study found that 68 percent of women agreed that advertisers use models that present an image of beauty that women find unattainable. The findings had Dove marketers wondering if it was time to change the definition of beauty. Dove recently launched an advertising campaign that used real women instead of models.

Dove's Campaign for Real Beauty, showed real women in their underwear, celebrating—and advertising—their own unique beauty. The women modelling for Dove loved challenging skinny stereotypes.

Lauren, a 25-year-old Vancouver disability-insurance examiner, could hardly wait to take her clothes off. For Dove, that is. Lauren was chosen as a model for Dove's Campaign for Real Beauty. When she first saw the campaign Lauren thought: "Wouldn't it be fun to be part of something like that!" Yvonne, a 37-year-old Fraser Valley-based writer and mother of a teenager, felt the same way. "I believed in what they were doing," she says. "I like that they say, 'Real women have real curves.' They do!" It's not surprising that these strong, opinionated women (last names withheld by Dove) headed down to the casting call last November to audition to be in the new all-Canadian Dove billboards.

"I just wondered how it would feel to participate in something that had meaning," says Lauren. "I could be in an ad for watches or jewellery or a car, but that wouldn't say anything about me or my values. But these ads do make a difference. They're getting people to buy into themselves. Nobody can give you confidence but you."

Adds Yvonne: "I feel good about being part of saying, 'Stop it! Every woman should feel beautiful. Don't hate yourself or abuse your body!'"

Both Lauren and Yvonne say they worry about the effect skinny stereotypes are having on younger women today. "If I were a teenager today, I wouldn't know who to look to as a role model," says Lauren. "As far as mainstream in-your-face role models—I don't think there is one."

How do you feel about Dove's campaign for Real Beauty? Is it a step in the right direction as far as breaking down stereotypes about real beauty?[7]

INTEGRATED DIRECT-RESPONSE PROMOTION IS VERY TARGETED

The challenge of developing promotions that reach *specific* target customers has prompted many firms to turn to direct marketing—direct communication between a seller and an individual customer using a promotion method other than face-to-face personal selling. Most direct marketing communications are designed to prompt immediate feedback—a direct response—by customers. That's why this type of communication is often called *direct-response promotion*.

Early efforts in the direct-response area focused on direct-mail advertising. A carefully selected mailing list—perhaps from the firm's customer relationship management (CRM) database—allowed advertisers to reach customers with specific interests. And direct-mail advertising proved to be very effective when the objective was to get a direct response from the customer.

Now it's more than direct-mail advertising

Achieving a measurable, direct response from specific target customers is still the heart of direct promotion. But direct-response media now include telephone, print, e-mail, a Web site, broadcast, and even interactive video. The customer's response may be a purchase (or donation), a question, or a request for more information. At a Web site, the response may be a simple mouse-click to link to more information, a click to put an item in a virtual shopping cart, or a click to purchase.

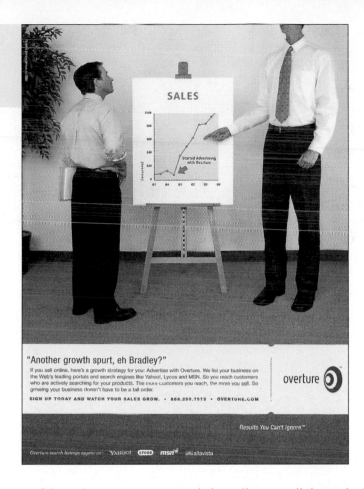

Often the customer responds by calling a toll-free telephone number or, in the case of business markets, by sending a fax or an e-mail. Then a salesperson calls and follows up. That might involve filling an order or scheduling a personal visit with a prospect. There are, however, many variations on this approach. For example, some firms route incoming information-request calls to a computerized answering system. The caller indicates what information is required by pushing a few buttons on the telephone keypad. Then the computer instantly sends requested information to the caller's fax machine.

Direct-response promotion is often an important component of integrated marketing communications programs and is closely tied to other elements of the marketing mix. However, what distinguishes this general approach is that the marketer targets more of its promotion effort at specific individuals who respond directly.[8] A promotion campaign developed by BMW illustrates these ideas. BMW uses the Internet to promote new models and provide interested consumers with information. In the past, BMW sent videotapes to selected consumers. Now, consumers can access BMW online films and books featuring BMW products (www.bmwusa.com/uniquelybmw—click on BMW Art). Interested consumers can sign up for e-mail updates and new product information.

Target customer directly with a CRM database

Direct-response promotion usually relies on a customer relationship management (CRM) database to target specific prospects. The computerized database includes customers' names and addresses (or telephone numbers) as well as past purchases and other segmenting characteristics. Greenpeace and the Cousteau Society send mail advertisements to people interested in environmental issues. They ask for donations or other types of support. Individuals (or segments) who respond to direct promotion are the target for additional promotion. For example, a customer who buys lingerie from a catalogue or a Web site once is a good candidate for a follow-up. The follow-up might extend to other types of clothing. Many Web sites, such as Amazon.ca, remember orders and provide offers tailored to these individual consumers.

Direct-response methods raise ethical concerns

Direct-response promotion and CRM database targeting have become an important part of many marketing mixes. But critics argue that thousands of acres of trees are consumed each week just to make the paper for direct-response "junk mail" that consumers don't want. In addition, many consumers don't like getting direct-promotion telephone solicitations at any time, but especially during evening mealtimes when these calls are particularly frequent. Similarly, most e-mail users resent that they need to waste time dealing with a constant flow of "spam" that floods their e-mail boxes; there's so much spam that it slows down the whole Internet. Worse, some firms have been criticized for creating Web sites that secretly install "spyware" on customers' computers; then, unknown to the user, the program gathers information about the user and sends it back to the firm over the Internet. There are many other privacy issues related to how a direct-response database might be used, especially if it includes details of a consumer's purchases.

Most firms that use direct-response promotion are very sensitive to these concerns and take steps to address them. However, many people feel that solutions to these problems require other steps, and laws in these areas are changing. A host of new regulations concerning consumer privacy are also being considered by lawmakers. So marketers who do not heed warnings about consumer concerns in this area may find themselves in trouble—not only with customers but in the courts.[9]

THE CUSTOMER MAY INITIATE THE COMMUNICATION PROCESS

Traditional thinking about promotion—and for that matter about the communication process—has usually been based on the idea that it's the seller ("source") who initiates the communication. Of course, for decades consumers have been looking in the Yellow Pages for information or asking retail salespeople for help. Similarly, it's not news that organizational buyers contact potential vendors to ask questions or request bids.

In the past, a marketer usually viewed the buyer as a passive message receiver—at least until the marketer has done something to stimulate attention, interest, and desire. That's one reason that targeting is so important—so that the promotion expense isn't wasted on someone who isn't interested. Moreover, most mass-selling messages are based on the idea that you can get a customer's attention and interest for only a minute or two. Even with direct-response promotion, the marketer typically has taken the first step.

New electronic media enable interactive communication

However, this is changing. Buyers can now access a great deal of information (including pictures, video, and audio, as well as text) and place an order without the seller having been directly involved at all. The interactive technologies enabling this change take many different forms. Some of the most important are Web sites, e-mail list-servers, caller-controlled fax-on-demand, computerized telephone voice-messaging systems, video kiosks in malls, CD and DVD disks on personal computers, and MSN TV.

For example, England has had interactive cable TV for over a decade. Consumers can use a standard TV and remote control to get information that ranges from local weather to specials at the local supermarket. Similar systems are becoming more available in other countries as government regulations change and as cable companies upgrade their equipment.

When a Web surfer uses the search engine at Yahoo, one or more pop-up ads may appear. The advertising revenue pays for the service that Yahoo provides free to users, and some consumers click on interesting ads to get more information. However, some critics argue that pop-ups are too obtrusive.

INTERNET EXERCISE

Visit the Campbell's Soup Web site (www.campbellsoup.ca). Does the Web site make it easy for you to get information? Does it make you want to spend more time and get more information? Explain your answer.

Work is underway on interactive cable systems in which icons will appear on-screen as consumers watch a program or movie. For example, an icon might appear on a jacket worn by a talk show guest. A consumer who is interested in the product will be able to press a button on a remote control to pause the show and get more information about the product and where to buy it—or even to place an order. The same concept is already implemented on DVDs for some movies. When this type of system is available via cable (or with streaming video over the Internet), it will reshape the way many marketing communications are handled.

Consider the simple model of customer ("receiver") initiated interactive communication shown in Exhibit 13-5. At first it doesn't seem very different from the traditional communication model we considered earlier (Exhibit 13-4). However, the differences are significant.

Consumer initiates communication with a search process

In the model in Exhibit 13-5, a customer initiates the communication process with a decision to search for information in a particular message channel. The most far-reaching message channel to search is the Internet. The message channel is still the carrier of the message, as was the case before, but "searchable" message channels usually feature an archive of existing messages on a number of topics. There may be many available topics—even millions.

In the next step, the consumer selects one specific topic on which to receive a message. Selecting a topic might be done in one of a variety of ways, depending on the message channel. The most typical approaches involve using a mouse,

Exhibit 13-5
A Model of Customer-
Initiated Interactive
Communication

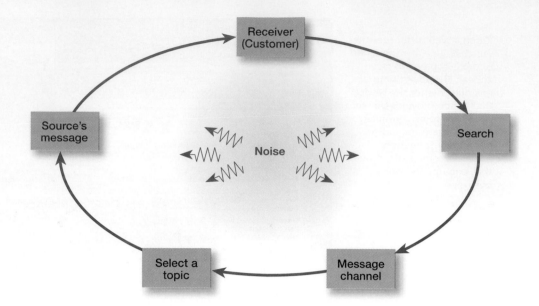

remote control device, or keypad to highlight a selection from an initial list (like a table of contents or index). Of course, other approaches are common. Many dial-up telephone systems use voice-recognition. Or, in the case of the Internet, you might type a phrase and have the computer search for a list of topics that include it.

Consumer decides how much information to get

Once a specific topic is selected, the message for that topic is displayed. Typically, the message is brief. But it may include a simple way to get more detailed information, select another related topic, return to the original selection process, or quit the search. Thus, after each message the consumer can decide whether to search further (say, to get more detail). This interactive approach makes it easy for the consumer to get as much information as desired. However, noise may still be a problem. For example, a consumer may waste time and still not find what is needed—because it is not available or is too hard to find. So some firms offer consumers a Web site choice that establishes communication with a real person at a 24-hour-a-day service centre. Some of these systems use instant messaging so that the consumer and a customer service person can chat online. With other systems, like AT&T's "Interactive Answers" approach, a service person immediately phones the customer to provide the information or help needed. Other firms are using variations of this approach, including live teleconferencing or messaging over the Internet. The *Globe and Mail* allows consumers to customize their news on www.globeandmail.ca.

Action, including purchase, may be immediate

The action required to make a purchase by interactive media is usually fast and easy. At many Internet sites, such as www.chapters.indigo.ca for example, a consumer can click on an item to place it in a virtual shopping cart, charge it to a credit card, and arrange for shipping.

Custom communications will be more personalized

The traditional principles of communication discussed earlier in the chapter are still important in customer-initiated interactive communication. At the same time, the interactive approach allows the marketer to customize communication to the needs and responses of the consumer. As new approaches develop in this arena, we are seeing more promotion targeted at single-person "segments."[10]

HOW TYPICAL PROMOTION PLANS ARE BLENDED AND INTEGRATED

There is no one right blend

There is no one *right* promotion blend for all situations. Each one must be developed as part of a marketing mix and should be designed to achieve the firm's promotion objectives in each marketing strategy. So let's take a closer look at typical promotion blends in different situations.

Get a push in the channel with promotion to middlemen

When a channel of distribution involves middlemen, their cooperation can be crucial to the success of the overall marketing strategy. **Pushing** (a product through a channel) means using normal promotion effort—personal selling, advertising, and sales promotion—to help sell the whole marketing mix to possible channel members. This approach emphasizes the importance of securing the wholehearted cooperation of channel members to promote the product in the channel and to the final user.

Producers usually take on much of the responsibility for the pushing effort in the channel. However, wholesalers often handle at least some of the promotion to retailers. Similarly, retailers often handle promotion in their local markets. The overall effort is most likely to be effective when all of the individual messages are carefully integrated.

Promotion to middlemen emphasizes personal selling

Salespeople handle most of the important communication with middlemen. Middlemen don't want empty promises. They want to know what they can expect in return for their cooperation and help. A salesperson can answer questions about what promotion will be directed toward the final consumer, each channel member's part in marketing the product, and important details on pricing, markups, promotion assistance, and allowances. A salesperson can also help the firm determine when it should adjust its marketing mix from one middleman to another.

When suppliers offer similar products and compete for attention and shelf space, middlemen usually pay attention to the one with the best profit potential. So sales promotions targeted at middlemen usually focus on short-term arrangements that will improve the middleman's profits. For example, a soft-drink bottler might offer a convenience store a free case of drinks with each two cases it buys. The free case improves the store's profit margin on the whole purchase.

The Hanes ad (on the left) is targeted at parents and kids and designed to stimulate demand and help pull Hanes' popular products through the channel of distribution. The Hanes trade ad (on the right) is targeted at retailers and designed to inform them about the consumer promotion and encourage them to carry Hanes brand products.

Exhibit 13-6
Promotion May Encourage
Pushing in the Channel,
Pulling by Customers, or
Both

Firms run ads in trade magazines to recruit new middlemen or to inform channel members about a new offering. Trade ads usually encourage middlemen to contact the supplier for more information, and then a salesperson takes over.

Push within a firm—with promotion to employees

Some firms emphasize promotion to their own employees—especially salespeople or others in contact with customers. This type of *internal marketing* effort is basically a variation on the pushing approach. One objective of an annual sales meeting is to inform reps about important elements of the marketing strategy—so they'll work together as a team to implement it. Some firms use promotion to motivate employees to provide customer service or achieve higher sales. This is typical in services where the quality of the employees' efforts is a big part of the product. Some ads, for example, use the theme "we like to see you smile." The ads communicate to customers, but also remind employees that the service they provide is crucial to customer satisfaction.

Pulling policy—customer demand pulls the product through the channel

Most producers focus a significant amount of promotion on customers at the end of the channel. This helps to stimulate demand and pull the product through the channel of distribution. **Pulling** means getting customers to ask middlemen for the product.

Pulling and pushing are usually used in combination. Refer to the Hanes ads and Exhibit 13-6. However, if middlemen won't work with a producer—perhaps because they're already carrying a competing brand—a producer may try to use a pulling approach by itself. This involves highly aggressive promotion to final consumers or users—perhaps using coupons or samples—temporarily bypassing middlemen. If the promotion works, the middlemen are forced to carry the product to satisfy customer requests. However, this approach is risky. Customers may lose interest before reluctant middlemen make the product available. At minimum, middlemen should be told about the planned pulling effort—so they can be ready if the promotion succeeds.

Who handles promotion to final customers at the end of the channel varies in different channel systems, depending on the mix of pushing and pulling. Further, the promotion blend typically varies depending on whether customers are final consumers or business users.[11]

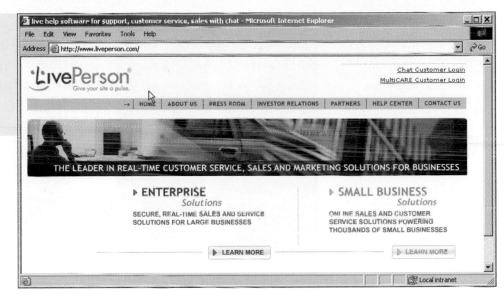

LivePerson helps firms identify the best prospects who visit the firm's Web site so that a salesperson can then immediately reach out and move them through the sales process.

Promotion to final consumers

The large number of consumers almost forces producers of consumer products and retailers to emphasize advertising and sales promotion. Sales promotion—such as coupons, contests, or free samples—builds consumer interest and short-term sales of a product. Effective mass selling may build enough brand familiarity so that little personal selling is needed, as in self-service and discount operations.[12]

Personal selling can be effective too. But aggressive personal selling to final consumers usually is found in expensive channel systems, such as those for higher-priced speciality goods, financial services, furniture, consumer electronics, designer clothing, and automobiles such as BMW's Mini.

Promotion to business customers

Producers and wholesalers that target business customers often emphasize personal selling. This is practical because there are fewer of these customers and their purchases are typically larger. Sales reps can be more flexible in adjusting their companies' appeals to suit each customer—and personal contact is usually required to close a sale. A salesperson is also able to call back later to follow up, resolve any problems, and nurture the relationship with the customer.

While personal selling dominates in business markets, mass selling is necessary too. A typical sales call on a business customer costs about $200.[13] That's because salespeople spend less than half their time actually selling. The rest is consumed by such tasks as travelling, paperwork, sales meetings, and strictly service calls. So it's seldom practical for salespeople to carry the whole promotion load.

Ads in trade magazines or at a B2B e-commerce Web site, for instance, can inform potential customers that a product is available. Most trade ads give a toll-free telephone number, fax number, or Web site address to stimulate direct inquiries. Domestic and international trade shows also help identify prospects. Even so, most sellers who target business customers spend only a small percentage of their promotion budget on mass selling and sales promotion.

Each market segment may need a unique blend

Knowing what type of promotion is typically emphasized with different targets is useful in planning the promotion blend. But each unique market segment may need a separate marketing mix and a different promotion blend. You should be careful not to slip into a shotgun approach when what you really need is a rifle approach—with a more careful aim.

PROMOTION BLENDS VARY OVER THE LIFE CYCLE

Stage of product in its life cycle

The adoption curve helps explain why a new product goes through the product life-cycle stages described in Chapter 10. Promotion blends usually have to change to achieve different promotion objectives at different life-cycle stages.

Market introduction stage—"this new idea is good"

During market introduction, the basic promotion objective is informing. If the product is a really new idea, the promotion must build **primary demand**—demand for the general product idea—not just for the company's own brand. The Mini promotion campaign informed consumers about the advantages of a small car. Video phone service and "smart" appliances (that connect to the Internet) are good examples of product concepts where primary demand is just beginning to grow. There may be few potential innovators during the introduction stage, and personal selling can help find them. Firms also need salespeople to find good channel members and persuade them to carry the new product. Sales promotion may be targeted at salespeople or channel members to get them interested in selling the new product. And sales promotion may also encourage customers to try it.

Market growth stage—"our brand is best"

In the market growth stage, more competitors enter the market, and promotion emphasis shifts from building primary demand to stimulating **selective demand**—demand for a company's own brand. The main job is to persuade customers to buy, and keep buying, the company's product.

Now that there are more potential customers, mass selling becomes more economical. But salespeople and personal selling must still work in the channels, expanding the number of outlets and cementing relationships with channel members.

Market maturity stage—"our brand is better, really"

In the market maturity stage, mass selling and sales promotion may dominate the promotion blends of consumer products firms. Business products may require more aggressive personal selling—perhaps supplemented by more advertising. The total dollars allocated to promotion may rise as competition increases.

If a firm already has high sales—relative to competitors—it may have a real advantage in promotion at this stage. For example, sales of Tylenol tablets are about four times the sales of Motrin's competing tablets. If both Tylenol and Motrin spend the same percentage of sales (say 35 percent) on promotion, Tylenol will spend four times as much as its smaller competitor and will probably communicate to more people.

Firms that have differentiated their marketing mixes may favour mass selling because they have something to talk about. For instance, a firm with a strong brand may use reminder-type advertising or target frequent-buyer promotions at current customers to strengthen the relationship and keep customers loyal. This may be more effective than costly efforts to win customers away from competitors.

However, as a market drifts toward pure competition, some companies resort to price-cutting. This may temporarily increase the number of units sold, but it is also likely to reduce total revenue and the money available for promotion. The temporary sales gains disappear and prices are dragged down even lower when competitors retaliate with their own short-term sales promotions, like price-off coupons. As cash flowing into the business declines, spending may have to be cut back.[14]

Sales decline stage—"let's tell those who still want our product"

During the sales decline stage, the total amount spent on promotion usually decreases as firms try to cut costs to remain profitable. Since some people may still want the product, firms need more targeted promotion to reach these customers.

On the other hand, some firms may increase promotion to try to slow the cycle, at least temporarily. Crayola had almost all of the market for children's crayons, but sales were slowly declining as new kinds of markers came along. Crayola increased ad spending to urge parents to buy their kids a "fresh box."

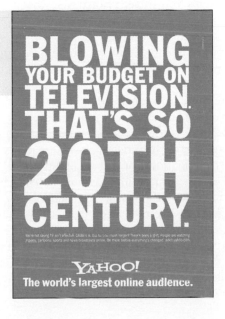

SETTING THE PROMOTION BUDGET

Size of budget affects promotion efficiency and blend

There are some economies of scale in promotion. An ad on national TV might cost less *per person* reached than an ad on local TV. Similarly, citywide radio, TV, and newspapers may be cheaper than neighbourhood newspapers or direct personal contact. But the *total cost* for some mass media may force small firms, or those with small promotion budgets, to use promotion alternatives that are more expensive per contact. For example, a small retailer might want to use local television but find that there is only enough money for a Web page, an ad in the Yellow Pages, and an occasional newspaper ad.

Find the task, budget for it

The most common method of budgeting for promotion expenditures is to compute a percentage of either past sales or sales expected in the future. The virtue of this method is its simplicity. However, just because this mechanical approach is common doesn't mean that it's smart. It leads to expanding marketing expenditures when business is good and cutting back when business is poor. When business is poor, this approach may just make the problem worse—if weak promotion is the reason for declining sales.

Other common methods of budgeting for marketing expenditures are:

1. Match expenditures with competitors.
2. Set the budget as a certain number of cents or dollars per sales unit (by case, by thousand, or by ton) using the past year or estimated year ahead as a base.
3. Base the budget on any uncommitted revenue, perhaps including budgeted profits. Companies with limited resources may use this approach. Or a firm may be willing to sacrifice some or all of its current profits for future sales—that is, it looks at promotion spending as an *investment* in future growth.
4. Base the budget on the job to be done. For example, the spending level might be based on the number of new customers desired and the percentage of current customers that the firm must retain to leverage investments in already established relationships. This is called the **task method**—basing the budget on the job to be done.

Task method can lead to budgeting without agony

In the light of our continuing focus on planning marketing strategies to reach objectives, the most sensible approach to budgeting promotion expenditures is the task method. It helps you to set priorities so that the money you spend produces specific results. In fact, this approach makes sense for *any* marketing expenditure, but here we'll focus on promotion.

A practical approach is to determine which promotion objectives are most important and which promotion methods are most economical and effective for the communication tasks relevant to each objective. The costs of these tasks are then totalled—to determine how much should be budgeted for promotion (just as money is allocated for other marketing activities required by the strategy). In other words, the firm can assemble its total promotion budget directly from detailed plans rather than by simply relying on historical patterns or ratios. The Mini campaign created awareness in a cost-effective manner, avoiding costly TV ads.

This method also helps to eliminate budget fights between managers responsible for different promotion methods who see themselves as pitted against each other for limited budget dollars. The specialists may still make their own suggestions about how to perform tasks. But then the budget allocations are based on the most effective ways of getting things done, not on what the firm did last year, what some competitor does, or even on internal politics. With this approach, different promotion specialists are also more likely to recognize that they must all work together to achieve truly integrated marketing communications.[15]

CONCLUSION

Promotion is an important part of any marketing mix. Most consumers and intermediate customers can choose from among many products. To be successful, a producer must not only offer a good product at a reasonable price but also inform potential customers about the product and where they can buy it. Further, producers must tell wholesalers and retailers in the channel about their product and their marketing mix. These middlemen, in turn, must use promotion to reach their customers.

The promotion blend should fit logically into the strategy being developed to satisfy a particular target market. Strategy planning needs to state *what* should be communicated to the target market and *how*. The overall promotion objective is to affect buying behaviour, but the basic promotion objectives are informing, persuading, and reminding.

Three basic promotion methods can be used to reach these objectives. Behavioural science findings can help firms combine various promotion methods for effective communication.

An action-oriented framework called AIDA can help marketing managers plan promotion blends. But the marketing manager has the final responsibility for combining the promotion methods into one integrated promotion blend for each marketing mix. The task method of budgeting is practical for most promotional campaigns.

In this chapter, we considered some basic concepts that apply to all areas of promotion. In the next two chapters, we'll discuss personal selling, advertising, and sales promotion in more detail.

KEY TERMS

promotion, 358

integrated marketing communications, 361

AIDA model, 363

communication process, 363

source, 363

receiver, 363

noise, 364

encoding, 364

decoding, 364

message channel, 364

pushing, 371

pulling, 372

primary demand, 374

selective demand, 374

task method, 376

QUESTIONS AND PROBLEMS

1. Briefly explain the nature of the three basic promotion methods available to a marketing manager. What are the main strengths and limitations of each?

2. In your own words, discuss the integrated marketing communications concept. Explain what its emphasis on "consistent" and "complete" messages implies with respect to promotion blends.

3. Relate the three basic promotion objectives to the four jobs (AIDA) of promotion using a specific example.

4. Discuss the communication process in relation to a producer's promotion of an accessory product—say, a new electronic security system businesses use to limit access to areas where they store confidential records.

5. If a company wants its promotion to appeal to a new group of target customers in a foreign country, how can it protect against its communications being misinterpreted?

6. Promotion has been the target of considerable criticism. What specific types of promotion are probably the object of this criticism? Give a specific example that illustrates your thinking.

7. With direct-response promotion, customers provide feedback to marketing communications. How can a marketing manager use this feedback to improve the effectiveness of the overall promotion blend?

8. How can a promotion manager target a message to a certain target market with electronic media (like the Internet) when the customer initiates the communication? Give an example.

9. What promotion blend would be most appropriate for producers of the following established products? Assume average- to large-sized firms in each case and support your answer.

  a. Chocolate candy bar.
  b. Car batteries.
  c. Pantyhose.
  d. Castings for truck engines.
  e. A special computer used by manufacturers for control of production equipment.
  f. Inexpensive plastic rainhats.

10. A small company has developed an innovative new spray-on glass cleaner that prevents the buildup of electrostatic dust on computer screens and TVs. Give examples of some low-cost ways the firm might effectively promote its product. Be certain to consider both push and pull approaches.

11. Would promotion be successful in expanding the general demand for: (a) almonds, (b) air travel, (c) golf clubs, (d) walking shoes, (e) high-octane unleaded gasoline, (f) single-serving, frozen gourmet dinners, and (g) bricks? Explain why or why not in each case.

12. If a marketing manager uses the task method to budget for marketing promotions, are competitors' promotion spending levels ignored? Explain your thinking and give an example that supports your point of view.

13. Discuss the potential conflict among the various promotion managers. How could this be reduced?

COMPUTER–AIDED PROBLEM

13. Selecting a Communications Channel

RESOURCE REMINDER

Helen Troy, owner of three Sound Haus stereo equipment stores, is deciding what message channel (advertising medium) to use to promote her newest store. Her current promotion blend includes direct-mail ads that are effective for reaching her current customers. She also has knowledgeable salespeople who work well with consumers once they're in the store. However, a key objective in opening a new store is to attract new customers. Her best prospects are professionals in the 25–44 age range with incomes over $38,000 a year. But only some of the people in this group are audiophiles who want the top-of-the-line brands she carries. Troy has decided to use local advertising to reach new customers.

Troy narrowed her choice to two advertising media: an FM radio station and a biweekly magazine that focuses on entertainment in her city. Many of the magazine's readers are out-of-town visitors interested in concerts, plays, and restaurants. They usually buy stereo equipment at home. But the magazine's audience research shows that many local professionals do subscribe to the magazine. Troy doesn't think that the objective can be achieved with a single ad. However, she believes that ads in six issues will generate good local awareness with her target market. In addition, the magazine's colour format will let her present the prestige image she wants to convey in an ad. She thinks that will help convert aware prospects to buyers. Specialists at a local advertising agency will prepare a high-impact ad for $2,000, and then Troy will pay for the magazine space.

The FM radio station targets an audience similar to Troy's own target market. She knows repeated ads will be needed to be sure that most of her target audience is exposed to her ads. Troy thinks it will take daily ads for several months to create adequate awareness among her target market. The FM station will provide an announcer and prepare a tape of Troy's ad for a one-time fee of $200. All she has to do is tell the station what the message content for the ad should say.

Both the radio station and the magazine gave Troy reports summarizing recent audience research. She decides that comparing the two media in a spreadsheet will help her make a better decision.

a. Based on the data displayed on the initial spreadsheet, which message channel (advertising medium) would you recommend to Troy? Why?

b. The agency that offered to prepare Troy's magazine ad will prepare a fully produced radio ad—including a musical jingle—for $2,500. The agency claims that its musical ad will have much more impact than the ad the radio station will create. The agency says its ad should produce the same results as the station ad with 20 percent fewer insertions. If the agency claim is correct, would it be wise for Troy to pay the agency to produce the ad?

c. The agency will not guarantee that its custom-produced radio ad will reach Troy's objective—making 80 percent of the prospects aware of the new store. Troy wants to see how lower levels of awareness—between 50 percent and 70 percent—would affect the advertising cost per buyer and the cost per aware prospect. Use the analysis feature to vary the percent of prospects who become aware. Prepare a table showing the effect on the two kinds of costs. What are the implications of your analysis?

If you want to read the cases and view the video cases that accompany this chapter, visit the *Basic Marketing* Online Learning Centre at: **www.mcgrawhill.ca/olc/perreault**. Along with these cases and video cases, the OLC also has the software and user guide for this chapter's Computer-Aided Problem, as well as exercises, quizzes, articles, links, and other *interactive* content that will help you with your studies.

WHEN YOU FINISH THIS CHAPTER, YOU SHOULD

1. Understand the importance and nature of personal selling.

2. Know the three basic sales tasks and what the various kinds of salespeople can be expected to do.

3. Know how sales technology affects the way sales are performed.

4. Know what the sales manager must do—including selecting, training, and organizing salespeople—to carry out the personal selling job.

5. Understand how the right compensation plan can help motivate and control salespeople.

6. Understand when and where to use the three types of sales presentations.

Personal Selling

Salespeople are communicators who build relationships. And there's nobody better at doing that than Harry Rosen. Soon after Harry Rosen opened his first menswear store in Toronto in 1954, he began filling out note cards to record not only the purchase history but also the favourite hobbies and other personal tidbits about each client. It was just one of his methods for building customer relationships.

Today, Harry Rosen Inc. (HRI), run by Harry Rosen's eldest son Larry, still relies on close-knit customer relationships to drive its business, but it operates on a much larger scale. The HRI enterprise now encompasses 16 stores across Canada, employs 600 associates, and rings up more than $150 million in annual sales, commanding about 40 percent of the Canadian market for high-end men's clothing.

"Customer service is the omnipresent buzz term these days," says chairman and CEO Larry Rosen. "The reality is that everybody talks about it, but very few do it. We don't perceive ourselves as being in the clothing business. We don't just sell suits and sport jackets. It's a relationship-based business. My business is to get to know you, to have you build a relationship with one of my highly trained associates. I want to be your clothier for life. The whole key to our business is loyal clients. I strongly believe we have a corporate culture that has a love of quality and a love of clients. And building customer relationships is a managed process."

How does HRI maintain its "one client at time" service levels while dealing with so many clients? Larry Rosen hands much of the credit to a customer relationship management information system, developed by the software firm GERS Retail Systems. The technology enables HRI to capture "tremendous amounts of personal information" that associates continually use to build relationships with customers, he says. "We want to know about them —not just their sizes, but where they work, their family structure, their lifestyle and so on—all so we can advise them," says Rosen. HRI also uses the system to profile clients in order to alert them of special store events. For example, one of Harry Rosen's stores recently invited about 500 key customers to an in-store concert with Adam Cohen, the son of folk legend Leonard Cohen. Associates

also use data from the system to alert customers about when a shipment of one of their favourite brands arrives.

HRI is continually reaching out to its customer base, whether through phone calls and personal e-mails or its quarterly o mail newsletter and biannual catalogue. It's all a part of the retailer's strategy to convert prospects into clients and build lifelong bonds with frequent clients.

"We want to have that ongoing relationship with them," says Rosen. "We want our associates to grow with him [the customer] and the store to grow with him. It's not about selling him the max, but selling him the right stuff and consulting with him in the right way to make him into a Harry Rosen fanatic." Rosen says HRI invests more than $1 million annually in associate training on its customer relationship management IT systems, as well as in proper selling techniques. The sales associate success rate at HRI is evident in the firm's low employee turnover. In fact, several associates have worked the floor at a Harry Rosen store for more than 20 years, and a few for more than 40 years, says Rosen. "Once you've been with us for two or three years, the turnover is negligible," he notes.

On Saturdays, Harry Rosen, the man who epitomizes the brand, can usually be found at his Bloor Street or Yorkdale store in Toronto, serving customers. But the company's chairman doesn't limit his in-store presence to Toronto. Harry also travels across the country each season promoting made-to-measure clothing from his house label, J.P. Tilford by Samuelsohn. This event, the J.P. Tilford by Samuelsohn Made-to-Measure Trunk Show, provides customers a chance to meet and discuss their clothing needs with Harry himself. He takes their measurements personally and recommends the most appropriate garment based on their needs and tastes.[1]

THE IMPORTANCE AND ROLE OF PERSONAL SELLING

Salespeople are communicators who build relationships

Promotion is communicating with potential customers. As the Harry Rosen case suggests, personal selling is often the best way to do it. While face-to-face with prospects, salespeople can get more attention than an advertisement or a display. They can adjust what they say or do to the prospect's interests, needs, questions, and feedback. If, and when, the prospect is ready to buy, the salesperson is there to ask for the order. And afterward, the salesperson works to be certain that the customer is satisfied and will buy again in the future.

Personal selling requires strategy decisions

In this chapter, we'll discuss the importance and nature of personal selling at the manufacturer, wholesale, and retail level so you'll understand the strategy decisions sales and marketing managers face. These strategy decisions are shown in Exhibit 14-1.

We'll also discuss a number of frameworks and how-to approaches that guide these strategy decisions. Because these approaches apply equally to domestic and international markets, we won't emphasize that distinction in this chapter. This does not mean, however, that personal selling techniques don't vary from one country to

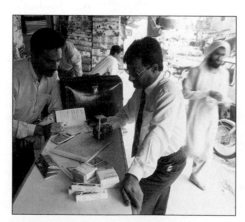

another. To the contrary, in dealing with *any* customer, the salesperson must adjust for cultural influences and other factors that might affect communication. For example, a Japanese customer and an Arab customer might respond differently to subtle aspects of a salesperson's behaviour. The Arab customer might expect to be very close to a salesperson, perhaps only two feet away, while they talk. The Japanese customer might consider that distance rude. Similarly, what topics of discussion are considered sensitive, how messages are interpreted, and which negotiating styles

Exhibit 14-1   Strategy Planning for Personal Selling

are used vary from one country to another. A salesperson must know how to communicate effectively with each customer—wherever and whoever that customer is.[2]

Personal selling is important

Personal selling is absolutely essential in the promotion blends of some firms. Consider how you would feel if you regularly had to meet payrolls and somehow, almost miraculously, your salespeople kept coming in with orders just in time to keep the business profitable.

Personal selling is often a company's largest single operating expense. This is another reason why it is important to understand sales management decisions. Bad ones are costly in both lost sales and in actual out-of-pocket expenses.

Helping to buy is good selling

Good salespeople don't just try to *sell* the customer. Rather, they try to *help the customer buy*—by understanding the customer's needs and presenting the advantages and disadvantages of their products. The opening case on Harry Rosen exemplifies this type of thinking. Such helpfulness results in satisfied customers and long-term relationships. And strong relationships often form the basis for a competitive advantage, especially in business markets.

You may think in terms of an old-time stereotype of a salesperson: a bag of wind with no more to offer than a funny story, a big expense account, and an engaging grin. But that isn't true anymore. Old-time salespeople are being replaced by real professionals—problem solvers—who have something definite to contribute to their employers *and* their customers.

Salespeople represent the whole company—and customers too

The salesperson is often a representative of the whole company—responsible for explaining its total effort to customers rather than just pushing products. The salesperson may provide information about products, explain company policies, and even negotiate prices or diagnose technical problems.

The sales rep is often the only link between the firm and its customers, especially if customers are far away. When a number of people from the firm work with the customer organization—which is common when suppliers and customers form close relationships—it is usually the sales rep who coordinates the relationship for his or her firm.

The salesperson also represents the *customer* back inside the selling firm. Recall that feedback is an essential part of both the communication process *and* the basic management process of planning, implementing, and control. For example, it's likely to be the sales rep who explains to the production manager why a customer is unhappy with product quality or to the e-commerce specialist how better order status information available on the Web site could cut the customer's costs.

As evidence of these changing responsibilities, some companies give their salespeople such titles as account representative, field manager, sales consultant, market specialist, or sales engineer.

Sales force aids in market information function as well

The sales force can aid in the marketing information function too. The sales rep may be the first to hear about a new competitor or a competitor's new strategy. And sales reps who are well attuned to customers' needs can be a key source of ideas for new products or new uses for existing products.

Material Sciences Corporation developed a product called Quiet Steel, two thin layers of steel bonded together to absorb vibration so that it doesn't rattle. A sales rep who worked with the Ford team developing the new F-150 truck probed to understand where Ford was trying to reduce noise and recommended how Quiet Steel could help. Feedback to the company about the most promising applications helps Quiet Steel reps who call on other car makers pursue similar applications. And the R&D department for Quiet Steel benefits from hearing from the sales reps about applications where the current product isn't quite right, but where there might be an opportunity for a new product.[3]

CRM—an ongoing process

A good salesperson cultivates an ongoing relationship with their customers. This relationship must be built and nurtured over time. The concept of customer relationship management (CRM) refers to this ongoing process. Just as buyers invest in the products a company offers, so must the salespeople invest in their customers. Good customer relationship management takes time but is crucial to the success of the selling effort.

Salespeople can be strategy planners too

Some salespeople are expected to be marketing managers in their own territories. And some become marketing managers by default because top management hasn't provided detailed strategy guidelines. Either way, the salesperson may have choices about (1) what target customers to aim at, (2) which particular products to emphasize, (3) which middlemen to rely on or help, (4) how to use promotion money, and (5) how to adjust prices. A salesperson who can put together profitable strategies and implement them well can rise very rapidly. The opportunity is there for those prepared and willing to work.[4]

WHAT KINDS OF PERSONAL SELLING ARE NEEDED?

If a firm has too few salespeople, or the wrong kind, some important personal selling tasks may not be completed. And having too many salespeople wastes money. In addition, the balance that is right may change over time with other changes in strategy or the market environment. That's why many firms have to restructure their sales forces.

One of the difficulties of determining the right number and kind of salespeople is that every sales job is different. While an engineer or accountant can look forward to fairly specific duties, the salesperson's job changes constantly. However, there are three basic types of sales tasks. This gives us a starting point for understanding what selling tasks need to be done and how many people are needed to do them.

Personal selling is divided into three tasks

The three **basic sales tasks** are order-getting, order-taking, and supporting. For convenience, we'll describe salespeople by these terms—referring to their primary task—*although one person may do all three tasks in some situations*.

ORDER GETTERS DEVELOP NEW BUSINESS RELATIONSHIPS

Order getters are concerned with establishing relationships with new customers and developing new business. **Order-getting** means seeking possible buyers with a well-organized sales presentation designed to sell a good, service, or idea.

Order getters must know what they're talking about, not just be personal contacts. Order-getting salespeople normally are well paid—many earn more than $80,000 a year.

Producers' order getters—find new opportunities

Producers of all kinds of products, especially business products, have a great need for order getters. They use order getters to locate new prospects, open new accounts, see new opportunities, and help establish and build channel relationships.

Top-level customers are more interested in ways to save or make more money than in technical details. Good order getters cater to this interest. They help the customer identify ways to solve problems; then they sell concepts and ideas, not just physical products. The goods and services they supply are merely the means of achieving the customer's end.

To be effective at this sort of "solutions selling," an order getter often needs to understand a customer's whole business as well as technical details about the product and its applications. For example, a salesperson for automated manufacturing equipment must understand a prospect's production process as well as the technical details of converting to computer-controlled equipment.

Order getters for professional services—and other products where service is a crucial element of the marketing mix—face a special challenge. The customer usually can't inspect a service before deciding to buy. The order getter's communication and relationship with the customer may be the only basis on which to evaluate the quality of the supplier.

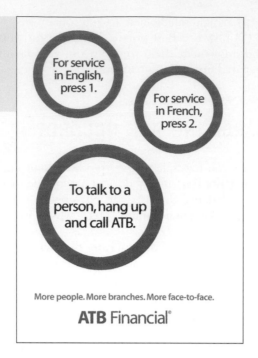

For service
in English,
press 1.

For service
in French,
press 2.

To talk to a
person, hang up
and call ATB.

More people. More branches. More face-to-face.

ATB Financial®

Wholesalers' order getters—almost hand it to the customer

Agent middlemen often are order getters—particularly the more aggressive manufacturers' agents and brokers. They face the same tasks as producers' order getters. But, unfortunately for them, once the order-getting is done and the customers become established and loyal, producers may try to eliminate the agents and save money with their own order takers.

Progressive merchant wholesaler sales reps should be consultants and store advisors rather than just order takers. Such order getters become retailers' partners in the job of moving goods from the wholesale warehouse through the retail store to consumers. These order getters almost become a part of the retailer's staff—helping to solve consumers' problems, train employees, conduct demonstrations, and plan advertising, special promotions, and other retailing activities.

| Retail order getters influence consumer behaviour | Convincing consumers about the value of products they haven't seriously considered takes a high level of personal selling ability. Order getters for unsought consumer products must help customers see how a new product can satisfy needs now being filled by something else. Without order getters, many common products—ranging from mutual funds to air conditioners—might have died in the market introduction stage. The order getter helps bring products out of the introduction stage into the market growth stage. |

Order getters are also helpful for selling *heterogeneous* shopping products. Consumers shop for many of these items on the basis of suitability and value. They welcome useful information.

ORDER TAKERS NURTURE RELATIONSHIPS TO KEEP THE BUSINESS COMING

Order takers sell to the regular or established customers, complete most sales transactions, and maintain relationships with their customers. After a customer becomes interested in a firm's products through an order getter or supporting salesperson or through advertising or sales promotion, an order taker usually answers any final questions and completes the sale. **Order-taking** is the routine completion of sales made regularly to target customers. It usually requires ongoing follow-up to make certain that the customer is totally satisfied.

| Producers' order takers—train, explain, and collaborate | Order takers work on improving the whole relationship with their accounts, not just on completing a single sale. Even in e-commerce, where customers place routine orders with computerized order systems and EDI, order takers do a variety of important jobs that are essential to the business relationship. Someone has to explain details, make adjustments, handle complaints, explain new prices or terms, place sales promotion materials, and keep customers informed of new developments. An order taker who fails to meet a customer's expectations on any of these activities might jeopardize the relationship and future sales. Dell computers uses well-trained order takers to sell successfully. |

| Friendly and capable retail order takers can play an important role in building good relations with customers. | |

Producers' order takers often have a regular route with many calls. To handle these calls well, they must have energy, persistence, and a friendly personality that wears well over time. They sometimes have to take the heat when something goes wrong with some other element of the marketing mix.

Firms sometimes use order-taking jobs to train potential order getters and managers. Such jobs give them an opportunity to meet customers and better understand their needs. And frequently, they run into some order-getting opportunities. Order takers who are alert to order-getting possibilities can make the big difference in generating new sales. Some firms lose sales just because no one ever asks for the order.

Wholesalers' order takers—not getting orders but keeping them

While producers' order takers usually handle relatively few items, wholesalers' order takers often sell thousands of items. Sales reps who handle that many items may single out a few of the newer or more profitable items for special attention, but it's not possible to give aggressive sales effort to many. So the main job of wholesalers' order takers is to maintain close contact with customers, place orders, and check to be sure the company fills orders promptly. Order takers also handle any adjustments or complaints and generally act as liaisons between the company and its customers.

Retail order takers—often they are poor salesclerks

Order-taking may be almost mechanical at the retail level—for example, at the supermarket checkout counter. Some retail clerks perform poorly because they aren't paid much—often only the minimum wage. Even so, retail order takers play a vital role in a retailer's marketing mix. Customers expect prompt and friendly service. They will find a new place to shop, or to do their banking or have their car serviced, rather than deal with a salesclerk who is rude or acts annoyed by having to complete a sale.

SUPPORTING SALES FORCE INFORMS AND PROMOTES IN THE CHANNEL

Supporting salespeople help the order-oriented salespeople—but they don't try to get orders themselves. Their activities are aimed at enhancing the relationship with the customer and getting sales in the long run. For the short run, however, they are ambassadors of goodwill who may provide specialized services and information. Almost all supporting salespeople work for producers or middlemen who do this supporting work for producers. There are two types of supporting salespeople: missionary salespeople and technical specialists.

Missionary salespeople can increase sales

Missionary salespeople are supporting salespeople who work for producers—calling on their middlemen and their customers. They try to develop goodwill and stimulate demand, help the middlemen train their salespeople, and often take orders for delivery by the middlemen. In the pharmaceutical industry, sales reps call on doctors on a regular basis. Missionary salespeople are sometimes called *merchandisers* or *detailers*.

Producers who rely on merchant wholesalers or e-commerce to obtain widespread distribution often use missionary salespeople. The sales rep can give a promotion boost to a product that otherwise wouldn't get much attention because it's just one of many. A missionary salesperson for Vicks' cold remedy products, for example, might visit druggists during the cold season and encourage them to use a special end-of-aisle display for Vicks' cough syrup—and then help set it up. The wholesaler that supplies the drugstore would benefit from any increased sales, but might not take the time to urge use of the special display.

An imaginative missionary salesperson can double or triple sales. Naturally, this doesn't go unnoticed. Missionary sales jobs are often a route to order-oriented jobs.

Technical specialists are experts who know product applications

Technical specialists are supporting salespeople who provide technical assistance to order-oriented salespeople. Technical specialists are often science or engineering graduates with the know-how to understand the customer's applications and explain the advantages of the company's product. They are usually more skilled in showing the technical details of their product than in trying to persuade customers to buy it. Before the specialist's visit, an order getter probably has stimulated interest. The technical specialist provides the details. Bombardier Aerospace uses technical specialists on their sales force—essential in such a complex industry.

Three tasks may have to be blended

We have described three sales tasks—order-getting, order-taking, and supporting. However, a particular salesperson might be given two, or all three, of these tasks. Ten percent of a particular job may be order-getting, 80 percent order-taking, and the additional 10 percent supporting. Another company might have many different people handling the different sales tasks. This can lead to **team selling**—when different people work together on a specific account. Sometimes members of a sales team are not from the sales department at all. If improving the relationship with the customer calls for inputs from the quality control manager, then that person becomes a part of the team, at least temporarily.

Producers of high-ticket items often use team selling. Bell uses team selling to sell office communications systems for a whole business. Different specialists handle different parts of the job—but the whole team coordinates its efforts to achieve the desired result.[5] SNC-Lavalin uses team selling for their engineering and infrastructure management services.

THE RIGHT STRUCTURE HELPS ASSIGN RESPONSIBILITY

A sales manager must organize the sales force so that all the necessary tasks are done well. A large organization might have different salespeople specializing by different selling tasks *and* by the target markets they serve.

Different target markets need different selling tasks

Sales managers often divide sales force responsibilities based on the type of customer involved. For example, Bigelow—a company that makes quality carpet for homes and office buildings—divided its sales force into two groups of specialists. Some Bigelow salespeople call only on architects to help them choose the best type of carpet for new office buildings. These reps know all the technical details, such as how well a certain carpet fibre will wear or its effectiveness in reducing noise from office equipment. Often no selling is involved because the architect only suggests specifications and doesn't actually buy the carpet.

Other Bigelow salespeople call on retail carpet stores. These reps encourage the store manager to keep a variety of Bigelow carpets in stock. They also introduce new products, help train the store's salespeople, and try to solve any problems that occur.

Big accounts get special treatment

Very large customers often require special selling effort—and relationships with them are treated differently. Moen, a maker of plumbing fixtures, has a regular sales force to call on building material wholesalers and an elite **major accounts sales force** that sells directly to large accounts—like RONA or other major retail chains that carry plumbing fixtures.

You can see why this sort of special attention is justified when you consider Procter & Gamble's relationship with Wal-Mart. Wal-Mart accounts for one-fourth or more of the total North American sales in many of the product categories in which P&G competes. For instance, Wal-Mart sells about one-third of the toothpaste in the U.S. If P&G wants to grow its 23 percent share of the toothpaste market, it has to make certain that it stimulates an effective sales effort with Wal-Mart. It's understandable why the P&G sales team that calls on Wal-Mart lives in Bentonville, Arkansas, where Wal-Mart is based.[6]

Some salespeople specialize in telephone selling

Some firms have a group of salespeople who specialize in **telemarketing**—using the telephone to "call" on customers or prospects. In Chapter 13, we highlighted the consumer backlash to the use of "cold call" telemarketing for prospecting. However, the reception to telemarketing in business markets is often quite different.

In business markets, a telemarketing sales force can often build profitable relationships with small or hard-to-reach customers the firm might otherwise have to ignore. Telemarketing is also used to extend personal selling efforts to new target markets or increase the frequency of contact with current customers. The big advantage of telemarketing in these situations is that it saves time and money for the seller, and it gives customers a fast and easy way to solve a purchasing problem. For example, many firms use toll-free telephone lines to make it convenient for customers to call the telemarketing sales force for assistance or to place an order. Firms also rely heavily on telemarketing to provide support a customer may need in an e-commerce situation.[7]

Sales tasks are done in sales territories

Often companies organize selling tasks on the basis of a **sales territory**—a geographic area that is the responsibility of one salesperson or several working together. A territory might be a region of a country, a state, or part of a city, depending on the market potential. An airplane manufacturer like Boeing might consider a whole country as *part* of a sales territory for one salesperson.

Carefully set territories can reduce travel time and the cost of sales calls. Assigning territories can also help reduce confusion about who has responsibility for a set of selling tasks. Consider the Hyatt Hotel chain. A few years ago, each hotel had its own salespeople to get bookings for big conferences and business meetings. That meant that people who had responsibility for selecting meeting locations might be called on by sales reps from 20 or 30 different Hyatt hotels. Now, the Hyatt central office divides up responsibility for working with specific accounts; one rep calls on an account and then tries to sell space in the Hyatt facility that best meets the customer's needs.

Sometimes simple geographic division isn't easy. A company may have different products that require very different knowledge or selling skills—even if products sell in the same territory or to the same customer. For example, Du Pont makes special films for hospital X-ray departments as well as chemicals used in laboratory blood tests.

Size of sales force depends on workload

Once the important selling tasks are specified and the responsibilities divided, the sales manager must decide how many salespeople are needed. The first step is estimating how much work can be done by one person in some time period. Then the sales manager can make an educated guess about how many people are required in total.

Some managers forget that over time the right number of salespeople may change as selling tasks change. Then when a problem becomes obvious, they try to change everything in a hurry—a big mistake. Consideration of what type of salespeople and how many should be ongoing. If the sales force needs to be reduced, it doesn't make sense to let a lot of people go all at once, especially when that could be avoided with some planning.

Exhibit 14-2
Examples of Possible
Personal Selling Emphasis in
Some Different Business-
Market Selling Situations

Standardized information
exchanged on a recurring basis
(orders, invoices, delivery status,
product information, prices)

High — Emphasis on standardized e-commerce (with customer service) | Emphasis on both personal selling & customized e-commerce

Low — Emphasis on digital self-service | Emphasis on personal selling

Low | High

Relationship building required
(problem solving, coordination, support, cooperation)

**E-commerce
sometimes
substitutes for
personal selling**

Some tasks that have traditionally been handled by a salesperson can now be handled effectively and at lower cost by e-commerce systems. The nature of the selling situation that the firm faces may influence which approach makes the most sense and how many salespeople are really needed. See Exhibit 14-2.

A salesperson is required in important selling situations where there is a need to create and build relationships. Here the salesperson focuses on tasks like creative problem solving, persuading, coordinating among people who do different jobs, and finding ways to support the customer—Harry Rosen sales personnel solve wardrobe problems for their customers. On the other hand, information technology is cost effective for handling needs related to the recurring exchange of standardized information (such as inventory, orders, and delivery status). Similarly, details of product specifications and prices can be organized at a Web site. Of course, there should be some way to provide good customer service when needs arise. In a complex relationship, using technology for standard information frees the sales rep to spend time on value-added communication.

When relationship building by a sales rep is not required and there is not a recurring need for routine information, a firm may be able to meet customer needs best by providing digital self-service. This is basically the role of ATMs for banks—to service customers who don't want to wait until a teller is available. Similarly, Amazon's virtual shopping carts play this role. But digital self-service can be more sophisticated. Some firms provide "intelligent agents" at their Web sites. An intelligent agent is a computer program that helps customers solve their own problems. Similarly, a wholesaler's Web site might provide an agent to help retailers forecast demand for a new product based on information about their local market areas.

The total amount of personal selling effort justified in any of these situations may depend on other factors, including how important the customer is. Further, we've focused on technology that substitutes for personal contact by a salesperson. But marketing managers also need to make decisions about providing sales technology support to help salespeople communicate more effectively.

INFORMATION TECHNOLOGY PROVIDES TOOLS TO DO THE JOB

**Changes in how
sales tasks are
handled**

How sales tasks and responsibilities are planned and handled is changing in many companies because of the new sales technology tools that are available. It is usually the sales manager's job—perhaps with help from specialists in technology—to decide what types of tools are needed and how they will be used.

SALESPEOPLE WORK SMARTER —WITH THEIR FINGERTIPS

Tablet PCs, PDAs, BlackBerrys, and laptops help more salespeople work smarter, not just harder. Salespeople use computers in many different ways.

Without a laptop, it was impossible for a wholesaler's salespeople to master Cincinnati Milacron's product line. Now a computer asks a series of questions and then helps the salesperson figure out which of 65,000 grinding wheels and hundreds of cutting fluids to sell to each metal shop. After adding this system, Milacron doubled its market share—without adding any new salespeople.

Sales reps for Crown Beer Distributors found that laptops were too bulky to take with them when they called on accounts along their routes. However, a handheld tablet PC was just right for the task. The sales reps enter inventory data and orders right into the tablet. The screen is small, but they can instantly pull up whatever information a customer may want to see. With everything at their fingertips, some salespeople save an hour each day—and in the process handle required administrative reporting without it becoming tedious. As the president of the firm noted, "When you start to multiply that out for distributors with 20 or 30 salespeople, that's a significant amount of savings."

Salespeople for Metropolitan Life Insurance company use laptops to help customers analyze the financial implications of different investments. For example, when the manager of a pension fund wanted to see what would happen if she switched money from one investment to another, the salesperson used spreadsheet software on the laptop to do the analysis—on the spot. The customer was convinced, and the sales rep closed a $633,000 sale.

Herman Miller, the office equipment company, provides dealers who sell its furniture with software that allows their sales reps to do a better job in a variety of tasks ranging from competitor analysis to preparation of realistic three-dimensional graphics that show an arrangement of furniture in a customer's office space. The competitor database provides very useful information about the limitations of office furniture available from many other firms. For instance, a sales rep learned that a prospect was leaning toward buying a competitor's office cubicles. She got back on track when the database revealed that the cubicles had no electrical outlets.

Results like these explain why the number of companies equipping salespeople with computers is growing so rapidly. New computers that feature built-in DVD drives (to handle massive amounts of information, including full-motion video for demonstrations and presentations), wireless Internet access, and the power to handle e-commerce applications are attracting even more attention. Further, Web-enabled PDAs and cell phones now offer capabilities once reserved only for computers, providing a link to company databases and all the resources of the Internet.[8]

To get a sense of what is involved, consider a day in the life of a sales rep for a large consumer packaged goods firm. Over a hasty breakfast, she plans the day's sales calls on her laptop's organizer, logs onto the company network, and sorts through a dozen e-mail messages she finds there. One is from a buyer for a supermarket chain. Sales in the chain's paper towel category are off 10 percent, and he wants to know if the rep can help. The rep downloads sales trend data for the chain and its competitors from her firm's intranet. A spreadsheet analysis of the data reveals that the sales decline is due to new competition from warehouse clubs. After a conference call with a brand manager and a company sales promotion specialist to seek advice, she prepares a PowerPoint presentation, complete with a proposed shelf-space plan, that recommends that the buyer promote larger size packages of both her company's and competitors' brands. Before leaving home, the rep e-mails an advance copy of the report to the buyer and her manager. In her car, she calls the buyer to schedule an appointment.

New software and hardware provide a competitive advantage

As in the example given above, sales reps today rely on support from an array of software and hardware that was hardly imaginable even a decade ago. Software for spreadsheet sales analysis, digital presentations, time management, sales forecasting, customer contact, and shelf-space management is at the salesperson's fingertips.

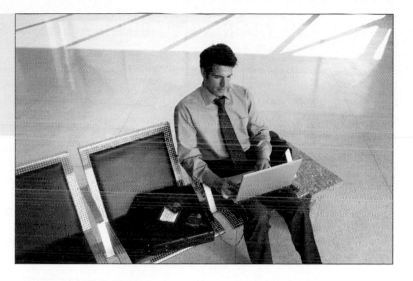

Information technology is making the modern sales force more efficient and giving salespeople new ways to meet the needs of their customers while achieving the objectives of their jobs.

Commonplace hardware includes everything from PDAs with wireless Internet access to personal videoconferencing systems. In many situations, these technologies give sales reps new ways to meet customers' needs while achieving the objectives of their jobs. Sales representatives from McGraw-Hill Ryerson bring their technical equipment on sales calls to university and college professors. This allows the sales rep to access the most up-to-date information during a sales call.

The basic sales tasks are not different, but the tools change how well the job is done. Yet this is not simply a matter that is best left to individual sales reps. Use of these tools may be necessary just to compete effectively. For example, if a customer expects a sales rep to access data on past sales and provide an updated sales forecast, a sales organization that does not have this capability will be at a real disadvantage in keeping that customer's business.

On the other hand, these tools have costs. There is an obvious expense of buying the technology. But there is also the training cost of keeping everyone up-to-date. Often that is not a simple matter. Some salespeople who have done the sales job well for a long time "the old-fashioned way" resent being told that they have to change what they are doing, even if it's what customers expect. So if a firm expects salespeople to be able to use these technologies, that requirement needs to be included in selecting and training people for the job.[9]

Customers who rent heavy construction equipment want to deal with a knowledgeable salesperson. So Cat selects salespeople who have experience with the applications for which the equipment will be used and gives them training on Cat products and new developments in the market.

SOUND SELECTION AND TRAINING TO BUILD A SALES FORCE

Selecting good salespeople takes judgment, plus

It is important to hire *well-qualified* salespeople who will do a good job. But selection in many companies is done without serious thought about exactly what kind of person the firm needs. Managers may hire friends and relations, or whoever is available, because they feel that the only qualifications for sales jobs are a friendly personality. This approach leads to poor sales and costly sales force turnover.

Progressive companies are more careful. They constantly update a list of possible job candidates. They invite applications at the company's Web site. They schedule candidates for multiple interviews with various executives and do thorough background checks. Unfortunately, such techniques don't guarantee success. But a systematic approach based on several different inputs results in a better sales force.

One problem in selecting salespeople is that two different sales jobs with identical titles may involve very different selling tasks and require different skills. A carefully prepared job description helps avoid this problem.

Job descriptions should be in writing and specific

A **job description** is a written statement of what a salesperson is expected to do. It might list 10 to 20 specific tasks—as well as routine prospecting and sales report writing. Each company must write its own job specifications. And it should provide clear guidelines about what selling tasks the job involves. This is critical to determine the kind of salespeople who should be selected—and later it provides a basis for seeing how they should be trained, how well they are performing, and how they should be paid.

Good salespeople are trained, not born

The idea that good salespeople are born may have some truth—but it isn't the whole story. A salesperson needs to be taught about the company and its products, about giving effective sales presentations, and about building relationships with customers. But this isn't always done. Many salespeople do a poor job because they haven't had good training. Firms often hire new salespeople and immediately send them out on the road, or the retail selling floor, with no grounding in the basic selling steps and no information about the product or the customer. They just get a price list and a pat on the back. This isn't enough!

All salespeople need some training

It's up to sales and marketing management to be sure that salespeople know what they're supposed to do and how to do it. Hewlett-Packard Co. recently faced this problem. For years the company was organized into divisions based on different product lines—printers, networks servers, and the like. However, sales reps who specialized in the products of one division often couldn't compete well against firms that could offer customers total solutions to computing problems. When a new top executive came in and reorganized the company, all sales reps needed training in their new responsibilities, how they would be organized, and what they should say to their customers about the benefits of the reorganization.[10]

Sales training should be modified based on the experience and skills of the group involved. But the company's sales training program should cover at least the following areas: (1) company policies and practices, (2) product information, (3) building relationships with customer firms, and (4) professional selling skills.

Selling skills can be learned

Many companies spend the bulk of their training time on product information and company policy. They neglect training in selling techniques because they think selling is something anyone can do. But training in selling skills can pay off. Estée Lauder, for example, has selling skills for the "beauty advisors" who sell its cosmetics down to a fine art—and its training manual and seminars cover every detail. Its advisors who take the training seriously immediately double their sales.[11] Training can also help salespeople learn how to be more effective in cold calls on new prospects, in listening carefully to identify a customer's real objections, and in closing the sale.

The Motivating Tape Company sells various sales training videos. Go to the firm's Web site (www.achievement.com) and then scroll down and select *Sales Training Videos*. Review the list of sales training videos offered. If a sales manager were going to rely on some of these tapes for training people just moving into a sales career, what key areas of sales training would he have to cover by some other approach?

Training on selling techniques often starts in the classroom with lectures, case studies, and videotaped trial presentations and demonstrations. But a complete training program adds on-the-job observation of effective salespeople and coaching from sales supervisors. Many companies also use Web-based training, weekly sales meetings or work sessions, annual conventions, and regular e-mail messages and newsletters, as well as ongoing training sessions, to keep salespeople up-to-date and motivated.[12] The Canadian Professional Sales Association (CPSA) offers many training tools (www.cpsa.com).

COMPENSATING AND MOTIVATING SALESPEOPLE

To recruit, motivate, and keep good salespeople, a firm has to develop an effective compensation plan. Ideally, sales reps should be paid in such a way that what they want to do—for personal interest and gain—is in the company's interest too. Most companies focus on financial motivation—but public recognition, sales contests, and simple personal recognition for a job well done can be highly effective in encouraging greater sales effort.[13] Our main emphasis here, however, will be on financial motivation.[14]

Two basic decisions must be made in developing a compensation plan: (1) the level of compensation and (2) the method of payment.

Compensation varies with job and needed skills

To build a competitive sales force, a company must pay at least the going market wage for different kinds of salespeople. To be sure it can afford a specific type of salesperson, the company should estimate—when the job description is written—how valuable such a salesperson will be. A good order getter may be worth $50,000 to $100,000 to one company but only $15,000 to $25,000 to another—just because the second firm doesn't have enough to sell! In such a case, the second company should rethink its job specifications, or completely change its promotion plans, because the going rate for order getters can often be much higher than $15,000 a year.

If a job requires extensive travel, aggressive pioneering, or contacts with difficult customers, the pay may have to be higher. But the salesperson's compensation level should compare, at least roughly, with the pay scale of the rest of the firm. Normally, salespeople earn more than the office or production force but less than top management.

Payment methods vary

Given some competitive level of compensation, there are three basic methods of payment: (1) *straight salary*, (2) *straight commission*, or (3) a *combination plan*. Straight salary normally supplies the most security for the salesperson—and straight commission, the most incentive. Most companies want to offer their salespeople some balance between incentive and security, so the most popular method is a combination plan that includes some salary and some commission. Bonuses, profit sharing, pensions, stock plans, insurance, and other fringe benefits may be included too.

Salary gives control—if there is close supervision

A salesperson on straight salary earns the same amount regardless of how he or she spends time. So the salaried salesperson is expected to do what the sales manager asks—whether it is order-taking, supporting sales activities, solving customer problems, or completing sales call reports. However, the sales manager maintains control *only* by close supervision. As a result, straight salary or a large salary element in the compensation plan increases the amount of sales supervision needed.

Commissions can both motivate and direct

If personal supervision would be difficult, a firm may get better control with a compensation plan that includes some commission, or even a straight commission plan, with built-in direction. One trucking company, for example, has a sales incentive plan that pays higher commissions on business needed to balance freight shipments—depending on how heavily traffic has been moving in one direction or another. Another company that wants to motivate its salespeople to devote more time to developing new accounts could pay higher commissions on shipments to a new customer. However, a salesperson on a straight commission tends to be his or her own boss. The sales manager is less likely to get help on sales activities that won't increase the salesperson's earnings.

An incentive compensation plan can help motivate salespeople, but incentives must be carefully aligned with the firm's objectives. For example, IBM at one time had a sales commission plan that resulted in IBM salespeople pushing customers to buy expensive computers that were more powerful than they needed. The sales reps got sales and increased their income, but later many customers were dissatisfied and switched to other suppliers. Now most IBM sales reps receive incentive pay that is in part based on satisfaction ratings they earn from their customers. Many firms use variations of this approach—because incentives that just focus on short-term sales objectives may not motivate sales reps to develop long-term, need-satisfying relationships with their customers.

Incentives should link efforts to results

The incentive portion of a sales rep's compensation should be large only if there is a direct relationship between the salesperson's effort and results. Otherwise, a salesperson in a growing territory might have rapidly increasing earnings, while the sales rep in a poor area will have little to show for the same amount of work. Such a situation isn't fair, and it can lead to high turnover and much dissatisfaction. A sales manager can take such differences into consideration when setting a salesperson's **sales quota**—the specific sales or profit objective a salesperson is expected to achieve.

Sometimes it is difficult to make such adjustments. For example, the relationship between a salesperson's efforts and sales results is less direct if a number of other people—engineers, top management, or supporting salespeople—are involved in the sale. In this case, each one's contribution is less obvious, and greater emphasis on salary may make more sense.

Commissions reduce need for working capital

Small companies that have limited working capital or uncertain markets often prefer straight commission, or combination plans with a large commission element. When sales drop off, costs do too. Such flexibility is similar to using manufacturers' agents who get paid only if they deliver sales. This advantage often dominates in selecting a sales compensation method. Exhibit 14-3 shows the general relation between personal selling expense and sales volume for each of the basic compensation alternatives.

Exhibit 14-3
Relation between Personal
Selling Expenses and Sales
Volume—for Three Basic
Personal Selling
Compensation Alternatives

Compensation plans should be clear	Salespeople are likely to be dissatisfied if they can't see the relationship between the results they produce and their pay. A compensation plan that includes different commissions for different products or types of customers can become quite complicated. Simplicity is best achieved with straight salary. But in practice, it's usually better to sacrifice some simplicity to gain some incentive, flexibility, and control. The best combination of these factors depends on the job description and the company's objectives.

To make it easier for a sales rep to see the relationship between effort and compensation, some firms provide the rep with that information online. For example, Oracle, a company that sells database systems, developed a system that allows sales reps, at any point, to check a Web site and see how they are doing. As new sales results come in, the report at the Web site is updated. Sales managers can also make changes quickly—for example, by putting a higher commission on a product or more weight on customer satisfaction scores. Other firms use the same idea but just give their sales reps a spreadsheet so that they can keep their own information up-to-date.[15]

Sales managers must plan, implement, and control	Managers must regularly evaluate each salesperson's performance and be certain that all the needed tasks are being done well. The compensation plan may have to be changed if the pay and work are out of line. And by evaluating performance, firms can also identify areas that need more attention—by the salesperson or management.[16]

PERSONAL SELLING TECHNIQUES—PROSPECTING AND PRESENTING

We've stressed the importance of training in selling techniques. Now let's discuss these ideas in more detail so you understand the basic steps each salesperson should follow—including prospecting and selecting target customers, planning sales presentations, making sales presentations, and following up after the sale. Exhibit 14-4 shows the steps we'll consider. You can see that the salesperson is just carrying out a planned communication process, as we discussed in Chapter 13.[17]

Prospecting— narrowing down to the right target	Narrowing the personal selling effort down to the right target requires constant, detailed analysis of markets and much prospecting. Basically, **prospecting** involves following all the leads in the target market to identify potential customers.

Finding live prospects who will help make the buying decision isn't as easy as it sounds. In business markets, for example, the salesperson may need to do some hard detective work to find the real purchase decision makers.

Some companies provide prospect lists or a customer relationship management (CRM) database to make this part of the selling job easier. Inquiries that come

Exhibit 14-4
Key Steps in the Personal
Selling Process

in at the firm's Web site, for example, can be passed along to a sales rep for follow-up. A more indirect approach may be required. For example, one insurance company checks the local newspaper for marriage announcements—then a salesperson calls to see if the new couple is interested in finding out more about life insurance.

All customers are not equal

While prospecting focuses on identifying new customers, established customers require attention too. It's often time-consuming and expensive to establish a relationship with a customer, so once established it makes sense to keep the relationship healthy. That requires the rep to routinely review active accounts, rethink customers' needs, and reevaluate each customer's long-term business potential. Some small accounts may have the potential to become big accounts, and some accounts that previously required a lot of costly attention may no longer warrant it. So a sales rep may need to set priorities both for new prospects and existing customers.

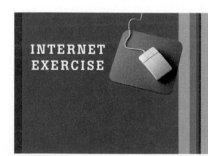

INTERNET EXERCISE

Maximizer, a CRM company, sells various software products, including personal management software that is used by many salespeople to organize information about their customers, sales calls, and tasks they need to do. Visit the Maximizer Web site (www.maximizer.com) for information about this product. Give a few specific examples of ways that a salesperson could use Maximizer software to build better relationships with customers.

How long to spend with whom?

Once a set of prospects and customers who need attention have been identified, the salesperson must decide how much time to spend with each one. A sales rep must qualify customers—to see if they deserve more effort. The salesperson usually makes these decisions by weighing the potential sales volume as well as the likelihood of a sale. This requires judgment. But well-organized salespeople usually develop some system because they have too many demands on their time.[18]

Many firms provide their reps with computer programs to help with this process. Most of them use some grading scheme. A sales rep might estimate how much each prospect is likely to purchase and the probability of getting and keeping the business given the competition. The computer then combines this information and grades each prospect. Attractive accounts may be labelled A—and the salesperson may plan to call on them weekly until the sale is made, the relationship is in good shape, or the customer is moved into a lower category. B customers might offer somewhat lower potential and be called on monthly. C accounts might be called on only once a year—unless they happen to contact the salesperson. And D accounts might be transferred to a telemarketing group.[19]

Three kinds of sales presentations may be useful

Once the salesperson selects a target customer, it's necessary to make a **sales presentation**—a salesperson's effort to make a sale or address a customer's problem. But someone has to plan what kind of sales presentation to make. This is a strategy decision. The kind of presentation should be set before the sales rep goes calling. And in situations where the customer comes to the salesperson—in a retail store, for instance—planners have to make sure that prospects are brought together with salespeople.

A marketing manager can choose two basically different approaches to making sales presentations: the prepared approach or the consultative selling approach. Another approach, the selling formula approach, is a combination of the two. Each of these has its place.

The prepared sales presentation

The **prepared sales presentation** approach uses a memorized presentation that is not adapted to each individual customer. This approach says that a customer faced with a particular stimulus will give the desired response—in this case, a yes answer to the salesperson's prepared statement, which includes a **close**, the salesperson's request for an order.

If one trial close doesn't work, the sales rep tries another prepared presentation and attempts another closing. This can go on for some time—until the salesperson runs out of material or the customer either buys or decides to leave. Exhibit 14-5 shows the relative participation of the salesperson and customer in the prepared approach. Note that the salesperson does most of the talking.

Firms may rely on this canned approach when only a short presentation is practical. It's also sensible when salespeople aren't very skilled. The company can control what they say and in what order. For example, Novartis uses missionary salespeople to tell doctors about new drugs when they're introduced. Doctors are busy, so they only give the rep a minute or two. That's just enough time to give a short, prepared pitch and leave some samples. To get the most out of the presentation, Novartis refines it based on feedback from doctors whom it pays to participate in focus groups.[20]

But a canned approach has a weakness. It treats all potential customers alike. It may work for some and not for others. A prepared approach may be suitable for simple order-taking—but it is no longer considered good selling for complicated situations.

Exhibit 14-5
Prepared Approach to Sales Presentation

Exhibit 14-6
Consultative Selling Approach to Sales Presentation

Exhibit 14-7
Selling Formula Approach to Sales Presentation

Consultative selling—builds on the marketing concept

The **consultative selling approach** involves developing a good understanding of the individual customer's needs before trying to close the sale. This name is used because the salesperson is almost acting as a consultant to help identify and solve the customer's problem. With this approach, the sales rep makes some general benefit statements to get the customer's attention and interest. Then the salesperson asks questions and *listens carefully* to understand the customer's needs. Once they agree on needs, the seller tries to show the customer how the product fills those needs and to close the sale. This is a problem-solving approach—in which the customer and salesperson work together to satisfy the customer's needs. That's why it's sometimes called the need-satisfaction approach. Exhibit 14-6 shows the participation of the customer and the salesperson during such a sales presentation.

The consultative selling approach takes skill and time. The salesperson must be able to analyze what motivates a particular customer and show how the company's offering would help the customer satisfy those needs. The sales rep may even conclude that the customer's problem is really better solved with someone else's product. That might result in one lost sale, but it also is likely to build real trust and more sales opportunities over the life of the relationship with the customer. That's why this kind of selling is typical in business markets when a salesperson already has established a close relationship with a customer. IBM Canada uses consultative selling effectively to build relationships with their customers.

Selling formula approach—some of both

The **selling formula approach** starts with a prepared presentation outline—much like the prepared approach—and leads the customer through some logical steps to a final close. The prepared steps are logical because we assume that we know something about the target customer's needs and attitudes.

Exhibit 14-7 shows the selling formula approach. The salesperson does most of the talking at the beginning of the presentation—to communicate key points early. This part of the presentation may even have been prepared as part of the marketing strategy. As the sales presentation moves along, however, the salesperson brings the customer into the discussion to help clarify just what needs this customer has. The salesperson's job is to discover the needs of a particular customer to know how to proceed. Once it is clear what kind of customer this is, the salesperson comes back to show how the product satisfies this specific customer's needs and to close the sale. This approach is common in the retail marketplace, especially for technical products, such as electronics.

AIDA helps plan sales presentations

AIDA—Attention, Interest, Desire, Action: Most sales presentations follow this AIDA sequence. The time a sales rep spends on each of the steps varies depending on the situation and the selling approach being used. But it is still necessary to begin

Keebler salespeople use an interactive tool called Instant Data Evaluation Access ("IDEA") Wizard on their laptop computers. It provides research data related to the marketing of cookies and crackers on topics such as shelf space management and consumer purchase patterns. The sales rep can use the Wizard to support a consultative selling approach in working to develop closer relationships with retailers.

a presentation by getting the prospect's *attention* and, hopefully, to move the customer to *action*.[21]

Each sales manager and salesperson needs to think about this sequence in deciding what sales approach to use and in evaluating a possible presentation. Does the presentation get the prospect's attention quickly? Will it be interesting? Will the benefits be clear? Does the presentation consider likely objections so the sales rep can close the sale when the time is right? These may seem like simple things. But too frequently they aren't done at all—and a sale is lost.

PERSONAL SELLING TECHNIQUES—CLOSING THE SALE

Most sales are lost because the salesperson does not successfully close the sale. Many sales are lost because a sales close is not even attempted. Although attempting a sales close does create the potential for rejection, a salesperson must attempt the close—it is crucial to making a sale.

Different sales closes are suitable for different individuals and selling situations. Exhibit 14-8 describes a few of the most popular closes. To be successful, sales personnel should choose a close they are comfortable with that suits the selling situation.

Ethical issues may arise

As in every other area of marketing communications, ethical issues arise in the personal selling area. The most basic issue, plain and simple, is whether a salesperson's presentation is honest and truthful. But addressing that issue is a no-brainer. No company is served well by a salesperson who lies or manipulates customers to get their business.

On the other hand, most sales reps sooner or later face a sales situation in which they must make more difficult ethical decisions about how to balance company interests, customer interests, and personal interests. Conflicts are less likely to arise

Pepsi Cola route sales representatives have to follow an unshakeable rule: no consumer must ever see a stale-dated product on any store shelf. Donald Chester, a 20-year route sales representative, delivered Hostess Frito-Lay products (owned by Pepsi) to retail outlets. Pepsi expected Chester to ensure its products were removed from stores before their best-before date expired. Most of the time, Chester honoured Pepsi's rule, but occasionally he slipped up. Pepsi made it perfectly clear what it expected, and the consequence was termination if Chester failed.

When his superiors performed their spot checks, they detected 39 bags of stale chips. Chester was dismissed. Chester then commenced a claim for wrongful dismissal and won. The Saskatchewan trial judge reviewed Pepsi's expectations and found that the standard Pepsi expected of Chester was neither reasonable nor attainable. Chester was awarded 14 months of severance pay plus his cost of suing. The court continued that perfection is a laudable goal but not likely attainable by many.

Do you feel that the verdict in this case was the correct one? [22]

if the firm's marketing mix really meets the needs of its target market. Similarly, they are less likely to arise when the firm sees the value of developing a longer-term relationship with the customer. Then the salesperson is arranging a happy marriage. By contrast, ethical conflicts are more likely when the sales rep's personal outcomes (such as commission income) or the selling firm's profits hinge on making sales to customers whose needs are only partially met by the firm's offering. This chapter's Marketing Ethically illustrates the type of problem a company can face motivating and managing its sales force.

Ideally, companies can avoid the whole problem by supporting their salespeople with a marketing mix that really offers target customers unique benefits. Moreover, top executives, marketing managers, and sales managers set the tone for the ethical climate in which a salesperson operates. If they set impossible goals or project a "do-what-you-need-to-do" attitude, a desperate salesperson may yield to the pressure of the moment. When a firm clearly advocates ethical selling behaviour and makes it clear that manipulative selling techniques are not acceptable, the salesperson is not left trying to swim "against the flow."[23]

Exhibit 14-8
Popular Sales Closes

Sales Close	Description
Assumptive	A very aggressive close that assumes a sale is made and concentrates on the details of implementation (e.g., When would you like this delivered?).
Alternative	A variation on the assumptive close that is less aggressive. Offers a choice between two alternatives that both indicate acceptance of the deal (e.g., Would you like a red one or a blue one?).
Direct	A straightforward close that simply asks for the business (e.g., Shall we sign the deal?).
Concession	A last-ditch attempt to make the sale by offering something extra as an incentive to close the sale (e.g., How about if we throw in three DVDs?).
Silence	A simple close that can be used repeatedly (e.g., Say nothing. Let the consumer think for a few moments while remaining close by—but not too close!).

CONCLUSION

In this chapter, we discussed the importance and nature of personal selling. Selling is much more than just getting rid of the product. In fact, a salesperson who is not given strategy guidelines may have to become the strategy planner for the market he or she serves. Ideally, however, the sales manager and marketing manager work together to set some strategy guidelines: the kind and number of salespersons needed, what sales technology support will be provided, the kind of sales presentation desired, and selection, training, and motivation approaches.

We discussed the three basic sales tasks: (1) order-getting, (2) order-taking, and (3) supporting. Most sales jobs combine at least two of these three tasks. Once a firm specifies the important tasks, it can decide on the structure of its sales organization and the number of salespeople it needs. The nature of the job and the level and method of compensation also depend on the blend of these tasks. Firms should develop a job description for each sales job. This, in turn, provides guidelines for selecting, training, and compensating salespeople.

Once the marketing manager agrees to the basic plan and sets the budget, the sales manager must implement the plan, including directing and controlling the sales force. This includes assigning sales territories and controlling performance. You can see that the sales manager has more to do than jet around the country sipping martinis and entertaining customers. A sales manager is deeply involved with the basic management tasks of planning and control—as well as ongoing implementation of the personal selling effort.

We also reviewed some basic selling techniques and identified three kinds of sales presentations. Each has its place—but the consultative selling approach seems best for higher-level sales jobs. In these kinds of jobs, personal selling is achieving a new, professional status because of the competence and level of personal responsibility required of the salesperson. The day of the old-time glad-hander is passing in favour of the specialist who is creative, industrious, persuasive, knowledgeable, highly trained, and therefore able to help the buyer. This type of salesperson always has been, and probably always will be, in short supply. And the demand for high-level salespeople is growing.

KEY TERMS

basic sales tasks, 385

order getters, 385

order-getting, 385

order takers, 387

order-taking, 387

supporting salespeople, 388

missionary salespeople, 388

technical specialists, 389

team selling, 389

major accounts sales force, 389

telemarketing, 390

sales territory, 390

job description, 394

sales quota, 396

prospecting, 397

sales presentation, 399

prepared sales presentation, 399

close, 399

consultative selling approach, 400

selling formula approach, 400

QUESTIONS AND PROBLEMS

1. What strategy decisions are needed in the personal selling area? Why should the marketing manager make these strategy decisions?

2. What kind of salesperson (or what blend of the basic sales tasks) is required to sell the following products? If there are several selling jobs in the channel for each product, indicate the kinds of salespeople required. Specify any assumptions necessary to give definite answers.

   a. Laundry detergent.
   b. Costume jewellery.
   c. Office furniture.
   d. Dry cleaning.
   e. Mattresses.
   f. Corn.
   g. Life insurance.

3. Distinguish among the jobs of producers', wholesalers', and retailers' order-getting salespeople. If one order getter is needed, must all the salespeople in a channel be order getters? Illustrate.

4. Discuss the future of the specialty shop if producers place greater emphasis on mass selling because of the inadequacy of retail order-taking.

5. Compare and contrast missionary salespeople and technical specialists.

6. Explain how a compensation plan could be developed to provide incentives for experienced salespeople and yet make some provision for trainees who have not yet learned the job.

7. Cite an actual local example of each of the three kinds of sales presentations discussed in the chapter.

Explain for each situation whether a different type of presentation would have been better.

8. Are the benefits and limitations of a canned presentation any different if it is supported with a slide show or videotape than if it is just a person talking? Why or why not?

9. Describe a consultative selling sales presentation that you experienced recently. How could it have been improved by fuller use of the AIDA framework?

10. How would our economy operate if personal salespeople were outlawed? Could the economy work? If so, how? If not, what is the minimum personal selling effort necessary? Could this minimum personal selling effort be controlled by law?

COMPUTER-AIDED PROBLEM

14. Sales Compensation

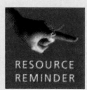

RESOURCE REMINDER

Franco Welles, sales manager for Nanek Inc., is trying to decide whether to pay a sales rep for a new territory with straight commission or a combination plan. He wants to evaluate possible plans—to compare the compensation costs and profitability of each. Welles knows that sales reps in similar jobs at other firms make about $36,000 a year.

The sales rep will sell two products. Welles is planning a higher commission for Product B—because he wants it to get extra effort. From experience with similar products, he has some rough estimates of expected sales volume under the different plans and various ideas about commission rates. The details are found in the spreadsheet. The program computes compensation and how much the sales rep will contribute to profit. "Profit contribution" is equal to the total revenue generated by the sales rep minus sales compensation costs and the costs of producing the units.

a. For the initial values shown in the spreadsheet, which plan—commission or combination—would give the rep the highest compensation, and which plan would give the greatest profit contribution to Nanek Inc.?

b. Welles thinks a sales rep might be motivated to work harder and sell 1,100 units of Product B if the commission rate (under the commission plan) were increased to 10 percent. If Welles is right (and everything else stays the same), would the higher commission rate be a good deal for Nanek? Explain your thinking.

c. A sales rep interested in the job is worried about making payments on her new car. She asks if Welles would consider paying her with a combination plan but with more guaranteed income (an $18,000 base salary) in return for taking a 3 percent commission on Products B and A. If this arrangement results in the same unit sales as Welles originally estimated for the combination plan, would Nanek Inc., be better off or worse off under this arrangement?

d. Do you think the rep's proposal will meet Welles' goals for Product B? Explain your thinking.

If you want to read the cases and view the video cases that accompany this chapter, visit the *Basic Marketing* Online Learning Centre at: **www.mcgrawhill.ca/olc/perreault**. Along with these cases and video cases, the OLC also has the software and user guide for this chapter's Computer-Aided Problem, as well as exercises, quizzes, articles, links, and other *interactive* content that will help you with your studies.

Advertising, Publicity, and Sales Promotion

In the summer of 1965, 17-year-old Fred DeLuca was trying to figure out how to pay for college. A family friend suggested that Fred open a sandwich shop—and then the friend invested $1,000 to help get it started. Within a month, they opened their first sandwich shop. From that humble start grew the Subway franchise chain with over 20,000 outlets in 70 countries.

Targeted advertising and sales promotion have been important to Subway's growth. Some memorable Subway ads featured Jared Fogle, a college student who was overweight but lost over 110 kilograms by only eating Subway's low-fat sandwiches, like the "Veggie Delite." Jared says it was a fluke that he ended up in Subway's ads. After all, he was recruited to do the ads because of good publicity that Subway got after national media picked up a story that Jared's friend wrote about him in a college newspaper. On the other hand, Subway's strategy at that time focused on its line of seven different sandwiches with under 6 grams of fat. The objective was to set Subway apart from other fast food in a way that would appeal to health-conscious eaters and spark new sales growth. Jared walked past a nearby Subway every day, but what pulled him in the first time was Subway's point-of-purchase promotion for the "7 under 6" menu. So maybe it wasn't as random as it seems to Jared.

As soon as Jared's ads began to run, word of his inspiring story spread and consumer awareness of Subway and its healthy fare increased. It's always hard to isolate the exact impact of ads on sales, but sales grew more than 18 percent that year. Another benefit was that the ads attracted attention from potential franchisees. Many of them followed up by requesting the franchise brochure, which explains how Subway's strategy works and why it is profitable for franchisees. For instance, it describes how franchisees elect a group to help manage advertising and media buying decisions—so that Subway outlets get the most return from their advertising dollars. Subway headquarters also supports franchisees by providing materials and guidance for the local advertising and sales promotion they do to reach their own target customers.

Recently, Subway has been squeezed at the high end by rival sandwich shops like Quiznos' Sub and Panera Bread. So Subway has to balance its menu and promotion. Balance is needed to appeal to the segment of customers who are most interested in taste as well as the low-fat segment. Subway balances the menu with a line of "Subway Selects" sandwiches made with zesty sauces and special breads. It turned to a new ad agency, Fallon Worldwide, to create new ads that would balance the copy thrust. Subway can also expect cooperative promotional support from Coca-Cola now that it is taking over as the exclusive supplier for all Subway outlets.

Subway includes many other elements in its promotion blend. For example, it is involved with many charities. It also has contests and games to keep its customers interested. One is a trivia contest in which customers can win a boxed set of recordings. The contest ties in with a section of Subway's Web site that keeps customers coming back by providing handy reviews of current movies and music. The Web site also provides tips on dieting and exercise as well as nutritional details about its sandwiches. These details help consumers who want all the health-related facts.

Subway is in a very competitive, dynamic market. More change is sure to come. But so far, Subway has achieved profitable growth with a targeted strategy that includes effective use of promotion.[1]

ADVERTISING, SALES PROMOTION, AND MARKETING STRATEGY DECISIONS

The Subway case shows that carefully planned advertising and sales promotion are often critical elements in the success or failure of a strategy. They can provide an inexpensive way—on a per-contact or per-sale basis—to inform, persuade, and activate customers. Advertising and sales promotion often play a central role in efforts to position a firm's marketing mix as the one that meets customers' needs. They can help motivate channel members or a firm's own employees, as well as final customers.

Unfortunately, the results that marketers *actually achieve* with advertising and sales promotion are very uneven. It's often said that half of the money spent on these activities is wasted—but that too few managers know which half. Mass selling can be exciting and involving, or it can be downright obnoxious. Sometimes it's based on careful research, yet much of it is just based on someone's pet idea. A creative idea may produce great results or be a colossal waste of money. Ads can stir deep emotions or go unnoticed.

Many managers do a poor job with advertising and sales promotion. So just copying how lots of other firms handle these important strategy decisions is not "good enough." There's no sense in imitating bad practices. Instead, it makes sense to understand the important strategy decisions involved in each of these areas.

As the Subway case illustrates, marketing managers and the advertising agencies that work with them have important advertising decisions to make, including (1) who their target audience is, (2) what kind of advertising to use, (3) how to reach customers (via which types of media), (4) what to say to them (the copy thrust), and (5) who will do the work—the firm's own advertising department or outside agencies. See Exhibit 15-1.

International dimensions are important

The basic strategy planning decisions for advertising and sales promotion are the same regardless of where in the world the target market is located. However, the look and feel of advertising and sales promotion vary a lot in different countries. The choices available to a marketing manager within each of the decision areas may also vary dramatically from one country to another.

Commercial television may not be available. If it is, government rules may limit the type of advertising permitted or when ads can be shown. Radio broadcasts in a market area may not be in the target market's language. The target audience may not be able to read. Access to interactive media like the Internet may be nonexistent. Cultural influences may limit ad messages. Ad agencies who already know a nation's unique advertising environment may not be available.

International dimensions also impact sales promotion. Trade promotion may be difficult, or even impossible, to manage. A typical Japanese grocery retailer with only 75 square metres of space, for example, doesn't have room for *any* special end-of-aisle displays. Consumer promotions may be affected too. Many Polish consumers, for example, are skeptical about product samples; they figure that if it's free something's

Exhibit 15-1 Strategy Planning for Advertising

amiss. In some developing nations, samples can't be distributed through the mail, because they're routinely stolen before they get to target customers. And some countries ban consumer sweepstakes because they see it as a form of gambling.

In this chapter we'll consider a number of these international issues, but we'll focus on the array of choices available in Canada and other advanced economies.[2]

Total spending is big—and growing internationally

As an economy grows, advertising becomes more important—because more consumers have income and advertising can get results. But good advertising results cost money. And spending on advertising is significant. In 2006, almost $12 billion will be spent on advertising in Canada.

Traditional media choices are more limited in some international markets, so marketers must be creative to communicate their messages. In North Africa and the Middle East, Coke uses hot-air balloons. The 12-stories-tall Ariel shirt was mounted on a building in China.

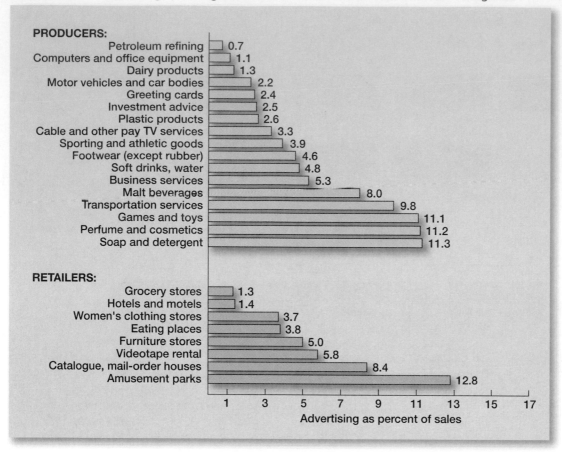

PRODUCERS:

Category	
Petroleum refining	0.7
Computers and office equipment	1.1
Dairy products	1.3
Motor vehicles and car bodies	2.2
Greeting cards	2.4
Investment advice	2.5
Plastic products	2.6
Cable and other pay TV services	3.3
Sporting and athletic goods	3.9
Footwear (except rubber)	4.6
Soft drinks, water	4.8
Business services	5.3
Malt beverages	8.0
Transportation services	9.8
Games and toys	11.1
Perfume and cosmetics	11.2
Soap and detergent	11.3

RETAILERS:

Category	
Grocery stores	1.3
Hotels and motels	1.4
Women's clothing stores	3.7
Eating places	3.8
Furniture stores	5.0
Videotape rental	5.8
Catalogue, mail-order houses	8.4
Amusement parks	12.8

Advertising as percent of sales

During the last decade, the rate of advertising spending has increased rapidly in other countries. Advertising in the U.S. accounts for roughly half of worldwide ad spending. Europe accounts for about 23 percent, and Asia about 22 percent. For most countries in other regions, advertising spending has traditionally been quite low.[3]

Most advertisers aren't really spending that much

While total spending on advertising seems high, it represents a small portion of what people pay for the goods and services they buy. Corporations spend an average of only about 2.5 percent of their sales dollar on advertising. Worldwide, the percentage is even smaller.

Exhibit 15-2 shows, however, that advertising spending as a percent of sales dollars varies significantly across product categories. Producers of consumer products generally spend a larger percent than firms that produce business products. For example, companies that make soap and detergent spend a whopping 11.3 percent. However, companies that sell plastics to manufacturers spend only about 2.6 percent on advertising. Some business products companies—those that depend on e-commerce or personal selling—may spend less than $1/10$ of 1 percent.

In general, the percent is smaller for retailers and wholesalers than for producers. Large chains like The Bay may spend as much as 3 percent, but many retailers and wholesalers spend 1 percent or less. Individual firms may spend more or less than others in the industry, depending on the role of advertising in their promotion blend.

Of course, percentages don't tell the whole story. Nissan, which spends less than 1 percent of sales on advertising, is among the top 20 advertisers worldwide. The really big spenders are very important to the advertising industry because they account for a large share of total advertising spending. Worldwide, the top 100 global advertisers spend about $65 billion a year. At, or near, the top of that list in most years are the three biggest consumer packaged goods companies (P&G, Unilever, and Nestlé) and major car companies, including GM, Toyota, and Ford.[4]

Advertising spending is very important in certain markets, especially final consumer markets. Nevertheless, in total, advertising costs much less than personal selling and sales promotion.

Advertising doesn't employ that many people

While total advertising expenditures are large, the advertising industry itself employs relatively few people. The major expense is for media time and space. In Canada, the largest share of this—26 percent—goes for television (including cable). Newspapers take about 17 percent of the total and direct mail about 15 percent. The shares for radio (11 percent), the Yellow Pages (10 percent), magazines (5 percent), outdoor (3 percent), and the Internet (2 percent) are much smaller.[5]

ADVERTISING OBJECTIVES ARE A STRATEGY DECISION

Advertising objectives must be specific

Every ad and every advertising campaign should have clearly defined objectives. These should grow out of the firm's overall marketing strategy and the promotion jobs assigned to advertising. It isn't enough for the marketing manager to say "Promote the product." The marketing manager must decide exactly what advertising should do.

Advertising objectives should be more specific than personal selling objectives. One of the advantages of personal selling is that a salesperson can shift the presentation for a specific customer. Each ad, however, must be effective not just for one customer but for thousands, or millions, of them.

The marketing manager sets the overall direction

The marketing manager might give the advertising manager one or more of the following specific objectives, along with the budget to accomplish them:

1. Help position the firm's brand or marketing mix by informing and persuading target customers or middlemen about its benefits.
2. Help introduce new products to specific target markets.
3. Help obtain desirable outlets and tell customers where they can buy a product.
4. Provide ongoing contact with target customers, even when a salesperson isn't available.
5. Prepare the way for salespeople by presenting the company's name and the merits of its products.
6. Get immediate buying action.
7. Help to maintain relationships with satisfied customers and encourage more purchases.

If you want half the market, say so!

The objectives listed above highlight that a balancing act may be required. The first objective is quite broad and relates to the basic decisions about how the marketing manager wants to differentiate and position the whole marketing mix. That should guide decisions about what other specific objectives are most important. In fact, some of the objectives listed are not as specific as they could be. If a marketing manager really wants specific results, they should be clearly stated. A general objective is "To help expand market share." This could be rephrased more specifically: "To increase shelf space in our cooperating retail outlets by 25 percent during the next three months."

Awareness	Interest	Evaluation and trial	Decision	Confirmation
Teaser campaigns Pioneering ads Jingles/slogans Internet banners Announcements	Informative or descriptive ads Image/celebrity ads Flash ads Demonstration of benefits	Competitive ads Persuasive copy Comparative ads Testimonials	Direct-action retail ads Point-of-purchase ads Price deal offers	Reminder ads Informative "why" ads

Objectives guide implementation too

The specific objectives obviously affect what type of advertising is best. Exhibit 15-3 shows that the type of advertising that achieves objectives for one stage of the adoption process may be off target for another. For example, most advertising for cameras in Canada, the United States, Germany, and Japan focuses on foolproof pictures or state-of-the-art digital designs because most consumers in these countries already own *some* camera. In Africa, where only about 20 percent of the population owns a camera, ads must sell the whole concept of picture-taking.

OBJECTIVES DETERMINE THE KINDS OF ADVERTISING NEEDED

The advertising objectives largely determine which of two basic types of advertising to use—product or institutional.

Product advertising tries to sell a product. It may be aimed at final users or channel members.

Institutional advertising tries to promote an organization's image, reputation, or ideas rather than a specific product. Its basic objective is to develop goodwill or improve an organization's relations with various groups—not only customers but also current and prospective channel members, suppliers, shareholders, employees, and the general public. The British government, for instance, uses institutional advertising to promote England as a place to do business.

Hoechst's attention-getting institutional ad is effective in promoting the company's name and image, rather than trying to sell just one of its many specific product lines.

Product advertising—know us, like us, remember us

Product advertising falls into three categories: pioneering, competitive, and reminder advertising.

Pioneering advertising—builds primary demand

Pioneering advertising tries to develop primary demand for a product category rather than demand for a specific brand. Pioneering advertising is usually done in the early stages of the product life cycle; it informs potential customers about the new product and helps turn them into adopters. When digital cameras first came out, consumers didn't know their benefits or why they might want one—and at the same time they worried about how they could get printed pictures. So advertising for the early products in the market had to explain these basics and build primary demand. Now that there are a hundred brands of digital cameras, each brand's ads try to highlight its own advantages—like the number of megapixels, amount of memory, or ease of use.

Competitive advertising—emphasizes selective demand

Competitive advertising tries to develop selective demand for a specific brand. A firm is forced into competitive advertising as the product life cycle moves along—to hold its own against competitors.

Competitive advertising may be either direct or indirect. The **direct type** aims for immediate buying action. The **indirect type** points out product advantages to affect future buying decisions.

Subway ads emphasize their competitive product advantage—a healthier choice for consumers desiring fast food. WestJet uses competitive advertising with a focus on price as well as the overall customer experience.

Comparative advertising is even rougher. **Comparative advertising** means making specific brand comparisons—using actual product names. Many countries forbid comparative advertising, but that situation is changing. For example, Japan banned comparative advertising until about 15 years ago, when the restrictions were relaxed. Japan's move followed an earlier change in the United States. After banning them for years, the U.S. decided to encourage comparative ads—because it was thought they would increase competition and provide consumers with more useful information.

Superiority claims are supposed to be supported by research evidence—but the guidelines aren't clear. When P&G's Dryel did not fare well in independent test

Comparative ads make direct comparisons with other brands using actual product names. The Baby Orajel ad touts its fast relief compared to Children's Tylenol.

comparisons with stain removal by professional dry cleaners, P&G changed its ad claims. However, some firms just keep running tests until they get the results they want. Others talk about minor differences that don't reflect a product's overall benefits. Comparative ads can also backfire by calling attention to competing products that consumers had not previously considered.[6] Hence, they are not that common in Canada.

Reminder advertising—reinforces a favourable relationship

Reminder advertising tries to keep the product's name before the public. It may be useful when the product has achieved brand preference or insistence, perhaps in the market maturity or sales decline stages. It is used primarily to reinforce previous promotion. Here the advertiser may use soft-sell ads that just mention or show the name—as a reminder. Hallmark, for example, often relies on reminder ads because most consumers already know the brand name and, after years of promotion, associate it with high product quality.

Institutional advertising—remember our name

Institutional advertising usually focuses on the name and prestige of an organization or industry. It may seek to inform, persuade, or remind. Many Japanese firms, like Hitachi, emphasize institutional advertising, in part because they often use the company name as a brand name.

Companies sometimes rely on institutional advertising to present the company in a favourable light, perhaps to overcome image problems. General Electric recently launched a $100 million institutional ad campaign, along with the new tagline "innovation at work." A new team of executives at GE felt that many of the people who influence big purchase decisions in the varied business markets where GE competes associated GE with products like light bulbs and refrigerators and that the familiar "we bring good things to life" tagline just reinforced an old-fashioned image. The purpose of the new TV spots—which feature jet engines, high-tech plastics, and medical systems—is to reposition GE as a company that produces revolutionary innovations.[7]

Some organizations use institutional advertising to advocate a specific cause or idea. Insurance companies and organizations like Mothers Against Drunk Driving, for example, use these advocacy ads to encourage people not to drink and drive.[8]

COORDINATING ADVERTISING EFFORTS WITH COOPERATIVE RELATIONSHIPS

Vertical cooperation—advertising allowances, cooperative advertising

Sometimes a producer knows that an advertising job can be done more effectively or more economically by someone further along in the channel. Alternatively, a retail chain like Future Shop may approach a manufacturer like Panasonic with an ad program and tell them how much it will cost to participate. In either case, the producer may offer **advertising allowances**—price reductions to firms further along in the channel to encourage them to advertise or otherwise promote the firm's products locally.

Cooperative advertising involves middlemen and producers sharing in the cost of ads. This helps wholesalers and retailers compete in their local markets. It also helps the producer get more promotion for the advertising dollar because media usually give local advertisers lower rates than national or international firms. In addition, a retailer or wholesaler who is paying a share of the cost is more likely to follow through.

Integrated communications from cooperative relationships

Coordination and integration of ad messages in the channel is another reason for cooperative advertising. One big, well-planned, integrated advertising effort is often better than many different, perhaps inconsistent, local efforts. Many franchise operations like the idea of communicating with one voice. KFC, for example, encourages its franchises to use a common advertising program. Before, many developed their own local ads—with themes like "Eight clucks for four bucks"—that didn't fit with the company's overall marketing strategy.

To get this coordination, producers often provide a master of an ad on a DVD, CD, Web site, or printed sheets. The middlemen add their identification before turning the ad over to local media.

However, allowances and support materials alone don't ensure cooperation. When channel members don't agree with the advertising strategy, it can be a serious source of conflict. For example, Wendy's strategy includes an objective to be the late-night, quick-serve restaurant of choice for its target market. This requires staying open late at night and advertising the longer hours. However, some Wendy's restaurants are franchise operations rather than company-owned. A franchise operator who does not think that late-night hours will be profitable in his or her local market may not want to stay open for the longer hours or pay franchise fees to support the national ad campaign. If a situation like this affected only a few restaurants, it might not be a big problem. However, if concerns about the campaign are widespread, it might require that the whole strategy be revisited.[9]

Ethical concerns may arise

Ethical issues sometimes arise concerning advertising allowance programs. For example, a retailer may run one producer's ad to draw customers to the store but then try hard to sell them another brand. Is this unethical? Some producers think it is. A different view is that retailers are obligated to the producer to run the ad but obligated to consumers to sell them what they want, no matter whose brand it may be. A producer can often avoid the problem by setting the allowance amount as a percent of the retailer's *actual purchases*. Smart producers also insist on proof that the advertising was really done. That way, a retailer who doesn't produce sales—or even run the ads—doesn't get the allowance.[10]

CHOOSING THE "BEST" MEDIUM—HOW TO DELIVER THE MESSAGE

What is the best advertising medium? There is no simple answer to this question. Effectiveness depends on how well the medium fits with the rest of a marketing strategy—that is, it depends on (1) your promotion objectives, (2) what target

Kinds of Media	Sales Volume, 2001 ($ millions)	Typical Costs	Advantages	Disadvantages
Television	$2,561	$8,000 for a 30-second spot, prime time	Demonstrations, good attention, wide reach	Expensive in total, "clutter," less-selective audience
Newspaper	$1,678	$50,850 for one-page, *The Globe and Mail*	Flexible, timely, local market	May be expensive, short life, no "pass-along"
Direct mail	$1,489	$215 per 1,000 for listing of 114,000 Human Resource executives by industry or employee size	Selected audience, flexible, can personalize	Relatively expensive per contact, "junk mail"—hard to retain attention
Radio	$1,063	$100–$400 or more for one-minute drive time	Wide reach, segmented audience, inexpensive	Weak attention, many different rates, short exposure
Magazine	$541	$41,750 for one-page, four-colour in *Chatelaine* (national)	Very targeted, good detail, good "pass-along"	Inflexible, long lead times
Outdoor and transit	$310	$100,000 for over 300 exterior transit ads for one month	Flexible, repeat exposure, inexpensive	"Mass market," very short exposure
Internet	$120	Banner ads average about $30 for every 1,000 ad impressions on a site	Ads link to more detailed Web site, some "pay for results"	Hard to compare costs with other media

markets you want to reach, (3) the funds available for advertising, and (4) the nature of the media, including who they *reach*, with what *frequency*, with what *impact*, and at what *cost*.

Exhibit 15-4 shows some pros and cons of major kinds of media and some examples of costs. However, some of the advantages noted in this table may not apply in all markets. For example, direct mail may not be a flexible choice in a country with a weak postal system. Internet ads might be worthless if few target customers have access to the Internet. Similarly, TV audiences are often less selective and targeted, but a special-interest cable TV show may reach a very specific audience.[11]

Specific promotion objectives

The medium should support the promotion objectives. If the objective requires demonstrating product benefits, TV may be the best alternative. If the objective is to inform, telling a detailed story and using precise pictures, then Internet advertising might be right. Alternatively, with a broad target market, print media like magazines and newspapers may be better. For example, Jockey switched its advertising to magazines from television when it decided to show the variety of styles of its men's briefs. Jockey worried that there were problems with modelling men's underwear on television. However, Jockey might have stayed with TV if it had been targeting consumers in France or Brazil, where nudity in TV ads is common.[12]

Match your market with the media

To guarantee good media selection, the advertiser first must *clearly* specify its target market. Then the advertiser can choose media that reaches those target customers.

The Yellow Pages reaches a broad audience, but for many firms it is a "must buy" element in an integrated marketing communications plan.

The media available in a country may limit the choices. In less-developed nations, for example, radio is often the only way to reach a broad-based market of poor consumers who can't read or afford television.

In most cases, however, the major problem is to match media with the target audience. Most media firms use marketing research to develop profiles of their audiences. Generally, this research focuses on demographic characteristics rather than the segmenting dimensions specific to the planning needs of *each* different advertiser. The problem is even worse in some countries because available media don't provide any information.

Advertisers pay for the whole audience

Another problem is that the audience for media that *do* reach your target market may also include people who are *not* in the target group. But *you pay for the whole audience the media delivers*, including those who aren't potential customers. For example, breweries such as Molson or Labatt often run male-orientated ads during hockey telecasts. These ads do not generally appeal to women—but many women watch hockey. The breweries pay to reach the whole audience, both men and women.

The cost of reaching the real target market goes up fastest when the irrelevant audience is very large. For example, the last episode of the wildly popular *Seinfeld* sitcom drew about 75 million viewers and NBC charged $1.5 million or more for a 30-second ad slot. It may have been worth that for Visa to reach such a large, mainly adult, audience.[13] On the other hand, tiny Gardenburger Inc., bought an ad slot in a shoot-for-the-moon effort to turn the audience on to its veggie patties. Yet only about 8 percent of consumers have ever tasted a veggie burger. A 30-second ad, even a memorable one, isn't likely to change a basic mindset for most people. So in betting the farm on its *Seinfeld* ad, Gardenburger had to pay to reach a very large audience, most of whom were not interested in what the company had to offer.[14]

Because it's hard to pick the best media, media analysts often focus on cost per thousand of audience size or circulation. This may seem an objective approach, but advertisers preoccupied with keeping these costs down may ignore the relevant segmenting dimensions and slip into mass marketing.

Some media help zero in on specific target markets

Today, the major media direct more attention to reaching smaller, more defined target markets. The most obvious evidence of this is in the growth of spending on direct-mail advertising to consumers in databases. However, other media, even traditional ones, are becoming more targeted as well.

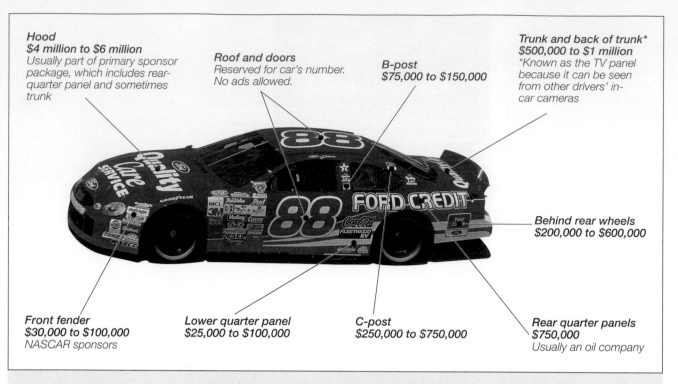

Hood
$4 million to $6 million
Usually part of primary sponsor package, which includes rear-quarter panel and sometimes trunk

Roof and doors
Reserved for car's number. No ads allowed.

B-post
$75,000 to $150,000

Trunk and back of trunk*
$500,000 to $1 million
**Known as the TV panel because it can be seen from other drivers' in-car cameras*

Behind rear wheels
$200,000 to $600,000

Front fender
$30,000 to $100,000
NASCAR sponsors

Lower quarter panel
$25,000 to $100,000

C-post
$250,000 to $750,000

Rear quarter panels
$750,000
Usually an oil company

Advertising space on a race car reaches racing fans and often benefits from extended TV coverage. But the cost for primary sponsors can be millions of dollars.

TV is a good example of this fragmentation. Cable TV channels—like CNN, TSN, and MTV—are taking advertisers away from the networks because they target specific audiences. TSN, for example, has an audience heavily weighted toward affluent, male viewers. Moreover, being specialized doesn't necessarily mean that the target market is small. MTV appeals most strongly to young viewers, but its programming is seen in nearly 400 million homes worldwide—more than any other programmer.

Infomercials—long commercials that are broadcast with a TV show format—are a reminder of how targeted cable TV has become now that many consumers have access to hundreds of TV channels. With many channels competing for attention, most will succeed only if they offer programs and commercials specific to the interests of smaller, more homogeneous target markets.

Radio has also become a more specialized medium. Some stations cater to particular ethnic and racial groups, such as Asians or French Canadians. Others aim at specific target markets with rock, country, or classical music. Now that radio stations can get their programming to a larger number of consumers over the Internet and via satellite broadcast systems, expect even more targeting.

Many magazines serve only special-interest groups, such as fishermen, new parents, and personal computer users. In fact, the most profitable magazines seem to be the ones aimed at clearly defined markets. Many specialty magazines also have international editions that help marketers reach consumers with similar interests in different parts of the world. *PC Magazine*, for example, offers European, Japanese, and other editions.

There are also trade magazines in many fields, such as chemical engineering, furniture retailing, electrical wholesaling, farming, and the aerospace market. *Canadian Advertising Rates and Data* provides a guide to the thousands of magazines now available. Similar guides exist in most other countries.

DOES ADVERTISING THAT'S EVERYWHERE GET US ANYWHERE?

It's everywhere. You get to the beach, look down, and huge versions of the Skippy peanut butter logo are embossed in the sand. You roll your eyes in dismay and catch a view of a plane pulling a 30-metre-long banner ad with Catherine Zeta-Jones urging you to "Sign up for T-Mobile's free Friday minutes." You go in the bathroom to change into your swimsuit, but the walls are adorned with posters for Good Humor ice cream bars. Forget that. Maybe you should just eat your picnic lunch. Oops, the whole back of the bench you're going to sit on is an ad for a cheque-cashing service—and just for good measure the banana you pull out of your lunch bag has a sticker advertising Florida oranges. You look up just as a baby carriage rolls by with ads on its side. So you jump in your car to escape the onslaught. But when you stop to pump gas a miniature video screen by the credit card slot urges you to get a Visa debit card from a bank. The billboards you ignore along the way seem pretty civilized compared to the towering trucks whose trailers are rolling billboards. Back at the ranch, at last, you know you can watch the Grammy Awards show in peace because you have TiVo—so you can zap past the ads. But no, you can't see the celebrities arrive without staring at virtual logos digitally superimposed on the entry canopy and sidewalk by the front door. So there's no alternative but to pull the plug on the TV and check for e-mail from your sweetie. Wrong move. A pop-up ad for a video cam covers half of the screen—and why can't you make it go away? You can drag it to the side, but then there's so much spam in your mailbox that you've run out of disk space.

There are certainly many cases where promotion benefits both the consumer and the firm, and after all it is revenues from advertising that cover the cost of lots of great stuff consumers get for free. Yet sometimes you can't help but wish that you were not the target that somebody else is aiming at![15]

Specialized media are small, but gaining rapidly	The advertising media listed in Exhibit 15-4 are attracting the vast majority of advertising media budgets. But advertising specialists always look for cost-effective new media that will help advertisers reach their target markets. For example, one company successfully sells space for signs on bike racks that it places in front of 7-Eleven stores. In Eastern Europe, where major media are still limited, companies like Campbell's pay to put ads on bus shelters. A new generation of ATMs show video ads while customers wait to get their money. Some gas station pumps have similar displays.[16] And, of course, the Internet is a medium that can be highly targeted.
"Must buys" may use up available funds	Selecting which media to use is still pretty much an art. The media buyer starts with a budgeted amount and tries to buy the best blend to reach the target audience.

Some media are obvious "must buys," like *the* local newspaper for a retailer in a small town. Most firms serving local markets view a Yellow Pages listing as a must buy. Web site advertising is increasingly seen as a must buy. It may be the only medium for firms trying to reach business buyers in overseas markets. Must buy ads may even use up the available funds.

For many firms, even national advertisers, the high cost of television may eliminate it from the media blend. The average cost just to produce a national TV ad is now about $250,000—and a big impact ad can easily cost twice that. In the United States, a 30-second commercial on a popular prime-time show like *Grey's Anatomy* is well over $400,000. The price goes up rapidly for "big event" shows that attract the largest audiences. Thirty seconds of advertising on the 2004 Super Bowl cost sponsors about $2.3 million.[17]

ADVERTISING ON THE INTERNET—NEW OPPORTUNITIES AND NEW CHALLENGES

Internet advertising is taking hold

Even though Internet advertising accounts for a small proportion of total ad spending, many firms are experimenting to figure out what works and does not work. Spending on Internet advertising shot up during the 1990s until it peaked at around $8 million in 2000. However, much of that early Internet advertising was to promote dot-com firms. When technology stocks plummeted, so did spending on Internet ads. However, in 2003, Internet advertising started to come back as mainstream advertisers increased both their spending and the percentage of it going to the Internet.

Most Internet ads seek a direct response

Advertising on the Internet takes a variety of forms—like buttons, banners, animations, and pop-ups—but the purpose of an ad is usually just to attract the interest of people in the advertiser's target market so that they'll click through to the firm's Web site. It is the Web site that does the heavy lifting, not the ads. But ads are the path to the site.

Web site advertising tends to be more interactive than traditional advertising. Increasingly, the content moves beyond the text and pictures typical of print ads and instead includes videos, sound, a product database, and order-entry shopping carts. The Web site advertiser can also offer a great deal more information and allow customers to self-direct to pages that interest them the most. In addition, the Web site can provide links to other outside sources of information. Or it can invite the viewer to e-mail or start a chat session for more detailed information. Further, it can offer a sign-up for e-mail updates when there is some sort of news.

But many consumers don't want to respond

We talked about the benefits of this sort of interactive communication in Chapter 13. However, it can also have a downside if it interferes with what the customer wants to do on the Internet. Pop-ups that won't go away, loud music that starts unexpectedly, and animations that take over the computer while they load often just create aggravation rather than interest. It's no wonder that some of the most popular free downloads on the Internet are programs to block pop-ups, turn off interactive features at a Web site, and prevent advertisers' "cookies" from tracking customers. Internet advertisers face the challenge of figuring out how to stimulate customer interest in ways that are acceptable to the customer.

Advertising managers are always looking for cost-effective new media that will help them reach their specific target markets.

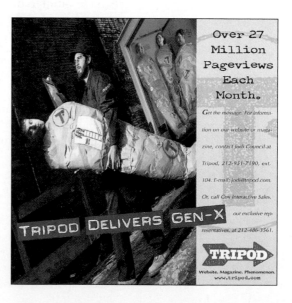

Some Web sites generate more exposure

Some advertisers are primarily interested in placing ads on Web sites that will give their ads more exposure, almost without regard to the content of the Web site or who visits it. Although there are millions of Web sites on the Internet, a small subset accounts for a large percentage of the potential audience. For example, many people start at the AOL, MSN, or Yahoo portal each time they use the Internet.

These Web sites are becoming for the Internet what the networks once were for television: *the* place where an advertiser is willing to pay high rates because they are uniquely able to reach a very large, broad market. For example, Dell might want its computer ads on the AOL or Yahoo home page so they will be viewed by the large number of computer user visitors. But what makes sense for Dell in that situation might not make sense for a firm with a different strategy. As with traditional media, getting lots of exposure for an Internet ad doesn't help if viewers are not in the firm's target market. At many Web sites, rates are set based on number of exposures, and you pay for an exposure regardless of who it is.

Some Web sites are better for reaching target customers

Bristol-Myers Squibb's experiment with Web advertising is typical of what many other firms do—place ads on Web sites that attract the desired target market. In the middle of income tax season, Bristol-Myers Squibb ran ads on financial Web sites extolling Excedrin as "the tax headache medicine." The ads offered a free sample of Excedrin. Within a month, more than 30,000 people clicked on the ad and typed their names into the firm's customer database. The cost of obtaining those names was half that of traditional methods. Now the firm can follow up the Excedrin samples with other database-directed promotions, either by e-mail or other methods.

Context advertising links ad to content being viewed

Targeting on the Internet can be even more precise. For example, ads for PerfumeOutlet.net pop up when an Internet user does a search on a term such as *perfume* or *Estée Lauder*. This approach is called *context advertising*—monitoring the content a net surfer is viewing and then serving up related ads. For example, if a consumer visits a Web site with information about cars, an ad for Amazon.ca might appear and note that it carries books on buying a car. If the consumer clicks on the Amazon ad, a list of links to relevant books appears on screen.

Pointcasting determines which customers see an ad

Another approach that offers more precise targeting is **pointcasting**. Pointcasting means displaying an ad *only* to an individual who meets certain qualifications, perhaps a person who has previously expressed direct interest in the topic of the advertising. A pointcasting ad is usually included with other information that the customer wants and that a pointcasting service provides for free. An example shows how this works. A woman who is interested in financial planning might sign up with Time-Warner Cable's Road Runner service and request that it routinely send her newly published articles on independent retirement accounts. When the service sends her that information over the Internet, it might include an ad from a mutual fund company. Many advertisers like this concept but worry that pointcasting overwhelms the recipient with too much clutter.

In response to rising consumer resentment, many firms send ads directly to the target customer via e-mail. A limitation of e-mail is that a person's e-mail software may reformat messages in different ways. That is changing with increased use of e-mail in HTML format and high-speed connections. However, a different problem will continue: Most people resent being "spammed" with a lot of unsolicited e-mail, and spam can become a big problem. Many firms send e-mail only to people who have given the firm permission to send it.

Some viewers get benefits if they agree to look at ads

Some Web sites offer people a benefit—like free e-mail or a chance to enter a contest—if they provide information about themselves and agree to view ads selected to match their interests. Juno offers free Internet and e-mail service when people sign up and provide detailed information about themselves. The information might include demographics as well as interests, what products they use, where they shop, and where they live. Then when a person checks for e-mail messages, ads are displayed. Each ad is selected specifically for that person based on his or her characteristics. For example, a cosmetics firm might specify that its ads be shown only to females who are 16 or older and who routinely wear nail polish.

While some consumers are willing to be targeted with advertising in exchange for free services, it is an ethical concern when many firms capture personal information about consumers without their knowledge. Even a brand-new computer may come with "spyware" already installed. Stealth tracking programs can be installed just by visiting a Web site or opening an e-mail. The intent of these advertisers may be to target more effectively, but in the process they impose costs on consumers. Invasion of privacy is one cost. Another is that a computer bogged down by a number of tracking programs slows to a crawl. Some stealth systems even divert consumers to Web sites they did not want to visit. The consumer backlash against these abuses is growing, and marketers who do not exercise judgment are likely to suffer the consequences.

At some Web sites, ads are free if they don't get results

Many Web sites charge advertisers a fee based on how frequently or how long an ad is shown. However, competition for advertisers has prompted some Web sites to display an ad for free and charge a fee only if the ad gets results. The fee the advertiser pays is sometimes based on "clickthrough"—the number of people who actually click on the ad and link to the advertiser's Web site. Some Web sites set fees based on actual sales that result from the clickthrough. This is a big shift from traditional media where firms have to pay for their ads whether they work or not. A lot more firms will put ads on Web sites if there is a direct relationship between costs and results. Moreover, this arrangement gives a Web site more incentive to attract an audience that some specific advertiser wants to reach.[18]

Another form of e-mail marketing is **viral marketing**. Viral marketing occurs when a firm sends e-mail to potential consumers in the hope those consumers will pass the e-mail along to their friends. Essentially this is the Internet version of the word-of-mouth advertising. To encourage viral marketing to happen, companies must create an e-mail message that is highly entertaining. Although it works best in consumer markets, it is possible for business-to-business firms to conduct a viral marketing campaign. Entertainment value in this market has an information-based focus.

The right copy thrust helps an ad clearly communicate to its target market.

PLANNING THE "BEST" MESSAGE—WHAT TO COMMUNICATE

Specifying the copy thrust

Once you decide *how* the messages will reach the target audience, you have to decide on the **copy thrust**—what the words and illustrations should communicate.

Carrying out the copy thrust is the job of advertising specialists. But the advertising manager and the marketing manager need to understand the process to be sure that the job is done well.

Let AIDA help guide message planning

Basically, the overall marketing strategy should determine *what* the message should say. Then management judgment, perhaps aided by marketing research, can help decide how to encode this content so it will be decoded as intended.

As a guide to message planning, we can use the AIDA concept: getting Attention, holding Interest, arousing Desire, and obtaining Action.

Getting attention

Getting attention is an ad's first job. Many readers leaf through magazines without paying attention to any of the ads, and viewers get snacks during TV commercials. When watching a program on TiVo, they may zap past the commercial with a flick of a button. On the Internet, they may use a pop-up blocker or click on the next Web site before the ad message finishes loading onto the screen.

Many attention-getting devices are available. A large headline, computer animations, shocking statements, attractive models, animals, special effects—anything different or eye-catching—may do the trick. However, the attention-getting device can't detract from, and hopefully should lead to, the next step, holding interest. The Dove advertising campaign garnered attention by using individuals rather than models in the ads.

Holding interest

Holding interest is more difficult. A humorous ad, an unusual video effect, or a clever photo may get your attention—but once you've seen it, then what? If there is no relation between what got your attention and the marketing mix, you'll move on. To hold interest, the tone and language of the ad must fit with the experiences and attitudes of the target customers and their reference groups. As a result, many advertisers develop ads that relate to specific emotions. They hope that the good feeling about the ad will stick, even if its details are forgotten.

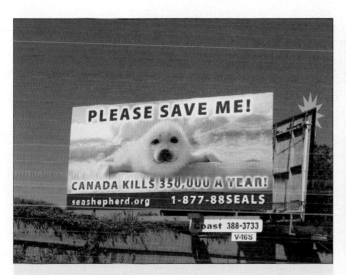

Billboards are good for getting attention with a simple copy thrust.

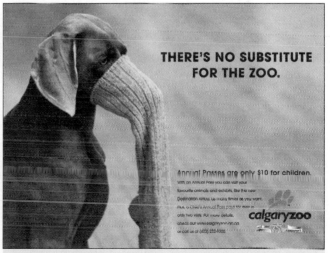

An unusual graphic captures attention. This ad was part a a series based on the same concept: Identify that animal!

The Dove Real Beauty Campaign featured real women of varying body sizes and types instead of the typical models normally used in advertisements.

New Dove Firming Lotion. Put your best behind forward.

To hold interest, informative ads need to speak the target customer's language. Persuasive ads must provide evidence that convinces the customer. For example, TV ads often demonstrate a product's benefits.

Layouts for print ads should be arranged to encourage the eye to move smoothly through the ad—perhaps from a headline that starts in the upper left-hand corner to the illustration or body copy in the middle and finally to the lower right corner where the ad's "signature" usually gives the company or brand name, toll-free number, and Web site address. If all of the elements of the ad work together as a whole, they will help to hold interest and build recall.[19] The Dove Real Beauty campaign related to the consumers' beliefs to hold interest. A reality focus differentiated their message.

Arousing desire

Arousing desire to buy a particular product is one of an ad's most difficult jobs. The ad must convince customers that the product can meet their needs. Testimonials may persuade a consumer that other people with similar needs like the product. Product comparisons may highlight the advantages of a particular brand.

Although products may satisfy certain emotional needs, many consumers find it necessary to justify their purchases on some logical basis. Snickers candy bar ads helped ease the guilt of calorie-conscious snackers by assuring them that "Snickers satisfies you when you need an afternoon energy break."

An ad should usually focus on a unique selling proposition that aims at an important unsatisfied need. This can help differentiate the firm's marketing mix and position its brand as offering superior value to the target market. For example, Altoids has used humour in its ads to highlight the "curiously strong" flavour of its mints. Too many advertisers ignore the idea of a unique selling proposition. Rather than using an integrated blend of communications to tell the whole story, they cram too much into each ad—and then none of it has any impact. Cold-Fx uses hockey personality Don Cherry to extoll the benefits of their unique product.

Obtaining action

Getting action is the final requirement—and not an easy one. From communication research, we now know that prospective customers must be led beyond considering how the product *might* fit into their lives to actually trying it.

Direct-response ads can sometimes help promote action by encouraging interested consumers to do *something* even if they are not ready to make a purchase. For example, an ad that includes a toll-free telephone number or Web site address might prompt some consumers to at least follow up for more information. Then follow-up brochures or a telephone salesperson can attempt to prompt another action—perhaps a visit to a store or a "satisfaction guaranteed" trial period. This approach seeks to get action one step at a time, where the first step provides a "foot in the door" for subsequent communication efforts. The Cold-Fx Web site carries product endorsements from athletes such as Clara Hughes and Jason Smith.

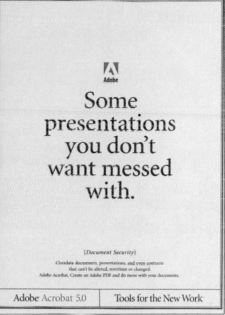

Ads that feature a unique selling proposition help consumers focus on what is different and better about a firm's marketing mix. This ad highlights the fact that Adobe's Acrobat 5.0 allows users to create electronic documents that can't be altered.

Subway uses their Web site to provide interested consumers with nutritional information.

Careful research on attitudes in the target market may help uncover strongly felt *unsatisfied* needs. Appealing to important needs can get more action and also provide the kind of information buyers need to confirm the correctness of their decisions. Some customers seem to read more advertising *after* a purchase than before.

Can global messages work?

Many international consumer products firms try to use one global advertising message all around the world. Of course, they translate the message or make other minor adjustments—but the focus is one global copy thrust. Some do it to cut the cost of developing different ads for each country. Others feel their customers' basic needs are the same, even in different countries. Some just do it because it's fashionable to "go global."

This approach works for some firms. Coca-Cola and IBM, for example, feel that the needs their products serve are very similar for customers around the world. They focus on the similarities among customers who make up their target market rather than the differences. However, most firms who use this approach experience terrible results. They may save money by developing fewer ads, but they lose sales because they don't develop advertising messages, and whole marketing mixes, aimed at specific target markets. They just try to appeal to a global "mass market." McDonald's global campaign tag line—"I'm lovin' it" has mass market appeal.

Combining smaller market segments into a single, large target market makes sense if the different segments can be served with a single marketing mix. But when that is not the case, the marketing manager should treat them as different target markets and develop different marketing mixes for each target.[20]

ADVERTISING AGENCIES OFTEN DO THE WORK

An advertising manager manages a company's advertising effort. Many advertising managers, especially those working for large retailers, have their own advertising departments that plan specific advertising campaigns and carry out the details. Others turn over much of the advertising work to specialists—the advertising agencies.

Ad agencies are specialists

Advertising agencies are specialists in planning and handling mass-selling details for advertisers. Agencies play a useful role. They are independent of the advertiser and have an outside viewpoint. They bring experience to an individual client's problems because they work for many other clients. They can often do the job more economically than a company's own department. And if an agency isn't doing a good job, the client can select another. However, ending a relationship with an agency is a serious decision. Too many marketing managers just use their advertising agency as a scapegoat. Whenever anything goes wrong, they blame the agency.

Some full-service agencies handle any activities related to advertising, publicity, or sales promotion. They may even handle overall marketing strategy planning as well as marketing research, product and package development, and sales promotion. Other agencies are more specialized. For example, in recent years there has been rapid growth of firms that specialize in developing Web sites and Internet ads. Critical Mass, a Calgary agency, specializes in Internet advertising for clients such as Dell, Mercedes-Benz, Hyatt Hotels, and NASA. Similarly, creative specialists just handle the artistic elements of advertising but leave media scheduling and buying, research, and related services to other specialists or full-service agencies.

The biggest agencies handle much of the advertising

The vast majority of advertising agencies are small, with 10 or fewer employees. But the largest agencies account for most of the billings. Over the past decade many of the big agencies merged, creating mega-agencies with worldwide networks. The move toward international marketing is a key reason behind the mergers. Two of the largest are Omnicom and Interpublic, handling accounts for PepsiCo, FedEx, and John Deere, among others.

The mega-agency can offer varied services, wherever in the world a marketing manager needs them. This may be especially important for managers in large corporations—like Toyota, Renault, Unilever, NEC, and PepsiCo—that advertise worldwide.[21]

The really big agencies are less interested in smaller accounts. Smaller agencies will continue to appeal to customers who want more personal attention and a close relationship that is more attuned to their marketing needs.

Are they paid too much?

Traditionally, advertising agencies have been paid a commission of about 15 percent on media and production costs. This arrangement evolved because media usually have two prices: one for national advertisers and a lower rate for local advertisers, such as local retailers. The advertising agency gets a 15 percent commission on national rates but not on local rates. This makes it worthwhile for producers and national middlemen to use agencies. National advertisers have to pay the full media rate anyway, so it makes sense to let the agency experts do the work and earn their commission. Local retailers—allowed the lower media rate—seldom use agencies.

Many firms—especially big producers of consumer packaged goods—resist the idea of paying agencies the same way regardless of the work performed or *the results achieved.* The commission approach also makes it hard for agencies to be completely objective about inexpensive media. But agencies don't always like a commission arrangement, either. Some try to charge additional fees when advertisers spend relatively little on media or need extra services, like preparation of materials to support a Web site or the personal selling effort. About half of all advertisers now pay agencies some sort of labour-based fee.

Firms that spend huge amounts for help from advertising agencies are increasingly involving their purchasing departments in the process of negotiating agency compensation and other terms of the agency-client relationship. Procurement specialists may also set up procedures to audit agency charges for "billable hours" or other expenses. Auditing may become even more common in the future because of a few highly publicized cases in which agency executives have been accused of padding their time sheets.

Some firms pay the agency based on results

A number of advertisers now grade the work done by their agencies—and the agencies' pay depends on the grade. General Foods was the first to do this. It lowered its basic commission to about 13 percent. However, it paid the agency a bonus of about 3 percent on campaigns that earned an A rating. If the agency only earned a B, it lost the bonus. If it earned a C, it had to improve fast or GF removed the account.

Variations on this approach are becoming common. For example, Carnation directly links its agency's compensation with how well its ads score in market research tests. Gillette uses a sliding scale, and the percentage of compensation declines with increased advertising volume. And some agencies develop their own plans in which they guarantee to achieve the results expected or give the advertiser a partial refund. This approach forces the advertiser and agency to agree on very specific objectives for their ads and what they expect to achieve. It also reduces the likelihood of the creative people in an agency focusing on ads that will win artistic approval in their industry rather than ads that do what the firm needs done.[22]

Ethical conflicts may arise

Ad agencies usually work closely with their clients, and they often have access to confidential information. This can create ethical conflicts if an agency is working with two or more competing clients. Most agencies are sensitive to the potential problems and keep people and information from competing accounts separated. Even so, that doesn't always happen. For example, PepsiCo got a restraining order to stop an ad agency from assigning four people who had worked on advertising for its Aquafina bottled water to the account for Coca-Cola's competing brand, Dasani. Coca-Cola, in turn, yanked the account away from the agency. In another case, the part of General Motors' ad agency that handles ads for archrival Toyota hired an employee away from GM to work on the Toyota account. GM's marketing managers were outraged by the agency's lack of loyalty. Because of situations like these, many advertisers refuse to work with any agency that handles any competing accounts, even if they are handled in different offices.[23]

MEASURING ADVERTISING EFFECTIVENESS IS NOT EASY

Success depends on the total marketing mix

It would be convenient if we could measure the results of advertising by looking at sales. Some breakthrough ads do have a very direct effect on a company's sales—and the advertising literature is filled with success stories that "prove" advertising increases sales. Similarly, market research firms like Information Resources can sometimes compare sales levels before and after the period of an ad campaign. Yet we usually can't measure advertising success just by looking at sales. The total marketing mix—not just advertising—is responsible for the sales result. Sales results are also affected by what competitors do and by other changes in the external marketing environment. Only with direct-response advertising can a company make a direct link between advertising and sales results.

Research and testing can improve the odds

Ideally, advertisers should pretest advertising before it runs rather than relying solely on their own guesses about how good an ad will be. The judgment of creative people or advertising experts may not help much. They often judge only on the basis of originality or cleverness of the copy and illustrations.

Many progressive advertisers now demand laboratory or market tests to evaluate an ad's effectiveness. For example, split runs on cable TV systems in test markets are an important approach for testing ads in a normal viewing environment. Scanner sales data from retailers in those test markets can provide an estimate of how an ad is likely to affect sales. This approach will become even more powerful in the future as more cable systems allow viewers to provide immediate feedback to an ad as it appears on TV or on the Internet.

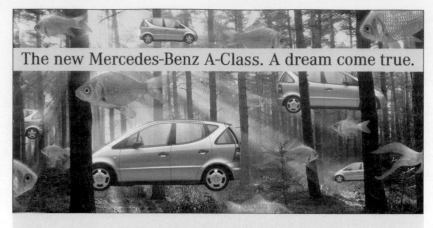

The new Mercedes-Benz A-Class. A dream come true.

Mercedes used this ad (above) to help introduce its new model and attract younger customers in Latin America. A bad economy dampened sales, but the ad did pull the target market into showrooms. This increased names in the dealers' customer database, used to target other promotions, by 50 percent. Firms like QuickTake.com do research to help advertisers determine if a creative ad is also effective.

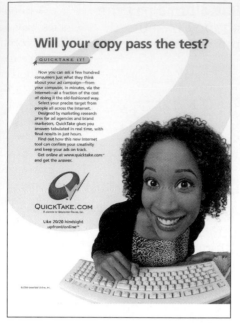

Hindsight may lead to foresight

After ads run, researchers may try to measure how much consumers recall about specific products or ads. The response to radio or television commercials or magazine readership can be estimated using various survey methods to check the size and composition of audiences (the Nielsen and Starch reports are examples). Similarly, most Internet advertisers keep track of how many "hits" on the firm's Web site come from ads placed at other Web sites.[24]

HOW TO AVOID UNFAIR ADVERTISING

Government agencies may say what is fair

In most countries, the government takes an active role in deciding what kinds of advertising are allowable, fair, and appropriate. For example, France and Japan limit the use of cartoon characters in advertising to children. In Canada, Quebec bans *any* advertising targeted directly at children. Greece and Sweden have similar policies and want the rest of the European Union to adopt them. In Switzerland, an advertiser cannot use an actor to represent a consumer. New Zealand and Switzerland limit political ads on TV. In the United States, print ads must be identified so they aren't confused with editorial matter; in other countries ads and editorial copy can be intermixed. Most countries limit the number and length of commercials on broadcast media.

What is seen as positioning in one country may be viewed as unfair or deceptive in another. For example, when Pepsi was advertising its cola as "the choice of the new generation" in most countries, Japan's Fair Trade Committee didn't allow it—because in Japan Pepsi was not "the choice." Similarly, Hungary's Economic Competition Council fined Unilever $25,000 for running an ad that claimed that its OMO detergent removed stains better than ordinary detergent. The Council said the ad was unfair because Hungarian consumers would interpret the phrase "ordinary detergent" as a reference to a locally produced detergent.[25]

Differences in rules mean that a marketing manager may face very specific limits in different countries, and local experts may be required to ensure that a firm doesn't waste money developing ads that will never be shown or which consumers will think are deceptive.

Industry Canada controls unfair practices in Canada

In Canada, Industry Canada (via the Competition Act) has the power to control unfair or deceptive business practices, including deceptive advertising—which they have been policing for many years. And it may be getting results now that advertising agencies as well as advertisers must share equal responsibility for false, misleading, or unfair ads. The possibility of large financial penalties or the need to pay for corrective ads has caused more agencies and advertisers to stay well within the law.

However, sometimes ad claims seem to get out of hand anyway. For example, there have been many ads and infomercials that tout various gadgets and dietary supplements as effective for weight loss. For most of these products there is no evidence that they work (unless used while training to compete in a marathon). Industry Canada will force advertisers to pull ads that cannot substantiate their claims.

What is unfair or deceptive is changing

What constitutes unfair and deceptive advertising is a difficult question. The law provides some guidelines, but the marketing manager must make personal judgments as well. The social and political environment is changing worldwide. Practices considered acceptable some years ago are now questioned or considered deceptive. Saying or even implying that your product is best may be viewed as deceptive.

Supporting ad claims is a fuzzy area

It's really not hard to figure out how to avoid criticisms of being unfair and deceptive. A little puffing is acceptable, and probably always will be. But marketing managers need to put a stop to the typical production-oriented approach of trying to use advertising to differentiate me-too products that are not different and don't offer customers better value.[26]

PUBLICITY

Publicity stimulates consumer demand

Publicity is a nonpersonal, nonpaid form of stimulating consumer demand. Public relations is an image-directed, planned effort to generate publicity for a company or a product. The two terms, although different, are often used interchangeably in the practice of marketing. Companies want to manage publicity to ensure that this component of the promotion strategy is integrated with the advertising, sales promotion, and personal selling efforts.

Tools of the trade include news releases, media coverage of sponsored events, press conferences, and interviews. Media coverage for events such as the CIBC Run For The Cure or the Forzani's Mother's Day Run generates positive publicity for their sponsors. New product introductions may also generate publicity. The Dove Real Beauty advertising campaign generated a lot of publicity for Dove. Ads were discussed on TV talk shows, by radio personalities, and covered in newspaper and magazine articles.

Free media space is an advantage

Publicity has many advantages for a company. Although managing the public relations effort does involve paying for people to do the work, the media space is free. The company does not pay for the message or the media.

Due to the nature of publicity, it has high credibility with consumers. Consumers generally do not perceive publicity to be advertising. More likely, they will perceive the message as news. Hence the audience may be much more attentive than if watching an advertisement.

Lack of message control is not

Although publicity comes without a media cost, there are definite drawbacks to using publicity. Companies have little control over the message, the timing of the message, the placement, or even the media used. A concerted public relations effort is needed to ensure that negative publicity is minimized and the desired messages are communicated to the audience in a timely manner.

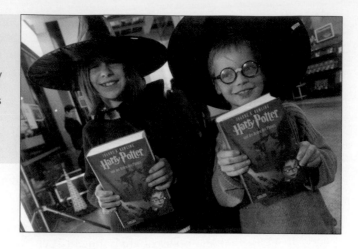

Publicity generated for *Harry Potter and the Order of the Phoenix* is a classic example. There was already huge interest in the Potter series. Every new book had increased sales. But Raincoast Books, the distributor, got an even bigger bang—and worldwide media coverage—by keeping the plot shrouded in secrecy and notifying bookstores and the media that no store could sell the book before 12:01 A.M. Saturday, June 21. Print runs and deliveries were scheduled to make that stick. As word of the secrecy spread, national media picked up on the story and devoted a huge amount of attention to it. For example, the week the book came out, Harry was on the cover of *Time* and a feature article explained all of the reasons it was going to be one of the fastest-selling books in history. Local newspapers got in on the action with their own stories on late-night Harry parties planned by local retailers. With publicity like that, even people who had never heard of the series wanted to find out what they were missing.[27] A few books "leaked" (sold) in Quebec in advance of the launch also created publicity for the Harry Potter book.

If a firm has a really new message, publicity may be more effective than advertising. Trade magazines, for example, may carry articles featuring the newsworthy products of regular advertisers—in part because they *are* regular advertisers. The firm's publicity people write the basic copy and then try to convince magazine editors to print it. A consumer might carefully read a long magazine story but ignore an ad with the same information.

Some companies prepare videotapes designed to get free publicity for their products on TV news shows. For example, after learning that Seattle Mariner Jay Buhner loves Cheerios, a General Mills marketing manager had 162 boxes of the cereal stuffed into his spring-training locker and videotaped Buhner's surprise on opening his locker. TV news programs in 12 major markets showed the video. It would have cost hundreds of thousands of dollars to get as much attention with advertising.[28]

One problem with publicity is that the media don't always say or show what the firm intends. Heinz ran into this problem when it introduced Blastin' Green EZ Squirt Ketchup. The media covered it earlier than Heinz intended, so in-store displays were not yet stocked and there wasn't enough inventory to fill the orders that flowed in from retailers. Heinz also wanted publicity to focus more on the bottle's design and how it was easy for kids to use, but the green colour got the attention. In Heinz' case, the media coverage was still a positive.[29] That isn't always the case. When Segway got an order from the vice president of the United States, it seemed like a perfect opportunity for publicity. It looked even better at the White House when President Bush got on to take a ride—until he fell off the Segway with photographers snapping pictures.[30]

Sony's interactive kiosk provides special in-store sales promotion support for memory sticks used by portable electronic devices like the new MS Walkman.

SALES PROMOTION—DO SOMETHING DIFFERENT TO STIMULATE CHANGE

The nature of sales promotion

Sales promotion refers to those promotion activities—other than advertising, publicity, and personal selling—that stimulate interest, trial, or purchase by final customers or others in the channel. Exhibit 13-2 shows examples of typical sales promotions targeted at final customers, channel members, or a firm's own employees.

Sales promotion is generally used to complement the other promotion methods. While advertising campaigns and sales force strategy decisions tend to have longer-term effects, a particular sales promotion activity usually lasts for only a limited time period. But sales promotion can often be implemented quickly and get sales results sooner than advertising. Further, sales promotion objectives usually focus on prompting some short-term action. For a middleman, such an action might be a decision to stock a product, provide a special display space, or give the product extra sales emphasis. For a consumer, the desired action might be to try a new product, switch from another brand, or buy more of a product. The desired action by an employee might be a special effort to satisfy customers.

Sales promotion objectives and situation should influence decision

There are many different types of sales promotion, but what type is appropriate depends on the situation and objectives. For example, Exhibit 15-5 shows some possible ways that a short-term promotion might affect sales. The sales pattern in the graph on the left might occur if Hellmann's issues coupons to help clear its excess mayonnaise inventory. Some consumers might buy earlier to take advantage of the coupon, but unless they use extra mayonnaise their next purchase will be delayed. In the centre graph, kids might convince parents to eat more Big Macs while McDonald's has a *Lord of the Rings* promotion, but when it ends things go back to normal. The graph on the right shows a Burger King marketer's dream come true: Free samples of a new style of french fries quickly pull in new customers who like what they try and keep coming back after the promotion ends. This is also the kind of long-term result that is the aim of effective advertising. From these examples, you can see that the situation and the objective of the promotion should determine what specific type is best.

Exhibit 15-5   Some Possible Effects of a Sales Promotion on Sales

Sales temporarily increase, then decrease, then return to regular level

Sales temporarily increase and then return to regular level

Sales increase and then remain at higher level

Sales promotion spending has grown in mature markets

Sales promotion involves so many different types of activities that it is difficult to estimate accurately how much is spent in total. There is general consensus, however, that the total spending on sales promotion exceeds spending on advertising. Companies that sell frequently purchased consumer products shifted their promotion blends to put more emphasis on sales promotion during the 1990s.[31]

One reason for increased use of sales promotion by many consumer products firms is that they are generally competing in mature markets. There's only so much soap that consumers want to buy, regardless of how many brands there are vying for their dollars. There's also only so much shelf space that retailers will allocate to a particular product category.

The competitive situation is intensified by the growth of large, powerful retail chains. They have put more emphasis on their own dealer brands and also demanded more sales promotion support for the manufacturer brands they do carry. Canadian Tire encourages store loyalty be offering customers Canadian Tire money with purchases. The Canadian Tire money can later be redeemed for merchandise or donated to charity. Exhibit 15-6 outlines a variety of promotional tools.

A number of firms that specialize in different aspects of consumer promotion, ranging from in-store ideas to games, are available to create solutions for marketing managers.

Exhibit 15-6
Examples of Consumer Sales
Promotion Tools

Contests	Coupons	Sweepstakes
Samples	Rebates	Loyalty Programs
Lotteries	Referral Gifts	Demonstrations
Gift with Purchase	Point of Purchase Displays	Trade-in Allowances

Perhaps in part because of this competition, many consumers have become more price sensitive. Many sales promotions, like coupons, have the effect of lowering the prices consumers pay. So sales promotion has been used as a tool to overcome consumer price resistance.

Changes in technology have also made sales promotion more efficient. For example, scanners at retail checkout counters instantly pinpoint a customer who is the target for a particular coupon. If a customer buys a bottle of Kraft salad dressing, Kraft can have the retailer's cash register print out a coupon, on the spot, to encourage the customer to buy Kraft again the next time.

The growth of sales promotion has also been fostered by the availability of more ad agencies and specialists who plan and implement sales promotion programs. Of course, the most basic reason for the growth of spending on sales promotion is that it can be very effective if it is done properly. But there are problems in the sales promotion area.

PROBLEMS IN MANAGING SALES PROMOTION

Does sales promotion erode brand loyalty?

Some experts think that marketing managers—especially those who deal with consumer packaged goods—put too much emphasis on sales promotion. They argue that the effect of most sales promotion is temporary and that money spent on advertising and personal selling helps the firm more over the long term. Their view is that most sales promotion doesn't help develop close relationships with consumers and instead erodes brand loyalty.

There is heavy use of sales promotion in mature markets where competition for customers and attention from middlemen is fierce. When the market is not growing, sales promotion may just encourage "deal-prone" customers (and middlemen) to switch back and forth among brands. Here, all the expense of the sales promotion simply contributes to lower profits. It also increases the prices that consumers pay because it increases selling costs.

However, once a marketing manager is in this situation there may be little choice other than to continue. In mature markets, frequent sales promotions may be needed just to offset the effects of competitors' promotions. One escape from this competitive rat race is for the marketing manager to seek new opportunities—with a strategy that doesn't rely solely on short-term sales promotions for competitive advantage.

There are alternatives

Procter & Gamble is a company that changed its strategy, and promotion blend, to decrease its reliance on sales promotion targeted at middlemen. It is offering middlemen lower prices on many of its products and supporting those products with more advertising and promotion to final consumers. P&G believes that this approach builds its brand equity, serves consumers better, and leads to smoother-running relationships in its channels. Not all retailers are happy with P&G's changes. However, many other producers are following P&G's lead.[32]

Sales promotion is hard to manage

Another problem in the sales promotion area is that it is easy to make big, costly mistakes. Because sales promotion includes such a wide variety of activities, it's difficult for the typical company to develop skill in managing all of them. Even large

MARKETING ETHICALLY

Ethical questions come into play when consumers provide their names for a contest, for example, and then are hounded by telemarketers and other direct marketers who buy that list from the original company. CBC's *Marketplace* looked at this situation on one of its episodes. The episode starts with Kerri-Lynn G. who lives in St. John's, Newfoundland. A few years ago, she was looking forward to being a new mom. Shortly after her baby was due to be born, Kerri-Lynn got a call from a company selling RESPs (Registered Education Savings Plans) for kids.

Kerri-Lynn had no idea how they got her name. She'd never heard of the company. "They said, 'Congratulations on the birth of your baby,'" recalls Kerri-Lynn. What the RESP company didn't know was that Kerri-Lynn had had a miscarriage months before. Kerri-Lynn was very upset getting this call. To add insult to injury, Kerri-Lynn started getting a barrage of brochures and coupons dealing with baby items in the mail. Kerri-Lynn suspects she could have been added to the RESP seller's lists when she signed up for a contest at a clothing store. Her name, along with others who entered the contest, was sold to other direct marketing companies.

Another example from this episode was Kelly, who was called by someone who sounded official, such as a government agency, but who in reality was selling RESPs. The call upset Kelly who, having given birth a few days previous, was in no mood to talk to a telemarketer.

Marketplace found out that her name and phone number were obtained underhandedly. It turns out that Kelly's hospital allows photo companies into the maternity ward to take pictures of the new babies. They take more than photographs—they take personal data: children's birth dates, names, and home phone numbers. The photo company sells that information to other companies who want to pitch products to new parents.

What suggestions do you have to stop unethical marketers from engaging in underhanded practices such as those explained above?[33]

firms and agencies that specialize in sales promotion run into difficulties because each promotion is typically custom-designed and then used only once. Yet mistakes caused by lack of experience can be costly or hurt relationships with customers.

In a promotion for Pampers diapers that was designed to reward loyal buyers and steal customers away from competing Huggies, marketing managers offered parents Fisher-Price toys if they collected points printed on Pampers' packages. At first the promotion seemed to be a big success because so many parents were collecting points. But that turned into a problem when Fisher-Price couldn't produce enough toys to redeem all the points. Pampers had to add 50 toll-free phone lines to handle all the complaints, and a lot of mad parents stopped buying Pampers for good. Burger King has also had problems with toys. Several times in recent years it has had to issue recalls because toys included in its Kid's Meal promotions were not safe. McDonald's had a different problem. An employee of an outside firm hired to run McDonald's Monopoly game promotion was accused of rigging the top prizes. McDonald's sued the outside firm, but in the meantime it had to offer an additional $10 million game to fulfill its promises to customers. These are not isolated examples. Such problems are common.[34] Tim Hortons' Roll Up the Rim To Win campaign generated a lawsuit regarding who "owned" a winning cup found discarded on the street. This did, however, generate publicity for Tim Hortons!

Not a sideline for amateurs

Sales promotion mistakes are likely to be worse when a company has no sales promotion manager. If the personal selling or advertising managers are responsible for sales promotion, they often treat it as a "stepchild." They allocate money to sales promotion if there is any "left over" or if a crisis develops.

Making sales promotion work is a learned skill, not a sideline for amateurs. That's why specialists in sales promotion have developed, both inside larger firms and as outside consultants. Some of these people are real experts. But it's the marketing manager's responsibility to set sales promotion objectives and policies that will fit in with the rest of each marketing strategy.[35]

DIFFERENT TYPES OF SALES PROMOTION FOR DIFFERENT TARGETS

Sales promotion for final consumers or users

Much of the sales promotion aimed at final consumers or users tries to increase demand, perhaps temporarily, or speed up the time of purchase. Such promotion might involve developing materials to be displayed in retailers' stores, including banners, sample packages, calendars, and various point-of-purchase materials. It might include sweepstakes contests as well as coupons designed to get customers to buy a product by a certain date. Coupon distribution has dropped off some in recent years but still averages about 3,000 coupons per household! However, only about 1 percent of all coupons are redeemed.[36]

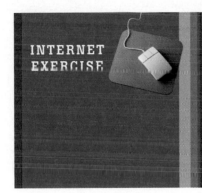

INTERNET EXERCISE

AM/PM Service is a Canadian company offering retailers a variety of point-of-sale tools. Many of these tools are compatible with the promotion mix retailers desire to offer. Check out their Web site (ampmservice.com) to see what's available. Click on *Grocery Store Checkout Systems*. Click *Fujitsu U-Scan Self-Checkout Information* to see what can be integrated into a new self-checkout system. Then compare those features to the standard shopper features on a regular checkout system such as the Fujitsu ISS 45. Which system works better for a retailer with a customer loyalty program?

All of these sales promotion efforts are aimed at specific objectives. For example, if customers already have a favourite brand, it may be hard to get them to try anything new. A free trial-sized bottle of mouthwash might be just what it takes to get cautious consumers to try the new product. Samples might be distributed house to house, by mail, at stores, or attached to other products sold by the firm. In this type of situation, sales of the product might start to pick up as soon as customers try the product and find out that they like it. And sales will continue at the higher level after the promotion is over if satisfied customers make repeat purchases. Thus, the cost of the sales promotion in this situation might be viewed as a long-term investment. Many retail stores, such as Fruits & Passion, offer point-of-purchase testers so consumers can try new products without having to purchase them.

Once a product is established, consumer sales promotion usually focuses on short-term sales increases. For example, after a price-off coupon for a soft drink is distributed, sales might temporarily pick up as customers take advantage of buying at a lower price. When the objective of the promotion is focused primarily on producing a short-term increase in sales, it's sensible for the marketing manager to evaluate the cost of the promotion relative to the extra sales expected. If the increase in sales won't at least cover the cost of the promotion, it probably doesn't make sense to do it. Otherwise, the firm is "buying sales" at the cost of reduced profit. Longer-term promotions often focus on loyalty programs, such as Air Canada's Aeroplan or The Bay's Hbc Rewards.

Sales promotion directed at industrial customers might use the same kinds of ideas. In addition, the sales promotion people might set up and staff trade show exhibits. Here, attractive models are often used to encourage buyers to look at a firm's product, especially when it is displayed near other similar products in a circuslike atmosphere. Trade shows are a cost-effective way to reach target customers and generate a list of "live" prospects for sales rep follow-up. However, many firms handle these leads badly. One study indicated that 85 percent of leads never got followed up by anybody.

Some sellers give promotion items—pen sets, watches, or clothing (perhaps with the firm's brand name on them)—to remind business customers of their products. This is common, but it can be a problem. Some companies do not allow buyers to take any gifts.[37]

Sales promotion for middlemen

Sales promotion aimed at middlemen—sometimes called *trade promotion*—emphasizes price-related matters. The objective may be to encourage middlemen to stock new items, buy in larger quantity, buy early, or stress a product in their own promotion efforts.

The tools used here include merchandise allowances, promotion allowances, and perhaps sales contests to encourage retailers or wholesalers to sell specific items or the company's whole line. Offering to send contest winners to Hawaii, for example, may increase sales.

About half of the sales promotion spending targeted at middlemen has the effect of reducing the price that they pay for merchandise. So we'll go into more detail on different types of trade discounts and allowances in the next chapter.[38]

Sales promotion for own employees

Sales promotion aimed at the company's own sales force might try to encourage providing better service, getting new customers, selling a new product, or selling the company's whole line. Depending on the objectives, the tools might be contests, bonuses on sales or number of new accounts, and holding sales meetings at fancy resorts to raise everyone's spirits.

Ongoing sales promotion work might also be aimed at the sales force—to help sales management. Sales promotion might be responsible for preparing sales portfolios, digital videos or PowerPoint presentations on new products, displays, and other sales aids, as well as sales training material.

Service-oriented firms such as hotels and restaurants use sales promotions targeted at their employees. Some, for example, give a monthly cash prize for the employee who provides the "best service." And the employee's picture is displayed to give recognition.[39]

CONCLUSION

It may seem simple to develop an advertising campaign. Just pick the medium and develop a message. But it's not that easy. Effectiveness depends on using the "best" available medium and the "best" message considering (1) promotion objectives, (2) the target markets, and (3) the funds available for advertising.

Specific advertising objectives determine what kind of advertising to use—product or institutional. If product advertising is needed, then the particular type must be decided—pioneering, competitive (direct or indirect), or reminder. And advertising allowances and cooperative advertising may be helpful.

Many technical details are involved in mass selling, and specialists—advertising agencies—handle some of

these jobs. But specific objectives must be set for them, or their advertising may have little direction and be almost impossible to evaluate.

Effective advertising should affect sales. Using Jared in Subway ads did increase sales for Subway. But the whole marketing mix affects sales—and the results of advertising usually can't be measured by sales changes alone. By contrast, sales promotion tends to be more action-oriented.

Sales promotion spending is big and growing. This approach is especially important in prompting action—by customers, middlemen, or salespeople. There are many different types of sales promotion, and it is a problem area in many firms because it is difficult for a firm to develop expertise with all of the possibilities.

Companies must also keep up to date with advances in the use of the Internet for both advertising and sales promotion.

Advertising and sales promotion are often important parts of a promotion blend—but in most blends personal selling also plays an important role. Further, promotion is only a part of the total marketing mix a marketing manager must develop to satisfy target customers. So to broaden your understanding of the four Ps and how they fit together, in the next two chapters we'll go into more detail on the role of Price in strategy decisions.

KEY TERMS

product advertising, 412

institutional advertising, 412

pioneering advertising, 413

competitive advertising, 413

direct type advertising, 413

indirect type advertising, 413

comparative advertising, 413

reminder advertising, 414

advertising allowances, 415

cooperative advertising, 415

pointcasting, 421

viral marketing, 422

copy thrust, 423

advertising agencies, 426

QUESTIONS AND PROBLEMS

1. Identify the strategy decisions a marketing manager must make in the advertising area.

2. Discuss the relation of advertising objectives to marketing strategy planning and the kinds of advertising actually needed. Illustrate.

3. List several media that might be effective for reaching consumers in a developing nation with low per capita income and a high level of illiteracy. Briefly discuss the limitations and advantages of each medium you suggest.

4. Give three examples where advertising to middlemen might be necessary. What are the objective(s) of such advertising?

5. What does it mean to say that "money is invested in advertising"? Is all advertising an investment? Illustrate.

6. Find advertisements to final consumers that illustrate the following types of advertising: (a) institutional, (b) pioneering, (c) competitive, and (d) reminder. What objective(s) does each of these ads have? List the needs each ad appeals to.

7. Describe the type of media that might be most suitable for promoting: (a) tomato soup, (b) greeting cards, (c) a business component material, and (d) playground equipment. Specify any assumptions necessary to obtain a definite answer.

8. Briefly discuss some of the pros and cons an advertising manager for a producer of sports equipment might want to think about in deciding whether to advertise on the Internet.

9. Discuss the use of testimonials in advertising. Which of the four AIDA steps might testimonials accomplish? Are they suitable for all types of products? If not, for which types are they most suitable?

10. Find a magazine ad that you think does a particularly good job of communicating to the target audience. Would the ad communicate well to an audience in another country? Explain your thinking.

11. Johnson & Johnson sells its baby shampoo in many different countries. Do you think baby shampoo would be a good product for Johnson & Johnson to advertise with a single global message? Explain your thinking.

12. Discuss the future of smaller advertising agencies now that many of the largest are merging to form mega-agencies.

13. Does advertising cost too much? How can this be measured?

14. How would your local newspaper be affected if local supermarkets switched their weekly advertising and instead used a service that delivered weekly, free-standing ads directly to each home?

15. Is it unfair to criticize a competitor's product in an ad? Explain your thinking.

16. Consider Exhibit 15-2. Why do you think ad spending is so variable across different product-markets?

17. Explain why P&G and other consumer packaged goods firms are trying to cut back on some types of sales promotion like coupons for consumers and short-term trade promotions such as "buy a case and get a case free."

18. Discuss some ways that a firm can link its sales promotion activities to its advertising and personal selling efforts—so that all of its promotion efforts result in an integrated effort.

19. Indicate the type of sales promotion that a producer might use in each of the following situations and briefly explain your reasons:

    a. A firm has developed an improved razor blade and obtained distribution, but customers are not motivated to buy it.
    b. A competitor is about to do a test market for a new brand and wants to track sales in test market areas to fine tune its marketing mix.

    c. A big grocery chain won't stock a firm's new pop-corn-based snack product because it doesn't think there will be much consumer demand.

20. Why wouldn't a producer of toothpaste just lower the price of its product rather than offer consumers a price-off coupon?

21. If sales promotion spending continues to grow—often at the expense of media advertising—how do you think this might affect the rates charged by mass media for advertising time or space? How do you think it might affect advertising agencies?

22. Discuss how Petro-Canada could use each element of the promotion mix in an integrated communication program.

COMPUTER-AIDED PROBLEM

15. Sales Promotion

RESOURCE REMINDER

As a community service, disc jockeys from radio station WMKT formed a basketball team to help raise money for local nonprofit organizations. The host organization finds or fields a competing team and charges $5 admission to the game. Money from ticket sales goes to the nonprofit organization.

Ticket sales were disappointing at recent games, averaging only about 300 people per game. When WMKT's marketing manager, Bruce Miller, heard about the problem, he suggested using sales promotion to improve ticket sales. The PTA for the local high school—the sponsor for the next game—is interested in the idea but is concerned that its budget doesn't include any promotion money. Miller tries to help them by reviewing his idea in more detail.

Specifically, he proposes that the PTA give a free T-shirt (printed with the school name and date of the game) to the first 500 ticket buyers. He thinks the T-shirt giveaway will create a lot of interest. In fact, he says he is almost certain the promotion would help the PTA sell 600 tickets, double the usual number. He speculates that the PTA might even have a sellout of all 900 seats in the school gym. Further, he notes that the T-shirts will more than pay for themselves if the PTA sells 600 tickets.

A local firm that specializes in sales promotion items agrees to supply the shirts and do the printing for $2.40 a shirt if the PTA places an order for at least 400 shirts. The PTA thinks the idea is interesting but wants to look at it more closely to see what will happen if the promotion doesn't increase ticket sales. To help the PTA evaluate the alternatives, Miller sets up a spreadsheet with the relevant information.

a. Based on the data from the initial spreadsheet, does the T-shirt promotion look like a good idea? Explain your thinking.

b. The PTA treasurer worries about the up-front cost of printing the T-shirts and wants to know where they would stand if they ordered the T-shirts and still sold only 300 tickets. He suggests it might be safer to order the minimum number of T-shirts (400). Evaluate his suggestion.

c. The president of the PTA thinks the T-shirt promotion will increase sales but wonders if it wouldn't be better just to lower the price. She suggests $2.60 a ticket, which she arrives at by subtracting the $2.40 T-shirt cost from the usual $5.00 ticket price. How many tickets would the PTA have to sell at the lower price to match the money it would make if it used the T-shirt promotion and actually sold 600 tickets? (Hint: Change the selling price in the spreadsheet and then vary the quantity using the analysis feature.)

If you want to read the cases and view the video cases that accompany this chapter, visit the *Basic Marketing* Online Learning Centre at: **www.mcgrawhill.ca/olc/perreault**. Along with these cases and video cases, the OLC also has the software and user guide for this chapter's Computer-Aided Problem, as well as exercises, quizzes, articles, links, and other *interactive* content that will help you with your studies.

Pricing Objectives and Policies

In the early 1960s, the electric toothbrush was a new idea. A number of brands were on the market, and the American Dental Association declared that electric brushes were better at cleaning teeth. Yet when Consumers' Union found that the available models created an electric shock hazard, demand fizzled. In the 1990s, SonicCare introduced a safe, rechargeable unit at a premium price. Braun and other competitors followed its lead. But demand was limited. Few consumers saw an electric brush priced at more than $50 as a good value.

In 1998, John Osher and his three business partners had an idea for a battery-powered toothbrush that has changed the market. Even before 1998, Osher had been successful developing new-product ideas and then selling them to big companies. One hit was the Spin Pop, a spinning lollipop attached to a battery-powered plastic handle. After selling Spin Top to Hasbro, Osher and his partners searched for their next big idea. While looking at the toothbrush display at a Wal-Mart store, they realized that they could adapt the Spin Pop idea to create an electric toothbrush. They reasoned that many consumers would trade up to their product if it was more effective than the premium manual brushes—and not much more expensive. So they spent the next year and a half researching, designing, and sourcing a high-quality brush that could sell for $5, including the batteries.

Their next challenge was to prove that the brush would sell. Large firms typically support new-product introductions with a hefty advertising budget and by giving retailers introductory deals or allowances. Then, to cover all the costs, they charge a premium price—at least until competition heats up. But Osher's small firm wanted to penetrate the market at a low initial price, where demand would be the greatest. And at a low price it couldn't afford all of the promotion. Instead, they decided to build interest at the point of purchase with packaging that said "Try me" and that left the button exposed so consumers could see the brush work. With the help of a salesperson who had experience working with big discount chains, they set up a test market. In the test, their new SpinBrush outsold the leading manual brush nearly 3 to 1. Using that sales data as evidence of the profit a retailer could make selling

SpinBrush, they persuaded other retailers to carry it. Within a year, by the end of 2000, their new SpinBrush had expanded sales in the electric toothbrush market by 300 percent.

With that track record, Osher approached Procter & Gamble about buying SpinBrush. The timing was good. Price competition was making it tough for P&G's Crest oral care line to meet its profit objectives. Worse, Colgate had just launched its $19.95 ActiBrush electric toothbrush and it was off to a fast start. So P&G quickly struck a deal and soon was selling the SpinBrush with the Crest brand name. P&G kept the suggested retail price of the SpinBrush at $5.99, and relied on its sales reps to expand distribution. Even without TV ads, sales took off like a rocket.

ActiBrush suffered in comparison, so by 2002 Colgate cut its price to $12 and also introduced a brush like the SpinBrush at the same $5.99 price. However, by then marketing managers for SpinBrush had introduced new models, including new colours and designs to appeal to kids. They also offered an improved $7.99 SpinBrush Pro with dual action heads and replaceable brushes. The higher price on the Pro model gave P&G a better profit margin and gave retailers greater incentive to give it more shelf space. Consumers saw SpinBrush as a good value, and that was confirmed when *Consumer's Digest* declared it a best buy.

Oral-B didn't want to sit by while SpinBrush took customers from its regular brushes and high-end electrics, so it added a battery brush in the middle of its line. To help fend off the increasing competition, P&G came out with testimonial ads for SpinBrush that also included a toll-free number for a $1-off coupon. The price-off coupons didn't leave much profit margin, but they attracted customers who will bolster profits each time they buy replacement brushes, in a package of two for $5.95. Penetration of battery-powered brushes is now about 12 percent of households, but here and in overseas markets—where SpinBrush is already building strong distribution—there appears to be room for more profitable growth.[1]

PRICE HAS MANY STRATEGY DIMENSIONS

Price is one of the four major strategy decision variables a marketing manager controls. Price decisions affect both the number of sales a firm makes and how much money it earns. Price is what a customer must give up to get the benefits offered by the rest of a firm's marketing mix, so it plays a direct role in shaping customer value.

Guided by the company's objectives, marketing managers must develop a set of pricing objectives and policies. They must spell out what price situations the firm will face and how it will handle them. These policies should explain (1) how flexible prices will be, (2) at what level they will be set over the product life cycle, (3) to whom and when discounts and allowances will be given, and (4) how transportation costs will be handled. See Exhibit 16-1. These Price-related strategy decision areas are the focus of this chapter. After we've looked at specific decision areas, we will discuss how they combine to impact customer value as well as laws that are relevant. In the next chapter, we will discuss how specific prices are set.

It's not easy to define price in real-life situations because price reflects many dimensions. People who don't realize this can make big mistakes.

Suppose you've been saving to buy a new car and you see in an ad that, after a $1,000 rebate, the base price for the new-year model is $16,494—5 percent lower than the previous year. At first this might seem like a real bargain. However, your view of this deal might change if you found out you also had to pay a $400 transportation charge and an extra $480 for an extended service warranty. The price might look even less attractive if you discovered that the fancy stereo, side air bags, and moonroof that were standard the previous year are now options that cost $1,400. The cost of the higher interest rate on the car loan and the sales tax on all of this might come as an unpleasant surprise too. Further, how would you feel if you bought the car anyway and then learned that a friend who just bought the exact same model got a much lower price from the dealer by using a broker he found on the Internet?[2]

Exhibit 16-1
Strategy Planning for Price

The price equation: Price equals something of value

This example emphasizes that when a seller quotes a price, it is related to *some* assortment of goods and services. So **Price** is the amount of money that is exchanged for "something" of value. Of course, price may be called different things in different settings. Universities and colleges charge tuition. Landlords collect rent. Motels post a room rate. Country clubs get dues. Banks ask for interest when they loan money. Airlines have fares. Employees want a wage. People may call it different things, but *almost every business transaction in our modern economy involves an exchange of money—the Price—for something.*

The something can be a physical product in various stages of completion, with or without supporting services, with or without quality guarantees, and so on. Or it could be a pure service—dry cleaning, a lawyer's advice, or insurance on your car.

The nature and extent of this something determines the amount of money exchanged. Some customers pay list price. Others obtain large discounts or allowances because something is *not* provided. Exhibit 16-2 summarizes some possible variations for consumers or users, and Exhibit 16-3 does the same for channel members. These variations are discussed more fully, and then we'll consider the customer value concept—in terms of competitive advantage. But here it should be clear that Price has many dimensions. How each of these dimensions is handled affects customer value. If a customer sees greater value in spending money in some other way, no exchange will occur.

Exhibit 16-2
Price as Seen by Consumers or Users

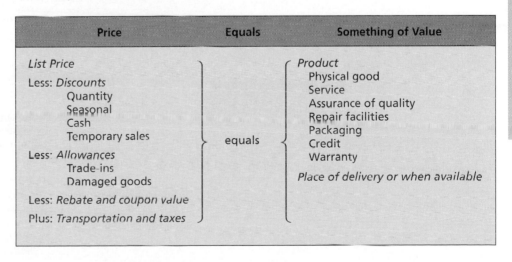

Exhibit 16-3
Price as Seen by Channel
Members

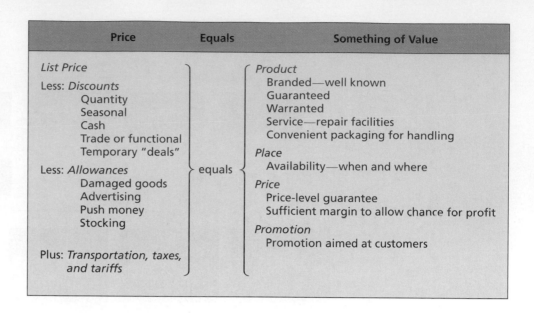

Price	Equals	Something of Value

List Price
 	
Less: *Discounts*
    Quantity
    Seasonal
    Cash
    Trade or functional
    Temporary "deals"
 	
Less: *Allowances*
    Damaged goods
    Advertising
    Push money
    Stocking
 	
Plus: *Transportation, taxes,
    and tariffs*
	equals	*Product*
		    Branded—well known
		    Guaranteed
		    Warranted
		    Service—repair facilities
		    Convenient packaging for handling
		Place
		    Availability—when and where
		Price
		    Price-level guarantee
		    Sufficient margin to allow chance for profit
		Promotion
		    Promotion aimed at customers

OBJECTIVES SHOULD GUIDE STRATEGY PLANNING FOR PRICE

Pricing objectives should flow from, and fit in with, company-level and marketing objectives. Pricing objectives should be *explicitly stated* because they have a direct effect on pricing policies as well as the methods used to set prices. Exhibit 16-4 shows the various types of pricing objectives we'll discuss.

PROFIT-ORIENTED OBJECTIVES

**Target returns
provide specific
guidelines**

A **target return objective** sets a specific level of profit as an objective. Often this amount is stated as a percentage of sales or of capital investment. A large manufacturer like Motorola might aim for a 15 percent return on investment. The target for Sobeys and other supermarket chains might be a 1 percent return on sales.

Exhibit 16-4
Possible Pricing Objectives

Some politicians want to control the prices of drugs, but that may not be in the public interest if it reduces the incentive for firms to make the big investment required to develop innovative new medicines that people need. That, in turn, would reduce consumer choices.

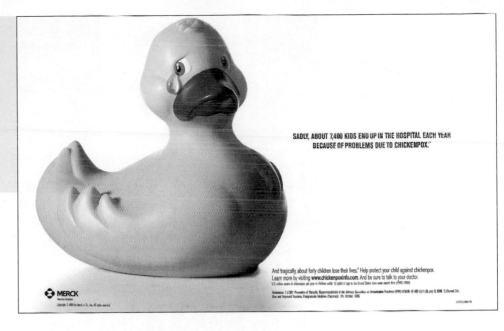

SADLY, ABOUT 7,400 KIDS END UP IN THE HOSPITAL EACH YEAR BECAUSE OF PROBLEMS DUE TO CHICKENPOX."

And tragically, about forty children lose their lives.¹ Help protect your child against chickenpox. Learn more by visiting **www.chickenpoxinfo.com**. And be sure to talk to your doctor.

MERCK
Vaccine Division

A target return objective has administrative advantages in a large company. Performance can be compared against the target. Some companies eliminate divisions, or drop products, that aren't yielding the target rate of return. For example, General Electric sold its small appliance division to Black & Decker because it felt it could earn higher returns in other product-markets.

Some just want satisfactory profits

Some managers aim for only satisfactory returns. They just want returns that ensure the firm's survival and convince shareholders they're doing a good job. Similarly, some small family-run businesses aim for a profit that will provide a comfortable lifestyle.[3]

Many private and public nonprofit organizations set a price level that will just recover costs. In other words, their target return figure is zero. For example, a government agency may charge motorists a toll for using a bridge but then drop the toll when the cost of the bridge is paid.

Similarly, firms that provide critical public services—including many utility and insurance companies, transportation firms, and defence contractors—sometimes pursue only satisfactory long-run targets. They are well aware that the public expects them to set prices that are in the public interest. They may also have to face public or government agencies that review and approve prices.[4]

Profit maximization can be socially responsible

A **profit maximization objective** seeks to get as much profit as possible. It might be stated as a desire to earn a rapid return on investment—or, more bluntly, to charge all the traffic will bear.

Pricing to achieve profit maximization doesn't always lead to high prices. Low prices may expand the size of the market and result in greater sales and profits. For example, when prices of cell phones were very high, only businesses and wealthy people bought them. When producers lowered prices, nearly everyone bought one.

If a firm is earning a very large profit, other firms will try to copy or improve on what the company offers. Frequently, this leads to lower prices. In 1981, IBM unveiled the first 1-gigabyte disk drive. It was the size of a school locker, weighed 500 pounds, and cost $40,000. It was very profitable. Twenty years later, IBM offered a 1-gigabyte drive the size of a matchbox. It weighed 1 ounce and cost about $350. Now customers can buy a tiny flash memory card with that much memory for less than half that price, and the prices continue to drop.[5]

When the price of a barrel of crude oil suddenly doubled, gasoline prices at the pump jumped 10 cents a litre almost overnight. In this situation, a customer may have no choice but to pay the "arm and leg" price. However, if prices stayed high for a longer period of time many consumers might switch to more energy efficient vehicles or perhaps to public transportation.

SALES-ORIENTED OBJECTIVES

A **sales-oriented objective** seeks some level of unit sales, dollar sales, or share of market—*without referring to profit.*

Sales growth doesn't necessarily mean big profits

Some managers are more concerned about sales growth than profits. They think sales growth always leads to more profits. This kind of thinking causes problems when a firm's costs are growing faster than sales. Some major corporations have had declining profits in spite of growth in sales. At the extreme, many dot-coms kept lowering prices to increase market share but never earned any profits. Pets.com had growing sales until it burned through investors' money and went bankrupt. Generally, however, business managers now pay more attention to profits, not just sales.[6]

Some nonprofit organizations set prices to increase market share—precisely because they are *not* trying to earn a profit. For example, many cities set low fares to fill up their buses. Buses cost the same to run empty or full, and there's more benefit when they're full even if the total revenue is no greater.

Market share objectives are popular

Many firms seek to gain a specified share (percent) of a market. If a company has a large market share, it may have better economies of scale than its competitors. In addition, it's usually easier to measure a firm's market share than to determine if profits are being maximized.

A company with a longer-run view may aim for increased market share when the market is growing. The hope is that future volume will justify sacrificing some profit in the short run. Companies as diverse as 3M and Coca-Cola look at opportunities in Eastern Europe this way.

Of course, market share objectives have the same limitations as straight sales growth objectives. A larger market share, if gained at too low a price, may lead to profitless "success." This is a too-common symptom of death-wish marketing.

Unfortunately, profitless market share is exactly what the Ford Taurus achieved. In the late 1990s, it was the family sedan with the highest market share. When

446

WestJet's decision to advertise price pushed Air Canada into price competition in the airline industry.

competitors started to take away customers, Ford kept its market share high by selling thousands of cars at highly discounted rates to rental car companies and corporate fleets. That made things look better for a while, but profits were poor. Worse, when all of those cars flooded into the used-car market, the resale value of the Taurus went down the tubes. Consumers who had bought a new Taurus expecting the value of their investment to hold up felt betrayed, and many said they'd never buy another Ford.[7]

STATUS QUO PRICING OBJECTIVES

Don't-rock-the-boat objectives

Managers satisfied with their current market share and profits sometimes adopt **status quo objectives**—don't-rock-the-*pricing*-boat objectives. Managers may say that they want to stabilize prices, or meet competition, or even avoid competition. This don't-rock-the-boat thinking is most common when the total market is not growing. Gasoline retailers such as Petro-Canada and Esso regularly meet the competition's price, a don't-rock-the-boat approach.

Or stress nonprice competition instead

A status quo pricing objective may be part of an aggressive overall marketing strategy focusing on **nonprice competition**—aggressive action on one or more of the Ps other than Price. Fast-food chains like McDonald's, Wendy's, and Burger King experienced very profitable growth by sticking to nonprice competition for many years. However, when Taco Bell and others started to take away customers with price-cutting, the other chains also turned to price competition. WestJet ads stressing price pushed Air Canada to cut prices and turn to price competition.

Some Internet firms originally thought that they'd compete with low prices and still earn high profits from volume. However, when they didn't get the sales volume they hoped for, they realized that there were also some nonprice ways to compete.

MOST FIRMS SET SPECIFIC PRICING POLICIES—TO REACH OBJECTIVES

Administered prices help achieve objectives

Price policies usually lead to **administered prices**—consciously set prices. In other words, instead of letting daily market forces (or auctions) decide their prices, most firms set their own prices. They may hold prices steady for long periods of time or change them more frequently if that's what's required to meet objectives.

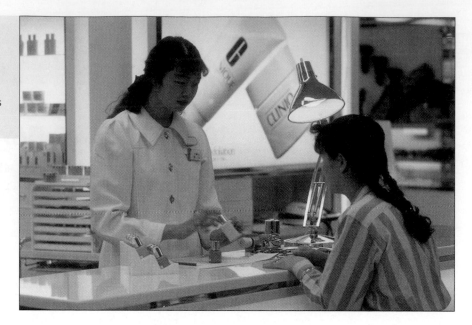

Cosmetics manufacturers such as Estée Lauder, who also own Clinique, consciously set price (manufacturer suggested retail price) to ensure profits for all channel members.

If a firm doesn't sell directly to final customers, it usually wants to administer both the price it receives from middlemen and the price final customers pay. After all, the price final customers pay will ultimately affect the quantity it sells. Yet it is often difficult to administer prices throughout the channel. Other channel members may also wish to administer prices to achieve their own objectives.

Some firms don't even try to administer prices. They just meet competition—or worse, mark up their costs with little thought to demand. They act as if they have no choice in selecting a price policy.

Remember that Price has many dimensions. Managers usually *do* have many choices. They *should* administer their prices. And they should do it carefully because, ultimately, customers must be willing to pay these prices before a whole marketing mix succeeds. In the rest of this chapter, we'll talk about policies a marketing manager must set to do an effective job of administering Price.[8]

PRICE FLEXIBILITY POLICIES

One-price policy— the same price for everyone

One of the first decisions a marketing manager has to make is whether to use a one-price or a flexible-price policy. A **one-price policy** means offering the same price to all customers who purchase products under essentially the same conditions and in the same quantities. The majority of firms use a one-price policy—mainly for administrative convenience and to maintain goodwill among customers. P & G used a one-price policy for SpinBrush.

A one-price policy makes pricing easier. But a marketing manager must be careful to avoid a rigid one-price policy. This can amount to broadcasting a price that competitors can undercut, especially if the price is somewhat high. One reason for the growth of mass-merchandisers is that conventional retailers rigidly applied traditional margins and stuck to them.

Flexible-price policy—different prices for different customers

A **flexible-price policy** means offering the same product and quantities to different customers at different prices. When computers are used to implement flexible pricing, the decisions focus more on what type of customer will get a price break.

To reach its objectives, Carnival uses flexible pricing—including discounts for retired people. By contrast, *Professional Carwashing & Detailing*, a trade magazine, wants advertisers to know that it charges everyone the same price for ad space.

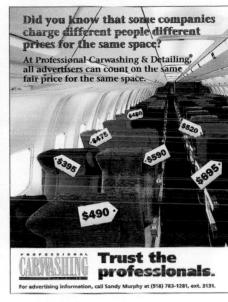

Pricing databases make flexible pricing easier

Various forms of flexible pricing are more common now that most prices are maintained in a central computer database. Frequent changes are easier. You see this when supermarket chains give frequent-shopper club members reduced prices on weekly specials. The checkout scanner reads the code on the package, then the computer looks up the club price or the regular price depending on whether a club card has been scanned.

Some marketing managers have set up relationships with Internet companies whose ads invite customers to "set your own price." For example, Priceline operates a Web site at www.priceline.com. Visitors to the Web site specify the desired schedule for an airline flight and what price they're willing to pay. Priceline electronically forwards the information to airlines and if one accepts the offer the consumer is notified.

It may appear that these marketing managers have given up on administering prices. Just the opposite is true. They are carefully administering a flexible price. Most airlines, for example, set a very high list price. Not many people pay it. Travellers who plan ahead or who accept nonpeak flights get a discount. Business travellers who want high-demand flights on short notice pay the higher prices. However, it doesn't make sense to stick to a high price and fly the plane half empty. So the airline continuously adjusts the price on the basis of how many seats are left to fill. If seats are still empty at the last minute, the Web site offers a rock-bottom fare. Other firms, especially service businesses, use this approach when they have excess capacity.[9]

Salespeople can adjust prices to the situation

Flexible pricing is most common in the channels, in direct sales of business products, and at retail for expensive shopping products. Retail shopkeepers in less-developed economies typically use flexible pricing. These situations usually involve personal selling, not mass selling. The advantage of flexible pricing is that the salesperson can adjust price—considering prices charged by competitors, the relationship with the customer, and the customer's bargaining ability. Flexible-price policies often specify a *range* in which the actual price charged must fall.[10]

Too much price-cutting erodes profits

Some sales reps let price-cutting become a habit. This can lead to a lower price level and lower profit. A small price cut may not seem like much; but keep in mind that all of the revenue that is lost would go to profit. If salespeople for a producer that usually earns profits equal to 15 percent of its sales cut prices by an average of about 5 percent, profits would drop by a third!

Disadvantages of flexible pricing	Flexible pricing does have disadvantages. A customer who finds that others paid lower prices for the same marketing mix will be unhappy. This can cause real conflict in channels.

If buyers learn that negotiating is in their interest, the time needed for bargaining will increase. This can increase selling costs and reduce profits. It can also frustrate customers. For example, most auto dealers use flexible pricing and bargain for what they can get. Inexperienced consumers, reluctant to bargain, often pay hundreds of dollars more than the dealer is willing to accept. By contrast, Toyota has earned high customer-satisfaction ratings by offering haggle-weary consumers a one-price policy.[11]

PRICE-LEVEL POLICIES—OVER THE PRODUCT LIFE CYCLE

Marketing managers who administer prices must consciously set a price-level policy. As they enter the market, they have to set introductory prices that may have long-run effects. They must consider where the product life cycle is and how fast it's moving. And they must decide if their prices should be above, below, or somewhere in between relative to the market.

Let's look for a moment at a new product in the market introduction stage of its product life cycle. There are few (or no) direct substitute marketing mixes. So the price-level decision should focus first on the nature of market demand. A high price may lead to higher profit from each sale but also to fewer units sold. A lower price might appeal to more potential customers. With this in mind, should the firm set a high or low price?

Skimming pricing— feeling out demand at a high price

A **skimming price policy** tries to sell the top (skim the cream) of a market—the top of the demand curve—at a high price before aiming at more price-sensitive customers. Skimming may maximize profits in the market introduction stage for an innovation, especially if there are few substitutes or if some customers are not price sensitive. Skimming is also useful when you don't know very much about the shape of the demand curve. It's sometimes safer to start with a high price that customers can refuse and then reduce it if necessary.

Skimming has critics

Some critics argue that firms should not try to maximize profits by using a skimming policy on new products that have important social consequences—a patent-protected, life-saving drug or a technique that increases crop yields, for example. Many of those who need the product may not have the money to buy it. This is a serious concern. However, it's also a serious problem if firms don't have any incentive to take risks and develop new products.[12]

Price moves down the demand curve

A skimming policy usually involves a slow reduction in price over time. See Exhibit 16-5. Note that as price is reduced, new target markets are probably being sought. So as the price level steps down the demand curve, new Place, Product, and Promotion policies may be needed too.

This is happening with hang-on-the-wall, flat-panel TVs. In 2000, the average selling price for a plasma TV was $12,000. Most of these units were sold by dealers who sell commercial lines to business customers who are less price sensitive. For instance, a firm that wanted a plasma TV to display product demo videos at a trade show was more likely to focus on picture quality, saving space, and the "wow factor." Yet by 2001, about 16,000 of these pricey plasma TVs had been sold to early-adopter consumers. When Sony, Mitsushita (Panasonic), and other firms saw that trend, they came out with consumer models and distributed them through electronics superstores, like Future Shop. These retailers used a lower markup (about 30 percent) than the commercial dealers. Their lower prices stimulated consumer demand, so producers built more factories. Then, with more production capacity

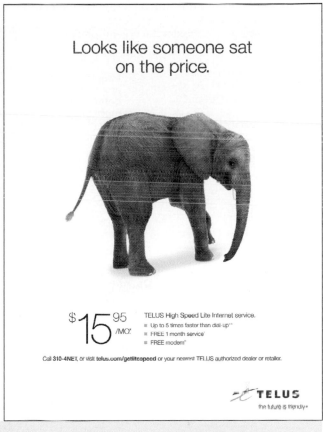

DuPont Corian, a solid countertop material, was costly to develop. When Corian was introduced, there was little direct competition and a premium price helped to recover development costs. Now that there is more competition, discounted prices are sometimes available. Telus has reduced their price for high-speed Internet service to gain market share.

than demand, price competition increased—and producers came out with new models to appeal to different market segments. As the demand for flat-panel TVs surged, manufacturers of computer LCD displays added TV tuners and improved the picture quality on their large screens. By 2004, general-merchandise retailers like Sears and Wal-Mart were selling flat-panel TVs, and firms like Dell and HP had added them to their lines. At that point, prices were only about 60 percent of where they had started—and they continue to fall as demand grows and more firms switch from producing traditional TVs to flat-panel ones.[13]

Penetration pricing—get volume at a low price

A **penetration pricing policy** tries to sell the whole market at one low price. This approach might be wise when the elite market—those willing to pay a high price—is small. This is the case when the whole demand curve is fairly elastic. SpinBrush appealed to a much larger market than SonicCare due to a penetration price level. See Exhibit 16-5. A penetration policy is even more attractive if selling larger quantities results in lower costs because of economies of scale. Penetration pricing may be wise if the firm expects strong competition very soon after introduction.

When the first version of the PalmPilot was introduced, competitors were close behind. In addition, Apple had failed when it tried to introduce the Newton personal information manager at a skimming price of $1,000. So the focus for Palm was on a combination of features and price that would be a good value and help penetrate the market quickly. The initial price of about $250 resulted in sales of a million units in 24 months. A $250 retail price may not seem that low now that the PDA market is maturing and the Palm Zire, for example, is priced at about $70

Exhibit 16-5 Alternative Introductory Pricing Policies

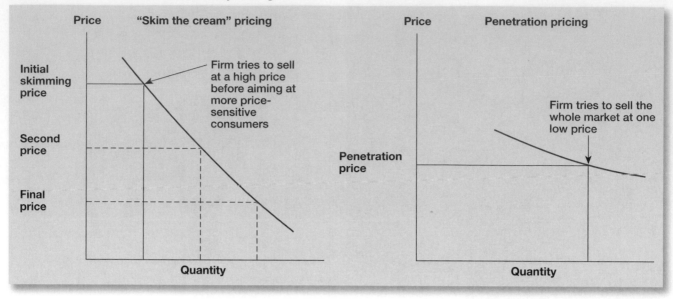

to appeal to first-time PDA buyers. However, Palm's initial price was low enough to discourage some competitors from quickly entering the market.

Even a very low penetration price usually won't keep competitors out of a growth market permanently—and product life cycles do march on. For instance, competition is now intense among firms that sell PDAs, and different models appeal to different segments. Higher-priced PDAs that combine a cell phone, digital camera, and Internet access as well as MP3 and video players compete with single-use products in other product categories.[14]

Introductory price dealing—temporary price cuts

Low prices do attract customers. Therefore, marketers often use **introductory price dealing**—temporary price cuts—to speed new products into a market and get customers to try them. However, don't confuse these *temporary* price cuts with low penetration prices. The plan here is to raise prices as soon as the introductory offer is over. By then, hopefully, target customers will have decided it is worth buying again at the regular price.

Marketers often use introductory price dealing—in the form of temporary price cuts or introductory coupons—to speed new products into a market.

Exhibit 16-6 Exchange Rates for Various Currencies against the U.S. Dollar over Time

	Number of Units of Base Currency per U.S. Dollar*								
Base Currency	**1989**	**1991**	**1993**	**1995**	**1997**	**1999**	**2001**	**2003**	**2005**
British pound	0.62	0.57	0.67	0.67	0.61	0.62	0.70	0.64	0.53
Thai baht	25.72	25.53	25.33	24.92	31.07	37.40	45.65	42.89	39.65
Japanese yen	138.07	134.59	111.08	94.11	121.09	117.86	124.58	120.04	107.64
Australian dollar	1.26	1.32	1.47	1.35	1.34	1.55	1.96	1.64	1.30
Canadian dollar	1.18	1.15	1.29	1.37	1.38	1.49	1.56	1.46	1.24
German mark	1.88	1.66	1.65	1.43	1.73				
Euro						1.07	1.13	0.92	0.77

*Units shown are the average for each year 1989–1997. For 1999, 2001, 2003, and 2005 units shown are for April 16, 1999, April 16, 2001, April 16, 2003, and April 15, 2005.

Established competitors often choose not to meet introductory price dealing—as long as the introductory period is not too long or too successful. However, some competitors match introductory price deals with their own short-term sale prices to discourage customers from shopping around.

Different price-level policies through the channel

The price of a product sold to channel members should be set so that channel members can cover their costs and make a profit. For example, a producer of a slightly better product might set a price level that is low relative to competitors when selling to retailers but suggest an above-the-market retail price. This encourages retailers to emphasize the product because it yields higher profits. Canadian companies must also ensure that they allow for the exchange rate when producers and other channel members are not located in Canada. Check out the Internet Exercise to see how current exchange rates can influence the cost, and hence price, of a product in Canada.

PayPal is an online financial service that makes it easier and less risky for firms or individuals who sell over the Internet to receive payment from a distant buyer.

MOST PRICE STRUCTURES ARE BUILT AROUND LIST PRICES

Prices start with a list price

Most price structures are built around a base price schedule or list price. **Basic list prices** are the prices final customers or users are normally asked to pay for products. In this book, unless noted otherwise, list price refers to basic list price.

In the next chapter, we discuss how firms set these list prices. For now, however, we'll consider variations from list price and why they are made.

DISCOUNT POLICIES—REDUCTIONS FROM LIST PRICES

Discounts are reductions from list price given by a seller to buyers who either give up some marketing function or provide the function themselves. Discounts can be useful in marketing strategy planning. In the following discussion, think about what function the buyers are giving up, or providing, when they get each of these discounts.

Quantity discounts encourage volume buying

Quantity discounts are discounts offered to encourage customers to buy in larger amounts. This lets a seller get more of a buyer's business, or shifts some of the storing function to the buyer, or reduces shipping and selling costs—or all of these. There are two kinds of quantity discounts: cumulative and noncumulative.

454

HOW MUCH DOES IT REALLY COST TO RENT A VIDEO?

The price a customer actually pays to rent a video at Blockbuster isn't always easy to figure out. At first glance, it seems that everyone pays one price for a New Release and a lower price for Favourites. But that's not the whole story. Members of the $10-a-year Blockbuster Rewards program get a free movie each month—and another one free when they rent five during a month. They also get a free Favourite when they rent a movie Monday to Wednesday—and there are other special offers, like three-for-one deals some weekends. The Blockbuster Rewards Web site (www.blockbuster.ca) provides a special online calculator so movie buffs can plug in their own rental numbers and figure out how many free movies they would get with the Rewards program. But, oops, the calculator does not include a way to plug in how often a customer is late in returning movies. A late fee can apply even if the rental was free. Some cynics think that Blockbuster offers its Rewards Gold membership—and even more free movies—to customers who return a lot of movies late. Those late fees add up to more than 10 percent of Blockbuster revenues. The recent "No Late Fees" campaign, where consumers were instead offered a chance to buy the movie, contributed to this view.

In the United States, Netflix (www.netflix.com) and Wal-Mart (www.walmart.com) both compete with Blockbuster by offering a subscription service that has no late fees. Subscribers pay a fixed fee of about $20 a month and can request as many DVDs as they want (with prepaid postage both ways) but with a limit of three out at a time. Given a fixed fee, the most profitable customers are the ones who don't view many movies. Netflix and Wal-Mart have both offered free trial periods to pull in subscribers. Prompted by this competition, Blockbuster has experimented with its own subscription approach. However, Netflix hopes that its customers will be loyal because many of them like Netflix's free online movie reviews. In Canada, Rogers Video has recently introduced Rogers Video Direct to compete in this market. Consumers can rent DVDs online with no return dates or late fees as long as they pay their monthly flat membership fee.

Some experts think that video-on-demand movies—distributed over the Internet or from cable services—will be tough competition for all these firms. Yet current rental firms will probably also offer video-on-demand if that is what their customers want. Either way, if things continue on the current path, customers still won't know what it actually costs to see a movie.[15]

Cumulative quantity discounts apply to purchases over a given period—such as a year—and the discount usually increases as the amount purchased increases. Cumulative discounts encourage *repeat* buying by reducing the customer's cost for additional purchases. This is a way to develop loyalty and ongoing relationships with customers. For example, a RONA lumberyard might give a cumulative quantity discount to a building contractor who is not able to buy all of the needed materials at once. RONA wants to reward the contractor's patronage and discourage shopping around.

A cumulative quantity discount is often attractive to business customers who don't want to run up their inventory costs. They are rewarded for buying large quantities, even though individual orders may be smaller.

Noncumulative quantity discounts apply only to individual orders. Such discounts encourage larger orders but do not tie a buyer to the seller after that one purchase. RONA may resell insulation products made by several competing producers. Roxul might try to encourage RONA to stock larger quantities of its Flexibatt insulation by offering a noncumulative quantity discount.

While quantity discounts are usually given as price cuts, sometimes they are given as free or bonus products. RBC Rewards uses this approach.

Quantity discounts can be a very useful tool for the marketing manager. Some customers are eager to get them. But marketing managers must use quantity discounts carefully. In business markets, they must offer such discounts to all customers on equal terms—to avoid price discrimination.

Noncumulative discounts sometimes produce unexpected results. If the discount is too big, wholesalers or retailers may buy more than they can possibly sell to their own customers—to get the low price. Then they sell the excess at a low price to whoever will buy it—as long as the buyer doesn't compete in the same market area. These grey-market channels often take customers away from regular channel members, perhaps with a selling price even lower than what most channel members pay. This problem plagues channels for products ranging from electronic components to toilet paper. To avoid these problems, a marketing manager must consider the effect of discounts on the whole strategy, not just the effect on sales to a given middleman.

Seasonal discounts—buy sooner

Seasonal discounts are discounts offered to encourage buyers to buy earlier than present demand requires. If used by a manufacturer, this discount tends to shift the storing function further along in the channel. It also tends to even out sales over the year. For example, Kyota offers wholesalers a lower price on its garden tillers if they buy in the fall, when sales are slow.

Service firms that face irregular demand or excess capacity often use seasonal discounts. For example, some tourist attractions, like ski resorts, offer lower weekday rates when attendance would otherwise be down.

Payment terms and cash discounts set payment dates

Most sales to businesses are made on credit. The seller sends a bill (invoice) by mail or electronically, and the buyer's accounting department processes it for payment. Some firms depend on their suppliers for temporary working capital (credit). Therefore, it is very important for both sides to clearly state the terms of payment—including the availability of cash discounts—and to understand the commonly used payment terms.

Net means that payment for the face value of the invoice is due immediately. These terms are sometimes changed to net 10 or net 30, which means payment is due within 10 or 30 days of the date on the invoice.

Cash discounts are reductions in price to encourage buyers to pay their bills quickly. The terms for a cash discount usually modify the net terms.

2/10, net 30 means the buyer can take a 2 percent discount off the face value of the invoice if the invoice is paid within 10 days. Otherwise, the full face value is due within 30 days. And it usually is stated or understood that an interest charge will be added after the 30-day free-credit period.

INVOICE NO.		4238
ORDER NO.	INVOICE DATE	
179642	1/8/200x	
DATE SHIPPED	SHIPPED VIA	
1/1/200x	Truck	
NO. PCS WT.	FOB	TERMS
5 300	Lansing, MI	2/10 net 30

0 34100 0600 0

Why cash discounts are given and should be evaluated

Smart buyers carefully evaluate cash discounts. A discount of 2/10, net 30 may not look like much at first. But the buyer earns a 2 percent discount for paying the invoice just 20 days sooner than it should be paid anyway. By not taking the discount, the company in effect is borrowing at an annual rate of 36 percent. That is, assuming a 360-day year and dividing by 20 days, there are 18 periods during which the company could earn 2 percent—and 18 times 2 equals 36 percent a year.

Consumers say "charge it"

Credit sales are also important to retailers. Most retailers use credit card services, such as Visa or MasterCard, and pay a percent of the revenue from each credit sale for this service. For this reason, some retailers offer discounts to consumers who pay cash.

Many consumers like the convenience of credit card buying. But some critics argue that the cards make it too easy for consumers to buy things they really can't afford. Credit card interest rates can increase the total costs to consumers.

Trade discounts often are set by tradition

A **trade (functional) discount** is a list price reduction given to channel members for the job they are going to do.

A manufacturer, for example, might allow retailers a 30 percent trade discount from the suggested retail list price to cover the cost of the retailing function and their profit. Similarly, the manufacturer might allow wholesalers a *chain* discount of 30 percent and 10 percent off the suggested retail price. In this case, the wholesalers would be expected to pass the 30 percent discount on to retailers.[16]

Special sales reduce list prices— temporarily

A **sale price** is a temporary discount from the list price. Sale price discounts encourage immediate buying. In other words, to get the sale price, customers give up the convenience of buying when they want to buy and instead buy when the seller wants to sell.

Special sales provide a marketing manager with a quick way to respond to changing market conditions without changing the basic marketing strategy. For example, a retailer might use a sale to help clear extra inventory or to meet a competing store's price.

In recent years, sale prices and deals have become much more common. Some retailers have sales so often that consumers just wait to purchase when there's a sale. Others check out Web sites to figure out where the product they want is already on sale. At first it may seem that consumers benefit from all this. But prices that change constantly erode brand loyalty.

To avoid these problems, some firms that sell consumer convenience products offer **everyday low pricing (EDLP)**—setting a low list price rather than relying on frequent sales, discounts, or allowances. Many supermarkets use this approach. Along with Real Canadian Superstores (Loblaws), other retailers such as Wal-Mart have been very successful with EDLP.

Sale prices should be used carefully, consistent with well-thought-out pricing objectives and policies. A marketing manager who constantly uses temporary sales to adjust the price level probably has not done a good job setting the normal price.[17]

ALLOWANCE POLICIES—OFF LIST PRICES

Allowances, like discounts, are given to final consumers, customers, or channel members for doing something or accepting less of something.

Advertising allowances— something for something

Advertising allowances are price reductions given to firms in the channel to encourage them to advertise or otherwise promote the supplier's products locally. For example, Sony might give an allowance (3 percent of sales) to its retailers. They, in turn, are expected to spend the allowance on local advertising.

Stocking allowances—get attention and shelf space

Stocking allowances—sometimes called *slotting allowances*—are given to a middleman to get shelf space for a product. For example, a producer might offer a retailer cash or free merchandise to stock a new item. Stocking allowances are used mainly to get supermarket chains to handle new products. Supermarkets are more willing to give space to a new product if the supplier will offset their handling costs and risks. With a big stocking allowance, the middleman makes extra profit—even if a new product fails and the producer loses money.

Are stocking allowances ethical?

Critics say that retailer demands for big stocking allowances slow new product introductions and make it hard for small producers to compete. Some producers feel that retailers' demands are unethical—just a different form of extortion. Retailers, on the other hand, point out that the fees protect them from producers that simply want to push more and more me-too products onto their shelves. Perhaps the best way for a producer to cope with the problem is to develop new products that really do offer consumers superior value. Then it benefits everyone in the channel, including retailers, to get the products to the target market.[18]

PMs—push for cash

Push money (or prize money) allowances—sometimes called *PMs* or *spiffs*—are given to retailers by manufacturers or wholesalers to pass on to the retailers' salesclerks for aggressively selling certain items. PM allowances are used for new items, slower-moving items, or higher-margin items. They are often used for pushing furniture,

Coupons for consumer products are popular and prompt customers to action.

clothing, consumer electronics, and cosmetics. A salesclerk, for example, might earn an additional $5 for each new model Panasonic DVD player sold.

Bring in the old, ring up the new—with trade-ins

A **trade-in allowance** is a price reduction given for used products when similar new products are bought. Trade-ins give the marketing manager an easy way to lower the effective price without reducing list price. Proper handling of trade-ins is important when selling durable products. A classic example is the Ford new car dealer that takes the buyer's old vehicle as a trade-in, giving credit toward the new car purchase price.

SOME CUSTOMERS GET SOMETHING EXTRA

Clipping coupons— more for less

Many producers and retailers offer discounts (or free items) through coupons distributed in packages, mailings, print ads, or at the store. By presenting a coupon to a retailer, the consumer is given a discount off list price. This is especially common in the consumer packaged goods business—but the use of price-off coupons is growing in other lines of business too.

Retailers are willing to redeem producers' coupons because it increases their sales—and they usually are paid for the trouble of handling the coupons. For example, a retailer that redeems a 50 cents off coupon might be repaid 75 cents.

Couponing is so common that firms have been set up to help repay retailers for redeeming manufacturers' coupons. The total dollar amounts involved are so large that crime has become a big problem. Some dishonest retailers have gone to jail for collecting on coupons they redeemed without requiring customers to buy the products.

INTERNET EXERCISE

Consumers interested in finding deals such as coupons, special offers, and more can check out the Frugalshopper Web site (www.frugalshopper.ca). Frugalshopper offers freebies, coupons, and contests as well as many sponsored links to other deals. For example, HBC has a link via dealsoutlet.ca. Check out a few links to see what kinds of deals you can find. Do you think the password system used for coupons on the site will prevent coupon fraud?

Cash rebates when you buy

Some firms offer **rebates**—refunds paid to consumers after a purchase. Sometimes the rebate is very large. Some automakers offer rebates of $500 to $6,000 to promote sales of slow-moving models. Rebates are also used on lower-priced items, ranging from Duracell batteries to Memorex CD-Rs to Logitech Webcams. Rebates give a producer a way to be certain that final consumers actually get the price reduction. If the rebate amount were just taken off the price charged middlemen, they might not pass the savings along to consumers.

However, what explains the big increase in the use of rebates is that many consumers buy because of the rebate but then don't request the refund. That's why some retailers lure consumers with their own mail-in rebates rather than just lowering prices at checkout. However, many consumers resent sellers who make it an unnecessary hassle to claim a rebate. So don't be surprised if there is a consumer backlash against some of the current rebate practices.[19]

LIST PRICE MAY DEPEND ON GEOGRAPHIC PRICING POLICIES

Retail list prices sometimes include free delivery. Or free delivery may be offered to some customers as an aid to closing the sale. But deciding who pays the freight charge is more important on sales to business customers than to final consumers because more money is involved. Purchase orders usually specify place, time, method of delivery, freight costs, insurance, handling, and other charges. There are many possible variations for an imaginative marketing manager, and some specialized terms have developed.

F.O.B. pricing is easy

A commonly used transportation term is **F.O.B.**—which means free on board some vehicle at some place. Typically, F.O.B. pricing names the place—often the location of the seller's factory or warehouse—as in F.O.B. Taiwan or F.O.B. mill. This means that the seller pays the cost of loading the products onto some vehicle, then title to the products passes to the buyer. The buyer pays the freight and takes responsibility for damage in transit.

If a firm wants to pay the freight for the convenience of customers, it can use F.O.B. delivered or F.O.B. buyer's factory. In this case, title does not pass until the products are delivered. If the seller wants title to pass immediately but is willing to prepay freight (and then include it in the invoice), F.O.B. seller's factory-freight prepaid can be used.

F.O.B. shipping point pricing simplifies the seller's pricing—but it may narrow the market. Since the delivered cost varies depending on the buyer's location, a customer located farther from the seller must pay more and might buy from closer suppliers.

Zone pricing smooths delivered prices

Zone pricing means making an average freight charge to all buyers within specific geographic areas. The seller pays the actual freight charges and bills each customer for an average charge. For example, a company in Vancouver, BC might divide Canada into four zones (Western Canada, Ontario, Quebec, and the Maritimes), then bill all customers in the same zone the same amount for freight even though actual shipping costs might vary.

Zone pricing reduces the wide variation in delivered prices that results from an F.O.B. shipping point pricing policy. It also simplifies transportation charges.

Uniform delivered pricing—one price to all

Uniform delivered pricing means making an average freight charge to all buyers. It is a kind of zone pricing—an entire country may be considered as one zone— that includes the average cost of delivery in the price. Uniform delivered pricing is most often used when (1) transportation costs are relatively low and (2) the seller wishes to sell in all geographic areas at one price, perhaps a nationally advertised price.

Freight-absorption pricing—competing on equal grounds in another territory

When all firms in an industry use F.O.B. shipping point pricing, a firm usually competes well near its shipping point but not farther away. As sales reps look for business farther away, delivered prices rise and the firm finds itself priced out of the market.

This problem can be reduced with **freight-absorption pricing**—which means absorbing freight cost so that a firm's delivered price meets the nearest competitor's. This amounts to cutting list price to appeal to new market segments. Some firms look at international markets this way; they just figure that any profit from export sales is a bonus.

PRICING POLICIES COMBINE TO IMPACT CUSTOMER VALUE

Look at Price from the customer's viewpoint

We've discussed pricing policies separately so far, but from the customer's view they all combine to impact customer value. So when we talk about Price we are really talking about the whole set of price policies that define the real price level. On the other hand, superior value isn't just based on having a lower price than some competitor but rather on the whole marketing mix.

Value pricing leads to superior customer value

Smart marketers look for the combination of Price decisions that result in value pricing. **Value pricing** means setting a fair price level for a marketing mix that really gives the target market superior customer value.

Value pricing doesn't necessarily mean cheap if cheap means bare-bones or low-grade. It doesn't mean high prestige either if the prestige is not accompanied by the right quality goods and services. Rather, the focus is on the customer's requirements and how the whole marketing mix meets those needs.

Toyota is a firm that has been effective with value pricing. It has different marketing mixes for different target markets. But from the $15,000 Yaris to the $37,000 FJ Cruiser, the Japanese automaker consistently offers better quality and lower prices than its competitors. Among fast-food restaurants, Wendy's has a good reputation for value pricing.

Companies that use value pricing deliver on their promises. They try to give the consumer pleasant surprises—like an unexpected service—because it increases value and builds customer loyalty. They return the price if the customer isn't completely satisfied. They avoid unrealistic price levels—prices that are high only

When a customer rents a car, both the rental fee and the quality of the car influence the customer value. Thrifty wants customers to know that it offers both great rates and great cars.

460

Marketers for Luvs diapers want consumers to know that Luvs' value price, compared to the pricey brands, is equivalent to getting 275 diapers a year for free. The ad for Liquidation World emphasizes 30–80% off regular retail prices.

because consumers already know the brand name. They build relationships so customers will come back time and again.

There are Price choices in most markets

Some marketing managers miss the advantages of value pricing. They've heard economists say that in perfect competition it's foolish to offer products above or below the market price. But most firms *don't* operate in perfect competition where what firms offer is exactly the same.

Most operate in monopolistic competition, where products and whole marketing mixes are *not* exactly the same. This means that there are pricing options. At one extreme, some firms are clearly above the market—they may even brag about it. Tiffany's is well known as one of the most expensive jewellery stores in the world. Other firms emphasize below-the-market prices in their marketing mixes. Prices offered by discounters and mass-merchandisers, such as Wal-Mart and Tesco, illustrate this approach. They may even promote their pricing policy with catchy slogans like "guaranteed lowest prices."

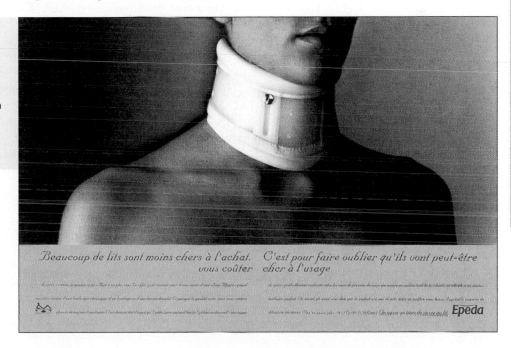

Epeda sells high-quality mattresses. It wants customers to know that its higher price is worth it. This ad says, "Lots of mattresses are cheap to buy. The reason is to make you forget how much sleeping on them is going to cost you."

Value pricers define the target market and the competition

In making price decisions and using value pricing, it is important to clearly define the *relevant target market* and *competitors* when making price comparisons.

Consider Zellers' prices again from this view. Zellers may have lower camera prices than conventional camera retailers, but it offers less help in the store, less selection, and it won't take old cameras in trade. Zellers may be appealing to budget-oriented shoppers who compare prices *and* value among different mass-merchandisers. But a specialty camera store may be trying to appeal to different customers and not even be a direct competitor!

A camera producer with this point of view might offer the specialty store models that are not available to Zellers—to ensure that customers don't view price as the only difference between the two stores.

Further, the specialty store needs to communicate clearly to its target market *how* it offers superior value. Zellers is certainly going to communicate that it offers low prices. If that's all customers hear, it's no wonder that they just focus on price. The specialty retailer has to be certain that consumers understand that price is not the only thing of value that is different. This same logic applies to comparisons between Internet sellers and brick-and-mortar competitors. Each may have advantages or disadvantages that relate to value.

Meeting competitors' prices may be necessary

In a mature market there is downward pressure on both prices and profit margins. Moreover, differentiating the value a firm offers may not be easy when competitors can quickly copy new ideas. Extending our camera example, if our specialty store is in a city with a number of similar stores with the same products, there may not be a way to convince consumers that one beats all of the others. In such circumstances there may be no real pricing choice other than to "meet the competition." With profit margins already thin, they would quickly disappear or turn into losses at a lower price. And a higher price would simply prompt competitors to promote their price advantage.[20]

Similarly, a B2B supplier may have a better marketing mix than competitors; but if buyers have decided to use a procurement hub and reverse auction as the only way to buy, the supplier may not have any choice but to decide what the lowest price is that it will bid to get the business. Winning the bid at a profit-losing price doesn't help.

Even though competition can be intense, too many marketers give up too easily. They often can find a way to differentiate, even if it's something that competitors dismiss as less important. For example, Kellogg was facing soggy sales and tough competition in the dry cereal category. Dealer brands made price competition even tougher. However, when Kellogg added freeze-dried fruit to create Special K Red Berries, it attracted many customers away from competing brands. The berries did increase costs, but Kellogg's profits still improved. In Europe, where price sensitivity was greatest, Kellogg kept the price the same but reduced the size of the Red Berries box. In the U.S., the size of the box is standard but the price was increased enough to provide profit margins. Even though General Mills later copied the idea, Kellogg had a head start and quickly came out with other fruit-added cereals. And both producers benefited by having a way to differentiate from the low-price store brands in their category.[21]

There may be little choice about Price in oligopoly situations. Pricing at the market—that is, meeting competition—may be the only sensible policy. To raise prices might lead to a large loss in sales, unless competitors adopt the higher price too. And cutting prices would probably lead to similar reductions by competitors—downward along an inelastic industry demand curve. This can only lead to a decrease in total revenue for the industry and probably for each firm.

To avoid these problems, each oligopolist may choose a status quo pricing objective and set its price at the competitive level. Some critics call this pricing behaviour conscious parallel action, implying it is unethical and the same as intentional conspiracy among firms. As a practical matter, however, that criticism seems overly harsh. It obviously isn't sensible for firms to ignore their competitors.

Value pricing fits with market-oriented strategy planning

There are times when the marketing manager's hands are tied and there is little that can be done to differentiate the marketing mix. However, most marketing managers do have choices—many choices. They can vary strategy decisions with respect to all of the marketing mix variables, not just Price, to offer target customers superior value. And when a marketer's hands are really tied, it's time to look for new opportunities that offer more promise.

LEGALITY OF PRICING POLICIES

This chapter discusses the many pricing decisions that must be made. However, some pricing decisions are limited by government legislation. The first step to understanding pricing legislation is to know the thinking of legislators and the courts. To get a better idea of the "why" of legislation, we'll focus on Canadian legislation here, but many other countries have similar pricing laws.[22]

Canadian laws protect the consumer

In Canada, the Competition Act regulates pricing practices. Canadian companies must conform to the pricing laws or risk investigation by the Competition Bureau and potentially serious consequences.

Predatory pricing laws in Canada specify that companies may not charge very low prices (below cost) over a long period of time with the objective to drive competitors out of the marketplace. They must also avoid doing so to deter new entrants into the marketplace. In general, companies must also avoid pricing products below cost. Some exceptions are allowed for short-term sales.

The Competition Act also specifies how companies may advertise sale and regular prices. Products must be offered for sale at a regular price before a sale price may be advertised. If this is not done, penalties will be incurred.

Recently, Grafton-Fraser Inc. was investigated by the Competition Bureau for just such a concern. The Competition Bureau "believes that Grafton-Fraser's ordinary

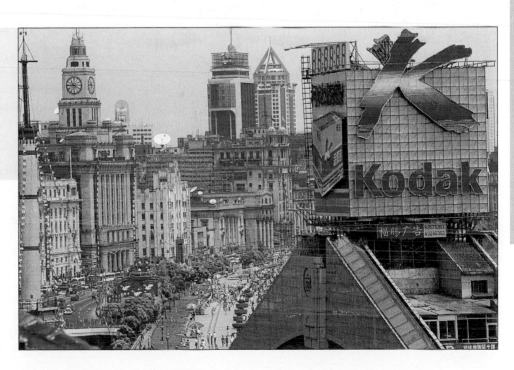

Local media in China claimed that both Fuji from Japan and Kodak from the U.S. were dumping their products in China, even though China's Lucky brand of film and paper had a price that was 50 percent lower.

Marketing Ethically

Many people feel that there is price fixing in the gasoline industry. Price fixing means that competitors get together to raise, lower, or stabilize prices. The federal agency in Canada that oversees this and similar issues is the Competition Bureau. Since 1990, this agency has conducted six major investigations into allegations of collusion in the gasoline industry. It has consistently found no evidence that periodic price increases resulted from conspiracy to limit competition.

If there is no collusion, why do retail prices always seem to be similar? Similar prices do not constitute an offence under the Competition Act—there must be evidence that companies have made an illegal agreement to set the prices.

What are your thoughts on gasoline prices? Do you still feel that price fixing is going on?[23]

price representations misled consumers and that certain menswear products were never offered for sale or sold at these prices." Grafton-Fraser is primarily a menswear retailer with over 180 retail stores operating under such banners as Grafton & Co., Britches, Jack Fraser, Mr. Big & Tall, and Tip Top Tailors. As a result of this ruling, Grafton-Fraser faced a number of penalties, including:

- Pay a $1 million dollar monetary penalty;
- Contribute $200,000 towards the cost of the investigation; and
- Develop a corporate compliance program to ensure there are no further violations of the Competition Act.[24]

The **Consumer Protection Act** also provides buyers of consumer goods with protection. This act also deals with the fair disclosure of the cost of credit and specifies that lenders much disclose the full cost of borrowing in their advertisements.

Even very high prices may be OK

Generally speaking, firms can charge high prices—even outrageously high prices— as long as they don't conspire with their competitors to fix prices, discriminate against some of their customers, or lie.

Of course, there are exceptions. Firms in regulated businesses may need to seek approval for their prices. For example, some provinces regulate automobile insurance rates. Some countries impose more general price controls—to reduce inflation or try to control markets. However, most countries have followed the move toward a market-directed economy. That doesn't mean, however, that there aren't important regulations in the pricing area.

Price fixing is illegal—you can go to jail

Difficulties with pricing—and violations of pricing legislation—usually occur when competing marketing mixes are quite similar. When the success of an entire marketing strategy depends on price, there is pressure (and temptation) to make agreements with competitors (conspire). And **price fixing**—competitors getting together to raise, lower, or stabilize prices—is common and relatively easy. *But it is also completely illegal in Canada.* To discourage price fixing, the Competition Act provides for both individual managers and companies to be held responsible. However, it is very difficult to prosecute such cases in Canada. This chapter's Marketing Ethically refers to such a case.

Different countries have different rules concerning price fixing, and this has created problems in international trade. Japan, for example, allows price fixing, especially if it strengthens the position of Japanese producers in world markets.

Price discrimination

Price discrimination is also illegal in Canada under the Competition Act. A notable exception is that price discrimination on the basis of the quantity of goods purchased is legal. Other forms of offering different prices to different buyers (such as offering a discount to one buyer but not another) are illegal. Note that some price discrimination is regularly tolerated in the retail marketplace—students and seniors are often given discounts.

How to avoid discriminating

Because price discrimination laws are complicated and penalties for violations heavy, many business managers follow the safest course by offering few or no quantity discounts and the same cost-based prices to *all* customers. This is *too* conservative a reaction. But when firms consider price differences, they may need a lawyer involved in the discussion!

CONCLUSION

The Price variable offers an alert marketing manager many possibilities for varying marketing mixes. What pricing policies should be used depends on the pricing objectives. We looked at profit-oriented, sales-oriented, and status quo-oriented objectives.

A marketing manager must set policies about price flexibility, price levels over the product life cycle, who will pay the freight, and who will get discounts and allowances. While doing this, the manager should be aware of legislation that affects pricing policies.

In most cases, a marketing manager must set prices—that is, administer prices. For example, P & G administered a penetration pricing policy for the SpinBrush.

Starting with a list price, a variety of discounts and allowances may be offered to adjust for the something of value being offered in the marketing mix.

The Competition Act in Canada regulates pricing to protect the consumer.

Throughout this chapter, we talk about what may be included or excluded in the something of value and what objectives a firm might set to guide its pricing policies. We discuss how pricing policies combine to impact customer value. Price setting itself is not discussed. It will be covered in the next chapter, where we show ways to carry out the various pricing objectives and policies.

KEY TERMS

price, 443

target return objective, 444

profit maximization objective, 445

sales-oriented objective, 446

status quo objectives, 447

nonprice competition, 447

administered prices, 447

one-price policy, 448

flexible-price policy, 448

skimming price policy, 450

penetration pricing policy, 451

introductory price dealing, 452

basic list prices, 454

discounts, 454

quantity discounts, 454

cumulative quantity discounts, 455

noncumulative quantity discounts, 455

seasonal discounts, 456

net, 456

cash discounts, 456

2/10, net 30, 456

trade (functional) discount, 456

sale price, 457

everyday low pricing (EDLP), 457

allowances, 457

stocking allowances, 457

push money (or prize money) allowances, 457

trade-in allowance, 458

rebates, 459

F.O.B., 459

zone pricing, 459

uniform delivered pricing, 459

freight-absorption pricing, 460

value pricing, 460

predatory pricing, 463

Consumer Protection Act, 464

price fixing, 464

QUESTIONS AND PROBLEMS

1. Identify the strategy decisions a marketing manager must make in the Price area. Illustrate your answer for a local retailer.

2. How should the acceptance of a profit-oriented, a sales-oriented, or a status quo-oriented pricing objective affect the development of a company's marketing strategy? Illustrate for each.

3. Distinguish between one-price and flexible-price policies. Which is most appropriate for a hardware store? Why?

4. What pricing objective(s) is a skimming pricing policy most likely implementing? Is the same true for a penetration pricing policy? Which policy is probably most appropriate for each of the following products: (a) a new type of home lawn-sprinkling system, (b) a skin patch drug to help smokers quit, (c) a DVD of a best-selling movie, and (d) a new children's toy?

5. How would differences in exchange rates between different countries affect a firm's decisions concerning the use of flexible-price policies in different foreign markets?

6. Are seasonal discounts appropriate in agricultural businesses (which are certainly seasonal)?

7. What are the effective annual interest rates for the following cash discount terms: (a) 1/10, net 20; (b) 1/5, net 10; and (c) net 25?

8. Do stocking allowances increase or reduce conflict in a channel of distribution? Explain your thinking.

9. Why would a manufacturer offer a rebate instead of lowering the suggested list price?

10. How can a marketing manager change a firm's F.O.B. terms to make an otherwise competitive marketing mix more attractive?

11. What type of geographic pricing policy is most appropriate for the following products (specify any assumptions necessary to obtain a definite answer): (a) a chemical by-product, (b) nationally advertised candy bars, (c) rebuilt auto parts, and (d) tricycles?

12. How would a ban on freight absorption (that is, requiring F.O.B. factory pricing) affect a producer with substantial economies of scale in production?

13. Give an example of a marketing mix that has a high price level but that you see as a good value. Briefly explain what makes it a good value.

14. Think about a business from which you regularly make purchases even though there are competing firms with similar prices. Explain what the firm offers that improves value and keeps you coming back.

15. Cite two examples of continuously selling above the market price. Describe the situations.

16. Explain the types of competitive situations that might lead to a meeting-competition pricing policy.

17. How would our marketing system change if manufacturers were required to set fixed prices on *all* products sold at retail and *all* retailers were required to use these prices? Would a manufacturer's marketing mix be easier to develop? What kind of an operation would retailing be in this situation? Would consumers receive more or less service?

18. Is price discrimination involved if a large oil company sells gasoline to taxicab associations for resale to individual taxicab operators for 2½ cents a litre less than the price charged to retail service stations? What happens if the cab associations resell gasoline not only to taxicab operators but to the general public as well?

19. Do you think the Internet will lead more firms to use administered or flexible pricing? Why?

20. Are Canadian consumers well protected by the Consumer Protection Act and the Competition Act? What areas do you feel are still a problem for pricing in Canada?

21. Telus lowered the price of high-speed Internet access. How should they handle their current customers who have contracts at a higher rate? How will this affect their profitablilty?

COMPUTER–AIDED PROBLEM

16. Cash Discounts

RESOURCE REMINDER

Joe Tulkin owns Tulkin Wholesale Co. He sells paper, tape, file folders, and other office supplies to about 120 retailers in nearby cities. His average retailer customer spends about $900 a month. When Tulkin started business in 1991, competing wholesalers were giving retailers invoice terms of 3/10, net 30. Tulkin never gave the issue much thought—he just used the same invoice terms when he billed customers. At that time, about half of his customers took the discount. Recently, he noticed a change in the way his customers were paying their bills. Checking his records, he found that 90 percent of the retailers were taking the cash discount. With so many retailers taking the cash discount, it seems to have become a price reduction. In addition, Tulkin learned that other wholesalers were changing their invoice terms.

Tulkin decides he should rethink his invoice terms. He knows he could change the percent rate on the cash discount, the number of days the discount is offered, or the number of days before the face amount is due. Changing any of these, or any combination, will change the interest rate at which a buyer is, in effect, borrowing money if he does not take the discount. Tulkin decides that it will be easier to evaluate the effect of different invoice terms if he sets up a spreadsheet to let him change the terms and quickly see the effective interest rate for each change.

a. With 90 percent of Tulkin's customers now taking the discount, what is the total monthly cash discount amount?

b. If Tulkin changes his invoice terms to 1/5, net 20, what interest rate is each buyer paying by not taking the cash discount? With these terms, would fewer buyers be likely to take the discount? Why?

c. Tulkin thinks 10 customers will switch to other wholesalers if he changes his invoice terms to 2/10, net 30, while 60 percent of the remaining customers will take the discount. What interest rate does a buyer pay by not taking this cash discount? For this situation, what will the total gross sales (total invoice) amount be? The total cash discount? The total net sales receipts after the total cash discount? Compare Tulkin's current situation with what will happen if he changes his invoice terms to 2/10, net 30.

If you want to read the cases and view the video cases that accompany this chapter, visit the *Basic Marketing* Online Learning Centre at: **www.mcgrawhill.ca/olc/perreault**. Along with these cases and video cases, the OLC also has the software and user guide for this chapter's Computer-Aided Problem, as well as exercises, quizzes, articles, links, and other *interactive* content that will help you with your studies.

**WHEN YOU FINISH
THIS CHAPTER,
YOU SHOULD**

1. Understand how
   most wholesalers and
   retailers set their
   prices—using
   markups.

2. Know how to use
   break-even analysis
   to evaluate possible
   prices.

3. Understand the
   advantages of
   marginal analysis and
   how to use it for
   price setting.

4. Understand the
   various factors that
   influence customer
   price sensitivity.

5. Know the many ways
   that price setters use
   demand estimates in
   their pricing.

Price Setting in the Business World

Wal-Mart International is the largest retailer in the world. It currently has sales revenues of $316 billion. That's well over ten times the sales it had in 1990. Wal-Mart sells more food than any supermarket chain and more toys than Toys "R" Us. Procter & Gamble and Kimberly-Clark are giants in consumer packaged goods, but more than 10 percent of their sales are at Wal-Mart; for many major producers, it's more than 20 percent of sales.

When Wal-Mart arrived in Canada other department stores—especially those in the discount end of the price spectrum—began to have a tough time with losses in market share and profitability. Wal-Mart passed Zellers to become the largest department store in Canada in the late 1990s.

How did they manage to take market share away from the old discount leader? After all, Zellers was well entrenched having been started in Canada in 1931. Part of the answer is that the size of their sales volume means Wal-Mart commands incredible buying power among its suppliers. That drives down their B2B purchase price for inventory, which in turn means they can be an extremely aggressive price competitor at the retail level. And that's very important if you want to be a successful discount department store because your target market are price sensitive consumers.

Wal-Mart's huge sales volume also reduces its fixed operating costs as a percentage of sales. That means it can add a smaller markup, still cover its operating expenses, and make a larger profit. And as ongoing price rollbacks pull in more and more customers, its percentage of overhead costs to sales revenue goes down.

Wal-Mart has become even more efficient in cutting unnecessary inventory. In one sweeping set of improvements a few years ago, Wal-Mart cut more than $2 billion in average inventory, thereby saving $150 million in carrying costs and reducing the need for markdowns. Now Wal-Mart turns over its inventory close to 10 times each year, while most other mass-merchandisers average about 7. Wal-Mart also works closely with producers to reduce costs in the channel. For example, Wal-Mart was one of the first major retailers to insist that all orders be placed by computer and more recently has been one of the first to use radio frequency ID "smart tags" to precisely track the flow of goods from vendors through its distribution centres to stores. That reduces stock-outs on store shelves and lost sales at the checkout counter. Wal-Mart also works with vendors to create quality private-label brands, like Sam's Choice Cola. Its low price—about 15 percent below what consumers expect to pay for well-known colas—doesn't leave a big profit margin. Yet when customers come in to buy it, they also pick up other, more profitable, products.

Even with its lower costs, Wal-Mart isn't content to take the convenient route to price setting by just adding a standard percentage markup on different items. The company was one of the first retailers to give managers in every department in every store frequent, detailed information about what is selling and what isn't. Managers drop items that are collecting dust and roll back prices on the ones with the fastest turnover and highest margins. That not only increases stockturns but also puts the effort behind products with the most potential. For instance, Wal-Mart's analysis of checkout-scanner sales data revealed that parents often pick up more than one kid's video at a time. So now managers make certain that special displays feature several videos and that the rest of the selection is close by. And while many stores carry DVDs instead of videotapes, Wal-Mart carries both because it knows that its parent-customers often prefer VHS for kids' movies.

Wal-Mart was the first major retailer to move to online selling (www.walmart.com). Its online sales still account for only a small percentage of its total sales, so there's lots of room to grow there too. Further, Wal-Mart is aggressively taking its low-price approach to other countries, ranging from Mexico to Japan. It lists its current international growth strength as coming from Argentina, China, and Canada. Look for more openings near you.

So where does all this leave Zellers and the other discount department stores? Clearly it will be worth their while to copy Wal-Mart's innovations and minimize their costs.

However, Wal-Mart has such advantages on sales volume, unit costs, and margins that it will be difficult for Zellers or any other price discounter to win in any price war—unless Wal-Mart somehow stumbles because of its enormous size. But don't bet on that anytime soon.[1]

PRICE SETTING IS A KEY STRATEGY DECISION

In the previous chapter, we discussed the idea that pricing objectives and policies should guide pricing decisions. We accepted the idea of a list price and went on to discuss variations from list and how they combine to impact customer value. Now we'll see how the basic list price is set in the first place—based on information about costs, demand, and profit margins. See Exhibit 17-1.

There are many ways to set list prices. But for simplicity they can be reduced to two basic approaches: *cost-oriented* and *demand-oriented* price setting. We will discuss cost-oriented approaches first because they are most common. Also, understanding

Exhibit 17-1
Key Factors That Influence
Price Setting

the problems of relying only on a cost-oriented approach shows why a marketing manager must also consider demand to make good Price decisions. Let's begin by looking at how most retailers and wholesalers set cost-oriented prices.

SOME FIRMS JUST USE MARKUPS

Markups guide pricing by middlemen

Some firms, including most retailers and wholesalers, set prices by using a **markup**—a dollar amount added to the cost of products to get the selling price. For example, suppose that a Shoppers Drug Mart drugstore buys a bottle of Pert Plus shampoo and conditioner for $2. To make a profit, the drugstore obviously must sell Pert Plus for more than $2. If it adds $1 to cover operating expenses and provide a profit, we say that the store is marking up the item $1.

Markups, however, usually are stated as percentages rather than dollar amounts. And this is where confusion sometimes arises. Is a markup of $1 on a cost of $2 a markup of 50 percent? Or should the markup be figured as a percentage of the selling price—$3.00—and therefore be 33⅓ percent? A clear definition is necessary.

Markup percent is based on selling price—a convenient rule

Unless otherwise stated, markup (percent) means percentage of selling price that is added to the cost to get the selling price. So the $1 markup on the $3.00 selling price is a markup of 33⅓ percent. Markups are related to selling price for convenience.

There's nothing wrong with the idea of markup on cost. However, to avoid confusion, it's important to state clearly which markup percent you're using.

A manager may want to change a markup on selling price to one based on cost, or vice versa.[2]

Marketing Ethically

Canadian retailers are committed to accurate scanner pricing. Incorrect prices can result in poor customer relations and legal sanctions. Consequently, many retailers are now implementing a variety of procedures that were developed to help achieve and maintain accurate scanner pricing.

The Scanner Price Accuracy Voluntary Code works as follows: on a claim being presented by the customer, where the scanned price of a product at checkout is higher than the price displayed in the store or than advertised by the store, the lower price will be honoured, and the product will be given free of charge if the correct price is $10 or less; or if the correct price of the product is higher than $10, the retailer will give the customer a discount of $10 off the corrected price.

This policy is an honourable way of dealing with incorrectly scanned prices. Unfortunately, not many consumers are aware of this policy. There is the temptation that the retail person who is faced with a customer who is unaware of the policy to just give back the difference in price instead of giving the item to the customer for free. It's also possible that not every clerk is aware of the policy in the first place.

What can retailers do to make consumers more aware of this policy?[3]

Many use a standard markup percent

Many middlemen select a standard markup percent and then apply it to all their products. This makes pricing easier. When you think of the large number of items the average retailer and wholesaler carry—and the small sales volume of any one item—this approach may make sense. Spending the time to find the best price to charge on every item in stock (day to day or week to week) might not pay.

Moreover, different companies in the same line of business often use the same markup percent. There is a reason for this: Their operating expenses are usually similar. So they see a standard markup as acceptable as long as it's large enough to cover the firm's operating expenses and provide a reasonable profit.

Markups are related to gross margins

How does a manager decide on a standard markup in the first place? A standard markup is often set close to the firm's *gross margin*. Managers regularly see gross margins on their operating (profit and loss) statements. The gross margin is the amount left—after subtracting the cost of sales (cost of goods sold) from net sales—to cover the expenses of selling products and operating the business. Our Shoppers Drug Mart

Kohler is an example of a specialized product that relies on selective distribution and sells in smaller volumes usually offering retailers higher markups, in part to offset the retailer's higher carrying costs and marketing expenses. Bic is an example of a product that relies on intensive distribution and sells in larger volumes offering retailers smaller markups.

manager knows that there won't be any profit if the gross margin is not large enough. For this reason, Shoppers might accept a markup percent on Pert Plus that is close to the store's usual gross margin percent.

Smart producers pay attention to the gross margins and standard markups of middlemen in their channel. They usually allow trade (functional) discounts similar to the standard markups these middlemen expect.

Markup chain may be used in channel pricing

Different firms in a channel often use different markups. A markup chain—the sequence of markups firms use at different levels in a channel—determines the price structure in the whole channel. The markup is figured on the *selling price* at each level of the channel.

For example, Black & Decker's selling price for an electric drill becomes the cost the Home Depot wholesaler pays. The wholesaler's selling price becomes the hardware retailer's cost. And this cost plus a retail markup becomes the retail selling price. Each markup should cover the costs of running the business and leave a profit.

Exhibit 17-2 illustrates the markup chain for an electric drill at each level of the channel system. The production (factory) cost of the drill is $21.60. In this case, the producer takes a 10 percent markup and sells the product for $24. The markup is 10 percent of $24 or $2.40. The producer's selling price now becomes the wholesaler's cost—$24. If the wholesaler is used to taking a 20 percent markup on selling price, the markup is $6—and the wholesaler's selling price becomes $30. The $30 now becomes the cost for the hardware retailer. And a retailer who is used to a 40 percent markup adds $20, and the retail selling price becomes $50.

High markups don't always mean big profits

Some people, including many conventional retailers, think high markups mean big profits. Often this isn't true. A high markup may result in a price that's too high—a price at which few customers will buy. You can't earn much if you don't sell much, no matter how high your markup on a single item. So high markups may lead to low profits.

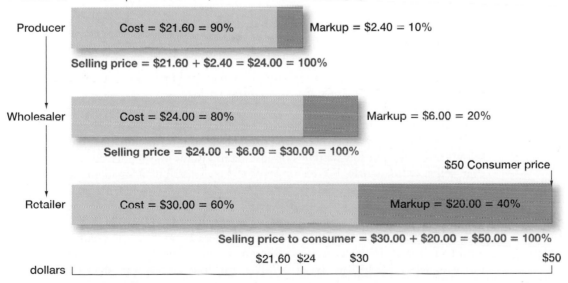

Exhibit 17-2   Example of a Markup Chain and Channel Pricing

Lower markups can speed turnover and the stockturn rate

Some retailers and wholesalers, however, try to speed turnover to increase profit—even if this means reducing their markups. They realize that a business runs up costs over time. If they can sell a much greater amount in the same time period, they may be able to take a lower markup and still earn higher profits at the end of the period. In the opening vignette this strategy was used by Zellers and by Wal-Mart. The problem of course is that the sales volumes have to be substantial because the markups are very low. If the company fails to attract a sufficient level of sales they can encounter rough financial circumstances. This was the problem that plagued the discount department store Army and Navy.

An important idea here is the stockturn rate—the number of times the average inventory is sold in a year. A low stockturn rate may be bad for profits.

At the very least, a low stockturn increases inventory carrying cost and ties up working capital. If a firm with a stockturn of 1 (once per year) sells products that cost it $100,000, it has that much tied up in inventory all the time. But a stockturn of 5 requires only $20,000 worth of inventory ($100,000 cost ÷ 5 turnovers a year). If annual inventory carrying cost is about 20 percent of the inventory value, that reduces costs by $16,000 a year. That's a big difference on $100,000 in sales!

Whether a stockturn rate is high or low depends on the industry and the product involved. An electrical parts wholesaler may expect an annual rate of 2—while a supermarket might expect 8 stockturns on average but 20 stockturns for soaps and 70 stockturns for fresh fruits and vegetables.

Mass-merchandisers run in fast company

Although some middlemen use the same standard markup percent on all their products, this policy ignores the importance of fast turnover. Mass-merchandisers know this. They put low markups on fast-selling items and higher markups on items that sell less frequently. For example, Wal-Mart may put a small markup on fast-selling health and beauty aids (like toothpaste or shampoo) but higher markups on appliances and clothing.

Where does the markup chain start?

Some markups eventually become standard in a trade. Most channel members tend to follow a similar process—adding a certain percentage to the previous price. But who sets price in the first place? The firm that brands a product is usually the one that sets its basic list price. It may be a large retailer, a large wholesaler, or most often, the producer.

Some producers just start with a cost per unit figure and add a markup—perhaps a standard markup—to obtain their selling price. Or they may use some rule-of-thumb formula such as:

$$\text{Selling price} = \text{Average production cost per unit} \times 3$$

A producer who uses this approach might develop rules and markups related to its own costs and objectives. Yet even the first step—selecting the appropriate cost per unit to build on—isn't easy. Let's discuss several approaches to see how cost-oriented price setting really works.

AVERAGE-COST PRICING IS COMMON AND CAN BE DANGEROUS

Average-cost pricing means adding a reasonable markup to the average cost of a product. A manager usually finds the average cost per unit by studying past records. Dividing the total cost for the last year by all the units produced and sold in that period gives an estimate of the average cost per unit for the next year. If the cost was $32,000 for all labour and materials and $30,000 for fixed overhead expenses—such as selling expenses, rent, and manager salaries—then the total cost is $62,000. If the company produced 40,000 items in that time period, the average cost is $62,000 divided by 40,000 units, or $1.55 per unit. To get the price, the producer decides how much profit per unit to add to the average cost per unit. If the company considers 45 cents a reasonable profit for each unit, it sets the new price at $2.00. Exhibit 17-3A shows that this approach produces the desired profit if the company sells 40,000 units.

It does not make allowances for cost variations as output changes

It's always a useful input to pricing decisions to understand how costs operate at different levels of output. Further, average-cost pricing is simple. But it can also be dangerous. It's easy to lose money with average-cost pricing. To see why, let's follow this example further.

Exhibit 17-3 Results of Average-Cost Pricing

A. Calculation of Planned Profit if 40,000 Items Are Sold		B. Calculation of Actual Profit if Only 20,000 Items Are Sold	
Calculation of Costs:		**Calculation of Costs:**	
Fixed overhead expenses	$30,000	Fixed overhead expenses	$30,000
Labour and materials ($0.80 a unit)	32,000	Labour and materials ($0.80 a unit)	16,000
Total costs	$62,000	Total costs	$46,000
"Planned" profit	18,000		
Total costs and planned profit	$80,000		
Calculation of Profit (or Loss):		**Calculation of Profit (or Loss):**	
Actual unit sales × price ($2.00*)	$80,000	Actual unit sales × price ($2.00*)	$40,000
Minus: total costs	62,000	Minus: total costs	46,000
Profit (loss)	$18,000	Profit (loss)	($6,000)
Result:		**Result:**	
Planned profit of $18,000 is earned if 40,000 items are sold at $2.00 each.		Planned profit of $18,000 is not earned. Instead, $6,000 loss results if 20,000 items are sold at $2.00 each.	

*Calculation of "reasonable" price: $\dfrac{\text{Expected total costs and planned profit}}{\text{Planned number of items to be sold}} = \dfrac{\$80,000}{40,000} = \$2.00$

First, remember that the average cost of $2.00 per unit was based on output of 40,000 units. But if the firm is only able to produce and sell 20,000 units in the next year, it may be in trouble. Twenty thousand units sold at $2.00 each ($1.55 cost plus 45 cents for expected profit) yield a total revenue of only $40,000. The overhead is still fixed at $30,000, and the variable material and labour cost drops by half to $16,000—for a total cost of $46,000. This means a loss of $6,000, or 30 cents a unit. The method that was supposed to allow a profit of 45 cents a unit actually causes a loss of 30 cents a unit! See Exhibit 17-3B.

The basic problem with the average-cost approach is that it doesn't consider cost variations at different levels of output. In a typical situation, costs are high with low output, and then economies of scale set in—the average cost per unit drops as the quantity produced increases. This is why mass production and mass distribution often make sense. It's also why it's important to develop a better understanding of the different types of costs a marketing manager should consider when setting a price.

MARKETING MANAGERS MUST CONSIDER VARIOUS KINDS OF COSTS

Average-cost pricing may lead to losses because there are a variety of costs—and each changes in a *different* way as output changes. Any pricing method that uses cost must consider these changes. To understand why, we need to define six types of costs.

There are three kinds of total cost

1. **Total fixed cost** is the sum of those costs that are fixed in total—no matter how much is produced. Among these fixed costs are rent, depreciation, managers' salaries, property taxes, and insurance. Such costs stay the same even if production stops temporarily. Heavy industry firms like Dofasco and Petro-Canada have a huge amount of capital tied up in plant and equipment and their overhead cost continues whether they are producing at full capacity or producing nothing.

2. **Total variable cost**, on the other hand, is the sum of those changing expenses that are closely related to output—expenses for parts, wages, packaging materials, outgoing freight, and sales commissions.

Average fixed costs are lower when a larger quantity is produced.

JETBLUE'S PROFIT TAKES OFF IN SPITE OF TURBULENCE

JetBlue Airways just got its start in 2000, but it has achieved profitable growth while major airlines have been fighting just to survive. JetBlue offers a low-cost, high-quality flying experience—so it's not exactly an "economy" carrier. JetBlue offers each passenger seat-back DirectTV and high-touch service. Its sleek look on everything from fashionable blue uniforms to comfortable leather seats—sends the signal that low fares don't preclude high style. Its strategy is to excel at the things that can really distinguish the airline but cost relatively little—such as comfort, punctuality, and courtesy—while dispensing with things that can't, like airline grub. For example, when delays do occur, JetBlue goes out of its way to keep passengers fully informed.

JetBlue's quality service and low fares explain why it attracts customers. Yet its small fleet limits the quantity of customers it can serve. So how can JetBlue make higher profits when it has lower prices and lower quantity? The answer is that JetBlue earns an above-average 16 percent profit margin on the revenue it takes in. For that to happen, its costs must be, on a relative basis, even lower than its fares. And that's the case. For example, JetBlue's operating cost per "seat mile" is just over 5 cents. American and Delta are close to 9 cents per seat mile. JetBlue's new planes are fuel efficient, and with fewer types of planes, its costs for training and maintenance are lower. The planes are also the right size to match demand on the routes that JetBlue picks; empty seats would mean missed revenue. JetBlue picks routes where competing airlines have high fares, but it ignores expensive-to-serve "feeder routes." Some of JetBlue's advantages accrue because it is small and new. As JetBlue grows and others copy or improve its approach, it may need to modify its strategy. But for now it is flying high.[4]

At zero output, total variable cost is zero. As output increases, so do variable costs. If Roots doubles its output of sweatshirts in a year, its total cost for cloth also (roughly) doubles.

3. **Total cost** is the sum of total fixed and total variable costs. Changes in total cost depend on variations in total variable cost, since total fixed cost stays the same.

There are three kinds of average cost

The pricing manager usually is more interested in cost per unit than total cost because prices are usually quoted per unit.

1. **Average cost (per unit)** is obtained by dividing total cost by the related quantity (that is, the total quantity that causes the total cost).
2. Average fixed cost (per unit) is obtained by dividing total fixed cost by the related quantity.
3. Average variable cost (per unit) is obtained by dividing total variable cost by the related quantity.

An example shows cost relations

Exhibit 17-4 shows the six types of cost and how they vary at different levels of output. The line for 40,000 units is highlighted because that was the expected level of sales in our average-cost pricing example. For simplicity, we assume that average variable cost is the same for each unit. Notice, however, that total variable cost increases when quantity increases.

Exhibit 17-5 shows the three average cost curves from Exhibit 17-4. Notice that average fixed cost goes down steadily as the quantity increases. Although the average variable cost remains the same, average cost decreases continually too. This is because average fixed cost is decreasing. With these relations in mind, let's reconsider the problem with average-cost pricing.

Exhibit 17-4 Cost Structure of a Firm

Quantity (Q)	Total Fixed Costs (TFC)	Average Fixed Costs (AFC)	Average Variable Costs (AVC)	Total Variable Costs (TVC)	Total Cost (TC)	Average Cost (AC)
0	$30,000	—	—	—	$ 30,000	—
10,000	30,000	$3.00	$0.80	$ 8,000	38,000	$3.80
20,000	30,000	1.50	0.80	16,000	46,000	2.30
30,000	30,000	1.00	0.80	24,000	54,000	1.80
40,000	30,000	0.75	0.80	32,000	62,000	1.55
50,000	30,000	0.60	0.80	40,000	70,000	1.40
60,000	30,000	0.50	0.80	48,000	78,000	1.30
70,000	30,000	0.43	0.80	56,000	86,000	1.23
80,000	30,000	0.38	0.80	64,000	94,000	1.18
90,000	30,000	0.33	0.80	72,000	102,000	1.13
100,000	30,000	0.30	0.80	80,000	110,000	1.10

$$\begin{bmatrix} 110,000 \text{ (TC)} \\ -80,000 \text{ (TVC)} \\ \hline 30,000 \text{ (TFC)} \end{bmatrix}$$

$$\text{(Q) } 100,000 \overline{\left| \begin{array}{c} 0.30 \text{ (AFC)} \\ 30,000 \text{ (TFC)} \end{array} \right.}$$

$$\begin{bmatrix} 100,000 \text{ (Q)} \\ \times 0.80 \text{ (AVC)} \\ \hline 80,000 \text{ (TVC)} \end{bmatrix} \begin{bmatrix} 30,000 \text{ (TFC)} \\ +80,000 \text{ (TVC)} \\ \hline 110,000 \text{ (TC)} \end{bmatrix}$$

$$\text{(Q) } 100,000 \overline{\left| \begin{array}{c} 1.10 \text{ (AC)} \\ 110,000 \text{ (TC)} \end{array} \right.}$$

Ignoring demand is the major weakness of average-cost pricing

Average-cost pricing works well if the firm actually sells the quantity it used to set the average-cost price. Losses may result, however, if actual sales are much lower than expected. On the other hand, if sales are much higher than expected, then profits may be very good. But this will only happen by luck—because the firm's demand is much larger than expected.

Unless your company is like Sifto Canada who produce salt or Rogers Sugar it is best to be wary of average-cost pricing. Products like salt and sugar enjoy relatively stable and predictable demand (at least in the short run) so the firm can realistically estimate the quantity it expects to sell.

To use average-cost pricing, a marketing manager must make *some* estimate of the quantity to be sold in the coming period. Without a quantity estimate, it isn't possible to compute average cost. But unless this quantity is related to price—that is, unless the firm's demand curve is considered—the marketing manager may set a price

Exhibit 17-5
Typical Shape of Cost (per unit) Curves When Average Variable Cost per Unit Is Constant

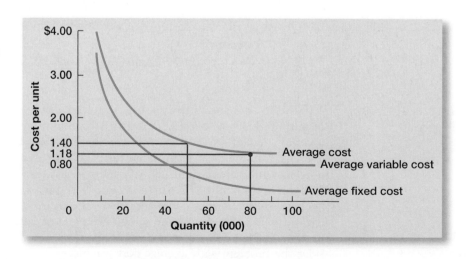

Exhibit 17-6
Evaluation of Various Prices along a Firm's Demand Curve

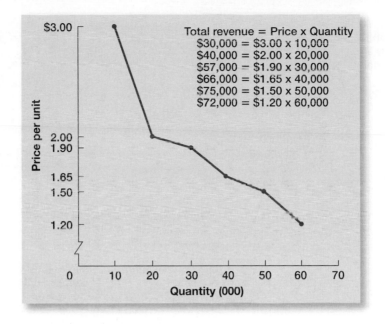

that doesn't even cover a firm's total cost! You saw this happen in Exhibit 17-3B, when the firm's price of $2.00 resulted in demand for only 20,000 units and a loss of $6,000.

The demand curve is still important even if a manager doesn't take time to think about it. For example, Exhibit 17-6 shows the demand curve for the firm we're discussing. This demand curve shows *why* the firm lost money when it tried to use average-cost pricing. At the $2.00 price, quantity demanded is only 20,000. With this demand curve and the costs in Exhibit 17-4, the firm will incur a loss whether management sets the price at a high $3 or a low $1.20. At $3, the firm will sell only 10,000 units for a total revenue of $30,000. But total cost will be $38,000—for a loss of $8,000. At the $1.20 price, it will sell 60,000 units—at a loss of $6,000. However, the curve suggests that at a price of $1.65 consumers will demand about 40,000 units, producing a profit of about $4,000.

In short, average-cost pricing is simple in theory but often fails in practice. In stable situations, prices set by this method may yield profits but not necessarily *maximum* profits. And note that such cost-based prices may be higher than a price that would be more profitable for the firm, as shown in Exhibit 17-6. When demand conditions are changing, average-cost pricing is even more risky.

Exhibit 17-7 summarizes the relationships discussed above. Cost-oriented pricing requires an estimate of the total number of units to be sold. That estimate determines the *average* fixed cost per unit and thus the average total cost. Then the firm adds the desired profit per unit to the average total cost to get the cost-oriented selling price. How customers react to that price determines the actual quantity the firm will be able to sell. But that quantity may not be the quantity used to compute the average cost![5]

Experience curve pricing is even riskier

Some aggressive firms use a variation of average-cost pricing called experience curve pricing. **Experience curve pricing** is average-cost pricing using an estimate of *future* average costs. This approach is based on the observation that over time—as an industry gains experience in certain kinds of production—managers learn new ways to reduce costs. In some industries, costs decrease about 15 to 20 percent each time cumulative production volume (experience) doubles. So a firm might set average-cost prices based on where it expects costs to be when products are sold in the future—not where costs actually are when the strategy is set. This approach is more common in rapidly growing markets because cumulative production volume (experience) grows faster.

If costs drop as expected, this approach works. But it has the same risks as regular average-cost pricing. The price setter has to estimate what quantity will be sold to be able to read the right price from the experience-based average-cost curve.[6]

**Don't ignore
competitors' costs**

Another danger of average-cost pricing is that it ignores competitors' costs and prices. Just as the price of a firm's own product influences demand, the price of available substitutes may impact demand. We saw this operate in our Wal-Mart case at the start of this chapter. By finding ways to cut costs, Wal-Mart was able to offer prices lower than competitors and still make an attractive profit.

SOME FIRMS ADD A TARGET RETURN TO COST

**Target return pricing
scores sometimes**

Target return pricing—adding a target return to the cost of a product—has become popular in recent years. With this approach, the price setter seeks to earn (1) a percentage return (say, 10 percent per year) on the investment or (2) a specific total dollar return.

This method is a variation of the average-cost method since the desired target return is added into total cost. As a simple example, if a company had $180,000 invested and wanted to make a 10 percent return on investment, it would add $18,000 to its annual total costs in setting prices.

This approach has the same weakness as other average-cost pricing methods. If the quantity actually sold is less than the quantity used to set the price, then the company doesn't earn its target return, even though the target return seems to be part of the price structure. In fact, we already saw this in Exhibit 17-3. Remember that we added $18,000 as an expected profit, or target return. But the return was much lower when the expected quantity was not sold. (It could be higher too—but only if the quantity sold is much larger than expected.) Target return pricing clearly does not guarantee that a firm will hit the target.

Hitting the target in the long run

Managers in some larger firms who want to achieve a long-run target return objective use another cost-oriented pricing approach—**long-run target return pricing**—adding a long-run average target return to the cost of a product. Instead of estimating the quantity they expect to produce in any one year, they assume that during several years' time their plants will produce at, say, 80 percent of capacity. They use this quantity when setting their prices.

Companies that take this longer-run view assume that there will be recession years when sales drop below 80 percent of capacity. For example, Owens-Corning Fiberglas sells insulation. In years when there is little construction, output is low, and the firm does not earn the target return. But the company also has good years when it sells more insulation and exceeds the target return. Over the long run, Owens-Corning managers expect to achieve the target return. And sometimes they're right—depending on how accurately they estimate demand!

BREAK-EVEN ANALYSIS CAN EVALUATE POSSIBLE PRICES

Some price setters use break-even analysis in their pricing. **Break-even analysis** evaluates whether the firm will be able to break even—that is, cover all its costs—with a particular price. This is important because a firm must cover all costs in the long run or there is not much point being in business. This method focuses on the break-even point (BEP)—the quantity where the firm's total cost will just equal its total revenue.

Break-even charts help find the BEP

To help understand how break-even analysis works, look at Exhibit 17-8, an example of the typical break-even chart. *The chart is based on a particular selling price*—in this case $1.20 a unit. The chart has lines that show total costs (total variable plus total fixed costs) and total revenues at different levels of production. The break-even point on the chart is at 75,000 units, where the total cost and total revenue lines intersect. At that production level, total cost and total revenue are the same—$90,000.

The difference between the total revenue and total cost at a given quantity is the profit—or loss! The chart shows that below the break-even point, total cost is higher than total revenue and the firm incurs a loss. The firm would make a profit above the break-even point. However, the firm would only reach the break-even point, or get beyond it into the profit area, *if* it could sell at least 75,000 units at the $1.20 price.

Break-even analysis can be helpful if used properly, so let's look at this approach more closely.

Exhibit 17-8
Break-Even Chart for a
Particular Situation

How to compute a break-even point

A break-even chart is an easy-to-understand visual aid, but it's also useful to be able to compute the break-even point.

The BEP, in units, can be found by dividing total fixed costs (TFC) by the **fixed-cost (FC) contribution per unit**—the assumed selling price per unit minus the variable cost per unit. This can be stated as a simple formula:

$$\text{BEP (in units)} = \frac{\text{Total fixed cost}}{\text{Fixed cost contribution per unit}}$$

This formula makes sense when we think about it. To break even, we must cover total fixed costs. Therefore, we must figure the contribution each unit will make to covering the total fixed costs (after paying for the variable costs to produce the item). When we divide this per-unit contribution into the total fixed costs that must be covered, we have the BEP (in units).

To illustrate the formula, let's use the cost and price information in Exhibit 17-8. The price per unit is $1.20. The average variable cost per unit is 80 cents. So the FC contribution per unit is 40 cents ($1.20 − 80 cents). The total fixed cost is $30,000 (see Exhibit 17-8). Substituting in the formula:

$$\text{BEP} = \frac{\$30,000}{.40} = 75,000 \text{ units}$$

From this you can see that if this firm sells 75,000 units, it will exactly cover all its fixed and variable costs. If it sells even one more unit, it will begin to show a profit—in this case, 40 cents per unit. Note that once the fixed costs are covered, the part of revenue formerly going to cover fixed costs is now *all profit*.

BEP can be stated in dollars too

The BEP can also be figured in dollars. The easiest way is to compute the BEP in units and then multiply by the assumed per-unit price. If you multiply the selling price ($1.20) by the BEP in units (75,000) you get $90,000—the BEP in dollars.

Each possible price has its own break-even point

Often it's useful to compute the break-even point for each of several possible prices and then compare the BEP for each price to likely demand at that price. The marketing manager can quickly reject some price possibilities when the expected quantity demanded at a given price is way below the break-even point for that price.

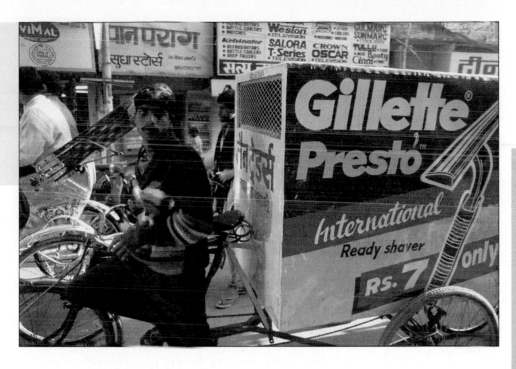

The money that a firm spends on marketing and other expenses must be at least covered by a firm's price if it is to make a profit. That's why Gillette enjoys big economies of scale by selling the same razors in many markets around the world.

A target profit can be included

So far in our discussion of BEP we've focused on the quantity at which total revenue equals total cost—where profit is zero. We can also vary this approach to see what quantity is required to earn a certain level of profit. The analysis is the same as described above for the break-even point in units, but the amount of target profit is added to the total fixed cost. Then when we divide the total fixed cost plus profit figure by the contribution from each unit, we get the quantity that will earn the target profit.

Break-even analysis shows the effect of cutting costs

Break-even analysis makes it clear why managers must constantly look for effective new ways to get jobs done at lower costs. For example, if a manager can reduce the firm's total fixed costs—perhaps by using computer systems to cut out excess inventory carrying costs—the break-even point will be lower and profits will start to build sooner. Similarly, if the variable cost to produce and sell an item can be reduced, the fixed-cost contribution per unit increases; that too lowers the break-even point and profit accumulates faster for each product sold beyond the break-even point.

Break-even analysis is helpful—but not a pricing solution

Break-even analysis is helpful for evaluating alternatives. It is also popular because it's easy to use. Yet break-even analysis is too often misunderstood. Beyond the BEP, profits seem to be growing continually. And the graph—with its straight-line total revenue curve—makes it seem that any quantity can be sold at the assumed price. But this usually isn't true. It is the same as assuming a perfectly horizontal demand curve at that price. In fact, most managers face down-sloping demand situations. And their total revenue curves do *not* keep going up.

The firm and costs we discussed in the average-cost pricing example earlier in this chapter illustrate this point. You can confirm from Exhibit 17-4 that the total fixed cost ($30,000) and average variable cost (80 cents) for that firm are the same ones shown in the break-even chart (Exhibit 17-8). So this break-even chart is the one we would draw for that firm assuming a price of $1.20 a unit. But the demand curve for that case showed that the firm could only sell 60,000 units at a price of $1.20. So that firm would never reach the 75,000 unit break-even point at a $1.20 price. It would only sell 60,000 units, and it would lose $6,000! A firm with a different demand curve—say, one where the firm could sell 80,000 units at a price of $1.20—would in fact break even at 75,000 units.

Break-even analysis is a useful tool for analyzing costs and evaluating what might happen to profits in different market environments. But it is a cost-oriented approach. Like other cost-oriented approaches, it does not consider the effect of price on the quantity that consumers will want—that is, the demand curve.

So to really zero in on the most profitable price, marketers are better off estimating the demand curve itself and then using marginal analysis, which we'll discuss next.[7]

MARGINAL ANALYSIS CONSIDERS BOTH COSTS AND DEMAND

Marginal analysis helps find the right price

The best pricing tool marketers have for looking at costs and revenue (demand) at the same time is marginal analysis. **Marginal analysis** focuses on the changes in total revenue and total cost from selling one more unit to find the most profitable price and quantity. Marginal analysis shows how costs, revenue, and profit change at different prices. The price that maximizes profit is the one that results in the greatest difference between total revenue and total cost.[8]

Demand estimates involve "if-then" thinking

Since the price determines what quantity will be sold, a manager needs an estimate of the demand curve to compute total revenue. A practical approach here is for managers to think about a price that appears to be too high and one that is too low. Then, for a number of prices between these two extremes, the manager estimates what quantity it might be possible to sell. You can think of this as a summary of the answers to a series of what-if questions—*What* quantity will be sold *if* a particular price is selected?

Profit is the difference between total revenue and total cost

The first two columns in Exhibit 17-9 give quantity and price combinations (demand) for an example firm. Total revenue in column 3 of Exhibit 17-9 is equal to a price multiplied by its related quantity. Costs at the different quantities are also shown. The profit at each quantity and price is the difference between total revenue and total cost. In this example, the best price is $79 (and a quantity of six units sold) because that combination results in the highest profit ($106). Now let's look at this example in more detail.

Exhibit 17-9 Revenue, Cost, and Profit at Different Prices for a Firm

(1) Quantity (Q)	(2) Price (P)	(3) Total Revenue (TR)	(4) Total Variable Cost (TVC)	(5) Total Cost (TC)	(6) Profit (TR − TC)	(7) Marginal Revenue (MR)	(8) Marginal Cost (MC)	(9) Marginal Profit (MR − MC)
0	$150	$ 0	$ 0	$200	$−200			
1	140	140	96	296	−156	$140	$96	$ + 44
2	130	260	116	316	− 56	120	20	+100
3	117	351	131	331	+ 20	91	15	+ 76
4	105	420	144	344	+ 76	69	13	+ 56
5	92	460	155	355	+105	40	11	+ 29
6	79	474	168	368	+106	14	13	+ 1
7	66	462	183	383	+ 79	−12	15	− 27
8	53	424	223	423	+ 1	−38	40	− 78
9	42	378	307	507	−129	−46	84	−130
10	31	310	510	710	−400	−68	203	−271

Marginal revenue can be negative

This firm faces a demand curve that slopes down. That means that the marketer can expect to increase sales volume by lowering the price. Yet the lower price required to sell the larger quantity may reduce total revenue. Therefore, it's important to evaluate the likely effect of alternative prices on total revenue and profit. The way to do this is to look at marginal revenue.

Marginal revenue is the change in total revenue that results from the sale of one more unit of a product. At a price of $105, the firm in this example can sell four units for total revenue of $420. By cutting the price to $92, it can sell five units for total revenue of $460. Thus, the marginal revenue for the fifth unit is $460 − $420, or $40. But will total revenue continue to rise if the firm sells more units at lower prices? Exhibit 17-9 shows that total revenue goes down at price levels lower than $79. Note in the table that marginal revenue is negative when total revenue decreases. Profit depends on both revenue and costs, so let's look at costs next.

The marginal cost of just one more can be important

Column 5 in Exhibit 17-9 shows the total cost increasing as quantity increases. Remember that total cost is the sum of fixed cost (in this example, $200) and total variable cost. The fixed cost does not change over the entire range of output. However, total variable costs increase as more units are produced. So it's the increases in variable cost that explain the increase in total cost.

There is another kind of cost that is vital to marginal analysis. **Marginal cost** is the change in total cost that results from producing one more unit. In Exhibit 17-9, you can see that it costs $355 to produce five units of a product but only $344 to produce four units. Thus, the marginal cost for the fifth unit is $11. In other words, marginal cost is the additional cost of producing one more specific unit. By contrast, average cost is the average for *all* units (total cost divided by the number of units).

Profit is largest when marginal revenue = marginal cost

To maximize profit, a manager generally wants to lower the price and sell more units as long as the marginal revenue from selling them is at least equal to the marginal cost of the extra units. From this we get the following rule for maximizing profit: The highest profit is earned at the price where marginal cost is just less than or equal to marginal revenue.*

You can see this rule operating in Exhibit 17-9. As the price is cut from $140 down to $79, the quantity sold increases to six units and the profit increases to its maximum level, $106. At that point, marginal revenue and marginal cost are about equal. However, beyond that point further price cuts result in lower profits (or losses).

At the point where marginal revenue (MR) equals marginal cost (MC), **marginal profit**—the extra profit on the last unit—is near zero. So when the firm is looking for the best price to charge, it should lower the price—to increase the quantity it will sell—as long as the last unit it sells will yield extra profit.

Profit maximization with total revenue and total cost curves

Exhibit 17-10 graphs the total revenue, total cost, and total profit relationships for the numbers we've been working with in Exhibit 17-9. The highest point on the total profit curve is at a quantity of six units. This is also the quantity where we find the greatest vertical distance between the total revenue curve and the total cost curve. Exhibit 17-9 shows that it is the $79 price that results in selling six units, so $79 is the price that leads to the highest profit. A price lower than $79 would result in a higher sales volume. But you can see that the total profit curve declines beyond a quantity of six units. So a profit-maximizing marketing manager would not be interested in setting a lower price.

A profit range is reassuring

Marginal analysis focuses on the price that earns the *highest* profit. But a slight miss doesn't mean failure because demand estimates don't have to be exact. There

---

*This rule applies in typical situations where the curves are shaped similarly to those discussed here. As a technical matter, however, we should add the following to the rule for maximizing profit: The marginal cost must be increasing, or decreasing, at a lesser rate than marginal revenue.

Exhibit 17-10
Graphic Determination of
the Price Giving the Greatest
Total Profit for a Firm

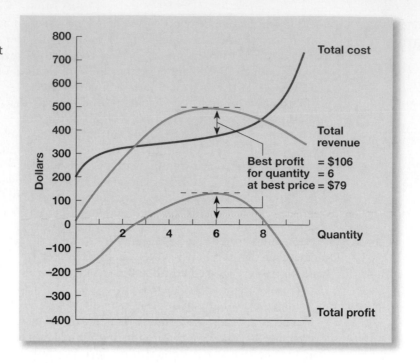

is usually a range of profitable prices. You can see this in Exhibit 17-9 and in the section of Exhibit 17-10 shown in yellow. Although the price that would result in the highest profit is $79, the firm's strategy would be profitable all the way from a price of $53 to $117. So the effort of trying to estimate demand will probably lead to being some place in the profitable range. In contrast, mechanical use of average-cost pricing could lead to a price that is much too high—or much too low.

How to lose less, if you must

In a weak market, demand may fall off and there may be no way to operate at a profit. If this is a permanent situation—as might occur in the decline stage of the product life cycle—there may be no choice other than to go out of business or do something totally different. However, if it appears that the situation is temporary, it may be best to sell at a low price, even if it's not profitable.

Why would you sell at a price that is unprofitable? Marginal analysis provides the answer. Most fixed costs will continue even if the firm doesn't sell anything. So if the firm can charge a price that at least recovers the marginal cost of the last unit (or more generally, the variable cost of the units being considered), the extra income would help pay the fixed costs and reduce the firm's losses.

Marginal analysis applies in oligopoly too

In Chapter 16 we noted that marketing managers who compete in oligopoly situations often just set a price that meets what competitors charge. Marginal analysis also helps to explain why they do this.

Exhibit 17-11 shows a demand curve and marginal revenue curve typical of what a marketing manager in an oligopoly situation faces. The demand curve is kinked, and the current market price is at the kink. The dashed part of the marginal revenue line in Exhibit 17-11 shows that marginal revenue drops sharply at the kinked point.

Even if costs change somewhat, the marginal revenue curve drops so fast that the marginal cost curve is still likely to cross the marginal revenue curve (that is, marginal cost will be equal to marginal revenue) someplace along the drop in the marginal revenue curve. In other words, marginal costs and marginal revenue will continue to be equal to each other at a price and quantity combination that is close to where the kink occurs already. So even though the change in costs seems to be a reason for changing the price, prices are relatively "sticky" at the kinked point. Setting the price at the level of the kink maximizes profit.

Exhibit 17-11
Marginal Revenue Drops
Fast in an Oligopoly

A price leader usually sets the price

Most managers who compete in oligopoly markets (or markets headed toward oligopoly) are aware of the economics of their situation, at least intuitively. As a result, a **price leader** usually sets a price for all to follow, perhaps to maximize profits or to get a certain target return on investment. Without any collusion, other members of the industry follow. The price leader is usually the firm with the lowest costs. That may give it more flexibility than competitors. This price may be maintained for a long time.

Sometimes, however, a price leader tries to lower the price, and a competitor lowers it even further. This can lead to price wars. You sometimes see this in competition between major computer companies. But price wars usually pass quickly because they are unprofitable for each firm and the whole industry.

A rough demand estimate is better than none

Some managers don't take advantage of marginal analysis because they think they can't determine the exact shape of the demand curve. But that view misses the point of marginal analysis. Marginal analysis encourages managers to think carefully about what they *do know* about costs and demand. Only rarely is either type of information exact. So in practice, the focus of marginal analysis is not on finding the precise price that will maximize profit. Rather, the focus is on getting an estimate of how profit might vary across a *range of relevant prices*. Further, a number of practical demand-oriented approaches can help a marketing manager do a better job of understanding the likely shape of the demand curve for a target market. We'll discuss these approaches next.

DEMAND-ORIENTED APPROACHES FOR SETTING PRICES

Evaluating the customer's price sensitivity

A manager who knows what influences target customers' price sensitivity can do a better job estimating the demand curve that the firm faces. Marketing researchers have identified a number of factors that influence price sensitivity across many different market situations.

The first is the most basic. When customers have *substitute ways* of meeting a need, they are likely to be more price sensitive. A cook who wants a cappuccino

Hallmark's ad prompts consumers to think of the reference price for a greeting card in terms of the value it creates for the person who receives the card. Abbey National ads highlight its low monthly insurance rates. The total expenditure might seem larger—and consumers might be even more price sensitive—if rates were for a whole year instead of just a month.

maker to be able to serve something distinctive to guests at a dinner party may be willing to pay a high price. However, if different machines are available and our cook sees them as pretty similar, price sensitivity will be greater. It's important not to ignore dissimilar alternatives if the customer sees them as substitutes. If a machine for espresso were much less expensive than one for cappuccino, our cook might decide that an espresso machine would meet her needs just as well.

The impact of substitutes on price sensitivity is greatest when it is easy for customers to *compare prices*. For example, unit prices make it easier for our cook to compare the prices of espresso and cappuccino grinds on the grocery store shelf. Many people believe that the ease of comparing prices on the Internet increases price sensitivity and brings down prices. If nothing else, it may make sellers more aware of competing prices.

INTERNET EXERCISE

Bizrate.com is a Web site that makes it easy to find different brands of products from different sellers and compare prices. Go to www.bizrate.com and search for *popcorn poppers*. Review the products and prices listed and check a few of the links to related information. How useful is this sort of service? Is there more variety in features and prices than you expected? Do you think that this sort of comparison makes people more price sensitive? Why or why not?

People tend to be less price sensitive when someone else pays the bill or *shares the cost*. Perhaps this is just human nature. Insurance companies think that consumers would reject high medical fees if they were paying all of their own bills. And executives might plan longer in advance to get better discounts on airline flights if their companies weren't footing the bills.

Customers tend to be more price sensitive the greater the *total expenditure*. Sometimes a big expenditure can be broken into smaller pieces. Mercedes knows this. When its ads focused on the cost of a monthly lease rather than the total price of the car, more consumers got interested in biting the bullet.

Customers are less price sensitive the greater the *significance of the end benefit* of the purchase. Computer makers will pay more to get Intel processors if they believe that having an "Intel inside" sells more machines. Positioning efforts often focus on emotional benefits of a purchase to increase the significance of a benefit. Ads for L'Oréal hair colour, for example, show closeups of beautiful hair while popular celebrities like Heather Locklear tell women to buy it "because you're worth it." A consumer who cares about the price of a bottle of hair colour might still have no question that she's worth the difference in price.

Customers are sometimes less price sensitive if they already have a *sunk investment* that is related to the purchase. This is especially relevant with business customers. For example, once managers of a firm have invested to train employees to use Microsoft Excel, they are less likely to resist the high price of a new version of that software.

These factors apply in many different purchase situations, so it makes sense for a marketing manager to consider each of them in refining estimates of how customers might respond at different prices.[9]

Value in use pricing—how much will the customer save?

Organizational buyers think about how a purchase will affect their total costs. Many marketers who aim at business markets keep this in mind when estimating demand and setting prices. They use **value in use pricing**—which means setting prices that will capture some of what customers will save by substituting the firm's product for the one currently being used.

Value in use pricing considers what a customer will save by buying a product. Axilok's ad reminds its business customers that its wheel bearing nut system can cut labour costs by 50 percent. Similarly, Emerson Electric invites prospective customers to use computer models available on the PlantWeb Internet site to calculate project savings for their plants.

For example, a producer of computer-controlled machines used to assemble cars knows that the machine doesn't just replace a standard machine. It also reduces labour costs, quality control costs, and—after the car is sold—costs of warranty repairs. The marketer can estimate what each auto producer will save by using the machine—and then set a price that makes it less expensive for the auto producer to buy the computerized machine than to stick with the old methods. The number of customers who have different levels of potential savings also provides some idea about the shape of the demand curve.

Creating a superior product that could save customers money doesn't guarantee that customers will be willing to pay a higher price. To capture the value created, the seller must convince buyers of the savings—and buyers are likely to be skeptical. A salesperson needs to be able to show proof of the claims.[10]

Auctions show what a customer will pay

Auctions have always been a way to determine exactly what some group of potential customers would pay, or not pay, for a product. However, the use of online auctions has dramatically broadened the use of this approach for both consumer and business products. About 5 million auctions are on eBay each day. And some firms are setting up their own auctions, especially for products in short supply.

Some sellers use sequential price reductions

Some sellers are taking the auction approach and adapting it by using sequential price reductions over time. The basic idea is that the seller starts with a relatively high price and sells as much of the product as possible at that price, but plans from the start on a series of step-by-step price reductions until the product is sold out. This approach is most commonly used with products that have a short life or are in short supply, but which would just run up inventory costs if they are not sold. Retailers like SportChek use this approach with sporting goods, and grocery stores use it with perishable food like fruits and vegetables. Cruise lines sell space this way; they don't want the ship to sail with empty cabins. Some people may think of this as a "clearance" sale. But the difference here is that the plan from the outset is to work down the demand curve in steps—appealing to segments who are least price sensitive first—until all of a product is sold. However, sellers hope that if they offer the right products they'll never get to price reductions (which earn lower margins). Rather, they prefer to be bringing in the next round of products to start the process over again.

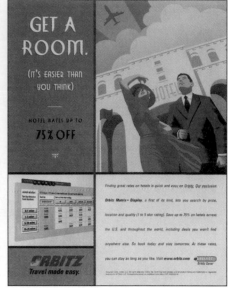

Customers may have reference prices

Some people don't devote much thought to what they pay for the products they buy, including some frequently purchased goods and services. But consumers often have a **reference price**—the price they expect to pay—for many of the products they purchase. And different customers may have different reference prices for the same basic type of purchase. For example, a person who really enjoys reading might have a higher reference price for a popular paperback book than another person who is only an occasional reader.[11]

If a firm's price is lower than a customer's reference price, customers may view the product as a better value and demand may increase. Sometimes a firm will try to position the benefits of its product in such a way that consumers compare it with a product that has a higher reference price. Public Broadcasting System TV stations do this when they ask viewers to make donations that match what they pay for "just one month of cable service." Insurance companies frame the price of premiums for homeowners' coverage in terms of the price to repair flood damage—and advertising makes the damage very vivid. Some retailers just want consumers to use the manufacturer's list price as the reference price, even if no one anywhere actually pays that list price.

Loss-leader pricing—make it low to attract customers

Loss-leader pricing means setting some very low prices—real bargains—to get customers into retail stores. The idea is not only to sell large quantities of the loss-leader items but also to get customers into the store to buy other products. Certain products are picked for their promotion value and priced low. In food stores, the loss-leader prices are the "specials" that are advertised regularly to give an image of low prices. This approach is normally used with products for which consumers do have a specific reference price. Home Hardware and Home Depot also use loss-leader pricing to draw traffic to their stores.

Loss-leader pricing can backfire if customers buy only the low-priced leaders. To avoid hurting profits, managers often select leader items that aren't directly competitive with major lines—as when bargain-priced blank CDs are a leader for an electronics store like Future Shop.[12]

Bait-and-switch pricing—offer a steal, but sell under protest

Bait-and-switch pricing is setting some very low prices to attract customers but trying to sell more expensive models or brands once the customer is in the store. For example, a furniture store may advertise a colour TV for $199. That's the bait. But once bargain hunters come to the store, salespeople point out the disadvantages

490

of the low-priced TV and try to convince (switch) them to trade up to a better, and more expensive, set. Bait-and-switch pricing is something like loss-leader pricing. But here the seller *doesn't* plan to sell many at the low price.

If bait-and-switch pricing is successful, the demand for higher-quality products expands. This approach may be a sensible part of a strategy to trade up customers. And customers may be well served if—once in the store—they find a higher-priced product offers features better suited to their needs. But bait-and-switch pricing is also criticized as unethical.

Is bait-and-switch pricing ethical?

Extremely aggressive and sometimes dishonest bait-and-switch advertising has given this method a bad reputation. Some stores make it very difficult to buy the bait item. The federal government considers this type of pricing a deceptive act and has banned its use in Canada. Even well-known chains like Sears have been criticized for bait-and-switch pricing.

Psychological pricing—some prices just seem right

Psychological pricing means setting prices that have special appeal to target customers. Some people think there are whole ranges of prices that potential customers see as the same. So price cuts in these ranges do not increase the quantity sold. But just below this range, customers may buy more. Then, at even lower prices, the quantity demanded stays the same again—and so on. Exhibit 17-12 shows the kind of demand curve that leads to psychological pricing. Vertical drops mark the price ranges that customers see as the same. Pricing research shows that there *are* such demand curves.[13]

Exhibit 17-12
Demand Curve When Psychological Pricing Is Appropriate

Odd-even pricing is setting prices that end in certain numbers. For example, products selling below $50 often end in the number 5 or the number 9—such as 49 cents or $24.95. Prices for higher-priced products are often $1 or $2 below the next even dollar figure—such as $99 rather than $100.

Some marketers use odd-even pricing because they think consumers react better to these prices—perhaps seeing them as "substantially" lower than the next highest even price. Marketers using these prices seem to assume that they have a rather jagged demand curve—that slightly higher prices will substantially reduce the quantity demanded. Long ago, some retailers used odd-even prices to force their clerks to make change. Then the clerks had to record the sale and could not pocket the money.[14]

Price lining—a few prices cover the field

Price lining is setting a few price levels for a product line and then marking all items at these prices. This approach assumes that customers have a certain reference price in mind that they expect to pay for a product. For example, many neckties are priced between $20 and $50. In price lining, there are only a few prices within this range. Ties will not be priced at $20, $21, $22, $23, and so on. They might be priced at four levels—$20, $30, $40, and $50.

Price lining has advantages other than just matching prices to what consumers expect to pay. The main advantage is simplicity—for both salespeople and customers. It is less confusing than having many prices. Some customers may consider items in only one price class. Their big decision, then, is which item(s) to choose at that price.

For retailers, price lining has several advantages. Sales may increase because (1) they can offer a bigger variety in each price class and (2) it's easier to get customers to make decisions within one price class. Stock planning is simpler because demand is larger at the relatively few prices. Price lining can also reduce costs because inventory needs are lower.

Demand-backward pricing and prestige pricing

Demand-backward pricing is setting an acceptable final consumer price and working backward to what a producer can charge. It is commonly used by producers of consumer products, especially shopping products such as women's clothing and appliances. It is also used with gift items for which customers will spend a specific amount—because they are seeking a $10 or a $15 gift. Here a reverse cost-plus pricing process is used. This method has been called market-minus pricing.

The producer starts with the retail (reference) price for a particular item and then works backward—subtracting the typical margins that channel members expect. This gives the approximate price the producer can charge. Then the average or planned marketing expenses can be subtracted from this price to find how much can be spent producing the item. Candy companies do this. They alter the size of the candy bar to keep the bar at the expected price.

Prestige pricing is setting a rather high price to suggest high quality or high status. Some target customers want the best, so they will buy at a high price. But if the price seems cheap, they worry about quality and don't buy. Prestige pricing is most common for luxury products such as furs, jewellery, and perfume.

It is also common in service industries, where the customer can't see the product in advance and relies on price to judge its quality. Target customers who respond to prestige pricing give the marketing manager an unusual demand curve. Instead of a normal down-sloping curve, the curve goes down for a while and then bends back to the left again.[15] See Exhibit 17-13.

Exhibit 17-13
Demand Curve Showing a Prestige Pricing Situation

PRICING A FULL LINE

Our emphasis has been, and will continue to be, on the problem of pricing an individual product mainly because this makes our discussion clearer. But most marketing managers are responsible for more than one product. In fact, their "product" may be the whole company line! So we'll discuss this matter briefly.

Full-line pricing— market- or firm- oriented

Full-line pricing is setting prices for a whole line of products. How to do this depends on which of two basic situations a firm is facing.

In one case, all products in the company's line are aimed at the same general target market, which makes it important for all prices and value to be logically related. This is a common approach with shopping products. A producer of TV sets might offer several models with different features at different prices to give its target customers some choice. The difference among the prices and benefits should appear reasonable when the target customers are evaluating them. Customer perceptions can be important here. A low-priced item, even one that is a good value at that price, may drag down the image of the higher end of the line. Alternatively, one item that consumers do not see as a good value may spill over to how they judge other products in the line.

In other cases, the different products in the line are aimed at entirely different target markets so there doesn't have to be any relation between the various prices. A chemical producer of a wide variety of products with several target markets, for example, probably should price each product separately.

Costs are complicated in full-line pricing

The marketing manager must try to recover all costs on the whole line—perhaps by pricing quite low on more competitive items and much higher on ones with unique benefits. However, estimating costs for each product is a challenge because there is no single right way to assign a company's fixed costs to each of the products. Regardless of how costs are allocated, any cost-oriented pricing method that doesn't consider demand can lead to very unrealistic prices. To avoid mistakes, the marketing manager should judge demand for the whole line as well as demand for each individual product in each target market.

Complementary product pricing

Complementary product pricing is setting prices on several products as a group. This may lead to one product being priced very low so that the profits from another product will increase, thus increasing the product group's total profits. When Gillette introduced the M3Power battery-powered wet-shaving system, the shaver, two blade cartridges, and a Duracell battery had a relatively low suggested retail price of $14.99. However, the blade refill cartridges, which must be replaced frequently, come in a package of four at a hefty price of $10.99.

Complementary product pricing differs from full-line pricing because different production facilities may be involved—so there's no cost allocation problem. Instead, the problem is really understanding the target market and the demand curves for each of the complementary products. Then various combinations of prices can be tried to see what set will be best for reaching the company's pricing objectives.

Product-bundle pricing—one price for several products

A firm that offers its target market several different products may use **product-bundle pricing**—setting one price for a set of products. Firms that use product-bundle pricing usually set the overall price so that it's cheaper for the customer to buy the products at the same time than separately. Drugstores sometimes bundle the cost of a roll of film and the cost of the processing. A bank may offer a product-bundle price for a safe-deposit box, traveller's cheques, and a savings account. Bell bundles wireless minutes and long distance. Bundling encourages customers to spend more and buy products that they might not otherwise buy—because the added cost of the extras is not as high as it would normally be, so the value is better.

Most firms that use product-bundle pricing also set individual prices for the unbundled products. This may increase demand by attracting customers who want one item in a product assortment but don't want the extras. Many firms treat services this way. A software company may have a product-bundle price for its software and access to a toll-free telephone assistance service. However, customers who don't need help can pay a lower price and get just the software.[16]

BID PRICING AND NEGOTIATED PRICING DEPEND HEAVILY ON COSTS

A new price for every job

We introduced the issue of competitive bidding and reverse auctions in Chapter 7. But now let's take a closer look at bid pricing. **Bid pricing** means offering a specific price for each possible job rather than setting a price that applies for all customers. In an e-commerce reverse auction for a standardized product, this may just require that the manager decide the firm's lowest acceptable selling price. But in many situations bid pricing is more complicated. For example, building contractors usually must bid on possible projects. And many companies selling services (like cleaning or data processing) must submit bids for jobs they would like to have.

A big problem in bid pricing on a complicated job is estimating all the costs that will apply. This may sound easy, but a complicated bid may involve thousands of cost components. Further, management must include an overhead charge and a charge for profit.

Because many firms use an e-mail distribution list or Web site to solicit bids, the process is fast and easy for the buyer. But a seller has to be geared up to set a price and respond quickly. However, this system does allow the seller to set a price based on the precise situation and what marginal costs and marginal revenue are involved.

Bids are usually based on purchase specifications provided by the customer. The specs may be sent as an attachment to an e-mail message, or increasingly, they are posted on a Web site. Sometimes the seller can win the business, even with a higher bid price, by suggesting changes in the specs that save the customer money.

At times it isn't possible to figure out specs or costs in advance. This may lead to a negotiated contract where the customer agrees to pay the supplier's total cost plus an agreed-on profit figure (say, 10 percent of costs or a dollar amount)—after the job is finished.

Ethical issues in cost-plus bid pricing

Some unethical sellers give bid prices based on cost-plus contracts a bad reputation by faking their records to make costs seem higher than they really are. In other cases, there may be honest debate about what costs should be allowed. We've already considered, for instance, the difficulties in allocating fixed costs.

Demand must be considered too

Competition must be considered when adding in overhead and profit for a bid price. Usually, the customer will get several bids and accept the lowest one. So unthinking addition of typical overhead and profit rates should be avoided. Some bidders use the same overhead and profit rates on all jobs, regardless of competition, and then are surprised when they don't get some jobs.[17]

The Internet is making it fast and easy for customers to communicate their needs to a larger number of suppliers to solicit competitively based bid prices.

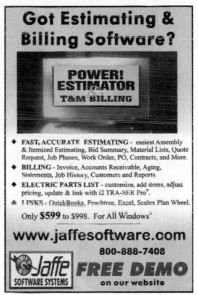

Negotiated prices—what will a specific customer pay?

Sometimes the customer asks for bids and then singles out the company that submits the *most attractive* bid, not necessarily the lowest, for further bargaining. What a customer will buy—if the customer buys at all—depends on the **negotiated price**, a price set based on bargaining between the buyer and seller. As with simple bid pricing, negotiated pricing is most common in situations where the marketing mix is adjusted for each customer—so bargaining may involve the whole marketing mix, not just the price level. Through the bargaining process, the seller tries to determine what aspects of the marketing mix are most important—and worth the most—to the customer.

Sellers must know their costs to negotiate prices effectively. However, negotiated pricing is a demand-oriented approach. Here the seller analyzes very carefully a particular customer's position on a demand curve, or on different possible demand curves based on different offerings, rather than the overall demand curve for a group of customers.

CONCLUSION

In this chapter, we discussed various approaches to price setting. Generally, retailers and wholesalers use markups. Some just use the same markups for all their items. Others find that varying the markups increases turnover and profit. In other words, they consider demand and competition.

Many firms use average-cost pricing to help set their prices. But this approach sometimes ignores demand completely. In the opening case about Wal-Mart you saw this demand-oriented approach to price setting in their policy of giving managers up-to-date information on the sale of individual products. This allowed managers to fine tune their prices to make the best use of customer demand. The result is more stockturns and better margins on selected items.

Break-even analysis is useful for evaluating possible prices. But management must estimate demand to evaluate the chance of reaching these possible break-even points.

The major difficulty with demand-oriented pricing is estimating the demand curve. But experienced managers, aided perhaps by marketing research, can estimate the nature of demand for their products. Such estimates are useful even if they aren't exact. They get you thinking in the right ballpark. Sometimes, when all you need is a decision about raising or lowering price, even rough demand estimates can be very revealing. Further, a firm's demand curve does not cease to exist simply because it's ignored. Some information is better than none at all. And marketers should consider demand in their pricing. We see this with value in use pricing, online auctions, loss-leader pricing, bait-and-switch pricing, psychological pricing, odd-even pricing, full-line pricing, and even bid pricing. Understanding the factors that influence price sensitivity can make these approaches more effective.

Throughout the book, we stress that firms must consider the customer before they do anything. This certainly applies to pricing. It means that when managers are setting a price, they have to consider what customers will be willing to pay. This isn't always easy. But it's nice to know that there is usually a profit range around the best price. Therefore, even rough estimates about what potential customers will buy at various prices will probably lead to a better price than mechanical use of traditional markups or cost-oriented formulas.

KEY TERMS

markup, 471

average-cost pricing, 475

total fixed cost, 476

total variable cost, 476

total cost, 477

average cost (per unit), 477

experience curve pricing, 479

target return pricing, 480

long-run target return pricing, 481

break-even analysis, 481

fixed-cost (FC) contribution per unit, 482

marginal analysis, 484

marginal revenue, 485

marginal cost, 485

marginal profit, 485

price leader, 487

value in use pricing, 488

reference price, 490

loss-leader pricing, 490

bait-and-switch pricing, 490

psychological pricing, 491

odd-even pricing, 491

price lining, 491

prestige pricing, 492

full-line pricing, 493

complementary product pricing, 493

product-bundle pricing, 494

bid pricing, 494

negotiated price, 495

QUESTIONS AND PROBLEMS

1. A department store and a discount house both buy an electric drill from DeWALT for $30.00. The department store retails it for $75.00 while the discounter sells it for $60.00. What might account for the differences in the markups?

2. A producer distributed its riding lawn mowers through wholesalers and retailers. The retail selling price was $800, and the manufacturing cost to the company was $312. The retail markup was 35 percent and the wholesale markup 20 percent. (a) What was the cost to the wholesaler? To the retailer? (b) What percentage markup did the producer take?

3. Relate the concept of stock turnover to the growth of mass-merchandising. Use a simple example in your answer.

4. If total fixed costs are $200,000 and total variable costs are $100,000 at the output of 20,000 units, what are the probable total fixed costs and total variable costs at an output of 10,000 units? What are the average fixed costs, average variable costs, and average costs at these two output levels? Explain what additional information you would want to determine what price should be charged.

5. Explain how experience curve pricing differs from average-cost pricing.

6. Construct an example showing that mechanical use of a very large or a very small markup might still lead to unprofitable operation while some intermediate price would be profitable. Draw a graph and show the break-even point(s).

7. The Davis Company's fixed costs for the year are estimated at $200,000. Its product sells for $250. The variable cost per unit is $200. Sales for the coming year are expected to reach $1,250,000. What is the break-even point? Expected profit? If sales are forecast at only $875,000, should the Davis Company shut down operations? Why?

8. Discuss the idea of drawing separate demand curves for different market segments. When is it a good idea and when is it a bad idea?

9. Distinguish between loss-leader pricing and bait-and-switch pricing. What do they have in common? How can their use affect a marketing mix?

10. Cite a local example of psychological pricing and evaluate whether it makes sense.

11. Cite a local example of odd-even pricing and evaluate whether it makes sense.

12. How does a prestige pricing policy fit into Tiffany's marketing mix? Would exclusive distribution be necessary?

13. Is a full-line pricing policy available only to producers? Cite local examples of full-line pricing. Why is full-line pricing important?

14. HP sell their printers at incredibly low prices. Check the prices for their replacement ink tanks. What kind of pricing strategy is being followed?

15. If Bell Canada supplies your telephone, Internet, and television signal why do they like to follow a bundled pricing strategy? Would you prefer to buy each of these services individually or do you like their bundled pricing approach?

16. What are the problems of full-line pricing when you consider fixed costs?

17. What kind of problems does the seller encounter when participating in competitive bidding on a buyer's Internet Web site?

COMPUTER-AIDED PROBLEM

17. Break-Even/Profit Analysis

RESOURCE REMINDER

This problem lets you see the dynamics of break-even analysis. The starting values (costs, revenues, etc.) for this problem are from the break-even analysis example in this chapter (see Exhibit 17-8).

The first column computes a break-even point. You can change costs and prices to figure new break-even points (in units and dollars). The second column goes further. There you can specify target profit level, and the unit and dollar sales needed to achieve your target profit level will be computed. You can also estimate possible sales quantities, and the program will compute costs, sales, and profits. Use this spreadsheet to address the following issues.

a. Vary the selling price between $1.00 and $1.40. Prepare a table showing how the break-even point (in units and dollars) changes at the different price levels.

b. If you hope to earn a target profit of $15,000, how many units would you have to sell? What would total cost be? Total sales dollars? (Note: Use the right-hand ["profit analysis"] column in the spreadsheet.)

c. Using the "profit analysis" column (column 2), allow your estimate of the sales quantity to vary between 64,000 and 96,000. Prepare a table that shows, for each quantity level, what happens to average cost per unit and profit. Explain why average cost changes as it does over the different quantity values.

If you want to read the cases and view the video cases that accompany this chapter, visit the *Basic Marketing* Online Learning Centre at: **www.mcgrawhill.ca/olc/perreault**. Along with these cases and video cases, the OLC also has the software and user guide for this chapter's Computer-Aided Problem, as well as exercises, quizzes, articles, links, and other *interactive* content that will help you with your studies.

18

CHAPTER

1. Understand the elements of the planning process and the related strategy decisions for the 4 Ps.

2. Understand how and why both your marketing strategy and plan will likely need to change over different stages of the product life cycle.

3. Understand the basic forecasting approaches and how they are used to evaluate different strategies.

4. Understand how sales analysis can aid marketing strategy planning.

5. Understand how planning and control can be combined to improve the marketing management process.

6. Understand what a marketing audit is and when and where it should be used.

Marketing Plans and Controls

BEN & JERRY'S BRINGS ITS SWEET-TOOTH FANS A LOT OF PLEASURE WITH UNIQUE ICE CREAM CONCOCTIONS LIKE UNCANNY CASHEW. THERE MAY BE A FEW MOMENTS OF PAIN IF YOUR FAVOURITE FLAVOUR DISAPPEARS FROM STORE SHELVES TO JOIN A FEW HUNDRED OTHERS ON BEN & JERRY'S

"dearly departed flavours list." But the odds are that the flavour that replaces it will be even more popular. In fact, that doesn't happen by chance. A key strategy behind the Ben & Jerry's brand is to maintain a high degree of flexibility. Their marketing plan is designed to respond to the changing demands of their target markets—and those demands can change over time as well as differ by geographic region.

Ben & Jerry's produces and distributes only about 30 different flavours at a time. Its down-home image might make you think that's all it can handle. But that image belies the fact that massive pipes in the Ben & Jerry's factory pump out over 100,000 litres of ice cream each day. Tractor-trailer loads of half-litre containers continuously flow into depots and from there are shipped to hundreds of scoop shops as well 50,000 grocery stores in 13 countries.

Ben & Jerry's marketing managers use an information system that tracks every container—from what ingredients went into it to where it sells. They constantly study sales to see if Cherry Garcia is still in the number 1 sales spot or if Chunky Monkey is moving up or down the top 10 sellers list. And if sales of a flavour are not doing as well in Western Canada as in Eastern Canada, they alter the mix that goes to that region. If sales of a flavour start to slip in one channel of distribution, they watch to see if it's a onetime blip or if it's the start of a trend that spreads. And if it is a trend, they replace that flavour with a new one before the drop in sales turns into a problem.

Everyone at Ben & Jerry's is obsessed with the quality they offer customers. It's a key to their marketing plan and a key to their customers' loyalty. Each time a call or an e-mail with a comment or complaint comes into the customer service people, they follow up and match it to the particular container that's a problem to determine when it was produced and where it was sold. They receive more than 200 calls and e-mails each week, so they sort all the inputs to see if they bring to light undetected problems— whether it's the milk from a particular supplier, a specific production batch in the factory, or how the product is stored in the channel. This means their marketing control system has to be fast and able to track problems down through reams of data. Sometimes it reveals surprising information.

In one such case, the customer service people were getting a lot of complaints from customers that their Cherry Garcia ice cream pops didn't have enough cherries. After the service people matched the complaints with sales records, they concluded it wasn't a regional problem—complaints pointed to units that were sold all over the country. There wasn't a quality problem with just certain production batches either. Finally they discovered that the photo on the box was not of ice cream but of frozen yogourt treats—a product with more cherries. The difference wasn't great, but customers expected more cherries than they were getting. When Ben & Jerry's fixed the image on the box, the complaints melted away.

Ben & Jerry's faces a lot of competition from other premium brands. Some consumers have increased concern about fat in their diets, and that impacts the market too. Whether it's changes in competitors' strategies or changes in consumer tastes, the market environment is continually impacting and forcing alterations to a firm's marketing plan. That's why marketing managers at Ben & Jerry's have access to the data they need to get fast feedback that helps them constantly improve their strategy and how it is controlled.[1]

MARKETING PLANNING PROCESS IS MORE THAN ASSEMBLING THE FOUR Ps

Developing a successful marketing plan is a creative process. But it is also a logical process. And the logic that leads to a sound strategy may need to change as the marketing environment and target customers change.

Even so, the strategy planning process is guided by basic principles. The marketing concept emphasizes that all of a firm's activities should focus on its target markets. Further, a firm should try to find a competitive advantage in meeting the needs of some target market(s) that it can satisfy very well. If it can do that, it provides target customers with superior value. The target market(s) should be large enough to support the firm's efforts and yield a profit. And ideally, the strategy should take advantage of trends in the external market, not buck them. Vancouver-based Business Objects has become a world leader in supplying business intelligence reporting systems. Their products, such as their Crystal Reports series software, successfully address companies' needs to gather and analyze information used for market planning and strategy. Business Objects appear to have anticipated the

Bali Blinds come in a large variety of colours to give consumers nearly unlimited choices for interior design. There's usually nothing very interesting about a photo of even the nicest blinds. But this ad builds interest in the firm's positioning by matching the colour of the blinds to the colour of the fish in the bowl. Similarly, when Mr. Clean brand managers wanted to differentiate their cleaner with a new line of scents, this clever picture of a lemon slice, adorned with Mr. Clean's earring, helped to convey the message.

target market's needs. The business intelligence and analytics market is currently $8.5 billion and expected to grow to $13 billion in the next five years.

As we explained in Chapter 2, the marketing strategy planning process involves narrowing down from a broad set of possible marketing opportunities to a specific strategy the firm will pursue. A marketing *strategy* consists of a target market and a marketing mix; it specifies what a firm will do in some target market. A marketing *plan* includes the time-related details—including expected costs and revenues—for that strategy. In most firms, the marketing manager must ultimately combine the different marketing plans into an overall marketing *program*.

BLENDING THE FOUR Ps TAKES UNDERSTANDING OF A TARGET MARKET

Marketing strategy planning process brings focus to efforts

Developing a good marketing strategy and turning the strategy into a marketing plan requires blending the ideas we've discussed throughout this text. Exhibit 18-1 provides a broad overview of the major areas we've been talking about. Now we must integrate ideas about these different areas to narrow down to logical marketing mixes, marketing strategies, marketing plans—and a marketing program.

As suggested in Exhibit 18-1, developing an effective marketing strategy involves a process of narrowing down to a specific target market and marketing mix that represents a real opportunity. This narrowing-down process requires a thorough understanding of the market. That understanding is enhanced by careful analysis of customers' needs, current or prospective competitors, and the firm's own objectives and resources. Similarly, favourable or unfavourable factors and trends in the external marketing environment may make a potential opportunity more or less attractive.

There are often more different strategy possibilities than a firm can pursue. Each possible strategy usually has a number of different potential advantages and disadvantages. This can make it difficult to zero in on the best target market and marketing mix. However, developing a set of specific qualitative and quantitative screening criteria—to define what business and markets the firm wants to compete in—can help eliminate potential strategies that are not well suited for the firm.

Exhibit 18-1
Overview of Marketing Strategy Planning Process

Narrowing down to focused strategy with quantitative and qualitative screening criteria

Customers
Needs and Other Segmenting Dimensions

Company
Objectives and Resources

Competitors
Current and Prospective

S. W. O. T.

Segmentation & Targeting

Differentiation & Positioning

Product   Place
Target Market
Price   Promotion

External Market Environment
Technological   Political and Legal   Cultural and Social   Economic

Another useful aid for zeroing in on a feasible strategy is **S.W.O.T. analysis**—which identifies and lists the firm's strengths and weaknesses and its opportunities and threats. A good S.W.O.T. analysis helps the manager focus on a strategy that takes advantage of the firm's opportunities and strengths while avoiding its weaknesses and threats to its success. These can be compared with the pros and cons of strategies that are considered. For example, if a firm is considering a strategy that focuses on a target market that is already being served by several strong competitors, success will usually hinge on some sort of competitive advantage. Such a competitive advantage might be based on a better marketing mix—perhaps an innovative new product, improved distribution, more effective promotion, or a better price. Just offering a marketing mix that is like what is available from competitors usually doesn't provide superior value—or any real basis for the firm to position or differentiate its marketing mix as better for customers.

Marketing mix flows from target market dimensions

Ideally, the ingredients of a good marketing mix flow logically from all the relevant dimensions of a target market. The market definition and segmenting approaches help the marketing manager identify which dimensions are qualifying and which are determining in customers' choices.

Product benefits must match needs. If and how customers search for information helps to define the promotion blend. Demographic dimensions reveal where customers are located and if they have the income to buy. Where customers shop for or buy products helps define channel alternatives. The value of the whole marketing mix and the urgency of customer needs, combined with an understanding of what customers see as substitute ways of meeting needs, help companies estimate price sensitivity. Rogers Video has to consider the price structure for it movie rentals in the face of competitors like Telus and Bell ExpressVu who deliver pay-per-view movie programming through their new technologies. These are substitute products that pose dangerous competition for Rogers because of the convenience they offer consumers who want video on demand without the inconvenience of a trip to the local video rental shop.

It would seem that if we fully understand the needs and attitudes of a target market, then combining the four Ps should be easy. Yet there are three important gaps in this line of reasoning. (1) We don't always know as much as we would like to about the needs and attitudes of our target markets. (2) Competitors are also trying to satisfy these or similar needs—and their efforts may force a firm to shift its

Treif's marketing mix, targeted at firms that process meat, includes this ad for its high-quality slicing equipment, which uses the brand name Zebra-CE. The brand name and the picture of zebras with thick and thin stripes are intended to highlight the thick and thin cutting technology of the equipment, but a potential customer might miss the point and instead be distracted with thoughts of sliced zebra meat. Gardenburger's ad takes a humorous approach, which might appeal to consumers who are cynical about advertisers' sales pitches. On the other hand, Hindu consumers (who would logically be potential customers for Gardenburger products) might find it offensive that the ad alludes to Hindu religious beliefs.

marketing mix. (3) The other dimensions of the marketing environment may be changing, which may require more changes in marketing mixes. These points warrant further consideration.

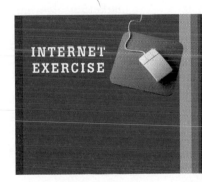

INTERNET EXERCISE

The Atlantic Canada Opportunities Agency (www.acoa-apeca.gc.ca) provides a template for creating a marketing plan. Visit the site and on the home page menu at the top, select *Business Info*. On the Business Info page, select *Business Tools* and then choose *How to Prepare a Marketing Plan*. Why does the situational analysis precede a discussion of the 4 Ps in their action plan and why does all of that information precede the break-even analysis and cash flow projections at the end of their template?

Product classes suggest typical marketing mixes

Even if you don't or can't know all you would like to about a potential target market, you usually know enough to decide whether the product is a consumer product or a business product and which product class is most relevant.

Identifying the proper product class helps because it suggests how a typical product should be distributed and promoted. So if you don't know as much as you'd like about potential customers' needs and attitudes, at least knowing how *they* would view the company's product can give you a head start on developing a marketing mix. A convenience product, for example, usually needs more intensive distribution, and the producer usually takes on more responsibility for promotion. A specialty product needs a clear brand identity, which may require a more extensive positioning effort. A new unsought product will need a mix that leads customers through the adoption process.

It's reassuring to see that product classes do summarize some of what you would like to know about target markets and what marketing mixes are relevant. After all, knowing what others have done in similar situations can serve as a guide to get started. From that base you may see a better way to meet needs that is *not* typical and that provides a competitive advantage.

Typical is not necessarily right

The typical marketing mix for a given product class is not necessarily right for all situations. To the contrary, some marketing mixes are profitable because they depart from the typical—to satisfy some target markets better. In fact, it is often through differentiation of the firm's product or other elements of the marketing mix that the marketing manager can offer target customers unique value.

Superior mixes may be breakthrough opportunities

When marketing managers fully understand their target markets, they may be able to develop marketing mixes that are superior to competitors' mixes. Such understanding may provide breakthrough opportunities. Taking advantage of these opportunities can lead to large sales and profitable growth. This is why we stress the importance of looking for breakthrough opportunities rather than just trying to imitate competitors' offerings. Alarm Force was able to create a unique position in the home alarm business by introducing its two-way voice communication system. Does it work better than ADT? Who knows, but Alarm Force appears to have found a target market that values their marketing mix and the competitors haven't found a way to match their two-way voice system.

Inferior mixes are easy to reject

Just as some mixes are superior, some mixes are clearly inferior—or unsuitable. For example, a national TV advertising campaign might make sense for a large company like Honda—but it could quickly be screened out by a small firm that only has the resources to put a Web page on the Internet and perhaps get some help from manufacturers' agents.

Marketing manager must blend the four Ps

Exhibit 18-2 reviews the major marketing strategy decision areas organized by the four Ps. Each of these requires careful decision making. Yet marketing planning involves much more than just independent decisions and assembling the parts into a marketing mix. The four Ps must be creatively *blended*—so the firm develops the best mix for its target market. In other words, each decision must work well with all of the others to make a logical whole.

Throughout the text, we've given the job of integrating the four Ps strategy decisions to the marketing manager. The title of that person might vary, but now you

Exhibit 18-2
Strategy Decision Areas Organized by the Four Ps

Product	Place	Promotion	Price
Physical good	Objectives	Objectives	Objectives
Service	Channel type	Promotion blend	Flexibility
Features	Market exposure	Salespeople	Level over
Benefits	Kinds of	Kind	product life
Quality level	middlemen	Number	cycle
Accessories	Kinds and	Selection	Geographic terms
Installation	locations of	Training	Discounts
Instructions	stores	Motivation	Allowances
Warranty	How to handle	Advertising	
Product lines	transporting	Targets	
Packaging	and storing	Kinds of ads	
Branding	Service levels	Media type	
	Recruiting	Copy thrust	
	middlemen	Prepared by	
	Managing	whom	
	channels	Sales promotion	
		Publicity	

WHY THE WIRELESS PHONE SERVICE FOR CAB DRIVERS HAS BEEN A WINNER

It's no accident that Telus Mobility joined forces with Nextel a few years back. For years, Nextel had been out of step with other firms that offer wireless service. But recently its atypical strategy has earned better profits and had the highest revenue per customer of any firm in the business. In the wake of a new rule that allowed customers to switch their cell phone numbers to a new carrier, most firms were scrambling to hang on to subscribers, but Nextel increased subscribers by 20 percent. And while people often view wireless as a commodity and shop on price, many of Nextel's subscribers see its Direct Connect service as essential. Direct Connect is a walkie-talkie-like feature that allows a cell phone user to push a button and instantly talk with someone else who has the same service carrier. Nextel has had this service since the early 1990s, and it has set Nextel apart. It has been especially popular with construction workers, delivery drivers, firefighters, and others accustomed to working with two-way radios. Ninety percent of Nextel customers use Direct Connect.

However, freed by a change in regulations, other cell phone firms that once derided Nextel as the service for "cab drivers" are now imitating its proprietary technology. What they offer doesn't work as well so far. For example, conversations with Verizon's service are punctuated with pauses because there is a five-second delay between when a message is spoken and when it is heard. However, within a few years competitors will catch up. And Sprint PCS will sell push-to-talk service as part of a comprehensive set of business services, including high-speed wireless Internet access for laptops.

Push-to-talk used to work only within a local service area. To broaden the appeal of its service, Telus and Nextel have made it available internationally, which makes it more attractive to professionals. Nextel is also testing strategies to reach other target markets, including government agencies, with homeland security applications. At the same time it is expanding its profitable wireless data service. For example, its @Road service helps truck fleet operators locate vehicles with a global positioning system. Nextel will feel the impact of competitors nipping at its heels, but with new strategy planning it may be able to keep its edge over rivals.[2]

should see the need for this integrating role. It is easy for specialists to focus on their own areas and expect the rest of the company to work for or around them. This is especially true in larger firms like Ford—where specialists are needed—just because the size of the whole marketing job is too big for one person. Yet the ideas of the product manager, the advertising manager, the sales manager, the logistics manager, and whoever makes pricing decisions may have to be adjusted to improve the whole mix. It's critical that each marketing mix decision work well with all of the others. A breakdown in any one decision area may doom the whole strategy to failure.

Product life cycle guides planning

Careful consideration of where a firm's offering fits in the product life cycle can also be a big help in evaluating the best marketing mix. We introduced Exhibit 18-3 in Chapter 10 to summarize how marketing mix variables typically change over the product life cycle. Now you can see that this exhibit is a good review of many topics we've discussed throughout the text. Certainly, the pioneering effort required for a really new product concept is different from the job of taking market share away from an established competitor late in the market growth stage.

Further, when you're thinking about the product life cycle don't forget that markets change continually. This means you must plan strategies that can adjust to changing conditions. The original marketing plan for a new marketing strategy may even include details about what adjustments in the marketing mix or target market will be required as the nature of competition and the adoption process evolve.[3]

FORECASTING TARGET MARKET POTENTIAL AND SALES

Effective strategy planning and developing a marketing plan require estimates of future sales, costs, and profits. Without such information, it's hard to know if a strategy is potentially profitable.

The marketing manager's estimates of sales, costs, and profits are usually based on a forecast (estimate) of target **market potential**—what a whole market segment might buy—and a **sales forecast**—an estimate of how much an industry or firm hopes to sell to a market segment. Usually we must first try to judge market potential before we can estimate what share a particular firm may be able to win with its particular marketing mix.

Three levels of forecasts are useful

We're interested in forecasting the potential in specific market segments. To do this, it helps to make three levels of forecasts.

Some economic conditions affect the entire global economy. Others may influence only one country or a particular industry. And some may affect only one company or one product's sales potential. For this reason, a common top-down approach to forecasting is to

1. Develop a *national income forecast* (for each country in which the firm operates) and use this to
2. Develop an *industry sales forecast,* which then is used to
3. Develop forecasts for a *specific company*, its *specific products*, and the *segments* it targets.

Alcan for example, would produce a national income forecast for Japan to gain insight into its general economic outlook over the coming two- to three-year period. Next it would focus that forecast down to the industry specific level. In this case, the construction industry for multiple residential housing and commercial buildings. Finally, Alcan would produce forecasts for the major contractors and industry manufacturers to whom it supplies aluminum. These customers produce extruded aluminum products like window and door frames that are used in high-rise apartment and office tower construction.

Exhibit 18-3
Typical Changes in Marketing Variables over the Product Life Cycle

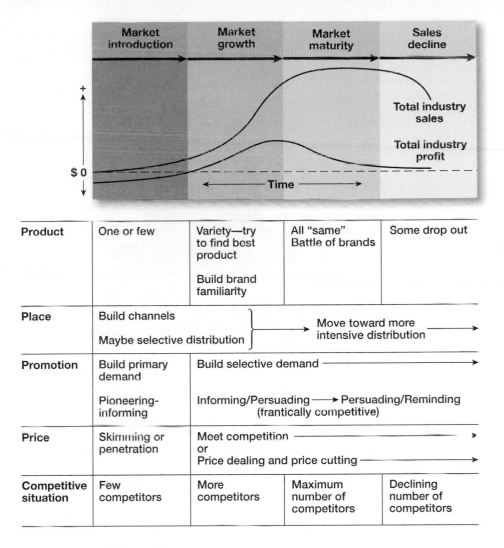

	Market introduction	Market growth	Market maturity	Sales decline
Product	One or few	Variety—try to find best product Build brand familiarity	All "same" Battle of brands	Some drop out
Place	Build channels Maybe selective distribution	Move toward more intensive distribution →		
Promotion	Build primary demand Pioneering-informing	Build selective demand ————————→ Informing/Persuading ——→ Persuading/Reminding (frantically competitive)		
Price	Skimming or penetration	Meet competition ——————————→ or Price dealing and price cutting ——————→		
Competitive situation	Few competitors	More competitors	Maximum number of competitors	Declining number of competitors

Generally, a marketing manager doesn't have to make forecasts for a national economy or the broad industry. This kind of forecasting—basically trend projecting—is a specialty in itself. Such forecasts are available in business and government publications, and large companies often have their own technical specialists. Managers can use just one source's forecast or combine several. Unfortunately, however, the more targeted the marketing manager's earlier segmenting efforts have been, the less likely that industry forecasts will match the firm's product-markets. So managers have to move directly to estimating potential for their own companies and for their specific products.

Two approaches to forecasting

Many methods are used to forecast market potential and sales, but they can all be grouped into two basic approaches: (1) extending past behaviour and (2) predicting future behaviour. The large number of methods may seem confusing at first, but this variety has an advantage. Forecasts are so important that managers often develop forecasts in two or three different ways and then compare the differences before preparing a final forecast.

Extending past behaviour can miss important turning points

When we forecast for existing products, we usually have some past data to go on. The basic approach, called **trend extension**, extends past experience into the future. With existing products, for example, the past trend of actual sales may be extended into the future. See Exhibit 18-4.

Ideally, when extending past sales behaviour, we should decide why sales vary. This is the difficult and time-consuming part of sales forecasting. Usually we can gather a lot of data about the product or market or about changes in the marketing environment. But unless we know the *reason* for past sales variations, it's hard to predict in what direction, and by how much, sales will move. Graphing the data and statistical techniques—including correlation and regression analysis—can be useful here. (These techniques, which are beyond our scope, are discussed in beginning statistics courses.)

Once we know why sales vary, we can usually develop a specific forecast. Sales may be moving directly up as population grows in a specific market segment, for example. So we can just estimate how population is expected to grow and project the impact on sales. Plavix is sold in Canada as a drug for treating heart and stroke victims. The pharmaceutical manufacturers have a pretty good idea of how prevalent those pathologies are in the Canadian population and in what age brackets the diseases are most common. They forecast how much the Canadian population will grow and in particular how much the seniors' population will increase because that is what drives the demand for their drug. With that forecast in hand they have a reasonable estimate for projecting the impact on their sales.

The weakness of the trend extension method is that it assumes past conditions will continue unchanged into the future. In fact, the future isn't always like the past. An agent wholesaler's business may have been on a steady path, but the development of the Internet added a totally new factor. The past trend for the agent's sales changed because now the agent can quickly reach a broader market.

Exhibit 18-4
Straight-Line Trend Projection—Extends Past Sales into the Future

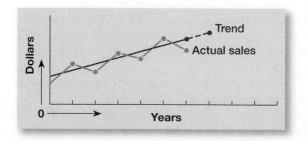

As another example, for years the trend in sales of disposable diapers moved closely with the number of new births. However, as the number of women in the workforce increased and as more women returned to jobs after babies were born, use of disposable diapers increased, and the trend changed. As in these examples, trend extension estimates will be wrong whenever big changes occur. For this reason—although they may extend past behaviour for one estimate—most managers look for another way to help them forecast sharp market changes.

Predicting future behaviour takes judgment

When we try to predict what will happen in the future, instead of just extending the past, we have to use other methods and add more judgment. Some of these methods (to be discussed later) include juries of executive opinion, salespeople's estimates, surveys, panels, and market tests.

FORECASTING COMPANY AND PRODUCT SALES BY EXTENDING PAST BEHAVIOUR

Past sales can be extended

At the very least, a marketing manager ought to know what the firm's present markets look like and what it has sold to them in the past. A detailed sales analysis for products and geographic areas helps to project future results.

Just extending past sales into the future may not seem like much of a forecasting method. But it's better than just assuming that next year's total sales will be the same as this year's.

Factor method includes more than time

A simple extension of past sales gives one forecast. But it's usually desirable to tie future sales to something more than the passage of time.

The factor method tries to do this. The **factor method** tries to forecast sales by finding a relation between the company's sales and some other factor (or factors). The basic formula is: something (past sales, industry sales, etc.) *times* some factor *equals* sales forecast. A **factor** is a variable that shows the relation of some other variable to the item being forecast. For instance, in our example above, both the birthrate and the number of working mothers are factors related to sales of disposable diapers.

Times series and leading series may help estimate a fluctuating future

Not all past economic or sales behaviour can be neatly extended with a straight line or some manipulation. Economic activity has ups and downs, and other uncontrollable factors change. To cope with such variation, statisticians have developed time series analysis techniques. **Time series** are historical records of the fluctuations in economic variables. We can't give a detailed discussion of these techniques here, but note that there are techniques to handle daily, weekly, monthly, seasonal, and annual variations.[4]

All forecasters dream of finding an accurate **leading series**—a time series that changes in the same direction *but ahead of* the series to be forecast. For example, car producers watch trends in the Index of Consumer Sentiment, which is based on regular surveys of consumers' attitudes about their likely future financial security. People are less likely to buy a car or other big-ticket item if they are worried about their future income. As this suggests, a drop in the index usually "leads" a drop in car sales. It is important that there be some logical relation between the leading series and what is being forecast.

Sometimes a number of these leading series or leading indicators are strung together to give the marketer and the manufacturer as much lead time as possible in order to estimate future demand. Forest products manufacturers in Ontario and BC need as much lead time as possible to plan their production of framing lumber for residential construction. First they monitor the interest rate because that affects the applications for residential mortgages (which are monitored next). Then they monitor building permit applications and finally housing starts—which ultimately creates the demand for framing lumber.

No single series has yet been found that leads GDP or other national figures. Lacking such a series, forecasters develop indices—statistical combinations of several time series—in an effort to find some time series that will lead the series they're trying to forecast. Government agencies publish some indices of this type. And business publications, like *BusinessWeek* and *The London Financial Times,* publish their own indices.

PREDICTING FUTURE BEHAVIOUR CALLS FOR MORE JUDGMENT AND SOME OPINIONS

These past-extending methods use quantitative data—projecting past experience into the future and assuming that the future will be like the past. But this is risky in competitive markets. Usually, it's desirable to add some judgment to other forecasts before making the final forecast yourself.

Jury of executive opinion adds judgment

One of the oldest and simplest methods of forecasting—the **jury of executive opinion**—combines the opinions of experienced executives, perhaps from marketing, production, finance, purchasing, and top management. Each executive estimates market potential and sales for the *coming years.* Then they try to work out a consensus.

The main advantage of the jury approach is that it can be done quickly and easily. On the other hand, the results may not be very good. There may be too much extending of the past. Some of the executives may have little contact with outside market influences. But their estimates could point to major shifts in customer demand or competition.

Estimates from salespeople can help too

Using salespeople's estimates to forecast is like the jury approach. But salespeople are more likely than home office managers to be familiar with customer reactions and what competitors are doing. Their estimates are especially useful in some business markets where the few customers may be well known to the salespeople. But this approach may be useful in any type of market.

Kellogg's used market testing to develop a sales forecast and provide evidence to retailers that its new Snack 'Ums would be profitable. Online surveys and concept tests are a faster and less expensive way to develop an initial forecast; however, they are also likely to be less accurate.

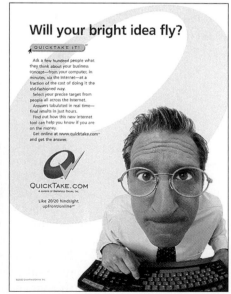

However, managers who use estimates from salespeople should be aware of the limitations. For example, new salespeople may not know much about their markets. Even experienced salespeople may not be aware of possible changes in the economic climate or the firm's other environments. And if salespeople think the manager is going to use the estimates to set sales quotas, the estimates may be low!

Surveys, panels, and market tests

Special surveys of final buyers, retailers, or wholesalers can show what's happening in different market segments. Some firms use panels of stores—or final consumers—to keep track of buying behaviour and to decide when just extending past behaviour isn't enough.

Surveys are sometimes combined with market tests when the company wants to estimate customers' reactions to possible changes in its marketing mix. A market test might show that a product increased its share of the market by 10 percent when its price was dropped 1 cent below competition. But this extra business might be quickly lost if the price were increased 1 cent above competition. Such market experiments help the marketing manager make good estimates of future sales when one or more of the four Ps is changed.

Accuracy depends on the marketing mix

Forecasting can help a marketing manager estimate the size of possible market opportunities. But the accuracy of any sales forecast depends on whether the firm selects and implements a marketing mix that turns these opportunities into sales and profits.[5]

THE MARKETING PLAN BRINGS ALL THE DETAILS TOGETHER

Marketing plan provides a blueprint for implementation

Once the manager has selected the target market, decided on the (integrated) marketing mix to meet that target market's needs, and developed estimates of the costs and revenue for that strategy, it's time to put it all together in the marketing plan. The plan basically serves as a blueprint for what the firm will do.

Exhibit 18-5 provides a summary outline of the different sections of a complete marketing plan. You can see that this outline is basically an abridged overview of the topics we've covered throughout the text and highlighted in this chapter. Thus, you can flesh out your thinking for any portion of a marketing plan by reviewing the section of the book where that topic is discussed in more detail.

Marketing plan spells out the timing of the strategy

Some time schedule is implicit in any strategy. A marketing plan simply spells out this time period and the time-related details. Usually, we think in terms of some reasonable length of time—such as six months, a year, or a few years. But it might be only a month or two in some cases, especially when rapid changes in fashion or technology are important. Or a strategy might be implemented over several years, perhaps the length of a product life cycle or at least the early stages of the product's life.

Although the outline in Exhibit 18-5 does not explicitly show a place for the time frame for the plan or the specific costs for each decision area, these should be included in the plan—along with expected estimates of sales and profit— so that the plan can be compared with *actual performance* in the future. In other words, the plan not only makes it clear to everyone what is to be accomplished and how—it also provides a basis for the control process after the plan is implemented.

A complete plan spells out the reasons for decisions

The plan outline shown in Exhibit 18-5 is quite complete. It doesn't just provide information about marketing mix decisions—it also includes information about customers (including segmenting dimensions), competitors' strategies, other aspects of the marketing environment, and the company's objectives and resources.

Exhibit 18-5 Summary Outline of Different Sections of Marketing Plan

Name of Product-Market

Major screening criteria relevant to product-market opportunity selected
  Quantitative (ROI, profitability, risk level, etc.)
  Qualitative (nature of business preferred, social responsibility, etc.)
  Major constraints

Analysis of Other Aspects of External Market Environment (favourable and unfavourable factors and trends)

Economic environment
Technological environment
Political and legal environment
Cultural and social environment

Customer Analysis (organizational and/or final consumer)

Possible segmenting dimensions (customer needs, other characteristics)
  Identification of qualifying dimensions and determining dimensions
Identification of target market(s) (one or more specific segments)
  Operational characteristics (demographics, geographic locations, etc.)
  Potential size (number of people, dollar purchase potential, etc.) and likely growth
Key psychological and social influences on buying
Type of buying situation
Nature of relationship with customers

Competitor Analysis

Nature of current/likely competition
Current and prospective competitors (or rivals)
  Current strategies and likely responses to plan
Competitive barriers to overcome and sources of potential competitive advantage

Company Analysis

Company objectives and overall marketing objectives
Company resources
S.W.O.T.: Identification of major *strengths, weaknesses, opportunities,* and *threats* (based on above analyses of company resources, customers, competitors, and other aspects of external market environment)

Marketing Information Requirements

Marketing research needs (with respect to customers, marketing mix effectiveness, external environment, etc.)
Secondary data and primary data needs
Marketing information system needs, models to be used, etc.

Product

Product class (type of consumer or business product)
Current product life cycle stage
New-product development requirements (people, dollars, time, etc.)
  Product liability, safety and social responsibility considerations
Specification of core physical good or service
  Features, quality, etc.
Supporting customer service(s) needed
Warranty (what is covered, timing, who will support, etc.)
Branding (manufacturer versus dealer, family brand versus individual brand, etc.)
Packaging
  Promotion and labelling needs
  Protection needs
Cultural sensitivity of product
Fit with product line

Place

Objectives
  Degree of market exposure required
  Distribution customer service level required
Type of channel (direct, indirect)
  Other channel members or facilitators required
  Type/number of wholesalers (agent, merchant, etc.)
  Type/number of retailers

(continued)

Place (continued)
  How discrepancies and separations will be handled
  How marketing functions will be shared
Coordination needed in company, channel, and supply chain
  Information requirements (EDI, the Internet, e-mail, etc.)
Transportation requirements
Inventory product-handling requirements
Facilities required (warehousing, distribution centres, etc.)
Reverse channels (for returns, recalls, etc.)

Promotion

Objectives
Major message theme(s) for integrated marketing communications (desired "positioning")
Promotion blend
  Advertising (type, media, copy thrust, etc.)
  Personal selling (type and number of salespeople, how compensated, how effort will be allocated, etc.)
  Sales promotion (for channel members, customers, employees)
  Publicity
  Interactive media
Mix of push and pull required
Who will do the work

Price

Nature of demand (price sensitivity, price of substitutes)
Demand and cost analyses (marginal analysis)
Markup chain in channel
Price flexibility
Price level(s) (under what conditions) and impact on customer value
Adjustments to list price (geographic terms, discounts, allowances, etc.)

Special Implementation Problems to Be Overcome

People required
Manufacturing, financial, and other resources needed

Control

Marketing information system needs
Criterion measures comparison with objectives (customer satisfaction, sales, cost, performance analysis, etc.)

Forecasts and Estimates

Costs (all elements in plan, over time)
Sales (by market, over time, etc.)
Estimated operating statement (pro forma)

Timing

Specific sequence of activities and events, etc.
Likely changes over the product life cycle

This material provides important background information relevant to the "why" of the marketing mix and target market decisions.

Too often, managers do not include this information; their plans just lay out the details of the target market and the marketing mix strategy decisions. This short-cut approach is more common when the plan is really just an update of a strategy that has been in place for some time. However, that approach can be risky.

Managers too often make the mistake of casually updating plans in minor ways—perhaps just changing some costs or sales forecasts—but otherwise sticking with what was done in the past. A big problem with this approach is that it's easy to lose sight of why those strategy decisions were made in the first place. When the market situation changes, the original reasons may no longer apply. Yet if the logic for those strategy decisions is not retained, it's easy to miss changes taking place that should result in a plan being reconsidered. For example, a plan that was established in the growth stage of the product life cycle may have been very successful for a number of years. But a marketing manager can't be complacent and assume that success will continue forever. When market maturity hits, the firm may be in for big trouble—unless the basic strategy and plan are modified. If a plan spells out the details of the market analysis and logic for the marketing mix and target market selected, then it is a simple matter to routinely check and update it. Remember: The idea is for all of the analysis and strategy decisions to fit together as an integrated whole. Thus, as some of the elements of the plan or marketing environment change, the whole plan may need a fresh approach. Ben & Jerry's evaluation and control system is designed to catch market trend changes quickly so that the firm can adjust its plans for a wide range of different regional markets.

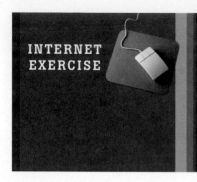

INTERNET EXERCISE

Go to the Health Canada Web site at www.hc-sc.gc.ca. Select *About Health Canada* from the menu on the left. From here, choose *Activities & Responsibilities*. From the Topic list in the box on this page, select *Social Marketing*. Now, from the Topic list, select *Seven Steps Tutorial*.

How does this social nonprofit marketing plan differ from your for-profit business marketing plan? How would you evaluate the success of a social nonprofit marketing plan?

CONTROL PROVIDES FEEDBACK TO IMPROVE PLANS AND IMPLEMENTATION

Keeping a firmer hand on the controls

Although information technology speeds up the flow of feedback and allows managers to improve plans and implementation continuously, the basic control questions that a marketing manager wants to answer are pretty similar to what they've always been.

A good manager wants to know which products' sales are highest and why, which products are profitable, what is selling where, and how much the marketing process is costing. Managers need to know what's happening, in detail, to improve the bottom line.

Unfortunately, traditional accounting reports are usually too general to be much help in answering these questions. A company may be showing a profit, while 80 percent of its business comes from only 20 percent of its products—or customers. The other 80 percent may be unprofitable. But without special analyses, managers won't know it. This 80/20 relationship is fairly common—and it is often referred to as the *80/20 rule*.

What happened at Allegiance Healthcare Corporation (AHC), which recently became part of CardinalHealth, is a good example. As a major distributor of hospital supplies, AHC carried over 100,000 products—everything a hospital might need from scalpels and skin markers to gowns and bandages. The huge array of products was complicated, but AHC was doing well with its strategy of being a "single source" for hospitals. However, careful analysis of sales and costs by region and product line revealed that AHC's profitable level of sales was masking a problem: 57 percent of its products accounted for just 2 percent of sales.

In a similar situation, the sales efficiency of a large Canadian steel producer was impeded by just too many customers. Sales analysis of their customer base revealed that out of roughly 1750 customers only 200 accounted for approximately 75 percent of their sales revenue.

As these examples show, it *is* possible for marketing managers to get detailed information about how marketing plans are working—but only if they ask for and analyze the necessary data. In this section, we'll discuss the kinds of information that can be available and how to use it. The techniques are not really complicated. They basically require only simple arithmetic—and of course computers easily take care of that when a large volume of sorting, adding, and subtracting is required.

SALES ANALYSIS SHOWS WHAT'S HAPPENING

Sales analysis looks at the details

Marketers are always interested in what sort of sales results they're achieving, but it's usually not enough to just know totals or summary information. Marketing executives need more detailed sales data to keep in touch with what's happening in the market. They get this detail by turning to **sales analysis**—a detailed breakdown of a company's sales records.

There is no one best way to break down or analyze sales data. Several breakdowns may be useful, depending on the nature of the company and product and what dimensions are relevant. Typical breakdowns include:

1. Product category, brand, package size, grade, or colour.
2. Geographic region—country, province, city, or sales rep's territory.
3. Customer characteristics (new or existing account, frequency of purchases, etc.).
4. Channel of distribution (type of middlemen involved, target markets served, etc.).
5. Price or discount class.
6. Method of sale—online, telephone, or sales rep.
7. Financial arrangement—cash or charge.
8. Order size.

Sales analysis is easy to do, and usually it's inexpensive because the data for the analysis can easily be obtained as a by-product of basic billing and accounts receivable procedures. However, the manager must make sure the company captures identifying information on important dimensions such as territory, sales reps, product model,

Information Resources Inc. developed the DataServer Analyzer Software, illustrated here, to easily do sales analysis and produce graphs that clearly illustrate patterns that might otherwise be hidden in a table of numbers.

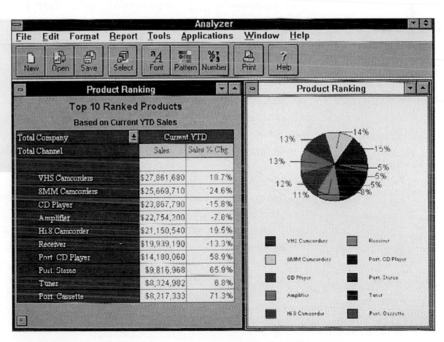

customer, and so forth in a database. Then the marketing information system can easily provide detailed sales analyses broken down by any variable (or combination of variables) in the database.

Sales analyses over time highlight trends

When sales analyses are routinely prepared over time (every day, week, month, or quarter), they show trends and help managers develop more accurate sales forecasts. A manager who ignores trends may not be able to spot shifts in the market that point to new opportunities or alternatively, problems. This is critical because today's profit is no guarantee that you'll make money tomorrow.

A graph is worth a thousand numbers

While detailed and timely sales analysis can be very useful, information that is too detailed or complex can drown a manager. Information systems can spew out more data than a manager can absorb. Well-designed information systems provide managers with colour graphs and charts that make it easy to see patterns that otherwise might be hidden scrolling through online tables with a browser. For example, a sales analysis breakdown of sales by product might show a bar graph for each product, where the height of the bar reflects the level of sales and where increases from the previous period are in green and decreases are in red.

While graphs can help a manager sort through raw sales data, another way to identify what data is most relevant and really needs attention is *performance analysis*.

PERFORMANCE ANALYSIS LOOKS FOR DIFFERENCES

Numbers are compared

Performance analysis looks for exceptions or variations from planned performance. In simple sales analysis, the figures are merely listed or graphed—they aren't compared against standards. In performance analysis, managers make comparisons. They might compare one territory against another, against the same territory's performance last year, or against expected performance.

The purpose of performance analysis is to improve operations. The salesperson, territory, or other factors showing poor performance can be identified and singled out for detailed analysis and corrective action. Or outstanding performances can be analyzed to see if the successes can be explained and made the general rule.

Performance analysis doesn't have to be limited to sales. Other data can be analyzed too. This data may include the frequency of stock-outs, the number of sales calls made, the number of orders, customer satisfaction ratings, or the cost of various tasks.

A performance analysis can be quite revealing, as shown in the following example.

Straight performance analysis—an illustration

A manufacturer of business products sells to wholesalers through five sales reps, each serving a separate territory. Total net sales for the year amount to $2,386,000. Sales force compensation and expenses come to $198,000, yielding a direct-selling expense ratio of 8.3 percent—that is, $198,000 ÷ $2,386,000 × 100.

This information—taken from a profit and loss statement—is interesting, but it doesn't explain what's happening from one territory to another. To get a clearer picture, the manager compares the sales results with other data *from each territory*. See Exhibits 18-6 and 18-7. Keep in mind that exhibits like these and others that follow in this chapter are easy to generate with programs like Microsoft Office. Larger companies make such analysis available at a Web site so the manager can sort out whatever is needed.

The reps in sales areas D and E aren't doing well. Sales are low and marketing costs are high. Perhaps more aggressive sales reps could do a better job, but the number of customers suggests that sales potential might be low. Perhaps the whole plan needs revision.

Exhibit 18-6 Comparative Performance of Sales Reps

Sales Area	Total Calls	Total Orders	Order-Call Ratio	Sales by Sales Rep	Average Sales Rep Order	Total Consumers
A	1,900	1,140	60.0%	$ 912,000	$800	195
B	1,500	1,000	66.7	720,000	720	160
C	1,400	700	50.0	560,000	800	140
D	1,030	279	27.1	132,000	478	60
E	820	165	20.1	62,000	374	50
Total	6,650	3,284	49.3%	$2,386,000	$634	605

Exhibit 18-7 Comparative Cost of Sales Reps

Sales Area	Annual Compensation	Expense Payments	Total Sales Rep Cost	Sales Produced	Cost-Sales Ratio
A	$ 22,800	$11,200	$ 34,000	$ 912,000	3.7%
B	21,600	14,400	36,000	720,000	5.0
C	20,400	11,600	32,000	560,000	5.7
D	19,200	24,800	44,000	132,000	33.3
E	20,000	32,000	52,000	62,000	83.8
Total	$104,000	$94,000	$198,000	$2,386,000	8.3%

The figures themselves, of course, don't provide the answers. But they do reveal the areas that need improvement. This is the main value of performance analysis. It's up to management to find the remedy, either by revising or changing the marketing plan.

PERFORMANCE INDEXES SIMPLIFY HUMAN ANALYSIS

Comparing against "what ought to have happened"

With a straight performance analysis, the marketing manager can evaluate the variations among sales reps to try to explain the "why." But this takes time. And poor performances are sometimes due to problems that bare sales figures don't reveal. Some uncontrollable factors in a particular territory—tougher competitors or ineffective middlemen—may lower the sales potential. Or a territory just may not have much potential.

To get a better check on performance effectiveness, the marketing manager compares what did happen with what ought to have happened. This involves the use of performance indexes.

A performance index is like a batting average

When a manager sets standards—that is, quantitative measures of what ought to happen—it's relatively simple to compute a **performance index**—a number like a baseball batting average that shows the relation of one value to another.

Baseball batting averages are computed by dividing the actual number of hits by the number of times at bat (the possible number of times the batter could have had a hit) and then multiplying the result by 100 to get rid of decimal points. A sales performance index is computed the same way—by dividing actual sales by expected sales for the area (or sales rep, product, etc.) and then multiplying by 100. If a sales rep is batting 82 percent, the index is 82.

Exhibit 18-8 Development of a Measure of Sales Performances (by region)

Regions	(1) Population as Percent of Total	(2) Expected Distribution of Sales Based on Population	(3) Actual Sales	(4) Performance Index
Atlantic	20	$ 200,000	$ 210,000	105
Quebec	25	250,000	250,000	100
Ontario	35	350,000	420,000	120
Western	20	200,000	120,000	60
Total	100	$1,000,000	$1,000,000	

A simple example shows where the problem is

We show how to compute a performance index in the following example, which assumes that population is an effective measure of sales potential.

In Exhibit 18-8, the population is broken down by region as a percent of the total population. The regions are Atlantic, Quebec, Ontario, and Western.

A firm already has $1 million in sales and now wants to evaluate performance in each region. Column 2 shows the actual sales of $1 million broken down in proportion to the population in the four regions. This is what sales *should* be if population were a good measure of future performance. Column 3 in Exhibit 18-8 shows the actual sales for the year for each region. Column 4 shows measures of performance (performance indexes)—Column 3 ÷ Column 2 × 100.

In our hypothetical example, the Western region isn't doing as well as expected. It has 20 percent of the total population—and expected sales (based on population) are $200,000. Actual sales, however, are only $120,000. This means that the Western region's performance index is only 60—(120,000 ÷ 200,000) × 100— because actual sales are much lower than expected on the basis of population. If population is a good basis for measuring expected sales (an important *if*), the poor sales performance should be analyzed further. Perhaps sales reps in the Western region aren't working as hard as they should. Perhaps promotion there isn't as effective as elsewhere. Or competitive products may have entered the market.

Whatever the cause, it's clear that performance analysis does not solve problems. Managers do that. But performance analysis does point out potential problems— and it does this well.

INTERNET EXERCISE SPSS sells software that can be used for a variety of purposes, including analyses of sales, cost, and customer data. Browse the SPSS Web site (www.spss.com) and identify three ways that SPSS could make it easier for a manager to do a performance analysis.

A SERIES OF PERFORMANCE ANALYSES MAY FIND THE REAL PROBLEM

Performance analysis helps a marketing manager see if the firm's marketing plans are working properly—and, if they aren't, it can lead to problem solving. But a marketing manager may need a series of performance analyses, as shown in the following example.

To get a feel for how performance analysis can be part of a problem-solving process, follow this example carefully—one exhibit at a time. Try to anticipate the marketing manager's decision.

The case of CarAudio Inc.

CarAudio's sales manager finds that sales for the Western region are $130,000 below the quota of $14,500,000 (that is, actual sales are $14,370,000) for the January through June period. The quota is based on forecast sales of the various types of replacement car audio equipment the company sells. Specifically, the quota is based on forecasts for each product type in each store in each sales rep's territory.

Pam Dexter, the sales manager, thinks this difference isn't too large (1.52 percent) and is inclined to forget the matter—especially since forecasts usually err to some extent. But she thinks about sending an e-mail message to all sales reps and district supervisors in the region—a message aimed at stimulating sales effort.

Exhibit 18-9 shows the overall picture of CarAudio's sales in the Western sales region. What do you think the manager should do?

Edmonton has the poorest performance—but it isn't too bad. Before writing a "let's get with it" letter to Edmonton and then relaxing, the sales manager decides to analyze the performance of the four sales reps in the Edmonton district. Exhibit 18-10 shows a breakdown of the Edmonton figures by sales rep. What conclusion or action do you suggest now?

Since Shanna Smith previously was the top sales rep, the sales manager wonders if Smith is having trouble with some of her larger customers. Before making a drastic move, she does an analysis of Smith's sales to the five largest customers. See Exhibit 18-11. What action could the sales manager take now? Should Smith be fired?

Smith's sales in all the large stores are down significantly, although her sales in many small stores are holding up well. Smith's problem seems to be general. Perhaps she just isn't working. Before calling her, the sales manager decides to look at Smith's sales of the four major products. Exhibit 18-12 shows Smith's sales. What action is indicated now?

Smith is having real trouble with radio receivers. Was the problem Smith or the radios?

Further analysis by product for the whole region shows that everyone in the Western region is having trouble with radio receivers because customers there are buying new satellite radios that come from another company. But higher sales on other products hid this fact. Since radio sales are doing all right nationally, the problem is only now showing up. You can see that this is the *major* problem. If CarAudio doesn't offer a satellite radio, it will just slowly lose sales as more customers shift to satellite.

Exhibit 18-9
Sales Performance—
Western Region,
January–June ($000)

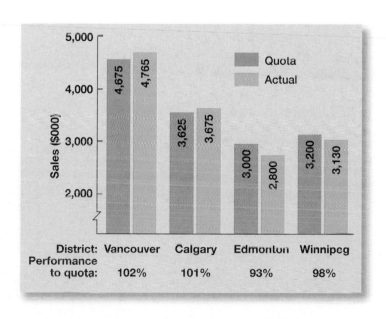

Exhibit 18-10
Sales Performance—
Edmonton District,
January–June ($000)

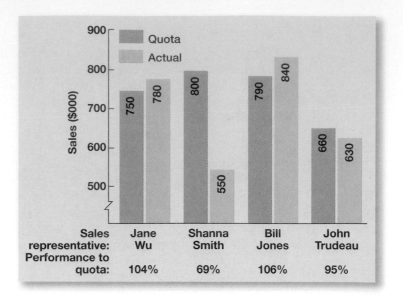

Since overall company sales are fairly good, many sales managers wouldn't bother with this analysis. Some might trace the problem to Smith. But without detailed sales records and performance analysis, they might assume that Smith—rather than the missed opportunity to add a new product—is at fault. And Smith herself might not be able to pinpoint what's happening.

The iceberg principle—90 percent is below the surface

The CarAudio case illustrates the **iceberg principle**—much good information is hidden in summary data. Icebergs show only about 10 percent of their mass above water level. The other 90 percent is below water level, and not directly below either. The submerged portion almost seems to search out ships that come too near.

The same is true of much business and marketing data. Since total sales may be large and company activities varied, problems in one area may hide below the surface. Everything looks calm and peaceful. But closer analysis may reveal jagged edges that can severely damage or even sink the business. The 90:10 ratio—or the 80/20 rule we mentioned earlier—must not be ignored. Averaging and summarizing data are helpful, but be sure summaries don't hide more than they reveal. Marketing managers need facts to avoid rash judgments based on incomplete information. Some students want to fire Smith after they see the store-by-store data (Exhibit 18-11).

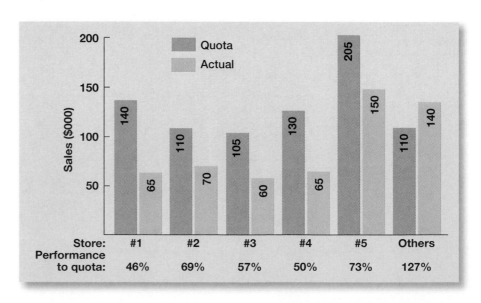

Exhibit 18-12
Sales Performance by Product for Shanna Smith in Edmonton District, January–June ($000)

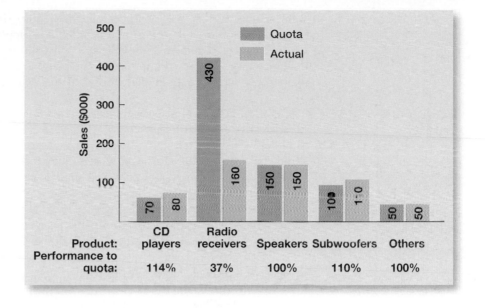

Product:	CD players	Radio receivers	Speakers	Subwoofers	Others
Performance to quota:	114%	37%	100%	110%	100%

MARKETING COST ANALYSIS—CONTROLLING COSTS TOO

So far we've emphasized sales analysis. But sales come at a cost. And costs can and should be analyzed and controlled too. You can see why in the case of Watanake Packaging Ltd. (WPL). WPL developed a new strategy to target the packaging needs of producers of high-tech electronic equipment. WPL designed unique Styrofoam inserts to protect electronic equipment during shipping. It assigned order getters to develop new accounts and recruited agent middlemen to develop overseas markets. WPL's marketing mix was well received and led to good profits. But over time as marketing managers at WPL analyzed costs, they realized their once-successful strategy was slipping. Personal selling expense as a percent of sales had doubled because it took longer to find and sell new accounts. It was costly to design special products for the many customers who purchased only small quantities. Profit margins

For a restaurant to be profitable, the manager needs to worry not only about satisfying customers but also about how much each item contributes to overall costs.

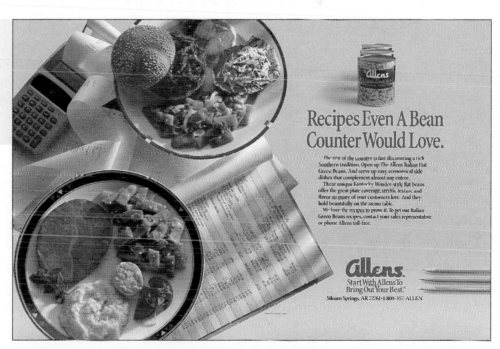

were falling too because of increased price competition. In contrast, the analysis showed that online sales of ordinary cardboard shipping boxes for agricultural products were very profitable. So WPL stopped calling on *small* electronics firms and developed a new plan to improve its Web site and build the firm's share of the less glamorous, but more profitable, cardboard box business.

Marketing costs have a purpose

Detailed cost analysis is very useful in understanding production costs—but much less is done with *marketing cost analysis*.[6] One reason is that many accountants show little interest in their firm's marketing process—or they don't understand the different marketing activities. They just treat marketing as overhead and forget about it. For now, however, you should see that careful analysis of most marketing costs shows that the money is spent for a specific purpose—for example, to develop or promote a particular product or to serve particular customers.

Let's reconsider Exhibit 18-7 from this perspective. It shows that the company's spending on sales compensation and sales expenses varies by salesperson and market area. By breaking out and comparing the costs of different sales reps, the marketing manager has a much better idea of what it costs to implement the strategy in each sales area. In this example, it's clear that the sales reps in sales areas D and especially E are not only falling short in sales, but also that their costs are high relative to other reps who are getting more results. The table shows that the difference isn't due to annual compensation; that's lower. Rather, these reps have expenses that are two or three times the average. The smaller number of total customers in these sales areas (Exhibit 18-6) might explain the lower levels of sales, but it probably doesn't explain the higher expenses. Perhaps the customers are more spread out and require more travel to reach. Here again, the cost analysis doesn't explain *why* the results are as they are—but it does direct the manager's attention to a specific area that needs improvement. A more detailed breakdown of costs may help pinpoint the specific cause.

Allocate costs to specific customers and products

Because marketing costs have a purpose, it usually makes sense to allocate costs to specific market segments, or customers, or to specific products. In some situations, companies allocate costs directly to the various geographical market segments they serve. This may let managers directly analyze the profitability of the firm's target markets. In other cases, companies allocate costs to specific customers or specific products and then add these costs for market segments depending on how much of which products each customer buys.

Should all costs be allocated?

So far we've discussed general principles. But allocating costs is tricky. Some costs are likely to be fixed for the near future, regardless of what decision is made. And some costs are likely to be *common* to several products or customers, making allocation difficult.

There are two basic approaches to handling this allocating problem: the full-cost approach and the contribution-margin approach.

Full-cost approach— everything costs something

In the **full-cost approach**, all costs are allocated to products, customers, or other categories. Even fixed costs and common costs are allocated in some way. Because all costs are allocated, we can subtract costs from sales and find the profitability of various customers, products, and so on. This *is* of interest to some managers.

The full-cost approach requires that difficult-to-allocate costs be split on some basis. Here the managers assume that the work done for those costs is equally beneficial to customers, to products, or to whatever group they are allocated. Sometimes this allocation is done mechanically. But often logic can support the allocation—if we accept the idea that marketing costs are incurred for a purpose. For example, advertising costs not directly related to specific customers or products might be allocated to *all* customers based on their purchases—on the theory that advertising helps bring in the sales.

Contribution-margin—ignores some costs to get results

When we use the **contribution-margin approach**, all costs are not allocated in *all* situations. Why?

When we compare various alternatives, it may be more meaningful to consider only the costs directly related to specific alternatives. Variable costs are relevant here.

The contribution-margin approach focuses attention on variable costs rather than on total costs. Total costs may include some fixed costs that do not change in the short run and can safely be ignored or some common costs that are more difficult to allocate.[7]

PLANNING AND CONTROL COMBINED

We've been treating sales and cost analyses separately up to this point. But management often combines them to keep a running check on its activities—to be sure the plans are working—and to see when and where new strategies are needed.

Sales + Costs + Everybody helps = $163,000

Let's see how this works at Cindy's Fashions, a small-town apparel retailer. This firm netted $155,000 last year. Cindy Reve, the owner, expects no basic change in competition and slightly better local business conditions. So she sets this year's profit objective at $163,000—an increase of about 5 percent.

Next she develops tentative plans to show how she can make this higher profit. She estimates the sales volumes, gross margins, and expenses—broken down by months and by departments in her store—that she would need to net $163,000.

Exhibit 18-13 is a planning and control chart Reve developed to show the contribution each department should make each month. At the bottom of Exhibit 18-13, the plan for the year is summarized. Note that space is provided to insert the

Exhibit 18-13   Planning and Control Chart for Cindy's Fashions

| | Contribution to Store | | | | | Store Expense | Operating Profit | Cumulative Operating Profit |
	Dept. A	Dept. B	Dept. C	Dept. D[*]	Total			
January								
Planned	27,000	9,000	4,000	−1,000	39,000	24,000	15,000	15,000
Actual								
Variation								
February								
Planned	20,000	6,500	2,500	−1,000	28,000	24,000	4,000	19,000
Actual								
Variation								
November								
Planned	32,000	7,500	2,500	0	42,000	24,000	18,000	106,500
Actual								
Variation								
December								
Planned	63,000	12,500	4,000	9,000	88,500	32,000	56,500	163,000
Actual								
Variation								
Total								
Planned	316,000	70,000	69,000	−4,000	453,000	288,000	163,000	163,000
Actual								
Variation								

*The objective of minus $4,000 for this department was established on the same basis as the objectives for the other departments—that is, it represents the same percentage gain over last year when Department D's loss was $4,200. Plans call for discontinuance of the department unless it shows marked improvement by the end of the year.

actual performance and a measure of variation. So this chart can be used to do both planning and control.

Exhibit 18-13 shows that Reve is focusing on the monthly contribution to overhead and profit by each department. The purpose of monthly estimates is to get more frequent feedback and allow faster adjustment of plans. Generally, the shorter the planning and control period, the easier it is to correct problems before they become emergencies.

In this example, Reve uses a modified contribution-margin approach—some of the fixed costs can be allocated logically to particular departments. On this chart, the balance left after direct fixed and variable costs are charged to departments is called Contribution to Store. The idea is that each department will contribute to covering *general* store expenses—such as top-management salaries and holiday decorations—and to net profits.

In Exhibit 18-13, we see that the whole operation is brought together when Reve computes the monthly operating profit. She totals the contribution from each of the four departments, then subtracts general store expenses to obtain the operating profit for each month.

As time passes, Reve can compare actual sales with what's projected. If actual sales were less than projected, corrective action could take either of two courses: improving implementation efforts or developing new, more realistic strategies.

THE MARKETING AUDIT

While crises pop up, planning and control must go on

The analyses we've discussed so far are designed to help a firm plan and control its operations. They can help a marketing manager do a better job. Often, however, the control process focuses on short-run problems and adjustments.

To make sure that the whole marketing program is evaluated *regularly*, marketing specialists developed the marketing audit. A marketing audit is similar to an accounting audit or a personnel audit, which businesses have used for some time.

The **marketing audit** is a systematic, critical, and unbiased review and appraisal of the basic objectives and policies of the marketing function and of the organization, methods, procedures, and people employed to implement the policies.[8]

A marketing audit requires a detailed look at the company's current marketing plans to see if they are still the best plans the firm can offer. Customers' needs and attitudes change—and competitors continually develop new and better plans. Plans more than a year or two old may be out-of-date or even obsolete. Sometimes marketing managers are so close to the trees that they can't see the forest. An outsider can help the firm see whether it really focuses on some unsatisfied needs and offers appropriate marketing mixes. Basically, the auditor uses our strategy planning framework. But instead of developing plans, the auditor works backward and evaluates the plans being implemented. The consultant-auditor also evaluates the quality of the effort, looking at who is doing what and how well. This means interviewing customers, competitors, channel members, and employees. A marketing audit can be a big job. But if it helps ensure that the company's strategies are on the right track and being implemented properly, it can be well worth the effort.

An audit shouldn't be necessary—but often it is

A marketing audit takes a big view of the business—and it evaluates the whole marketing program. It might be done by a separate department within the company, perhaps by a marketing controller. But to get both expert and objective evaluation, it's probably better to use an outside organization such as a marketing consulting firm.

Ideally, a marketing audit should not be necessary. Good managers do their best in planning, and controlling—and they should continually evaluate the effectiveness of the operation. In practice, however, managers often become identified with certain strategies, and pursue them blindly, when other strategies might be more effective. Since an outside view can give needed perspective, marketing audits may be more common in the future.

CONCLUSION

In this chapter, we stressed the importance of developing whole marketing mixes—not just developing policies for the individual four Ps and hoping they will fit together into some logical whole. As a starting place for developing new marketing mixes, a manager can use the product classes that have served as a thread through this text. Even if the manager can't fully describe the needs and attitudes of target markets, it is usually possible to select the appropriate product class for a particular product. This, in turn, will help set Place and Promotion policies. It may also clarify what type of marketing mix is typical for the product. However, just doing what is typical may not give a firm any competitive advantage. Creative strategies are often the ones that identify new and better ways of uniquely giving target customers what they want or need. Similarly, seeing where a firm's offering fits in the product life cycle helps to clarify how current marketing mixes are likely to change in the future.

Developing and evaluating marketing strategies and plans usually requires that the manager use some approach to forecasting. We talked about two basic approaches to forecasting market potential and sales: (1) extending past behaviour and (2) predicting future behaviour. The most common approach is to extend past behaviour into the future. This gives reasonably good results if market conditions are fairly stable. Methods here include extension of past sales data and the factor method. We saw that projecting the past into the future is risky when big market changes are likely. To make up for this possible weakness, marketers predict future behaviour using their own experience and judgment. They also bring in the judgment of others, using the jury of executive opinion method and salespeople's estimates. And they may use surveys, panels, and market tests. Of course, any sales forecast depends on the marketing mix the firm actually selects.

A marketing program must also be controlled. This helps the manager locate and correct weak spots as well as identify strengths that can be applied in the rest of the marketing program. Controls work hand in hand with planning. We reviewed a number of performance-based techniques that can help track down problems so they can be corrected quickly—before they become major threats. We saw in the Ben & Jerry's case how their control system caught a problem that was not connected to product quality as they thought, but rather to something as basic (but crucial) as their packaging that made customers expect more cherries in their ice cream than they were getting.

KEY TERMS

market potential, 506

sales forecast, 506

trend extension, 507

factor method, 509

factor, 509

time series, 509

leading series, 509

jury of executive opinion, 510

sales analysis, 515

performance analysis, 516

performance index, 517

iceberg principle, 520

full-cost approach, 522

contribution-margin approach, 523

marketing audit, 524

QUESTIONS AND PROBLEMS

1. How would Rogers Video use S.W.O.T. analysis to position itself against Star Choice pay-per-view?

2. Give some examples of how you would incorrectly combine elements of the 4 Ps in a marketing plan targeted at selling laptops to university students.

3. Why do we care about competitors when developing a marketing plan?

4. How would you choose among several possible marketing plans if you had limited resources? Would the job be easier in the consumer product or business product area? Why?

5 How does understanding the product classes help a manager develop a strategy for a really new product that is unlike anything currently available?

6. Distinguish between competitive marketing mixes and superior mixes that leads to breakthrough opportunities.

7. What is the difference between a forecast of market potential and a sales forecast?

8. Suggest some plausible explanations for sales fluctuations of:
   (a) computers, *(b)* ice cream, *(c)* washing machines, *(d)* tennis rackets, *(e)* oats, *(f)* disposable diapers, and *(g)* latex for rubber-based paint.

9. Various breakdowns can be used for sales analysis depending on the nature of the company and its products. Describe a situation (one for each) where each of the following breakdowns would yield useful information. Explain why.

   a. By geographic region.
   b. By product.
   c. By customer.
   d. By size of order.
   e. By size of sales rep commission on each product or product group.

10. Distinguish between a sales analysis and a performance analysis.

11. Carefully explain what the iceberg principle should mean to the marketing manager.

12. Explain the meaning of the comparative performance and comparative cost data in Exhibits 18-6 and 18-7. Why does it appear that eliminating sales areas D and E would be profitable?

13. Most sales forecasting is subject to some error (perhaps 5 to 10 percent). Should we then expect variations in sales performance of 5 to 10 percent above or below quota? If so, how should we treat such variations in evaluating performance?

14. Why is there controversy between the advocates of the full-cost and the contribution-margin approaches to cost analysis?

COMPUTER-AIDED PROBLEM

18. Marketing Cost Analysis

RESOURCE REMINDER

This problem emphasizes the differences between the full-cost approach and contribution-margin approach to marketing cost analysis.

Tapco Inc., currently sells two products. Sales commissions and unit costs vary with the quantity of each product sold. With the full-cost approach, Tapco's administrative and advertising costs are allocated to each product based on its share of total sales dollars. Details of Tapco's costs and other data are given in the spreadsheet. The first column shows a cost analysis based on the full-cost approach. The second column shows an analysis based on the contribution-margin approach.

a. If the number of Product A units sold were to increase by 1,000 units, what would happen to the allocated administrative expense for Product A? How would the

change in sales of Product A affect the allocated administrative expense for Product B? Briefly discuss why the changes you observe might cause conflict between the product managers of the two different products.

b. What would happen to total profits if Tapco stopped selling Product A but continued to sell 4,000 units of Product B? What happens to total profits if the firm stops selling Product B but continues to sell 5,000 units of Product A? (Hint: To stop selling a product means that the quantity sold would be zero.)

c. If the firm dropped Product B and increased the price of Product A by $2.00, what quantity of Product A would it have to sell to earn a total profit as large as it was originally earning with both products? (Hint: Change values in the spreadsheet to reflect the changes the firm is considering, and then use the What If analysis to vary the quantity of Product A sold and display what happens to total profit.)

> If you want to read the cases and view the video cases that accompany this chapter, visit the *Basic Marketing* Online Learning Centre at: **www.mcgrawhill.ca/olc/perreault**. Along with these cases and video cases, the OLC also has the software and user guide for this chapter's Computer-Aided Problem, as well as exercises, quizzes, articles, links, and other *interactive* content that will help you with your studies.

APPENDIX A

Economics Fundamentals

WHEN YOU FINISH THIS APPENDIX, YOU SHOULD

1. Understand the "law of diminishing demand."

2. Understand demand and supply curves and how they set the size of a market and its price level.

3. Know about elasticity of demand and supply.

4. Know why demand elasticity can be affected by availability of substitutes.

The economist's traditional analysis of demand and supply is a useful tool for analyzing markets. In particular, you should master the concepts of a demand curve and demand elasticity. A firm's demand curve shows how the target customers view the firm's Product—really its whole marketing mix. And the interaction of demand and supply curves helps set the size of a market and the market price. The interaction of supply and demand also determines the nature of the competitive environment, which has an important effect on strategy planning. These ideas are discussed more fully in the following sections.

PRODUCTS AND MARKETS AS SEEN BY CUSTOMERS AND POTENTIAL CUSTOMERS

The law of diminishing demand

Suppose that consumers buy Thai Jasmine rice in 1 kilogram bags at the same time they buy other foods such as bread and cheese. If the consumers are mainly interested in buying a certain amount of food and the price of the rice drops, it seems reasonable to expect that they will switch some of their food money to rice and away from some other foods. But if the price of Thai rice rises, you expect our consumers to buy less rice and more of other foods.

The general relationship between price and quantity demanded illustrated by this food example is called the **law of diminishing demand**—which says that if the price of a product is raised, a smaller quantity will be demanded and if the price of a product is lowered, a greater quantity will be demanded. Experience supports this relationship between price and total demand in a market, especially for broad product categories or commodities such as rice.

The relationship between price and quantity demanded in a market is what economists call a "demand schedule." An example is shown in Exhibit A-1. For each row in the table, column 2 shows the quantity consumers will want (demand) if they have to pay the price given in column 1. The third column shows that the total revenue (sales) in the rice market is equal to the quantity demanded at a given price times that price. Note that as prices drop, the total *unit* quantity increases, yet the total *revenue* decreases. Fill in the blank lines in the third column and observe the behaviour of total revenue, an important number for the marketing manager. We will explain what you should have noticed, and why, a little later.

The demand curve— usually down-sloping

If your only interest is seeing at which price the company will earn the greatest total revenue, the demand schedule may be adequate. But a demand curve shows more. A **demand curve** is a graph of the relationship between price and quantity

Exhibit A-1
Demand Schedule for Thai Jasmine Rice (1 kilogram bag)

Point	(1) Price of Thai Jasmine Rice per Bag (P)	(2) Quantity Demanded (bags per month) (Q)	(3) Total Revenue per Month (P × Q = TR)
A	$1.60	8,000,000	$12,800,000
B	1.30	9,000,000	_____
C	1.00	11,000,000	11,000,000
D	0.70	14,000,000	_____
E	0.40	19,000,000	_____

Exhibit A-2
Demand Curve for
Thai Jasmine Rice
(1 kilogram bag)

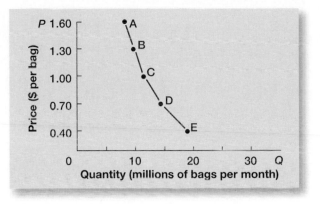

demanded in a market, assuming that all other things stay the same. Exhibit A-2 shows the demand curve for rice—really just a plotting of the demand schedule in Exhibit A-1. It shows how much rice potential customers will demand at various possible prices. This is a "down-sloping demand curve." Most demand curves are down-sloping. This just means that if prices are decreased, the quantity customers demand will increase.

Note that the demand curve only shows how customers will react to various possible prices. In a market, we see only one price at a time, not all of these prices. The curve, however, shows what quantities will be demanded, depending on what price is set.

Microwave oven demand curve looks different

To get a more complete picture of demand-curve analysis, let's consider another product that has a different demand schedule and curve. A demand schedule for standard 1-cubic-foot microwave ovens is shown in Exhibit A-3. Column (3) shows the total revenue that will be obtained at various possible prices and quantities. Again, as the price goes down, the quantity demanded goes up. But here, unlike the rice example, total revenue increases as prices go down—at least until the price drops to $150.

Every market has a demand curve for some time period

These general demand relationships are typical for all products. But each product has its own demand schedule and curve in each potential market, no matter how small the market. In other words, a particular demand curve has meaning only for a particular market. We can think of demand curves for individuals, groups of individuals who form a target market, regions, and even countries. And the time period covered really should be specified, although this is often neglected because we usually think of monthly or yearly periods.

Exhibit A-3
Demand Schedule for
1-Cubic-Foot Microwave
Ovens

Point	(1) Price per Microwave Oven (P)	(2) Quantity Demanded per Year (Q)	(3) Total Revenue (TR) per Year (P × Q = TR)
A	$300	20,000	$6,000,000
B	250	70,000	15,500,000
C	200	130,000	26,000,000
D	150	210,000	31,500,000
E	100	310,000	31,000,000

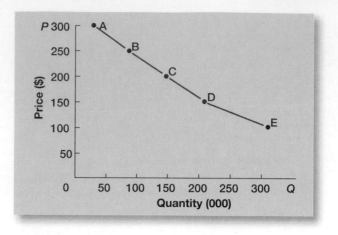

The difference between elastic and inelastic

The demand curve for microwave ovens (see Exhibit A-4) is down-sloping—but note that it is flatter than the curve for rice. It is important to understand what this flatness means.

We will consider the flatness in terms of total revenue, since this is what interests business managers.*

When you filled in the total revenue column for rice, you should have noticed that total revenue drops continually if the price is reduced. This looks undesirable for sellers and illustrates inelastic demand. **Inelastic demand** means that although the quantity demanded increases if the price is decreased, the quantity demanded will not "stretch" enough—that is, it is not elastic enough—to avoid a decrease in total revenue.

In contrast, **elastic demand** means that if prices are dropped, the quantity demanded will stretch (increase) enough to increase total revenue. The upper part of the microwave oven demand curve is an example of elastic demand.

But note that if the microwave oven price is dropped from $150 to $100, total revenue will decrease. We can say, therefore, that between $150 and $100, demand is inelastic—that is, total revenue will decrease if price is lowered from $150 to $100.

Thus, elasticity can be defined in terms of changes in total revenue. *If total revenue will increase if price is lowered, then demand is elastic. If total revenue will decrease if price is lowered, then demand is inelastic.* (Note: A special case known as "unitary elasticity of demand" occurs if total revenue stays the same when prices change.)

Total revenue may increase if price is raised

A point often missed in discussions of demand is what happens when prices are raised instead of lowered. With elastic demand, total revenue will *decrease* if the price is *raised*. With inelastic demand, however, total revenue will *increase* if the price is *raised*.

The possibility of raising price and increasing dollar sales (total revenue) at the same time is attractive to managers. This only occurs if the demand curve is inelastic. Here total revenue will increase if price is raised, but total costs probably will not increase—and may actually go down—with smaller quantities. Keep in mind that profit is equal to total revenue minus total costs. So when demand is inelastic, profit will increase as price is increased!

The ways total revenue changes as prices are raised are shown in Exhibit A-5. Here total revenue is the rectangular area formed by a price and its related quantity. The larger the rectangular area, the greater the total revenue.

---

*Strictly speaking, two curves should not be compared for flatness if the graph scales are different, but for our purposes now we will do so to illustrate the idea of "elasticity of demand." Actually, it would be more accurate to compare two curves for one product on the same graph. Then both the shape of the demand curve and its position on the graph would be important.

P_1 is the original price here, and the total potential revenue with this original price is shown by the area with blue shading. The area with red shading shows the total revenue with the new price, P_2. There is some overlap in the total revenue areas, so the important areas are those with only one colour. Note that in the left-hand figure—where demand is elastic—the revenue added (the red-only area) when the price is increased is less than the revenue lost (the blue-only area). Now let's contrast this to the right-hand figure, when demand is inelastic. Only a small blue revenue area is given up for a much larger (red) one when price is raised.

An entire curve is not elastic or inelastic

It is important to see that it is *wrong to refer to a whole demand curve as elastic or inelastic*. Rather, elasticity for a particular demand curve refers to the change in total revenue between two points on the curve, not along the whole curve. You saw the change from elastic to inelastic in the microwave oven example. Generally, however, nearby points are either elastic or inelastic—so it is common to refer to a whole curve by the degree of elasticity in the price range that normally is of interest—the *relevant range*.

Demand elasticities affected by availability of substitutes and urgency of need

At first, it may be difficult to see why one product has an elastic demand and another an inelastic demand. Many factors affect elasticity, such as the availability of substitutes, the importance of the item in the customer's budget, and the urgency of the customer's need and its relation to other needs. By looking more closely at one of these factors—the availability of substitutes—you will better understand why demand elasticities vary.

Substitutes are products that offer the buyer a choice. For example, many consumers see grapefruit as a substitute for oranges and hot dogs as a substitute for hamburgers. The greater the number of "good" substitutes available, the greater will be the elasticity of demand. From the consumer's perspective, products are "good" substitutes if they are very similar (homogeneous). If consumers see products as extremely different, or heterogeneous, then a particular need cannot easily be satisfied by substitutes. And the demand for the most satisfactory product may be quite inelastic.

Exhibit A-5
Changes in Total Revenue as Prices Increase

As an example, if the price of hamburger is lowered (and other prices stay the same), the quantity demanded will increase a lot, as will total revenue. The reason is that not only will regular hamburger users buy more hamburger, but some consumers who formerly bought hot dogs or steaks probably will buy hamburger too. But if the price of hamburger is raised, the quantity demanded will decrease, perhaps sharply. Still, consumers will buy some hamburger, depending on how much the price has risen, their individual tastes, and what their guests expect (see Exhibit A-6).

In contrast to a product with many "substitutes"—such as hamburger—consider a product with few or no substitutes. Its demand curve will tend to be inelastic. Motor oil is a good example. Motor oil is needed to keep cars running. Yet no one person or family uses great quantities of motor oil. So it is not likely that the quantity of motor oil purchased will change much as long as price changes are *within a reasonable range*. Of course, if the price is raised to a staggering figure, many people will buy less oil (change their oil less frequently). If the price is dropped to an extremely low level, manufacturers may buy more—say, as a lower-cost substitute for other chemicals typically used in making plastic (Exhibit A-7). But these extremes are outside the relevant range.

Demand curves are introduced here because the degree of elasticity of demand shows how potential customers feel about a product—and especially whether they see substitutes for the product. But to get a better understanding of markets, we must extend this economic analysis.

MARKETS AS SEEN BY SUPPLIERS

Customers may want some product—but if suppliers are not willing to supply it, then there is no market. So we'll study the economist's analysis of supply. And then we'll bring supply and demand together for a more complete understanding of markets.

Economists often use the kind of analysis we are discussing here to explain pricing in the marketplace. But that is not our intention. Here we are interested in how and why markets work and the interaction of customers and potential suppliers.

Supply curves reflect supplier thinking

Generally speaking, suppliers' costs affect the quantity of products they are willing to offer in a market during any period. In other words, their costs affect their supply schedules and supply curves. While a demand curve shows the quantity of products customers will be willing to buy at various prices, a **supply curve** shows the quantity of products that will be supplied at various possible prices. Eventually, only one quantity will be offered and purchased. So a supply curve is really a hypothetical (what-if) description of what will be offered at various prices. It is, however, a very important curve. Together with a demand curve, it summarizes the attitudes and probable behaviour of buyers and sellers about a particular product in a particular market—that is, in a product-market.

Some supply curves are vertical

We usually assume that supply curves tend to slope upward—that is, suppliers will be willing to offer greater quantities at higher prices. If a product's market price is very high, it seems only reasonable that producers will be anxious to produce more of the product and even put workers on overtime or perhaps hire more workers to increase the quantity they can offer. Going further, it seems likely that producers of other products will switch their resources (farms, factories, labour, or retail facilities) to the product that is in great demand.

On the other hand, if consumers are only willing to pay a very low price for a particular product, it's reasonable to expect that producers will switch to other products, thus reducing supply. A supply schedule (Exhibit A-8) and a supply curve (Exhibit A-9) for rice illustrates these ideas. This supply curve shows how much rice would be produced and offered for sale at each possible market price in a given month.

In the very short run (say, over a few hours, a day, or a week), a supplier may not be able to change the supply at all. In this situation, we would see a vertical supply curve. This situation is often relevant in the market for fresh produce. Fresh strawberries, for example, continue to ripen, and a supplier wants to sell them quickly—preferably at a higher price—but in any case, they must be sold.

If the product is a service, it may not be easy to expand the supply in the short run. Additional barbers or medical doctors are not quickly trained and licensed, and they only have so much time to give each day. Further, the prospect of much higher prices in the near future cannot easily expand the supply of many services. For example, a hit play or an "in" restaurant or nightclub is limited in the amount of product it can offer at a particular time.

Exhibit A-8
Supply Schedule for
Rice (1 kilogram bag)

Point	Possible Market Price per 1 kg Bag	Number of Bags Sellers Will Supply per Month at Each Possible Market Price
A	$1.60	17,000,000
B	1.30	14,000,000
C	1.00	11,000,000
D	0.70	8,000,000
E	0.40	3,000,000

Note: This supply curve is for a month to emphasize that farmers might have some control over when they deliver their rice. There would be a different curve for each month.

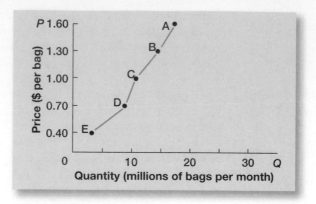

Elasticity of supply

The term *elasticity* also is used to describe supply curves. An extremely steep or almost vertical supply curve, often found in the short run, is called **inelastic supply** because the quantity supplied does not stretch much (if at all) if the price is raised. A flatter curve is called **elastic supply** because the quantity supplied does stretch more if the price is raised. A slightly up-sloping supply curve is typical in longer-run market situations. Given more time, suppliers have a chance to adjust their offerings, and competitors may enter or leave the market.

DEMAND AND SUPPLY INTERACT TO DETERMINE THE SIZE OF THE MARKET AND PRICE LEVEL

We have treated market demand and supply forces separately. Now we must bring them together to show their interaction. The *intersection* of these two forces determines the size of the market and the market price—at which point (price and quantity) the market is said to be in *equilibrium*.

The intersection of demand and supply is shown for the rice data discussed above. In Exhibit A-10, the demand curve for rice is now graphed against the supply curve in Exhibit A-9.

In this rice market, demand is inelastic—the total revenue of all the rice producers would be greater at higher prices. But the market price is at the **equilibrium point**—where the quantity and the price sellers are willing to offer are equal to the quantity and price that buyers are willing to accept. The $1.00 equilibrium price for rice yields a smaller *total revenue* to rice producers than a higher price would. This lower equilibrium price comes about because the many producers are willing to supply enough rice at the lower price. *Demand is not the only determiner of price level. Cost also must be considered—via the supply curve.*

Exhibit A-10
Equilibrium of Supply and
Demand for Rice
(1 kilogram bag)

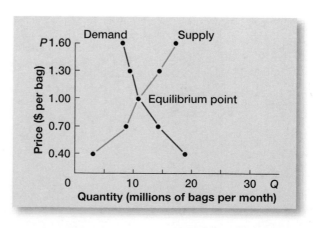

Some consumers get a surplus

Presumably, a sale takes place only if both buyer and seller feel they will be better off after the sale. But sometimes the price a consumer pays in a sales transaction is less than what he or she would be willing to pay.

The reason for this is that demand curves are typically down-sloping, and some of the demand curve is above the equilibrium price. This is simply another way of showing that some customers would have been willing to pay more than the equilibrium price—if they had to. In effect, some of them are getting a bargain by being able to buy at the equilibrium price. Economists have traditionally called these bargains the **consumer surplus**—that is, the difference to consumers between the value of a purchase and the price they pay.

Some business critics assume that consumers do badly in any business transaction. In fact, sales take place only if consumers feel they are at least getting their money's worth. As we can see here, some are willing to pay much more than the market price.

CONCLUSION

The economist's traditional demand and supply analysis provides a useful tool for analyzing the nature of demand and competition. It is especially important that you master the concepts of a demand curve and demand elasticity. How demand and supply interact helps determine the size of a market and its price level.

The nature of supply and demand is very important in marketing strategy planning. We discuss these topics more fully in Chapters 3 and 4 and then build on them throughout the text. This appendix provides a good foundation on these topics.

KEY TERMS

law of diminishing demand, 528

demand curve, 528

inelastic demand, 530

elastic demand, 530

substitutes, 531

supply curve, 533

inelastic supply, 534

elastic supply, 534

equilibrium point, 534

consumer surplus, 535

QUESTIONS AND PROBLEMS

1. Explain in your own words how economists look at markets and arrive at the "law of diminishing demand."

2. Explain what a demand curve is and why it is usually down-sloping. Then give an example of a product for which the demand curve might not be down-sloping over some possible price ranges. Explain the reason for your choice.

3. What is the length of life of the typical demand curve? Illustrate your answer.

4. If the general market demand for men's shoes is fairly elastic, how does the demand for men's dress shoes compare to it? How does the demand curve for

women's shoes compare to the demand curve for men's shoes?

5. If the demand for perfume is inelastic above and below the present price, should the price be raised? Why or why not?

6. If the demand for shrimp is highly elastic below the present price, should the price be lowered?

7. Discuss what factors lead to inelastic demand and supply curves. Are they likely to be found together in the same situation?

8. Why would a marketing manager prefer to sell a product that has no close substitutes? Are high profits almost guaranteed?

Marketing Arithmetic

WHEN YOU FINISH THIS APPENDIX, YOU SHOULD

1. Understand the components of an operating statement (profit and loss statement).

2. Know how to compute the stockturn rate.

3. Understand how operating ratios can help analyze a business.

4. Understand how to calculate markups and markdowns.

5. Understand how to calculate return on investment (ROI) and return on assets (ROA).

Marketing students must become familiar with the essentials of the language of business. Businesspeople commonly use accounting terms when talking about costs, prices, and profit. And using accounting data is a practical tool in analyzing marketing problems.

THE OPERATING STATEMENT

An **operating statement** is a simple summary of the financial results of a company's operations over a specified period of time. Some beginning students may feel that the operating statement is complex, but as we'll soon see, this really isn't true. *The main purpose of the operating statement is determining the net profit figure and presenting data to support that figure.* This is why the operating statement is often referred to as the *profit and loss statement.*

Exhibit B-1 shows an operating statement for a wholesale or retail business. The statement is complete and detailed so you will see the framework throughout the discussion, but the amount of detail on an operating statement is *not* standardized. Many companies use financial statements with much less detail than this one. They emphasize clarity and readability rather than detail. To really understand an operating statement, however, you must know about its components.

Only three basic components

The basic components of an operating statement are *sales*—which come from the sale of goods and services; *costs*—which come from the producing and selling process; and the balance—called *profit or loss*—which is just the difference between sales and costs. So there are only three basic components in the statement: sales, costs, and profit (or loss). Other items on an operating statement are there only to provide supporting details.

Time period covered may vary

There is no one time period an operating statement covers. Rather, statements are prepared to satisfy the needs of a particular business. This may be at the end of each day or at the end of each week. Usually, however, an operating statement summarizes results for one month, three months, six months, or a full year. Since the time period does vary, this information is included in the heading of the statement as follows:

> **Perry Company**
> Operating Statement
> For the (Period) Ended (Date)

Also see Exhibit B-1.

Management uses of operating statements

Before going on to a more detailed discussion of the components of our operating statement, let's think about some of the uses for such a statement. Exhibit B-1 shows that a lot of information is presented in a clear and concise manner. With this information, a manager can easily find the relation of net sales to the cost of sales, the gross margin, expenses, and net profit. Opening and closing inventory figures are available—as is the amount spent during the period for the purchase of goods for resale. Total expenses are listed to make it easier to compare them with previous statements and to help control these expenses.

All this information is important to a company's managers. Assume that a particular company prepares monthly operating statements. A series of these statements is a valuable tool for directing and controlling the business. By comparing results from one month to the next, managers can uncover unfavourable trends in the sales, costs, or profit areas of the business and take any needed action.

Perry Company
Operating Statement
For the Year Ended December 31, 200X

Gross sales			$540,000
Less: Returns and allowances			40,000
Net sales			$500,000
Cost of sales:			
Beginning inventory at cost		$ 80,000	
Purchases at billed cost	$310,000		
Less: Purchase discounts	40,000		
Purchases at net cost	270,000		
Plus: freight-in	20,000		
Net cost of delivered purchases		290,000	
Cost of goods available for sale		370,000	
Less: Ending inventory at cost		70,000	
Cost of sales			300,000
Gross margin (gross profit)			200,000
Expenses:			
Selling expenses:			
Sales salaries	60,000		
Advertising expense	20,000		
Web site updates	10,000		
Delivery expense	10,000		
Total selling expense		100,000	
Administrative expense:			
Office salaries	30,000		
Office supplies	10,000		
Miscellaneous administrative expense	5,000		
Total administrative expense		45,000	
General expense:			
Rent expense	10,000		
Miscellaneous general expenses	5,000		
Total general expense		15,000	
Total expenses			160,000
Net profit from operation			$ 40,000

A skeleton statement gets down to essential details

Let's refer to Exhibit B-1 and begin to analyze this seemingly detailed statement to get first-hand knowledge of the components of the operating statement.

As a first step, suppose we take all the items that have dollar amounts extended to the third, or right-hand, column. Using these items only, the operating statement looks like this:

Gross sales	$540,000
Less: Returns and allowances	40,000
Net sales	500,000
Less: Cost of sales	300,000
Gross margin	200,000
Less: Total expenses	160,000
Net profit (loss)	$ 40,000

Is this a complete operating statement? The answer is *yes*. This skeleton statement differs from Exhibit B-1 only in supporting detail. All the basic components are included. In fact, the only items we must list to have a complete operating statement are

Net sales	$500,000
Less: Costs	460,000
Net profit (loss)	$ 40,000

These three items are the essentials of an operating statement. All other subdivisions or details are just useful additions.

Meaning of sales

Now let's define the meaning of the terms in the skeleton statement.

The first item is sales. What do we mean by sales? The term **gross sales** is the total amount charged to all customers during some time period. However, there is always some customer dissatisfaction or just plain errors in ordering and shipping goods. This results in returns and allowances, which reduce gross sales.

A **return** occurs when a customer sends back purchased products. The company either refunds the purchase price or allows the customer dollar credit on other purchases.

An **allowance** usually occurs when a customer is not satisfied with a purchase for some reason. A department store might give you a price reduction for a scratch on your new appliance rather than have it shipped back to the warehouse. You're happy and they avoid return shipping costs and the problem of dealing with a used and scratched appliance. The company gives a price reduction on the original invoice (bill), but the customer keeps the goods and services.

These refunds and price reductions must be considered when the firm computes its net sales figure for the period. Really, we're only interested in the revenue the company manages to keep. This is **net sales**—the actual sales dollars the company receives. Therefore, all reductions, refunds, cancellations, and so forth made because of returns and allowances are deducted from the original total (gross sales) to get net sales. This is shown below.

Gross sales	$540,000
Less: Returns and allowances	40,000
Net sales	$500,000

Meaning of cost of sales

The next item in the operating statement—**cost of sales**—is the total value (at cost) of the sales during the period. We'll discuss this computation later. Meanwhile, note that after we obtain the cost of sales figure, we subtract it from the net sales figure to get the gross margin.

Meaning of gross margin and expenses

Gross margin (gross profit) is the money left to cover the expenses of selling the products and operating the business. Firms hope that a profit will be left after subtracting these expenses.

Selling expense is commonly the major expense below the gross margin. Note that in Exhibit B-1, **expenses** are all the remaining costs subtracted from the gross margin to get the net profit. The expenses in this case are the selling, administrative, and general expenses. (Note that the cost of purchases and cost of sales are not included in this total expense figure—they were subtracted from net sales earlier to get the gross margin. Note, also, that some accountants refer to cost of sales as cost of goods sold.)

Net profit—at the bottom of the statement—is what the company earned from its operations during a particular period. It is the amount left after the cost of sales and the expenses are subtracted from net sales. *Net sales and net profit are not the same.* Many firms have large sales and no profits—they may even have losses! That's why understanding costs, and controlling them, is important.

DETAILED ANALYSIS OF SECTIONS OF THE OPERATING STATEMENT

Cost of sales for a wholesale or retail company

The cost of sales section includes details that are used to find the cost of sales ($300,000 in our example).

In Exhibit B-1, you can see that beginning and ending inventory, purchases, purchase discounts, and freight-in are all necessary to calculate cost of sales. If we pull the cost of sales section from the operating statement, it looks like this:

Cost of sales:		
Beginning inventory at cost		$ 80,000
Purchases at billed cost	$310,000	
Less: Purchase discounts	40,000	
Purchases at net cost	270,000	
Plus: Freight-in	20,000	
Net cost of delivered purchases		290,000
Cost of goods available for sale		370,000
Less: Ending inventory at cost		70,000
Cost of sales		$300,000

Cost of sales is the cost value of what is *sold*, not the cost of goods on hand at any given time.

Inventory figures merely show the cost of goods on hand at the beginning and end of the period the statement covers. These figures may be obtained by physically counting goods on hand on these dates or estimated from perpetual inventory records that show the inventory balance at any given time. The methods used to determine the inventory should be as accurate as possible because these figures affect the cost of sales during the period and net profit.

The net cost of delivered purchases must include freight charges and purchase discounts received since these items affect the money actually spent to buy goods and bring them to the place of business. A **purchase discount** is a reduction of the original invoice amount for some business reason. For example, a cash discount may be given for prompt payment of the amount due. We subtract the total of such discounts from the original invoice cost of purchases to get the *net* cost of purchases. To this figure we add the freight charges for bringing the goods to the place of business. This gives the net cost of *delivered* purchases. When we add the net cost of delivered purchases to the beginning inventory at cost, we have the total cost of goods available for sale during the period. If we now subtract the ending inventory at cost from the cost of the goods available for sale, we get the cost of sales.

One important point should be noted about cost of sales. The way the value of inventory is calculated varies from one company to another—and it can cause big differences in the cost of sales and the operating statement. (See any basic accounting textbook for how the various inventory valuation methods work.)

Cost of sales for a manufacturing company

Exhibit B-1 shows the way the manager of a wholesale or retail business arrives at his cost of sales. Such a business *purchases* finished products and resells them. In a manufacturing company, the purchases section of this operating statement is replaced by a section called cost of production. This section includes purchases of

Exhibit B-2
Cost of Sales Section of an
Operating Statement for a
Manufacturing Firm

Cost of sales:		
Finished products inventory (beginning)	$ 20,000	
Cost of production (Schedule 1)	100,000	
Total cost of finished products available for sale	120,000	
Less: Finished products inventory (ending) ...	30,000	
Cost of sales		$ 90,000

Schedule 1, Schedule of cost of production

Beginning work in process inventory		15,000
Raw materials:		
Beginning raw materials inventory	10,000	
Net cost of delivered purchases	80,000	
Total cost of materials available for use	90,000	
Less: Ending raw materials inventory	15,000	
Cost of materials placed in production	75,000	
Direct labour	20,000	
Manufacturing expenses:		
Indirect labour $4,000		
Maintenance and repairs 3,000		
Factory supplies 1,000		
Heat, light, and power 2,000		
Total manufacturing expenses	10,000	
Total manufacturing costs		105,000
Total work in process during period		120,000
Less: Ending work in process inventory		20,000
Cost of production		$100,000

raw materials and parts, direct and indirect labour costs, and factory overhead charges (such as heat, light, and power) that are necessary to produce finished products. The cost of production is added to the beginning finished products inventory to arrive at the cost of products available for sale. Often, a separate cost of production statement is prepared, and only the total cost of production is shown in the operating statement. See Exhibit B-2 for an illustration of the cost of sales section of an operating statement for a manufacturing company.

Expenses

Expenses go below the gross margin. They usually include the costs of selling and the costs of administering the business. They do not include the cost of sales, either purchased or produced.

There is no right method for classifying the expense accounts or arranging them on the operating statement. They can just as easily be arranged alphabetically or according to amount, with the largest placed at the top and so on down the line. In a business of any size, though, it is clearer to group the expenses in some way and use subtotals by groups for analysis and control purposes. This was done in Exhibit B-1.

Summary on operating statements

The statement presented in Exhibit B-1 contains all the major categories in an operating statement—together with a normal amount of supporting detail. Further detail can be added to the statement under any of the major categories without changing the nature of the statement. The amount of detail normally is determined by how the statement will be used. A shareholder may be given a sketchy operating statement—while the one prepared for internal company use may have a lot of detail. Even so, in the post-financial meltdown of companies like Nortel and Enron, full and detailed disclosure of accounting information is drawing much more attention than previously from organizations like the Toronto Stock Exchange.

COMPUTING THE STOCKTURN RATE

A detailed operating statement can provide the data needed to compute the **stockturn rate**—a measure of the number of times the average inventory is sold during a year. Note that the stockturn rate is related to the *turnover during a year,* not the length of time covered by a particular operating statement.

The stockturn rate is a very important measure because it shows how rapidly the firm's inventory is moving. Some businesses typically have slower turnover than others. But a drop in turnover in a particular business can be very alarming. It may mean that the firm's assortment of products is no longer as attractive as it was. Also, it may mean that the firm will need more working capital to handle the same volume of sales. Most businesses pay a lot of attention to the stockturn rate, trying to get faster turnover (and lower inventory costs).

Three methods, all basically similar, can be used to compute the stockturn rate. Which method is used depends on the data available. These three methods, which usually give approximately the same results, are shown below.*

(1) $$\frac{\text{Cost of Sales}}{\text{Average Inventory at Cost}}$$

(2) $$\frac{\text{Net Sales}}{\text{Average Inventory at Selling Price}}$$

(3) $$\frac{\text{Sales in Units}}{\text{Average Inventory in Units}}$$

Computing the stockturn rate will be illustrated only for Formula 1, since all are similar. The only difference is that the cost figures used in Formula 1 are changed to a selling price or numerical count basis in Formulas 2 and 3. Note: Regardless of the method used, you must have both the numerator and denominator of the formula in the same terms.

If the inventory level varies a lot during the year, you may need detailed information about the inventory level at different times to compute the average inventory. If it stays at about the same level during the year, however, it's easy to get an estimate. For example, using Formula 1, the average inventory at cost is computed by adding the beginning and ending inventories at cost and dividing by 2. This average inventory figure is then divided into the cost of sales (in cost terms) to get the stockturn rate.

For example, suppose that the cost of sales for one year was $1,000,000. Beginning inventory was $250,000 and ending inventory $150,000. Adding the two inventory figures and dividing by 2, we get an average inventory of $200,000. We next divide the cost of sales by the average inventory ($1,000,000 ÷ $200,000) and get a stockturn rate of 5.

OPERATING RATIOS HELP ANALYZE THE BUSINESS

Many businesspeople use the operating statement to calculate **operating ratios**—the ratio of items on the operating statement to net sales—and to compare these ratios from one time period to another. They can also compare their own operating ratios with those of competitors. Such competitive data is often available through trade associations. Each firm may report its results to a trade association,

---

*Differences occur because of varied markups and nonhomogeneous product assortments. In an assortment of tires, for example, those with low markups might have sold much better than those with high markups. But with Formula 3, all tires would be treated equally.

which then distributes summary results to its members. These ratios help managers control their operations. If some expense ratios are rising, for example, those particular costs are singled out for special attention.

Operating ratios are computed by dividing net sales into the various operating statement items that appear below the net sales level in the operating statement. The net sales is used as the denominator in the operating ratio because it shows the sales the firm actually won.

We can see the relation of operating ratios to the operating statement if we think of there being another column to the right of the dollar figures in an operating statement. This column contains percentage figures, using net sales as 100 percent. This approach can be seen below.

Gross sales	$540,000	
Less: Returns and allowances	40,000	
Net sales	500,000	100%
Less: Cost of sales	300,000	60
Gross margin	200,000	40
Less: Total expenses	160,000	32
Net profit	$ 40,000	8%

$$\frac{\text{Gross Margin}}{\text{Net Sales}} = \frac{200,000}{500,000} = 40\%$$

In the above example, the 40 percent ratio of gross margin to net sales shows that 40 percent of the net sales dollar is available to cover sales expenses and administering the business to provide a profit.

$$\frac{\text{Total Expenses}}{\text{Net Sales}} = \frac{160,000}{500,000} = 32\%$$

$$\frac{\text{Net Profit}}{\text{Net Sales}} = \frac{40,000}{500,000} = 8\%$$

The ratio of total expenses of sales (32 percent) added to the ratio of net profit to sales (8 percent) equals the 40 percent gross margin ratio.

The net profit ratio shows that 8 percent of the net sales dollar is left for profit.

The value of percentage ratios should be obvious. The percentages are easily figured and much easier to compare than large dollar figures.

Note that because these operating statement categories are interrelated, only a few pieces of information are needed to figure the others. In this case, for example, knowing the gross margin percent and net profit percent makes it possible to figure the expenses and cost of sales percentages. Further, knowing just one dollar amount and the percentages lets you figure all the other dollar amounts.

MARKUPS

A markup is the dollar amount added to the cost of sales to get the selling price. The markup usually is similar to the firm's gross margin because the markup amount added onto the unit cost of a product by a retailer or wholesaler is expected to cover the selling and administrative expenses and to provide a profit. A simple example illustrates the idea. If a retailer buys an article that costs $1 when delivered to his store, he must sell it for more than this cost if he hopes to make a profit. So he might add 50 cents onto the cost of the article to cover his selling and other costs and, hopefully, to provide a profit. The 50 cents is the markup.

The 50 cents is also the gross margin or gross profit from that item *if* it is sold. But note that it is *not* the net profit. Selling expenses may amount to 35 cents, 45 cents, or even 55 cents. In other words, there is no guarantee the markup will cover costs. Further, there is no guarantee customers will buy at the marked-up price. This may require markdowns, which are discussed later.

Markup conversions

Often it is convenient to use markups as percentages rather than focusing on the actual dollar amounts. But markups can be figured as a percent of cost or selling price. To have some agreement, *markup (percent)* will mean percentage of selling price unless stated otherwise. So the 50-cent markup on the $1.50 selling price is a markup of 33 ⅓ percent. On the other hand, the 50-cent markup is a 50 percent markup on cost.

Some retailers and wholesalers use markup conversion tables or spreadsheets to easily convert from cost to selling price, depending on the markup on selling price they want. To see the interrelation, look at the two formulas below. They can be used to convert either type of markup to the other.

(4) $\quad \dfrac{\text{Percent markup}}{\text{on selling price}} = \dfrac{\text{Percent markup on cost}}{100\% + \text{Percent markup on cost}}$

(5) $\quad \dfrac{\text{Percent markup}}{\text{on cost}} = \dfrac{\text{Percent markup on selling price}}{100\% - \text{Percent markup on selling price}}$

In the previous example, we had a cost of $1, a markup of 50 cents, and a selling price of $1.50. We saw that the markup on selling price was 33 ⅓ percent—and on cost, it was 50 percent. Let's substitute these percentage figures—in Formulas 4 and 5—to see how to convert from one basis to the other. Assume first of all that we only know the markup on selling price and want to convert to markup on cost. Using Formula 5, we get

$$\text{Percent markup on cost} = \frac{33\,⅓\%}{100\% - 33\,⅓\%} = \frac{33\,⅓\%}{66\,⅔\%} = 50\%$$

On the other hand, if we know only the percent markup on cost, we can convert to markup on selling price as follows:

$$\text{Percent markup on selling price} = \frac{50\%}{100\% + 50\%} = \frac{50\%}{150\%} = 33\,⅓\%$$

These results can be proved and summarized as follows:

Markup $0.50 = 50\%$ of cost, or 33 ⅓% of selling price

$\dfrac{+ \text{ Cost } \$1.00 = 100\% \text{ of cost, or } 66\,⅔\% \text{ of selling price}}{\text{Selling price } \$1.50 = 150\% \text{ of cost, or } 100\% \text{ of selling price}}$

Note that when the selling price ($1.50) is the base for a markup calculation, the markup percent (33 ⅓ percent = $.50/$1.50) must be less than 100 percent. As you can see, that's because the markup percent and the cost percent (66 ⅔ percent = $1.00/$1.50) sums to exactly 100 percent. So if you see a reference to a markup percent that is greater than 100 percent, it could not be based on the selling price and instead must be based on cost.

MARKDOWN RATIOS HELP CONTROL RETAIL OPERATIONS

The ratios we discussed above were concerned with figures on the operating statement. Another important ratio, the **markdown ratio**, is a tool many retailers use to measure the efficiency of various departments and their whole business. But note that it is *not directly related to the operating statement*. It requires special calculations.

A **markdown** is a retail price reduction required because customers won't buy some item at the originally marked-up price. This refusal to buy may be due to a variety of reasons—soiling, style changes, fading, damage caused by handling, or an original price that was too high. Sears may have to mark down its lawn mowers in August because it doesn't want to be caught with excess inventory at the end of the summer season. To get rid of these products, the retailer offers them at a lower price.

Markdowns are generally considered to be due to business errors, perhaps because of poor buying, original markups that are too high, and other reasons. (Note, however, that some retailers use markdowns as a way of doing business rather than a way to correct errors. For example, a store that buys out overstocked fashions from other retailers may start by marking each item with a high price and then reduce the price each week until it sells. Heavy discounters like Liquidation World use this strategy.) Regardless of the reason, however, markdowns are reductions in the original price—and they are important to managers who want to measure the effectiveness of their operations.

Markdowns are similar to allowances because price reductions are made. Thus, in computing a markdown ratio, markdowns and allowances are usually added together and then divided by net sales. The markdown ratio is computed as follows:

$$\text{Markdown \%} = \frac{\text{\$ Markdowns} + \text{\$ Allowances}}{\text{\$ Net sales}} \times 100$$

The 100 is multiplied by the fraction to get rid of decimal points.

Returns are *not* included when figuring the markdown ratio. Returns are treated as consumer errors, not business errors, and therefore are not included in this measure of business efficiency.

Retailers who use markdown ratios usually keep a record of the amount of markdowns and allowances in each department and then divide the total by the net sales in each department. Over a period of time, these ratios give management one measure of the efficiency of buyers and salespeople in various departments.

It should be stressed again that the markdown ratio is not calculated directly from data on the operating statement since the markdowns take place before the products are sold. In fact, some products may be marked down and still not sold. Even if the marked-down items are not sold, the markdowns—that is, the reevaluations of their value—are included in the calculations in the time period when they are taken.

The markdown ratio is calculated for a whole department (or profit center), *not* individual items. What we are seeking is a measure of the effectiveness of a whole department, not how well the department did on individual items.

RETURN ON INVESTMENT (ROI) REFLECTS ASSET USE

Another off-the-operating-statement ratio is **return on investment (ROI)**—the ratio of net profit (after taxes) to the investment used to make the net profit, multiplied by 100 to get rid of decimals. Investment is not shown on the operating statement. But it is on the **balance sheet** (statement of financial condition), another accounting statement, which shows a company's assets, liabilities, and net worth. It may take some digging or special analysis, however, to find the right investment number.

Investment means the dollar resources the firm has invested in a project or business. For example, a new product may require $4 million in new money—for inventory, accounts receivable, promotion, and so on—and its attractiveness may be judged by its likely ROI. If the net profit (after taxes) for this new product is expected to be $1 million in the first year, then the ROI is 25 percent—that is, ($1 million ÷ $4 million) × 100.

There are two ways to figure ROI. The *direct* way is

$$\text{ROI (in \%)} = \frac{\text{Net profit (after taxes)}}{\text{Investment}} \times 100$$

The *indirect* way is

$$\text{ROI (in \%)} = \frac{\text{Net profit (after taxes)}}{\text{Sales}} = \frac{\text{Sales}}{\text{Investment}} \times 100$$

This way is concerned with net profit margin and turnover—that is,

$$\text{ROI (in \%)} = \text{Net profit margin} \times \text{Turnover} \times 100$$

This indirect way makes it clearer how to *increase* ROI. There are three ways:

1. Increase profit margin (with lower costs or a higher price).
2. Increase sales.
3. Decrease investment.

Effective marketing strategy planning and implementation can increase profit margins or sales, or both. And careful asset management can decrease investment.

ROI is a revealing measure of how well managers are doing. Most companies have alternative uses for their funds. If the returns in a business aren't at least as high as outside uses, then the money probably should be shifted to the more profitable uses.

Some firms borrow more than others to make investments. In other words, they invest less of their own money to acquire assets—what we called *investments*. If ROI calculations use only the firm's own investment, this gives higher ROI figures to those who borrow a lot—which is called *leveraging*. To adjust for different borrowing proportions—to make comparisons among projects, departments, divisions, and companies easier—another ratio has come into use. **Return on assets (ROA)** is the ratio of net profit (after taxes) to the assets used to make the net profit—times 100. Both ROI and ROA measures are trying to get at the same thing—how effectively the company is using resources. These measures became increasingly popular as profit rates dropped and it became more obvious that increasing sales volume doesn't necessarily lead to higher profits—or ROI or ROA. Inflation and higher costs for borrowed funds also force more concern for ROI and ROA. Marketers must include these measures in their thinking or top managers are likely to ignore their plans and requests for financial resources.

KEY TERMS

QUESTIONS AND PROBLEMS

1. Distinguish between the following pairs of items that appear on operating statements: (*a*) gross sales and net sales, and (*b*) purchases at billed cost and purchases at net cost.

2. How does gross margin differ from gross profit? From net profit?

3. Explain the similarity between markups and gross margin. What connection do markdowns have with the operating statement?

4. Compute the net profit for a company with the following data:

Beginning inventory (cost)	$ 150,000
Purchases at billed cost	330,000
Sales returns and allowances	250,000
Rent	60,000
Salaries	400,000
Heat and light	180,000
Ending inventory (cost)	250,000
Freight cost (inbound)	80,000
Gross sales	1,300,000

5. Construct an operating statement from the following data:

Returns and allowances	$150,000
Expenses	20%
Closing inventory at cost	600,000
Markdowns	2%
Inward transportation	30,000
Purchases	1,000,000
Net profit (5%)	300,000

6. Compute net sales and percent of markdowns for the data given below:

Markdowns	$ 40,000
Gross sales	400,000
Returns	32,000
Allowances	48,000

7. (*a*) What percentage markups on cost are equivalent to the following percentage markups on selling price: 20, 37½, 50, and 66⅔? (*b*) What percentage markups on selling price are equivalent to the following percentage markups on cost: 33⅓, 20, 40, and 50?

8. What net sales volume is required to obtain a stock-turn rate of 20 times a year on an average inventory at cost of $100,000 with a gross margin of 25 percent?

9. Explain how the general manager of a department store might use the markdown ratios computed for her various departments. Is this a fair measure? Of what?

10. Compare and contrast return on investment (ROI) and return on assets (ROA) measures. Which would be best for a retailer with no bank borrowing or other outside sources of funds (that is, the retailer has put up all the money that the business needs)?

Notes

CHAPTER 1

1. For more on Starbucks, see "The Virtually Cashless Society," *BusinessWeek*, November 17, 2003, p. 125; "Starbucks Unwired," *BusinessWeek*, November 10, 2003, pp. A20–A21; "Starbucks Brews Up New Prepaid Card," *USA Today*, October 13, 2003, p. 2B; "Not a Johnny-Come-Latte," *USA Today*, September 9, 2003, p. 3B; "Starbucks Gives Chile a Chance to Wake Up and Smell the Coffee," *The Wall Street Journal*, August 27, 2003, p. B3A; "At Starbucks, the Future Is in Plastic," *Business 2.0*, August 2003, p. 56; "Tea, Coffee Energizing Multiple Retail Segments," *Food Retailing Today*, July 21, 2003, p. 10; "Starbucks' Road to China," *The Wall Street Journal*, July 14, 2003, p. B1; "In Japan, Adding Beer, Wine to Latte List," *The Wall Street Journal*, July 14, 2003, p. B1; "Another Overpriced Coffee Option," *The Wall Street Journal*, June 17, 2003, p. D1; "We've Jumped the Shark," *Brandweek*, June 2, 2003, p. 28; "Starbucks Adds Buzz to DoubleShot, Frappuccino Drinks with New Push," *Brandweek*, May 12, 2003, p. 9; "Mr. Coffee," *Fortune*, April 14, 2003, p. 139; "Marketers of the Next Generation," *Brandweek*, April 7, 2003, p. 40; "Chain Brewing Rewards for Latte Lovers," *Investor's Business Daily*, April 2, 2003, p. A6; "America's Most Admired Companies," *Fortune*, March 3, 2003, p. 87; "Starbucks Plans to Offer Its Own Credit Card in Fall," *The New York Times*, February 21, 2003, p. C6; "Wi-Fi Connects as a Marketing Tool," *Advertising Age (Special Report Technology Marketing)*, January 27, 2003, p. S2; "Counting Beans: Despite the Jitters, Most Coffeehouses Survive Starbucks," *The Wall Street Journal*, September 24, 2002, p. A1; "Starbucks' Asian Tea Party," *BusinessWeek*, September 23, 2002, p. 14; "Planet Starbucks," *BusinessWeek*, September 9, 2002, p. 100; "Starbucks May Indeed Be a Robust Staple," *The Wall Street Journal*, July 26, 2002, p. B4; "Starbucks Corp. Overseas Growth Plan Should Have Its Perks," *Investor's Business Daily*, June 14, 2002, p. A7; "Starbucks Goes to Europe . . . with Humility and Respect," *The Wall Street Journal*, April 9, 2002, p. B16; "The Best Global Brands," *BusinessWeek*, August 6, 2001, p. 56; "Starbucks Fills Asia's Cup," *USA Today*, June 7, 2000, p. 10B; "Now, Starbucks Uses Its Bean," *BusinessWeek*, February 14, 2000, p. 92; "Trouble Brewing," *Newsweek*, July 19, 1999, p. 40; "Battle Grounds," *Inc.*, July 1999, p. 52; "Still Perking after All These Years," *Fortune*, May 24, 1999, p. 203; "Starbucks.com Will Let Coffee Drinkers Get Wired," *Brandweek*, April 27, 1998, p. 33; "Starbucks: Making Values Pay," *Fortune*, September 29, 1997, p. 261; "Restaurant Brands Fill Supermarkets," *USA Today*, August 26, 1997, p. 1B.

2. Eric H. Shaw, "A Review of Empirical Studies of Aggregate Marketing Costs and Productivity in the United States," *Journal of the Academy of Marketing Science*, Fall, 1990, p. 285; Christopher H. Lovelock and Charles B. Weinberg, *Marketing for Public and Nonprofit Managers* (New York: John Wiley & Sons, 1984).

3. Gregory D. Upah and Richard E. Wokutch, "Assessing Social Impacts of New Products: An Attempt to Operationalize the Macromarketing Concept," *Journal of Public Policy and Marketing* 4 (1985), p. 166.

4. An American Marketing Association committee developed a similar—but more complicated—definition of marketing: "Marketing is the process of planning and executing conception, pricing, promotion, and distribution of ideas, goods, and services to create exchanges that satisfy individual and organizational objectives." See *Marketing News*, March 1, 1985, p. 1. See also Ernest F. Cooke, C. L. Abercrombie, and J. Michael Rayburn, "Problems With the AMA's New Definition of Marketing Offer Opportunity to Develop an Even Better Definition," *Marketing Educator*, Spring 1986, p. 1.

5. George Fisk, "Editor's Working Definition of Macromarketing," *Journal of Macromarketing* 2, no. 1 (1982), p. 3; Shelby D. Hunt and John J. Burnett, "The Macromarketing/ Micromarketing Dichotomy: A Taxonomical Model," *Journal of Marketing*, Summer 1982, p. 11.

6. Fang Wu, Vijay Mahajan, and Sridhar Balasubramanian, "An Analysis of E-Business Adoption and its Impact on Business Performance," *Journal of the Academy of Marketing Science*, Fall 2003, p. 425; Peter R. Dickson, "Understanding the Trade Winds: the Global Evolution of Production, Consumption, and the Internet," *Journal of Consumer Research*, June 2000, p. 115; Hans H. Bauer, Mark Grether, and Mark Leach, "Building Customer Relations over the Internet," *Industrial Marketing Management*, February 2002, p. 155; Roger A. Layton, "Measures of Structural Change in Macromarketing Systems," *Journal of Macromarketing*, Spring 1989, p. 5.

7. Graham Hooley, Tony Cox, John Fahy, David Shipley et al. "Market Orientation in the Transition Economies of Central Europe: Tests of the Narver and Slater Market Orientation Scales," *Journal of Business Research*, December 2000, p. 273; Saeed Samiee, "Globalization, Privatization, and Free Market Economy," *Journal of the Academy of Marketing Science*, Summer 2001, p. 319; Robert A. Peterson and Ashutosh Prasad, "A General Theory of Competition: Resources, Competencies, Productivity, Economic Growth," *Journal of the Academy of Marketing Science*, Fall 2001, p. 422; Robert W. Nason and Phillip D. White, "The Visions of Charles C. Slater: Social Consequences of Marketing," *Journal of Macromarketing* 1, no. 2 (1981), p. 4.

8. "Making Sense of India," *Newsweek*, August 4, 1997, p. 41; "In Rural India, Video Vans Sell Toothpaste, and Shampoo," *The Wall Street Journal*, January 10, 1996, p. B1. See also "Good Reason for Smiles: Colgate Brings Dental Care to Brazilian Indian Tribes, Ravages of Tobacco and Rice," *The Wall Street Journal*, July 23, 2003, p. B1.

9. Dave Webb, Cynthia Webster, and Areti Krepapa, "An Exploration of the Meaning and Outcomes of a Customer-Defined Market Orientation," *Journal of Business Research*, May 2000, p. 101; Jagdish N. Sheth, Rajendra S. Sisodia, and Arun Sharma, "The Antecedents and Consequences of Customer-Centric Marketing," *Journal of the Academy of Marketing Science*, Winter 2000, p. 55; Ken Matsuno, John T. Mentzer, and Aysegul Ozsomer, "The Effects of Entrepreneurial Proclivity and Market Orientation on Business Performance," *Journal of Marketing*, July 2002, p. 18; Karen Norman Kennedy, Jerry R. Goolsby, and Eric J. Arnould, "Implementing a Customer Orientation: Extension of Theory and Application," *Journal of Marketing*, October 2003, p. 67; Karen Norman Kennedy, Felicia G. Lassk, and Jerry R. Goolsby, "Customer Mind-Set of Employees Throughout the Organization," *Journal of the Academy of Marketing Science*, Spring 2002, p. 159. See also Charles R. Weiser, "Championing the Customer," *Harvard Business Review*, November–December 1995, p. 113; Stanley F. Slater and John C. Narver, "Market Orientation and the Learning Organization," *Journal of Marketing*, July 1995, p. 63; Regina F. Maruca, "Getting Marketing's Voice Heard," *Harvard Business Review*, January–February 1998, p. 10; Christine Steinman, "Beyond Market Orientation: When Customers and Suppliers Disagree," *Journal of the Academy of Marketing Science*, Winter 2000, p. 109; R.W. Ruekert, "Developing a Market Orientation: An Organizational Strategy Perspective," *International Journal of Research in Marketing*, August 1992,

p. 225; George J. Avlonitis and Spiros P. Gounaris, "Marketing Orientation and Company Performance: Industrial Vs. Consumer Goods Companies," *Industrial Marketing Management*, September 1997, p. 385; Bernard J. Jaworski and Ajay K. Kohli, "Market Orientation: Antecedents and Consequences," *Journal of Marketing*, July 1993, p. 53; Franklin S. Houston, "The Marketing Concept: What It Is and What It Is Not," *Journal of Marketing*, April 1986, p. 81.

10. For more on the marketing concept in the banking industry, see "Service Charge: As Banks Elbow for Consumers, Washington Mutual Thrives," *The Wall Street Journal*, November 6, 2003, p. A1; "Is This Any Way to Run a Bank?" *BusinessWeek*, October 13, 2003, p. 44; "The Hot News in Banking: Bricks and Mortar," *BusinessWeek*, April 21, 2003, p. 83; "Bank of the Americas," *Fortune*, April 14, 2003, p. 144; "A New Banking Model," *Fortune*, March 31, 2003, p. 102; "Doral Financial: Bank Grows New York Business by Luring One Client at a Time," *Investor's Business Daily*, March 27, 2003, p. A6; "Putting Banks in Touch with Their Retailer Side," *The New York Times*, March 9, 2003, Sect. 3, p. 4; "Buy a Toaster, Open a Bank Account," *BusinessWeek*, January 13, 2003, p. 54; "Welcome to the Un-Bank," *Brandweek*, November 4, 2002, p. 28; "Do You Really Need a Bank?" *The Wall Street Journal*, July 10, 2002, p. D1; "Why Banks Are Getting Nicer," *The Wall Street Journal*, May 29, 2002, p. D1; "A Mini-Mall in Your ATM," *Time*, April 8, 2002, p. 61; "Commerce Bancorp: It's a Bank, It's a Retail Firm, It's . . . Both?" *Investor's Business Daily*, February 4, 2002, p. A10; "Branching Out," *Business 2.0*, November 2001, p. 137; "Altering Course, Banks Welcome Check Cashers," *The Wall Street Journal*, July 6, 2001, p. B1; "Banks Cozy Up to Customers," *The Wall Street Journal*, April 26, 2001, p. B1. For more on the marketing concept and churches, see "The Glorious Rise of Christian Pop," *Newsweek*, July 16, 2001, p. 38; "God, Mammon and 'Bibleman,'" *Newsweek*, July 16, 2001, pp. 44–48: "Religious Advertising Converts, Moving Toward a Tougher Sell," *The Wall Street Journal*, February 24, 1998, p. B2. For more on the marketing concept and the academic community, see "Cash-Cow Universities," *BusinessWeek*, November 17, 2003, p. 70; "The New U: A Tough Market Is Reshaping Colleges," *BusinessWeek*, December 22, 1997, p. 96; "Some Small Colleges Hire Recruiters to Get Bigger Freshman Class," *The Wall Street Journal*, September 5, 1995, p. A1. For more on the marketing concept and the dental and medical professions, see "Massaging More than Your Gums," *The Wall Street Journal*, September 11, 2002, p. D1; "Hospitals Use TV Spots to Boost Business," *The Wall Street Journal*, September 26, 1996, p. B10; "Rx: Thirty Minutes on the StairMaster Twice Weekly," *Newsweek*, March 17, 1997, p. 46; "Offering Aerobics, Karate, Aquatics, Hospitals Stress Business of 'Wellness,'" *The Wall Street Journal*, August 9, 1993, p. B1. See also Gary D. Hailey, "The Federal Trade Commission, the Supreme Court and Restrictions on Professional Advertising," *International Journal of Advertising* 8, no. 1 (1989), p. 1.

11. "Remedies for an Economic Hangover," *Fortune*, June 25, 2001, p. 130; "The Best Little Grocery Store in America," *Inc.*, June 2001, p. 54; "Fanatics!" *Inc.*, April 2001, p. 36; "Internet Nirvana," *Ecompany*, December 2000, p. 99; "Why Women Find Lauder Mesmerizing," *Fortune*, May 25, 1998, p. 96; "Smart Managing: The Power of Reflection," *Fortune*, November 24, 1997, p. 291; "Why Some Customers Are More Equal than Others," *Fortune*, September 19, 1994, p. 215. See also Youn-Kyung Kim, "Consumer Value: an Application to Mall and Internet Shopping," *International Journal of Retail & Distribution Management*, (11) 2002, p. 595; Jillian C. Sweeney and Geoffrey N. Soutar, "Consumer Perceived Value: the Development of a Multiple Item Scale," *Journal of Retailing*, Summer 2001, p. 203; Ronald L. Hess, Jr. Shankar Ganesan, and Noreen M. Klein, "Service Failure and Recovery: the Impact of Relationship Factors on Customer Satisfaction," *Journal of the Academy of Marketing Science*, Spring 2003, p. 127; Ziv Carmon and Dan Ariely, "Focusing on the Forgone: How Value Can Appear So Different to Buyers and Sellers," *Journal of Consumer Research*, December 2000, p. 360; Mihaly Csikszentmihalyi, "The Costs and Benefits of Consuming," *Journal of Consumer Research*, September

2000, p. 267; Jaishankar Ganesh, Mark J. Arnold, and Kristy E. Reynolds, "Understanding the Customer Base of Service Providers: an Examination of the Differences Between Switchers and Stayers," *Journal of Marketing*, July 2000, p. 65; Wolfgang Ulaga and Samir Chacour, "Measuring Customer-Perceived Value in Business Markets: a Prerequisite for Marketing Strategy Development and Implementation," *Industrial Marketing Management*, August 2001, p. 525; Maria Jose Sanzo, Maria Leticia Santos, Rodolfo Vazquez and Luis Ignacio Alvarez, "The Effect of Market Orientation on Buyer-Seller Relationship Satisfaction," *Industrial Marketing Management*, May 2003, p. 327; C. B. Bhattacharya and Sankar Sen, "Consumer-Company Identification: a Framework for Understanding Consumers' Relationships with Companies," *Journal of Marketing*, April 2003, p. 76; George S. Day, "Managing Market Relationships," *Journal of the Academy of Marketing Science*, Winter 2000, p. 24; Deepak Sirdeshmukh, Jagdip Singh and Barry Sabol, "Consumer Trust, Value, and Loyalty in Relational Exchanges," *Journal of Marketing*, January 2002, p. 15; Denise D. Schoenbachler and Geoffrey L. Gordon, "Trust and Customer Willingness to Provide Information in Database-Driven Relationship Marketing," *Journal of Interactive Marketing*, Summer 2002, p. 2; Stanley F. Slater and John C. Narver, "Market Orientation, Customer Value, and Superior Performance," *Business Horizons*, March–April 1994, p. 22; Sharon E. Beatty, "Keeping Customers," *Journal of Marketing*, April 1994, p. 124; Thomas W. Gruen, "Relationship Marketing: The Route to Marketing Efficiency and Effectiveness," *Business Horizons*, November–December 1997, p. 32; Diana L. Deadrick, R. B. McAfee, and Myron Glassman, "'Customers for Life': Does It Fit Your Culture?" *Business Horizons*, July–August 1997, p. 11.

12. "Dot-Com Decline Turns into Lift for the Dot-Orgs," *The Wall Street Journal*, March 12, 2001, p. B1; "With Recruiting Slow, the Air Force Seeks a New Ad Campaign," *The Wall Street Journal*, February 14, 2001, p. A1; "Big Retailers Cutting into Nonprofits' Tree Sales," *The Wall Street Journal*, December 19, 2000, p. B1; "When Nonprofits Go After Profits," *BusinessWeek*, June 26, 2000, p. 173; "Army Enlists Net to Be All It Can Be," *USA Today*, April 19, 2000, p. 10B; "Modern Marketing Helps Sell Life as a Nun," *The Wall Street Journal*, May 11, 1999, p. B1; "Charities Draw Younger Donors with Hip Events and Door Prizes," *The Wall Street Journal*, April 25, 1994, p. B1. See also Thomas W. Gruen, John O. Summers, and Frank Acito, "Relationship Marketing Activities, Commitment, and Membership Behaviors in Professional Associations," *Journal of Marketing*, July 2000, p. 34; Glenn B. Voss and Zannie Giraud Voss, "Strategic Orientation and Firm Performance in an Artistic Environment," *Journal of Marketing*, January 2000, p. 67; Dennis B. Arnett, Steve D. German and Shelby D. Hunt, "The Identity Salience Model of Relationship Marketing Success: the Case of Nonprofit Marketing," *Journal of Marketing*, April 2003, p. 89; William A. Sutton, "Sports Marketing: Competitive Business Strategies for Sports," *Journal of the Academy of Marketing Science*, Spring 1996, p. 176; Russell W. Jones, Carolyn Marshall, and Thomas P. Bergman, "Can a Marketing Campaign Be Used to Achieve Public Policy Goals?" *Journal of Public Policy & Marketing*, Spring 1996, p. 98; C. Scott Greene and Paul Miesing, "Public Policy, Technology, and Ethics: Marketing Decisions for NASA's Space Shuttle," *Journal of Marketing*, Summer 1984, p. 56; Alan R. Andreasen, "Nonprofits: Check Your Attention to Customers," *Harvard Business Review*, May–June 1982, p. 105.

13. "The Black Market Vs. the Ozone," *BusinessWeek*, July 7, 1997, p. 128; "CFC-Span: Refrigerant's Reign Nears an End," *USA Today*, August 22, 1994, p. 5B; "Air-Conditioner Firms Put Chill on Plans to Phase Out Use of Chlorofluorocarbons," *The Wall Street Journal*, May 10, 1993, p. B1. See also Alan R. Andreasen, "Social Marketing: Its Definition and Domain," *Journal of Public Policy & Marketing*, Spring 1994, p. 108.

14. For more on Wal-Mart's efforts, see "Wrestling with Your Conscience," *Time*, November 15, 1999, p. 72; "Wal-Mart Provides Many an Introduction to Sport Shooting," *The Wall Street Journal*, April 15, 1999,

p. A1. For more on Kmart's efforts, see "Kmart Sells Out: Ammo Sales End, under Pressure from PC Prankster," *Investor's Business Daily*, July 10, 2001, p. A18. For more on Green Mountain, see "GreenMountain.com Makes Pitch for Clean Energy," *The Wall Street Journal*, May 1, 2000, p. A36; "Energy: Green Fees," *The Wall Street Journal Reports*, September 13, 1999, p. R12. For more on overseas sweatshops, see "Sweatshops: Finally, Airing the Dirty Linen," *BusinessWeek*, June 23, 2003, p. 100. See also Maria Piacentini, Lynn MacFadyen and Douglas Eadie, "Corporate Social Responsibility in Food Retailing," *International Journal of Retail & Distribution Management*, (11) 2000, p. 459.

15. Edward J. O'Boyle and Lyndon E. Dawson, Jr., "The American Marketing Association Code of Ethics: Instructions for Marketers," *Journal of Business Ethics*, December 1992, p. 921; Ellen J. Kennedy and Leigh Lawton, "Ethics and Services Marketing," *Journal of Business Ethics*, October 1993, p. 785; Michael R. Hyman, Robert Skipper, and Richard Tansey, "Ethical Codes Are Not Enough," *Business Horizons*, March/April, 1990, p. 15.

16. Lawrence B. Chonko and Shelby D. Hunt, "Ethics and Marketing Management: a Retrospective and Prospective Commentary," *Journal of Business Research*, December 2000, p. 235; Barry J. Babin, James S. Boles, and Donald P. Robin, "Representing the Perceived Ethical Work Climate among Marketing Employees," *Journal of the Academy of Marketing Science*, Summer 2000, p. 345; Peter J. Vander Nat and William W. Keep, "Marketing Fraud: an Approach for Differentiating Multilevel Marketing from Pyramid Schemes," *Journal of Public Policy & Marketing*, Spring 2002, p. 139; Jeffrey G. Blodgett, Long-Chuan Lu, Gregory M. Rose, and Scott J. Vitell, "Ethical Sensitivity to Stakeholder Interests: a Cross-Cultural Comparison," *Journal of the Academy of Marketing Science*, Spring 2001, p. 190; George G. Brenkert, "Ethical Challenges of Social Marketing," *Journal of Public Policy & Marketing*, Spring 2002, p. 14; Stanley J. Shapiro, "Ethical Decision Making in Marketing," *Journal of Public Policy & Marketing*, Fall 1996, p. 321; Oswald A. Mascarenhas, "Exonerating Unethical Marketing Executive Behaviors: A Diagnostic Framework," *Journal of Marketing*, April 1995, p. 43. For a discussion of some criticisms of advertising, see Banwari Mittal, "Public Assessment of TV Advertising: Faint Praise and Harsh Criticism," *Journal of Advertising Research*, January/February 1994, p. 35.

17. "Too Much Corporate Power?" *BusinessWeek*, September 11, 2000, p. 144; "Ad Nauseam," *Advertising Age*, July 10, 2000, p. 1; Stephen J. Arnold and Monika Narang Luthra, "Market Entry Effects of Large Format Retailers: a Stakeholder Analysis," *International Journal of Retail & Distribution Management*, (4) 2000, p. 139.

CHAPTER 2

1. Available from World Wide Web: <http://www.dell.com>; 2003 *Annual Report*, Dell; "New Products, Markets Boost Dell's Profit," *USA Today*, November 14, 2003, p. 3B; "Dell Pins Hopes on Services to Boost Profit," *The Wall Street Journal*, November 11, 2003, p. B1; "What You Don't Know about Dell," *BusinessWeek*, November 3, 2003, p. 76; "Slowing PC Sales Drive Computer Firms' Push to Consumer Gadgets," *Investor's Business Daily*, October 8, 2003, p. A1; "Dell Wants Your Home," *Time*, October 6, 2003, p. 48; "Dell to Dive into Consumer Electronics Market," *USA Today*, September 25, 2003, p. 1B; "Dell Blitz Surprises Printer Market," *Investor's Business Daily*, May 30, 2003, p. A4; "How IBM, Dell Managed to Build Crushing Tech Dominance," *USA Today*, May 21, 2003, p. 3B; "Dell Gets Greener," *BusinessWeek*, May 5, 2002, p. 97; "Taking Dell's Limelight HP Unveils Printers and New Web Site," *Investor's Business Daily*, April 2, 2003, p. A4; "After the Sale," *Brandweek*, March 31, 2003, p. 20; "The Dell Way," *Business 2.0*, February 2003, p. 61; "Dell Plans to Peddle PCs Inside Sears, Other Large Chains," *The Wall Street Journal*, January 30, 2003, p. B1; "Dell Business Model Turns to Muscle as Rivals Struggle," *USA Today*, January 20, 2003, p. 1B; "How to Thrive in a Sick Economy," *Business 2.0*, January 2003, p. 88; "The Upper Hand in Handhelds?" *BusinessWeek*, December 23, 2002, p. 20; "The 'Dude' You May Not Know," *Brandweek*, October 14, 2002, pp. M6–M11; "Dell Takes Time to Build," *USA Today*, October 10, 2002, p. 6B; "Dell Slashes Prices and Still Turns a Profit; Credit It to Planning," *Investor's Business Daily*, September 30, 2002, p. A4; "Integrated Marketing Success Stories" (Special Report), *BtoB*, June 10, 2002, p. 25; "Dell Does Domination," *Fortune*, January 21, 2002, p. 70; "The Net as a Lifeline," *BusinessWeek E.Biz*, October 29, 2001, pp. EB16–EB23; "Dell, the Conqueror," *BusinessWeek*, September 24, 2001, p. 92; "The Mother of All Price Wars," *BusinessWeek*, July 20, 2001, p. 32; "How Dell Fine-Tunes Its PC Pricing to Gain Edge in a Slow Market," *The Wall Street Journal*, June 8, 2001, p. A1; "Price War Squeezes PC Makers," *The Wall Street Journal*, March 26, 2001, p. B1; "How a Low-Cost Provider like Dell also Delivers Best Customer Service," *Investor's Business Daily*, November 13, 2000, p. A1; "Going Digital? Think First," *Fortune*, November 13, 2000, p. 190; "Dell Looks for Ways to Rekindle the Fire It Had as an Upstart," *The Wall Street Journal*, August 31, 2000, p. A1; "Dell to Offer Hosting of Small-Business Web Sites," *The Wall Street Journal*, February 22, 2000, p. B23; "Dell Cracks China," *Fortune*, June 21, 1999, p. 120; "Dell Builds an Electronics Superstore on the Web," *The Wall Street Journal*, March 3, 1999, p. B1; Joan Magretta, "The Power of Virtual Integration: An Interview With Dell Computer's Michael Dell," *Harvard Business Review*, March–April 1998, p. 72; "And Give Me an Extra-Fast Modem with That, Please," *BusinessWeek*, September 29, 1997, p. 38; "Now Everyone in PCs Wants to Be like Mike," *Fortune*, September 8, 1997, p. 91; "Dell Fights PC Wars by Emphasizing Customer Service," *The Wall Street Journal*, August 15, 1997, p. B4.

2. Charles H. Noble, Rajiv K. Sinha, and Ajith Kumar, "Market Orientation and Alternative Strategic Orientations: a Longitudinal Assessment of Performance Implications," *Journal of Marketing*, October 2002, p. 25; Mary Anne Raymond and Hiram C. Barksdale, "Corporate Strategic Planning and Corporate Marketing: Toward an Interface," *Business Horizons*, September/October, 1989, p. 41; George S. Day, "Marketing's Contribution to the Strategy Dialogue," *Journal of the Academy of Marketing Science*, Fall 1992, p. 323; P. Rajan Varadarajan and Terry Clark, "Delineating the Scope of Corporate, Business, and Marketing Strategy," *Journal of Business Research*, October–November 1994, p. 93.

3. "What Customers Want," *Fortune*, July 7, 2003, p. 122; "The Unprofitable Customers," *The Wall Street Journal Reports*, October 28, 2002, p. R7; "Will This Customer Sink Your Stock," *Fortune*, September 30, 2002, p. 126; "With the Telecom Industry on Hold, Nextel Sends Out a Different Signal," *Investor's Business Daily*, March 2, 2001, p. A1; "Keep 'Em Coming Back," *BusinessWeek E. Biz*, May 15, 2000, p. EB20; "Marketers Put a Price on Your Life," *USA Today*, July 7, 1999, p. 3B. See also Heinz K. Stahl, Kurt Matzler, and Hans H. Hinterhuber, "Linking Customer Lifetime Value with Shareholder Value," *Industrial Marketing Management*, May 2003, p. 267; Valarie A. Zeithaml, "Service Quality, Profitability, and the Economic Worth of Customers: What We Know and What We Need to Learn," *Journal of the Academy of Marketing Science*, Winter 2000, p. 67; Dipak Jain and Siddhartha S. Singh, "Customer Lifetime Value Research in Marketing: a Review and Future Directions," *Journal of Interactive Marketing*, Spring 2002, p. 34; Charlotte H. Mason, "Tuscan Lifestyles: Assessing Customer Lifetime Value," *Journal of Interactive Marketing*, Autumn 2003, p. 54; Vikas Mittal, "Driving Customer Equity: How Customer Lifetime Value Is Reshaping Corporate Strategy," *Journal of Marketing*, April 2001, p. 107; Werner J. Reinartz and V. Kumar, "The Impact of Customer Relationship Characteristics on Profitable Lifetime Duration," *Journal of Marketing*, January 2003, p. 77.

4. "Genesco Names New Executive of Children's Footwear Division," *Press Release*, Genesco, July 15, 1994; "Toddler University Ends Up in Westport," *Westport News*, March 8, 1991, p. A13; "Whiz Kid," *Connecticut*, August 1989, p. 56; "The Young and the Restless," *Children's Business*, May 1989, p. 29.

5. Orville C. Walker, Jr., and Robert W. Ruckert, "Marketing's Role in the Implementation of Business Strategies: A Critical Review and

Conceptual Framework," *Journal of Marketing*, July 1987, p. 15; Thomas V. Bonoma, "A Model of Marketing Implementation," *1984 AMA Educators' Proceedings* (Chicago: American Marketing Association, 1984), p. 185; Kevin Romer and Doris C. Van Doren, "Implementing Marketing in a High-Tech Business," *Industrial Marketing Management*, August 1993, p. 177.

6. *2003 Annual Report*, Gillette Company.

7. "What Was Dick Tracy's Monthly Fee," *BusinessWeek*, October 13, 2003, p. 14; "Now, Even Your Watch Can Help You Carry Your Computer Files," *The Wall Street Journal*, September 25, 2003, p. B1; "Good Timing," *Brandweek*, September 8, 2003, p. 28; "Fossil's New Watch Has Awkward PDA, but Cool Style Feature," *The Wall Street Journal*, July 17, 2003, p. B1; "Research a Bigger Part of Microsoft Mix," *Investor's Business Daily*, June 11, 2003, p. A6; "Bill Has Designs on Your Wrist," *BusinessWeek*, January 20, 2003, p. 68; "Are Profits in Gadgets for Sickness, or for Health?" *The Wall Street Journal*, August 10, 2001, p. B1; "For the Wrist that Has Everything," *Newsweek*, June 25, 2001, p. 80; "Now That's Good Timing," *BusinessWeek Small Biz*, April 23, 2001, p. 14; "Movado Winds Up Lifestyle Effort, Expanded Line, with $15M in Print," *Brandweek*, April 2, 2001, p. 4; "Timex Pursues Hip, Younger Set in Ads for Its New iControl Watch," *The Wall Street Journal*, May 19, 2000, p. B2; "Swatch: Ready for Net Time," *BusinessWeek*, February 14, 2000, p. 61; "Timex Puts 'Iron' into TV with $5M," *Brandweek*, September 22, 1997, p. 6; "Timex Back to Basics to Retro-fit Gen X," *Brandweek*, August 5, 1996, p. 3; "Swatch Adds Metal Watch," *Advertising Age*, November 7, 1994, p. 60; "Benetton Readies Watch Campaign," *Brandweek*, August 8, 1994, p. 5; "Indiglo Watch Lights Up Better Times for Timex," *Brandweek*, April 25, 1994, p. 30.

8. Mark B. Houston, "Competing for the Future: Breakthrough Strategies for Seizing Control of Your Industry and Creating the Markets of Tomorrow," *Journal of the Academy of Marketing Science*, Winter 1996, p. 77; George S. Day and Robin Wensley, "Assessing Advantage: A Framework for Diagnosing Competitive Superiority," *Journal of Marketing*, April 1988, p. 1; Kevin P. Coyne, "Sustainable Competitive Advantage—What It Is, What It Isn't," *Business Horizons*, January/February 1986, p. 54; Michael E. Porter, *Competitive Advantage—Creating and Sustaining Superior Performance* (New York: Free Press, MacMillan, 1986).

9. "GM Warms Up Its Branding Iron," *BusinessWeek*, April 16, 2001, p. 56; "GM Still Pushing Lame-Duck Oldsmobiles," *USA Today*, February 19, 2001, p. 4B; "One Last Look at Oldsmobile," *Brandweek*, January 8, 2001, p. 28; "GM: 'Out with the Olds' Is Just the Start," *BusinessWeek*, December 25, 2000, p. 57; "After Decades of Brand Bodywork, GM Parks Oldsmobile—for Good," *The Wall Street Journal*, December 13, 2000, p. B1.

10. Available from World Wide Web: <http://www.soapworks.com>; "Taking On Procter & Gamble," *Inc.*, October 2000, p. 66.

11. Stephen J. Arnold, "Lessons Learned from the World's Best Retailers," *International Journal of Retail & Distribution Management*, (11) 2002, p. 562; Ashesh Mukherjee and Wayne D. Hoyer, "The Effect of Novel Attributes on Product Evaluation," *Journal of Consumer Research*, December 2001, p. 462; Jin K. Han, Namwoon Kim and Hong-Bumm Kim, "Entry Barriers: a Dull-, One-, or Two-Edged Sword for Incumbents? Unraveling the Paradox from a Contingency Perspective," *Journal of Marketing*, January 2001, p. 1; Douglas W. Vorhies and Neil A. Morgan, "A Configuration Theory Assessment of Marketing Organization Fit with Business Strategy and its Relationship with Marketing Performance," *Journal of Marketing*, January 2003, p. 100; Jean L. Johnson, Ruby Pui-Wan Lee, Amit Saini, and Bianca Grohmann, "Market-Focused Strategic Flexibility: Conceptual Advances and an Integrative Model," *Journal of the Academy of Marketing Science*, Winter 2003, p. 74; Ian C. MacMillan and Rita G. McGrath, "Discovering New Points of Differentiation," *Harvard Business Review*, July–August 1997, p. 133; Des Thwaites, Keith Walley, and Steve Foots, "Systematic Management of Differential Advantage," *Industrial Marketing Management*, May 1996, p. 209.

12. For more on Coleman, see "The Grill of Their Dreams," *Business 2.0*, February 2002, p. 96; "Growing to Match Its Brand Name," *Fortune*, June 13, 1994, p. 114. See also Peter C. Verhoef, "Understanding the Effect of Customer Relationship Management Efforts on Customer Retention and Customer Share Development," *Journal of Marketing*, October 2003, p. 30; Youjae Yi and Hoseong Jeon, "Effects of Loyalty Programs on Value Perception, Program Loyalty, and Brand Loyalty," *Journal of the Academy of Marketing Science*, Summer 2003, p. 229.

13. For more on E-Z-Go, see "Off-Roading, Golf-Cart Style," *The Wall Street Journal*, June 14, 2001, p. B1. For more on McDonald's, see World Wide Web: <http://www.mcdonalds.com>; *2003 Annual Report*, McDonald's; "You Want Ambiance with That?" *USA Today*, October 30, 2003, p. 3B; "Will Ratatouille Bring Japanese to McDonald's?" *The Wall Street Journal*, August 14, 2003, p. B1; "100 Innovations: McD's Tests Wi-Fi, Self-Service and 'China,'" *Advertising Age*, August 11, 2003, p. 4; "McDonald's Salads Lure Women," *USA Today*, June 16, 2003, p. 7B; "It's Back to Basics for McDonald's," *USA Today*, May 21, 2003, p. 1B; "What's This? The French Love McDonald's?" *BusinessWeek*, January 13, 2003, p. 50; "McHaute Cuisine: Armchairs, TVs, and Espresso—Is It McDonald's?" *The Wall Street Journal*, August 30, 2002, p. A1; "How Mr. Bambang Markets Big Macs in Muslim Indonesia," *The Wall Street Journal*, October 26, 2001, p. A1; "Why You Won't Find Any Egg McMuffins for Breakfast in Brazil," *The Wall Street Journal*, October 23, 1997, p. A1; "Burger Wars Sizzle as McDonald's Clones the Whopper," *The Wall Street Journal*, September 17, 1997, p. B1. See also Michael S. Garver, "Best Practices in Identifying Customer-Driven Improvement Opportunities," *Industrial Marketing Management*, August 2003, p. 455; John H. Roberts, "Developing New Rules for New Markets," *Journal of the Academy of Marketing Science*, Winter 2000, p. 31.

14. For more on Heinz EZ Squirt, see *2003 Annual Report*, Heinz; "Heinz Picks Purple as New EZ Squirt Color," *Brandweek*, June 25, 2001, p. 7; "Kids Salivate for New, Yucky, Weirdly Colored Food," *USA Today*, April 23, 2001, p. 7B; "Do E-Ads Have a Future?" *BusinessWeek E.Biz*, January 22, 2001, pp. EB46–EB50; "Squeezing New from Old," *USA Today*, January 4, 2001, p. 1B. For more on ski resorts, see "Bikers Give Ski Resorts Summer Time Lift," *The Wall Street Journal*, July 7, 1994, p. B1. For more on Nike, see *2003 Annual Report*, Nike; "Nike Puts Its Swoosh on MP3 Players, Walkie-Talkies, Heart Monitors," *The Wall Street Journal*, May 10, 2000, p. B1. See also Sarah J. Marsh and Gregory N. Stock, "Building Dynamic Capabilities in New Product Development Through Intertemporal Integration," *The Journal of Product Innovation Management*, March 2003, p. 136; George C. Kingston and Beebe Nelson, "Leading Product Innovation: Accelerating Growth in a Product-Based Business," *The Journal of Product Innovation Management*, November 2001, p. 414.

15. For more on McDonald's and its hotel diversification effort, see World Wide Web: <http://www.goldenarcheshotel.com>; "Would You Like a Bed with Your Burger?" *Ad Age Global*, February 2001, p. 12; "The Golden Arches: Burgers, Fries and 4-Star Rooms," *The Wall Street Journal*, November 17, 2000, p. B1.

16. For more on Purafil, see "Small Businesses Find International Success," *USA Today*, June 30, 2000, p. 1B.

17. For more on JLG, see "The Secret of U.S. Exports: Great Products," *Fortune*, January 10, 2000, pp. 154C–J.

18. Peter N. Golder, "Insights from Senior Executives about Innovation in International Markets," *The Journal of Product Innovation Management*, September 2000, p. 326; Shaoming Zou and S. Tamer Cavusgil, "The GMS: a Broad Conceptualization of Global Marketing Strategy and its Effect on Firm Performance," *Journal of Marketing*, October 2002, p. 40; Susan P. Douglas, "Exploring New Worlds: the Challenge of Global

Marketing," *Journal of Marketing*, January 2001, p. 103; Catharine M. Curran, "Selling to Newly Emerging Markets," *Journal of the Academy of Marketing Science*, Summer 2001, p. 324; "Key Ingredient in Going Global Is Acquiring Local Tastes," *USA Today*, December 2, 1997, p. 15A; Judith Clair, "International Marketing: Your Company's Next Stage of Growth," *Journal of the Academy of Marketing Science*, Summer 1997, p. 257.

19. For more on global social responsibility, see Chapter 1, endnote 8, and Chapter 5, endnote 3.

20. For other environmental issues, see "The Race to Save a Rainforest," *BusinessWeek*, November 24, 2003, p. 125; "Cellphone Makers Connect for Recycling Program," *USA Today*, October 22, 2003, p. 6B; "The Information Age's Toxic Garbage," *BusinessWeek*, October 6, 2003, p. 54; "Offsetting Environmental Damage by Planes," *The New York Times*, February 18, 2003, p. C6; "Behind Roses' Beauty, Poor and Ill Workers," *The New York Times*, February 13, 2003, p. A1; "Industrial Evolution," *BusinessWeek*, April 8, 2002, p. 70; "Green Sales Pitch Isn't Moving Many Products," *The Wall Street Journal*, March 6, 2002, p. B1; "Brazilian Mahogany: Too Much in Demand," *The Wall Street Journal*, November 14, 2001, p. B1; "How Much Power Do You Use?" *The Wall Street Journal*, August 16, 2001, p. B1; "Choice of Evils: As a Tropical Scourge Makes a Comeback, So, Too, Does DDT," *The Wall Street Journal*, July 26, 2001, p. A1; "It May Be Time to Toss Old Ideas on Recycling," *USA Today*, July 2, 2001, p. 7D; "As BP Goes Green, the Fur Is Flying," *The Wall Street Journal*, April 16, 2001, p. A10; "Once Is Not Enough," *BusinessWeek*, April 16, 2001, p. 128B; "EarthShell Saw Big Macs and Big Bucks—Got Big Woes," *The Wall Street Journal*, April 10, 2001, p. B2; "Recycling Redefined," *The Wall Street Journal*, March 6, 2001, p. B1; "More Gas-Powered Autos on 'Green' List," *USA Today*, February 9, 2001, p. 3B; "Nonprofits—and Landfills—Deluged with Old PCs," *Investor's Business Daily*, November 27, 2000, p. A6; "Conservation: Been There, Doing That," *BusinessWeek*, November 27, 2000, p. 194F; "Recycler's Nightmare: Beer in Plastic," *The Wall Street Journal*, November 16, 1999, p. B1; "As Old Pallets Pile Up, Critics Hammer Them as a New Eco-Menace," *The Wall Street Journal*, April 1, 1998, p. A1. See also Lynette Knowles Mathur and Ike Mathur, "An Analysis of the Wealth Effects of Green Marketing Strategies," *Journal of Business Research*, November 2000, p. 193; Subhabrata Bobby Banerjee, Easwar S. Iyer, and Rajiv K. Kashyap, "Corporate Environmentalism: Antecedents and Influence of Industry Type," *Journal of Marketing*, April 2003, p. 106; Anil Menon and Ajay Menon, "Enviropreneurial Marketing Strategy: The Emergence of Corporate Environmentalism As Market Strategy," *Journal of Marketing*, January 1997, p. 51; William E. Kilbourne, "Green Advertising: Salvation or Oxymoron?" *Journal of Advertising*, Summer 1995, p. 7.

CHAPTER 3

1. Available from World Wide Web: <http://www.hallmark.com>; *2003 Annual Report*, Hallmark; "Hallmark Cards' Joyce C. Hall," *Investor's Business Daily*, October 14, 2003, p. A3; "Hallmark Hits the Mark," *USA Today*, June 14, 2001, p. 1D; "American Greetings Thinks Time for 'Anytime' Is Now," *The Wall Street Journal*, March 24, 1998, p. B9; "Old-Fashioned Sentiments Go High-Tech," *The Wall Street Journal*, November 9, 1992, p. B1.

2. Terri C. Albert, "Need-Based Segmentation and Customized Communication Strategies in a Complex-Commodity Industry: a Supply Chain Study," *Industrial Marketing Management*, May 2003, p. 281; Shelby D. Hunt and Robert M. Morgan, "Resource-Advantage Theory: A Snake Swallowing Its Tail or a General Theory of Competition?" *Journal of Marketing*, October 1997, p. 74; Stavros P. Kalafatis and Vicki Cheston, "Normative Models and Practical Applications of Segmentation in Business Markets," *Industrial Marketing Management*, November 1997, p. 519; Lisa R. Adam, "Nichecraft: Using Your Specialness to Focus Your Business, Corner Your Market, and Make Customers Seek You Out,"

Journal of the Academy of Marketing Science, Summer 1997, p. 259; George S. Day, A. D. Shocker, and R. K. Srivastava, "Customer-Oriented Approaches to Identifying Product-Markets," *Journal of Marketing*, Fall 1979, p. 8; Rajendra K. Srivastava, Mark I. Alpert, and Allan D. Shocker, "A Customer-Oriented Approach for Determining Market Structures," *Journal of Marketing*, Spring 1984, p. 32.

3. Sally Dibb and Lyndon Simkin, "Market Segmentation: Diagnosing and Treating the Barriers," *Industrial Marketing Management*, November 2001, p. 609; Terry Elrod and Russell S. Winer, "An Empirical Evaluation of Aggregation Approaches for Developing Market Segments," *Journal of Marketing*, Fall 1982, p. 32; Frederick W. Winter, "A Cost-Benefit Approach to Market Segmentation," *Journal of Marketing*, Fall 1979, p. 103.

4. C. Samuel Craig and Susan P. Douglas, "Configural Advantage in Global Markets," *Journal of International Marketing*, (1) 2000, p. 6; Ruth N. Bolton and Matthew B. Myers, "Price-Based Global Market Segmentation for Services," *Journal of Marketing*, July 2003, p. 108; Philip A. Dover, "Segmentation and Positioning for Strategic Marketing Decisions," *Journal of the Academy of Marketing Science*, Summer 2000, p. 438; John Hogan, "Defining Your Market: Winning Strategies for High-Tech, Industrial, and Service Firms," *Journal of the Academy of Marketing Science*, Summer 2000, p. 442; Alex Chernev, "The Effect of Common Features on Brand Choice: Moderating Role of Attribute Importance," *Journal of Consumer Research*, March 1997, p. 304; Robert L. Armacost and Jamshid C. Hosseini, "Identification of Determinant Attributes Using the Analytic Hierarchy Process," *Journal of the Academy of Marketing Science*, Fall 1994, p. 383; Joel S. Dubow, "Occasion-based vs. User-based Benefit Segmentation, A Case Study," *Journal of Advertising Research*, March/April 1992, p. 11; Peter R. Dickson and James L. Ginter, "Market Segmentation, Product Differentiation, and Marketing Strategy," *Journal of Marketing*, April 1987, p. 1; Russell I. Haley, "Benefit Segmentation—20 Years Later," *Journal of Consumer Marketing* 1, no. 2 (1984), p. 5.

5. For more on General Mills, see "General Mills Intends to Reshape Doughboy in Its Own Image," *The Wall Street Journal*, July 18, 2000, p. A1. See also "Food Marketing," *Brandweek*, April 30, 2001, p. 20.

6. "Marketers Find 'Tweens' Too Hot to Ignore," *USA Today*, July 10, 2001, p. 13A; "Yamada Card Gives Credit to Struggling Brazilians," *The Wall Street Journal*, March 27, 2001, p. B1; "Grown-Up Drinks for Tender Taste Buds," *BusinessWeek*, March 5, 2001, p. 96; "Boosting Diageo's Spirits," *The Wall Street Journal*, February 12, 2001, p. B1; "Soda Pop That Packs a Punch," *Newsweek*, February 19, 2001, p. 45; Suzanne Benet, Robert E. Pitts, and Michael LaTour, "The Appropriateness of Fear Appeal Use for Health Care Marketing to the Elderly: Is It OK to Scare Granny?" *Journal of Business Ethics*, January 1993, p. 45; "New Converse Shoe Named Run 'N Gun Is Angering Critics," *The Wall Street Journal*, February 8, 1993, p. B5; "Malt Liquor Makers Find Lucrative Market in the Urban Young," *The Wall Street Journal*, March 9, 1992, p. A1; Richard W. Pollay, S. Siddarth, Michael Siegel, Anne Haddix et al., "The Last Straw? Cigarette Advertising and Realized Market Shares Among Youths and Adults, 1979–1993," *Journal of Marketing*, April 1996, p. 1; N. C. Smith and Elizabeth Cooper-Martin, "Ethics and Target Marketing: The Role of Product Harm and Consumer Vulnerability," *Journal of Marketing*, July 1997, p. 1.

7. For more on new hotel features, see "Hotels Pump Up Their Gyms to Lure Execs Seeking Pecs," *The Wall Street Journal*, November 13, 2003, p. D1; "New Concepts in Lodging," *The Wall Street Journal*, October 8, 2003, p. B1; "New at the Inn: Remote-Control Curtains," *The Wall Street Journal*, April 27, 2001, p. W9; "Hotels Target Generation X," *USA Today*, February 10, 2000, p. 1B; "Sweet Dreams Are Made of This," *USA Today*, August 31, 1999, p. 1B. See also Per Vagn Freytag and Ann Hojbjerg Clarke, "Business to Business Market Segmentation," *Industrial Marketing Management*, August 2001, p. 473.

8. Girish Punj and David W. Stewart, "Cluster Analysis in Marketing Research: Review and Suggestions for Application," *Journal of Marketing*

Research, May 1983, p. 134; Fernando Robles and Ravi Sarathy, "Segmenting the Computer Aircraft Market with Cluster Analysis," *Industrial Marketing Management*, February 1986, p. 1.

9. For more on CRM, see Chapter 8, endnote 6. For more on Amazon, see "Reprogramming Amazon: Sure, It Still Sells Loads of Books and CDs, but . . . ," *BusinessWeek*, December 22, 2003, p. 82; "Amazon Moves to Front Line of Shaping Web Services," *USA Today*, September 30, 2003, p. 1B; "Amazon Plans a Search Service to Drive Sales," *The Wall Street Journal*, September 25, 2003, p. B1; "New Chapter: A Web Giant Tries to Boost Profits by Taking on Tenants," *The Wall Street Journal*, September 24, 2003, p. A1; "Mighty Amazon," *Fortune*, May 26, 2003, p. 60; "Amazon: Creative Coddling, Great Word of Mouth," *BusinessWeek E. Biz*, September 16, 2000; "Secrets of the New Brand Builders," *Fortune*, June 22, 1998, p. 167. See also Katherine N. Lemon, Tiffany Barnett White, and Russell S. Winer, "Dynamic Customer Relationship Management: Incorporating Future Considerations into the Service Retention Decision," *Journal of Marketing*, January 2002, p. 1; Richard A. Feinberg, Rajesh Kadam, Leigh Hokama, and Iksuk Kim, "The State of Electronic Customer Relationship Management in Retailing," *International Journal of Retail & Distribution Management*, (10) 2002, p. 470; Jonghyeok Kim, Euiho Suh, and Hyunseok Hwang, "A Model for Evaluating the Effectiveness of CRM Using the Balanced Scorecard," *Journal of Interactive Marketing*, Spring 2003, p. 5. For more on privacy, see Chapter 13, endnote 9.

10. "Return of the Middleman," *Business 2.0*, March 2003, p. 52.

11. Girish Punj and Junyean Moon, "Positioning Options for Achieving Brand Association: a Psychological Categorization Framework," *Journal of Business Research*, April 2002, p. 275; Kalpesh Kaushik Desai and S. Ratneshwar, "Consumer Perceptions of Product Variants Positioned on Atypical Attributes," *Journal of the Academy of Marketing Science*, Winter 2003, p. 22; Hans Muhlbacher, Angelika Dreher, and Angelika Gabriel-Ritter, "MIPS—Managing Industrial Positioning Strategies," *Industrial Marketing Management*, October 1994, p. 287; David A. Aaker and J. Gary Shansby, "Positioning Your Product," *Business Horizons*, May/June, 1982, p. 56; Al Ries and Jack Trout, *Positioning: The Battle for Your Mind* (New York: McGraw-Hill, 1981), p. 53. For some examples of positioning, see "Getting Corian Out of the Kitchen," *The Wall Street Journal*, December 12, 2000, p. B1; "Pie in the Sky," *Brandweek*, December 16, 1996, p. 23; "From the Horse's Mouth: Try a Little Hoof Fix on Your Nails," *The Wall Street Journal*, July 29, 1994, p. B1.

CHAPTER 4

1. Peter Koven, "Trying to reel them in," *National Post*, June 10, 2006; Richard Corliss, "Can This Man Save the Movies?" *Time*, March 20, 2006.

2. See Peter F. Drucker, *Management: Tasks, Responsibilities, Practices, and Plans* (New York: Harper and Row, 1973); Sev K. Keil, "The Impact of Business Objectives and the Time Horizon of Performance Evaluation on Pricing Behavior," *International Journal of Research in Marketing*, June 2001, p. 67; Kenneth E. Clow, "Marketing Strategy: The Challenge of the External Environment," *Journal of the Academy of Marketing Science*, Summer 2000, p. 437.

3. This point of view is discussed at much greater length in a classic article by T. Levitt, "Marketing Myopia," *Harvard Business Review*, September–October 1975, p. 1. See also David J. Morris, Jr., "The Railroad and Movie Industries: Were They Myopic?" *Journal of the Academy of Marketing Science*, Fall, 1990, p. 279.

4. Lance Leuthesser and Chiranjeev Kohli, "Corporate Identity: The Role of Mission Statements," *Business Horizons*, May–June 1997, p. 59; Christopher K. Bart, "Sex, Lies, and Mission Statements," *Business Horizons*, November–December 1997, p. 9; Christopher K. Bart, "Industrial

Firms and the Power of Mission," *Industrial Marketing Management*, July 1997, p. 371.

5. "Why Inflation Is Not Inevitable," *Fortune*, September 12, 1988, p. 117.

6. Available from World Wide Web: <http://www. harley-davidson. com>; *2003 Annual Report*, Harley-Davidson; "Hurdles on the Road to Hog Heaven," *BusinessWeek*, November 10, 2003, p. 96; "Harley-Davidson Merchandising Goes Full Throttle," *USA Today*, August 25, 2003, p. 1B; "Where Hundreds Failed, Harley-Davidson Succeeded," *USA Today*, August 25, 2003, p. 3B; "Harley-Davidson Sees Decrease in Registrations," *The Wall Street Journal*, May 14, 2003, p. B5A; "How Harley Revved Online Sales," *Business 2.0*, December 2002, p. 44; "Richer, Older Harley Riders 'Like Everyone Else,'" *USA Today*, March 8, 2002, p. 1A; "Gearing Up for the Cruiser Wars," *Fortune*, August 3, 1998, pp. 128B–L; "Motorcycle Maker Caters to the Continent," *USA Today*, April 22, 1998, p. 8B; "Killer Strategies that Make Shareholders Rich," *Fortune*, June 23, 1997, p. 70; "Aided by Research, Harley Goes Whole Hog," *Marketing News*, December 2, 1996, p. 16; "Tune-Up Time for Harley," *BusinessWeek*, April 8, 1996, p. 90; "The Rumble Heard Round the World," *BusinessWeek*, May 24, 1993, p. 58; "How Harley Beat Back the Japanese," *Fortune*, September 25, 1989, p. 155.

7. For more on Starbucks, see Chapter 1, endnote 1.

8. For more on patents, see "Would You Buy a Patent License from This Man?" *Ecompany*, April 2001, p. 104; "Eli Lilly Loses Prozac Patent-Protection Battle," *The Wall Street Journal*, August 10, 2000, p. A3; "Businesses Battle over Intellectual Property," *USA Today*, August 2, 2000, p. 1B; "Qualcomm Hits the Big Time," *Fortune*, May 15, 2000, p. 213; "New Teeth for Old Patents," *BusinessWeek*, November 30, 1998, p. 92; "What's Next—A Patent for the 401(K)?" *BusinessWeek*, October 26, 1998, p. 104; "Drug Pirates," *Fortune*, October 12, 1998, p. 146.

9. "PlayStation 2 to Rivals: Game On!" *Brandweek*, November 17, 2003, p. 1; "Microsoft's Xbox to Use IBM Chips," *The Wall Street Journal*, November 4, 2003, p. B4; "Fear Not, Hardcore Violence Fans: Game Maker's Not Going Soft," *Investor's Business Daily*, October 23, 2003, p. A10; "The Biggest Game in Town," *Fortune*, September 15, 2003, p. 132; "New Sony Videogame Camera Sells Well," *The Wall Street Journal*, August 29, 2003, p. B6; "Is Nintendo Playing the Wrong Game?" *Business 2.0*, August 2003, p. 110; "Pay and Play," *The Wall Street Journal Reports*, June 16, 2003, p. R6; "Xbox Problems? Microsoft's Not Singing the Blues," *BusinessWeek*, May 19, 2003, p. 64; "Hackers Use Xbox for More than Games," *USA Today*, May 15, 2003, p. 3B; "Choosing Sides: Videogame Giant Links with Sony, Snubbing Microsoft," *The Wall Street Journal*, May 12, 2003, p. A1; "On the Web, Word-of-Mouth Marketing Can Become Viral," *Investor's Business Daily*, January 30, 2003, p. A4; "Sony's Big Bazooka," *Fortune*, December 30, 2002, p. 111; "Marketer of the Year: Xbox, We Know What Guys Want," *Brandweek*, October 14, 2002, p. M48; "Why Videogame Makers Are Taking Aim at You," *The Wall Street Journal*, May 16, 2002, p. D1; "Sony to Cut Price of PlayStation 2 by a Third in U.S.," *The Wall Street Journal*, May 14, 2002, p. D8; "Showdown in Mario Land," *The Wall Street Journal*, April 19, 2002, p. A14; "Game Wars," *Time*, March 20, 2000, p. 44; "How Four Renegades Persuaded Microsoft to Make a Game Machine," *The Wall Street Journal*, March 10, 2000, p. B1.

10. Peter J. Williamson, "Asia's New Competitive Game," *Harvard Business Review*, September–October 1997, p. 55; David J. Collis and Cynthia A. Montgomery, "Competing on Resources: Strategy in the 1990s," *Harvard Business Review*, July–August 1995, p. 118; "Firms Analyze Rivals to Help Fix Themselves," *The Wall Street Journal*, May 3, 1994, p. B1; Thomas S. Gruca and D. Sudharshan, "A Framework for Entry Deterrence Strategy: The Competitive Environment, Choices, and Consequences," *Journal of Marketing*, July 1995, p. 44; Venkatram Ramaswamy, Hubert Gatignon, and David J. Reibstein, "Competitive

Marketing Behavior in Industrial Markets," *Journal of Marketing*, April 1994, p. 45; Z. S. Deligonul and S. T. Cavusgil, "Does the Comparative Advantage Theory of Competition Really Replace the Neoclassical Theory of Perfect Competition?" *Journal of Marketing*, October 1997, p. 65; J. S. Armstrong, "Co-Opetition," *Journal of Marketing*, April 1997, p. 92; John L. Haverty and Myroslaw J. Kyj, "What Happens when New Competitors Enter an Industry," *Industrial Marketing Management* 20, no. 1 (1991), p. 73; William W. Keep, Glenn S. Omura, and Roger J. Calantone, "What Managers Should Know about Their Competitors' Patented Technologies," *Industrial Marketing Management*, July 1994, p. 257.

11. Timothy B. Heath, Gangseog Ryu, Subimal Chatterjee, Michael S. McCarthy et al. "Asymmetric Competition in Choice and the Leveraging of Competitive Disadvantages," *Journal of Consumer Research*, December 2000, p. 291; *Kao* (Cambridge, MA: Harvard Business School Press, 1984); Bruce R. Klemz, "Managerial Assessment of Potential Entrants: Processes and Pitfalls," *International Journal of Research in Marketing*, June 2001, p. 37. For more on P&G's diaper competition in U.S., see "Opportunity Knocks: In Lean Times, Big Companies Make a Grab for Market Share," *The Wall Street Journal*, September 5, 2003, p. A1; "Rivals Take P&G to Court to Challenge Ads," *The Wall Street Journal*, June 17, 2003, p. B1; "Dueling Diapers," *Fortune*, February 17, 2003, p. 115. For a different competitor analysis in the cosmetics market, see "Face-Off: An Unlikely Rival Challenges L'Oreal in Beauty Market," *The Wall Street Journal*, January 9, 2003, p. A1; "L'Oreal's Global Makeover," *Fortune*, September 30, 2002, p. 141.

12. "A Whole New Wave of Japanese Exports Is Headed Westward," *The Wall Street Journal*, November 14, 1997, p. A1.

13. "Chinese Economic Engine Revs as Worldwide Low-Cost Leader," *Investor's Business Daily*, August 12, 2003, p. A1; "Follow the Leader: As U.S. Shows Signs of Strength, Global Economies Look Up, Too," *The Wall Street Journal*, August 12, 2003, p. A1; Rajdeep Grewal, "Building Organizational Capabilities for Managing Economic Crisis: The Role of Market Orientation and Strategic Flexibility," *Journal of Marketing*, April 2001, p. 67; "Daimler Thinks Small: With Gas Prices Soaring, Will Americans Get 'Smart'?" *Newsweek*, May 21, 2001, p. 48; "Europeans Unmoved by USA's Energy Plight," *USA Today*, May 17, 2001, p. 8A; "Wary Consumers Watch as Inflation Nudges Prices Up," *USA Today*, April 30, 2001, p. 1B; "Time for a Reality Check," *BusinessWeek*, December 2, 1996, p. 58.

14. "Technology: Emerging Technologies," *USA Today* (*Bonus Section E*), November 17, 2003; "What's Next," *Time*, September 8, 2003, p. 46; "The Future of Tech," *BusinessWeek*, August 25, 2003, p. 62; "Special Report: Digital Homes," *BusinessWeek*, July 21, 2003, p. 58; "Technology: There Goes the Status Quo," *The Wall Street Journal Reports*, May 19, 2003; "Six Technologies that Will Change the World," *Business 2.0*, May 2003, p. 116; "Special Report: Next Frontiers, Moving into the Future," *Newsweek*, April 29, 2002, p. 40; "Technology: What's Ahead," *The Wall Street Journal Reports*, June 25, 2001; "Technology: How Technology Has Changed the Way We . . . ," *The Wall Street Journal Reports*, November 13, 2000; "The Internet Age," *BusinessWeek*, October 4, 1999, p. 69. See also Gary S. Lynn, Sharon M. Lipp, Ali E. Akgun, and Alexander Cortex Jr., "Factors Impacting the Adoption and Effectiveness of the World Wide Web in Marketing," *Industrial Marketing Management*, January 2002, p. 35; P. Rajan Varadarajan and Manjit S Yadav, "Marketing Strategy and the Internet: an Organizing Framework," *Journal of the Academy of Marketing Science*, Fall 2002, p. 296; A. Parasuraman and George M Zinkhan, "Marketing to and Serving Customers Through the Internet: an Overview and Research Agenda," *Journal of the Academy of Marketing Science*, Fall 2002, p. 286; Guilherme D. Pires and Janet Aisbett, "The Relationship Between Technology Adoption and Strategy in Business-to-Business Markets: the Case of E-Commerce," *Industrial Marketing Management*, May 2003, p. 291; Edward U. Bond III and Mark B. Houston, "Barriers to Matching New Technologies and Market Opportunities in Established Firms," *The Journal of Product Innovation Management*, March

2003, p. 120; Paul Whysall, "Retailing and the Internet: a Review of Ethical Issues," *International Journal of Retail & Distribution Management*, (11) 2000, p. 481; Robert A. Peterson, Sridhar Balasubramanian, and Bart J. Bronnenberg, "Exploring the Implications of the Internet for Consumer Marketing," *Journal of the Academy of Marketing Science*, Fall 1997, p. 329; Karen A. Graziano, "The Innovator's Dilemma: When New Technologies Cause Great Firms to Fail," *Journal of Product Innovation Management*, January 1998, p. 95; Edward McDonough, "Strategic Management of Technology and Innovation," *Journal of Product Innovation Management*, November 1997, p. 533.

15. "Technology: A Tech To-Do List," *The Wall Street Journal Reports*, November 17, 2003; "Advances in Car Technology Bring High-Class Headaches," *USA Today*, November 12, 2003, p. 1B; "Epidemic: Crippling Computer Viruses and Spam Attacks Threaten the Information Economy," *BusinessWeek*, September 8, 2003, p. 28; "Technology: Just Make It Simpler," *BusinessWeek*, September 8, 2003, p. 38; "Getting Unplugged Sheds Light on What Is Wired These Days," *The Wall Street Journal*, August 18, 2003, p. A1; "Innovation on Hold," *The Wall Street Journal*, May 29, 2003, p. B1; "Chips: Breaking the Light Barrier," *BusinessWeek*, April 16, 2001, p. 74; "Handhelds That Do It All," *BusinessWeek*, February 12, 2001, p. 98; "Will Light Bulbs Go the Way of the Victrola?" *BusinessWeek*, January 22, 2001, p. 94H; "High-Tech Applications Transform Old Economy," *USA Today*, September 7, 2000, p. 3B; "In Japan, the World Goes Flat," *The Wall Street Journal*, June 29, 2000, p. B1; "The World Is Your Office," *Fortune*, June 12, 2000, p. 227; "Wireless Gets Easier and Faster," *BusinessWeek*, May 29, 2000, p. 34; "Wireless Option Opens Door to a New E-World," *USA Today*, February 18, 2000, p. 1A; "This Frame Fetches Photos from the Net, Staging a Slide Show," *The Wall Street Journal*, February 3, 2000, p. B1; "The Soul of a New Refrigerator," *BusinessWeek*, January 17, 2000, p. 42; Noel Capon and Rashi Glazer, "Marketing and Technology: A Strategic Coalignment," *Journal of Marketing*, July 1987, p. 1. For more on privacy, see Chapter 13, endnote 9.

16. "Lessons of a Crisis," *BusinessWeek*, April 23, 2001, p. 56; "Made in Japan? Not for Home Team," *The Wall Street Journal*, February 18, 1998, p. A6; "U.S. Backpedals on Law that Hung 'Made in China' Tag on European Goods," *The Wall Street Journal*, August 8, 1997, p. A2. See also George Balabanis and Adamantios Diamantopoulos, "Domestic Country Bias, Country-of-Origin Effects, and Consumer Ethnocentrism: a Multidimensional Unfolding Approach," *Journal of the Academy of Marketing Science*, Winter 2004, p. 80; Zeynep Gurhan-Canli and Durairaj Maheswaran, "Determinants of Country-of-Origin Evaluations," *Journal of Consumer Research*, Jun 2000, p. 96; Kent L. Granzin and John J. Painter, "Motivational Influences on 'Buy Domestic' Purchasing: Marketing Management Implications from a Study of Two Nations," *Journal of International Marketing*, (2) 2001, p. 73; Gopalkrishnan R. Iyer, "Anticompetitive Practices in Japan: Their Impact on the Performance of Foreign Firms," *Journal of Marketing*, October 1997, p. 97; Michael G. Harvey, 'Buy American': Economic Concept or Political Slogan?" *Business Horizons*, May–June 1993, p. 40; Terry Clark, "National Boundaries, Border Zones, and Marketing Strategy: A Conceptual Framework and Theoretical Model of Secondary Boundary Effects," *Journal of Marketing*, July 1994, p. 67.

17. Available from World Wide Web: <http://www.nafta.org>. For more on NAFTA, see "After NAFTA's Thaw, a New Chill," *The Wall Street Journal*, October 7, 2003, p. A18; "Border Crossing? No Problema," *BusinessWeek Small Biz*, July 16, 2001, p. 10; "NAFTA Scorecard: So Far, So Good," *BusinessWeek*, July 9, 2001, p. 54; "Mexican Trucks Won't Fill the U.S. Soon," *The Wall Street Journal*, February 16, 2001, p. C4; "Mexico Thrives under NAFTA, Seeks More," *USA Today*, August 28, 2000, p. 1B; "Mexico Pulls Off Another Trade Coup," *BusinessWeek*, February 7, 2000, p. 56; "In the Wake of NAFTA, a Family Firm Sees Business Go South," *The Wall Street Journal*, February 23, 1999, p. A1; "Mexican Makeover," *BusinessWeek*, December 21, 1998, p. 50; Kent Jones,

"NAFTA Chapter 19: Is There Hope for Bilateral Dispute Resolution of Unfair Trade Law Decisions?" *Journal of Public Policy & Marketing*, Fall 1994, p. 300.

18. Industry Canada Competition Bureau Web site: <http://www.ic.gc.ca/cmb/welcomeic.nsf/0/85256a5d006b9720852570f100602477?OpenDocument>.

19. For more on auto safety, see "U.S. Pushes for Wider Seat Belt Use," *USA Today*, May 20, 2003, p. 1A; "Shopping for Safety," *BusinessWeek*, April 14, 2003, p. 84; "Smash, Bang, Crunch, Screech—Wow, What a Car!" *The Wall Street Journal*, April 13, 2001, p. B1; "Safety First," *Newsweek*, October 30, 2000, p. 56; "Formula Predicts Rollover Risk," *USA Today*, July 17, 2000, p. 1B. For more on food and drug safety, see "The Big Gap at the FDA," *Fortune*, July 22, 2002, p. 113; "Product Recalls Are Rising Amid Concern the Public Ignores Them" *The Wall Street Journal*, March 22, 2002, p. B1; "Pills on a Pedestal," *USA Today*, February 6, 2001, p. 1D; "Complex Drug Labels Bury Safety Messages," *USA Today*, May 3, 2000, p. 1A.

20. "Marketing Law: A Marketer's Guide to Alphabet Soup," *Business Marketing*, January 1990, p. 56; Ray O. Werner, "Marketing and the Supreme Court in Transition, 1982–1984," *Journal of Marketing*, Summer 1985, p. 97; Ray O. Werner, "Marketing and the United States Supreme Court, 1975–1981," *Journal of Marketing*, Spring 1982, p. 73; Dorothy Cohen, "Trademark Strategy," *Journal of Marketing*, January 1986, p. 61.

21. "Green—and Red-Hot, Too," *BusinessWeek*, December 1, 2003, p. 116; "It's Easy Being Green," *Business 2.0*, December 2003, p. 132; "Can Anything Stop Toyota?" *BusinessWeek*, November 17, 2003, p. 114; "Automakers Think Outside the Hybrid," *USA Today*, November 17, 2003, p. 5E; "Japan's Power Play," *BusinessWeek*, October 13, 2003, p. 90; "GM'S Race to the Future," *Business 2.0*, October 2003, p. 86; "Ford Delays Hybrid and Faces Race with Toyota," *The Wall Street Journal*, September 24, 2003, p. D4; "It's Easy Being Green," *Time*, September 22, 2003, p. 81; "Toyota's Prius: No Plug Required," *The Wall Street Journal*, September 11, 2003, p. D6; "Pump Lets Natural Gas Civics Go to Market," *USA Today*, August 27, 2003, p. 2B; "Hybrid Autos May Proliferate but at a Price," *The Wall Street Journal*, August 22, 2003, p. B1; "Dude, Where's My Hybrid?" *Fortune*, April 28, 2003, p. 112; "$2.50 a Gallon Gas? Not a Problem," *Advertising Age*, April 14, 2003, p. S6; "Hybrid Cars Attract More Buyers," *The Wall Street Journal*, March 13, 2003, p. D3; "Hybrids: How Detroit Can Gun the Engines," *BusinessWeek*, February 17, 2003, p. 80; "When Hybrid Cars Collide," *The Wall Street Journal*, February 6, 2003, p. B1; "Police Vehicles Go Green and Help Save Green," *The Wall Street Journal*, February 6, 2003, p. B1; "The Hybrid Car Moves beyond Curiosity Stage," *The New York Times*, January 28, 2003, p. A1.

22. "Where the Girls Are," *The Wall Street Journal*, October 28, 2003, p. B1; "If You Build It, Will She Come?" *Brandweek*, September 29, 2003, p. 28; "Fisher-Price Courts Gen-X Mothers," *The Wall Street Journal*, September 19, 2003, p. B3; "Tractor Supply: Retail Chain Uses Horse Sense to Plow New Growth Avenues," *Investor's Business Daily*, September 4, 2003, p. A9; "Tech Companies Try Wooing Women with Girlie Marketing," *The Wall Street Journal*, August 26, 2003, p. B1; "Ads Remind Women They Have Two Hands," *The Wall Street Journal*, August 14, 2003, p. B1; "Lowe's: Retailer Improves Your Home, Its Financials," *Investor's Business Daily*, May 16, 2003, p. A5; "A Slim Gym's Fat Success," *Time* (*Inside Business Bonus Section*), May 2003; "Lowe's Is Sprucing Up Its House. . . by Appealing to Women," *BusinessWeek*, June 3, 2002, p. 56; "Tapping Girl Power," *Brandweek*, April 22, 2002, p. 26; "Tool Sellers Tap Their Feminine Side," *The Wall Street Journal*, March 29, 2002, p. B1; "The NFL Tackles Mom," *The Wall Street Journal*, February 1, 2002, p. W1; "Aiming to Please Women," *USA Today*, June 10, 1999, p. 1B; Patricia Braus, "The Mother Market," *American Demographics*, October 1996, p. 37. See also Kathleen Brewer Doran, "Lessons Learned in Cross-Cultural Research of Chinese and North American Consumers," *Journal of Business Research*, October 2002, p. 823; Craig J. Thompson and Maura Troester, "Consumer Value Systems in the Age of Postmodern Fragmentation: the Case of the Natural Health Microculture," *Journal of Consumer Research*, March 2002, p. 550; Inger L. Stole, "Stronger than Dirt: a Cultural History of Advertising: Personal Hygiene in America, 1875–1940," *Journal of Advertising*, Summer 2002, p. 93; Bert Rosenbloom and Trina Larsen, "Communication in International Business-to-business Marketing Channels: Does Culture Matter?," *Industrial Marketing Management*, May 2003, p. 309.

23. For more on the changing nature of families, see "Power: Do Women Really Want It," *Fortune*, October 13, 2003, p. 80; "She Works, He Doesn't," *Newsweek*, May 12, 2003, p. 44; "Gen X Moms Have It Their Way," *USA Today*, May 7, 2003, p. 1D; "Mommy Is Really Home from Work," *BusinessWeek*, November 25, 2002, p. 101; "How to Shrink the Pay Gap," *BusinessWeek*, June 24, 2002, p. 151; "Career Matters," *American Demographics*, April 2002, p. 18; "In 24-Hour Workplace, Day Care Is Moving to the Night Shift," *The Wall Street Journal*, July 6, 2001, p. A1; "Net Lets Japanese Women Join Work Force at Home," *The Wall Street Journal*, February 29, 2000, p. B1; "Ads that Portray Women," *USA Today*, September 9, 1996, p. 4B. For more on changing food habits, see "The Fine Art of Finding the Fat," *BusinessWeek*, October 13, 2003, p. 134; "Are They Safe? The Skinny on Fat and Sugar Substitutes," *The Wall Street Journal*, August 12, 2003, p. D1; "The End of Nesting," *The Wall Street Journal*, May 16, 2003, p. W1; "The New Kitchen—Your Car," *The Wall Street Journal*, April 11, 2003, p. W10; "America Adds Salsa to Its Burgers and Fries," *The Wall Street Journal*, January 2, 2003, p. A9; "Fleeing from Fast Food," *The Wall Street Journal*, November 11, 2002, p. B1; "Fast-Growing Casual Restaurants Have the Burger Joints Drooling," *Investor's Business Daily*, June 20, 2002, p. A1; "Upper Crust: Fast-Food Chains Vie to Carve Out Empire in Pricey Sandwiches," *The Wall Street Journal*, February 5, 2002, p. A1; "Can Tyson Fight 'Chicken Fatigue' with Pork, Beef?" *The Wall Street Journal*, January 10, 2001, p. B1. For more on poverty of time, see "America Untettered," *American Demographics*, March 2003, p. 34; "How Much Is Your Time Worth?" *The Wall Street Journal*, February 26, 2003, p. D1; "Can Workplace Stress Get Worse?" *The Wall Street Journal*, January 16, 2001, p. B1; "Telecommuters' Lament," *The Wall Street Journal*, October 31, 2000, p. B1; "The Price of Speed," *USA Today*, August 3, 2000, p. 10D; "The End of Leisure," *American Demographics*, July 2000, p. 50. See also Laura M. Milner and James M. Collins, "Sex-Role Portrayals and the Gender of Nations," *Journal of Advertising*, Spring 2000, p. 67; Eric Panitz, "Marketing in a Multicultural World: Ethnicity, Nationalism and Cultural Identity," *Journal of the Academy of Marketing Science*, Spring 1997, p. 169; Victoria D. Bush and Thomas Ingram, "Adapting to Diverse Customers: A Training Matrix for International Marketers," *Industrial Marketing Management*, September 1996, p. 373.

24. Frank R. Bacon, Jr., and Thomas W. Butler, Jr., *Planned Innovation*, rev. ed. (Ann Arbor: Institute of Science and Technology, University of Michigan, 1980).

25. Paul F. Anderson, "Marketing, Strategic Planning and the Theory of the Firm," *Journal of Marketing*, Spring 1982, p. 15; George S. Day, "Analytical Approaches to Strategic Market Planning," in *Review of Marketing 1981*, ed. Ben M. Enis and Kenneth J. Roering (Chicago: American Marketing Association, 1981), p. 89; Ronnie Silverblatt and Pradeep Korgaonkar, "Strategic Market Planning in a Turbulent Business Environment," *Journal of Business Research*, August 1987, p. 339.

26. Jimme A. Keizer, Johannes I. M. Halman, and Michael Song, "From Experience: Applying the Risk Diagnosing Methodology," *The Journal of Product Innovation Management*, May 2002, p. 213; Richard N. Cardozo and David K. Smith, Jr., "Applying Financial Portfolio Theory to Product Portfolio Decisions: An Empirical Study," *Journal of Marketing*, Spring 1983, p. 110; Yoram Wind, Vijay Mahajan, and Donald J. Swire, "An Empirical Comparison of Standardized Portfolio Models," *Journal of Marketing*, Spring 1983, p. 89; Philippe Haspeslagh, "Portfolio Planning: Uses and Limits," *Harvard Business Review*, January–February 1982, p. 58.

27. Keith B. Murray and Edward T. Popper, "Competing under Regulatory Uncertainty: A U.S. Perspective on Advertising in the Emerging European Market," *Journal of Macromarketing*, Fall 1992, p. 38; "Inside Russia—Business Most Unusual," *UPS International Update*, Spring 1994, p. 1; "Freighted with Difficulties," *The Wall Street Journal*, December 10, 1993, p. R4; "Russia Snickers after Mars Invades," *The Wall Street Journal*, July 13, 1993, p. B1; Michael G. Harvey and James T. Rothe, "The Foreign Corrupt Practices Act: The Good, the Bad and the Future," in *1983 American Marketing Association Educators' Proceedings*, ed. P. E. Murphy et al. (Chicago: American Marketing Association, 1983), p. 374.

28. "Sensitive Export: Seeking New Markets for Tampons, P&G Faces Cultural Barriers," *The Wall Street Journal*, December 8, 2000, p. A1; "Pizza Queen of Japan Turns Web Auctioneer," *The Wall Street Journal*, March 6, 2000, p. B1; "What Makes Italy Easier?" *Going Global—Italy* (supplement to *Inc.*), 1994; "Jean Cloning," *Brandweek*, May 30, 1994, p. 15; "Double Entendre: The Life and the Life of Pepsi Max," *Brandweek*, April 18, 1994, p. 40; "Global Ad Campaigns, After Many Missteps, Finally Pay Dividends," *The Wall Street Journal*, August 27, 1992, p. A1; Kamran Kashani, "Beware the Pitfalls of Global Marketing," *Harvard Business Review*, September–October 1989, p. 91.

CHAPTER 5

1. Based on U.S. Census data, including *Global Population Profile: 2000* and *World Population Profile: 1998* and *World Population at a Glance: 1998 and Beyond*, IB/98–4 (Washington, DC: Government Printing Office); and other Census data available from World Wide Web: <http://www.census.gov/ipc>.

2. Based on U.S. Census "International Data Base" available from World Wide Web: <http://www.census.gov/cgi-bin/ipc/idbsum? cty=??> and other U.S. Census data, including *An Aging World: 2001*, P95/01-1 and World Bank data including, *World Development Indicators: 2003* (Washington, DC: International Bank for Reconstruction and Development/The World Bank, 2003) and available from World Wide Web: <http://devdata.worldbank. org/data-query>; Central Intelligence Agency data and available from World Wide Web: <http://www.odci. gov/cia/publications/ factbook>; Population Reference Bureau data, including *2002 World Population Data Sheet* (Washington, DC: Population Reference Bureau, 2002) and available from World Wide Web: <http://www.prb.org/pubs/ wpds2002> and *World Population: More Than Just Numbers* (Washington, DC: Population Reference Bureau, 1999); and CountryWatch, available from World Wide Web: <http://www. countrywatch.com>; "To Put It in Perspective," *American Demographics*, June 2003, p. 9; "When Globalization Suffers, the Poor Take the Heat," *BusinessWeek*, April 21, 2003, p. 28; "Leveraging the Age Gap: Nations that Skew Young Have Small Window to Try to Catch Up with the Wealthy," *The Wall Street Journal*, February 27, 2003, p. B1; "Time for Marketers to Grow Up?" *The Wall Street Journal*, February 27, 2003, p. B1; "Going Gray: For Ailing Japan, Longevity Begins to Take a Toll," *The Wall Street Journal*, February 11, 2003, p. A1; "Global Baby Bust: Economic, Social Implications Are Profound as Birthrates Drop in Almost Every Nation," *The Wall Street Journal*, January 24, 2003, p. B1; "The Middle East Baby Boom," *American Demographics*, September 2002, p. 55; "Arrested Development: Botswana Watches Economic Success Destroyed by AIDS," *The Wall Street Journal*, August 29, 2002, p. A1; Tarun Khanna and Krishna Palepu, "Why Focused Strategies May Be Wrong for Emerging Markets," *Harvard Business Review*, July–August 1997, p. 41; Tamer S. Cavusgil, "Measuring the Potential of Emerging Markets: An Indexing Approach," *Business Horizons*, January–February 1997, p. 87; E. B. Keehn, "A Yen to Spend," *Harvard Business Review*, March–April 1996, p. 154.

3. "Two Ways to Help the Third World," *Fortune*, October 27, 2003, p. 187; "Good Reasons for Smiles: Colgate Brings Dental Care to Brazil-
ian Indian Tribes, Ravages of Tobacco and Rice," *The Wall Street Journal*, July 23, 2003, p. B1; "A Way to Help Africa Help Itself," *BusinessWeek*, July 21, 2003, p. 40; "Companies Market to India's Have-Littles," *The Wall Street Journal*, June 5, 2003, p. B1; "Tech Where It's Needed," *Business 2.0*, July 2003, p. 124; "With Little Loans, Mexican Women Overcome," *The New York Times*, March 19, 2003, p. A8; "CelPay Puts Africa on Wireless Map," *The Wall Street Journal*, December 2, 2002, p. B4; "Digital Divide: The Hunt for Globalization that Works," *Fortune*, October 28, 2002, pp. 163–176, "Special Report: Global Poverty," *BusinessWeek*, October 14, 2002, p. 108; "World Poverty Rates," *Investor's Business Daily*, June 12, 2002, p. A15; "Small Change: Bank that Pioneered Loans for the Poor Hits Repayment Snag," *The Wall Street Journal*, November 27, 2001, p. A1; "America's Future: Smart Globalization," *BusinessWeek*, August 27, 2001, p. 130; "Global Capitalism: Can It Be Made to Work Better?" *BusinessWeek*, November 6, 2000, p. 72; "The Fight Against Latin Poverty," *BusinessWeek*, May 1, 2000, p. 72; and World Bank statistical data available from World Wide Web: <http://devdata. worldbank.org>. See also Chapter 1, endnote 8.

4. "Pfizer Makes Aid Pledge, Breaks Aid Pact," *The Wall Street Journal*, November 12, 2003, p. B1; "African Gold Giant Finds History Impeded a Fight Against AIDS," *The Wall Street Journal*," June 26, 2001, p. A1; "Bottled Up: As UNICEF Battles Baby-Formula Makers, African Infants Sicken," *The Wall Street Journal*, December 5, 2000, p. A1; "Death of a Continent," *Fortune*, November 13, 2000, p. 258; "World Bank Is Targeting AIDS in Africa," *The Wall Street Journal*, September 12, 2000, p. A3; "American Home Infant-Formula Giveaway to End," *The Wall Street Journal*, February 4, 1991, p. B1.

5. Based on World Bank statistical data available from World Wide Web: <http://devdata.worldbank.org/data-query>; "The Lowdown on Literacy," *American Demographics*, June 1994, p. 6.

6. Based on U.S. Census data, including U.S. Bureau of the Census, *Statistical Abstract of the United States 2002* (Washington, DC: U.S. Government Printing Office, 2001), pp. 22–23 and available from World Wide Web: <http://www.census.gov/ statab> and *Census 2000 Special Reports: Demographic Trends in the 20th Century* CENSR-4 and "The Next 25 Years," *American Demographics* (Marketing Tools Sourcebook 2004), pp. D26–D29; "Moving West Is No Longer the Norm," *USA Today*, August 6, 2003, p. 1A; "Decade of Change for USA," *USA Today*, June 5, 2002, p. 3B; "The Census Report," *American Demographics*, January 2002, pp. S3–S6; "Snapshot of America 2000," *The Wall Street Journal*, August 6, 2001, p. B1; "Exploring a Nation of Extremes," *The Wall Street Journal*, May 25, 2001, p. B1; "Census Tracks Geographical Generation Gap," *USA Today*, May 25, 2001, p. 3A; "Lust for Statistics," *American Demographics*, March 2001, p. 68. Also based on data from Population Reference Bureau and Ameristat, available from World Wide Web: <http:// www.prb.org> and <http://www.ameristat.org>.

7. Based on U.S. Census data, including U.S. Bureau of the Census, *Statistical Abstract of the United States 2002* (Washington, DC: U.S. Government Printing Office, 2001), p. 9 and p. 59 and available from World Wide Web: <http://www.census.gov/ statab>.

8. Based on U.S. Census data, including U.S. Bureau of the Census, *Statistical Abstract of the United States 2002* (Washington, DC: U.S. Government Printing Office, 2001), p. 18, p. 20, and p. 25 and available from World Wide Web: <http://www.census.gov/statab> and *Census 2000 Special Reports: Demographic Trends in the 20th Century* CENSR-4 and "The Next 25 Years," *American Demographics*, April 2003, p. 24; "Gadgets Help Baby Boomers Navigate Old Age," *USA Today*, November 17, 2003, p. 1A; "The Dream Vacation: Go Home Younger," *The Wall Street Journal*, August 13, 2003, p. D1; Michael J. Weiss, "Great Expectations," *American Demographics*, May 2003, p. 26; "Boomers: A Forgotten Generation," *Brandweek*, October 7, 2002, p. 1; Carol M. Morgan and Doran J. Levy, "The Boomer Attitude," *American Demographics*, October 2002, p. 42; Michael Weiss, "Chasing Youth," *American Demographics*, October

2002, p. 34; Rebecca Gardyn, "Retirement Redefined," *American Demographics*, November 2000, p. 52. See also Linda L. Price, Eric J. Arnould and Carolyn Folkman Curasi, "Older Consumers' Disposition of Special Possessions," *Journal of Consumer Research*, September 2000, p. 179; William R. Swinyard and Heikki J. Rinne, "The Six Shopping Worlds of Baby Boomers," *Business Horizons*, September–October 1994, p. 64.

9. Based on U.S. Census data and "New Baby Boom Swamps Colleges," *USA Today*, January 2, 2003, p. 1A; Pamela Paul, "Echoboomerang," *American Demographics*, June 2001, p. 44; *Teen Fact Book* (Channel One Network, 2000) and available from World Wide Web: <http://www.TeenFactBook.com>; Susan Mitchell, "The Next Baby Boom," *American Demographics*, October 1995, p. 22; "Teens, the Most Global Market of All," *Fortune*, May 16, 1994, p. 90.

10. Adapted from "Hooking Up with Gen Y," *Business 2.0*, October 2003, p. 49; "Degree of Challenge," *American Demographics*," May 2003, p. 20.

11. Based on U.S. Census data, including U.S. Bureau of the Census, *Statistical Abstract of the United States 2002* (Washington, DC: U.S. Government Printing Office, 2001), p. 47, p. 48, and p. 53 and *Census 2000 Special Reports: Demographic Trends in the 20th Century CENSR-4*; "Unmarried America," *BusinessWeek*, October 20, 2003, p. 106; "Married with Children," *American Demographics*, March 2003, p. 17; "The American Family in the 21st Century," *American Demographics*, August 2001, p. 20; "Living Alone in America: Singleness Not the Same as Not Settled," *USA Today*, October 23, 2001, p. 1D; "Unmarried with Children," *Newsweek*, May 28, 2001, p. 46; "Census 2000: The New Demographics," *The Wall Street Journal*, May 15, 2001, p. B1; "Advertisers Are Cautious as Household Makeup Shifts," *The Wall Street Journal*, May 15, 2001, p. B1; Rebecca Gardyn, "Unmarried Bliss," *American Demographics*, December 2000, p. 56.

12. Based on U.S. Census data and "Population of Rural America Is Swelling," *The Wall Street Journal*, July 21, 1996, p. B1; "The Rural Rebound," *American Demographics*, May 1994, p. 24. See also Hugh M. Cannon and Attila Yaprak, "Will the Real-World Citizen Please Stand Up! The Many Faces of Cosmopolitan Consumer Behavior," *Journal of International Marketing*, (4) 2002, p. 30.

13. Based on U.S. Census data, including U.S. Bureau of the Census, *Statistical Abstract of the United States 2002* (Washington, DC: U.S. Government Printing Office, 2001), p. 30 and *Census 2000 Special Reports: Demographic Trends in the 20th Century CENSR-4* and "Minorities Reshape Suburbs," *USA Today*, July 9, 2001, p. 1A; "Counting Change," *Advertising Age*, May 14, 2001, p. 16; "U.S. Cities Buck Trend with Boom Downtown," *USA Today*, May 7, 2001, p. 1A; "Downtowns Make Cities Winners," *USA Today*, May 7, 2001, p. 3A; "Immigration Helped Restore Cities," *USA Today*, March 19, 2001, p. 3A.

14. Based on U.S. Census data, including U.S. Bureau of the Census, *Statistical Abstract of the United States 2002* (Washington, DC: U.S. Government Printing Office, 2001), p. 29 and "Geographical Mobility: March 1998 to March 1999 (Update), p. 20–531" and available from World Wide Web: <http://www.census.gov/population/www/socdemo/migrate>; Roberto Suro, "Movement at Warp Speed," *American Demographics*, August 2000, p. 61.

15. Based on U.S. Census data, including U.S. Bureau of the Census, *Statistical Abstract of the United States 2002* (Washington, DC: U.S. Government Printing Office, 2001), pp. 41–42 and pp. 441–442 and "Table F-1. Income Limits for Each Fifth and Top 5 Percent of Families (All Races): 1947 to 2001" and "Table F-2. Share of Aggregate Income Received by Each Fifth and Top 5 Percent of Families (All Races): 1947 to 2001" and "Table F-6. Regions—Families (All Races) by Median and Mean Income: 1953 to 2001" and all 3 tables available from World Wide Web: <http://www.census.gov/hhes/income/hitinc> and "Table 1. People and Families in Poverty by Selected Characteristics: 2000 and 2001" and available from World Wide Web: <http://www.census.gov/hhes/

poverty>. For more on income, see "Waking Up from the American Dream," *BusinessWeek*, December 1, 2003, p. 54; "Middle Class Barely Treads Water," *USA Today*, September 15, 2003, p. 1B; "Economic Inequality Grew in 90's Boom, Fed Reports," *The New York Times*, January 23, 2003, p. C1; "Defining the Rich in the World's Wealthiest Nation," *The New York Times*, January 12, 2003, Sect. 4, p. 1; "The Income Report," *American Demographics*, January 2003, p. 35; Peter Francese, "Older and Wealthier," *American Demographics*, November 2002, p. 40. For more on poverty, see "Is Poverty Rate Rise as Bad as It Looks?" *Investor's Business Daily*, September 29, 2003, p. A1; "Income Gap Steady, Poverty Spreads," *The Wall Street Journal*, September 29, 2003, p. A14; "Poverty Rate Rise Greater for Whites," *The Wall Street Journal*, September 25, 2002, p. D2; "Down and Out in the Midst of a Boom," *BusinessWeek*, May 28, 2001, p. 24; "Poverty in America," *BusinessWeek*, October 18, 1999, p. 156; "Income Gap between Rich and Poor Grows Nationwide," *The Wall Street Journal*, December 17, 1997, p. B2.

16. Ronald W. Hasty, Joseph A. Bellizzi, and Fernando R. Diaz, "A Cross-Cultural Study of Ethical Perceptions of Whites and Hispanics Toward 14 Questionable Retail Practices," *Journal of Marketing Theory & Practice*, Winter 1997, p. 135; "Nutrament, Debunked as a 'Fitness' Drink, Is Reborn in the Slums," *The Wall Street Journal*, November 2, 1994, p. B1; "Some Mortgage Firms Neglect Black Areas More Than Banks Do," *The Wall Street Journal*, August 9, 1994, p. A1; "A Marketing Giant Uses Its Sales Prowess to Profit on Poverty," *The Wall Street Journal*, September 22, 1993, p. A1.

17. "Chasing Viking," *Brandweek*, August 18, 2003, p. 20; Michael J. Weiss, "Inconspicuous Consumption," *American Demographics*, April 2002, p. 31; "Marketing to the New Millionaire," *The Wall Street Journal*, October 11, 2000, p. B1; "The Lure of the Entrepreneur," *American Demographics*, February 1998, p. 41; "Spending at Our Discretion," *American Demographics*, August 1997, p. 2; Peter K. Francese, "Big Spenders," *American Demographics*, August 1997, p. 51; "Disposable Dollars Determine Spending," *American Demographics*, June 1997, p. 18.

18. Pamela Paul, "Make Room for Granddaddy," *American Demographics*, April 2002, p. 40; "The Grandparent Industry," *The Wall Street Journal*, November 2, 2001, p. W1; Jan Larson, "The New Face of Homemakers," *American Demographics*, September 1997, p. 45; "Work & Family" (Special Section), *The Wall Street Journal*, March 31, 1997, p. 1; "A Snapshot of Younger Lifestage Group Purchases," *American Demographics*, November 9, 1992, p. 28. See also Richard G. Netemeyer, Thomas Brashear-Alejandro and James S. Boles, "A Cross-National Model of Job-Related Outcomes of Work Role and Family Role Variables: a Retail Sales Context," *Journal of the Academy of Marketing Science*, Winter 2004, p. 49; Patrick E. Murphy and William A. Staples, "A Modernized Family Life Cycle," *Journal of Consumer Research*, June 1979, p. 12.

19. Based on U.S. Census data and "Do Us Part," *American Demographics*, September 2002, p. 9; Joan Raymond, "The Ex-Files," *American Demographics*, February 2001, p. 60; "The Ties that Bind," *Time*, August 18, 1997, p. 48; Frank F. Fustenberg, Jr., "The Future of Marriage," *American Demographics*, June 1996, p. 34. See also James A. Roberts, Chris Manolis, and John F. Tanner Jr, "Family Structure, Materialism, and Compulsive Buying: a Reinquiry and Extension," *Journal of the Academy of Marketing Science*, Summer 2003, p. 300.

20. Based on U.S. Census data and "More Parents Are Leaving School Shopping to the Kids," *USA Today*, August 11, 2003, p. 1A; "Special Report: Kids, Tweens & Teens," *Advertising Age*, February 17, 2003, pp. S1–S6; "Just How Deep Are Those Teen Pockets?" *BusinessWeek*, July 30, 2001, p. 39; "Special Report: Teen Marketing," *Advertising Age*, June 25, 2001, p. S1; "To Reach the Unreachable Teen," *BusinessWeek*, September 18, 2000, p. 78; "Rushing to Cash In on the New Baby Boom," *The Wall Street Journal*, August 9, 2000, p. B1; "The Six Value Segments of Global Youth," *Brandweek*, May 22, 2000, p. 38; Elissa Moses, *The $100 Billion Allowance: Accessing the Global Teen Market* (John Wiley & Sons, 2000);

"Generation Y," *BusinessWeek*, February 15, 1999, p. 80; Soyeon Shim, "Adolescent Consumer Decision-Making Styles: The Consumer Socialization Perspective," *Psychology & Marketing*, September 1996, p. 547.

21. Based on U.S. Census data and "Mom and Dad, I'm Home—Again," *BusinessWeek*, November 3, 2003, p. 110; "Free at Last!" *Newsweek*, October 13, 2003, p. 62; "Bringing Up Adultolescents," *Newsweek*, March 25, 2002, p. 38; Joan Raymond, "The Joy of Empty Nesting," *American Demographics*, May 2000, p. 48; "Take My Stuff, Please!" *The Wall Street Journal*, March 31, 2000, p.W1; "Extreme Nesting," *The Wall Street Journal*, January 7, 2000, p. W1.

22. Based on Census data, including "The Older Population in the United States: March 1999, P20–532"; "Your New Neighbor: Mom," *The Wall Street Journal*, December 20, 2002, p. W1; "Take My Mother—Please!" *The Wall Street Journal*, October 4, 2002, p. W1; "The Exotic Travel Boom," *American Demographics*, June 2002, p. 48; "Senior Theses," *Brandweek*, August 4, 1997, p. 22; "The Ungraying of America," *American Demographics*, July 1997, p. 12; Linda J. Barton, "A Shoulder to Lean On: Assisted Living in the U.S.," *American Demographics*, July 1997, p. 45; "Brave Old World," *Newsweek*, June 30, 1997, p. 63; George P. Moschis, "Life Stages of the Mature Market," *American Demographics*, September 1996, p. 44.

23. Based on U.S. Census data, including *Census 2000 Special Reports: Demographic Trends in the 20th Century CENSR-4*. For an overview of ethnic populations in the U.S., see *Racial and Ethnic Diversity* (Ithaca, NY: New Strategist, 2000); "Ads for Ethnic Hair Care Show a New Face" *The Wall Street Journal*, July 21, 2003, p. B1; "Multicultural Marketing," *Advertising Age* (Special Report), July 7, 2003, p. S1; "Ethnic Marketing," *DSN Retailing Today* (Special Report), March 24, 2003, p. 13; Sean Kelly, "Race, Ethnicity, and the Way We Shop," *American Demographics*, February 2003, p. 30; Alison Stein Wellner, "Diversity in America," *American Demographics* (Supplement), November 2002, p. S1; "Ethnic Marketing," *DSN Retailing Today* (Special Report), May 6, 2002, p. 17; Geng Cui, "Marketing to Ethnic Minority Consumers: An Historical Journey (1932–1997)," *Journal of Macromarketing*, June 2001, Vol. 21, 1, p. 23; Marilyn Halter, *Shopping for Identity: The Marketing of Ethnicity* (Schocken Books, 2000); William H. Frey, "Micro Melting Pots," *American Demographics*, June 2001, p. 20; "Color Them Beautiful—and Visible," *USA Today*, May 2, 2001, p. 1B; "The New Age of Ethnic Marketing," *Brandweek*, March 19, 2001, p. 24; "The New America: The New Face of Race," *Newsweek*, September 18, 2000, p. 38; "Our New Look: The Colors of Race," *Newsweek*, January 1, 2000, p. 28. For more on the white population, see U.S. Census data, including "The White Population: August 2001, C2KBR/01-4." For more on the African-American market, see U.S. Census data, including "The Black Population in the United States: April 2003, P20–541" and available from World Wide Web: <http://www.census.gov/population/www/socdemo/race>; William H. Frey, "Revival," *American Demographics*, October 2003, p. 26; Sandra Yin, "Color Bind," *American Demographics*, September 2003, p. 22; "Card Crafter Uses Creativity to Carve Out Niche," *USA Today*, March 19, 2003, p. 7B; "The Black Gender Gap," *Newsweek*, March 3, 2003, p. 46; "Black Boom in the 'Burbs," *American Demographics*, July 2001, p. 20; "The New Demographics of Black Americans," *BusinessWeek*, December 4, 2000, p. 14; Carol M. Motley, "Aunt Jemima, Uncle Ben, and Rastus: Blacks in Advertising, Yesterday, Today, and Tomorrow," *Journal of Marketing*, April 1995, p. 111. For more on the Hispanic market, see U.S. Census data, including "The Hispanic Population: May 2001, C2KBR/01-3" and available from World Wide Web: <http://www.census.gov/population/www/socdemo/race>; "Once-Spurned Clamato Juice Is Big with Latinos, and Not Just for Its Taste," *The Wall Street Journal*, October 21, 2003, p. A17; "Marketing to Hispanics," *Advertising Age* (Special Report), September 15, 2003, p. S1; "39 Million Make Hispanics Largest Minority Group," *USA Today*, June 19, 2003, p. 1A; "New Brooklyns Replace White Suburbs," *USA Today*, May 19, 2003, p. 1A; "Buying Power of Hispanics Is Set to Soar," *The Wall*

Street Journal, April 18, 2003, p. B1; "Advertisers Point and Click to Find Hispanic Audiences," *Adweek*, April 7, 2003, p. 8, "Fresh from the Border," *Time* (Inside Business Supplement), April 2003; "Advertisers Tap into Hispanic Gold Mine," *USA Today*, February 21, 2003, p. 1B; "Prospecting: As Latinos Fan Out across America, Businesses Follow," *The Wall Street Journal*, November 26, 2002, p. A1; "Marketing to Hispanics," *Advertising Age* (Special Report), September 16, 2002, p. S1; "Goya Foods Leads an Ethnic Sales Trend," *The Wall Street Journal*, July 9, 2002, p. B4; "Big Advertising Firms Scoop Up Hispanic-Focused Agencies," *USA Today*, July 5, 2002, p. 2B; "Hispanic-Targeted Advertising Outpaces Overall Ad Growth," *The Wall Street Journal*, April 19, 2002, p. A17; Rebecca Gardyn, "Habla English?" *American Demographics*, April 2001, p. 54; M. Isabel Valdes, *Marketing to American Latinos* (Ithaca, NY: Paramount, 2000); "P&G Reaches Out to Hispanics," *The Wall Street Journal*, October 13, 2000, p. B1; "Why the Latino Market Is So Hard to Count," *The Wall Street Journal*, October 13, 2000, p. B1. For more on the Asian-American market, see U.S. Census data, including "The Asian Population: February 2002, C2KBR/01-16" and available from World Wide Web: <http://www.census.gov/population/www/socdemo/race>; "More Firms Reach Out to Asian Americans," *Investor's Business Daily*, September 29, 2003, p. A6; "Chinese at Home," *American Demographics*, February 2003, p. 12; "The Asian American Blind Spot," *American Demographics*, July 2001, p. 16; "U.S. Asian Population Grew and Diversified, Census Shows," *The Wall Street Journal*, May 15, 2001, p. B4; "Ford, Penney's Targeting Calif.'s Asian Populations," *Advertising Age*, January 4, 1999, p. 28; Charles R. Taylor and Barbara B. Stern, "Asian-Americans: Television Advertising and the 'Model Minority' Stereotype," *Journal of Advertising*, Summer 1997, p. 47; Charles R. Taylor and Ju Yung Lee, "Not in *Vogue*: Portrayals of Asian Americans in Magazine Advertising," *Journal of Public Policy & Marketing*, Fall 1994, p. 239. See also Lucette B. Comer and J. A. F. Nicholls, "Communication Between Hispanic Salespeople and Their Customers: A First Look," *The Journal of Personal Selling & Sales Management*, Summer 2000, p. 121; Scott D. Roberts and H. S. Hart, "A Comparison of Cultural Value Orientations As Reflected by Advertisements Directed at the General U.S. Market, the U.S. Hispanic Market, and the Mexican Market," *Journal of Marketing Theory & Practice*, Winter 1997, p. 91; Geng Cui, "Marketing Strategies in a Multi-Ethnic Environment," *Journal of Marketing Theory & Practice*, Winter 1997, p. 122; Michael Laroche, Chung K. Kim, and Madeleine Clarke, "The Effects of Ethnicity Factors on Consumer Deal Interests: An Empirical Study of French- and English-Canadians," *Journal of Marketing Theory & Practice*, Winter 1997, p. 100.

CHAPTER 6

1. Available from World Wide Web: <http://www.yoplait.com>; "Wacky Colors, Unconventional Flavors Appeal to the Savvy Younger Set," *DSN Retailing Today*, May 19, 2003, p. 18; "Down with Tubes?" *Brandweek*, March 3, 2003, p. 1; "Spread 'Em," *Brandweek*, June 3, 2002, p. 1; "'To Go' Becoming the Way to Go," *Advertising Age*, May 13, 2002, p. 73; "Marketers Get Creative to Fit Needs of Retailers, Time-Pressed Consumers," *Brandweek*, May 13, 2002, p. 13; "You've Got Surveys," *American Demographics*, November 2000, p. 42; "Marketers of the Year: Groove Tube," *Brandweek* (SuperBrands Issue), October 16, 2000, pp. M111–M116; "Yoplait's Revenge Is Portable Yogurt that Kids Slurp Up," *Advertising Age*, September 11, 2000, p. 28; "Dannon Struggles against Go-Gurt's Market Incursions," *Advertising Age*, September 11, 2000, p. 28; "Squeezable Yogurt? Eggs on a Stick? You Got It!" *USA Today*, March 31, 2000, p. 1D; *Annual Report 2000*, General Mills; "Yogurt Goes Tubular," *Newsweek*, October 11, 1999, p. 63.

2. Kristina D. Frankenberger, "Consumer Psychology for Marketing," *Journal of the Academy of Marketing Science*, Summer 1996, p. 279, K. H. Chung, *Motivational Theories and Practices* (Columbus, Ohio: Grid, 1977), p. 40; A. H. Maslow, *Motivation and Personality* (New York: Harper & Row, 1970).

3. "Features Drive Kitchen Gadget Evolution," *DSN Retailing Today*, May 19, 2003, p. 20; "What Works for One Works for All," *Business-Week*, April 20, 1992, p. 112.

4. See Fredrik Herzberg, *Work and the Nature of Man* (Cleveland: William Collins, 1966).

5. "Who Said That? Buyers Don't Recognize Some Slogans," *USA Today*, October 1, 2003, p. 1B; "Super Tags, Still Believers," *Brandweek*, February 3, 2003, p. 16; "Big Ideas for Ducks and Their Keepers," *Brandweek*, October 13, 2003, p. 24; "Advertising that Keeps Going and Going . . . ," *Adweek*, February 3, 2003, p. 38.

6. For more on Ben & Jerry's, see Chapter 18, endnote 1. See also Les Carlson, Russell N. Laczniak, and Ann Walsh, "Socializing Children about Television: an Intergenerational Study," *Journal of the Academy of Marketing Science*, Summer 2001, p. 276; Elizabeth Cowley and Andrew A. Mitchell, "The Moderating Effect of Product Knowledge on the Learning and Organization of Product Information," *Journal of Consumer Research*, December 2003, p. 443; Stacy L. Wood and John G. Lynch Jr, "Prior Knowledge and Complacency in New Product Learning," *Journal of Consumer Research*, December 2002, p. 416; Naomi Mandel and Eric J. Johnson, "When Web Pages Influence Choice: Effects of Visual Primes on Experts and Novices," *Journal of Consumer Research*, September 2002, p. 235; Elizabeth S. Moore and Richard J. Lutz, "Children, Advertising, and Product Experiences: a Multimethod Inquiry," *Journal of Consumer Research*, June 2000, p. 31; Julie A. Ruth, Frederic F. Brunel and Cele C. Otnes, "Linking Thoughts to Feelings: Investigating Cognitive Appraisals and Consumption Emotions in a Mixed-Emotions Context," *Journal of the Academy of Marketing Science*, Winter 2002, p. 44; Stijn M. J. Van Osselaer and Chris Janiszewski, "Two Ways of Learning Brand Associations," *Journal of Consumer Research*, September 2001, p. 202; William E. Baker, "When Can Affective Conditioning and Mere Exposure Directly Influence Brand Choice?," *Journal of Advertising*, Winter 1999, p. 31; Jaideep Sengupta and Gita Venkataramani Johar, "Effects of Inconsistent Attribute Information on the Predictive Value of Product Attitudes: Toward a Resolution of Opposing Perspectives," *Journal of Consumer Research*, Jun 2002, p. 39; J. Jeffrey Inman, "The Role of Sensory-Specific Satiety in Attribute-Level Variety Seeking," *Journal of Consumer Research*, Jun 2001, p. 105; Jennifer Gregan-Paxton and Deborah R. John, "Consumer Learning by Analogy: A Model of Internal Knowledge Transfer," *Journal of Consumer Research*, December 1997, p. 266; M. C. Macklin, "Preschoolers' Learning of Brand Names From Visual Cues," *Journal of Consumer Research*, December 1996, p. 251; Jaideep Sengupta, Ronald C. Goodstein, and David S. Boninger, "All Cues Are Not Created Equal: Obtaining Attitude Persistence Under Low-Involvement Conditions," *Journal of Consumer Research*, March 1997, p. 351; John Kim, Jeen-Su Lim, and Mukesh Bhargava, "The Role of Affect in Attitude Formation: A Classical Conditioning Approach," *Journal of the Academy of Marketing Science*, Spring 1998, p. 143; Paul S. Speck and Michael T. Elliott, "Predictors of Advertising Avoidance in Print and Broadcast Media," *Journal of Advertising*, Fall 1997, p. 61; Frances K. McSweeney and Calvin Bierley, "Recent Developments in Classical Conditioning," *Journal of Consumer Research*, September 1984, p. 619; Scott A. Hawkins and Stephen J. Hoch, "Low-Involvement Learning: Memory without Evaluation," *Journal of Consumer Research*, September 1992, p. 212.

7. "Secrets of That New-Car Smell," *Car and Driver*, November 2003, p. 141; "Battling the Inferior-Interior Complex," *The Wall Street Journal*, December 3, 2001, p. B1. See also Anna S. Mattila and Jochen Wirtz, "Congruency of Scent and Music as a Driver of In-Store Evaluations and Behavior," *Journal of Retailing*, Summer 2001, p. 273.

8. "Sweet Success," *Brandweek*, May 12, 2003, p. 22.

9. "Purina Dog Chow: Grand Effie Winner, Pet Care/Gold Winner," *Brandweek*, (Special Effies Winner Supplement), 1997. See also Edward Rosbergen, Rik Pieters, and Michel Wedel, "Visual Attention to Advertising: A Segment-Level Analysis," *Journal of Consumer Research*, December 1997, p. 305; Gavan J. Fitzsimons and Vicki G. Morwitz, "The Effect of Measuring Intent on Brand-Level Purchase Behavior," *Journal of Consumer Research*, June 1996, p. 1; Ellen C. Garbarino and Julie A. Edell, "Cognitive Effort, Affect, and Choice," *Journal of Consumer Research*, September 1997, p. 147.

10. "A New Oxymoron: Hip Minivan," *BusinessWeek*, October 20, 2003, p. 156; "Automakers Lavish Attention on Van Market," *USA Today*, August 6, 2003, p. 12B; "Nissan Attempts to Sex Up Quest," *Advertising Age*, August 4, 2003, p. 7; "Operation: Minivan," *The Wall Street Journal*, August 1, 2003, p. W1. See also Rohini Ahluwalia, "Examination of Psychological Processes Underlying Resistance to Persuasion," *Journal of Consumer Research*, September 2000, p. 217; Dena Cox and Anthony D. Cox, "Beyond First Impressions: the Effects of Repeated Exposure on Consumer Liking of Visually Complex and Simple Product Designs," *Journal of the Academy of Marketing Science*, Spring 2002, p. 119; J. Joseph Cronin Jr, Michael K Brady end G Tomas M Hult, "Assessing the Effects of Quality, Value, and Customer Satisfaction on Consumer Behavioral Intentions in Service Environments," *Journal of Retailing*, Summer 2000, p. 193; Yih Hwai Lee, "Manipulating Ad Message Involvement Through Information Expectancy: Effects on Attitude Evaluation and Confidence," *Journal of Advertising*, Summer 2000, p. 29; Vikas Mittal, William T. Ross, and Patrick M. Baldasare, "The Asymmetric Impact of Negative and Positive Attribute-Level Performance on Overall Satisfaction and Repurchase Intentions," *Journal of Marketing*, January 1998, p. 33; Mary F. Luce, "Choosing to Avoid: Coping With Negatively Emotion-Laden Consumer Decisions," *Journal of Consumer Research*, March 1998, p. 409; Calvin P. Duncan and Richard W. Olshavsky, "External Search: The Role of Consumer Beliefs," *Journal of Marketing Research*, February 1982, p. 32; M. Joseph Sirgy, "Self-Concept in Consumer Behavior: A Critical Review," *Journal of Consumer Research*, December 1982, p. 287.

11. "For Asian Women, Weight-Loss Rule 1 Is Skip the Gym," *The Wall Street Journal*, October 9, 2003, p. A1; "Unilever Expands Slim-Fast to Create a Diet Megabrand," *Advertising Age*, June 23, 2003, p. 8; "Living Larger," *USA Today*, March 16, 1998, p. 4D; "If Fat-Free Pork Is Your Idea of Savory, It's a Bright Future," *The Wall Street Journal*, January 29, 1998, p. A1.

12. "Chock Full of Peanuts," *American Demographics*, April 1997, p. 60.

13. "The Dirt on At-Home Dry Cleaning," *The Wall Street Journal*, September 15, 2000, p. W14; "P&G Shifts Strategy for Dryel," *Advertising Age*, January 24, 2000, p. 4; "Novel P&G Product Brings Dry Cleaning Home," *The Wall Street Journal*, November 19, 1997, p. B1.

14. For more on wrinkle-free clothing, see "Botox for Broadcloth," *The Wall Street Journal*, October 7, 2002, p. A19; "'Wrinkle-Free' Shirts Don't Live Up to the Name," *The Wall Street Journal*, May 11, 1994, p. B1. For more on stain-resistant clothing, see "A Tie You Can Wipe Your Mouth With," *The Wall Street Journal*, October 14, 2003, p. D1; "Look, Ma, No Stains," *Time*, December 9, 2002, p. 64. For more on service quality, see Chapter 9, endnote 3. For more on service expectations, see "Can I Get a Smile with My Burger and Fries?" *The Wall Street Journal*, September 23, 2003, p. D6; "After the Sale," *Brandweek*, March 31, 2003, p. 20; "Service—with a Side of Sales," *The Wall Street Journal Reports*, October 29, 2001, p. R13; "Why Service Stinks," *BusinessWeek*, October 23, 2000, p. 118; "Customer Service: Rewriting the Rules of the Road," *BusinessWeek E.Biz*, September 18, 2000, p. EB86; "It's the Service, Stupid," *BusinessWeek E.Biz*, April 3, 2000, p. EB118. See also A. Parasuraman, Valarie A. Zeithaml, and Leonard L. Berry, "Reassessment of Expectations As a Comparison Standard in Measuring Service Quality: Implications for Further Research," *Journal of Marketing*, January 1994, p. 111; Alain Genestre and Paul Herbig, "Service Expectations and Perceptions Revisited: Adding Product Quality to SERVQUAL," *Journal of Marketing Theory & Practice*, Fall 1996, p. 72; Valarie A. Zeithaml, Leonard L. Berry, and A. Parasuraman, "The Nature and Determinants of Customer Expectations of Service," *Journal of the Academy of Marketing Science*, Winter 1993, p. 1.

15. Harold H. Kassarjian and Mary Jane Sheffet, "Personality and Consumer Behavior: An Update," in H. Kassarjian and T. Robertson, *Perspectives in Consumer Behavior* (Glenview, IL: Scott, Foresman, 1981), p. 160; Todd A. Mooradian and James M. Olver, " 'I Can't Get No Satisfaction': The Impact of Personality and Emotion on Postpurchase Processes," *Psychology & Marketing*, July 1997, p. 379.

16. "It's Mind Vending . . . in the World of Psychographics," *Time (Inside Business Bonus Section)*, October 2003; "Lifestyles Help Shape Innovation," *DSN Retailing Today*, August 4, 2003, p. 20; "Generation Next," *Advertising Age*, January 15, 2001, p. 14; "Head Trips," *American Demographics*, October 2000, p. 38; "Join the Club," *Brandweek*, February 15, 1999, p. 26; Rebecca Piirto Heath, "The Frontier of Psychographics," *American Demographics*, July 1996, p. 38; Robert A. Mittelstaedt, "Economics, Psychology, and the Literature of the Subdiscipline of Consumer Behavior," *Journal of the Academy of Marketing Science*, Fall 1990, p. 303; W. D. Wells, "Psychographics: A Critical Review," *Journal of Marketing Research*, May 1975, p. 196.

17. Available from World Wide Web: <www.sric-bi.com>; Judith Waldrop, "Markets with Attitude," *American Demographics*, July 1994, p. 22; "New VALS 2 Takes Psychological Route," *Advertising Age*, February 13, 1989, p. 24; Lynn R. Kahle, Sharon E. Beatty, and Pamela Homer, "Alternative Measurement Approaches to Consumer Values: The List of Values (LOV) and Values and Life Styles (VALS)," *Journal of Consumer Research*, December 1986, p. 405.

18. "PRIZMCE" and links retrieved from: <http://www.environicsanalytics.ca>, July 2006.

19. For more on kids' influence in purchase decisions, see "My Two Front Teeth—and a Handheld," *BusinessWeek*, December 15, 2003, p. 42; "My First Handheld," *BusinessWeek*, September 1, 2003, p. 98; "Spending It All on the Kids," *Time*, July 14, 2003, p. 42; "Ads Put Kids in Minivan Spotlight," *USA Today*, June 30, 2003, p. 6B; "Targeting the Family's Chief Tech Officer," *Adweek*, June 16, 2003, p. 8; "Special Report: Kids, Tweens & Teens," *Advertising Age*, February 17, 2003, pp. S1–S6; "Deconstructing Cute," *Business 2.0*, December 2002, p. 47; "Family Secret: The Concierge Floor," *The Wall Street Journal*, September 27, 2002, p. W1; "Child's Play for Furniture Retailers," *The Wall Street Journal*, September 25, 2002, p. B1; "Catering to Kids," *The Wall Street Journal*, May 3, 2002, p. W1; "Peek-a Boo, I See You—Clearly," *The Wall Street Journal*, January 25, 2002, p. W1; "Marketers Find 'Tweens' Too Hot to Ignore," *USA Today*, July 10, 2001, p. 13A; "Marketers Call on Kids to Help Design Web Sites," *USA Today*, June 5, 2001, p. 1B; "Kid-Fluence," *USA Today*, December 29, 2000, p. 1E; "Young Girls Targeted by Makeup Companies," *Advertising Age*, November 27, 2000, p. 15; "Retailers Reaching Out to Capture Kids' Clout," *Advertising Age*, October 9, 2000, p. 16; Alison Stein Wellner, "Generation Z," *American Demographics*, September 2000, p. 60; "Foods Targeting Children Aren't Just Child Play," *Advertising Age*, March 1, 1999, p. 16; James U. McNeal, "Tapping the Three Kids' Markets," *American Demographics*, April 1998, p. 37; "Hey Kid, Buy This!" *BusinessWeek*, June 30, 1997, p. 62; Sharon E. Beatty and Salil Talpade, "Adolescent Influence in Family Decision Making: A Replication with Extension," *Journal of Consumer Research*, September 1994, p. 332. See also Ugur Yavas, Emin Babakus, and Nejdet Delener, "Family Purchasing Roles in Saudi Arabia: Perspectives from Saudi Wives," *Journal of Business Research*, September 1994, p. 75; Eric H. Shaw and Stephen F. I. Pirog, "A Systems Model of Household Behavior," *Journal of Marketing Theory & Practice*, Summer 1997, p. 17; Kay M. Palan and Robert E. Wilkes, "Adolescent-Parent Interaction in Family Decision Making," *Journal of Consumer Research*, September 1997, p. 159; Conway L. Lackman, David P. Hanson, and John M. Lanasa, "Social Relations in Culture and Marketing," *Journal of Marketing Theory & Practice*, Winter 1997, p. 144; Ellen R. Foxman, Patriya S. Tansuhaj, and Karin M. Ekstrom, "Adolescents' Influence in Family Purchase Decisions: A Socialization Perspective," *Journal of Business Research*, March 1989, p. 159; C. Lackman and J.M. Lanasa, "Family

Decision-Making Theory: An Overview and Assessment," *Psychology & Marketing*, March/April 1993, p. 81. For more on women's influence in purchase decisions, see U.S. Census data, including "Women in the United States: A Profile, March 2000," and available from World Wide Web: <http://www.census.gov/population/www/socdemo/women>; "A Guide to Who Holds the Purse Strings," *The Wall Street Journal*, June 22, 2000, p. A14; "How to Market to Women," *Advertising Age*, June 12, 2000, p. 24.

20. "PRIZMCE" retrieved from: <http://www.environicsanalytics.ca>, July 2006.

21. "Consumers Enjoy Lap of Luxury," *Investor's Business Daily*, October 27, 2003, p. A7; "Downsized Luxury," *The Wall Street Journal*, October 14, 2003, p. B1; "The Japanese Paradox," *The Wall Street Journal*, September 23, 2003, p. B1; "Luxury for the Masses," *Brandweek*, June 25, 2001, p. 16; "Special Report: Luxury Marketing," *Advertising Age*, June 11, 2001, p. S1; "Which Is Luxury?" *USA Today*, May 4, 2001, p. 1B; Hassan Fattah, "The Rising Tide," *American Demographics*, April 2001, p. 48; "Despite Downturn, Japanese Are Still Having Fits for Luxury Goods," *The Wall Street Journal*, April 24, 2001, p. B1; "The Rise of the Comfortable," *Advertising Age*, October 16, 2000, p. 60; "Class in America," *Fortune*, February 7, 1994, p. 114. See also Cornelia Pechmann and Susan J. Knight, "An Experimental Investigation of the Joint Effects of Advertising and Peers on Adolescents' Beliefs and Intentions about Cigarette Consumption," *Journal of Consumer Research*, Jun 2002, p. 5; Albert M. Muniz Jr and Thomas C. O'Guinn, "Brand Community," *Journal of Consumer Research*, March 2001, p. 412; Gary Cross, "Valves of Desire: a Historian's Perspective on Parents, Children, and Marketing," *Journal of Consumer Research*, December 2002, p. 441; Basil G. Englis and Michael R. Solomon, "To Be and Not to Be: Lifestyle Imagery, Reference Groups, and the Clustering of America," *Journal of Advertising*, Spring 1995, p. 13; Greg J. Duncan, Timothy M. Smeeding, and Willard Rodgers, "The Incredible Shrinking Middle Class," *American Demographics*, May 1992, p. 34; Dennis L. Rosen and Richard W. Olshavsky, "The Dual Role of Informational Social Influence: Implications for Marketing Management," *Journal of Business Research*, April 1987, p. 123; Terry L. Childers and Akshay R. Rao, "The Influence of Familial and Peer-based Reference Groups on Consumer Decisions," *Journal of Consumer Research*, September 1992, p. 198; Basil G. Englis and Michael R. Solomon, "To Be and Not to Be: Lifestyle Imagery, Reference Groups, and The Clustering of America," *Journal of Advertising*, Spring 1995, p. 13.

22. For more on opinion leaders and word-of-mouth publicity, see Chapter 10, endnote 17. See also "Auto Makers Find They Don't Want to Avoid Collisions in Movies," *The Wall Street Journal*, July 5, 2001, p. B1, "Small Wonder," *The Wall Street Journal*, June 25, 2001, p. R1; Rebecca Gardyn, "Granddaughters of Feminism," *American Demographics*, April 2001, p. 43; "A Wide Web of Advice," *BusinessWeek E.Biz*, January 22, 2001, pp. EB18–EB20; "How to Generate Buzz to Sell Your Product," *Investor's Business Daily*, October 3, 2000, p. A1; "Word of Mouth in the Digital Age: Marketers Win when Friends Hit 'Send,' " *Brandweek*, October 2, 2000, p. 24. See also Barbara Bickart and Robert M. Schindler, "Internet Forums as Influential Sources of Consumer Information," *Journal of Interactive Marketing*, Summer 2001, p. 31; Robert Madrigal, "The Influence of Social Alliances with Sports Teams on Intentions to Purchase Corporate Sponsors' Products," *Journal of Advertising*, Winter 2000, p. 13; Peter C. Verhoef, Philip Hans Franses and Janny C. Hoekstra, "The Effect of Relational Constructs on Customer Referrals and Number of Services Purchased from a Multiservice Provider: Does Age of Relationship Matter?" *Journal of the Academy of Marketing Science*, Summer 2002, p. 202.

23. "Overcoming the Stigma of Dishwashers in Japan," *The Wall Street Journal*, May 19, 2000, p. B1; Sydney Roslow, "International Consumer Behavior: Its Impact on Marketing Strategy Development," *Journal of the Academy of Marketing Science*, Summer 1996, p. 278; R. Mead, "Where is the Culture of Thailand?" *International Journal of Research in Marketing*, September 1994, p. 401.

24. "Does Class Count in Today's Land of Opportunity?" *The New York Times*, January 18, 2003, p. A17; John L. Graham, "How Culture Works," *Journal of Marketing*, April 1996, p. 134; Gary D. Gregory and James M. Munch, "Cultural Values in International Advertising: An Examination of Familial Norms and Roles in Mexico," *Psychology & Marketing*, March 1997, p. 99; Shiretta F. Ownbey and Patricia E. Horridge, "Acculturation Levels and Shopping Orientations of Asian-American Consumers," *Psychology & Marketing*, January 1997, p. 1; Jennifer L. Aaker and Durairaj Maheswaran, "The Effect of Cultural Orientation on Persuasion," *Journal of Consumer Research*, December 1997, p. 315; Grant McCracken, "Culture and Consumption: A Theoretical Account of the Structure and Movement of the Cultural Meaning of Consumer Goods," *Journal of Consumer Research*, June 1986, p. 71.

25. "Will the British Warm Up to Iced Tea? Some Big Marketers Are Counting on It," *The Wall Street Journal*, August 22, 1994, p. B1. See also "Starbucks Hits a Humorous Note in Pitching Iced Coffee to Brits," *The Wall Street Journal*, September 1, 1999, p. B7.

26. "No More Shoppus Interruptus," *American Demographics*, May 2001, p. 39; "No Buy? Then Bye-Bye," *BusinessWeek E.Biz*, April 16, 2001, p. EB6; "Ok, Forget the Whole Damn Thing," *Ecompany*, December 2000, p. 185; "Special Report: E-Tailing," *BusinessWeek E.Biz*, May 15, 2000, pp. EB103–EB118; "Many Web Shoppers Abandon Virtual Carts," *Investor's Business Daily*, May 11, 2000, p. A8. See also Rajneesh Suri and Kent B. Monroe, "The Effects of Time Constraints on Consumers' Judgments of Prices and Products," *Journal of Consumer Research*, Jun 2003, p. 92; Pratibha A. Dabholkar and Richard P. Bagozzi, "An Attitudinal Model of Technology-Based Self-Service: Moderating Effects of Consumer Traits and Situational Factors," *Journal of the Academy of Marketing Science*, Summer 2002, p. 184; Darren W. Dahl, Rajesh V. Manchanda and Jennifer J. Argo, "Embarrassment in Consumer Purchase: the Roles of Social Presence and Purchase Familiarity," *Journal of Consumer Research*, December 2001, p. 473; Charles S. Areni, Pamela Kiecker, and Kay M. Palan, "Is It Better to Give Than to Receive? Exploring Gender Differences in the Meaning of Memorable Gifts," *Psychology & Marketing*, January 1998, p. 81; Russell W. Belk, "Situational Variables and Consumer Behavior," *Journal of Consumer Research* 2, 1975, p. 157; John F. Sherry, Jr., "Gift Giving in Anthropological Perspective," *Journal of Consumer Research*, September 1983, p. 157.

27. Adapted and updated from James H. Myers and William H. Reynolds, *Consumer Behavior and Marketing Management* (Boston: Houghton Mifflin, 1967), p. 49. See also Ronald E. Goldsmith, "A Theory of Shopping," *Journal of the Academy of Marketing Science*, Fall 2000, p. 541; Judith Lynne Zaichkowsky, "Consumer Behavior: Yesterday, Today, and Tomorrow," *Business Horizons*, May/June 1991, p. 51.

28. Dawn Iacobucci, Phipps Arabie and Anand Bodapati, "Recommendation Agents on the Internet," *Journal of Interactive Marketing*, Summer 2000, p. 2; Dan Ariely, "Controlling the Information Flow: Effects on Consumers' Decision Making and Preferences," *Journal of Consumer Research*, September 2000, p. 233; Amitav Chakravarti and Chris Janiszewski, "The Influence of Macro-Level Motives on Consideration Set Composition in Novel Purchase Situations," *Journal of Consumer Research*, September 2003, p. 244; Mary Frances Luce, Jianmin Jia, and Gregory W. Fischer, "How Much Do You like It? Within-Alternative Conflict and Subjective Confidence in Consumer Judgments," *Journal of Consumer Research*, December 2003, p. 464; Ravi Dhar and Steven J. Sherman, "The Effect of Common and Unique Features in Consumer Choice," *Journal of Consumer Research*, December 1996, p. 193; Victor V. Cordell, "Consumer Knowledge Measures As Predictors in Product Evaluation," *Psychology & Marketing*, May 1997, p. 241; John V. Petrof and Naoufel Daghfous, "Evoked Set: Myth or Reality?" *Business Horizons*, May–June 1996, p. 72; Wayne D. Hoyer, "An Examination of Consumer

Decision Making for a Common Repeat Purchase Product," *Journal of Consumer Research*, December 1984, p. 822; James R. Bettman, *An Information Processing Theory of Consumer Choice* (Reading, MA.: Addison-Wesley Publishing, 1979); Richard W. Olshavsky and Donald H. Granbois, "Consumer Decision Making: Fact or Fiction?" *Journal of Consumer Research*, September 1979, p. 93.

29. Fuan Li, Paul W. Miniard, and Michael J. Barone, "The Facilitating Influence of Consumer Knowledge on the Effectiveness of Daily Value Reference Information," *Journal of the Academy of Marketing Science*, Summer 2000, p. 424; Robin A. Coulter, Linda L. Price, and Lawrence Feick, "Rethinking the Origins of Involvement and Brand Commitment: Insights from Postsocialist Central Europe," *Journal of Consumer Research*, September 2003, p. 151; Gal Zauberman, "The Intertemporal Dynamics of Consumer Lock-In," *Journal of Consumer Research*, December 2003, p. 405; Brian T. Ratchford, "The Economics of Consumer Knowledge," *Journal of Consumer Research*, March 2001, p. 397; Cele Otnes, Tina M. Lowrey, and L J. Shrum, "Toward an Understanding of Consumer Ambivalence," *Journal of Consumer Research*, June 1997, p. 80; Ronald E. Goldsmith, "Consumer Involvement: Concepts and Research," *Journal of the Academy of Marketing Science*, Summer 1996, p. 281; Jeffrey B. Schmidt and Richard A. Spreng, "A Proposed Model of External Consumer Information Search," *Journal of the Academy of Marketing Science*, Summer 1996, p. 246; Raj Arora, "Consumer Involvement—What It Offers to Advertising Strategy," *International Journal of Advertising* 4, no. 2 (1985), p. 119; J. Brock Smith and Julia M. Bristor, "Uncertainty Orientation: Explaining Differences in Purchase Involvement and External Search," *Psychology & Marketing*, November/December 1994, p. 587.

30. Adapted from E. M. Rogers, *Diffusion of Innovation* (New York: Free Press, 2003). For sampling examples, see "Mr., Mrs., Meet Mr. Clean," *The Wall Street Journal*, January 30, 2003, p. B1; "J&J Supports Marathon Runners at Point of Pain," *Brandweek*, December 2, 2002, p. 32; "Taking the Free Out of Free Samples," *The Wall Street Journal*, September 25, 2002, p. D1; "Marketers Revel with Spring Breakers," *USA Today*, March 12, 2002, p. 3B; "When Free Samples Become Saviors," *The Wall Street Journal*, August 14, 2001, p. B1; "Small Wonder," *The Wall Street Journal*, June 25, 2001, p. R1; "Use of Samples in Drug Industry Raises Concern," *The Wall Street Journal*, July 19, 2000, p. B1; "Try It. You'll Like It," *The Wall Street Journal*, September 27, 1999, p. 15. See also Michael A. Jones, David L. Mothersbaugh, and Sharon E. Beatty, "Switching Barriers and Repurchase Intentions in Services," *Journal of Retailing*, Summer 2000, p. 259; Kevin Mason, Thomas Jensen, Scot Burton, and Dave Roach, "The Accuracy of Brand and Attribute Judgments: the Role of Information Relevancy, Product Experience, and Attribute-Relationship Schemata," *Journal of the Academy of Marketing Science*, Summer 2001, p. 307; Jan-Benedict E. M. Steenkamp and Katrijn Gielens, "Consumer and Market Drivers of the Trial Probability of New Consumer Packaged Goods," *Journal of Consumer Research*, December 2003, p. 368; Stephen J. Hoch, "Product Experience Is Seductive," *Journal of Consumer Research*, December 2002, p. 448.

31. "PepsiCo Tries to Clarify Pepsi One's Image," *The Wall Street Journal*, February 25, 2000, p. B7.

32. J. Jeffrey Inman and Marcel Zeelenberg, "Regret in Repeat Purchase Versus Switching Decisions: the Attenuating Role of Decision Justifiability," *Journal of Consumer Research*, Jun 2002, p. 116; Michael Tsiros and Vikas Mittal, "Regret: A Model of its Antecedents and Consequences in Consumer Decision Making," *Journal of Consumer Research*, March 2000, p. 401; Thomas A. Burnham, Judy K. Frels, and Vijay Mahajan, "Consumer Switching Costs: a Typology, Antecedents, and Consequences," *Journal of the Academy of Marketing Science*, Spring 2003, p. 109; Ziv Carmon, Klaus Wertenbroch, and Marcel Zeelenberg, "Option Attachment: When Deliberating Makes Choosing Feel like Losing," *Journal of Consumer Research*, Jun 2003, p. 15; Alan D. J. Cooke, Tom Meyvis, and Alan Schwartz, "Avoiding Future Regret in Purchase-Timing

Decisions," *Journal of Consumer Research*, March 2001, p. 447; Anna S. Mattila, "The Impact of Cognitive Intertia on Postconsumption Evaluation Processes," *Journal of the Academy of Marketing Science*, Summer 2003, p. 287; William Cunnings and Mark Venkatesan, "Cognitive Dissonance and Consumer Behavior: A Review of the Evidence," *Journal of Marketing Research*, August 1976, p. 303; Sarah Fisher Gardial et al., "Comparing Consumers' Recall of Prepurchase and Postpurchase Product Evaluation Experience," *Journal of Consumer Research*, March 1994, p. 548.

33. Robert M. March, *The Honourable Customer: Marketing and Selling to the Japanese in the 1990s* (Melbourne, Vic.: Longman Professional, 1990); Robert Gottliebsen, "Japan's Stark Choices," *Business Review Weekly*, October 16, 1992. See also Annamma Joy, "Gift Giving in Hong Kong and the Continuum of Social Ties," *Journal of Consumer Research*, September 2001, p. 239.

34. "Fuel and Freebies," *The Wall Street Journal*, June 10, 2002, p. B1.

CHAPTER 7

1. Available from World Wide Web: <http://www.johndeere.com> and <http://www.jdparts.com> and <http://www.metokote.com>. See also "Outsourcing Is More than Cost Cutting," *Fortune*, October 26, 1998, p. 238C; *2003 Annual Report*, Deere & Company; *1999 Annual Report*, Deere & Company.

2. "Detroit to Suppliers: Quality or Else," *Fortune*, September 30, 1996, p. 134C. See also Thomas H. Stevenson and Frank C. Barnes, "What Industrial Marketers Need to Know Now about ISO 9000 Certification: a Review, Update, and Integration with Marketing," *Industrial Marketing Management*, November 2002, p. 695; Roger Calantone and Gary Knight, "The Critical Role of Product Quality in the International Performance of Industrial Firms," *Industrial Marketing Management*, November 2000, p. 493; Stanley E. Fawcett, Roger J. Calantone, and Anthony Roath, "Meeting Quality and Cost Imperatives in a Global Market," *International Journal of Physical Distribution & Logistics Management*, (6) 2000, p. 472; G. M. Naidu, V. K. Prasad, and Arno Kleimenhagen, "Purchasing's Preparedness for ISO 9000 International Quality Standards," *International Journal of Purchasing & Materials Management*, Fall 1996, p. 46; Wade Ferguson, "Impact of the ISO 9000 Series Standards on Industrial Marketing," *Industrial Marketing Management*, July 1996, p. 305.

3. "The Push to Streamline Supply Chains," *Fortune*, March 3, 1997, pp. 108C–R; P. F. Johnson, Michiel R. Leenders, and Harold E. Fearon, "Evolving Roles and Responsibilities of Purchasing Organizations," *International Journal of Purchasing & Materials Management*, Winter 1998, p. 2; Scott Elliott, "Collaborative Advantage: Winning Through Extended Enterprise Supplier Networks," *The Journal of Product Innovation Management*, September 2001, p. 352; Chris Howgego, "Maximizing Competitiveness Through the Supply Chain," *International Journal of Retail & Distribution Management*, (11) 2002, p. 603; Robert J. Trent and Robert M. Monczka, "Understanding Integrated Global Sourcing," *International Journal of Physical Distribution & Logistics Management*, (7) 2003, p. 607; Harry R. Page, "Revolution in Purchasing: Building Competitive Power Through Proactive Purchasing," *International Journal of Purchasing & Materials Management*, Fall 1996, p. 56; Joseph R. Carter and Ram Narasimhan, "A Comparison of North American and European Future Purchasing Trends," *International Journal of Purchasing & Materials Management*, Spring 1996, p. 12.

4. Jae H. Pae, Namwoon Kim, Jim K. Han, and Leslie Yip, "Managing Intraorganizational Diffusion of Innovations: Impact of Buying Center Dynamics and Environments," *Industrial Marketing Management*, November 2002, p. 719; Jeffrey E. Lewin, "The Effects of Downsizing on Organizational Buying Behavior: An Empirical Investigation," *Journal of the Academy of Marketing Science*, Spring 2001, p. 151; Larry C. Giunipero and Judith F. Vogt, "Empowering the Purchasing Function: Moving to

Team Decisions," *International Journal of Purchasing & Materials Management*, Winter 1997, p. 8; Jerome M. Katrichis, "Exploring Departmental Level Interaction Patterns in Organizational Purchasing Decisions," *Industrial Marketing Management*, March 1998, p. 135; Robert D. McWilliams, Earl Naumann, and Stan Scott, "Determining Buying Center Size," *Industrial Marketing Management*, February 1992, p. 43; Ajay Kohli, "Determinants of Influence in Organizational Buying: A Contingency Approach," *Journal of Marketing*, July 1989, p. 50; Melvin R. Mattson, "How to Determine the Composition and Influence of a Buying Center," *Industrial Marketing Management*, August 1988, p. 205; Barbara C. Perdue, "The Size and Composition of the Buying Firm's Negotiation Team in Rebuys of Component Parts," *Journal of the Academy of Marketing Science*, Spring 1989, p. 121; R. Venkatesh, Ajay K. Kohli, and Gerald Zaltman, "Influence Strategies in Buying Centers," *Journal of Marketing*, October 1995, p. 71.

5. Daniel J. Flint, Robert B. Woodruff, and Sarah Fisher Gardial, "Exploring the Phenomenon of Customers' Desired Value Change in a Business-to-Business Context," *Journal of Marketing*, October 2002, p. 102; E. Stephen Grant, "Buyer-Approved Selling: Sales Strategies from the Buyers Side of the Desk," *Journal of the Academy of Marketing Science*, Winter 2004, p. 99; W. E. I. Patton, "Use of Human Judgment Models in Industrial Buyers' Vendor Selection Decisions," *Industrial Marketing Management*, March 1996, p. 135; Minette E. Drumwright, "Socially Responsible Organizational Buying: Environmental Concern As a Noneconomic Buying Criterion," *Journal of Marketing*, July 1994, p. 1; Lisa M. Ellram, "A Structured Method for Applying Purchasing Cost Management Tools," *International Journal of Purchasing & Materials Management*, Winter 1996, p. 11; Morgan P. Miles, Linda S. Munilla, and Gregory R. Russell, "Marketing and Environmental Registration/Certification: What Industrial Marketers Should Understand About ISO 14000," *Industrial Marketing Management*, July 1997, p. 363; Sime Curkovic and Robert Handfield, "Use of ISO 9000 and Baldrige Award Criteria in Supplier Quality Evaluation," *International Journal of Purchasing & Materials Management*, Spring 1996, p. 2; M. Bixby Cooper, Cornelia Droge, and Patricia J. Daugherty, "How Buyers and Operations Personnel Evaluate Service," *Industrial Marketing Management* 20, no. 1 (1991), p. 81.

6. Richard F. Beltramini, "Exploring the Effectiveness of Business Gifts: Replication and Extension," *Journal of Advertising*, Summer 2000, p. 75; Dong-Jin Lee, M. Joseph Sirgy, James R. Brown and Monroe Murphy Bird, "Importers' Benevolence Toward Their Foreign Export Suppliers," *Journal of the Academy of Marketing Science*, Winter 2004, p. 32; Jeanette J. Arbuthnot, "Identifying Ethical Problems Confronting Small Retail Buyers During the Merchandise Buying Process," *Journal of Business Ethics*, May 1997, p. 745; Gail K. McCracken and Thomas J. Callahan, "Is There Such a Thing As a Free Lunch?" *International Journal of Purchasing & Materials Management*, Winter 1996, p. 44; Robert W. Cooper, Garry L. Frank, and Robert A. Kemp, "The Ethical Environment Facing the Profession of Purchasing and Materials Management," *International Journal of Purchasing & Materials Management*, Spring 1997, p. 2; I. Fredrick Trawick, John E. Swan, Gail W. McGee, and David R. Rink, "Influence of Buyer Ethics and Salesperson Behavior on Intention to Choose a Supplier," *Journal of the Academy of Marketing Science*, Winter 1991, p. 17; J. A. Badenhorst, "Unethical Behaviour in Procurement: A Perspective on Causes and Solutions," *Journal of Business Ethics*, September 1994, p. 739.

7. Michael D. Smith, "The Impact of Shopbots on Electronic Markets," *Journal of the Academy of Marketing Science*, Fall 2002, p. 446; Carol C. Bienstock, "Understanding Buyer Information Acquisition for the Purchase of Logistics Services," *International Journal of Physical Distribution & Logistics Management*, (8) 2002, p. 636; David Tucker and Laurie Jones, "Leveraging the Power of the Internet for Optimal Supplier Sourcing," *International Journal of Physical Distribution & Logistics Management*, (3) 2000, p. 255; H. L. Brossard, "Information Sources Used by an Organization During a Complex Decision Process: An

Exploratory Study," *Industrial Marketing Management*, January 1998, p. 41; Michele D. Bunn, "Taxonomy of Buying Decision Approaches," *Journal of Marketing*, January 1993, p. 38; Patricia M. Doney and Gary M. Armstrong, "Effects of Accountability on Symbolic Information Search and Information Analysis by Organizational Buyers," *Journal of the Academy of Marketing Science*, Winter 1996, p. 57; Thomas G. Ponzurick, "International Buyers Perspective Toward Trade Shows and Other Promotional Methods," *Journal of Marketing Theory & Practice*, Winter 1996, p. 9; Mark A. Farrell and Bill Schroder, "Influence Strategies in Organizational Buying Decisions," *Industrial Marketing Management*, July 1996, p. 293; Richard G. Newman, "Monitoring Price Increases With Economic Data: A Practical Approach," *International Journal of Purchasing & Materials Management*, Fall 1997, p. 35; Barbara Kline and Janet Wagner, "Information Sources and Retailer Buyer Decision-Making: The Effect of Product-Specific Buying Experience," *Journal of Retailing*, Spring 1994, p. 75; Ellen Day and Hiram C. Barksdale, Jr., "How Firms Select Professional Services," *Industrial Marketing Management*, May 1992, p. 85; Edward F. Fern and James R. Brown, "The Industrial/Consumer Marketing Dichotomy: A Case of Insufficient Justification," *Journal of Marketing*, Spring 1984, p. 68; Rowland T. Moriarty, Jr. and Robert E. Spekman, "An Empirical Investigation of the Information Sources Used During the Industrial Buying Process," *Journal of Marketing Research*, May 1984, p. 137.

8. "With Promise of Big Savings, Net Bill Paying Could Soon Win Fans among U.S. Businesses," *Investor's Business Daily*, February 26, 2001, p. A7; "How Baxter, PNC, Pratt & Whitney Make the Internet Work for Them," *Investor's Business Daily*, February 12, 2001, p. A1; "Look, Ma, No Humans," *BusinessWeek E.Biz*, November 20, 2000, p. EB132; "Hewlett-Packard's Slick Procurement System," *Ecompany*, November 2000, p. 236; "Setting Standards for Corporate Purchasing on the Internet," *Fortune*, September 8, 1997, p. 156; "Invoice? What's an Invoice?" *BusinessWeek*, June 10, 1996, p. 110. See also Werner Delfmann, Sascha Albers and Martin Gehring, "The Impact of Electronic Commerce on Logistics Service Providers," *International Journal of Physical Distribution & Logistics Management*, (3) 2002, p. 203; Daniel Knudsen, "Aligning Corporate Strategy and E-procurement Tools," *International Journal of Physical Distribution & Logistics Management*, (8) 2003, p. 720; Earl D. Honeycutt, Theresa B. Flaherty, and Ken Benassi, "Marketing Industrial Products on the Internet," *Industrial Marketing Management*, January 1998, p. 63.

9. "The Push to Streamline Supply Chains," *Fortune*, March 3, 1997, p. 108C; "Push from Above," *The Wall Street Journal*, May 23, 1996, p. R24; "The New Golden Rule of Business," *Fortune*, February 21, 1994, p. 60.

10. For other examples of big/small partnerships, see "A Fruitful Relationship," *BusinessWeek E.Biz*, November 20, 2000, pp. EB94–EB96; "Automating an Automaker," *Inc. Tech 2000*, No. 4, p. 86. See also "Polaroid Corp. Is Selling Its Technique for Limiting Supplier Price Increases," *The Wall Street Journal*, February 13, 1985, p. 36; "Making Honda Parts, Ohio Company Finds, Can Be Road to Ruin," *The Wall Street Journal*, October 5, 1990, p. A1. See also Paul N. Bloom and Vanessa G. Perry, "Retailer Power and Supplier Welfare: the Case of Wal-Mart," *Journal of Retailing*, Fall 2001, p. 379.

11. "A Blaze in Albuquerque Sets Off Major Crisis for Cell-Phone Giants," *The Wall Street Journal*, January 29, 2001, p. A1; "Toyota's Fast Rebound after Fire at Supplier Shows Why It Is Tough," *The Wall Street Journal*, May 8, 1997, p. A1; Larry R. Smeltzer and Sue P. Siferd, "Proactive Supply Management: The Management of Risk," *International Journal of Purchasing & Materials Management*, Winter 1998, p. 38; Paul D. Larson and Jack D. Kulchitsky, "Single Sourcing and Supplier Certification: Performance and Relationship Implications," *Industrial Marketing Management*, January 1998, p. 73; Cathy Owens Swift, "Preferences for Single Sourcing and Supplier Selection," *Journal of Business Research*, February 1995, p. 105.

12. "You Buy My Widgets, I'll Buy Your Debt," *BusinessWeek*, August 1, 1988, p. 85; Robert E. Weigand, "The Problems of Managing Reciprocity," *California Management Review*, Fall 1973, p. 40.

13. Available from World Wide Web: <http://www.getradeweb.com> and <http://www.gegxs.com>. See also "Why EDI Won't Die," *Business 2.0*, August 2003, p. 68; "Sales Are Clicking on Manufacturing's Internet Mart," *Fortune*, July 7, 1997, pp. 136C–T.

14. Available from World Wide Web: <http://www.national.com>. See also "Web Masters," *Sales & Marketing Management*, 2000 and 2001.

15. Available from World Wide Web: <http://www.naics.com>. See also "Classified Information," *American Demographics*, July 1999, p. 16; "SIC: The System Explained," *Sales and Marketing Management*, April 22, 1985, p. 52; "Enhancement of SIC System Being Developed," *Marketing News Collegiate Edition*, May 1988, p. 4.

16. U.S. Bureau of the Census, *Statistical Abstract of the United States 2002* (Washington, DC: U.S. Government Printing Office, 2001); U.S. Bureau of the Census, *County Business Patterns 1998, United States* (Washington, DC: U.S. Government Printing Office, 2000). For more on targeting small business, see "Small Firms Enjoy Courtship of Big Suppliers," *The Wall Street Journal*, June 24, 2003, p. B9. For more on Canon, see "Perfecting the Pitch," *The Wall Street Journal*, May 23, 1996, p. R26; *1996 Annual Report*, Canon; "Can Anyone Duplicate Canon's Personal Copiers' Success?" *Marketing and Media Decisions*, Special Issue, Spring 1985, p. 97.

17. *2003 Annual Report*, Super Valu; *1996 Annual Report*, Super Valu.

18. *2003 Annual Report*, Safeway; *2003 Annual Report*, Food Lion; *2003 Annual Report*, Winn-Dixie; *2003 Annual Report*, A&P; Daulatram B. Lund, "Retail Scanner Checkout System: How Buying Committees Functioned," *Industrial Marketing Management* 18, no. 3 (1989), p. 179; Janet Wagner, Richard Ettenson, and Jean Parrish, "Vendor Selection Among Retail Buyers: An Analysis by Merchandise Division," *Journal of Retailing*, Spring 1989, p. 58.

19. "Create Open-to-Buy Plans the Easy Way," *Retail Control*, December 1984, p. 21.

20. Based on U.S. Census data and "Uncle Sam Is a Tough Customer," *Investor's Business Daily*, October 20, 2003, p. A8; "Hand-Helds' New Frontier," *The Wall Street Journal*, August 8, 2003, p. B1; "Super Soldiers," *BusinessWeek*, July 28, 2003, p. 62; "For G.I. Joe, Smart Uniforms via Nanotech," *BusinessWeek*, June 9, 2003, p. 125; "Supplier's Armor Plates Find a Ready Market," *Investor's Business Daily*, May 8, 2003, p. A7; "The Humvee of Laptops," *BusinessWeek*, April 21, 2003, p. 74; "Invented to Save Gas, Kevlar Now Saves Lives," *USA Today*, April 16, 2003, p. 1B; "Raytheon on Target," *Business 2.0*, February 2003, p. 79; "Mickey Mouse, Nike Give Advice on Air Security," *The Wall Street Journal*, January 24, 2002, p. B1; "The Marines Learn New Tactics—from Wal-Mart," *BusinessWeek*, December 24, 2001, p. 74; Sheryl B. Ball and Catherine C. Eckel, "Buying Status: Experimental Evidence on Status in Negotiation," *Psychology & Marketing*, July 1996, p. 381; Robert Gulbro and Paul Herbig, "Negotiating Successfully in Cross-Cultural Situations," *Industrial Marketing Management*, May 1996, p. 235; William C. Perkins, James C. Hershauer, Abbas Foroughi, and Michael M. Delaney, "Can a Negotiation Support System Help a Purchasing Manager?" *International Journal of Purchasing & Materials Management*, Spring 1996, p. 37.

CHAPTER 8

1. Available from World Wide Web: <http://www.whitestrips.com>; "The New and Improved P&G," *Brandweek*, November 17, 2003, p. 44; "Crest Biting Back with Whiter Strips," *Brandweek*, September 8, 2003, p. 6; "P&G: New and Improved," *BusinessWeek*, July 7, 2003, p. 52; "P&G Seeks Rejuvenating Effect for New Crest Line," *Brandweek*, June

16, 2003, p. 7; "The Cranky Consumer Works on Its Smile," *The Wall Street Journal*, January 14, 2003, p. D1; "Information, Please," *The Wall Street Journal Reports*, October 29, 2001, p. R6; "How Do You Feel about a $44 Tooth-Bleaching Kit?" *Business 2.0*, October 2001, p. 126.

2. "Winging into Wireless," *BusinessWeek E.Biz*, February 18, 2002, pp. EB8–EB9; "How an Intranet Opened Up the Door to Profits," *BusinessWeek E.Biz*, July 26, 1999, pp. EB32–EB38; "Here Comes the Intranet," *BusinessWeek*, February 26, 1996, p. 76. See also Dale D. Achabal, Shelby H. McIntyre, Stephen A. Smith and Kirthi Kalyanam, "A Decision Support System for Vendor Managed Inventory," *Journal of Retailing*, Winter 2000, p. 430.

3. Gary L. Lilien, Arvind Rangaswamy, Gerrit H. van Bruggen, and Berend Wierenga, "Bridging the Marketing Theory-Practice Gap with Marketing Engineering," *Journal of Business Research*, February 2002, p. 111; "Virtual Management," *BusinessWeek*, September 21, 1998, p. 80; John T. Mentzer and Nimish Gandhi, "Expert Systems in Marketing: Guidelines for Development," *Journal of the Academy of Marketing Science*, Winter, 1992, p. 73; William D. Perreault, Jr., "The Shifting Paradigm in Marketing Research," *Journal of the Academy of Marketing Science*, Fall 1992, p. 367; J.M. McCann, W.G. Lahti, and J. Hill, "The Brand Manager's Assistant: A Knowledge-Based System Approach to Brand Management," *International Journal of Research in Marketing*, April 1991, p. 51.

4. Available from World Wide Web: <http://www.lenscrafters.com>; "LensCrafters Hits One Billion in Sales," *Business Wire*, February 3, 1998; "LensCrafters Polishes Image with Style," *Chain Store Age Executive*, October 1996, p. 144; "'SuperOpticals' Edge out the Corner Optician," *Adweek's Marketing Week*, October 1, 1990, p. 36; "LensCrafters Takes the High Road," *Adweek's Marketing Week*, April 30, 1990, p. 26.

5. Ram Narasimhan and Soo Wook Kim, "Information System Utilization Strategy for Supply Chain Integration," *Journal of Business Logistics*, (2) 2001, p. 51; Stanley F. Slater and John C. Narver, "Intelligence Generation and Superior Customer Value," *Journal of the Academy of Marketing Science*, Winter 2000, p. 120; Mark Peyrot, Nancy Childs, Doris Van Doren, and Kathleen Allen, "An Empirically Based Model of Competitor Intelligence Use," *Journal of Business Research*, September 2002, p. 747; Bruce H. Clark, "Business Intelligence Using Smart Techniques," *Journal of the Academy of Marketing Science*, Fall 2003, p. 488; Philip B. Evans and Thomas S. Wurster, "Strategy and the New Economics of Information," *Harvard Business Review*, September–October 1997, p. 70; Deborah Utter, "Information-Driven Marketing Decisions: Development of Strategic Information Systems," *Journal of the Academy of Marketing Science*, Spring 1998, p. 157; James M. Sinkula, "Market Information Processing and Organizational Learning," *Journal of Marketing*, January 1994, p. 35; Lawrence B. Chonko, John F. Tanner, Jr., and Ellen Reid Smith, "The Sales Force's Role in International Marketing Research and Marketing Information Systems," *Journal of Personal Selling and Sales Management*, Winter, 1991, p. 69; James C. Bondra and Tim R. V. Davis, "Marketing's Role in Cross-Functional Information Management," *Industrial Marketing Management*, May 1996, p. 187.

6. For more on CRM, see Chapter 3, endnote 9. See also "Study Finds High CRM Success Rate," *BtoB*, December 9, 2002, p. 19; "Data Mining: Welcome to Harrah's," *Business 2.0*, April 2002, p. 48; "The Net as a Lifeline," *BusinessWeek E.Biz*, October 29, 2001, pp. EB16–EB23; "Moving Up to CRM," *Business 2.0*, August/September 2001, p. 149; "Marketers Hone Targeting," *Advertising Age*, June 18, 2001, p. T16; "Data Miners Reel after Wal-Mart Snub," *Brandweek*, May 21, 2001, p. 9; "Closer Than Ever," *BusinessWeek Small Biz*, May 21, 2001, p. 14; "CRM: Shooting Holes in the Hype," *Advertising Age*, April 16, 2001, p. 1; "Firms See Value of CRM Software, but Adoption Can Be Costly," *Investor's Business Daily*, April 4, 2001, p. A7; "A Singular Sensation," *Brandweek*, February 28, 2001, p. 32; "The New Software Whizzes,"

BusinessWeek E.Biz, December 11, 2000, pp. EB30–EB42; "Looking for Patterns," *The Wall Street Journal*, June 21, 1999, p. R16; "Know Your Customer," *The Wall Street Journal*, June 21, 1999, p. R18. See also Kim Bartel Sheehan and Mariea Grubbs Hoy, "Dimensions of Privacy Concern among Online Consumers," *Journal of Public Policy & Marketing*, Spring 2000, p. 62; Siva K. Balasubramanian, "The New Marketing Research Systems—How to Use Strategic Database Information for Better Marketing Decisions," *Journal of the Academy of Marketing Science*, Spring 1996, p. 179; "What's the Best Source of Market Research?" *Inc.*, June 1992, p. 108. For more on privacy, see Chapter 13, endnote 9.

7. For a discussion of ethical issues in marketing research, see "Name, Please: Surveyor Quietly Sells Student Information to Youth Marketer," *The Wall Street Journal*, December 13, 2001, p. A1; "How 'Tactical Research' Muddied Diaper Debate: a Case," *The Wall Street Journal*, May 17, 1994, p. B1. See also Rita Marie Cain, "Supreme Court Expands Federal Power to Regulate the Availability and Use of Data," *Journal of the Academy of Marketing Science*, Fall 2001, p. 425; Malcolm Kirkup and Marylyn Carrigan, "Video Surveillance Research in Retailing: Ethical Issues," *International Journal of Retail & Distribution Management*, (11) 2000, p. 470; Brian Carroll, "Price of Privacy: Selling Consumer Databases in Bankruptcy," *Journal of Interactive Marketing*, Summer 2002, p. 47; Eve M. Caudill and Patrick E. Murphy, "Consumer Online Privacy: Legal and Ethical Issues," *Journal of Public Policy & Marketing*, Spring 2000, p. 7; John R. Sparks and Shelby D. Hunt, "Marketing Researcher Ethical Sensitivity: Conceptualization, Measurement, and Exploratory Investigation," *Journal of Marketing*, April 1998, p. 92; Naresh K. Malhotra and Gina L. Miller, "An Integrated Model for Ethical Decisions in Marketing Research," *Journal of Business Ethics*, February 1998, p. 263; Stephen B. Castleberry, Warren French and Barbara A. Carlin, "The Ethical Framework of Advertising and Marketing Research Practitioners: A Moral Development Perspective," *Journal of Advertising*, June 1993, p. 39.

8. Linda I. Nowak, Paul D. Boughton, and Arun J. A. Pereira, "Relationships Between Businesses and Marketing Research Firms," *Industrial Marketing Management*, November 1997, p. 487; Peter M. Chisnall, "The Effective Use of Market Research: A Guide for Management to Grow the Business," *International Journal of Market Research*, Summer 2000, Vol. 42, 3, p. 359; Seymour Sudman and Edward Blair, *Marketing Research: A Problem Solving Approach* (Burr Ridge, IL: Irwin/McGraw-Hill, 1998). See also Christine Moorman, Rohit Deshpande, and Gerald Zaltman, "Factors Affecting Trust in Market Research Relationships," *Journal of Marketing*, January 1993, p. 81.

9. "Special Report: 2001 David Ogilvy Research Awards," *American Demographics*, March 2001, p. S1; "Special Report: 2000 David Ogilvy Research Awards," *American Demographics*, March 2000, p. S1; "What Consumer Research Won't Tell You," *Brandweek*, November 1, 1999, p. 40; "Intelligence Agents," *American Demographics*, March 1999, p. 52; "Grandma Got Run Over by Bad Research," *Inc.*, January 1998, p. 27.

10. For more on Google, see "Can Google Grow Up?" *Fortune*, December 8, 2003, p. 102; "Seeking Growth, Search Engine Google Acts like Ad Agency," *The Wall Street Journal*, October 18, 2003, p. B1; "Google: The Search Engine that Could," *USA Today*, August 26, 2003, p. 1D; "Search Star: Rising Clout of Google Prompts Rush by Internet Rivals to Adapt," *The Wall Street Journal*, July 16, 2003, p. A1; "The World According to Google," *Newsweek*, December 16, 2002, p. 46. For more on search engines, see World Wide Web: <http://www.windweaver.com/searchtools> and <http://www.windweaver.com/searchengines>; "Sharpen Your Internet Search," *BusinessWeek*, November 3, 2003, p. 106; "Web Searches: The Fix Is In," *BusinessWeek*, October 6, 2003, p. 89; "No Excuse for Rigging Searches," *BusinessWeek*, October 6, 2003, p. 168; "Ask Jeeves Gets 'Intuitive' in Ads, without Butler's Help," *Adweek*, August 11, 2003, p. 12; "Battle of the Search Bots," *BtoB*, August 11, 2003, p. 1; "Technical Adviser: Making the Most of Searches," *The Wall Street Journal Reports*, June 16, 2003, p. R10.

11. For more on Census data, see "The National Headcount," *American Demographics*, March 2001, p. S12; "Counting on the Census," *The Wall Street Journal*, February 14, 2001, p. B1. See also "Library Sites Can Be Useful when Doing Online Research," *Investor's Business Daily*, April 5, 2001, p. A13.

12. Available from World Wide Web: <http://www.burke.com/ ice/online>; "A Face Any Business Can Trust," *Business 2.0*, December 2003, p. 58; "No Focus Groups Here," *Investor's Business Daily*, November 19, 2003, p. A4; "Is Viagra Vulnerable?" *BusinessWeek*, October 27, 2003, p. 70; "How the Roomba Was Realized," *BusinessWeek*, October 6, 2003, pp. IM10–IM12; "Borders Sets Out to Make the Book Business Businesslike," *The Wall Street Journal*, May 20, 2002, p. B1; "Quite Contrary: How Gingham and Polyester Rescued a Retailer," *The Wall Street Journal*, May 9, 2003, p. A1; "The New Science of Focus Groups," *American Demographics*, March 2003, p. 29; "Selling Cellphone with Mixed Messages," *The Wall Street Journal*, February 27, 2003, p. B5; "Botox for Broadcloth," *The Wall Street Journal*, October 7, 2002, p. A19; "Heinz Picks Purple as New EZ Squirt Color," *Brandweek*, June 25, 2001, p. 7; "Web Enhances Market Research," *Advertising Age*, June 18, 2001, p. T18. See also William J. McDonald, "Focus Group Research Dynamics and Reporting: An Examination of Research Objectives and Moderator Influences," *Journal of the Academy of Marketing Science*, Spring 1993, p. 161; Thomas Kiely, "Wired Focus Groups," *Harvard Business Review*, January–February 1998, p. 12.

13. "How Big Blue Is Turning Geeks into Gold," Fortune, June 9, 2003, p. 133.

14. "Selling Sibelius Isn't Easy," *American Demographics*, The 1994 Directory, p. 24; "Symphony Strikes a Note for Research as It Prepares to Launch a New Season," *Marketing News*, August 29, 1988, p. 12.

15. Available from World Wide Web: <http://www.sawtooth.com/pages/glossary>; "A New Style: QB Net. . . Japanese Consumers," *The Wall Street Journal Reports*, September 22, 2003, p. R3; "Marketers Re-Evaluate Research," *BtoB*, February 10, 2003, p. 1; "Today, Brawny Men Help with the Kids and the Housework," *The Wall Street Journal*, October 4, 2002, p. B2; "Educated Guesses: Sampling Is Taboo, but the Census Does Plenty of Imputing," *The Wall Street Journal*, August 30, 2001, p. A1; "You've Got Surveys," *American Demographics*, November 2000, p. 42; "A Matter of Opinion," *The Wall Street Journal Reports*, October 23, 2000, p. R46; "Online Testing Rated," *Advertising Age*, May 8, 2000, p. 64; "The Surfer in the Family," *American Demographics*, April 2000, p. 34; "Market Research for the Internet Has Its Drawbacks," *The Wall Street Journal*, March 2, 2000, p. B4; "High Level of Comfort Leads to Truthful Research Worth a Mint," *USA Today*, May 17, 1999, p. 1A. See also Stanley E. Griffis, Thomas J. Goldsby, and Martha Cooper, "Web-Based and Mail Surveys: a Comparison of Response, Data, and Cost," *Journal of Business Logistics*, (2) 2003, p. 237; Christine M. Fox, K. L. Robinson, and Debra Boardley, "Cost-Effectiveness of Follow-Up Strategies in Improving the Response Rate of Mail Surveys," *Industrial Marketing Management*, March 1998, p. 127; Kathy E. Green, "Sociodemographic Factors and Mail Survey Response," *Psychology & Marketing*, March 1996, p. 171; Terry L. Childers and Steven J. Skinner, "Toward a Conceptualization of Mail Survey Response Behavior," *Psychology & Marketing*, March 1996, p. 185.

16. Available from World Wide Web: <http://www.whirlpool.com> and <http://acsi.asqc.org>; " Like, What's a Spin Cycle?" The Wall Street Journal, June 4, 2002, p. B1; "Firms Hope to Clean Up Taking Housework High-Tech," *The Wall Street Journal*, March 16, 2001, p. B4; "As I Was Saying to My Refrigerator. . .," *BusinessWeek E.Biz*, September 18, 2000, p. EB40; "Now Are You Satisfied?" Fortune, February 16, 1998, p.161; "Product Pampering," *Brandweek*, June 16, 1997, p. 29; Deborah Duarte and Nancy Snyder, "From Experience: Facilitating Global Organizational Learning in Product Development at Whirlpool Corporation," *Journal of Product Innovation Management*, January 1997, p. 48.

17. "Red, White, and Blue," *Beverage Industry*, February 2002, p. 20.

18. For more on types of observation, see "Sharpening the Focus," *Brandweek*, November 3, 2003, p. 28; "Rear Window," *Business 2.0*, August 2003, p. 72; "U.S. Satellite May Play 'I Spy' with Brazil Citrus Industry," *The Wall Street Journal*, January 28, 2003, p. B1; "Shop, You're on Candid Camera," *USA Today*, November 6, 2002, p. 1B; "Special Report Ethnographic Research: Watch Me Now," *American Demographics*, October 2002, pp. S1–S8; "McDonald's Asks Mysetery Shoppers What Ails Sales," *The Wall Street Journal*, December 17, 2001, p. B1; "P&G Checks Out Real Life," *The Wall Street Journal*, May 17, 2001, p. B1; "Research on a Shoestring," *American Demographics*, April 2001, p. 38; "Attention Shoppers: This Man Is Watching You," *Fortune*, July 19, 1999, p. 131; "The New Market Research," *Inc.*, July 1998, p. 87. See also Stephen J. Grove and Raymond P. Fisk, "Observational Data Collection Methods for Services Marketing: An Overview," *Journal of the Academy of Marketing Science*, Summer 1992, p. 217; Magid M. Abraham and Leonard M. Lodish, "An Implemented System for Improving Promotion Productivity Using Store Scanner Data," *Marketing Science*, Summer 1993, p. 248.

19. "Will Your Web Business Work? Take It for a Test Drive," *Ecompany*, May 2001, p. 101; "Ads Awaken to Fathers' New Role in Family Life," *Advertising Age*, January 10, 1994, p. S8; "AT&T's Secret Multi-Media Trials Offer Clues to Capturing Interactive Audiences," *The Wall Street Journal*, July 28, 1993, p. B1; "Experimenting in the U.K.: Phone, Cable Deals Let U.S. Test Future," *USA Today*, June 28, 1993, p. 1B. See also Raymond R. Burke, "Virtual Shopping: Breakthrough in Marketing Research," *Harvard Business Review*, March–April 1996, p. 120; Glen L. Urban, Bruce D. Weinberg, and John R. Hauser, "Premarket Forecasting of Really-New Products," *Journal of Marketing*, January 1996, p. 47.

20. For more on Nielsen's people meters, see "Nielsen's Feud with TV Networks Shows Scarcity of Marketing Data," *The Wall Street Journal*, October 29, 2003, p. A1; "Nielsen Adapts Its Methods as TV Evolves," *The Wall Street Journal*, September 29, 2003, p. B1; "People Meters Push Right Button," *Advertising Age*, May 12, 2003, p. S22; "Confessions of a Nielsen Household," *American Demographics*, May 2001. See also "Trying to Clean Up Sweeps," *American Demographics*, May 2001, p. 42; "The Metrics System," *Brandweek*, November 13, 2000, p. 106; "Special Report: Top 25 Global Research Organizations," *Advertising Age*, August 24, 2000; "We're Being Watched," *American Demographics*, October 1998, p. 52; "Special Report: 100 Leading Research Companies," *Advertising Age*, May 19, 1997; Peter J. Danaher and Terence W. Beed, "A Coincidental Survey of People Meter Panelists: Comparing What People Say with What They Do," *Journal of Advertising Research*, January/February 1993, p. 86.

21. For more detail on data analysis techniques, see Joe Hair, Rolph Anderson, Ron Tatham, and William Black, *Multivariate Data Analysis* (New York: Prentice-Hall, 1998) or other marketing research texts. See also "Merry Maids Clean Up Territories with MapInfo System," *Investor's Business Daily*, February 20, 2001, p. A8; Michael D. Johnson and Elania J. Hudson, "On the Perceived Usefulness of Scaling Techniques in Market Analysis," *Psychology & Marketing*, October 1996, p. 653; Milton D. Rosenau, "Graphing Statistics and Data: Creating Better Charts," *Journal of Product Innovation Management*, March 1997, p. 144.

22. "Careful What You Ask For," *American Demographics*, July 1998, p. 8; See also John G. Keane, "Questionable Statistics," *American Demographics*, June 1985, p. 18. Detailed treatment of confidence intervals is beyond the scope of this text, but it is covered in most marketing research texts, such as Donald R. Lehmann and Russ Winer, *Analysis for Marketing Planning* (Burr Ridge, IL: Irwin/McGraw-Hill, 2001).

23. "Chinese Puzzle: Spotty Consumer Data," *The Wall Street Journal*, October 15, 2003, p. B1. See also Thomas Tsu Wee Tan and Tan Jee Lui,

"Globalization and Trends in International Marketing Research in Asia," *Journal of Business Research*, October 2002, p. 799; Masaaki Kotabe, "Using Euromonitor Database in International Marketing Research," *Journal of the Academy of Marketing Science*, Spring 2002, p. 172.

24. Alan R. Andreasen, "Cost-Conscious Marketing Research," *Harvard Business Review*, July–August, 1983, p. 74; A. Parasuraman, "Research's Place in the Marketing Budget," *Business Horizons*, March/April 1983, p. 25; Jack J. Honomichl, "Point of View: Why Marketing Information Should Have Top Executive Status," *Journal of Advertising Research*, November/December 1994, p. 61; Jim Bessen, "Riding the Marketing Information Wave," *Harvard Business Review*, September–October 1993, p. 150.

CHAPTER 9

1. Eric Giguere, "Getting Your Tools Ready," from Mobilized Software site at: <http://www.mobilizedsoftware.com/showArticle.jhtml?articleId=18200576&printableArticle=true>; Gail Kachadourian, "BlackBerry: Source of freedom, or crack for the work addict?" *Automotive News*, April 3, 2006; Arik Hesseldahl, Heather Green, "BlackBerry Won't Get Squashed," *BusinessWeek Online*, March 6, 2006; Todd Wasserman "The Fruits of His Labor," *Brandweek New York*, October 15, 2001.

2. R. Kenneth Teas and Sanjeev Agarwal, "The Effects of Extrinsic Product Cues on Consumers' Perceptions of Quality, Sacrifice, and Value," *Journal of the Academy of Marketing Science*, Spring 2000, p. 278; Amna Kirmani and Akshay R. Rao, "No Pain, No Gain: a Critical Review of the Literature on Signaling Unobservable Product Quality," *Journal of Marketing*, April 2000, p. 66; Neil A. Morgan and Douglas W. Vorhies, "Product Quality Alignment and Business Unit Performance," *The Journal of Product Innovation Management*, November 2001, p. 396; Joseph M. Juran, "Made In U.S.A.: A Renaissance in Quality," *Harvard Business Review*, July–August 1993, p. 42; "Measuring Quality Perception of America's Top Brands," *Brandweek*, April 4, 1994, p. 24; Neil A. Morgan and Nigel F. Piercy, "Market-Led Quality," *Industrial Marketing Management*, May 1992, p. 111.

3. For more on service expectations, see Chapter 6, endnote 14. For more on service quality, see *2003 Annual Report*, MCI; *2003 Annual Report*, Merrill Lynch. For an excellent example on Avis, see "The Payoff for Trying Harder," *Business 2.0*, July 2002, p. 84; "Avis to Try Even Harder with Ads Touting High Quality of Service," *The Wall Street Journal*, February 18, 2000, p. B9. For more on air service, see "Paved Paradise: The New Airport Parking Lots," *The Wall Street Journal*, November 12, 2003, p. D1; "Flat-Out Winners," *BusinessWeek*, October 27, 2003, p. 132. See also "The Demise of Free Pizza Delivery," *The Wall Street Journal*, August 19, 2003, p. D1; "Pizza Chains Deliver . . . Fees," *USA Today*, September 4, 2002, p. 3B. See also Neeli Bendapudi and Robert P. Leone, "Psychological Implications of Customer Participation in Co-Production," *Journal of Marketing*, January 2003, p. 14; Leonard L. Berry, Kathleen Seiders and Dhruv Grewal, "Understanding Service Convenience," *Journal of Marketing*, July 2002, p. 1; Matthew L. Meuter, Amy L. Ostrom, Robert I. Roundtree, and Mary Jo Bitner, "Self-Service Technologies: Understanding Customer Satisfaction with Technology-Based Service Encounters," *Journal of Marketing*, July 2000, p. 50; Valarie A. Zeithaml, A. Parasuraman and Arvind Malhotra, "Service Quality Delivery Through Web Sites: a Critical Review of Extant Knowledge," *Journal of the Academy of Marketing Science*, Fall 2002, p. 362; James L. Thomas, Scott J. Vitell, Faye W. Gilbert, and Gregory M. Rose, "The Impact of Ethical Cues on Customer Satisfaction with Service," *Journal of Retailing*, Fall 2002, p. 167; Mary Jo Bitner, Stephen W. Brown and Matthew L. Meuter, "Technology Infusion in Service Encounters," *Journal of the Academy of Marketing Science*, Winter 2000, p. 138; Valerie S. Folkes and Vanessa M. Patrick, "The Positivity Effect in Perceptions of Services: Seen One, Seen Them All?," *Journal of Consumer Research*, June 2003, p. 125; Dwayne D. Gremler, "Discovering the Soul of Service: The

Nine Drivers of Sustainable Business Success," *Journal of the Academy of Marketing Science*, Spring 2000, p. 311; James Golleher, "Value-Added Customer Service," *Journal of Personal Selling & Sales Management*, Spring 1997, p.71; James Reardon, Chip Miller, Ronald Hasty, and Blaise J. Waguespack, "A Comparison of Alternative Theories of Services Marketing," *Journal of Marketing Theory & Practice*, Fall 1996, p. 61; James C. Anderson and James A. Narus, "Capturing the Value of Supplementary Services," *Harvard Business Review*, January–February 1995, p. 75; Mary Jo Bitner, Bernard H. Booms, and Lois A. Mohr, "Critical Service Encounters: The Employee's Viewpoint," *Journal of Marketing*, October 1994, p. 95.

4. Edward M. Tauber, "Why Do People Shop?" *Journal of Marketing*, October 1972, p. 46; Christopher H. Lovelock, "Classifying Services to Gain Strategic Marketing Insights," *Journal of Marketing*, Summer 1983, p. 9. Tom Boyt and Michael Harvey, "Classification of Industrial Services," *Industrial Marketing Management*, July 1997, p. 291.

5. Dennis W. Rook, "The Buying Impulse," *Journal of Consumer Research*, September 1987, p. 189; Cathy J. Cobb and Wayne D. Hoyer, "Planned Versus Impulse Purchase Behavior," *Journal of Retailing*, Winter 1986, p. 384.

6. For example, see "Russian Maneuvers Are Making Palladium Ever More Precious," *The Wall Street Journal*, March 6, 2000, p. A1. See also William S. Bishop, John L. Graham, and Michael H. Jones, "Volatility of Derived Demand in Industrial Markets and Its Management Implications," *Journal of Marketing*, Fall 1984, p. 95.

7. William B. Wagner and Patricia K. Hall, "Equipment Lease Accounting in Industrial Marketing Strategy," *Industrial Marketing Management* 20, no. 4 (1991), p. 305; Robert S. Eckley, "Caterpillar's Ordeal: Foreign Competition in Capital Goods," *Business Horizons*, March/April 1989, p. 80; M. Manley, "To Buy or Not to Buy," *Inc.*, November 1987, p. 189.

8. P. Matthyssens and W. Faes, "OEM Buying Process for New Components: Purchasing and Marketing Implications," *Industrial Marketing Management*, August 1985, p. 145; Paul A. Herbig and Frederick Palumbo, "Serving the Aftermarket in Japan and the United States," *Industrial Marketing Management*, November 1993, p. 339; Timothy L. Wilson and Frank E. Smith, "Business Services 1982–1992: Growth, Industry Characteristics, Financial Performance," *Industrial Marketing Management*, March 1996, p. 162.

9. Ruth H. Krieger and Jack R. Meredith, "Emergency and Routine MRO Part Buying," *Industrial Marketing Management*, November 1985, p. 277; Warren A. French et al., "MRO Parts Service in the Machine Tool Industry," *Industrial Marketing Management*, November 1985, p. 283. See also "The Web's New Plumbers," *Ecompany*, March 2001, p. 126.

10. For more on Listerine PocketPaks, see "The Strip Club," *Business 2.0*, June 2003, p. 36; "Marketer of the Year: PocketPaks, a Breath of Minty Fresh Air," *Brandweek*, October 14, 2002, pp. M42–M46. For more on brand extensions, see "Hershey Has a Taste for Line Extensions," *Brandweek*, October 27, 2003, p. 4; Kellogg Milks Vanilla Trend for Special K," *Brandweek*, September 15, 2003, p. 4; "Mr. Clean Gets $50M Push," *Advertising Age*, August 18, 2003, p. 3; "Great for Combat and Camping," *BusinessWeek*, May 12, 2003, p. 12. For more on brand equity and brand value, see "Hard Lesson Learned: Premium and No-Frills Don't Mix," *The Wall Street Journal*, November 3, 2003, p. B1; "Nonprofits Can Provide a Brand Name that Sells," *The Wall Street Journal*, September 23, 2003, p. B11; "Rip Van Brands," *Brandweek*, July 14, 2003, p. 24; "Tyson: Is There Life Outside the Chicken Coop?" *BusinessWeek*, March 10, 2003, p. 77; "Can GE Make Lexan as Famous as Teflon?" *The Wall Street Journal*, March 7, 2003, p. B1; "The Art of Brand Revival," *Business 2.0*, September 2002, p. 45; "New ABCs of Branding," *The Wall Street Journal*, August 26, 2002, p. B1; "Cookware Heavyweights," *The Wall Street Journal*, June 21, 2002, p. B1; "Big Brands (Small Companies)," *BusinessWeek Small Biz*, August 13, 2001, p. 17; "When Designers

Attack!" *Ecompany*, June 2001, p. 45. See also Arjun Chaudhuri and Morris B. Holbrook, "The Chain of Effects from Brand Trust and Brand Affect to Brand Performance: the Role of Brand Loyalty," *Journal of Marketing*, April 2001, p. 81; Boonghee Yoo, Naveen Donthu and Sungho Lee, "An Examination of Selected Marketing Mix Elements and Brand Equity," *Journal of the Academy of Marketing Science*, Spring 2000, p. 195; Zeynep Gurhan-Canli, "The Effect of Expected Variability of Product Quality and Attribute Uniqueness on Family Brand Evaluations," *Journal of Consumer Research*, June 2003, p. 105; Russell Casey, "Designing Brand Identity: A Complete Guide to Creating, Building, and Maintaining Strong Brands," *Journal of the Academy of Marketing Science*, Winter 2004, p. 100; Subramanian Balachander and Sanjoy Ghose, "Reciprocal Spillover Effects: a Strategic Benefit of Brand Extensions," *Journal of Marketing*, January 2003, p. 1; Rashmi Adaval, "How Good Gets Better and Bad Gets Worse: Understanding the Impact of Affect on Evaluations of Known Brands," *Journal of Consumer Research*, December 2003, p. 352; Stijn M. J. Van Osselaer and Joseph W. Alba, "Consumer Learning and Brand Equity," *Journal of Consumer Research*, June 2000, p. 1; Sheri Bridges, Kevin Lane Keller and Sanjay Sood, "Communication Strategies for Brand Extensions: Enhancing Perceived Fit by Establishing Explanatory Links," *Journal of Advertising*, Winter 2000, p. 1; Elizabeth S. Moore, William L. Wilkie, and Richard J. Lutz, "Passing the Torch: Intergenerational Influences as a Source of Brand Equity," *Journal of Marketing*, April 2002, p. 17; Rohini Ahluwalia and Zeynep Gurhan-Canli, "The Effects of Extensions on the Family Brand Name: An Accessibility-Diagnosticity Perspective," *Journal of Consumer Research*, December 2000, p. 371; Kevin P. Gwinner and John Eaton, "Building Brand Image Through Event Sponsorship: the Role of Image Transfer," *Journal of Advertising*, Winter 1999, p. 47; Susan Mudambi, "Branding Importance in Business-To-Business Markets: Three Buyer Clusters," *Industrial Marketing Management*, September 2002, p. 525; James H. McAlexander, John W. Schouten, and Harold F. Koening, "Building Brand Community," *Journal of Marketing*, January 2002, p. 38; Richard C. Leventhal, "Branding Strategy," *Business Horizons*, September–October 1996, p. 17; Deborah R. John, Barbara Loken, and Christopher Joiner, "The Negative Impact of Extensions: Can Flagship Products Be Diluted?" *Journal of Marketing*, January 1998, p. 19; Cathy J. Cobb-Walgren, Cynthia A. Ruble, and Naveen Donthu, "Brand Equity, Brand Preference, and Purchase Intent," *Journal of Advertising*, Fall 1995, p. 25; Vijay Vishwanath and Jonathan Mark, "Your Brand's Best Strategy," *Harvard Business Review*, May–June 1997, p. 123; John A. Quelch and David Kenny, "Extend Profits, Not Product Lines," *Harvard Business Review*, September 1994–October 1994, p. 153; Linda B. Samuels and Samuels Jeffery M, "Famous Marks Now Federally Protected Against Dilution," *Journal of Public Policy & Marketing*, Fall 1996, p. 307; Pamela W. Henderson and Joseph A. Cote, "Guidelines for Selecting or Modifying Logos," *Journal of Marketing*, April 1998, p. 14; Erich Joachimsthaler and David A. Aaker, "Building Brands Without Mass Media," *Harvard Business Review*, January–February 1997, p. 39.

11. "Long Live the Dudes," *Adweek*, June 2, 2003, p. 32; "Pepsi Is Planning Promotions to Put Some Fizz into Summer," *The Wall Street Journal*, May 1, 2003, p. B5; "Pepsi Plans New Mountain Dew Flavor," *The Wall Street Journal*, March 12, 2003, p. B9A; "Call It the Pepsi Blue Generation," *BusinessWeek*, February 3, 2003, p. 96; "On the Web, Word-of-Mouth Marketing Can Become Viral," *Investor's Business Daily*, January 30, 2002, p. A4; "Cracking the Code for Pepsi," *Brandweek*, October 14, 2002, p. M13; "Beat Is On for Pepsi," *USA Today*, August 28, 2002, p. 3B" Pepsi Adds Blue-Hued Beverage to Spectrum of Colored Sodas," *The Wall Street Journal*, May 8, 2002. B2; "Code Red: PepsiCo's Guerrilla Conquest," *The Wall Street Journal*, August 17, 2001, p. B5.

12. "Global Products Require Name-Finders," *The Wall Street Journal*, April 11, 1996, p. B8; Martin S. Roth, "Effects of Global Market Conditions on Brand Image Customization and Brand Performance," *Journal of Advertising*, Winter 1995, p. 55.

13. Available from World Wide Web: <http://www.yahoo.com>. See also "Coterie of Early Hires Made Yahoo! A Hit but an Insular Place," *The Wall Street Journal*, March 9, 2001, p. A1; "Voulez-vous Yahoo Avec Moi?" *Fortune*, October 16, 2000, p. 245; "The Two Grown-Ups behind Yahoo!'s Surge," *The Wall Street Journal*, April 10, 1998, p. B1.

14. "Road to Foreign Franchises Is Paved with New Problems," *The Wall Street Journal*, May 14, 2001, p. B10; "Tiger Fight Sees Kellogg, ExxonMobil Clash in Court," *Ad Age Global*, November 2000; "Wrestling, Wildlife Fund Battle over WWF Site," *USA Today*, October 25, 2000, p. 1A; "More Firms Flash New Badge," *USA Today*, October 4, 2000, p. 3B; "Name Lawsuit Prompts AppleSoup to Become Flycode," *USA Today*, September 11, 2000, p. 6B. See also Karen Gantt, "Revisiting the Scope of Lanham Act Protection," *Journal of the Academy of Marketing Science*, Winter 2004, p. 102; Maureen Morrin and Jacob Jacoby, "Trademark Dilution: Empirical Measures for an Elusive Concept," *Journal of Public Policy & Marketing*, Fall 2000, p. 265; Chris Janiszewski and Tom Meyvis, "Effects of Brand Logo Complexity, Repetition, and Spacing on Processing Fluency and Judgment," *Journal of Consumer Research*, June 2001, p. 18; F. C. Hong, Anthony Pecotich and Clifford J. Schultz II, "Brand Name Translation: Language Constraints, Product Attributes, and Consumer Perceptions in East and Southeast Asia," *Journal of International Marketing*, (2) 2002, p. 29; Daniel J. Howard, Roger A. Kerin, and Charles Gengler, "The Effects of Brand Name Similarity on Brand Source Confusion: Implications for Trademark Infringement," *Journal of Public Policy & Marketing*, Fall 2000, p. 250; Charles H. Schwepker, "Trademark Problems and How to Avoid Them," *Journal of the Academy of Marketing Science*, Winter 1997, p. 89; Lee B. Burgunder, "Trademark Protection of Product Characteristics: A Predictive Model," *Journal of Public Policy & Marketing*, Fall 1997, p. 277; Itamar Simonson, "Trademark Infringement from the Buyer Perspective: Conceptual Analysis and Measurement Implications," *Journal of Public Policy & Marketing*, Fall 1994, p. 181; "Asian Trademark Litigation Continues," *The Wall Street Journal*, February 16, 1994, p. B8.

15. Wendy Leung, "The Goods On Fakes," *The Vancouver Sun*, May 8, 2006, p. E1; Diane Francis, "Counterfeit laws too lax in Canada: Black market in bogus goods worth $30B annually," *National Post*, May 6, 2006, p. FP2.

16. "From Betamax to Kazaa: The Real War over Piracy," *Fortune*, October 27, 2003, p. 148; "Debate Heats Up as Student Spots Hole in CD Protection," *USA Today*, October 27, 2003, p. 1A; "Can Copyright Be Saved?" *The Wall Street Journal Reports*, October 20, 2003, p. R1; "Striking Back," *BusinessWeek*, September 29, 2003, p. 94; "Hollywood's Burning Issue," *The Wall Street Journal*, September 18, 2003, p. B1; "Hammering Away at Piracy," *USA Today*, September 11, 2003, p. 1D; "Music Industry Doesn't Know What Else to Do as It Lashes Out at File-Sharing," *USA Today*, September 10, 2003, p. 3B; "Indonesia Turns to Trademark Piracy," *The Wall Street Journal*, September 9, 2003, p. A20; "Increase in Software Piracy Could Blight Financial Future," *USA Today*, August 1, 2002, p. 1B; "Road Warriors: Motorcycle Makers from Japan Discover Piracy Made in China," *The Wall Street Journal*, July 25, 2001, p. A1; "Beijing's Phony War on Fakes," *Fortune*, October 30, 2000, p. 188; "Knocking Out the Knockoffs," *Fortune*, October 2, 2000, p. 213. See also Laurence Jacobs, A. Coskun Samli and Tom Jedlik, "The Nightmare of International Product Piracy: Exploring Defensive Strategies," *Industrial Marketing Management*, August 2001, p. 499; Janeen E. Olsen and Kent L. Granzin, "Using Channels Constructs to Explain Dealers' Willingness to Help Manufacturers Combat Counterfeiting," *Journal of Business Research*, June 1993, p. 147; Ronald F. Bush, Peter H. Bloch, and Scott Dawson, "Remedies for Product Counterfeiting," *Business Horizons*, January–February 1989, p. 59; Alexander Nill and Clifford J. Schultz II, "The Scourge of Global Counterfeiting," *Business Horizons*, November–December 1996, p. 37.

17. For more on licensing, see "Testing Limits of Licensing: SpongeBob-Motif Holiday Inn," *The Wall Street Journal*, October 9, 2003, p. B1ff,;

"Making Tracks beyond Tires," *Brandweek*, September 15, 2003, p. 16; "Candy Cosmetics: Licensing's Sweet Spot," *DSN Retailing Today*, August 4, 2003, p. 24; "The Creative License," *Brandweek*, June 9, 2003, p. 36; "Procter & Gamble Deals License Several Brand Names," *USA Today*, April 18, 2003, p. 3B; "Whoa, Cool Shirt. Yeah, It's a Pepsi," *Business-Week*, September 10, 2001, p. 84; "In Europe, Hot New Fashion for Urban Hipsters Comes from Peoria," *The Wall Street Journal*, August 8, 2001, p. B1; "Washed Up at Warnaco?" *Time*, June 25, 2001, p. 36; "Brand New Goods," *Time*, November 1, 1999; "Brand Builders: Licensing, the Color of Money," *Brandweek*, September 15, 1997, p. 22.

18. For more on branding organic foods, see "Health-Food Maker Hain Faces Rivals," *The Wall Street Journal*, August 13, 2003, p. B5B; "Big Brand Logos Pop Up in Organic Aisle," *The Wall Street Journal*, July 29, 2003, p. B1; "USDA Enters Debate on Organic Label Law," *The New York Times*, February 26, 2003, p. D1; "Food Industry Gags at Proposed Label Rule for Trans Fat," *The Wall Street Journal*, December 27, 2002, p. B1; "Curbs Are Eased on Food Makers' Health Claims," *The Wall Street Journal*, December 19, 2002, p. D4; "Organic Rules!" *Brandweek*, October 21, 2002, p. 3; "In Natural Foods, a Big Name's No Big Help," *The Wall Street Journal*, June 7, 2002, p. B1. See also Amitabh Mungale, "Managing Product Families," *Journal of Product Innovation Management*, January 1998, p. 102; Gloria Barczak, "Product Management," *Journal of Product Innovation Management*, September 1997, p. 425.

19. "Ten Years May Be Generic Lifetime," *Advertising Age*, March 23, 1987, p. 76; Brian F. Harris and Roger A. Strang, "Marketing Strategies in the Age of Generics," *Journal of Marketing*, Fall 1985, p. 70.

20. "Brand Killers," *Fortune*, August 11, 2003, p. 88; "Going Private (Label), *The Wall Street Journal*, June 12, 2003, p. B1; "7-Eleven Cracks Open a Private-Label Brew," *The Wall Street Journal*, May 2, 2003, p. B1; "Retailers Create Own-Label PCs as Brand Names Dwindle," *The Wall Street Journal*, May 3, 2002, p. B1; "White Clouds Could Bring Rain on P&G," *Advertising Age*, July 2, 2001, p. 4; "National Tool Brands Vie for Maximum Exposure," *DSN Retailing Today*, March 5, 2001, p. 26; "New Private-Label Alternatives Bring Changes to Supercenters, Clubs," *DSN Retailing Today*, February 5, 2001, p. 66; "Popularity of PL Toys Stems from Benefits in Cost, Exclusivity," *DSN Retailing Today*, November 20, 2000, p. 4; "Wal-Mart Stores Go Private (Label)," *Advertising Age*, November 29, 1999, p. 1. See also Rajeev Batra and Indrajit Sinha, "Consumer-Level Factors Moderating the Success of Private Label Brands," *Journal of Retailing*, Summer 2000, p. 175; John Low and Keith Blois, "The Evolution of Generic Brands in Industrial Markets: the Challenges to Owners of Brand Equity," *Industrial Marketing Management*, August 2002, p. 385; Judith A. Garretson, Dan Fisher, and Scot Burton, "Antecedents of Private Label Attitude and National Brand Promotion Attitude: Similarities and Differences," *Journal of Retailing*, Summer 2002, p. 91; Kusum L. Ailawadi, Scott A. Neslin and Karen Gedenk, "Pursuing the Value-Conscious Consumer: Store Brands Versus National Brand Promotions," *Journal of Marketing*, January 2001, p. 71; R. Sethuraman and J. Mittelstaedt, "Coupons and Private Labels: A Cross-Category Analysis of Grocery Products," *Psychology & Marketing*, November/December 1992, p. 487; John A. Quelch and David Harding, "Brands Versus Private Labels: Fighting to Win," *Harvard Business Review*, January–February 1996, p. 99.

21. For more on SoupatHand, see "Demand for Convenient Foods Continues to Rise," *Brandweek*, November 18, 2002, p. 8. For another example, milk packaging, see "Dean Foods: Dairy Processor Looks to Milk Other Products," *Investor's Business Daily*, March 28, 2003, p. A6; "Dean Foods: Dairy Firm Milks New Products for Growth, though Cows Still Account for Most Sales," *Investor's Business Daily*, September 18, 2002, p. A8; "Milk Chug Sweetens Double Chocolate Push," *Brandweek*, February 25, 2002, p. 9; "Many-Flavored Milk Competes with Sodas," *USA Today*, January 26, 2001, p. 1D.

22. "Thinking Outside the Can," *Brandweek*, October 13, 2003, p. 13; "Are Your Competitors Packing?" *Business 2.0*, July 2003, p. 52;

"Packaging Is the Capper," *Advertising Age*, May 5, 2003, p. 22; "Here's the Beef. So, Where's the Butcher?" *The New York Times*, February 15, 2003, p. B1; "Salad in Sealed Bags Isn't So Simple, It Seems," *The New York Times*, January 14, 2003, p. A1; "Finger Food: Marketers Push Individual Portions and Families Bite," *The Wall Street Journal*, July 23, 2002, p. A1; "Getting a Grip on Consumer Tastes," *BusinessWeek*, July 16, 2001, p. 12; "Color Me Popular: Marketers Shape Up Packaging," *USA Today*, February 8, 2001, p. 7B; "Heinz Puts Squeeze on Places Refilling Its Ketchup Bottles," *The Wall Street Journal*, June 22, 2000, p. A1; "What's Foiling the Aluminum Can," *BusinessWeek*, October 6, 1997, p. 106; "Breakthrough Bottles," *Brandweek*, May 20, 1996, p. 32. See also Brian Wansink and Koert van Ittersum, "Bottoms Up! The Influence of Elongation on Pouring and Consumption Volume," *Journal of Consumer Research*, December 2003, p. 455; Brian Wansink, "Can Package Size Accelerate Usage Volume?" *Journal of Marketing*, July 1996, p. 1.

23. "Bar Codes: Beyond the Checkout Counter," *BusinessWeek*, April 8, 1985, p. 90; Ronald C. Goodstein, "UPC Scanner Pricing Systems: Are They Accurate?" *Journal of Marketing*, April 1994, p. 20.

24. Paula Fitzgerald, Bone Corey, and Robert J. Corey, "Ethical Dilemmas in Packaging: Beliefs of Packaging Professionals," *Journal of Macromarketing*, Spring 1992, p. 45. For more on package volume, see "Pay the Same, Get Less as Package Volume Falls," *USA Today*, March 17, 2003, p. 3B; "Taking the Value Out of Value-Sized," *The Wall Street Journal*, August 14, 2002, p. D1; "Critics Call Cuts in Package Size Deceptive Move," *The Wall Street Journal*, February 5, 1991, p. B1; "Disposing of the Green Myth," *Adweek's Marketing Week*, April 13, 1992, p. 20; "The Waste Land," *Adweek*, November 11, 1991, p. 26.

25. Anthony D. Miyazaki, David E. Sprott, and Kenneth C. Manning, "Unit Prices on Retail Shelf Labels: an Assessment of Information Prominence," *Journal of Retailing*, Spring 2000, p. 93; J. E. Russo, "The Value of Unit Price Information," *Journal of Marketing Research*, May 1977, p. 193; David A. Aaker and Gary T. Ford, "Unit Pricing Ten Years Later: A Replication," *Journal of Marketing*, Winter 1983, p. 118.

26. For more on Hyundai warranty, see "Hyundai's Reliability Rankings Now Tie Honda's," *USA Today*, March 11, 2003, p. 2B; "Hyundai's Reputation Is Rising, as It's Proving in India and U.S.," *The Wall Street Journal*, November 12, 2002, p. D3; "Garfield's Ad Review: Hyundai Brand Work Ahead of Its Time," *Advertising Age*, October 14, 2002, p. 57. For more on warranties and service guarantees, see "The Best Car Deal Around: Never Paying for Repairs," *The Wall Street Journal*, November 12, 2002, p. D1; "Forbes.com Offers Brand Guarantee," *BtoB*, October 14, 2002, p. 14; "Sheraton Plans to Pay Guests for Bad Service," *The Wall Street Journal*, September 6, 2002, p. B1; "Guaranteed to Last a Whole 90 Days," *The Wall Street Journal*, July 16, 2002, p. D1; "Best Buy Co.: Retailer's 'Guaranteed' Strategy for Growth," *Investor's Business Daily*, May 21, 2002, p. A10; "Amtrak Rolls Out Service Guarantee, New Logo," *Investor's Business Daily*, July 7, 2000, p. A7. See also Jennifer Hamilton and Ross D. Petty, "The European Union's Consumer Guarantees Directive," *Journal of Public Policy & Marketing*, Fall 2001, p. 289; M. E. Blair and Daniel E. Innis, "The Effects of Product Knowledge on the Evaluation of Warranteed Brands," *Psychology & Marketing*, August 1996, p. 445; Ellen M. Moore and F. Kelly Shuptrine, "Warranties: Continued Readability Problems After the 1975 Magnuson-Moss Warranty Act," *Journal of Consumer Affairs*, Summer 1993, p. 23; M.A.J. Menezes and I.S. Currim, "An Approach for Determination of Warranty Length," *International Journal of Research in Marketing*, May 1992, p. 177.

CHAPTER 10

1. "America Zooms In on Camera Phones," *BusinessWeek*, December 22, 2003, p. 44; "Windows on a Phone: Not Bad for a First Foray," *BusinessWeek*, December 1, 2003, p. 26; "Plantronics Hears Sound of New Opportunities as Core Sales Slow," *Investor's Business Daily*, November 17, 2003, p. A8; "Motorola Makes Good," *BusinessWeek*, October 27,

2003, p. 52; "A Motorola Spin-Off," *BusinessWeek,* October 20, 2003, p. 56; "Cordless—and Hands-Free, Too," *BusinessWeek,* October 20, 2003, p. 157; "Motorola Needs a Revolutionary," *BusinessWeek,* October 6, 2003, p. 52; "Cell Phone Motorists Driving Headset Sales," *Investor's Business Daily,* August 8, 2003, p. A4; "Box Makers Putting Their Stamp on Looks," *Investor's Business Daily,* August 4, 2003, p. A4; "Can Mike Z Work More Magic at Motorola?" *BusinessWeek,* April 14, 2003, p. 58; "Tech Companies Scramble to Fill Military Orders," *The Wall Street Journal,* March 24, 2003, p. B1; "Cutting the Cell Phone Cord," *Business-Week,* February 10, 2003, p. 84; "Can You Hear Me?" *Time,* December 30, 2002, p. 156; "Great-Looking Product (Too Bad Nobody Wants It)," *Business 2.0,* April 2002, p. 120.

2. Alina B. Sorescu, Rajesh K. Chandy, and Jaideep C. Prabhu, "Sources and Financial Consequences of Radical Innovation: Insights from Pharmaceuticals," *Journal of Marketing,* October 2003, p. 82; Ulrike de Brentani, "Innovative Versus Incremental New Business Services: Different Keys for Achieving Success," *The Journal of Product Innovation Management,* May 2001, p. 169; Erik Jan Hultink and Fred Langerak, "Launch Decisions and Competitive Reactions: an Exploratory Market Signaling Study," *The Journal of Product Innovation Management,* May 2002, p. 199; Barry L. Bayus, "The Languages of Edison's Light," *The Journal of Product Innovation Management,* May 2000, p. 254; Marion Debruyne, Rudy Moenaert, Abbie Griffin, Susan Hart et al. "The Impact of New Product Launch Strategies on Competitive Reaction in Industrial Markets," *The Journal of Product Innovation Management,* March 2002, p. 159; X. Michael Song, C. Anthony Di Benedetto and Lisa Z. Song, "Pioneering Advantage in New Service Development: a Multi-Country Study of Managerial Perceptions," *The Journal of Product Innovation Management,* September 2000, p. 378; Beverly B. Tyler and Devi R. Gnyawali, "Mapping Managers' Market Orientations Regarding New Product Success," *The Journal of Product Innovation Management,* July 2002, p. 259; Christopher M. McDermott and Gina Colarelli O'Connor, "Managing Radical Innovation: an Overview of Emergent Strategy Issues," *The Journal of Product Innovation Management,* November 2002, p. 424; George J. Avlonitis, Paulina G. Papastathopoulou and Spiros P. Gounaris, "An Empirically-Based Typology of Product Innovativeness for New Financial Services: Success and Failure Scenarios," *The Journal of Product Innovation Management,* September 2001, p. 324; Ronald W. Niedrich and Scott D. Swain, "The Influence of Pioneer Status and Experience Order on Consumer Brand Preference: a Mediated-Effects Model," *Journal of the Academy of Marketing Science,* Fall 2003, p. 468; Rajesh K. Chandy and Gerard J. Tellis, "The Incumbent's Curse? Incumbency, Size, and Radical Product Innovation," *Journal of Marketing,* July 2000, p. 1; Robert W. Veryzer, "Key Factors Affecting Customer Evaluation of Discontinuous New Products," *Journal of Product Innovation Management,* March 1998, p. 136; Frank H. Alpert and Michael A. Kamins, "An Empirical Investigation of Consumer Memory, Attitude and Perceptions Toward Pioneer and Follower Brands," *Journal of Marketing,* October 1995, p. 34; Neil A. Morgan, "Managing Imitation Strategies: How Later Entrants Seize Market Share From Pioneers," *Journal of Marketing,* October 1995, p. 104; David M. Szymanski, Lisa C. Troy, and Sundar G. Bharadwaj, "Order of Entry and Business Performance: An Empirical Synthesis and Reexamination," *Journal of Marketing,* October 1995, p. 17; George Day, "The Product Life Cycle: Analysis and Applications Issues," *Journal of Marketing,* Fall 1981, p. 60; Igal Ayal, "International Product Life Cycle: A Reassessment and Product Policy Implications," *Journal of Marketing,* Fall 1981, p. 91; Mary Lambkin and George S. Day, "Evolutionary Processes in Competitive Markets: Beyond the Product Life Cycle," *Journal of Marketing,* July 1989, p. 4.

3. Jorge Alberto Sousa De Vasconcellos, "Key Success Factors in Marketing Mature Products," *Industrial Marketing Management* 20, no. 4 (1991), p. 263; Paul C.N. Michell, Peter Quinn, and Edward Percival, "Marketing Strategies for Mature Industrial Products," *Industrial Marketing Management* 20, no. 3 (1991), p. 201; Peter N. Golder and Gerard J.

Tellis, "Pioneer Advantage: Marketing Logic or Marketing Legend?" *Journal of Marketing Research,* May 1993, p. 158.

4. For more on Xbox, see Chapter 4, endnote 9.

5. U.S. Bureau of the Census, *Statistical Abstract of the United States 2002* (Washington, DC: U.S. Government Printing Office, 2001), p. 605; U.S. Bureau of the Census, *Statistical Abstract of the United States 2000* (Washington, DC: U.S. Government Printing Office, 2000), p. 726.

6. "DVD: It Pays to Spend a Little More," *USA Today,* December 3, 2003, p. 10D; "Backseat Movies: Car DVD Entertainment Systems . . . ," *BusinessWeek,* May 26, 2003, p. 108; "High-Definition Discs Aim to Outshine DVDs," *Investor's Business Daily,* May 6, 2003, p. A6; "Safe at Home and All Plugged In," *USA Today,* January 8, 2002, p. 1D; "Pioneer, Panasonic Drive toward Recordable DVD," *Investor's Business Daily,* June 26, 2001, p. A7; "Blockbuster Tests Postvideo Future," *The Wall Street Journal,* June 18, 2001, p. B1; "DVDs' Popularity Gives Studio Earnings Much-Needed Spin," *USA Today,* April 30, 2001, p. 4B; "Sales of DVD Players Boom, but Makers Record Little Profit," *Investor's Business Daily,* January 22, 2001, p. A6; "DVD Makers Battle over Recording Standard," *The Wall Street Journal,* November 9, 2000, p. B6; "To DVD—or Not to DVD?" *The Wall Street Journal,* November 3, 2000, p. W1.

7. For more on Cisco, see "Cisco: In Hot Pursuit of a Chinese Rival," *BusinessWeek,* May 19, 2003, p. 62; "Cisco: Making a Federal Case of it," *BusinessWeek,* February 10, 2003, p. 36. See also "Would You Buy a Patent License from This Man?" *Ecompany,* April 2001, p. 104; "Rivals Square Off Toe to Toe," *USA Today,* August 24, 1993, p. 1B; "Is It Time to Reinvent the Patent System?" *BusinessWeek,* December 2, 1991, p. 110; C. C. Baughn, Michael Bixby, and L. S. Woods, "Patent Laws and the Public Good: IPR Protection in Japan and the United States," *Business Horizons,* July–August 1997, p. 59.

8. For more on EV1, see "An Electric Car Propelled by Star Power?" *BusinessWeek,* December 9, 1996, p. 40; "GM Energizes EV1 Launch with $8 Mil Ad Blitz," *Advertising Age,* December 2, 1996, p. 12; "A Big Charge for Electric Vehicles," *BusinessWeek,* November 18, 1996, p. 102; "Batteries Not Included," *BusinessWeek,* September 23, 1996, p. 78. For more on Toyota and Honda hybrids, see Chapter 4, endnote 21. See also Sigvald J. Harryson, "How Canon and Sony Drive Product Innovation Through Networking and Application-Focused R&D," *Journal of Product Innovation Management,* July 1997, p. 288; M. Lambkin, "Pioneering New Markets: A Comparison of Market Share Winners and Losers," *International Journal of Research in Marketing,* March 1992, p. 5.

9. For more on Zara, see "Fashion Fast Forward," *Business 2.0,* May 2002, p. 61; "Just-in-Time Fashion," *The Wall Street Journal,* May 18, 2001, p. B1; "The Fashion Cycle Hits High Gear," *BusinessWeek E.Biz,* September 18, 2000, p. EB66; "Zara Has a Made-to-Order Plan for Success," *Fortune,* September 4, 2000, p. 80; "The Mark of Zara," *Business-Week,* May 29, 2000, p. 98.

10. "UGG Boots a Fashion Kick," *USA Today,* December 11, 2003, p. 3B; "Fashion Tip: Get Online," *The Wall Street Journal,* October 31, 2003, p. B1; "Denim Gets Daring in Asia," *The Wall Street Journal,* July 7, 2003, p. A9; "Care Bears' Second Act," *The Wall Street Journal,* June 11, 2003, p. B1; "Fashion Emergency: Duct Tape Makes a Fine Prom Dress," *The Wall Street Journal,* February 28, 2003, p. A1; "The Skinny on the Mini," *The Wall Street Journal,* February 4, 2003, p. B1; "Nothing Comes Between Teens and Their Jeans—Not Even Cost," *USA Today,* September 5, 2002, p. 1D; "Fashion Flip-Flop: Lowly Sandal Leaves the Shower Behind," *The Wall Street Journal,* August 8, 2002, p. A1; "Too Trendy for You?" *The Wall Street Journal,* May 17, 2002, p. W1; "Recipe for a Fashion Brand?" *The Wall Street Journal,* June 25, 2001, p. B1; "Dusting Off Fashion's Old Bags," *Time* (Special Issue: Your Business), June 2001, pp. Y2–Y4; "Designers Howl for Fur," *The Wall Street Journal,* September 22, 2000, p. B1. See also Martin G. Letscher, "How to Tell Fads from Trends," *American Demographics,* December 1994, p. 38; R.E. Goldsmith,

J.B. Freiden, and J.C. Kilsheimer, "Social Values and Female Fashion Leadership: A Cross-Cultural Study," *Psychology & Marketing*, September/October 1993, p. 399; "Special Report: Fashion Marketing," *Advertising Age*, August 22, 1994, p. 23; Craig J. Thompson and Diana L. Haytko, "Speaking of Fashion: Consumers' Uses of Fashion Discourses and the Appropriation of Countervailing Cultural Meanings," *Journal of Consumer Research*, June 1997, p. 15.

11. "DVD Acceptance Picks Up Pace," *Discount Store News*, August 9, 1999, p. 29; "DVD and Conquer: Why One Technology Prevailed," *BusinessWeek*, July 5, 1999, p. 34; "Divx: The Video Technology That Geeks Love to Hate," *Fortune*, June 21, 1999, p. 177; "Circuit City Pulls the Plug on Its Divx Videodisk Venture," *The Wall Street Journal*, June 17, 1999, p. B10; "8-Tracks, Betamax—and Divx?" *BusinessWeek*, November 9, 1998, p. 108.

12. "Big Brands (Small Companies)," *BusinessWeek Small Biz*, August 13, 2001, p. 13.

13. *2003 Annual Report*, RJR Nabisco; "Oreo, Ritz Join Nabisco's Low-Fat Feast," *Advertising Age*, April 4, 1994, p. 3; "They're Not Crying in Their Crackers at Nabisco," *BusinessWeek*, August 30, 1993, p. 61; "Nabisco Unleashes a New Batch of Teddies," *Adweek's Marketing Week*, September 24, 1990, p. 18.

14. For more on Tide, see *2003 Annual Report*, Procter & Gamble; "Detergent Tablets of the '70s Make a Comeback," *USA Today*, July 27, 2000, p. 9B; "Boom in Liquid Detergents Has P&G Scrambling," *The Wall Street Journal*, September 25, 1997, p. B1; "Ultra-Clean—Retail Cheers Still More P&G Concentrates," *Advertising Age*, August 22, 1994, p. 1; "Detergent Industry Spins into New Cycle," *The Wall Street Journal*, January 5, 1993, p. B1; "P&G Unleashes Flood of New Tide Products," *Advertising Age*, June 16, 1986, p. 3. See also "The Hard Life of Orphan Brands," *The Wall Street Journal*, April 13, 2001, p. B1; "Orphan Relief," *Advertising Age*, March 19, 2001, p. 3.

15. Brian Wansink, "Making Old Brands New," *American Demographics*, December 1997, p. 53; "Classic Roller Skates Return as Safety Fears Dull Blades," *The Wall Street Journal*, October 24, 1997, p. B1; "Dusting Off the *Britannica*," *BusinessWeek*, October 20, 1997, p. 143; "At Du Pont, Time to Both Sow and Reap," *BusinessWeek*, September 29, 1997, p. 107; "A Boring Brand Can Be Beautiful," *Fortune*, November 18, 1991, p. 169; "Teflon Is 50 Years Old, but Du Pont Is Still Finding New Uses for Invention," *The Wall Street Journal*, April 7, 1988, p. 34; Stephen W. Miller, "Managing Imitation Strategies: How Later Entrants Seize Markets From Pioneers," *Journal of the Academy of Marketing Science*, Summer 1996, p. 277; Regina Fazio Maruca and Amy L. Halliday, "When New Products and Customer Loyalty Collide," *Harvard Business Review*, November–December 1993, p. 22.

16. John Gustavson, Guest Column Section, *Financial Post*: May 12, 2006, p. FP7; WOMMA (Word Of Mouth Marketing Association) available at <http://www.womma.org>.

17. For an example of TiVo's targeting innovators and early adopters, see "TiVo Creating Program Glut for Some Users," *Investor's Business Daily*, November 12, 2003, p. A7; "PVRs to Hit 20% by '07," *Advertising Age*, September 29, 2003, p. 6; "Switching Channels: TiVo Revamps Strategy," *Investor's Business Daily*, July 23, 2003, p. A4; "PVRs: A Shift in Time," *The Wall Street Journal Reports*, March 31, 2003, p. R10; "Time to Jettison the Old VCR? Set-Top Recorder Battle Looms," *Investor's Business Daily*, March 13, 2003, p. A1; "Couch Potato Crisis: Is It Time to Get TiVo?" *The Wall Street Journal*, November 13, 2002, p. D1; "The Ad Zappers," *Time (Inside Business Bonus Section)*, June 2002. For more on opinion leaders and word-of-mouth publicity, see Chapter 6, endnote 22. See also "The Influentials: Movers and Shakers," *Brandweek*, February 3, 2003, p. 27; "How Does This Work?" *American Demographics*, December 2002, p. 18; "Companies Fawn over Reviewers of Hand-Helds," *The Wall Street Journal*, April 1, 2002, p. B1; "Can You Set Your VCR?"

American Demographics, March 2002, p. 8; "Auto Makers Find They Don't Want to Avoid Collisions in Movies," *The Wall Street Journal*, July 5, 2001, p. B1; "Small Wonder," *The Wall Street Journal*, June 25, 2001, p. R1; "Word of Mouth Makes Nike Slip-On Sneakers Take Off," *The Wall Street Journal*, June 7, 2001, p. B1; "Bristol-Myers Builds Buzz for True Intense Color Line," *Advertising Age*, April 23, 2001, p. 18; "How an Idea Spreads Like Flu," *Advertising Age*, May 8, 2000, p. 42; "Street Marketing Hits the Internet," *Advertising Age*, May 1, 2000, p. 32; "Ad Budget: Zero. Buzz: Deafening," *The Wall Street Journal*, December 29, 1999, p. B1; "Word of Mouth Makes Kansas Store a Star," *The Wall Street Journal*, November 7, 1997, p. B1; "Why the Veterinarian Really Recommends that 'Designer' Chow," *The Wall Street Journal*, November 3, 1997, p. A1. See also Jyh-Shen Chiou and Cathy Cheng, "Should a Company Have Message Boards on its Web Sites?," *Journal of Interactive Marketing*, Summer 2003, p. 50; Raji Srinivasan, Gary L. Lilien, and Arvind Rangaswamy, "Technological Opportunism and Radical Technology Adoption: an Application to E-Business," *Journal of Marketing*, July 2002, p. 47; Suman Basuroy, Subimal Chatterjee, and S. Abraham Ravid, "How Critical Are Critical Reviews? The Box Office Effects of Film Critics, Star Power, and Budgets," *Journal of Marketing*, October 2003, p. 103; Jeffrey G. Blodgett, Donald H. Granbois, and Rockney G. Walters, "The Effects of Perceived Justice on Complainants' Negative Word-of-Mouth Behavior and Repatronage Intentions," *Journal of Retailing*, Winter 1993, p. 399; Paula Fitzgerald Bone, "Word-of-Mouth Effects on Short-term and Long-term Product Judgments," *Journal of Business Research*, March 1995, p. 213; Bruce MacEvoy, "Change Leaders and the New Media," *American Demographics*, January 1994, p. 42; Dale F. Duhan, Scott D. Johnson, James B. Wilcox, and Gilbert D. Harrell, "Influences on Consumer Use of Word-of-Mouth Recommendation Sources," *Journal of the Academy of Marketing Science*, Fall 1997, p. 283; Russell N. Laczniak, Thomas E. DeCarlo, and Carol M. Motley, "Retail Equity Perceptions and Consumers' Processing of Negative Word-of-Mouth Communication," *Journal of Marketing Theory & Practice*, Fall 1996, p. 37.

18. Hokey Min and William P. Galle, "E-Purchasing: Profiles of Adopters and Nonadopters," *Industrial Marketing Management*, April 2003, p. 227; Yikuan Lee and Gina Colarelli O'Connor, "The Impact of Communication Strategy on Launching New Products: the Moderating Role of Product Innovativeness," *The Journal of Product Innovation Management*, January 2003, p. 4; David R. Fell, Eric N. Hansen, and Boris W. Becker, "Measuring Innovativeness for the Adoption of Industrial Products," *Industrial Marketing Management*, May 2003, p. 347; Subin Im, Barry L. Bayus and Charlotte H. Mason, "An Empirical Study of Innate Consumer Innovativeness, Personal Characteristics, and New-Product Adoption Behavior," *Journal of the Academy of Marketing Science*, Winter 2003, p. 61; Eric Waarts, Yvonne M. van Everdingen, and Jos van Hillegersberg, "The Dynamics of Factors Affecting the Adoption of Innovations," *The Journal of Product Innovation Management*, November 2002, p. 412; Meera P. Venkatraman, "Opinion Leaders, Adopters, and Communicative Adopters: A Role Analysis," *Psychology and Marketing*, Spring 1989, p. 51; S. Ram and Hyung-Shik Jung, "Innovativeness in Product Usage: A Comparison of Early Adopters and Early Majority," *Psychology & Marketing*, January/February 1994, p. 57; Robert J. Fisher and Linda L. Price, "An Investigation into the Social Context of Early Adoption Behavior," *Journal of Consumer Research*, December 1992, p. 477; Leisa R. Flynn, Ronald E. Goldsmith, and Jacqueline K. Eastman, "Opinion Leaders and Opinion Seekers: Two New Measurement Scales," *Journal of the Academy of Marketing Science*, Spring 1996, p. 137; Everett M. Rogers and F. Floyd Shoemaker, *Communication of Innovations: A Cross-Cultural Approach* (New York: Free Press, 1971), p. 203.

19. For more on Logitech, see "The Fastest-Growing Technology Companies," *Business 2.0*, October 2002, p. 81. For more on Gatorade, see "Gatorade Gallon Goes Rectangular," *Packaging Digest*, June 2003, p. 2; "Latest Gatorade Bottle Edges toward Ergonomics," *Packaging Digest*, November 1999, p. 15.

20. "Reposition: Simplifying the Customer's Brandscape," *Brandweek*, October 2, 2000, p. 36; "Consumers to GM: You Talking to Me?" *BusinessWeek*, June 19, 2000, p. 213; "How Growth Destroys Differentiation," *Brandweek*, April 24, 2000, p. 42; "P&G, Seeing Shoppers Were Being Confused, Overhauls Marketing," *The Wall Street Journal*, January 15, 1997, p. A1; "Make It Simple," *BusinessWeek*, September 9, 1996, p. 96; "Diaper Firms Fight to Stay on the Bottom," *The Wall Street Journal*, March 23, 1993, p. B1.

21. "Too Many Choices," *The Wall Street Journal*, April 20, 2001, p. B1; "Special Report: New Products," *Ad Age International*, April 13, 1998, p. 17; "The Ghastliest Product Launches," *Fortune*, March 16, 1998, p. 44; "New and Improved," *American Demographics*, March 1998, p. 32; "Flops: Too Many New Products Fail. Here's Why—and How to Do Better," *BusinessWeek*, August 16, 1993, p. 76; Brian D. Ottum and William L. Moore, "The Role of Market Information in New Product Success/Failure," *Journal of Product Innovation Management*, July 1997, p. 258.

22. "Makers of Chicken Tonight Find Many Cooks Say, 'Not Tonight,'" *The Wall Street Journal*, May 17, 1994, p. B1; "Failure of Its Oven Lovin' Cookie Dough Shows Pillsbury Pitfalls of New Products," *The Wall Street Journal*, June 17, 1993, p. B1; Sharad Sarin and Gour M. Kapur, "Lessons From New Product Failures: Five Case Studies," *Industrial Marketing Management*, November 1990, p. 301.

23. "Design Tools Move into the Fast Lane," *BusinessWeek*, June 2, 2003, pp. 84B–84C; "How Top Software Firms Dominate," *Investor's Business Daily*, June 12, 2001, p. A1; "Opening the Spigot," *BusinessWeek E.Biz*, June 4, 2001, pp. EB16–Eb20; "Digital Workflow Speeds Time to Shelf," *Brand Packaging*, March/April 2001, p. 24; "How Fast Can This Baby Go?" *BusinessWeek*, April 10, 2000, p. 38. See also Muammer Ozer, "Process Implications of the Use of the Internet in New Product Development: a Conceptual Analysis," *Industrial Marketing Management*, August 2003, p. 517; J. Daniel Sherman, William E. Souder, and Svenn A. Jenssen, "Differential Effects of the Primary Forms of Cross Functional Integration on Product Development Cycle Time," *The Journal of Product Innovation Management*, July 2000, p. 257; Greg Githens, "Successful Product Development: Speeding from Opportunity to Profit," *The Journal of Product Innovation Management*, May 2000, p. 250; Daniel J. Flint, "Compressing New Product Success-to-Success Cycle Time: Deep Customer Value Understanding and Idea Generation," *Industrial Marketing Management*, July 2002, p. 305; Cornelia Droge, Jayanth Jayaram, and Shawnee K. Vickery, "The Ability to Minimize the Timing of New Product Development and Introduction: an Examination of Antecedent Factors in the North American Automobile Supplier Industry," *The Journal of Product Innovation Management*, January 2000, p. 24; Ajay Menon, Jhinuk Chowdhury and Bryan A. Lukas, "Antecedents and Outcomes of New Product Development Speed: an Interdisciplinary Conceptual Framework," *Industrial Marketing Management*, July 2002, p. 317; Kathleen M. Eisenhardt and Shona L. Brown, "Time Pacing: Competing in Markets That Won't Stand Still," *Harvard Business Review*, March–April 1998, p. 59; Richard Bauhaus, "Developing Products in Half the Time," *Journal of Product Innovation Management*, January 1997, p. 68. For more on P&G's efforts to bring products to market faster, see "Brands in a Bind," *BusinessWeek*, August 28, 2000, p. 234; "Warm and Fuzzy Won't Save Procter & Gamble," *BusinessWeek*, June 26, 2000, p. 48.

24. "Building a Better R&D Mousetrap," *Business 2.0*, September 2003, p. 50; "Critical Curds: At Kraft, Making Cheese Fun Is Serious Business," *The Wall Street Journal*, May 31, 2002, p. A1; "Stuck on You: P&G's New Outlast Lipstick Is Nothing to Pout About," *The Wall Street Journal*, May 9, 2002, p. B1; "Bleeding Cash: Pfizer Youth Pill Ate Up $71 Million before It Flopped," *The Wall Street Journal*, May 2, 2002, p. A1; "How Burger King Got Burned in Quest to Make the Perfect Fry," *The Wall Street Journal*, January 16, 2001, p. A1; "Tailoring World's Cars to U.S. Tastes," *The Wall Street Journal*, January 15, 2001, p. B1; "From Research Dollars to Riches," *Investor's Business Daily*, December 5, 2000,

p. A1; "Why Dow Chemical Finds Slime Sublime," *The Wall Street Journal*, November 15, 1999, p. B1. See also Lisa C. Troy, David M. Szymanski and P. Rajan Varadarajan, "Generating New Product Ideas: an Initial Investigation of the Role of Market Information and Organizational Characteristics," *Journal of the Academy of Marketing Science*, Winter 2001, p. 89; Rajesh Sethi, "New Product Quality and Product Development Teams," *Journal of Marketing*, April 2000, p. 1; Mark A. A. M. Leenders and Berend Wierenga, "The Effectiveness of Different Mechanisms for Integrating Marketing and R&D," *The Journal of Product Innovation Management*, July 2002, p. 305; George J. Avlonitis, Susan J. Hart, and Nikolaos X. Tzokas, "An Analysis of Product Deletion Scenarios," *The Journal of Product Innovation Management*, January 2000, p. 41; Elliot Maltz, William E. Souder, and Ajith Kumar, "Influencing R&D/Marketing Integration and the Use of Market Information by R&D Managers: Intended and Unintended Effects of Managerial Actions," *Journal of Business Research*, April 2001, p. 69; Angel Martinez Sanchez and Manuela Perez Perez, "Cooperation and the Ability to Minimize the Time and Cost of New Product Development Within the Spanish Automotive Supplier Industry," *The Journal of Product Innovation Management*, January 2003, p. 57; Robert Polk, Richard E. Plank, and David A. Reid, "Technical Risk and New Product Success: An Empirical Test in High Technology Business Markets," *Industrial Marketing Management*, November 1996, p. 531; X. M. Song and Mark E. Parry, "A Cross-National Comparative Study of New Product Development Processes: Japan and the United States," *Journal of Marketing*, April 1997, p. 1; Robert G. Cooper, "Overhauling the New Product Process," *Industrial Marketing Management*, November 1996, p. 465; Jeffrey B. Schmidt and Roger J. Calantone, "Are Really New Product Development Projects Harder to Shut Down?" *Journal of Product Innovation Management*, March 1998, p. 111; Cheryl Nakata and K. Sivakumar, "National Culture and New Product Development: An Integrative Review," *Journal of Marketing*, January 1996, p. 61; Gary S. Lynn, Joseph G. Morone, and Albert S. Paulson, "Marketing and Discontinuous Innovation: The Probe and Learn Process," *California Management Review*, Spring 1996, p. 8; Gary L. Ragatz, Robert B. Handfield, and Thomas V. Scannell, "Success Factors for Integrating Suppliers into New Product Development," *Journal of Product Innovation Management*, May 1997, p. 190; X. M. Song and Mitzi M. Montoya-Weiss, "Critical Development Activities for Really New Versus Incremental Products," *Journal of Product Innovation Management*, March 1998, p. 124.

25. "Pickups Get Women's Touch," *USA Today*, June 13, 2001 p. 1B; "Windstar's Designing Women," *USA Today*, July 19, 1999, p. 3B; "Where Great Ideas Come From," *Inc.*, April 1998, p. 76; "Seeing the Future First," *Fortune*, September 5, 1994, p. 64. See also Edward F. McDonough III, Kenneth B. Kahn and Gloria Barczak, "An Investigation of the Use of Global, Virtual, and Colocated New Product Development Teams," *The Journal of Product Innovation Management*, March 2001, p. 110; Ari-Pekka Hameri and Jukka Nihtila, "Distributed New Product Development Project Based on Internet and World Wide Web: A Case Study," *Journal of Product Innovation Management*, March 1997, p. 77.

26. "It Was a Hit in Buenos Aires—So Why Not Boise?" *BusinessWeek*, September 7, 1998, p. 56. See also Rudy K. Moenaert, Filip Caeldries, Annouk Lievens and Elke Wauters, "Communication Flows in International Product Innovation Teams," *The Journal of Product Innovation Management*, September 2000, p. 360; Vittorio Chiesa, "Global R&D Project Management and Organization: a Taxonomy," *The Journal of Product Innovation Management*, September 2000, p. 341; Jinhong Xie, Michael Song and Anne Stringfellow, "Antecedents and Consequences of Goal Incongruity on New Product Development in Five Countries: a Marketing View," *The Journal of Product Innovation Management*, May 2003, p. 233; John J. Cristiano, Jeffrey K. Liker, and Chelsea C. White III, "Customer-Driven Product Development Through Quality Function Deployment in the U.S. and Japan," *The Journal of Product Innovation Management*, July 2000, p. 286; Don R. Graber, "How to Manage a Global Product Development Process," *Industrial Marketing Management*,

November 1996, p. 483; "U.S. Companies Shop Abroad for Product Ideas," *The Wall Street Journal*, March 14, 1990, p. B1.

27. Erik L. Olson and Geir Bakke, "Implementing the Lead User Method in a High Technology Firm: a Longitudinal Study of Intentions Versus Actions," *The Journal of Product Innovation Management*, November 2001, p. 388; Eric von Hippel, *The Sources of Innovation* (New York: Oxford University Press, 1988).

28. "Shielding the Shield Makers," *The Wall Street Journal*, November 26, 2003, p. B1; "Gun Makers to Push Use of Gun Locks," *The Wall Street Journal*, May 9, 2001, p. B12; "U.S. Recalls Millions of Evenflo 'Joyride' Infant Seats, Carriers," *The Wall Street Journal*, May 2, 2001, p. B6; "Stand Up and Fight," *BusinessWeek*, September 11, 2000, p. 54; "Why One Jury Dealt a Big Blow to Chrysler in Minivan-Latch Case," *The Wall Street Journal*, November 19, 1997, p. A1; "Chinese Discover Product-Liability Suits," *The Wall Street Journal*, November 13, 1997, p. B1; Paula Mergenhagen, "Product Liability: Who Sues?" *American Demographics*, June 1995, p. 48; "How a Jury Decided that a Coffee Spill Is Worth $2.9 Million," *The Wall Street Journal*, September 1, 1994, p. A1; Paul A. Herbig and James E. Golden, "Innovation and Product Liability," *Industrial Marketing Management*, July 1994, p. 245; Robert N. Mayer and Debra L. Scammon, "Caution: Weak Product Warnings May Be Hazardous to Corporate Health," *Journal of Business Research*, June 1992, p. 347.

29. "Want Shelf Space at the Supermarket? Ante Up," *BusinessWeek*, August 7, 1989, p. 60; "Grocer 'Fee' Hampers New-Product Launches," *Advertising Age*, August 3, 1987, p. 1.

30. "This Bright Idea Could Make GE a Billion," *BusinessWeek*, December 4, 1989, p. 120.

31. Joseph M. Bonner, Robert W. Ruekert, and Orville C. Walker, Jr. "Upper Management Control of New Product Development Projects and Project Performance," *The Journal of Product Innovation Management*, May 2002, p. 233; Madeleine E. Pullman, William L. Moore, and Don G. Wardell, "A Comparison of Quality Function Deployment and Conjoint Analysis in New Product Design," *The Journal of Product Innovation Management*, September 2002, p. 354; Harold Z. Daniel, Donald J. Hempel and Narasimhan Srinivasan, "A Model of Value Assessment in Collaborative R&D Programs," *Industrial Marketing Management*, November 2002, p. 653; Sundar Bharadwaj and Anil Menon, "Making Innovations Happen in Organizations: Individual Creativity Mechanisms, Organizational Creativity Mechanisms or Both?" *The Journal of Product Innovation Management*, November 2000, p. 424; Kwaku Atuahene-Gima and Haiyang Li, "Marketing's Influence Tactics in New Product Development: a Study of High Technology Firms in China," *The Journal of Product Innovation Management*, November 2000, p. 451; Preston G. Smith, "Mastering Virtual Teams: Strategies, Tools, and Techniques That Succeed," *The Journal of Product Innovation Management*, March 2001, p. 127; Eugene Sivadas and F. Robert Dwyer, "An Examination of Organizational Factors Influencing New Product Success in Internal and Alliance-Based Processes," *Journal of Marketing*, January 2000, p. 31; Gregory D. Githens, "Customer Centered Products: Creating Successful Products Through Smart Requirements Management," *The Journal of Product Innovation Management*, September 2001, p. 350; Fred Langerak, Ed Peelen, and Harry Commandeur, "Organizing for Effective New Product Development," *Industrial Marketing Management*, May 1997, p. 281; Keith Goffin, "Evaluating Customer Support During New Product Development—An Exploratory Study," *Journal of Product Innovation Management*, January 1998, p. 42; Paul S. Adler, Avi Mandelbaum, Vien Nguyen, and Elizabeth Schwerer, "Getting the Most Out of Your Product Development Process," *Harvard Business Review*, March–April 1996, p. 134; Frank R. Bacon, Jr., and Thomas W. Butler, Jr., *Planned Innovation*, rev. ed. (Ann Arbor: Institute of Science and Technology, University of Michigan, 1980).

32. "Torture Testing," *Fortune*, October 2, 2000, pp. 244B–X; "Industry's Amazing New Instant Prototypes," *Fortune*, January 12, 1998, pp. 120E–L;

"Secrets of Product Testing," *Fortune*, November 28, 1994, p. 166; "A Smarter Way to Manufacture," *BusinessWeek*, April 30, 1990, p. 110.

33. For more on Gillette's razor costs, see "Cutting Edge," *Brandweek*, February 4, 2002, p. 16; "Gillette's Edge," *Brandweek*, May 28, 2001, p. 5; "No New CEO, but Gillette Does Have a New Product," *Advertising Age*, November 6, 2000, p. 25; "Brands in a Bind," *BusinessWeek*, August 28, 2000, p. 234; "How Gillette Brought Its MACH3 to Market," *The Wall Street Journal*, April 15, 1998, p. B1.

34. "Oops! Marketers Blunder Their Way Through the 'Herb Decade,'" *Advertising Age*, February 13, 1989, p. 3.

35. "An Rx for Drug Trials," *BusinessWeek E.Biz*, December 11, 2000, p. EB66; "Web Sites Give Retailers Better Way to Test-Market Products," *USA Today*, August 29, 2000, p. 3B; "Can Procter & Gamble Change Its Culture, Protect Its Market Share, and Find the Next Tide?" *Fortune*, April 26, 1999, p. 146; "To Test or Not to Test . . . ," *American Demographics*, June 1998, p. 64; John R. Dickinson and Carolyn P. Wilby, "Concept Testing With and Without Product Trial," *Journal of Product Innovation Management*, March 1997, p. 117; "Born to Be a Little Too Wild," *BusinessWeek*, December 18, 2000, p. 69.

36. Jeffrey B. Schmidt and Roger J. Calantone, "Escalation of Commitment During New Product Development," *Journal of the Academy of Marketing Science*, Spring 2002, p. 103; Ely Dahan and V. Srinivasan, "The Predictive Power of Internet-Based Product Concept Testing Using Visual Depiction and Animation," *The Journal of Product Innovation Management*, March 2000, p. 99; Erwin Danneels and Elko J. Kleinschmidt, "Product Innovativeness from the Firm's Perspective: Its Dimensions and Their Relation with Project Selection and Performance," *The Journal of Product Innovation Management*, November 2001, p. 357; R. Jeffrey Thieme, Michael Song and Geon-Cheol Shin, "Project Management Characteristics and New Product Survival," *The Journal of Product Innovation Management*, March 2003, p. 104; William E. Souder, David Buisson, and Tony Garrett, "Success Through Customer-Driven New Product Development: A Comparison of U.S. and New Zealand Small Entrepreneurial High Technology Firms," *Journal of Product Innovation Management*, November 1997, p. 459; Artemis March, "Usability: The New Dimension of Product Design," *Harvard Business Review*, September–October 1994, p. 144; Peter H. Bloch, "Seeking the Ideal Form: Product Design and Consumer Response," *Journal of Marketing*, July 1995, p. 16; Alan Flaschner, "Technology Fountainheads: The Management Challenge of R&D Consortia," *Journal of Product Innovation Management*, July 1997, p. 309; William Q. Judge, Gerald E. Fryxell, and Robert S. Dooley, "The New Task of R&D Management: Creating Goal-Directed Communities for Innovation," *California Management Review*, Spring 1997, p. 72; John P. Workman, Jr., "Marketing's Limited Role in New Product Development in One Computer Systems Firm," *Journal of Marketing Research*, November 1993, p. 405.

37. Available from World Wide Web: <http://www.3m.com>; 2003 *Annual Report*, 3M; "How Leader at 3M Got His Employees to Back Big Changes," *The Wall Street Journal*, April 23, 2002, p. B1; "3M: A Lab for Growth?" *BusinessWeek*, January 21, 2002, p. 50; "How to Get the Most Out of R&D. Balance Funds against Risk, Timing" *Investor's Business Daily*, May 11, 2001, p. A1; "3M: Glued to the Web," *BusinessWeek E.Biz*, November 20, 2000, p. EB65; "Steel Wool Dino Roars a Powerful Message," *Advertising Age*, September 16, 1996, p. 55; "How 3M, by Tiptoeing into Foreign Markets, Became a Big Exporter," *The Wall Street Journal*, March 29, 1991, p. A1.

38. "Brands at Work," *Brandweek*, April 13, 1998, p. 27; "Special Report: Auto Marketing & Brand Management," *Advertising Age*, April 6, 1998, p. S1; "P&G Redefines the Brand Manager," *Advertising Age*, October 13, 1997, p. 1. See also Sanjay K. Dhar, Stephen J. Hoch, and Nanda Kumar, "Effective Category Management Depends on the Role of the Category," *Journal of Retailing*, Summer 2001, p. 165; Don Frey, "Learning the Ropes: My Life as a Product Champion," *Harvard Business Review*, September/October 1991, p. 46; Stephen K. Markham, "New Products Management," *Journal of Product Innovation Management*, July 1997, p. 312; Manfred F. Maute and William B. Locander, "Innovation as a Socio-Political Process: An Empirical Analysis of Influence Behavior among New Product Managers," *Journal of Business Research*, June 1994, p. 161.

CHAPTER 11

1. Available from World Wide Web: <http://www.friedas. com>; "How Lower-Tech Gear Beat Web 'Exchanges' at Their Own Game," *The Wall Street Journal*, March 16, 2001, p. A1; "Family Firms Confront Calamities of Transfer," *USA Today*, August 29, 2000, p. 1B; "Business, Too Close to Home," *Time*, July 17, 2000, pp. B24–B27; "The Kiwi to My Success," *Hemispheres*, July 1999; "Searching for the Next Kiwi: Frieda's Branded Produce," *Brandweek*, May 2, 1994, p. 46; "Strange Fruits," *Inc.*, November 1989, p. 80; "The Produce Marketer," *Savvy*, June 1988, p. 26.

2. *2003 Annual Report*, Colgate-Palmolive; *2003 Annual Report*, Procter & Gamble; "For Petco, Success Is a Bitch," *Business 2.0*, November 2003, p. 54; "Petsmart: Why Dogs Don't Worry about a Soft Economy," *Investor's Business Daily*, October 30, 2003, p. A12; "P&G Is Set to Unleash Dental Adult-Pet Food," *The Wall Street Journal*, December 12, 2002, p. B4; "Petco: Pet Supplies Retailer Marks Its Territory in a Dog-Eat-Dog World," *Investor's Business Daily*, December 5, 2002, p. A7; "The Money in Creature Comforts," *BusinessWeek*, September 23, 2002, p. 128; "Well, Doggone! Pet Suppliers Survived the Dot-Bombs," *Investor's Business Daily*, September 9, 2002, p. A5; "For Online Pet Stores, It's Dog-Eat-Dog," *BusinessWeek*, March 6, 2000, p. 78; "P&G Is Out to Fetch Distribution Gains for Iams Pet Food," *The Wall Street Journal*, January 6, 2000, p. A6; "Big Pet-Supply Retailers Try to Tame the Competition," *The Wall Street Journal*, August 20, 1999, p. B4; "Pet Superstores Collar Customers from Supermarkets, Small Shops," *The Wall Street Journal*, November 18, 1993, p. B12.

3. S. Chan Choi, "Expanding to Direct Channel: Market Coverages as Entry Barrier," *Journal of Interactive Marketing*, Winter 2003, p. 25; David Shipley, Colin Egan, and Scott Edgett, "Meeting Source Selection Criteria: Direct versus Distributor Channels," *Industrial Marketing Management* 20, no. 4 (1991), p. 297; Thomas L. Powers, "Industrial Distribution Options: Trade-Offs to Consider," *Industrial Marketing Management* 18, no. 3 (1989), p. 155.

4. For more on Avon, see "Avon's Makeover," *Time (Inside Business Bonus Section)*, December 2003; "Avon Calling—Lots of New Reps," *BusinessWeek*, June 2, 2003, p. 53; "Avon Tries Knocking on Dorm Doors," *The Wall Street Journal*, March 28, 2003, p. B2; "Avon Is Set to Call on Teens," *The Wall Street Journal*, October 17, 2002, p. B1; "Sears Says Stores Won't Sell Makeup, a Setback for Avon's New Line," *The Wall Street Journal*, July 11, 2001, p. B1; "Avon Thinks Younger, Wealthier," *Advertising Age*, October 2, 2000, p. 69; "Ding-Dong, Avon Calling (on the Web, Not Your Door)," *The Wall Street Journal*, December 28, 1999, p. B4; "Deck the Mall with Kiosks," *BusinessWeek*, December 13, 1999, p. 86; "Is the Bell Tolling for Door-to-Door Selling?" *BusinessWeek E.Biz*, November 1, 1999, pp. EB58–EB60; "Avon's New Calling: Sell Barbie in China," *The Wall Street Journal*, May 1, 1997, p. B1. For other examples of direct channels, see "Catwalk to Coffee Table," *The Wall Street Journal*, November 7, 2003, p. B1; "India's Retailing Makeover," *The Wall Street Journal*, October 28, 2003, p. A14; "Amway in China: Once Barred, Now Booming," *The Wall Street Journal*, March 12, 2003, p. B1; "Knock, Knock: In Brazil, an Army of Underemployed Goes Door-to-Door," *The Wall Street Journal*, February 19, 2003, p. A1; "Skechers: Savvy Marketing Keeps Shoe Firm Hopping," *Investor's Business Daily*, August 27, 2002, p. A8. See also Mitzi M. Montoya-Weiss, Glenn B. Voss and Dhruv Grewal, "Determinants of Online Channel Use and Overall Satisfaction with a Relational, Multichannel Service Provider," *Journal of the Academy of Marketing Science*, Fall 2003, p. 448; Inge Geyskens, Katrijn Gielens and Marnik G. Dekimpe, "The Market Valuation of Internet Channel Additions," *Journal of Marketing*, April 2002, p. 102; Stewart Brodie, John Stanworth and Thomas R. Wotruba, "Comparisons of Salespeople in Multilevel Vs. Single Level Direct Selling Organizations," *The Journal of Personal Selling & Sales Management*, Spring 2002, p. 67.

5. Edward L. Nash, *Direct Marketing* (New York: McGraw-Hill, 1986).

6. For an example of a Levi Strauss' new indirect channels via discount stores, see "Lessons from a Faded Levi Strauss," *BusinessWeek*, December 15, 2003, p. 44; "At Levi Strauss, Trouble Comes from All Angles," *The Wall Street Journal*, October 13, 2003, p. B1; "Levi's Adds Signature," *Advertising Age*, October 6, 2003, p. 24; "Wal-Mart Adds Touch of Hip to Fashion Choices," *USA Today*, July 22, 2003, p. 3B; "Levi's Won't Fly Signature Ads," *Brandweek*, June 16, 2003, p. 18; "Mass Levi's, Class Levi's," *The Wall Street Journal*, October 31, 2002, p. B1. For other examples of new indirect channels, see "Health-Food Maker Hain Faces Rivals," *The Wall Street Journal*, August 13, 2003, p. B5B; "TRU, Albertsons Launch Toy Box," *DSN Retailing Today*, June 23, 2003, p. 1. For a discussion of indirect channel systems, see Richard Parker and G. R. Funkhouser, "The Consumer As an Active Member of the Channel: Implications for Relationship Marketing," *Journal of Marketing Theory & Practice*, Spring 1997, p. 72; Lou E. Pelton, David Strutton, and James R. Lumpkin, *Marketing Channels: A Relationship Management Approach* (Burr Ridge, IL: Irwin/McGraw-Hill, 2002). See also Bert Rosenbloom and Trina L. Larsen, "How Foreign Firms View Their U.S. Distributors," *Industrial Marketing Management*, May 1992, p. 93; Frank Lynn, "The Changing Economics of Industrial Distribution," *Industrial Marketing Management*, November 1992, p. 355. For more on intermediaries and their functions, see Richard Greene, "Wholesaling," *Forbes*, January 2, 1984, p. 226; Elizabeth J. Wilson and Arch G. Woodside, "Marketing New Products with Distributors," *Industrial Marketing Management*, February 1992, p. 15; W. Benoy et al., "How Industrial Distributors View Distributor-Supplier Partnership Arrangements," *Industrial Marketing Management*, January 1995, p. 27.

7. For a classic discussion of the discrepancy concepts, see Wroe Alderson, "Factors Governing the Development of Marketing Channels," in *Marketing Channels for Manufactured Goods*, ed. Richard M. Clewett (Homewood, IL: Richard D. Irwin, 1954), p. 7.

8. "13,000 and Counting: Cell Stores Multiply Even as Sign-Ups Slow," *Investor's Business Daily*, June 4, 2002, p. A1; "Cellular Carriers Bypass Dealers, Creating Static," *The Wall Street Journal*, March 9, 1998, p. B1; "Mobile Warfare," *Time*, May 26, 1997, p. 52; "Cell-Phone Service May Be Getting Cheaper," *The Wall Street Journal*, January 11, 1996, p. B1.

9. For some examples on how channels change to adjust discrepancies, see "Selling Literature like Dog Food Gives Club Buyer Real Bite," *The Wall Street Journal*, April 10, 2002, p. A1. See also Robert Tamilia, Sylvain Senecal, and Gilles Corriveau, "Conventional Channels of Distribution and Electronic Intermediaries: a Functional Analysis," *Journal of Marketing Channels*, (3,4) 2002, p. 27; Robert A. Mittelstaedt and Robert E. Stassen, "Structural Changes in the Phonograph Record Industry and Its Channels of Distribution, 1946–1966," *Journal of Macromarketing*, Spring 1994, p. 31; Arun Sharma and Luis V. Dominguez, "Channel Evolution: A Framework for Analysis," *Journal of the Academy of Marketing Science*, Winter 1992, p. 1.

10. Arne Nygaard and Robert Dahlstrom, "Role Stress and Effectiveness in Horizontal Alliances," *Journal of Marketing*, April 2002, p. 61; M. B. Sarkar, Raj Echambadi, S. Tamer Cavusgil and Preet S. Aulakh, "The Influence of Complementarity, Compatibility, and Relationship Capital on Alliance Performance," *Journal of the Academy of Marketing Science*, Fall 2001, p. 358; Jakki J. Mohr, Robert J. Fisher, and John R. Nevin, "Collaborative Communication in Interfirm Relationships: Moderating Effects of Integration and Control," *Journal of Marketing*, July 1996, p. 103; Joseph P. Cannon, "Contracts, Norms, and Plural Form Governance,"

Journal of the Academy of Marketing Science, Spring 2000, p. 180; Amy E. Cox and Orville C. Walker, "Reactions to Disappointing Performance in Manufacturer-Distributor Relationships: The Role of Escalation and Resource Commitments," *Psychology & Marketing*, December 1997, p. 791; Rajiv P. Dant and Patrick L. Schul, "Conflict Resolution Processes in Contractual Channels of Distribution," *Journal of Marketing*, January 1992, p. 38.

11. "What's Wrong with Selling Used CDs?" *BusinessWeek*, July 26, 1993, p. 38.

12. "Get Great Results from Salespeople by Finding What Really Moves Them," *Investor's Business Daily*, July 2, 2001, p. A1.

13. "How Goodyear Blew Its Chance to Capitalize on a Rival's Woes," *The Wall Street Journal*, February 19, 2003, p. A1; "For Two Tire Makers, a Flat-Out Pitch for Safer Wheels," *The Wall Street Journal*, July 3, 1997, p. B4; "Goodyear Revs Image," *Brandweek*, February 10, 1997, p. 12; "Goodyear Wins Court Dispute with Dealers," *The Wall Street Journal*, July 2, 1996, p. B6; "Stan Gault's Designated Driver," *BusinessWeek*, April 8, 1996, p. 128; "Goodyear Expands Just Tires by Converting Full Service Centers," *Discount Store News*, May 16, 1994, p. 6. See also David I. Gilliland, "Toward a Business-to-business Channel Incentives Classification Scheme," *Industrial Marketing Management*, January 2003, p. 55; Keysuk Kim and Changho Oh, "On Distributor Commitment in Marketing Channels for Industrial Products: Contrast Between the United States and Japan," *Journal of International Marketing*, (1) 2002, p. 72; Pierre Berthon, Leyland F. Pitt, Michael T. Ewing and Gunnar Bakkeland, "Norms and Power in Marketing Relationships: Alternative Theories and Empirical Evidence," *Journal of Business Research*, September 2003, p 699; Rajiv Mehta, Alan J. Dubinsky, and Rolph E. Anderson, "Marketing Channel Management and the Sales Manager," *Industrial Marketing Management*, August 2002, p. 429; Wujin Chu and Paul R. Messinger, "Information and Channel Profits," *Journal of Retailing*, Winter 1997, p. 487; Donald V. Fites, "Make Your Dealers Your Partners," *Harvard Business Review*, March–April 1996, p. 84; John F. Tanner, Rick E. Ridnour, and Stephen B. Castleberry, "Types of Vertical Exchange Relationships: An Empirical Re-Examination of the Cadre/ Hired-Hand Distinction," *Journal of Marketing Theory & Practice*, Summer 1997, p. 109; Zhan G. Li and Rajiv P. Dant, "An Exploratory Study of Exclusive Dealing in Channel Relationships," *Journal of the Academy of Marketing Science*, Summer 1997, p. 201.

14. See G. Peter Dapiran and Sandra Hogarth-Scott, "Are Co-operation and Trust Being Confused with Power? An Analysis of Food Retailing in Australia and the UK," *International Journal of Retail & Distribution Management*, (4) 2003, p. 256; David I. Gilliland and Daniel C. Bello, "Two Sides to Attitudinal Commitment: the Effect of Calculative and Loyalty Commitment on Enforcement Mechanisms in Distribution Channels," *Journal of the Academy of Marketing Science*, Winter 2002, p. 24; Keysuk Kim, "On Interfirm Power, Channel Climate, and Solidarity in Industrial Distributor-Supplier Dyads," *Journal of the Academy of Marketing Science*, Summer 2000, p. 388; "Making the Middleman an Endangered Species," *BusinessWeek*, June 6, 1994, p. 114; Jule B. Gassenheimer et al., "Models of Channel Maintenance: What Is the Weaker Party to Do?" *Journal of Business Research*, July 1994, p. 225; Gregory T. Gundlach, Ravi S. Achrol, and John T. Mentzer, "The Structure of Commitment in Exchange," *Journal of Marketing*, January 1995, p. 78; Jan B. Heide, "Interorganizational Governance in Marketing Channels," *Journal of Marketing*, January 1994, p. 71; Jean L. Johnson et al., "The Exercise of Interfirm Power and Its Repercussions in U.S.-Japanese Channel Relationships," *Journal of Marketing*, April 1993, p. 1.

15. "Kimberly-Clark Keeps Costco in Diapers, Absorbing Costs Itself," *The Wall Street Journal*, September 7, 2000, p. A1. For another example, see "Made to Measure: Invisible Supplier Has Penney's Shirts All Buttoned Up," *The Wall Street Journal*, September 11, 2003, p. A1.

16. Kevin L. Webb, "Managing Channels of Distribution in the Age of Electronic Commerce," *Industrial Marketing Management*, February 2002, p. 95; Carolyn Y. Nicholson, Larry D. Compeau and Rajesh Sethi, "The Role of Interpersonal Liking in Building Trust in Long-Term Channel Relationships," *Journal of the Academy of Marketing Science*, Winter 2001, p. 3; Charles A. Ingene and Mark E. Parry, "Is Channel Coordination All it Is Cracked up to Be?," *Journal of Retailing*, Winter 2000, p. 511; Kenneth H. Wathne and Jan B. Heide, "Opportunism in Interfirm Relationships: Forms, Outcomes, and Solutions," *Journal of Marketing*, October 2000, p. 36; James R. Brown, Chekitan S. Dev, and Dong-Jin Lee, "Managing Marketing Channel Opportunism: the Efficacy of Alternative Governance Mechanisms," *Journal of Marketing*, April 2000, p. 51; Ashwin W. Joshi and Alexandra J. Campbell, "Effect of Environmental Dynamism on Relational Governance in Manufacturer-Supplier Relationships: a Contingency Framework and an Empirical Test," *Journal of the Academy of Marketing Science*, Spring 2003, p. 176; Kersi D. Antia and Gary L. Frazier, "The Severity of Contract Enforcement in Interfirm Channel Relationships," *Journal of Marketing*, October 2001, p. 67; Ravi S. Achrol, "Changes in the Theory of Interorganizational Relations in Marketing: Toward a Network Paradigm," *Journal of the Academy of Marketing Science*, Winter 1997, p. 56; Aric Rindfleisch and Jan B. Heide, "Transaction Cost Analysis: Past, Present, and Future Applications," *Journal of Marketing*, October 1997, p. 30; Robert F. Lusch and James R. Brown, "Interdependency, Contracting, and Relational Behavior in Marketing Channels," *Journal of Marketing*, October 1996, p. 19; Robert D. Buzzell, "Is Vertical Integration Profitable?" *Harvard Business Review*, January–February 1983, p. 92.

17. "Crowded House: With the Web Shaking Up Music, a Free-for-All in Online Songs," *The Wall Street Journal*, November 19, 2003, p. A1; "Microsoft Plans to Sell Music over the Web," *The Wall Street Journal*, November 17, 2003, p. B1; "Ads Aim to Sell That Tune," *The Wall Street Journal*, November 10, 2003, p. B1; "Everybody Wants a Piece of the iPod," *BusinessWeek*, October 27, 2003, p. 48; "Pumping Up the Volume," *Newsweek*, October 27, 2003, p. 52; "Walt Rocks: Rating the New Music Sites," *The Wall Street Journal*, October 22, 2003, p. D1; "Apple Opens Door of E-Music Store to Windows Users," *The Wall Street Journal*, October 17, 2003, p. B2; "Music Industry Presses 'Play' on Plan to Save Its Business," *The Wall Street Journal*, September 9, 2003, p. A1; "Best Buy Gets Jump on Retailers," *Investor's Business Daily*, August 27, 2003, p. A4; "Special Report: Music Marketing," *Advertising Age*, July 28, 2003, pp. S1–S8; "Lawsuits May Help Net Song Sellers," *USA Today*, June 30, 2003, p. 2B; "Taps for Music Retailers?" *BusinessWeek*, June 23, 2003, p. 40; "Free Samples at the Record Store," *The Wall Street Journal*, June 12, 2003, p. D1; "Music Sites Launch Battle of the Brands," *Advertising Age*, May 12, 2003, p. 3; "Apple Brings Its Flair for Smart Designs to Digital Music Player," *The Wall Street Journal*, November 1, 2001, p. B1.

18. "Special Report: Partners," *BusinessWeek*, October 25, 1999, p. 106.

19. "A Talk with the Man Who Got Rayovac All Charged Up," *BusinessWeek*, February 21, 2000, p. 32F.

20. "Can Esprit Be Hip Again?" *The Wall Street Journal*, June 17, 2002, p. B1; "Esprit's Spirited Style Is Hot Seller," *USA Today*, March 25, 1986, p. B5. See also Carol J. Johnson, Robert E. Krapfel, Jr. and Curtis M. Grimm, "A Contingency Model of Supplier-Reseller Satisfaction Perceptions in Distribution Channels," *Journal of Marketing Channels*, (1,2) 2001, p. 65; Inge Geyskens and Jan-Benedict E. M. Steenkamp, "Economic and Social Satisfaction: Measurement and Relevance to Marketing Channel Relationships," *Journal of Retailing*, Spring 2000, p. 11; Gary L. Frazier and Walfried M. Lassar, "Determinants of Distribution Intensity," *Journal of Marketing*, October 1996, p. 39; Adam J. Fein and Erin Anderson, "Patterns of Credible Commitments: Territory and Brand Selectivity in Industrial Distribution Channels," *Journal of Marketing*, April 1997, p. 19.

21. For more on Reebok, see *2003 Annual Report*, Reebok; "Reebok's Direct Sales Spark a Retail Revolt," *Adweek's Marketing Week*, December 2, 1991, p. 7. See also Saul Sands and Robert J. Posch, Jr., "A Checklist of Questions for Firms Considering a Vertical Territorial Distribution Plan," *Journal of Marketing*, Summer 1982, p. 38; Debra L. Scammon and Mary Jane Sheffet, "Legal Issues in Channels Modification Decisions: The Question of Refusals to Deal," *Journal of Public Policy and Marketing* 5 (1986), p. 82.

22. Gregory T. Gundlach and Patrick E. Murphy, "Ethical and Legal Foundations of Relational Marketing Exchanges," *Journal of Marketing*, October 1993, p. 35; Craig B. Barkacs, "Multilevel Marketing and Antifraud Statutes: Legal Enterprises or Pyramid Schemes?" *Journal of the Academy of Marketing Science*, Spring 1997, p. 176; Robert A. Robicheaux and James E. Coleman, "The Structure of Marketing Channel Relationships," *Journal of the Academy of Marketing Science*, Winter 1994, p. 38; Brett A. Boyle and F. Robert Dwyer, "Power, Bureaucracy, Influence and Performance: Their Relationships in Industrial Distribution Channels," *Journal of Business Research*, March 1995, p. 189.

23. For more on online return policies, see "I Ordered That? Web Retailers Make It Easier to Return Goods," *The Wall Street Journal*, September 4, 2003, p. D1; "Gone Today, Here Tomorrow," *Business 2.0*, December 2001, p. 116; "Happy Returns," *BusinessWeek Small Biz*, October 8, 2001, p. 12. For more on in-store return policies, see "I Take Thee . . . Back to the Store," *The Wall Street Journal*, May 30, 2002, p. D1; "The Point of No Return," *The Wall Street Journal*, May 14, 2002, p. D1. See also Andy A. Tsay, "Risk Sensitivity in Distribution Channel Partnerships: Implications for Manufacturer Return Policies," *Journal of Retailing*, Summer 2002, p. 147; Sara Lonn and Julie Ann Stuart, "Increasing Service Through Aggressive Dealer Inventory Return Policies," *International Journal of Physical Distribution & Logistics Management*, (6) 2003, p. 519.

24. Charles Fishman, "The Wal-Mart You Don't Know," *Fast Company*, December 2003.

25. See, for example, "P&G to Stores: Keep the Dented Crisco Cans," *The Wall Street Journal*, March 21, 1997, p. B1. See also "Cellphone Makers Connect for Recycling Program," *USA Today*, October 22, 2003, p. 6B; "The Information Age's Toxic Garbage," *BusinessWeek*, October 6, 2003, p. 54. See also Rene B. M. de Koster, Marisa P. de Brito and Masja A. van de Vendel, "Return Handling: an Exploratory Study with Nine Retailer Warehouses," *International Journal of Retail & Distribution Management*, (8) 2002, p. 407; Ronald S. Tibben-Lembke, "Life after Death: Reverse Logistics and the Product Life Cycle," *International Journal of Physical Distribution & Logistics Management*, (3) 2002, p. 223; A. Michael Knemeyer, Thomas G. Ponzurick, and Cyril M. Logar, "A Qualitative Examination of Factors Affecting Reverse Logistics Systems for End-of-Life Computers," *International Journal of Physical Distribution & Logistics Management*, (6) 2002, p. 455; Chad W. Autry, Patricia J. Daugherty, and R. Glenn Richey, "The Challenge of Reverse Logistics in Catalog Retailing," *International Journal of Physical Distribution & Logistics Management*, (1) 2001, p. 26; Dale S. Rogers and Ronald Tibben-Lembke, "An Examination of Reverse Logistics Practices," *Journal of Business Logistics*, (2) 2001, p. 129.

26. For an excellent example of EDI, see "To Sell Goods to Wal-Mart, Get on the Net," *The Wall Street Journal*, November 21, 2003, p. B1. See also Cornelia Droge and Richard Germain, "The Relationship of Electronic Data Interchange with Inventory and Financial Performance," *Journal of Business Logistics*, (2) 2000, p. 209; Lisa R. Williams, Avril Nibbs, Dimples Irby, and Terence Finley, "Logistics Integration: The Effect of Information Technology, Team Composition, and Corporate Competitve Positioning," *Journal of Business Logistics*, 1997, p. 31; Paul R. Murphy and James M. Daley, "International Freight Forwarder Perspectives on Electronic Data Interchange and Information Management Issues," *Journal of Business Logistics*, 1996, p. 63; Ira Lewis and Alexander Talalayevsky, "Logistics and Information Technology: A Coordination Perspective," *Journal of Business Logistics*, 1997, p. 141.

27. "A Smart Cookie at Pepperidge," *Fortune*, December 22, 1986, p. 67.

28. Douglas Lambert, James R. Stock, and Lisa M. Ellram, *Fundamentals of Logistics* (Burr Ridge, IL: Irwin/McGraw-Hill, 1998).

29. "Next Stop: The 21st Century," *Business 2.0*, September 2003, p. 152; "Back on Track: Left for Dead, Railroads Revive by Watching Clock," *The Wall Street Journal*, July 25, 2003, p. A1; "Trains: Industry Report," *Investor's Business Daily*, May 7, 2001, p. B6; "America's Railroads Struggle to Recapture Their Former Glory," *The Wall Street Journal*, December 5, 1997, p. A1; "The Rails: Trouble Behind, Trouble Ahead," *BusinessWeek*, November 24, 1997, p. 40.

30. "Costs of Trucking Seen Rising under New Safety Rules," *The Wall Street Journal*, November 12, 2003, p. A1; "Trucker Rewards Customers for Good Behavior," *The Wall Street Journal*, September 9, 2003, p. B4; "Trucking: Rig and Roll," *The Wall Street Journal*, October 23, 2000, p. R51; "Trucking Gets Sophisticated," *Fortune*, July 24, 2000, p. T270B; "Forward Air Corp.: Hauler Gets Freight from Jets to Businesses," *Investor's Business Daily*, June 6, 2000, p. A14; "Making Sure Big Rigs Have Something to Carry," *BusinessWeek*, June 12, 2000, p. 168F; "Trucking Finds the Internet," *Heavy Duty Trucking*, October 1999, p. 116; "Riding the Data Highway," *Newsweek*, March 21, 1994, p. 54; "E-Commerce's Newest Portals: Truck Drivers," *The Wall Street Journal*, January 3, 2000, p. A11; "Getting the Goods," *The Wall Street Journal*, November 22, 1999, p. R39.

31. For more on overnight carriers, see "Why FedEx Is Gaining Ground," *Business 2.0*, October 2003, p. 56; "FedEx Recasts Itself on the Ground," *The Wall Street Journal*, September 4, 2003, p. B7; "UPS, FedEx Wage Handheld Combat," *Investor's Business Daily*, May 19, 2003, p. A6; "Shipping Firms' Web Sites Help You Track Items," *Investor's Business Daily*, July 6, 2001, p. A6; "UPS Puts Its Back into It," *BusinessWeek*, October 27, 1997, p. 50.

32. *2003 Annual Report*, Du Pont; *2003 Annual Report*, Matlack; *2003 Annual Report*, Shell; *2003 Annual Report*, FedEx; *2003 Annual Report*, UPS; "FedEx and Brown Are Going Green," *BusinessWeek*, August 11, 2003, p. 60; "Conservation Power," *BusinessWeek*, September 16, 1991, p. 86. See also Lawrence Christensen, "The Environment and its Impact on the Supply Chain," *International Journal of Retail & Distribution Management*, (11) 2002, p. 571.

33. Anita Lahey, "Brand Revolution," from World Wide Web: <http://www.fmi.org>.

34. "New Warehouses Take On a Luxe Look," *The Wall Street Journal*, June 18, 2003, p. B6; Arnold B. Maltz, "Outsourcing the Warehousing Function: Economics and Strategic Considerations," *The Logistics and Transportation Review*, September 1994, p. 245; Patricia J. Daugherty, Dale S. Rogers, and Theodore P. Stank, "Benchmarking: Strategic Implications for Warehousing Firms," *The Logistics and Transportation Review*, March 1994, p. 55.

35. "Down, but Far from Out: RFID Technology Is Off to a Disappointing Start, but Retailers Are Convinced," *The Wall Street Journal Reports*, January 12, 2004, p. R5; "Wal-Mart Keeps the Change," *Fortune*, November 10, 2003, p. 46; "Sensor Revolution: Bugging the World," *BusinessWeek*, August 25, 2003, p. 100; "Cutting Navy Hospital Paperwork," *Investor's Business Daily*, May 22, 2003, p. A7; "Bar Codes Better Watch Their Backs," *BusinessWeek*, July 14, 2003, p. 42; "Radio ID Tags Take on Bar Codes," *Investor's Business Daily*, March 13, 2003, p. A7; "A Radio Chip in Every Consumer Product," *The New York Times*, February 25, 2003, *p. C1*.

CHAPTER 12

1. Available from the World Wide Web: <http://www.roots.com>, retrieved April 12, 2006; "Gretzky gives Roots an Olympic edge," *National Post*, February 16, 2006.

2. Available from World Wide Web: <http://www.census.gov>; U.S. Bureau of the Census, *Statistical Abstract of the United States 2002* (Washington, DC: U.S. Government Printing Office, 2001); U.S. Bureau of the Census, *County Business Patterns 1998, United States* (Washington, DC: U.S. Government Printing Office, 2000); "Annual Industry Report, Top 150," *DSN Retailing Today*, July 7, 2003, p. 15; "Just Take the Money!" *Time (Inside Business Bonus Section)*, July 2003; "Paying Less for Prada," *The Wall Street Journal*, April 29, 2003, p. D1; "When Is a Mall Not Just a Mall? When Sign Says Shoppingtown," *Investor's Business Daily*, April 28, 2003, p. A1; "Point-of-Sale Technology Is Changing the Retailing Industry," *Investor's Business Daily*, February 25, 2003, p. A4; "Islands in the Mall: Pushcarts as Revenue Streams," *The New York Times*, January 22, 2003, p. C6; "Hunter Gatherer: Rare Retailer Scores by Targeting Men Who Hate to Shop," *The Wall Street Journal*, December 17, 2002, p. A1; "The 40 People and Events That Have Shaped Mass Market Retailing," *DSN Retailing Today (Special Issue)*, August 2002; "Retail Reckoning," *BusinessWeek*, December 10, 2001, p. 72; "Remedies for an Economic Hangover," *Fortune*, June 25, 2001, p. 130; "Outlet Centers Go Upmarket with Amenities," *The Wall Street Journal*, June 6, 2001, p. B12.

3. "Small Retailers Outfox Big Rivals," *Investor's Business Daily*, November 28, 2000, p. A1; "Urban Rarity: Stores Offering Spiffy Service," *The Wall Street Journal*, July 25, 1996, p. B1; "Airports: New Destination for Specialty Retailers," *USA Today*, January 11, 1996, p. 5B; Sharon E. Beatty, Morris Mayer, James E. Coleman, Kristy E. Reynolds, and Jungki Lee, "Customer-Sales Associate Retail Relationships," *Journal of Retailing*, Fall 1996, p. 223.

4. Available from World Wide Web: <http://www.census.gov>; U.S. Bureau of the Census, *County Business Patterns 1998, United States*; U.S. Bureau of the Census, *1997 Census of Retail Trade, Subject Series, Establishment and Firm Size* (Washington, DC: U.S. Government Office, 2000). For more on department stores, see "It's Not Your Mom's Department Store," *BusinessWeek*, December 1, 2003, p. 98; "Department Stores Embrace Toy Chains as Holiday Lure," *The Wall Street Journal*, October 8, 2003, p. B1; "Department Stores Ring Up Centralized Checkouts," *USA Today*, June 6, 2002, p. 5B; "Idle Aisles: Department Stores Fight an Uphill Battle Just to Stay Relevant," *The Wall Street Journal*, March 12, 2002, p. A1; "Department Stores and Designer Tenants Jockey Over Real Estate," *The Wall Street Journal*, October 31, 2000, p. A1.

5. David Appel, "The Supermarket: Early Development of an Institutional Innovation," *Journal of Retailing*, Spring 1972, p. 39.

6. "How Growth Destroys Differentiation," *Brandweek*, April 24, 2000, p. 42.

7. For more on Wal-Mart's Neighborhood Markets, see "Neighborhood Market Caps Year with Round of New Market Entries," *DSN Retailing Today*, January 27, 2003, p. 1; "For America's Big Retailers, Small Is Beautiful, Sometimes," *The New York Times*, January 22, 2003, p. C1; "Wal-Mart: Lengthening Its Lead," *DSN Retailing Today*, June 10, 2002, p. 83; "Meet Your New Neighborhood Grocer," *Fortune*, May 13, 2002, p. 93; "Wal-Mart Is Eating Everyone's Lunch," *BusinessWeek*, April 15, 2002, p. 43.

8. For more on superstores, see "Wal-Mart, the Category King," *DSN Retailing Today*, June 9, 2003, p. 65; "Price War in Aisle 3," *The Wall Street Journal*, May 27, 2003, p. B1; "Supershoppers," *American Demographics*, May 2003, p. 17; "Wal-Mart, Target Gain Supercenter Share," *Food Retailing Today*, February 24, 2003, p. 4; "Supercenters Take Lead in Food Retailing," *Food Retailing Today*, May 6, 2002, p.8. "How Grocers Are Fighting Giant Rivals," *The Wall Street Journal*, March 27, 1997, p. B1.

9. For more on warehouse clubs, see "The Only Company Wal-Mart Fears," *Fortune*, November 24, 2003, p. 158; "Clubs Expand Despite Each Other," *Food Retailing Today*, July 21, 2003, p. 6; "Warehouse Stores Aren't Just for Those Pinching Pennies," *USA Today*, June 20, 2003, p. 1B; "Wal-Mart, the Category King," *DSN Retailing Today*, June 9, 2003, p. 65; "Retailers Try New Venues to Boost Sales," *USA Today*, May 13, 2003, p. 3B; "Out of the Box Thinking," *Newsweek*, May 12, 2003, p. 40; "Sam's Club: Back to Business," *DSN Retailing Today (Special Issue)*, April 2003; "Costco Home Poised to Revolutionize High-End Furniture," *DSN Retailing Today*, January 6, 2003, p. 5.

10. For more on category killers, see "Toys 'R' Us: Taking the Family of Brands to New Heights," *DSN Retailing Today (Special Issue)*, October 2003; "Category Killers Go from Lethal to Lame in the Space of a Decade," *The Wall Street Journal*, March 9, 2000, p. A1; "U.S. Superstores Find Japanese Are a Hard Sell," *The Wall Street Journal*, February 14, 2000, p. B1; "Office-Supply Superstores Find Bounty in the Boonies," *The Wall Street Journal*, September 1, 1998, p. B1; "Health-Care Superstores Experience Growing Pains," *The Wall Street Journal*, May 12, 1997, p. B1; "New Sneaker Superstores Aim to Step on Their Competition," *The Wall Street Journal*, March 19, 1997, p. B1; "Bridal Superstores Woo Couples with Miles of Gowns and Tuxes," *The Wall Street Journal*, February 14, 1996, p. B1.

11. For more on 7-Eleven in the U.S., see "At 7-Eleven, Fresh-Food Fix Is Focus," *The Wall Street Journal*, August 21, 2002, p. B3B; "7-Eleven Cracks the Code on Elusive Sugar-Free Slurpee," *The Wall Street Journal*, October 29, 2001, p. B9; "New Banking Hours: From 7 a.m. to 11 p.m.," *Newsweek*, May 7, 2001, p. 79; "Mobile Phone with That Slurpee? Holiday Shoppers Buy on the Run," *USA Today*, December 15, 2000, p. 1B. For more on 7-Eleven in Japan, see "From Convenience Store to Online Behemoth?" *BusinessWeek*, April 10, 2000, p. 64; "Japan Goes Web Crazy," *Fortune*, February 7, 2000, p. 115; "In Japan, the Hub of E-Commerce Is a 7-Eleven," *The Wall Street Journal*, November 1, 1999, p. B1.

12. For more on vending and wireless, see "Want a Soda? Call the Machine," *Investor's Business Daily*, November 13, 2002, p. A4; "Speedpass Use Shows Demand for Wireless Payments," *Investor's Business Daily*, April 19, 2002, p. A6; "Thirsty? Soon You May Be Able to Charge and Chug," *USA Today*, December 21, 2001, p. 7B; "Kodak Rages in Favor of the Machines," *Brandweek*, February 26, 2001, p. 6.

13. "Major Retailers to Stuff Mailboxes with Catalogs," *USA Today*, November 11, 2003, p. 6B; "New Page in E-Retailing: Catalogs," *The Wall Street Journal*, November 30, 2000, p. B1; "Beyond Mail Order: Catalogs Now Sell Image, Advice," *The Wall Street Journal*, July 29, 1997, p. B1; "Catalogers Expand in Asia," *USA Today*, October 18, 1996, p. 4B; "U.S. Catalogers Test International Waters," *The Wall Street Journal*, April 19, 1994, p. B1. See also Charla Mathwick, Naresh K. Malhotra, and Edward Rigdon, "The Effect of Dynamic Retail Experiences on Experiential Perceptions of Value: an Internet and Catalog Comparison," *Journal of Retailing*, Spring 2002, p. 51; C.R. Jasper and P.N.R. Lan, "Apparel Catalog Patronage: Demographic, Lifestyle, and Motivational Factors," *Psychology & Marketing*, July/August 1992, p. 275.

14. "Getting Ready for Prime Time," *Inc.*, November 2003, p. 17; "Is There a Future for the TV Mall?" *Brandweek*, March 25, 1996, p. 24; "QVC Draws Wares from Everywhere," *USA Today*, November 1, 1994, p. 1D; "Battling for Buck$," *Profiles*, November 1994, p. 49.

15. "Making Bank on Small Change," *Business 2.0*, November 2003, p. 56; "PayPal Pushes for Business Use," *Investor's Business Daily*, October 24, 2003, p. A4; "Marketer of the Year: The EBay Way, Brand It Now," *Brandweek*, October 20, 2003, p. M20; "Hitching a Ride on eBay," *The Wall Street Journal Reports*, October 20, 2003, p. R4; "Despite Auto-Unit Caution Flag, EBay Remains in the Fast Lane," *Investor's Business Daily*, October 16, 2003, p. A1; "Chic at a Click: EBay Fashions a Deal with Designers," *The Wall Street Journal*, September 15, 2003, p. B1; "Buying in Bulk: EBay Recasts Itself as Wholesaler Source," *Investor's Business Daily*, September 4, 2003, p. A5; "Meg and the Machine," *Fortune*, September 1, 2003, p. 68; "The eBay Economy," *BusinessWeek*, August 25, 2003, p. 124; "eBay's Worst Nightmare," *Fortune*, May 26, 2003, p. 89;

"EBay Earnings More than Double," *The Wall Street Journal*, April 23, 2003, p. B7; "EBAY Rules," *BusinessWeek* (The BusinessWeek 50), Spring 2003, p. 172; "Clicking the Tires: EBay Is Emerging as Unlikely Giant in Used-Car Sales," *The Wall Street Journal*, February 7, 2003, p. A1; "Take a Lesson from EBay in Buying, Selling," *Investor's Business Daily*, February 3, 2003, p. A4; "How eBay Spurred Sellers to Grab Hot Toys," *The Wall Street Journal*, December 13, 2002, p. B1; "eBay Bids on B-to-B Business," *BtoB*, December 9, 2002, p. 1; "Why EBay Keeps Growing," *Investor's Business Daily*, November 15, 2002, p. A3; "Are You Satisfied?" *The Wall Street Journal Reports*, September 16, 2002, p. R7; "What eBay Isn't Telling You," *Business 2.0*, August 2002, p. 56.

16. "Web Shopping Gains Popularity," *USA Today*, November 26, 2003, p. 3B; "Online Comparison Shopping's on a Spree," *Investor's Business Daily*, October 22, 2003, p. A4; "He Turned Website in the Rough into Online Jewel," *USA Today*, October 20, 2003, p. 5B; "Online Shoppers Still Fear Security Issues," *Investor's Business Daily*, June 3, 2003, p. A4; "Can You Really Buy a Couch Online?" *The Wall Street Journal Reports*, April 28, 2003, p. R9; "Cruising the Online Mall," *Time (Inside Edition Bonus Section)*, April 2003; "Net vs. Not: Which Offers Better Shopping?" *USA Today*, March 10, 2003, p. 3B; "Merlot by Mail: Ordering Wine Online Gets Easier," *The Wall Street Journal*, August 21, 2002, p. D1; "Sears Enhances Service for Customers in Stores and on Web," *Investor's Business Daily*, August 5, 2002, p. A4; "Click and. . . Drive?" *The Wall Street Journal Reports*, July 15, 2002, p. R11; "Internet Firms Fish for Revenue from Fees," *USA Today*, June 11, 2002, p. 1B; "Retailers Discover Leap to Web's a Doozy," *USA Today*, December 18, 2001, p. 3B; "Making the Sale," *The Wall Street Journal Reports*, September 24, 2001, p. R6; "An Internet Model That Works," *Inc.*, May 2001, p. 25; "Battle-Tested Rules of Online Retail," *Ecompany*, April 2001, p. 72; Matthew L. Meuter, "Self-Service Technologies: Understanding Customer Satisfaction with Technology-Based Service Encounters," *Journal of Marketing*, July 2000, p. 50; "Special Report: Rethinking the Internet," *BusinessWeek*, March 26, 2001, p. 117; "Online America," *American Demographics* March 2001, p. 53; "Bricks vs. Clicks," *The Wall Street Journal*, December 11, 2000, p. R10; "Wooing the Newbies," *BusinessWeek E.Biz*, May 15, 2000, p. 116; "The Lessons Learned," *The Wall Street Journal*, April 17, 2000, p. R6. See also Fang-Fang Tang and Xiaolin Xing, "Will the Growth of Multi-Channel Retailing Diminish the Pricing Efficiency of the Web?," *Journal of Retailing*, Fall 2001, p. 319; Gerald L. Lohse, Steven Bellman and Eric J. Johnson, "Consumer Buying Behavior on the Internet: Findings from Panel Data," *Journal of Interactive Marketing*, Winter 2000, p. 15; Jonathan Reynolds, "Charting the Multichannel Future: Retail Choices and Constraints," *International Journal of Retail & Distribution Management*, (11) 2002, p. 530; Jennifer Rowley, "Shopping Bots: Intelligent Shopper or Virtual Department Store?" *International Journal of Retail & Distribution Management*, (7) 2000, p. 297; Sung-Joon Yoon, "The Antecedents and Consequences of Trust in Online-Purchase Decisions," *Journal of Interactive Marketing*, Spring 2002, p. 47; David M. Szymanski and Richard T. Hise, "E-Satisfaction: an Initial Examination," *Journal of Retailing*, Fall 2000, p. 309; Charla Mathwick, "Understanding the Online Consumer: a Typology of Online Relational Norms and Behavior," *Journal of Interactive Marketing*, Winter 2002, p. 40; Satya Menon and Barbara Kahn, "Cross-Category Effects of Induced Arousal and Pleasure on the Internet Shopping Experience," *Journal of Retailing*, Spring 2002, p. 31; Vijay Mahajan, Raji Srinivasan, and Jerry Wind, "The Dot.com Retail Failures of 2000: Were There Any Winners?," *Journal of the Academy of Marketing Science*, Fall 2002, p. 474; Kirthi Kalyanam and Shelby McIntyre, "The E-Marketing Mix: A Contribution of the E-Tailing Wars," *Journal of the Academy of Marketing Science*, Fall 2002, p. 487; Terry L. Childers, Christopher L. Carr, Joann Peck, and Stephen Carson, "Hedonic and Utilitarian Motivations for Online Retail Shopping Behavior," *Journal of Retailing*, Winter 2001, p. 511; Brian T. Ratchford, Xing Pan and Venkatesh Shankar, "On the Efficiency of Internet Markets for Consumer Goods," *Journal of Public Policy & Marketing*, Spring 2003, p. 4; Raymond R. Burke, "Technology and the Customer Interface:

What Consumers Want in the Physical and Virtual Store," *Journal of the Academy of Marketing Science*, Fall 2002, p. 411; Joseph Alba, John Lynch, Barton Weitz, Chris Janiszewski et al., "Interactive Home Shopping: Consumer, Retailer, and Manufacturer Incentives to Participate in Electronic Marketplaces," *Journal of Marketing*, July 1997, p. 38.

17. Chip E. Miller, "The Effects of Competition on Retail Structure: an Examination of Intratype, Intertype, and Intercategory Competition," *Journal of Marketing*, October 1999, p. 107; "A Quart of Milk, a Dozen Eggs, and a 2.6-GHz Laptop," *Business 2.0*, October 2003, p. 58; "Jordan's Puts Imax in Its Furniture Picture," *The Wall Street Journal*, October 4, 2002, p. B6; "Latest Supermarket Special—Gasoline," *The Wall Street Journal*, April 30, 2001, p. B1; "Levi's Doesn't Fancy Selling with Cukes," *The Wall Street Journal*, April 10, 2001, p. B10; "Barnes & Noble Finds Grinch Effect in Games Strategy," *The Wall Street Journal*, December 20, 2000, p. B4; "Savoring Chocolate," *Advertising Age*, September 4, 2000, p. 24; "In Aisle 10, Soup, Tea—and Bikinis?" *The Wall Street Journal*, June 28, 2000, p. B1; Jack M. Cadeaux, "Industry Product Volatility and Retailer Assortments," *Journal of Macromarketing*, Fall 1992, p. 28; Ronald Savitt, "The 'Wheel of Retailing' and Retail Product Management," *European Journal of Marketing* 18, no. 6/7 (1984), p. 43.

18. National Public Radio online at <http://www.npr.org/templates/story/story.php?storyId=5368068>; American Apparel Web site at <http://store.americanapparel.ca/>.

19. "How Did Sears Blow This Gasket?" *BusinessWeek*, June 29, 1992, p. 38; "An Open Letter to Sears Customers," *USA Today*, June 25, 1992, p. 8A; see also John Paul Fraedrich, "The Ethical Behavior of Retail Managers," *Journal of Business Ethics*, March 1993, p. 207.

20. Statistics Canada 2004: "Department Store Sales by Province," retrieved March 2, 2006 from: <http://www.statcan.caezproxy.lib.ucalgary.ca>.

21. For an excellent example of AutoZone as successful chain, see "An Auto-Parts Store Your Mother Could Love," *Fortune*, November 10, 2003, p. 163; "Auto Accessories Still in the Fast Lane," *DSN Retailing Today*, May 5, 2003, p. 32; "AutoZone: The Hottest Growth Concept in Retailing," *DSN Retailing Today (Special Report)*, November 11, 2002; "In Corporate America It's Clean Up Time," *Fortune*, September 16, 2002, p. 62. See also "European Inns Take the Hilton Route," *The Wall Street Journal*, April 23, 2001, p. B1; "Forging Ahead with Custom Contracts," *Foodservice Equipment & Supplies Specialist*, June 1994, p. 52; "CLOUT! More and More, Retail Giants Rule the Marketplace," *BusinessWeek*, December 21, 1992, p. 66. See also Gary K. Rhoads, William R. Swinyard, Michael D. Geurts and William D. Price, "Retailing as a Career: A Comparative Study of Marketers," *Journal of Retailing*, Spring 2002, p. 71; Marilyn Lavin, ""Not in My Neighborhood": Resistance to Chain Drug-Stores," *International Journal of Retail & Distribution Management*, (6) 2003, p. 321.

22. "Why Subway Is 'The Biggest Problem in Franchising,'" *Fortune*, March 16, 1998, p. 126; "Fast-Food Fight," *BusinessWeek*, June 2, 1997, p. 34; "Rattling the Chains," *Brandweek*, April 21, 1997, p. 28; "Chicken and Burgers Create Hot New Class: Powerful Franchisees," *The Wall Street Journal*, May 21, 1996, p. A1. See also Surinder Tikoo, "Franchiser Influence Strategy Use and Franchisee Experience and Dependence," *Journal of Retailing*, Fall 2002, p. 183; Mika Tuunanen, "An Ounce of Prevention Is Worth a Pound of Cure: Findings from National Franchisee (Dis-)Satisfaction Study," *Journal of Marketing Channels*, (2) 2002, p. 57; Patrick J. Kaufmann and Rajiv P. Dant, "The Pricing of Franchise Rights," *Journal of Retailing*, Winter 2001, p. 537; Ram C. Rao and Shuba Srinivasan, "An Analysis of Advertising Payments in Franchise Contracts," *Journal of Marketing Channels*, (3,4) 2001, p. 85; Madhav Pappu and David Strutton, "Toward an Understanding of Strategic Inter-Organizational Relationships in Franchise Channels," *Journal of Marketing Channels*, (1,2) 2001, p. 111; Rajiv P. Dant and Patrick J. Kaufmann, "Structural and Strategic Dynamics in Franchising," *Journal of Retailing*,

(2) 2003, p. 63; Robert Dahlstom, "Franchising: Contemporary Issues and Research," *Journal of Public Policy & Marketing*, Spring 1996, p. 159; Roger D. Blair and Jill B. Herndon, "Franchise Supply Agreements: Quality Control or Illegal Tying?" *Journal of the Academy of Marketing Science*, Spring 1997, p. 177.

23. "China's Rush to Convenience," *The Wall Street Journal*, November 3, 2003, p. A13; "Making the Cuts," *The Wall Street Journal Reports*, September 22, 2003, p. R3; "Big German Retailer Metro AG Brings Superstores to Vietnam," *The Wall Street Journal*, August 13, 2002, p. B3B; "Germans Put Stock in Store of Future," *The Wall Street Journal*, June 19, 2003, p. A10; "Western Stores Woo Chinese Wallets," *The Wall Street Journal*, November 26, 2002, p. B1; "To Russia, with Love: The Multinationals' Song," *BusinessWeek*, September 16, 2002, p. 44; "European Inns Take the Hilton Route," *The Wall Street Journal*, April 23, 2001, p. B1; "U.S. Superstores Find Japanese Are a Hard Sell," *The Wall Street Journal*, February 14, 2000, p. B1; "How's This for a Cultural Revolution? Chinese Are Getting Home Shopping," *The Wall Street Journal*, January 4, 1996, p. A6; "Retailers Go Global," *Fortune*, February 20, 1995, p. 102. See also T. Wing-Chun Lo, Ho-Fuk Lau, and Gong-Shi Lin, "Problems and Prospects of Supermarket Development in China," *International Journal of Retail & Distribution Management*, (2) 2001, p. 66; Paul T. McGurr, "The Largest Retail Firms: a Comparison of Asia-, Europe- and US-based Retailers," *International Journal of Retail & Distribution Management*, (2) 2002, p. 145; Barry Quinn and Nicholas Alexander, "International Retail Franchising: a Conceptual Framework," *International Journal of Retail & Distribution Management*, (5) 2002, p. 264; Marieke de Mooij and Geert Hofstede, "Convergence and Divergence in Consumer Behavior: Implications for International Retailing," *Journal of Retailing*, Spring 2002, p. 61; Valerie Severin, Jordan J. Louviere, and Adam Finn, "The Stability of Retail Shopping Choices over Time and Across Countries," *Journal of Retailing*, Summer 2001, p. 185; Jozefina Simova, Colin M. Clarke-Hill, and Terry Robinson, "A Longitudinal Study of Changes in Retail Formats and Merchandise Assortment in Clothing Retailing in the Czech Republic in the Period 1994–1999," *International Journal of Retail & Distribution Management*, (6) 2003, p. 352; Arieh Goldman, "The Transfer of Retail Formats into Developing Economies: the Example of China," *Journal of Retailing*, Summer 2001, p. 221; Herbert Kotzab and Maria Madlberger, "European Retailing in E-Transition? An Empirical Evaluation of Web-Based Retailing—Indications from Austria," *International Journal of Physical Distribution & Logistics Management*, (6) 2001, p. 440; Nicholas Alexander and Marcelo de Lira e Silva "Emerging Markets and the Internationalisation of Retailing: the Brazilian Experience," *International Journal of Retail & Distribution Management*, (6) 2002, p. 300.

24. "Why the Web Can't Kill the Middleman," *Ecompany*, April 2001, p. 75; "Not Dead Yet," *Inc. Tech*, No. 1, 2001, p. 58; "Electronics Distributors Are Reporting Record Profits," *The Wall Street Journal*, July 13, 2000, p. B4; "Chow (On)Line," *BusinessWeek E.Biz*, June 5, 2000, p. EB84; "Why Online Distributors—Once Written Off—May Thrive," *Fortune*, September 6, 1999, p. 270; "Middlemen Find Ways to Survive Cyberspace Shopping," *The Wall Street Journal*, December 12, 1996, p. B6; "Invoice? What's an Invoice?" *BusinessWeek*, June 10, 1996, p. 110. See also Susan Mudambi and Raj Aggarwal, "Industrial Distributors: Can They Survive in the New Economy?" *Industrial Marketing Management*, May 2003, p. 317; Das Narayandas, Mary Caravella, and John Deighton, "The Impact of Internet Exchanges on Business-to-Business Distribution," *Journal of the Academy of Marketing Science*, Fall 2002, p. 500; Amrik S. Sohal, Damien J. Power, and Mile Terziovski, "Integrated Supply Chain Management from the Wholesaler's Perspective: Two Australian Case Studies," *International Journal of Physical Distribution & Logistics Management*, (1) 2002, p. 96.

25. "Cold War: Amana Refrigeration Fights Tiny Distributor," *The Wall Street Journal*, February 26, 1992, p. B2. For another example, see "Quickie-Divorce Curbs Sought By Manufacturers' Distributors," *The*

Wall Street Journal, July 13, 1987, p. 27; "Merger of Two Bakers Teaches Distributors a Costly Lesson (3 parts)," *The Wall Street Journal*, September 14, 1987, p. 29; October 19, 1987, p. 35; November 11, 1987, p. 33.

26. Available from World Wide Web: <http://www.census. gov>; U.S. Bureau of the Census, *County Business Patterns 1998*, *United States*; U.S. Bureau of the Census, *1997 Census of Wholesale Trade, Geographic Area Series, United States* (Washington, DC: U.S. Government Printing Office, 2000); "Why Manufacturers Are Doubling as Distributors," *Business-Week*, January 17, 1983, p. 41. See also "Who Is Bob Kierlin—and Why Is He So Successful?" *Fortune*, December 8, 1997, p. 245; Robert F. Lusch, Deborah S. Coykendall, and James M. Kenderdine, *Wholesaling in Transition: An Executive Chart Book* (Norman, OK: Distribution Research Program, University of Oklahoma, 1990).

27. Available from World Wide Web: <http://www.fastenal. com>; "Fastenal: In This Sluggish Market, You Gotta Have Faith," *Investor's Business Daily*, August 13, 2001, p. A12.

28. "Revolution in Japanese Retailing," *Fortune*, February 7, 1994, p. 143; Arieh Goldman, "Evaluating the Performance of the Japanese Distribution System," *Journal of Retailing*, Spring 1992, p. 11; "Japan Begins to Open the Door to Foreigners, a Little," *Brandweek*, August 2, 1993, p. 14.

29. Available from World Wide Web: <http://www.inmac. com> and <http://www.grainger.com>; "B2B: Yesterday's Darling," *The Wall Street Journal*, October 23, 2000, p. R8; "W.W. Grainger's Web Investments: Money Well Spent? Don't Ask Street," *Investor's Business Daily*, September 19, 2000, p. A1.

30. For more on manufacturers' agents being squeezed, see "Philips to End Long Relations with North American Reps—Will Build Internal Sales Force Instead," *EBN*, November 10, 2003, p. 8; "Wal-Mart Draws Fire: Reps, Brokers Protest Being Shut Out by New Policy," *Advertising Age*, January 13, 1992, p. 3; Daniel H. McQuiston, "A Conceptual Model for Building and Maintaining Relationships Between Manufacturers' Representatives and Their Principals," *Industrial Marketing Management*, February 2001, p. 165; Patrick R. Mehr, "Identifying Independent Reps," *Industrial Marketing Management*, November 1992, p. 319. For more discussion on wholesaling abroad, see "Japan Rises to P&G's No. 3 Market," *Advertising Age*, December 10, 1990, p. 42; "'Papa-Mama' Stores in Japan Wield Power to Hold Back Imports," *The Wall Street Journal*, November 14, 1988, p. 1. See also Yoo S. Yang, Robert P. Leone, and Dana L. Alden, "A Market Expansion Ability Approach to Identify Potential Exporters," *Journal of Marketing*, January 1992, p. 84; Daniel C. Bello and Ritu Lohtia, "The Export Channel Design: The Use of Foreign Distributors and Agents," *Journal of the Academy of Marketing Science*, Spring 1995, p. 83; D. Steven White, "Behind the Success and Failure of U.S. Export Intermediaries: Transactions, Agents and Resources," *Journal of the Academy of Marketing Science*, Summer 2001, p. 18.

31. "Keep the Excess Moving," *BusinessWeek E.Biz*, November 20, 2000, p. EB78; "Good-Bye to Fixed Pricing?" *BusinessWeek*, May 4, 1998, p. 71; "Sales Are Clicking on Manufacturing's Internet Mart," *Fortune*, July 7, 1997, p. 136C.

32. "Delivering the Goods," *The Wall Street Journal Reports*, February 11, 2002, p. R14; "Sick of Checkout Lines? These Guys Can Help," *Investor's Business Daily*, July 9, 2001, p. A7; "What's Ahead for Retailing," *The Wall Street Journal*, June 25, 2001, p. R16; "Digital ID Cards," *The Wall Street Journal*, June 25, 2001, p. R16; "Now, Harried Shoppers Can Take Control at Supermarkets," *USA Today*, June 7, 2001, p. 1A; "Leave It in the Box," *BusinessWeek E.Biz*, December 11, 2000, p. EB82. See also Enrico Colla, "International Expansion and Strategies of Discount Grocery Retailers: The Winning Models," *International Journal of Retail & Distribution Management*, (1) 2003, p. 55; Robert A. Peterson and Sridhar Balasubramanian, "Retailing in the 21st Century: Reflections and Prologue to Research," *Journal of Retailing*, Spring 2002, p. 9; Elliot Rabinovich and Philip T. Evers, "Product Fulfillment in Supply Chains

Supporting Internet-Retailing Operations," *Journal of Business Logistics*, (2) 2003, p. 205; Alan C. McKinnon and Deepak Tallam, "Unattended Delivery to the Home: an Assessment of the Security Implications," *International Journal of Retail & Distribution Management*, (1) 2003, p. 30; Hannu Yrjola, "Physical Distribution Considerations for Electronic Grocery Shopping," *International Journal of Physical Distribution & Logistics Management*, (9) 2001, p. 746; Stacy L. Wood, "Future Fantasies: a Social Change Perspective of Retailing in the 21st Century," *Journal of Retailing*, Spring 2002, p. 77.

CHAPTER 13

1. Available from World Wide Web: <http://www.mini-cooper.com>; "Mags Put Pedal to Mini's Metal," *Brandweek*, September 22, 2003; "Hot Off the Lot," *The Wall Street Journal*, September 10, 2003, p. D4; "Mini Ads Throw Tradition Aside," *Advertising Age*, September 8, 2003, p. M7; "Crispin Porter + Bogusky," *Adweek*, June 23, 2003, pp. SR6–SR7; "Mini's Wild Ride," *Adweek*, June 2, 2003, p. 24; "Mini Fever Spawns Line of Accessories," *The New York Times*, March 6, 2003, p. D13; "What Went Right," *Fortune*, December 30, 2002, p. 164; "Giving a Small Car Big 'Tude," *Brandweek*, December 9, 2002, p. 31; "Creating Max Buzz for New BMW Mini," *Advertising Age*, June 17, 2002, p. 12; "Most Innovative Campaign," *Business 2.0*, May 2002, p. 98; "Big Enough to Turn Heads," *BusinessWeek*, April 22, 2002, p. 100; "BMW's Mini Driven to Generate Maximum Impact for Sub-Compact," *Brandweek*, April 15, 2002; "BMW 'Mini' Campaign: Odd to the Max," *The Wall Street Journal*, March 1, 2002, p. B5; "High Style in a Tiny Package," *The Wall Street Journal*, October 17, 2001, p. B1.

2. For more on Reebok's Terrible Terry Tate campaign, see "Grabbing Market Share," *Adweek Interactive Quarterly*, November 24, 2003, pp. IQ1–IQ5. For more on Tylenol 8 Hour campaign, see "Tylenol Hits the Gym for Launch," *Advertising Age*, May 26, 2003, p. 30. See also "Small Wonder," *The Wall Street Journal*, June 25, 2001, p. R1; "Minute Maid Opens Juicy Site to Promote New Drink," *Brandweek*, April 30, 2001; "PMA Reggie Awards 2001," *Brandweek* (Supplement), March 12, 2001, p. R1; "Mystery Shoppers," *American Demographics*, December 2000, p. 41; "Sweet Deals," *Inc. Tech*, No. 4, 2000, p. 98; "Hot Wheels," *American Demographics*, August 2000, p. 48; "Calling All Car Worms," *Brandweek*, March 6, 2000, p. 22; "Sharp Curves Ahead for Car Marketers," *Brandweek*, January 3, 2000, p. 18; "Talbots Mounting Its Biggest Integrated Marketing Push," *Advertising Age*, August 11, 1997, p. 29; "Olds' Intrigue Stars in Web Game Based on NBC TV Show," *Advertising Age*, July 28, 1997, p. 16; "Promotion Marketing," *Brandweek*, March 4, 1996, p. 22. See also X. Michael Song, Jinhong Xile, and Barbara Dyer, "Antecedents and Consequences of Marketing Managers' Conflict-Handling Behaviors," *Journal of Marketing*, January 2000, p. 50; David A. Griffith, Aruna Chandra and John K. Ryans, Jr. "Examining the Intricacies of Promotion Standardization: Factors Influencing Advertising Message and Packaging," *Journal of International Marketing*, (3) 2003, p. 30; Kim Bartel Sheehan and Caitlin Doherty, "Re-Weaving the Web: Integrating Print and Online Communications," *Journal of Interactive Marketing*, Spring 2001, p. 47; J. R. Shannon, "The New Promotions Mix: A Proposed Paradigm, Process, and Application," *Journal of Marketing Theory & Practice*, Winter 1996, p. 56; Kathleen J. Kelly, "Integrated Marketing Communication: Putting It Together & Making It Work," *Journal of the Academy of Marketing Science*, Winter 1997, p. 83.

3. "High-Tech Branding: Pushing Digital PCS," *Brandweek*, August 4, 1997, p. 30; "Brand Builders: Delivery Guy Chic," *Brandweek*, June 30, 1997, p. 18; "Eye-Catching Logos All Too Often Leave Fuzzy Images in Minds of Consumers," *The Wall Street Journal*, December 5, 1991, p. B1. See also George S. Low and Jakki J. Mohr, "Factors Affecting the Use of Information in the Evaluation of Marketing Communications Productivity," *Journal of the Academy of Marketing Science*, Winter 2001, p. 70; David I. Gilliland and Wesley J. Johnston, "Toward a Model of Business-to-Business Marketing Communications Effects," *Industrial Marketing Management*, January 1997, p. 15; Michel T. Pham and Gita V. Johar, "Contingent Processes of Source Identification," *Journal of Consumer Research*, December 1997, p. 249; Louisa Ha and Barry R. Litman, "Does Advertising Clutter Have Diminishing and Negative Returns?" *Journal of Advertising*, Spring 1997, p. 31; Barbara B. Stern, "A Revised Communication Model for Advertising: Multiple Dimensions of the Source, the Message, and the Recipient," *Journal of Advertising*, June 1994, p. 5; Ronald E. Dulek, John S. Fielden, and John S. Hill, "International Communication: An Executive Primer," *Business Horizons*, January/February 1991, p. 20; Kaylene C. Williams, Rosann L. Spiro, and Leslie M. Fine, "The Customer-Salesperson Dyad: An Interaction/Communication Model and Review," *Journal of Personal Selling and Sales Management*, Summer 1990, p. 29; Richard F. Beltramini and Edwin R. Stafford, "Comprehension and Perceived Believability of Seals of Approval Information in Advertising," *Journal of Advertising*, September 1993, p. 3.

4. "Finally, Some Help at the Health-Food Store," *The Wall Street Journal*, July 10, 2002, p. D1; "Good Housekeeping Unveils Web Site Review Program," *Brandweek*, May 29, 2000, p. 52; "Good Housekeeping to Offer 'Seal' to Autos," *Advertising Age*, June 29, 1998, p. 18; "Marketing in Which We Bash a Baby Seal," *Fortune*, September 8, 1997, p. 36.

5. "Global Branding: Same, But Different," *Brandweek*, April 9, 2001, p. 25; "When You Translate 'Got Milk' for Latinos, What Do You Get?" *The Wall Street Journal*, June 3, 1999, p. A1; "Cash, Cache, Cachet: All 3 Seem to Matter When You Buy a PC," *The Wall Street Journal*, December 18, 1998, p. A1; "Hey, #!@*% Amigo, Can You Translate the Word 'Gaffe'?" *The Wall Street Journal*, July 8, 1996, p. B2; "Lost in Translation: How to 'Empower Women' in Chinese," *The Wall Street Journal*, September 13, 1994, p. A1; "In World Cup Games, Words Get Lost and Gained in Translation," *The Wall Street Journal*, July 14, 1994, p. B1; "Too Many Computer Names Confuse Too Many Buyers," *The Wall Street Journal*, June 29, 1994, p. B1; "Go Ask Alice," *Adweek*, January 17, 1994, p. 32.

6. For more on video publicity releases, see "The Corruption of TV Health News," *BusinessWeek*, February 28, 2000, p. 66; "Collagen Corp.'s Video Uses News Format," *The Wall Street Journal*," March 29, 1994, p. B8; "'News' Videos That Pitch Drugs Provoke Outcry for Regulations," *The Wall Street Journal*, February 8, 1990, p. B6; Thomas H. Bivins, "Public Relations, Professionalism, and the Public Interest," *Journal of Business Ethics*, February 1993, p. 117; Siva K. Balasubramanian, "Beyond Advertising and Publicity: Hybrid Messages and Public Policy Issues," *Journal of Advertising*, December 1994, p. 47. For more on celebrity endorsements, see "Marketers Drool over a Jordan Return," *USA Today*, April 11, 2001, p. 1B; "The Jordan Effect," *Fortune*, June 22, 1998, p. 124; "Yao Ming's Super Deals," *USA Today*, January 23, 2003, p. 3B; "Full-Court Press for LeBron," *The Wall Street Journal*, May 21, 2003, p. B1; "Biking Champ Armstrong to Get $12M to Peddle Subaru," *USA Today*, February 3, 2003, p. 3B; "Brand It like Beckham," *Time*, June 30, 2003, p. 49; "Woods' Latest Trophy: $100 Million Nike Deal," *USA Today*, September 15, 2000, p. 1A; "Phat News: Rappers Choose Reebok Shoes," *The Wall Street Journal*, November 14, 2003, p. B1; "The CEO of Hip Hop," *BusinessWeek*, October 27, 2003, p. 90; "In the NBA, Shoe Money Is No Longer a Slam-Dunk," *The Wall Street Journal*, May 14, 1998, p. B1. See also Therese A. Louie and Carl Obermiller, "Consumer Response to a Firm's Endorser (Dis)association Decisions," *Journal of Advertising*, Winter 2002, p. 41; Marla Royne Stafford, Thomas F. Stafford, and Ellen Day, "A Contingency Approach: the Effects of Spokesperson Type and Service Type on Service Advertising Perceptions," *Journal of Advertising*, Summer 2002, p. 17; Dwane Hal Dean and Abhijit Biswas, "Third-Party Organization Endorsement of Products: an Advertising Cue Affecting Consumer Prepurchase Evaluation of Goods and Services," *Journal of Advertising*, Winter 2001, p. 41; Ronald E. Goldsmith, Barbara A. Lafferty and Stephen J. Newell, "The Impact of Corporate Credibility and Celebrity Credibility on Consumer Reaction to Advertisements and Brands," *Journal of Advertising*, Fall 2000, p. 43; Ron Coulter, "High Visibility: The Making and Marketing of Professionals into Celebrities," *Journal* of the *Academy of Marketing Science*, Winter 2001, p. 105; Jagdish Agrawal and Wagner A. Kamakura, "The Economic Worth of Celebrity Endorsers: An Event Study Analysis," *Journal of Marketing*, July 1995, p. 56; David J. Moore, John C. Mowen, and Richard Reardon, "Multiple Sources in Advertising Appeals: When Product Endorsers Are Paid by the Advertising Sponsor," *Journal of the Academy of Marketing Science*, Summer 1994, p. 234.

7. Jeani Read, "Don't Hate or Abuse Your Body," *Calgary Herald*, May 15, 2006; Rebecca Harris, "Keeping It Real," *Marketing Magazine*, November 8, 2004.

8. "Direct Marketing Special Report," *BtoB*, October 13, 2003, p. 24; "DMA Benchmarks Response Rates," *BtoB*, July 14, 2003, p. 13; "Direct Marketing Gets Cannes Do Spirit," *USA Today*, June 17, 2002, p. 4B; "Escalade Got Game," *Advertising Age*, June 11, 2001, p. 42; "All Juiced Up," *American Demographics*, January 2001, p. 42. For an electronic direct mail example, see "Web Slice," *Brandweek*, May 26, 1997, p. 22. See also Sally J. McMillan and Jang-Sun Hwang, "Measures of Perceived Interactivity: an Exploration of the Role of Direction of Communication, User Control, and Time in Shaping Perceptions of Interactivity," *Journal of Advertising*, Fall 2002, p. 29; Carrie M. Heilman, Frederick Kaefer, and Samuel D. Ramenofsky, "Determining the Appropriate Amount of Data for Classifying Consumers for Direct Marketing Purposes," *Journal of Interactive Marketing*, Summer 2003, p. 5; Mark J. Arnold and Shelley R. Tapp, "The Effects of Direct Marketing Techniques on Performance: an Application to Arts Organizations," *Journal of Interactive Marketing*, Summer 2001, p. 41; Patrick Barwise and Colin Strong, "Permission-Based Mobile Advertising," *Journal of Interactive Marketing*, Winter 2002, p. 14; Tito Tezinde, Brett Smith, and Jamie Murphy, "Getting Permission: Exploring Factors Affecting Permission Marketing," *Journal of Interactive Marketing*, Autumn 2002, p. 28; Charles R. Taylor, George R. Franke, and Michael L. Maynard, "Attitudes Toward Direct Marketing and its Regulation: a Comparison of the United States and Japan," *Journal of Public Policy & Marketing*, Fall 2000, p. 228; Jennifer Rowley and Frances Slack, "Kiosks in Retailing: the Quiet Revolution," *International Journal of Retail & Distribution Management*, (6) 2003, p. 329; David W. Stewart and Paul A. Pavlou, "From Consumer Response to Active Consumer: Measuring the Effectiveness of Interactive Media," *Journal of the Academy of Marketing Science*, Fall 2002, p. 376; Yuping Liu and L. J. Shrum, "What Is Interactivity and Is it Always Such a Good Thing? Implications of Definition, Person, and Situation for the Influence of Interactivity on Advertising Effectiveness," *Journal of Advertising*, Winter 2002, p. 53; Fusun F. Gonul, Byung-Do Kim, and Mengze Shi, "Mailing Smarter to Catalog Customers," *Journal of Interactive Marketing*, Spring 2000, p. 2; Judy F. Davis, "Maintaining Customer Relationships Through Effective Database Marketing: A Perspective for Small Retailers," *Journal of Marketing Theory & Practice*, Spring 1997, p. 31; Craig A. Conrad, "Response! The Complete Guide to Direct Marketing," *Journal of the Academy of Marketing Science*, Winter 1998, p. 70; Kapil Bawa, "Influences on Consumer Response to Direct Mail Coupons: An Integrative Review," *Psychology & Marketing*, March 1996, p. 129; William J. Carner, "Direct Marketing Through Broadcast Media: TV, Radio, Cable, Infomercials, Home Shopping, and More," *Journal of the Academy of Marketing Science*, Winter 1997, p. 86.

9. For more on regulation of spam, junk mail, and telemarketing calls, see "The Taming of the Internet," *BusinessWeek*, December 15, 2003, p. 78; "Telemarketing after Do Not Call," *Inc.*, November 2003, p. 32; "Silence of the Spams," *Brandweek*, October 20, 2003, p. 14; "Closing Lid on Spam May Cause Problems," *Investor's Business Daily*, October 13, 2003, p. A1; "The Bad News: Telemarketers Will Still Call," *The Wall Street Journal*, October 9, 2003, p. D1; "America Hangs Up on Telemarketers," *Fortune*, October 13, 2003, p. 58; "FTC Told to Enforce Do-Not-Call List," *USA Today*, October 8, 2003, p. 1B; "A Stab at Stemming Spam," *BusinessWeek*, October 6, 2003, p. 115; "Most Big Companies Stop Calling," *USA Today*, October 2, 2003, p. 3B, "It's FCC to the Rescue of Do-Not-Call List," *USA Today*, September 30, 2003, p. 1B; "The

Do-Not-Call Law Won't Stop the Calls," *BusinessWeek*, September 29, 2003, p. 89; "When E-Mail Ads Aren't Spam," *BusinessWeek*, October 16, 2000, p. 112; "Special Report: Direct and Database Marketing," *Advertising Age*, October 16, 2000, p. S1; "E-Mail Direct," *Brandweek*, April 10, 2000, p. 108; "You've Got Snail Mail!" *American Demographics*, March 2000, p. 54; George R. Milne and Mary Ellen Gordon, "Direct Mail Privacy-Efficiency Trade-Offs Within an Implied Social Contract Framework," *Journal of Public Policy & Marketing*, Fall 1993, p. 206.

10. Monica Perry and Charles D. Bodkin, "Fortune 500 Manufacturer Websites: Innovative Marketing Strategies or Cyberbrochures?" *Industrial Marketing Management*, February 2002, p. 133; Nicole Coviello, Roger Milley and Barbara Marcolin, "Understanding IT-Enabled Interactivity in Contemporary Marketing," *Journal of Interactive Marketing*, Autumn 2001, p. 18; Donna L. Hoffman and Thomas P. Novak, "Marketing in Hypermedia Computer-Mediated Environments: Conceptual Foundations," *Journal of Marketing*, July 1996, p. 50; Pierre Berthon, Leyland Pitt, and Richard T. Watson, "Marketing Communication and the World Wide Web," *Business Horizons*, September–October 1996, p. 24.

11. For more on direct-to-consumer drug advertising, see "Introducing the All-Purpose Pill," *Brandweek*, July 28, 2003, p. 24; "Net Grows as DTC Platform," *Advertising Age*, May 12, 2003, p. 60; "DTC Ads Influence Majority of Consumers, Say Doctors," *Advertising Age*, January 20, 2003, p. 6; "Patient Channel to Blast Ads at Bedridden," *The Wall Street Journal*, September 26, 2002, p. B1; "Drug Markers Find New Way to Push Pills," *The Wall Street Journal*, June 14, 2002, p. B1; "Special Report: DTC Marketing," *Advertising Age*, May 27, 2002, p. S1; "Wearing Off: Schering-Plough Faces a Future with Coffers Unfortified by Claritin," *The Wall Street Journal*, March 22, 2002, p. A1; "Reining In Drug Advertising," *The Wall Street Journal*, March 13, 2002, p. B1; "Drug Makers Offer Coupons for Free Prescriptions," *The Wall Street Journal*, March 13, 2002, p. B1; "Spotlight Falls on Drug Ads," *USA Today*, December 11, 2001, p. 9D; "While Critics May Fret, Public Likes DTC Ads," *Advertising Age*, March 26, 2001, p. 24; "The Fine Print," *The Wall Street Journal*, October 19, 1998, p. R6. See also Steven W. Kopp and Mary J. Sheffet, "The Effect of Direct-to-Consumer Advertising of Prescription Drugs on Retail Gross Margins: Empirical Evidence and Public Policy Implications," *Journal of Public Policy & Marketing*, Fall 1997, p. 270; Mary C. Gilly and Mary Wolfinbarger, "Advertising's Internal Audience," *Journal of Marketing*, January 1998, p. 69; S. A. Erdem and L. J. Harrison-Walker, "Managing Channel Relationships: Toward an Identification of Effective Promotional Strategies in Vertical Marketing Systems," *Journal of Marketing Theory & Practice*, Spring 1997, p. 80.

12. "Decker Scores with Sweepstakes to Promote Days Inn," *USA Today*, November 6, 1997, p. B10; "Biore: The Nose Knew at Lilith Fair," *Brandweek*, September 15, 1997, p. 28; "Brand Builders: Progresso Warriors," *Brandweek*, June 23, 1997, p. 20; "Advertisers Often Cheer the Loudest," *USA Today*, March 27, 1997, p. 1A; "Crossing the Border," *Brandweek*, December 16, 1996, p. 17; "Brand Builders: Pie in the Sky," *Brandweek*, December 16, 1996, p. 23; "Tractor Dealers Get Down in the Dirt Promoting Machines," *The Wall Street Journal*, July 16, 1996, p. A1; "Pepsi Cancels an Ad Campaign as Customers Clamor for Stuff," *The Wall Street Journal*, June 27, 1996, p. B1.

13. "Compensation and Expenses," *Sales & Marketing Management*, June 28, 1993, p. 65; "The Cost of Selling Is Going Up," *Boardroom Reports*, December 15, 1991, p. 15; "An In-House Sales School," *Inc.*, May 1991, p. 85.

14. Kusum L. Ailawadi, Paul W. Farris and Mark E. Parry, "Share and Growth Are Not Good Predictors of the Advertising and Promotion/Sales Ratio," *Journal of Marketing*, January 1994, p. 86.

15. Kissan Joseph and Vernon J. Richardson, "Free Cash Flow, Agency Costs, and the Affordability Method of Advertising Budgeting," *Journal*

of Marketing, January 2002, p. 94; John A. Weber, "Managing the Marketing Budget in a Cost-Constrained Environment," *Industrial Marketing Management*, November 2002, p. 705; Deborah Utter, "Marketing on a Budget," *Journal of the Academy of Marketing Science*, Summer 2000, p. 441; Kim P. Corfman and Donald R. Lehmann, "The Prisoner's Dilemma and the Role of Information in Setting Advertising Budgets," *Journal of Advertising*, June 1994, p. 35; C.L. Hung and Douglas West, "Advertising Budgeting Methods in Canada, the UK and the USA," *International Journal of Advertising* 10, no. 3 (1991), p. 239; Pierre Filiatrault and Jean-Charles Chebat, "How Service Firms Set Their Marketing Budgets," *Industrial Marketing Management*, February 1990, p. 63; James E. Lynch and Graham J. Hooley, "Industrial Advertising Budget Approaches in the U.K.," *Industrial Marketing Management* 18, no. 4 (1989), p. 265; "Beat the Budgeting Blues," *Business Marketing*, July 1989, p. 48; Douglas J. Dalrymple and Hans B. Thorelli, "Sales Force Budgeting," *Business Horizons*, July/August 1984, p. 31; Peter J. Danaher and Roland T. Rust, "Determining the Optimal Level of Media Spending," *Journal of Advertising Research*, January/February 1994, p. 28.

CHAPTER 14

1. Thomas J. Ryan, "All Star Salute," *Apparel* Web site, Dec. 1, 2005 at <http://www.apparelmag.com/index.shtml>; Candice Weber, "On the Road With Harry Rosen," *Marketing*, April 30, 2001.

2. "The Seoul Answer to Selling," *Going Global* (supplement to *Inc.*), March 1994; "AIG Sells Insurance in Shanghai, Testing Service Firms' Role," *The Wall Street Journal*, July 21, 1993, p. A1; "Hungarians Seeking to Find a New Way Find Instead Amway," *The Wall Street Journal*, January 15, 1993, p. A1; "The Secret to Northern's Japanese Success: When in Tokyo . . . ," *BusinessWeek*, July 27, 1992, p. 57; "U.S. Companies in China Find Patience, Persistence and Salesmanship Pay Off," *The Wall Street Journal*, April 3, 1992, p. B1; Paul A. Herbig and Hugh E. Kramer, "Do's and Don'ts of Cross-Cultural Negotiations," *Industrial Marketing Management*, November 1992, p. 287; Alan J. Dubinsky et al., "Differences in Motivational Perceptions among U.S., Japanese, and Korean Sales Personnel," *Journal of Business Research*, June 1994, p. 175; Carl R. Ruthstrom and Ken Matejka, "The Meanings of 'YES' in the Far East," *Industrial Marketing Management*, August 1990, p. 191.

3. "Shhh!" *Forbes*, November 24, 2003, p. 84; "Deliver More Value to Earn Loyalty," *Selling*, May 2003; "Hush: Improving NVH through Improved Material," *Automotive Design and Production*, July 2003, p. 42.

4. Julie T. Johnson, Hiram C. Barksdale, Jr., and James S. Boles, "The Strategic Role of the Salesperson in Reducing Customer Defection in Business Relationships," *The Journal of Personal Selling & Sales Management*, Spring 2001, p. 123; Artur Baldauf, David W. Cravens, and Nigel F. Piercy, "Examining Business Strategy, Sales Management, and Salesperson Antecedents of Sales Organization Effectiveness," *The Journal of Personal Selling & Sales Management*, Spring 2001, p. 109; Michael Beverland, "Contextual Influences, and the Adoption and Practice of Relationship Selling in a Business-to-Business Setting: an Exploratory Study," *The Journal of Personal Selling & Sales Management*, Summer 2001, p. 207; Sandy D. Jap, "The Strategic Role of the Salesforce in Developing Customer Satisfaction Across the Relationship Lifecycle," *The Journal of Personal Selling & Sales Management*, Spring 2001, p. 95; John E. Swan, Cathy Goodwin, Michael A. Mayo and Lynne D. Richardson, "Customer Identities: Customers as Commercial Friends, Customer Coworkers or Business Acquaintances," *The Journal of Personal Selling & Sales Management*, Winter 2001, p. 29; Neeli Bendapudi and Robert P. Leone, "Managing Business-to-Business Customer Relationships Following Key Contact Employee Turnover in a Vendor Firm," *Journal of Marketing*, April 2002, p. 83; Michael J. Dorsch, Les Carlson, Mary Anne Raymond and Robert Ranson, "Customer Equity Management and Strategic Choices for Sales Managers," *The Journal of Personal Selling & Sales Management*, Spring 2001, p. 157; Thomas W. Leigh, Ellen Bolman

Pullins and Lucette B. Comer, "The Top Ten Sales Articles of the 20th Century," *The Journal of Personal Selling & Sales Management*, Summer 2001, p. 217; Thomas Tellefsen and Nermin Eyuboglu, "The Impact of a Salesperson's In-House Conflicts and Influence Attempts on Buyer Commitment," *The Journal of Personal Selling & Sales Management*, November 2002, p. 157; Charles H. Schwepker, Jr. "Customer-Oriented Selling: a Review, Extension, and Directions for Future Research," *The Journal of Personal Selling & Sales Management*, Spring 2003, p. 151; Thomas R. Wotruba, "The Transformation of Industrial Selling: Causes and Consequences," *Industrial Marketing Management*, September 1996, p. 327; William M. Strahle, Rosann L. Spiro, and Frank Acito, "Marketing and Sales: Strategic Alignment and Functional Implementation," *Journal of Personal Selling & Sales Management*, Winter 1996, p. 1; Paul Boughton, "Winning Customers, Building Accounts: Some Do It Better Than Others," *Journal of the Academy of Marketing Science*, Spring 1996, p. 175; Jerome A. Colletti and Lawrence B. Chonko, "Change Management Initiatives: Moving Sales Organizations From Obsolescence to High Performance," *Journal of Personal Selling & Sales Management*, Spring 1997, p. 1; Douglas M. Lambert, Howard Marmorstein, and Arun Sharma, "Industrial Salespeople as a Source of Market Information," *Industrial Marketing Management*, May 1990, p. 141.

5. "Specialized Training Can Improve Sales Force Focus," *Investor's Business Daily*, January 16, 2003, p. A7; "Joe Galli's Army," *Fortune*, December 30, 2002, p. 134; Mark A. Moon and Susan F. Gupta, "Examining the Formation of Selling Centers: A Conceptual Framework," *Journal of Personal Selling & Sales Management*, Spring 1997, p. 31; S. Joe Puri and Pradeep Korgaonkar, "Couple the Buying and Selling Teams," *Industrial Marketing Management* 20, no. 4 (1991), p. 311; "P&G Rolls Out Retailer Sales Teams," *Advertising Age*, May 21, 1990, p. 18.

6. Sanjit Sengupta, Robert E. Krapfel and Michael A. Pusateri, "An Empirical Investigation of Key Account Salesperson Effectiveness," *The Journal of Personal Selling & Sales Management*, Fall 2000, p. 253; Christian Homburg, John P. Workman, Jr. and Ove Jensen, "A Configurational Perspective on Key Account Management," *Journal of Marketing*, April 2002, p. 38; Andrea L. Dixon, Jule B. Gassenheimer and Terri Feldman Barr, "Bridging the Distance Between Us: How Initial Responses to Sales Team Conflict Help Shape Core Selling Team Outcomes," *The Journal of Personal Selling & Sales Management*, Fall 2002, p. 247; Jim Blythe, "Using Trade Fairs in Key Account Management," *Industrial Marketing Management*, October 2002, p. 627; Michael G. Harvey, Milorad M. Novicevic, Thomas Hench and Matthew Myers, "Global Account Management: a Supply-Side Managerial View," *Industrial Marketing Management*, October 2003, p. 563; Roberta J. Schultz and Kenneth R. Evans, "Strategic Collaborative Communication by Key Account Representatives," *The Journal of Personal Selling & Sales Management*, Winter 2002, p. 23; Dan C. Weilbaker and William A. Weeks, "The Evolution of National Account Management: A Literature Perspective," *Journal of Personal Selling & Sales Management*, Fall 1997, p. 49; C. J. Lambe and Robert E. Spekman, "National Account Management: Large Account Selling or Buyer-Supplier Alliance?" *Journal of Personal Selling & Sales Management*, Fall 1997, p. 61; Catherine Pardo, "Key Account Management in the Business to Business Field: The Key Account's Point of View," *Journal of Personal Selling & Sales Management*, Fall 1997, p. 17; Sanjit Sengupta, Robert E. Krapfel, and Michael A. Pusateri, "Switching Costs in Key Account Relationships," *Journal of Personal Selling & Sales Management*, Fall 1997, p. 9; Paul Dishman and Philip S. Nitse, "National Accounts Revisited: New Lessons From Recent Investigations," *Industrial Marketing Management*, January 1998, p. 1.

7. For more on telemarketing and attempts to regulate it, see Chapter 13, endnote 9. See also "Telephone Sales Reps Do Unrewarding Jobs that Few Can Abide," *The Wall Street Journal*, September 9, 1993, p. A1; Brett A. Boyle, "The Importance of the Industrial Inside Sales Force: A Case Study," *Industrial Marketing Management*, September 1996, p. 339; "How to Unite Field and Phone Sales," *Inc.*, July 1992, p. 115.

8. "The Task at Hand," *Beverage World*, December 15, 2003, p. 46; "Sales Force Effectiveness through E-Learning," *Pharmaceutical Executive*, October 2003, p. 106; "The Biggest Mouth in Silicon Valley," *Business 2.0*, September 2003, p. 107; "Software that Actually Useful," *Sales & Marketing Management*, August 2003, p. 25; Scott M. Widmier, Donald W. Jackson, Jr., and Deborah Brown McCabe, "Infusing Technology into Personal Selling," *The Journal of Personal Selling & Sales Management*, November 2002, p. 189; "Salespeople Say Automation Software Still Lacking," *Investor's Business Daily*, January 18, 2001, p. A4; "MarketSoft Tailors Products to Solve Problems," *The Wall Street Journal*, November 30, 2000, p. B8; "New Software's Payoff? Happier Salespeople," *Investor's Business Daily*, May 23, 2000, p. A8; "Making the Sale," *The Wall Street Journal*, November 15, 1999, p. R16; "Offices Goin' Mobile," *USA Today*, May 17, 1999, p. 3D; "Bob Schmonsees Has a Tool for Better Sales and It Ignores Excuses," *The Wall Street Journal*, March 26, 1999, p. B1; "New Software Is Helping Reps Fill Custom Orders without Glitches," *The Wall Street Journal*, August 11, 1992, p. B6; "Salespeople on Road Use Laptops to Keep in Touch," *The Wall Street Journal*, April 25, 1991, p. B1.

9. Amy J. Morgan and Scott A. Inks, "Technology and the Sales Force: Increasing Acceptance of Sales Force Automation," *Industrial Marketing Management*, July 2001, p. 463; Mary E. Shoemaker, "A Framework for Examining IT-Enabled Market Relationships," *The Journal of Personal Selling & Sales Management*, Spring 2001, p. 177; Robert C. Erffmeyer and Dale A. Johnson, "An Exploratory Study of Sales Force Automation Practices: Expectations and Realities," *The Journal of Personal Selling & Sales Management*, Spring 2001, p. 167; Cheri Speier and Viswanath Venkatesh, "The Hidden Minefields in the Adoption of Sales Force Automation Technologies," *Journal of Marketing*, July 2002, p. 98; Eli Jones, Suresh Sundaram and Wynne Chin, "Factors Leading to Sales Force Automation Use: a Longitudinal Analysis," *The Journal of Personal Selling & Sales Management*, November 2002, p. 145; Mary Jo Bitner, "Technology Infusion in Service Encounters," *Journal of the Academy of Marketing Science*, Winter 2000, p. 138; Michael J. Swenson and Adilson Parrella, "Sales Technology Applications: Cellular Telephones and the National Sales Force," *Journal of Personal Selling & Sales Management*, Fall 1992, p. 67; Paul Dishman and Kregg Aytes, "Exploring Group Support Systems in Sales Management Applications," *Journal of Personal Selling & Sales Management*, Winter 1996, p. 65.

10. "HP Adapting to a New," *CRN*, March 29, 2004, p. 18; "Fiorina Whips H-P into Fighting Shape," *USA Today*, June 5, 2001, p. 3D; "H-P Profit Drops 66% But Tops Forecast," *The Wall Street Journal*, May 17, 2000, p. A3; "H-P Woes Are Deeper Than the Downturn," *BusinessWeek*, May 7, 2001, p. 48; "The Radical: Carly Fiorina's Bold Management Experiment at HP," *BusinessWeek*, February 19, 2001, p. 68; "The Boss," *BusinessWeek*, August 2, 1999, p. 76.

11. "Selling Salesmanship," *Business 2.0*, December 2002, p. 66; "The Art of the Sale," *The Wall Street Journal*, January 11, 2001, p. B1.

12. Available from World Wide Web: <http://www.achievement. com/sales>; Brian P. Matthews and Tom Redman, "Recruiting the Wrong Salespeople: Are the Job Ads to Blame?," *Industrial Marketing Management*, October 2001, p. 541; R. Edward Bashaw, Thomas N. Ingram and Bruce D. Keillor, "Improving Sales Training Cycle Times for New Trainees: an Exploratory Study," *Industrial Marketing Management*, July 2002, p. 329; Ellen Bolman Pullins and Leslie M. Fine, "How the Performance of Mentoring Activities Affects the Mentor's Job Outcomes," *The Journal of Personal Selling & Sales Management*, Fall 2002, p. 259; Greg W. Marshall, Thomas H. Stone, and I. M. Jawahar, "Selection Decision Making by Sales Managers and Human Resource Managers: Decision Impact, Decision Frame and Time of Valuation," *The Journal of Personal Selling & Sales Management*, Winter 2001, p. 19; Phillip H. Wilson, David Strutton and, M. Theodore Farris II, "Investigating the Perceptual Aspect of Sales Training," *The Journal of Personal Selling & Sales Management*, Spring 2002, p. 77; Hiram C. Barksdale, Jr. Danny N. Bellenger, James S. Boles, and Thomas G. Brashear, "The Impact of Realistic Job

Previews and Perceptions of Training on Sales Force Performance and Continuance Commitment: a Longitudinal Test," *The Journal of Personal Selling & Sales Management*, Spring 2003, p. 125; Ashraf M. Attia, Earl D. Honeycutt, Jr., and Magdy Mohamed Attia, "The Difficulties of Evaluating Sales Training," *Industrial Marketing Management*, April 2002, p. 253; Earl D. Honeycutt, Jr. Kiran Karande, Ashraf Attia, and Steven D. Maurer, "An Utility Based Framework for Evaluating the Financial Impact of Sales Force Training Programs," *The Journal of Personal Selling & Sales Management*, Summer 2001, p. 229; Ellen B. Pullins, Leslie M. Fine, and Wendy L. Warren, "Identifying Peer Mentors in the Sales Force: An Exploratory Investigation of Willingness and Ability," *Journal of the Academy of Marketing Science*, Spring 1996, p. 125; Alan J. Dubinsky, "Some Assumptions About the Effectiveness of Sales Training," *Journal of Personal Selling & Sales Management*, Summer 1996, p. 67; Patrick L. Schul and Brent M. Wren, "The Emerging Role of Women in Industrial Selling: A Decade of Change," *Journal of Marketing*, July 1992, p. 38; William A. Weeks and Carl G. Stevens, "National Account Management Sales Training and Directions for Improvement: A Focus on Skills/Abilities," *Industrial Marketing Management*, September 1997, p. 423; Earl D. Honeycutt, Jr., John B. Ford, and John F. Tanner, Jr., "Who Trains Salespeople? The Role of Sales Trainers and Sales Managers," *Industrial Marketing Management*, February 1994, p. 65.

13. Ken Grant, David W. Cravens, George S. Low, and William C. Moncrief, "The Role of Satisfaction with Territory Design on the Motivation, Attitudes, and Work Outcomes of Salespeople," *Journal of the Academy of Marketing Science*, Spring 2001, p. 165; Balaji C. Krishnan, Richard G. Netemeyer and James S. Boles, "Self-Efficacy, Competitiveness, and Efforts as Antecedents of Salesperson Performance," *The Journal of Personal Selling & Sales Management*, Fall 2002, p. 285; Guangping Wang and Richard G. Netemeyer, "The Effects of Job Autonomy, Customer Demandingness, and Trait Competitiveness on Salesperson Learning, Self-Efficacy, and Performance," *Journal of the Academy of Marketing Science*, Summer 2002, p. 217; Joseph O. Rentz, C. David Shepherd, Armen Tashchian, Pratibha A. Dabholkar and Robert T. Ladd, "A Measure of Selling Skill: Scale Development and Validation," *The Journal of Personal Selling & Sales Management*, Winter 2002, p. 13; Erin Anderson and Thomas S. Robertson, "Inducing Multiline Salespeople to Adopt House Brands," *Journal of Marketing*, April 1995, p. 16; Stephen B. Knouse and David Strutton, "Molding a Total Quality Salesforce Through Managing Empowerment, Evaluation, and Reward and Recognition Processes," *Journal of Marketing Theory & Practice*, Summer 1996, p. 24; Ajay K. Kohli and Bernard J. Jaworski, "The Influence of Coworker Feedback on Salespeople," *Journal of Marketing*, October 1994, p. 82; William L. Cron, Alan J. Dubinsky, and Ronald E. Michaels, "The Influence of Career Stages on Components of Salesperson Motivation," *Journal of Marketing*, January 1988, p. 78.

14. "The Sales Commission Dilemma," *Inc.*, May 2003, p. 49; "Creating Incentives Down in Ranks: Marriott Ties Pay to Guest Replies," *Investor's Business Daily*, July 6, 2001, p. A1; "Get Great Results from Salespeople by Finding What Really Moves Them," *Investor's Business Daily*, July 2, 2001, p. A1; "Medical Gear Sales Force Works on Commission," *Investor's Business Daily*, July 25, 2000, p. A14; R. Venkatesh, Goutam Challagalla and Ajay K. Kohli, "Heterogeneity in Sales Districts: Beyond Individual-Level Predictors of Satisfaction and Performance," *Journal of the Academy of Marketing Science*, Summer 2001, p. 238; Ellen Bolman Pullins, "An Exploratory Investigation of the Relationship of Sales Force Compensation and Intrinsic Motivation," *Industrial Marketing Management*, July 2001, p. 403; Sridhar N. Ramaswami and Jagdip Singh, "Antecedents and Consequences of Merit Pay Fairness for Industrial Salespeople," *Journal of Marketing*, October 2003, p. 46; Goutam Ghallagalla, "Supervisory Orientations and Salesperson Work Outcomes: the Moderating Effect of Salesperson Location," *The Journal of Personal Selling & Sales Management*, Summer 2000, p. 161; Kissan Joseph and Manohar U. Kalwani, "The Role of Bonus Pay in Salesforce Compensation Plans," *Industrial Marketing Management*, March 1998,

p. 147; Rene Y. Darmon, "Selecting Appropriate Sales Quota Plan Structures and Quota-Setting Procedures," *Journal of Personal Selling & Sales Management,* Winter 1997, p. 1; Thomas E. Tice, "Managing Compensation Caps in Key Accounts," *Journal of Personal Selling & Sales Management,* Fall 1997, p. 41; Arun Sharma, "Customer Satisfaction-Based Incentive Systems: Some Managerial and Salesperson Considerations," *Journal of Personal Selling & Sales Management,* Spring 1997, p. 61.

15. "New Software's Payoff? Happier Salespeople," *Investor's Business Daily,* May 23, 2000, p. A8.

16. Thomas G. Brashear, James S. Boles, Danny N. Bellenger, and Charles M. Brooks, "An Empirical Test of Trust-Building Processes and Outcomes in Sales Manager-Salesperson Relationships," *Journal of the Academy of Marketing Science,* Spring 2003, p. 189; Kwaku Atuahene-Gima and Haiyang Li, "When Does Trust Matter? Antecedents and Contingent Effects of Supervisee Trust on Performance in Selling New Products in China and the United States," *Journal of Marketing,* July 2002, p. 61; Andrea L. Dixon, Rosann L. Spiro and Lukas P. Forbes, "Attributions and Behavioral Intentions of Inexperienced Salespersons to Failure: an Empirical Investigation," *Journal of the Academy of Marketing Science,* Fall 2003, p. 459; Mark C. Johlke, Dale F. Duhan, Roy D. Howell and Robert W. Wilkes, "An Integrated Model of Sales Managers' Communication Practices," *Journal of the Academy of Marketing Science,* Spring 2000, p. 263; Dominique Rouzies and Anne Macquin, "An Exploratory Investigation of the Impact of Culture on Sales Force Management Control Systems in Europe," *The Journal of Personal Selling & Sales Management,* Winter 2002–2003, p. 61; Scott B. MacKenzie, Philip M. Podsakoff, and Gregory A. Rich, "Transformational and Transactional Leadership and Salesperson Performance," *Journal of the Academy of Marketing Science,* Spring 2001, p. 115; Cengiz Yilmaz and Shelby D. Hunt, "Salesperson Cooperation: the Influence of Relational, Task, Organizational, and Personal Factors," *Journal of the Academy of Marketing Science,* Fall 2001, p. 335; Richard L. Oliver and Erin Anderson, "An Empirical Test of the Consequences of Behavior- and Outcome-Based Sales Control Systems," *Journal of Marketing,* October 1994, p. 53; Susan K. DelVecchio, "The Salesperson's Operating Freedom: A Matter of Perception," *Industrial Marketing Management,* January 1998, p. 31; Vlasis Stathakopoulos, "Sales Force Control: A Synthesis of Three Theories," *Journal of Personal Selling & Sales Management,* Spring 1996, p. 1; Gregory A. Rich, "The Constructs of Sales Coaching: Supervisory Feedback, Role Modeling and Trust," *Journal of Personal Selling & Sales Management,* Winter 1998, p. 53; Steven P. Brown and Robert A. Peterson, "The Effect of Effort on Sales Performance and Job Satisfaction," *Journal of Marketing,* April 1994, p. 70; Frederick A. Russ, Kevin M. McNeilly, and James M. Comer, "Leadership, Decision Making and Performance of Sales Managers: A Multi-Level Approach," *Journal of Personal Selling & Sales Management,* Summer 1996, p. 1; Jhinuk Chowdhury, "The Motivational Impact of Sales Quotas on Effort," *Journal of Marketing Research,* February 1993, p. 28; Douglas N. Behrman and William D. Perreault, Jr., "A Role Stress Model of the Performance and Satisfaction of Industrial Salespersons," *Journal of Marketing,* Fall 1984, p. 9.

17. "Chief Executives Are Increasingly Chief Salesmen," *The Wall Street Journal,* August 6, 1991, p. B1; Joe F. Alexander, Patrick L. Schul, and Emin Babakus, "Analyzing Interpersonal Communications in Industrial Marketing Negotiations," *Journal of the Academy of Marketing Science,* Spring 1991, p. 129.

18. Kirk Smith, Eli Jones, and Edward Blair, "Managing Salesperson Motivation in a Territory Realignment," *The Journal of Personal Selling & Sales Management,* Fall 2000, p. 215; Andris A. Zoltners, "Sales Territory Alignment: An Overlooked Productivity Tool," *The Journal of Personal Selling & Sales Management,* Summer 2000, p. 139; Ken Grant, "The Role of Satisfaction with Territory Design on the Motivation, Attitudes, and Work Outcomes of Salespeople," *Journal of the Academy of Marketing Science,* Spring 2001, p. 165; J. David Lichtenthal, Saameer Sikri, and

Karl Folk, "Teleprospecting: An Approach for Qualifying Accounts," *Industrial Marketing Management,* February 1989, p. 11.

19. "How to Get Your Company Where You Want It," *The American Salesman,* December 2003, p. 12; "When Should I Give Up on a Sales Prospect?" *Inc.,* May 1998, p. 129; "Downloading Their Dream Cars," *BusinessWeek,* March 9, 1998, p. 93; "The New Wave of Sales Automation," *Business Marketing,* June 1991, p. 12. See also Sean Dwyer, John Hill and Warren Martin, "An Empirical Investigation of Critical Success Factors in the Personal Selling Process for Homogenous Goods," *The Journal of Personal Selling & Sales Management,* Summer 2000, p. 151; L. Brent Manssen, "Using PCs to Automate and Innovate Marketing Activities," *Industrial Marketing Management,* August 1990, p. 209; Doris C. Van Doren and Thomas A. Stickney, "How to Develop a Database for Sales Leads," *Industrial Marketing Management,* August 1990, p. 201.

20. "Novartis' Marketing Doctor," *BusinessWeek,* March 5, 2001, p. 56.

21. For more on sales presentation approaches, see "Trapped in the Sales Presentation from Hell," *Information Week,* November 10, 2003, p. 122; "Advise and Conquer," *Brandweek,* May 14, 2001, p. 1; "Rick Francolini, TV Guide," *Brandweek,* October 25, 1999, p. 22; "The 60-Second Sales Pitch," *Inc.,* October 1994, p. 87. See also Daniel M. Eveleth and Linda Morris, "Adaptive Selling in a Call Center Environment: a Qualitative Investigation," *Journal of Interactive Marketing,* Winter 2002, p. 25; Thomas W. Leigh and John O. Summers, "An Initial Evaluation of Industrial Buyers' Impressions of Salespersons' Nonverbal Cues," *The Journal of Personal Selling & Sales Management,* Winter 2002, p. 41; Kalyani Menon and Laurette Dube, "Ensuring Greater Satisfaction by Engineering Salesperson Response to Customer Emotions," *Journal of Retailing,* Fall 2000, p. 285; Susan K. DelVecchio, James E. Zemanek, Roger P. McIntyre and Reid P. Claxton, "Buyers' Perceptions of Salesperson Tactical Approaches," *The Journal of Personal Selling & Sales Management,* Winter 2002–2003, p. 39; Alfred M. Pelham, "An Exploratory Model and Initial Test of the Influence of Firm Level Consulting-Oriented Sales Force Programs on Sales Force Performance," *The Journal of Personal Selling & Sales Management,* Spring 2002, p. 97; Annie H. Liu and Mark P. Leach, "Developing Loyal Customers with a Value-Adding Sales Force: Examining Customer Satisfaction and the Perceived Credibility of Consultative Salespeople," *The Journal of Personal Selling & Sales Management,* Spring 2001, p. 147; Richard S. Jacobs, Kenneth R. Evans, Robert E. Kleine III and Timothy D. Landry, "Disclosure and its Reciprocity as Predictors of Key Outcomes of an Initial Sales Encounter," *The Journal of Personal Selling & Sales Management,* Winter 2001, p. 51; Gary L. Frankwick, Stephen S. Porter, and Lawrence A. Crosby, "Dynamics of Relationship Selling: a Longitudinal Examination of Changes in Salesperson-Customer Relationship Status," *The Journal of Personal Selling & Sales Management,* Spring 2001, p. 135; Willemijn van Dolen, Jos Lemmink, Ko de Ruyter and Ad de Jong, "Customer-Sales Employee Encounters: a Dyadic Perspective," *Journal of Retailing,* Winter 2002, p. 265; Willem Verbeke and Richard P. Bagozzi, "Sales Call Anxiety: Exploring What it Means When Fear Rules a Sales Encounter," *Journal of Marketing,* July 2000, p. 88; Michael D. Hartline, James G. Maxham III and Daryl O. McKee, "Corridors of Influence in the Dissemination of Customer-Oriented Strategy to Customer Contact Service Employees," *Journal of Marketing,* April 2000, p. 35; David M. Szymanski, "Modality and Offering Effects in Sales Presentations for a Good Versus a Service," *Journal of the Academy of Marketing Science,* Spring 2001, p. 179; Cathy Waters, "Customer Centered Selling: Eight Steps to Success from the World's Best Sales Force," *Journal of the Academy of Marketing Science,* Fall 2000, p. 546; Jon M. Hawes, James T. Strong, and Bernard S. Winick, "Do Closing Techniques Diminish Prospect Trust?" *Industrial Marketing Management,* September 1996, p. 349; Morgan P. Miles, Danny R. Arnold, and Henry W. Nash, "Adaptive Communication: The Adaption of the Seller's Interpersonal Style to the Stage of the Dyad's Relationship and the Buyer's Communication Style," *Journal of Personal Selling & Sales Management,* Winter 1990, p. 21; Harish Sujan, Barton A. Weitz, & Nirmalya Kumar,

"Learning Orientation, Working Smart, and Effective Selling," *Journal of Marketing*, July 1994, p. 39.

22. Howard Levitt, "Make sure employees can meet set standard," *National Post*, July 20, 2005.

23. For more on pharmaceutical company selling tactics, see "Side Effects: As Drug-Sales Teams Multiply, Doctors Start to Tune Them Out," *The Wall Street Journal*, June 13, 2003, p. A1; "New Prescription: Its Rivals in Funk, Novartis Finds a Way to Thrive," *The Wall Street Journal*, August 23, 2002, p. A1; "Swallow This: How Drug Makers Use Pharmacies to Push Pricey Pills," *The Wall Street Journal*, May 1, 2002, p. A1; "Sorry, Doc, No Dinners-to-Go," *The Wall Street Journal*, April 23, 2002, p. D4; "More than Ads, Drug Makers Rely on Sales Reps," *The Wall Street Journal*, March 14, 2002, p. B1; "Pushing Pills: Drug Firms' Incentives to Pharmacists in India Fuel Mounting Abuse," *The Wall Street Journal*, August 16, 2001, p. A1; "Doctors Step Out; Drug Salesmen Step In," *USA Today*, July 5, 2001, p. 11A; "Sales Pitch: Drug Firms Use Perks to Push Pills," *USA Today*, May 16, 2001, p. 1B. For more on Oracle's selling tactics, see "Learning to Be a Great Host," *Business 2.0*, May 2003, p. 70; "Oracle Puts Priority on Customer Service," *The Wall Street Journal*, January 21, 2003, p. B5; "Out of Control," *Business 2.0*, August 2002, p. 38. See also Terry W. Loe and William A. Weeks, "An Experimental Investigation of Efforts to Improve Sales Students' Moral Reasoning," *The Journal of Personal Selling & Sales Management*, Fall 2000, p. 243; Lawrence B. Chonko, Thomas R. Wotruba, and Terry W. Loe, "Direct Selling Ethics at the Top: an Industry Audit and Status Report," *The Journal of Personal Selling & Sales Management*, Spring 2002, p. 87; Eugene Sivadas, Susan Bardi Kleiser, James Kellaris, and Robert Dahlstrom, "Moral Philosophy, Ethical Evaluations, and Sales Manager Hiring Intentions," *The Journal of Personal Selling & Sales Management*, Winter 2002–2003, p. 7; John Cherry and John Fraedrich, "Perceived Risk, Moral Philosophy and Marketing Ethics: Mediating Influences on Sales Managers' Ethical Decision-Making," *Journal of Business Research*, December 2002, p. 951; Bulent Menguc, "Organizational Consequences, Marketing Ethics and Salesforce Supervision: Further Empirical Evidence," *Journal of Business Ethics*, March 1998, p. 333; David Strutton, J. B. I. Hamilton, and James R. Lumpkin, "An Essay on When to Fully Disclose in Sales Relationships: Applying Two Practical Guidelines for Addressing Truth-Telling Problems," *Journal of Business Ethics*, April 1997, p. 545; Lawrence B. Chonko, John F. Tanner, and William A. Weeks, "Ethics in Salesperson Decision Making: A Synthesis of Research Approaches and an Extension of the Scenario Method," *Journal of Personal Selling & Sales Management*, Winter 1996, p. 35.

CHAPTER 15

1. "Subway to Sell Kids Pak Meal that Focuses on Health," *USA Today*, September 26, 2003, p. 1B; "Subway on Track to Bow a Pair of Healthy Efforts," *Brandweek*, September 22, 2003, p. 5; "Subway Orders Weightier Campaign," *The Wall Street Journal*, August 21, 2003, p. B6; "Creative: Ordinary People," *Adweek*, August 11, 2003, p. 24; "Fast-Food Firms' Big Budgets Don't Buy Consumer Loyalty," *The Wall Street Journal*, July 24, 2003, p. B4; "Why Subway Chose Fallon," *Advertising Age*, July 21, 2003, p. 4; "Fallon Takes Home Subway after All-Star Shootout," *Adweek*, July 21, 2003, p. 7; "Subway Seeing Double in Trio of New Spots," *Adweek*, July 7, 2003, p. 9; "Subway Seeks Better Creative," *Adweek*, May 19, 2003, p. 7; "Marketers of the Year: Subway, in Search of Fresh Ideas," *Brandweek*, October 15, 2001, pp. M54–M63.

2. "Special Report: U.S. Multinationals," *Ad Age International*, January 1998, p. 17; "Colgate-Palmolive Is Really Cleaning Up in Poland," *BusinessWeek*, March 15, 1993, p. 54. See also Carolyn A. Lin, "Cultural Values Reflected in Chinese and American Television Advertising," *Journal of Advertising*, Winter 2001, p. 83; Christophe Collard, Michael Pustay, Christophe Roquilly and Asghar Zardkoohi, "Competitive Cross-Couponing: a Comparison of French and U.S. Perspectives," *Journal of*

Public Policy & Marketing, Spring 2001, p. 64; Charles R. Taylor, Gordon E. Miracle, and R. D. Wilson, "The Impact of Information Level on the Effectiveness of U.S. and Korean Television Commercials," *Journal of Advertising*, Spring 1997, p. 1; Ann M. Barry, "Advertising and Culture: Theoretical Perspectives," *Journal of the Academy of Marketing Science*, Winter 1998, p. 67; Siew M. Leong, Sween H. Ang, and Leng L. Tham, "Increasing Brand Name Recall in Print Advertising Among Asian Consumers," *Journal of Advertising*, Summer 1996, p. 65; Ronald E. Taylor, Mariea G. Hoy, and Eric Haley, "How French Advertising Professionals Develop Creative Strategy," *Journal of Advertising*, Spring 1996, p. 1; Nan Zhou and Mervin Y. T. Chen, "A Content Analysis of Men and Women in Canadian Consumer Magazine Advertising: Today's Portrayal, Yesterday's Image?" *Journal of Business Ethics*, April 1997, p. 485; Johny K. Johansson, "The Sense of 'Nonsense': Japanese TV Advertising," *Journal of Advertising*, March 1994, p. 17; Yong Zhang and Betsy D. Gelb, "Matching Advertising Appeals to Culture: The Influence of Products' Use Conditions," *Journal of Advertising*, Fall 1996, p. 29; John L. Graham, Michael A. Kamins and Djoko S. Oetomo, "Content Analysis of German and Japanese Advertising in Print Media from Indonesia, Spain, and the United States," *Journal of Advertising*, June 1993, p. 5; Bob D. Cutler, and Rajshekhar G. Javalgi, "A Cross-Cultural Analysis of the Visual Components of Print Advertising: The United States and the European Community," *Journal of Advertising Research*, January/February 1992, p.71.

3. Available from World Wide Web: <http://www.adage.com>; "Ad Spending Soothsayers Optimistic on Year Ahead," *Advertising Age*, December 15, 2003, p. 8; "Forecaster Trims View, Sees Upturn," *The Wall Street Journal*, June 18, 2003, p. B9; "The Top 5 Rules of the Ad Game," *BusinessWeek*, January 20, 2003, p. 72; "Analysts See a Rise in Ad Spending as Firms Look to Spread the Word," *Investor's Business Daily*, January 3, 2003, p. A6; "Advertisers Compete to Become Pride of Lions," *USA Today*, June 18, 2002, p. 1B.

4. Available from World Wide Web: <http://www.adage.com>; "AdAge Feature: Global Marketing," *Advertising Age*, November 10, 2003, p. 26; "Ad Spenders Loosen Purse Strings," *The Wall Street Journal*, October 15, 2003, p. B3; "AdAge Feature: Megabrands," *Advertising Age*, October 13, 2003, p. 23; "Special Report: Top Advertisers," *BtoB*, September 15, 2003, p. 19; "2003 Fact Pack," *Advertising Age (supplement)*, September 2003; "Ad Spending in U.S. Climbs 6.8%," *The Wall Street Journal*, August 29, 2003, p. B6; AdAge Special Report: Megabrands," *Advertising Age*, July 21, 2003, p. S1; "AdAge Special Report: 100 Leading National Advertisers," *Advertising Age*, June 23, 2003, p. S1; "2001 Advertising-to-Sales Ratios for the 200 Largest Ad Spending Industries," *Advertising Age*, June 2001.

5. Available from European Advertising & Media Forecast Databook, p. 23. Published by World Advertsing Research Centre, Oxfordshire, U.K., 2006.

6 For more on Dryel, see "The Dirt on At-Home Dry Cleaning," *The Wall Street Journal*, September 15, 2000, p. W14. See also "Industry Wrestles with Comparative Ads," *Advertising Age*, October 27, 2003, p. 10; "Sour Dough: Pizza Hut v. Papa John's," *Brandweek*, May 21, 2001, p. 26; "Irate Firms Take Comparisons to Court," *The Wall Street Journal*, December 22, 1999, p. B8; "Survey: Comparative Ads Can Dent Car's Credibility," *Advertising Age*, May 4, 1998, p. 26. For more on AT&T, MCI, and Sprint's comparative ads, see "Best Phone Discounts Go to Hardest Bargainers," *The Wall Street Journal*, February 13, 1997, p. B1; "Fighting for Customers Gets Louder," *USA Today*, January 9, 1995, p. 1B. For other examples of comparative advertising, see "Allergy Drugs Wage a Bitter War of the Noses," *The Wall Street Journal*, May 23, 1996, p. B1; "New Drug Ads Give Doctors Heartburn," *The Wall Street Journal*, April 25, 1996, p. B9. See also Kenneth C. Manning, Paul W. Miniard, Michael J. Barone, and Randall L. Rose, "Understanding the Mental Representations Created by Comparative Advertising," *Journal of Advertising*, Summer 2001, p. 27; Paschalina Ziamou and S. Ratneshwar, "Innovations in Product Functionality: When and Why Are Explicit

Comparisons Effective?" *Journal of Marketing,* April 2003, p. 49; Patrick Meirick, "Cognitive Responses to Negative and Comparitive Political Advertising," *Journal of Advertising,* Spring 2002, p. 49; Bruce E. Pinkleton, Nam-Hyun Um and Erica Weintraub Austin, "An Exploration of the Effects of Negative Political Advertising on Political Decision Making," *Journal of Advertising,* Spring 2002, p. 13; Diana L. Haytko, "Great Advertising Campaigns: Goals and Accomplishments," *Journal of Marketing,* April 1995, p. 113; Carolyn Tripp, "Services Advertising: An Overview and Summary of Research, 1980–1995," *Journal of Advertising,* Winter 1997, p. 21; Dhruv Grewal, Sukumar Kavanoor, Edward F. Fern, Carolyn Costley, and James Barnes, "Comparative Versus Noncomparative Advertising: A Meta-Analysis," *Journal of Marketing,* October 1997, p. 1; Thomas E. Barry, "Comparative Advertising: What Have We Learned in Two Decades?" *Journal of Advertising Research,* March/April 1993, p. 19; Naveen Donthu, "Comparative Advertising Intensity," *Journal of Advertising Research,* November/December 1992, p. 53.

7. "G.E. to Spend $100 Million Promoting Itself as Innovative," *The New York Times,* January 16, 2003, p. C1.

8. "The Selling of Breast Cancer," *Business 2.0,* February 2003, p. 88; "Seeking Cause and Effect," *Brandweek,* November 11, 2002, p. 18; "Brands Step Up to Battle Breast Cancer," *USA Today,* September 5, 2001, p. 3B; "Spiffing up the Corporate Image," *Fortune,* July 21, 1986, p. 68. See also T. Bettina Cornwell, Donald P. Roy, and Edward A. Steinard II, "Exploring Managers' Perceptions of the Impact of Sponsorship on Brand Equity," *Journal of Advertising,* Summer 2001, p. 41; Michael J. Barone, Anthony D. Miyazaki, and Kimberly A. Taylor, "The Influence of Cause-Related Marketing on Consumer Choice: Does One Good Turn Deserve Another?" *Journal of the Academy of Marketing Science,* Spring 2000, p. 248; Minette E. Drumwright, "Company Advertising With a Social Dimension: The Role of Noneconomic Criteria," *Journal of Marketing,* October 1996, p. 71; Eric Haley, "Exploring the Construct of Organization As Source: Consumer's Understandings of Organizational Sponsorship of Advocacy Advertising," *Journal of Advertising,* Summer 1996, p. 19.

9. For more on Wendy's, see "The Year in 2003—Review," *Nation's Restaurant News,* December 22, 2003, p. 51. For more on Cadillac, see "Cadillac Steers Dealers toward Unified Messages," *Brandweek,* October 6, 2003, p. 77. For more on Benetton, see "Store Owners Rip into Benetton," *Advertising Age,* February 6, 1995, p. 1; "Benetton, German Retailers Squabble," *Advertising Age,* February 6, 1995, p. 46. For more on Intel, see "Intel Inside at 10," *Advertising Age,* April 30, 2001, p. 4; "Co-op Crossroads," *Advertising Age,* November 15, 1999, p. 1. For more on GM, see "Still Pulling the Strings, But Locally, Too," *Brandweek,* April 17, 2000, p. 34; "GM Dealers Rebel Against Local Ad Structure," *Advertising Age,* January 24, 2000, p. 3. See also Steffen Jorgensen, Simon Pierre Sigue, and Georges Zaccour, "Dynamic Cooperative Advertising in a Channel," *Journal of Retailing,* Spring 2000, p. 71.

10. For more on co-op ads, see "Appeals Court Rules against Pork Council," *Advertising Age,* October 27, 2003, p. 4; "Big Blue Offers Solutions with $60 Mil Co-op Effort," *Advertising Age,* April 30, 2001, p. 8; "Revlon Plans Another Makeover," *The Wall Street Journal,* November 21, 2000, p. B1; "Joint Marketing with Retailers Spreads," *The Wall Street Journal,* October 24, 1996, p. B6; "H&R Block, Excedrin Discover Joint Promotions Can Be Painless," *The Wall Street Journal,* February 28, 1991, p. B3; John P. Murry and Jan B. Heide, "Managing Promotion Program Participation Within Manufacturer-Retailer Relationships," *Journal of Marketing,* January 1998, p. 58.

11. *Standard Rate and Data,* 2003; "What Makes Them Buy?" *Brandweek,* November 3, 2003, p. 22; "Marketers Slap Network TV in Survey on ROI," *Advertising Age,* October 13, 2003, p. 1; "POP Sharpens Its Focus," *Brandweek,* June 16, 2003, p. 31; "Special Report: Media Outlook 2001," *Adweek,* September 25, 2000. For more on the Yellow Pages medium, see "Print Yellow Pages Are Still Profitable," *The Wall Street Journal,* May 22, 2000, p. B16; Gerald L. Lohse and Dennis L. Rosen, "Signaling Quality and Credibility in Yellow Pages Advertising: the Influence of Color and Graphics on Choice," *Journal of Advertising,* Summer 2001, p. 73; "The Truth About Yellow Pages: Making Them Work for You," *Journal of the Academy of Marketing Science,* Winter 1998, p. 71. For more on the outdoor medium, see "Adidas Introduces Human Billboards," *Advertising Age,* September 1, 2003, p. 11; "Adidas' Billboard Ads Give a Kick to Japanese Pedestrians," *The Wall Street Journal,* August 29, 2003, p. B1; "Special Section: Introduce Yourself to Outdoor Advertising," *Advertising Age,* June 9, 2003, pp. C1–C13; "Firms Pitch Stuff Outside," *USA Today,* July 19, 2001, p. 3B; "A Market on the Move," *Ad Age Global,* April 2001, p. 38; "New Technology, Improved Image Draw Companies to Billboard Ads," *The Wall Street Journal,* July 31, 2000, p. B10. See also Charles R. Taylor and John C. Taylor, "Regulatory Issues in Ourdoor Advertising: A Content Analysis of Billboards," *Journal of Public Policy & Marketing,* Spring 1994, p. 97. For more on the radio medium, see "Old Media Get a Web Windfall," *The Wall Street Journal,* September 17, 1999, p. B1. See also Darryl W. Miller and Lawrence J. Marks, "Mental Imagery and Sound Effects in Radio Commercials," *Journal of Advertising,* December 1992, p. 83. For more on the newspaper medium, see "Special Report: Newspapers," *Advertising Age,* April 29, 2002, pp. S1–S7; "How Newspaper Overcame Loss of Big Advertisers," *The Wall Street Journal,* January 25, 2002, p. A13; "Special Report: Newspaper Industry," *Advertising Age,* April 30, 2001, p. S1; "Special Report: Newspapers," *Adweek,* April 30, 2001, p. SR1. See also Lawrence C. Soley and Robert L. Craig, "Advertising Pressures on Newspapers: A Survey," *Journal of Advertising,* December 1992, p. 1; Srini S. Srinivasan, Robert P. Leone, and Francis J. Mulhern, "The Advertising Exposure Effect of Free Standing Inserts," *Journal of Advertising,* Spring 1995, p. 29; Karen W. King, Leonard N. Reid, and Margaret Morrison, "Large-Agency Media Specialists' Opinions on Newspaper Advertising for National Accounts," *Journal of Advertising,* Summer 1997, p. 1. For more on the magazine medium, see "Special Report: Magazines, the A-List," *Advertising Age,* October 20, 2003, pp. S1–S14; "Adweek Magazines Special Report," *Adweek,* October 13, 2003, pp. SR1–SR22; "Special Report: Magazines 300," *Advertising Age,* September 22, 2003, pp. S1–S8; "Special Section: Magazines 2003," *Advertising Age,* September 8, 2003, pp. M1–M62; "Adweek Magazines Special Report," *Adweek,* June 9, 2003, pp. SR1–SR28; "Special Report: Magazines 300," *Advertising Age,* September 23, 2002, pp. S1–S11; "To Sell Ad Pages, Magazines Offer Extra Services," *The Wall Street Journal,* July 9, 2001, p. B1. For more on the television and cable medium, see "Special Report: Cable TV," *Advertising Age,* June 9, 2003, pp. S1–S14; "Special Report: TV's Upfront," *Advertising Age,* May 14, 2001, p. S1; "Special Report: Cable TV," *Ad Age Global,* May 1, 2001, p. 25; "Special Report: Cable TV," *Advertising Age,* April 16, 2001, p. S1. See also James R. Coyle and Esther Thorson, "The Effects of Progressive Levels of Interactivity and Vividness in Web Marketing Sites," *Journal of Advertising,* Fall 2001, p. 65; Mandeep Singh, Siva K. Balasubramanian and Goutam Chakraborty, "A Comparative Analysis of Three Communication Formats: Advertising, Infomercial, and Direct Experience," *Journal of Advertising,* Winter 2000, p. 59; Jean L. Rogers, "Mail Advertising and Consumer Behavior," *Psychology & Marketing,* March 1996, p. 211; Elizabeth C. Hirschman and Craig J. Thompson, "Why Media Matter: Toward a Richer Understanding of Consumers' Relationships With Advertising and Mass Media," *Journal of Advertising,* Spring 1997, p. 43; Richard J. Fox and Gary L. Geissler, "Crisis in Advertising?" *Journal of Advertising,* December 1994, p. 79.

12. "Staid U.S. Marketers Try Racier Ads," *The Wall Street Journal,* July 31, 2003, p. B6; "A Leap for Advertising," *Adweek,* June 16, 2003, p. 28; "Sex-Themed Ads Often Don't Travel Well," *The Wall Street Journal,* March 31, 2000, p. B7; "U.S. Admakers Cover It Up; Others Don't Give a Fig Leaf," *USA Today,* June 27, 1997, p. 1B; "Mars Inc. Dips into Sex to Lure Consumers into Arms of M&M's," *The Wall Street Journal,* January 21, 1997, p. B9; "Underwear Ads Caught in Bind over Sex Appeal," *Advertising Age,* July 8, 1996, p. 27.

13. "Yech and Yada in 'Seinfeld' Ads," *Advertising Age*, May 18, 1998, p. 63; "'Seinfeld' Finale Advertisers Put on Game Faces," *USA Today*, April 29, 1998, p. 1B; "NBC May Get Only $1.5 Million for Ad Spots on 'Seinfeld' Finale," *The Wall Street Journal*, March 4, 1998, p. B6.

14. "Gardenburger's Ad May Help Its Rival," *The Wall Street Journal*, May 20, 1998, p. B8; "Gardenburger Bets the (Soybean) Farm on the Last 'Seinfeld,'" *The Wall Street Journal*, April 13, 1998, p. A1.

15. "Hey, Shoppers: Ads on Aisle 7!" *Fortune*, November 24, 2003, p. 50; "Asics Sneaks Are 'Kill Bill' Sleeper Hit," *Advertising Age*, November 10, 2003, p. 4; "Gone in 30 Seconds," *Business 2.0*, November 2003, p. 68; "Your Ad Should Be in Pictures," *Fortune*, October 27, 2003, p. 60; "Turn on '24' and You'll Also Catch a 6-Min. Film-ercial," *USA Today*, October 27, 2003, p. 1B; "Instant Messaging Programs Are No Longer Just for Messages," *USA Today*, October 20, 2003, p. 5D; "Why the Great American Brands Are Doing Lunch," *Business 2.0*, September 2003, p. 146; "Cue the Stapler!" *Time (Inside Business Bonus Section)*, September 2003; "Getting a Piece of the 'Eye,'" *Advertising Age*, August 4, 2003, p. 4; "The Wider World of Advertising," *Adweek*, June 23, 2003, p. 24; "Captive Marketing: There's No Escape," *Time (Time Bonus Section)*, June 2003; "Ads Invade Videogames!" *Fortune*, May 26, 2003, p. 46; "Consumers Give Movie Ads a Thumbs Up," *Adweek*, May 19, 2003, p. 10; "Your Ad Could Be Here!" *Business 2.0*, May 2003, p. 76; "Advertising: Altered Reality," *The New York Times*, March 12, 2003, p. C7; "Growing Pains for Placements," *Advertising Age*, February 3, 2003, p. S2; "Lights, Camera, Commercial," *American Demographics*, February 2003, p. 34; "Ad Intrusion Up, Say Consumers," *Advertising Age*, January 6, 2003, p. 1; "Clear Channel to Take the 'V' Train," *The Wall Street Journal*, December 23, 2002, p. B3; "Guerrilla Marketers of the Year: Brand's Best Friend," *Brandweek*, December 9, 2002, p. 28; "Cities Plan to Put Ads on Police Cars," *USA Today*, October 31, 2002, p. 1A; "The New Billboards: Buggies," *Advertising Age*, August 19, 2002, p. 11; "Pitch at the Pump: Talking Audio Ads Run at Gas Stations," *Advertising Age*, August 5, 2002, p. 16; "Bank of America Puts Ads in ATMs," *The Wall Street Journal*, July 25, 2002, p. B8; "Roxy Builds TV, Book Series around Its Own Surf Wear," *The Wall Street Journal*, February 19, 2002, p. B1; "Outdoor Interactive," *American Demographics*, August 2001, p. 32; "Advertisers Pepper Reality Shows with Product Placements," *USA Today*, July 23, 2001, p. 5B; "Firms Pitch New Place to Park Ads," *The Wall Street Journal*, July 11, 2001, p. B10; "Look Up, Down, All Around—Ads Fill Airports, Planes," *USA Today*, July 10, 2001, p. 12B; "It's an Ad, Ad, Ad, Ad World," *Time*, July 9, 2001, p. 17; "Ads Are Here, There, Everywhere," *USA Today*, June 19, 2001, p. 1B; "Ahh, the Sun, the Surf. . . and Tons of Ads," *USA Today*, May 24, 2001, p. 3B; "Ads Show Up in Unexpected Places," *USA Today*, March 23, 2001, p. 1B; "From Elevators to Gas Stations, Ads Multiplying," *Advertising Age*, November 13, 2000, p. 40; "Moving Targets," *American Demographics*, October 2000, p. 32; "From Cell Phones to Sell Phones," *BusinessWeek*, September 11, 2000, p. 88; "Advertisers Find One of the Last Clutter-Free Places," *The Wall Street Journal*, June 15, 2000, p. B1; "Virtual Ads Grab More Attention from Marketers," *Advertising Age*, May 29, 2000. See also Cristel Antonio Russell, "Investigating the Effectiveness of Product Placements in Television Shows: the Role of Modality and Plot Connection Congruence on Brand Memory and Attitude," *Journal of Consumer Research*, December 2002, p. 306.

16. For more on ATM ads, see "Ads on Automated Teller Machines Multiply as Technology Improves," *Investor's Business Daily*, October 5, 2000, p. A6; "ATMs Are Latest Place-Based Medium," *Advertising Age*, November 24, 1997, p. 1. For more on Nascar ads, see "Hotel Rides with Race Fans," *USA Today*, November 4, 2003, p. 3B; "Nextel Link Takes Nascar to New Level," *Advertising Age*, October 27, 2003, p. S7; "The Changing Face of Nascar," *USA Today (Bonus Section E)*, August 29, 2003; "Space for Rent," *Brandweek*, June 2, 2003, p. 30; "Nascar's Image May Be In for a Wild Ride," *USA Today*, November 15, 2002, p. 1A.

17. "Friends' Tops TV Price Chart," *Advertising Age*, September 15, 2003, p. 1; "P&G Snaps Up Super Bowl Ad at $2.4 Million," *Advertising Age*, June 30, 2003, p. 1; "Low CPM Can Spell Bargain for Buyers," *Advertising Age*, May 19, 2003, p. 10; "Ad Buyers Back Off Reality Programs," *USA Today*, May 12, 2003, p. 1B; "Ad Meter," *USA Today*, January 27, 2003, p. 5B; "Name Brands: Super Bowl Ads Cost Plenty, but the Message Lasts Forever," *The New York Times*, January 24, 2003, p. 6; "A Super Sunday for Football and for Madison Avenue," *The New York Times*, January 24, 2003, p. C1.

18. "Long-Derided Banner Web Ads Could Be Worthwhile after All," *Investor's Business Daily*, November 11, 2003, p. A6; "Online Ad Sales Continue Upswing," *The Wall Street Journal*, November 11, 2003, p. B8; "FTC Clamps Down on Stealth Pop-Ups Today," *USA Today*, November 6, 2003, p. 1B; "Pop-Up Ads Explode in Popularity," *The Wall Street Journal*, October 28, 2003, p. B7; "Pop-Ups Assail through Windows," *USA Today*, September 25, 2003, p. 3B; "Stalk Market: New Battleground in Web Privacy War, Ads that Snoop," *The Wall Street Journal*, August 27, 2003, p. A1; "Web Ads on the Rebound," *The Wall Street Journal*, August 25, 2003, p. B1; "Contextual Ads Gather Steam," *Advertising Age*, August 11, 2003, p. 34; "Net Marketing: Top 5 Rich-Media Mistakes Advertisers Should Avoid," *BtoB*, July 14, 2003, p. 14; "Beyond the Banner," *Adweek*, May 12, 2003, p. 30; "Advertising: As an Alternative to Pop-Up Ads, Marketers Are Trying to Create Useful Web Sites to Draw Viewers," *The New York Times*, February 11, 2003, p. C8; "Behind the Wheel Driving the Web," *Advertising Age*, July 23, 2001, p. 10; "Web Ads Getting in Your Way? Try Blocking Software," *Investor's Business Daily*, July 12, 2001, p. A6; "Do e-Ads Have a Future?" *BusinessWeek E.Biz*, January 22, 2001, pp. EB46–EB50; "Beyond the Banner Ad," *BusinessWeek E.Biz*, December 11, 2000, p. EB16; "As Ads Fail to Heat Up, Sites Turning to Paid Subscribers," *Investor's Business Daily*, December 11, 2000, p. A8; "Clicks for Free," *American Demographics*, February 1999, p. 54; "Ads Click for Net Retailers," *USA Today*, January 28, 1999, p. 3B; "Web Sites Say: Your Ad Sells or It's on Us," *The Wall Street Journal*, June 27, 1997, p. B9. See also Kim Bartel Sheehan, "Re-Weaving the Web: Integrating Print and Online Communications," *Journal of Interactive Marketing*, Spring 2001, p. 47; Lee Sherman, "Banner Advertising: Measuring Effectiveness and Optimizing Placement," *Journal of Interactive Marketing*, Spring 2001, p. 60; Satya Menon and Dilip Soman, "Managing the Power of Curiosity for Effective Web Advertising Strategies," *Journal of Advertising*, Fall 2002, p. 1; Steven M. Edwards, Hairong Li, and Joo-Hyun Lee, "Forced Exposure and Psychological Reactance: Antecedents and Consequences of the Perceived Intrusiveness of Pop-Up Ads," *Journal of Advertising*, Fall 2002, p. 83; Xavier Dreze and Francois-Xavier Hussherr, "Internet Advertising: Is Anybody Watching?" *Journal of Interactive Marketing*, Autumn 2003, p. 8; Erik L. Olson and Robert E. Widing II, "Are Interactive Decision Aids Better than Passive Decision Aids? A Comparison with Implications for Information Providers on the Internet," *Journal of Interactive Marketing*, Spring 2002, p. 22; Richard T. Watson, Sigmund Akselsen, and Leyland F. Pitt, "Attractors: Building Mountains in the Flat Landscape of the World Wide Web," *California Management Review*, Winter 1998, p. 36; W. W. Kassaye, "Global Advertising and the World Wide Web," *Business Horizons*, May–June 1997, p. 33.

19. For some creative and controversial ads, see "Special Report: Marketers of the Year," *Brandweek*, October 20, 2003; "How to Sell a Strange Idea," *Adweek*, July 14, 2003, p. 22; "Downloading the Future of TV Advertising," *Business 2.0*, July 2003, p. 46; "Cheers and Jeers," *Adweek*, June 30, 2003, p. 20; "Ikea's 'Lamp' Wins Cannes," *Advertising Age*, June 23, 2003, p. 1; "A Leap for Advertising," *Adweek*, June 16, 2003, p. 28; "The Lowest Moments in Advertising," *Adweek*, June 9, 2003, p. 38; "Special Report: Best Awards," *Advertising Age*, May 26, 2003, pp. S1–S6; "Man behind Nike Ads Wants Innovation Rewarded," *USA Today*, June 17, 2003, p. 7B; "Special Report: Marketers of the Year," *Brandweek*, October 14, 2002; "You-Are-There Advertising," *The Wall Street Journal*,

August 5, 2002, p. B1; "Special Report: Marketers of the Year," *Brandweek*, October 15, 2001; "Dip Ad Stirs Church Ire," *Advertising Age*, July 2, 2001, p. 8; "Duck Ads Have New Customers," *USA Today*, September 18, 2000, p. 13B; "Cough Syrup Touts 'Awful' Taste in U.S.," *The Wall Street Journal*, December 15, 1999, p. B10. See also Barbara J. Phillips and Edward F. McQuarrie, "The Development, Change, and Transformation of Rhetorical Style in Magazine Advertisements 1954–1999," *Journal of Advertising*, Winter 2002, p. 1; Susan E. Morgan and Tom Reichert, "The Message Is in the Metaphor: Assessing the Comprehension of Metaphors in Advertisements," *Journal of Advertising*, Winter 1999, p. 1; Parthasarathy Krishnamurthy and Anuradha Sivaraman, "Counterfactual Thinking and Advertising Responses," *Journal of Consumer Research*, March 2002, p. 650; Kineta Hung, "Framing Meaning Perceptions with Music: the Case of Teaser Ads," *Journal of Advertising*, Fall 2001, p. 39; Jennifer Edson Escalas and Barbara B. Stern, "Sympathy and Empathy: Emotional Responsed to Advertising Dramas," *Journal of Consumer Research*, March 2003, p. 566; Amanda B. Bower, "Highly Attractive Models in Advertising and the Women Who Loathe Them: the Implications of Negative Affect for Spokesperson Effectiveness," *Journal of Advertising*, Fall 2001, p. 51; Tom Reichert, Susan E. Heckler and Sally Jackson, "The Effects of Sexual Social Marketing Appeals on Cognitive Processing and Persuasion," *Journal of Advertising*, Spring 2001, p. 13; Barbara J. Phillips, "The Impact of Verbal Anchoring on Consumer Response to Image Ads," *Journal of Advertising*, Spring 2000, p. 15; Anne M. Brumbaugh, "Source and Nonsource Cues in Advertising and Their Effects on the Activation of Cultural and Subcultural Knowledge on the Route to Persuasion," *Journal of Consumer Research*, September 2002, p. 258; David Luna and Laura A. Peracchio, "Moderators of Language Effects in Advertising to Bilinguals: a Psycholinguistic Approach," *Journal of Consumer Research*, September 2001, p. 284; Erik L. Olson, "How Magazine Articles Portrayed Advertising From 1900 to 1940," *Journal of Advertising*, Fall 1995, p. 41; Audhesh K. Paswan, "Marketing to the Mind: Right Brain Strategies for Advertising and Marketing," *Journal of the Academy of Marketing Science*, Winter 1998, p. 68; Avery M. Abernethy and George R. Franke, "The Information Content of Advertising: A Meta-Analysis," *Journal of Advertising*, Summer 1996, p. 1; James H. Leigh, "The Use of Figures of Speech in Print Ad Headlines," *Journal of Advertising*, June 1994, p. 17; Bruce A. Huhmann and Timothy P. Brotherton, "A Content Analysis of Guilt Appeals in Popular Magazine Advertisements," *Journal of Advertising*, Summer 1997, p. 35; Margaret F. Callcott and Wei-Na Lee, "A Content Analysis of Animation and Animated Spokes-Characters in Television Commercials," *Journal of Advertising*, December 1994, p. 1; Alan J. Bush and Victoria D. Bush, "The Narrative Paradigm As a Perspective for Improving Ethical Evaluations of Advertisements," *Journal of Advertising*, September 1994, p. 31; L. W. Turley and Scott W. Kelley, "A Comparison of Advertising Content: Business to Business Versus Consumer Services," *Journal of Advertising*, Winter 1997, p. 39; Eleonora Curlo and Robert Chamblee, "Ad Processing and Persuasion: The Role of Brand Identification," *Psychology & Marketing*, May 1998, p. 279; Noel M. Murray and Sandra B. Murray, "Music and Lyrics in Commercials: A Cross-Cultural Comparison Between Commercials Run in the Dominican Republic and in the United States," *Journal of Advertising*, Summer 1996, p. 51; Barbara B. Stern, "Advertising Intimacy: Relationship Marketing and the Services Consumer," *Journal of Advertising*, Winter 1997, p. 7; Baba Shiv, Julie A. Edell, and John W. Payne, "Factors Affecting the Impact of Negatively and Positively Framed Ad Messages," *Journal of Consumer Research*, December 1997, p. 285; Harlan E. Spotts, Marc G. Weinberger, and Amy L. Parsons, "Assessing the Use and Impact of Humor on Advertising Effectiveness: A Contingency Approach," *Journal of Advertising*, Fall 1997, p. 17; Martha Rogers and Kirk H. Smith, "Public Perceptions of Subliminal Advertising: Why Practitioners Shouldn't Ignore This Issue," *Journal of Advertising Research*, March/April 1993, p. 10; Kathryn T. Theus, "Subliminal Advertising and the Psychology of Processing Unconscious Stimuli: A Review of Research," *Psychology & Marketing*, May/June 1994, p. 271; Carolyn A. Lin, "Cultural Differences in Message Strategies: A Comparison between American and Japanese TV Commercials," *Journal of Advertising Research*, July/August 1993, p. 40.

20. "One Size Doesn't Fit All," *The Wall Street Journal*, October 1, 2003, p. B1; "Exxon Centralizes New Global Campaign," *The Wall Street Journal*, July 11, 2001, p. B6; "McCann Finds Global a Tough Sell in Japan," *The Wall Street Journal*, June 19, 1997, p. B2. See also Fahad S. Al-Olayan, "A Content Analysis of Magazine Advertisements from the United States and the Arab World," *Journal of Advertising*, Fall 2000, p. 69; Bongjin Cho, Up Kwon, James W. Gentry, Sunkyu Jun and Fredric Kropp, "Cultural Values Reflected in Theme and Execution: a Comparative Study of U.S. and Korean Television Commercials," *Journal of Advertising*, Winter 1999, p. 59; Michael G. Harvey, "A Model to Determine Standardization of the Advertising Process in International Markets," *Journal of Advertising Research*, July/August 1993, p. 57; Barbara Mueller, "Standardization vs. Specialization: An Examination of Westernization in Japanese Advertising," *Journal of Advertising Research*, January/February 1992, p. 15; Dana L. Alden, Wayne D. Hoyer, and Chol Lee, "Identifying Global and Culture-Specific Dimensions of Humor in Advertising: A Multinational Analysis," *Journal of Marketing*, April 1993, p. 64; "International Special Report: Global Media," *Advertising Age International*, July 18, 1994, p. I11; Ali Kanso, "International Advertising Strategies: Global Commitment to Local Vision," *Journal of Advertising Research*, January/February 1992, p. 10; Theodore Levitt, "The Globalization of Markets," *Harvard Business Review*, May–June 1983, p. 92; Kamran Kashani, "Beware the Pitfalls of Global Marketing," *Harvard Business Review*, September/October 1989, p. 91; William L. Shanklin and David A. Griffith, "Crafting Strategies for Global Marketing in the New Millennium," *Business Horizons*, September–October 1996, p. 11.

21. "China's Edgy Advertising," *The Wall Street Journal*, October 27, 2003, p. B1; "How Tiny German Shop Landed McDonald's," *The Wall Street Journal*, August 6, 2003, p. B1; "Still in the Hunt," *BusinessWeek*, July 7, 2003, p. 42; "WPP's Sorrell Bests Publicis in Cordiant Bid," *The Wall Street Journal*, June 18, 2003, p. B1; "Are Holding Companies Obsolete?" *Adweek*, June 9, 2003, p. 30; "Special Report: Integrated Agencies," *Advertising Age*, May 19, 2003, pp. S1–S5; "Agency Report: Top 100 National Agencies," *Adweek*, April 7, 2003; "The Rise of the Superagency," *Advertising Age*, January 28, 2002, p. 1; "Will Ad Agencies Survive Slowdown?" *Investor's Business Daily*, May 8, 2001, p. A1; "A Chill Hits Madison Avenue," *The Wall Street Journal*, March 19, 2001, p. B1; "Culture Shock," *Advertising Age*, January 8, 2001, p. 1. See also Gerard Prendergast, Yizheng Shi and Douglas West, "Organizational Buying and Advertising Agency-Client Relationships in China," *Journal of Advertising*, Summer 2001, p. 61; George C. Hozier, Jr. and John D. Schatzberg, "Advertising Agency Terminations and Reviews: Stock Returns and Firm Performance," *Journal of Business Research*, November 2000, p. 169; Douglas West and John Ford, "Advertising Agency Philosphies and Employee Risking Taking," *Journal of Advertising*, Spring 2001, p. 77; Mark Davies and Mel Prince, "Examining the Longevity of New Agency Accounts: a Comparative Study of U.S. and U.K. Advertising Experiences," *Journal of Advertising*, Winter 1999, p. 75; Louise Ripley, "Why Industrial Advertising is Often Done in House," *Industrial Marketing Management*, November 1992, p. 331; Murray Young and Charles Steilen, "Strategy-Based Advertising Agency Selection: An Alternative to 'Spec' Presentations," *Business Horizons*, November–December 1996, p. 77; Douglas C. West, "Purchasing Professional Services: The Case of Advertising Agencies," *International Journal of Purchasing & Materials Management*, Summer 1997, p. 2; Douglas W. LaBahn and Chiranjeev Kohli, "Maintaining Client Commitment in Advertising Agency-Client Relationships," *Industrial Marketing Management*, November 1997, p. 497.

22. "Agencies Face New Accountability," *The Wall Street Journal*, October 2, 2003, p. B4; "Interpublic May Become More Open," *The Wall Street Journal*, September 10, 2003, p. B4; "Kraft Rethinks Agency Pay, Brand Duties," *Adweek*, August 18, 2003, p. 6; "GM Overhauls Compensation," *Advertising Age*, March 17, 2003, p. 1; "Up Close and Personal,"

Adweek, March 17, 2003, p. 26; "Adweek Adspend Survey: What Clients Think," *Adweek*, December 16, 2002, p. 21; "Nestle Move on Fees Will Rattle Agencies," *The Wall Street Journal*, October 8, 2001, p. A21; "Feeling the Squeeze," *Advertising Age*, June 4, 2001, p.1; "Unilever Reviews the Way It Pays for Ads," *The Wall Street Journal*, April 27, 2001, p. B6; "Performance Pays," *Advertising Age*, February 28, 2000, pp. S14–S16; "Dot-Compensation: Ad Agencies Feel Net Effect," *Advertising Age*, February 7, 2000, p. 1; "P&G Expands Its Program to Tie Agency Pay to Brand Performance," *The Wall Street Journal*, September 16, 1999, p. B12. See also R. Susan Ellis and Lester W. Johnson, "Agency Theory as a Framework for Advertising Agency Compensation Decisions," *Journal of Advertising Research*, September/October 1993, p. 76; Thorolf Helgesen, "Advertising Awards and Advertising Agency Performance Criteria," *Journal of Advertising Research*, July/August 1994, p. 43.

23. "GM to Publicis: Loyalty Matters," *Advertising Age*, May 26, 2003, p. 16; "Foote Cone Loses Two Accounts from Coke in Wake of Pepsi Suit," *The Wall Street Journal*, November 12, 2001, p. B3; "The Rise of the Superagency," *Advertising Age*, January 28, 2002, p. 1; "Commercial Break: An Ad Mega-Agency Faces Harsh Realities of a Shaken Industry," *The Wall Street Journal*, October 31, 2001, p. A1; "Can An Agency Be Guilty of Malpractice?" *Advertising Age*, January 31, 2000, p. 24.

24. For Got Milk? campaign, see "Got Milk? A Decade of Lessons Pours In," *Brandweek*, June 2, 2003, p. 24; "Dairy's Queen," *Adweek*, April 14, 2003, p. 32; "Borrowed Time," *Adweek*, November 18, 2002, p. 24; "Got Milk? An Campaign to Take On a Tough Target: Hispanic Teens," *The Wall Street Journal*, December 28, 2001, p. A9. For Taco Bell campaign, see "Dog-Gone Days: FCB Creates Ads for Taco Bell Acc't," *Advertising Age*, July 24, 2000, p. 4; "Taco Bell Drops the Chihuahua in Management Shuffle," *USA Today*, July 19, 2000, p. 1B; "Taco Bell Ads to Focus on Food, Not Dog," *The Wall Street Journal*, October 11, 1999, p. B10. For U.S. government's anti-drug campaign, see "Drug Czar Says Ad Campaign Has Flopped," *The Wall Street Journal*, May 14, 2002, p. B1. See also "How Terrific Ads Propelled Colgate, Dethroned Longtime Leader P&G," *Investor's Business Daily*, April 20, 2001, p. A1. See also "Budweiser Spot Sheds Tradition of Family-Friendly Advertising," *The Wall Street Journal*, September 11, 2003, p. B7; "At Last a Way to Measure Ads," *The Wall Street Journal Reports*, June 16, 2003, p. R4; "The Top 5 Rules of the Ad Game," *BusinessWeek*, January 20, 2003, p. 72; "Buyers Seek Hard-to-Find Tostitos Gold," *USA Today*, January 10, 2003, p. 5B; "Consumers May Notice the Ads, but Will They Buy the Product?" *Investor's Business Daily*, December 19, 2002, p. A4; "Marketer of the Year: Dove's Key Softening Agents," *Brandweek*, October 15, 2001, p. M32; "Cautious Used Car Buyers Trust Carfax," *USA Today*, August 20, 2001, p. 7B; "Does Creativity Count?" *Brandweek*, December 11, 2000, p. 32; "The Metrics System," *Brandweek*, November 13, 2000, p. 106. See also Subodh Bhat, Michael Bevans, and Sanjit Sengupta, "Measuring Users' Web Activity to Evaluate and Enhance Advertising Effectiveness," *Journal of Advertising*, Fall 2002, p. 97; Ann Marie Barry, "How Advertising Works: the Role of Research," *Journal of the Academy of Marketing Science*, Winter 2001, p. 103; Els Gijsbrechts, Katia Campo, and Tom Goossens, "The Impact of Store Flyers on Store Traffic and Store Sales: a Geo-Marketing Approach," *Journal of Retailing*, (1) 2003, p. 1; Fuyuan Shen, "Banner Advertisement Pricing, Measurement, and Pretesting Practices: Perspectives from Interactive Agencies," *Journal of Advertising*, Fall 2002, p. 59; DeAnna S. Kempf and Russell N. Laczniak, "Advertising's Influence on Subsequent Product Trial Processing," *Journal of Advertising*, Fall 2001, p. 27; Gerald J. Tellis and Doyle L. Weiss, "Does TV Advertising Really Affect Sales? The Role of Measures, Models, and Data Aggregation," *Journal of Advertising*, Fall 1995, p. 1; John H. Holmes, "When Ads Work," *Journal of the Academy of Marketing Science*, Winter 1997, p. 88; Karen Whitehill King, John D. Pehrson, and Leonard N. Reid, "Pretesting TV Commercials: Methods, Measures, and Changing Agency Roles," *Journal of Advertising*, September 1993, p. 85; Erik du Plessis, "Recognition versus Recall," *Journal of Advertising Research*, May/June 1994, p. 75.

25. "McDonald's Arches Outlawed in Beijing," *USA Today*, March 5, 2002, p. 7B; "In Asia, It's Not a Wide-Open Web," *The Wall Street Journal*, July 9, 2001, p. B1; "Chinese Officials Force Magazines to Go Without Famous Names," *The Wall Street Journal*, February 2, 2000, p. B1; "Sweden Presses EU for Further Ad Restrictions," *Advertising Age*, April 12, 1999, p. 2; "Vietnamese Police Raid Bates' Ho Chi Minh Office," *Advertising Age*, May 4, 1998, p. 6; "Pakistan Cracks Whip," *Ad Age International*, February 9, 1998, p. 26; "Indian Court Tells Lever to Clean Up Ad Claims," *Ad Age International*, January 1998, p. 32; "PepsiCo's Pitch in Japan Has New Twist," *The Wall Street Journal*, May 23, 1997, p. B10. See also Young Sook Moon and George R. Franke, "Cultural Influences on Agency Practitioners' Ethical Perceptions: a Comparison of Korea and the U.S.," *Journal of Advertising*, Spring 2000, p. 51; Kim Bartel Sheehan, "Balancing Acts: an Analysis of Food and Drug Administration Letters about Direct-to-Consumer Advertising Violations," *Journal of Public Policy & Marketing*, Fall 2003, p. 159; J. Howard Beales III, "The Federal Trade Commission's Use of Unfairness Authority: its Rise, Fall, and Resurrection," *Journal of Public Policy & Marketing*, Fall 2003, p. 192; Alexander Simonson, "The Impact of Advertising Law on Business and Public Policy," *Journal of Marketing*, October 1994, p. 123; Ross D. Petty, "Advertising Law in the United States and European Union," *Journal of Public Policy & Marketing*, Spring 1997, p. 2; Steve Lysonski and Michael F. Duffy, "The New Zealand Fair Trading Act of 1986: Deceptive Advertising," *Journal of Consumer Affairs*, Summer 1992, p. 177; "Drop That Remote! In Britain, Watching TV Can Be a Crime," *The Wall Street Journal*, September 27, 1993, p. A1; "East Europeans Adjust to Western Ads; Information after Years of Propaganda," *The Wall Street Journal*, July 17, 1993, p. A5B; Albert Schofield, "International Differences in Advertising Practices: Britain Compared with Other Countries," *International Journal of Advertising* 10, no. 4 (1991), p. 299.

26. Ivan L. Preston, "Regulatory Positions Toward Advertising Puffery of the Uniform Commercial Code and the Federal Trade Commission," *Journal of Public Policy & Marketing*, Fall 1997, p. 336; Claude R. Martin, Jr., "Ethical Advertising Research Standards: Three Case Studies," *Journal of Advertising*, September 1994, p. 17; William K. Darley and Robert E. Smith, "Advertising Claim Objectivity: Antecedents and Effects," *Journal of Marketing*, October 1993, p. 100; George M. Zinkhan, "Advertising Ethics: Emerging Methods and Trends," *Journal of Advertising*, September 1994, p. 1.

27. "Potter Book Brews Up Sales Magic," *DSN Retailing Today*, July 7, 2003, p. 1; "That Old Black Magic," *Time*, June 30, 2003, p. 60; "Harry Potter and—What Else?" *BusinessWeek*, June 20, 2003, p. 79; "Wizard's Return," *The Wall Street Journal*, June 27, 2003, p. W13; "The Real Magic of Harry Potter," *Time*, June 23, 2003, p. 60; "Harry Potter Casts a Record-Breaking Spell," *USA Today*, June 23, 2003, p. 1D; "Booksellers Get Ready for Harry," *USA Today*, June 19, 2003, p. 3B; "Transportation," *BusinessWeek*, January 8, 2001, p. 130; "Buzzmeisters of the Year," *Brandweek* (Marketers of the Year Special Issue), October 16, 2000, pp. M8–M18; "Harry Potter, Meet 'Ha-li Bo-te,'" *The Wall Street Journal*, September 21, 2000, p. B1; "Creative Coddling, Great Word of Mouth," *BusinessWeek E.Biz*, September 18, 2000; "Wizard of Marketing," *BusinessWeek*, July 24, 2000, p. 84; "Web Booksellers Give Potter Fans Rush Delivery," *The Wall Street Journal*, June 22, 2000, p. B1.

28. "Old-Fashioned PR Gives General Mills Advertising Bargains," *The Wall Street Journal*, March 20, 1997, p. A1. See also "Name That Chintz! How Shelter Magazines Boost Brands," *The Wall Street Journal*, March 14, 1997, p. B1; "Rosie and 'Friends' Make Drake's Cakes a Star," *The Wall Street Journal*, February 10, 1997, p. B1; "Toy Story: How Shrewd Marketing Made Elmo a Hit," *The Wall Street Journal*, December 16, 1996, p. B1; "PR Shouldn't Mean 'Poor Relations,'" *Industry Week*, February 3, 1992, p. 51; Siva K. Balasubramanian, "Beyond Advertising and Publicity: Hybrid Messages and Public Policy Issues," *Journal of Advertising*, December 1994, p. 29; Thomas H. Bivins, "Ethical Implications of the Relationship of Purpose to Role and Function in Public Relations," *Journal of Business Ethics*, January 1989, p. 65.

29. "The Potatoes Were Smiling; the Fries Were Blue," *The New York Times*, March 13, 2003, p. C1; "Marketing Tactics: Ries' Thesis, Ads Don't Build Brands, PR Does," *Advertising Age*, July 15, 2002, p. 14; "Want Some Blue Fries with That Shake?" *USA Today*, March 21, 2002, p. 8D; "Edible Entertainment," *The Wall Street Journal*, October 24, 2001, p. B1; "Marketers of the Year: Grand Marketer, Heinz," *Brandweek*, October 15, 2001, p. M6.

30. "President's Tumble Off a Segway Seems a Tiny Bit Suspicious," *USA Today*, June 18, 2003, p. 3B; "Watch Your Step: Segways Ahead," *USA Today*, June 17, 2003, p. 1A; "Segway Book: Inventor No 'Deep Throat,'" *Investor's Business Daily*, June 13, 2003, p. A4.

31. "P&G Breaks Out of Its Slump," *USA Today*, October 14, 2003, p. 3B; "Ads Mmm, Junk Mail," *Newsweek*, August 18, 2003, p. 12; "Road Shows Take Brands to the People," *The Wall Street Journal*, May 14, 2003, p. A10; "Offbeat Marketing Sells," *Investor's Business Daily*, March 27, 2002, p. A4; "Events & Promotions," *Advertising Age*, March 17, 1997, p. S1; "Special Report: Promotional Marketing," *Advertising Age*, March 21, 1994, p. S1. See also D. C. Gilbert and N. Jackaria, "The Efficacy of Sales Promotions in UK Supermarkets: A Consumer View," *International Journal of Retail & Distribution Management*, (6) 2002, p. 315; Pierre Chandon, Brian Wansink, and Gilles Laurent, "A Benefit Congruency Framework of Sales Promotion Effectiveness," *Journal of Marketing*, October 2000, p. 65; Andrew G. Parsons, "Assessing the Effectiveness of Shopping Mall Promotions: Customer Analysis," *International Journal of Retail & Distribution Management*, (2) 2003, p. 74; Nancy Spears, "Time Pressure and Information in Sales Promotion Strategy: Conceptual Framework and Content Analysis," *Journal of Advertising*, Spring 2001, p. 67; K. Sivakumar, "Tradeoff Between Frequency and Depth of Price Promotions: Implications for High- and Low-Priced Brands," *Journal of Marketing Theory & Practice*, Winter 1996, p. 1.

32. "Too Many Choices," *The Wall Street Journal*, April 20, 2001, p. B1; "Reposition: Simplifying the Customer's Brandscape," *Brandweek*, October 2, 2000, p. 36; "Make It Simple," *BusinessWeek*, September 9, 1996, p. 96; "Pay for Performance Picking Up Speed," *Advertising Age*, August 9, 1993, p. 19. See also Page Moreau, Aradhna Krishna and Bari Harlam, "The Manufacturer-Retailer-Consumer Triad: Differing Perceptions Regarding Price Promotions," *Journal of Retailing*, Winter 2001, p. 547; Donald R. Lichtenstein, Scot Burton, and Richard G. Netemeyer, "An Examination of Deal Proneness Across Sales Promotion Types: A Consumer Segmentation Perspective," *Journal of Retailing*, Summer 1997, p. 283; Donald R. Glover, "Distributor Attitudes Toward Manufacturer-Sponsored Promotions," *Industrial Marketing Management* 20, no. 3 (1991), p. 241.

33. CBC *Marketplace*, "Mining Your Own Business," broadcast date October 24, 2004.

34. For more on Pampers example, see "P&G Promotion Is Too Successful, Angering Buyers," *The Wall Street Journal*, April 2, 2002, p. B1. For another example, see "Shopper Turns Lots of Pudding into Free Miles," *The Wall Street Journal*, January 24, 2000, p. B1; "The Pudding Guy Flies Again (and Again) Over Latin America," *The Wall Street Journal*, March 16, 2000, p. B1.

35. George E. Belch and Michael E. Belch, *Advertising and Promotion, an Integrated Marketing Communication Perspective* (Burr Ridge, IL: McGraw-Hill, 2004).

36. "Designated Shopper," *Brandweek*, February 4, 2002, p. 34; "Cyber-coupons," *Discount Store News*, March 9, 1998, p. 18; "The Scoop on Coupons," *Brandweek*, March 17, 1997, p. 34; "Many Companies Are Starting to Wean Shoppers Off Coupons," *The Wall Street Journal*, January 22, 1997, p. B1; "Internet Coupons offer H.O.T! Deals," *USA Today*, December 13, 1996, p. 17D; "First, Green Stamps. Now, Coupons?" *BusinessWeek*, April 22, 1996, p. 68; "P&G Ad Chief Plots Demise of the Coupon," *The Wall Street Journal*, April 17, 1996, p. B1; Judy F.

Graham, "Increasing Repurchase Rates: A Reappraisal of Coupon Effects," *Psychology & Marketing*, November/December 1994, p. 533; A. Krishna and R.W. Shoemaker, "Estimating the Effects of Higher Coupon Face Values on the Timing of Redemptions, the Mix of Coupon Redeemers, and Purchase Quality," *Psychology & Marketing*, November/December 1992, p. 453; Venkatram Ramaswamy and Srini S. Srinivasan, "Coupon Characteristics and Redemption Intentions: A Segment-Level Analysis," *Psychology & Marketing*, January 1998, p. 59.

37. "The Show Goes On: Online Trade Shows," *The Wall Street Journal Reports*, April 28, 2003, p. R4; "The Cyber-Show Must Go On," *Trade Media*, May 7, 2001, p. SR3; "Getting the Most from a Trade-Show Booth," *Investor's Business Daily*, April 25, 2000, p. 1. See also Marnik G. Dekimpe, Pierre Francois, Srinath Gopalakrishna, Gary L. Lilien, and Christophe Van den Bulte, "Generalizing About Trade Show Effectiveness: A Cross-National Comparison," *Journal of Marketing*, October 1997, p. 55; Scott Barlass, "How to Get the Most Out of Trade Shows," *Journal of Product Innovation Management*, September 1997, p. 423; Srinath Gopalakrishna, Gary L. Lilien, Jerome D. Williams, and Ian K. Sequeira, "Do Trade Shows Pay Off?" *Journal of Marketing*, July 1995, p. 75; "Trade Promotion Rises," *Advertising Age*, April 3, 2000, p. 24; "Getting Tough on Trade," *Adweek*, April 13, 1992, p. 20.

38. "A Shift in Direction?" *Adweek's Marketing Week*, April 13, 1992, p. 26; Sunil Gupta, "Impact of Sales Promotions on When, What, and How Much to Buy," *Journal of Marketing Research*, November 1988, p. 342.

39. "Creating Incentives Down in Ranks: Marriott Ties Pay to Guest Replies," *Investor's Business Daily*, July 6, 2001, p. A1; "Get Great Results from Salespeople by Finding What Really Moves Them," *Investor's Business Daily*, July 2, 2001, p. A1.

CHAPTER 16

1. "If the Pros Use a Tool or a Toothbrush, It Will Sell," *USA Today*, December 17, 2003, p. 1A; "Power Brushes a Hit at Every Level," *Advertising Age*, May 26, 2003, p. 10; "Less Power to You," *Newsweek*, January 27, 2003, p. 73; "Toothbrush Wars: Group's Findings Spark Another Battle," *The Wall Street Journal*, January 14, 2003, p. D4; "Do You Really Need a Turbo Toothbrush?" *The Wall Street Journal*, October 1, 2002, p. D1; "New SpinBrush Line Backed by $30 Mil," *Advertising Age*, September 9, 2002, p. 3; "Why P&G's Smile Is So Bright," *BusinessWeek*, August 12, 2002, p. 58; "SpinBrush Cost P&G a Hefty $475 Million," *Advertising Age*, May 13, 2002, p. 4; "Colgate Adds Motion to Brush Market," *Marketing Magazine*, April 8, 2002, p. 2; "All About Gadgets and Gizmosity," *Fortune*, February 19, 2002, p. 264; "Think Small: Procter & Gamble Takes a New Approach to Tackling the Competition," *Advertising Age*, January 21, 2002, p. 1; "D'Arcy Switches Sonicare Ads' Focus to Technology," *Adweek*, October 8, 2001, p. 4; "What's Hot: Powered-Up Toothbrushes," *DSN Retailing Today*, April 16, 2001, p. 35; "Retailers Are Brushing Up on the Latest Oral Care Advances," *DSN Retailing Today*, April 16, 2001, p. 35; "Gillette Lines Up Oral-B Ad Push," *Advertising Age*, December 4, 2000, p. 22; "Fashionable Mouths Bristle at the Ordinary," *USA Today*, May 10, 2000, p. 5D; "Colgate Challenges Gillette Dominance in Electric Brushes," *Advertising Age*, April 3, 2000, p. 10.

2. "Detroit's Latest Offer: Pay More, Get Less," *The Wall Street Journal*, July 24, 2002, p. D1; "Did You Overpay for Your Car? States Sue Dealers over Fees," *The Wall Street Journal*, June 20, 2002, p. D1; "Sticker Shock: Detroit's Hidden Price Hikes," *The Wall Street Journal*, April 10, 2002, p. D1; "Adding Options Helps Car Firms Increase Prices," *The Wall Street Journal*, December 27, 1993, p. 9; "Car Makers Seek to Mask Price Increases," *The Wall Street Journal*, August 16, 1989, p. B1.

3. Alfred Rappaport, "Executive Incentives versus Corporate Growth," *Harvard Business Review*, July–August 1978, p. 81; David M. Szymanski, Sundar G. Bharadwaj, and P. Rajan Varadarajan, "An Analysis of the Market Share-Profitability Relationship," *Journal of Marketing*, July 1993, p. 1.

4. "EU Court Backs Resale of Drugs," *The Wall Street Journal*, April 2, 2004, p. B3; "The Telecom Follies," *The Wall Street Journal*, March 26, 2004, p. A8; "It's Time to Look at Rx Pricing," *Modern Healthcare*, March 15, 2004, p. 18; "The New Drug War," *Fortune*, March 8, 2004, p. 144; "Rethinking Restructuring," *Public Utilities Fortnightly*, February 2004, p. 12; "The Economy: Steel Prices Jump, Spurring Protests from Customers," *The Wall Street Journal*, January 23, 2004, p. A2.

5. "Tiny Storage Makes Big Impact," *Investor's Business Daily*, October 4, 2001, p. A6.

6. For more on the dot-com bust, see "Applying Old Pricing Lessons to a New Investing World," *The Wall Street Journal*, May 21, 2001, p. C1; Stephen E. Frank, *Net Worth* (2001); "E-Assets for Sale," *BusinessWeek E.Biz*, May 14, 2001, p. EB20; "Last Guys Finish First," *Ecompany*, May 2001, p. 93; "After the Wild Ride," *BusinessWeek E.Biz*, April 16, 2001, p. EB29; "Study: Net Start-Ups Ignored Economics 101," *Investor's Business Daily*, March 2, 2001, p. A8; "12 Months When the Dot Turned into a Dark Period," *Investor's Business Daily*, January 2, 2001, p. A6; "We're Heading into Something Big—but What?" *USA Today*, December 29, 2000, p. 1B; "What Detonated Dot-Bombs?" *USA Today*, December 4, 2000, p. 1B; "Dot-Bombs," *Brandweek*, November 27, 2000, p. IQ16.

7. For more on Taurus, see "How Detroit Is Ruining Your Car's Value," *The Wall Street Journal*, October 8, 2002, p. D1. For more on GM's recent attempts to add market share, see "GM Revs Incentives: $3,000 or 0% on 5-year Loans," *USA Today*, April 1, 2003, p. 1B.; "Rick Wagoner's Game Plan," *BusinessWeek*, February 10, 2003, p. 52; "Record Sales Incentives Drive GM's Market Share," *USA Today*, January 17, 2003, p. 1B; "GM Raises Market Share and Increases Sales by 36%," *The New York Times*, January 4, 2003, p. B1; "For GM, Sweet Deals Are Smarter than They Look," *BusinessWeek*, August 26, 2002, p. 44; "Job Accelerator: GM's 0% Finance Plan Is Good for Economy, Risky for the Company," *The Wall Street Journal*, October 30, 2001, p. A1. See also Robert Jacobson and David A. Aaker, "Is Market Share All That It's Cracked Up to Be?" *Journal of Marketing*, Fall 1985, p. 11; Carolyn Y. Woo, "Market-Share Leadership—Not Always So Good," *Harvard Business Review*, January–February 1984, p. 50; "Reichhold Chemicals: Now the Emphasis Is on Profits Rather than Volume," *BusinessWeek*, June 20, 1983, p. 178.

8. Kissan Joseph, "On the Optimality of Delegating Pricing Authority to the Sales Force," *Journal of Marketing*, January 2001, p. 62; Michael V. Marn and Robert L. Rosiello, "Managing Price, Gaining Profit," *Harvard Business Review*, September–October 1992, p. 84; Subhash C. Jain and Michael B. Laric, "A Framework for Strategic Industrial Pricing," *Industrial Marketing Management* 8 (1979), p. 75; Peter R. Dickson and Joel E. Urbany, "Retailer Reactions to Competitive Price Changes," *Journal of Retailing*, Spring 1994, p. 1; Mary Karr, "The Case of the Pricing Predicament," *Harvard Business Review*, March–April, 1988, p. 10; Saeed Samiee, "Pricing in Marketing Strategies of U.S. and Foreign-Based Companies," *Journal of Business Research*, February 1987, p. 17; Gerard J. Tellis, "Beyond the Many Faces of Price: An Integration of Pricing Strategies," *Journal of Marketing*, October 1986, p. 146.

9. For more on Priceline, see "A Humbler, Happier Priceline," *BusinessWeek*, August 11, 2003, p. 34; "Inside Jay Walker's House of Cards," *Fortune*, November 13, 2000, p. 127; "Letting the Masses Name Their Price," *BusinessWeek E.Biz*, September 18, 2000, p. EB44; "Name Your Price—for Everything?" *BusinessWeek*, April 17, 2000, p. 72. See also "The Discount Cards that Don't Save You Money," *The Wall Street Journal*, January 21, 2003, p. D1; "Beating Retailers at the Discount Game," *The Wall Street Journal*, November 27, 2002, p. D1; "Lessons from a Grocer," *Investor's Business Daily*, April 3, 2002, p. A4; "Ways to Boost Sales Right Now: Price Wisely, Do What You Know," *Investor's Business Daily*, October 15, 2001, p. A1. For more on other online travel sites, see "Scoring a Travel Discount Gets Easier," *The Wall Street Journal*, Novem-

ber 4, 2003, p. D1; "The Travel Agent Bosses Love," *BusinessWeek*, October 27, 2003, p. 134; "Convention Hotels Hurt by Web Bookings," *Investor's Business Daily*, August 21, 2003, p. A4; "When Hotel Discounts Are No Bargain," *The Wall Street Journal*, August 6, 2003, p. D1; "Expedia: Changing Pilots in Mid-Climb," *BusinessWeek*, February 24, 2003, p. 120; "How to Get a Four-Star Hotel at Two-Star Prices," *The Wall Street Journal*, January 30, 2003, p. D1.

10. For more on EBay and its flexible pricing, see Chapter 13, endnote 18. See also "Will Auction Frenzy Cool?" *BusinessWeek E. Biz*, September 18, 2000, p. EB140; "Going, Going, Gone," *BusinessWeek*, April 12, 1999, p. 30; "Good-Bye to Fixed Pricing," *BusinessWeek*, May 4, 1998, p. 71; "One-Price Deals Save Time, Hassles, but Not Money," *USA Today*, March 11, 1998, p.1B. See also Eric Matson, "Customizing Prices," *Harvard Business Review*, November– December 1995, p. 13; Sanjay K. Dhar and Stephen J. Hoch, "Price Discrimination Using in-Store Merchandising," *Journal of Marketing*, January 1996, p. 17; Michael H. Morris, "Separate Prices as a Marketing Tool," *Industrial Marketing Management*, May 1987, p. 79; P. Ronald Stephenson, William L. Cron, and Gary L. Frazier, "Delegating Pricing Authority to the Sales Force: The Effects on Sales and Profit Performance," *Journal of Marketing*, Spring 1979, p. 21.

11. For more on Amazon offering different prices to different customers, see "Price? For You, $2; For the Rich Guy, $5," *Investor's Business Daily*, September 29, 2000, p. A8. For more on car haggling, see "CarMax: Psst, Wanna Buy a Used Car, Hassle-Free?" *Investor's Business Daily*, January 30, 2002, p. A9; "Haggling in Cyberspace Transforms Car Sales," *The Wall Street Journal*, December 30, 1997, p. B1; "Car Hagglers May Still Drive Best Car Deals," *The Wall Street Journal*, October 12, 1994, p. B1. See also <http://www.toyota.ca>.

12. "What's a Fair Price for Drugs?" *BusinessWeek*, April 30, 2001, p. 105; "AIDS Gaffes in Africa Come Back to Haunt Drug Industry at Home," *The Wall Street Journal*, April 23, 2001, p. A1; "Vaccine's Price Drives a Debate about Its Use," *The Wall Street Journal*, February 16, 2000, p. B1; "Breakthrough in Birth Control May Elude Poor," *The Wall Street Journal*, March 4, 1991, p. B1; "Burroughs Wellcome Reaps Profits, Outrage from Its AIDS Drug," *The Wall Street Journal*, September 15, 1989, p. A1; Richard A. Spinello, "Ethics, Pricing and the Pharmaceutical Industry," *Journal of Business Ethics*, August 1992, p. 617.

13. "In a Sleek Flat Set, Plasma's Price Plunges," *The New York Times*, January 8, 2004, p. E3; "For Digital TVs, the Future Is Now," *USA Today*, December 3, 2003, p. 10D; "The Skinny on Flat Screens," *The Wall Street Journal*, November 26, 2003, p. D1; "Rise of Flat-Screen TVs Reshapes Industry," *The Wall Street Journal*, November 20, 2003, p. B8; "I Want My Big TV . . . ," *The Wall Street Journal*, November 13, 2003, p. B1; "Consumer Spending Gives Tech Extra Push," *USA Today*, September 8, 2003, p. 1B; "Maker of Flat Screens Rounds Out Its Lines," *Investor's Business Daily*, August 6, 2003, p. A8; "Mirror, Mirror, on the Wall, Which Big-Screen TV Is Fairest of All?" *Fortune*, July 7, 2003, p. 145; "Prices of Flat-Panel Monitors, TVs to Drop," *The Wall Street Journal*, April 3, 2003, p. B4; "Flat Screens: Looking Good," *The Wall Street Journal*, March 31, 2003, p. R9; "Hit Show of the Season: The Revival of Digital TV," *The Wall Street Journal*, August 1, 2002, p. D1; "It's the Screens, Not the Sales, That Are Flat for Digital TVs," *Investor's Business Daily*, September 27, 2002, p. A6.

14. Available from World Wide Web: <http://www.palm.com>; "Stiff Competition, New Technology Mean Great Gadget Deals," *USA Today*, November 10, 2003, p. 3B; "Palm Reaches Out for a Hand," *BusinessWeek*, November 3, 2003, p. 74; "Palm Hopes Breaking in Two Will Juice Its Sluggish Sales," *The Wall Street Journal*, October 28, 2003, p. B1; "Hand-Helds' New Frontier," *The Wall Street Journal*, August 8, 2003, p. B1; "Tower Buyers Giving the Big Thumbs-Up to Handheld PC Gear," *Investor's Business Daily*, November 27, 2002, p. A5; "New Palms Offer Something for Every Pocketbook," *USA Today*, November 13, 2002, p. 5D.; "An Address Book that Shoots Movies," *The Wall Street Journal*,

October 2, 2002, p. D1; "Palm, Seeking Business Clients, Targets Corporate Executives," *The Wall Street Journal*, May 13, 2002, p. B6; "Start-Up Joins Hand-Held-Device Battle," *The Wall Street Journal*, May 9, 2002, p. B5; "Price Wars Hit PDAs: Is It Time to Buy One Yet?" *The Wall Street Journal*, May 9, 2002, p. D1; "Pilot Error: How Palm Tumbled from Star of Tech to Target of Microsoft," *The Wall Street Journal*, September 7, 2001, p. A1; "Palm Slips to No. 2 in Revenue as iPaq Grabs the Top Spot," *Investor's Business Daily*, June 19, 2001, p. A6; "Palm Shares Sink as One-Time Star Says Sales Fading," *Investor's Business Daily*, May 21, 2001, p. A6; "HandEra's Hand-Held Puts Some New Twists on the Usual Formula," *The Wall Street Journal*, May 10, 2001, p. B1; "Hand-Helds that Are Less of a Handful," *BusinessWeek*, April 9, 2001, p. 18; "PDA Wars: Round 2," *Time*, April 2, 2001, p. 40; "New Devices Shrink Difference in Price for Palm, Pocket PC," *Investor's Business Daily*, March 21, 2001, p. A6; "Seeding Demand for Handspring," *Advertising Age*, November 6, 2000, p. S36; "Palm Hopes to Blaze a New Image in Major Campaign," *The Wall Street Journal*, November 1, 2000, p. B10; "Hard Cell," *Fortune*, October 30, 2000, p. 305; "If at First You Don't Succeed . . . ," *BusinessWeek*, April 24, 2000, p. 120; "3Com Tries to Solve Its Palm Problem," *Fortune*, October 11, 1999, p. 167; "Palm Has the Whole World in Its Hand," *USA Today*, September 14, 1999, p. 1B; "The Palm Pilot Sequel Is a Hit," *Fortune*, April 13, 1998, p. 154; "3Com Again Changes Name of Hot-Selling PalmPilot," *Advertising Age*, March 9, 1998, p. 4; "Apple Drops Newton, an Idea Ahead of Its Time," *The Wall Street Journal*, March 2, 1998, p. B1; "Little Computers, Big New Marketing Battle," *The Wall Street Journal*, November 17, 1997, p. B1; "How Palm Computing Became an Architect," *Harvard Business Review*, September–October 1997, p. 89. "A Rocket in Its Pocket," *BusinessWeek*, September 9, 1996, p. 111.

15. "Netflix Expects Fast Subscriber, Earnings Gain," *Investor's Business Daily*, January 5, 2004, p. A7; "DVD-Rental Firm May be Victim of Its Success," *The Wall Street Journal*, November 20, 2003, p. C1; "Cable Fights for Its Movie Rights," *BusinessWeek*, October 27, 2003, p. 88; "Blockbuster's Poor Sales Results Cast Shadow over a Rise in Net," *The Wall Street Journal*, October 22, 2003, p. B3; "For Netflix, It's So Far, So Good," *USA Today*, October 15, 2003, p. 3B; "No Late Fees: Disney to 'Beam' Rental Movies to Homes," *The Wall Street Journal*, September 29, 2003, p. B1; "The Next DTC: DVD Explodes," *Advertising Age*, September 1, 2003, p. 1; "90,000 DVDs. No Shelves," *Fast Company*, September 2003, p. 38; "The Transition from Rental to Retail Bodes Well for Blockbuster Sales," *DSN Retailing Today*, July 21, 2003, p. 4; "Netflix Bets on DVD Rental Market," *The Wall Street Journal*, April 30, 2003, p. B6B; "Can Netflix Keep Spinning Gold?" *BusinessWeek*, April 21, 2003, p. 112; "Online DVD Rental Service Netflix Eyes Starring Role with Consumers," *Investor's Business Daily*, March 18, 2003, p. A4; "Future Looks Less than Stellar for Video Rental Firms," *USA Today*, January 23, 2003, p. 6B; "DVD Is Killing the Video Star," *Fortune*, January 20, 2003, p. 181; "DVD Sales Surge Puts Crimp in Blockbuster's Profit," *USA Today*, December 19, 2002, p. 4B; "Getting the Video-Store Guy Out of Your Life," *The Wall Street Journal*, October 24, 2002, p. D1; "DVDs Conquer the Movie World," *USA Today*, October 18, 2002, p. 1E; "Blockbuster Borrows from Netflix's Playbook, but Stays Offline," *Investor's Business Daily*, August 12, 2002, p. A4; "Blockbuster Bolsters Games Section," *DSN Retailing Today*, June 10, 2002, p. 8; "DVD Take Wind Out of Sails for Video on Demand," *USA Today*, May 7, 2002, p. 3B; "The Meteoric Rise of the DVD," *Business 2.0*, May 2002, p. 34; "At $70 a Pop, Consumers Put Discount DVD Players on Holiday List," *The Wall Street Journal*, December 13, 2001, p. B1.

16. "Fliers' Dilemma: Save Now or Later?" *BusinessWeek*, October 13, 2003, p. 138; "Pizza Hut Adds Videos, Loyalty Cards to Recipe," *Brandweek*, September 29, 2003, p. 9; "Plastic's New Pitch: Something for Nothing," *The Wall Street Journal*, July 31 2003, p. D1; "Frequent Flier to Rental Driver Has Its Price," *The New York Times*, January 14, 2003, p. C4; "The Holy Grail: Getting Miles for Your Mortgage," *The Wall Street Journal*, December 5, 2002, p. D1; "Road Warriors' Secret: Hotel Points

Trump Miles," *The Wall Street Journal*, November 14, 2002, p. D1; "Discounts Follow Dip in Business Travel," *USA Today*, June 21, 2001, p. 1B; "Sailing on Sale: Travelers Ride a Wave of Discounts on Cruise Ships," *The Wall Street Journal*, July 17, 2000, p. B1; "Competing Online, Drugstore Chains Virtually Undersell Themselves," *The Wall Street Journal*, January 10, 2000, p. B1; "Prescription: Cash Only, Some Doctors Offer Discounts," *USA Today*, December 22, 1999, p. 1B; "Owens Corning: Back from the Dead," *Fortune*, May 26, 1997, p. 118. See also Andy A. Tsay, "Managing Retail Channel Overstock: Markdown Money and Return Policies," *Journal of Retailing*, Winter 2001, p. 457; David E. Sprott, Kenneth C. Manning and Anthony D. Miyazaki, "Grocery Price Setting and Quantity Surcharges," *Journal of Marketing*, July 2003, p. 34; Douglas D. Davis and Charles A. Holt, "List Prices and Discounts: The Interrelationship Between Consumer Shopping Patterns and Profitable Marketing Strategies," *Psychology & Marketing*, July 1996, p. 341; David W. Arnesen, C. P. Fleenor, and Rex S. Toh, "The Ethical Dimensions of Airline Frequent Flier Programs," *Business Horizons*, January–February 1997, p. 47; K.J. Blois, "Discounts in Business Marketing Management," *Industrial Marketing Management*, April 1994, p. 93; James B. Wilcox et al., "Price Quantity Discounts: Some Implications for Buyers and Sellers," *Journal of Marketing*, July 1987, p. 60; Mark T. Spriggs and John R. Nevin, "The Legal Status of Trade and Functional Price Discounts," *Journal of Public Policy & Marketing*, Spring 1994, p. 61; "Cash Discounts," *Electrical Wholesaling*, May 1989, p. 90.

17. For more on P&G's everyday low pricing, see "P&G, Others Try New Uses for Coupon-Heavy Media," *Advertising Age*, September 22, 1997, p. 20; "Move to Drop Coupons Puts Procter & Gamble in Sticky PR Situation," *The Wall Street Journal*, April 17, 1997, p. A1; "Zeroing In on Zero Coupons," *Brandweek*, June 3, 1996, p. 30; "Company Makes Big Cuts to Stay Fit," *USA Today*, July 16, 1993, p. 1B; "P&G Plays Pied Piper on Pricing," *Advertising Age*, March 9, 1992, p. 6. See also Kusum L. Ailawadi, Donald R. Lehmann, and Scott A. Neslin, "Market Response to a Major Policy Change in the Marketing Mix: Learning from Procter & Gamble's Value Pricing Strategy," *Journal of Marketing*, January 2001, p. 44; Monika Kukar-Kinney and Rockney G. Walters, "Consumer Perceptions of Refund Depth and Competitive Scope in Price-Matching Guarantees: Effects on Store Patronage," *Journal of Retailing*, Fall 2003, p. 153; Stephen J. Hoch, Xavier Dreze, and Mary E. Purk, "EDLP, Hi-Lo, and Margin Arithmetic," *Journal of Marketing*, October 1994, p. 16; George S. Bobinski, Dena Cox, and Anthony Cox, "Retail 'Sale' Advertising, Perceived Retailer Credibility, and Price Rationale," *Journal of Retailing*, Fall 1996, p. 291; Francis J. Mulhern and Daniel T. Padgett, "The Relationship Between Retail Price Promotions and Regular Price Purchases," *Journal of Marketing*, October 1995, p. 83.

18. For more on slotting fees, see "Kraft Speeds New Product Launch Times," *Advertising Age*, November 18, 2002, p. 1; "The Hidden Cost of Shelf Space," *BusinessWeek*, April 15, 2002, p. 103. See also Ramarao Desiraju, "New Product Introductions, Slotting Allowances, and Retailer Discretion," *Journal of Retailing*, Fall 2001, p. 335; David Balto, "Recent Legal and Regulatory Developments in Slotting Allowances and Category Management," *Journal of Public Policy & Marketing*, Fall 2002, p. 289; William L. Wilkie, Debra M. Desrochers and Gregory T. Gundlach, "Marketing Research and Public Policy: the Case of Slotting Fees," *Journal of Public Policy & Marketing*, Fall 2002, p. 275; Paul N. Bloom, Gregory T. Gundlach and Joseph P. Cannon, "Slotting Allowances and Fees: Schools of Thought and the Views of Practicing Managers," *Journal of Marketing*, April 2000, p. 92; J. Chris White, Lisa C. Troy and R. Nicholas Gerlich, "The Role of Slotting Fees and Introductory Allowances in Retail Buyers' New-Product Acceptance Decisions," *Journal of the Academy of Marketing Science*, Spring 2000, p. 291; Paul N. Bloom, "Slotting Allowances and Fees: Schools of Thought and the Views of Practicing Managers," *Journal of Marketing*, April 2000, p. 92.

19. For more on coupons, see "The Latest Craze in Coupon-Clipping: Free Trial Offers for Prescription Drugs," *The Wall Street Journal*, April

16, 2002, p. D1; "Penny-Pinchers' Paradise," *BusinessWeek E.Biz*, January 22, 2001, p. EB12; "E-Tailers Missing the Mark with Flood of Web Coupons," *Advertising Age*, September 25, 2000, p. 104; Gail Ayala Taylor, "Coupon Response in Services," *Journal of Retailing*, Spring 2001, p. 139. For more on rebates, see "Let's Make a (Tough) Deal," *Newsweek*, June 23, 2003, p. 48; "Ford Tames the Rebate Monster," *BusinessWeek*, May 5, 2003, p. 38; "Rejected! Rebates Get Harder to Collect," *The Wall Street Journal*, June 11, 2002, p. D1; "Free-with-Rebate Costs Web Buyers Some Big Bucks," *The Wall Street Journal*, May 18, 2001, p. B1. See also William D. Diamond, "Just What Is a 'Dollar's Worth'? Consumer Reactions to Price Discounts vs. Extra Product Promotions," *Journal of Retailing*, Fall 1992, p. 254; Kenneth A. Hunt and Susan M. Keaveney, "A Process Model of the Effects of Price Promotions on Brand Image," *Psychology & Marketing*, November/December 1994, p. 511; "Rebates' Secret Appeal to Manufacturers: Few Consumers Actually Redeem Them," *The Wall Street Journal*, February 10, 1998, p. B1; Peter K. Tat, "Rebate Usage: A Motivational Perspective," *Psychology & Marketing*, January/February 1994, p. 15.

20. "America's Pricing Paradox," *The Wall Street Journal*, May 16, 2003, p. B1; "Ideas + Innovations: How to Thrive When Prices Fall," *Fortune*, May 12, 2003, p. 130; "Why Some Companies Can Levy Premium Prices and Others Not," *Investor's Business Daily*, April 15, 2003, p. A1; "Survival Strategies: After Cost Cutting, Companies Turn toward Price Rises," *The Wall Street Journal*, September 18, 2002, p. A1; "Stepping Up: Middle Market Shrinks as Americans Migrate toward the High End," *The Wall Street Journal*, March 29, 2002, p. A1; "Two-Tier Marketing," *BusinessWeek*, March 17, 1997, p. 82; "Makeup Ads Downplay Glamour for Value," *The Wall Street Journal*, June 20, 1994, p. B5; "Value Pricing Kicks off Model Year," *USA Today*, October 1, 1993, p. 1B; "Value Pricing Comes to Funerals," *USA Today*, July 14, 1993, p. 5B; "Tide, Cheer Join P&G 'Value Pricing' Plan," *Advertising Age*, February 15, 1993, p. 3; "More Stores Switch from Sales to 'Everyday Low Prices,'" *The Wall Street Journal*, November 12, 1992, p. B1; "Value Marketing," *BusinessWeek*, November 11, 1991, p. 132; Louis J. De Rose, "Meet Today's Buying Influences with Value Selling," *Industrial Marketing Management* 20, no. 2 (1991), p. 87.

21. "Freeze-Dried Berries Heat Up Cereal Duel," *The Wall Street Journal*, May 15, 2003, p. B2; "Garfield's AdReview: A Few Spoons of Truth Tossed into Special K Red Berries Spot," *Advertising Age*, May 12, 2003, p. 65.

22. For an excellent discussion of laws related to pricing, see Louis W. Stern and Thomas L. Eovaldi, *Legal Aspects of Marketing Strategy: Antitrust and Consumer Protection Issues* (Englewood Cliffs, NJ: Prentice-Hall, 1984); Joseph P. Guiltinan and Gregory T. Gundlach, "Aggressive and Predatory Pricing: A Framework for Analysis," *Journal of Marketing*, July 1996, p. 87.

23. Consumer Fact Sheet on Gasoline Prices, March 2006, retrieved from Competition Bureau Web site: <http://www.competitionbureau.gc.ca>.

24. See World Wide Web sites: <http://www.competitionbureau.gc.ca> and <http://www.ct-tc.gc.ca>, and *Calgary Herald*, August 12, 2006, p. A5.

CHAPTER 17

1. For more on Wal-Mart in the U.S., see *2003 Annual Report*, Wal-Mart; "Wal-Mart Fires the First Shot in Holiday Toy Pricing War," *The Wall Street Journal*, November 19, 2003, p. B1; "Retail Giant Wal-Mart Faces Challenges on Many Fronts," *USA Today*, November 11, 2003, p. 1B; "Running the Gauntlet at Wal-Mart," *Inc.*, November 2003, p. 92; "Wal-Mart Eating Away at Big Supermarkets' Already Wilting Sales," *Investor's Business Daily*, October 14, 2003, p. A1; "Wal-Mart Continues Unabated Expansion," *DSN Retailing Today*, October 13, 2003, p. 1; "Wal-Mart Gains on a Feast of Advantages," *Food Retailing*, October 13, 2003, p. 1; "Is Wal-Mart Too Powerful?" *BusinessWeek*, October 6, 2003, p. 100;

"Wal-Mart Report," *Advertising Age*, October 6, 2003, p. 1; "Minn. Small Town Just Says No to Starbucks Nation," *USA Today*, October 1, 2003, p. 4A; "Wal-Mart Uber Alles," *American Demographics*, October 2003, p. 38; "Wal-Mart Debuts a More Contemporary Design," *DSN Retailing Today*, July 21, 2003, p. 5; "Call It Mall-Wart," *BusinessWeek*, July 14, 2003, p. 40; "Price War in Aisle 3," *The Wall Street Journal*, May 27, 2003, p. B1; "One Nation under Wal-Mart," *Fortune*, March 3, 2003, p. 64; "Can Wal-Mart Get Any Bigger?" *Time*, January 13, 2003, p. 38; "The World's Largest Focus Group," *Business 2.0*, October 2002, p. 58; "Pinstripes and Motor Oil?" *The Wall Street Journal*, September 3, 2002, p. B1; "Like My Pants? Pssst, They're Wal-Mart," *The Wall Street Journal*, September 3, 2002, p. B1; "Wal-Mart Consolidates Home into Destination Department," *DSN Retailing Today*, August 26, 2002, p. 1; "Wal-Mart: Lengthening Its Lead," *DSN Retailing Today*, June 10, 2002, p. 83; "Wal-Mart's Move into Banking Sparks New Worry on Main Street," *Investor's Business Daily*, December 27, 2001, p. A1; "Kmart, Wal-Mart Face Off in Price-Cutting Fight," *USA Today*, June 8, 2001, p. 1B; "How Wal-Mart Transfers Power," *The Wall Street Journal*, March 27, 2001, p. B1; Sharon M. Davidson and Amy Rummel, "Retail Changes Associated with Wal-Mart's Entry into Maine," *International Journal of Retail & Distribution Management*, (4) 2000, p. 162; "Wal*Mart, Retailer of the Century," *Discount Store News* (Special Issue), October 1999; "Logistics Whiz Rises at Wal-Mart," *The Wall Street Journal*, March 11, 1999, p. B1. See also Norman W. Hawker, "Wal-Mart and the Divergence of State and Federal Predatory Pricing Law," *Journal of Public Policy & Marketing*, Spring 1996, p. 141. For more on Wal-Mart International, see "Pacific Aisles: Wal-Mart's Foray into Japan Spurs a Retail Upheaval," *The Wall Street Journal*, September 19, 2003, p. A1; "Wal-Mart Adds to Global Reach with Tokyo Supermarket Stake," *Investor's Business Daily*, March 15, 2002, p. A1; Angela da Rocha and Luis Antonio Dib, "The Entry of Wal-Mart in Brazil and the Competitive Responses of Multinational and Domestic Firms," *International Journal of Retail & Distribution Management*, (1) 2002, p. 61, John Fernie and Stephen J. Arnold, "Wal-Mart in Europe: Prospects for Germany, the UK and France," *International Journal of Retail & Distribution Management*, (2) 2002, p. 92; "How Well Does Wal-Mart Travel?" *BusinessWeek*, September 3, 2001, p. 82; "Wal-Mart de Mexico to Grow Stores by 10%," *DSN Retailing Today*, March 19, 2001, p. 3; "Wal-Mart Fumes at Argentine Legislation," *The Wall Street Journal*, November 28, 2000, p. A23; "Stores Told to Lift Prices in Germany," *The Wall Street Journal*, September 11, 2000, p. A27; "The Wal-Mart Way Sometimes Gets Lost in Translation Overseas," *The Wall Street Journal*, October 8, 1997, p. A1.

2. Ritu Lohtia, Ramesh Subramaniam and Rati Lohtia, "Are Pricing Practices in Japanese Channels of Distribution Finally Changing?" *Journal of Marketing Channels*, (1,2) 2001, p. 5; Marvin A. Jolson, "A Diagrammatic Model for Merchandising Calculations," *Journal of Retailing*, Summer 1975, p. 3; C. Davis Fogg and Kent H. Kohnken, "Price-Cost Planning," *Journal of Marketing*, April 1978, p. 97.

3. Retail Council of Canada Web site at: <http://www.retailcouncil.org/membersonly/govrelations/codes/scanner_acc/scanner_accuracy02_eng.asp>.

4. "Look Who's Buzzing the Discounters," *BusinessWeek*, November 24, 2003, p. 48; "Unlike Rivals, JetBlue Won't Do the Bump," *USA Today*, October 24, 2003, p. 1B; "Cheaper Flights, Better Service: JetBlue Flies against the Wind," *Investor's Business Daily*, October 15, 2003, p. A9; "Off We Go into the Wild (Jet)Blue Yonder," *Brandweek*, September 22, 2003, p. 36; "JetBlue Gains on Its Competition," *USA Today*, August 13, 2003, p. 3B; "Discount Airlines Go Shopping for Jetliners," *USA Today*, July 2, 2003, p. 1B; "Is This the Future of Air Travel?" *Time* (Inside Business Bonus Section), July 2003; "JetBlue's Focus on Customers Pushes Airline's Sales Skyward," *Investor's Business Daily*, June 20, 2003, p. A1; "Delta Hopes Fliers Think It's Playing Their Song," *USA Today*, April 14, 2003, p. 6B; "How to Shake Up a Calcified Industry," *Business 2.0*, December 2002, p. 92; "Special Report: Marketer of the Year, JetBlue," *Advertising Age*, December 9, 2002, pp. S1–S6; "Lofty Goals: JetBlue Is

Taking Technology to New Heights," *The Wall Street Journal Reports*, December 9, 2002, p. R8; "JetBlue Soars on CEO's Creativity," *USA Today*, October 8, 2002, p. 1B; "Something Stylish, Something Blue," *Business 2.0*, February 2002, p. 94.

5. "The Little Extras That Count (Up)," *The Wall Street Journal*, July 12, 2001, p. B1; "Battle-Tested Rules of Online Retail," *Ecompany*, April 2001; "The Return of Pricing Power," *BusinessWeek*, May 8, 2000, p. 50; "The Power of Smart Pricing," *BusinessWeek*, April 10, 2000, p. 160. See also Mary L. Hatten, "Don't Get Caught with Your Prices Down: Pricing in Inflationary Times," *Business Horizons*, March 1982, p. 23; Douglas G. Brooks, "Cost Oriented Pricing: A Realistic Solution to a Complicated Problem," *Journal of Marketing*, April 1975, p. 72; Steven M. Shugan, "Retail Product-Line Pricing Strategy When Costs and Products Change," *Journal of Retailing*, Spring 2001, Vol. 77, 1, p. 17.

6. John C. Lere, "Your Product-Costing System Seems to Be Broken: Now What?" *Industrial Marketing Management*, October 2001, p. 586; William W. Alberts, "The Experience Curve Doctrine Reconsidered," *Journal of Marketing*, July 1989, p. 36; G. Dean Kortge et al., "Linking Experience, Product Life Cycle, and Learning Curves: Calculating the Perceived Value Price Range," *Industrial Marketing Management*, July 1994, p. 221.

7. G. Dean Kortge, "Inverted Breakeven Analysis for Profitable Marketing Decisions," *Industrial Marketing Management*, October 1984, p. 219; Thomas L. Powers, "Breakeven Analysis with Semifixed Costs," *Industrial Marketing Management*, February 1987, p. 35.

8. Approaches for estimating price-quantity relationships are reviewed in Kent B. Monroe, *Pricing: Making Profitable Decisions* (New York: McGraw-Hill, 2003). For specific examples see Gordon A. Wyner, Lois H. Benedetti, and Bart M. Trapp, "Measuring the Quantity and Mix of Product Demand," *Journal of Marketing*, Winter 1984, p. 101. See also Michael F. Smith and Indrajit Sinha, "The Impact of Price and Extra Product Promotions on Store Preference," *International Journal of Retail & Distribution Management*, (2) 2000, p. 83; Michael H. Morris and Mary L. Joyce, "How Marketers Evaluate Price Sensitivity," *Industrial Marketing Management*, May, 1988, p. 169. David E. Griffith and Roland T. Rust, "The Price of Competitiveness in Competitive Pricing," *Journal of the Academy of Marketing Science*, Spring 1997, p. 109; Frank D. Jones, "A Survey Technique to Measure Demand under Various Pricing Strategies," *Journal of Marketing*, July 1975, p. 75; Robert J. Dolan, "How Do You Know When the Price Is Right?" *Harvard Business Review*, September–October 1995, p. 174; S. C. Choi, "Price Competition in a Duopoly Common Retailer Channel," *Journal of Retailing*, Summer 1996, p. 117.

9. "Getting Skewered by Shrimp Prices," *The Wall Street Journal*, October 16, 2003, p. D1; "Secret in the Dairy Aisle: Milk Is a Cash Cow," *The Wall Street Journal*, July 28, 2003, p. B1; "New Status Symbol: Overpaying for Your Minivan," *The Wall Street Journal*, July 23, 2003, p. D1; "No More Free Lunch . . . Please?" *The Wall Street Journal Reports*, September 24, 2001, p. R13; "Who Really Needs a Pentium 4?" *Fortune*, January 8, 2001, p. 217; "Marriott International: A Hotel That Clicks with Guests," *BusinessWeek E.Biz*, September 18, 2000, p. EB58; "The Paradox of Value," *Brandweek*, June 5, 2000, p. 40; Watts Wacker and Jim Taylor, *The Visionary's Handbook: Nine Paradoxes That Will Shape the Future of Your Business* (HarperCollins, 2000). See also Kristin Diehl, Laura J. Kornish, and John G. Lynch Jr, "Smart Agents: When Lower Search Costs for Quality Information Increase Price Sensitivity," *Journal of Consumer Research*, Jun 2003, p. 56; Amir Heiman, Bruce McWilliams, Jinhua Zhao and David Zilberman, "Valuation and Management of Money-Back Guarantee Options," *Journal of Retailing*, Fall 2002, p. 193; Dhruv Grewal, Kent B. Monroe, and R. Krishnan, "The Effects of Price-Comparison Advertising on Buyers' Perceptions of Acquisition Value, Transaction Value, and Behavioral Intentions," *Journal of Marketing*, April 1998, p. 46; John T. Gourville, "Pennies-a-Day: The Effect of Temporal Reframing on Transaction Evaluation," *Journal of Consumer*

Research, March 1998, p. 395; Joel E. Urbany, Rosemary Kalapurakal, and Peter R. Dickson, "Price Search in the Retail Grocery Market," *Journal of Marketing*, April 1996, p. 91; Venkatesh Shankar and Lakshman Krishnamurthi, "Relating Price Sensitivity to Retailer Promotional Variables and Pricing Policy: An Empirical Analysis," *Journal of Retailing*, Fall 1996, p. 249; Chakravarthi Narasimhan, Scott A. Neslin, and Subrata K. Sen, "Promotional Elasticities and Category Characteristics," *Journal of Marketing*, April 1996, p. 17; K. Sivakumar and S. P. Raj, "Quality Tier Competition: How Price Change Influences Brand Choice and Category Choice," *Journal of Marketing*, July 1997, p. 71.

10. Thomas T. Nagle and Reed R. Holder, *The Strategy and Tactics of Pricing* (Englewood Cliffs, NJ: Prentice-Hall, 2002); "Fram Pays Up Now," *Brandweek*, July 20, 1998, p. 16; "New Long-Life Bulbs May Lose Brilliance in a Crowded Market," *The Wall Street Journal*, June 2, 1992, p. B4; Benson P. Shapiro and Barbara P. Jackson, "Industrial Pricing to Meet Customer Needs," *Harvard Business Review*, November–December 1978, p. 119; "The Race to the $10 Light Bulb," *BusinessWeek*, May 19, 1980, p. 124; see also Michael H. Morris and Donald A. Fuller, "Pricing an Industrial Service," *Industrial Marketing Management*, May 1989, p. 139.

11. "The Price Is Really Right," *BusinessWeek*, March 31, 2003, p. 62; "New Software Manages Price Cuts," *Investor's Business Daily*, March 31, 2003, p. A4; "The Power of Optimal Pricing," *Business 2.0*, September 2002, p. 68; "Priced to Move: Retailers Try to Get Leg Up on Markdowns with New Software," *The Wall Street Journal*, August 7, 2001, p. A1; "The Price Is Right," *Inc.*, July 2001, p. 40. See also Marc Vanhuele and Xavier Dreze, "Measuring the Price Knowledge Shoppers Bring to the Store," *Journal of Marketing*, October 2002, p. 72; Rashmi Adaval and Kent B. Monroe, "Automatic Construction and Use of Contextual Information for Product and Price Evaluations," *Journal of Consumer Research*, March 2002, p. 572; Sangman Han, Sunil Gupta and Donald R. Lehmann, "Consumer Price Sensitivity and Price Thresholds," *Journal of Retailing*, Winter 2001, p. 435; David Ackerman and Gerard Tellis, "Can Culture Affect Prices? A Cross-Cultural Study of Shopping and Retail Prices," *Journal of Retailing*, Spring 2001, p. 57; David M. Hardesty and William O. Bearden, "Consumer Evaluations of Different Promotion Types and Price Presentations: the Moderating Role of Promotional Benefit Level," *Journal of Retailing*, (1) 2003, p. 17; Rajesh Chandrashekaran and Dhruv Grewal, "Assimilation of Advertised Reference Prices: the Moderating Role of Involvement," *Journal of Retailing*, (1) 2003, p. 53; Thomas Jensen, Jeremy Kees, Scot Burton and Fernanda Lucarelli Turnipseed, "Advertised Reference Prices in an Internet Environment: Effects on Consumer Price Perceptions and Channel Search Intentions," *Journal of Interactive Marketing*, Spring 2003, p. 20; Joel E. Urbany, Peter R. Dickson and Alan G. Sawyer, "Insights into Cross- and Within-Store Price Search: Retailer Estimates vs. Consumer Self-Reports," *Journal of Retailing*, Summer 2000, p. 243; Merrie Brucks, Valarie A. Zeithaml and Gillian Naylor, "Price and Brand Name as Indicators of Quality Dimensions for Consumer Durables," *Journal of the Academy of Marketing Science*, Summer 2000, p. 359; Joydeep Srivastava and Nicholas Lurie, "A Consumer Perspective on Price-Matching Refund Policies: Effect on Price Perceptions and Search Behavior," *Journal of Consumer Research*, September 2001, p. 296; Ronald W. Niedrich, Subhash Sharma and Douglas H. Wedell, "Reference Price and Price Perceptions: a Comparison of Alternative Models," *Journal of Consumer Research*, December 2001, p. 339; Erica Mina Okada, "Trade-Ins, Mental Accounting, and Product Replacement Decisions," *Journal of Consumer Research*, March 2001, p. 433; Aradhna Krishna, Richard Briesch, Donald R. Lehmann and Hong Yuan, "A Meta-Analysis of the Impact of Price Presentation on Perceived Savings," *Journal of Retailing*, Summer 2002, p. 101; Valerie A. Taylor and William O. Bearden, "The Effects of Price on Brand Extension Evaluations: the Moderating Role of Extension Similarity," *Journal of the Academy of Marketing Science*, Spring 2002, p. 131; James K. Binkley and John Bejnarowicz, "Consumer Price Awareness in Food Shopping: the Case of Quantity Surcharges," *Journal of Retailing*, (1) 2003,

p. 27; Lesa E. Bolton, Luk Warlop and Joseph W. Alba, "Consumer Perceptions of Price (Un)fairness," *Journal of Consumer Research*, March 2003, p. 474; Amir Heiman, Bruce McWilliams and David Zilberman, "Demonstrations and Money-Back Guarantees: Market Mechanisms to Reduce Uncertainty," *Journal of Business Research*, October 2001, p. 71; Edward A. Blair, Judy Harris and Kent B. Monroe, "Effects of Shopping Information on Consumers' Responses to Comparative Price Claims," *Journal of Retailing*, Fall 2002, p. 175; Hooman Estelami, "The Impact of Research Design on Consumer Price Recall Accuracy: An Integrative Review," *Journal of the Academy of Marketing Science*, Winter 2001, p. 36; Richard A. Briesch, Lakshman Krishnamurthi, Tridib Mazumdar, and S. P. Raj, "A Comparative Analysis of Reference Price Models," *Journal of Consumer Research*, September 1997, p. 202; Tracy A. Suter and Scot Burton, "Believability and Consumer Perceptions of Implausible Reference Prices in Retail Advertisements," *Psychology & Marketing*, January 1996, p. 37; K. N. Rajendran and Gerard J. Tellis, "Contextual and Temporal Components of Reference Price," *Journal of Marketing*, January 1994, p. 22; Abhijit Biswas, Elizabeth J. Wilson, and Jane W. Licata, "Reference Pricing Studies in Marketing: A Synthesis of Research Results," *Journal of Business Research*, July 1993, p. 239; Daniel S. Putler, "Incorporating Reference Price Effects into a Theory of Consumer Choice," *Marketing Science*, Summer 1992, p. 287; Kristina D. Frankenberger and Ruiming Liu, "Does Consumer Knowledge Affect Consumer Responses to Advertised Reference Price Claims?" *Psychology & Marketing*, May/June 1994, p. 235.

12. For a classic example applied to a high-price item, see "Sale of Mink Coats Strays a Fur Piece from the Expected," *The Wall Street Journal*, March 21, 1980, p. 30.

13. K. Douglas Hoffman, L. W. Turley and Scott W. Kelley, "Pricing Retail Services," *Journal of Business Research*, December 2002, p. 1015; Steven M. Shugan and Ramarao Desiraju, "Retail Product-Line Pricing Strategy When Costs and Products Change," *Journal of Retailing*, Spring 2001, p. 17; Noel M. Noel and Nessim Hanna, "Benchmarking Consumer Perceptions of Product Quality With Price: An Exploration," *Psychology & Marketing*, September 1996, p. 591; Niraj Dawar and Philip Parker, "Marketing Universals: Consumers' Use of Brand Name, Price, Physical Appearance, and Retailer Reputation As Signals of Product Quality," *Journal of Marketing*, April 1994, p. 81; Tung-Zong Chang and Albert R. Wildt, "Impact of Product Information on the Use of Price As a Quality Cue," *Psychology & Marketing*, January 1996, p. 55; B. P. Shapiro, "The Psychology of Pricing," *Harvard Business Review*, July–August 1968, p. 14; Lutz Hildebrandt, "The Analysis of Price Competition Between Corporate Brands," *International Journal of Research in Marketing*, June 2001, p. 139.

14. Lee C. Simmons and Robert M. Schindler, "Cultural Superstitions and the Price Endings Used in Chinese Advertising," *Journal of International Marketing*, (2) 2003, p. 101; Robert M. Schindler and Thomas M. Kibarian, "Image Communicated by the Use of 99 Endings in Advertised Prices," *Journal of Advertising*, Winter 2001, p. 95; Robert M. Schindler and Patrick N. Kirby, "Patterns of Rightmost Digits Used in Advertised Prices: Implications for Nine-Ending Effects," *Journal of Consumer Research*, September 1997, p. 192; Mark Stiving and Russell S. Winer, "An Empirical Analysis of Price Endings With Scanner Data," *Journal of Consumer Research*, June 1997, p. 57; Robert M. Schindler and Alan R. Wiman, "Effects of Odd Pricing on Price Recall," *Journal of Business Research*, November 1989, p. 165.

15. "Tiffany & Co. Branches Out under an Alias," *The Wall Street Journal*, July 23, 2003, p. B1; "The Cocoon Cracks Open," *Brandweek*, April 28, 2003, p. 32; "Goodbye, Mr. Goodbar; Chocolate Gets Snob Appeal," *The Wall Street Journal*, February 13, 2003, p. D1; "Special Report: Luxury Marketing," *Advertising Age*, March 11, 2002, pp. S1–S10; "Keeping the Cachet," *The Wall Street Journal*, April 23, 2001, p. R28; "Luxury Sites Get Scrappy," *The Wall Street Journal*, December 4, 2000, p. B1; "Online Luxury Has Limits," *BusinessWeek E.Biz*, September 18, 2000, p.

EB24; "Special Report: Luxury Marketing," *Advertising Age*, August 14, 2000, p. S1; "The Galloping Gourmet Chocolate," *Brandweek*, July 31, 2000, p. 32. See also Xing Pan, Brian T. Ratchford and Venkatesh Shankar, "Can Price Dispersion in Online Markets Be Explained by Differences in E-Tailer Service Quality?" *Journal of the Academy of Marketing Science*, Fall 2002, p. 433; Kusum L. Ailawadi, Donald R. Lehmann and Scott A. Neslin, "Revenue Premium as an Outcome Measure of Brand Equity," *Journal of Marketing*, October 2003, p. 1; Rebecca Piirto Heath, "Life on Easy Street," *American Demographics*, April 1997, p. 33; G. Dean Kortge and Patrick A. Okonkwo, "Perceived Value Approach to Pricing," *Industrial Marketing Management*, May 1993, p. 133.

16. "Can Gillette Regain Its Edge?" *BusinessWeek*, January 26, 2004, p. 46; "Adobe Turns Page with New Software Line," *Investor's Business Daily*, November 13, 2003, p. A4; "The Allure of Bundling," *The Wall Street Journal*, October 7, 2003, p. B1; "Computer Deals Hit New Lows," *The Wall Street Journal*, August 13, 2003, p. D1. For more on phone bundling, see "Internet Phone Calls Could Squeeze Prices," *Investor's Business Daily*, December 12, 2003, p. A1; "Circuit Breaker: Battered Telecoms Face New Challenge: Internet Calling," *The Wall Street Journal*, October 9, 2003, p. A1; "BellSouth Hooks Up with DirecTV," *The Wall Street Journal*, August 27, 2003, p. B7; "Honey, I Shrunk the Phone Bill," *BusinessWeek*, June 9, 2003, p. 132; "Cellphone Giveaways Get an Upgrade," *The Wall Street Journal*, May 20, 2003, p. D1; "A Nickel Here, a Buck There Add Up to Big Local Bills," *USA Today*, February 28, 2003, p. 1B; "Phone, Cable Cos. Use Bundling to Keep Users from Switching," *Investor's Business Daily*, December 13, 2002, p. A1. For more on airline food unbundling, see "Dining Out at 32,000 Feet," *The Wall Street Journal*, June 3, 2003, p. D1; "Food Flights," *USA Today*, January 17, 2003, p. 1D. See also Andrea Ovans, "Make a Bundle Bundling," *Harvard Business Review*, November–December 1997, p. 18; Preyas S. Desai and Kannan Srinivasan, "Aggregate Versus Product-Specific Pricing: Implications for Franchise and Traditional Channels," *Journal of Retailing*, Winter 1996, p. 357; Manjit S. Yadav and Kent B. Monroe, "How Buyers Perceive Savings in a Bundle Price: An Examination of a Bundle's Transaction Value," *Journal of Marketing Research*, August 1993, p. 350; Dorothy Paun, "When to Bundle or Unbundle Products," *Industrial Marketing Management*, February 1993, p. 29.

17. Mary Anne Raymond, John F. Tanner, Jr. and Jonghoon Kim, "Cost Complexity of Pricing Decisions for Exporters in Developing and Emerging Markets," *Journal of International Marketing*, (3) 2001, p. 19; Peter E. Connor and Robert K. Hopkins, "Cost Plus What? The Importance of Accurate Profit Calculations in Cost-Plus Agreements," *International Journal of Purchasing & Materials Management*, Spring 1997, p. 35; Daniel T. Ostas, "Ethics of Contract Pricing," *Journal of Business Ethics*, February 1992, p. 137; J. Steve Davis, "Ethical Problems in Competitive Bidding: The Paradyne Case," *Business and Professional Ethics Journal*, 7, no. 2 (1988), p. 3; David T. Levy, "Guaranteed Pricing in Industrial Purchases: Making Use of Markets in Contractual Relations," *Industrial Marketing Management*, October 1994, p. 307; Akintola Akintoye and Martin Skitmore, "Pricing Approaches in the Construction Industry," *Industrial Marketing Management*, November 1992, p. 311.

CHAPTER 18

1. *2003 Annual Report*, Ben & Jerry's; "Economic Crunch," *Fortune*, December 8, 2003, p. 64; "Vermont's Latest," *Dairy Foods*, September 2003, p. 50; "Ice Cream Rivals Prepare to Wage a New Cold War," *The Wall Street Journal*, June 26, 2003, p. B1; "Summer of the Smush-In: 31 Flavors in a Single Cone," *The Wall Street Journal*, May 8, 2003, p. D1; "Looking for Intelligence in Ice Cream," *Fortune*, March 17, 2003, p. 114; "A Sweet Marketing Campaign," *Sales & Marketing Management*, November 2001, p. 14; "Ben & Jerry's Keeps Its Folksy Focus," *Advertising Age*, February 12, 2001, p. 4; "Ben & Jerry's: Surviving the Big Squeeze," *Food Business*, May 6, 1991, p. 10; "The Peace Pop Puzzle," *Inc.*, March 1990, p. 25.

2. Available from World Wide Web: <http://www.nextel. com>; "That Loud Squawk May Come from a Walkie-Talkie Phone," *The Wall Street Journal,* November 21, 2003, p. B1; "Eyeing Nextel's Success, Sprint PCS to Offer Push-to-Talk Service," *Investor's Business Daily,* November 17, 2003, p. A5; "Sprint PCS Plans to Unveil a New Walkie-Talkie Service," *The Wall Street Journal,* November 17, 2003, p. B4; "Cellphones Go Walkie-Talkie," *USA Today,* October 27, 2003, p. 4B; "Push-to-Talk: Nextel Is Still the One to Beat," *BusinessWeek,* October 13, 2003, p. 24; "Push to Talk: New Twist on Cellular Is Connecting," *USA Today,* October 13, 2003, p. 1D; "Guarding Nextel's Niche," *Fortune,* September 29, 2003, p. 133; "Nextel Execs Bullish on Growth Prospects," *Investor's Business Daily,* July 23, 2003, p. A6; "Nextel Wins the Race to Sponsor NASCAR," *BtoB,* July 14, 2003, p. 3; "Why Rivals Want Nextel's Number," *BusinessWeek,* May 5, 2003, p. 74; "Nextel's Users Connect with Push to Talk," *Investor's Business Daily,* May 2, 2003, p. A6; "Business Customers Buoy Nextel," *Investor's Business Daily,* December 13, 2002, p. A6; "In Front: Barry West, the Great Communicator," *Business 2.0,* November 2002, p. 25; "Free-Spending Nextel Customers Help It Pull Away from the Rest," *Investor's Business Daily,* September 18, 2002, p. A1.

3. "Good Product. Sound Plans. No Sure Thing," *The New York Times,* January 18, 1998, Sect. 3, p. 1; John E. Smallwood, "The Product Life Cycle: A Key to Strategic Marketing Planning," *MSU Business Topics,* Winter 1973, p. 29; Richard F. Savach and Laurence A. Thompson, "Resource Allocation within the Product Life Cycle," *MSU Business Topics,* Autumn 1978, p. 35; Peter F. Kaminski and David R. Rink, "PLC: The Missing Link between Physical Distribution and Marketing Planning," *International Journal of Physical Distribution and Materials Management* 14, no. 6 (1984), p. 77.

4. See most basic statistics textbooks under time series analysis.

5. Checking the accuracy of forecasts is a difficult subject. See "Can This Weatherman See Your Future?" *Business 2.0,* August 2003, p. 96; Kenneth B. Kahn, "An Exploratory Investigation of New Product Forecasting Practices," *The Journal of Product Innovation Management,* March 2002, p. 133; Manoj K. Agarwal, "Developing Global Segments and Forecasting Market Shares: a Simultaneous Approach Using Survey Data," *Journal of International Marketing,* (4) 2003, p. 56; Jonathon T. Fite, G. Don Taylor, John S. Usher, John R. English, and John N. Roberts, "Forecasting Freight Demand Using Economic Indices," *International Journal of Physical Distribution & Logistics Management,* (3) 2002, p. 299; John B. Mahaffie, "Why Forecasts Fail," *American Demographics,* March 1995, p. 34; "Don't Be Trapped By Past Success," *Nation's Business,* March 1992, p. 52; Margaret K. Ambry, "States of the Future," *American Demographics,* October 1994, p. 36; Marcus O'Connor, William Remus, and Ken Griggs, "Going Up—Going Down: How Good Are People at Forecasting Trends and Changes in Trends?" *Journal of Forecasting,* May 1997, p. 165; Marshall L. Fisher, Janice H. Hammond, Walter R. Obermeyer, and Ananth Raman, "Making Supply Meet Demand in an Uncertain World," *Harvard Business Review,* May–June 1994, p. 83; Craig S. Galbraith and Gregory B. Merrill, "The Politics of Forecasting: Managing the Truth," *California Management Review,* Winter 1996, p. 29; Larry D. Compeau, "Forecasting and Market Analysis Techniques:

A Practical Approach," *Journal of the Academy of Marketing Science,* Spring 1996, p. 181; Richard H. Evans, "Analyzing the Potential of a New Market," *Industrial Marketing Management,* February 1993, p. 35; Shelby H. McIntyre, Dale D. Achabal, and Christopher M. Miller, "Applying Case-Based Reasoning to Forecasting Retail Sales," *Journal of Retailing,* Winter 1993, p. 372; Paul A. Berbig, John Milewicz, and James E. Golden, "The Do's and Don'ts of Sales Forecasting," *Industrial Marketing Management,* February 1993, p. 49; David L. Kendall and Michael T. French, "Forecasting the Potential for New Industrial Products," *Industrial Marketing Management* 20, no. 3 (1991), p. 177; F. William Barnett, "Four Steps to Forecast Total Market Demand," *Harvard Business Review,* July–August 1988, p. 28; D. M. Georgoff and R. G. Murdick, "Manager's Guide to Forecasting," *Harvard Business Review,* January–February 1986, p. 110.

6. "The Numbers Game," *BusinessWeek,* May 14, 2001, p. 100; "Accounting Gets Radical," *Fortune,* April 16, 2001, p. 184; "Kmart's Bright Idea," *BusinessWeek,* April 9, 2001, p. 50; "Manufacturing Masters Its ABCs," *BusinessWeek,* August 7, 2000, p. 86J. See also Joseph P. Cannon and Christian Homburg, "Buyers-Supplier Relationships and Customer Firm Costs," *Journal of Marketing,* January 2001, p. 29; Robin Cooper and W. B. Chew, "Control Tomorrow's Costs Through Today's Designs," *Harvard Business Review,* January–February 1996, p. 88; Robin Cooper and Robert S. Kaplan, "Profit Priorities From Activity-Based Costing," *Harvard Business Review,* May/June 1991, p. 130; Douglas M. Lambert and Jay U. Sterling, "What Types of Profitability Reports Do Marketing Managers Receive?" *Industrial Marketing Management,* November 1987, p. 295; Nigel F. Piercy, "The Marketing Budgeting Process: Marketing Management Implications," *Journal of Marketing,* October 1987, p. 45; Michael J. Sandretto, "What Kind of Cost System Do You Need?" *Harvard Business Review,* January–February 1985, p. 110; Patrick M. Dunne and Harry I. Wolk, "Marketing Cost Analysis: A Modularized Contribution Approach," *Journal of Marketing,* July 1977, p. 83.

7. Technically, a distinction should be made between variable and direct costs, but we will use these terms interchangeably. Similarly, not all costs that are common to several products are fixed costs, and vice versa. But the important point here is to recognize that some costs are fairly easy to allocate, and other costs are not. See Stewart A. Washburn, "Establishing Strategy and Determining Costs in the Pricing Decision," *Business Marketing,* July 1985, p. 64.

8. Neil A. Morgan, Bruce H. Clark and Rich Gooner, "Marketing Productivity, Marketing Audits, and Systems for Marketing Performance Assessment: Integrating Multiple Perspectives," *Journal of Business Research,* May 2002, p. 363; James T. Rothe, Michael G. Harvey, and Candice E. Jackson, "The Marketing Audit: Five Decades Later," *Journal of Marketing Theory & Practice,* Summer 1997, p. 1; Douglas Brownlie, "The Conduct of Marketing Audits," *Industrial Marketing Management,* January 1996, p. 11; Leonard L. Berry, Jeffrey S. Conant, and A. Parasuraman, "A Framework for Conducting a Services Marketing Audit," *Journal of the Academy of Marketing Science,* Summer 1991, p. 255; John F. Grashof, "Conducting and Using a Marketing Audit," in *Readings in Basic Marketing,* eds. E. J. McCarthy, J. J. Grashof, and A. A. Brogowicz (Homewood, IL: Richard D. Irwin, 1984).

Glossary

Accessories Short-lived capital items—tools and equipment used in production or office activities.

Accumulating Collecting products from many small producers.

Administered channel systems Various channel members informally agree to cooperate with each other.

Administered prices Consciously set prices aimed at reaching the firm's objectives.

Adoption curve Shows when different groups accept ideas.

Adoption process The steps individuals go through on the way to accepting or rejecting a new idea.

Advertising Any *paid* form of nonpersonal presentation of ideas, goods, or services by an identified sponsor.

Advertising agencies Specialists in planning and handling mass-selling details for advertisers.

Advertising allowances Price reductions to firms in the channel to encourage them to advertise or otherwise promote the firm's products locally.

Agent middlemen Wholesalers who do not own (take title to) the products they sell.

AIDA model Consists of four promotion jobs: (1) to get *Attention*, (2) to hold *Interest*, (3) to arouse *Desire*, and (4) to obtain *Action*.

Allowance (accounting term) Occurs when a customer is not satisfied with a purchase for some reason and the seller gives a price reduction on the original invoice (bill), but the customer keeps the goods or services.

Allowances Reductions in price given to final consumers, customers, or channel members for doing something or accepting less of something.

Assorting Putting together a variety of products to give a target market what it wants

Attitude A person's point of view toward something.

Auction companies Agent middlemen that provide a place where buyers and sellers can come together and complete a transaction.

Auction sites Usually seller-driven e-commerce sites popular for used, surplus, or perishable items that are unique and only available for sale once.

Automatic vending Selling and delivering products through vending machines.

Average-cost pricing Adding a reasonable markup to the average cost of a product.

Average cost (per unit) The total variable cost divided by the related quantity.

Baby boom The largest age group, born in the fifteen years following World War II.

Bait-and-switch pricing Setting some very low prices to attract customers but trying to sell more expensive models or brands once the customer is in the store.

Balance sheet An accounting statement that shows a company's assets, liabilities, and net worth.

Basic list prices The prices that final customers or users are normally asked to pay for products.

Basic sales tasks *Order-getting, order-taking, and supporting*

Battle of the brands The competition between dealer brands and manufacturer brands.

Belief A person's opinion about something.

Bid pricing Offering a specific price for each possible job rather than setting a price that applies for all customers.

Birthrate The number of babies per 1,000 people.

"Bot" A search engine or robot used by managers to find and monitor Web sites that mention specific products, services, or sources of information.

Brand equity The value of a brand's overall strength in the market.

Brand familiarity How well customers recognize and accept a company's brand.

Brand insistence Customers insist on a firm's branded product and are willing to search for it.

Brand managers Manage specific products, often taking over the jobs formerly handled by an advertising manager—sometimes called *product managers*.

Brand name A word, letter, or a group of words or letters.

Brand preference Target customers usually choose the brand over other brands, perhaps because of habit or favourable past experience.

Brand recognition Customers remember the brand.

Branding The use of a name, term, symbol, or design—or a combination of these—to identify a product.

Break-even analysis An approach to determine whether the firm will be able to break even—that is, cover all its costs—with a particular price.

Breakthrough opportunities Opportunities that help innovators develop hard-to-copy marketing strategies that will be very profitable for a long time.

Brokers Agent middlemen who specialize in bringing buyers and sellers together.

Bulk-breaking Dividing larger quantities into smaller quantities as products get closer to the final market.

Business and organizational customers Any buyers who buy for resale or to produce other goods and services.

Business products Products meant for use in producing other products.

Buying centre All the people who participate in or influence a purchase.

Buying function Looking for and evaluating goods and services.

Cash-and-carry wholesalers Like service wholesalers, except that the customer must pay cash.

Cash discounts Reductions in the price to encourage buyers to pay their bills quickly.

Catalogue wholesalers Sell out of catalogues that may be distributed widely to smaller industrial customers or retailers that might not be called on by other middlemen.

Category killers A single-line mass-merchandiser, sometimes referred to as a big box store.

Census metropolitan area (CMA) An integrated economic and social unit with a large population nucleus.

Chain of supply The complete set of firms and facilities and logistics activities that are involved in procuring materials, transforming them into intermediate and finished products, and distributing them to customers.

Channel captain A manager who helps direct the activities of a whole channel and tries to avoid, or solve, channel conflicts.

Channel of distribution Any series of firms or individuals who participate in the flow of products from producer to final user or consumer.

Close The salesperson's request for an order.

Clustering techniques Approaches used to try to find similar patterns within sets of data.

Combination export manager A blend of manufacturers' agent and selling agent—handling the entire export function for several producers of similar but noncompeting lines.

Combined target market approach Combining two or more submarkets into one larger target market as a basis for one strategy.

Combiners Firms that try to increase the size of their target markets by combining two or more segments.

Communication process A source trying to reach a receiver with a message.

Comparative advertising Advertising that makes specific brand comparisons using actual product names.

Competition Act Federal laws that govern the way business is conducted in Canada.

Competitive advantage A firm has a marketing mix that the target market sees as better than a competitor's mix.

Competitive advertising Advertising that tries to develop selective demand for a specific brand rather than a product category.

Competitive barriers The conditions that may make it difficult, or even impossible, for a firm to compete in a market.

Competitive bids Terms of sale offered by different suppliers in response to the buyer's purchase specifications.

Competitive environment The number and types of competitors the marketing manager must face, and how they may behave.

Competitive rivals A firm's closest competitors.

Complementary product A product commonly used with another product, e.g., coffee and sugar.

Complementary product pricing Setting prices on several related products as a group.

Components Processed expense items that become part of a finished product.

Concept testing Getting reactions from customers about how well a new product idea fits their needs.

Confidence intervals The range on either side of an estimate from a sample that is likely to contain the true value for the whole population.

Consideration set The list of potential choices that a consumer will actually consider buying.

Consultative selling approach A type of sales presentation in which the salesperson develops a good understanding of the individual customer's needs before trying to close the sale.

Consumer panel A group of consumers who provide information on a continuing basis.

Consumer Packaging and Labelling Act A federal statute requiring bilingual labels and standard product packaging.

Consumer Protection Act A federal statute that provides protection to consumers and governs the fair disclosure of the cost of credit and borrowing in advertisements.

Consumer products Products meant for the final consumer.

Consumer surplus The difference to consumers between the value of a purchase and the price they pay.

Consumerism A social movement that seeks to increase the rights and powers of consumers.

Containerization Grouping individual items into an economical shipping quantity and sealing them in protective containers for transit to the final destination.

Contractual channel systems Various channel members agree by contract to cooperate with each other.

Contribution-margin approach A cost analysis approach in which all costs are not allocated in *all* situations.

Convenience (food) stores A convenience-oriented variation of the conventional limited-line food stores.

Convenience products Products a consumer needs but isn't willing to spend much time or effort shopping for.

Cooperative advertising Middlemen and producers sharing in the cost of ads.

Copy thrust What the words and illustrations of an ad should communicate.

Corporate chain A firm that owns and manages more than one store—and often it's many.

Corporate channel systems Corporate ownership all along the channel.

Corrective advertising Ads to correct deceptive advertising.

Cost of sales Total value (at cost) of the sales during the period.

Cues Products, signs, ads, and other stimuli in the environment.

Cultural and social environment Affects how and why people live and behave as they do.

Culture The whole set of beliefs, attitudes, and ways of doing things of a reasonably homogeneous set of people.

Cumulative quantity discounts Reductions in price for larger purchases over a given period, such as a year.

Customer relationship management (CRM) An approach where the seller fine-tunes the marketing effort with information from a detailed customer database.

Customer satisfaction The extent to which a firm fulfills a consumer's needs, desires, and expectations.

Customer value The difference between the benefits a customer sees from a market offering and the costs of obtaining those benefits.

Data warehouse A place where databases are stored so that they are available when needed.

Dealer brands Brands created by middlemen—sometimes referred to as *private brands*.

Decision support system (DSS) A computer program that makes it easy for marketing managers to get and use information *as they are making decisions*.

Decoding The receiver in the communication process translating the message.

Demand curve A graph of the relationship between price and quantity demanded in a market, assuming all other things stay the same.

Department stores Larger stores that are organized into many separate departments and offer many product lines.

Derived demand Demand for business products derives from the demand for final consumer products.

Determining dimensions The dimensions that actually affect the customer's purchase of a *specific* product or brand in a *product-market*.

Differentiation The marketing mix is distinct from and better than what's available from a competitor.

Direct marketing Direct communication between a seller and an individual customer using a promotion method other than face-to-face personal selling.

Direct type advertising Competitive advertising that aims for immediate buying action.

Discount retailers Stores that sell hard goods (cameras, TVs, appliances) at substantial price cuts to customers who go to discounter's low-rent store, pay cash, and take care of any service or repair problems themselves.

Discounts Reductions from list price given by a seller to buyers, who either give up some marketing function or provide the function themselves.

Discrepancy of assortment The difference between the lines a typical producer makes and the assortment final consumers or users want.

Discrepancy of quantity The difference between the quantity of products it is economical for a producer to make and the quantity final users or consumers normally want.

Discretionary income What is left of disposable income after paying for necessities.

Disposable income Income that is left after taxes.

Dissonance Tension caused by uncertainty about the rightness of a decision.

Distribution centre A special kind of warehouse designed to speed the flow of goods and avoid unnecessary storing costs.

Diversification Moving into totally different lines of business—perhaps entirely unfamiliar products, markets, or even levels in the production-marketing system.

Door-to-door selling Going directly to the consumer's home.

Drive A strong stimulus that encourages action to reduce a need.

Drop-shippers Wholesalers that own (take title to) the products they sell but do not actually handle, stock, or deliver them.

Dual distribution When a producer uses several competing channels to reach the same target market—perhaps using several middlemen in addition to selling directly (sometimes called *multichannel distribution*).

Early adopters The second group in the adoption curve to adopt a new product; these people are usually well respected by their peers and often are opinion leaders.

Early majority A group in the adoption curve that avoids risk and waits to consider a new idea until many early adopters try it and like it.

E-commerce Exchanges between individuals or organizations—and activities that facilitate those exchanges—based on applications of information technology.

Economic and technological environment Affects the way firms, and the whole economy, use resources.

Economic buyers People who know all the facts and logically compare choices to get the greatest satisfaction from spending their time and money.

Economic needs Needs concerned with making the best use of a consumer's time and money—as the consumer judges it.

Elastic demand If prices are dropped, the quantity demanded will stretch enough to increase total revenue.

Elastic supply The quantity supplied does stretch more if the price is raised.

Electronic data interchange (EDI) An approach that puts information in a standardized format easily shared between different computer systems.

Emergency products Products that are purchased immediately when the need is great.

Empty nesters People whose children are grown and who are now able to spend their money in other ways.

Encoding The source in the communication process deciding what it wants to say and translating it into words or symbols that will have the same meaning to the receiver.

Equilibrium point The quantity and the price sellers are willing to offer are equal to the quantity and price that buyers are willing to accept.

Everyday low pricing Setting a low list price rather than relying on frequent sales, discounts, or allowances.

Exclusive distribution Selling through only one middleman in a particular geographic area.

Expectation An outcome or event that a person anticipates or looks forward to.

Expenses All the remaining costs that are subtracted from the gross margin to get the net profit.

Experience curve pricing Average-cost pricing using an estimate of *future* average costs.

Experimental method A research approach in which researchers compare the responses of two or more groups that are similar except on the characteristic being tested.

Export agents Manufacturers' agents who specialize in export trade.

Export brokers Brokers who specialize in bringing together buyers and sellers from different countries.

Extensive problem solving The type of problem solving consumers use for a completely new or important need—when they put much effort into deciding how to satisfy it.

Facilitators Firms that provide one or more of the marketing functions other than buying or selling.

Factor A variable that shows the relation of some other variable to the item being forecast.

Factor method An approach to forecast sales by finding a relation between the company's sales and some other factor (or factors).

Fad An idea that is fashionable only to certain groups who are enthusiastic about it—but these groups are so fickle that a fad is even more short-lived than a regular fashion.

Family brand A brand name that is used for several products.

Family life cycle The stages a person might "flow" through during a lifetime.

Fashion Currently accepted or popular style.

Financing Provides the necessary cash and credit to produce, transport, store, promote, sell, and buy products.

Fixed-cost (FC) contribution per unit The selling price per unit minus the variable cost per unit.

Flexible-price policy Offering the same product and quantities to different customers at different prices.

F.O.B. A transportation term meaning free on board some vehicle at some point.

Focus group interview An interview of 6 to 10 people in an informal group setting.

Franchise operation A franchisor develops a good marketing strategy, and the retail franchise holders carry out the strategy in their own units.

Freight-absorption pricing Absorbing freight cost so that a firm's delivered price meets the nearest competitor's.

Full-cost approach All costs are allocated to products, customers, or other categories.

Full-line pricing Setting prices for a whole line of products.

General merchandise wholesalers Service wholesalers that carry a wide variety of nonperishable items such as hardware, electrical supplies, furniture, drugs, cosmetics, and automobile equipment.

Generic market A market with *broadly* similar needs—and sellers offering various and *often diverse* ways of satisfying those needs.

Generic products Products that have no brand at all other than identification of their contents and the manufacturer or middleman.

Gold-collar segment An emerging demographic of working-class youth, aged 18–24, who live at home to minimize living expenses and maximize disposable income.

Gross domestic product (GDP) The total market value of all goods and services provided in a country's economy in a year by both residents and nonresidents of that country.

Gross sales The total amount charged to all customers during some time period.

Heterogeneous shopping products Shopping products the customer sees as different and wants to inspect for quality and suitability.

Homogeneous shopping products Shopping products the customer sees as basically the same and wants at the lowest price.

Hypotheses Educated guesses about the relationships between things or about what will happen in the future.

Iceberg principle Much good information is hidden in summary data.

Ideal market exposure When a product is available widely enough to satisfy target customers' needs but not exceed them.

Implementation Putting marketing plans into operation.

Import agents Manufacturers' agents who specialize in import trade.

Import brokers Brokers who specialize in bringing together buyers and sellers from different countries.

Impulse products Products that are bought quickly as *unplanned* purchases because of a strongly felt need.

Indirect type advertising Competitive advertising that points out product advantages—to affect future buying decisions.

Individual brands Separate brand names used for each product.

Individual product A particular product within a product line.

Inelastic demand Although the quantity demanded increases if the price is decreased, the quantity demanded will not stretch enough to avoid a decrease in total revenue.

Inelastic supply The quantity supplied does not stretch much (if at all) if the price is raised.

Innovation The development and spread of new ideas, goods, and services.

Innovators The first group to adopt new products.

Installations Important capital items such as buildings, land rights, and major equipment.

Institutional advertising Advertising that tries to promote an organization's image, reputation, or ideas rather than a specific product.

Integrated marketing communications The intentional coordination of every communication from a firm to a target customer to convey a consistent and complete message.

Intensive distribution Selling a product through all responsible and suitable wholesalers or retailers who will stock or sell the product.

Intermediary Someone who specializes in trade rather than production, sometimes called a *middleman*.

Internet retailing An e-commerce growth area primarily concerned with moving information, and which currently accounts for less than 2 percent of retailing sales dollars.

Intranet A system for linking computers within a company.

Introductory price dealing Temporary price cuts to speed new products into a market and get customers to try them.

Inventory The amount of goods being stored.

ISO 9000 A way for a supplier to document its quality procedures according to internationally recognized standards.

Job description A written statement of what a salesperson is expected to do.

Jury of executive opinion Forecasting by combining the opinions of experienced executives, perhaps from marketing, production, finance, purchasing, and top management.

Laggards Prefer to do things the way they have been done in the past and are very suspicious of new ideas; sometimes called *nonadopters*—see *adoption curve*.

Late majority A group of adopters who are cautious about new ideas—see *adoption curve*.

Law of diminishing demand If the price of a product is raised, a smaller quantity will be demanded—and if the price of a product is lowered, a greater quantity will be demanded.

Leading series A time series that changes in the same direction *but ahead of* the series to be forecast.

Learning A change in a person's thought processes caused by prior experience.

Licensed brand A well-known brand that sellers pay a fee to use.

Lifestyle analysis The analysis of a person's day-to-day pattern of living as expressed in that person's Activities, Interests, and Opinions—sometimes referred to as AIOs or *psychographics*.

Limited-function wholesalers Merchant wholesalers that provide only *some* wholesaling functions.

Limited-line stores Stores that specialize in certain lines of related products rather than a wide assortment—sometimes called *single-line stores*.

Limited problem solving When a consumer is willing to put *some* effort into deciding the best way to satisfy a need.

Logistics The transporting, storing, and handling of goods to match target customers' needs with a firm's marketing mix—both within individual firms and along a channel of distribution (i.e., another name for *physical distribution*).

Long-run target return pricing Pricing to cover all costs and over the long run achieve an average target return.

Loss-leader pricing Setting some very low prices—real bargains—to get customers into retail stores.

Low-involvement purchases Purchases that have little importance or relevance for the customer.

Macro-marketing A social process that directs an economy's flow of goods and services from producers to consumers in a way that effectively matches supply and demand and accomplishes the objectives of society.

Major accounts sales force Salespeople who sell directly to large accounts such as major retail chain stores.

Manufacturer brands Brands created by producers.

Manufacturers' agents Agent middlemen who sell similar products for several noncompeting producers for a commission on what is actually sold.

Manufacturers' sales branches Separate warehouses that producers set up away from their factories.

Marginal analysis Evaluating the change in total revenue and total cost from selling one more unit to find the most profitable price and quantity.

Marginal cost The change in total cost that results from producing one more unit.

Marginal profit Profit on the last unit sold.

Marginal revenue The change in total revenue that results from the sale of one more unit of a product.

Markdown A retail price reduction that is required because customers won't buy some item at the originally marked-up price.

Markdown ratio A tool used by many retailers to measure the efficiency of various departments and their whole business.

Market A group of potential customers with similar needs who are willing to exchange something of value with sellers offering various goods or services—that is, ways of satisfying those needs.

Market development Trying to increase sales by selling present products in new markets.

Market growth A stage of the product life cycle when industry sales grow fast—but industry profits rise and then start falling.

Market information function The collection, analysis, and distribution of all the information needed to plan, carry out, and control marketing activities.

Market introduction A stage of the product life cycle when sales are low as a new idea is first introduced to a market.

Market maturity A stage of the product life cycle when industry sales level off and competition gets tougher.

Market penetration Trying to increase sales of a firm's present products in its present markets—probably through a more aggressive marketing mix.

Market potential What a whole market segment might buy.

Market segmentation A two-step process of (1) *naming* broad product-markets and (2) *segmenting* these broad product-markets in order to select target markets and develop suitable marketing mixes.

Marketing audit A systematic, critical, and unbiased review and appraisal of the basic objectives and policies of the marketing function and of the organization, methods, procedures, and people employed to implement the policies.

Marketing concept The idea that an organization should aim *all* its efforts at satisfying its *customers*—at a *profit*.

Marketing ethics The moral standards that guide marketing decisions and actions.

Marketing information system (MIS) An organized way of continually gathering, accessing, and analyzing information that marketing managers need to make decisions.

Marketing management process The process of (1) *planning* marketing activities, (2) directing the *implementation* of the plans, and (3) *controlling* these plans.

Marketing mix The controllable variables that the company puts together to satisfy a target group.

Marketing model A statement of relationships among marketing variables.

Marketing orientation Trying to carry out the marketing concept.

Marketing plan A written statement of a marketing strategy *and* the time-related details for carrying out the strategy.

Marketing program Blends all of the firm's marketing plans into one big plan.

Marketing research Procedures to develop and analyze new information to help marketing managers make decisions.

Marketing research process A five-step application of the scientific method that includes (1) defining the problem, (2) analyzing the situation, (3) getting problem-specific data, (4) interpreting the data, and (5) solving the problem.

Marketing strategy Specifies a target market and a related marketing mix.

Markup A dollar amount added to the cost of products to get the selling price.

Mass marketing The typical production-oriented approach that vaguely aims at everyone with the same marketing mix.

Mass-merchandisers Large, self-service stores with many departments that emphasize soft goods (housewares, clothing, and fabrics) and staples (like health and beauty aids) and selling on lower margins to get faster turnover.

Mass-merchandising concept The idea that retailers should offer low prices to get faster turnover and greater sales volume by appealing to larger numbers.

Mass selling Communicating with large numbers of potential customers at the same time.

Merchant wholesalers Wholesalers who own (take title to) the products they sell.

Message channel The carrier of the message.

Micro-macro dilemma What is good for some producers and consumers may not be good for society as a whole.

Micro-marketing The performance of activities that seek to accomplish an organization's objectives by anticipating customer or client needs and directing a flow of need-satisfying goods and services from producer to customer or client.

Middleman An intermediary.

Mission statement Sets out the organization's basic purpose for being.

Missionary salespeople Supporting salespeople who work for producers by calling on their middlemen and their customers.

Modified rebuy The in-between process where some review of the buying situation is done—though not as much as in new-task buying or as little as in straight rebuys.

Multichannel distribution When a producer uses several competing channels to reach the same target market—perhaps using several middlemen in addition to selling directly (sometimes called *dual distribution*).

Multiple buying influence Several people share in making a purchase decision—perhaps even top management.

Multiple target market approach Segmenting the market and choosing two or more segments, then treating each as a separate target market needing a different marketing mix.

Nationalism An emphasis on a country's interests before everything else.

Needs The basic forces that motivate a person to do something.

Negotiated price A price that is set based on bargaining between the buyer and seller.

Net An invoice term meaning that payment for the face value of the invoice is due immediately—also see *cash discounts*.

Net profit What the company earns from its operations during a particular period.

Net sales The actual sales dollars the company receives.

New product A product that is new *in any way* for the company concerned.

New-task buying When an organization has a new need and the buyer wants a great deal of information.

New unsought products Products offering really new ideas that potential customers don't know about yet.

Noise Any distraction that reduces the effectiveness of the communication process.

Nonadopters Prefer to do things the way they have been done in the past and are very suspicious of new ideas; sometimes called *laggards*—see *adoption curve*.

Noncumulative quantity discounts Reductions in price when a customer purchases a larger quantity on an *individual order*.

Nonprice competition Aggressive action on one or more of the Ps other than Price.

North American Free Trade Agreement (NAFTA) Lays out a plan to reshape the rules of trade among Canada, the U.S., and Mexico.

North American Industry Classification System (NAICS) codes Codes used to identify groups of firms in similar lines of business.

Odd-even pricing Setting prices that end in certain numbers.

One-price policy Offering the same price to all customers who purchase products under essentially the same conditions and in the same quantities.

Open to buy A buyer has budgeted funds that he can spend during the current time period.

Operating ratios Ratios of items on the operating statement to net sales.

Operating statement A simple summary of the financial results of a company's operations over a specified period of time.

Operational decisions Short-run decisions to help implement strategies.

Opinion leader A person who influences others.

Order getters Salespeople concerned with establishing relationships with new customers and developing new business.

Order-getting Seeking possible buyers with a well-organized sales presentation designed to sell a good, service, or idea.

Order takers Salespeople who sell to regular or established customers, complete most sales transactions, and maintain relationships with their customers.

Order-taking The routine completion of sales made regularly to target customers.

Packaging Promoting, protecting and enhancing the product.

Penetration pricing policy Trying to sell the whole market at one low price.

Perception How we gather and interpret information from the world around us.

Performance analysis Analysis that looks for exceptions or variations from planned performance.

Performance index A number that shows the relation of one value to another.

Personal needs An individual's need for personal satisfaction unrelated to what others think or do.

Personal selling Direct spoken communication between sellers and potential customers, usually in person but sometimes over the telephone or even via a video conference over the Internet.

Physical distribution (PD) The transporting, storing, and handling of goods to match target customers' needs with a firm's marketing mix—both within individual firms and along a channel of distribution (i.e., another name for *logistics*).

Physiological needs Biological needs such as the need for food, drink, rest, and sex.

Piggyback service Loading truck trailers or flatbed trailers carrying containers on railcars to provide both speed and flexibility.

Pioneering advertising Advertising that tries to develop primary demand for a product category rather than demand for a specific brand.

Place Making goods and services available in the right quantities and locations—when customers want them.

Pointcasting Displaying an ad only to an individual who meets certain qualifications, such as a previously expressed interest in the topic of the ad.

Population In marketing research, the total group you are interested in.

Portfolio management Treats alternative products, divisions, or strategic business units (SBUs) as though they are stock investments to be bought and sold using financial criteria.

Positioning An approach that refers to how customers think about proposed or present brands in a market.

Predatory pricing The practice of charging a below-cost price over a long period with the objective to drive competitors out of the market.

Prepared sales presentation A memorized presentation that is not adapted to each individual customer.

Prestige pricing Setting a rather high price to suggest high quality or high status.

Price The amount of money that is charged for "something" of value.

Price fixing Competitors illegally getting together to raise, lower, or stabilize prices.

Price leader A seller who sets a price that all others in the industry follow.

Price lining Setting a few price levels for a product line and then marking all items at these prices.

Primary data Information specifically collected to solve a current problem.

Primary demand Demand for the general product idea, not just the company's own brand.

Private brands Brands created by middlemen—sometimes referred to as *dealer brands*.

Private warehouses Storing facilities owned or leased by companies for their own use.

Procurement hub An e-commerce site, usually industry specific, that directs suppliers to companies that need to make purchases.

Product The need-satisfying offering of a firm.

Product advertising Advertising that tries to sell a specific product.

Product assortment The set of all product lines and individual products that a firm sells.

Product-bundle pricing Setting one price for a set of products.

Product development Offering new or improved products for present markets.

Product liability The legal obligation of sellers to pay damages to individuals who are injured by defective or unsafe products.

Product life cycle The stages a new product idea goes through from beginning to end.

Product line A set of individual products that are closely related.

Product managers Manage specific products, often taking over the jobs formerly handled by an advertising manager—sometimes called *brand managers*.

Product-market A market with very similar needs—and sellers offering various *close substitute* ways of satisfying those needs.

Production Actually *making* goods or *performing* services.

Production orientation Making whatever products are easy to produce and *then* trying to sell them.

Professional services Specialized services that support a firm's operations.

Profit maximization objective An objective to get as much profit as possible.

Promotion Communicating information between seller and potential buyer or others in the channel to influence attitudes and behavior.

Prospecting Following all the leads in the target market to identify potential customers.

Psychographics The analysis of a person's day-to-day pattern of living as expressed in that person's Activities, Interests, and Opinions—sometimes referred to as *AIOs* or *lifestyle analysis*.

Psychological pricing Setting prices that have special appeal to target customers.

Public warehouses Independent storing facilities.

Publicity Any *unpaid* form of nonpersonal presentation of ideas, goods, or services.

Pulling Using promotion to get consumers to ask middlemen for the product.

Purchase discount A reduction of the original invoice amount for some business reason.

Purchasing managers Buying specialists for their employers.

Purchasing power parity An approximation of the purchasing power of consumers.

Purchasing specifications A written (or electronic) description of what the firm wants to buy.

Pure subsistence economy Each family unit produces everything it consumes.

Push money (or prize money) allowances Allowances (sometimes called *PMs* or *spiffs*) given to retailers by manufacturers or wholesalers to pass on to the retailers' salesclerks for aggressively selling certain items.

Pushing Using normal promotion effort—personal selling, advertising, and sales promotion—to help sell the whole marketing mix to possible channel members.

Qualifying dimensions The dimensions that are relevant to including a customer type in a product-market.

Qualitative research Seeks in-depth, open-ended responses, not yes or no answers.

Quality A product's ability to satisfy a customer's needs or requirements.

Quantitative research Seeks structured responses that can be summarized in numbers—like percentages, averages, or other statistics.

Quantity discounts Discounts offered to encourage customers to buy in larger amounts.

Rack jobbers Merchant wholesalers that specialize in hard-to-handle assortments of products that a retailer doesn't want to manage—and they often display the products on their own wire racks.

Random sampling Each member of the research population has the *same* chance of being included in the sample.

Rebates Refunds to consumers after a purchase.

Receiver The target of a message in the communication process, usually a potential customer.

Reciprocity Trading sales for sales—that is, "if you buy from me, I'll buy from you."

Reference group The people to whom an individual looks when forming attitudes about a particular topic.

Reference price The price a consumer expects to pay.

Regrouping activities Adjusting the quantities or assortments of products handled at each level in a channel of distribution.

Regularly unsought products Products that stay unsought but not unbought forever.

Reinforcement Occurs in the learning process when the consumer's response is followed by satisfaction—that is, reduction in the drive.

Relationship marketing A campaign to build a profitable long-term relationship with each customer.

Reminder advertising Advertising to keep the product's name before the public.

Requisition A request to buy something.

Research proposal A plan that specifies what marketing research information will be obtained and how.

Response An effort to satisfy a drive.

Response rate The percent of people contacted in a research sample who complete the questionnaire.

Retailing All of the activities involved in the sale of products to final consumers.

Return When a customer sends back purchased products.

Return on assets (ROA) The ratio of net profit (after taxes) to the assets used to make the net profit—multiplied by 100 to get rid of decimals.

Return on investment (ROI) Ratio of net profit (after taxes) to the investment used to make the net profit—multiplied by 100 to get rid of decimals.

Reverse channels Channels used to retrieve products that customers no longer want.

Risk taking Bearing the uncertainties that are part of the marketing process.

Routinized response behaviour When consumers regularly select a particular way of satisfying a need when it occurs.

Safety needs Needs concerned with protection and physical well-being.

Sale price A temporary discount from the list price.

Sales analysis A detailed breakdown of a company's sales records.

Sales decline A stage of the product life cycle when new products replace the old.

Sales forecast An estimate of how much an industry or firm hopes to sell to a market segment.

Sales-oriented objective An objective to get some level of unit sales, dollar sales, or share of market—without referring to profit.

Sales presentation A salesperson's effort to make a sale or address a customer's problem.

Sales promotion Those promotion activities—other than advertising, publicity, and personal selling—that stimulate interest, trial, or purchase by final customers or others in the channel.

Sales quota The specific sales or profit objective a salesperson is expected to achieve.

Sales territory A geographic area that is the responsibility of one salesperson or several working together.

Sample A part of the relevant population.

Scientific method A decision-making approach that focuses on being objective and orderly in *testing* ideas before accepting them.

Scrambled merchandising Retailers carrying any product lines that they think they can sell profitably.

Search engine A computer program that helps a marketing manager find information that is needed.

Seasonal discounts Discounts offered to encourage buyers to buy earlier than present demand requires.

Secondary data Information that has been collected or published already.

Segmenters Aim at one or more homogeneous segments and try to develop a different marketing mix for each segment.

Selective demand Demand for a company's own brand rather than a product category.

Selective distribution Selling through only those middlemen who will give the product special attention.

Selective exposure Our eyes and minds seek out and notice only information that interests us.

Selective perception People screen out or modify ideas, messages, and information that conflict with previously learned attitudes and beliefs.

Selective retention People remember only what they want to remember.

Selling agents Agent middlemen who take over the whole marketing job of producers, not just the selling function.

Selling formula approach A sales presentation that starts with a prepared presentation outline—much like the prepared approach—and leads the customer through some logical steps to a final close.

Selling function Promoting the product.

Service A deed performed by one party for another.

Service mark Those words, symbols, or marks that are legally registered for use by a single company to refer to a service offering.

Service wholesalers Merchant wholesalers that provide all the wholesaling functions.

Shopping products Products that a customer feels are worth the time and effort to compare with competing products.

Single-line (or general-line) wholesalers Service wholesalers that carry a narrower line of merchandise than general merchandise wholesalers.

Single-line stores Stores that specialize in certain lines of related products rather than a wide assortment—sometimes called *limited-line stores*.

Single target market approach Segmenting the market and picking one of the homogeneous segments as the firm's target market.

Situation analysis An informal study of what information is already available in the problem area.

Skimming price policy Trying to sell the top of the market—the top of the demand curve—at a high price before aiming at more price-sensitive customers.

Social class A group of people who have approximately equal social position as viewed by others in the society.

Social needs Needs concerned with love, friendship, status, and esteem—things that involve a person's interaction with others.

Social responsibility A firm's obligation to improve its positive effects on society and reduce its negative effects.

Sorting Separating products into grades and qualities desired by different target markets.

Source The sender of a message.

Specialty products Consumer products that the customer really wants and makes a special effort to find.

Specialty shop A type of conventional limited-line store—usually small and with a distinct personality.

Specialty wholesalers Service wholesalers that carry a very narrow range of products and offer more information and service than other service wholesalers.

Standardization and grading Sorting products according to size and quality.

Staples Products that are bought often, routinely, and without much thought.

Statistical packages Easy-to-use computer programs that analyze data.

Status quo objectives "Don't-rock-the-*pricing*-boat" objectives.

Stocking allowances Allowances given to middlemen to get shelf space for a product—sometimes called *slotting allowances*.

Stockturn rate The number of times the average inventory is sold during a year.

Storing The marketing function of holding goods.

Storing function Holding goods until customers need them.

Straight rebuy A routine repurchase that may have been made many times before.

Strategic business unit (SBU) An organizational unit (within a larger company) that focuses its efforts on some product-markets and is treated as a separate profit center.

Strategic (management) planning The managerial process of developing and maintaining a match between an organization's resources and its market opportunities.

Substitutes Products that offer the buyer a choice.

Supercentres Very large stores that try to carry not only food and drug items, but all goods and services that the consumer purchases routinely (also called *hypermarkets*).

Supermarkets Large stores specializing in groceries—with self-service and wide assortments.

Supplies Expense items that do not become part of a finished product.

Supply chain management Focuses on how logistics should be coordinated to meet end-of-channel customers.

Supply curve The quantity of products that will be supplied at various possible prices.

Supporting salespeople Salespeople who help the order-oriented salespeople but don't try to get orders themselves.

Switching costs Costs and risks incurred when buyers or sellers drop an established exchange partner and have to reconfigure their products or operations in order to work with a new exchange partner.

S.W.O.T. analysis Identifies and lists the firm's strengths and weaknesses and its opportunities and threats.

Target marketing A marketing mix is tailored to fit some specific target customers.

Target return objective A specific level of profit as an objective.

Target return pricing Pricing to cover all costs and achieve a target return.

Task method An approach to developing a budget—basing the budget on the job to be done.

Team selling Different sales reps working together on a specific account.

Technical specialists Supporting salespeople who provide technical assistance to order-oriented salespeople.

Telemarketing Using the telephone to call on customers or prospects.

Telephone and direct-mail retailing Allows consumers to shop at home—usually placing orders by mail or a toll-free long-distance telephone call and charging the purchase to a credit card.

Test marketing A multicycle process for testing models and early versions of a product in the market.

Time series Historical records of the fluctuations in economic variables.

Total cost The sum of total fixed and total variable costs.

Total fixed cost The sum of those costs that are fixed in total—no matter how much is produced.

Total variable cost The sum of those changing expenses that are closely related to output—such as expenses for parts, wages, packaging materials, outgoing freight, and sales commissions.

Trade (functional) discount A list price reduction given to channel members for the job they are going to do.

Trade-in allowance A price reduction given for used products when similar new products are bought.

Trademark Those words, symbols, or marks that are legally registered for use by a single company.

Trademark Act A federal statute that protects a company from other firms using trademarks or brand names that could be confused with the company's own.

Traditional channel systems A channel in which the various channel members make little or no effort to cooperate with each other.

Transactional marketing Interactions between buyers and sellers where no loyalty or customer relationship management exists and bargaining is usually based on distributive (adversarial) negotiations.

Transporting The marketing function of moving goods.

Transporting function The movement of goods from one place to another.

Trend extension Extends past experience to predict the future.

Truck wholesalers Wholesalers that specialize in delivering products that they stock in their own trucks.

Tweens The preteen age group.

2/10, net 30 Allows a 2 percent discount off the face value of the invoice if the invoice is paid within 10 days.

Uniform delivered pricing Making an average freight charge to all buyers.

Unique selling proposition A statement that tells a target audience why they should buy the product.

Unit-pricing Placing the price per ounce (or some other standard measure) on or near the product.

Universal functions of marketing Buying, selling, transporting, storing, standardizing and grading, financing, risk taking, and market information.

Universal product code (UPC) Special identifying marks for each product readable by electronic scanners.

Unsought products Products that potential customers don't yet want or know they can buy.

Validity The extent to which data measures what it is intended to measure.

Value in use pricing Setting prices that will capture some of what customers will save by substituting the firm's product for the one currently being used.

Value pricing Setting a fair price level for a marketing mix that really gives the target market superior customer value.

Vendor analysis Formal rating of suppliers on all relevant areas of performance.

Vertical integration Acquiring firms at different levels of channel activity.

Vertical marketing systems Channel systems in which the whole channel focuses on the same target market at the end of the channel.

Viral marketing This Internet version of word-of-mouth advertising occurs when a firm sends e-mail to potential consumers in the hope they will pass it along to friends.

Wants Needs that are learned during a person's life.

Warranty What the seller promises about its product.

Wheel of retailing theory New types of retailers enter the market as low-status, low-margin, low-price operators and then, if successful, evolve into more conventional retailers offering more services with higher operating costs and higher prices.

Wholesalers Firms whose main function is providing *wholesaling activities*.

Wholesaling The *activities* of those persons or establishments that sell to retailers and other merchants, or to industrial, institutional, and commercial users, but who do not sell in large amounts to final consumers.

Zone pricing Making an average freight charge to all buyers within specific geographic areas.

Illustration Credits

CHAPTER 1

Exhibits: Exhibit 1-1, adapted from William McInnes, "A Conceptual Approach to Marketing," in *Theory in Marketing*, 2d ser., ed. Reavis Cox, Wroe Alderson, and Stanley J. Shapiro (Homewood, IL: Richard D. Irwin, 1964), pp. 51–67. Exhibit 1-3, adapted from R. F. Vizza, T. E. Chambers, and E. J. Cook, *Adoption of the Marketing Concept—Fact or Fiction* (New York: Sales Executive Club, Inc., 1967), pp. 13–15. Exhibit 1-5, adapted from the Web site for the Canadian Marketing Association, <www.the-cma.org>.

Photos/ads: Zuma Press/Marianna Day Massey; GLAD and STAND & ZIP are trademarks of The Glad Products Company. Advertisement ©2000 The Glad Products Company. Used with permission; Courtesy Pfizer, Inc.; Courtesy SAP AG; ©2003 PeopleSoft, Inc. PeopleSoft is a registered trademark of PeopleSoft, Inc.; Courtesy Maryland Aviation Administration; Courtesy Bob Theisz, www.canadianmade.com; Courtesy john st. advertising; Courtesy AllBusiness; ©William D. Perreault, Jr., Ph.d.; CLOROX® is a registered trademark of The Clorox Company. Used with permission. ©1994 The Clorox Company. Reprinted with permission; Courtesy Toyota Motor Sales, U.S.A., Inc.; agency: Oasis Advertising/New York.

CHAPTER 2

Exhibits: Exhibit 2-9, Copernicus: The Marketing Investment Strategy Group, Inc., 450 Lexington Street, Auburndale, MA 02166. Exhibit 2-11, Igor Ansoff, *Corporate Strategy* (New York: McGraw-Hill, 1965).

Photos/ads: AP Photo/Harry Cabluck. All Courtesy Penzoil-Quaker State Co.to/Car @ Jiffy Lube. All Courtesy Toddler University.sity ad. Courtesy Timex Corporation. Courtesy of Zippo Manufacturing Company, Inc. Courtesy Sara Lee Bakery Group. Courtesy of Audi of Norway; Agency: Bates Reklamebyra/ Oslo. Used with permission from McDonald's Corporation. Used with permission from McDonald's Corporation; Agency: DDB Chicago. Courtesy Unilever P.L.C. ©1999 Barry Lewis/Network.

CHAPTER 3

Exhibits: Exhibit 3-11, Russell I. Haley, "Benefit Segmentation: A Decision-Oriented Research Tool," *Journal of Marketing*, July 1968, p. 33.

Photos/ads: Courtesy Olympus America, Inc; Courtesy of Vivitar Corporation; Polter, Katz, Postal & Ferguson; MGI Software, Inc. Courtesy Samsung Electronics America. Courtesy Hallmark Cards, Inc. CLOROX CLEAN-UP® is a registered trademark of The Clorox Company. Used with permission. ©2002 The Clorox Company. Reprinted with permission. READYMOP® is a registered trademark of The Clorox Company.

Used with permission. ©2002 The Clorox Company. NADbank 2005. Courtesy CNN. ©The Procter & Gamble Company. Used by permission. Courtesy Del Laboratories. Photographer: Steve Bonini; Courtesy Orange Glo International; Courtesy Grey Worldwide/Thailand; Courtesy Roots Canada.

CHAPTER 4

Exhibits: Exhibit 4-3, this material is condensed from information provided by the Government of Canada. A full description of the acts as well as their interpretation and enforcement can be seen on the Competition Bureau Web site. Exhibit 4-4, these advertising "Dos and Don'ts" were created by the Competition Bureau of Canada and placed on their Web site to alert businesses and consumers to deceptive marketing practices. Source: The Competition Bureau of Canada Web site: <www.competitionbureau.gc.ca>. Exhibit 4-7, adapted from M. G. Allen, "Strategic Problems Facing Today's Corporate Planner," speech given at the Academy of Management, 36th Annual Meeting, Kansas City, Missouri, 1976.

Photos/ads: Courtesy REI; Courtesy Harley-Davidson Motor Company; Courtesy Royal Appliance Mfg. Co.; Used with permssion of Rogers Communications Inc. All rights reserved. Courtesy Accenture; Courtesy Smart Money; Ad created by: DiMassimo Brand Advertising/New York; Courtesy MSNBC; Microsoft Corporation; Courtesy Springer & Jacoby UK Ltd.; Photography by: F.A. Cesar; Courtesy Adero, Inc.; Courtesy adidas America; Photo by: Bob Allen; Nutri-Grain® is a registered trademark of Kellogg Company. ©2003 Kellogg Co.; Courtesy Con Agra Foods, Inc. – Snack Foods Group; Both Courtesy American Honda Motor Co.; Courtesy Honda North America, Inc.; Courtesy Baldor Electric; Courtesy Click 2 Asia.

CHAPTER 5

Exhibits: Exhibit 5-1, adapted from Statistics Canada, *Estimates of population, by age group and sex, Canada, provinces and territories, annual (Persons)*. Statistics Canada CANSIM Database, Table 051-0001, using E-STAT (distributor), available at: <http://estat.statcan.ca/cgi-win/CNSMCGI.EXE?CANSIMFILE =EStat\English\CII_1_E.htm>; retrieved March 16, 2006. Exhibit 5-2, "Changes in Canadian Birth Rate, 1935–2002," data is adapted in part from the Statistics Canada CANSIM Database, Table 102-4505, using E-STAT (distributor), available at: <http://estat.statcan.ca/cgi-win/CNSMCGI. EXE?CANSIMFILE=EStat\English\CII_1_E.htm>; retrieved March 16, 2006. Exhibit 5-3: "Population by Age Group for Different 10 Year Periods," adapted from the Statistics Canada CANSIM Database, Tables 052-0004 and 051-0001, using E-STAT (distributor), available at: <http://estat.statcan.ca/cgiwin/CNSMCGI.EXE?CANSIMFILE= EStat\English\CII_1_E.htm>; retrieved March 16, 2006.

Exhibit 5-4: "Median Total Income of Economic Family Type in Constant Dollars," adapted from the Statistics Canada CANSIM Database, Table 202-0411, using E-STAT (distributor), available at: <http://estat.statcan.ca/cgi-win/CNSMCGI. EXE?CANSIMFILE=EStat\English\CII_1_E.htm>; retrieved March 16, 2006. Exhibit 5-5, adapted from Patrick E. Murphy and William A. Staples, "A Modern Family Life Cycle," *Journal of Consumer Research*, June 1979, p. 17. Exhibit 5-6, "Population by Selected Ethnic Origins, by Province and Territories in Millions," adapted from the Statistics Canada Web site: <http://www40.statcan.ca/l01/cst01/demo26a.htm>. Information retrieved March 16, 2006.

Photos/ads: Courtesy Charles Schwab & Co.; Courtesy SRC; Courtesy Leo Burnett Advertising Sdn Bhd; ©Setboun Michel/Corbis Sygma; Courtesy Accenture; Courtesy Turner Broadcasting System; Courtesy DiMassimo Brand Advertising; Creative Director: Mark DiMassimo; Art Director: Christian Hasford; Courtesy of CBS Television Network; Courtesy element79partners; Courtesy of T & T Supermarket Inc., <www.tnt-supermaket.com>.

CHAPTER 6

Exhibits: Exhibit 6-2, adapted from C. Glenn Walters, *Consumer Behavior*, 3d ed. (Homewood, IL: Richard D. Irwin, 1979). Exhibit 6-5, Joseph T. Plummer, "The Concept and Application of Life-Style Segmentation," *Journal of Marketing*, January 1974, pp. 33–37.

Photos/ads: Copyright 2001 USA TODAY. Reprinted with permission; The Wendy's name, design and logo are registered trademarks of Oldemark, LLC and are licensed to Wendy's International, Inc.; Courtesy of ConAgra Foods; Courtesy DDB Singapore; Courtesy Bates Hong Kong Ltd.; Courtesy Belairdirect Insurance, Inc. Title: "Crash-Proof Policy"; Agency: Diesel; Courtesy Stride Rite Corporation; Lifestyle Photo: Peggy Sirota; Product Photo: John Lawler; All ©The Procter & Gamble Company. Used by permission; Courtesy Harley-Davidson, Inc.; Agency: Carmichael Lynch/ Minneapolis; Photo: ©Chris Wimpey; ©M. Hruby; ©2000 Jockey International, Inc. World Rights Reserved; ©2006 Bombardier Recreational Products Inc. All rights reserved. ® is trademark of Bonbardier Recreational Products Inc. or its affiliates; Courtesy A.T. Cross Company; AP Photo/Hasan Jamali; Christopher Morris/VII Photo Agency.

CHAPTER 7

Exhibits: Exhibit 7-1, U.S. Bureau of the Census, *Statistical Abstract of the United States 2000*; U.S. Bureau of the Census, *County Business Patterns 1998, United States* (Washington, DC: U.S. Government Printing Office, 2000). Exhibit 7-6, adapted from Rowland T. Moriarty, Jr., and Robert E. Spekman, "An Empirical Investigation of the Information Sources Used During the Industrial Buying Process, *Journal of Marketing Research*, May 1984, pp. 137–47. Exhibit 7-8, available from World Wide Web: <http://www.naics.com>.

Photos/ads: Photo courtesy of Deere & Company/Moline, Illinois; Both ©Roger Ball Photography; Courtesy Yellow Freight Systems, Inc.; Courtesy Canon USA, Inc.; Courtesy Ingersoll-Rand; Reproduced with permission of Yahoo! Inc. ©2003 by

Yahoo! Inc. YAHOO! and the YAHOO! logo are trademarks of Yahoo! Inc. Photo: Doug Adesko; Courtesy Google; Courtesy DoveBid.com; Courtesy National Semiconductor; All photos: Courtesy of Alcoa; Courtesy Hertz Corporation; Courtesy Savin Corporation; Courtesy SDI Technologies; Courtesy Cisco Systems, Inc.

CHAPTER 8

Exhibits: Exhibit 8-5, adapted from Paul E. Green, Frank J. Carmone, and David P. Wachpress,"On the Analysis of Qualitative Data in Marketing Research," *Journal of Marketing Research*, February 1977, pp. 52–59.

Photos/ads: ©The Procter & Gamble Company. Used by permission; Courtesy Oracle; Courtesy of MapInfo; Courtesy Find/SVP; Created by Sonnenberg, Haviland & Partners, Ridgewood, N.J.; Courtesy JRP Marketing Research Services; Courtesy Decision Analyst, Inc.; Courtesy Focus Vision Worldwide, ™Inc.; Courtesy Focus World International; Courtesy Zero knowledge Systems, Inc.; Courtesy Greenfield Online; Courtesy Royal Appliance Mfg. Co.; Courtesy Office Depot, Inc.; ©John Harding; Both Courtesy Simmons Company; Courtesy Abacus B2B/A Division of DoubleClick, Inc.; Courtesy of W Network; Courtesy SPSS, Inc.; Copyright 2002, SAS Institute Inc., Cary, NC, USA. All Rights Reserved. Reproduced with permission of SAS Institute Inc. Cary, NC, USA; Courtesy Survey Sampling, Inc.; Courtesy Simmons Custom Research; Courtesy P. Robert & Partners; Courtesy Quality Controlled Services – St. Louis, MO.

CHAPTER 9

Exhibits: Exhibit 9-5, Courtesy Dole Food Company; Courtesy Volkswagen of America, Agency: arnoldworldwide/Boston; Michelin and Tire Man logo are registered trademarks of Michelin North America, Inc., and are used here by permission; Courtesy FedEx Service; Linux: Created by Larry Ewing and The Gimp.

Photos/ads: Courtesy Garrity Industries; Reproduced courtesy of the Workrite Uniform Company/Oxnard, CA.; Agency: Applied Concepts/Ventura, CA; Courtesy The Hertz Corporation; The McGraw-Hill Companies Inc./Andrew Resek, photographer; Courtesy 3M; Courtesy Crate & Barrel; Courtesy GE Plastics; Courtesy ADP; Both Courtesy Unilever United States, Inc.; Courtesy Del Monte Fresh Produce N.A., Inc.; Courtesy GE Lighting; Courtesy Saatchi & Saatchi/Paris; Art Director: Benoit Raynert; Copywriter: Jean-Francois Fournon; ©M. Hruby; ©2003 KCWW Reprinted with Permission; Courtesy Colgate-Palmolive Company; These materials have been reproduced with the permission of eBay Inc. COPYRIGHT© EBAY INC. ALL RIGHTS RESERVED; Courtesy Sears Roebuck & Co.

CHAPTER 10

Exhibits: Exhibit 10-5, adapted from Frank R. Bacon, Jr., and Thomas W. Butler, *Planned Innovation* (Ann Arbor: University of Michigan Institute of Science and Technology, 1980). Exhibit 10-6, adapted from Philip Kotler, "What Consumerism Means for Marketers," *Harvard Business Review*, May–June 1972, pp. 55–56.

Name Index

Company Index

Subject Index